Sustainable Develo
in the Decisions of
Courts and Tribunals

The 2002 New Delhi Declaration of Principles of International Law relating to Sustainable Development set out seven principles on sustainable development, as agreed in treaties and soft-law instruments from before the 1992 Rio 'Earth Summit' UNCED, to the 2002 Johannesburg World Summit on Sustainable Development, to the 2012 Rio UNCSD. Recognition of the New Delhi principles is shaping the decisions of dispute settlement bodies with jurisdiction over many subjects: the environment, human rights, trade, investment, and crime, among others.

This book explores the expanding international jurisprudence incorporating principles of international law on sustainable development. Through chapters by respected experts, the volume documents the application and interpretation of these principles, demonstrating how courts and tribunals are contributing to the world's Sustainable Development Goals, by peacefully resolving disputes. It charts the evolution of these principles in international law from soft law standards towards recognition as customary law in certain instances, assessing key challenges to further judicial consideration of the principles, and discussing, for instance, how their relevance for compliance and disputes related to the 2015 Paris Agreement on climate change. The volume provides a unique contribution of great interest to law and policy-makers, judges, academics, students, civil society and practitioners concerned with sustainable development and the law, globally.

Marie-Claire Cordonier Segger is Senior Director, Centre for International Sustainable Development Law; Full Professor of Law, University of Waterloo; Advisor and Fellow of C-EENRG and LCIL, University of Cambridge; and Rapporteur, ILA Committee on Sustainable Resources Management. She also served as IDLO Senior Legal Expert, as Senior Legal Advisor to the UNFCCC CoP22 Presidency and Ramsar Convention and as A/Director, Canadian Government. She has authored/edited 21 books and over 120 papers, and assisted the UN and over 70 countries in legal education and reform on sustainable development.

H.E. Judge C. G. Weeramantry was former Vice-President of the International Court of Justice and Founder of the Weeramantry International Centre for Peace Education and Research. Over five decades as lawyer, legal educator, domestic judge, international judge, author and lecturer, the Judge pioneered international law on sustainable development. He was laureate of the UNESCO Peace Education Prize 2006 in recognition of his commitment and concrete undertakings in support of peace.

Routledge Research in International Environmental Law

Sustainable Development Principles in the Decisions of International Courts and Tribunals

1992–2012

Edited by
Marie-Claire Cordonier Segger with
H.E. Judge C.G. Weeramantry

Routledge
Taylor & Francis Group

LONDON AND NEW YORK

First published 2017 by Routledge

2 Park Square, Milton Park, Abingdon, Oxfordshire OX14 4RN
52 Vanderbilt Avenue, New York, NY 10017

Routledge is an imprint of the Taylor & Francis Group, an informa business

First issued in paperback 2018

British Library Cataloguing in Publication Data
A catalogue record for this book is available from the British Library

Library of Congress Cataloging in Publication Data
Names: Cordonier Segger, Marie-Claire, 1973- editor. | Weeramantry, C. G., editor.
Title: Sustainable development principles in the decisions of international courts and tribunals, 1992-2012 / edited by Marie-Claire Cordonier Segger and H.E. Judge C.G. Weeramantry.
Description: Abingdon, Oxon ; New York, NY : Routledge,2017. | Series: Routledge research in international environmental law | Includes bibliographical references and index.
Identifiers: LCCN 2016042602| ISBN 9781138780057 (hbk) | ISBN 9781315769639(ebk)
Subjects: LCSH: Sustainable development—Law and legislation—Cases. | International courts.
Classification: LCC K3585 .S8685 2017 | DDC 343.07—dc23
LC record available at https://lccn.loc.gov/2016042602

ISBN: 978-1-138-78005-7 (hbk)
ISBN: 978-0-367-19339-3 (pbk)

Typeset in ITC Galliard Std
by Swales & Willis Ltd, Exeter, Devon, UK

Contents

Table of cases

African Commission on Human and People's Rights

Aarhus Compliance Committee

European Court of Human Rights

European Court of Justice

ICJ Cases

Inter-American Court of Human Rights

International Arbitration Cases

ICSID

ITLOS Cases

North American Agreement on Environmental Cooperation

NAFTA Arbitrations

Other International Arbitrations

Seabed Disputes Chamber

UNHRC

WTO Cases

Miscellaneous Cases

National Cases

Table of treaties and declarations

Abbreviations and acronyms

ACP	African Caribbean and Pacific
AOSIS	Alliance of Small Island States
ASEAN	Association of Southeast Asian Nations
ATCA	Alien Tort Claims Act
ATS	Antarctic Treaty System
BAP	Bali Action Plan
BIT	Bilateral Investment Treaty
CAFTA-DR	Dominican Republic-Central America Free Trade Agreement
CAN	Andean Community (Spanish: *Comunidad Andina*)
CARICOM	Caribbean Community
CBD	Convention on Biological Diversity
CBDR	common but differentiated responsibility
CCAD	Central American Commission for Environment and Development
CCAP	Climate Change Action Plan
CDM	Clean Development Mechanism
CEP	Committee on Environmental Policy
CER	Certified Emission Reduction
CERD	Committee on the Elimination of Racial Discrimination
CEPAL	Economic Commission for Latin America and the Caribbean (ECLAC) (Spanish: *Comisión Económica para América Latina* or CEPAL)
CETA	Comprehensive Economic and Trade Agreement
CIL	customary international law
CISDL	Centre for International Sustainable Development Law
CITES	Convention on International Trade in Endangered Species of Wild Fauna and Flora
CJEU	Court of Justice of the European Union
CMP	Conference of the Parties serving as the meeting of the Parties to the Kyoto Protocol
COMESA	Common Market for Eastern and Southern Africa
COP	Conference of the Parties
CPRS	Carbon Pollution Reduction Scheme
CSD	Commission for Sustainable Development
CSR	corporate social responsibility

CTE	Committee on Trade and Environment
DSU	The Understanding on Rules and Procedures Governing the Settlement of Disputes, or Dispute Settlement Understanding
EA	environmental assessment
EC	European Community
ECA	Environmental Cooperation Agreement
ECACC	Enhancing Capacity for Adaptation to Climate Change
ECE	Economic Commission for Europe
ECHR	European Convention on Human Rights
ECJ	European Court of Justice
ECLAC	Economic Commission for Latin America and the Caribbean
ECO	Environmental Citizens' Organizations
ECOSOC	Economic and Social Council
ECT	Energy Charter Treaty
ECtHR	European Court of Human Rights
EEC	European Economic Community
EEZ	exclusive economic zone
EIA	environmental impact assessment
ETS	Emissions Trading Scheme
EU	European Union
EU ETS	European Union Emissions Trading Scheme
FAO	Food and Agriculture Organization
FDI	foreign direct investment
FIDA	Inter-American Forum on Environmental Law
FTA	Free Trade Agreement
G-77	Group of 77
GATS	General Agreement on Trade in Services
GATT	General Agreement on Tariffs and Trade
GEF	Global Environment Facility
GHGs	greenhouse gases
GMOs	genetically modified organisms
GNI	gross national income
GNP	gross national product
HCFC	hydrochlorofluorocarbons
HDI	Human Development Index
HFC	hydrofluorocarbon
IAEA	International Atomic Energy Agency
ICCAT	International Convention on the Conservation of Atlantic Tunas
ICCPR	International Covenant on Civil and Political Rights
ICESCR	International Covenant on Economic, Social and Cultural Rights
ICJ	International Court of Justice

ICRW	International Convention for the Regulation of Whaling
ICSID	International Centre for the Resolution of Investment Disputes
ICTSD	International Centre on Trade and Sustainable Development
ICTY	International Criminal Tribunal for Yugoslavia
IDP	internally displaced person
IEA	International Energy Agency
IEL	international environmental law
IADB	Inter-American Development Bank
IGC	intergovernmental committee
IGO	intergovernmental organization
IIA	International Investment Agreement
IISD	International Institute for Sustainable Development
IJC	International Joint Commission
ILA	International Law Association
ILC	International Law Commission
ILO	International Labour Organization
IMF	International Monetary Fund
IMO	International Maritime Organization
IPCC	Intergovernmental Panel on Climate Change
IPF	Intergovernmental Panel on Forests
IR	international relations
ISI	import substitution industrialisation
ITLOS	International Tribunal for the Law of the Sea
IUCN	International Union for Conservation of Nature
JI	Joint Implementation
LAC	Latin America and the Caribbean
LCA	long-term cooperative action
LCIL	Lauterpacht Centre for International Law
LMOs	living modified organisms
LOSC	United Nations Convention on the Law of the Sea
LULUCFG	Land Use, Land Use Change and Forestry Guidelines
MACC	Mainstreaming Adaptation on Climate Change
MARPOL	International Convention for the Prevention of Pollution from Ships
MDB	multilateral development bank
MDGs	Millennium Development Goals
MEA	Multilateral Environmental Accords/Agreements
MERCOSUR	Southern American Common Market
MFN	most favoured nation
MNC	multinational corporation
MNE	multinational enterprise
MOP	Meeting of the Parties
MRC	Mekong River Commission

MRV	measurement, reporting and verification
MSY	maximum sustainable yield
MTR	multilateral treaty regimes
NAAEC	North American Agreement on Environmental Cooperation
NAFTA	North American Free Trade Agreement
NAMAs	Nationally Appropriate Mitigation Actions
NAP	national action programme
NATO	North Atlantic Treaty Organization
NCP	national contact point
NGOs	non-governmental organizations
NIEO	New International Economic Order
NPT	Treaty on the Non-Proliferation of Nuclear Weapons
NZ	New Zealand
NZ ETS	New Zealand Emissions Trading Scheme
OAS	Organization of American States
OAU	Organization of African Unity
ODA	official development aid or overseas development assistance
OECD	Organisation for Economic Co-operation and Development
PCA	Permanent Court of Arbitration
PCIJ	Permanent Court of International Justice
PCF	Prototype Carbon Fund
PCT	Patent Cooperation Treaty
PES	payment for ecosystem services
PFM	Participatory Forest Management
PIC	prior informed consent
PIL	public interest litigation
PLT	Patent Law Treaty
PPMs	process and production methods
PPP	public-private partnership
PRTR	Pollutant Release and Transfer Register
R&D	research and development
REAs	sub-regional or bilateral environmental agreements
REDD	Reducing Emissions from Deforestation and Forest Degradation
RRACC	Reducing Risk to Human and Natural Assets Resulting from Climate Change
RTA	regional trade agreement
SADC	South African Development Community
SBSTA	Subsidiary Body for Scientific and Technological Advice
SCM Agreement	Agreement on Subsidies and Countervailing Measures
SFM	sustainable forest management
SIA	sustainability impact assessment
SIDS	Small Island Developing States
SPACC	Special Programme on Adaptation to Climate Change
SPS Agreement	Agreement on the Application of Sanitary and Phytosanitary Measures

TBT Agreement	Agreement on Technical Barriers to Trade
TEU	Treaty on European Union
TFEU	Treaty on the Functioning of the European Union
TNCs	transnational corporations
TRIPS	Agreement on Trade-Related Aspects of Intellectual Property Rights
UDRME	Universal Declaration on the Rights of Mother Earth
UK	United Kingdom
UN	United Nations
UNCCD	United Nations Convention to Combat Desertification
UNCED	United Nations Conference on Environment and Development
UNCHR	United Nations Commission on Human Rights
UNCITRAL	United Nations Commission on International Trade Law
UNCLOS	United Nations Convention on the Law of the Sea
UNCSD	United Nations Commission on Sustainable Development
UNCTAD	United Nations Conference on Trade and Development
UNDP	United Nations Development Programme
UNDRIP	United Nations Declaration on the Rights of Indigenous Peoples
UNECE	United Nations Economic Commission for Europe
UNEP	United Nations Environment Programme
UNESCO	United Nations Educational, Scientific and Cultural Organization
UNFCCC	United Nations Framework Convention on Climate Change
UNFF	United Nations Forum on Forests
UNGA	United Nations General Assembly
UNIDROIT	International Institute for the Unification of Private Law
UNTS	United Nations Treaty System
UPOV	International Convention for the Protection of New Varieties of Plants
US	United States
USD	US Dollars
VCLT	Vienna Convention on the Law of Treaties
WCED	World Commission on Environment and Development
WHO	World Health Organization
WIPO	World Intellectual Property Organization
WMO	World Meteorological Organization
WSSD	World Summit on Sustainable Development
WTO	World Trade Organization
WWF	World Wide Fund for Nature

Notes on contributors

Editors and Preface authors

Justice Antonio Herman Benjamin, of the National High Court of Brazil, has co-drafted several major Brazilian statutes, including on consumer protection, anti-corruption, environmental protection and environmental crimes. He has published over 30 books and articles in Brazil and abroad. During the 2012 Rio+20 Conference, he served as Secretary-General of the UNEP World Congress on Justice, Governance and Law for Environmental Sustainability.

Prof. Marie-Claire Cordonier Segger DPhil (Oxon), MEM (Yale), BCL and LL.B (McGill) and B.A. Hons. (Car.) is Senior Director of the Centre for International Sustainable Development Law (CISDL), Affiliated Fellow of the Lauterpatcht Centre for International Law at the University of Cambridge and Full Professor of Law at the University of Waterloo. She has also served as Executive Secretary to the Climate Law and Governance Initiative, Senior Legal Advisor to the Presidency of the UNFCCC COP22, and the Ramsar Convention on Wetlands, and Senior Legal Expert, Sustainable Development, for the International Development Law Organization. She has published over 140 books and papers on sustainable development law and policy in six languages.

H.E. Judge James Crawford, JD (Budapest), LL.D (Cantab), DPhil (Oxon), LL.B Hons and BA (Adelaide), serves on the International Court of Justice, and is former Whewell Professor of International Law at the University of Cambridge and Fellow in Law at Jesus College, Cambridge. He also served as Director of Lauterpacht Centre for International Law (LCIL). He has written widely on public international law, law of international responsibility and human rights.

H.E. Judge C.G. Weeramantry was former Judge and Vice-President of the International Court of Justice. As a lawyer, legal educator, domestic judge, international judge, and author, he touched on a wide variety of topics essential to peace, cross-cultural understanding and education, wrote over 20 books and lectured extensively on these topics in over 40 countries. He received the UNESCO Peace Education Prize 2006 in recognition of his commitment and concrete undertakings in support of the concept and culture of peace through his career.

Authors

Mr. Andriy Andrusevych, MIR, is a Senior Policy Expert at Resource and Analysis Center Society and Environment, an environmental think tank organization in Ukraine. He has worked with environmental public interest law organizations and participated in the work of various working groups and task forces within the Aarhus and Espoo Conventions, such as the Task Force on Public Participation in International Forums, the Task Force on Access to Justice and general Working Groups of the Parties.

Prof. Sumudu Atapattu, PhD (Cantab) and LL.M (Cantab), is Director, Research Centres at University of Wisconsin Law School and the Executive Director of the UW-Madison Human Rights Program. She is also the Lead Counsel for Human Rights at CISDL, and an Attorney-at-Law of the Supreme Court of Sri Lanka. She has published widely and her latest book, *Human Rights Approaches to Climate Change: Challenges and Opportunities* was published by Routledge in 2015.

Dr. Freya Baetens, PhD (Cantab), LL.M (Columbia), Cand.Jur./Lic.Jur. (Ghent), is Professor of Public International Law at the PluriCourts Centre (Faculty of Law, Oslo University). In addition to her academic activities, she regularly acts as counsel or expert in international disputes.

Dr. Jonathan Bonnitcha, DPhil, MPhil, and BCL (University of Oxford) and LL.B and BEc (University of Sydney), is a Visiting Fellow in International Investment Law and Policy at the Australian National University, and a Senior Lawyer in the Australian Government's Office of International Law. He has advised both developing and developed country governments on investment treaties, and published a monograph and several articles on the subject.

Ms. Francesse Joy Cordon, MPhil (Cantab), JD Hons. (University of the Philippines), BS *magna cum laude* (University of the Philippines) is an Associate Fellow and International Law on Sustainable Development Project Coordinator at the CISDL. She worked for the Asian Development Bank as a legal consultant, handling projects on environmental justice, environmental and wildlife crime, as well as energy and water. She was also engaged in projects with the University of the Philippines Collesge of Law Institute of Human Rights/WHO.

Mr. Antony Crockett, BSc and LL.B (Hons) (University of Melbourne), LL.M (Dist) (LSE) is an International Counsel with Hiswara Bunjamin & Tandjung in Jakarta, Indonesia, on secondment from the international law firm Herbert Smith Freehills. He is admitted to practice as a solicitor in England & Wales and Victoria, Australia. He has extensive experience in international dispute resolution, particularly international arbitration, as well as public international law.

Ms. Stephanie Forte, LL.B Hons (UWI), LEC Merit (NMLS), LL.M (Cantab), is Crown Counsel in the International Affairs Division of the Attorney General's Chambers of Jamaica. She previously practiced civil and commercial litigation and is a tutor in Public International Law at the University of the West Indies. She is a former editor of the Cambridge Journal of International and Comparative Law, Pegasus Scholar and Publications Officer with CISDL, and has also worked with an environmental NGO in Jamaica and as a legal intern at the Caribbean Court of Justice.

Prof. David Freestone, LL.B (University of Hull), LL.M (KCL), LL.D (University of Hull), is the Executive Secretary of the Sargasso Sea Commission, Co-Rapporteur of the International Law and Sea Level Rise Committee of the International Law Association, and Editor-in-Chief of the *International Journal of Marine and Coastal Law*. He served as the Lobingier Visiting Professor of Comparative Law and Jurisprudence at the George Washington University Law School.

Prof. Duncan French, LL.B (East Anglia), LL.M (Nottingham), and PhD (Wales, Cardiff), Head of the Lincoln Law School, is a leading academic on international environmental law and the international legal implications of sustainable development. He has written extensively in these areas, as well as writing generally on both broader questions of public international law (e.g. treaty interpretation), international economic and investment law and the interaction between international law and European Union law. He has secondary research interests in international law of the sea and Antarctica. As a key figure in the global debate on sustainable development, he has been co-rapporteur of the International Law Association Committee on the International Law on Sustainable Development for 10 years. He is currently Chairman of the ILA Working Group on International Law and Due Diligence and a senior research fellow of the CISDL.

Prof. Markus Gehring, JSD (Yale), MA (Cantab), LL.M (Yale), Dr.jur (Hamburg) is Lecturer in Law at the University of Cambridge and Director of Studies at Hughes Hall, Cambridge. He also serves Lead Counsel for Trade, Investment and Financial Law with the CISDL, BIICL Arthur Watts Senior Research Fellow, and holds an ad personam Jean Monnet Chair in Sustainable Development Law, and is former Vice-Dean of Research at the University of Ottawa Faculty of Law. He has published 30 books and articles on various aspects of trade, European and climate change law, sustainable development, and constitutional law.

Mr. Alexandre Genest MPA (Paris-Dauphine), DPA-CIL (ÉNA) and LL.B (Montréal) is a Canadian lawyer (Québec Bar) and an Associate at Volterra Fietta in London. He is in the final stages of a Double PhD with the University of Ottawa and the University of Leiden. He previously clerked with His Excellency Judge Peter Tomka at the International Court of Justice and acted as Counsel at Canada's Department of Foreign Affairs. He also served as Part-time Professor at the University of Ottawa and as Visiting Lecturer at Leiden University College.

Dr. Armelle Gouritin is currently Visiting Professor at the Centro de Investigación y Docencia Económicas, A.C. and Maitre de Conférences at the Université libre de Bruxelles where she lectures on environmental law. She joined the IES in 2007. Initially trained as a lawyer, she holds a maîtrise in public and European law (Université Paris I Panthéon-Sorbonne), a master's in public international law (Université Libre de Bruxelles), a specialization in international environmental law (Université Libre de Bruxelles), and a master's in human rights law (Université Saint Louis, Brussels).

Prof. Joyeeta Gupta is Professor of Environment and Development in the Global South at the Amsterdam Institute for Social Science Research of the University of Amsterdam and at the UNESCO-IHE Institute for Water Education, Delft.

Dr. Alexandra Harrington, PhD (McGill), J.D., LL.M, D.C.L. (McGill) is Lead Counsel for the CISDL's Cross-Cutting Programme. She is an international law scholar, Adjunct Professor at Albany Law School, and affiliated faculty at the Global Institute for Health and Human Rights. Her publications address a variety of fields relating to international law, including environmental law, legal issues relating to climate change, natural resources regulation, international organizations, international human rights law, international child's rights, international trade law, corporate social responsibility, and criminal law, as well as domestic fields such as constitutional law and military law. Dr. Harrington routinely presents her works at domestic and international conferences. She also serves as a member of the CISDL Board of Directors and a member of the Global Health Committee of the Global Health Center at the SUNY Albany School of Public Health. She has served as a professor at the University of Montreal Centre d'Etudes et de Recherches Internationales summer programs and as a Consultant to the Commission for Environmental Cooperation of the North American Agreement on Environmental Cooperation.

Dr. Jarrod Hepburn, DPhil, MPhil and BCL (University of Oxford) and LL.B and BE (University of Melbourne) is a Lecturer in Law at the University of Exeter, UK, and Legal Research Fellow at the CISDL. He has been a visiting researcher at the Max Planck Institute for Comparative and International Private Law in Hamburg, and his writings appear in journals including the *International and Comparative Law Quarterly* and the *Journal of International Dispute Settlement*. He is qualified to practise law in Australian federal and state jurisdictions.

Prof. Zsuzanna Horváth, PhD (EC Environmental Policy and Law), is an associate professor in the Department of International and European Law of the University of Pécs, Faculty of Law, Jean Monnet Professor of European Law and European Environmental Law, and the director of special training programme in EU Law. She also teaches Sustainable Production and Consumption, the Integrated Product Policy of the EU for Erasmus students.

Dr. Kamal Hossain is a practising barrister, much of whose work involves international law, constitutional law, and human rights. He served the Government of Bangladesh as Minister of Law (1972–1973), Foreign Affairs (1973–1975), and Petroleum and Minerals (1974–1975). More recently, he has been the UN

Special Rapporteur on Afghanistan (1998–2003) and is currently a Member of the UN Compensation Commission.

Prof. Phan Tuan Hung is the Deputy Director General of the Department of Legal Affairs, Ministry of Natural Resources and Environment of Vietnam. He served as the Legal Specialist and Asia Coordinator for the Legal Preparedness Climate Change Initiative in Vietnam, Environment and Sustainable Development Law Programs of the International Development Law Organization.

Ms. Aline Jaeckel, PhD (UNSW), LL.M (Leiden), LL.B (UWE Bristol) is a Research Fellow at Macquarie Law School where she is a recipient of the Macquarie University Research Fellowship. Her work focuses on the regulation of deep seabed mineral mining in areas beyond national jurisdiction. She is the author of *The International Seabed Authority and the Precautionary Principle* (Brill: Nijhoff, 2017) as well as articles and book chapters on law of the sea, international law, and international environmental law.

Ms. Caroline Jo, MPhil Environmental Policy (Cantab), BA Woodrow Wilson School (Princeton), is an Associate Fellow for CISDL and currently works at SunEdison. She previously taught at the China Foreign Affairs University in Beijing and worked at the Environment and Natural Resources Division at the US Department of Justice.

Dr. Sébastien Jodoin, PhD (Yale), MIR (Cantab), LL.M. (LSE) and BCL and LL.B (McGill) is an Assistant Professor in the Faculty of Law of McGill University. He is also a Faculty Associate of the Governance, Environment and Markets Initiative at Yale University. His research seeks to understand law and public policy in the context of the manifold forces associated with globalization, processes of social change, new and evolving forms of public and private governance, and the pursuit of sustainability at various levels.

Ms. Alexandra Keenan, LL.B (Dalhousie), LL.L (University of Ottawa). She holds a Certificate in Environmental Law and practices law in Ottawa, Ontario and the Eeyou Istchee (James Bay) region of Quebec, with an emphasis on indigenous governance and economic development.

Mr. Alexander Kenny, BA (McGill), MA (Université de Montréal), is an Associate Fellow with the CISDL. His work has focused primarily on the economics of the environment and development. He has rendered consultancy services to country governments, non-government organizations and international organizations on green growth, sustainable investment financing, biodiversity and climate change policy, and socio-economic and environmental impact.

Dr. Avidan Kent, PhD (Cantab), LL.M (McGill) and LL.B (Haifa), is a Lecturer at the University of East Anglia and a Legal Research Fellow with the CISDL. His research interests include public international law, international economic law, international environmental law, and international dispute resolution.

He currently teaches public international law and international trade law. He previously supervised in European Union Environmental Law at Cambridge University.

Prof. Jennifer McKay is Professor of Business Law, School of Law UniSA and holds a Bachelor of Arts (BA) Hons and a PhD from the University of Melbourne, a Bachelor of Laws (LL.B) from Adelaide University, a Graduate Diploma of Legal Practice from UniSA, and a Diploma of Human Rights and Humanitarian Law from the Washington College of Law at American University. In 2008 Professor McKay was recognised with a Fulbright Senior Fellowship at the University of California Berkeley (UCB). She publishes in sustainable development law, governance and protecting the public interest in private sector provision of water supply services and promotes a new war crime of ecocide.

Prof. Jorge Cabrera Medaglia, BCL (University of Costa Rica), LL.M (University of Costa Rica), MBA (National University of Costa Rica), is Lead Counsel for International Sustainable Biodiversity Law with the CISDL. He is also a Professor of Environmental Law in Postgraduate Studies of Agrarian and Environmental Law at University of Costa Rica, and a Professor of International Trade for the School of Business Administration, University of Costa Rica.

Valentina Durán Medina, LLB (Universidad de Chile), Master (DEA) in Environmental Law (University of Paris I Panthéon) is an environmental law clinic professor at Universidad de Chile and Research Coordinator at Centro de Derecho Ambiental (University of Chile Law School) CDA. She is a professor at the Environmental Law Master program (Universidad de Chile) and is the Director of the Universidad de Chile Centre for Environmental Law. Prof. Duran leads research projects and consultancy in the private and public sector in environmental law topics, such as: international environmental law, environmental compliance and enforcement, environmental policy, biodiversity, environmental instruments. She is the author of articles and coeditor of books, and is an alternate director of the environmental law journal (Universidad de Chile), a board member on the Domeyko Program on Biodiversity, a member of AJDE (Association des Juristes du DEA de Droit de l'Environnement des Universités de Paris I et de Paris II) and of Sociedad Chilena de Derecho Ambiental. Additionally, Prof. Duran has participated as a trainer in courses addressed to enterprises and public servants in environmental matters.

Ms. Danielle Turnquest Moulton, LL.B (University of the West Indies), BA (Macalester College), is an attorney-at-law at Turnquest-Wilson & Franklin. She worked in Washington, DC as the Voter Mobilisation Training Coordinator at the Center for Progressive Leadership. She has received public interest fellowships including a Wellstone Organising Fellow. She hopes to practice in the fields of maritime, environmental and energy law.

Mr. Freedom-Kai Phillips, MA (Seton Hall), LL.B (Dalhousie), LL.M (Ottawa) is a Legal Research Fellow, Biosafety and Biodiversity Law Programme at the CISDL. His research focuses on market mechanisms to biodiversity conservation, access and benefit sharing regimes, and developing strategies to integrate biodiversity and sustainability goals into organizational framework.

Mr. Dane Ratliff was until recently Director of the Commission for Environmental Cooperation (CEC) Submissions on Enforcement Matters (SEM) Unit, where he processed citizen submissions asserting that a NAAEC party has failed to effectively enforce its environmental law, spearheaded the CEC's online portal for submissions, and was instrumental in drafting the revised Guidelines for the NAAEC Articles 14 & 15 SEM process. Prior to that he was Legal Counsel at the Permanent Court of Arbitration (PCA) in The Hague, where he, inter alia, played a lead role in the development and promotion of the (PCA) environmental dispute resolution facilities, and acted as registrar in state-state arbitrations such as the Eritrea-Ethiopia Boundary Commission, and also assisted tribunals on several early international environmental law related cases such as the OSPAR and MOX Plant tribunals (Ireland/UK), and the Barbados/Trinidad and Tobago, and Guyana/Suriname, maritime boundary delimitation tribunals. He is pursuing a doctorate and holds degrees in law, and environmental philosophy from US and European universities. He currently advises governments and private parties on matters of international environmental law and policy, dispute resolution, and international business, as well as teaching environmental studies courses at Emory and Henry college.

Ms. Cairo Robb, MA (Cantab), Lic. spéc. dr. eur. (ULB), was called to the Bar of England and Wales in 1993. She edited the *International Environmental Law Reports* (CUP), including volumes on trade and environment, human rights and environment and international environmental law in national courts. On secondment from the University of Cambridge to the UK Department for Environment, Food and Rural Affairs (DEFRA) in London, Cairo spent two years working as a Policy Advisor at DEFRA's Sustainable Development Unit.

Dr. Henning Grosse Ruse-Khan is a University Lecturer in Intellectual Property Law at the University of Cambridge and a Fellow at King's College. He is also a Fellow at the Lauterpacht Centre for International Law and the Centre for Intellectual Property and Information Law. He also holds positions at the Max Planck Institute for Intellectual Property and Competition Law in Munich (Germany) and the CISDL (McGill University, Montreal).

Ms. Stephanie Safdi, JD and MEM (Yale), MPhil (Cantab), AB (Harvard), is an environmental lawyer specializing in environmental justice, land use, and indigenous rights. She currently practices with the public interest law firm Shute, Mihaly & Weinberger in San Francisco, California. She has clerked on the U.S. Court of Appeals for the Ninth Circuit and the U.S. District Court for the Western District of Washington.

Mr. Miguel Saldivia Olave, JD (Chile), is a member of the Legal Research Group of the Centre for International Sustainable Development Law (CISDL). He is an associate at Carey in Chile, while also working as Professor of Right to Information and as Teaching Assistant of Environmental Law at the Universidad de Chile. Additionally, he is Research Assistant at the Centre of Environmental Law and at the Solar Energy Research Centre, both from the Universidad de Chile.

Ms. Nadia Sanchez Castillo, LL.M (Advanced Studies in PIL) (Leiden) and JD (Pontificia Universidad Católica de Chile), is a researcher and author on issues related to international environmental law and the law of the atmosphere. She is currently a PhD candidate at Leiden University. She has also given lectures on international and environmental law related topics.

Prof. Sabine Schlemmer-Schulte, SJD (Saarland), LL.M (American), LL.M (Saarland), LL.B (Kiel), LED (Toulon), is a visiting professor of law at the British Institute of International and Comparative Law. She has also taught at the University of the Pacific McGeorge School of Law, after working as senior counsel at the World Bank.

Prof. Nico Schrijver is Professor of International Law and Academic Director of the Grotius Centre for International Legal Studies, Leiden University and a member of the Senate of the Dutch house of Parliament. He is a member and vice-chair of the UN Committee on Economic, Social and Cultural Rights, member of the Permanent Court of Arbitration and associate member of the Institut de droit international.

Prof. Tim Stephens, PhD (Sydney), MPhil (Cantab), BA (Hons) and LL.B (Hons) (Sydney), is Professor of International Law and Australian Research Council Future Fellow at the Faculty of Law, University of Sydney. He teaches and researches in public international law, with his work focusing on the law of the sea, international environmental law and international dispute settlement.

Prof. Hennie Strydom, B Iuris, LL.B, LL.M (University of the Free State), LL.D (UNISA), is a Professor in International Law and the National Research Foundation (NRF) Research Chair in International Law at the University of Johannesburg. He has published extensively on environmental and humanitarian law and is currently the president of the South African Branch of the International Law Association.

Prof. Marcel Szabó, JD (ELTE), PhD (PPCU), Dr. Habil. (legal and political sciences, PPCU), is an Associate Professor and Head of the Chair of the European Law Department at the Pázmány Péter Catholic University. After being the Deputy Commissioner for Fundamental Rights Responsible for the Protection of the Interests of Future Generations at the Office of the Commissioner for Fundamental Rights for four years, he was elected as a member of the Constitutional Court with an effective date of December 1st, 2016.

Prof. Dire Tladi, PhD (Rotterdam), LL.M (Connecticut), LL.B (Pretoria), is a Professor of International Law at the University of Pretoria and a member of the International Law Commission. He also serves as Special Adviser to the Minister of International Relations and Cooperation of South Africa. He was previously a legal adviser in the South African foreign ministry and legal counselor to the South African Permanent Mission to the United Nations in New York.

Researchers

Ms. Aleks Bojovic is doing her PhD dissertation on the World Trade Organization and Tanzania, particularly the relationship between increased global trade and environmental degradation, at the London School of Economics and Political Science. Her research interests include international economic law issues, WTO trade policies, bilateral and regional trade agreements, environmental agreements and policies.

Ms. Rina Kuusipalo, BA Hons (Harvard), is a law student at the University of Cambridge focusing on international environmental and human rights law. She has worked at the UN Climate Change Secretariat, Leigh Day, Delegation of Finland to UNESCO, Cambridge Institute for Sustainability Leadership, and served as Education Officer for CISDL.

Mr. Patrick Reynaud, BCL/LL.B (McGill), BA Hons (Concordia), DUECODEV (Université Marc Bloch), is the Senior Manager of CISDL. Patrick is an expert and practices in the area of tax law, including international tax law. Patrick has conducted research on sustainable development in regional trade agreements, and has acted as a Program Specialist in Sustainable Development and Environmental Law for the International Development Law Organization.

Ms. Yolanda Saito, BASc (University of British Columbia), JD (University of Ottawa). Yolanda is the Senior Program Coordinator, Strategic Initiatives at the International Development Law Organization (IDLO) where she focuses on biodiversity, climate change and sustainable development issues. She is also an Attorney Member of the New York State Bar.

Ms. Claudette van Zyl, BC./LL.B candidate and BA Hons. (McGill), served as Editor-in-Chief of the *McGill Journal of Dispute Resolution*, a legal researcher at CISDL, and legal consultant at the International Development Law Organization.

Ms. Krista Zeman, LL.B/BCL (McGill) and BA (Alberta), is counsel at the Trade Law Bureau of the Foreign Affairs, Trade and Development Canada. She served as law clerk at Cogan & Partners LLP, intern at the International Court of Arbitration, research assistant at McGill University, intern at the Trade Law Bureau of the Foreign Affairs and International Trade Canada, and judicial law clerk at the Federal Court of Appeal Canada.

Foreword

H.E. Judge C.G. Weeramantry

After nearly seven decades spent in learning and observing the law – as law student, practising lawyer, domestic judge, law professor and international judge – it has been my good fortune to see the law in operation in a variety of settings. All of this has given me the opportunities of seeing the law at every level, from the village council to the International Court of Justice, from the power centres of the rich world to the depths of poverty in the poor world, from the tremors and palpitations of a young lawyer handling his first brief, to the authority and definitiveness of a superior court judge and from the legally blind regime of apartheid to the breadth of vision of a free and open society. I have thus seen the law at work in all its forms and forums.

The achievements of the law over the centuries have been one of the greatest contributions to modern civilization. One notes with pride the contributions of the law towards a just world order, such as the development of the principles of equality and freedom, the curbing of tyrannical and arbitrary rule and the flowering of human rights, concepts and procedures.

However, the concentration on the letter of the law operates as an instrument of oppression to the developing world by the developed world, because the letter of the law is cited in justification. Without a rejection of this attitude, the peaceful world we seek would be impossible, for justice lies at the very heart of peace, just as justice lies at the very heart of government. All legal systems are so structured that they only protect the rights of those who are alive, here and now. This is in total contrast to the concept of justice, which applies not only to us and our children, but should take account of future generations as well. It is totally contrary to the notion of justice that the rights of future generations should be plundered without some awareness at least of the duty of lawyers and legal systems to protect them.

I remember taking a walk through a wooded area in Melbourne with two of my granddaughters when we found the remains of a beautiful tree that had been been felled by a woodcutter. The branches with their lovely leaves and flowers were lying across our path. One of them observed "if only this tree could talk, how sadly it would have pleaded with the woodcutter not to hurt it". Such a remark opens up whole avenues of thought one could ponder on.

Today, on massive scale, the earth's resources are being depleted and the environment is being polluted for thousands of generations yet to come. Our generation is polluting the environment with a degree of irresponsibility never shown by any generation since the human race began. We are doing so with full knowledge of the consequences and it is time legal professionals and legal systems moved into action to prevent this. An enlightened legal profession geared to the high ideals of a noble calling has the potential and the obligation to render this service to the community today. This is an enormous trust. It is a tragedy of our time that this trust is not being adequately discharged.

It is a pleasure to provide the foreword to this volume, and to commend it to you, as a project that I have found it a delight to inspire and to guide. Convened and edited by the Centre for International Sustainable Development Law (CISDL), which has been a focal point of my activities since retirement given its activity to advance scholarship and education in international law on sustainable development through research and CISDL. The CISDL addresses a range of sustainable development goals, including poverty eradication, climate change, health, trade and investment, and biodiversity, and has an impressive programme of action worked out for the succeeding years. Among CISDL's projects is the preparation of this book on sustainable development in international courts and tribunals.

The volume, like much of my work over the last two decades, is a call to lawyers, both present and future, to shake themselves out of their insularity and their molecular vision and rise triumphant towards their time-honoured role. They must lead their communities towards patterns of conduct based upon the quintessential principles which were the original inspiration of that learned body of persons who were custodians of the accumulated wisdom of their communities. All that has been said thus far about lawyers applies *a fortiori* to the judges. In this volume, by exploring how the principles of international law on sustainable development are being reflected in judicial reasoning in various courts, tribunals and other international dispute settlement mechanisms, we hope to assist those engaged in the law with this momentous task.

C.G. Weeramantry
Colombo, Sri Lanka
2016

Preface

H.E. Judge James Crawford

Among other things, international law allows States to be held responsible for their actions, pursuant to a web of obligations owed to each other and to other actors. In this respect, the latter part of the twentieth century has seen considerable developments: an enduring international organization of universal membership, the process of decolonization, the codification and progressive development of international law, the growth of international courts and tribunals, the emergence of new fields and specializations and the consolidation of old ones – human rights, the law of the sea, sustainable development, investment protection and criminal law.

Within the international system, States must shoulder a variety of responsibilities if international law is to work. At its most basic level, this entails an obligation of observation, a notion inherent within the concept of 'law' itself. But a further corollary is that of participation. States are more than mere subjects of international law; they are also its primary lawmakers.

Fraternity – as a political concept – is tied up with questions of boundaries: at what point does the community in question become something else to which (or to whom) the benefits of fraternity do not extend? This point was recognized by Justice C.D. Gonthier, to whom this volume is in part dedicated. After seventeen years on the Supreme Court of Canada, Justice Gonthier saw fraternity as a neglected pillar of democracy, one that informed a wide variety of legal doctrines though values such as empathy, commitment, fairness and cooperation.

The term 'sustainability' has several meanings, two of which are relevant here. In the first place, there is the question of the sustainability of international law itself as a normative system observed across time. In the second, there is sustainability as an outcome in its own right, towards which States may be guided by international law – including international environmental, economic and human rights law – as well as by enlightened self-interest.

As to the first, there are limits to the ability of international law to develop outside of the mandates conferred by states. If international law is to be perceived as sustainable – in that its system of rules are observed, adjusted and maintained – it cannot ignore the constraints of consent and acceptability.

As to the second, questions of environmental protection and economic development in international law can be approached from a variety of angles: concepts of property, of no-fault liability, of trusteeship, of treaty interpretation and implementation may be implicated. While agreements on specific topics and regions are important for the preservation of the environment, sustainability concerns arise as part of an interconnected web of issues. Realization of these interconnections led, *inter alia*, to the 1992 UN Conference on Environment and Development. The Rio Declaration on Environment and Development set out a series of principles designed to reconcile the needs of the environment on the one hand, and development on the other. Indeed, running through the Rio Declaration is the concept of sustainable development. The concept is stated most directly in Principle 4, which provides:

> In order to achieve sustainable development, environmental protection shall constitute an integral part of the development process and cannot be considered in isolation from it.

Justice Gonthier, as founding Chair of the Centre for International Sustainable Development Law, gave sustained attention to the concept of sustainable development, writing that:

> Sustainable development law seeks to bring together, rationalize, reconcile and harmonize the various strands of the law; of legal rules needed to govern the environment and human activity, economic and social. [. . .] Its special concern is with 'cross-cutting' issues. It is thus concerned with the proper role of law in governance as distinguished from, though in complement with, ethics: the law is the guardian of liberty, and ethics its inspiration – for liberty calls for responsibility.

This volume, with contributions from distinguished judges, experts, specialists and scholars of international law, brings together diverse views on how, over several decades from the 1972 Stockholm Conference to the 2012 Rio Conference, international courts and tribunals have sought to resolve international disputes related to sustainable development. It builds upon nearly three decades of analysis, dialogue and exchange within the International Law Association, and represents a serious effort to monitor and understand the progressive development of international law.

I am pleased to be able to call this volume to the attention of jurists and other interested readers.

James Crawford
The Hague
9 March 2016

Preface

Justice Antonio Herman Benjamin

This volume, *Sustainable Development Principles in the Decisions of International Courts and Tribunals: 1992–2012* offers a vision for development in harmony with others and with nature. In the face of a changing climate, the destruction of global resources, the pollution of our environment and injustices in our human family, the younger generation represented in this volume offers a playful, creative voice, which carries hope for a better future. It is a gentle reminder that courage, kindness, innovation and responsibility are the keystones on which civilization flourishes. This is also the central message of the 2012 Rio+20 Conference, which I served as Secretary-General of the UNEP World Congress on Justice, Governance and Law for Environmental Sustainability.

Indeed, there are various criticisms leveled at judges ruling on environmental conflicts. First, environmental conservation as a limitation on private property can be perceived as an illegitimate state intrusion, regardless of the constitutional mandate authorizing the intrusion. Second is that environmental laws serve a redistributive function in terms of values and interests as such legislation determines state assets and limits their functions. Third, access to environmental justice is increased by legal provisions and procedural rules that relax the *locus standi* requirement to file environmental cases. Lastly, when judges decide cases at the trial court level and the losing parties elevate their cases to appellate courts, local issues are brought to the forefront and become national concerns. While judges are undoubtedly latecomers in the environmental debate arena, the judiciary's role in this arena has been greatly expanded.

There are two models of viewing the judiciary's role in environmental protection: the judiciary spectator and the active judiciary.

The judiciary spectator model, which I believe must be rejected, appears based on the following rationale: (i) environmental conflict issues, which are highly complex and require technical expertise, should be settled by congress and the administration, and not by the judiciary, which is ill-equipped to handle such issues; (ii) judges, not having been elected by the public and thus considered nondemocratic state agents, should not make policy decisions on behalf of society; and (iii) judges are unable to speedily adjudicate environmental cases.

The active judiciary model, on the other hand, is anchored first and foremost on the constitution, which expressly provides for the people's right to a clean and safe environment and the correlative duty of the state's institutions, the judiciary included, to protect such right, and legitimizes the judiciary's intervention in this sphere. Besides, the promotion of ecological sustainability is a legal role, which judges must serve.

As a judge for one of Brazil's highest courts, the founding President of the Green Planet Institute, Chair of the IUCN World Commission on Environmental Law and a longstanding member of the Brazilian Environmental Council (CONAMA), I find myself contemplating our future with both concern and optimism.

This book offers insightful perspectives on these questions. I warmly commend the *Sustainable Development Principles in the Decisions of International Courts and Tribunals: 1992–2012* to your attention, as we continue our journey toward sustainability.

Justice Antonio Herman Benjamin
Brasilia
2016

Acknowledgements

The editors wish to express all their thanks and warm appreciation to their kind, patient and brilliant extended families, particularly the spouses, parents, children, god-children, and grandchildren (present and future), for their continuing support and inspiration.

Sincere thanks and acknowledgments are further due to the partners which made this volume possible over the past two decades of international legal scholarship, with formal and invaluable informal support and guidance, especially the leaders, experts, and colleagues of the Centre for International Development Law, the International Law Association, the Lauterpacht Centre for International Law, the International Development Law Organization and the Weeramantry Centre for International Peace Education Research. Finally, we must thank and recognise the tireless efforts and collaboration of our Routledge colleagues.

Tribute to H.E. Judge C.G. Weeramantry

Judge Christopher Gregory Weeramantry was an extraordinary and international inspiring jurist, an insightful scholar, a talented educator, a kind and gracious gentleman, and a deeply beloved mentor and friend.

His creativity, engagement and deep sense of responsibility, ethics and history were well known and deeply appreciated in our field.

His vision, insight, and dedication has made a lasting impression on international law, inspiring many young scholars and jurists to work towards peace, justice, and sustainable development. Across the world, and across generations, his works will be remembered and cherished. The Judge truly made a difference to our world, advancing peace, education, and research, and reminding us of the spirit of the law, with our responsibilities towards the most vulnerable peoples and our Earth.

Judge Weeramantry will be deeply missed and honoured by many. It is very hard to imagine him gone.

We deeply appreciate that it was possible to contribute to a special manuscript for him, together with many others, and to learn that the messages sent brought joy to the Judge and his family over the final months of his life. This volume will provide a testament to his legacy as a jurist and humanitarian, with a special dedication to honour his memory.

1 Introduction

Marie-Claire Cordonier Segger and
H.E. Judge C.G. Weeramantry

> We can be the first generation to succeed in ending poverty; just as we may be the
> last to have a chance of saving the planet.
>
> (*Transforming our World*, United Nations General Assembly
> Res 70/1 2015, Para 50)

In the United Nations General Assembly on the 25–27 September 2015, heads of
State and leaders from over 150 countries adopted a new global agenda for sustain-
able development. Entitled *Transforming our World: The 2030 Agenda for Sustainable
Development*, this Agenda aims to provide a plan of action for 'people, planet and
prosperity.'[1] The Agenda builds on the Millennium Development Goals, and reflects
the outcomes of nearly 50 years of international policy debate through the 1972
Stockholm UN Conference on the Human Environment (UNCHE), the 1992 Rio UN
Conference on Environment and Development (UNCED),[2] the 2002 Johannesburg
World Summit on Sustainable Development (WSSD), the 2012 Rio UN Conference
on Sustainable Development (UNCSD), and beyond, recognizing that the eradication of poverty is an indispensable requirement for sustainable development.

As recognized in the Agenda, in this time of immense challenge to sustainable
development, billions of the world's citizens continue to live in poverty and are
denied a life of dignity. Indeed, heads of State admit:

> [t]here are rising inequalities within and among countries. There are
> enormous disparities of opportunity, wealth and power. Gender inequality
> remains a key challenge. Unemployment, particularly youth unemploy-
> ment, is a major concern. Global health threats, more frequent and intense
> natural disasters, spiralling conflict, violent extremism, terrorism and related
> humanitarian crises and forced displacement of people threaten to reverse
> much of the development progress made in recent decades. Natural resource

1 *Transforming our World: The 2030 Agenda for Sustainable Development*, UNGA A/Res/70/1,
Preamble.
2 Report of the United Nations Conference on Environment and Development, Rio de Janeiro,
3–14 June 1992, vol. I, Resolutions Adopted by the Conference (United Nations publication,
Sales No. E.93.I.8 and corrigendum), resolution 1, annex I.

depletion and adverse impacts of environmental degradation, including desertification, drought, land degradation, freshwater scarcity and loss of biodiversity, add to and exacerbate the list of challenges which humanity faces. Climate change is one of the greatest challenges of our time and its adverse impacts undermine the ability of all countries to achieve sustainable development. Increases in global temperature, sea level rise, ocean acidification and other climate change impacts are seriously affecting coastal areas and low-lying coastal countries, including many least developed countries and small island developing States.

In essence, the Agenda notes, "the survival of many societies, and of the biological support systems of the planet, is at risk."[3]

The Agenda also recognizes and celebrates a time of immense opportunity. Heads of State point to significant progress in meeting many development challenges. They note that:

> [w]ithin the past generation, hundreds of millions of people have emerged from extreme poverty. Access to education has greatly increased for both boys and girls. The spread of information and communications technology and global interconnectedness has great potential to accelerate human progress, to bridge the digital divide and to develop knowledge societies, as does scientific and technological innovation across areas as diverse as medicine and energy.[4]

In this context, on the UN's Seventieth Anniversary, countries and many thousands of others resolved to work together to meet 17 integrated Sustainable Development Goals, backed by 169 targets which balance the environmental, social and economic dimensions of sustainable development. They seek to end poverty and hunger everywhere; to combat inequalities within and among countries; to build peaceful, just and inclusive societies; to protect human rights and promote gender equality and the empowerment of women and girls; and to ensure the lasting protection of the planet and its natural resources. They also resolved to create conditions for sustainable, inclusive and sustained economic growth, shared prosperity and decent work for all, taking into account different levels of national development and capacities.[5]

These Sustainable Development Goals invoke a commitment from all countries and all stakeholders, acting in collaborative partnership, to "take the bold and transformative steps which are urgently needed to shift the world on to a sustainable and resilient path."[6] As noted by the UNGA, it is an "Agenda of unprecedented scope and significance . . . accepted by all countries and is applicable to all . . . universal goals and targets which involve the entire world, developed and developing countries alike."[7]

---

3 *Transforming our World, supra* note 1 at Para 14.
4 Ibid. at Para 15.
5 Ibid. at Para 3.
6 Ibid. at Preamble.
7 Ibid. at Para 5.

As further noted at Paragraph 10, the new Agenda is grounded in the Universal Declaration of Human Rights,[8] international human rights treaties, the Millennium Declaration[9] and the 2005 World Summit Outcome,[10] and informed by other instruments such as the Declaration on the Right to Development,[11] and will be "guided by the purposes and principles of the Charter of the United Nations, including full respect for international law."[12] Further, as declared firmly at Paragraph 12, through the Agenda, countries "reaffirm all the principles of the Rio Declaration on Environment and Development, including, *inter alia*, the principle of common but differentiated responsibilities . . ."[13]

World leaders commit to implement the Agenda for the full benefit of all, for today's generation and for future generations. At Paragraph 21, countries pledge to "work to implement the Agenda within our own countries and at the regional and global levels, taking into account different national realities, capacities and levels of development and respecting national policies and priorities."[14] In doing so, as stated in Paragraph 18, they reaffirm their "commitment to international law and emphasize that the Agenda is to be implemented in a manner that is consistent with the rights and obligations of States under international law."[15]

As the United Nations Secretary-General noted in the World Summit on Sustainable Development in Johannesburg, South Africa, in 2002 it was already time to face an uncomfortable truth. "[T]he model of development we are accustomed to has been fruitful for the few, but flawed for the many. A path to prosperity that ravages the environment and leaves a majority of humankind behind in squalor will soon prove to be a dead-end road for everyone." In academia or professional practice, it is not enough to simply recognize the immensity of this challenge and then stand aside. It is necessary to debate, develop and implement innovative, integrated solutions on all levels. The Secretary-General continued: "Unsustainable practices are woven deeply into the fabric of modern life. Some say we should rip up that fabric . . . I say we can and must weave in new strands of knowledge and cooperation."[16]

A very important aspect of this 'fabric of modern life' is found in our evolving laws and justice systems. These systems are intricately woven upon the shared values, morals and ethics of an increasingly interconnected and interdependent world. Among the shared values, there is found a growing sense of respect for the common interest of all, a sense of responsibility for our common future. This responsibility, in certain instances recognized as a duty, engenders special attention to the needs of the most vulnerable and voiceless, especially the world's poor, and its shared environment.

8 Resolution 217 A (III).
9 Resolution 55/2.
10 Resolution 60/1.
11 Resolution 41/128, annex.
12 *Transforming our World, supra* note 1 at Para 10.
13 Ibid. at Para 12.
14 Ibid. at Para 21.
15 Ibid. at Para 18.
16 UN Secretary General, World Summit on Sustainable Development, Johannesburg, 2002.

Indeed, the need for more sustainable development has been the subject of important international treaty negotiations for several decades since identification of this global objective in the 1987 Brundtland Report and its recognition by the international community in the 1992 Rio Declaration. The precise contours of what kind of development is most sustainable, however, remained difficult to define for many years, leaving many States committed to implementation with little guidance. Legal scholarship contributed some clarity, analysing 'soft law' declarations and standards, also 'hard law' treaties in the field. The Sustainable Development Goals provide further guidance, outlining universal targets for more sustainable development that all countries can aspire to support.

It has been observed that a great transition is currently occurring in international law.[17] Though this transformation is still opposed by many, it is to be hoped that international law is shifting, through transnational legal process and the development of governance regimes, from the era of state 'individualism' to the era of the collective community of states. Most rules of past international law have been based on preserving the individual desires and interests of states. The international law of the future may, instead, focus on preserving the collective rights of the community of states, as co-stewards of the planet Earth.

For this to occur, a new system of international law, and international justice, must emerge and develop, slowly informing and transforming the current rudimentary rules and procedures. The norms which make up this system, it is hoped, will be based on an aspiration of freedom and equality for all. As Judge Charles D. Gonthier has proposed, there is a need to develop a sense of common responsibility for all members of our community, as symbolized in the third, often under-represented value of the famous French revolutionary cry: 'liberté, égalité, fraternité'.[18] A spirit of common responsibility for our increasingly interdependent societies and economies, for our shared environment and natural resources, and for the condition of humanity can inform the development of these norms. If the world can begin to move towards a more 'sustainable justice', such justice will be founded upon good faith recognition of a duty towards the present generation throughout the world, so that their needs can be equitably met, and also respect for the interests of future generations.

Sustainable development, as a concept, emerges from a global aspiration to meet these collective moral obligations and emerging international law realities.

The 1987 Brundtland Report describes sustainable development as "development which meets the needs of the present without compromising the ability of future generations to meet their own needs."[19] The 1992 Rio Declaration states, in Principle 3, that the right to development must be fulfilled so as to equitably meet

---

17 See Christopher Gregory Weeramantry, *Universalising International Law* (Leiden: Martinus Nijhoff, 2004).

18 See G. Canivet, "De la valeur de fraternite en droit francais," Proceedings of Responsibility, fraternity and sustainability in law: A conference in honour of Charles D. Gonthier 20–21 May 2011, McGill University, Montreal, Canada <www.cisdl.org>.

19 World Commission on Environment and Development, *Our Common Future* (Oxford: Oxford University Press, 1987).

the development and environmental needs of present and future generations.[20] It identifies an imperative to meet the development needs of the present and future equitably, and to simultaneously meet environmental needs. Sustainable development provides a 'conceptual bridge' between the right to social and economic development, and the need to protect the environment. Accommodation, reconciliation and integration are emphasized.

While certainly inspiring, this global concept of sustainable development suffers from a certain degree of vagueness.[21] This vagueness may well have been deliberate, in order to ensure its acceptability to many different local and global perspectives, from many cultures and regions.[22] However, the lack of conceptual clarity, coupled with obstacles from many powerful economic interest groups, has made it quite difficult to implement sustainable development in international policy and especially in binding international law.

The time has come to seek greater clarity. In 1992 at the United Nations Conference on Environment and Development, heads of State recognized the "need to clarify and strengthen the relationship between existing international instruments or agreements in the field of environment and relevant social and economic agreements or instruments, taking into account the special needs of the developing countries."[23]

Over the past decade, scholars and practitioners from national and international agencies, courts and law faculties around the world have examined and sought to define the relationship between sustainable development and international law.[24] Clarity is now urgently needed. It is needed to help avoid or resolve bewildering conflicts and overlaps between economic, environmental and social treaties. It is also needed to make implementation of international law possible, in the many treaties and regimes that have set sustainable development as an object

---

20 Rio Declaration, Report of the United Nations Conference on Environment and Development (1992) UN Doc. A/CONF.151/26/Rev. 1 (1992) 31 ILM 874.

21 See B. Simma, "Foreword" in N. Schrijver and F. Weiss, *International Law and Sustainable Development* (Leiden: Martinus Nijhoff, 2004) [hereinafter *Schrijver & Weiss*] at vi, where he states ". . . perhaps it is inevitable that . . . an integrative concept such as that of sustainable development which was endorsed as such by the world community as a whole, lacks the kind of clarity . . . one might be accustomed to in a more limited homogenous group of states . . . that need not necessarily be considered a disadvantage. Indeed, it may well have been the very lack of conceptual rigor which permitted the entire world community to embrace it."

22 See M.C. Cordonier Segger and A. Khalfan, *Sustainable Development Law: Principles, Practices and Prospects* (Oxford: Oxford University Press, 2004) [hereinafter *Cordonier Segger & Khalfan*].

23 *Supra* note 5.

24 See *Schrijver & Weiss, supra* note 21. For a careful legal examination of the status of sustainable development in international law, see V. Lowe, "Sustainable Development and Unsustainable Arguments" in A. Boyle and D. Freestone, eds., *International Law and Sustainable Development: Past Achievements and Future Challenges* (Oxford: Oxford University Press, 1999). See also W. Lang, ed., *Sustainable Development and International Law* (Boston: Graham & Trotman/Martinus Nijhoff, 1995); K. Ginther, E. Denters and Paul JIM de Waart, eds., *Sustainable Development and Good Governance* (Norwell, MA: Kluwer Academic Publishers, 1995); M. McGoldrick, "Sustainable Development: The Challenge to International Law" (1994) *Review of the European Community and International Environmental Law* (RECIEL*)* 3; and P. Sands, "International Law in the Field of Sustainable Development" (1994) 65 *Brit. Y.B. of Int'l L.* 303.

or purpose. And it is needed to provide judiciaries, in domestic courts and international tribunals, with guidance to resolve disputes in this area.

At the 2002 World Summit for Sustainable Development, heads of State agreed to continue "to promote coherent and coordinated approaches to institutional frameworks for sustainable development at all national levels, including, as appropriate, the establishment or strengthening of existing authorities and mechanisms necessary for policy-making, coordination and implementation and enforcement of laws."[25] They mandated the United Nations Commission on Sustainable Development to take "into account significant legal developments in the field of sustainable development, with due regard to the role of relevant intergovernmental bodies in promoting the implementation of *Agenda 21* relating to international legal instruments and mechanisms."[26]

Indeed, international law has a great deal to contribute to the implementation of the pressing global sustainable development agenda, including through the peaceful resolution of disputes. The increasingly significant contributions of such tribunals were confirmed a decade after the Johannesburg World Summit on Sustainable Development in the outcomes of the 2012 UN 'Rio+20' Conference on Sustainable Development (UN CSD), *The Future We Want*, which highlighted the essential role of judicial and administrative proceedings in the promotion of sustainable development.[27]

1.1 Integrated international law on sustainable development

Irrational exploitation of natural resources, without regard for the future or the rights of others, is one of the principal contemporary causes of global tension. In many circumstances, it is the seed of future conflicts.[28] Sustainable development law can be described as an insurance against these otherwise inevitable wars. Justice has the working tools with which to handle this enormous responsibility. The basic concepts and procedures are present. Using legal scholarship, new technologies and practical wisdom, judges can access the traditions of thousands of years of human experience in dealing with natural resources, and can rely upon considerable,

25 Johannesburg Plan of Implementation, Report of the World Summit on Sustainable Development, Johannesburg (South Africa) (4 Sept. 2002) UN Doc. A/CONF.199/20, available online: <http://www.un.org/esa/sustdev/documents/WSSD_POI_PD/English/POIToc.htm>
26 Johannesburg Declaration on Sustainable Development and Johannesburg Plan of Implementation, Report of the World Summit on Sustainable Development, Johannesburg (South Africa) (4 Sept. 2002) UN Doc. A/CONF.199/20.
27 Rio+12 The Future We Want, Report of the United Nations Conference on Sustainable Development, Rio de Janiero (Brazil) (24 July 2012) UN Doc. A/CONF.216/16.
28 See Christopher Gregory Weeramantry, *Universalising International Law* (Leiden: Martinus Nijhoff, 2004) at 447, which states: "True peace is impossible without justice. A principal element of justice is economic justice. Economic justice is impossible without sustainable development. Sustainable development is thus an important prerequisite to peace. If peace is an indispensable object of international law, sustainable development is indispensable to the attainment by international law of its most important goal."

often underused, equitable jurisdiction. Judges can elevate the legal standing of the sustainable development concept by moving it up the hierarchy of legal norms and principles, preventing it from being lightly dismissed by political, commercial or other interests which seek to advance 'development', whatever the cost.

The law, including international and domestic law, can play a very important role in the realization of more sustainable justice. And in recent years, as is canvassed in timely literature[29] and in the chapters of this book, international legal principles have emerged to help. These principles provide an increasingly firm backbone for a more effective, coherent sustainable development law. International, regional and bi-lateral courts, tribunals and other dispute settlement mechanisms are seeking to balance overlapping economic, social and environmental interests and needs. International regimes, including – and on occasions led by – the tribunals and courts of the world, can contribute an independent, long term perspective to sustainable development decision-making.

Elements of a renewed global sustainable development governance system, as identified by the 2002 Johannesburg World Summit for Sustainable Development and the 2012 UNCSD Rio+20 Declaration on *The Future We Want*, continue to be saddled with the nearly impossible – but vitally necessary – role of coordinating these myriad complex efforts. As a result of this activity, some of which will be canvassed in this volume, the field of sustainable development law is being practically moulded and adapted to meet a variety of diverse situations and problems, taking it far from a merely academic and theoretical concept. The next few decades have been offered the exciting task of constructing a law of sustainable development which will help not one geographical region but all, draw upon the nuances not only of one cultural tradition but of all, advance the interests of not merely one section of the global economy but of all and protect the environment not merely for this generation but for others yet unborn.

1.2 Sustainable progress in international law and policy debates

In the 2002 Johannesburg Summit on Sustainable Development (the 'Johannesburg Summit'), the need for a coherent approach to sustainable development law was identified and advanced by 202 international scholars, law professors, legal professionals and judges.[30] It was argued that an international law of sustainable

---

29 *Cordonier Segger & Khalfan, supra* note 22. See also *Schrijver & Weiss, supra* note 21 at 699.

30 "International Jurists Mandate for the Implementation of International Sustainable Development Law" in M.C. Cordonier Segger and A. Khalfan, eds., Conference Report from *Sustainable Justice 2002: Implementing International Sustainable Development Law*, co-hosted by the Centre for International Sustainable Development Law, the United Nations Environment Programme, the World Bank, and the International Law Association (13–15 June 2002, Montreal), available online: <http://www.cisdl.org>. See also M.C. Cordonier Segger, A. Khalfan and S. Nakjhavani, *Weaving the Rules for Our Common Future: Principles, Practices and Prospects of an International Sustainable Development Law* (Montreal: CISDL, 2002), which was launched at the 2002 World Summit for Sustainable Development in Johannesburg, South Africa.

development is now emerging.[31] Indeed, a growing corpus of legal provisions and instruments can be identified which integrate international environmental, social and economic law into a variety of laws at the international, regional and domestic levels.[32]

International jurists, professionals and scholars have made great strides in the definition and analysis of legal principles and practices related to sustainable development.[33] International law provides a framework for regimes of cooperation – deliberately woven, implemented, financed and monitored by state actors and many other stakeholders. International law on sustainable development invokes historic, indeed ancient traditions of responsible, sustainable use of natural resources, respect for the earth and consideration for its peoples, for the past, the present and the future. It has important procedural elements related to consultations between environment and socio-economic decision-makers, transparency, participation of civil society and major stakeholders, and impact assessment. It includes a collection of legal instruments for sustainable use of shared resources, bi-lateral, regional and global regimes which set sustainable development as their object and purpose.

As recognized in the Johannesburg Summit, States have assumed "a collective responsibility to advance and strengthen the interdependent and mutually reinforcing pillars of sustainable development – economic development, social development and environmental protection – at the local, national, regional and global levels."[34] At this Summit, States expressed support for "the leadership role of the United Nations as the most universal and representative organization in the world, which is best placed to promote sustainable development."[35] In the 2015 Sustainable Development Goals, the reasons for this confidence were realized, and States also reaffirmed their "commitment to the principles and purposes of the Charter of the United Nations and international law."

There are several ways that these global policy statements on the value of international law to sustainable development can be understood. First, of course, a growing body of international treaty law on sustainable development is being implemented by States, and when States commit to sustainable development in a treaty or international legal process, this is not legally meaningless. States are accepting an obligation to seek balance between sometimes conflicting economic, environmental and social priorities in the development process, in the interests of future generations. The balance can be achieved through procedures and

---

31 On the process of developing norms, see J. Brunnée and S.J. Toope "International Law and Constructivism: Elements of an Interactional Theory of International Law" (2000) 39(1) *Col. J. Trans'l. Law* 19.

32 See *Cordonier Segger & Khalfan, supra* note 22.

33 Reviews are provided in *Cordonier Segger & Khalfan, supra* note 22, and in *Schrijver & Weiss, supra* note 21. See also A. Boyle and D. Freestone, eds., *International Law and Sustainable Development: Past Achievements and Future Challenges* (Oxford: Oxford University Press, 1999).

34 Johannesburg Declaration on Sustainable Development, Report of the World Summit on Sustainable Development, Johannesburg (South Africa) (4 Sept. 2002) UN Doc. A/CONF.199/20, available online: <http://www.un.org/esa/sustdev/documents/WSSD_POI_PD/English/POIToc.htm>

35 Ibid.

substantive obligations which differ depending on the treaty instrument and the area of law and policy that is regulated.

Second, the normative consequences of a commitment to sustainable development may not be the same as a straightforward prohibition or prescription. However, if one adopts a more complex view of international law as part of a series of inter-actional regimes, a legal commitment to sustainable development has interstitial meaning and normative force both in international treaties, and in 'soft law' cooperation arrangements. This interstitial normative character may well encourage States and tribunals to adopt and implement sustainable development related principles and measures, both inside existing treaty regimes, and even in their efforts to resolve disputes among themselves, or between States and third parties.

Third, and most important for the purposes of this present volume, the resolution of international disputes on sustainable development can serve to strengthen multilateralism, to aid in delivery of the principles and purposes of the Charter and of international law, especially with regard to its three 'pillars' – economic development, social development and environmental protection. A balanced accommodation, reconciliation and even integration of these priorities and norms is increasingly necessary, indeed essential, to achieve development that can last. This proposal is both ancient and new. Many courts and tribunals at a number of levels have fully acknowledged a connection between environmental protection, economic development and human rights.[36] On the international level, in binding decisions and awards, it is clear that the world's judiciaries increasingly perceive these objectives as complementary rather than unrelated or opposing disciplines.

However, as was implicitly recognized in the Johannesburg Plan of Implementation, these laws are not always coherent, either internationally or in the national context. International trade, investment and other economic laws aim mainly to achieve economic growth and progress. International law related to human rights, health, indigenous peoples and other social concerns seeks to achieve social justice. International environmental law aims to protect the environment, including the interests of all species. All three must meet the needs of present and future generations for a development that can last over the long term. Principle 4 of the 1992 Rio Declaration states that in "order to achieve sustainable development, environmental protection shall constitute an integral part of the development process and cannot be considered in isolation from it."[37] Perhaps not all economic or social law requires environmental expertise, nor vice

---

36 For example, see Indian cases such as *Charan Lal Sadhu v Union of India* AIR 1990 SC 1480 and *Koolwal v Rajasthan* AIR 1998, Raj.2, which address environmental pollution as an issue affecting the human right to life. See also *Leatch v National Parks and Wildlife Service and Shoalhaven City Council*, 81 LGERA 270 (1993) (NSW Land and Environment Court, Australia); *Vellore Citizens Welfare Forum v Union of India* [1996] 5 SCC 647 (Supreme Court, India); *Balankulama v The Secretary, Ministry of Industrial Development, SAER*, vol. 7(2) June 2000 (Supreme Court, Sri Lanka.

37 Rio Declaration on Environment and Development, United Nations Conference on Environment and Development, UN Doc. A/CONF.151/6/Rev.1 (1992), reprinted in 31 ILM 874 (1992) at Principle 4.

versa.[38] But certain instruments in each regime do need to integrate the priorities of others at the intersections. Sustainable development law focuses on these intersections between social, economic and environmental fields of law.[39]

Social, environmental and economic obligations can overlap or even conflict. When they do, they are not sustainable. As witnessed in recent years, public protests and global tensions, popular struggles against the privatization of essential services, against new rules for trade and investment liberalization, against decisions of international financial institutions, are centred on this concern. Economic laws and policies which do not take social and environmental elements into account are unlikely to be successful in a democratic society. Similarly, environmental laws that ignore social and economic realities, and social laws that violate environmental or economic principles, can waste valuable political and material resources, also leading to failure. The need for a balanced integration of socio-economic development and environment priorities and norms permeates international law and policy on sustainable development.

These tangled obligations, institutions and issues may inspire grand controversy, international debate, tension and conflict, but they are not impossible to resolve. Indeed, reconciliation and accommodation is taking place every day: in treaty negotiations and implementation, in the drafting or challenging of new regulations, in international organizations, and especially, as is the focus of this volume, in courtrooms and tribunals around the world. Indeed, significant progress has been made in international courts and tribunals over recent decades for the resolution of disputes related to sustainable development.

1.3 Principles of international law on sustainable development

Great debates have raged as to which legal principles (and underlying these, which values) will guide the reconciliation, accommodation and integration of

---

38 This means that not all aspects of international environmental law are international sustainable development law. For example, animal rights, the conservation of 'charismatic mega-fauna', and transboundary environmental disputes do not necessarily address sustainable development problems. See A. Boyle and D. Freestone, eds., *Sustainable Development and International Law: Past Achievements and Future Challenges* (Oxford: Oxford University Press, 1999). It is important to be clear on this point. Sustainable development is not about the environment alone. It is not a 'softer' word for international environmental law, and is not simply a euphemism for environmental law in developing countries. International environmental law programming is extremely important and must be strengthened. But sustainable development is focused on human communities inasmuch as they depend on their environment, their economy and their society. It addresses a key concept of "needs, in particular the essential needs of the world' poor, to whom overwhelming priority should be given." It requires an accommodation between social, economic and environmental objectives, on all levels. As such, multilateral environmental agreements (MEAs) are only a third of the locus of sustainable development efforts. Other aspects of the United Nations system, powerful international actors, particularly those with economic and social mandates, must seek ways to deliver on the overall Sustainable Development Goals.

39 *Supra* note 18. See also M.C. Cordonier Segger, "Significant Developments in Sustainable Development Law and Governance: A Proposal" (2004) *United Nations Natural Resources Forum* 28:1.

environmental, social and economic priorities. Based on prior work by the United Nations Commission for Sustainable Development and others,[40] the International Law Association Committee on the Legal Aspects of Sustainable Development has elaborated a set of Principles of International Law for Sustainable Development. The International Law Association's 2002 *New Delhi Declaration of Principles of International Law Relating to Sustainable Development* [New Delhi Declaration/ Principles] marks a significant milestone in the legal analytical scholarship, setting out seven principles of sustainable development found in treaties on sustainable development, and reflected in soft law instruments such as the 1992 UNCED Rio Principles, which are beginning to assert certain persuasive legal force in the decisions of international courts and tribunals. The Centre for International Sustainable Development Law (CISDL) surveys of international treaty and customary sources of international law have indicated that many became more widely accepted after the 2002 Johannesburg WSSD.[41] Recognition of these principles has been increasingly widespread, occurring across the international human rights, economic and environmental fields of law in dispute settlement bodies with diverse jurisdictions over human rights, international trade, investment, and international crimes, amongst others.

The seven *New Delhi Principles of International Law on Sustainable Development* contribute to the achievement of sustainable development in many diverse contexts, and are further explained in the ILA's 2012 *Sofia Guiding Statements on the Judicial Elaboration of the 2002 New Delhi Declaration of Principles of International Law Relating to Sustainable Development* [2012 Sofia Guiding Statements]. In this context, judicial interpretation of these principles within the context of sustainable development represents an invaluable source of guidance for all those whose work deals with the promotion and realization of sustainable development at all levels of society and across the

---

40 These included, *inter alia*, World Commission on Environment and Development (WCED), "Report by the World Commission on Environment and Development Experts Group on Environmental Law" in *Our Common Future* (Oxford: Oxford University Press, 1987); Rio Declaration on Environment and Development (1992) 31 ILM 874 (adopted 14 June 1992); the concluding Declarations of various large UN Conferences, including the 18th *UNGA Special Session on International Economic Co-operation* (1990); the Vienna *World Conference on Human Rights* (1993), the Cairo *UN Conference on Population and Development* (1994); the Beijing *UN Women's Conference* (1995) and the Copenhagen *Social Summit* (1995); the Agenda for Development by the UN Secretary General (1995); the IUCN *Draft Covenant on Environment and Development* (Gland: IUCN, 2000 rev.); the *Report of the Expert Group Meeting on Identification of Principles of International Law for Sustainable Development* (New York: United Nations, September 1995); International Law Association Committee on Legal Aspects of Sustainable Development research reports, including *The Right to Development in International Law* (1992), *Sustainable Development and Good Governance* (1995), and *International Economic Law with a Human Face* (1997); the UNEP *Position Papers on International Environmental Law Aimed at Sustainable Development* (Nairobi: UNEP, 1997 and 2000) (Montevideo Programmes II and III), and the *Earth Charter* (Costa Rica: Earth Council, 2000).

41 M.C. Cordonier Segger, A. Khalfan, M. Gehring and M. Toering, "Prospects for Principles of International Sustainable Development Law: Common but Differentiated Responsibilities, Precaution and Participation" (2003) RECIEL 12:1 at 45–69.

multiple sectors of human rights, investment, trade, law of the sea, and the environment.

Certain principles which aim to contribute to and achieve sustainable development *as an objective* may come to be used so often, and to be accepted so generally, that they do, indeed, gain recognition as customary international rules themselves, binding on all States that have not persistently objected.[42] The ILA New Delhi Declaration thus notes that "sustainable development is now widely accepted as a global objective and that the concept has been amply recognized in various international and national legal instruments, including treaty law and jurisprudence at international and national levels . . ."[43] Given the comprehensive and balanced decade of study and analysis conducted by the Committee and the relative normative clarity of their findings, the 2002 New Delhi Declaration provides the most current benchmark of the important principles of international law on sustainable development.[44] These principles can be found in a later chapter of this volume, and need only be briefly mentioned here.

First, the New Delhi Principles recognize a duty of states to ensure sustainable use of natural resources whereby States have sovereign rights over their natural resources, and a duty not to cause (or allow) undue damage to the environment of other States in the use of these resources. Second, they recognize a principle of equity and the eradication of poverty. Third, they recognize a principle of common but differentiated obligations. Fourth, they recognize the principle of the precautionary approach to human health, natural resources and ecosystems. Fifth, they underline the principle of public participation and access to information and

42 In the 1972 Stockholm Declaration, the 1987 Brundtland Commission's Legal Experts Group on Principles of International Law for the Protection of the Environment and Sustainable Development, the 1992 Rio Declaration, the 2002 World Summit on Sustainable Development Johannesburg Plan of Implementation, several international experts reports and other processes, States and legal scholars sought to identify principles of international law related to sustainable development. In 2002, the International Law Association's Committee on the Legal Aspects of Sustainable Development released its New Delhi ILA Declaration on Principles of International Law relating to Sustainable Development as a Resolution of the 70th Conference of the International Law Association in New Delhi India, 2–6 April 2002. See "ILA New Delhi Declaration of Principles of International Law Relating to Sustainable Development" (2002) 2 *Int'l Environmental Agreements* 209; N. Schrijver and F. Weiss, "Editorial Introduction" (2002) 2 *Int'l Environmental Agreements* 105; see also International Law Association, *Report of the Expert Group on Identification of Principles of International Law for Sustainable Development* (ILA, London 1995); International Law Association, *Report of the Sixty-Second Conference* (ILA, Seoul 1987) 1–11, 409–87.

43 N. Schrijver and F. Weiss, *International Law and Sustainable Development: Principles and Practice* (Lieden: Martinus Nijhoff, 2004) 1–152, 699–706; *Cordonier Segger & Khalfan (supra note 22)* 95–191; D. French, *International Law and Policy of Sustainable Development* (Manchester: Manchester University Press, 2005); See also 7 CISDL Legal Working Papers detailing the meaning, scope and existing status in international law of each proposed ILA New Delhi Declaration Principle, online: <http://www.cisdl.org/projects001.html>.

44 M.C. Cordonier Segger, "Significant Developments in Sustainable Development Law and Governance: A Proposal" (2004) 28 *Natural Resources Forum* 61; M.C. Cordonier Segger et al., "Prospects for Principles of International Sustainable Development Law after the WSSD: Common but Differentiated Responsibilities, Precaution and Participation" (2003) 12:1 *R. Eur. Community Int'l Envtl. L.* 54.

justice. Sixth, a principle of good governance is posited, noting that development activities become meaningless if the benefits are lost through waste, corruption or other governance challenges. Seventh, the Declaration recognizes a principle of integration and interrelationship, in particular in relation to human rights and social, economic and environmental objectives. This last may indeed be simply another more accurate name for a norm sometimes described in shorthand a 'principle of sustainable development.' This list is not exhaustive. And not all are yet recognized as binding rules of customary international law. In some cases, they might never be. However, they are increasingly forming part of international law and policy in the field of sustainable development. As such, certain rather functional principles are gaining recognition by States, and may be relevant to future decisions of courts and tribunals.

In summary, as noted by Boyle and Freestone, "[e]ven if there is no legal obligation to develop sustainably, there may nevertheless be, through incremental development, law 'in the field of sustainable development'."[45]

Indeed, though more remains to be done, over the past decade in these areas of intersection and conflict, there have been striking international advances in sustainable development law. This volume seeks to canvass, from the perspective of authors and experts from many areas of law, and many regions of the world, the recent experiences of international courts, tribunals and other dispute settlement measures that have sought to set this difficult balance, in the interests of present and future generations.

1.4 Sustainable development in the world's courts

Some may still argue that the concept of sustainable development is only an aspiration, and not really law – and hence our courts should not concern themselves with it. However, as is demonstrated in the chapters of this book, the concept of sustainable development is a substantive part of international law in a very real sense. It is an object and purpose of many treaties and legal instruments. It has even been suggested that sustainable development has an interstitial normative force.[46] It can drive law-makers (including judges, treaty negotiators and others) to accommodate, to reconcile, and even to integrate intersecting and conflicting social, economic and environmental priorities towards development that can last. And it encompasses a body of principles and practices that are gaining increasing recognition in international law on sustainable development or, in short, in 'sustainable development law.'

Sustainable development must, at least in part, be achieved through law. The judiciary, being such an important part of the legal establishment, must necessarily be involved in this. This involvement must be sensitive, and sensible.

---

45 *Boyle and Freestone, supra* note 24 [17], citing P. Sands, *International Law in the Field of Sustainable Development.*

46 V. Lowe, "The Politics of Law-Making: Are the Method and Character of Norm Creation Changing?" in M. Byers, ed., *The Role of Law in International Politics: Essays in International Relations and International Law* (Oxford: Oxford University Press, 2000) at 214–15, where it is proposed that sustainable development can be considered an interstitial norm to resolve conflicting economic development and environmental claims.

Sustainable development is currently one of the vibrant topics in the development of both domestic and international law. It is also probably one of the least developed among the myriad legal topics that come up before the courts. In international law, this is even more so. Sustainable development law is one of the least developed areas of international law. It is, as yet, a concept that has only begun to mature, so far as modern law is concerned. As a young idea, it needs to be fostered and nurtured. Treaties and legislation cannot anticipate the nuances of the myriad practical problems that could arise. When cases involving sustainable development arise, tribunals will often find themselves called upon to apply a broad general approach, the detailed implications of which have not yet been considered by scholars or regulators. It is very much like the situation of common law judges, who with only the broadest of general guiding principles, fashioned an intricately nuanced system of law to meet a number of situations which the formal law giver had not and could not have anticipated.

Justice systems are at the cutting edge of the development of sustainable development. Both domestically and internationally, judges will need to show imagination, initiative and vision in handling a matter so deeply fraught with implications for the global future. Only this imagination, initiative and vision can move us toward 'sustainable justice.' A poignant circumstance is associated with this need to develop more sustainable justice. Disregard for the balance between economic development, social justice and environmental protection causes harm to two classes of humanity in particular – the poor, and the unborn. Neither of these groups has more than a fledgling ability to assert its rights. Justice systems take up a very particular task in this regard. They must play a role to hold the balance true between powerful interests, on the one hand, and the voiceless, on the other. Justice could be seen to hold an extremely significant fiduciary duty, a trusteeship, in this regard.

1.5 Overview of this volume

Existing literature discusses the decisions of international tribunals on particular disputes, often from within the 'silo' of one pillar of sustainable development, be it economic, environmental or human rights. An expanding and under-studied body of jurisprudence balances and integrates these aspects of sustainable development, particularly through activation of the New Delhi Principles of Sustainable Development. This collection aims to fill the current knowledge gap on how sustainable development principles are being recognized and used in judicial decisions.

In this volume, the application and interpretation of the principles of international law on sustainable development by international and regional courts, tribunals and dispute settlement bodies is documented and considered, highlighting the leading judicial cases and statements for each of the seven New Delhi Principles. This analysis can contribute to academic debates, but might also serve as a tool for practising jurists preparing to make arguments based on the sustainable development principles in order to resolve future disputes.

Such international law research can also inform policy-makers and other stake-holders on the growing use of sustainable development principles in reasoned deliberations of courts and tribunals around the world to resolve real and pressing disputes. The growing acceptance of sustainable development principles may also inform multi-level efforts to implement the global Sustainable Development Goals. As a contribution to the international discussion surrounding the current status and areas for future focus regarding the New Delhi Principles of Sustainable Development, it is hoped that this analysis will be useful for judges, jurists, scholars, academics and students, but also policy-makers, civil-society organizations and other actions concerned with sustainable development around the world. In particular, this volume aims to provide an overview and analysis of decisions by international courts and tribunals that have applied and interpreted legal principles of sustainable development outlined in the 2002 New Delhi Declaration.

In doing so, the works of learned authors collected herein are seeking to achieve several objectives. First, the research monitors the evolution of principles on sustainable development in international law from soft law standards towards recognition as customary law in certain instances. Second, it analyses the judicial interpretation of principles on sustainable development by leading international and regional courts, tribunals and dispute settlement bodies. Third, it highlights the leading dispute settlement decisions that exhibit significant progress made in the interpretation of principles on sustainable development. As such, it examines the differences and commonalities in application amongst courts with jurisdiction over the environment, human rights, trade, investment and international crime, amongst others. Fourth, it assesses remaining practical, legal, political and economic challenges to further judicial consideration and acceptance of the principles. Fifth, it seeks to facilitate and support the application and interpretation of the principles by practising jurists in helping to resolve future disputes that touch upon sustainable development matters.

The book can be described with reference to its six principal sections.

First, the Foreword is provided by H.E. Judge C.G. Weeramantry (former Vice-President of the International Court of Justice; founder, Weeramantry International Centre for Peace Education and Research; and laureate of the UNESCO Prize for Peace Education). Two Prefaces are also kindly provided, by H.E. Judge James Richard Crawford (former Whewell Professor of International Law, University of Cambridge and Member of the International Court of Justice) and Justice Antonio Herman Benjamin, Judge of the Federal High Court of Brazil, and Chair of the IUCN World Commission on Environmental Law.

This introduction opens the volume, establishes the relevance of the sustainable development issues considered in today's emerging global context, positions the volume in related legal scholarship, introduces the structure and logic of the volume, and provides an overview of the chapters to come.

Part I then explains the concept of sustainable development, and the historical international law and policy context leading to the 2002 New Delhi Declaration. It also sets out the content and legal foundations of the seven principles of the

New Delhi Declaration of Principles of International Law relating to Sustainable Development. In Part I, Chapter 2 by Professor Marie-Claire Cordonier Segger provides an introduction to the origins and concept of sustainable development, surveying how it has been characterized in international treaties and tribunals on global, regional and bi-lateral levels. It explains that in the past 30 years, sustainable development has been increasingly recognized as an objective in international and regional treaties related to the environment, but also related to natural resources, trade and investment, and human rights of indigenous peoples, amongst others. It comments on the continuing gaps in legal scholarship and practice related to sustainable development, considering the challenges of implementing treaties on sustainable development at the national and local levels, and demonstrates how a better understanding of the legal principles related to sustainable development, including in specific disputes and cases, could contribute to both clarity and practical progress.

Then, in Chapter 3, with an introduction by Professor Nico Schrijver, the International Law Association's Committee on International Law on Sustainable Development's 2012 Report is reprinted, examining the historical, political and legal context within international affairs leading to the 2002 pronouncement of the New Delhi Principles. It recognizes the emergence of sustainable development as a key objective of the international community with the Brundtland Commission report in 1987 and Rio Declaration in 1992, and places the development of the concept of sustainable development in context with critical global trends. The Chapter suggests that these principles may be discerned to be gaining recognition in both treaty law and the decisions of international courts and tribunals.

Chapter 4 by H.E. Judge C.G. Weeramantry explores the basic characteristics of a global justice system, setting out a vision for international law that the author believes should be articulated, advanced and respected in order to achieve global sustainable development building on earlier works.

Part II explains the architecture and context of the international and regional courts, tribunals and dispute settlement bodies whose decisions are covered in the volume, explaining both *state to state* dispute settlement in international law, and also recent developments in international bodies mandated to consider disputes between *state and non-state actors.* It surveys recent debates on the potential to consider international judicial decisions as a relevant source of international law as it evolves, taking into account their value in providing reasoned responses to disputes on emerging global issues.

In Part II, Chapter 5 by Ms. Cairo Robb and Dr. Alexandra Harrington covers the mandates of the key state-to-state dispute settlement mechanisms in international law, and also recent developments in international bodies mandated to consider disputes between state and non-state actors. It surveys recent debates on the potential to consider international judicial decisions as a relevant source of international law as it evolves, taking into account their value in providing reasoned responses to disputes on emerging global issues that overlap in their economic, environmental and human rights aspects.

Then, Chapter 6 by Ms. Cairo Robb, Professor Marie-Claire Cordonier Segger and Ms. Caroline Jo surveys how international courts, tribunals and dispute settlement bodies are currently engaged in resolving disputes on trade and investment related to sustainable development, on human rights related to sustainable development, and on the environment related to sustainable development. The types of disputes, the mandates of the specific tribunals and the most significant cases are discussed and explained, providing essential background for the analytical chapters which follow.

Part III contains several chapters by leading international experts on sustainable development that discuss the application and interpretation of the New Delhi Principles in state-to-state dispute settlement mechanisms. These include decisions related to sustainable development from the International Court of Justice, the Permanent Court of Arbitration, the International Tribunal on the Law of the Sea, the World Trade Organization Dispute Settlement Mechanism, and other international and regional tribunals.

First, Chapter 7, with an introduction by Professor Duncan French, provides the main work of the International Law Association's Committee on International Law on Sustainable Development, the 2012 *Sofia Guiding Statements on the Judicial Elaboration of the 2002 New Delhi Declaration of Principles of International Law Relating to Sustainable Development.* Drawing on several ILA Reports, it examines the groundbreaking judicial statements of the International Court of Justice (ICJ) on the application and interpretation of the principles of sustainable development from 1992 to 2012. The ICJ jurisprudence addresses all seven principles, and is most developed with relation to the principles of sustainable use of natural resources, equity, precaution and integration. Sustainable use of natural resources has been proclaimed by the ICJ as relevant in international humanitarian law in the 1996 *Advisory Opinion on the Legality of the Threat or Use of Nuclear Weapons,* and military law in the 2004 *Advisory Opinion on the Legal Consequences of the Construction of a Wall in the Occupied Palestinian Territory.* Several ICJ decisions have noted the need for the just allocation of resources considering the interest of future generations under the principle of equity. Despite early ICJ jurisprudence that exhibited reluctance to incorporate the principle of precaution, the 2009 *Pulp Mills on the River Uruguay (Argentina v Uruguay)* decision declared that environmental impact assessments (EIAs) are necessary for major development projects under obligations of general international law, including customary international law. It suggests that this is a major step forward for the field of EIAs, and the precautionary principle has been strongly applied by the ICJ in subsequent cases. Finally, it suggests that a principle of integration is recognized in several key decisions of the ICJ, and demonstrates how the ICJ sought to achieve balance between environmental conservation, economic development and social needs, objectives that all fall together under the overarching concept of sustainable development.

Second, Chapter 8 by Professor Dire Tladi discusses the development of the sustainable development principles in the *Pulp Mills* case, a case which reveals the complexities of sustainable development and the approach of the ICJ. This chapter provides an analysis of the Court's consideration of the principles relevant to sustainable development in the *Pulp Mills* case and, in particular, assesses the contribution of the case to the evolution of sustainable development. It concludes that the Court's statement that the requirement to conduct EIAs is part of customary international law is a significant contribution to the law on sustainable development. However, the decision did not set the parameters to determine the 'quality' of the mandated EIAs, and by and large the Court chose to decide the case without consideration of sustainable development principles. Overall the decision contains a number of minority and separate opinions, one or two of which are destined to receive significant scholarly attention in the future.

Third, Chapter 9 by Professor Jorge Cabrera Medaglia and Mr. Miguel Saldivia Olave analyses the application of the principles of sustainable development in the 2011 *Certain Activities carried out by Nicaragua in the Border Area (Costa Rica v Nicaragua)* ICJ decision. Costa Rica instituted proceedings in the ICJ alleging Nicaragua's Army violated Costa Rica's territorial integrity, and further, Nicaragua breached their international treaty obligations by constructing and dredging along the San Juan River, causing serious damage to protected rainforests and wetlands within Costa Rica. The chapter outlines the environmental implications and legal framework of the dispute and discusses the ICJ's decision regarding Costa Rica's request for provisional measures. It highlights that this case established that States must be capable of preventing irreparable prejudice to natural resources, and the need for good governance and precaution to reduce tension and hostility in political disputes over territory and natural resources.

Next, Chapter 10 by Professor and Judge Marcel Szabó discusses the judicial statements relevant to the principles of sustainable development made in reference to the seminal *Gabčíkovo-Nagymaros* case, and in the context of other later cases in the ICJ. It analyses how the decision reflects both the principles of equity and of sustainable use of natural resources, as well as transparency and public participation, and integration. The chapter, provided by an esteemed international law expert and the Commissioner for Future Generations of Hungary, suggests the impacts of one of the most important cases for development of international legal reasoning in this field, while also commenting briefly on how these principles have carried forward in future ICJ reasoning.

The volume then turns to the decisions of the Permanent Court of Arbitration (PCA). First, in Chapter 11 by Professor Jennifer McKay provides a detailed analysis of the 2009 *Abyei Arbitration* and analyses the outcome of the case reflecting on the seven New Delhi Principles. It discusses how three principles – equity, public participation and access to information and justice, and good governance – are embedded as fundamental premises of the entire process due to their inclusion in the agreements underlying the dispute. The author then proposes the use of an adaptation of a legal content analysis to uncover nuances referencing other principles, outlines the methodology, and uncovers examples of the principle of public participation through this analysis. The chapter concludes that the New Delhi Principles are making their way into the jurisprudence of the PCA.

Second, Chapter 12 by Professor Freya Baetens examines the 2005 *Iron Rhine Arbitration* between Belgium and the Netherlands. The case concerned Belgium's request to reactivate the Iron Rhine train line which crosses Dutch territory and is authorized under the Iron Rhine Treaty of 1873. The Dutch Government opposed the reopening as the railway track passes through a nature reserve, and raises threats of habitat loss for endangered species. The chapter discusses the PCA's consideration of the principle of sustainable use of natural resources by other international courts and tribunals and the European Commission. It analyses the PCA's rejection of the Dutch request to make the reopening of the railway conditional upon the construction of a tunnel under the nature reserve with Belgium's cooperation.

The volume then discusses certain ground-breaking decisions of the International Tribunal for the Law of the Sea. First, Chapter 13 by Professor David Freestone and Mr. Freedom-Kai Phillips provides a brief overview of the 1982 United Nations Convention on the Law of the Sea (LOSC),[47] with a focus on its contributions to sustainable development principles and practices as seen in recent jurisprudence. Through a synopsis of key provisions of the LOSC and related international instruments, a discussion of the 2009 *Southern Bluefin Tuna* case, the 2011 Advisory Opinion of the Seabed Disputes Chamber of the International Tribunal on the Law of the Sea (ITLOS) on the Responsibilities and Obligations of States Sponsoring Persons and Entities with Respect to Activities in the Area,[48] and the Request for an Advisory Opinion Submitted by the Sub-regional Fisheries Commission (SRFC) of 2015, the chapter illustrates the evolving international legal responsibility of States for fishing vessels flying their flags and further developing the application of the 'due diligence' requirements,[49] providing a few conclusions relating to the contributions to sustainable development made by the LOSC and respective jurisprudence.

Second, Chapter 14 by Dr. Aline Jaeckel and Professor Tim Stephens also critically examines the jurisprudence of the ITLOS, highlighting leading international judicial statements on the interpretation of the principles of sustainable development. It provides an overview of the Tribunal's environmental competence and the classification of its cases, the majority of which have engaged with questions of environmental protection or sustainable resource management in some way. The chapter pays particular attention to the evolution of the precautionary

---

47 *United Nations Convention on the Law of the Sea*, (10 December 1982), UNTS No. 31363, <http://www.un.org/depts/los/convention_agreements/texts/unclos/unclos_e.pdf>. [LOSC, *Convention*]

48 Responsibilities and Obligations of States Sponsoring Persons and Entities with Respect to Activities in the Area, Case No. 17, Advisory Opinion (ITLOS Seabed Disputes Chamber Feb. 1, 2011), 50 ILM (2011), <https://www.itlos.org/fileadmin/itlos/documents/cases/case_no_17/adv_op_010211.pdf>. [ITLOS Advisory Opinion 2011]

49 Request for an Advisory Opinion Submitted by the Sub-regional Fisheries Commission (SRFC), Case No. 21, Advisory Opinion (ITLOS, 2 April 2015), <https://www.itlos.org/fileadmin/itlos/documents/cases/case_no.21/advisory_opinion/C21_AdvOp_02.04.pdf>. [ITLOS Advisory Opinion 2015]

principle in ITLOS decisions, from the nascent references to 'prudence and caution' in early decisions, to the strongest endorsement to date by any international court or tribunal of the precautionary principle in the Deep Seabed Advisory Opinion. The chapter contends that ITLOS, and the broader dispute settlement system under Part XV of the UN Convention on the Law of the Sea, is of critical importance for the development and implementation of a sustainable development agenda for the world's oceans.

Then the volume turns to the decisions of the World Trade Organization (WTO) Dispute Settlement Mechanism.

First, in Chapter 15 by Professor Markus Gehring and Mr. Alexandre Genest the decisions from the WTO Dispute Settlement Mechanism are examined for evidence of the application and interpretation of principles of sustainable development. It discusses alternative perspectives of the intersection between sustainable development and globalization. The WTO has identified the concept of sustainable development as a relevant factor in the interpretation of the WTO Agreement. The chapter examines the interpretation of four principles in particular: the precautionary principle, sustainable use of natural resources, common but differentiated responsibilities and integration. The WTO has accepted the precautionary principle as a principle of international environmental law and applied the principle to its decisions. However, it has refrained from recognizing it as a principle of customary law, and thus its legal status remains unsettled. The WTO decisions recognize the remaining three principles to some degree, but there is much space for more substantive integration of these principles.

Second, Chapter 16 by Dr. Jarrod Hepburn considers how aspects of the principle of good governance has manifested in the case law of the WTO over the last 20 years. It analyses the decisions of the WTO dispute settlement panels and the Appellate Body to assess the WTO's utility or instrumental success as a tool for achieving good governance at the national level. It focuses specifically on two aspects of good governance: the concepts of transparency and due process. The cases indicate that duties of transparency must be implemented carefully by national authorities to avoid provoking tension with other aspects of good governance such as impartial administration. Due process is examined through the lens of cases relating to the duty to give reasons for national administrative decisions. WTO case law can be seen to encourage improvement in the quality of national decision-making, but also emphasize the WTO's own position as part of the national decision-making structure, via its role of international review. The chapter concludes by noting the despite the fact that WTO case law addressing these concepts is not extensive, the existing decisions provide proactive application of the good governance principle and overall support for sustainable development.

Third, Chapter 17 by Dr. Henning Grosse Ruse-Khan analyses the extent to which WTO jurisprudence concerning the Agreement on Trade Related Aspects of Intellectual Property Rights (TRIPS) has utilized the principles of integration in addressing the manifold intersections between intellectual property (IP) protection and other economic, social and environmental concerns. Articles 7 and 8 of TRIPS represent IP-specific expressions of the sustainable development objective and its principle of integration. Panels have a legal obligation to interpret TRIPS in light of Articles 7 and 8 TRIPS. The chapter conducts an empirical analysis of the relevant TRIPS cases where the principle of integration was addressed, mentioned or applied. It concludes that the results paint a picture of a quantitatively limited, and qualitatively rather arbitrary use of TRIPS object and purpose in the interpretation exercise.

Fourth, Chapter 18 by Professor Joyeeta Gupta and Ms. Nadia Sanchez analyses the interpretation of the CBDR principle in the environmental literature and in WTO cases. The literature shows that the meaning of the common but differentiated responsibilities (CBDR) principle is contested; some argue that this is an inevitable translation of justice principles, others that this principle does not help to address environmental problems. The WTO's key principle is trade without discrimination. And yet, there is an emergence of ideas of differentiation between countries which are being tested in cases before WTO Panels. The WTO Panel clearly recognizes the need to differentiate in terms of capabilities. It also sets precedents on the scope and limits of differentiation and argues in favour of seeing differentiation as temporary and context dependent. The literature and precedents thus provide a first step towards articulating the boundaries of interpretation of the CBDR principle.

In Part IV, the volume turns away from State-to-State disputes, and considers decisions and awards relating to sustainable development in state-to-other dispute settlement mechanisms. In particular, Part IV offers chapters discussing the interpretation of the principles of sustainable development in dispute settlement mechanisms that involve non-state actors, including human rights courts, investor-state arbitral tribunals, regional courts that accept submissions from individuals, the Aarhus Convention Compliance Committee, and the World Bank Inspection Panel.

The volume considers several decades of decisions by human rights courts. First, Chapter 19 by Ms. Stephanie Safdi and Dr. Sébastien Jodoin examines the interpretation of the principles of sustainable development in the international human rights regime. It provides an overview of the foundations in international human rights law for economic, social, and cultural rights and environmental protection, and the relation of these rights to the principles of sustainable development. The United Nations has set up several general and treaty-based bodies with the mandate to promote and investigate the achievement of human rights. The chapter analyses the reports and decisions of these bodies to reveal a rich and growing body of interpretation of the principles of sustainable development.

Second, Chapter 20 by Professor Hennie Strydom examines two cases of the African Commission, namely *SERAC v Nigeria* and *Centre for Minority Rights Development (Kenya) v Kenya*. In both cases, the Commission has broken its long-standing silence on socio-economic rights and in doing so has also ventured into the applicability of sustainable development principles in factual situations where environmental rights and the right to development have played a major role. The Commission has invoked case law developments in other regions of the world,

notably in the Americas. The chapter concludes that this comparative method
has the added value that environmental law principles and notions of sustainable development will increasingly assume a universal meaning and importance in
determining whether states have acted with due diligence in responding to the
environmental and development rights and interests of their citizens.

Third, Chapter 21 by Ms. Alexandra Keenan examines the main sources of
law and constituted bodies of the Inter-American Human Rights system and
discusses instances and potential for incorporation of the principles of sustainable development. The American Declaration on the Rights and Duties of Man
is the world's first human rights instrument of a general nature. The Declaration
gives competence to two adjudicating bodies: the Inter-American Commission
on Human Rights and the Inter-American Court of Human Rights. The Court
is a source of progressive statements of law on several principles of sustainable
development, including sustainable use of resources, integration and openness.
The chapter discusses the progress within the Court's jurisprudence, notes that
the key concepts are developed in relation to indigenous and tribal rights, and
asks whether these concepts can translate to a broader societal context.

Fourth, Chapter 22 by Dr. Armelle Gouritin examines the extent to which
the European Convention of Human Rights as it is applied and interpreted
by the European Court of Human Rights endorses and applies the New Delhi
Principles. It is demonstrated that, even though the Convention does not mention the word 'environment', the Court has had a very dynamic approach and
endorses some elements of the Principles (either in substance or formally). The
chapter will focuses on the duty of states to ensure sustainable use of natural resources, the principle of the precautionary approach to human health,
natural resources and ecosystems, the principle of participation and access to
information and justice, and the principle of integration and interrelationship,
in particular in relation to human rights and social, economic and environmental
objectives. It is then demonstrated that the Court's dynamism is nevertheless limited: the Court cannot endorse the intrinsic approach to the environment. This
limit is explained and illustrated with regard to the Principles.

Then, in a second section, the volume turns to Investor-State Arbitral
Tribunals.

First, Chapter 23 by Mr. Antony Crockett analyses the statements related
to the principle of integration made in arbitral tribunals established under the
International Convention on the Settlement of Investment Disputes (ICSID).
It discusses cases involving investor claims of harm due to uncompensated
expropriation when host governments take measures ostensibly in pursuit of
environmental or social objectives. It finds that arbitral tribunals undertake a
balancing exercise that assesses the proportionality between the legitimate and
reasonable expectations and the host State's legitimate regulatory interest in
regulating domestic matters in the public interest.

Second, Chapter 24 by Dr. Avidan Kent examines the application of the
principle of public participation both within the tribunals' own processes and in
the substantive issues between parties dealt with under ICSID. It traces the history

of investment tribunals, from the initial intention to create a non-politicized, commercially natured dispute settlement mechanism to the more recent conflicts between this mandate and the increasingly public nature of investment treaty arbitration. Notably, the tribunals have no specific mandate to examine issues of sustainable development and are in fact limited by ICSID to deciding disputes in accordance with the rules of law agreed by the parties. The chapter notes that the principle has little acceptance in the substantive matters of the court. However, there is growing acceptance of its applicability in the court process itself, which reflects an evolution of the principle from an application only to decision-making processes by states to becoming relevant to quasi-private tribunals on matters that affect the public interest. The chapter concludes that this could be part of the changing nature of global governance, in which transnational corporations and civil organizations are increasingly involved in national and international governance.

Third, Chapter 25 by Dr. Jonathan Bonnitcha examines the extent to which arbitral tribunals have invoked the principle of good governance, as understood in the New Delhi Declaration, in resolving investor-state disputes arising under international investment treaties. It analyses the relevant jurisprudence and describes the findings of specific arbitrations that apply sub-principles of good governance, specifically transparency, corruption and due process. It concludes that that integration of the principle of good governance into the reasoning of investor-state arbitral tribunals is partial and incomplete, and, to the extent it has occurred, that there is considerable complexity in the nature of integration.

Next, the volume turns to the diverse approaches of different Regional Courts and Dispute Settlement mechanisms.

First, Chapter 26 by Professor Marie-Claire Cordonier Segger and Professor Markus Gehring provides an overview of the incorporation of the concept of sustainable development within the European Community, and its judicial application by the European Court of Justice. It traces the evolution of the concept from its first enunciation as 'harmonious development' in the 1957 Treaty of Rome to the most recent pronouncement as both a principle and primary objective of the 2009 Lisbon Treaty. A European definition of 'sustainable development' has emerged in policy documents and in an *ad hoc* manner in secondary European Union law. The European Court of Justice itself, however, provides a rich body of law under which the concept of sustainable development has continually been applied, interpreted and evolved. The Court has taken a cautious approach, limiting its judicial review to findings of manifest error and applying a high, but not technically the highest, standard to its review of legislative decisions. Despite this, the chapter outlines a strong development of many of the New Delhi Principles of Sustainable Development.

Second, Chapter 27 by Professor Zsuzanna Horváth discusses the emergence of two principles, environmental integration and precaution, in European Union law, and their meaning and interpretation by EU institutions, scholars and EU Courts. It examines the EU Treaties and the case law of the European Court of Justice and the General Court (the former Court of First Instance). It concludes that environmental integration and precaution can be considered general principles of EU law. They serve as instruments for the interpretation of law, contribute to the assessment of the validity of secondary norms, and form binding obligations for EU institutions in the exercise of their competencies. The case law shows that the principles are not yet fully fledged and require further clarification for more effective application but nonetheless play a key role in the strengthening of EU environmental policy.

Third, Chapter 28 by Professor Sumudu Atapattu discusses the emergence of sustainable development jurisprudence in South Asia. The courts in South Asia have been instrumental in expanding the concept of rights in South Asia by interpreting existing rights in a very expansive manner. This chapter discusses some of the seminal cases in South Asian courts in India, Pakistan, Bangladesh, Nepal and Sri Lanka, and evaluates to what extent the cases have contributed to the development of a sustainable development jurisprudence in the region. This chapter looks at a region that boasts of an ancient civilization that led a very sustainable way of life many centuries ago. Notably, the Supreme Court of India has been a most active judiciary in the region and its influence on other courts in the region has been considerable.

Fourth, Chapter 29 by Ms. Danielle Turnquest Moulton and Ms. Stephanie Forte discusses the emergence of sustainable development jurisprudence in the Caribbean, with particular relevance to how the precautionary principle has been reflected in regimes and disputes relating to management of fisheries and oceans resources in the region. The new regional Caribbean Court of Justice has only begun to build up its own jurisprudence. This chapter discusses some of the seminal cases in the Caribbean, and evaluates to what extent principles such as transparency and public participation, sustainable use of natural resources, precaution and integration have contributed to the resolution of disputes. It considers potential future directions for the Caribbean Court of Justice, drawing on key jurisprudence from the region, and analysing how important cases have reflected these important principles.

Fifth, Chapter 30 by Mr. Phan Tuan Hung and Mr. Alexander Kenny analyses the cooperation principles of the Agreement on the Cooperation for the Sustainable Development of the Mekong River Basin in comparison to the principles of sustainable development in the New Delhi Declaration. Although this agreement, which was created to resolve disputes among countries, is primarily inter-state, it includes participation of individuals and civil society, among others, in its 'soft' dispute resolution modalities. The Agreement commits four countries, Thailand, Laos, Cambodia and Vietnam, to jointly manage the shared water resource and develop the economic potential of the river. The chapter describes the current legal and institutional framework for cooperation and dispute settlement in the Mekong River basin in accordance with the Agreement. It concludes that although the principles of sustainable development are largely embedded into the Agreement, the role of the dispute settlement mechanisms is still limited and there is a need for further practical implementation.

Further, the volume considers dispute resolution mechanisms in international organizations

First, Chapter 31 by Mr. Andriy Andrusevych and Ms. Caroline Jo examines the application of the principles of sustainable development in the practice of the Compliance Committee of the Aarhus Convention. As a leading international text on participation rights, the Committee's decisions on access to information and access to justice and participation rights provide leading and innovative interpretations of this principle.

Second, Chapter 32 by Professor Sabine Schlemmer-Schulte analyses the decisions of the World Bank Inspection Panel for evidence of the principles of sustainable development. The Panel provides a forum for persons who believe that they may be adversely affected by Bank-financed operations to bring their concerns to the highest levels of the World Bank. The Panel's mandate is to ensure accountability and that Bank-financed operations provide social and environmental benefits while avoiding harm to people and the environment. The chapter assesses the evidence from the Panel in relation to the World Bank's success in achieving these goals on integration, good governance and public participation.

Third, Chapter 33 by Mr. Dane Ratliff examines the application of the principles of sustainable development in the practice of the Non-Enforcement of Environmental Law Article 14 and 15 Factual Reports Process of the North American Commission for Environmental Cooperation between Mexico, the US and Canada. As a key international mechanism to examine claims of non-enforcement of environmental regulations related to trade, environment, and a special process for participation rights, the Committee's decisions on enforcement of environmental laws provide leading and innovative interpretations of several sustainable development principles.

Fourth, Chapter 34 by Dr. Alexandra Harrington and Dr. Valentina Duran considers how the principles of access to information, public participation and access to justice are reflected in the accountability mechanism established by the Inter-American Development Bank.

Finally, the Part V Conclusion offers scholarly and practical legal analysis of the judicial application and interpretation of the New Delhi Principles of Sustainable Development. Building on the analysis in the volume, it provides a focused overview and comparative analysis of the judicial breakthroughs and trends. It provides tools for immediate use for those aiming at understanding the current status of these principles and furthering their application in courts and tribunals worldwide. It summarizes key conclusions on the strengths and weaknesses of the juridical interpretations of the principles that are discussed in the book, and offers advice to the law-makers and legal practitioners around the world seeking to further the application of these principles in national and international regimes.

In particular, the final chapter by Marie-Claire Cordonier Segger, Ms. Francesse J. Cordon and Dr. Alexandra Harrington provides a concise and focused overview that discusses and analyses the key findings and ground-breaking cases discussed in the volume. It argues that the principles of sustainable development are at the cutting edge of international law. They provide new legal foundations that have served to guide and support States designing more equitable and sustainable access to information laws, judges called upon to decide on complex issues of sharing of natural resources, and citizens petitioning for access to clean water and air. The chapter discusses each of the seven New Delhi Principles in turn, taking special account of the 2012 Sofia Guiding Statements developed by the International Law Association's Committee on International Law on Sustainable Development from 2002–2012, and highlighting the leading judicial statements and their implications in international law and global affairs. It also provides a scholarly and practical legal analysis of the application and interpretation of the principles of sustainable development in the New Delhi Declaration. It summarizes key conclusions on the strengths and weaknesses of the juridical statements discussed in the book, and offers advice to the law-makers and legal practitioners around the world seeking to further the application of these principles in national and international regimes.

Part I

Evolution of international law and policy on sustainable development

2 Commitments to sustainable development through international law and policy

Marie-Claire Cordonier Segger

> We assume a collective responsibility to advance and strengthen the interdependent and mutually reinforcing pillars of sustainable development – economic development, social development and environmental protection – at the local, national, regional and global levels.
>
> *2002 Johannesburg Declaration*, World Summit on
> Sustainable Development

2.1 Introduction

Of nearly 200 countries that exist today,[1] a vast majority are considered 'developing countries'.[2] What exactly constitutes development, however, remains unclear in fact and in law. Many economic development decisions have significant environmental and social implications, and the notion of 'sustainable development' has gained a great deal of currency in international debates over the past two decades since the World Commission on Environment and Development's report, *Our Common Future*, was released in 1987. However, sustainable development remains hard to define in a universal way. When states commit 'to promote sustainable development' in a treaty, or agree to conduct their economic relations 'in accordance with a principle of sustainable development', the implications of this commitment are not always clear.

In this chapter, the origins of sustainable development as a concept are reviewed and its meaning in international law is examined. Definitions of 'development', 'sustainability' and 'sustained yield' in current literature are discussed, along with their inception in natural resource management and economics. It

---

1 James Richard Crawford, *The Creation of States*, 2nd edn (Oxford: Oxford University Press, 2006) at 727.

2 The World Bank, "World Bank list of economies (July 2007)", online: The World Bank <http://siteresources.worldbank.org/DATASTATISTICS/Resources/CLASS.XLS>; Organisation for Economic Co-operation and Development, "*Development Assistance Committee's List of Recipients of Official Development Assistance*", online: Organisation for Economic Co-operation and Development <www.oecd.org/dac/stats/daclist>; United Nations Development Programme "2007/2008 Human Development Index rankings", online: United Nations Development Program <http://hdr.undp.org/en/statistics/>.

is argued that sustainable development, as a concept, bridges between the need for increased attention to development in order to end poverty, and the need to assess and respect the environmental limits and social impacts of economic growth. The international concept of sustainable development is briefly described and analysed.[3] It is argued that international consensus on this concept is emerging through global policy debates, from the 1972 United Nations Conference on the Human Environment (UNCHE), the 1987 Brundtland Report, the 1992 United Nations Conference on Environment and Development (UNCED), the 1997 United Nations General Assembly Special Session on Sustainable Development, the 2002 World Summit on Sustainable Development, and the 2012 United Nations Conference on Sustainable Development (UNCSD), as reflected in the outcomes of the 2015 Sustainable Development Summit, the world's global Sustainable Development Goals.[4]

In the context of these global policy debates, stretching across nearly five decades, it is suggested that sustainable development, as a common goal and 'bridging concept', plays an important role in reconciling tensions between economic growth, social development and environmental protection activities. For instance, this normative function is particularly apparent in links between international trade, investment rules, and sustainable development.

The chapter then turns to how sustainable development is reflected in international law. It considers the evidence, in UN General Assembly resolutions, international tribunal decisions, treaties, and international environmental law literature, that sustainable development could be characterized as an emerging 'principle of customary international law'. Briefly explaining how such principles are usually identified in international law, it is discussed whether sustainable development might be defined as an emerging customary principle. It is argued that while there is a great deal of state practice related to sustainable development, it is not clear that as yet, States consider themselves to be bound by sustainable development as a legal principle, and it is also not clear that sustainable development in itself holds the 'fundamentally normative character' to be conceived as a customary principle *per se*. This is not due to some inherent lack of clarity and specificity of the concept, but rather because sustainable development has different implications for diverse resources and regions.

A second, more nuanced, option is then considered, that sustainable development is better characterized as an objective of international law and our interactive international system of governance, as an 'object and purpose' of many different treaties, one which has certain 'interstitial' characteristics. In support of this

---

3 This chapter shares thoughts with previous works of the Centre for International Sustainable Development Law, of which the author serves as Senior Director, and the author's work in M. C. Cordonier Segger and A. Khalfan *Sustainable Development Law* (Oxford: Oxford University Press, 2004) 95–191; M. C. Cordonier Segger, "Sustainable Development in International Law" in D. Armstrong and other works. See also <www.cisdl.org> for notes on how each principle has been reflected in international treaty law on sustainable development over several decades.

4 *Transforming our World: The 2030 Agenda for Sustainable Development*, UNGA A/Res/70/1, Preamble.

view, recent international treaty law is surveyed, along with unanimously agreed statements about international law on sustainable development, and the views of international scholars. After considering these examples, the *New Delhi Principles of International Law Relating to Sustainable Development* [New Delhi Principles] are briefly discussed, laying the foundations for the rest of this volume.

2.2 Making development sustainable

Sustainable development refers to State efforts to achieve progress (development), qualified by the condition that the efforts should be possible to maintain over the long term ('sustainable'). International understanding of both concepts has evolved a great deal in recent decades, and like other important terms (peace, democracy, human rights), they can mean different things in diverse contents. Finding one accepted definition is like trying to hit a series of moving targets in all regions of the world, simultaneously.

2.2.1 Evolving definitions of development

First, it is useful to consider what is meant by 'development'. Scholarship and practice in this area has evolved in recent years. Originally, development efforts were intensely focused on increasing economic growth, and development policies aimed mainly to increase a State's gross domestic product (GDP). In the era of post-World War II reconstruction, it was believed that modernization and economic progress could help 'backward, traditional societies' to end poverty.[5] Not surprisingly, however, attempts to impose one model of development on many diverse countries and cultures were not entirely successful. Fierce debates raged between those who espoused modernization and industrialization as the path to development, and those who critiqued these theories as colonial impositions leading to under-development in the global south, or the majority world.[6] In the late 1980s and 1990s, inspired by *Our Common Future* (the Brundtland Report) and other international processes, a new model emerged which focuses on a human-centred approach, where development is seen as an iterative process which seeks to improve human conditions and find viable livelihoods for peoples in developing countries. This view is found in the Preamble to the 1986 Declaration on the Right to Development, which defines development as "a comprehensive, economic, social and cultural process which aims at the constant improvement and well-being of the entire population and of all individuals on the basis of their active, free and meaningful participation in

5 Frans J. Schuurman, ed., *Beyond the Impasse: New Directions in Development Theory* (London: Zed Press, 1993); Arturo Escobar, *Encountering Development: The Making and Unmaking of the Third World* (Princeton, NJ: Princeton University Press, 1995).
6 Fernando Henrique Cardoso and Enzo Faletto, *Dependency and Development in Latin America* (Berkeley: University of California Press, 1979); James D. Cockcroft, Andre Gunder Frank and Dale L. Johnson, eds., *Dependence and Underdevelopment: Latin America's Political Economy* (New York: Anchor Books, 1972).

development and in the fair distribution of the benefits resulting therefrom."[7] While debates do persist in some contexts, most international institutions active in development theory and practice, including the United Nations Development Programme, the World Bank, the International Monetary Fund, the Organisation for Economic Co-operation and Development (OECD), as well as many developed country international aid agencies, have now adopted a variation of this approach.[8] Development efforts focus on poverty reduction and on the socio-economic strategies and programmes of States which seek to improve livelihoods and promote better quality of life for communities and individuals, especially in developing countries.[9] In 2000, the Millennium Development Goals provided an important global set of targets that countries agreed to with respect to international development.[10]

As such, development can be defined as the processes of expanding people's choices, enabling improvements in collective and individual quality of life, and in the exercise of full freedoms and rights. Indian Nobel Laureate Professor Amartya Sen, in *Development as Freedom*, provides theoretical underpinnings for this approach. As he describes it, development is a process of expanding the real personal freedoms that people might enjoy.[11] The expansion of freedoms, as Sen notes, can be explained through recognition of the 'instrumental' and 'constitutive' roles of development (the means and the ends). There are, according to Sen, five particular instrumental freedoms,[12] areas in which the individual opportunities and capabilities of citizens living in developing countries could be improved. Sen's second category of 'economic facilities' refers to the opportunities that individuals might enjoy to utilize economic resources for the purposes of consumption, production or exchange.[13] In this context, Sen argues, the rules and regimes which open and stabilize the markets of a developing country, in a way that respects other aspects of development, can improve the general respect for the exercise of fundamental rights and freedoms.

7　The Declaration on the Right to Development, adopted 4 Dec. 1986, G.A. Res. 41/128, UN GAOR, 41st Sess., at 3, Annex, UN Doc. A/Res/41/128/Annex (1987) at Preamble.

8　For instance, UNDP focus areas include Democratic Governance, Poverty Reduction, Crisis Prevention and Recovery, Energy and Environment and HIV/AIDS, *United Nations Development Programme Focus Areas*, online: United Nations Development Programme <http://www.undp.org/focusareas/>. The OECD works on the areas of Economy, Society, Governance, Finance, Innovation and Sustainability, *OECD Topics*, online: OECD <http://www.oecd.org/maintopic/0, 3348,en_2649_201185_1_1_1_1_1,00.html>.

9　See, e.g., United Nations Development Programme, *Human Development Reports*, online: United Nations Development Programme <http://hdr.undp.org/>; see also Gustavo Esteva, "Development" in Wolfgang Sachs, ed., *The Development Dictionary: A Guide to Knowledge as Power* (London: Zed Press, 1992).

10　*United Nations Millennium Development Goals*, online: United Nations <http://www.un.org/millenniumgoals/> [*Millennium Development Goals*]; see also United Nations Millennium Declaration, G.A. Res. 55/2, UN GAOR, 55th Sess., Supp. No. 49, at 4, UN Doc. A/55/49 (2000).

11　Amartya Sen, *Development as Freedom* (Oxford: Oxford University Press, 1999) at 35.

12　Ibid. at 38 (the five sub-categories are (1) political freedoms, (2) economic facilities, (3) social opportunities, (4) transparency guarantees and (5) protective security).

13　Ibid. at 39.

While many indicators exist for development, the Human Development Index (HDI) is the most widely accepted. It provides a comparative measure of life expectancy, literacy, education, and standard of living among countries, seeking to assess human well-being rather than economic ranking. It is used by the UNDP in its annual Human Development Report to determine and indicate whether a country can be considered developed or 'still developing,' by estimating the average quality of life for citizens of the country. The HDI was developed in the 1990s by international development economists such as Sen and Pakistani economist Mahbub ul Haq. It focuses attention on three basic dimensions of human development: a long and healthy life (as measured by life expectancy at birth); knowledge (as measured by the adult literacy rate and the combined primary, secondary, and tertiary gross enrollment ratio); and a decent standard of living (as measured by the log of gross domestic product per capita at purchasing power parity in USD). Each year, UN Member States are listed and ranked according to these measures. A HDI of 0.8 or more is considered to represent a high level of development, and is found in all developed countries, including North America, Western Europe, Oceania and Eastern Asia, as well as some developing countries.

From a pragmatic point of view, there are nearly 200 countries in the world, and around 34 countries, as members of the OECD, are considered developed countries.[14] Another 25 non-members participate as regular observers or full participants in OECD Committees. According to the UNDP Human Development Reports, the great majority of the world's population lives in self-described 'developing countries' – at least 114 countries. Indeed, over 4 billion people live in countries ranking below 0.8 on the HDI. Further, a HDI ranking below 0.5 represents very low development. In 2006, there were 31 countries in this category, with 28 located in Africa, representing 568 million people.[15] In the 14 December 2015 HDI, it was found that 51 per cent, just over half of the world's population, live in countries with 'medium human development', while 18 per cent, nearly a fifth of the world's population, live in countries falling in the 'low human development' category. As such, a great deal remains to be done.

2.2.2 Origins of 'sustainable development'

While development means much more than mere economic growth, growth (measured in increases of per capita GDP) is still a central factor in development theory, indicators and practice. This focus on economic growth, however, has

---

14 As testimony to the evolving nature of development, in May 2007, OECD countries agreed to invite Chile, Estonia, Israel, Russia and Slovenia to open discussions for membership of the organization and offered enhanced engagement, with a view to possible membership, to Brazil, China, India, Indonesia and South Africa. Many of these countries, along with several small island states which enjoy a very high standard of living, have specific historical or geographical circumstances which make them difficult to categorize 'pragmatically'.

15 UNDP, Human Development Report 2006 (New York: UNDP, 2006); UNDP, Human Development Report 2015 (New York: UNDP, 2015).

become a subject of considerable international debate. Certain critiques were ethical – disagreement with the anthropocentric and utilitarian nature of the development concept, as it focuses on using the earth's resources to improve only human quality of life, rather than to improve conditions for all species of life on earth.[16] An important criticism of the economic growth aspect of development, however, has emerged in global debates on the nature of development. The concern is that if populations continue to increase and all human beings adopt the extraction, production, consumption and pollution patterns that are currently common in developed countries, humanity will quickly exceed the carrying capacity of the world's resources, leading to collapse. In short, these voices argued, current models of economic development are unsustainable. They cannot be maintained and hence their benefits will not last over time. The sustainability critique was initially brought forward by developed country scientists, economists and environmentalists, but the arguments quickly gained political currency and became reflected in international discourse. It was countered by developing countries. As States hold sovereignty over their own natural resources, most were unwilling to accept internationally imposed limits on the exploitation of these resources. They argued that if developed countries achieved their present standard of living due to such exploitation (unsustainable or not), it is patently unreasonable (and unworkable) to seek to prevent developing countries from adopting the same patterns, no matter the impact on the environment or long term global survival. This was, essentially, a claim of inequity. In some United Nations General Assembly (UNGA) debates, it has been described as a 'right to development'.[17]

In certain sectors of natural resource development, where the common resource has a clear transboundary nature and can be studied scientifically (such as fish stocks, oceans and perhaps shared watercourses), the potential for depletion and collapse creates a very practical imperative for States to negotiate rational common management of the resource itself. But in other areas, particularly where impacts are diffused, global and cumulative over time (e.g. depletion of the common atmosphere, loss of global biological diversity, depletion of soil or water resources) and result from economic development patterns which are diffused, it is much more difficult to find a common starting point and develop an agreement on the goal of these new management regimes.

The global concept of sustainable development emerged in the 1980s as a way to bridge between these deadlocked views in developed and developing

16 The first concern, which relates to ethics, and the need for greater recognition of the intrinsic worth of all species of life, is common to many cultures and continues to be a basis for critiques of development decisions. It is often an objective of national and international environmental law on the conservation and preservation of nature, and protection of endangered species, which is not the topic of this chapter.

17 Declaration on the Establishment of a New International Economic Order, UNGA Res. 3201 (S-VI) of May 1, 1974, UN Doc.A/Res.3201(S-VI); See also Declaration on the Right to Development, UNGA Res. 41/128, annex, 41 UN GAOR Supp. (No. 53) at 186, UN Doc. A/41/53 (1986).

countries, to address these concerns about the long term sustainability of international, national and local development policy objectives. In its simplest form, the concept of 'sustainable development' provides that common global objective, which permits States to co-operatively design policies to improve the quality of life of their populations in ways that have the potential to last over the long term. This is not without international legal relevance. Indeed, during this same period, States have set new international policy directions, while also conducting negotiations in particular areas which have resulted in international law.

In order to understand what sustainable development means, and whether there is an international consensus on its principal elements and scope, it is useful to trace the origins of the concept, and the main debates about it in international relations. This provides a basis to put forward a stipulated definition of 'sustainable development' as it is currently understood in international relations, and to then carefully examine the status of sustainable development in international law, before focusing on the evolution of a global trade and sustainable development agenda.

2.2.2.1 Prior to the 1987 Report of the UN Commission on Environment and Development

The term 'sustainable development' is first documented in laws governing forest industry management practices (*Forstordnungen*) in Europe toward the end of the eighteenth century.[18] According to these laws, only as much of the forest was permitted to be harvested as would grow again each year, so that the forest as a whole (the natural capital stocks) would be maintained. Gifford Pinchot, a noted American forester who founded the Yale School of Forestry in the early 1900s, later built on these ideas to advance a strategy of 'wise use' of natural resources. As such, it is important to note that the concept of sustainable development, from inception, did not involve stopping economic activity but rather a *re-direction* of such activity, in order to ensure the potential for long-term, *sustained* yields.[19]

The need for societies to develop while living within certain environmental limits has been recognized since ancient times and across diverse civilizations.[20] However, global concern about the direction of economic development practices increased dramatically in the recent century.[21] As noted in the writings of early political economists Thomas Malthus and David Ricardo, in the early 1900s concerns were raised about the prospect for economic growth to continue over the long-term. As Malthus argued, partly in reaction to the 'social contract' philosophies of

18 See *Lexikon der Nachhaltigkeit*, online: <http://www.nachhaltigkeit.aachener-stiftung.de>.
19 D. W. Pearce and R. K. Turner, *Economics of Natural Resources and the Environment* (Baltimore: John Hopkins University Press, 1990) at 6–7.
20 See *Case Concerning the Gabčíkovo-Nagymaros Project (Hungary/Slovakia), Separate Opinion of Vice President Weeramantry*, [1997] ICJ Rep. 7, 37 ILM 162 (where the concept of sustainable development is traced to the practices of ancient tribes in Sri-Lanka, Eastern Africa, America and Europe, and in Islamic legal traditions) [herinafter, *Gabčíkovo-Nagymaros*].
21 See, e.g., Human Development Reports, *supra* note 9.

Jean-Jacques Rousseau and others, there exists a danger that populations could simply continue to increase until diminishing returns from agricultural production, due to the fixed quantity of land, forces standards of living down to subsistence levels (or worse).[22] Similarly, as Ricardo noted, economic growth will be limited by the scarcity of natural resources, hence effective conservation measures are essential if human survival is to be assured.[23]

These early debates on the sustainability of development patterns gained currency and began to influence public opinion in many countries. The discourse focused at first on the need to preserve natural resources, flora and fauna. In 1962, the UN General Assembly, building upon an earlier 1961 UNESCO statement, passed a Resolution that called for natural resource, flora and fauna protection measures to be taken at the earliest possible moment simultaneously with economic development, noted that such development may jeopardize irreplaceable natural resources, flora and fauna, underlined the importance of economic development and the need for 'rational use' of natural resources, and called for fullest technical assistance and cooperation to be provided to developing countries in this respect.[24] In 1972, a seminal report, *Limits to Growth*, was released by the Club of Rome, forecasting widespread economic, social and environmental collapse if countries did not learn to recognize and respect absolute limits to growth, especially population control.[25] The 1973 oil crisis fueled the debates, as did growing awareness of endangered species and large scale pollution. In many developed countries, discourse shifted to focus on the need for protection of the environment, more broadly. Many national environmental authorities were established at this time.

In 1972, the United Nations called an international Conference on the Human Environment (UNCHE), which resulted in the *Stockholm Declaration on the Human Environment*,[26] the creation of the United Nations Environment Programme, and increased impetus to agree on certain multilateral environmental agreements (MEAs) such as the 1973 *Convention on International Trade in Endangered Species* (CITES).[27] The Stockholm Declaration implicitly recognizes, in Principle 14, the need to reconcile conflicts "between the needs of

---

22 Thomas Robert Malthus, *An Essay on the Principle of Population* (Oxford: Oxford University Press, 1999).

23 David Ricardo, *On the Principles of Political Economy and Taxation*, 3rd ed. (London: John Murray, 1821).

24 *Economic Development and the Conservation of Nature*, G.A. res. 1831, UN GAOR, 17th Sess. (1962).

25 D. W. Pearce and R. K. Turner, *Economics of Natural Resources and the Environment* (Baltimore: John Hopkins University Press, 1990) at 6–7.

26 *Stockholm Declaration of the United Nations Conference on the Human Environment*, UN Doc. A/C. 48/14 (1972), 11 ILM 1461 (1972) [hereinafter Stockholm Declaration]. For discussion, see, e.g. G. D. Meyers and S. C. Muller, "The Ethical Implications, Political Ramifications and Practical Limitations of Adopting Sustainable Development as National and International Policy" (1996) 4 *Buff. Envtl. L. J.* 1. And see A. Geisinger, "Sustainable Development and the Domination of Nature: Spreading the Seed of the Western Ideology of Nature" (1999) 27 *B.C. Envtl Aff. L. Rev.* 43.

27 *Convention on International Trade in Endangered Species of Wild Fauna and Flora*, (adopted 3 March 1973), 993 UNTS 243, 12 ILM 1085.

development and the need to protect and improve the environment." Several elements of the Declaration underline the deep divides between developed and developing countries on a global environmental protection agenda. For instance, States agreed in Principle 11 that the "environmental policies of all States should enhance and not adversely affect the present or future development potential of developing countries . . ." and in Principle 23 which demands that ". . . it will be essential in all cases to consider the systems of values prevailing in each country, and the extent of the applicability of standards which are valid for the most advanced countries but which may be inappropriate and of unwarranted social cost for the developing countries."[28]

By the release of the 1980 *World Conservation Strategy* of the International Union for the Conservation of Nature (IUCN), which defines "the modification of the biosphere and the application of human, financial, living and non-living resources to satisfy human needs and improve the quality of human life," the term sustainable development was more generally recognized in global debates.[29] The *World Charter for Nature*, adopted by the UN General Assembly two years later, calls for 'optimum sustainable productivity,' affirming that in "formulating long-term plans for economic development, population growth and the improvement of standards of living, due account shall be taken of the long-term capacity of natural systems to ensure the subsistence and settlement of the populations concerned, recognizing that this capacity may be enhanced through science and technology."[30]

In 1983, responding to increasingly heated debates between developed and developing countries, the UNGA established the World Commission on the Environment and Development (WCED). While UNGA Resolution A/38/161 on the Process of Preparation of the Environmental Perspective to the Year 2000 and Beyond was understandably focused on the environment, the UNGA required equal representation of developing and developed countries on the special commission, and significantly, directed the commission to report both to the UNEP Governing Council and to the UNGA itself. The Resolution referred specifically to the need for sustainable development in the terms of reference for the Commission, which included:

(a) To propose long-term environmental strategies for achieving sustainable development to the year 2000 and beyond;

(b) To recommend ways in which concern for the environment may be translated into greater co-operation among developing countries and

---

28 Stockholm Declaration, *supra* note 26.

29 It contained a section entitled 'Towards Sustainable Development' which linked ecological destruction with poverty, population pressure, social inequity and trade relationships, laying out the need for a new international development strategy which could establish a more dynamic and stable world economy, stimulate accelerating economic growth, counter the worst impacts of poverty and promote greater equity.

30 *World Charter for Nature*, G.A. Res. 37/7, UN GAOR, 37th Sess., Supp. No. 51, UN Doc. A/37/7 (1983); 22. ILM 455 at para. 8.

between countries at different stages of economic and social development and lead to the achievement of common and mutually supportive objectives which take account of the interrelationships between people, resources, environment and development;

(c) To consider ways and means by which the international community can deal more effectively with environmental concerns, in the light of the other recommendations in its report;

(d) To help to define shared perceptions of long-term environmental issues and of the appropriate efforts needed . . .[31]

The WCED, chaired by Prime Minister Gro Harlem Brundtland of Norway, embarked on a global series of consultations and through an Experts Group on Environmental Law also designed a series of legal principles and recommendation on environmental protection and sustainable development, which will be discussed later in this chapter.

In 1987, the Commission delivered its Report to the UNGA, *Our Common Future*.[32] The most generally accepted definition of sustainable development is found in this 'Brundtland Report' where it is defined as ". . . development that meets the needs of the present without compromising the ability of future generations to meet their own needs,"[33] which was drafted by a small working group of the World Commission in two hours.[34] The Brundtland Report found that the critical objectives for environment and development policies, which "follow from the need for sustainable development must include preserving peace, reviving growth and changing its quality, remedying the problems of poverty and satisfying human needs, addressing the problems of population growth and of conserving and enhancing the resource base, reorienting technology and managing risk, and merging environment and economics in decision-making."

The *Brundtland* definition of sustainable development, and the contents of the Report, were accepted by the UNGA in Resolution 42/187, 'Report of the World Commission on Environment and Development', which reiterates the concerns of the UNGA about the "accelerating deterioration of the human environment and natural resources and the consequences of that deterioration for economic and social development," and states that:

---

31 *Process of Preparation of the Environmental Perspective to the Year 2000 and Beyond*, Meeting no. 102, UN GAOR, 19 December 1983, UN Doc. A/RES/38/161.

32 World Commission on Environment and Development, *Our Common Future* (Oxford: Oxford University Press, 1987) at ix.

33 Ibid. at 43.

34 Interview with Prof. Hans-Christian Bugge, University of Oslo Faculty of Law, and former legal staff to the World Commission, notes on file with author.

Believing that sustainable development, which implies meeting the needs of the present without compromising the ability of future generations to meet their own needs, should become a central guiding principle of the United Nations, Governments and private institutions, organizations and enterprises . . .

The Resolution recognized a "common interest of all countries to pursue policies aimed at sustainable and environmentally sound development" – differentiating the two. It also noted the importance of "a reorientation of national and international policies towards sustainable development patterns" and emphasized "the need for a new approach to economic growth, as an essential prerequisite for eradication of poverty and for enhancing the resource base on which present and future generations depend."

Significantly, the UNGA also agreed with the Commission that "while seeking to remedy existing environmental problems, it is imperative to influence the sources of those problems in human activity, and economic activity in particular, and thus to provide for sustainable development", orienting the focus of future work on sustainable development toward economic activities. Following the recommendations of the Brundtland Report, the UNGA agreed that "an equitable sharing of the environmental costs and benefits of economic development between and within countries and between present and future generations is a key to achieving sustainable development", and called upon all Governments to "ask their central and sectoral economic agencies to ensure that their policies, programmes and budgets encourage sustainable development and to strengthen the role of their environmental and natural resource agencies in advising and assisting central and sectoral agencies in that task." It also called upon the "governing bodies of the organs, organizations and programmes of the United Nations system to review their policies, programmes, budgets and activities aimed at contributing to sustainable development" and upon "other relevant multilateral development assistance and financial institutions to commit their institutions more fully to pursuing sustainable development in establishing their policies and programmes in accordance with the national development plans, priorities and objectives established by the recipient Governments themselves . . ."

Finally, the Resolution requested the "Secretary-General, through the appropriate existing mechanisms, including the Administrative Committee on Co-ordination, to review and co-ordinate on a regular basis the efforts of all the organs, organizations and bodies of the United Nations system to pursue sustainable development, and to report thereon to the General Assembly through the Governing Council of the United Nations."

A few points should be highlighted with regards to both this definition, and the UNGA Resolution which adopted it. First, the Resolution differentiates between the objective of sustainable development and the objective of environmental protection, though it considers them linked. In the mandates that it sets out, both the UNEP and environment ministries on one hand, and the Economic and Social Council (ECOSOC), other development institutions of the UN and economic ministries on the other, are tasked with different specific duties. Second, the Brundtland definition grounds the need for sustainable development with a claim for equitable opportunities for development between and among generations, rather than, for instance, a claim about the need to prevent environmental damage as such.[35] It focuses on 'needs', especially the essential needs of the world's poor, to which overriding priority should be given.[36] It can be suggested that these elements, as the concept has evolved, provide a basis to integrate a stronger social and human rights aspect into the concept of sustainable development. Third, the Brundtland Report found that there are 'carrying capacity' limits to development which must be understood and respected, indeed, it showed that some of these limits were already being stretched nearly to breaking point in the 1980s. However, these limits are imposed not by the actual environment *per se*, which is always changing, but instead by the current state of technology and social organization on the environment's ability to meet human needs.

Overall, the Resolution makes it clear that in 1987, the UNGA did not see the concept of sustainable development as merely a 'compromise term' for more environmentally sound exploitation of natural resources, or a softer, more 'development-friendly' way to refer to new environmental policies in developing countries. It meant a new objective for governments and the international system, a common goal to design and implement a 'new kind of development' in certain specific economic sectors (such as agriculture, forestry, fisheries), one that can last over the long term. It called for new efforts at international and national levels to reorient economic programming and policies toward sustainable development. However, the Resolution also identifies the need for sustainable development to become a 'central guiding principle' of the UN, governments and other institutions. The question of whether sustainable development is an objective, a principle or somehow both will be discussed in greater depth in the rest of this chapter.

---

35   Edith Brown Weiss, *In Fairness to Future Generations: International Law, Common Patrimony and Intergenerational Equity* (Tokyo/New York: UNU/Transnational Publishers, 1989) at 17–26.

36   Ibid. In particular, the WCED stated that:

> "Sustainable development must be viewed in a global context, not as just applicable in the Third World. Rather, it requires changes in the domestic and international policies of every nation. *Sustainable development is development that meets the needs of the present without compromising the ability of future generations to meet their own needs.* It contains within it two key concepts. The concept of 'needs', in particular, the essential needs of the world's poor, to which overriding priority should be given; and, the idea of limitations imposed by the state of technology and social organization in the environment's ability to meet present and future needs . . . Even the narrow notion of physical sustainability implies a concern for social equity between generations, a concern that must logically be extended to equity within each generation . . . Perceived needs are socially and culturally determined, and sustainable development requires the promotion of values that encourage consumption standards that are within the bounds of the ecological possible and to which all can reasonably aspire . . ." (Emphasis added).

2.2.2.2 The 1992 UN Conference on the Environment and Development and the UNCSD

In 1992, in response to the Brundtland Report, the UN convened a global conference in Rio de Janeiro – the United Nations Conference on Environment and Development (UNCED, or the Rio Earth Summit).[37] The very name of the conference reflected a change in approach since the Conference on the Human Environment in Stockholm. While the focus had once been on the human impact on the environment and assessing the relevance of the environment in terms of human need, the UNCED's approach presented a marked contrast. Here, in accordance with the issues signalled in the Brundtland Report and the UNGA Resolution which accepted it, the focus was on development needs, and how to integrate environmental considerations into development planning and economic decision-making. In 1992, public awareness about environmental issues had reached an extremely high level, and it was also becoming clear that traditional strategies for development were not yielding adequate results in developing countries. Developed country leaders were anxious to show their political concern, and developing country leaders were increasingly frustrated with what was perceived as attempts to limit their sovereign decisions concerning the use of natural resources for development. A scene of high tensions, vigorous debates and extremely active participation from civil society, scientists, business leaders and many others, the UNCED was broadly viewed as a global success. Specific outcomes included the 1992 Rio Declaration, a short consensus declaration agreed by the Heads of State assembled in Rio; the 1992 *Agenda 21,* which is annexed to the Declaration and contains an extensive global action plan on specific environment and development issues; and three international treaties signed by a record number of countries: the 1992 *United Nations Framework Convention on Climate Change,*[38] the 1992 *United Nations Convention on Biological Diversity,*[39] and the 1994 *United Nations Convention to Combat Desertification,*[40] which was only released two years later but had been negotiated in the framework of UNCED.

The Rio Declaration, a short document of twenty-seven principles, has a composite character.[41] These principles reflect the work of the World Commission

---

37 A. Kiss and D. Shelton, *International Environmental Law,* 2nd edn (New York: Transnational Publishers, 1994) at 67 [hereinafter *Kiss & Shelton*].

38 *United Nations Framework Convention on Climate Change,* opened for signature June 4, 1992 (entered into force March 21, 1994), 1771 UNTS 107, 31 ILM 849.

39 *United Nations Convention on Biological Diversity,* opened for signature June 5, 1992, 1760 UNTS 79, 143; 31 ILM 1004.

40 *United Nations Convention to Combat Desertification in those Countries Experiencing Serious Drought and/or Desertification, Particularly in Africa,* opened for signature 14 October 1994 (entered into force 26 December 1996), 1954 UNTS 3, 33 ILM 1328.

41 Rio Declaration on Environment and Development, Report of the United Nations Conference on Environment and Development, UN Doc. A/CONF.151/6/Rev.1, (1992), 31 ILM 874; *Agenda 21,* Report of the UNCED, I (1992) UN Doc. A/CONF.151/26/Rev.1, (1992) 31 ILM 874 [hereinafter *Agenda 21*].

on Environment and Development's Experts Group on Environmental Law,[42] which is discussed further in this chapter. Here, it is simply useful to note that the Rio Declaration affirms the focus on human development that is central to the concept of sustainable development, and lays out a series of 'principles' which can help to achieve sustainable development. It does not, significantly, provide one universal definition for the concept. However, there are several key elements of the Rio Declaration which can elucidate key elements of the 'new kind of development' that was being contemplated by the world community. In particular, the Declaration focuses on procedural changes, such as building scientific knowledge, undertaking impact assessment and promoting public participation in decision-making, which permit governments to take environmental concerns into account in development planning.

Agenda 21, which was negotiated by the States engaged in the UNCED process, complements the Rio Declaration by providing an 800 page 'blueprint' for sustainable development. It contains hundreds of recommendations specific to various different sectors of economic and other activities that States can undertake in order to turn the principles agreed in the Declaration into strategies and programmes.[43] The purpose of this 'blueprint' was to halt and reverse the effects of environmental degradation and to promote sustainable development in all countries.[44] The text of *Agenda 21* comprises four sections and a preamble. Its four sections are entitled "Social and Economic Dimensions,"[45] "Conservation and Management of Resources for Development,"[46] "Strengthening the Role of Major Groups"[47] and "Means of Implementation."[48] When they left the Earth Summit, States had agreed on many broad recommendations and policy directions which, it was hoped, could guide environment and development decision-making in the future.

---

42 Experts Group on Environmental Law of the World Commission on Environment and Development, *Environmental Protection and Sustainable Development* (London: Graham & Trotman/Martinus Nijhoff, 1987).

43 M. McCoy and P. McCully, *The Road From Rio: An NGO Action Guide to Environment and Development* (Amsterdam: Utrecht International Books, 1993) at 29.

44 Nicholas A. Robinson, ed., "*Agenda 21*: Earth's Action Plan" IUCN Environmental Policy and Law Paper No. 27 (1993).

45 Containing chapters on international cooperation to accelerate sustainable development in developing countries, poverty, consumption patterns, demographic dynamics, human health, human settlements and integrating environment and development in decision-making.

46 This section deals with the more traditional environmental problems and contains chapters concerning atmosphere, land resources, deforestation, desertification and drought, mountain ecosystems, sustainable agriculture and rural development, biological diversity, biotechnology, oceans and seas, fresh waters, toxic chemicals, hazardous wastes, solid and sewage wastes and radioactive wastes.

47 Section 3 contains chapters pertaining to the roles in achieving sustainable development to be played by women, children and youth, indigenous people, non-governmental organizations, local authorities, workers and trade unions, business and industry, science and technology, and farmers.

48 This section addresses financing mechanisms, technology transfers, science, education, capacity building in developing countries, international institutional arrangements, international legal instruments and information for decision-making.

However, most of the details on sustainable development goals and standards, as well as commitments meant to achieve this objective, remained to be worked out through the specific conventions signed at the UNCED, and the new institutions recommended by the Conference.[49] In particular, the global treaties signed at the UNCED became one of the principal areas where new standards, rules and regimes helped to clarify the content of a commitment to sustainable development.

The Earth Summit, therefore, contributed to global understanding of the concept of sustainable development. First, the package of outcomes (Declaration, Plan of Action and three treaties), taken together, were designed to influence not only the policies of environmental authorities, but additionally the policies of economic development authorities, and even cover the responsibilities of some departments in charge of the social aspects of development such as health and education. As such, the Rio process clarified that the concept of sustainable development is different from, and goes beyond, an environmental agenda alone. Second, the Brundtland definition, which grounds the need for sustainable development with a claim for equitable opportunities for development between and among generations, rather than, for instance, a claim about the need to prevent environmental damage as such, was adopted and affirmed in Rio. Further, the outcomes contain specific provisions in which developed countries accept responsibilities vis-à-vis developing countries in this regard. Further, the UNCED outcomes strongly reaffirm the need to change procedural aspects of development decision-making.[50] While a stronger social and human rights aspect was not yet fully brought into the concept of sustainable development in Rio, the social development agenda itself was recognized and affirmed. All Rio outcomes recognize and accept the Brundtland recommendations that 'carrying capacity' limits to development which must be understood and respected, indeed, they underline, with a sense of urgency, that some of these limits were reached in the early 1990s. However, the focus of policy-making and international cooperation to address this challenge was further investment into new technology and new forms of social organization in order to permit further development that could meet human needs. The outcomes of Rio cannot be described as a set of global agreements to forego unsustainable development in exchange for a commitment to invest in sustainable development. However, the Rio Declaration, *Agenda 21* and the three treaties do present a great deal of guidance for key sectors of national economies, and do contain commitments from developed countries to provide cooperation and technical assistance in these areas. This premise/promise was a key part of the concept of sustainable development itself in Rio.

One follow-up mechanism, which was recommended by the Brundtland Report and *Agenda 21*, was the creation of a specialized United Nations institution to carry the international sustainable development policy agenda forward. Its purpose would be to ensure the effective follow-up of decisions made at the Earth Summit, enhance international cooperation toward integration on environment

---

49 Brown Weiss, *supra* note 35 at 200.
50 Ibid.; see also *supra* note 36.

and development, and examine progress in the implementation of *Agenda 21*.[51] It was meant to address questions of sustainable development which went beyond cooperation on environmental issues, as these were being undertaken by the UN Environment Programme. A second, equally important mechanism involved the UNCED's recommendation to create a global environmental fund which would support the incremental costs of ensuring that development initiatives were also environmentally sound, in four main areas agreed at the Rio Earth Summit.

The UN responded by creating a Global Environment Facility (GEF), hosted by the World Bank, the UNEP, and the UNDP (as implementing agencies), which was funded by voluntary contributions from States. The UNGA also created the United Nations Commission for Sustainable Development (CSD) on 25 November 1992.[52] Its membership was limited to 53 countries each year on a rotational basis among all UN Members States, with non-members of the Committee having observer status.[53] Meeting on a yearly basis, the CSD was to review implementation of the *Agenda 21* at national, regional and international levels. In this manner, the CSD was to address all chapters every three years.[54] If an issue required a stronger legal framework, initial discussions might take place at the CSD, but would then be designated to an appropriate body to negotiate legally binding actions. After Rio, the CSD mandate was fairly broad.[55] The CSD made some progress over the next decade, but also faced many challenges.

In the years of the CSD's operations between 1992 and 2002, several critiques were raised by developing countries and others. These had expected the CSD to provide an effective body to monitor progress towards the target of 0.7 per cent GNP, ensuring adequate financing and the transfer of sustainable-development related technologies, but this was perceived not to have happened adequately. Rather, the CSD looked at finance and technology transfer themes in isolation from issues that might have enabled an effective argument for new funds. In addition, while occasionally development, transport, energy or agriculture Ministers would attend if a relevant sector was being discussed, CSD was not seriously attended by Ministers with budgets to deliver the promised 'additional

---

51   *Agenda 21*, *supra* note 41 at 38.11.

52   McCoy and McCully, *supra* note 43 at 45; Robinson, *supra* note 44 at 655.

53   The allocation of seats is 13 from Africa, 11 from Asia, six from Eastern Europe, 10 from Latin America and the Caribbean and 13 from Western Europe and North America. The Secretariat is the Division of Sustainable Development in the UN Department of Economic and Social Affairs (DESA). One of the interesting aspects of elections to the CSD is that they have been actively pursued by countries, unlike some other UN Commissions.

54   Ibid.

55   See Resolution A/1993/207. The mandate includes: to monitor progress on the implementation of *Agenda 21* and activities related to the integration of environmental and developmental goals by governments, NGOs and other UN bodies; to monitor progress towards the target of 0.7 per cent GNP from developed countries for Overseas Development Aid; to review the adequacy of financing and the transfer of technologies as outlined in *Agenda 21*; to enhance dialogue with NGOs, the independent sector, and other entities outside the UN system, within the UN framework; and to provide recommendations to the General Assembly through ECOSOC. McCoy and McCully, *supra* note 43 at 45.

financing for sustainable development.' This raised several critiques: the CSD was described as a 'talk shop' with excessive focus on environmental interests, without enough participation of development Ministries, or with limited machinery for implementation. The CSD had a record of certain achievements for international sustainable development policy, as opposed to law. Others argued that the CSD actually achieved much in the first decade of its mandate (Dodds, 2000).[56] The involvement of major groups at the CSD also increased each year, with innovative formal and informal participation procedures being developed.[57] There was a high level of involvement of civil society organizations and major groups in the 2002 World Summit on Sustainable Development (WSSD) process, where concrete steps were taken to ensure participation through many different channels. The CSD provided a platform for cross-sectoral dialogue, coordination and eventual cooperation which leads to international instruments in the long term.

Between 1992 and 2002, many countries began to implement specific commitments on sustainable development from the Rio outcomes. For instance, many governments have developed national or sub-national *Agenda 21*s, authorized special bodies to implement *Agenda 21*,[58] or even negotiated regional blueprints for sustainable development, such as the 1996 Santa Cruz de la Sierra Summit of the Americas on Sustainable Development for the Organization of American States, or indeed the complex treaty processes of the European Union.

Further, international organizations adopted sustainable development policies or objectives through their own internal decision-making procedures. These included

56 It produced recommendations to codify Prior Informed Consent procedures (1994); the establishment of an Inter-Governmental Panel on Forests (1995) and an International Forum on Forests (1997); support the Washington Global Plan of Action on protecting the marine environment from land-based activities (1996); the replenishment of the Global Environmental Facility (GEF) (1997); setting a firm date of 2002 for governments to produce their National Sustainable Development Strategies (1997); establishment of a new process in the General Assembly to discuss oceans (1999); agreement that new consumer guidelines would include sustainable development (1999); and development of an International Work Programme on Sustainable Tourism (1999).

57 In 1993, civil society groups gained rights of participation in informal and formal meetings and were allowed to speak. In 1994, NGOs were granted the right to ask their governments questions on their national presentations in front of their peer groups. In 1997, Dialogue Sessions were introduced as a series of 5 half-day Major Group presentations for ministers and officials, and representatives of Major Groups were invited to speak at the Heads of State meeting of the UN General Assembly Special Session for the first time. In 1999, Dialogue Session outcomes were included by the UN CSD Chair as part of the materials for Ministerial discussions, and as part of official UN CSD Intersessional documents for governments to draw upon in formulating their positions.

58 United Nations Commission on Sustainable Development, *National Information Report of the Secretary-General*, UN SECOR, March 5, 1996, UN Doc. E/CN.17/1996/19 (This document consists of a table summarizing national level co-ordination of actions pursuant to *Agenda 21*, and a matrix summarizing national priorities assigned to the various issues and current status. According to CSD, nations having taken these steps towards implementation include Australia, Benin, Belgium, Cameroon, Cuba, Canada, China, Egypt, Germany, Italy, Korea, Malaysia, Mongolia, New Zealand, Netherlands, Norway, Niger, Philippines, Portugal, Peru, Senegal, Switzerland, Sweden, United Kingdom and Zaire. In addition, over 55 nations are submitting reports to the CSD on *Agenda 21* implementation).

international economic development institutions such as the World Bank, the Organisation for Economic Co-operation and Development, the United Nations regional economic commissions, and the regional development banks, in addition to environmental organizations such as the World Conservation Union (IUCN) and the UNEP. Many of these institutions worked to implement particular recommendations from the UNCED, undertaking programmes on identification of scientific 'indicators' for measuring progress towards sustainable development;[59] design of operational guidelines which can curb worst excesses in development processes; identification and marketing of more 'sustainable' goods and services; and definition of what exactly the 'needs' of present and future generations might be. As will be discussed in greater detail below, *Agenda 21* also noted, as means of implementation of sustainable development, the need for international action to codify and develop 'international law on sustainable development.'[60]

2.2.2.3 The 1997 UN General Assembly Special Session on Sustainable Development

In 1997, a special session of the United Nations General Assembly, widely referred to as 'Earth Summit+5', was held in New York to review progress toward the objectives set in Rio. The session was attended by heads of state and governments from across the world. A relatively modest event, it reviewed and appraised implementation of *Agenda 21* and other commitments adopted by the 1992 Earth Summit. It sought to assess global progress made in sustainable development since Rio; to demonstrate the effectiveness of sustainable development by highlighting 'success stories' from around the world; to identify reasons why certain goals set in Rio had been met and suggest corrective action; and to highlight special issues; and to identify priorities for future action.

The UNGA called on governments, international organizations and major groups to renew their commitment to sustainable development. In the resulting Declaration, the *Programme of Further Action to Implement Agenda 21*, priorities were focused on particular sectors and issues where further work was needed, such as finance and technology transfer, patterns of production and consumption, use of energy and transportation, and scarcity of freshwater. The focus was on assessing progress since Rio, and calling attention to areas where action to implement *Agenda 21* recommendations was still slow, rather than further definition of the concept of sustainable development.

However, certain elements can be highlighted. First, in terms of procedural innovations, the 1997 UNGASS included formal mechanisms to engage civil

---

59   It not always clear that 'needs' are self-evident or capable of being discerned, and it is extremely difficult to discern how development can take place without compromising the ability of future generations to meet these needs. T. C. Trzyna, ed., *A Sustainable World: Defining and Measuring Sustainable Development* (Sacramento: California Institute of Public Affairs, 1995) at 23.

60   See in particular, *Agenda 21*, *supra* note 41 at Chapter 39, International Legal Mechanisms and Instruments, from paras 39.1–39.10.

society groups, through the 'major groups' identified in *Agenda 21*, in direct dialogue with State representatives, with space allotted to them in the official programme. Second, rather than States identifying sustainable development as a bridge between environment and development priorities, the texts began to emphasize that economic development, social development and environmental protection are three interdependent and mutually reinforcing 'pillars' of sustainable development.[61] As such, the social development aspect of the concept gained prominence. Further, as discussed below, in identifying the priorities for action to promote sustainable development worldwide, the need to further strengthen and codify international law related to sustainable development was highlighted.[62] The CSD continued to meet annually from 1997 to 2002, while States embarked on a cycle of global Conferences of Parties and global conferences.

Parallel to the UNGA-led global Summits and Special Sessions which adopted non-binding policy outcomes aimed at identifying points of global consensus on sustainable development issues, a track of legally binding negotiations on specific sustainable development challenges began to emerge. The treaties themselves are discussed in greater detail in the next sections of this chapter. However, it is important to note that over 180 States Parties to the 1992 UN Framework Convention on Climate Change, after five years of extremely arduous negotiations held in the context of annual Conferences of the Parties (COPs), in 1997 adopted the Kyoto Protocol for the reduction of greenhouse gases. The commitment to develop and adopt binding targets for such reductions was one of the important Rio Earth Summit outcomes. Similarly, over 180 States Parties to the 1992 UN Convention on Biological Diversity negotiated and adopted, through a parallel series of Conferences of the Parties, the *Cartagena Protocol on Biosafety* in 2000. This was another key commitment from Rio. And in the Conferences of the Parties to the *UN Convention to Combat Desertification and Drought*, States negotiated and adopted a series of regional and national Action Plans to define and address major challenges in this area while also linked to national Poverty Reduction Strategies. Further, another three international agreements were negotiated and entered into force. In particular, in the *UN Convention on the Law of the Sea*, the Straddling Stocks Agreement was finally signed. The *Stockholm Convention* and the *Rotterdam Convention* were also agreed, and entered into force. These agreements, and their contributions to our understanding of the concept of sustainable development, are discussed in the next section of this chapter.

The global Conferences, hosted by the United Nations, focused on building global consensus on a new meaning of 'development for all.' As part of the re-conceptualization of 'development', the United Nations negotiated and adopted

---

61 *Programme for the Further Implementation of Agenda 21*, General Asembly Resolution S-19/2. UN GAOR, 19th Special Sess. (1997), UN Doc. A/RES/S-19/2.

62 Ibid. at 109–10.

the Millennium Development Goals (2000), which provided a series of specific social, economic and environmental targets as reference points for achieving global development goals.[63] Further, the World Trade Organization (WTO) hosted a Meeting of World Trade Ministers in Doha, Qatar (2001), launching a new round of trade and economic liberalization negotiations, the so-called 'Doha Development Agenda', and while negotiations were not proceeding rapidly, many States were engaged in analysing the potential impacts and opportunities of these plans.[64] These developments are more carefully analysed in the next section of this chapter. Finally, the International Conference on Financing for Development in Monterrey, Mexico (2002) led to concrete commitments for new and additional developed country resources, earmarked for development spending.[65] As noted informally by one international expert, in the lead-up to the World Summit on Sustainable Development, "Monterrey committed new resources, but the WSSD still needs to decide how to spend them."[66]

2.2.2.4 The 2002 World Summit on Sustainable Development

The World Summit on Sustainable Development, held from 26 August to 4 September 2002, brought together an estimated 45,000 participants in Johannesburg, South Africa. Over 100 heads of state, and over 22,000 government delegates, international experts and non-governmental organizations and media representatives attended the Summit itself, from more than 189 countries.[67] Another 23,000 were represented at parallel events for business, scientists, civil

---

63 *United Nations Reform: Measures and proposals; and strengthening of the United Nations system,* General Assembly Res. 53/239, UN GAOR (5 September 2000), UN.Doc. A/RES/53/239; See also *Millennium Development Goals, supra* note 10.

64 The results of the WTO Ministerial Meeting in Doha, Qatar, November 2002, included the Ministerial Declaration WT/MIN(01)/DEC/1 (20 November 2001); A Declaration on the TRIPS Agreement and Public Health, a Decision on implementation-related issues and concerns, a Decision on Subsidies related to procedures for extensions under Article 27.4 (of the Subsidies and Countervailing Measures Agreement) for certain developing country members, a Decision on a waiver for EU-ACP Partnership Agreement, and a Decision on the EU transitional regime for banana imports. See WTO, online: <http://www.wto.org/english/thewto_e/minist_e/min01_e/min01_e.htm#declarations>.

65 Report of the International Conference on Financing for Development, A/Conf.198/11 (18–22 March 2002) See also Financing for Development, online: <http://www.un.org/esa/ffd/>.

66 Notes from interview with Mr. Richard Ballhorn, Director General, Environment and Sustainable Development Affairs Bureau, Canadian Department of Foreign Affairs and International Trade, on file with authors.

67 The official documents from the World Summit for Sustainable Development (WSSD) are available from the WSSD Secretariat, online: <http://www.johannesburgsummit.org/html/documents/summit_docs.html>. See also the *Johannesburg Declaration on Sustainable Development* and *Johannesburg Plan of Implementation* [hereinafter JPOI], in Report of the World Summit on Sustainable Development, Johannesburg, South Africa, 26 August to 4 Sept 4 2002, A/CONF.199/L.1. A full report is available from the Earth Negotiations Bulletin, online: <http://www.iisd.ca/linkages/2002/wssd/>.

society and other major groups.[68] The United Nations objectives for the Summit were to review the 1992 UN Conference on Environment and Development (UNCED) and reinvigorate global commitment to sustainable development.[69]

States hoped to focus on how best to *implement* sustainable development in a context of globalization and renewed commitments to international development assistance. The nature of the WSSD outcomes reflects this new focus. The Summit did produce a 2002 Johannesburg Declaration, and the *Johannesburg Plan of Implementation* (JPOI). Further, however, the Johannesburg outcomes built on the 1992 and 1997 changes in the procedural aspects of development decision-making. Johannesburg witnessed the launch of more than 200 'Type II Outcomes.' These were specific sustainable development partnerships between governments, civil society and industry, agreed under the auspices of the WSSD process and supported by the CSD, to achieve a set of measurable objectives and results focused on the implementation of sustainable development in specific areas.

The 2002 Johannesburg Declaration, rather than laying out principles as the Stockholm and Rio Declarations, simply provides a collective political commitment by States to sustainable development.[70] It outlines the path taken from UNCED to the WSSD, highlights present challenges, expresses a commitment to sustainable development, and then underscores the importance of multilateralism and emphasizes the need for States (and their international institutions), in partnership with civil society, the business community and others, to focus on the implementation of more sustainable development policies and programmes.

The JPOI is designed as a framework for action to implement the commitments originally agreed at UNCED, and address several additional issues that had arisen since the 1992 Conference. It includes eleven chapters. After an introduction, substantive chapters cover poverty eradication; consumption and production; the natural resource base; health; small island developing States (SIDS); Africa; other regional initiatives; means of implementation and the institutional framework (governance). The JPOI contains over thirty specific time-bound targets for action (including many that were already agreed in the Millennium Development

---

68 A full report is available from the Earth Negotiations Bulletin, online: <http://www.iisd.ca/linkages/2002/wssd/>.

69 In December 2000, the UN General Assembly decided to convene a ten-year review of progress since UNCED (A/RES/55/199). Despite ongoing efforts since the Stockholm Conference in 1972 to protect the environment and natural resources, the UNGA expressed concern about continuing deterioration. Therefore, UNGA called for the World Summit on Sustainable Development to focus on the status of *Agenda 21*'s implementation and the other Earth Summit outcomes. The WSSD's mandate was to identify further measures to implement the Rio agreements, accomplishments and areas where more effort and action-oriented decisions were needed, as well as new challenges and opportunities. The WSSD was to ensure balance among economic, social and environmental concerns and reinvigorate the global commitment to sustainable development.

70 2002 Johannesburg Declaration, in *Report of the World Summit on Sustainable Development*, 26 August to 4 September 2002, UN Doc. A/AC.257/32 at 5.

Goals and other agreements).[71] It shifts the focus to an integrated social and development agenda, one which highlights strategies to address poverty eradication, sanitation and health. New resources were committed to the Global Environment Facility, which agreed that desertification would be henceforth funded, as a new focal area. Specific attention was focused on certain important priorities identified by the UN Secretary-General, in the areas of water and sanitation, energy, health, agriculture and biodiversity (the so-called 'WEHAB' issues). By the end of the Summit a number of the WEHAB commitments set out in the JPOI had been linked to new 'voluntary' partnerships and financial commitments.[72]

The WSSD process did accomplish a further task. It set in place a broadened institutional architecture for sustainable development, to further implement *Agenda 21* and the WSSD outcomes, and to meet emerging sustainable development challenges.[73] JPOI Chapter XI lays out a multi-tiered international architecture for sustainable development governance, through which States seek to provide a strengthened and linked system of international bodies and organizations working toward sustainable development. The framework of this sustainable development regime is organized on three principal levels:

71 The other significant commitments from the meeting include: using and producing chemicals in ways that do not harm human health and the environment; reducing biodiversity loss by 2010; restoring fisheries to their maximum sustainable yields by 2015; establishing a representative network of marine protected areas by 2012; improving developing countries' access to environmentally-sound alternatives to ozone depleting chemicals by 2010; and undertaking initiatives by 2004 to implement the Global Programme of Action for the protection of the Marine Environment from Land Based Sources.

72 For example, a number of initiatives publicized at the Summit will support the JPOI commitment to halve the proportion of people without access to sanitation by 2015 together with the Millennium Declaration Goal to halve the proportion without access to safe drinking water by 2015. The US has announced US$970 million in investments on water and sanitation projects; the EU announced its "Water for Life" initiative; and the UN has received an additional 21 water- and sanitation-related initiatives worth at least US$20 million. Similarly, the JPOI commitment on energy access will be accompanied by financial commitments from the EU (US$700 million), the US (US$43 million), and 32 separate partnership initiatives worth up to US$26 million.

73 This process was initiated pursuant to a mandate from the UNGA. Ten-year review of progress achieved in the implementation of the outcome of the United Nations Conference on Environment and Development, UNGA Resolution A/RES/55/199 20 Dec 2000. The United Nations World Summit on Sustainable Development, Draft Plan of Implementation of the World Summit on Sustainable Development, A/CONF.199/L.1 26 Aug to 4 Sept 2002 can be found online: <http://www.johannesburgsummit.org/html/documents/summit_docs.html>. See also "Sustainable Development Governance", a paper prepared by the Vice-Chairs, Ositadinma Anaedu and Lars-Goran Engfeldt, online: <www.johannesburgsummit.org/html/documents/ prepcom3docs/governance30.3.rev1.doc>. This section shares thoughts with M. C. Cordonier Segger and M. Ivanova, "Sustainable Development Governance: Take Two", a concept paper prepared at the request of the South African Chair of CSD 11, April–May, 2003, on file with author.

- international (including the UNGA, the ECOSOC, and the CSD, but also other agencies and international organizations),[74]
- regional and sub-regional (including the United Nations Regional Commissions and other regional and sub-regional bodies, such as the regional development banks) and
- national (which includes different governments ministries, sub-national and local authorities).

The JPOI emphasized the need to strengthen and better integrate the social, economic and environmental dimensions of sustainable development into policies and programmes on all these levels. Sustainable development governance was clearly differentiated from international environmental governance (IEG), which is addressed elsewhere in the UN system.[75] In the JPOI, the international architecture for sustainable development was broadened, existing fragmentation was recognized, and a rather complex grouping of mechanisms was identified to coordinate coherence.[76]

First, the JPOI encouraged collaboration between facilitated by the United Nations Chief Executive Board (CEB), the UN Development Group, the Environmental Management Group (EMG) and other high level inter-agency coordinating bodies. In particular, the Secretary-General of the United Nations was asked to use the CED to further promote system-wide inter-agency cooperation and coordination on sustainable development, to take appropriate measures to facilitate exchange of information, and to keep ECOSOC and CSD informed of actions being taken to implement *Agenda 21*.

74 Further information on the United Nations Commission on Sustainable Development and its relationship to other international organizations can be found at the UN CSD website online: <http://www.un.org/esa/sustdev/csd.htm>. Further information on the broader United Nations system of agencies, and their relationship to other international organizations, can be found at the UN website, online: <http://www.un.org>.

75 A decision of the UNEP governing council addresses issues and options for strengthening international environmental governance. The decision includes: UNEP is to be greatly strengthened and given adequate, more secured financing; there is a special role for the Global Environmental Facility (GEF) in terms of financing environmental projects; coordination will be enhanced, including the further development of an Environmental Management Group (EMG) composed of relevant international organizations and treaty secretariats; there will be clustering of Multilateral Environmental Agreements (MEAs) along functional and programmatic lines; the General Assembly was invited, in 2002, to consider the important but complex issue of establishing universal membership for the Governing Council/Global Ministerial Environment Forum. Further information on the United Nations Environment Programme, and the international environmental governance negotiations, can be found at the UNEP website, online: <http://www.unep.org/IEG>. See also M. C. Cordonier Segger, A. Khalfan and M. Gehring, "International Environmental Governance for Sustainable Development", Centre for International Sustainable Development Law (CISDL), online: <http://www.cisdl.org>.

76 Further information on the International Conference on Financing for Development, held in Monterrey, Mexico from 18–22 March, 2002, can be found at the ECOSOC website, online: <http://www.un.org/esa/ffd>.

Second, to address existing fragmentation and segmentation of mandates, the UNGA was asked to adopt sustainable development as a key element of the overarching framework for UN activities. This sets a global mandate in place, and the JPOI refers directly to the contributions of different UN agencies to sustainable development.[77] It also, rather significantly, refers to the need for increased collaboration by those outside the UN system, such as the international financial institutions (IFIs) and the World Trade Organization (WTO).

Third, the JPOI also grants a stronger role to the ECOSOC, especially in matters of coordination. ECOSOC was asked to increase its role in overseeing system-wide coordination, and to balance integration of economic, social and environmental aspects of the United Nations policies and programmes aimed at promoting sustainable development. As such, ECOSOC is to provide coordination and integration. It was mandated to promote greater coordination, complementarity, effectiveness and efficiency of those activities of its functional commissions and its other subsidiary bodies, those relevant to the implementation of *Agenda 21*.

The WSSD mandated the CSD to focus on reviewing and monitoring progress, and on fostering coherence of implementation, initiatives and partnerships.[78] For the next decade, the CSD would still develop recommendations, but only every two years, and the number of themes addressed at each session would be constrained. A UN Secretary-General Report on Follow-up to Johannesburg and the Future Role of the CSD[79] served to further refine the CSD, and mandated a shift from reporting and supportive normative discussions to tracking implementation, with a greater emphasis on specific sectors and mechanisms, and on promotion of overall integration of the three dimensions of sustainable development. In later years, after further reviews undertaken in the context of the 2012 UN Conference on Sustainable Development in Rio de Janeiro, and after the adoption in 2015 of 'Transforming our World: The 2030 Agenda for Sustainable Development' and its 17 inter-related Sustainable Development Goals, the CSD would be further transformed into a high level political forum on sustainable development. Such further evolutions of the global governance structure for sustainable development, perhaps intended to give greater weight to all three environmental, social and economic dimensions of the sustainable development, and also to provide a

---

77 The JPOI stresses that UNDP has capacity building programmes for sustainable development. It commits to strengthen cooperation among UNEP and other UN bodies and specialized agencies, the Bretton Woods institutions and the WTO, within their mandates. The UNEP, UN-Habitat, UNDP and UNCTAD are also expected to strengthen their contribution to sustainable development programmes and the implementation of *Agenda 21* at all levels, particularly in the area of promoting capacity building.

78 <http://www.earthsummit2002.org/es/issues/Governance/governance.html#Sustainable%20 Governance>. For more civil society and expert reviews of the functioning of the United Nations Commission on Sustainable Development, see the International Institute for Environment and Development (IIED) series on the World Summit for Sustainable Development, online: <http://www.iied.org/wssd/index.html>. See also the International Institute for Sustainable Development (IISD), online: <http://www.iisd.org>, and the Centre for International Sustainable Development Law (CISDL), online: <http://www.cisdl.org>. And for the official structure, see the Johannesburg Plan of Implementation of the WSSD, online: <www.johannesburgsummit.org>.

79 *Johannesburg and the Future Role of the CSD.* UN Doc. E/CN.17/2003/2.

more comprehensive and politically higher profile platform for debates within the United Nations, were already foreshadowed by the discussions at the WSSD, and the resulting reforms.

The CSD Chair and secretariat host 'Partnerships Fairs' in each CSD session.[80] Third, the JPOI mandates the CSD to review capacity-building, financial assistance and transfer of technology for sustainable development, an important point for developing countries. Fourth, the JPOI mandates the CSD to provide a forum for analysis and exchange of experience on measures that assist sustainable development planning, decision-making and the implementation of sustainable development strategies. The fifth of the new functions highlighted in the JPOI is the international mandate at 148 (e) to "[t]ake into account significant legal developments in the field of sustainable development, with due regard to the role of relevant intergovernmental bodies in promoting the implementation of *Agenda 21* relating to international legal instruments and mechanisms."

2.2.2.5 The 2012 United Nations Conference on Sustainable Development

As explained by the United Nations, the UN Conference on Sustainable Development – or Rio+20 – took place in Rio de Janeiro, Brazil on 20–22 June 2012, and resulted in a focused political outcome document laying out clear and practical measures for implementing sustainable development.[81] In Rio, Member States launched a process to develop a set of Sustainable Development Goals (SDGs), which will build upon the Millennium Development Goals and converge with the post-2015 development agenda. The Conference also adopted guidelines on green economy policies. Governments also decided to establish an intergovernmental process under the UNGA to prepare options on a strategy for sustainable development financing. Governments also agreed to strengthen the United Nations Environment Programme (UNEP) on several fronts with action to be taken during the 67th session of the UNGA. They agreed to establish a high-level political forum for sustainable development. Decisions on this entity's detailed form were taken during the upcoming session of the UNGA, with the aim of having the first session of the forum at the beginning of the 68th session of the UNGA. Governments also requested the United Nations Statistical Commission, in consultation with relevant United Nations system entities and other relevant organizations, to launch a programme of work in the area of measures of progress to complement gross domestic product in order to better inform policy decisions. Governments also adopted the 10-year framework of programmes on sustainable consumption and production patterns, as contained in document A/CONF.216/5,

---

80 See the UN Division for Sustainable Development website at www.un.org under 'Partnerships Fair.' The Partnerships Fair provides a venue to hear of the progress in WSSD and UNCSD partnerships, as well as an opportunity to network, identify or launch new partnerships and exchange lessons learned.

81 See 2012 United Nations Conference on Sustainable Development website at sustainable development.un.org/rio20, from which this section is directly cited.

and invited the UNGA, at its 67th session, to designate a Member State body to take any necessary steps to fully operationalize the framework. Further, the Conference also took forward-looking decisions on a number of thematic areas, including energy, food security, oceans and cities, and decided to convene a Third International Conference on SIDS in 2014. The Rio+20 Conference also galvanized the attention of thousands of representatives of the UN system and major groups. It resulted in over 700 voluntary commitments and witnessed the formation of new partnerships to advance sustainable development.

The focus on technical implementation in specific sectors of development, rather than general principles or new international instruments, has become evident in the international outcomes of the 2002 World Summit on Sustainable Development and the 2012 Rio+20 Conference. Unlike in the 1992 Rio Earth Summit, the Johannesburg World Summit on Sustainable Development and the Rio+20 UN Conference on Sustainable Development processes did not produce new international treaties. However, in the JPOI, States specifically named over 60 international agreements in economic, environmental and social fields, at bi-lateral, regional and international levels, all of which play a role in achieving sustainable development, and mentioned more than 200 others, ratifications announced at the World Summit permitted the entry into force of the *Kyoto Protocol* to the *UN Framework for Climate Change*. Further, specific commitments in the JPOI resulted in the development of a dedicated area of funding within the Global Environment Facility for the implementation of the *UN Convention to Combat Desertification*, as well as the launch of negotiations within the *UN Convention on Biological Diversity* on access to genetic resources and the sharing of its benefits, and reinforcement of the sustainable development elements of FAO negotiations on plant genetic resources for food and agriculture which later led to the FAO *International Treaty on Plant Genetic Resources for Food and Agriculture*. In *The Future We Want*, the negotiated declaration that was the outcome of the 2012 UNCSD, similarly, over 40 treaties and international instruments are specifically recognized, and the contributions of the judiciary are also highlighted.

The global policy debates have contributed certain further refinements to international understanding of the concept of sustainable development, and certainly popularized it. First, the Brundtland definition of sustainable development, and its nature as a 'new kind of development' were reaffirmed in Johannesburg, and in Rio+20, negotiations were launched for the world's new Sustainable Development Goals, later to be agreed in 2015 at a further Summit event. Second, these global events gave strong emphasis to the need to "advance and strengthen the interdependent and mutually reinforcing pillars of sustainable development – economic development, social development and environmental protection – at the local, national, regional and global levels." The outcomes of the global events, taken together, were clearly designed to influence not only economic and environmental authorities, but also those in charge of social issues such as human health, in a balanced way.

In Johannesburg, Rio and New York the social and human rights aspects of the sustainable development agenda were recognized and strongly affirmed. For instance, the 2015 Sustainable Development Goals integrate international 'social development' institutions such as the World Health Organization, the International Labour Organization, and the UN Development Programme to play a strong role in sustainable development. They focus on how to implement sustainable development, concluding that this requires the integration and reconciliation of social, economic and environmental policies related to development. As another example, *The Future We Want*, from 2012 Rio+20, clearly sought to combine priorities from all three sets of global regimes, to address challenges of poverty eradication; unsustainable consumption and production patterns; sustainable management of natural resources; a 'globalizing' world economy; and human health. It set in place a sustainable development 'governance' structure, which includes new clarity on the roles of international environmental, social and economic institutions, but also clearer sustainable development mandates for the UNGA, the ECOSOC and a High Level Political Forum on Sustainable Development. And it recognized that international efforts to achieve global sustainable development had moved beyond general principles and broad conceptual debates into specific projects for joint scientific research, education and programming in specific technical areas of cooperation (through, for instance, the Type II Partnerships) and in many other cases, through particular internationally agreed legal regimes (including several global, regional and even bi-lateral treaties).

2.3 An international meaning for 'sustainable development'?

Where does this review of global policy-making processes leave international law? The World Commission on Environment and Development sought to bridge between developed and developing countries in order to resolve serious problems of environmental degradation and lack of social and economic development. The concept of sustainable development provided that bridge. However, neither the 1992 Rio Declaration and *Agenda 21*, nor the 2002 Johannesburg Declaration and Plan of Implementation, nor 2012 *The Future We Want*, provide one universal definition of sustainable development that is agreed among States and covers all resources, all regions and all situations. The most accepted short description continues to be the one recommended in the 1987 Brundtland Report, which was adopted by the UNGA, when it stated that sustainable development "implies meeting the needs of the present without compromising the ability of future generations to meet their own needs."

This definition is not particularly helpful to determine the exact parameters of an international treaty commitment to 'sustainable development,' or the precise normative content of sustainable development in international law. As noted by Vaughan Lowe, how can one determine the needs of present generations? Are these needs also rights or entitlements? And how can one predict what will be the needs of generations to come?[82]

The world's thousands of societies have diverse traditions and cultures, livelihoods, climates and living conditions. Economists, scientists and development scholars are working to develop the necessary indicators and instruments which might help to answer these questions in diverse conditions and contexts. Above, it was noted that there is no single universal definition for 'development.' International development objectives continue to evolve, as does our understanding of sustainability for different sectors, societies and conditions. This makes it highly unlikely that there is one globally recognized definition for what constitutes 'sustainable development'.

And indeed, in global policy-making processes, especially through the two Summits in Rio and Johannesburg, States have not agreed on one definition for sustainable development. Rather, they have focused on developing greater global consensus on how to achieve it, signing and ratifying international treaties where necessary.

One international treaty attempts a more precise legal definition of sustainable development. In Article 3(1)(a) of the 2002 *Convention for Cooperation in the Protection and Sustainable Development of the Marine and Coastal Environment of the Northeast Pacific*. At Art 3(1)(a), States adopt:

> . . . [S]ustainable development means the process of progressive change in the quality of life of human beings, which places them as the center and primary subjects of development, by means of economic growth with social equity and transformation of production methods and consumption patterns, sustained by the ecological balance and life support systems of the region. This process implies respect for regional, national and local ethnic and cultural diversity, and full public participation, peaceful coexistence in harmony with nature, without prejudice to and ensuring the quality of life of future generations.[83]

The original treaty language is Spanish and a straightforward translation cannot do justice to the central concepts. With relation to 'development,' it focuses on a process of improvements in quality of life for human beings. With relation to 'sustainable,' it calls for economic growth which respects social equity, carried out through the transformation of production methods and consumption patterns, in such a way that there is respect for the ecological balance and life support systems of a particular area (in this context, the 'region' refers to Central

---

82 V. Lowe, "Sustainable Development and Unsustainable Arguments" in A. Boyle and D. Freestone, eds., *International Law and Sustainable Development: Past Achievements and Future Challenges* (Oxford: Oxford University Press, 1999) at 27. He references, further, "Agora: What Obligation Does Our Generation Owe to the Next? An Approach to Global Environmental Responsibility" (1990) 84 AJIL 190.

83 The 2002 *Convention for Cooperation in the Protection and Sustainable Development of the Marine and Coastal Environment of the Northeast Pacific*, 18 February 2002, City of Antigua, Guatemala. (Translation provided by author). Online: <http://www.cep.unep.org/services/nepregseas/Convention_English_NEP.doc>.

America and the regional sea in question). It also provides for other elements: respect for diversity, public participation, peaceful coexistence with nature and inter-generational equity.

Without further reviewing the many recommendations and targets found in the Brundtland Report, the outcomes of the Stockholm, Johannesburg, Rio and New York Conferences and Summits, and the new global Sustainable Development Goals, a general definition of sustainable development can be distilled which emphasizes certain key elements for the purposes of this volume.

In essence, sustainable development can be defined as a new type of development that does not irreversibly deplete essential natural capital, one that reconciles social, economic and environmental policies to enable improvements in present generations' quality of life, in a way that takes the interests of the future into account.

This definition emphasizes certain aspects of the concept that have been recognized by States in the global policy-making process. First, it focuses on sustainable development as human-centred, in that it involves finding new ways to improve quality of life for people. Second, it focuses on the need to reconcile and integrate environmental protection and social development with economic development. As such, sustainable development decision-making needs to take all three sets of priorities and rules into account in a balanced way. This can be done through procedures such as consultation among environment, social and economic development authorities; impact assessment; scientific collaboration and education; technical assistance and capacity building; and transparency and public participation. Third, development that is sustainable should be able to last over the long term. In order to do this, States need to determine and respect the environmental limits of ecosystems and resources. However, these limits are not static but rather are dynamic, and the relevant time horizon depends on the resource and ecosystem in question.

Over the past five decades, there has been an extensive policy-making process related to sustainable development, including the debates and outcomes of the 1992 UNCED, the 2002 WSSD, and the 2012 UNCSD, which has engaged nearly all countries of the world. The concept of sustainable development has served to bridge deep divisions between developed and developing countries. In Johannesburg and in Rio, States assumed "a collective responsibility to advance and strengthen the interdependent and mutually reinforcing pillars of sustainable development – economic development, social development and environmental protection – at the local, national, regional and global levels." Certain fields of resource development and other economic activity, especially in relation to sustainable management of the common atmosphere, biodiversity, energy, forests, agriculture, water and fisheries which appear in every global sustainable development declaration, are testimony to the focus of the sustainable development policy agenda. Relevant long-term focused development activities in these areas can involve sustaining yields, recycling, restoring or re-investing, rather than simple exploitation or preservation of a resource.

More specifically for international law, building on the conclusions of the 1987 Brundtland Report, in the 1992 *Agenda 21* States highlight the need for further efforts to develop and strengthen international law on sustainable development through procedural and substantive steps. At 108, they agree that "[a]ccess to information and broad public participation in decision-making are fundamental to sustainable development. Further efforts are required to promote, in the light of country-specific conditions, the integration of environment and development policies, through appropriate legal and regulatory policies, instruments and enforcement mechanisms at the national, state, provincial and local levels . . ." And at 109, they note that ". . . it is necessary to continue the progressive development and, as and when appropriate, codification of international law related to sustainable development. Relevant bodies in which such tasks are being undertaken should co-operate and coordinate in this regard." Further, at 110, they state that "[i]mplementation of and compliance with commitments made under international treaties and other instruments in the field of the environment remain a priority. Implementation can be promoted by secure, sustained and predictable financial support, sufficient institutional capacity, human resources and adequate access to technology. Cooperation on implementation between States on mutually agreed terms may help reduce potential sources of conflict between States . . ."[84] This direction was reaffirmed in the 2002 Johannesburg Declaration and Plan of Implementation, where States provided a further political commitment to sustainable development,[85] building on the outcomes of other recent global events, in the 2012 UNCSD, and in the global Sustainable Development Goals.

2.4 Sustainable development in international law: re-conceptualizing the debate

While the concept of sustainable development, like development, may have no single simple accepted universal definition, this does not require that the status of sustainable development in international law must also remain unclear. International law, as noted in the *Western Sahara* case, must be able to take note of different legal traditions and cultures, yet still continue to advance, and ". . . in the development of the international legal system it may be more important to

---

84 Under "International legal instruments and the Rio Declaration on Environment and Development"; further, at 110, States mention "[i]t is also important to further improve reporting and data-collection systems and to further develop appropriate compliance mechanisms and procedures, on a mutually agreed basis, to help and encourage States to fulfil all their obligations . . . under multilateral environmental agreements. Developing countries should be assisted to develop these tools according to country-specific conditions."

85 The 2002 Johannesburg Declaration states, at 5, "Accordingly, we assume a collective responsibility to advance and strengthen the interdependent and mutually reinforcing pillars of sustainable development – economic development, social development and environmental protection – at the local, national, regional and global levels." It notes "14. Globalization has added a new dimension to these challenges. The rapid integration of markets, mobility of capital and significant increases in investment flows around the world have opened new challenges and opportunities for the pursuit of sustainable development. But the benefits and costs of globalization are unevenly distributed, with developing countries facing special difficulties in meeting this challenge."

stress the imperative need to develop international law to comprehend within itself the rich diversity of cultures, civilizations and legal traditions . . ."[86]

Sustainable development has been the topic of a World Summit and the subject matter of at least a dozen international treaties. Sustainable development has also been part of the arguments before nearly all prominent international tribunals to date. In certain treaties and decisions, sustainable development has been characterized as an emerging principle of international law. In others, it can be described as a policy objective of international law, as the object and purpose of international treaties rather than a norm in itself.

While one does not necessarily preclude the other, the final section of this chapter discusses the differences between these views below, as an introduction to the rest of the volume which explores how various principles of sustainable development are reflected in the decisions of international courts, tribunals and dispute settlement mechanisms.

2.4.1 Defining sustainable development in international law

International environmental advocates have argued that sustainable development is a new customary principle of international law, one that is in the process of being established as binding upon States.[87] Scholars have suggested that it is a "general principle that states should ensure the development and use of their natural resources in a manner which is sustainable,"[88] stating that "there can be little doubt that the concept of sustainable development has entered the corpus of international customary law . . ."[89] H.E. Judge C. G. Weeramantry, while Vice-President of the International Court of Justice, also argued that sustainable development was a principle of international law in his Separate Opinion in the *Gabčíkovo-Nagymaros* case. In particular, he stated that he considers sustainable development to be "more than a mere concept, but as a principle with normative value which is crucial to the determination of this case."[90] Indeed, as he further explains, after reviewing many international commitments:

> The concept of sustainable development is thus a principle accepted not merely by the developing countries, but one which rests on a basis of world-wide acceptance. In 1987, the Brundtland Report brought the concept of

---

86 Sir Robert Y. Jennings, "Universal International Law in a Multicultural World" in T.M.C. Asser Institute, ed., *International Law and the Grotian Heritage: A Commemorative Colloquium on the Occasion of the Fourth Centenary of the Birth of Hugo Grotius* (The Hague: T.M.C. Asser Institute, 1985) at 195; cited with approval by H.E. Judge C. G. Weeramantry in his Separate Opinion, *Gabčíkovo-Nagymaros, supra* note 20 at 93.

87 D. Hunter, D. Zaelke, and J. Salzman, *International Environmental Law and Policy* (New York: Foundation Press, 2001); A. Kiss and D. Shelton, *International Environmental Law* (New York: Transnational Publishers, 2000); Philippe Sands, *Principles of International Environmental Law*, 2nd edn (Cambridge: Cambridge University Press, 2003).

88 Sands, *supra* note 87 at 252–66.

89 See generally Sands, *supra* note 87 at 252–66.

90 *Gabčíkovo-Nagymaros, supra* note 20.

sustainable development to the forefront of international attention. In 1992, the Rio Conference made it a central feature of its Declaration, and it has been a focus of attention in all questions relating to development in the developing countries. The principle of sustainable development is thus a part of modern international law by reason not only of its inescapable logical necessity, but also by reason of its wide and general acceptance by the global community.

In the 2005 *Iron Rhine* (*Belgium v Netherlands*) award, the Arbitral Tribunal struck under the auspices of the Permanent Court of Arbitration, considered sustainable development an emerging principle in international law, without prejudice to its status, noting that:

> There is considerable debate as to what, within the field of environmental law, constitutes "rules" or "principles"; what is "soft law"; and which environmental treaty law or principles have contributed to the development of customary international law. Without entering further into those controversies, the Tribunal notes that in all of these categories "environment" is broadly referred to as including air, water, land, flora and fauna, natural ecosystems and sites, human health and safety, and climate. The emerging principles, whatever their current status, make reference to conservation, management, notions of prevention and of sustainable development, and protection for future generations.

As argued by the parties to several recent cases in international human rights tribunals, and as was recently proposed by Uruguay to the International Court of Justice, there may even be an international customary rule which grants a "right to sustainable economic development" to States or indigenous peoples under international law.

Others have been less convinced of this approach, arguing that sustainable development itself is not necessarily one customary principle, as such. From this view, international law on sustainable development has mainly emerged in international treaties and accords. It can be seen as a second, sometimes marginalized objective of multilateral environmental accords, phrased in different ways depending on the specific problem being addressed or resource being managed. It can also be seen as one objective of international economic treaties, where States often note, in the Preamble, their joint commitment to promote sustainable development. It can be found in new treaties on social concerns such as corruption. And in some cases, such as recent treaties related to energy, desertification or food and agriculture, it might even be seen as a primary object of the international agreements themselves. From this view, sustainable development is an object or purpose of treaty law rather than a principle in itself, though States may agree on certain principles in order to achieve their sustainable development goal.

These two views provide different pictures of the status of sustainable development in international law, and have different normative consequences. As this volume considers the normative consequences of a commitment to sustainable development in the decisions of international courts, tribunals and other dispute settlement bodies over the last fifty years, it is helpful to first introduce the differences between these approaches with reference to other recent developments in international law more broadly.

2.4.2 A principle versus a policy objective

To discuss whether sustainable development can be characterized as a principle of international law, the nature of legal principles – in particular customary principles of international law – must be briefly introduced.

Present jurisprudence debates on the nature of legal norms range far beyond the scope of this chapter. However, as maintained by Ronald Dworkin, a legal obligation can exist whenever the case supporting such an obligation, in terms of binding legal principles of different sorts, is as strong that the case against it. Black letter laws reflect legal norms, but as Dworkin notes, principles, policies and other standards also have normative value.[91] Principles embody legal standards or norms, but "the norms they contain are more general than commitments and do not specify particular actions," unlike rules.[92]

In international law, the question of consequences that flow from characterizing a norm as a legal rule or principle has, according to Phillipe Sands, not been sufficiently addressed by courts and tribunals. However, as he notes, the 1903 *Gentini* case presages Dworkin's views on the legal effect of principles and their relationship to rules, stating that a rule "is essentially practical and moreover, binding . . ." while a principle "expresses a general truth, which guides our action, serves as a theoretical basis for the various acts of our life, and the application of which to reality produces a given consequence."[93]

A further distinction is possible among principles versus policies. As noted by Dworkin, it is possible to distinguish policies as standards that set out goals to be reached, generally improvements in some economic, political or social situation deemed desirable by the community.[94] Arguments of policy justify a political decision by showing that the decision advances or protects a collective goal of the community as a whole.[95] Principles, in contrast, provide normative standards to be observed because it is a requirement of justice, fairness or some other dimension of morality,[96] so that arguments of principle justify a political decision by showing that the decision respects or secures some individual or group right.[97] These other

---

91   Ronald Dworkin, *Taking Rights Seriously* (London: Duckworth, 1977), 22–31.
92   Ibid. as cited in Sands, *supra* note 87 at 233.
93   *Gentini* case (*Italy* v *Venezuela*) M.C.C. (1903), J. H. Ralston and W. T. S. Doyle, Venezuelan Arbitrations of 1903 etc. (1904), 720, 725, cited in B. Cheng, *General Principles of Law as Applied by International Courts and Tribunals* (Cambridge: Grotius Publications, 1953) at 376, and cited in Sands, *supra* note 87 at 233.
94   Ibid.
95   Dworkin, *supra* note 91 at 82–130.
96   Ibid. at 22–31.
97   Ibid. at 82–130.

types of norms (principles and policies) have a dimension that rules do not – the dimension of weight and importance.[98] If two rules conflict, as Dworkin argues, one of them cannot be a valid rule, but when other norms intersect (for example, if a policy and a principle conflict), those resolving the conflict must take the relative weight of each into account. 'Policies' are not necessarily legally binding on judges, but principles often are. This last point is important. In international law, following Dworkin's argument, a principle could be binding upon an international tribunal or judge, while a policy would be taken into account by the tribunal, but not necessarily fulfil a normative legal function in determining the outcome.

In international law, principles of Dworkin's 'binding' sort may best be characterized as principles of international customary law. Such principles are important as they can establish obligations for all States except those which have persistently objected to a practice and its legal consequences. Article 38(1)(b) of the Statute of the International Court of Justice, which was incorporated into the UN Charter by Article 92, explains the basis for recognition of customary law by an international tribunal, stating that:

> The Court, whose function is to decide in accordance with international law such disputes as are submitted to it, shall apply . . . international custom, as evidence of a general practice accepted as law;[99]

In essence, customary international law rules can be derived from the consistent conduct of States acting in the belief that international law required them to so act. Jurists, to rely upon an international customary principle, must show State practice, by demonstrating the widespread repetition by States of similar international acts over time. Such acts must be taken by a significant number of States, and not be rejected by too many others.[100] The ICJ has stated that "it might be that, even without the passage of any considerable period of time, a very widespread and representative participation in the convention might suffice of itself, provided it included states whose interest were specifically affected."[101] The ICJ has also found that it is sufficient that the conduct of States should, in general, be consistent with a customary principle, and that instance of inconsistent conduct have been generally treated as breaches of the rule rather than indications of a new rule having emerged.[102]

---

98 Ibid. at 22–31.
99 Statute of the International Court of Justice, June 26, 1945, at art 38.1; Malcom Shaw, *International Law*, 5th edn (Cambridge: Cambridge University Press, 2003), at 68–88.
100 Anthony D'Amato, *The Concept of Custom in International Law* (Ithaca, NY: Cornell University Press, 1971); Michael Akehurst, "Custom as a Source of International Law" (1974–75) 47 BYIL 1; Maurice H. Mendelson, "The Formation of Customary International Law" in Hague Academy of International Law, *Collected Courses of the Hague Academy*, tome 272 (The Hague: Martinus Nijhoff, 1999) at 155.
101 *North Sea Continental Shelf* cases, 1969 ICJ Rep. 3, 8 ILM 340, at para. 73.
102 *Case Concerning Military and Paramilitary Activities in and against Nicaragua*, 1986 ICJ Rep. 98, 25 ILM 1023 at para. 186.

To prove that a norm has been accepted as a principle of customary international law, jurists must also show that these international acts have occurred out of sense of legal obligation (*opinio juris*). The ICJ, in the *North Sea Continental Shelf* cases, stated in this regard:

> Not only must the acts concerned amount to a settled practice, but they must also be such, or be carried out in such a way, as to be evidence of a rule of law requiring it. The need for such a belief, i.e. the existence of a subjective element, is implicit in the very notion of the *opinio juris sive necessitates.* The states concerned must therefore feel that they are conforming to what amounts to a legal obligation.[103]

Further, if a norm that is enshrined in a treaty is followed in the practice of non-parties, it can, provided that there is *opinio juris*, lead to the evolution of a customary rule which will be applicable between states that are not party to the treaty and between parties and non-parties. This can happen even before the treaty has entered into force.[104]

There are two further points to be made about establishing that a concept is a principle or a rule of international customary law, even in a brief summary. First, as was demonstrated in the *Ango-Norwegian Fisheries* case at the ICJ, a state can avoid being bound by a customary rule if it persistently objects to that rule.[105] Second, as has been observed by the ICJ in reference to a discussion of whether a treaty norm had also been transformed into a customary principle, it is in the first place necessary "that the provision concerned should, at all events potentially, be of a fundamentally norm-creating character such as could be regarded as forming the basis of a general rule . . ."[106]

2.4.3 Sustainable development as a customary principle

2.4.3.1 A significant weight of general state practice on sustainable development

State practice demonstrating that sustainable development is now a principle of international law could be discerned from many sources, including broad ratification of treaties on sustainable development; the records or *travaux preparatoires* of international negotiations and conferences which document formal notes or statements by State representatives; votes and other acts in the UNGA and other international organizations; the pleadings of states before national and

---

103   *North Sea Continental Shelf* cases, *supra* note 101 at 44.
104   Hugh Thirlway, "The Law and Procedure of the International Court of Justice" (1990) 60 BYIL 1 at 87.
105   *Anglo-Norwegian Fisheries* case, 1951 ICJ Rep. 131.
106   *North Sea Continental Shelf* cases, *supra* note 101 at 41–2.

international tribunals and legal opinions by government lawyers; and national legislation and the decisions of national courts.[107]

And indeed, the evidence of an international commitment by States with regards to sustainable development is significant and weighty. There have been near-universal ratifications of treaties such as the *UN Framework Convention on Climate Change*, the *UN Convention on Biological Diversity,* and the *UN Convention to Combat Desertification and Drought*, all of which contain significant commitments to sustainable development, though the actual language of the commitment differs depending on the treaty, as will be seen below. There is evidence of State announcements supporting the notion of sustainable development from Stockholm, Rio and Johannesburg. There are records of statements and formal notes from Ministers and senior officials expressing their country's commitments to sustainable development through fifteen years of meetings by the CSD in New York.

There are also records of votes adopting sustainable development policies, strategies and objectives in many international institutions, including the UNGA, the UNEP Governing Council, and the European Commission, even when such a vote implied the designation of new or additional resources. States have directed the World Bank Group, the Asian Development Bank, the African Development Bank, the Inter-American Development Bank and the European Bank for Reconstruction and Development, among others, to implement policies which ensure that their programmes will promote sustainable development.

A brief survey of State pleadings (and the decisions of judges) from the *Nuclear Tests* cases,[108] the *Case Concerning Certain Phosphate Lands in Nauru*,[109] the *Gabčíkovo-Nagymaros* case,[110] the *Iron Rhine* arbitration,[111] and the recent *Argentina-Uruguay Pulp Mills* case[112] demonstrates that a broad array of States are willing to appeal to arguments related to sustainable development in international tribunal processes, and that in some cases, tribunals are even willing to use the concept for legal reasoning. For instance, Belgium argued in the *Iron Rhine* case that:

> Belgium views the upgrading of the Iron Rhine railway also as a significant step towards the realization of the policy of so-called "modal shift" from road to rail transportation advocated by the EC and thus towards sustainable development. The need for this modal shift, Belgium argues, will help reduce

---

107 See *Yearbook of the International Law Commission* (1950-II), 368–72.

108 *Nuclear Tests* case, Judgment, 1974 ICJ Rep. 457.

109 *Certain Phosphate Lands in Nauru*, Preliminaty Objections, Judgment, 1992 ICJ Rep. 240, 32 ILM 1471.

110 *Gabčíkovo-Nagymaros, supra* note 20.

111 *The Iron Rhine Arbitration* (Belgium/Netherlands) Award of 24 May 2005, online: Permanent Court of Arbitration <http://www.pca-cpa.org/showfile.asp?fil_id=377> [*Iron Rhine*].

112 *Pulp Mills on the River Uruguay*, Request for the Indication of Provisional Measures, Order, 46 ILM 314.

greenhouse gas emissions and is recognized and supported in various EC official documents, as well as in statements of the Netherlands Government itself (BM, p. 26, para. 20).[113]

The Netherlands also replied that the "The Habitats Directive aims at reconciling the maintenance of biodiversity with sustainable development by developing a coherent European ecological network ('Natura 2000')."[114]

There is also increasing State practice in national legislation on sustainable development, and a growing number of domestic court decisions. Nearly every State has, at the least, some form of environmental law in place which commits to sustainable development, and several States have now also set further laws in place, at national or sub-national levels, that are specifically aimed at sustainable development.

In sum, there is ample, significant and voluminous evidence of State practice making commitments to sustainable development. There is even a certain weight of evidence that States take this to mean that they have committed to take environmental factors into account in economic development decision-making. Indeed, as will be discussed in the following sections of this chapter, there appears to be a great deal of State practice on sustainable development simply in the arena of global, regional and bi-lateral trade law. The answer to the question of *opinio juris* is, however, not quite so straightforward. And an assessment of the final element of customary law is even more difficult.

2.4.3.2 Opinio juris *on whether states are bound by international law to develop sustainably or to promote sustainable development*

It is not always straightforward to find evidence of *opinio juris*, as this requires demonstrating the actual motives underlying a State's words and actions. As noted by Sands, such evidence can be found in expressions of belief regarding acts of international organizations and other international meetings; statements made by representatives of States; and the conclusion of treaties.[115] It can also be found in the same sources which provide evidence of State practice. The problem, here, is uncovering specific statements which evince that States have committed to either realize, or even promote, sustainable development, believing their decision to have been required by a binding international obligation rather than a commitment to a common global objective.

One statement on State beliefs is found in the UNGA Resolution which accepted the Brundtland Report, in which UN Member States solemnly note the "accelerating deterioration of the human environment and natural resources and the consequences of that deterioration for economic and social development," and then declare:

---

113   *Iron Rhine, supra* note 111 at para. 114.
114   Ibid. at para. 126.
115   Sands, *supra* note 87.

Believing that sustainable development, which implies meeting the needs of the present without compromising the ability of future generations to meet their own needs, should become a central guiding principle of the United Nations, Governments and private institutions, organizations and enterprises . . .[116]

This Resolution, however, uses hortatory language – 'should become' rather 'is now recognized as.' This implies that the members of UNGA, in 1987 at least, did not yet recognize sustainable development as a guiding principle. Further, the UNGA does not actually declare that sustainable development should become a binding principle of customary international law. Rather, it uses slightly different terms – a "central guiding principle" and casts its net wider than States to include private institutions, organizations and enterprises. This suggests that the UNGA was not necessarily seeking to recognize sustainable development as binding law in the *opinio juris* sense.

However, one could argue that a commitment to sustainable development has emerged since the days in 1987 when the UNGA stated that it *should become* a central guiding principle of Governments and others. To do this successfully, it is necessary to show that while sustainable development was not yet accepted in 1987, it has since (quite rapidly) evolved into a customary principle of international law.

Certain evidence can be found in the pleadings and decisions of international tribunals since 1987. For instance, in the 1997 *Gabčíkovo-Nagymaros* (*Hungary* v *Slovakia*) case, Hungary states in its pleadings that: "Hungary and Slovakia agree that the principle of sustainable development, as formulated in the Brundtland Report, the Rio Declaration and *Agenda 21* is applicable to this dispute . . ."[117]

And indeed, in the more recent *Iron Rhine* arbitral award, the tribunal stated that with regards interpretative principles:

Since the Stockholm Conference on the Environment in 1972 there has been a marked development of international law relating to the protection of the environment. Today, both international and EC law require the integration of appropriate environmental measures in the design and implementation of economic development activities. Principle 4 of the Rio Declaration on Environment and Development, adopted in 1992[118] which reflects this trend, provides that "environmental protection shall constitute an integral part of the development process and cannot be considered in isolation from it." Importantly, these emerging principles now integrate environmental protection into the development process. Environmental

---

116   Resolution 42/187, 'Report of the World Commission on Environment and Development.'
117   *Gabčíkovo-Nagymaros, supra* note 20 at 90.
118   Rio Declaration, Report of the United Nations Conference on Environment and Development (1992) 31 ILM 874, at p. 877.

law and the law on development stand not as alternatives but as mutually reinforcing, integral concepts, which require that where development may cause significant harm to the environment there is a duty to prevent, or at least mitigate, such harm . . . This duty, in the opinion of the Tribunal, has now become a principle of general international law.

This principle applies not only in autonomous activities but also in activities undertaken in implementation of specific treaties between the Parties. The Tribunal recalled the observation of the ICJ in the *Gabčíkovo-Nagymaros* case that "[t]his need to reconcile economic development with protection of the environment is aptly expressed in the concept of sustainable development."[119] And, in that context, the ICJ further clarified that "new norms have to be taken into consideration, and . . . new standards given proper weight, not only when States contemplate new activities but also when continuing with activities begun in the past."[120] In the view of the Tribunal this dictum applies equally to the Iron Rhine railway. The Tribunal found this aspect of the ICJ's opinion to be applicable to the *Iron Rhine* arbitration as well.[121]

This determination was directly relevant for the decision of the Tribunal in this case:

> As the Tribunal has already observed above . . . economic development is to be reconciled with the protection of the environment, and, in so doing, new norms have to be taken into consideration, including when activities begun in the past are now expanded and upgraded.[122]
>
> Applying the principles of international environmental law, the Tribunal . . . is of the view that, by analogy, where a state exercises a right under international law within the territory of another state, considerations of environmental protection also apply. The exercise of Belgium's right of transit, as it has formulated its request, thus may well necessitate measures by the Netherlands to protect the environment to which Belgium will have to contribute as an integral element of its request. The reactivation of the Iron Rhine railway cannot be viewed in isolation from the environmental protection measures necessitated by the intended use of the railway line. These measures are to be fully integrated into the project and its costs.[123]

As noted above, further claims that there exists a 'sovereign right to implement sustainable economic development projects' were used by States in the 2007 *Pulp Mills on the River Uruguay* case. For instance, in pleadings on Provisional Measures of July 2006, the ICJ notes that:

---

119 *Gabčíkovo-Nagymaros, supra* note 20 at 78, para. 140.
120 Ibid.
121 *Iron Rhine, supra* note 111 at para. 59.
122 Ibid. at 222.
123 Ibid. at 223.

> Uruguay . . . asks the Court in particular to preserve its sovereign right, pending a decision of the Court on the merits of the case, to implement sustainable economic development projects on its own territory . . .[124]

Similarly, there is evidence from statements of State representatives in recent international treaty negotiations related to climate change, biological diversity, desertification, food security and other concerns, that even if States do not consider themselves bound by a legal obligation to develop sustainably in every instance, they do feel bound by a moral obligation to promote sustainable development generally.

Indeed, if it was formulated as a binding legal obligation "to promote sustainable development" or to promote "sustainable use of natural resources," it is possible to argue that several treaties actually recognize sustainable development as a principle of international law among the Parties. One of the most significant is the *UN Framework Convention on Climate Change* (UNFCCC). This treaty recognizes that the climate system is a shared resource whose stability can be affected by industrial and other emissions of carbon dioxide and other greenhouse gases, and sets an overall framework for intergovernmental efforts to tackle the challenge posed by climate change. It entered into force on 21 March 1994, and enjoys near universal membership, with 191 countries having ratified. Under the UNFCCC, governments gather and share information on greenhouse gas emissions, national policies and best practices; launch national strategies for addressing greenhouse gas emissions and adapting to expected impacts, including the provision of financial and technological support to developing countries; and co-operate in preparing for adaptation to the impacts of climate change. Article 3 of the UNFCCC, entitled Principles, recognizes:

> 4. The Parties have a right to, and should, promote sustainable development. Policies and measures to protect the climate system against human-induced change should be appropriate for the specific conditions of each Party and should be integrated with national development programmes, taking into account that economic development is essential for adopting measures to address climate change.

In the UNFCCC, therefore, the promotion of sustainable development is framed as one of the 'Principles' of the treaty, where it is described as a 'right.' It is also, however, framed as a hortatory ('should' rather than 'shall') commitment to 'promote.' And immediately qualified by the caveat that climate protection measures need to be appropriate for different Parties and integrated into development programmes, and the recognition that economic development is still 'essential.'

A second relevant treaty is the 1994 *United Nations Convention to Combat Desertification and Drought, especially in Africa* (UNCCD). In 1977, the United

---

124 *Case Concerning Pulp Mills on the River Uruguay (Argentina v Uruguay)*, Request for the Indication of Provisional Measures, Order of 13 July 2006 at 67.

Nations Conference on Desertification (UNCOD) adopted a Plan of Action to Combat Desertification (PACD). Unfortunately, the problem of land degradation in arid, semi-arid and dry sub-humid areas continued to intensify. As a result, the question of how to tackle desertification was still a major concern for the 1992 UNCED. According to the UNCCD materials, the UNCED "supported a new, integrated approach to the problem, emphasizing action to promote sustainable development at the community level." It also called on the UNGA to establish an Intergovernmental Negotiating Committee (INCD) to prepare, by June 1994, a Convention to Combat Desertification, particularly in Africa. In December 1992, the UNGA agreed and adopted resolution 47/188. Working to a tight schedule, the Committee completed its negotiations in five sessions. The Convention was adopted in Paris on 17 June 1994 and opened for signature on 14–15 October 1994. It entered into force on 26 December 1996, 90 days after the fiftieth ratification was received. Over 179 countries are Parties to the UNCCD.

Sustainable use is formulated as a Principle in Article 3 of the UNCCD which states "[p]rinciples: c) the Parties should develop, in a spirit of partnership, cooperation among all levels of government, communities, non-governmental organizations and landholders to establish a better understanding of the nature and value of land and scarce water resources in affected areas and to work towards their sustainable use . . ." Here, it is a principle which recognizes that Parties will co-operate to work towards the sustainable use of land and water resources. As will be seen below, there are other references to sustainable development in the UN FCCC and in the UNCCD which do not appear to be 'principles' of these treaties.

The bar to rapidly transform a principle agreed in a treaty into a principle agreed in customary law, as set by the ICJ in the *North Sea Continental Shelf* cases, is relatively high:

> an indispensable requirement would be that within the period in question, short though it might be, state practice, including that of states whose interests are specially affected, should have been both extensive and virtually uniform in the sense of the provision invoked; and should moreover have occurred in such a way as to show a general recognition that a rule of law or legal obligation is involved.[125]

As such, beyond state practice and *opinio juris*, there is a 'precondition' which should also be addressed.

2.4.3.3 A fundamentally normative character to develop sustainably

To prove a norm of customary law, there is a need to show that state practice and *opinio juris* has been extensive and virtually uniform *in the sense of the provision invoked*. This element relates to the need for a "fundamentally norm-creating character such as could be regarded as forming the basis of a general rule."

125 *North Sea Continental Shelf* cases (1969) ICJ Reports 3 at 43.

It is here, as observed by Vaughan Lowe, that the concept of sustainable development might currently encounter difficulties in being recognized as a principle of customary law in itself. Lowe and others have argued that 'sustainable development' is difficult to accurately describe as a single emerging customary principle that can, through demonstrable state practice and *opinio juris*, be accepted as binding on all states. Gunter Handl stated baldly, in 1990, that "[n]ormative uncertainty, coupled with the absence of justiciable standards for review, strongly suggest that there is as yet no international legal obligation that development must be sustainable,"[126] and that "decisions on what constitutes sustainability rest primarily with individual governments."[127] Together, Lowe and Handl suggest that sustainable development may not be sufficiently specific and normative to become a customary norm of international law, in itself. Lowe notes wryly that "the argument that sustainable development is a norm of customary international law, binding on and directing the conduct of states, and which can be applied by tribunals, is not sustainable."[128]

What would such a fundamentally norm-creating character entail? An international legal norm, whether derived from an international treaty or international customary law, can be understood in reference to its function, according to Hans Kelsen.[129] In international law, Kelsen explains, most norms have one of four functions. Either they impose an obligation on states to do something, as a command (prescriptive norms) or they impose an obligation on states not to do something, as a prohibition (prohibitive norms). They can also grant a right to a state not to do something, as an exemption (exempting norms), or grant a right to a state to do something, as a permission (permissive norms).[130]

If sustainable development were to be accepted as a principle of customary law, it needs to be clear what a commitment "to promote sustainable development" prescribes, prohibits, exempts or permits. A commitment to promote sustainable development would need to be specific and normative enough to form the basis of a claim against a State, in the sense that a prohibition against armed attack or a prescription to use equidistance to determine legal boundaries might be customary law. It seems unlikely that States accept a prohibition against developing unsustainably in general. Or even against action to promote unsustainable development.

---

126 See G. Handl, 'Environmental Security and Global Change: The Challenge to International Law' (1990) 1 YbIEL 25. For the same reasons Handl also rejects the possibility that sustainable development is a peremptory norm of international law. See also G. Handl, 'The Legal Mandate of Multilateral Development Banks as Agents for Change Towards Sustainable Development' (1998) 92 AJIL 641.

127 A. Boyle and D. Freestone, *International Law and Sustainable Development: Past Achievements and Future Challenges* (Oxford: Oxford University Press, 1999) at 16.

128 V. Lowe, "Sustainable Development and Unsustainable Arguments" in A. Boyle and D. Freestone, eds., *International Law and Sustainable Development: Past Achievements and Future Challenges* (Oxford: Oxford University Press, 1999) at 30.

129 H. Kelsen, *Theorie Generale des Normes* (Paris Presses Universitaires de France, 1996) at 1.

130 Ibid. at 1.

But perhaps sustainable development might be characterized as a permissive norm – a right of States to promote sustainable development (also found in Principle 4 of the UNFCCC). As noted by Wesley Hohfeld, such a right, to mean more than a privilege, would need to impose a corresponding duty upon another State or individual.[131] For instance, another State would be under a duty not to prevent, through their action or inaction, the sustainable development of the first. And perhaps States have accepted, over time, a prescription not to prevent the efforts of other States to promote sustainable development, in certain circumstances (the hortatory duty that states 'should' promote sustainable development, from UNFCCC Principle 4).

Indeed, certain elements of such a right, held by indigenous peoples against their own countries, and by States against other States, may be gaining recognition recently in regional human rights tribunals.[132] And it may even be that such a formulation formed part of the ICJ's reasoning in its first Order with regards to Provisional Measures in the *Pulp Mills on the River Uruguay* case,[133] where it stated:

> Whereas the present case highlights the importance of the need to ensure environmental protection of shared natural resources while allowing for sustainable economic development; whereas it is in particular necessary to bear in mind the reliance of the Parties on the quality of the water of the River Uruguay for their livelihood and economic development; whereas from this point of view account must be taken of the need to safeguard the continued conservation of the river environment and the rights of economic development of the riparian States; . . .[134]

For a state obligation on sustainable development, it is necessary to define the specific legal norm that States must respect, even if this were simply to be defined in the context of one type of economic activity, or in the exploitation of a particular natural resource.

What would be the content of such a norm? Would it be that States should ensure that certain development activities will not affect sustainability? That States must balance between the needs of present and future generations when taking development decisions? Or that States shall identify and abandon unsustainable development policies, programmes or projects? Much legal work remains.

At present, if a sustainable development principle exists in international law, its clearest expression is as a label for a principle requiring the integration of environment and socio-economic development: that States shall take environmental

---

131 Wesley Newcomb Hohfeld, *Fundamental Legal Conceptions, As Applied in Judicial Reasoning and Other Legal Essays* (Aldershot: Ashgate, 2001).

132 See *Case of the Sawhoyamaxa Community (Paraguay)* (2006), Inter-Am. Ct. H.R. (ser. C) No. 146 at para. 137–41; *Case of the Saramaka Peoples (Suriname)* (2007) Inter-Am. Ct. H.R. (ser. C) No. 172 at para. 93–5, 122, 129–32; *Case of the Ogoni People (Nigeria)* African Court of Human Rights.

133 *Pulp Mills* case, *supra* note 124.

134 Ibid. at 80.

protection into account in the development process and *vice versa* (as stated in the *Iron Rhine Railway* arbitration). There is clearly a great deal of general State practice committing to sustainable development, and there appears to be a certain weight of *opinio juris* which supports the proposal that *certain* States do this because they feel bound by some form of international commitment to sustainable development. Europe, in particular, appears to have accepted an integration principle labelled 'principle of sustainable development.' However, there is a lingering lack of clarity as to whether *most* States undertake such a commitment due to a sense of legal obligation, or simply due to a common commitment to a noble goal. It is not clear, essentially, that a principle of 'sustainable development' has yet emerged in international customary law yet.

2.4.4 Sustainable development as an object and purpose of international law

A search for one agreed customary norm of sustainable development might actually be a search in the wrong direction. Another possibility is that sustainable development could be characterized as an objective of States, and even an internationally recognized objective of the world community as a whole. As a global objective, similar to 'world peace,' 'respect for human rights' and 'conservation of nature,' sustainable development could be recognized as object and purpose of international treaty law.

2.4.4.1 The meaning and effect of an 'object and purpose' in international law

Both principles and policy objectives have a dimension that rules do not – the dimension of weight and importance.[135] As noted by Ronald Dworkin, policy objectives set out goals to be reached, generally improvements in some economic, political or social situation deemed desirable by the community.[136] Arguments of policy justify a political decision by showing that the decision advances or protects a collective goal of the community as a whole.[137] When

---

135   Dworkin, *supra* note 91 at 22–31.
136   Ibid. See also M. Koskenniemi, "What is International Law For?" in M. Evans, ed., *International Law* (Oxford: Oxford University Press, 2006), where he argues ". . . we do not honour the law because of the sacred aura of its text or its origin but because it enables us to reach valuable human purposes . . . In domestic society, abstract law-obedience can be defended in view of the routine nature of the cases that arise, and the dangers attached to entitling citizens to think for themselves. Such arguments are weak in the international realm where situations of law-application are few, and disadvantages of disobedience often significant." However, as he argues later, "there never are simple, well-identified objectives behind formal rules. Rules are legislative compromises, open-ended and bound in clusters expressing conflicting considerations." M. Koskenniemi, *The Politics of International Law* (Oxford:Oxford University Press, 2011)
137   Dworkin, *supra* note 91 at 82–130.

such norms intersect, those resolving the conflict must take the relative weight of each into account.[138]

In international law, particular relevance is given to policy objectives when agreed in a treaty by States. Article 31 of *Vienna Convention on the Law of Treaties*,[139] as the general rule of interpretation, provides in (1) that "A treaty shall be interpreted in good faith in accordance with the ordinary meaning to be given to the terms of the treaty in their context and in the light of its object and purpose."*And in (2) the Convention further states that: "The context for the purpose of the interpretation of a treaty shall comprise, in addition to the text, including its preamble and annexes . . ."[140] In essence, the terms of the treaty, in context and in accordance with its object and purpose, are taken together to guide a lawyer in understanding the intentions of the Parties, and are the prevailing elements for interpretation. These elements are not just legally relevant, but actually essential – *inter pares* to an international agreement, in any case. If sustainable development is object and purpose of more than thirty treaties which explicitly commit to achieve it (including many trade and investment agreements) since the Rio UNCED, it is also relevant in the regimes to implement further treaties that are related to sustainable development (such as the several hundred agreements highlighted by States as 'delivery mechanisms' for the priorities outlined in the JPOI). As an object and purpose of these treaties alone, the concept could be extremely important and influential in international law. It could affect interpretation of treaty obligations in a dispute related to the environment or development issues, and would also guide the implementation of the agreements and even the further evolution of the treaty regimes themselves.

This is important because few international treaties today, particularly in the field of sustainable development, are simply contracts among States. As John Ruggie and Stephen Krasner have suggested, to understand the norms found in international treaties and how they are implemented, it is important to analyse the implicit understandings between a broad range of actors, not necessarily only States.[141] A 'regime' is an institution that might coalesce or be structured around certain legal

---

138   Ibid.

139   (Adopted 23 May 1969, entered into force 27 January 1980) 1155 UNTS 331.

140   Ibid. at art 31(2). Note also the relevance of ". . . (b) any instrument which was made by one or more parties in connection with the conclusion of the treaty and accepted by the other parties as an instrument related to the treaty . . . (b) any subsequent practice in the application of the treaty which establishes the agreement of the parties regarding its interpretation; . . . 4. A special meaning shall be given to a term if it is established that the parties so intended." Also, Ibid. art 32 permits recourse to supplementary means of interpretation, including the preparatory work of the treaty and the circumstances of its conclusion. These reflect pre-existing customary international law, applying to treaties concluded before the *Vienna Convention* and also to non-Parties: *Case Concerning the Territorial Dispute (Libyan Arab Jamahiriya v Chad)* (Judgment) General List No 83 [1994] ICJ 6; *Kasikili/Sedudu Island (Botswana/Namibia)* (Judgment) General List No 99 [1999] ICJ 1045; *Case Concerning Sovereignty over Pulau Ligitan and Pulau Sipadan (Indonesia v Malaysia)* (Judgment) General List No 102 [2002] ICJ 625 37–8.

141   J. G. Ruggie, "International Responses to Technology: Ideas and Trends" (1975) 29 *Int'l Organization* 557, 557–83. See also J. G. Ruggie, "Reconstituting the Global Public Domain–Issues, Actors, and Practices" (2004) 10 *Eur. J. Int'l Relations* 499, 499–531.

rules and certain formal organizations, but goes well beyond them, and develops iteratively. Such regimes, as posited by John Vogler, can be defined as "sets of implicit or explicit principles, norms, rules and decision-making procedures around which actors' expectations converge in a given area of international relations."[142] Principles, norms, rules and decision-making procedures are all necessary parts of an international treaty regime which exists to achieve the common object and purpose of States and other international actors.[143]

Regimes, therefore, in international relations theory, can be described as governing subject matter of international interest in an interactive way. This distinguishes them from broader 'international orders' which imply an authority superintending over a wide range of institutions and issues.[144] As such, regimes are more "specialised arrangements that pertain to well defined activities, resources or geographical areas and often involve only some subset of the members of international society."[145] As John Vogler observes, the boundaries of a regime are thus determined partly by perceptions of the extent and linkage between issues.

Regimes call attention to the way that principles, rules and decision-making procedures develop, interact and evolve in one 'sub-system', focusing on the converging expectations of a group of international actors. As Stephen Toope and Jutta Brunnée suggest, regime analysis can serve the study of international law, drawing on the 'inter-actional' behaviours of legal subjects and rules originally observed by Lon L. Fuller.[146] International regimes, as they note, can coalesce around international treaty commitments, which evolve and 'deepen' over time through interactions between states and non-state actors, shaping and being shaped by the norms and rules, knowledge and networks generated by the regime.[147]

From this perspective, both 'hard' and 'soft' law between Parties to a treaty (or a series of treaties) also evolves with the regime, and involves more than States

---

142 J. Vogler, *The Global Commons: Environmental and Technological Governance*, 2nd edn (Chicester: John Wiley and Sons, 2000) 20–43.

143 See especially J. G. Ruggie, "International Regimes, Transactions and Change: Embedded Liberalism in the Postwar Economic Order" in S. Krasner, ed., *International Regimes* (Ithaca, NY: Cornell University Press, 1983); see also S. Haggard and B. A. Simmons, "Theories of International Regimes" (1987) 41 *Int'l Organization* 491; O. S. Stokke, "Regimes as Governance Systems" in O. R. Young, ed., *Global Governance: Drawing Insights from the Environmental Experience* (Boston: MIT Press, 1997) at 27–64.

144 Vogler, *supra* note 142 at 20–43.

145 O. R. Young, *International Cooperation: Building Regimes for Natural Resources and The Environment* (Ithaca, NY: Cornell University Press 1989) as cited in Vogler, *supra* note 142 at 23.

146 On inter-actional accounts of international law, see J. Brunée and S. J. Toope, *Legitimacy and Legality in International Law* (Cambridge: Cambridge University Press, 2010). See also J. Brunnée and S. J. Toope, "International Law and Constructivism: Elements of an Interactional Theory of International Law" (2000) 39 *Colu. J. Trans'l L.* 19, 19–74; J. Brunnée and S. J. Toope, "The Changing Nile Basin Regime: Does Law Matter?" (2002) 43 *Harvard Int'l L. J.* 105, 105–59.

147 Ibid. See also J. Brunee and S. J. Toope, "Persuasion and Enforcement: Explaining Compliance with International Law" (2002) XIII *Finnish Ybk Int'l L.* 1, 1–23. And see J. Brunnée, 'Coping with Consent: Lawmaking under Multilateral Environmental Agreements' (2002) 15 *Leiden J. Int'l L.* 1, 1–52.

in its implementation.[148] A regime may start with a legally binding agreement with broad participation but shallow substantive commitments, then deepen in substantive content and engagement of more and better informed actors, leading to greater compliance over time. As such, the emergence, evolution and effects of normative systems can coalesce around a particular object and purpose in international law, reinforced by 'epistemic communities' which share scientific information and data.[149] In certain circumstances, it may be undesirable to negotiate seemingly strong international treaties without first going through a careful, incremental process of regime-building. Without it, formal legal commitments are unlikely to be meaningful; states may simply assent with no intention of complying, or no capacity to comply.[150] As Jutta Brunnée and Stephen Toope argue, once a contextual agreement (such as a framework convention) initiates the development of self-reinforcing norms and institutions, regimes can then evolve in the direction of deeper substantive legal commitments. A steady building process, focused on the object and purpose of the treaty, may yield increasingly complex and sophisticated regimes of nearly universal application.[151] In many treaties on sustainable development, both the CBD and the UNFCCC for instance, States essentially establish framework agreements which commit to certain common objectives, and a process by which further more detailed and specific protocols are negotiated.

2.4.4.2 Sustainable development as an 'object and purpose' of international law

The 'soft law' from the Stockholm Declaration, the UNGA Resolution on the Brundtland Report, the Rio Declaration and *Agenda 21*, and the Johannesburg Declaration and JPOI provide convincing evidence to justify finding sustainable development to be the object and purpose of international treaty law. This view is found, for instance, in Chapter 39 of *Agenda 21*, entitled International Legal Mechanisms and Instruments, at para. 39.1, which states that:

> the following vital aspects of the universal, multilateral and bilateral treaty-making process should be taken into account:
>
> (a)   The further development of *international law on sustainable development*, giving special attention to the delicate balance between environmental and developmental concerns; . . .
> (c)   At the global level, the essential importance of the participation in and the contribution of all countries, including the developing countries, to treaty making *in the field of international law on sustainable development* . . .;[152]

---

148   Boyle and Freestone, *supra* note 82.
149   Ibid. See also J Brunnée, 'Coping with Consent: Lawmaking under Multilateral Environmental Agreements' (2002) 15 *Leiden J. Int'l L.* 1, 1–52.
150   Ibid.
151   Ibid.
152   See also *Agenda 21*, *supra* note 41, para. 39.10 (on the avoidance and settlement of disputes in the field of sustainable development).

By referring to international law in this context, as 'international law on sustainable development,' as 'international law concerning sustainable development,' 'in the field of international law sustainable development' and as 'treaties relating to sustainable development,' States do appear to set sustainable development as a goal or subject matter of international law, rather than as a principle of international law in itself. Further evidence can be found in the decisions taken in the 1997 UNGASS Programme of Further Implementation of *Agenda 21*. In particular, at paragraph 109 States agreed that:

> Taking into account the provisions of chapter 39, particularly paragraph 39.1, of *Agenda 21*, it is necessary to continue the progressive development and, as and when appropriate, codification of *international law related to sustainable development*. Relevant bodies in which such tasks are being undertaken should cooperate and coordinate in this regard.

The UNGASS continues at paragraph 110 by referring specifically to implementation of environmental law as a different field entirely.[153] In the 2002 World Summit on Sustainable Development, this characterization of 'international law in the field of sustainable development' was not overturned, nor significantly modified. Rather, as noted above, the focus was on implementation. States agreed, in the JPOI at paragraph 148 (e) to mandate the CSD to "[t]ake into account *significant legal developments in the field of sustainable development*, with due regard to the role of relevant intergovernmental bodies in promoting the implementation of *Agenda 21* relating to international legal instruments and mechanisms" (emphasis added).

2.4.4.3 Sustainable development as object and purpose of treaty regimes

A survey of the way that sustainable development is characterized in the grand majority of treaties which make specific reference to the concept further supports a characterization of sustainable development as 'purpose' of treaty law, whether or not it is also a 'principle.' First, as noted above, the UNFCCC sets the overall framework for intergovernmental efforts to tackle the challenge posed by climate change. In spite of the Principle discussed above, an operational reference to sustainable development is also found in Article 2, which states that:

> The ultimate objective of this Convention and any related legal instruments . . . is to achieve . . . stabilization of greenhouse gas concentrations in the atmosphere at a level that would prevent dangerous anthropogenic interference with the climate system. Such a level should be achieved within a time-frame sufficient . . . to enable economic development to proceed *in a sustainable manner* (emphasis added).

The UNFCCC Preamble also affirms that "responses to climate change should be coordinated with social and economic development in an integrated manner with

---

153   See *Programme for the Further Implementation of Agenda 21* (*supra* note 61).

a view to avoiding adverse impacts on the latter, taking into full account the legitimate priority needs of developing countries for *the achievement of sustained economic growth* and the eradication of poverty" (emphasis added), recognizes that "all countries, especially developing countries, need access to resources required *to achieve sustainable social and economic development . . .*" (emphasis added) and states that Parties are "determined to protect the climate system for present and future generations." The 1997 Kyoto Protocol and the 2015 Paris Agreement,[154] share UNFCCC objectives, principles and institutions, and recognise sustainable development as an objective in clear and straightforward way. Indeed, both accords offer clear guidance for measures that States can take 'in order to promote sustainable development' in the area of climate change. The treaties aim to promote a different, more sustainable type of development of the world's natural resources and infrastructure, in a manner that attempts to take environmental, social and economic factors into account.

> At Article 2, the Kyoto Protocol provides: "Each Party included in Annex 1 . . . in order to promote sustainable development, shall: (a) Implement . . . measures such as: (i) Enhancement of energy efficiency . . . (ii) . . . promotion of sustainable forms of agriculture . . . (iv) Research on, and promotion, development and increased use of, new and renewable forms of energy . . ." Parties to the Paris Agreement, in its Preamble, emphasized "the intrinsic relationship that climate change actions, responses and impacts have with equitable access to sustainable development and eradication of poverty," and at Article 2.1, further agreed that the accord:
> "aims to strengthen the global response to the threat of climate change, in the context of sustainable development . . . (c) Making finance flows consistent with a pathway towards low greenhouse gas emissions and climate-resilient development."

At Article 6, through the Paris Agreement, Parties establish a mechanism to contribute to the mitigation of greenhouse gas emissions and support sustainable development, also agree on a framework for non-market mechanisms to sustainable development.

In the context of the UNFCCC, taking account of regime theory, it can be argued that while an uneasy agreement existed to permit recognition of the right to promote sustainable development as a Principle, in the UNFCCC negotiations of 1991-92, from 1997–2015, consensus had sufficiently evolved among the Parties to recognise sustainable development as part of the 'object and purpose' of the regime, and to establish actual mechanisms to operationalise this commitment.

As a second example, the UNCCD addresses desertification as a major economic, social and environmental problem of concern to many countries in all regions of the world. In the UNCCD, States make over forty references to 'sustainable' development, use, management, exploitation, production and

---

154 *Kyoto Protocol to the United Nations Framework Convention on Climate Change* (adopted 11 December 1997, entered into force 16 February 2005) (1998) 37 ILM 22; Paris Agreement (adopted 12 December 2015, entered into force 04 November 2016) Report FCCC/CP/2015/L.9/Rev.1.

practices and/or unsustainable development and exploitation practices. While the Parties refer to sustainable use of land and water resources in the section on Principles at Article 3, States also clearly incorporated sustainable development as an 'Objective' of the UNCCD. In the Prologue, States note that they are: "Conscious that sustainable economic growth, social development and poverty eradication are priorities of affected developing countries, particularly in Africa, and are essential to *meeting sustainability objectives . . .*" (emphasis added). In Article 2, titled 'Objective', States agree that the:

> objective of this Convention is to combat desertification and mitigate the effects of drought in countries experiencing serious drought and/or desertification, particularly in Africa, through effective action at all levels, supported by international cooperation and partnership arrangements, in the framework of an integrated approach which is consistent with *Agenda 21*, with a view *to contributing to the achievement of sustainable development in affected areas* (emphasis added).

As such, in the treaty States speak both to their intention that an integrated approach will "contribute to the achievement of sustainable development" in particular areas, and that the adoption of integrated strategies will focus on "sustainable management of land and water resources" leading to "improved living conditions". This resonates well with the concepts discussed in Chapter 1 of this book, in terms of integration of environmental, social and economic priorities in the development process, and in terms of the focus on human well-being. In the UNCCD there is also some effort by States to specify how the objective will be realized. For instance in Part II, General Provisions, at Article 4.2, States agree that "In pursuing the objective of this Convention, the Parties shall: . . . (b) give due attention . . . to the situation of affected developing country Parties with regard to international trade, marketing arrangements and debt with a view to establishing an *enabling international economic environment conducive to the promotion of sustainable development . . .*" (emphasis added). Further, at Article 18.1, the Parties commit to a number of obligations regarding the transfer, acquisition, adaptation and development of "environmentally sound, economically viable and socially acceptable technologies . . . *with a view to contributing to the achievement of sustainable development* in affected areas . . ." (emphasis added). Interestingly, the different regional annexes refer to sustainable development in slightly different ways. For instance, in the African Annex at Article 6.1, States lay out a strategic planning framework for sustainable development, establishing that: "National action programmes shall be a central and integral part of a broader process of formulating national policies for the sustainable development of affected African country Parties." In the Asian Annex at Article 2, paragraph (f), States commit to taking into consideration, *inter alia*, their need, in varying degrees, "for international cooperation to pursue sustainable development objectives relating to combating desertification and mitigating the effects of drought." In the Latin America and Caribbean Annex at Article 2 States highlight that:

(b) the frequent use of unsustainable development practices in affected areas as a result of complex interactions . . . including international economic factors such as . . . deteriorating terms of trade and trade practices which affect markets for agricultural, fishery and forestry products; and (c) . . . . from the social point of view, the results are impoverishment, migration, internal population movements, and the deterioration of the quality of life; *the region will therefore have to adopt an integrated approach* to problems of desertification and drought by *promoting sustainable development models that are in keeping with the environmental, economic and social situation in each country* (emphasis added).

In a third example, 190 countries have ratified the CBD,[155] which recognizes that the conservation of biological diversity is "a common concern of humankind" and is an integral part of the development process, and covers all ecosystems, species, and genetic resources. It links traditional conservation efforts to the economic goal of using biological resources sustainably. It establishes principles for the fair and equitable sharing of the benefits arising from the use of genetic resources, notably those destined for commercial use. It also covers the rapidly expanding field of biotechnology, addressing technology development and transfer, benefit-sharing and biosafety. In Article 1, titled 'Objectives,' States agree that the:

> *objectives* of this Convention, to be pursued in accordance with its relevant provisions, are the conservation of biological diversity, *the sustainable use of its components* and the fair and equitable sharing of the benefits arising out of the utilization of genetic resources . . . (emphasis added).

As noted in CBD materials, the treaty seeks to remind "decision-makers that natural resources are not infinite and sets out a new philosophy for the twenty-first century, that of sustainable use."[156] In Article 2, on the Use of Terms, States agreed on the following definition for sustainable use of biological diversity: "'Sustainable use' means the use of components of biological diversity in a way and at a rate that does not lead to the long-term decline of biological diversity, thereby maintaining its potential to meet the needs and aspirations of present and future generations." Furthermore, Article 8 states that each Party shall as far as possible and as appropriate:

> (c) Regulate or manage biological resources important for the conservation of biological diversity whether within or outside protected areas, *with a view to ensuring their conservation and sustainable use*; . . . (e) *Promote environmentally sound and sustainable development* in areas adjacent to protected areas with a view to furthering protection of these areas; . . .

---

155 UNCBD, *supra* note 39.
156 Ibid.

As such, in the CBD, States appear not only to clearly adopt sustainable use of biological diversity as a treaty objective, but also define fairly precisely what is meant by sustainable use, and what types of measures and activities are needed to ensure that use is, indeed, sustainable in the context of biological resources.

A fourth example is the *Cartagena Protocol on Biosafety,*[157] adopted by the COP of the CBD in 2000. This Protocol builds on Article 8 (g) of the CBD, in which States agreed (as appropriate) to:

> Establish or maintain means to regulate, manage or control the risks associated with the use and release of living modified organisms resulting from biotechnology which are likely to have adverse environmental impacts *that could affect the conservation and sustainable use of biological diversity,* taking also into account the risks to human health . . .

In the Protocol, States seek to protect biological diversity from the potential risks posed by living modified organisms resulting from modern biotechnology. They establish an advance informed agreement (AIA) procedure for ensuring that countries are provided with the information necessary to make informed decisions before agreeing to the import of such organisms into their territory. They also establish a Biosafety Clearing-House to facilitate the exchange of information on living modified organisms and to assist countries in the implementation of the Protocol. There are twenty references to the term 'sustainable' in the *Cartagena Protocol.* In Article 1, clearly titled Objective, Parties agree that:

> In accordance with the precautionary approach contained in Principle 15 of the Rio Declaration on Environment and Development, the objective of this Protocol is to contribute to ensuring an adequate level of protection in the field of the safe transfer, handling and use of living modified organisms resulting from modern biotechnology that may have adverse effects on the conservation and *sustainable use of biological diversity,* taking also into account risks to human health, and specifically focusing on transboundary movements (emphasis added).

In Article 26, on Socio-Economic Considerations, the term appears in the context of awarding special consideration to "the value of biological diversity to indigenous and local communities." In this regard, at Article 26.2, the Parties agreed that they: "are encouraged to cooperate on research and information exchange on any socio economic impacts of living modified organisms, especially on indigenous and local communities." As such, in the *Cartagena Protocol,* Parties clearly considered 'sustainable use' to be a second objective to conservation, and furthermore, consider the object relevant to social and economic (not just environmental) priorities such as the needs of indigenous and

---

157 *Cartagena Protocol on Biosafety to the Convention on Biological Diversity* (adopted 29 January 2000, entered into force 11 September 2003) 39 ILM 1027.

local communities. This highlights the point raised earlier, that there are important social and economic dimensions to sustainable development. Sustainable development, as an objective of international law, cannot simply be conflated with environmental protection in developing countries.

A fifth example offers certain further guidance. After seven years of negotiations, the FAO Conference (through Resolution 3/2001) adopted the International Treaty on Plant Genetic Resources for Food and Agriculture[158] in November 2001. The Seed Treaty covers all plant genetic resources relevant for food and agriculture, and is vital in ensuring the continued availability of the plant genetic resources that countries will need to feed their people. In the Seed Treaty, States seek to conserve for future generations the genetic diversity that is essential for food and agriculture. They defined "plant genetic resources for food and agriculture" as "any genetic material of plant origin of actual or potential value for food and agriculture." In the Seed Treaty, States establish a Multilateral System for Access and Benefit-Sharing that is meant to provide an efficient, effective and transparent framework to facilitate access to plant genetic resources for food and agriculture, and to share the benefits in a fair and equitable way.[159] There are 24 references to 'sustainable' agricultural development, use and systems in the Seed Treaty. Sustainable use of genetic resources is clearly recognized as an 'Objective' of the treaty. First, in the Preamble, Parties clearly acknowledge that "the conservation, exploration, collection, characterization, evaluation and documentation of plant genetic resources for food and agriculture are essential for . . . sustainable agricultural development for this and future generations . . ." They also recognize that this "Treaty and other international agreements relevant to this Treaty should be mutually supportive with a view to sustainable agriculture and food security . . ." In Part 1, which establishes objectives at Article 1.1, States agree that the "objectives of this Treaty are the conservation and sustainable use of plant genetic resources for food and agriculture and the fair and equitable sharing of the benefits arising out of their use, in harmony with the Convention on Biological Diversity, *for sustainable agriculture and food security.*" It is a clear recognition of 'sustainable use' as an objective of an international law, and furthermore, sets sustainable agriculture as one of two ultimate purposes of the treaty. This has particular implications. In Article 6, the Parties actually define fairly clearly what is meant by sustainable use of plant genetic resources. And sustainable use, in this context, involves the development and maintenance of legal measures. At Article 6.1, the Contracting Parties accept the duty that they "shall develop and maintain appropriate policy and legal measures that promote the sustainable use of plant genetic resources for food and agriculture." In Article 6.2, the Parties further define this as:

158 (Adopted 3 November 2001, entered into force 29 June 2004) 33 ILM 81 ftp://ftp.fao.org/
    ag/cgrfa/it/ITPGRe.pdf [Seed Treaty].
159 The Multilateral System applies to over 64 major crops and forages. Resources may be obtained
    from the Multilateral System for utilization and conservation in research, breeding and train-
    ing. When a commercial product is developed using these resources, equitable contributions are
    made to the System. The Governing Body sets out conditions for access and benefit-sharing in a
    'Material Transfer Agreement'.

sustainable use of plant genetic resources for food and agriculture may include such measures as: (a) pursuing fair agricultural policies that promote, as appropriate, the development and maintenance of diverse farming systems . . .; (b) strengthening research which enhances and conserves biological diversity . . . (c) promoting, as appropriate, plant breeding efforts . . .; (d) broadening the genetic base of crops . . .; (e) promoting . . . the expanded use of local and locally adapted crops, varieties and underutilized species; (f) supporting . . . the wider use of diversity of varieties and species in on-farm management, conservation and sustainable use of crops and creating strong links to plant breeding and agricultural development . . .; (g) reviewing, and . . . adjusting breeding strategies and regulations concerning variety release and seed distribution.

This is important for two reasons. First, the Seed Treaty is a recent instrument, and therefore offers an insight into States' most current conception of the legal status of sustainable development. Second, in the treaty, States focus on 'sustainable use' in one particular context, that of plant genetic resources for food and agriculture. In this specific sector, it appears possible to pinpoint fairly precisely the meaning of sustainable use of the resource, and the type of measures that are required to ensure that it takes place.

The commitment "to promote sustainable development" is also found in international trade treaties,[160] and indeed, has been interpreted by decisions of the Appellate Body (AB) of the WTO and other trade tribunals, as has been discussed elsewhere.[161]

While certain tribunal decisions, noted above, appear to support the contention that sustainable development is a customary principle of international law, others appear to adopt the second approach. For instance, in the often-quoted *Gabčíkovo-Nagymaros* case,[162] the ICJ majority stated that:

Throughout the ages, mankind has, for economic and other reasons, constantly interfered with nature. In the past, this was often done without consideration of the effects upon the environment. Owing to new scientific insights and to a growing awareness of the risks for mankind – for present and future generations – of pursuit of such interventions at an unconsidered and unabated pace, new norms and standards have been developed, set forth in a great number of instruments during the last two decades. Such new norms have to be taken into consideration, and such new standards given proper weight, not only when States contemplate new activities but also when continuing with activities begun in the past. This need to

160 M. Gehring and M. C. Cordonier Segger, eds., *Sustainable Development in World Trade Law* (London: Kluwer Law International, 2005). See also M. C. Cordonier Segger, "Sustainable Development in Regional Trade Agreements" in L. Bartels and F. Ortino, eds., *Regional Trade Agreements and the WTO Legal System* (Oxford: Oxford University Press, 2006) 313–39.

161 Ibid.

162 *Gabčíkovo-Nagymaros, supra* note 20 140.

reconcile economic development with protection of the environment is aptly expressed in *the concept of sustainable development*. For the purposes of the present case, this means that the Parties together should look afresh at the effects on the environment of the operation of the Gabčíkovo power plant. In particular they must find a satisfactory solution for the volume of water to be released into the old bed of the Danube and into the side-arms on both sides of the river (emphasis added).

Due to the specific facts of this case, it appears at first glance that only procedural requirements were imposed on the Parties in connection with the 'concept' of sustainable development. However, the Court did, essentially, order the Parties to integrate environmental protection into their development project by requesting them to "look afresh at the effects on the environment . . ." and "find a satisfactory solution." The majority could be said to be taking a principle of *integration* into account in order to address the 'need' to reconcile economic development with the protection of the environment *for sustainable development* – an objective. The *Nuclear Tests* case,[163] the *Kasikili/Sedudu* case (especially H.E. Judge C. G. Weeramantry's Dissent),[164] the findings in the Tribunal Award of the *Iron Rhine* arbitration[165] and the Order on Provisional Measures in the ICJ *Pulp Mills* case[166] could also be interpreted in a way that supports this characterization. For instance, in the *Iron Rhine* arbitration as mentioned above, the Arbitral Tribunal does note that "[t]he emerging principles, whatever their current status, make reference to conservation, management, notions of prevention and of sustainable development." As the Tribunal states: "[I]mportantly, these emerging principles now integrate environmental protection into the development process." This could be read to mean that the emerging principles *achieve the objective of* integrating environmental protection into the development process. The actual legal principle would be that duty to "require that where development may cause significant harm to the environment there is a duty to prevent, or at least mitigate, such harm . . ." As the Tribunal affirms, "[t]his duty, in the opinion of the Tribunal, has now become a principle of general international law."[167] Similarly, in the *Pulp Mills on the River Uruguay* case, the ICJ does state that ". . . the present case highlights the importance of the need to ensure environmental protection of shared natural resources while allowing for sustainable economic development . . ."[168] A 'need' can be an objective, not a principle. Such decisions and their implications are discussed in greater detail in other chapters of this volume.

---

163 *Nuclear Tests* case, *supra* note 108 at 341–4.
164 *Kasikili/Sedudu Island*, *supra* note 140 at 87–8 (Dissenting Opinion by H. E. Judge C. G. Weeramantry).
165 *Iron Rhine*, *supra* note 111 at 58–9.
166 *Pulp Mills*, *supra* note 112 at 80.
167 *Iron Rhine*, *supra* note 111 at 58–9.
168 *Pulp Mills*, *supra* note 112 at 80.

2.5 Proposed principles of international law on sustainable development

Sustainable development could therefore be recognized as an object and purpose of many international treaties. A great amount of legal scholarship remains to determine whether this is the best or the only way to characterize the legal status of the concept of sustainable development in international law.

As noted above, however, should sustainable development be recognized as a treaty objective, this does not preclude the existence of international legal norms (including treaty rules or customary principles) which serve to realize the treaty purpose. For instance, a requirement that development decision-making integrate environmental protection objectives might have a specific normative character, and serve the overall sustainable use objective of the UNCBD. Such operational principles may gain recognition as customary international law, binding on all States that have not persistently objected, in order to achieve sustainable development. Their universal adoption in the context of particular resources or conditions, moreover, might support a contention that in the specific context, they have already reached such a status. The practical implications of such a contention, in some treaties which have near-universal membership and commit to these principles in their context, might be minimal, but it does not discount the value of examining the principles themselves.

2.5.1 The process of agreeing international principles on sustainable development

In global governance structures, particularly with regard to the environment, consensus is still forming on which legal principles (and in the end, which values) will provide orientation for the integration of environmental, social and economic law. The process of uncovering principles of international law related to sustainable development has been reasonable, complex and comprehensive. The most important undertakings ran parallel to the global policy making events outlined above, and included the process of elaborating the 1972 Stockholm Declaration, which sets out a series of (mainly environmental) principles, the 1987 Brundtland Commissions's Legal Experts Group on Principles of International Law for the Protection of the Environment and Sustainable Development, which built on the Stockholm Declaration but included a detailed commentary and a clear 'norm-generating' facet to each proposed Principles.

The 1992 Rio Declaration echoes many of the Principles recommended by the Brundtland Report. The central concept of the 1992 Rio Declaration[169] is sustainable development, as defined by the Brundtland Report. These views are also reflected in Principle 1, which states that "[h]uman beings are at the centre of concerns for sustainable development. They are entitled to a healthy and productive life in harmony with nature." Several procedural and substantive principles agreed in the 1992 Rio Declaration are relevant to international

169 Rio Declaration, *supra* note 41 at 70–1

trade policy, as will be further discussed later in this chapter. Principle 12 is straightforward: "States should cooperate to promote a supportive and open international economic system that would lead to economic growth and sustainable development in all countries, to better address the problems of environmental degradation." According to the Principle, trade measures should not constitute a means for arbitrary or unjustifiable discrimination or a disguised restriction on international trade, unilateral actions should be avoided, and environmental measures should be based as far as possible on international consensus. Principle 3 states that "[t]he right to development must be fulfilled so as to equitably meet developmental and environmental needs of present and future generations." Principle 4 states that "[i]n order to achieve sustainable development, environmental protection shall constitute an integral part of the development process and cannot be considered in isolation from it." Further, Principle 10 maintains that "States shall facilitate and encourage public awareness and participation by making information widely available. Effective access to judicial and administrative proceedings, including redress and remedy, shall be provided." Principle 14 reads "States should effectively cooperation to discourage or prevent the relocation and transfer to other States of any activities and substances that cause severe environmental degradation or are found to be harmful to human health." Principle 15 states that "the precautionary approach shall be widely applied by States according to their capabilities. Where there are threats of serious or irreversible damage, lack of full scientific certainty shall not be used as a reason for postponing cost-effective measures to prevent environmental degradation." Finally, Principle 16 states that "National authorities should endeavour to promote the internalization of environmental costs and the use of economic instruments, taking into account the approach that the polluter should, in principle, bear the cost of pollution, with due regard to the public interest and without distorting international trade and investment." These principles are reaffirmed and specifically mentioned throughout the 1992 *Agenda 21*.

The Rio Declaration was followed by the *Report of the Expert Group Meeting on Identification of Principles of International Law for Sustainable Development*, which was commissioned by the UN Secretariat and released in September 1995. In 1997, States provided further guidance, stating at para. 14, in the *Programme of Action for Further Implementation of Agenda 21* that:

> [p]rogress has been made in incorporating the principles contained in the Rio Declaration on Environment and Development – including the principle of common but differentiated responsibilities, which embodies the important concept of and basis for international partnership; the precautionary principle; the polluter pays principle; and the environmental impact assessment principle – in a variety of international and national legal instruments. While some progress has been made in implementing United Nations Conference on Environment and Development commitments through a variety of international legal instruments, much remains to be done to embody the Rio principles more firmly in law and practice.

In 2002, the International Law Association Committee on the Legal Aspects of Sustainable Development released the *New Delhi Declaration of Principles of International Law Relating to Sustainable Development* [New Delhi Principles][170] which were included as a submission from the Netherlands in the outcomes of the 2002 World Summit on Sustainable Development. These seven Principles are found throughout the 2002 *Johannesburg Plan of Implementation*. Though a detailed analysis is beyond the scope of this short survey, these principles are also reflected in many international treaties related to sustainable development.

2.5.2 *The* ILA New Delhi Declaration of Principles of International Law Relating to Sustainable Development

The New Delhi Principles mentioned both above and below, highlight seven principles of international law in the field of sustainable development.[171]

2.5.2.1 *The duty of states to ensure sustainable use of natural resources*

In essence, this principle evokes a duty of states to ensure sustainable use of natural resources. States have sovereign rights over their natural resources, and a duty not to cause (or allow) undue damage to the environment of other States in the use of these resources. States have sovereign rights over their natural resources, but shall not cause undue damage to the global environment through their use of these resources. This has evolved into a positive obligation to ensure that natural resources are used in a sustainable manner, in many areas of transboundary resources management. This principle has been reflected and strongly reaffirmed in several international treaties on sustainable development with extremely broad membership in the past two decades.[172]

---

170   See "ILA New Delhi Declaration of Principles of International Law Relating to Sustainable Development" in *International Environmental Agreements: Politics, Law and Economics* (The Hague: Kluwer Academic Publishers), 2, 2 2002, 209–16, online: <http://www.kluweronline.com/issn/1567-9764/current>. And see N. Schrijver and F. Weiss, *"Editorial"* in ibid. at 2, 2 2002, 105–08, online: <http://www.kluweronline.com/issn/1567-9764/current>. See also *Report of the Expert Group on Identification of Principles of International Law for Sustainable Development* (London: ILA, 1995), International Law Association (ILA); *Report of the Sixty-Second Conference* (Seoul: ILA, 1987) at 1–11, 409–87.

171   See, e.g. "ILA New Delhi Declaration of Principles of International Law Relating to Sustainable Development", supra note 170 at 2, 2 2002, 209–16, online: <http://www.kluweronline.com/issn/1567-9764/current>. And see N. Schrijver and F. Weiss, *supra* note 170 at 2, 2 2002, 105–08, online: <http://www.kluweronline.com/issn/1567-9764/current>.

172   See UNFCCC, Preamble; UNCBD, art 3,10; UNCCD, *supra* note 40 art 3(c), 10.4, 11, 17.1(a) and 19.1(c) and (e); *Marrakesh Agreement Establishing the World Trade Organization,* signed 15 April 1994, entry into force 1 January 1995, 1867 UNTS 4 (WTO Agreement), Preamble; Seed Treaty, art 1.1.

The principle was recognized in Stockholm Declaration Principle 21 and the Rio Declaration Principle 2.[173] Principle 2 of the 1992 Rio Declaration, for instance, provides "States have, in accordance with the Charter of the United Nations and the principles of international law, the sovereign right to exploit their own resources pursuant to their own environmental and developmental policies, and the responsibility to ensure that activities within their jurisdiction or control do not cause damage to the environment of other States or of areas beyond the limits of national jurisdiction." Certain goods are also considered as part of the global commons, which implies related obligations of non-appropriation, international management, sharing of benefits and exclusive use for peaceful purposes. This duty also recognizes the importance of common concerns for states, as respect for (and protection of) such concern is often the legal basis of sustainable development regulations that impose obligations on state, regional and local authorities.

2.5.2.2 *The principle of equity and the eradication of poverty*

As part of sustainable development, States shall promote a just distribution of resources among members of the present generation. These aspirations should focus in particular on meeting the basic needs of the poor, who have the greatest priority in sustainable development. States which are in a position to do so have a further responsibility to assist other States. In addition, the present generation has the obligation to refrain from depriving future generations of the means to meet their own environmental, social and economic needs. States shall take into account the needs of future generations in making decisions about allocations of resources. Furthermore, States have a duty to progressively reduce poverty. According to the New Delhi Principles, the principle of equity includes a duty to co-operate to secure development opportunities of developed and developing countries, and a duty to co-operate for the eradication of poverty, as noted in Chapter IX on International Economic and Social Cooperation of the UN Charter. The Declaration argues that whilst it is the primary responsibility of the State to aim for its own conditions of equity, all States which are in a position to do so have a responsibility to assist.[174] This principle is also clearly reflected in international treaty law on sustainable development.[175]

---

173 Cordonier Segger and Khalfan, *supra* note 3 109–22 both central norms are likely customary rules. K. Bottriel and D. French, "The Duty of States to Ensure Sustainable Use of Natural Resources," *CISDL Legal Working Papers* (CISDL Montreal 2005) <http://www.cisdl.org/pdf/sdl/SDL_Sustainable_Use.pdf>.

174 Cordonier Segger and Khalfan, *supra* note 3 122–32 not a clear customary norm. J. Hepburn and A. Khalfan, 'The Principle of Equity and the Eradication of Poverty', *CISDL Legal Working Papers* (CISDL Montreal 2005) <http://www.cisdl.org/pdf/sdl/SDL_Equity.pdf>.

175 See UNFCCC, *supra* note 38 Preamble; UNCBD, *supra* note 39 art 3,10; UNCCD, *supra* note 40 art 3(c), 10.4, 11, 17.1(a) and 19.1(c) and (e); WTO Agreement, *supra* note 172 Preamble; Seed Treaty, *supra* note 158 art 1.1, 10–13.

2.5.2.3 The principle of common but differentiated resonsibilities

The common responsibility of states for the protection of the environment at the national, regional and global levels shall be balanced by the need to take account of different circumstances, particularly in relation to each State's historical contribution to the creation of a particular problem, as well as its ability to prevent, reduce and control the threat. Developed countries bear a special burden of responsibility in reducing unsustainable patterns of consumption and providing assistance to developing countries to meet global sustainable development goals. According to the New Delhi Principles, this principle holds that the common responsibility of states for the protection of the environment at the national, regional and global levels shall be balanced by the need to take account of different circumstances, particularly in relation to each state's historical contribution to the creation of a particular problem, as well as its ability to prevent, reduce and control the threat.[176] This principle is reflected in a number of treaties,[177] including the *Paris Agreement on Climate Change* that was concluded in December 2015 at the 21st Conference of the Parties to the UNFCCC.

2.5.2.4 The principle of the precautionary approach to human health, natural resources and ecosystems

In order to protect the environment, natural resources and human health, the precautionary approach shall be widely applied by States according to their capabilities. Where there are threats of serious or irreversible damage, lack of full scientific certainty shall not be used as a reason for postponing cost-effective measures to prevent degradation. The precautionary principle shifts the burden of proof to those proposing activities which might cause serious harm. The precautionary principle shifts the burden of proof to those proposing activities which might cause serious harm.[178] This principle is a central component of a number of international agreements.[179] It favours prevention over re-mediation, focuses on

---

176 Cordonier Segger and Khalfan, *supra* note 3 at 132–43 may be emerging rule, I. Ahmad, "The Principle of Common but Differentiated Responsibilities", *CISDL Legal Working Papers* (CISDL Montreal 2005) <http://www.cisdl.org/pdf/sdl/SDL_Common_but_Diff.pdf>.

177 UNFCCC, Preamble, art 3 and 4; Kyoto Protocol, *supra* note 154 art 10 and 12; UNCCD, *supra* note 40 art 3–7; Seed Treaty, *supra* note 158 art 7.2(a), 8, 15.1(b)iii and 18.4(d).

178 Cordonier Segger and Khalfan, *supra* note 3 at 143–55 may be emerging customary norm, J. Hepburn, M. C. Cordonier Segger and M. Gehring, "The Principle of the Precautionary Approach to Human Health, Natural Resources and Ecosystems", *CISDL Legal Working Papers* (CISDL Montreal 2005) <http://www.cisdl.org/pdf/sdl/SDL_Precaution.pdf>.

179 UNCBD, *supra* note 39 art 14.1(b); *Cartagena Protocol, supra* note 157 Preamble, art 1, 7, 10.6, 11.8 and 15; UNFCCC, *supra* note 38 art 3; 1998 Rotterdam Convention on the Prior Informed Consent Procedure for Certain Hazardous Chemicals and Pesticides in International Trade (adopted 10 September 1998, entered into force 24 February 2004), UN Doc. UNEP/FAO/PIC/CONF/5, art 14(3) and Annex V; Stockholm Convention on Persistent Organic Pollutants (adopted 22 May 2001, entered into force 17 May 2004) 40 ILM 531., Preamble, art 1 and 8 and Part V(B) of Annex C; Agreement for the Implementation of the Provisions of the UN Convention on the Law of the Sea of 10 December 1982 relating to the Conservation and

the relevance and robustness of scientific data to development decision-making and carries an obligation to use precautionary measures in proportion to potential damage and the likelihood or degree of risk involved in each case.

2.5.2.5 The principle of public participation and access to information and justice

Sustainable development issues are best handled with participation of all concerned citizens, at the relevant level. States shall ensure at the national level that each individual shall have appropriate access to information concerning sustainable development that is held by public authorities and the opportunity to participate in decision-making processes. States shall facilitate and encourage public awareness and participation by making information widely available. Effective access to judicial and administrative proceedings, including redress and remedy, shall be provided. Essentially, this principle holds that people should be able to participate in decision-making processes which affect and impact their lives and well-being. In order to participate fully, the public must have access to adequate information. And in different ways, citizens should have access to independent appeal if their concerns are not addressed. According to this principle, States have a duty to ensure that individuals have appropriate access to 'appropriate, comprehensible and timely' information concerning sustainable development that is held by public authorities, and the opportunity to participate in decision-making processes. There are three main elements. First, this principle holds that people should be able to participate in decision-making processes which affect and impact their lives and well-being. Second, in order to participate fully, the public must have access to adequate information. And third, citizens should have access to independent review if their concerns are not addressed.[180] This principle is included in a great many international legal instruments.[181] In particular, as discussed late in this volume, the 1998 *Aarhus Convention on Access to Information, Public Participation in Decision-making and Access to Justice in Environmental Matters*, which relates mainly to the

Management of Straddling Fish Stocks and Highly Migratory Fish Stocks, (adopted 4 August 1995, entered into force 11 December 2001) UN Doc A/CONF.164/38 (1995), 34 ILM 1542, art 6. In addition, according to the WTO Appellate Body, the WTO Agreement on the Application of Sanitary and PhytoSanitary Measures art 5.7, as per *EC – Measures Concerning Meat and Meat Products (Hormones) (Compliance USA and Canada)* (13 February 1998), WTO Doc WT/DS26/AB/R, WT/DS48/AB/R (Appellate Body Report) 124.

180 Cordonier Segger and Khalfan, *supra* note 3 at 156–66. This may be an emerging customary principle, K. Bottriel and M. C. Cordonier Segger, "The Principle of Public Participation and Access to Information and Justice", *CISDL Legal Working Papers* (*CISDL Montreal* 2005) <http://www.cisdl.org/pdf/sdl/SDL_Participation.pdf>.

181 *Agenda 21*, paragraphs 8.18–8.19; UNCBD, art 13; *Cartagena Protocol, supra* note 157 art 23; UNCCD, *supra* note 40 art 3(a) and 10.2(f); WTO Agreement, *supra* note 172 art V.2; Seed Treaty, *supra* note 158 art 9.2(c); North American Agreement on Environmental Cooperation, 32 ILM (1993) 1480 at arts 14, 15; *Convention on Access to Information, Public Participation in Decision-Making and Access to Justice in Environmental Matters*, (open for signature 25 June 1998, entry into force on 30 October 2001) 2161 UNTS 447.

environment, is an example of an international legal instrument based on this principle, and many international human rights instruments also provide specifically for public participation, access to information and access to justice.

2.5.2.6 *The principle of good governance*

States shall take measures to combat corruption, taking into account the negative effects of corruption on sustainable development. Good governance is based on respect for the rule of law, democracy, political accountability, government flexibility and responsiveness for its citizens. Good governance means that institutions and processes seek to serve a strategic vision and include significant stakeholders, structures are oriented toward building consensus, ensuring efficiency, coherence and coordination among institutional actors. Good governance mediates differing interests to reach a broad consensus on what is in the best interests of the community and, where possible, on policies and procedures. Interrelated, these core characteristics are mutually reinforcing. Good governance is, on many levels, almost a pre-condition for effective law and regulation in any area, and is specifically prioritized in the JPOI as well as other international legal instruments. In essence, this means that States shall take measures to combat corruption, and encourage corporate social responsibility and socially responsible investment among private actors.[182] International treaties are beginning to incorporate such obligations.[183] According to State Parties to the *UN Convention Against Corruption,* corruption threatens the political stability and sustainable development of States.

2.5.2.7 *The principle of integration and interrelationship, in particular in relation to human rights and social, economic and environmental objectives*

As stated in Principle 4 of the Rio Declaration, in order to achieve sustainable development, environmental protection shall constitute an integral part of the development process and cannot be considered in isolation from it. States should strive to resolve apparent conflicts between competing economic and financial, social and environmental considerations. If a customary international rule *named* sustainable development were to emerge, the principle of "integration in order to achieve sustainable development" is the most likely candidate. However, as the New Delhi Principles themselves recommend, such a norm could just as easily be characterized as the 'integration principle.' The New Delhi Principles strongly emphasize recent developments in international consensus, such as the need to recognize social and

---

182   Cordonier Segger and Khalfan, *supra* note 3 at 166–70. This functional principle may not require recognition as a customary rule. N. Chowdry and C. E. Skarstedt, "The Principle of Good Governance", *CISDL Legal Working Papers* (CISDL Montreal 2005) <http://www.cisdl. org/pdf/sdl/SDL_Good_Governance.pdf>.

183   *UN Convention Against Corruption* (adopted 31 October 2003, entry into force 14 December 2005), Preamble, art 5.1, 62.1; UNCCD, *supra* note 40 art 3(c), 10.2(e) and 11–12.

human rights pillar of sustainable development, essentially by advocating an integration principle which requires States to take social and human rights, as well as environmental priorities, into account in the development process.[184] The principle is essential to international treaties on sustainable development.[185]

These New Delhi Principles, taken together, provide considerable guidance for jurists seeking ways to balance conflicting or overlapping social, environmental and economic obligations. They are generating increasing interest in academic, legal and policy debates.

2.5.3 A principled approach to international law on sustainable development

2.5.3.1 Functional principles of treaty law

While these rather functional principles may appear in most treaties related to sustainable development, it is not yet clear whether all are customary norms, both due to a lack of practice/*opinio juris*, and in some cases, a lack of specificity and 'normativity' in their formulation.[186] However, these seven principles, along with several of the others identified in earlier process, are present in nearly all international treaties which recognize sustainable development as an objective. As such, it is possible that they represent part of the corpus of international law on sustainable development.

There is, however, a second type of principle of international law that has been proposed in international legal scholarship, one which can be analysed from a combined international relations and international law perspective, and fits well with the concept of a regime discussed earlier.

2.5.3.2 Sustainable development as an interstitial norm

Sustainable development appears, often as an objective or preambular reference, in most international statements and declarations related to environmental, social and economic issues since the 1992 Rio de Janeiro Earth Summit. It has

---

184 Cordonier Segger and Khalfan, *supra* note 3 at 102–09, this principle is fast becoming recognized as a rule of customary international law. See also S. Jodoin, "The Principle of Integration and Interrelationship in International Sustainable Development Law" in A. Usha, ed., *Environmental Law: Principles and Governance* (Hyderabad, India: ICFAI University Press, 2008) at 83.

185 UNCBD, *supra* note 39 art 6; *Cartagena Protocol, supra* note 157 Preamble, art 2.4–2.5; Seed Treaty, *supra* note 158 Preamble, art 5.1. See also, e.g. *North American Free Trade Agreement* (adopted 17 December 1992, entered into force 1 January 1994) Can. T.S. 1994 No. 2, 32 ILM 289 (NAFTA) arts 103, 104, 104.1, 1114, 2101.

186 M. C. Cordonier Segger and A. Khalfan, *Sustainable Development Law: Principles, Practices and Prospects* (Oxford: Oxford University Press, 2004). See also M. C. Cordonier Segger, "Significant Developments in Sustainable Development Law and Governance: A Proposal" (2004) United Nations *Natural Resources Forum* 28:1. And see FAO, *International Law and Sustainable Development Since Rio* (Rome: FAO, 2002); or see M. C. Cordonier Segger, A. Khalfan, M. Gehring and M. Toering, "Prospects for Principles of International Sustainable Development Law after Johannesburg: Common but Differentiated Responsibilities, Precaution and Participation" (2003) 12:3 RECIEL.

also featured as a purpose in some economic, social and environmental treaties involving developed and developing countries, and as principle in others, and as both by judges in national courts around the world.[187]

This chapter has considered the normative status of sustainable development in international law. Is sustainable development a binding principle of international customary law? Is it simply a broad policy goal, found in certain international treaties but without specific meaning? Or is it more?

As mentioned above, it is not clear that 'sustainable development', as such, can be accurately described as a single emerging principle of international law, or as a customary norm that can eventually, through demonstrable state practice and *opinio juris*, be accepted as binding on all states. It is not certain that sustainable development is becoming a customary norm of international law in itself. International legal obligations of sustainable development may, however, have been assumed with regard to certain economic development sectors, regional cooperation initiatives, or resource management challenges, in treaties and in international practice. As such, it is difficult, at present, to describe 'sustainable development' as a binding principle of customary law in the traditional sense.

But neither is it accurate to describe sustainable development as simply a vague international policy goal, void of normative value outside the confines of treaties. As observed by H.E. Judge C. G. Weeramantry in his extraordinary Separate Opinion in the *Case Concerning the Gabčíkovo-Nagymaros Dam* (Hungary/ Slovakia),[188] there is "wide and general acceptance by the global community" of sustainable development. There is also emerging global consensus on the need to strengthen 'international law on sustainable development', and on the need for further implementation of this law. The sheer weight of legal instruments and treaties which have been set in place to implement the sustainable development obligations, and its significant procedural elements, argue against such a facile dismissal.

Neither of these two options serves to accurately characterize sustainable development in international law, especially after the 2015 release of the Sustainable Development Goals for the world. Rather, recent developments in international law on sustainable development can be understood through a combination of two complementary approaches.

---

187 National cases applying the concept of sustainable development include: *Vellore Citizens Welfare Forum* v *Union of India* (1996, Supreme Court of India) and *Bulankulame* v *Secretary, Ministry of Industrial Development and Others* (the Eppawela *Case*) (2000, Supreme Court of Sri Lanka). In *Rajendra Parajuli and Others v Shree Distillery Pvt. Ltd. & Others*, the Supreme Court of Nepal (Writ No. 3259, 1996) stated that sustainable development means "every industry has an obligation to run its development activities without creating environmental deterioration. The environment should not be viewed narrowly. It is imperative for any industry to be cautious towards the environment while it is in operation." The Court ordered the company to comply with a prior agreement to keep the environment free of pollution in the affected area.

188 (1997) ICJ Reports, 7.

First, 'international law on sustainable development' describes a 'group of congruent norms,'[189] a corpus of international legal principles and treaties which address the areas of intersection between international economic law, international environmental law and international human rights law,[190] in order to achieve the object and purpose of sustainable development. Certain procedural and substantive norms and instruments, which help to balance or integrate these fields, form part of this international law and play a role in its implementation.

Second, as an objective of international law, sustainable development may serve as a different type of norm in its own right,[191] one that exerts a certain pull between conflicting international norms relating to environmental protection, social development and economic growth. Sustainable development, when applied in treaty negotiation or dispute settlement, can be analysed as a "meta-principle, acting upon other legal rules and principles – a legal concept exercising a kind of interstitial normativity, pushing and pulling the boundaries of true primary norms when they threaten to overlap or conflict with each other."[192] This characterization is in accordance with the one relevant majority decision of the ICJ on this issue to date.[193]

The substantive aspect of this 'interstitial norm' is the requirement that all three sets of priorities be reflected in the substantive outcomes of a given dispute or conflict. While there are few bright lines, and no hard and fast rule, it is not 'sustainable' to allow one or the other priority to be ignored or undermined in situations where common international concerns are at stake. Viewed in this way, sustainable development can serve as a decision-making concept to help judges to curb the worst social and environmental excesses of nations in economic development activities,[194] and in treaty law, it can exert persuasive pressure for the internalization of otherwise externalized or marginalized social, economic or environmental concerns.

As Lowe observes, there is "an immense gravitational pull exerted by concepts such as sustainable development, regardless of their standing as rules or principles

189 V. Lowe, "Sustainable Development and Unsustainable Arguments" in A. Boyle and D. Freestone, eds., *International Law and Sustainable Development: Past Achievements and Future Challenges* (Oxford: Oxford University Press, 1999) at 26.

190 M. C. Cordonier Segger, "Significant Developments in Sustainable Development Law and Governance: A Proposal" (2004) United Nations *Natural Resources Forum* 28:1. See FAO, *International Law and Sustainable Development Since Rio* (Rome: FAO, 2002). See also M. C. Cordonier Segger, A. Khalfan, M. Gehring and M. Toering "Prospects for Principles of International Sustainable Development Law after Johannesburg: Common but Differentiated Responsibilities, Precaution and Participation" (2003) 12:3 RECIEL.

191 V. Lowe, "The Politics of Law-Making: Are the Method and Character of Norm Creation Changing?" in M. Byers, ed., *The Role of Law in International Politics: Essays in International Relations and International Law* (Oxford: Oxford University Press, 2000) at 214–15.

192 V. Lowe, "Sustainable Development and Unsustainable Arguments" in A. Boyle and D. Freestone, eds., *International Law and Sustainable Development: Past Achievements and Future Challenges* (Oxford: Oxford University Press, 1999) at 31.

193 *Gabčíkovo-Nagymaros, supra* note 20 at para. 140.

194 M. Decleris, *The Law of Sustainable Development: General Principles, A Report for the European Commission* (Luxembourg: Office for Official Publications of the European Communities, 2000) at 40.

of *lex lata*. That is plain when they are used by judges as modifiers; but it is also true when they are used in the same way by States as they negotiate (either with other states, or within their own governmental apparatus) on ways of reconciling conflicting principles."[195]

2.6 Conclusion

In conclusion, it is not clear whether a legally binding 'principle of sustainable development' has been agreed to by States as such.[196] However, a growing body of 'international law in the field of sustainable development' exists and is being implemented by States. As noted by Alan Boyle and David Freestone, "[e]ven if there is no legal obligation to develop sustainably, there may nevertheless be, through incremental development, law 'in the field of sustainable development'."[197]

As discussed above, the recognition of international law on sustainable development is supported by many references made by governments in agreed consensus statements, from the 1992 Rio Declaration and Chapters 38 and 39 of the 1992 *Agenda 21*, from the 1997 Programme of Further Implementation of *Agenda 21*, from the 2002 Johannesburg Declarations and Plan of Action from the World Summit for Sustainable Development from the 2012 Rio Declaration, the Future We Want, and from the 2015 Sustainable Development Goals. In response to the 1987 Brundtland Report, in 1992 governments committed to the "further development of international law on sustainable development, giving special attention to the delicate balance between environmental and developmental concerns."[198] Governments also recognized the "need to clarify and strengthen the relationship between existing international instruments or agreements in the field of environment and relevant social and economic agreements or instruments, taking into account the special needs of the developing countries . . ."[199] *Agenda 21* is clear on

---

195 V. Lowe, "Sustainable Development and Unsustainable Arguments" in A. Boyle and D. Freestone, eds., *International Law and Sustainable Development: Past Achievements and Future Challenges* (Oxford: Oxford University Press, 1999) at 35.

196 For different views on this point, see Phillipe Sands, "International Law in the Field of Sustainable Development: Emerging Legal Principles" in W. Lang, ed., *Sustainable Development and International Law* (Oxford: Oxford University Press, 1999); D. Ginthers, M. Denters and P. de Waart, eds., *Sustainable Development and Global Governance* (London: 1995); M. McGoldrick, "Sustainable Development: The Challenge to International Law" in *Review of European Community and International Environmental Law*, 3 (1994) or P. Sands, "International Law in the Field of Sustainable Development" (1994) 65 *Brit. Y.B. of Int'l L.* 303.

197 A. Boyle and D. Freestone, *International Law and Sustainable Development: Past Achievements and Future Challenges* (Oxford: Oxford University Press, 1999), at 17 citing P. Sands, "International Law in the Field of Sustainable Development" (1994) 65 BYIL 303.

198 Rio Declaration on Environment and Development, Report of the United Nations Conference on Environment and Development, UN Doc. A/CONF.151/6/Rev.1, (1992), 31 ILM 874 (1992), especially at Principle 27 on international law; *Agenda 21, supra* note 41 at chapter 39, on international law.

199 Ibid.

this point,[200] and emphasizes the importance of ensuring that developing countries can participate in "treaty making in the field of international law on sustainable development." They further called for action to, for instance, make laws and regulations more effective. At paragraph 8.17, they stated that "Governments, with the support, where appropriate, of competent international organizations, should regularly assess the laws and regulations enacted and the related institutional/administrative machinery established at the national/state and local/municipal level in the field of environment and sustainable development, with a view to rendering them effective in practice . . ." With regards to the establishment of judicial and administrative procedures, they noted at paragraph 8.18 that "Governments and legislators, with the support, where appropriate, of competent international organizations, should establish judicial and administrative procedures for legal redress and remedy of actions affecting environment and development that may be unlawful or infringe on rights under the law, and should provide access to individuals, groups and organizations with a recognized legal interest." And with regards to the provision of legal reference and support services, they stated at paragraph 8.19 that "Competent intergovernmental and non-governmental organizations could co-operate to provide Governments and legislators, upon request, with an integrated programme of environment and development law (sustainable development law) services, carefully adapted to the specific requirements of the recipient legal and administrative systems." Further, they recognized the need to establish "a cooperative training network for sustainable development law," stating at paragraph 8.20 that "[c]ompetent international and academic institutions could, within agreed frameworks, cooperate to provide, especially for trainees from developing countries, postgraduate programmes and in-service training facilities in environment and development law."

The 1997 *Plan of Further Implementation of Agenda 21*, similarly states that "it is necessary to continue the progressive development and, as and when appropriate, codification of international law related to sustainable development."[201]And the 2002 Johannesburg Plan of Implementation requests the CSD to track, and take into account, "significant legal developments in the field of sustainable development, with due regard to the role of relevant intergovernmental bodies in promoting the implementation of *Agenda 21* relating to international legal instruments and mechanisms."[202]

What is international law on sustainable development? In this volume, it is defined as the body of legal principles, treaties and instruments in the field of

---

200 At Chapter 39, entitled International Legal Mechanisms and Instruments, at para. 39.1, a basis for action is identified.
201 In particular, see paras 109 and 110, G.A. Res. S-19/2. UN GAOR, 19th Special Sess. (1997). A/RES/S-19/2.
202 Plan of Implementation of the World Summit on Sustainable Development at para. 148, in Report of the World Summit on Sustainable Development, A/CONF.199/20 Johannesburg, South Africa, 26 August to 4 September 2002.

sustainable development which govern the area of intersection between social, economic and environmental law.[203] Though the role of international law in sustainable development is still in process of definition, much progress has been made in recent decades.

At national and international levels, in binding 'hard law' treaties and international judgments, and in the persuasive authority of 'soft law' declarations and state practice, countries increasingly perceive economic, social and environmental protection as complementary rather than as unrelated or opposing disciplines. Sustainable development requires coherence between social, economic and environmental law, at the international level. Governments in many treaties and regimes have found themselves under pressure to link with, or take into account, significant developments in other areas of law related to sustainable development. For some, the decision of governments may be that further linkage or 'integration' is not a priority – often, the key to effectiveness is focus, adopting a relatively narrow mandate and fulfilling it. But for many others, progress toward a different 'degree of integration' with other fields might become a desirable goal. For such instruments, 'inter-locking mechanisms' must be developed to take into account relevant aspects of social, economic or environmental law, where lack of integration, coordination or coherence is affecting the ability of the institution or law to achieve its goals. These 'inter-locking mechanisms', which facilitate integration, are found in social, economic or environmental treaties and institutions, and are part of and governed by sustainable development law.

In the past, sustainable development has been seen as a legal concept of certain vagueness.[204] It needed to be relevant in different local and global contexts, from many cultures and regions. This approach has outlived its usefulness, particularly in international law. In this volume, sustainable development can be defined as a new type of development that does not irreversibly deplete essential natural capital, one that reconciles social, economic and environmental policies to enable improvements in present generations' quality of life, in a way that takes the interests of the future into account. The normative consequences of a commitment to sustainable development may not be the same as a straightforward prohibition or prescription. In Dworkin's terms, sustainable development might fit better

203 M. C. Cordonier Segger and A. Khalfan, *Sustainable Development Law: Principles, Practices and Prospects* (Oxford: Oxford University Press, 2004). On the process of development of international law in this manner, see J. Brunnée and S. J. Toope "International Law and Constructivism: Elements of an Interactional Theory of International Law" (2000) 39(1) *Col. J. Trans'l. Law* 19. See also V. Lowe, "The Politics of Law-Making: Are the Method and Character of Norm Creation Changing?" in M. Byers, ed., *The Role of Law in International Politics: Essays in International Relations and International Law* (Oxford: Oxford University Press, 2000) at 214–15.

204 One of the most compelling explanations for the early lack of clarity was presented by C. D. Stone, in "Deciphering Sustainable Development" (1994) 69 *Chi.-Kent L. Rev.* 977. "The term sustainable development is not merely vague – a masker of failed consensus – the way key terms in the U.S. Constitution are vague and require case by case elaboration. 'Sustainable development' functions to gloss over not only failed consensus, but a latent collision course."

into the category of a 'policy' objectives rather than legal rights or principles.[205] However, if one adopts a more complex view of international law informed by both legal theorists such as Fuller,[206] and also by international relations theorists such as Krasner,[207] which sees international law as part of the structure governing the relationships of States and other international actors, a sustainable development objective can have normative force that is different in distinct specific contexts. Indeed, many States have begun to focus on implementation in different contexts, committing to the sustainable use or management of a particular resource, or to promote sustainable development by re-directing a specific type of economic activity. If today's interactional treaty regimes are recognized as part of international law, a legal commitment to sustainable development has meaning and normative force both in the implementation of international treaties, and in 'soft law' cooperation arrangements which support them, and may be taken up by international courts, tribunals and other dispute settlement mechanisms that implement those treaties and that cooperative compliance.

A commitment to sustainable development requires States to find a balance between overlapping international economic, social and environmental priorities and obligations, in the interest of development that can last over the long term. Such overlaps seldom result in direct conflicts, taking into account Wesley Hohfeld's approach of co-related norms,[208] and the established conflict rules of the *Vienna Convention on the Law of Treaties*.[209] However, in specific areas of law and policy, such overlaps can create constraints on regulatory and other efforts to promote sustainable development. Principles of international law on sustainable development are emerging and gaining recognition to address such overlaps. In order to realize sustainable development, States have agreed *inter alia* to cooperate on certain matters of common global concern, to jointly manage certain transboundary natural resources in a way that is equitable and sustainable; to ensure that social and economic development decision-making and environmental protection is integrated; to respect the common but differentiated responsibilities of developed and developing countries; to use precaution in the face of scientific uncertainty; and to undertake development decision-making in a way that is transparent and participatory. State commitments to sustainable development, as an objective of international law, may also have a residual normative force which can best be described as an interstitial norm.

A great deal of progress has been made since the 1987 Brundland Report, though much more is needed. When States commit to sustainable development

---

205 Dworkin, *supra* note 91.
206 Lon L. Fuller, *The Morality of Law*, rev. edn (New Haven, CT: Yale University Press, 1969).
207 Stephen D. Krasner, *Sovereignty: Organized Hypocrisy* (Princeton, NJ: Princeton University Press, 1999).
208 Hohfeld, *supra* note 131.
209 Vienna Convention on the Law of Treaties, entered into force 27 Jan. 1980, 1155 UNTS 331, 8 ILM 679 at art 31.3.c.

in a treaty or international legal process, as international courts and tribunals are increasingly finding that this is not legally meaningless. It involves an obligation to seek balance between sometimes conflicting priorities in the development process, and in the interests of future generations. The balance can be achieved through procedures and substantive obligations which differ depending on the treaty instrument, the area of law and policy that it regulates, and the nature of the dispute in question. The challenge for future legal scholarship – and action – is to develop the understanding, wisdom and courage that is necessary to implement this global commitment in the interest of a common future.*

---

* With grateful thanks to Dr. Kamal Hossain for his insights, guidance and advice.

3 Advancements in the principles of international law on sustainable development[1]

Introduced by Nico Schrijver

Professor Nico Schrijver is Chair of the ILA Committee on International Law on Sustainable Development, and was Rapporteur of the ILA Committee on the Legal Aspects of Sustainable Development which, through ten years of intense international scholarly review and debate, developed the 2002 New Delhi Declaration of Principles of International Law Relating to Sustainable Development. This brief commentary shares some of his thoughts on the concept of sustainable development, and the process of developing the ILA New Delhi Declaration of Principles.[2]

The concept of 'sustainable development' has attracted considerable attention in recent years and has become of pivotal importance in scientific and political discourse. Increasingly, it has also gained importance in the practice of states and of relevant international organizations concerned with environmental conservation and development.

Following its introduction into international politics by the *World Commission on Environment and Development* in 1987, the concept of sustainable development rapidly acquired a prominent place on the international political agenda.[3] The documents resulting from the 1992 United Nations Conference on Environment and Development, held at Rio de Janeiro in 1992, were focused on sustainable development as their ultimate objective.

---

1 See "ILA New Delhi Declaration of Principles of International Law Relating to Sustainable Development" in 2 *International Environmental Agreements: Politics, Law and Economics* (Netherlands: Springer, 2002) at 209–16, available online: <http://www.kluweronline.com/issn/1567-9764/current>. For a comprehensive discussion of principles and practices related to sustainable development and international law, see N. Schrijver and F. Weiss, eds., *International Law and Sustainable Development: Principles and Practice* (Leiden: Martinus Nijhoff Publishers, 2004) at 699.

2 See N. Schrijver and F. Weiss, "Editorial" in 2 *International Environmental Agreements: Politics, Law and Economics* (Netherlands: Springer, 2002) at 105–8, available online: <http://www.kluweronline.com/issn/1567-9764/current>. This chapter is based on editorial comments made by Professors Schrijver and Weiss, providing a commentary to the Principles in order to offer an insight into the views of the international experts who participated in the elaboration of the ILA Principles that are reproduced herein, with permission of the authors. All errors are responsibility of the editors.

3 Ibid.

Since then and within a remarkably short period of time, sustainable development has been securely endorsed, and has been recognized in a number of instruments of international law. Thus, various environmental treaties incorporate sustainable development, for example the *UN Framework Convention on Climate Change* (1992), the *UN Convention on Biological Diversity* (1992), the *UN Convention to Combat Desertification and Drought* (1994) and the *International Tropical Timber Agreement* (1994). Sustainable development also features in the *Straddling Stocks Convention* (1995) as well as in the preamble to the 1994 *Agreement on the Establishment of the World Trade Organization* (WTO) according to which Members should, in their trade and economic relations, allow for the 'optimal use of the world's resources in accordance with the objective of sustainable development'. In the Doha Declaration of the Fourth Ministerial Conference of 14 November 2001, Ministers confirmed their commitment to the objective of sustainable development. They stated: "We are convinced that the aims of upholding and safeguarding an open and non-discriminatory multilateral trading system, and acting for the protection of the environment and the promotion of sustainable development can and must be mutually supportive."[4]

Reference may also be made to the clear policy response by the European Union and by the European Community to the call for 'sustainable development' as formulated at the UN Conference on Environment and Development. Indeed, both the *Treaty on European Union* and the *European Community Treaty*, as amended by the 1997 *Treaty of Amsterdam*, have given the objective of sustainable development a prominent place. Thus, in Article 2 the *European Community Treaty* includes objectives such as "economic and social progress and a high level of employment and to achieve balanced and sustainable development". Furthermore, Article 6 of the revised *European Community Treaty* stipulates the integration of environmental protection requirements in all Community policies and activities "with a view to promoting sustainable development." Sustainable development is also an over-arching objective in the various development co-operation treaties of the EU, such as the 2001 *Cotonou Agreement*.

Sustainable development or related concepts also feature in a number of international judicial decisions of the 1990s, for example those of the International Court of Justice in the *Nuclear Tests* case (*New Zealand* v *France*, 1995), in its Advisory Opinion to the UN General Assembly on *The Legality of the Threat or Use of Nuclear Weapons* (1996) and in the *Gabčíkovo-Nagymaros* case (*Hungary/ Slovakia*, 1997) concerning a dam project in the river Danube. Reference must also be made to the recognition by the WTO Appellate Body of the objective of sustainable development, most notably in the *United States-Import Prohibition of Certain Shrimp and Shrimp Products* case (1998), commonly known as the *Shrimp-Turtles* case. Many of these decisions and treaties are analysed in this volume, and other scholarly work.[5]

---

4 Ibid.
5 See, e.g. N. Schrijver and F. Weiss, eds., *International Law and Sustainable Development: Principles and Practices* (Leiden: Martinus Nijhoff, 2004).

It follows that sustainable development has become an established objective of the international community, arguably one vested with some degree of normative rather than merely exhortatory status in international law.[6]

However, the fact of its broad acceptance and use does not affirm that its scope and contents are clear. As such, it may be ranged alongside the economic paradigm of 'comparative advantage' which has come to be regarded and accepted as the '*Grundnorm*' of trade, or for that matter with the political promise of greater benefits from 'trade not aid', a slogan which brought many developing countries into the GATT/WTO. However, though its lack of precision must be recognized, various dimensions of the concept of sustainable development may be distinguished, covering a number of domains. As has been stated elsewhere, these include "sustainable use of natural resources; sound economic development, both of developing and industrialized countries; integration of developmental and environmental concerns; inter- and intra-generational equity; a temporal dimension; and respect for human rights and public participation."[7]

All these elements are aptly reflected in the description of sustainable development as formulated in the *New Delhi Declaration of Principles of International Law Relating to Sustainable Development*, adopted by the International Law Association in April 2002. The New Delhi Principles are not, of course, an international legal treaty, or even a non-binding 'soft law' declaration between States. Rather, they were the result of ten years of joint scholarship and investigation by the International Law Association (ILA) Committee on Legal Aspects of Sustainable Development, under the chairmanship of Dr. Kamal Hossain, former Minister of Foreign Affairs of Bangladesh. These scholars came to a joint resolution on seven indivisible principles of international law related to sustainable development, though these were not intended as an exhaustive list.

The New Delhi Principles recognize that the objective of sustainable development involves a comprehensive and integrated approach to economic, social and political processes, which aims at the sustainable use of natural resources of the Earth and the protection of the environment on which nature and human life, as well as social and economic development, depend and which seeks to realize the right of all human beings to an adequate living standard on the basis of their active, free and meaningful participation in development and in the fair distribution of benefits resulting therefrom, with due regard to the needs and interests of future generations.[8]

The 2002 *Johannesburg World Summit on Sustainable Development*, where the New Delhi Principles were presented, provided an important opportunity for addressing the role of international law in the pursuance of sustainable development. However, for now, one may conclude soberly that although the chief elements of a future global regime of governance for sustainable development might currently

6 *Supra* note 2.
7 Ibid.
8 Ibid.

be in place (including consensus on problems, objectives, principles, institutional underpinning and on the crucial role of civil society in all its diversity), much remains to be accomplished.

Moving forward from the Johannesburg Summit and the Rio UNCSD, one might chance the tentative prediction that the unflagging commitment to sustainable development as demonstrated by key players of any future global partnership for a regime of governance for sustainable development (governments, IGOs, NGOs, enterprises, segments of civil society) since 1992 will, over time, crystallize into a more sophisticated normative prescription of international law. It would be reasonable to expect that all the efforts already made, through standard setting, studies, conferences, consultation papers and guidelines, would in the end contribute to the shaping and enhancement of international law in this area of global concern.[9]

As this volume turns to a consideration of future directions, it can be observed that the 2002 New Delhi Principles of International Law Relating to Sustainable Development, as the product of nearly ten years of shared academic work, provide a first crucial and definitive tool for scholars, courts, national and international policy-makers and legal professionals, in relation to guiding principles of international law on sustainable development.

Resolution 3/2002

SUSTAINABLE DEVELOPMENT

NEW DELHI DECLARATION OF PRINCIPLES OF INTERNATIONAL LAW RELATING TO SUSTAINABLE DEVELOPMENT[10]

The 70th Conference of the International Law Association, held in New Delhi, India, 2–6 April 2002,

HAVING CONSIDERED the five consecutive reports (1994–2002) of the Committee on Legal Aspects of Sustainable Development and its efforts to identify existing and emerging principles of international law in the field of sustainable development,

HAVING BEEN INFORMED about the Committee's research seminar on *International Law and Sustainable Development. Principle and Practice*, held in Amsterdam with close cooperation from the Amsterdam Institute for International Development of the Free University, Amsterdam and the University of Amsterdam, 29 November-1 December 2001,

---

9 Ibid.

10 See "ILA New Delhi Declaration of Principles of International Law Relating to Sustainable Development" in 2 *International Environmental Agreements: Politics, Law and Economics* (Netherlands: Springer, 2002) at 209–16, available online: <http://www.kluweronline.com/issn/1567-9764/current>. See also N. Schrijver and F. Weiss, eds., *International Law and Sustainable Development: Principles and Practice* (Leiden: Martinus Nijhoff Publishers, 2004) at 699.

TAKING NOTE of the books resulting from research seminars under the auspices of the Committee on *The Right to Development in International Law* (1992), *Sustainable Development and Good Governance* (1995), *International Economic Law with a Human Face* (1998) and *International Law and Sustainable Development: Principle and Practice* (2002),

WELCOMING the initiative 'Sustainable Justice 2002: Implementing International Sustainable Development Law' of the Centre for International Sustainable Development Law, Montréal,

ADOPTS the New Delhi ILA Declaration on Principles of International Law relating to Sustainable Development, as annexed to this resolution,

REQUESTS the Secretary-General to forward the Report of the Committee and this Declaration to the UN Commission on Sustainable Development, the UN Secretary-General and his Special Representative on Sustainable Development, UNCTAD, UNEP, the WTO, the World Bank and other relevant intergovernmental and non-governmental organizations for their consideration, including organizations at the regional level.

NEW DELHI DECLARATION OF PRINCIPLES OF INTERNATIONAL LAW RELATING TO SUSTAINABLE DEVELOPMENT

The 70th Conference of the International Law Association, held in New Delhi, India, 2–6 April 2002,

NOTING that sustainable development is now widely accepted as a global objective and that the concept has been amply recognized in various international and national legal instruments, including treaty law and jurisprudence at international and national levels,

EMPHASIZING that sustainable development is a matter of common concern both to developing and industrialized countries and that, as such, it should be integrated into all relevant fields of policy in order to realize the goals of environmental protection, development and respect for human rights, emphasizing the critical relevance of the gender dimension in all these areas and recognizing the need to ensure practical and effective implementation,

TAKING THE VIEW that there is a need for a comprehensive international law perspective on integration of social, economic, financial and environmental objectives and activities and that enhanced attention should be paid to the interests and needs of developing countries, particularly least developed countries, and those adversely affected by environmental, social and developmental considerations,

RECALLING that in its Report on *Our Common Future* (1987), the World Commission on Environment and Development identified the objective of sustainable development as being '. . . to ensure that it meets the needs of the present without compromising the ability of future generations to meet their own needs',

CONCERNED about growing economic and social inequalities between and within States as well as about the ability of many developing countries, particularly least developed countries, to participate in the global economy,

RECOGNIZING the need to further develop international law in the field of sustainable development, with a view to according due weight to both the developmental and environmental concerns, in order to achieve a balanced and comprehensive international law on sustainable development, as called for in Principle 27 of the Rio Declaration and Chapter 39 of *Agenda 21* of the UN Conference on Environment and Development as well as in the various resolutions on legal aspects of sustainable development of the International Law Association . . .

EXPRESSES the view that the objective of sustainable development involves a comprehensive and integrated approach to economic, social and political processes, which aims at the sustainable use of natural resources of the Earth and the protection of the environment on which nature and human life as well as social and economic development depend and which seeks to realize the right of all human beings to an adequate living standard on the basis of their active, free and meaningful participation in development and in the fair distribution of benefits resulting therefrom, with due regard to the needs and interests of future generations,

IS OF THE OPINION that the realization of the international bill of human rights, comprising economic, social and cultural rights, civil and political rights and peoples' rights, is central to the pursuance of sustainable development,

CONSIDERS that the application and, where relevant, consolidation and further development of the following principles of international law relevant to the activities of all actors involved would be instrumental in pursuing the objective of sustainable development in an effective way:

NEW DELHI DECLARATION OF PRINCIPLES OF INTERNATIONAL LAW RELATING TO SUSTAINABLE DEVELOPMENT

1.   The duty of States to ensure sustainable use of natural resources

It is a well-established principle that, in accordance with international law, all States have the sovereign right to manage their own natural resources pursuant to their own environmental and developmental policies, and the responsibility to ensure that activities within their jurisdiction or control do not cause significant damage to the environment of other States or of areas beyond the limits of national jurisdiction.

States are under a duty to manage natural resources, including natural resources solely within their own territory or jurisdiction, in a rational, sustainable and safe way so as to contribute to the development of their peoples, with particular regard for the rights of indigenous peoples, and to the conservation and sustainable use of natural resources and the protection of the environment, including ecosystems. States must take into account the needs of future generations in determining the rate of use of natural resources. All relevant actors (including States, industrial concerns and other components of civil society) are under a duty to avoid wasteful use of natural resources and promote waste minimization policies.

The protection, preservation and enhancement of the natural environment, particularly the proper management of climate system, biological diversity and fauna and flora of the Earth, are the common concern of humankind. The resources of outer space and celestial bodies and of the sea-bed, ocean floor and subsoil thereof beyond the limits of national jurisdiction are the common heritage of humankind.

2. The principle of equity and the eradication of poverty

The principle of equity is central to the attainment of sustainable development. It refers to both inter-generational equity (the rights of future generations to enjoy a fair level of the common patrimony) and intra-generational equity (the rights of all peoples within the current generation of fair access to the current generation's entitlement to the Earth's natural resources).

The present generation has a right to use and enjoy the resources of the Earth but is under an obligation to take into account the long-term impact of its activities and to sustain the resource base and the global environment for the benefit of future generations of humankind. 'Benefit' in this context is to be understood in its broadest meaning as including, *inter alia*, economic, environmental, social and intrinsic benefit.

The right to development must be implemented so as to meet developmental and environmental needs of present and future generations in a sustainable and equitable manner. This includes the duty to co-operate for the eradication of poverty in accordance with Chapter IX on International Economic and Social Co-operation of the Charter of the United Nations and the Rio Declaration on Environment and Development as well as the duty to co-operate for global sustainable development and the attainment of equity in the development opportunities of developed and developing countries.

Whilst it is the primary responsibility of the State to aim for conditions of equity within its own population and to ensure, as a minimum, the eradication of poverty, all States which are in a position to do so have a further responsibility, as recognised by the Charter of the United Nations and the Millennium Declaration of the United Nations, to assist States in achieving this objective.

3. The principle of common but differentiated responsibilities

States and other relevant actors have common but differentiated responsibilities. All States are under a duty to co-operate in the achievement of global sustainable development and the protection of the environment. International organizations, corporations (including in particular transnational corporations), non-governmental organizations and civil society should co-operate in and contribute to this global partnership. Industrial concerns have also responsibilities pursuant to the polluter pays principle.

Differentiation of responsibilities, whilst principally based on the contribution that a State has made to the emergence of environmental problems, must also take into account the economic and developmental situation of the State, in accordance with paragraph 3.3.

The special needs and interests of developing countries and of countries with economies in transition, with particular regard to least developed countries and those affected adversely by environmental, social and developmental considerations, should be recognized.

Developed countries bear a special burden of responsibility in reducing and eliminating unsustainable patterns of production and consumption and in contributing to capacity-building in developing countries, *inter alia* by providing financial assistance and access to environmentally sound technology. In particular, developed countries should play a leading role and assume primary responsibility in matters of relevance to sustainable development.

4. The principle of the precautionary approach to human health, natural resources and ecosystems

A precautionary approach is central to sustainable development in that it commits States, international organizations and the civil society, particularly the scientific and business communities, to avoid human activity which may cause significant harm to human health, natural resources or ecosystems, including in the face of scientific uncertainty.

Sustainable development requires that a precautionary approach with regard to human health, environmental protection and sustainable utilization of natural resources should include accountability for harm caused (including, where appropriate, State responsibility), planning based on clear criteria and well-defined goals, consideration of all possible means in an environmental impact assessment to achieve an objective (including, in certain instances, not proceeding with an envisaged activity) and, in respect of activities which may cause serious long-term or irreversible harm, establishing an appropriate burden of proof on the person or persons carrying out (or intending to carry out) the activity.

Decision-making processes should endorse a precautionary approach to risk management and in particular should proceed to the adoption of appropriate precautionary measures even when the absence of risk seems scientifically assured.

Precautionary measures should be based on up-to-date and independent scientific judgment and be transparent. They should not result in economic protectionism. Transparent structures should be established which involve all interested parties, including non-state actors, in the consultation process. Appropriate review by a judicial body or administrative action should be available.

5. The principle of public participation and access to information and justice

Public participation is essential to sustainable development and good governance in that it is a condition of responsive, transparent and accountable governments as well a condition for the active engagement of equally responsive, transparent and accountable civil society organizations, including industrial concerns and trade unions. The vital role of women in sustainable development should be recognised.

Public participation in the context of sustainable development requires effective protection of the human right to hold and express opinions and to seek, receive and impart ideas. It also requires a right of access to appropriate, comprehensible and timely information held by governments and commerce on economic and social policies regarding the sustainable use of natural resources and the protection of the environment, without imposing undue financial burdens upon the applicants and with due consideration for privacy and adequate protection of business confidentiality.

The empowerment of peoples in the context of sustainable development requires access to effective judicial or administrative procedures in the State where efforts have been taken to challenge such measure and to claim compensation. States should ensure that where transboundary harm has been, or is likely to be, caused, individuals and peoples affected have non-discriminatory access to the same judicial and administrative procedures as would individuals and peoples of the State from which the harm is caused if such harm occurred in that State.

6. The principle of good governance

The principle of good governance is essential to the progressive development and codification of international law relating to sustainable development. It commits States and international organizations:

(a) to adopt democratic and transparent decision-making procedures and financial accountability;
(b) to take effective measures to combat official or other corruption;
(c) to respect due process in their procedures and to observe the rule of law and human rights; and
(d) to implement a public procurement approach according to the WTO Code on Public Procurement.

Civil society and non-governmental organizations have a right to good governance by States and international organizations. Non-state actors should be subject to internal democratic governance and to effective accountability.

Good governance requires full respect for the principles of the 1992 Rio Declaration on Environment and Development as well as the full participation of women in all levels of decision-making. Good governance also calls for corporate social responsibility and socially responsible investments as conditions for the existence of a global market aimed at a fair distribution of wealth among and within communities.

7. The principle of integration and interrelationship, in particular in relation to human rights and social, economic and environmental objectives

The principle of integration reflects the interdependence of social, economic, financial, environmental and human rights aspects of principles and rules of international law relating to sustainable development as well as of the needs of current and future generations of humankind.

All levels of governance – global, regional, national, sub-national and local – and all sectors of society should implement the integration principle, which is essential to the achievement of sustainable development.

States should strive to resolve apparent conflicts between competing economic, financial, social and environmental considerations, whether through existing institutions or through the establishment of appropriate new ones.

In their interpretation and application, the above principles are interrelated and each of them should be construed in the context of the other principles of this Declaration. Nothing in this Declaration shall be construed as prejudicing in any manner the provisions of the Charter of the United Nations and the rights of peoples under that Charter.

4 Achieving sustainable justice through international law

H. E. Judge C. G. Weeramantry[1]

4.1 Introduction

This chapter explores the basic characteristics of a global justice system, setting out a vision for the international law that the author believes should be articulated, advanced and respected in order to achieve global sustainable development.

4.2 International law in the world community

In human history, it is clear that power and privilege are rarely, if ever, ceded, except under the compulsion of necessity. Wars, the like of which humanity had not known in thirty centuries, provided this compulsion in the twentieth century. These wars demonstrated the need for a more effective system to govern the conduct of nations. There was the need for the power of a concept to rank above raw power, for the force of a system of cooperation to rank above brute force, for the majesty of a global order to stand above the majesty of the State. These were the thoughts that gripped the minds of practical statesmen at that time, though they had not always been receptive to such ideas.

The desire for the formation of a true international community based not on warfare, but on global cooperation resulted in the birth of the League of Nations out of the carnage of the First World War. The League was the first global assembly in the long history of recognized States. Unfortunately, one major war was not enough to compel States into giving up certain privileges. Certain imbalances existed which ultimately prevented the League from becoming an effective international organization that would work towards the advancement of equality and justice for all peoples of the globe.[2]

After a further devastating loss of life in the Second World War, the United Nations was conceived from the ashes of the League. The Charter that bound it together achieved the status of a supreme legal instrument effective among all nation states, producing a universally recognized system of positive law that every member of the world community accepted as binding, with all the force of law.

---

1 This chapter shares thoughts with the author's piece appearing in M. C. Cordonier Segger and C. G. Weeramantry, eds., *Sustainable Justice: Reconciling Economic, Social & Environmental Law* (The Hague: Martinus Nijhoff, 2004).

2 See E. H. Carr, *The Twenty Year's Crisis* (New York: Harper and Row, 1964).

Two giant steps had thus been taken – one towards establishing a universal body of nation states, and the other towards establishing a universally binding body of legal principles. The international rule of law had descended from the realm of aspiration to the real world. The first step had been taken in the tortuous history of humanity's quest for a legal order which was globally accepted. No longer could such ideas be dismissed as purely visionary. International law had made a quantum leap from utopian vision and non-law towards binding law.

The 'realists' and cynics then lowered the timbre of their questioning. No longer did they ask the question 'does international law exist?', but came down a notch and instead asked 'even if international law does exist, does it matter?' They pointed to the vast spectrum of arenas where power still continued to disport itself as though international law did not exist.[3] It is an indication of how far we have travelled along this road towards the advancement of international law that today scarcely anyone asks the question 'does international law exist?' Today its existence is largely assumed. However, the international community continues to struggle to ensure that international law is given the respect and authority that is needed in order to promote peace and the advancement of humanity.

It is a sobering thought that this giant leap forward was not the result of an ordered progression of human thought, but was forced upon the international community by the brutalities of two world wars. Once the thresholds were passed, these wars demonstrated to a disbelieving world the depths of barbarism to which civilized nations can descend, when State sovereignty is free to function without the restraints of a superior legal system to which it owes allegiance. They forced the world to come to its senses on this great issue.

This is where we are now. We are standing at the dawn of a new century and millennium, facing a new series of challenges to the survival of humanity. These challenges, as serious and immediate as the thresholds of the wars last century, relate to hazardous social, economic and ecological thresholds.

4.3 Current challenges for international law

There are several key crisis points which present future challenges for international law.

Almost every day, the international news features problems of refugees in many parts of the world. The tragedies of Somalia, Vietnam and Yugoslavia are well known throughout the international community. Thousands stream across national borders, leaving behind their lifetime's memories, their possessions, and sometimes their loved ones who are too aged or infirm to travel.[4]

Refugee problems are not the problems of refugees alone. They are the problems of the entire civilized world, for we cannot, with any claim to decency or civilization, leave other human beings in the filth and squalor of the refugee

---

3 H. Morgenthau, *Politics among Nations*, 5th edn (New York: Knopf, 1973).

4 See E. Feller, V. Türk and F. Nicholson, *Refugee Protection in International Law – UNHCR's Global Consultations on International Protection* (Cambridge: Cambridge University Press, 2003).

camps and the cloud of uncertainty that hangs over their entire future, without some form of international assistance. The international legal system should have some form of relief to offer to them.

Indeed, in recent times, a body of international law has been developed in an effort to protect them. For example, the 1951 *Convention* and the 1967 *Protocol* relating to the status of refugees proscribe required standards of treatment.[5] The United Nations has set up the Office of the United Nations High Commissioner for Refugees.[6] The absolute discretion of States to refuse entry of any foreigners into their countries has to a considerable extent been curtailed by international law in relation to refugees.[7] However, the current framework is still extremely inadequate. While there is insufficient space to enter into details here, this body of law is still far short of the level of achievement required, and it remains very much a crisis area.

The international community also has a related problem foreshadowed for the future – the problem of environmental refugees. International scientific studies have shown that global climate change and the rising of sea levels could pass a certain threshold, flooding a number of low-lying islands in another 50 years or less, so that the occupants of such islands will become refugees, seeking admittance into other States.[8] Desertification, drought and extreme temperature change will also lead to the displacement of thousands, if not millions of people.[9] The problem of environmental refugees may be with us even sooner than we expect. The justice systems of this world must not be caught unprepared.

Indeed, the international environmental pillar of sustainable development is also in crisis. It has been widely acknowledged throughout the world that humanity continues to be endangered by the depletion of the ozone layer, climate change, species extinction and the pollution of the oceans, rivers and lakes of this world.[10] Human beings, as self-interested consumers, have used our inheritance of land and water spaces throughout the world as if these were our private preserves, the absolute property of the present generation.

However, the current generation actually serves as a trustee for the generations yet to come. Unless humanity looks after its environment, it is possible that, through environmental degradation, we might damage our eco-system beyond recovery. We may even drag the future of humanity into destruction – because there is, especially in such fields as nuclear waste, nuclear reactors, nuclear

---

5 Convention Relating to the Status of Refugees, 28 July 1951, 189 UNTS 150 (entered into force 22 April 1954) and Protocol Relating to the Status of Refugees, 31 January 1967, 606 UNTS 267 (entered into force 4 October 1967).

6 See UNHCR, available online: <http://www.unhcr.ch>.

7 See generally, G. Goodwin-Gill, *The Refugee in International Law,* 2nd edn (Oxford: Oxford University Press, 1996).

8 See for example United Nations Environment Programme, *Global Environmental Outlook* (Nairobi: UNEP, 2000), and United Nations Development Programme, *Human Development Report* (New York: UNDP, 2001).

9 Ibid.

10 See *supra* note 7.

armaments, the destruction of the rainforests, the pollution of the seas and the damage to the ozone layer, the possibility of irreparable and irreversible damage to the life support system which sustains all of humanity.

The 1972 *Stockholm Declaration on the Environment*,[11] with its 26 principles which offer a foundation for international environmental law, ought to be better known throughout the world. These environmental principles contain an important philosophy for our time. Principle 1 stresses that man has a fundamental right to freedom, equality and adequate conditions of life, not in the abstract, but in an environment of quality that permits a life of dignity and well-being.[12] All the other human rights become worthless if the environment is so damaged as to deny this quality of life, and take away the health of our people. Similarly, the *World Charter for Nature*[13] and the later *Earth Charter* could easily and effectively be brought to the attention of children in schools, as a reminder to them of their duties to the world.

Further, international law must adapt to the fact that we are living in an age dominated by technology. This technology is changing every facet of domestic and international life, and the rate of change is increasing exponentially. Consequently, international law, a slow-moving discipline in the past, has to speed up its rate of change and adaptation. Where formerly international lawyers had two or three generations in which to cogitate upon a major social or technological change, they now must do so in only a number of months or years. Changes in communications technology, computerization and bio-medical engineering provide but a few examples.[14]

Some of these changes affect the very foundations on which certain legal principles have been built. The response of the international legal community to such new technology is illustrated in its response to space law and the exploration of the celestial bodies. Had international lawyers not thought as early as 1979 to construct a *Treaty on the Activities of States on the Moon and other Celestial Bodies* (commonly known as the *Moon Treaty*), we may well have had a new race for colonization of the moon and other celestial bodies.[15] As it currently stands, certain States are currently attempting to manipulate or even break the existing international treaty structure in order to militarize space in a new type of arms race. Similar problems are arising with regard to computer privacy, data banks, trans-border data flow, recombinant DNA experimentation, global warming, new drugs and chemicals and other issues. International

11 Stockholm Declaration on the Human Environment, 16 June 1972, UN Doc. A/CONF.48/14, 11 ILM 1461 (1972) at Principle 1.
12 Ibid. at Principle 1.
13 World Charter for Nature, G.A. Res. 37/7, UN GOAR, 37th Sess., Supp. No. 51, UN Doc. A/37/51 (1983); 23 ILM 455.
14 See generally, C. G. Weeramantry, *Impact of Technology on Human Rights: Global Case Studies* (Tokyo: United Nations University Press, 1993).
15 Treaty on Principles Governing the Activities of States in the Exploration and Use of Outer Space, Including the Moon and Other Celestial Bodies, 27 January 1967, 610 UNTS 205, 18 UST 2410 (entered into force 10 October 1967).

law must keep abreast of science, or it will watch helplessly from the sidelines while unrestrained technology transgresses all social controls.[16]

A fourth factor is also important, and presents a significant future challenge. Often economic pressures can operate just as compulsively as physical force in compelling a country to a particular course of conduct. Economic power can be so great as to enable it to break through the walls of sovereignty. It can influence, even in the minutest detail, the lives of every citizen in every State. It can become an instrument of exploitation from afar, unrestrained by the usual principle that power must be accompanied by responsibility.[17]

In particular, foreign investment is one field in which much work is required to transform the current state of the law and international practice. Throughout the world, there appear to be many unfair, even 'unconscionable', contracts between investors or investor countries and debtor countries. There are numerous ways that such contracts can affect human rights, potentially leading to human rights deprivations in certain countries, and even revolutions.[18] Such contracts are drafted by lawyers trained in intricate knowledge of corporate law. However, a proper knowledge and use of broader public international law is needed to address the equitable and human rights aspects of these agreements.

In an age of increasing economic power, of a global marketplace that is steadily increasing its grip on every aspect of peoples' lives, such imbalances can exacerbate severe problems of malnutrition, exploitation of labour, environmental damage, foreign debt, loss of national autonomy and deprivations of social, economic and cultural rights.[19] However, they appear to pass unnoticed, presenting the appearance of agreements made under firm contractual conditions.

This area requires the most careful and urgent attention. As international law develops, it must recognize the need to develop new principles to address these issues. It will need to recognize the analogy between economic force and physical force. The prohibitions against the illegitimate use of physical force would, where appropriate, be attracted to the illegitimate use of economic force.

This opens up a vast area in which international law will be a prime instrument of service to the global community. New principles and standards will have to be formulated. Much intellectual rigour is required for this task, for such a concept presents another revolutionary departure from classical principles of international law as articulated by Loewenfeld, among others.[20] While one must move with great caution, the constraint of illegitimate economic power may be an essential area of focus for international law in the future. As with most legal principles

---

16 For an early elaboration of this theme by the author, see C. G. Weeramantry, *The Slumbering Sentinels: Law and Human Rights in the Wake of Technology* (London: Penguin Books, 1984).

17 J. J. Rousseau, *The Social Contract and Discourses* (New York: Dutton, 1950).

18 See generally, S. R. Ratner, "Corporations and Human Rights: A Theory of Legal Responsibility" (2001) 111 *Yale L. J.* 443.

19 See generally, J. Stiglitz, *Globalization and Its Discontents* (London: Norton, 2003). See also A. Sen, *Development as Freedom* (New York: Knopf, 1999).

20 H. P. de Vries and A. Loewenfeld, "Jurisdiction in Personal Actions – A Comparison of Civil Law Views" (1959) 44 *Iowa L. Rev.* 306.

which have evolved through balancing competing principles, so also will this task involve a fine sense of judgment between legal principle and practical reality. The changing face of State sovereignty is a concurrent thread throughout this discussion. In the many strands that make up the concept of sovereignty, not the least important is the economic strand. Many concentrations of economic force wield more power than most sovereign States. This aspect of sovereignty is being gravely eroded today. While we must acknowledge that in today's world no State can regulate its economic affairs in total freedom from external factors, it is also clear that dependence on external factors can at a certain stage reach such a level as to amount to a negation of sovereignty.

A final major trend of the future that can be identified here is the tendency of international law to break through the barriers imposed upon it by narrow concepts of individual rights. International law cannot be constrained by the narrow focus on individual rights which flourished in domestic systems under individualist and positivist theories of the nature and functions of law. Under the combined influence of vulnerability and urgency for many of the world's people, ecological problems of global dimensions, a view of Planet Earth as a limited shared resource of all people, and a growing vision of the short-sightedness of current economic planning, the focus of the law's attention has broadened. It can no longer afford to concentrate on the individual, the isolated State and the present generation. It needs to set its sights further and broaden the narrow aperture of the lens through which it views the world.[21]

The concept of sustainable development, which looks beyond the mere present into the long-term future and mitigates against maximum, immediate exploitation of common resources at the cost of poor countries, vulnerable groups and future generations, is acquiring a central place in international law. International law must reflect very strongly the need to develop, define and implement this concept. These will be some of the principal formative influences over the international law of the future.

4.4 Sustainable development law in international tribunals

There are many reasons for the growing importance of treaty law and it is vital to examine customary international law in the light of the strengths and weaknesses of treaty law.

A considerable strength of treaty law in a world order still based on the sovereign state system is that it postulates the express consent of States and therefore conserves their sovereignty and autonomy. Another source of strength is the specificity of the obligations assumed, thus avoiding to some extent the difficulties attendant on determining whether a given situation falls within the reach of a general principle that is invoked.

But a world whose survival will increasingly depend in the future on active cooperation rather than mere co-existence has need of a system whereby rules

21 This idea is central to the concept of preserving our present global community and its resources for use by future generations.

that bind the international community do not need to have the specific individual consent of each and every one of the nearly 200 states comprising the community of nations. If this were the *sine qua non* for a binding rule of international law, we could never obtain the rules that are required to handle the problems of our global village. Treaty law will find itself hopelessly inadequate to handle such matters as the urgent environmental problems which are already on our hands. We must have resort to a set of principles that do not owe their existence to an act of specific State consent but reach beyond State consent to the primordial verities and principles on which the international order is founded. Customary international law provides such a source, which will need to be increasingly relied upon in a future where unexpected and urgent problems of an unprecedented nature will keep arising, for which treaty law cannot provide the solutions

Even if unanimous consent to a treaty can be obtained, a total global consensus will take time to achieve, and consent at the level of sovereign states is a slow and ponderous process. Moreover, even in the context of a treaty there will be uncertainties in interpretation and application, as well as gaps, and there must be a supplementary source from which these lacunae and interstices in the law can be filled.

The fact that treaty-making is a slow and involved process, that treaties are not all-embracing and do not specifically cover all relevant eventualities, and that treaties involve formality in the mode by which they come into existence – all of these combine to highlight the importance of customary international law which postulates a set of principles already in existence, wherefrom one may draw the specific rules which may be necessary for handling a given problem or situation. In the words of Oscar Schachter:

> However, treaties have not fully met the needs of new law. For one thing, the processes of treaty negotiation are often slow and cumbersome. It is easy to see why. The increase in the number of States, the diversity of interests, the novelty of the problems faced, the shortage of competent officials, are factors which combine to delay and complicate the treaty-drafting negotiations and ratifications. The difficulty of obtaining ratifications and accessions, even for States that had supported and signed the treaties has been a discouraging feature. Even when multilateral treaties obtained the requisite number of parties, a substantial number of countries remained outside the treaty, though they had no significant substantive objections and voted for its adoption by the drafting conference.[22]

If treaties require time to evolve, what happens in the time between the rising of the need and the achievement of the treaty? In the world of sustainable development law in particular, we shall have progressively less time in the future than we have had in the past to attend to these issues because they are growing increasingly urgent.

---

22 O. Schachter, "New Custom: Power, Opinio Juris and Contrary Practice" in *Theory of International Law at the Threshold of the 21st Century, Essays in Honour of Krzysztof Skubiszsweski* (Cambridge: Cambridge University Press, 1995) at 531.

There must be a body of legal principle that fills that gap. And customary international law provides these principles. Treaties involve formality, and customary international law does not suffer from this impediment. The latter is still a valuable instrument to us.

A sterling example to illustrate this aspect can be drawn from the field of the law relating to modern weapons. To arrive at an international treaty which pronounces that the use of nuclear weapons in any circumstances amounts to a violation of the law is well-nigh impossible under current circumstances. Yet the corpus of customary international law is replete with basic principles which point to this conclusion.[23] What could be more necessary for the survival of humanity than the establishment of such a proposition and what could be more urgent? Yet treaties as a source of the necessary principles are silent whilst customary international law speaks loud and clear. The voice must not be muted. There is therefore, a growing future for customary international law rather than a future of diminishing utility and stature.

The fertility of customary international law as a source of law in domestic jurisdictions that accept international law as part of their legal systems can be well illustrated from numerous jurisdictions.[24] If customary international law has played such a vital formative role in assisting domestic legal systems to handle such a variety of problems, it certainly has the potential in the milieu of international law proper to assist the international legal system to adapt itself to the numerous fundamental changes that system is currently facing.[25]

The World Court, as the principal judicial organ of the United Nations, must be empowered to state and apply international law with an authority matched by no other tribunal and must, in its jurisprudence, pay due recognition to the rights of future generations.[26] If there is any tribunal that can recognize and protect their interests under the law, it is this Court.

It is to be noted in this context that the rights of future generations have passed the stage when they were merely an embryonic right struggling for recognition. They have woven themselves into international law through major treaties, through juristic opinion and through general principles of law recognized by civilized nations. Among treaties that may be mentioned, the 1979 *London Ocean Dumping Convention*, the 1973 *Convention on International Trade in Endangered Species of Flora and Fauna*, and the 1972 *Convention Concerning the Protection of the World Cultural and Natural Heritage* expressly incorporate the principle of protecting the natural environment for future generations, and elevate the concept to the level of binding state obligation.

---

23 See generally, the author's Dissenting Opinion in *Legality of the Threat or Use of Nuclear Weapons*, July 8 1996, ICJ Rep. 226 (Advisory Opinion).

24 For an overview, see *supra* note 22, at Chapter 2.

25 H. H. Koh, "Why Do Nations Obey?" (1997) 106 *Yale L. J.* 2259. See also H. H. Koh, "The Globalization of Freedom" (2001) 26 *Yale J. Int'l L.* 305 at 306.

26 Weeramantry International Centre for Peace Education and Research (WICPER), *The World Court: Its Conception, Constitution and Contribution* (Ratmalana: Vishva Lekha, 2001).

Juridical opinion is now abundant, with several major treatises appearing upon the subject and with such concepts as intergenerational equity and the common heritage of mankind being academically well established.[27] Moreover, there is a growing awareness of the ways in which a multiplicity of traditional legal systems across the globe protect the environment for future generations. To these must be added a series of major international declarations commencing with the 1972 *Stockholm Declaration on the Human Environment*, and continuing through the 1992 *Rio Declaration on Environment and Development* and the 2002 *Johannesburg Declaration of the World Summit on Sustainable Development*.

When incontrovertible scientific evidence speaks of pollution of the environment on a scale that spans hundreds of generations, it is the opinion of this author that the World Court would fail in its trust if it did not take serious note of the ways in which the distant future is protected by present law. The ideals of the United Nations Charter do not limit themselves to the present, for they look forward to the promotion of social progress and better standards of life, and they fix their vision, not only on the present, but on 'succeeding generations'. This one factor of impairment of the environment over such a seemingly infinite time span would by itself be sufficient to call into operation the protective principles of international law which the Court, as the pre-eminent authority empowered to state them, must necessarily apply.

4.5 Developing sustainable development law

The concept of sustainable development is one of those forward-looking legal concepts on which the future of the human family very heavily depends. The betterment of the economic and social conditions of every individual is one of the cardinal missions of all legal systems. 'Development' aims at achieving this result at a practical level through such measures as development of economies, development of skills, development of wealth, development of utilization of resources, development of necessary infrastructures, development of living conditions, development of health, and development of the overall quality of life.

These are much-desired objectives which all too often have been much delayed. International lawyers and policy makers can and must contribute to achieving them and the law needs to help towards this result. Unfortunately, 'development' can take place at the expense of the environment. It can take place at the expense of future generations. It can take place at the expense of the poor and disadvantaged. It can take place at the expense of destroying cultural inheritances and traditional ways of life which have taken thousands of years to achieve. This is the crux of the problem. These values are not disposable, nor are they commodities to be purchased for a pittance. Each of these sets of values is important. Each of these represents a human right. Each of these is vital to the human future.

---

27 E. Brown Weiss, *In Fairness to Future Generations: International Law, Common Patrimony and Intergenerational Equity* (New York: Transnational, 1989).

Legal systems, both domestic and international, are expected to foster and advance all of these sets of concerns. Strong legal arguments can be advanced in favour of each of these. Legal systems are thus involved in a delicate balance of competing interests.

There is no longer any room for denying the legal aspects of development. Nor is there room any longer for denying the legal status of sustainability. Out of this juxtaposition of opposing considerations has arisen the concept of sustainable development. It is time that it becomes widely recognized that there is no denying the legal status of the concept of sustainable development – a new synthesis that must result from the clash of opposing interests.

Why can we suggest that sustainable development is part of international law? International law arises initially from the realm of aspiration. All its principles are formulations of aspirations. This formulated idea gradually hardens into concrete law. One excellent example is presented by the *Universal Declaration of Human Rights*,[28] which began with the formulation of a series of aspirations. As time went on, these aspirations became firmer, they crystallized, they became part of accepted international law and in that way they injected themselves into domestic law, often into constitutions of countries, recognized and enforced by courts and national justice systems. As this chapter seeks to demonstrate, such a process has been initiated for sustainable development. It begins in the realm of the aspirational but as time progresses and its importance becomes clearer, through an iterative process, it becomes more and more a part of the established international legal order and infuses itself into the domestic legal order as well.

It must be recognized that the concept of sustainable development, its place in international and domestic law, and its principles, are still highly contested. There remain several important barriers to the full recognition and enforcement of this concept.

First, it is still very strongly entrenched in modern law that only the living generation have rights under the law. The great majority of our current legal systems, whether Common Law or Civil Law, concentrate almost exclusively on the rights of those who are living here and now. These appear to be the only bearers of rights in modern legal systems. However, this is a very limited view. It does not accord with the philosophies that traditional wisdom has bequeathed to us. Those philosophies teach us that there is a duty on the present generation to look beyond itself to those who are to come after us, as well as to look back at the past and respect those who went before us. This is very beautifully expressed in the traditional African concept which Bishop Desmond Tutu has explained in his sermons – that the human community consists of three elements – those who went before us, those who are with us here and now, and those who are yet to come.[29] All three together constitute

---

28 Dec. 10, 1948, G.A. Res. 217A, UN GAOR, 3rd Sess., UN Doc. A/810 (1948).

29 D. Tutu, *The Rainbow People of God: South Africa's Victory Over Apartheid* (London: Doubleday, 1994). See also Sermon given by Arch Bishop Desmond Tutu, available online: <http://www.heureka.clara.net/books/tutu-sermon.htm>.

the human community. If one loses sight of any one of those component parts of the trinity, one gains only a lopsided view of the human endeavour. That is a very important tradition which international lawyers must weave into our environmental law framework.

Second, another rather narrow attitude of modern law is to hold that it is only human beings that have any recognizable rights. No other creatures which inhabit this planet which is our common home have any rights recognized by modern legal systems. That was not the case in traditional law. Especially in the Eastern part of the world, there was a very deep understanding of the rights of other living creatures to this planet which we all share. In the traditions of many indigenous peoples there were very strong items of State conduct which showed recognition of this principle. The establishment by indigenous rulers of hospitals for animals, as early as the fourth century,[30] showed that there was a strong understanding that human duties are not concentrated on human beings alone, and that one must, in devising a legal system, think a little beyond the confined vision that human beings are the only creatures that matter on this planet.

Third, modern law still seems to concentrate almost exclusively on the rights of individuals. There is a great stress on individualism as though only individuals have rights. However, traditional societies flourished not only on the basis of individual rights but also on the basis of group rights.[31] The group was very important and as one knows even from the history of Europe, the group, whether it be the guild or the manor or the parish, was very important to the life of every individual. There were groups to which every individual belonged and through which the individual felt secure and protected. If you destroy the group, to quote Edmund Burke in his description of the French Revolution, and wipe the State clean of the traditional group organizations, you leave the individual naked and alone to face the might of an all-encompassing State.[32] The individual, once he is broken away from the group, has to sink or swim on his own.

Ancient society, in contrast to modern society, recognized that groups had definitive rights. The village had rights. The church or temple had rights. The guild had rights. The manor community had rights. Those important rights were dimmed during the concentration on individualism that occurred after the European Revolutions. Indeed, when the Indian Constitution was established, Mahatma Gandhi strove hard to obtain recognition of group rights, though he was not successful in the face of the strength of Western individualism which provided the basic background thinking for many.

The old international law, if the international law that prevailed until the end of the Second World War can be so termed, was based upon individualism. It was based upon the individual sovereignty of the different States that are members

---

30 King Buddhadasa of Sri Lanka is recorded as having established such a hospital in the fourth century. See V. L. B. Mendis, *The Rulers of Sri Lanka* (Colombo: S. Godage & Bros., 2000) 239.

31 See generally, C. G. Weeramantry, *Universalising International Law* (Leiden: Martinus Nijhoff, 2004).

32 E. Burke, "Reflections on the Revolution in France" (Washington: Liberty Fund, 1999), available online: <http://www.baylor.edu/~BIC/WCIII/Essays/reflections.html>.

of the world community. But today's international law does not need to focus so excessively on the individual. It can and will become a socially-oriented international law.

Several pressures have forced this recognition, including the pressure of environmental needs, because with ozone depletion, global climate change, extinction of species, regional land degradation, collapse of fisheries and so forth, we face possible damage not merely to individual States but to the world at large. Environmental damage does not respect national boundaries. Pollution does not recognize the doctrine of state sovereignty and end at the boundaries of a nation state. Pollution proceeds beyond, and to stop such damage and waste we must act as a global community and not as a series of separate and individual States asserting sovereign rights alone.

In the past, States may have sought to function internationally on the basis of co-existence. Nation States tolerated the existence of the 'other' State as a necessity of life. The 'other' State was there and governments had to co-exist with one another whether it was desirable or not. States reconciled themselves to that situation and international law worked out rules for co-existence between those States. But humanity has now passed out of the era of co-existence into the era of cooperation; and not merely passive cooperation but active cooperation, because if we are to save our global inheritance we have to do so actively. Lawyers and policy makers need, for this purpose, to avoid dependence on ideas of sovereignty and the desire of each State to claim complete dominion over everything going on within its borders. States and their governments need to surrender some part of that sovereignty to the rest of the world and to accept common guidance by the global community. Hence, as the environment knows no territorial boundaries, the international community has to live as a cooperative group of States - at the very least so far as environmental law is concerned.

Similarly, the international vision must extend not only to States beyond national frontiers but it must extend in time beyond generational frontiers. The vision must be cast beyond the present generation and must look forward into the future. When lawyers and courts deal with sustainable development law, they are in the realm of future generations. What they are handling are the rights not only of themselves and the present generation, but of generations to come. In the argument of the General Assembly's request for an Advisory Opinion on the illegality of nuclear weapons, counsel appearing for one of the Parties argued that if people in the Stone Age had inflicted on natural resources the damage which we are inflicting upon it now, we would still be living with this damage from the Stone Age. Now it is the same with us. What we do now will affect future generations even more remote from us in the future than the Stone Age is remote from us in the past. Just as we would have blamed earlier civilizations for their lack of a sense of responsibility, a lack of moral sense and lack of civilized behaviour, so those arguments could be hurled against us by posterity if we do not take up our responsibilities, with dignity and consideration, now.

Another concept of importance to international law invokes *erga omnes* obligations i.e. an obligation owed towards the entire world and all its inhabitants.

Generally, disputes between two Parties are disputes *inter partes*, i.e. disputes between individual parties. There are two Parties who come before a judge and the judge's task is to determine between those individual Parties which Party should succeed. Sustainable development challenges are not merely *inter partes*, but may also affect other parties apart from those before the court. So the judge, whether domestically or internationally, has to have his eye also on the impact of the court's decision on the community. Although procedurally it is a matter between the two parties, in substance it is a matter which affects the world. It affects the rights of others outside the limited frame of the parties to the dispute. This *erga omnes* doctrine, which is now being developed in relation to sustainable development, may be useful for many courts and tribunals.

Another factor to be considered is that the forces of technology are advancing at an unprecedented rate. This is true of almost any kind of technology. But the rate of the advance of the law that tries to keep this technology in check, to harness it, is extremely slow. The gap between technology and law is continually widening.[33] Our ability therefore to control any technology through law is thus growing weaker day-by-day. This is a very important phenomenon which all judges and lawyers must take into consideration today. This phenomenon concerns the developing regions even more urgently than most others, because much of the technology used in those regions comes from the developed nations. Judges and lawyers must, as far as possible, assist in achieving appropriate regulation of new technology to ensure that it can serve the interests of all people.

Finally, international law must draw upon the principles of different civilizations. In the view of this author, this is not yet done adequately. International law on sustainable development might be a little further ahead than some areas. The international community must make a much greater commitment to this cause in the future, by drawing upon the thousands of years of wisdom in building up the concept of the common heritage of mankind. That is vital in the context of our ever-shrinking planet which is the common home of everybody. Whatever the forces may be that are resulting in our narrow view of law – be they monetarism or individualism – they are drawing us away from our cultural traditions. It is very important that we restore the links, for otherwise international law will grow further away from the people and the planet it is intended to serve. This is very important if we are to develop the international law of the future in a truly global sense.

Some time ago, the author was Chairman of the Nauru Commission of Inquiry which looked into the question of phosphate mining in Nauru.[34] In consequence of the mines, the land was devastated, unfit for any form of human activity. The philosophy behind this result is the idea that if an individual or corporation has certain property rights they can use them to the fullest extent without regard to the traditional ways in which land was respected and protected. There is much

---

33 See generally, C. G. Weeramantry, *Justice Without Frontiers: Protecting Human Rights in the Age of Technology* (The Hague: Kluwer Law International, 1998).

34 Statements and reports from the UN Nauru Mission, available online: <http://www.un.int/nauru/>.

guidance that can be gained from traditional wisdom which in these respects surpasses the rather limited vision of modern legal systems. Modern law, rich though it may be, is neglecting an important and fertile source of nourishment when it neglects the traditional wisdom of humanity. In environmental matters, the traditional wisdom of humanity can teach us how we can live in harmony with our environment without destroying it in the pursuit of legal concepts to the limit of their logic, without applying also the restraining influence of the traditional wisdom of the human family.

We must martial all our resources to this task. The international community has much access to traditional wisdom, and judges must see how they can best tap into that reservoir of wisdom. It will be very important to the international community in the future. When one analyses the rich history of these traditions, it is easy to see the force of the argument that humanity is neglecting its richest resource of wisdom if its members do not look back upon tradition and the lessons it can offer in both what should and should not be done. The human family has learnt to live in harmony with the environment for thousands of years and has achieved this in a very successful manner. If we fail to look to the past for its traditional wisdom in facing our environmental problems, we may be depriving ourselves of one of our richest resources. For example, many traditional peoples recognized that the land has a vitality of its own. Land lives and grows with the people. If the land withers and dies so also do the people, because the health of a community is dependent on the health of the land and the health of the land is lost unless we pay due regard and reverence to that land and look after it as we would look after a living thing. Another part of traditional wisdom involved ensuring that if a resource was used, this was done efficiently. Fauna and flora were comparatively meagre on the African and Australian continents, but every part of the plant and animal was used to maximum advantage. Nothing was discarded. There are many principles ingrained in traditional wisdom which lawyers, judges and policy makers can build into modern international law with great profit – the principle of sustainable use of resources, for example.

As one specific example, it is useful to consider the traditions of the Pacific. The previously mentioned Nauru Commission researched the customs relating to the land of the various islands in the Pacific.[35] It came across the evidence given by a Solomon Islander to a Land Reform Commission in the Solomon Islands. His evidence was to the effect that Pacific Islanders did not treat land like an article of merchandise – an article which, once it is purchased one can do with it what one will. Land has to be treated with reverence and respect and its 'owners' are obliged to use it in a manner that is respectful to the rights of future generations.

In another illustration, this idea was again encountered when the author was a visiting professor at the University of Papua New Guinea. In Port Moresby, there were pockets of land within the city (the capital) which were not developed. One day in the common room, the conversation turned to the reason why these lands were left undeveloped, lands belonging to various family groups.

35 See *supra* note 23.

One of the young lecturers in the Law Faculty was a family member of one of those groups and therefore one of the co-owners of this valuable piece of undeveloped land in the heart of the capital. The lecturer replied, "Do you not understand our traditions in this country? This land belonged to our ancestors and belongs to our posterity. How can you suggest that I have the right to sell it? I have to respect the rights of those who have come after me."[36] Such are examples of the traditions of the Pacific countries, traditional wisdom that can be woven into the fabric of modern international law.

This chapter will offer a further example, the Ancient Irrigation system of Sri Lanka, perhaps known from the author's Separate Opinion related to other large water projects. Sri Lanka is covered with a network of thousands of man-made lakes and ponds. As Arthur Clarke, the great futurist who lived in Sri Lanka, recognized, the system provides a textbook example of many modern dilemmas, including the dilemma of striking a balance between development and the environment. He stated that prior to "the Christian era, a series of tremendous irrigation works transformed the island's dry zone into what might have been a fertile paradise. Some of the artificial lakes created are kilometres in circumference and there are thousands of these tanks linked by intricate networks of canals."[37]

These enormous irrigation works – some of them enclosing an extent of water which might run to areas of up to 10 square miles had retaining structures sometimes several miles long and 50 feet high. The Sea of Parakrama for example has a retaining band 8.5 miles long. These enormous structures were linked to 25,000–35,000 small tanks. Sri Lankans call them tanks after the Portuguese word tanque, which means a reservoir. These 25,000–35,000 small tanks were linked by hundreds of miles of canals to these enormous reservoirs. It is clear that the rulers of that age were extremely concerned with what today is termed development. As development projects go, this network is even larger than many modern development projects. While they were aimed at development, at the same time they combined development with the protection of the environment. The early Sri-Lankan lawmakers and rulers did not neglect one or the other, but pursued both, striking a happy balance between the two concepts in a manner which has lasted for centuries.

That is precisely the concept which this chapter and text is trying to address: How do you strike a balance between social and economic development, and environmental protection? Respect and consideration for our common future is a part of the culture and responsibility of humanity. International legal scholars are looking for principles and formulas that can reconcile social and economic development and protection of the environment. We must work out these formulas using all the wisdom we can find. It is essential that we do not neglect the traditional wisdom of the many rich cultures of our region. We can draw upon this wisdom for the purpose of developing this very important area of future international law."

---

36 Ibid.
37 A. Clarke, *The View from Serendip* (New York: Ballantine Books, 1984) at 145.

4.6 Conclusion

The areas referred to in this chapter are representative of the vast field awaiting attention at the hands of international lawyers in the future. A greater interest in the growing discipline of international law is essential, for on its success are centred many of the hopes of humanity for the amelioration of its condition. If international law should fail us at this critical stage in human history, we risk a condition which can outdo the barbarisms of the past. Hence, if we neglect it we are sowing the seeds of our own destruction. Those who stand to lose most if the discipline of international law is neglected are the people of the poorest and most vulnerable countries. Their very survival depends upon financial and industrial agreements with the more affluent, and all these agreements are entered into in accordance with international law. If, through neglect, they face a situation where all the legal expertise is on the side of the lender or investor countries, they will necessarily suffer from bad bargains, for there will be no one to look after their interests.

The traditional neglect of international law at all levels can thus cost them dear as a nation, and it is from the legal profession itself that the impetus can best emerge to diffuse more information about international law and to ensure that more attention is paid to this aspect as well as to the training of more specialist international lawyers of the future. To students and young scholars, particularly, the message is addressed that it is from among your ranks that the international lawyers must emerge who will in the future guide countries and the world to a position of true equality in the community of nations. If one should fail in this responsibility, one would indeed be failing the world in the very area in which new talent can serve it to the greatest advantage.

Part II

Architecture of international dispute settlement related to sustainable development

5   A complex system of international courts and tribunals[1]

Cairo Robb and Alexandra Harrington

5.1 Introduction

The architecture and context of the international judicial and quasi-judicial bodies whose decisions are discussed in this volume has evolved and become more complex over time. While avoiding simplistic comparisons, and notwithstanding their differences, it is clear that international courts, tribunals and other dispute settlement mechanisms are implicitly and explicitly becoming cognizant of the principles of sustainable development.

This willingness is the outcome of a long, if somewhat less than obvious, history. Indeed, it has been noted that the obligation has existed for far longer than the contours of modern international law.[2] In the context of modern international law, the principles underlying sustainable development were raised as early as the 1880s. The *Bering Sea Fur-Seals* dispute[3] followed the suspension of negotiations that had aimed at safeguarding, by international cooperation, "the common interest of all nations in preventing the indiscriminate destruction and consequent extermination of an animal which contributes so importantly to the commercial wealth and general use of mankind". In agreeing to submit the dispute to arbitration, the parties in *Bering Sea Fur-Seals* asked the tribunal, in effect, whether the United States had exclusive jurisdiction over the area concerned specifically, and whether the United States had any right – and, if so, what the contours of the right would be – of protection or property in the fur-seals frequenting the islands of the United States in the Bering Sea when such seals are found outside the ordinary three-mile limit.

In its written argument, the United States asserted a property right in the seal herd "by reason of the nature and habits of the seals and their ownership of the breeding grounds to which the herds resort, and irrespective of the

---

1 We are grateful to the Centre for International Sustainable Development Law and its dedicated body of research assistants for their support.
2 H. E. Judge and Vice-President Weeramantry, Separate Opinion, *Case Concerning Gabčíkovo-Nagymaros Project (Hungary/Slovakia)* 1997 ICJ Reports 110 ("sustainable development is thus not merely a principle of modern international law. It is one of the most ancient of ideas in the human heritage").
3 1 IELR 43.

established industry".[4] The United States discussed the extent of dominion inherent in private ownership in the following terms: "[n]o possessor of property has an absolute title to it – his title is coupled with a trust for the benefit of mankind . . . things themselves are not given to him, but only the usufruct or increase – he holds the thing in trust for the present and future generations of man."[5]

The majority of the arbitrators decided that the United States had no right of protection or property in the fur-seals frequenting the islands of the United States in Bering Sea when such seals were found outside the ordinary three-mile limit. It did, however, go on to make detailed regulations setting out measures of protection and exceptions applicable to indigenous peoples in the area that relied on fur-seals for survival.[6] The arbitrators clearly saw it as their inherent duty to promote ideas that are now linked to sustainable development – upholding the value of commerce, the protection of the environment and protection of the rights of indigenous peoples in a balanced way.

More than one hundred years later, international law has made notable progress in favour of establishing sustainable development as a matter of law across a spectrum of fields. With growing international jurisprudence relating to the principles underlying sustainable development, and recognition that judicial elaboration of these principles plays a part in a comprehensive approach towards securing sustainable development goals and objectives, it is all the more imperative that scholarship and guidance in this field continue.[7] The 2012 ILA *Sofia Guiding Statements on the Judicial Elaboration of the 2002 New Delhi Declaration of Principles of International Law Relating to Sustainable Development* provide a vehicle for "still broader and better results". However it is imperative that there be a study of the academic and practice-based elements of the international dispute settlement landscape and how it relates to legitimization and advancing sustainable development principles.

5.2 International dispute settlement landscape

At the time the *Bering Sea Fur-Seals* case was decided, the only option for dispute settlement was arbitration between states by an *ad hoc* tribunal. Today we find the international dispute settlement landscape much wider and more varied, with a notable increase in fora available for use in dispute settlement in recent decades.

These fora have been categorized in various ways by different scholars, namely according to potential parties which can avail themselves of jurisdiction; according

---

4 1 IELR 56.

5 1 IELR 56.

6 Reproduced at 1 IELR 70–72.

7 See, e.g. the Online Legal Research Tool on International Court and Tribunal Decisions referring to Sustainable Development developed by the ILA Committee on International Law on Sustainable Development, the Centre for International Sustainable Development Law (CISDL) and the International Development Law Organization (IDLO), accessed at http://cisdl.org/tribunals/tool.html. See also notes 8 and 10.

to scope and compulsion of jurisdiction; according to subject matter jurisdiction; and according to different geographic factors.[8] There is no 'right' way to categorize them, and some fora will occupy multiple classifications and jurisdictional parameters.

In 1999, and again in its second edition in 2010, the *Manual* noted that:

> [T]here has been a sharp increase in the number of international adjudicatory bodies, a greater willingness to resort to them . . . Nevertheless, . . . knowledge about them, where they are, what they are, who sits on them, what they can do, how they relate to national proceedings – still remains limited even in well-informed legal circles. Many academics and practitioners in the field of international law are familiar with selected bodies, but few are informed about the range of international judicial and quasi-judicial bodies now available. And at the national level knowledge is opaque. In that sense, international courts – and practice – remain a somewhat exotic subject, and perhaps more marginal than it should be . . .[9]

Since then, interest in the variety, structure, interactions and impact of international judicial and quasi-judicial bodies has increased. The Project on International Courts and Tribunals has been at the forefront of this interest, and other academic and practice-based undertakings, such as the PluriCourts initiative, are also making significant contributions.[10]

When examining the international dispute settlement landscape and the issues that most often arise in its definition and application, it is essential to understand the areas in which there is often uncertainty or confusion. The *Manual on International Courts and Tribunals* explains that the most commonly asked questions relating to international dispute settlement mechanisms include those relating to the physical existence of specific courts and tribunals at the regional and international level and to issues of personal and subject matter jurisdiction related to these courts and tribunals. Other important aspects – and indeed distinguishing factors – of international courts and tribunals that require further explanation include the types of decisions and opinions that can be issued, the membership and composition of the decision-making body, and the rules that the courts and tribunals are subject to. At foundational levels, questions as to the

---

8 See Ibid. See also R. Mackenzie, Cesare P. R. Romano, Yuval Shany and Philippe Sands, *Manual on International Courts and Tribunals* (Oxford: OUP, 2010) [hereinafter MICT]; Project on International Courts and Tribunals Synoptic Chart and Matrix, accessed at http://www.pict-pcti.org; Tim Stephens, *International Courts and Environmental Protection.* Vol. 62 (Cambridge: CUP, 2009).

9 Repeated in the 2010 edition, MICT, *supra* note 8 at xxvi.

10 PluriCourts – Centre for the Study of the Legitimate Roles of the Judiciary in the Global Order, accessed at http://www.jus.uio.no/pluricourts/english/. Additionally, Oxford University Press has established an International Courts and Tribunals series of books to encourage the publication of independent and scholarly works which address, in critical and analytical fashion, the legal and policy aspects of the functioning of international courts and tribunals, including their institutional, substantive, and procedural aspects.

form of arguments and pleadings to be presented, the ability of third parties to intervene in some capacity, and the binding quality of decisions on the parties and as a matter of international and/or domestic law frequently occur and can form the fundamental underpinnings of decisions as to whether and where to bring a complaint.

As previously noted, over the past century the international judicial landscape has changed. There has been a shift from *ad hoc* and optional consensual jurisdiction towards more 'compulsory' jurisdiction,[11] while a proliferation of less adversarial procedures designed to support compliance with particular treaty regimes has also emerged.[12] Concomitantly, there has been a gradual opening of judicial and quasi-judicial processes to non-state actors, as well as a growing recognition of the importance of provisional measures as a way to protect the interests of these actors and state actors in appropriate circumstances.

With this increase in international dispute settlement measures and implementing bodies come challenges of jurisdictional coordination and the potential for pre-emption as well as forum shopping and simultaneous, or successive proceedings, which can not only increase the duration, cost and complexity of litigation but can also give rise to substantive problems.[13] In light of these possibilities, some commentators warn about a 'fragmentation' of international law through the functioning of multiple international dispute settlement mechanisms with overlapping jurisdictional concerns.[14]

---

11   For example, acceptance of compulsory dispute settlement jurisdiction is a requirement under the 1982 United Nations Convention on the Law of the Sea (UNCLOS), and the 1994 Agreement Establishing the World Trade Organization (WTO Agreement). The jurisdiction of the European Court of Human Rights over states parties to the European Convention on Human Rights has become compulsory by virtue of Protocol No 11.

12   See, for example, the compliance procedures and World Bank inspection panel described in Chapter 6. Martti Koskenniemi provides a thought provoking discussion of this development in "New Institutions and Procedures for Implementation Control and Reaction" *Greening International Institutions,* Earthscan (1996) 236–48.

13   For example, Tim Stephens refers to the undermining of some compulsory systems of environmental dispute settlement in *International Courts and Environmental Protection.* Vol. 62. (Cambridge: CUP, 2009) 17.

14   To demonstrate the breadth of views on this topic, Philippe Sands and Jaqueline Peel cite the following articles that refer to the issue of fragmentation in international law: P-M Dupuy, 'The Danger of Fragmentation or Unification of the International Legal System and the International Court of Justice', 31 *N.Y.U. J. Int'L L. & Pol.* 791 (1999); Martti Koskenniemi and Päivi Leino, 'Fragmentation of International Law? Postmodern Anxieties', 15 *Leiden J. Int'l L.* 552 (2002); Gerhard Hafner, 'Pros and Cons Ensuing from Fragmentation of International Law', 25 *Mich. U. J. Int'l L.* 849 (2004); Pemmaraju Rao, 'Multiple International Judicial Forums: A Reflection of the Growing Strength of International Law or Its Fragmentation?', 25 *Mich. U. J. Int'l L.* 929 (2004); Brunno Simma, 'Fragmentation in a Positive Light', 25 *Mich. U. J. Int'l L.* 845 (2004). See also Martti Koskenniemi, 'Fragmentation of International Law: Difficulties Arising from the Diversification and Expansion of International Law' (A/CN.4/L.682, International Law Commission, 206) as referred to in Philippe Sands and Jacqueline Peel, *Principles of International Environmental Law* (Cambridge: CUP, 2012) 183 fn 369 [hereinafter Sands and Peel, *Principles*].

5.3 Key features in international judicial and quasi-judicial proceedings[15]

To situate the details of any particular judicial or quasi-judicial body discussed in this volume in context, it is important to articulate certain key features of international judicial and quasi-judicial proceedings that form the basis of their existence and functioning prior to examining different tribunals themselves.

5.3.1 Types of proceedings

The types of proceedings occurring before the various international judicial and quasi-judicial bodies can, in general, be classified as either those: 1) relating to a contentious dispute that exists between two or more parties; or 2) relating to the request for an advisory opinion by one or several parties in advance of a contentious issue developing.

5.3.2 Parties to the proceedings

The question of who can be involved in proceedings involves many factors and varies greatly across the spectrum of international courts and tribunals. At a fundamental level, the question of allowable parties relates to the ability of legal and/or natural persons to bring an action against a particular party (or group of parties) before a particular court or tribunal. Once these matters have been determined, the focus of inquiry then shifts to secondary questions, such as the ability to involve outside parties, either as direct interveners or *amici* or as parties that provide scientific or other expert information.

Traditionally, international law has been concerned with proceedings between states. Reflecting this, the contentious jurisdiction of the International Court of Justice (ICJ), the International Tribunal for the Law of the Sea (with the exception of its Sea Bed Chamber) (ITLOS) and the World Trade Organization Dispute Settlement Body (WTO DSU) is limited to disputes between states. The jurisdiction of the Permanent Court of Arbitration (PCA) was originally limited to inter-state disputes but has been expanded to include disputes between: 1) a state and an international organization; 2) two international organizations; 3) a state and a private party; and 4) an international organization and a private party.

Standing in direct contrast to the standard international law focus on inter-state disputes, in recent years international tribunals and quasi-judicial bodies

---

15 The Project on International Courts and Tribunals Synoptic Chart describes 'international judicial bodies' as those entities that: 1) are permanent institutions; 2) are composed of independent judges; 3) adjudicate disputes between two or more entities, at least one of which is either a state or an international organization; 4) work on the basis of pre-determined rules of procedure; and 5) render decisions that are binding and 'quasi-judicial, implementation control and other dispute settlement bodies'. *Supra* note 8; see also PluriCourts – Centre for the Study of the Legitimate Roles of the Judiciary in the Global Order, accessed at http://www.jus.uio.no/pluricourts/english/. It should be noted that the following section draws heavily from the PluriCourt criteria and descriptions.

have been specifically designed for utilization by non-state actors in actions against states. For example, human rights tribunals may accept petitions from individuals against states. Additionally, the International Centre for Settlement of Investment Disputes (ICSID) provides facilities for arbitration of investment disputes between states and nationals of another state.

Inspection panels and non-compliance mechanisms have been created with varying provisions regarding parties and also address international disputes. The World Bank Inspection Panel, for example, is designed to be used by individuals against the World Bank, while compliance mechanisms under the *Montreal Protocol* can be invoked by other states, by the non-complying state itself, and by the Secretariat. The compliance mechanism under the *Aarhus Convention* goes further, and accepts communications from members of the public. On the regional plane, courts and other bodies relating to regional economic treaties have developed a range of practices in proceedings involving state and non-state actors.

A tribunal's jurisdiction to issue an advisory opinion, or a preliminary ruling, may differ for contentious cases. For example, the UNGA and the United Nations Security Council (UNSC) may request the ICJ render an advisory opinion on any legal question,[16] and other organs of the UN and specialized agencies authorized by the UNGA may request advisory opinions of the ICJ on legal questions arising within the scope of their activities.[17]

5.3.3 Consent, compulsory jurisdiction, and reciprocity[18]

Traditionally, dispute settlement jurisdiction has been based on consent, so that the exercise of jurisdiction depends upon consent being given by all parties to a case. Consent can be expressed on an *ad hoc* basis in relation to an existing dispute by way of a special agreement, or expressed *ex ante* by virtue of prior acceptance of jurisdiction.

Acceptance of dispute settlement jurisdiction may be an optional aspect of adherence to a particular treaty, or it may be a requirement of membership in an international agreement, as is the case with UNCLOS. Although the latter is typically

---

16   UN Charter art. 96(1) (1945).

17   Ibid. at art. 96(2).

18   Tim Stephens provides a list of examples of different types of dispute settlement provision in the context of multilateral environmental agreements as follows:

> 1) Instruments that include no provision for dispute settlement; 2) Instruments that provide that the parties agree to enter into consultations or negotiations whenever a dispute arises; 3) Instruments that provide that the parties agree to resolve disputes by a peaceful means of their own choice; 4) Instruments that provide not only that the parties agree to resolve disputes by peaceful means but also provide a list of available procedures including arbitration and judicial settlement; 5) Instruments that provide for the settlement of a dispute by compulsory but non-legal procedures such as mediation or conciliation; and 6) Instruments that provide for the settlement of a dispute by compulsory and binding adjudication (by arbitration or judicial settlement): a) . . . where the parties have 'opted in' to the procedure; b) . . . unless the parties have opted out of the procedure; and c) . . . which is automatically applicable

> T. Stephens *International Courts and Environmental Protection*. Vol. 62 (Cambridge: CUP, 2009) 25.

termed 'compulsory' jurisdiction, it still rests, ultimately, on consent in that the state has willingly consented to be bound by the treaty regime, including its compulsory jurisdiction. In both compulsory and non-compulsory regimes a state party may be permitted to specify limits to the jurisdiction, and in some cases – again under both compulsory and non-compulsory regimes – consent to dispute settlement jurisdiction may still leave the state party free to choose between various dispute settlement options. This is the case under the UNCLOS regime where there is a choice between submission to the ICJ, to different types of arbitral tribunal, or to ITLOS. Often jurisdiction will only exist on a reciprocal basis – that is where both parties have agreed to jurisdiction, and specifically to the same dispute settlement option. Sometimes a regime will be open to non-members as well.[19]

5.3.4 Subject matter jurisdiction

Whether a particular tribunal will have jurisdiction in a particular dispute will also depend on the subject matter of the dispute and how it correlates with the tribunal's inherent jurisdiction. In addition, limits set by the disputing parties' consent to jurisdiction may serve as bars.

In principle, the ICJ and the PCA have jurisdiction over any international law dispute involving appropriate parties. Other international judicial and quasi-judicial bodies have jurisdiction only over disputes in specific areas of law, generally relating to interpretation of and compliance with the provisions of a particular regime. ITLOS, for example, has specific jurisdiction over interpretation of and compliance with UNCLOS and related agreements. Human rights tribunals generally have jurisdiction over the interpretation of and compliance with the corresponding human rights agreements that establish and govern them. The WTO DSU has jurisdiction over interpretation and compliance with the relevant international trade law regimes. The mandate of the Court of Justice of the European Union is to ensure that the law is observed in the interpretation and application of the treaties involving issues arising in the European Union.

Concurrent jurisdiction can, of course, exist, where a treaty provides a range of options for dispute settlement. UNCLOS, for example, allows parties to choose between the ICJ, various arbitral tribunals and ITLOS in relation to much of the treaty, and thus all of them would potentially have jurisdiction.

In other instances a treaty may accord exclusive jurisdiction to one tribunal such that parties would breach the treaty were they to attempt to bring a dispute over its subject matter to another tribunal. For example, the Treaty on the Functioning of the European Union provides that: "Member States undertake not to submit a dispute concerning the interpretation or application of the Treaties to any method of settlement other than those provided for therein".[20]

---

19 Perhaps the most precedential example of this is the ability of states that are not members of the United Nations to join the Statute of the International Court of Justice on certain conditions or, subject to a distinct set of conditions, to participate in cases before the Court on an *ad hoc* basis without joining. Statute of the Court of International Justice art. 35 (1945) (ICJ Statute).

20 Treaty on the Functioning of the European Union art. 344 (2007).

5.3.5 *Other preconditions*

5.3.5.1 *Harm or prejudice*

Sometimes there is a requirement that the initiator has, or claims to have, suffered actual harm or prejudice.[21] This harm or prejudice will – if established – typically constitute a violation of the relevant treaty's terms.

5.3.5.2 *Exhaustion of domestic remedies*

Across a broad spectrum of subject matter jurisdiction and international dispute settlement bodies there is a requirement that the initiator exhaust domestic remedies prior to bringing the complaint before an international tribunal.[22] Exceptions to this requirement can be made in cases where domestic procedures do not meet appropriate standards or where seeking domestic remedies would endanger the safety of the complainant.

5.3.5.3 *Right to intervene*

A third state may wish to intervene in proceedings for a number of reasons. Indeed, in some circumstances such a state may actually have a right to intervene depending on the terms of a treaty regime. For example, in disputes relating to the interpretation of a convention to which states other than the states litigating are parties, those third states have a right to intervene in proceedings before the ICJ,[23] PCA[24] and the ITLOS.[25] In another example, states having a substantial interest in a matter have a right to intervene in WTO proceedings.[26] In other regimes, third party intervention may be permissible by agreement of the parties.

5.3.6 *Involvement of others in proceedings*

Rules of procedure frequently provide that the court or tribunal can be assisted through expert scientific or technical advice in addition to evidence from the parties.[27] This is very important in courts such as the Inter-American Court of Human Rights, where medical testimony is routinely used for determining the extent of damages and appropriate remedies. Increasingly, rules of procedure for

---

21 This is, for example, a requirement for individual complaints before human rights tribunals, and for complainants to the World Bank Inspection Panel. See International Bank for Reconstruction and Development, International Development Association, Res. No. IBRD 93–10, Res. No. IDA 93–6 (The World Bank Inspection Panel) (1993).
22 For example ECHR art. 35 (1950); UNCLOS art. 295 (1982); ICSID art. 26 (1966).
23 ICJ Statute, *supra* note 19 art. 63.
24 1899 Hague Convention art. 56; 1907 Hague Convention art. 84.
25 Statute of the International Tribunal for the Law of the Sea art. 32 (1982) (ITLOS).
26 Understanding on Rules and Procedures Governing the Settlement of Disputes arts 10, 17 (1991) (WTO DSU).
27 See MICT, *supra* note 8.

international dispute settlement bodies allow the submission of amicus curiae briefs to the tribunal, though these should not become a burden on the disputing parties.

5.4 Specific judicial and quasi-judicial bodies[28]

Key features of international judicial and quasi-judicial proceedings have been outlined above. Below follows a short description of the institutions whose decisions are heavily discussed in this volume, on a tribunal by tribunal basis. The goal of this section is to provide a basic understanding of these major entities and regimes, which in many cases have served as models to newly created international dispute settlement mechanisms.

5.4.1 International Court of Justice

The ICJ is the pre-eminent international judicial body.[29] It was established in 1945 as part of the United Nations Charter and is the UN's principle judicial organ. All members of the Statute of the ICJ may in principle bring contentious cases to the court, concerning the entire field of international law. It is possible for members of the United Nations to remove themselves from the jurisdiction of the ICJ.[30]

The ICJ is composed of 15 independent judges and can hear cases in plenary (the quorum is nine judges) or in chambers. The Statute of the ICJ provides for the establishment of permanent and *ad hoc* chambers. In July 1993 a permanent Chamber for Environmental Matters was formed, though it has not been utilized to date.[31] All questions before the ICJ are decided by

---

28 The following descriptions draw heavily on the work of MICT, *supra* note 8 and Marie-Claire Cordonier Segger 'Governing and Reconciling Economic, Social and Environmental Regimes' in Marie-Claire Cordonier Segger and H. E. Judge C. G. Weeramantry, eds., *Sustainable Justice: Reconciling Economic, Social and Environmental Law* (The Hague: Martinus Nijhoff, 2004) 592.

29 See generally, MICT, *supra* note 8, sect. 1.

30 See generally, ICJ Statute.

31 In her address of 26 October 2006 to the General Assembly Her Excellency Judge Rosalyn Higgins (then President of the ICJ) stated:

> The Court noted in recent times the growing interest of States, reflected in its docket, in issues relating to human rights, international humanitarian law, and environmental law. In 1993, a Chamber for Environmental Matters was created by the Court and has been periodically reconstituted. But in its 13 years of existence, no State has yet asked for a case to be heard by this Chamber. Cases such as the *Gabčíkovo-Nagymaros Project (Hungary/ Slovakia)* and *Pulp Mills on the River Uruguay (Argentina v Uruguay) have been submitted to the plenary Bench.* A survey of State practice suggests that States prefer environmental law not to be compartmentalized, but to find its place within international law as a whole. Indeed, environmental law has now become an important part of what we may term the mainstream of international law. Accordingly, this year the Court decided not to hold elections for a Bench for the Chamber for Environmental Matters. At the same time, *should parties in future cases request a chamber for a dispute involving environmental law, such a chamber could be constituted under Article 26, paragraph 2, of the Statute of the Court.*

a majority of the judges.[32] The judgments of the Court are final and binding and are not subject to appeal.[33]

Contentious jurisdiction at the ICJ is open only to states, and is dependent on consent of the parties under article 36 of its Statute. Consent may be manifested by special agreement, by jurisdictional clause in a bilateral or multilateral treaty, or by signing the ICJ Statute Optional Clause and accepting compulsory jurisdiction.[34] While parties may refer any legal dispute arising between them, the instrument constituting the basis for jurisdiction may restrict the subject matter competence of the ICJ.

The ICJ decides cases in accordance with international law and the terms of article 38(1) of its Statute providing:

1   The Court, whose function is to decide in accordance with international law such disputes as are submitted to it, shall apply: a. international conventions, whether general or particular, establishing rules expressly recognized by the contesting states; b. international custom, as evidence of a general practice accepted as law; c. the general principles of law recognized by civilized nations; d. subject to the provisions of Article 59, judicial decisions and the teachings of the most highly qualified publicists of the various nations, as subsidiary means for the determination of rules of law.

2   This provision shall not prejudice the power of the Court to decide a case *ex aequo et bono*, if the parties agree thereto.

The ICJ Statute and Rules contain procedures for submission of materials by international organizations, which may in some circumstances be conducive to settling pending cases. However, no NGO involvement in contentious cases is permitted. In relation to advisory opinions, Practice Direction XII[35] prescribes that written statements or documents submitted by NGOs do not constitute part of the case file, though states and international organizations may rely on them in their submissions.

The ICJ may indicate provisional measures where such measures are necessary to preserve the respective rights of the parties.[36] The UN Charter allows the UNGA or the UNSC to request that the ICJ give an advisory opinion on any legal question,[37] and allows other organs of the UN and specialized agencies

Press Release, International Court of Justice, accessed at http://www.icj-cij.org/presscom/index.php?%20p1=6&p2=1&pr=1874.

32   Ibid. at art. 55.
33   Ibid. at art. 60.
34   Under article 36(1) of its Statute, by special agreement whereby two or more states agree to refer a particular dispute to the ICJ, or by jurisdictional clause in a multilateral or bilateral treaty to which the states are party. This could be a treaty dealing generally with peaceful settlement of disputes or relations between the parties, or a treaty regulating a specific topic. Sands and Peel, *Principles, supra* note 14 at 172.
35   As amended 20 July 2004.
36   ICJ Statute arts 41(1), 75(1).
37   UN Charter art. 96(1).

authorized by the UNGA to request advisory opinions from the ICJ relating to legal questions that arise within the scope of their activities.[38] Advisory opinions are not binding upon the requesting body, although in practice they typically are accepted and acted upon by that body.[39]

5.4.2 Arbitration institutions and tribunals

As indicated earlier in this chapter, there was a time when submission of a dispute to an *ad hoc* arbitral tribunal was the only means of settlement of dispute between states. At present, the use of arbitral tribunals may still be viewed as an attractive means of resolving international disputes.[40]

Arbitral tribunals may be created on an *ad hoc* basis by agreement of the parties, independently of any existing regime or institution. These tribunals may also be established pursuant to a treaty regime allowing, or requiring, submission of related disputes to arbitration. Indeed, provision for the settlement of disputes through arbitration can be found in a wide range of existing treaties. The treaty may set out details for the establishment of an arbitral tribunal or may leave the details to the discretion of the parties. In some cases the parties may chose, or a treaty may specify, that disputes be referred to an arbitral tribunal under the auspices of a specific facilitative arbitration institution such as the PCA or ICSID, which are institutions through which *ad hoc* arbitral panels are arranged.

UNCLOS Annex VII arbitral tribunals and UNCLOS Annex VIII special arbitral tribunals may be chosen pursuant to the dispute settlement provisions of UNCLOS. A UNCLOS Annex VII tribunal is the default UNCLOS dispute settlement mechanism.[41] Such arbitral tribunals may use the administrative services of the PCA.[42]

5.4.3 Permanent Court of Arbitration[43]

The Permanent Court of Arbitration (PCA) is a facilitative arbitration institution.[44] It was established by the 1899 Hague Conference adopting the 1899

---

38 Ibid. at 96(2).
39 Sands and Peel, *Principles, supra* note 14 at 174
40 Ibid. at 169–70. As Sands points out "International arbitration has been described as having 'for its object the settlement of disputes between states by judges of their own choice and on the basis of respect for the law. Recourse to arbitration implies an engagement to submit in good faith to the award.'" 1907 Hague Convention on the Pacific Settlement of International Disputes art. 37.
41 See UNCLOS Annex VII; UNCLOS Annex VIII.
42 For example, NAFTA Chapter 11 tribunals are described under the heading Regional Economic Integration Bodies below, but could have been included here as they are arbitral tribunals. They sometimes use ICSID administrative services. See North American Free Trade Agreement chapter 11 (1994).
43 For example, 1999 Netherlands and France Dispute Concerning the 1976 Rhine Chloride Convention and its 1991 Protocol. 2003 Belgium and Netherlands Dispute Concerning Iron Rhine railway line; India and Pakistan Dispute Concerning the Indus River Treaty.
44 See generally, MICT, section 4, *supra* note 8.

Convention for the Pacific Settlement of International Disputes (revised in 1907).[45] The PCA is not actually a 'tribunal'. Rather, it comprises a permanent secretariat[46] that maintains a roster of potential arbitrators.[47] When a dispute is referred to arbitration under the auspices of the PCA, the parties to the dispute, with the assistance of the secretariat, establish an *ad hoc* arbitral tribunal of one, three or five arbitrators. It has adopted a number of sets of Optional Rules, including rules specifically designed to address needs arising from the arbitration of disputes relating to the environment and natural resources.[48]

The PCA was originally established with a view to the settlement of inter-state disputes, however the Optional Rules allow it to cater to arbitrations involving international actors other than states, such as international organizations and private parties.[49] Jurisdiction depends upon agreement of the parties, which can be made *ad hoc*, in a compromissory clause in a valid treaty, by way of a separate agreement, or through an arbitration clause in a contract or other legal instrument. The potential subject matter jurisdiction of the PCA is unlimited,[50] but its actual scope is determined in each case by the wording of the applicable arbitration clause or *compromis*.

An arbitral tribunal established under the PCA system generally is expected to apply the substantive law agreed upon by the parties. In the absence of an agreement, the tribunal will apply either the applicable rules of general international law or another body of law prescribed by choice of law rules. In cases involving international organizations, the tribunal is directed to take due account of the rules of the organization involved and of the law of international organizations generally. In cases involving private parties, the tribunal is directed to pay attention to use the contracts or agreements in question and take into account the

---

45 1907 Hague Convection.
46 Known as the International Bureau at the Peace Palace in The Hague.
47 Named in advance by the states parties to the 1899 and 1907 Hague Conventions for the Pacific Settlement of International Disputes. Arbitrators may, however, be drawn from outside this list.
48 Adopted 19 June 2001, accessed at www.pca-cpa.org. The Rules are available for the use of all parties who have agreed to use them, including states, intergovernmental organizations, non-governmental organizations and private entities. The Rules provide for the optional use of a panel of arbitrators with experience and expertise in environmental or conservation of natural resources law, who are nominated by the member states and the Secretary General, respectively, and a panel of environmental scientists nominated by the member states and the Secretary General, respectively. Ibid. at art. 8(3). The latter is able to provide expert scientific assistance to the parties and the arbitral tribunal. Ibid. at art. 27(5). The Rules also make provision for the submission to the arbitral tribunal of a document agreed to by the parties, summarizing and providing background to any scientific or technical issues which the parties may wish to raise in their memorials or at oral hearings, and empower the arbitral tribunal to order any interim measures necessary to prevent serious harm to the environment, unless the parties agree otherwise. Ibid. at arts 24, 26. Recognizing that time may be an important element in disputes concerning natural resources and the environment, the Rules provide for arbitration in a shorter period of time than under previous PCA Optional Rules or the UNCITRAL Rules.
49 See list at 4.2 of MICT, *supra* note 8. Optional Rules have also been adopted for conciliation and fact-finding procedures. PCA Optional Rules, accessed at http://www.pca-cpa.org/.
50 1899 Hague Convention art. 21; 1907 Hague Convention art. 42.

relevant terms of trade usage. Finally, with the agreement of the parties the tribunal may also apply laws of equity (i.e. *ex aequo et bono*).[51]

Under the Optional Rules the tribunal may order interim measures of protection at the request of a party if the tribunal deems it necessary to preserve the respective rights of the parties or the subject matter of the dispute. However, it is further provided in the Optional Rules that the parties may agree to restrict the power of the tribunal to issue interim awards.[52]

The decisions of the tribunal are issued by the majority of arbitrators. There is no right of appeal over PCA Arbitral awards and all awards are final and binding.[53] Such tribunals have contentious jurisdiction only. They do not give advisory opinions.

5.4.4 ICSID[54]

ICSID is one of the institutions of the World Bank Group and was established by the 1965 Convention on the Settlement of Investment Disputes between States and Nationals of Other States (the ICSID Convention).[55]

Like the PCA, ICSID is an administrative body under whose auspices arbitral tribunals may be established, in accordance with the provisions of the ICSID Convention. The ICSID Secretariat maintains lists of arbitrators and conciliators and provides institutional support to the initiation and conduct of arbitration proceedings under the ICSID Convention. Members of arbitral tribunals may be appointed from the lists and from outside them.

ICSID proceedings were designed specifically for non-state actors bringing proceedings against states. One of the parties must be a contracting state and the other party must be a 'national of another Contracting State'. This covers both natural and juridical persons.[56] ICSID facilities are not available for disputes between states.

There can be no recourse to arbitration under the ICSID Convention unless the parties have agreed to it and provided consent.[57] Consent may be given in

---

51   MICT, *supra* note 8 at 4.4.

52   Ibid. at 4.19.

53   See 1899 Hague Convention art. 54; 1907 Hague Convention art. 81.

54   See generally MICT section 5, *supra* note 8.

55   Convention on the Settlement of Investment Disputes between States and Nationals of Other States, 18 March 1965, 575 UNTS 159.

56   Ibid. at art. 25. Under article 25(2) a natural person is precluded from access to ICSID if in addition to being a national of another contracting state the person is also a national of the state party to the dispute. By contrast, a juridical person that is a national of the state party to the dispute may be a party to an ICSID proceeding if it and the state party to the dispute have agreed to treat the juridical person as a national of another contracting state because of foreign control. See A. Broches, 'The Convention on the Settlement of Investment Disputes Between States and Nationals of Other States' in Aron Broches, *Selected Essays* (Dordrecht: Martinus Nijhoff, 1995) at 201. MICT at 5.12, *supra* note 8.

57   The consent of both parties need not be in the same document. A government might in its investment promotion legislation offer to submit disputes arising out of certain classes of investment

regard to an existing dispute or with respect to a defined class of future disputes. For all disputes, the ICSID Convention requires that the dispute must be a 'legal dispute arising directly out of an investment'.[58]

An ICSID tribunal must decide a dispute in accordance with rules of law as may be agreed by the parties.[59] In the absence of such agreement, the tribunal will apply the law of the contracting state party to the dispute (including its rules on the conflicts of laws) and such rules of international law as may be applicable.[60] The tribunal may, if the parties so agree, decide a dispute *ex aequo et bono*.

Provisional measures may be prescribed for the preservation of rights. Parties to the ICSID Convention arbitration proceedings may request judicial or other authorities to order provisional measures, but only if the agreement recording their consent to arbitration allows.[61] The decisions of the tribunal are rendered by a majority of the votes of its members, and the award is binding on the parties.[62] Awards are not subject to appeal or to any remedy other than those provided for in the ICSID Convention,[63] such as rectification or supplementation of the award, interpretation of the award, revision of the award or annulment of the award.[64]

Under the ICSID 'Additional Facility Rules,'[65] the ICSID Secretariat may also, with consent of both parties, administer proceedings in cases where the state complained against, or the state of the national complaining, is not a Contracting Party to the ICSID Convention and where the dispute does not arise directly out of an investment. Neither the ICSID Convention nor the Additional Facility provide for advisory opinions.[66]

5.4.5 UNCLOS Annex VII arbitral tribunal

UNCLOS allows parties to choose from four possible dispute settlement mechanisms: ICJ, ITLOS, an Annex VII arbitral tribunal and an Annex VIII special arbitral tribunal.[67] An Annex VII arbitral tribunal is the default dispute settlement

to ICSID arbitration, and the investor might give their consent by accepting the offer in writing. See Broches, *supra* note 56 at 207. MICT 5.12, *supra* note 8. Once both parties have consented, neither may revoke its consent unilaterally. Convention on the Settlement of Investment Disputes between States and Nationals of Other States art. 25(1).

58 See Convention on the Settlement of Investment Disputes between States and Nationals of Other States art. 25.

59 Ibid. at art. 42.

60 Similar choice of law principles also applies in arbitrations conducted under the auspices of the Additional Facility. See Arbitration (Additional Facility) Rules, art. 55 MICT original p 89.

61 MICT original p 97.

62 Convention on the Settlement of Investment Disputes between States and Nationals of Other States art. 53(1).

63 Ibid. at art. 53(4).

64 Ibid.

65 Rules Governing the Additional Facility for the Administration of Proceedings by the Secretariat of the International Centre for Settlement of Investment Disputes (Additional Facility Rules).

66 Cases may however be brought for conciliation under the Convention or Additional Facility Rules or for fact finding under the Additional Facility Rules.

67 UNCLOS art. 287.

procedure under UNCLOS in cases where disputing parties have not chosen the same method, or have not chosen at all.[68]

An Annex VII arbitral tribunal is composed of five members[69] selected from a list held by the UN Secretary General, based on nominations from member states, and is free to determine its own procedure, unless the parties agree otherwise.[70] Potential parties are the states parties to UNCLOS and the entities listed in UNCLOS article 305.[71]

Like the other dispute settlement mechanisms listed under UNCLOS, an Annex VII arbitral tribunal has jurisdiction to deal with settlement of disputes concerning the interpretation or application of UNCLOS.[72] It also has jurisdiction over any dispute concerning the interpretation or application of an international agreement related to the purposes of UNCLOS, which is submitted to it in accordance with the agreement.[73]

An Annex VII tribunal applies UNCLOS and other rules of international law not incompatible with UNCLOS. The tribunal can also decide a case *ex aequo et bono*, if the parties so agree.[74] Provisional measures are possible, in cases where a tribunal considers that *prima facie* it has jurisdiction.[75] The tribunal may prescribe any provisional measures it considers appropriate under the circumstances to preserve the respective rights of the parties to the dispute or to prevent serious harm to the marine environment, pending the final decision.[76] It is also possible for one party to make a request for provisional measures to ITLOS (or, if the parties both agree, to another court or tribunal) pending the setting up of the Annex VII arbitral tribunal. This has happened on a number of occasions. Decisions are taken by majority of the tribunal, are final and are binding on all parties to the dispute.[77]

5.4.6 UNCLOS Annex VIII special arbitral tribunal

Where a dispute concerns the interpretation or application of the articles of UNCLOS relating to: 1) fisheries; 2) protection and preservation of the marine environment; 3) marine scientific research; or 4) navigation, including pollution from vessels and by dumping, UNCLOS parties may chose an Annex VIII special arbitration.

Arbitrators in such cases are drawn from a List of Experts nominated by member states and maintained in the fields of: fisheries by the Food and Agriculture Organization of the United Nations; protection and preservation of the marine

---

68 UNCLOS Annex VII.
69 One member can be nominated by each party (and can be its own national), and the remaining three are to be agreed between the parties. UNCLOS, Annex VII, art. 3.
70 UNCLOS, Annex VII, art. 5.
71 UNCLOS, art. 305.
72 UNCLOS, art. 288.
73 Ibid.
74 Ibid.
75 Ibid. at art. 290.
76 Ibid.
77 Ibid. at art. 296.

environment by the United Nations Environment Programme; marine scientific research by the Intergovernmental Oceanographic Commission; navigation, including pollution from vessels and by dumping, by the International Maritime Organization; or in each case by the appropriate subsidiary body concerned.

In many respects the operation of the arbitral tribunal is largely similar to Annex VII arbitral tribunals. However, there is special provision under Annex VIII in relation to the tribunal's fact-finding function. Under article 5 the parties may at any time agree to request a special arbitral tribunal to carry out an inquiry and establish the facts giving rise to the dispute. Unless the parties otherwise agree, the findings of fact of the special arbitral tribunal are conclusive as between the parties. If all the parties to the dispute request, the special arbitral tribunal may formulate recommendations which, without having the force of a decision, constitute the basis for a review by the parties of the questions giving rise to the dispute.

5.4.7 ITLOS[78]

The ITLOS was established pursuant to the 1982 UNCLOS. It is a permanent tribunal comprised of 21 elected members, out of which a quorum of eleven members is required. It has a permanent Seabed Disputes Chamber composed of 11 members, out of whom seven are needed for a quorum. Special chambers may be formed from three or more of the Tribunal's elected members for dealing with particular categories of dispute and also when requested by the parties. Similar to the ICJ, ITLOS has created a special chamber for Marine Environmental Disputes,[79] although it has not been used to date. A special chamber of five members, plus two substitutes, is elected annually to deal with summary proceedings.

ITLOS is open to States Parties to UNCLOS.[80] It is also open to entities other than UNCLOS States Parties in any case expressly provided for regarding the Area,[81] or in any case submitted pursuant to any other agreement conferring jurisdiction on the Tribunal which is accepted by all the parties to that case.[82]

The jurisdiction of the Tribunal includes all disputes and applications submitted to it in accordance with UNCLOS and all matters specifically provided for in any other agreement that confers jurisdiction on the Tribunal.[83] Jurisdiction is also available where all parties to a treaty or convention that is already in force and concerns the subject matter covered by UNCLOS have agreed that disputes concerning interpretation or application of the treaty may be submitted

---

78 MICT section 2, *supra* note 8 from which details provided here have been heavily drawn. UNCLOS Part V etc. UNCLOS Part XV addresses compulsory dispute settlement, allowing states at the time of signature, ratification or accession or at any time thereafter to designate any of the following four dispute settlement procedures, Sands and Peel, *Principles*, *supra* note 14 at 175, one of four dispute settlement procedures including ITLOS, see *infra* section 5.4.5.

79 See ITLOS Statute.

80 Ibid. at art. 20(1).

81 See UNCLOS Part XI.

82 ITLOS art. 20(2).

83 Ibid. at art. 21.

to ITLOS.[84] As a baseline, the Tribunal decides all disputes and applications in accordance with the substantive provisions of UNCLOS and other rules of international law not incompatible with UNCLOS.[85] If the parties agree ITLOS can decide a case *ex aequo et bono*.[86]

The ITLOS Seabed Disputes Chamber effectively has compulsory jurisdiction over disputes relating to the exploration and exploitation of the international seabed and ocean floor ('the Area').[87] The Seabed Disputes Chamber can acquire jurisdiction not just by virtue of and over the states involved, but also by a range of actors engaged in activities in the Area (e.g. state parties, the International Seabed Authority, state enterprises, legal or natural persons and prospective contractors). In addition to provisions of UNCLOS and principles of international law not incompatible with it, the Seabed Disputes Chamber can apply the rules, regulations and procedures of the International Seabed Authority, as well as terms of contracts concerning activities in matters relating to them.

The Tribunal and its Seabed Disputes Chamber have the power to prescribe provisional measures which are considered appropriate under the circumstances to preserve the respective rights of the parties to the dispute or to prevent serious harm to the marine environment, pending the final decision. Unusually, ITLOS also has jurisdiction to order provisional measures under UNCLOS, even when parties have chosen a different forum to resolve their disputes, in the absence of alternative agreement between the parties, and pending the constitution of the parties chosen forum.[88] This provision has been invoked on a number of occasions.

Decisions are issued by a majority of the members of the Tribunal who are present.[89] A judgment rendered by special chambers and by the Seabed Disputes Chamber is considered to have been rendered by the Tribunal.[90] The decision of the Tribunal is final and binding on all the parties to the dispute.[91] Additionally, ITLOS has the authority and ability to issue advisory opinions.[92]

---

84 Ibid. at art. 22.
85 UNCLOS art. 293(1); Statute of ITLOS art. 23.
86 Ibid.
87 Ibid. at sect 5.
88 See article 290(5), which states:

> Pending the constitution of an arbitral tribunal to which a dispute is being submitted under this section, any court or tribunal agreed upon by the parties or, failing such agreement within two weeks from the date of the request for provisional measures, the International Tribunal for the Law of the Sea or, with respect to activities in the Area, the Seabed Disputes Chamber, may prescribe, modify or revoke provisional measures in accordance with this article if it considers that *prima facie* the tribunal which is to be constituted would have jurisdiction and that the urgency of the situation so requires. Once constituted, the tribunal to which the dispute has been submitted may modify, revoke or affirm those provisional measures, acting in conformity with paragraphs 1 to 4.

89 ITLOS Statute, art. 29.
90 UNCLOS Annex VI, art. 15(5).
91 ITLOS Statute, art. 33(1)
92 In 2011 the Seabed Disputes Chamber rendered an opinion on *Responsibilities and Obligations of States Sponsoring Persons and Entities with Respect to Activities in the Area* at the request of the International Seabed Authority.

5.4.8 World Trade Organization[93]

The WTO is an international organization vested with powers and functions designed to promote and regulate international trade at a global level.

The WTO DSU[94] is Annexed to the 1994 Agreement Establishing the World Trade Organization[95] and sets out the terms of the WTO dispute settlement mechanism, which operates through the use of *ad hoc* panels, an Appellate Body and the WTO Dispute Settlement Body (DSB).

In the event of a dispute between WTO members, one member may request that the other enter into consultations with the goal of settling the matter. If such consultations fail, the complaining party may request the establishment of an *ad hoc* Panel.[96] Panels are constituted of three (or exceptionally five) members,[97] who conduct hearings on the dispute and issue a report and set of recommendations on the merits of the complaint. The Panel report may be appealed on legal grounds by either party, in which case the appeal is brought before the Appellate Body, which may uphold, modify or reverse the legal findings of the Panel. The Appellate Body is a permanent standing body and sits in divisions of three of its seven independent elected members.[98]

The Appellate Body is the most typically 'judicial' of the WTO dispute settlement mechanism bodies. Nevertheless, like Panel Reports, Reports of the Appellate Body are not binding on the parties to the disputes until they have been adopted by the WTO DSB, which sits at the apex of the WTO dispute settlement system, and is, effectively, a political body comprised of representatives of all members of the WTO.[99] However, because the WTO DSB operates on a reverse consensus basis, non-appealed Panel Reports and Reports of the Appellate Body are considered to be *de facto* binding on the parties since they will be adopted except in the highly unlikely event that the DSB decides otherwise by consensus.

All members of the WTO, including customs territories, are subject to the DSU's compulsory jurisdiction and may raise a dispute.[100] The subject matter jurisdiction of the WTO dispute settlement mechanism includes all disputes between members arising under the covered agreements listed in Appendix 1 to

93 See generally MICT, section 3, *supra* note 8, accessed at http://www.wto.org.

94 An Understanding on Rules and Procedures Governing the Settlement of Disputes.

95 Final Act Embodying the Results of the Uruguay Round of Trade Negotiations, concluded in Marrakech, 15 April 1994.

96 In addition, each party may propose that other dispute settlement procedures (good offices, conciliation or mediation) be employed between the parties, with the possible assistance of the Director-General (head of the WTO Secretariat). Where more than one member requests a panel in relation to the same matter, a single panel may be established DSU art. 9(1).

97 The Secretariat of the WTO proposes the nomination of members, usually on the basis of a list of prospective members maintained by the Secretariat, containing names put forward by the members and approved by the DSB(1). The parties are expected to agree to this composition, unless they have compelling reasons for objecting. DSU art. 8(7). No nationals of the disputing parties may serve as a panel member, unless the parties agree otherwise. Ibid. at art. 8(3).

98 Ibid. at art. 17(1).

99 See generally, DSU.

100 AB Report, EC-Bananas III, paras 132–38.

the DSU.[101] These Agreements constitute the trade-related laws that are created and enforced under the general auspices of the WTO.

Although the WTO system has supplanted the General Agreement on Tariffs and Trade (GATT) as a method of trade regulations, substantive conditions for initiation of proceeding set out in GATT 1947 are still generally adhered to by virtue of corresponding provisions. According to these provisions and the DSU procedure, a WTO member may present a claim based on evidence that: 1) a benefit accruing to it under a relevant agreement to which it is a party has been nullified or impaired;[102] or 2) the attainment of the objective of the agreement is being impeded.

This evidence alone is insufficient. It must also be demonstrated that the unwarranted result was caused by an act or omission on the part of the respondent member constituting one of the following: 1) failure to meet obligations under the relevant agreement; 2) application of a measure incompatible with the relevant agreement; or 3) any other situation.

The jurisdiction of a panel is limited by its terms of reference, which define the claims at issue in the dispute.[103] Article 3(2) of the DSU provides that the member states recognize that the dispute settlement system serves to preserve the rights and obligations of members under the covered agreements and to clarify the existing provisions of those agreements, in accordance with customary rules of interpretation of international law. In its first case, *US-Standards for Reformulated and Conventional Gasoline*, the Appellate Body affirmed that the rules of treaty interpretation in articles 31 and 32 of the Vienna Convention on the Law of Treaties had attained the status of a rule of customary international law, and that this required that trade rules were not to be read "in clinical isolation from public international law".[104]

Any member state having a substantial interest in a case pending before the Panel has the right to join the proceedings as a third party, under certain conditions.[105] WTO dispute panels may seek information or technical advice from any individual or body which it deems appropriate,[106] and may consult experts.[107] There are no provisions regarding acceptance of amicus curiae briefs, but the Appellate Body maintains that, in principle, both the Panels and the Appellate Body may accept and consider them.[108]

---

101 WTO Agreement, GATT agreements incl 1994, GATS, TRIPS, DSU as enumerated in Appendix 1 to the DSU. Others include Agreement on Trade in Goods, Agreement on Trade in Civil Aircraft, Agreement on Government Procurement, International Dairy Arrangement, Agreement on Bovine Meat.

102 DSU art. 3(3).

103 Ibid. at art. 7.

104 Case AB-1996-1, *US-Standards for Reformulated and Conventional Gasoline*, Report of the Appellate Body, 29 April 1996, at p. 18, WTO Doc WT/DS2/9.

105 DSU art. 10(2).

106 Ibid. at art. 13(1)

107 Ibid. at art. 13(2).

108 Appellate Body Report, *US – Shrimp*, paras 105–8; Appellate Body Report, *US – Lead and Bismuth II*, paras 41–42.

There are no provisions for preliminary measures. Usually a panel may be requested only after the expiration of sixty days from the day a party submits a request for consultations to the other party.[109] However, in urgent cases the establishment of a panel may be sought within twenty days,[110] and accelerated procedures may be instigated.[111] Panels only have contentious jurisdiction and cannot issue advisory opinions. Only the WTO Ministerial Conference has the authority to render authoritative interpretations of the WTO and related agreements.[112]

5.5 Conclusion

International law is an ever-evolving field in which the place of past decisions has served as a building block for current and future understandings. This chapter began with a discussion of the *Bering Sea Fur-Seals* case, which demonstrated that many of the core principles of sustainable development existed in nascent form in arbitral decisions from over a century ago. More than an interesting historical observation, this discussion emphasizes the role of arbitral panels in advancing the core elements of sustainable development.

This chapter highlights the growth of international dispute settlement mechanisms in modern international law and the many roles that such international judicial and quasi-judicial bodies have assumed. The chapter has also demonstrated the importance of international dispute settlement as a way to resolve disputes in a non-litigation venue while still creating regimes that have the potential to mould the future of international laws that impact sustainable development. Against this backdrop, examples such as the WTO DSU provide mechanisms through which a number of concerns – economic, political and environmental, to name only a few – converge and allow for the resolution of disputes by using laws and larger interpretive principles that may include sustainable development. Although there are critics of the use of international dispute settlement mechanisms, and those who find fault with the landscape in which they operate, such criticisms have failed to derail the progress of tribunals and courts throughout international law.

---

109 DSU art. 3(11).
110 Ibid. at art. 4(8).
111 Ibid. at art. 4(9).
112 WTO Agreement art. IX(2).

6 Sustainable development challenges in international dispute settlement

Cairo Robb, Marie-Claire Cordonier Segger and Caroline Jo

6.1 Introduction

At a time of debates over the fragmentation of international law,[1] challenges of global governance, treaty overload and stalled negotiations, international judicial and quasi-judicial bodies are in a position to play a crucial role. The ILA 2012 Sofia Guiding Statements on the Judicial Elaboration of the 2002 New Delhi Declaration of Principles of International Law relating to Sustainable Development ('Sofia Guiding Statements') may offer small support, in the interest of enhancing coherence. The Sofia Guiding Statements acknowledge and reaffirm the 2002 International Jurists Mandate on Sustainable Development, and provide a guide for decision makers to draw upon.

The Sofia Guiding Statements seek to assist and inspire courts and tribunals in their crucial tasks towards strengthening global governance by lending at least procedural and possibly normative coherence to decision making in harmony with the pursuit of the concept of sustainable development. The structure, jurisdiction and scope of various courts and tribunals are set out in this chapter. Human rights bodies, regional economic integration bodies, free trade agreements and multilateral environmental agreements (MEA) compliance procedures are surveyed in particular, given their frequent references to sustainable development objectives. This chapter concludes by considering the position of the judiciary and other legal decision makers in contemporary international context, and explores the possibilities and options at their disposal for discharging their responsibilities in harmony with the pursuit of the concept of sustainable development.

6.2 Human rights bodies

Human rights bodies interpret and determine States' compliance with the human rights instrument to which they are associated. While proceedings are designed

---

1 As H.E. Judge Sir Christopher Greenwood has noted "While such fragmentation is a danger against which international lawyers must be on their guard, it is a danger which can be met and is very far from being the present reality which some commentators have suggested." Greenwood, Christopher, 'Some Challenges of International Litigation', *Cambridge Journal of International and Comparative Law* (1)1: 7–22 (2012). See also *supra* Chapter 5, note 14.

to be instituted by non-state actors, usually by individuals, provisions also exist for State actors to raise compliance issues. Although the human rights bodies described hereunder share similarities, they differ notably in their structures, substantive rights enshrined, procedures, outputs and remedies.[2]

6.2.1 UN Human Rights Committee

The UN Human Rights Committee (UNHRC)[3] was established under the 1966 International Covenant on Civil and Political Rights (ICCPR).[4] It is an independent expert body entrusted with powers of supervision over the implementation of the ICCPR.[5] The Committee is comprised of 18 independent experts, each nationals of different States Party to the ICCPR.

The Committee may receive communications from States Parties that have accepted the jurisdiction of the Committee, States that have not, and individual victims of alleged human rights violations under the ICCPR. Communications to the UNHRC can address any violation of the rights enumerated in the ICCPR (in the case of individual communication)[6] or any failure to fulfil the obligations of the ICCPR (in the case of an inter-state communication).[7] There are no provisions for third party intervention, but multiple or joint proceedings may be possible. Meanwhile, there is no explicit provision that permits involvement by experts or the submission of amicus curiae briefs.

Decisions are taken by a majority of the members participating in the consideration of the communication. While there is no avenue for recourse against recommendations of the HRC,[8] the Committee's views are not binding on the States Parties.

6.2.2 European Court of Human Rights

The European Court of Human Rights (ECtHR)[9] is entrusted with monitoring the compliance of Member States of the Council of Europe with their obligations

---

2   For example the African Charter on Human and Peoples Rights contains article 21 on peoples' right to free disposal of wealth and natural resources which has no direct comparison in other human rights instruments.

3   See generally Mackenzie, Ruth, Cesare P. R. Romano, Yuval Shany and Philippe Sands. *Manual on International Courts and Tribunals* (Oxford: OUP, 2010) [hereinafter MICT] from which details provided here have been drawn, the PICT website.

4   Entered into force in 1976.

5   The Committee serves three main functions: 1) it receives periodic reports from the States parties to the ICCPR on their compliance with the ICCPR; 2) it issues 'general comments' on the provisions of the Covenant; and 3) it receives communications from individuals and/or States alleging violations of human rights by States parties to the ICCPR that have accepted the competence of the HRC to review such petitions.

6   ICCPR, arts 1, 2, 41(1) (1976).

7   Ibid. at 41(1).

8   However, decisions on admissibility may be revisited at the request of the concerned State Party. Rules of Procedure, r 99(4).

9   See generally MICT, *supra* note 3.

under the 1950 European Convention on Human Rights. Originally petitions from individuals, NGOs or States alleging violations of the Convention had to be brought before the European Commission on Human Rights ('Commission'). In 1998, the Commission was abolished with the entry into force of the 11th Protocol to the Convention, and individual applicants could submit applications directly to the Court.

The number of judges on the Court equals the number of parties to the Convention, and quorum for plenary is two-thirds of the judges.[10] The Court hears cases by a single judge[11] in chambers composed of five or seven judges and two substitutes.[12] When a case raises a serious question affecting the interpretation of the convention or Protocols, or a question that might result in a judgment inconsistent with previous judgments of the Court, the Chamber may relinquish its jurisdiction in favour of the Grand Chamber of 17 judges (and three substitutes).[13,14]

Any State Party may bring an action against another State Party for breach of the Convention. Individuals, NGOs and groups of individuals who claim to be victims of a human rights violation may also bring actions against the State Party they claim has committed the alleged violations.[15] Third party intervention by another State, including specifically the State of nationality of the victim, if different from the State complained of, is also possible.[16] In addition, the Court may permit any person concerned with the outcome of the case (including NGOs) to intervene as amicus curiae and submit written comments to the Court.[17]

The substantive law to be applied by the ECtHR consists of the rights and freedoms listed in Section I of the ECHR, and certain Protocols. The Court may only address complaints alleging a breach of the provisions by a State Party. To inform its decision, the Court may request and receive evidence from scientific and technical experts.[18]

Final judgments of the Court are binding on the States parties.[19] Interim measures may be indicated[20] when justified by the existence of an imminent risk of

---

10 ECHR, art 20.
11 Protocol 14.
12 The nine judges form a 'Section' composed with due regard to the need for geographical and gender balance, and should be representative of the different legal systems of the States parties.
13 ECHR, art 26.
14 Also in exceptional cases the judgment of a Chamber may be referred for second review by the Grand Chamber.
15 The ECtHR and Commission have construed the term 'victim' narrowly as implying the person directly affected by the challenged act or omission. There is no *actio popularis. Klass v Germany* (1978) 2 EHRR 214. This is rarely the case for NGOs. But victimhood can be established even if no prejudice was caused by the violation (*Aydin v Turkey*) 2000-III ECHR MICT, *supra* note 3, p. 342.
16 MICT, *supra* note 3, p. 351.
17 ECHR, art 36(2); Rules of Court, r44(2).
18 As of 2003, matters relating to expert testimony and reports are regulated by an Annex to the Rules Concerning Investigations.
19 ECHR, art 46(1).
20 At the request of a party, any other concerned person, or by the tribunal acting *proprio motu*.

irreparable damage,[21] and the consequent need to ensure effective exercise of the right of individual application to the Court, as well as the effective examination of the application by the latter.[22]

At the request of the Committee of Ministers, the Court may render an advisory opinion on the interpretation of the Convention and Protocols,[23] though the Court is limited to procedural questions and matters not concerning the scope of substantive rights and freedoms.

6.2.3 Inter-American Court of Human Rights and Inter-American Commission on Human Rights[24]

The Inter-American Court of Human Rights (IAHR Court) was inaugurated in 1979 and is the principle judicial body entrusted with monitoring and adjudicating the human rights practices of States parties to the 1969 American Convention on Human Rights, concluded under the auspices of the Organization of American States. It comprises seven judges who are nationals of the OAS States, of whom four make a quorum.[25]

The Inter-American Commission on Human Rights pre-dates the Court and has been active since 1959. It works alongside the IAHR Court. The Commission comprises seven members, of whom four make a quorum.[26] Some preparatory work may be done in working groups of not more than three members.

Any person, group of persons or NGO[27] may submit a petition to the Commission alleging a violation of the American Convention by a State Party. Claims may also be brought by one State Party against another State Party alleging a violation of the American Convention if both States have accepted the Commission's jurisdiction.[28]

Additionally, the Commission may receive from persons, groups of persons and NGOs, communications against OAS Member States not parties to the American Convention, alleging violations of fundamental human rights.[29] With regard to OAS Member States who are not parties to the American Convention, the IAHR Commission may review the observation of fundamental rights standards under general international law, with particular reference to the American Declaration of the Rights and Duties of Man.[30]

---

21   *Mamatkulov v Turkey*, 2005-I EurCtHR 293, para. 104.

22   Ibid. at para. 128.

23   ECHR at art 47(1). The power to issue advisory opinions was granted to the Court in Protocol No 2 to the Convention for the Protection of Human Rights and Fundamental Freedoms, 6 May 1963, ETS 44 (1963).

24   See generally MICT, section 12 364–86 from which details provided here draw are drawn, the PICT website and the Court and Commission's.

25   Not necessarily States that are party to the American Convention on Human Rights, art 52.

26   Of whom no two may be of the same nationality.

27   Recognized under the law of at least one Member State of the OAS.

28   American Convention at art 45(1), which acceptance may be made with restrictions.

29   IAHR Commission Statute at art 20.

30   Ibid. at art 20.

Following its review, the Commission issues a report on the merits including its conclusions of fact and law and determination on whether the Declaration, the Convention or another instrument has been violated. Only the Commission and States parties to the American Convention may bring a case before the Court, and only against States that have accepted the Court's jurisdiction.[31] The Court can receive cases only after proceedings at the Commission have failed to yield an appropriate result.[32] In the case of States parties that have accepted, or are willing to accept the jurisdiction of the Court *ad hoc*, the Commission may refer the case for adjudication to the Court, after giving the State Party time to consider its findings, and after consulting with the petitioners. Decisions of the Commission may be brought to the Court for an additional review by an unsatisfied State Party.

The Court issues its decisions in the form of judgments (decided by a majority of the judges). The decisions of the Court in contentious cases are final and binding. The IAHR Court may render non-binding advisory opinions at the request of any OAS Member State or authorized OAS organ, acting within the scope of its competence. The subject matter of such an opinion can encompass the interpretation of the American Convention and other human rights treaties applicable in the territory of the OAS Member State; the advisory jurisdiction also encompasses bilateral and multilateral treaties, treaties which are not primarily human rights treaties, and treaties whose membership includes non-OAS parties.[33]

Both the IAHR Court and Commission are competent to address all questions concerning the alleged violation or the interpretation and application of the human rights enumerated in the American Convention, in addition to some relevant provisions found in the San Salvador Protocol and in certain other human rights agreements.

Traditionally, procedures before the IAHR Court or Commission did not offer the possibility of third party intervention. However, the Commission appears as a representative of the 'public interest' in all cases,[34] and an amendment to the Court's rules of procedure now allows victims to intervene in the proceedings and submit pleadings, motions and evidence throughout the process.[35] In addition, the Court may hear any evidence, including expert testimony, it considers helpful. In practice the Court has long admitted amicus curiae briefs, now provided for explicitly in its rules of procedure.[36]

---

31 Consent may be made through a general declaration pursuant to article 62(1) of the Convention, through *ad hoc* declarations or through a special agreement. Acceptance of the Court's jurisdiction in respect of inter-state proceedings may be made subject to reciprocal acceptance by the other State.

32 American Convention at art 61(2).

33 Other treaties subject to the advisory opinion jurisdiction of the Court (Art. 64 American Convention on Human Rights), Advisory Opinion of 24 September 1982 I/A CHR (Ser A) No 1 at para. 25.

34 IACHR Court Statute, art 28.

35 IACHR Court Rules of Procedure at art 24.

36 Ibid. at arts 2(3), 41.

In urgent cases, when irreparable harm to persons is likely, the Commission may request the concerned government to take provisional precautionary measures.[37] Meanwhile, the Court is authorized to order provisional measures in cases of extreme gravity and urgency if such measures are necessary to avoid irreparable harm to persons.[38]

6.2.4 African Court on Human and Peoples' Rights and African Commission on Human and Peoples' Rights[39]

The African Court on Human and Peoples' Rights (ACtHPR or the Court) was established in 1998 to complement and reinforce the functions of the African Commission on Human and Peoples' Rights in promoting and protecting human and peoples' rights, freedoms and duties in African Union (AU)[40] Member States under the African Charter on Human and Peoples' Rights (ACHPR) and other human rights instruments. It comprises 11 judges, of whom seven make a quorum.

The African Commission on Human and Peoples' Rights (ACommHPR or the Commission) pre-dates the Court and has been active since 1987. It comprises 11 persons, of whom seven make a quorum, and can delegate some of its functions to working groups of three members.

The jurisdiction of the Commission encompasses all cases where a State Party or other competent applicant has good reason to believe that another State Party has violated the provisions of the African Charter on Human and Peoples' Rights and the Protocol on the Rights of Women in Africa.[41] The Commission may receive communications against States parties to the African Charter, which are submitted by another State Party,[42] or any other source. In the latter case, the Commission may consider the communication only if the majority of its members decides to do so.[43]

In investigating a communication the Commission may receive information from the AU Commission Chairperson or from any person capable of enlightening it.[44] A similar power can be found with regard to admitting information from interested States and specialized institutions of the AU.[45] The various

---

37   IAHR Commission Rules of Procedure at art 25.
38   American Convention at art 63(2). The Court may order measures at the request of a part, at the request of the Commission (in matters not yet submitted to the Court), at the request of the alleged victim, or acting on its own initiative.
39   See generally MICT section 13, *supra* note 3.
40   The African Union (AU) is the successor of the Organization of African Unity (OAU) which was founded in 1963 to provide a forum for independent States emerging from the dismantling of colonial empires.
41   Jurisdiction over the Protocol was given initially on a temporary basis, pending setting up of the Court.
42   African Charter at arts 47, 49.
43   Ibid. at art 55.
44   African Charter at art 46.
45   Commission Rules at rr 71, 73.

instruments regulating the work of the Commission do not specifically provide for, or exclude, third party intervention.

In cases brought by non-state applicants the Commission will normally prepare observations in the form of a judicial decision, including legal findings and specifying appropriate remedies. In cases brought by States the Commission will prepare a report within twelve months[46] with its decisions and conclusions on the merits of the case. Decisions of the Commission are not binding. The Commission may indicate its views on whether interim measures are needed to avoid irreparable damage to the alleged victim.[47]

The jurisdiction of the Court extends to all cases and disputes concerning the interpretation and application of the African Charter, the Protocol on the Court, or any human rights instrument ratified by the States concerned.[48] The Court has jurisdiction over cases brought by: 1) the Commission; 2) the State Party that lodged a complaint to the Commission; 3) the State Party against whom the complaint has been lodged; 4) the State Party whose citizen is a victim of human rights violations; and 5) any African intergovernmental organization.[49]

The Court is also authorized to receive cases brought directly to it by individuals or NGOs with observer status before the Commission,[50] if the State against whom the complaint has been made submitted a declaration under article 34(6) of the Protocol recognising the competence of the Court to receive such claims. Under the Protocol establishing the Court, any State Party with an interest in a case can make a request to join the proceedings.[51] Amicus curiae is not explicitly regulated in the constitutive documents of the Court.[52]

The Court provides decisions in the form of a reasoned judgment, which are binding on the parties and not subject to appeal. The Court may adopt provisional measures in cases of extreme gravity and urgency if such measures are needed to avoid irreparable harm to persons.[53] The African Court has the power to render advisory opinions at the request of AU Member States, the AU, any of its organs, or any African organization recognized by the AU,[54] provided the same matter is not being dealt with by the Commission. The African Court will be replaced by the African Court of Justice and Human Rights when the Protocol establishing it is ratified by 15 States parties.[55]

---

46   If no amicable settlement has been reached.
47   Commission Rules, r 111(1).
48   Court Protocol, art 3(1).
49   Ibid. at art 5(1)
50   Court Protocol, arts 5(3), 34(6). This is more stringent than applied in Commission proceedings which are open to all NGOs.
51   Court Protocol, art 5(2).
52   MICT, p. 13.27.
53   Court Protocol, art 27(2).
54   Ibid. at art 4.
55   Protocol on the Statute of the African Court of Justice and Human Rights, 1 July 2008.

6.3 Regional economic integration bodies and free trade agreements

The growing trend towards regional arrangements for economic cooperation and integration has resulted in dedicated dispute settlement arrangements pursuant to them.

Such bodies apply regional law, but are nevertheless of interest as supra-national dispute settlement bodies because, like national courts, these bodies have occasion to deal with questions of international law, and provide evidence of *opinio juris*.

The *Manual on International Courts and Tribunals* points out that the jurisdiction of the regional dispute settlement systems generally includes:

- Complaints against Member States of the relevant community for non-compliance with its rules, which may generally be brought by community institutions or by other Member States;
- complaints against the institutions of the community themselves, which may generally be brought by Member States or other institutions established within the community;
- preliminary references by domestic courts of the Member States for the interpretation of specific aspects of the law of the relevant community.[56]

A brief overview of dispute settlement mechanisms in these regional regimes is provided below.

6.3.1 *Court of Justice of the European Union*[57]

The European Court of Justice (ECJ), renamed the Court of Justice of the European Union (CJEU),[58] is the principal judicial organ of the European Union,[59] notably its component part, the European Community (EC). The CJEU, established in 1951,[60] has worked as a template for many other courts of regional economic integration agreements. TEU article 19 (formerly art. 220 EC) provides that the CJEU 'shall ensure that in the interpretation and application of the Treaties the law is observed'. In essence, within its jurisdiction, the CJEU reviews the legality of the acts of the institutions of the European Union; ensures that Member States comply with their obligations under EU law; and ensures uniform interpretation and implementation of EU law by ruling on requests for interpretation of EU law submitted by national courts.[61]

The Court consists of one judge per Member States, appointed by Member States' governments. The judges are assisted by 11 Advocates General who

---

56 MICT, Part IV, Introduction.
57 See generally MICT, from which details provided here have been drawn extensively.
58 After the entry into force of the Treaty of Lisbon.
59 See generally MICT section 9 and Part IV Introduction and Evaluation, which pre-dates the Treaty of Lisbon reforms, but nevertheless sheds light on the position and practice of the CJEU.
60 Treaty Establishing the European Coal and Steel Community, 18 April 1951, 261 UNTS 140.
61 See *supra* note 59.

propose to the Court, in complete independence, a legal solution to the cases for which they are responsible. The Advocate Generals' opinions are not binding on the Court, but are in fact often followed. The Court sits in a Grand Chamber of 15 judges in specified circumstances, or otherwise in Chambers of three or five judges. The court of first instance, the General Court, also consists of one judge per Member State. Decisions of the CJEU are taken by majority. Appeals may be brought before the Court of Justice against judgments and orders of the General Court, limited to points of law.

The Treaty of Maastricht, which established the European Union, divided EU policies into three main areas called 'pillars'. The CJEU's judicial supervision of legal acts of the EU is essentially limited to the first 'Community' pillar, the one inherited from the EC, and which concerns economic, social and environmental policies.[62] The CJEU has multiple heads of jurisdiction making a precise but succinct summary difficult. In short, cases can be brought before the CJEU either as 'direct actions' (for 'annulment'[63] 'failure to act'[64] and 'failure to fulfil obligations'[65]); or indirectly, as in the case of referrals for preliminary rulings from national courts,[66] or appeals of judgments decided by the General Court.

It is through the preliminary ruling jurisdiction that European citizens can challenge Community rules that affect them indirectly or not specifically. Although only the national court can make the reference, all the parties to the proceedings before the national court may take part in the proceedings before the Court of Justice. In cases other than referrals for preliminary rulings the Court of Justice may prescribe any necessary interim measures.[67] An expedited procedure for the main proceedings is also available under certain conditions, including for references for preliminary rulings.

62 Ibid.
63 By an action for annulment, the applicant seeks the annulment of a measure adopted by a Community institution (TFEU art 263, formerly WC Treaty art 230). Actions may be brought by a Member State, the European Parliament, the Council or the Commission on grounds of lack of competence, infringement of an essential procedural requirement, infringement of the Treaties or of any rule of law relating to their application or misuse of powers. For the purposes of protecting their own prerogatives, actions for annulment may also be brought by the Court of Auditors, the European Central Bank, and by the Committee of the Regions. Any natural or legal person, under certain conditions, may institute proceedings against an act addressed to that person, or which is of direct and individual concern to them, and against a regulatory act which is of direct concern to them and does not entail implementing measures.)
64 Procedurally, actions for failure to act against the European Parliament, the Council or Commission, for failing to act in infringement of the treaties, are similar to actions for annulment.
65 When a Member State fails to fulfil an obligation under the EC Treaty, another Member State (art 227) or the Commission (art 226) may bring an action before the ECJ. Natural or legal persons cannot bring actions for failure to fulfil obligations.
66 To ensure uniform application of community legislation and to prevent conflicting interpretations, when national courts have real and substantial doubts about the interpretation of EU law (and where it is relevant for the decision in the national proceedings), they may – and if it is a court of last instance, must – refer the matter to the Court of Justice 'for a preliminary ruling', asking the Court to clarify a point concerning the interpretation of Community Law. In recent years, preliminary rulings have become the largest part of the docket of the Court of Justice.
67 EC Treaty, art 243.

6.3.2 *Caribbean Court of Justice*[68]

The Caribbean Court of Justice is a hybrid judicial body established in 2001 by the Agreement Establishing the Caribbean Court of Justice (CCJ Agreement).[69] It settles disputes between contracting parties and community institutions over the interpretation and application of the 2001 Revised Treaty of Chaguaramas of the Caribbean Community (Revised Treaty) establishing the Caribbean Single Market and Economy (CSME). At the same time it is a national court of appeal, acting as last instance of jurisdiction for Caribbean States that have accepted its jurisdiction.

The Court is composed of the President and no more than nine judges, and is duly constituted with an odd number of no less than three judges, though a sole judge appointed by the Chairman can also be sufficient. The substantive law to be applied in the exercise of the Court's original jurisdiction is the applicable rules of international law.[70] The Court, however, may also employ other principles of law or equity where necessary.[71] Decisions, taken by majority of the judges hearing the case, are final and binding. The Court may also order interim measures

The original jurisdiction of the CCJ is very similar to that of other regional economic integration agreement courts, and in particular the CJEU. Much like the CJEU, the Court fulfils its role in two ways. First it settles disputes between contracting parties; or between contracting parties and the Community; or between individuals and contracting parties or Community institutions on the implementation of CSME law and regulations.[72] Standing of natural and legal persons is limited. It is granted only with special leave of the Court provided that the Court determines that the Treaty intended a right to be conferred for the benefit of the person directly; that the person has suffered a prejudice in respect to enjoyment of the benefit; that the contracting party entitled to espouse the claim of the person in question has either omitted or declined to do so, or expressly agreed that the person may bring the claim before the Court; and finally, that the Court finds that the interests of justice so requires.[73]

---

68   See generally MICT section 10, *supra* note 3. Available at: http://www.caribbeancourtofjustice.org/
69   Agreement Establishing the Caribbean Court of Justice (CCJ Agreement). See also the Revised Treaty of Chaguaramas Estabishing the Caribbean Community including the CARICOM Single Market and Economy, 5 July 2001, (Revised Treaty of Chaguaramas).

    A feature setting the CCJ apart from most other international courts is how judges are selected and appointed. With the exception of the President of the Court, who is appointed by the qualified majority vote of three-quarters of contracting parties, CCJ judges are appointed by a majority vote of an institution called the Regional Judicial and Legal Services Commission. The RJLSC is established by Article V of the CCJ Agreement, MICT 10.1.6 *supra* note 3.
70   CCJ Agreement, art XXIV.
71   Revised Treaty of Chaguaramas, art 217.
72   Art 211 of the Revised Treaty grants the CCJ compulsory and exclusive jurisdiction to hear and determine disputes concerning the interpretation and application of the Treaty.
73   CCJ Agreement, art XXIV.

In the exercise of the Court's original jurisdiction, whenever the construction of a convention to which Member States and persons other than those concerned in the case are parties is in question, the Registrar shall notify all such States and persons, and if they consider they have a substantial interest of a legal nature which may be affected by a decision of the Court, they may apply to intervene.

The CCJ also considers referrals for preliminary rulings from national courts facing an issue whose resolution involves a question concerning the interpretation or application of the Treaty, and if the national court in question determines that resolution of the issue is necessary to deliver a judgment it must refer the question to the CCJ for determination.[74]

The CCJ also has exclusive jurisdiction to deliver advisory opinions concerning the interpretation and application of the Treaty establishing the CARICOM and its revisions. Requests for advisory opinions can be made only by the contracting parties or the Community.

6.3.3 North American Free Trade Agreement (NAFTA)[75]

The North American Free Trade Agreement (NAFTA) was concluded by Canada, the USA and Mexico in 1992, establishing the North American Free Trade Area.

The agreement contains three sets of dispute settlement procedures: general dispute settlement procedures (Chapter 20); a separate dispute settlement mechanism for review of final administrative decisions by national authorities of the three Member States related to the imposition of anti-dumping and countervailing duties (Chapter 19); and specific, applicable procedures for investment disputes (Chapter 11). In addition, the separate NAFTA 'side agreements' on Environment (NAAEC) and Labour[76] contain their own dispute settlement and compliance mechanisms. However, where a matter is already in dispute in NAFTA proceedings, it cannot be raised in proceedings under the NAAEC side agreement.[77]

The general dispute settlement procedures apply to any dispute between the States parties concerning: 1) the interpretation or application of NAFTA; or 2) allegations that the application of an actual or proposed measure taken by a party is inconsistent with its NAFTA obligations, or would cause impairment or nullification of certain benefits that the complaining party expects to attain under NAFTA.[78]

Under this procedure if consultations between the parties are unsuccessful, a complaining party may request the convening of the Free Trade Commission, comprising Trade Ministers of the parties, which will put its good offices at the disposal of the parties to facilitate a settlement. If the parties fail to reach agreement within a certain time any party can request the Commission to establish an *ad hoc*

---

74 Revised Treaty of Chaguaramas, art 214; CCJ Agreement, art XVI.
75 See MICT 10.4, *supra* note 3.
76 NAALC.
77 See *infra* at 6.4.4.
78 NAFTA, art 2004.

arbitration panel,[79] which are roughly similar to GATT/WTO dispute settlement panels, except that the *ad hoc* arbitration panel's final report is binding on the parties, and not subject to appeal.

Where disputes address a matter arising under both NAFTA and GATT,[80] the matter may be settled in either forum at the discretion of the complaining party except in certain circumstances. One such circumstance would include instances where the responding party claims that its action is subject to Article 104 (relation to Environmental and Conservation Agreements) or in certain cases concerning: 1) a measure adopted or maintained by a party to protect its human, animal or plant life or health, or to protect its environment; or 2) that raises factual issues concerning the environment, and the responding States requests in writing that the dispute be considered under NAFTA, in which case the NAFTA dispute settlement procedure prevails.

Under Chapter 19 of NAFTA, *ad hoc* bi-national panels can be established to review domestic administrative determinations relating to anti-dumping and countervailing duties. A State Party to NAFTA may request the establishment of a bi-national panel where 1) another party has adopted a statutory amendment which is inconsistent with the GATT (or certain specified side agreements), the object and purpose of NAFTA, or has the function and effect of overturning a bi-national panel decision (and is also inconsistent with the GATT and/or NAFTA); and 2) if a determination of a competent domestic authority on antidumping or countervailing duties is incompatible with the domestic law of the importing State, as would have been applied by a domestic court of review. Such panels can also be established in relation to a dispute on antidumping or countervailing duties upon the request of its own initiative, or acting on the request of a person that would have had legal standing before equivalent domestic challenge procedures.[81]

Under Chapter 11 of NAFTA, a disputing investor may submit the claim to arbitration under the ICSID Convention, the Additional Facility Rules of ICSID, or under the UNCITRAL arbitration rules.

6.4 Multilateral environmental agreements (MEA) compliance procedures

Compliance procedures (also known as non-compliance procedures (NCPs)) are not courts or tribunals and do not comprise dispute resolution mechanisms as such.[82] They are invariably stated to be without prejudice to other dispute settlement procedures contained in the agreement establishing them.[83]

---

79 NAFTA, art 2008.
80 Or any agreement negotiated under it or any successor agreement.
81 NAFTA, art 1904.5.
82 MICT, Chapter 19 Introduction.
83 Ibid. Though M. Koskenniemi points out in relation to environmental treaties that "... this is more by way of ritual than any realistic belief that compliance problems should, or could, be dealt with through the doctrines of fault and attributability which characterize the legal doctrine

The function of NCPs is to promote compliance with agreement provisions, while recognizing the variety of reasons for failure of compliance, including lack of resources or capacity. They can review compliance, facilitate practical assistance with compliance, and in some cases initiate, instigate or propose sanctions.

MEA NCPs share similar characteristics with some judicial or quasi-judicial procedures in allowing States or non-state actors to raise complaints concerning another State's or international organization's performance of treaty obligations. However, whereas adjudication is an essentially confrontational and adversarial process, NCPs are more focused on promoting the overall objectives of the regime.[84]

A treaty may provide for the setting up of a compliance procedure by the Conference or Meeting of the Parties once the treaty enters into force. They can vary greatly in their mandate, design and functioning. In negotiations, differences often arise among parties as to the most basic elements of the compliance procedure, such as who should be entitled to trigger the mechanism, who should participate in it and what consequences are appropriate to a finding of non-compliance.[85]

Below are outlines of compliance mechanisms discussed in this volume. The first three are compliance procedures associated with MEAs – the Montreal Protocol, the Kyoto Protocol and the Aarhus Convention. The fourth example relates to a tripartite environmental agreement, the North American Agreement on Environmental Cooperation. The fifth differs in that it is directed not at compliance by States with their treaty undertakings, but at compliance by an international organization with its own stated operational policies and procedures – the World Bank Inspection Panel. Unlike the first two, the last three mentioned may be initiated by members of the public. The last two mentioned are limited to being fact finding mechanisms, and

---

of State responsibility." Koskenniemi, M. 'New Institutions and Procedures for Implementation Control and Reaction' in Werksman, J. *Greening International Institutions*, Public information (London: Routledge, 2014) 236 at 247.

84 In the context of international law in the field of "global public goods," Krisch States, "[w]e are witnessing a radical expansion of global regulation in general. This expansion often comes in forms other than formal law – especially through informal norms and institutions, which by all accounts have grown rapidly over the last few decades. But much of today's informality looks different from that of former times. Elaborate institutional structures for rulemaking and implementation have been developed, and as concerns about institutional legitimacy have grown, formalized procedures and participation rights have been established. Through these procedures, the informal realm slowly becomes more lawlike, and some commentators have suggested that informal norms should, under certain circumstances, be recognized as 'law'. This view faces significant obstacles, not least because the actors themselves typically do not understand informed norms as 'binding' in the same way as traditional legal norms. From a sociolegal or political science perspective, however, it is easier to understand law as a matter of degree and kind rather than exclusively in binary terms. And for purposes of understanding 'legalization' in global politics, it is useful to broaden the focus so that a variety of 'moves to law' can be better captured and explained. Regardless, however, of whether we are considering a shift within law or from law, the combined effect of a decrease in new multilateral treaties and a significant increase in informal regulation is certainly a shift away from classical, formal international law." Krisch, Nico, 'The Decay of Consent: International Law in an Age of Global Public Goods', 2014 *AJIL* vol 108:1 at pp. 35–6. (footnotes omitted)

85 MICT, sect. 19.

have no further tools or mandate to make recommendations to achieve compliance. Nonetheless, the investigation and public reporting process can create political pressure to achieve compliance.

6.4.1 Montreal Protocol

The Montreal Protocol on Substances that Deplete the Ozone Layer[86] non-compliance procedure was established in 1992 and revised in 1998. Its Implementation Committee consists of ten State representatives, elected by the Meeting of the Parties.[87]

Cases can be referred to the Implementation Committee by other States or by a State itself through the Secretariat, and by the Secretariat acting on its own motion.

The Implementation Committee considers the information before it, and may request further information, and undertake, with consent, on-site information gathering. The State Party whose compliance is called into question is entitled to participate in the proceedings before the Committee.[88]

The Committee submits its findings and recommendations in a report to the Meeting of the Parties, which has authority to take steps to bring about compliance with the Protocol.

An indicative list of measures agreed by parties includes the provision of special assistance to the non-complying State, issuing of cautions, and suspension of rights and privileges under the Protocol. In practice most actions have been aimed at facilitating compliance with the Protocol and monitoring measures to restore compliance, through, for example, the submission of action plans by the party concerned.[89]

6.4.2 Kyoto Protocol[90]

The Kyoto Protocol[91] NCP entered into force in 2005.[92] Its Compliance Committee is composed of 20 members serving in their personal capacity, and functions through a plenary of all Committee members, a supporting Bureau and two branches, the facilitative branch and the enforcement branch, consisting of ten Committee members each.

Decisions of the plenary and the facilitative branch may be taken by a three-quarters majority, while decisions of the enforcement branch require,

---

86 The Protocol was adopted pursuant to the 1985 Vienna Convention on Protection of the Ozone Layer.
87 In this it differs from other compliance mechanisms where members serve in their individual capacity.
88 1998 Non-Compliance Procedure, para. 10.
89 MICT, p. 504.
90 See generally MICT, *supra* note 3 from which details provided here have been extensively drawn; the PICT website at http://www.pict-pcti.org/
91 The Protocol was adopted under the auspices of the 1992 UN Framework Convention on Climate Change (UNFCCC).
92 Pursuant to art 18 of the Protocol.

in addition, a double majority of both Annex I and non-Annex I representative members.

Submissions may be made to the Committee through the Secretariat by a party with respect to its own compliance, by any part with respect to another party, with corroborating information. Questions of implementation in reports of expert review teams under article 8 of the Protocol may also be submitted to the Committee through the Secretariat.[93] The Bureau of the Committee allocates a question of implementation to the appropriate branch, based on their mandates.

If, after preliminary examination, a decision is taken to proceed the party concerned is informed and given an opportunity to comment, and to be represented during consideration of the matter (but not during elaboration and adoption of the decision). Each branch bases its decision on relevant information provided by: expert review team reports under article 8 of the Protocol; the party concerned; any party that has submitted a question of implementation concerning another party; reports of bodies of the UNFCCC and Kyoto protocol; and the other branch. In addition, each branch may seek expert advice, and competent inter-governmental and non-governmental organizations may submit relevant factual and technical data.

The Committee must take into account any degree of flexibility allowed by the CMP for Annex I Parties undergoing the process of transition to a market economy. In addition, the facilitative branch is to take into consideration the common but differentiated responsibilities of the Parties, and the circumstances pertaining to questions before it.[94]

There are additional detailed procedures with specific timetables for the enforcement branch, including the opportunity for a party facing the Compliance Committee to make formal written submissions and request a hearing where it can present its views and call on expert testimony.[95]

The compliance mechanism sets out the consequences of non-compliance, which may be applied by the facilitative branch and the enforcement branch. The facilitative branch remedies include the provision of advice and facilitation of assistance, including financial and technical assistance, technology transfer and capacity building.

The enforcement branch may apply a range of consequences depending upon the obligation with which the party concerned is found to be in non-compliance, including the requirement to develop a plan to analyze causes of non compliance and setting out measures to remedy it, including a timetable, suspending eligibility to aspects of the regime, and imposing a reduction in a party's emissions allocations for the next commitment period.

If a party's eligibility is withdrawn or suspended, it may request, either through an expert review team or directly to the enforcement branch, to have its eligibility restored if it believes it has rectified the problem and is again meeting the relevant criteria.

93 MICT, *supra* note 3.
94 UNFCCC website, *supra* note 90.
95 MICT 19.2.5 *supra* note 3 and the UNFCCC website.

As a general rule, decisions taken by the two branches of the Committee cannot be appealed. The exception is a decision of the enforcement branch relating to emissions targets. Even then, a party can only appeal if it believes it has been denied due process.[96] The 2015 Paris Agreement NCP is being detailed in negotiations to determine the modalities of implementation of the accord, a 'Paris Rulebook.'

6.4.3 Aarhus Convention [97]

The UNECE Aarhus Convention Compliance Committee consists of nine members who serve in their personal capacity, nominated by parties and signatories to the convention, and by certain types of non-governmental organization, and elected by the Meeting of the Parties.

It considers submissions, referrals or communications[98] from parties to the Convention regarding their own obligations or those of another party, from the Aarhus Convention Secretariat, and also from the public.

In addition, the Committee may examine compliance issues on its own initiative and make recommendations; prepare reports on compliance with or implementation of the provisions of the Convention at the request of the Meeting of the Parties; and monitor, assess and facilitate the implementation of and compliance with the reporting requirements under article 10, paragraph 2, of the Convention.

The Committee may seek the advice of experts, receive and request further information, and with consent gather on site information.

The party in question is entitled to participate in the discussions of the Committee, as is a member of public who has submitted a communication.

The final report of the Compliance Committee[99] is considered by the Meeting of the Parties, which may decide upon any measures to bring about full compliance with the Convention.

Pending consideration of the report by the Meeting of the Parties the Compliance Committee is entitled in consultation with the party concerned to provide advice and facilitate assistance, and with agreement, make recommendations to and requests to[100] the party concerned. The additional responses available to the

---

96 UNFCCC Decision 27/CMP.1 XI.1.
97 See generally MICT, *supra* note 3, from which details provided here have been drawn, the PICT website at http://www.pict-pcti.org/.
98 Made under the terms of Decision 1/7.
99 The presence of five members of the Committee is required for any decisions to be taken. The Committee makes every effort to reach its decisions by consensus. Decisions of a procedural nature can be taken by a simple majority of the members present and voting. Decisions on substantive matters can be taken only with the support of seven out of nine members present and voting; six out of eight members present and voting; six out of seven members present and voting; five out of six members present and voting; and four out of five members present and voting. Notwithstanding this, the Committee is generally sympathetic to the view that at least five members should be in support of any substantive decision being taken. Since Committee members are elected strictly in their personal capacity, an absent Committee member cannot designate a substitute (MP.PP/C.1/2003/2, para. 12).
100 Requests to submit a strategy including a time schedule.

Meeting of the Parties are to issue declarations of non-compliance; to issue cautions; to suspend the rights and privileges of the party under the Convention (in accordance with rules of treaty law); and consultative measures.

6.4.4 NAAEC[101]

The North American Agreement on Environmental Cooperation (NAAEC) was adopted in 1993 as part of the movement towards North American economic integration to ensure that conclusions of the NAFTA did not compromise domestic environmental standards. NAEEC established the Commission on Environmental Cooperation (CEC) to facilitate cooperation between States parties and monitor implementation of the NAAEC. The Commission comprises three organs: a Council composed of cabinet-level State representatives, the Secretariat, and the Joint Public Advisory Committee (JPAC), which consists of five citizens from each country.

The Council's role includes coordination of the settlement of inter-State disputes concerning the NAAEC. The Secretariat monitors compliance of the States parties with the provisions of NAAEC, supports the Council, and addresses submissions of persons and NGOs established or residing in the territory of a State Party alleging that a State Party is failing to enforce effectively its environmental laws. On the basis of the information presented by the parties, the Secretariat may request the approval of the Council for further investigation on the matter. If approval is granted, the Secretariat is to prepare a factual record on the matter, based, *inter alia*, on the information presented by NGOs, persons, the Joint Public Advisory Committee, or the parties or otherwise developed by the Secretariat or independent experts. The factual record is then to be submitted to the Council, which may decide to make it available to the public.[102, 103]

The Secretariat may not consider a complaint that a NAFTA party is not complying with its environmental obligations if this question is already the subject of NAFTA dispute settlement proceedings.[104]

6.4.5 *World Bank Inspection Panel*[105]

Established in 1993,[106] the World Bank Inspection Panel may receive complaints alleging non-compliance by the Bank's Management with the Bank's

---

101 See www.cec.org/about-us/NAAEC.

102 NAAEC, art 15(7).

103 In certain circumstances the Council can, upon written request and by a two thirds vote, convene an arbitral panel to consider the matter. NAAEC, art 24.

104 NAAEC, art 14(3)(a).

105 See generally MICT, *supra* note 3, from which details provided here have been drawn, the PICT website at http://www.pict-pcti.org/.

106 Resolution No IBRD 93–10, Resolution No IDA 93–6, The World Bank Inspection Panel, 34 ILM 520 (1995) (Panel Resolution). Available at http://www.world bank.org/inspectionpanel.

own operational policies and procedures, from groups of people who claim to be affected adversely by such non-compliance.

The request cannot be made by an individual but must be made two or more people with common interests and concerns including an organization, association, society or other grouping of individuals.[107] They must be from the territory of the borrowing State and be able to demonstrate that their rights and interests have been or are likely to be affected directly by an act or omission of the Bank, due to the Bank's failure to follow its operational policies and procedures in relation to a Bank-financed project.[108] A request for investigation may be also made by any Executive Director in special cases of serious alleged violations of policies and procedures, and, at any time, by the Executive Directors acting as a body.[109]

The scope of the Panel's jurisdiction covers requests relating to acts or omissions of the Bank resulting from a failure on the part of the Bank to follow operational policies and procedures pertaining to the design, appraisal and implementation of a project (including failure to require the borrower State to comply with its loan-related obligations with respect to such policies and procedures). Such failure must have had or must threaten to have a material adverse effect.[110,111] It is limited to the acts and omissions of the International Bank for Reconstruction and Development (IBRD) and the International Development Agency (IDA), and does not extend to other institutions of the World Bank Group. It does however extend to any project or programme financed in whole or part by the IBRD or IDA. It therefore includes, for example, projects funded through trust funds administered by the Bank, such as the Global Environment Facility.[112]

If the circumstances warrant a full investigation,[113] this is conducted by the Panel, which comprises three members of different nationalities from countries that are members of the Bank.

The applicable standards to be applied are the World Bank's operational policies and procedures. The Panel cannot rely upon non-binding policy Statements such as Guidelines and Best Practices, nor may the Panel examine the adequacy of the policies and procedures themselves.[114]

There is no provision for formal third party intervention. The Panel may request and receive information from a wide variety of State and non-state actors, including experts, Bank officials and NGOs. Any member of the public may provide a written document, not exceeding ten pages (including a one page summary) containing information that they believe is relevant to the investigation.

---

107 Ibid. at para. 12. The Executive Director's 1996 Clarification has explained that this implies any two or more persons who share some common interest or concerns.

108 Panel Resolution, para. 12.

109 Ibid.

110 Ibid.

111 The Panel is not charged with reviewing the appropriateness of the policies or procedures of the Bank, but merely with ensuring that the Bank observes them. MICT, *supra* note 3 at p. 469.

112 International Bank for Reconstruction and Development, *Accountability at the World Bank: The Inspection Panel at 15 Years* (2009) at 28.

113 The relevant Bank Manager is given an opportunity to respond, prior to a decision being made to conduct a full investigation (see MICT, pp. 471–3).

114 MICT, p. 466.

The Inspection Panel is not authorized to render provisional measures, nor does it have jurisdiction beyond review of requests for inspection.

The findings of the Panel are presented in the form of a report (adopted by majority) to the President of the Bank and the Executive Directors. It is the Board of Directors that may decide what action to take, if any, to implement the report.[115]

6.5 Decisions of international judicial and quasi-judicial bodies in contemporary international law context

It is well known that Article 38(1)(d) of the Statute of the International Court of Justice provides that the Court shall apply "judicial decisions . . . as a subsidiary means for the determination of rules of law".[116]

The Statute does not confine itself to judicial decisions of international tribunals. As has been noted by Bethlehem "[I]n the case of international law, the interpretation and application of law by States is an important part of the creation and development of the law – through State practice, through *opinio juris*, through the conduct of States in the interpretation and application of treaties".[117] Decisions of national and regional tribunals are clearly relevant in this context.

It is also well known that there is no general doctrine of precedent in international law.[118] Nevertheless international tribunals, including the ICJ, frequently make reference to their previous decisions, and there are increasing instances of one international tribunal drawing on, or making reference to, the jurisprudence of another.[119]

For the above reasons the ILA Committee on International Law on Sustainable Development focused much of its work, including its Final Report, on matters relating to sustainable development principles and the decision making of international courts and tribunals. Its biennial Reports chart is a pragmatic and realistic assessment of the current and future potential of the concept of sustainable development in judicial and quasi-judicial decision making, and also of the contribution that judicial and quasi-judicial decision

---

115 Several other international and regional financial institutions have established similar mechanisms, some with supplementary 'problem solving' and consultation-based approaches alongside the original inspection or compliance review functions. PICT 2010.
116 Whether these are sources of law or evidence of law is a subject of debate. For an overview see Zammit Borda, Aldo, 'A Formal Approach to Article 38(1)(d) of the ICJ Statute from the Perspective of the International Criminal Courts and Tribunals', *EU J. of Int'l L.* (2013), Vol 24 No. 2, 649–61 and references therein.
117 Bethlehem, Daniel. 'The Secret Life of International Law.' *Cambridge J. Int'l & Comp. L.* 1 (2012): 23 at 24.
118 ICJ Statute art 38(1)(c), for example, is subject to art 59 which provides decisions of the ICJ have no binding force except between the parties and in respect of that particular case.
119 See *infra* for examples. Philip Allot has commented that international courts and tribunals have increasingly relied upon their own, and other courts' previous decisions as a type of judge-made customary law; in *The Health of Nations. Society and Law Beyond the State* (Cambridge: CUP, 2002), Rosalyn Higgins has indicated that human rights courts "work consciously to co-ordinate their approaches", Higgins, Rosalyn, 'A Babel of Judicial Voices? Ruminations from the Bench', (2006) 55 *ICLQ* 791 at 798.

making bodies can make in the development and consolidation of the concept of sustainable development and its underlying principles.

There has been a concurrent increase in scholarly consideration of judicial and quasi-judicial jurisprudence in the context of sustainable development.[120]

The meaning and significance to be given to the concept of sustainable development and its underlying principles remain open to debate. Arguments continue to be made concerning the extent of their normative force, and discussion continues to focus on the extent to which they have relevance to substance as well as process.[121]

What is becoming clearer, however, is that judicial authorities have at their disposal a number of means by which they may incorporate the concept of sustainable development and its underlying principles into their decision-making, notwithstanding their own institutional background.

Acknowledging this background, the ILA Committee's 2010 Report points out:

> Inevitably, each court, tribunal and body adopts, as part of its reasoning process, its own juridical 'bias' – or lens – in which it considers matters of sustainable development. For instance, human rights courts would view many matters from a very different perspective and take into account a very distinctive range of principles than, invariably would, an investment tribunal. It is not the purpose of the Committee to either deny or homogenise these 'biases', but rather to recognise that despite them, there are general and systemic features of the sustainable development discourse [that] can be highlighted across courts and tribunals.[122]

As a result of its work the ILA Committee adopted the 2012 Sofia Guiding Statements,[123] which provide an accessible and fairly comprehensive and

---

120 See, for example, Cordonier Segger, Marie-Claire, 'Sustainable Development in International Law' in Bugge, Hans Christian and Christina Voigt, eds., *Sustainable Development in International and National Law*, Europa Law Publishing (2008) 87, 177–82; also Stephens, Tim, *International Courts and Environmental Protection*. Vol. 62, Cambridge University Press (2009). For example, Kotzé, Louis J. and Alexander R. Paterson, *The Role of the Judiciary in Environmental Governance: Comparative Perspectives*, Wolters Kluwer, in which the Head of the IUCN Environmental Law Programme and Director of the IUCN Environmental Law Centre, Dr. Alejandro Iza, States in the Foreward that it "focuses on the judiciary as an important component of developing environmental law in the broader quest for sustainability."

121 See, for example, Lowe, Vaughan, 'Sustainable Development and Unsustainable Arguments' in Boyle, Alan E. and David Freestone, eds., *International Law and Sustainable Development: Past Achievements and Future Challenges* (Oxford: OUP, 1999) 19–37; also Boyle, Alan, 'Between Process and Substance. Sustainable Development in the Jurisprudence of International Courts and Tribunals' in Bugge, Hans Christian and Christina Voigt, eds., *Sustainable Development in International and National Law* (Groningen: Europa Law Publishing, 2008) 201–16.

122 International Law Association Committee on International Law on Sustainable Development. Hague Conference Report (2010) at 19.

123 By Resolution No 7/2012 adopted the 2012 Sofia Guiding Statements on the Judicial Elaboration of the 2002 New Delhi Declaration of Principles of International Law Relating to Sustainable Development.

uncontroversial summary of what can be said to date on the subject and how decisions makers might approach the matter.

During the course of its work, the ILA Committee focused on the principle of integration. While this principle is relevant in terms of normative integration,[124] the Committee placed much emphasis on 'integration' as a judicial reasoning tool, available to judicial tribunals as part of the judicial reasoning process.

The ILA Committee noted that integration as a reasoning process is a technique that is *per se* unrelated to sustainable development, and cited the attempts by the International Court to bring together human rights law and international humanitarian law in recent advisory opinions and contentious cases as good examples of integrative reasoning, not specifically aimed at achieving sustainable development.[125]

The ILA Committee also pointed out that integrative judicial reasoning covers an array of techniques that a tribunal might use, including:

- attempting to reconcile various bodies of law (as in cases mentioned above);
- developing and using structural rules such as evolutive/dynamic interpretation (i.e. greater reliance on a treaty as a living document) and/or teleological interpretation (i.e. focusing on a treaty's object and purpose);[126, 127]
- incorporating other rules of law within the treaty process, for example pursuant to art 31(1)(c) 1969 Vienna Convention on the Law of Treaties and customary international law;[128] and
- utilizing notions of equity[129] and other considerations.[130]

124 I.e. in terms of the extent to which rules have incorporated sustainable development considerations within their meaning and provision and may assist, encourage or even mandate a tribunal to interpret rules in a more holistic manner.

125 The ILA Committee cites the *Advisory Opinion on Legality of the Threat or Use of Nuclear Weapons* ICJ Reports (1996) 240; *Legal Consequences of the Construction of a Wall in the Occupied Palestinian Territory* ICJ Reports (2004) 178; and *Armed Activities on the Territory of the Congo (Democratic Republic of the Congo v Uganda)* (2005), paragraph 216.

126 The Committee makes reference to the evolutionary approach to treaty interpretation in H.E. Judge C. G. Weeramantry's controversial dissent in *Case Concerning Kasikili/Sedudu Island (Botswana/Namibia)* ICJ Reports (1999) 1183 ("Environmental standards transcend temporal barriers . . . Consequently, in environmental matters, today's standards attach themselves to yesterday's transactions, and must be given due effect in judicial determinations stemming from them").

127 *Arbitration Regarding the Iron Rhine Railway (Belgium v The Netherlands)* (2005), para. 80 ("it seems that an evolutive interpretation, which would ensure an application of the treaty that would be effective in terms of its object and purpose, will be preferred to a strict application of the intertemporal rule").

128 Art 31(3)(c) 1969 Vienna Convention on the Law of Treaties provides: "[t]here shall be taken into account, together with the context: . . . any relevant rules of international law applicable in the relations between the parties." For discussion of this provision, see McLachlan C., 'The Principle of Systemic Integration and Article 31(3)(c) of the Vienna Convention' 54 *International and Comparative Law Quarterly* (2005) 279–319; and Sands, Philippe 'Sustainable Development: Treaty, Custom, and the Cross-fertilization of International law' in Boyle, Alan E. and David Freestone, eds., *International Law and Sustainable Development: Past Achievements and Future Challenges*, (Oxford: OUP, 1999) 39–60.

129 International tribunals often have provisions allowing them to decide cases on the basis of equity.

130 What the Committee had in mind as 'other' considerations is unclear. Of interest in this context, and more generally, is the recent article by Krisch in which he asserts:

Where sustainable development is explicit in the objects and purpose of international treaty law, it will be taken into account and will shape the interpretation of treaty rules, and the future development of these expanding treaty regimes. This involves an obligation to seek balance between sometimes conflicting priorities in the development process, in the interests of future generations.

Beyond treaty law, sustainable development can be invoked by judges and decision makers to curb the worst social and environmental excesses of nations in economic development activities and to exert persuasive pressure for the internalization of otherwise externalized or marginalized social, economic or environmental concerns.[131]

While the various international courts and tribunals all have their individual mandates, treaties and structures, they are still coping with cases that touch on broader issues, and recognizing that they do not sit in isolation, but in the context of an increasingly interdependent world.[132] It may be that specific preambular language, or specific treaty provisions, make it easier for courts and tribunals to incorporate the concept of sustainable development and its underlying principles into their decision making, but, as the discussion above makes clear it is it is also quite feasible[133] even in their absence.

Whether one adopts an approach based on normativity of principles and their relevance by virtue of Article 31(3)(c) of the Vienna Convention on the Law of Treaties, whereby 'other relevant rules of international law' must be taken into account in the interpretation of a treaty text;[134] or an approach based on an evolutive

> International law has never been based on consent in a pure form. It has long been influenced by natural law ideas; it has incorporated moral reasoning, most prominently in international humanitarian law and possibly in the *jus cogens* doctrine; and some of its traditional pillars, customary international law and general principles of law, cannot be fully explained on the basis of State consent. Moreover, institutions with lawmaking and adjudicatory powers act at one remove from States' consent. Their powers have always been subject to reinterpretation in ways that were not entirely controlled by the initial act of delegation. (footnotes omitted)

Krisch, Nico 'The Decay of Consent: International Law in an Age of Global Public Goods', 2014 *AJIL* vol 108:1 at 2–3.

131 Cordonier Segger, Marie-Claire, 'Sustainable Development in International Law' in Bugge, Hans Christian and Christina Voigt, eds., *Sustainable Development in International and National Law* (Groningen: Europa Law Publishing, 2008) 87.

132 As the ILA 2006 Report says at 14–15: "[t]he attempt to integrate both the concept and meaning of sustainable development within international agreements over the last fifteen years has become almost an act of faith. Whether it is the 1994 Marrakech Agreement which established the WTO, the 2000 Constitutive Act of the African Union or the 2003 WHO Framework Convention on Tobacco Control (to name but a few), as well as more obvious multilateral environmental agreements, some attempt to incorporate either the concept itself or, more ambitiously, its requirements can usually be found. While 'not all treaties, or actions of States in international law, integrate social, economic and environmental considerations to the same extent, or in the same way', the very fact that sincere attempts have been made is, at least, testimony to the rhetorical 'grip' and political endorsement of sustainable development."

133 And arguably 'necessary'. See note above.

134 As discussed by Sands, Philippe, 'Sustainable Development: Treaty, Custom, and the Cross-fertilization of International Law', in Boyle, Alan and David Freestone, eds., *International*

and dynamic interpretation viewing a treaty as a living instrument to be seen in its current context;[135] or an approach based on judicial reasoning, regardless of whether the principles of sustainable development themselves are *lex lata* or *lex ferenda*, or indeed a combination of the above, decision makers in courts and tribunals have the opportunity and responsibility to take the concept of sustainable development into account.

Lowe has pointed out:

> Unlike the natural sciences, where outdated theories are pushed out by new knowledge, the law has no self-cleansing mechanism. Constant judicial development and restatement of coherent doctrine are essential for the maintenance of an effective legal system.[136]
>
> Sustainable development can properly claim a normative status as an element of the process of judicial reasoning.' It is a meta-principle, acting upon other legal rules and principles – a legal concept exercising a kind of interstitial normativity, pushing and pulling the boundaries of true primary norms when they threaten to overlap or conflict with each other.[137]

As a modifying norm, the concept of sustainable development can be announced by judges in the exercise of an inherent judicial power and as part of the reasons for their decision. As Lowe says "The judges employ these modifying norms because they are judges, not because the law expressly requires them to be employed;" and in relation to the reference by the International Court of Justice to the concept of sustainable development in *Gabčíkovo*, he says:

> the Court could have managed without it; but it chose instead to refer to the concept and, but doing so, to open up the possibility of the development of the concept as a framework for the reconciliation of conflicts between development and environmental protection when they come before it.[138]

Law and Sustainable Development: Past Achievements and Future Challenges (1999); see also McLachlan, C. 'The Principle of Systemic Integration and Article 31(3)(c) of the Vienna Convention' 54 *Int'l & Comp. L.Q.* (2005) 279–319

135   Whether due to its 'fundamental character', or to the vagueness of its provisions, see Graham, Randal N. M., 'Right Theory, Wrong Reasons: Dynamic Interpretation, the Charter and Fundamental Laws' (2006), 34 SCLR (2d) 169–26, by analogy, at 197 and 224. For a recent paper discussing dynamic interpretation see Ulfstein, Geir, 'Interpretation of the ECHR in the Light of Other International Instruments' (June 17, 2015). Conference on 'The European Convention on Human Rights and General International Law', Strasbourg 5 June 2015; PluriCourts Research Paper No. 15–05. Available at SSRN: http://ssrn.com/abstract=2619592 or http://dx.doi.org/10.2139/ssrn.2619592

136   Lowe, Vaughan. 'Sustainable development and unsustainable arguments' in *International Law and Sustainable Development: Past Achievements and Future Challenges* (Oxford: OUP, 1999) 33.

137   Ibid. at 31.

138   Ibid. at 35.

As the concept is applied by tribunals and others, its content and its effect upon the application of other norms gradually becomes clearer.[139]

6.6 Conclusion

The international law of sustainable development seeks balance, and does not favour one or another international regime. As with the *Bering Sea Fur-Seals* case many years ago, a judicial or arbitral body may draw attention to what it perceives to be imbalance, and offer suggestions both where mandated (*Bering Sea Fur-Seals* Arbitral Tribunal 'Rules') and *proprio motu* (*Bering Sea Fur-Seals* Arbitral Tribunal 'Declarations') as to how balance may better be achieved. The content and implementation of normative regimes are determined by States, but judges have an important and unique role. Judicial bodies can offer a longer term and independent perspective, seeking balance and coherence in the interest of justice.

As Ulfstein concludes, on the independence of the international judiciary, of no less relevance in this context:

> It may be concluded that international courts and tribunals [ICs] serve essential governance functions in the international legal order. But in the absence of strong international enforcement powers, the effectiveness of [international courts] in fulfilling such functions is, to a great extent, a result of their perceived legitimacy. On the other hand, their success is also a source of legitimacy. The further expansion and use of the international judiciary, and thus its role in ensuring respect for the international rule of law, will depend on how the existing courts and tribunals accomplish their functions.[140]

In spite of the commonly cited fragmentation of international law, the diversity of courts and tribunals need not necessarily impede collective, integrated pursuit of the concept of sustainable development. One might ask how could judicial reasoning determine that a particular decision, or course of action, will contribute to sustainable development? It may be possible to consider elements of a useful juridical test, perhaps in several stages.

The jurist might first seek ways to accommodate between, or reconcile, competing economic, socio/cultural and environmental interests. Three principles of sustainable development law would be particularly relevant at first. First the jurist could inquire as to whether there is a particular renewable resource or common concern at stake, such as a particular fishery or forest, upon which societies, economies and ecosystems depend (the duty to ensure sustainable use of natural resources). Related to this it

139 Ibid. at 34.
140 Ulfstein, Geir, 'International Courts and Judges: Independence, Interaction, and Legitimacy' (2014) *N.Y.U. J. Int'l L. & Pol.* PluriCourts Research Paper No. 14–13; University of Oslo Faculty of Law Research Paper No. 2014–14. Available at SSRN: http://ssrn.com/abstract=2433584 10.

may also be necessary to determine whether all Parties have complied with the duty to notify each other of the proposed uses, to consult with environment and development decision makers in each country, and to negotiate solutions in good faith. Second, the jurist might inquire as to whether a science-based, objective, sustainability impact assessment has determined a certain threshold of exploitation beyond which the resource cannot be sustained, and where science is uncertain, to determine whether precautionary measures have been contemplated, so that lack of certain science is not used as a basis for postponing measures to mitigate or compensate for serious or irreversible damage (the principle of the precautionary approach to human health, natural resources and ecosystems). Third, public participation, including through consultation of all stakeholders, is essential in determining whether a society and economy depend on sustainable use of a resource. As such, the jurist might inquire as to whether appropriate levels of consultation and participation have been undertaken (the principle of public participation, access to information and justice).

Third, often, sustainable development conflicts are not very straightforward, and do not simply involve shared management of one natural resource. As such, two other principles might come into play to assist in a process of accommodation and reconciliation, at the moment of double-checking a solution proposed by the application of the other principles and the earlier two steps. First, the jurist might consider whether the resolution imposes burdens on countries or actors that have traditionally suffered from disadvantages, and have not benefited from past unsustainable practices. If it does, exceptions might need to be created for these countries or Parties (in accordance with the principle of common but differentiated responsibilities), or the resolution re-considered. Second, the jurist might need to specifically turn their mind towards the inter-relations and interdependence of the social, economic and environmental aspects of the dispute. Essentially, the jurist would need to ensure that neither the economic, nor the environmental, nor the social priorities had been ignored. While there are few clear bright lines, as each factual situation is different, it would not be 'sustainable' to allow one or the other dimension of sustainable development to be excluded (reflecting the principle of integration). Equity and good governance come into play throughout, as part of any court's mandate and overall responsibility.

As Cordonier Segger has concluded, such a principled approach, which is both substantive and procedural, might assist jurists, including treaty negotiators, judiciaries and arbitrators, in promoting more sustainable development in the interests of present and future generations.[141]

---

141 Cordonier Segger, Marie-Claire, 'Governing and Reconciling Economic, Social and Environmental Regimes' in Cordonier Segger, Marie-Claire and H.E. Judge C. G. Weeramantry, eds., *Sustainable Justice: Reconciling Economic, Social and Environmental Law*, Cambridge University Press (2014) 592.

Part III

Sustainable development principles in State-to-State dispute settlement mechanisms

International Court of Justice

7 The Sofia Guiding Statements on sustainable development principles in the decisions of international tribunals

Introduced by Duncan French

7.1 Introduction

It was an enormous privilege to act as co-rapporteur of the International Law Association (ILA) Committee on International Law on Sustainable Development between 2003 and 2012. In that capacity, I supported the Committee in its analysis of the normative implications of sustainable development,[1] which built on the work of the previous Committee on Legal Aspects of Sustainable Development. And as our Committee moved towards its principal output – namely the 2012 Sofia Guiding Statements on the Judicial Elaboration of Sustainable Development – it was a great honour to work with some of the most eminent scholars in the field to develop, and refine, the document.

So why focus on judicial elaboration? Why narrow down the rich discussion on the intergovernmental, institutional and political-legal interface that has always made studying sustainable development so intriguing for so many international lawyers? Certainly, there were genuine reasons not to do so: that the case-law (though notably increasing) was hardly abundant, that there were contemporaneous diplomatic aspects of sustainable development of equal interest, and that ten years was arguably too short a time to judge the success or otherwise of the seven international legal principles on sustainable development, which the previous Committee had so expertly enunciated in the 2002 New Delhi Declaration.[2]

Nevertheless, despite these concerns, the Committee pressed on and focused primarily on how sustainable development had developed and been elaborated primarily, though not exclusively, in international courts and tribunals. Of course, there were by 2012 several judgments of the International Court of Justice addressing environmental matters – two which had directly considered sustainable development (namely, *Gabčíkovo-Nagymaros Project (Hungary/Slovakia)*[3] and *Pulp Mills over the River Uruguay (Argentina v Uruguay)*[4]) – as well as judgments of the International Tribunal for the Law of the Sea (ITLOS) including its Seabed Disputes Chamber, awards of numerous arbitral tribunals,

---

1 For access to the Committee's reports, see http://www.ila-hq.org/en/committees/index.cfm/cid/1017
2 ILA resolution 3/2002, annex as published as UN Doc. A/57/329.
3 ICJ Reports (1997) 7 at 78.
4 ICJ Reports (2010) 14 at 74–5.

decisions of the World Trade Organization dispute settlement mechanism (notably from its Appellate Body), and an emerging human rights jurisprudence in human rights courts and committees. Thus, to the extent that international law ever has sufficient judicial material to analyse and deconstruct, environmental law and sustainable development no longer felt unduly lacking. No longer was it just *Trail Smelter*[5] and a somewhat extraneous reliance on the International Court discussing warship damage in the Adriatic![6]

The aim in developing the Sofia Guiding Statements – named after the venue for that ILA biennial conference – was remarkably simple, and stated perhaps most succinctly in the resolution of the ILA Conference which adopted the Guiding Statements. As the resolution noted, 'judicial elaboration of these principles is one element of a comprehensive approach to international law on sustainable development, which also includes treaty development, State practice, the practice of international and regional organizations, as well as reform of domestic law, which can itself be indicative of State practice'. Thus, the Guiding Statements were never intended to be either exhaustive or determinative of where the international law of sustainable development was invariably heading.

To some extent, it was – and could be no more than – a snapshot in time. As the resolution continued, 'it may be possible to determine more clearly in 2012 than it was in 2002 the formal legal status of a number of the principles, although cautioning against a formalistic delimitation between those principles that may now have obtained a more precise legal status and those that have not'. In conclusion to this short summary of the Guiding Statements, I will return to the question of whether the Sofia Guiding Statements remain extant and relevant.

In terms of the content and structure of the Guiding Statements, there are ten key statements built around, but extending beyond, the seven principles mentioned above, namely:

1) The duty of States to ensure sustainable use of natural resources
2) The principle of equity and the eradication of poverty
3) The principle of common but differentiated responsibility
4) The principle of the precautionary approach to human health, natural resources and ecosystems
5) The principle of public participation and access to justice and information
6) The principle of good governance
7) The principle of integration and interrelationship, in particular in relation to human rights and social, economic and environmental objectives

5 Reports of International Arbitral Awards, 16 April 1938 and 11 March 1941, Vol. III, 1905–1982.
6 Referring, of course, to *Corfu Channel (United Kingdom v Albania)* Merits, ICJ Reports (1949) 4 at 22: 'every State's obligation not to allow knowingly its territory to be used for acts contrary to the rights of other States'. See J. Viñuales, 'The Contribution of the International Court of Justice to the Development of International Environmental Law: A Contemporary Assessment' (2008) 32 *Fordham J. of Int'l L.* 232, 238.

Each of these principles has one statement in the Sofia document. For some, the period between 2002 and 2012 had indeed seen instances of judicial elaboration and even normative hardening. For others, the evidence was much more limited. An example (though not without controversy) of the former might be Guiding Statement 6 on the precautionary principle, in which the Committee felt confident – not only to refer to it as the precautionary principle rather than 'approach' – to state that it 'has significant and increasingly precise legal implications, notwithstanding ongoing debate surrounding its formal legal status'. This assessment sought to reflect both the advances achieved (notably by the Seabed Disputes Chamber in *Responsibilities and Obligations of States Sponsoring Persons and Entities with Respect to Activities in the Area* (2011)),[7] and yet the unwillingness by some courts or tribunals to grant it an autonomous status. In particular, there had not, nor has there yet, been, a definitive statement as to its status by the International Court.

For some principles, judicial elaboration had been – and arguably was always going to be – minimal. For instance, Guiding Statement 4 on equity had perhaps received less judicial attention than might have been hoped. Though there had been passing comment to future generations on numerous occasions,[8] intragenerational equity in particular had not been the subject of significant or discernible judicial discussion.[9] The statement thus recognized the innate political aspect of this principle but nevertheless felt confident to express, in normative terms, that although 'judicial bodies and quasi-judicial bodies cannot alone address the social, economic, governance and political issues that invariably form key aspects of such disputes, it is nevertheless incumbent upon [them] to further such principles of equity and fairness in exercising their judicial function'. In a similar way, the principle of good governance was not an immediate candidate for judicial elaboration, though even here there had been some notable judicial dicta – interestingly, again not by the International Court but by members of the ITLOS (in the guise of the Seabed Disputes Chamber).[10]

It is also worth noting the three additional guiding statements not directly linked to one of the seven New Delhi Principles, the inclusion of each said something, we believed, about how the debate had moved on in the ten years since 2002. First, Guiding Statement 1 on the legal status of sustainable development itself. In 2002, there had been no attempt to give normative substance to the concept *per se* other than through the manifestation of the seven principles; it remained an objective of political ambition. However by 2012, it was felt not

---

7   ITLOS Reports (2011) 10 at 47: 'The Chamber observes that the precautionary approach has been incorporated into a growing number of international treaties and other instruments, many of which reflect the formulation of Principle 15 of the Rio Declaration. In the view of the Chamber, this has initiated a trend towards making this approach part of customary international law'.

8   *Arbitration regarding the Iron Rhine Railway (Belgium v The Netherlands)* (2005) Award of 24 May 2005, para. 58.

9   Cf. D. French, 'From the Depths: Rich Pickings of Principles of Sustainable Development and General International Law on the Ocean Floor—the Seabed Disputes Chamber's 2011 Advisory Opinion' (2011) 26 *International Journal of Marine and Coastal Law* 525, 536.

10   Ibid. at 562–65.

unreasonable to attempt to articulate a legal conceptualization for sustainable development itself, relying in particular on the jurisprudence of the International Court and WTO Appellate Body. As the statement finally read: '[r]ecourse to the concept of 'sustainable development' in international case law may, over time, reflect a maturing of the concept into a principle of international law, despite a continued and genuine reluctance to formalise a distinct legal status'. It is a careful and cautious statement – certainly not radical in many respects, or even going as far as H.E. Judge C. G.Weeramantry in his separate opinion in *Gabčíkovo-Nagymaros* way back in 1997[11] – nevertheless the Committee felt it was appropriate to move beyond what had been considered possible before.

In a similar vein, Guiding Statement 2 sought to consider what many – at least I personally – had come to believe as sustainable development's principal function in judicial decision-making, namely interpretation and rule-development. Importantly, this not only concerned treaty interpretation but also the interpretation (to the extent this is the appropriate term to describe the methodology of discerning the evolution) of rules of customary international law. I had in mind, in particular, the International Court's synthesizing of sustainable development and the customary rule of equitable and reasonable utilization of a shared watercourse in *Pulp Mills*.[12] This seemed to me more than simple judicial rhetoric – as perhaps was the case with the International Court's use of the concept in *Gabčíkovo-Nagymaros* – rather this was relying on sustainable development to integrate and contemporise[13] normative ideas and obligations, which went beyond mere interpretation and certainly was more important than judicial obiter.

The wording in the end of this Guiding Statement was perhaps clumsier than I would have liked, but it reflected broadly the overall contribution sustainable development seemed capable of making as a judicial tool:

> Treaties and rules of customary international law should be interpreted in the light of principles of sustainable development; interpretations which might seem to undermine the goal of sustainable development should only take precedence where to do otherwise would undermine fundamental aspects of the global legal order, infringe the express wording of a treaty or breach a rule of *jus cogens;*

11 See *supra* note 3, 88 at 104: 'Happily for international law, there are plentiful indications, as recited earlier in this opinion, of that degree of "general recognition among States of a certain practice as obligatory" to give the principle of sustainable development the nature of customary law'.

12 See *supra* note 4, 75: 'The Court wishes to add that such utilization could not be considered to be equitable and reasonable if the interests of the other riparian State in the shared resource and the environmental protection of the latter were not taken into account. Consequently, it is the opinion of the Court that [the relevant treaty provision] embodies this interconnectedness between equitable and reasonable utilization of a shared resource and the balance between economic development and environmental protection that is the essence of sustainable development'.

13 See *supra* note 8, para. 80 'it seems that an evolutive interpretation, which would ensure an application of the treaty that would be effective in terms of its object and purpose, will be preferred to a strict application of the intertemporal rule'.

The third and final additional guiding statement was Guiding Statement 10 and reflected the enunciation by the International Court in *Pulp Mills* – endorsed, and its application broadened, by the Seabed Disputes Chamber in *Responsibilities and Obligations of States Sponsoring Persons and Entities with Respect to Activities in the Area* – of a customary obligation on States to assess the possible risks where a planned project within its territory or under its jurisdiction has the potential to cause significant transboundary harm. To the extent that this obligation was not just an aspect of the due diligence obligation on such States, but is a discrete and separate rule to undertake an environmental impact assessment, it was felt worthy of inclusion within the Sofia Guiding Statements. Taking into account the 2011 Advisory Opinion, Guiding Statement 10 also extended the obligation to activities which might cause harm to common resources and to protect against global environmental harm.

So how do the Guiding Statements look a number of years later? How far will they stand the test of time, be it for five years or further ahead? The first thing to note – reflecting on something already said – is that judicial elaboration is integrally related to treaty and diplomatic developments. Thus, changes (and challenges) in one sphere may affect the other. There are many examples in other areas of international law, for instance, where judicial innovation has prompted (directly or indirectly) treaty change (the law on reservations[14] or straight baselines[15] being two well-known examples) or diplomatic discourse, more generally. Equally, it must be recognized that intergovernmental shifts can produce change in judicial thinking, or retard future innovation. To outline briefly potential instances in sustainable development since 2012 of both how judicial innovation might evolve and slow down.

First, in terms of how judicial elaboration might affect how States understand their treaty obligations, the ITLOS Opinion in *Request for an Advisory Opinion Submitted by the Sub-Regional Fisheries Commission (SRFC)* (2015) is particularly instructive. The dicta on the due diligence obligations of flag States to seek to ensure their fishing vessels comply with a coastal State's regulations in its exclusive economic zone[16] not only makes apparent that which is arguably implicit in various provisions of the 1982 UN Convention of the Law of Sea but more than that it underlines the proactive and cooperative obligations on flag States and others to ensure the environmental and conservation objectives of the Convention.

Secondly, in terms of legal and diplomatic developments which may in due course affect judicial innovation in this area, nothing is certain but I would hesitantly put forward two examples. First, the International Law Commission's rejection of common concern as a normative principle in its work on protection

---

14 *Reservations to the Convention on the Prevention and Punishment of the Crime of Genocide,* ICJ Reports (1951) 15.

15 *Fisheries* case *(United Kingdom v Norway)* ICJ Reports (1951) 116.

16 *Advisory Opinion of 2 April 2015, supra* note 15 paras 133–40, in particular at para. 138: 'While the nature of the laws, regulations and measures that are to be adopted by the flag State is left to be determined by each flag State in accordance with its legal system, the flag State nevertheless has the obligation to include in them enforcement mechanisms to monitor and secure compliance with these laws and regulations'.

of the atmosphere[17] may prove indicative of a more general unwillingness to accept Sofia Guiding Statement 3's pronouncement that '[a]s a matter of common concern, the sustainable use of all natural resources represents an emerging rule of general customary international law'. Secondly, the shift away from common but differentiated responsibilities as a structural device between developed and developing countries in international environmental law towards a more individualized, contextual position (evidenced most clearly in the 2015 Paris Agreement on Climate Change) where each State's respective condition is increasingly determinative of the scope and extent of its own commitments, would also make me question how far it will be utilized in the future by international courts and tribunals. To some extent, the respective Sofia Guiding Statement had already foreseen this uncertainty with a relatively reticent assessment, noting that '[f]urther reliance upon it by judicial bodies would . . . allow[. . .] the legal principle to consolidate . . . as distinctive from the political discourse'. This was written in this way precisely because of the political arguments over the principle, but I wonder if this such reticence is now somewhat optimistic. To the extent that a court will ever engage with the underlying challenges of differentiation in international environmental law it is possible that more open-textured references to equity will provide a more useful conceptual tool. I am thinking in particular of H.E. Judge C. G. Weeramantry's magisterial discourse on equity in his separate opinion in *Maritime Delimitation in the Area between Greenland and Jan Mayen (Denmark v Norway)* (1993).[18]

The third and final point is to recognize that while judicial elaboration is innately seen as a good – that judicial endorsement is inherently viewed as a positive thing – this is not necessarily true. At the most basic level, one must remember that ultimately the purpose of dispute settlement is the resolution of the dispute itself. Thus, the decision by the parties in *Aerial Herbicide Spraying (Ecuador v Colombia)* to withdraw the case from the International Court and to put in place an agreed way forward must be preferable,[19] despite the missed opportunity for the International Court to expand on core principles. In this case, it would have been the first international case since *Trail Smelter* to consider the rules on transboundary atmospheric harm.

Moreover, judicial elaboration does not invariably mean the progressive development of the law. And while such negative engagement is most likely to mean the summary dismissal of environmental arguments or the non-reliance on seemingly relevant environmental principles, it might also arise through the misapplication or misinterpretation of environmental rules. In other words, instances where a court

---

17 See Report of the International Law Commission (Sixty-seventh session) (4 May–5 June and 6 July–7 August 2015) ILC Report, A/70/10, 2015, chap. V (Protection of the Atmosphere) para. 54: 'While a number of treaties and literature demonstrate some support for the concept of "common concern of humankind", the Commission decided not to adopt this language for the characterization of the problem, as the legal consequences of the concept of common concern of humankind remain unclear at the present stage of development of international law relating to the atmosphere. It was considered appropriate to express the concern of the international community as a matter of a factual statement, and not as a normative statement, as such, of the gravity of the atmospheric problems'.
18 ICJ Reports (1993) 38 at 211.
19 Order of 13 September 2013.

or tribunal utilizes environmental rules and principles but not necessarily in the way which will develop the law coherently or advance its underlying rationale.

On this point, one might point to the 2015 judgment of the International Court in the joined cases *Certain Activities Carried out by Nicaragua in the Border Area (Costa Rica v Nicaragua)/Construction of a Road in Costa Rica along the San Juan River (Nicaragua v Costa Rica)* (2015)[20] and, in particular, its discussion of the procedural obligations on States where there is a risk of significant transboundary harm. The International Court, relying on the ILC 2001 Articles on Prevention of Transboundary Harm from Hazardous Activities, sets out its view that obligations of notification and consultation with potentially affected States (altogether positive requirements) flow from, and after, the identification of risks subsequent to an impact assessment.[21] The lack of risk as identified by such an assessment would seem to negate the need for notification and consultation.

If indeed this were the intention of the International Court's reasoning, there is introduced a sequencing – a legal formalism – which has the potential to undermine the overall value of the obligations imposed. As Judge Donoghue notes in her separate opinion specifically on this matter – but the point is arguably of wider relevance – 'the fundamental duty of the State of origin is to exercise due diligence . . . The question whether due diligence calls for notification or consultation, as well as the details regarding the timing and content of such notification and consultation, *should be evaluated in light of particular circumstances*'.[22]

There has long been a tendency to place on international law the strictures of how processes work at the domestic level. This would seem instinctive in the ongoing development of international law. But we must avoid pitfalls in this approach, recognizing that international law starts from an altogether different premise. We must remain astute to potential wrong pathways in judicial decisions, just as we must remain critical of inconsistent State practice or poor drafting of treaty obligations, in our evaluations. The study of sustainable development has for a long time required a juxtaposition of legal advocacy, normative aspiration and critical thinking.

So, in conclusion, what is the ongoing contribution of the Sofia Guiding Statements? The Statements are a contribution to the debate as to the role of law in moving international society towards a social, political, economic – and legal – order premised around fair and sustainable development for all. They were indeed a snapshot as to the position in 2012, reflecting 'key trends and new themes'. Some of these may develop further, some may fall away, and others may be introduced. But the purpose of the Guiding Statements, as set out in the document itself, remains true, namely 'to support the continued application and development of the seven principles of the New Delhi Declaration'. Judicial elaboration is but one element of the wider endeavour, but international law on sustainable development has sufficiently matured that we can, and should, critically analyse the contribution of courts and tribunals in this matter.

20 Judgment of 16 December 2015.
21 Ibid. at 168.
22 Ibid. at para. 24 (emphasis added).

7.2 The Sofia Guiding Statements on the Principles of International Law on Sustainable Development

INTERNATIONAL LAW ASSOCIATION

SOFIA CONFERENCE (2012)

INTERNATIONAL LAW ON SUSTAINABLE DEVELOPMENT

Members of the Committee:

Professor Nicolaas J Schrijver (Netherlands): *Chair*
Professor Duncan French (UK): *Co-Rapporteur*
Dr Ximena Fuentes (Chile): *Co-Rapporteur*

Mr Donald K Anton (Australia)
Dr Karin Arts (Netherlands)
Professor Alan Boyle (Nominee of Chair)
Dr Tomer Broude (Israel)
Alternate: Professor Moshe Hirsch
Professor Hans Christian Bugge
(Norway) Professor Susana Camargo
Vieira (Brazil)
Professor Dr Marie-Claire Cordonier-
Segger (Canada)
Alternate: Kevin Gray
Professor P. J. I. M. de Waart (Netherlands)
Professor Joyeeta Gupta (Netherlands)
Professor Srecko Jelinic (Croatia)
Professor Maria Magdalena Kenig-
Witkowska (Poland)
Professor Jang Hie Lee (Korea)
Professor Maria Leichner Reynal
(Argentina)
Professor Jennifer McKay (Australia)

Professor Karl Meessen (Germany)
Professor Maki Nishiumi (Japan)
Professor Marc Pallemaerts
(Belgium)
Alternate: Professor Frank Maes
Dr M. C. W. Pinto (HQ)
Professor Georg Ress (Germany)
Alternate: Dr Markus Gehring
Professor Sabine Schlemmer-
Schulte (Germany)
Professor Jae Ho Seong (Korea)
Dr Tim Stephens (Australia)
Professor Surya P. Subedi OBE (UK)
Alternate: Mr Sunil Murlidhar
Shastri
Professor Dire Tladi (South Africa)
Adriana Beatriz Tripelli (Argentina)
Professor Rebecca Wallace (UK)
Dustin Kuan-Hsiung Wang (China
(Taiwan))

International Law on Sustainable Development

Final Report

1. Introduction

This is the fifth, and final, report of the Committee on International Law on Sustainable Development. The Committee was established by the ILA Executive Committee in 2003 under the chairmanship of Professor Nico Schrijver

(Dutch Branch) with the support of two co-rapporteurs: Professor Ximena Fuentes (Chilean Branch) and Professor Duncan French (British Branch). Members have been appointed from many different branches, reinforcing both the global nature of the issue under consideration and the strength of the Committee overall.

The mandate of the Committee adopted by the Executive Committee in May 2003 read as follows:

The objective of the Committee is to study the legal status and legal implementation of sustainable development. For this purpose the Committee's mandate includes:

(i) assessment of the legal status of principles and rules of international law in the field of sustainable development, with particular reference to the ILA New Delhi Principles (also published as UN Doc. A/57/329), as well as assessment of the practice of States and international organizations in this field;
(ii) the study of developing States in a changing global order, particularly the impact of globalization on the sustainable development opportunities of developing countries;
(iii) in the light of the principle of integration and interrelationship, a re-examination of certain topics of the international law of development, including analysis of:

    a   the position of the least developed countries in international law,
    b   the right to development, and
    c   the obligation to co-operate on matters of social, economic and environmental concern.

As the mandate implies, and as the work of this Committee has always made very apparent, this Committee owes a significant debt to the work of the previous Committee on Legal Aspects of Sustainable Development, as well as numerous members who have participated in both Committees, no more so than Dr Kamal Hossain who has provided untold support and guidance. In particular, the final output of that Committee – the drafting of the 2002 New Delhi Declaration of Principles of International Law relating to Sustainable Development – has rightly guided this Committee in its work; and as itself is coming to a closure, its own final output, the 'Sofia Guiding Statements', seeks to reinforce both the necessity for, and significance of, the New Delhi Declaration.

This final report focuses upon the significance of international courts and tribunals (and, in some instances, quasi-judicial bodies) in giving effect to the principles contained in the New Delhi Declaration. After some further words of introduction, both on the work of the Committee over the last decade and then to reintroduce the New Delhi Declaration itself, the report is divided into three sections. First, there is a summary of the relevant jurisprudence divided by court and tribunal. Though nearly all the cases discussed date after 1992, most have actually occurred more recently, itself indicating an important trend. Second, this jurisprudence is then analysed principle-by-principle to consider normative trends and developments that would not be apparent from a court/tribunal-specific analysis. Third, the report concludes by setting out the 2012 Sofia Guiding Statements, which seeks to provide further amplification of the principles of the New Delhi Declaration as now being interpreted, implemented and enforced by judicial tribunals. It is to be hoped that the Sofia Guiding Statements will be read alongside the New Delhi Declaration and give greater insight both into what sustainable development as a normative concept law has achieved, but also what it is still capable of achieving.

Work of the Committee 2004–2012

Since its first report in 2004 presented in Berlin, the Committee has submitted substantive reports to each biennial session of the International Law Association up to and including Sofia (2012). In addition, the Committee has met several times inter-sessionally in Pretoria (2007), Sheffield (2009) and Rome (2011).

Though it is not possible to revisit the contents of each of these reports, it is nevertheless worthwhile to highlight certain key themes. The 2004 Report was the first report since the 2002 World Summit on Sustainable Development, held in Johannesburg. The report's assessment of that summit remains both accurate and pertinent at a more general level: 'This is not to say that significant progress in certain areas was not made; rather, it is argued that the World Summit is better seen as simply part of the ongoing Rio process.'[23] As assessments come to be made as to the success of the 2012 UN Conf erence on Sustainable Development (Rio+20), such a sense of perspective and balanced judgment remains important.

The 2006 report of the Committee, presented in Toronto, focused upon the principle of integration, recognising that integration is a multi-faceted idea, which can be achieved at distinctive levels and by different means, including institutionally, legally and judicially. For the purposes of this report, integration as a judicial tool is particularly important. Nevertheless, as the 2006 report noted, 'integration needs to affect the entire spectrum of institutional, corporate, legal and individual behaviour if sustainable development is to have any chance of being meaningfully realised'.[24]

The 2008 report of the Committee, presented in Rio de Janeiro, sought to take this analysis further by examining in further detail the impact of, and relevance to, sustainable development of three discrete areas; namely, trade and investment, environmental governance and human rights. Though each topic raised its own distinctive questions, they equally contributed to a broader assessment of the current state of sustainable development in international affairs. The report's assessment on this matter was forceful and should infuse this Committee's final report and other debates on sustainable development. It is worth repeating in full:

23 ILA Report (2006) 496.
24 Ibid.

there continues to be a sizeable mismatch between the limited progress that can be evidenced in certain discrete areas and the lack of political will to achieve wholesale substantive change. Ultimately, until the necessary political will develops, innovations in law will have marginal impact in promoting lasting improvements.[25]

This must not, however, prompt a sense of pessimism. And the 2010 report of the Committee, presented in The Hague, sought to reflect upon broader ideas of justice, solidarity and collective responsibility – themes that infuse sustainable development. This is not just to accept such ideals as political dogma, but rather to question and seek to understand more clearly what role law plays in these broader societal and political endeavours. As the report noted, 'as lawyers, we should be wary of too easily conflating the normative with the actual'.[26]

The second section of the 2010 report focuses upon an analysis of recent jurisprudence, most notably the judgment of 2010 by the International Court of Justice in *Pulp Mills on the River Uruguay*. This section of the report acted as an important prelude to this final report, providing a first summary of how international judgments can demonstrate important trends either towards (or away from) sustainability considerations. The importance of such decisions cannot be underestimated; as the report makes clear:

> [t]he relationship between sustainable development and global justice is a nuanced one . . . However, between States with actual disputes, poised on the brink of either debilitating conflict or peaceful settlement of their differences, a commitment to global justice [alone] will not provide a sound legal basis for a decision, as such, to be taken by judges and lawyers.[27]

It was for that reason that the Committee decided in The Hague to focus its final report on the contribution of international jurisprudence to the achievement of sustainable development and to set out 'through a series of guiding statements, how international courts and tribunals have – and, as importantly, might more effectively – incorporate the concept of sustainable development and the principles reflected in the 2002 New Delhi Declaration'.[28]

2. Sustainable Development and the New Delhi Declaration

The ILA has been a singularly important non-governmental actor in the evolving debate on sustainable development, having previously made significant progress

---

25 ILA Report (2008) 904.
26 ILA Report (2010) 805.
27 Ibid. at 805.
28 Ibid. at 816. Particular thanks must be given to Tim Stephens, Tomer Broude, Marie-Claire Cordonier Segger and Markus Gehring who supported the Officers of the Committee as members of a final report steering group. Thanks are also expressed to Yolanda Saito, who undertook research on public participation.

on the legal aspects of the new international economic order (see the 1986 ILA Seoul Declaration on Progressive Development of Principles of Public International Law relating to a New International Economic Order) and, in the process, breaking down North-South divisions that had largely stymied debate. In a similar way, sustainable development allowed academics, jurists and other experts from around the world to consider matters of global importance in a non-parochial manner. The outcome of these discussions, the seven principles of the 2002 New Delhi Declaration of Principles of International Law relating to Sustainable Development, highlighted both the high degree of consensus that was necessary to draft such a declaration but also, once again, progress within the non-governmental forum of the ILA where at the intergovernmental level, attempts at such codification had long been abandoned.

This is not to say that the New Delhi Declaration is, or should be, considered the final word of the subject. Indeed, the Declaration itself recognises that the principles would, where relevant, be subject to consolidation and further development. Nevertheless, after consideration this Committee has found no need to seek formal amendment to the New Delhi Declaration endorsing both the definitional objective of sustainable development found therein and the seven principles which the Declaration reflected (both repeated for completeness below):

> *EXPRESSES* the view that the objective of sustainable development involves a comprehensive and integrated approach to economic, social and political processes, which aims at the sustainable use of natural resources of the Earth and the protection of the environment on which nature and human life as well as social and economic development depend and which seeks to realize the right of all human beings to an adequate living standard on the basis of their active, free and meaningful participation in development and in the fair distribution of benefits resulting therefrom, with due regard to the needs and interests of future generations,
>
> Principle 1: The duty of States to ensure sustainable use of natural resources
> Principle 2: The principle of equity and the eradication of poverty
> Principle 3: The principle of common but differentiated responsibilities
> Principle 4: The principle of the precautionary approach to human health, natural resources and ecosystems
> Principle 5: The principle of public participation and access to information and justice
> Principle 6: The principle of good governance
> Principle 7: The principle of integration and interrelationship, in particular in relation to human rights and social, economic and environmental objectives

A decade has passed since 2002, and emphasis has invariably shifted; changing political priorities, new challenges and greater understanding of pre-existing issues reveal a different political and legal landscape. In particular, the global financial crises of the last five years continue to absorb much of the political attention. Moreover, and clearly not unrelated, the overall conditions for sustainable development have worsened since 2002, environmentally, socially and in terms of the finance necessary to make the changes necessary. There are some glimmers of hope; some of the Millennium Development Goals are on course to be met, though equally others are not.

This report does not seek to belittle the enormity of the economic issues facing countries in any way, and certainly a healthy (as well as an equitable) global economy is a fundamental prerequisite for the progressive achievement of sustainable development, but equally a focus purely on current economic crises will ultimately marginalise and reduce still further the attention on other pressing matters. In a similar vein, as the international community continues to politicise the issue of climate change, it would seem to call into question the very ability of States to deliver not only on their continuing commitments in that context, but sustainable development more broadly.

In this light, how relevant is the jurisprudence of international courts and tribunals in the matter of sustainable development? For those who focus purely on the political and the systemic, individual judicial decisions carry little weight. But as the next section will highlight, the international rule of law, and the particular role of the judiciary in that regard, is increasingly important in matters of sustainable development. For that reason, judgments of international courts, tribunals and quasi-judicial bodies are of especial significance, both in what they say (and how they say it), what they include (and what they omit), and what trends their decisions may offer for future judicial interpretations and pronouncements.

Indeed, for those who remain unconvinced by the value of principles in the scheme of international law, a comment by Judge Cançado Trindade in his separate opinion in *Pulp Mills* is worthy of citation at length:

> Last but not least, it is not surprising to find that voluntarist-positivists, who have always attempted to minimize the role of general principles of law, have always met the opposition of those who sustain the relevance of those principles, as ensuing from the idea of an objective justice, and guiding the interpretation and application of legal norms and rules. This is the position that I sustain. It is the *principles* of the international legal system that can best ensure the cohesion and integrity of the international legal system as a whole. Those principles are intertwined with the very foundations of International Law, pointing the way to the universality of this latter, to the benefit of humankind.[29]

3. The significance of international courts and tribunals (and quasi-judicial bodies) in elaborating sustainable development

International courts and tribunals and quasi-judicial bodies are occupying an increasingly important role both in the conceptual development and practical

---

29 Ibid. at para. 217.

implementation of sustainable development and key related principles, including several of those enumerated in the New Delhi Declaration.[30]

The growing salience of 'sustainable development jurisprudence' in international law is a product of several related factors. First, states appear more willing than at any previous stage in history to litigate disputes concerning natural resources and environmental protection. After only a handful of cases in the previous century, the tempo of litigation on environmental questions accelerated from the 1970s onwards and such cases now comprise a substantial proportion of the dockets of several courts, most notably the International Court of Justice.

Of the cases in the International Court's docket, four are concerned with sustainable development. These include *Proceedings with Regard to "Violations of Nicaraguan Sovereignty and Major Environmental Damages to Its Territory" (Nicaragua v Costa Rica), Certain Activities carried out by Nicaragua in the Border Area (Costa Rica v Nicaragua), Aerial Herbicide Spraying (Ecuador v Colombia)* and *Whaling in the Antarctic (Australia v Japan)*. A fourth case, *Request for Interpretation of the Judgment of 15 June 1962 in the Case Concerning the Temple of Preah Vihear (Cambodia v Thailand)* also has some relevance as it is concerned in part with the protection of a culturally significant site inscribed on the World Heritage List in 2008. Most significantly, in 2010 the Court handed down a decision that made express reference to sustainable development in *Pulp Mills on the River Uruguay*.[31] In its judgment the Court recalled its statement in the *Gabčikovo-Nagymaros Project* case, in which it had first used the term, that the 'need to reconcile economic development with protection of the environment is aptly expressed in the concept of sustainable development'.[32]

As discussed below, although the Court did not seek to discuss sustainable development directly and substantively in the *Pulp Mills* case, it did nonetheless make a significant addition to the corpus of jurisprudence on sustainability through its focus on the procedural dimensions of sound transboundary environmental management. This reinvigoration of interest provides a new avenue for international judicial engagement with the practical implementation of sustainable development in a manner which avoids the need to address more fundamental questions about the concept that may be regarded by some States as politically contestable.

Even where the decisions reached by international courts on questions of sustainability are limited in scope (which is usually the case), the process of referring disputes to legal forums of dispute settlement is serving to build, even if only incrementally, a sizeable body of sustainable development jurisprudence. For the most part this had led to the strengthening and broadening of sustainable development rather than a weakening or narrowing of the field. However, it must be

---

30 See also N. J. Schrijver, *The Evolution of Sustainable Development in International Law: Inception, Meaning and Status* (Leiden: Martinus Nijhoff, 2008) at 141–53.

31 *Pulp Mills on the River Uruguay (Argentina v Uruguay)*, Judgment of 20 April 2010, available at www.icj-cij.org.

32 *Gabčikovo-Nagymaros Project (Hungary/Slovakia)* [1997] ICJ Rep 78, [140].

acknowledged that the direction of sustainable development jurisprudence is by no means pre-determined, and that courts and other dispute settlement bodies may take different views of what it requires. Sustainable development seeks integration of socio-economic development and ecological protection agendas without predetermining the terms of any balance, and accordingly, decision-making bodies are free to place more emphasis upon one value than the other. In light of the flexibility of the concept, it is more critical than ever for international courts to engage formally and informally in a dialogue on questions of sustainability to ensure both clarity and consistency, and so that the 'creative tension'[33] inherent in sustainable development advances not only academic and political discussion but also more coherent judicial understandings. Such inter-curia dialogue is able to be facilitated by the work of this Committee as set out in this report, and in its previous work, in synthesising and in analysing key lessons and trends in the 'international case law' on sustainability.

The second factor making possible the growing number of decisions relating to sustainable development is the substantial expansion in the content of public international law having relevance to environment and development questions. The existence of a body of international environmental law built upon multilateral agreements of universal importance (and widespread ratification) and on influential soft law instruments including the Rio Declaration,[34] makes it possible for international judicial bodies to refer with confidence to sustainable development and related principles as attracting the general support of States. The rules and principles can in this way be given meaning and effect by courts in the disputes brought before them, even where they are not themselves the core rights and obligations that are subject to litigation. This is seen in the way in which international courts and other bodies may turn to well-accepted contextual and teleological approaches in the interpretation of treaties codified in Articles 31 and 32 of the *Vienna Convention on the Law of Treaties*[35] to bring sustainability to bear upon areas such as international trade or investment law.[36]

However, while there has been a sizeable growth in international environmental law, such that commentators have warned for some time of the problems of 'treaty congestion',[37] there has in fact been little movement in the development of the legal foundations of sustainable development. The Committee observed in its report to the Rio Conference in 2008 that the question as to the legal status

---

33 11 ILA Committee on International Law on Sustainable Development, *Report to the Rio Conference* (2008) 7.

34 United Nations Declaration on Environment and Development, UN Doc. A/CONF.151/5/ Rev. 1 (1992).

35 Opened for signature 23 May 1969, 1155 UNTS 332 (entered into force 27 January 1980).

36 Markus Gehring and Marie-Claire Cordonier Segger, eds., *Sustainable Development in World Trade Law* (2005); Marie-Claire Cordonier Segger, Markus Gehring and Andrew Newcombe, eds., *Sustainable Development in World Investment Law* (2010).

37 See Donald K. Anton, '"Treaty Congestion" in International Environmental Law' in Shawkat Alam, Jahid Hossain Bhuiyan, Tareq M. R. Chowdhury and Erika J. Techera, eds., *Routledge Handbook of International Environmental Law* (Abingdon: Routledge, 2012).

of sustainable development was 'sterile',[38] a view the Committee continues to endorse, and that it was more important to inquire into the practical effect of sustainability as a *concept*. This entreaty to look to the discursive effect of sustainability remains no less relevant today than it was three years ago, yet the hurdles to achieving recognition of the value of this approach within international courts and tribunals appear as significant as they have ever been. While conceptually sustainable development can be released from the shackles of legal formalism in order to be given operational meaning, it cannot be gainsaid that international courts will recognise such flexibility. By virtue of their status in the international legal order (as discussed further below), international courts are inherently cautious in stepping beyond well-established legal norms and categories, meaning that international sustainability jurisprudence is likely to be advanced where concepts of sustainability are able to be argued within the boundaries of accepted norms.

Before turning to consider the contributions of specific international judicial bodies, some general observations may be made about the function of international courts in the development of the international law on sustainable development. Article 38(1)(d) of the *Statute of the International Court of Justice* establishes the formal position that international judicial decisions and arbitral awards are a subsidiary means for the determination of rules of international law, rather than courts being the originators of such rules. Moreover Article 59 of the *Statute* confines the binding character of decisions of the Court to the parties to a particular dispute. However these formal constraints upon the legal effect of international judicial decisions have in practice served to place few limits on the reach and influence of the Court's decisions both in terms of its subsequent decisions and the determinations of other international judicial bodies. This speaks to the authority that international courts have assumed in the international order above and beyond their formal status as arbiters of disputes between states, and instead their assumption of an effective role as authors of rules and principles of general relevance and application. In this regard the late Thomas Franck argued that in the absence of truly democratic political institutions, decisions of an international court such as the International Court of Justice, made according to a fair and 'principled process', carry particular global normative influence.[39] Such an approach by tribunals might, however, cause unforeseen political and legal implications.

Nonetheless it needs to be recognised that international courts occupy a position of particular sensitivity as law-making institutions on the international plane that places significant fetters on their capacity to develop the law. An appreciation of this dynamic is important as it tempers what might otherwise be unrealistic expectations as to the potential for international litigation generally,[40]

---

38 ILA Committee on International Law on Sustainable Development, *Report to the Rio Conference* (2008).

39 Thomas M. Franck, *Fairness in International Law and Institutions* (1995).

40 See Vaughan Lowe, 'The Function of Litigation in International Society' (2012) 61 *International and Comparative Law Quarterly* 209.

and in particular in relation to sustainable development. Such expectations have been fuelled in part because of perceived and actual roadblocks in the effective implementation of international law on sustainable development. They are also a product of the experience in domestic legal systems where citizens and other actors have turned (often successfully so) to the judiciary to address sustainable development issues where the other arms of government have failed to act. This emergence of public interest litigation for sustainable use of natural resources is highly variable between jurisdictions. Nonetheless landmark decisions, such as *Oposa v Secretary of the Department of Environment*,[41] while often isolated, do illustrate the potential for domestic courts, sure of their position within a political and legal system, to develop the law in innovative and significant ways. The same dynamic is not present to the same extent, if at all, for international courts which are constituted by the consent of states and enjoy jurisdiction over disputes only to the extent that states have consented to the process. Hence the prospects for truly public interest international litigation on the environment or development are far more limited. Neither the existing rules of standing in terms of jurisdiction *ratione personae* (which is limited in most cases to states alone) nor the grounds of admissibility of claims (which are limited in most cases to those directly affecting the complainant) are conducive to strategic litigation in international bodies to 'defend the environment' or 'fight poverty'.[42]

Nonetheless, the history of international disputation generally, and including the sustainable development context, is that international courts more assured of their jurisdiction are able to render more innovative and legally-significant decisions. In this respect the contrast is instructive between the *Nuclear Tests* cases[43] in which France did not accept the Court's jurisdiction (and did not appear in the proceedings) and the *Gabčikovo-Nagymaros* case in which Hungary and Slovakia jointly referred by *compromis* their dispute to the Court. Whereas in the *Nuclear Tests* cases the Court avoided a finding on the merits of Australia and New Zealand's claims concerning nuclear pollution, in the *Gabčikovo- Nagymaros* case the Court felt enabled to use for the first time in its history the express language of 'sustainable development'. Yet even in the *Gabčikovo-Nagymaros* case the Court was mindful of the precariousness of its place in the international legal order and declined to identify any specific obligations attached to the sustainable development principle. Although the International Court is a legal body deciding matters according to law, it operates in an inescapably political context in which there are pitfalls for being in the rearguard (witness the reaction of

---

41 *Juan Antonio Oposa et al., v The Honorable Fulgencio S. Factoran, Jr., in his capacity as the Secretary of the Department of Environment and Natural Resources* (1994) 33 ILM 173.

42 See Tim Stephens, *International Courts and Environmental Protection* (2009) 264.

43 *Nuclear Tests (Australia v France) (interim measures)* [1973] ICJ Rep 99, *(merits)* [1974] ICJ Rep 253; *(New Zealand v France) (interim measures)* [1973] ICJ Rep 135, *(merits)* [1974] ICJ Rep 457; *Nuclear Tests, request for an examination of the situation in accordance with paragraph 63 of the Court's judgment of 20 December 1974 in the Nuclear Tests (New Zealand v France) case* [1995] ICJ Rep 288.

many to the decision in *South-West Africa (Second Phase)*[44], for instance) or at the vanguard (as seen in the response by some states to the Advisory Opinions in *Legal Consequences of the Construction of a Wall in the Occupied Palestinian Territory*[45]) or *Accordance with International Law of the Unilateral Declaration of Independence in Respect of Kosovo*.[46] Necessarily the Court must walk a fine line between formalism and progressivism.

Against this background, the next section of this report examines key decisions of the International Court of Justice and the International Tribunal for the Law of the Sea (ITLOS) having a bearing on sustainable development in key jurisdictions. It is seen that any decision that makes specific reference to sustainable development is a *rara avis* indeed. In section 5 the report takes up the task of identifying how certain key principles have been taken forward, thus allowing the Committee 'to set out, through a series of guiding statements, how international courts and tribunals have – and, as important, might more effectively – incorporate the concept of sustainable development and the principles reflected in the 2002 New Delhi Declaration of Principles of International Law Relating to Sustainable Development.'[47]

4. Summary of sustainable development jurisprudence within the ICJ and the ITLOS

(a) The International Court of Justice

As the principal judicial organ of the United Nations with general jurisdiction *ratione materiae* the International Court of Justice has been seized of disputes addressing most areas of public international law since it began its work in 1946.

Given the generality of the Court's jurisdiction, it is remarkable that so substantial a proportion of its decisions and its current docket have involved either directly or indirectly issues of sustainable development. Moreover several of its decisions, while not directly relating to sustainable development, have been interpreted as having potential application to the concept. Indeed the very first decision of the Court, the *Corfu Channel* case,[48] in which the Court affirmed 'every State's obligation not to allow knowingly its territory to be used for acts contrary to the rights of other States'[49], was described by H.E. Judge C. G. Weeramantry in his dissenting opinion in the *1995 Nuclear Tests* case[50] as having 'laid down the environmentally important principle that, if a nation knows that harmful effects

---

44 *South West Africa (second phase) (Ethiopia v South Africa; Liberia v South Africa)* [1966] ICJ Rep 6.
45 [2004] ICJ Rep 134.
46 [2010] ICJ Rep 1.
47 International Committee on International Law on Sustainable Development, *Report to the Hague Conference (2010)* 18.
48 *Corfu Channel (United Kingdom v Albania) (merits)* [1949] ICJ Rep 4.
49 Ibid. at 22.
50 [1995] ICJ Rep 288.

may occur to other nations from facts within its knowledge and fails to disclose them, it will be liable to the nation that suffers damage'.[51]

However it must also be acknowledged that the International Court of Justice has not been utilised for environmental litigation to the extent that the Court itself appears to have anticipated. In 1993 the Court established a permanent, seven-member, Chamber for Environmental Matters, so that it would be 'prepared to the fullest extent possible to deal with any environmental case falling within its jurisdiction.'[52] Yet despite the flourishing of sustainability litigation in the Court since 1993 the Chamber was not used, and accordingly the Court decided in 2006 to cease holding elections for a Bench of the Chamber.

As of January 2012, 14 cases directly or indirectly involving environment and development questions had been (or were currently being) litigated in the Court. The purpose of this Report is not to furnish a comprehensive summary of the jurisprudence or the issues of sustainable development in the cases in the Court's docket, tasks that have been ably undertaken by the ILA and partners in another context, as is further discussed below.[53] Rather, it seeks to highlight key aspects and trends in this case law, and to explore the role that the Court may perform in implementing sustainability principles. A major test for the Court lies ahead in several of its cases where broad issues of sustainable development have been raised. The most significant is arguably the *Whaling in the Antarctic* case not only because of the substantive matters identified by Australia in its application, but also fundamental questions as to the enforceability of rights and obligations in areas beyond national jurisdiction. Australia's case against Japan relates to the latter's research whaling programme conducted in the Southern Ocean pursuant to Article VIII of the *1946 International Convention for the Regulation of Whaling*[54] (ICRW) and contends, among other things, that Japan has violated the commercial whaling moratorium under the ICRW, the prohibition under the *1973 Convention on International Trade in Endangered Species of Flora and Fauna* on 'introducing from the sea' an endangered species listed in Annex I of the Convention, and, perhaps most significantly in terms of general principle, the obligation under Article 3 of the *1992 Convention on Biological Diversity* (CBD) to ensure that activities do not cause damage to the environment of other states. Because the case involves both issues of a more technical character and also broad issues of sustainability relating to a core obligation in the CBD, it will be a litmus test for the Court's willingness to elaborate a sustainable development jurisprudence.

The case law of the International Court of Justice to date suggests that the Court is generally wary of entering into a discussion of either the formal status of sustainable development or cognate general concepts, let alone to identify any concrete demands that sustainable development makes of State behaviour. In the

---

51 Ibid. at 361.

52 Communiqué 93/20 on the Establishment of a Permanent Chamber for Environmental Matters (19 July 1993).

53 CISDL-IDLO-ILA Online Resource of Sustainable Development in International Courts and Tribunals, available at www.cisdl.org.

54 Opened for signature 2 December 1946, 161 UNTS 72 (entered into force 10 November 1948).

Gabčíkovo-Nagymaros case, the first occasion on which the court made express reference to sustainable development, no judgment was made on whether the joint project on the Danube between Hungary and Slovakia, or its unilateral variation by Slovakia, was, or was not, sustainable. This was despite the large body of evidence before the Court pointing to the damaging environmental impacts of the diversion of Danube waters from ecologically important floodplains. Instead the Court essentially deferred the adjustment of the balance between environmental protection and economic development to the parties themselves according to the bilateral treaty between them that set out the joint venture. This may be interpreted as the Court adopting a *procedural* approach to sustainable development, that is to say avoiding debates as to its substantive content and instead focussing on ways in which environmental government can be improved by improving the processes of that management in a transboundary context. Hence in the *Gabčíkovo-Nagymaros* case the Court required the parties to reassess the environmental consequences of the project and undertake comprehensive monitoring and protective measures in conformity with contemporary international environmental law. Yet even in this respect the Court did not refer to accepted procedural norms that could assist, most notably Environmental Impact Assessment (EIA). This deficiency was taken up by Judge Weeramantry in his separate opinion, in which he argued that a continuing obligation to carry out EIA was imported into the joint development treaty between the litigants. He also held that the obligation was a principle of international environmental law, namely a specific application of the more general principle of caution which must be read into treaties which have a significant impact upon the environment.[55] Judge Weeramantry's opinion proved to be harbinger of the change over a decade later in the *Pulp Mills* case, in which the Court did enter into a discussion of procedural norms, including EIA, in detail.

As noted in the Committee's Report to the 2010 Hague Conference, in the *Pulp Mills* case 'the Court did not view sustainable development as an operative rule of international law on the basis of which, and in the absence of other rules, it could decide about the legality or illegality of State behaviour'.[56] Nonetheless it is significant that the Court in its decision on the merits re-embraced the mainstream conception of sustainable development as set out in its *Gabčíkovo-Nagymaros* case. There were question marks hanging over the Court's approach to sustainability given its statement in response to Argentina's request for provisional measures to 'the present case highlights the importance of the need to ensure environmental protection of shared natural resources while allowing for *sustainable economic development*'.[57]

The primary significance of the *Pulp Mills* case is in the further development of the procedural dimensions of sustainable development. The case related primarily

55 [1997] ICJ Rep 7, separate opinion of Vice-President Weeramantry, 112.

56 International Committee on International Law on Sustainable Development, *Report to the Hague Conference* (2010), 11.

57 *Pulp Mills on the River Uruguay (Argentina v Uruguay) (request for provisional measures by Argentina)* (2006) 45 ILM 1025, [80] (emphasis added).

to the scope and operation of a bilateral river treaty, the *1975 Statute of the River Uruguay*[58] and the opportunities for venturing into an analysis of general principles somewhat limited. Argentina argued that Uruguay had breached the *1975 Statute* in authorising the construction of pulp mills that Argentina said would damage the River Uruguay by discharging pollutants. The ICJ examined the procedural and substantive obligations under the 1975 Statute and found that they were closely linked, in that satisfaction of the former assists in ensuring that the parties comply with the latter. The Court held that Uruguay had violated several procedural obligations including the requirement to notify Argentina of the environmental impact assessments that had been carried out before going ahead and authorising the mills.[59] Most significantly the Court found

> that it may now be considered a requirement under general international law to undertake an environmental impact assessment where there is a risk the proposed industrial activity may have a significant adverse impact in a transboundary context, in particular, on a shared resource.[60]

As the Committee noted in its Report to the 2010 Hague Conference '[t]he statement of the Court that environmental impact assessment can be considered a requirement under general international law in relation to activities that pose a risk of environmental harm is to be applauded.'[61]

However in dealing with the substantive obligations, such as the obligation to prevent pollution and preserve the aquatic environment in Article 41 of the 1975 Statute, the International Court of Justice found that Uruguay was not in breach. The Court concluded that the duty to notify of the EIA was a procedural obligation, but that EIA itself was part of the substantive obligation to act with due diligence in seeking to prevent pollution. This can be interpreted as the Court imbuing what is in essence a fairly narrow procedural obligation with broader and more meaningful content, and in so doing ensuring that EIA is not simply a 'rubber-stamping' exercise. However on the evidence before it, the Court was not satisfied that Uruguay's EIA was insufficient, and it found that Uruguay had complied with all of its substantive obligations under the 1975 Statute. As a consequence the Court concluded that the only remedy for Argentina was the declaration in the judgment that the procedural obligations had been violated. Moreover, as the Court expressly noted that international law does not specify the normative contents of an EIA, one must be left to wonder if the Court has given states too much leeway in ensuring respect for this new customary obligation.

The decision in the *Pulp Mills* case signals a potentially valuable direction for the evolution of the international jurisprudence of sustainable development. Rather

---

58 Opened for signature 26 February 1975, 1295 UNTS 340 (entered into force 18 September 1976).
59 See *infra* note 121.
60 *Pulp Mills* case, *infra* note 204.
61 International Committee on International Law on Sustainable Development, *Report to the Hague Conference* (2010), 12.

than grappling with overarching questions as to the adjustment of the innate competition between economic development and ecological protection, it may be more productive for Courts to develop the procedural or administrative dimensions of their supervision of State behaviour. However challenges remain for the effective linking of procedural and substantive obligations; there is no value in procedural rules if they do not assist in achieving a substantive objective, such as the prevention of transboundary environmental harm. In this respect the *Pulp Mills* case has attracted some criticism among commentators[62] and most significantly within the Court itself in the Joint Dissenting Opinion of Judges Al-Khasawneh and Simma that is deserving of extensive quotation for the deft way in which it identifies the tension between substance and procedure and the appropriate role of the Court:

> [26] ... in matters related to the use of shared natural resources and the possibility of transboundary harm, the most notable feature that one observes is the extreme elasticity and generality of the substantive principles involved. Permanent sovereignty over natural resources, equitable and rational utilization of these resources, the duty not to cause significant or appreciable harm, the principle of sustainable development, etc., all reflect this generality. The problem is further compounded by the fact that these principles are frequently, where there is a dispute, in a state of tension with each other. Clearly in such situations, respect for procedural obligations assumes considerable importance and comes to the forefront as being an essential indicator of whether, in a concrete case, substantive obligations were or were not breached. Thus, the conclusion whereby non-compliance with the pertinent procedural obligations has eventually had no effect on compliance with the substantive obligations is a proposition that cannot be easily accepted. For example, had there been compliance with the steps laid down in Articles 7 to 12 of the 1975 Statute, this could have led to the choice of a more suitable site for the pulp mills. Conversely, in the absence of such compliance, the situation that obtained was obviously no different from a *fait accompli*.
>
> [27]. The Court does recognize a functional link between procedural and substantive obligations laid down by the 1975 Statute (see Judgment, paragraph 79). However, the Court does not give full weight to this interdependence, neither when assessing whether a breach of Article 41 of the 1975 Statute has occurred nor in determining the appropriate remedies for the breach of Articles 7 to 12 thereof. According to the Court, as long as compliance with substantive obligations has been assured (or at least lack of it not proved), the breach of procedural obligations would not matter very much and hence a declaration to that effect constitutes appropriate satisfaction; this is not the proper way to pay due regard to the interrelation of procedure and substance.[63]

---

62 See Ilias Plakofelas, 'Current Legal Developments: International Court of Justice' (2011) 26 *Int'l J. Mar. Coast L.* 169, 180.

63 *Pulp Mills* case, *supra* notes 26–27.

(b) The International Tribunal for the Law of the Sea

In contrast to other international judicial and quasi-judicial bodies the International Tribunal for the Law of the Sea (ITLOS) possesses jurisdiction *ratione materiae* over issues of sustainable development as part of its mandate. This is by virtue of its central position within the system for resolving disputes under the *1982 United Nations Convention on the Law of the Sea*[64] (LOS Convention).

Not only does the LOS Convention have a strong environmental focus, as seen in Part XII on Protection of the Marine Environment and indeed throughout the text, but the function of ITLOS in preventing marine environmental damage is expressly recognised in its jurisdiction to grant provisional measures 'to preserve the respective rights of the parties to [a] dispute or to prevent serious harm to the marine environment, pending the final decision.'[65] ITLOS has also, like the International Court of Justice, created a Chamber for Marine Environmental Disputes under the special chambers mechanism of Annex VI to the LOS Convention. As with the International Court's Environmental Chamber, the ITLOS Chamber for Marine Environmental Disputes has never been used. This provides yet further confirmation that States prefer to have disputes involving sustainable development issues resolved by generalist rather than specialist bodies. This also underlines the critical importance of implementing the principle of integration as sustainability issues will almost inevitably be intertwined with other legal questions.

The jurisdiction of ITLOS, and the other dispute settlement bodies to which States parties to the LOS Convention may refer disputes under Part XV, is more 'stable' than that of the International Court of Justice. This is because the LOS Convention establishes a wide-ranging and generally compulsory system of dispute settlement. Most aspects of the LOS Convention, including key environmental protection and resource management obligations may be subject to compulsory settlement, allowing States to commence proceedings without seeking the specific consent of a respondent. Moreover as the newly elected President of ITLOS, Judge Shunji Yanai, observed in his address to the General Assembly in December 2011, 'a number of (multilateral or bilateral) conventions on, among other subjects, fisheries, protection and preservation of the marine environment, conservation of marine resources, underwater cultural heritage, and removal of wrecks refer to the Tribunal as the forum for the settlement of disputes.'[66]

For these reasons it can be expected that the Part XV system of dispute settlement will be one of the more important vehicles for the advancement of a jurisprudence of sustainable development. However, at least until its most recent decision of its Seabed Disputes Chamber (discussed below), since it began operating in 1996, ITLOS has in fact shown some caution in its approach to sustainability

---

64 Opened for signature 10 December 1982, 1833 UNTS 397 (entered into force 16 November 1994).

65 Art 290.

66 Available at http://www.itlos.org/fileadmin/itlos/documents/statements_of_president/yanai/Statement_Yanai_GA_061211.pdf

questions. This may be due in part to the criticism that the very creation of the Tribunal generated (and which, to some extent, it continues to provoke[67]). Nonetheless there is evidence of a significant evolution of the Tribunal's approach over time as the new judicial institution found its feet. This is seen in the changing tenor of its 'prompt release' cases. Of the 19 cases submitted to ITLOS, the vast majority have concerned the legality of the arrest of vessels, and nine have involved applications for the prompt release of vessels on the payment of a reasonable bond, as provided for under Article 292 of the LOS Convention. Most of the arrested vessels were apprehended for fisheries offences and raise directly questions of the sustainable management of marine living resources. None of the early decisions of ITLOS recognised the threat to the marine environment posed by illegal, unregulated and unauthorised (IUU) fishing and set fairly minimal bonds for the release of vessels. In contrast, in the *Volga* case[68] ITLOS made express reference to the problem and the efforts being made by states to control it. Indeed, IUU was a key background factor in ITLOS setting a hefty bond for the release of a vessel that had been apprehended fishing for Patagonian toothfish in sub-Antarctic waters near Heard and McDonald Islands (Australia).

So far, ITLOS has made use once use of its facilities under Art. 290 to prescribe provisional environmental measures. In the 2003 *Land Reclamation* case between Malaysia and Singapore, the Tribunal considered that "it cannot be excluded that, in the particular circumstances of this case, the land reclamation works may have adverse effects on the marine environment" and thus "given the possible implications of land reclamation on the marine environment, prudence and caution require that Malaysia and Singapore establish mechanisms for exchanging information and assessing the risks or effects of land reclamation works and devising ways to deal with them in the areas concerned".[69] The Tribunal consequently directed Singapore, by way of a provisional measure, not to conduct its land reclamation in ways that might cause irreparable prejudice to the rights of Malaysia or serious harm to the marine environment.

Without question, the most significant decision of ITLOS relating to sustainable development is the *Responsibilities and Obligations of States Sponsoring Persons and Entities with Respect to Activities in the Area (Seabed Mining Advisory Opinion)*.[70] The *Seabed Mining Advisory Opinion* has rightly been described as 'historic'[71] from the perspective of international law on sustainable development. The first advisory opinion of the Seabed Disputes Chamber of ITLOS, the decision was adopted unanimously. The opinion was sought by the International Seabed Authority Council on the prompting of Nauru and Tonga to ascertain the

---

67 Jillaine Seymour, 'The International Tribunal for the Law of the Sea: A Great Mistake?' (2006) 13 *Ind. J. Global Legal Stud.* 1.

68 *Volga* case *(Russian Federation v Australia) (prompt release)* (2003) 42 ILM 159

69 *Case Concerning Land Reclamation by Singapore in and around the Straits of Johor (Malaysia v Singapore)*, ITLOS Case No. 12 (2003).

70 (2011) 50 ILM 458.

71 David Freestone, 'Responsibilities and Obligations of States Sponsoring Persons and Entities with Respect to Activities in the Area' (2011) 105 *AJIL* 755, 759.

rights and duties of States, particularly developing countries, when they sponsor exploration of minerals on the deep seabed or the 'Area', which is declared by Part XI of the LOS Convention to be part of the common heritage of humankind.

Although the *Seabed Mining Advisory Opinion* does not make express reference to sustainable development, 'it is far from hyperbolic to suggest that in this Advisory Opinion we see discussion of each of the seven principles identified by the International Law Association (ILA) in its 2002 New Delhi Declaration of Principles of International Law relating to Sustainable Development, including the sustainable use of natural resources, the precautionary approach, common but differentiated responsibilities, and the principle of good governance.'[72] The contribution of the *Seabed Mining Advisory Opinion* in each of these areas is considered where relevant in Section 5 of this report.

The *Seabed Mining Advisory Opinion* turned on the interpretation of provisions of Part XI of the LOS Convention, the *1994 Implementation Agreement* (1994 Agreement), and regulations adopted by the International Seabed Authority (the Mining Code). These impose a range of stringent environmental controls on prospecting, exploration and mineral exploitation activities, and in its opinion the Seabed Disputes Chamber was able to confirm their scope and operation. As such care must be taken to understand the particular regulatory context of the *Seabed Mining Advisory Opinion* rather than rushing to judgment on its general significance.[73] Despite this caveat the decision will undoubtedly assume general importance in the implementing of sustainable development for several reasons. First there is much within the decision to inform understandings of the obligation of due diligence to prevent environmental harm. In relation to the obligation of due diligence under the LOS Convention to protect the marine environment when carrying out activities in the Area, as set out primarily in Article 139(1) of the LOS Convention, the Seabed Disputes Chamber identified several direct obligations on sponsoring states. These included obligations to assist ISA in controlling activities in the Area; to apply a precautionary approach (the Chamber said not only was the approach integral to the Mining Code, but also that there was a 'trend towards making this approach part of customary international law'); to apply best environmental practices; to assist in emergency to protect environment; to ensure recourse to compensation in respect of pollution damage; and to conduct environmental impact assessments.

Specifically in relation to environmental impact assessment (EIA), the Chamber found that states sponsoring mining contractors were under a due diligence obligation to ensure contractors conduct an EIA as required by the 1994 Agreement.[74] States were also under a direct obligation to conduct an EIA as this is required by the LOS Convention and by customary international law. In this

---

72 Duncan French, 'From the Depths: Rich Pickings of Principles of Sustainable Development and General International Law on the Ocean Floor – the Seabed Disputes Chamber's 2011 Advisory Opinion' (2011) 26 *Int'l J. Mar. Coast L.* 525, 526.

73 Ibid. at 566.

74 1994 Agreement, Annex s 1(7).

context the Chamber referred approvingly to the *Pulp Mills* case, a clear example of the way in which sustainable development jurisprudence may be reinforced when advanced through several different forums. It also confirms the important linkages between procedural and substantive obligations.

Another significant feature of the Chamber's reasoning was its engagement, albeit implicitly, with the principle of common but differentiated responsibilities. In this respect, the Chamber took a highly nuanced approach. In relation to marine environmental harm from deep seabed mining activities, the Chamber took the view that the overriding concern was to prevent the harm itself – a sensible conclusion that recognises that the marine ecosystem is indifferent to the economic or other capacity of the State responsible for inflicting damage upon it. Hence, the Chamber advised that the obligations on sponsoring states apply equally to developed and developing states such as Nauru and Tonga. However the Chamber noted that stringency of the obligations could be varied in specific provision. An example of such specific allowance is the precautionary principle as defined in Principle 15 of the Rio Declaration, and referred to in the Mining Code, according to which states may apply the precautionary approach 'according to their capabilities'.

Finally, an aspect of the Chamber's opinion that has attracted relatively little attention but which may prove to be among its most important elements is the discussion of *erga omnes* obligations and their enforceability.[75] The Chamber observed that there was no provision of the LOS Convention which allowed the ISA to pursue a claim for 'damage to the Area and its resources constituting the common heritage of mankind, and damage to the marine environment.' However, the Chamber went on to conclude that

> [180] . . . It may, however, be argued that such entitlement is implicit in Article 137, paragraph 2, of the Convention, which states that the Authority shall act "on behalf" of mankind. Each State Party may also be entitled to claim compensation in light of the erga omnes character of the obligations relating to the preservation of the environment of the high seas and in the Area. In support of this view, reference may be made to Article 48 of the ILC Articles on State Responsibility . . .

In this conclusion, the Seabed Disputes Chamber become the first international judicial body specifically to endorse Article 48 of the *Articles on State Responsibility*, thus accepting in principle the existence of an *actio popularis* for environmental harm. The Chamber also noted the capacity of both ISA *and* parties to the LOS Convention to instigate a claim. Additionally the Chamber recognised that an applicant would be entitled to seek compensation for *pure environmental harm*, i.e. damage to the marine environment beyond national jurisdiction that has no impact upon any particular state. Given the longstanding doubts over the status of Article 48 of the *Articles on State Responsibility* as *lex*

---

75 Ibid. at 546.

lata these conclusions, if followed, may prove to be a significant development in understanding the capacity of international courts to enforce environmental protection obligations.

Section 4 has provided an overview as to how certain judicial tribunals have approached matters of sustainable development and environmental protection. Earlier ILA Reports have made jurisprudence of other courts and tribunals (including human rights courts), arbitral tribunals, investor-State arbitrations, and quasi-judicial committees. Brevity prevents detailed analysis of each of these tribunals in this report, and indeed what would be revealed is a highly diverse, fragmented, even conflicting, picture. Investor-State arbitrations, in particular, have been particularly criticised for failing to reflect the public law aspects of environmental regulation in their decisions. The WTO Appellate Body, on the other hand, has been congratulated and chided in equal measure. Its willingness to give effect to the preambular reference to sustainable development, and its considered interpretation of the chapeau of Article XX (general exceptions) contrasts with its still overly-complex understandings of risk within the SPS Agreement and its continued failure to endorse a holistic

5. Analysis of normative trends and development of the New Delhi Declaration as evidence in judicial interpretations and applications

5.1 Sustainable use of natural resources

Significant analysis has already occurred above on the developments relating to the principle of sustainable use of natural resources. However, a number of comments may prove useful. First, though not without some controversy, the case-law of judicial bodies – alongside treaty development and other instances of State and institutional practice – would highlight that the sustainable use of natural resources is increasingly a rule of general customary international law, notwithstanding the geographical location and/or legal status of the natural resource involved. This is also demonstrated by the evolution of the principle of sovereignty over natural resources from a merely rights-based into a duties as well as rights-based principle. This development was reflected in the New Delhi Declaration, which put emphasis on the rational and sustainable management of natural resources and ecosystems including the protection of biological diversity and fresh water sources and the reversing of climate change, over-fishing and pollution.

Secondly, though the content of the general rule will vary depending upon whether it is a shared natural resource, a common resource or within the exclusive confines of the territory of a State, the general obligation of sustainable use is increasingly accepted. Moreover, this obligation becomes more precise and defined in particular circumstances, including (i) established treaty regimes on such matters as fisheries, marine living resources and specific ecosystems (e.g. wetlands), (ii) cooperative arrangements concerning transboundary and shared natural resources, especially watercourses, and (iii) the increasingly specific guidance on (if not also emerging customary law in) the rights of indigenous peoples and their management of local natural resources. The conservation of high seas fisheries is also becoming arguably more consistent and thus definable. A soft law example is also the 1995 FAO Code of Conduct for Responsible Fisheries, which requires from all those engaged in fisheries management – states, as well as fishing entities, organizations, and all persons concerned – to adopt measures for the long-term conservation and sustainable use of fisheries resources.[76]

Thirdly, the level and obligation of conservation required in the sustainable use of any particular natural resource will vary in light of all circumstances, though as a matter of the general obligation, a State is expected to act in accordance with precaution and due diligence and in the interests of both the long-term sustainability of the resource and the benefit of their peoples. It is increasingly expected that an ecological approach to natural resources will be integrated into resource conservation and this too will increasingly become a substantive element of any customary obligation.

5.2 The principle of equity and the eradication of poverty

The principle of equity and the eradication of poverty was a broadly-framed principle within the 2002 New Delhi Declaration of Principles. It contains a number of discrete, if closely related, concepts and arguments, held together by the conviction that 'the principle of equity is central to the attainment of sustainable development'. Within the wider principle, particular reference can be made to the inclusion of inter-generational equity, intra-generational equity, the right to development (phrased within the broader context of sustainable development, as reflected also in Principle 3 of the 1992 Rio Declaration on Environment and Development), a duty of cooperation on matters of global sustainable development and social and economic matters (as required by Article 56 of the United Nations Charter), and finally a recognition of the overall imperative of poverty eradication. Moreover, though not expressly referenced within the New Delhi Declaration *per se*, the reference to equity ties this principle with the first principle of sustainable utilisation of natural resources, particularly with regard to shared and transboundary resources, for which equitable utilization has become a fundamental, though partial, governing principle, and for which there has been significant case-law.

Nevertheless, despite such instances of judicial support, on the whole this remains a multi-layered principle for which jurisprudence remains sporadic, inchoate and ultimately not fully reflective of the broad-ambition of the New Delhi principle itself. As noted above, there has been important case-law on the equitable utilization of shared natural resources, as well as there being some important innovations in the judicial exploration of the right to development

---

76 FAO Code of Conduct for Responsible Fisheries (1995).

in addition to the often quoted references to the few cases that make mention of ideas of intergenerational equity. And though protecting the environment for future generations has a rhetorical attractiveness has invariably ensured its inclusion in the case-law, how far it has had normative effect remains less clear.

Where the international jurisprudence remains lacking, however, is in relation to general ideas of intra-generational equity ('the right of all peoples within the current generation of fair access to the current generation's entitlement to the Earth's natural resources') and the corresponding global duty to promote sustainable development and to eradicate poverty. Though even on these points, there is some evolution, reference being made to the Seabed Disputes Chamber's 2011 *Seabed Mining Advisory Opinion* and its emphasis of the importance of the full contribution of developing States to the resources of the Area and the contribution this makes to a 'just and equitable international economic order'.[77] And in relation to the duty of cooperation on matters of social and economic matters, the adoption of the 2008 Optional Protocol to the 1966 International Covenant on Economic, Social and Cultural Rights, which enshrines an individual communication procedure, may overtime lead to some further elaboration of the duty under article 2(1) of the Covenant by the Committee on Economic, Social and Cultural Rights.

Despite these limitations, it is nevertheless possible to discern certain key characteristics and trends in the case-law. First, reliance on equity within international jurisprudence continues to lack an overarching normative understanding, and consequently is highly context-dependent. The reliance on equitable principles within maritime delimitation,[78] for instance, is rarely placed alongside the use of equity as a basis to determine utilization of shared natural resources. Though a judge such as H. E. C. G. Weeramantry, when he served on the bench of the International Court of Justice, often sought to conceive equity within its widest span, as he memorably did in his separate opinion in *Maritime Delimitation in the Area between Greeland and Jan Mayen (Denmark v Norway)* (1993) in which he noted, 'International law throughout its history has been richly interwoven with equitable strands of thought',[79] most references to equity have been rather more circumscribed.

Nevertheless, despite reliance on equity being heavily context-dependent, it is important not to underplay the overarching importance of equity in individual disputes. As the International Court stated in the *Pulp Mills* case: 'the attainment of optimum and rational utilization requires a balance between the Parties' rights and needs to use the river for economic and commercial activities on the one hand, and the obligation to protect it from any damage to the environment that may be caused by such activities, on the other',[80] adding later that 'utilization could not

---

77 Advisory Opinion of 1 February 2011, para. 163 quoting the preamble to the 1982 UN Convention on the Law of the Sea.

78 Cf. *Barbados and Trinidad and Tobago* (Award of 11 April 2006): 'equitable considerations *per se* are an imprecise concept in the light of the need for stability and certainty in the outcome of the legal process' (para. 230).

79 ICJ Report (1993) 278.

80 Judgment of 20 April 2010, para. 175.

be considered to be equitable and reasonable if the interests of the other riparian State in the shared resource and the environmental protection of the latter were not taken into account'.[81]

Secondly, as noted above, reference has occasionally been made to the more explicit references to the intergenerational element of sustainable development. The International Court made mention of it in *Legality of Threat or Use of Nuclear Weapons* (1996): 'in order correctly to apply to the present case the Charter law on the use of force and the law applicable in armed conflict, in particular humanitarian law, it is imperative for the Court to take account of the unique characteristics of nuclear weapons, and in particular their destructive capacity, their capacity to cause untold human suffering, and their ability to cause damage to generations to come'.[82] Nevertheless, though prepared to reference the idea, the Court is reluctant to elaborate upon it to give it full effect. As Judge Cançado Trindade noted in his separate opinion in the *Pulp Mills* case, 'the Court should have expressly linked this important point [namely, the continuing obligation of monitoring] to inter-generational equity. As it did not, it unnecessarily and unfortunately deprived its own reasoning of the long-term temporal dimension, so noticeably present in the domain of environmental protection'.[83]

Thirdly, though there remains inadequate discussion of the right to development in international law, at least one judicial body has found it a useful concept, both to employ and to hold a State against. In the *Centre for Minority Rights Development (Kenya) and Minority Rights Group International on behalf of Endorois Welfare Council v Kenya*,[84] the African Commission on Human and Peoples' Rights found a violation of the right to development, a right enshrined in Article 22 of the 1981 African Charter of Human and People's Rights. Recognising the African Convention's endorsement of people's rights (and that the Endorois were such a people), the Commission went on to find a violation of the right to development, noting that

> the right to development is a two-pronged test, that it is both *constitutive* and *instrumental*, or useful as both a means and an end. A violation of either the procedural or substantive element constitutes a violation of the right to development. Fulfilling only one of the two prongs will not satisfy the right to development. The African Commission notes the Complainants' arguments that recognising the right to development requires fulfilling five main criteria: it must be equitable, non-discriminatory, participatory, accountable, and transparent, with equity and choice as important, over-arching themes in the right to development.[85]

---

81 Ibid. at para. 177.
82 ICJ Report (1996) 24.
83 Ibid. at para. 124.
84 Case 276/2003, May 2009.
85 Ibid. at para. 277.

Of particular significance was participation, which for the African Commission was not simply consultation in the democratic decision-making process, itself important, but in regard to development projects must include 'obtain[ing] their free, prior, and informed consent, according to their customs and traditions'.[86] This is a radical judgment, and one which should be subject to careful scrutiny, but it certainly belies the argument that the right to development cannot be subject to judicial consideration.

Fourthly, connected to that are recent maritime and land delimitation cases that have made reference to the need to respect and protect traditional fishing and pasture rights. Though often the discussion is incidental to the delimitation and rarely sets out a resource allocation regime, the very inclusion of the judicial dicta is to be noted. One example of this trend can be briefly referenced. In relation to grazing rights, the arbitral tribunal in *Government of Sudan and Sudan People's Liberation Movement/Army* (2009) had cause to say: 'The Tribunal's attention to territorial boundaries should not, however, be taken to imply that the Parties are entitled to disregard other territorial relationships that people living in and in the vicinity of the Abyei Area have historically maintained. Sovereign rights over territory are not, after all, the only relevant considerations in areas in which traditional land-use patterns prevail'.[87]

Fifthly, though broad understandings of intra-generational equity and global duties of cooperation (sometimes collectively categorised as an obligation of solidarity) remain ill-defined in the international case-law, this should not be taken they remain beyond the realms of judicial scrutiny or elaboration. As the Seabed Disputes Chamber had chance to remark in its 2011 *Seabed Mining Advisory Opinion*: 'the role of the sponsoring State is to contribute to the common interest of all States in the proper implementation of the principle of the common heritage of mankind'.[88] Much of the stringency of the tone of the Advisory Opinion is affected by the importance the Chamber gives to the Area as a common heritage of mankind, which elevates these particular natural resources, and this particular geographical region, to a special position in international law.

Finally, sixth, duties to tackle poverty eradication remain politically contentious and thus unsurprisingly there is a distinct lack of substantive judicial interrogation. Thus, it must be concluded that the principle of equity and the notion of justice that underpins it remains fragmented and constrained by both political and normatively-constituted parameters. What is true is that without equity, the ideal of sustainable developments lacks its moral compass. What remains to be determined is how far law and the courts should give effect, to operationalise and to concretise, these moral aspirations not just in certain discrete respects but more generally across the ambit of the wider principle.

---

86 Ibid. at para. 291.
87 Award of 22 July 2009, para. 748.
88 Advisory Opinion of 1 February 2011, para. 226.

5.3 Common but Differentiated Responsibilities (CBDR)

The third principle of the New Delhi Declaration is closely related to the equity principle in that it embodies the ability to pay principle, and the state responsibility principle in that it embodies the differentiated responsibilities of states if the Common but Differentiated Responsibilities and Respective Capabilities principle. This principle is explicitly included in the Rio Declaration on Environment and Development,[89] the United Nations Framework Convention on Climate Change (UNFCCC),[90] the Convention on Biological Diversity,[91] and the differential situation of developing countries is referred to many treaties including the 1982 United Nations Convention on the Law of the Sea,[92] and the (Article 5 countries of the) 1987 Montreal Protocol on Substance that Deplete the Ozone Layer.[93] The principle is also being applied within the European Union and the ECE countries in the 1988 EC Large Combustion Directive,[94] the 1991 VOC Protocol,[95] and the 1992 Maastricht Treaty[96].

The CBDR principle[97] is invoked when all countries face a common problem or a challenge to a shared environmental resource but when they have differential contributions to the problem and when they have differential capacities (irrespective of their contributions) to deal with the problem. In the run-up to the negotiations on the Rio Declaration and the UNFCCC treaty, there was growing recognition of the importance of this principle in addressing global environmental problems. Subsequently, the support for this principle has divided along two camps. Those supporting it argue that this principle flows from justice principles[98] – that differentiation between countries in relation to their contribution to causing the problem is logical and fair and that differentiation based on the ability to pay is also fair and is a common principle in most countries. Others are more negative about the effects of the principle. They see these principles as unlikely to improve the effectiveness of treaties in addressing the common problem, and that fast developing economies in the South need to be willing to take their responsibilities. For Weisslitz, "the use of territorial variation as a justification for differential standards ignores the significant likelihood of transboundary harm and is

89 Rio Declaration, Report of the United Nations Conference on Environment and Development (1992) UN Doc. A/CONF.151/26/Rev. 1 (1992) 31 ILM 874, *supra* note 34.

90 United Nations Framework Convention on Climate Change, 31 ILM 849 (1992).

91 United Nations Convention on the Law of the Sea, 21 ILM 1261 (1982).

92 United Nations Convention on the Law of the Sea (UNCLOS), 10 December 1982, UN Doc. A/CONF.62/122 21 ILM 1245, *supra* note 64.

93 Montreal Protocol on Substances the Deplete the Ozone Layer, 26 ILM 154 (1987)

94 88/609/EEC.

95 Protocol to the 1979 Convention on Long Range Transboundry Air Pollution Concerning the Control of Emissions of Volatile Organic Compounds and Their Transboundry Fluxes, 18 November 1991, 31 ILM 568

96 European Union Treaty, 1 February 1992, 31 ILM 247.

97 Duncan French, *Developing States and International Environmental Law – The Importance of Differentiated Responsibilities* (2000).

98 See, e.g. Lavanya Rajamani, *The Principle of Common but Differentiated Responsibility and the Balance of Commitments under the Climate Regime*, 9 RECIEL 120 (2000); Ruchi Anand, *International Environmental Justice: A North-South Dimension* (2004). Christine Batruch, *Hot Air as Precedent for Developing Countries' Equity Considerations*, 17 *UCLA J. of Envtl. L.* & Pol'y 45 (1988–89).

therefore an insignificant approach".[99] Adams explains that per capita emissions/ pollution are not the critical factor but totals of emissions.[100]

The argument of those opposing the CBDR principle can be summed up as follows: First, that common problems should not be assessed in terms of the per capita contribution of countries, but their gross contributions; this would be in line with the principle of sovereign equality of states.[101] Second, some of the countries claiming leniency under this principle are developed or developing rapidly and that this is not fair. In other words the classification of countries in the climate change regime[102] and in the ozone layer regime[103] does not really always justify the use and application of this principle always. Third, that in relation to large countries such as China, India and Brazil, allowing room for economic growth that is accompanied by emissions that lead to global problems is highly challenging as this can negate the effectiveness of the entire process of problem solving. Fourth, that making such differentiation may lead to provisions in favour of weak states that are subsequently unable to implement their responsibilities precisely because they are weak administratively.[104] Although the United States supports this principle, it has a difference of view about how it is to be interpreted and some of the above reasons were perhaps behind the United States disagreement with the principle as expressed in it's requirement for 'meaningful action' from key developing countries in the climate change regime just before the Kyoto Protocol was adopted.[105] The diversity of views on the interpretation of the CBDR is discussed in Honkonen.[106]

Some lessons emerge from the above discussion. A key issue in the interpretation of the CBDR is first, the need to apply this principle to differentiate between countries that is based on clear criteria.[107] Second, the differentiation of countries should be treated as temporary, allowing them to graduate in and out of categories.[108] Third, this implies that the developed countries will need to change their production and consumption patterns,[109] and fourth, that the assistance to the

99 Michael Weisslitz, 'Rethinking the Equitable Principle of Common but Differentiates Responsibility: Differential Versus Absolute Norms of Compliance and Contribution in the Global Climate Change Context', 13 *Colo. J. Int'l Envtl. L.& Pol'y* 473 (2005).

100 Todd B. Adams, 'Is there a Legal Future for Sustainable Development in Global Warming? Justice, Economics and Protecting the Environment', 16 *Geo. Int'l Envtl. L. Rev.* 77 (2003).

101 Nina E. Bafundo, 'Compliance with the Ozone Treaty: Weak States and the Principle of Common but Differentiated Responsibilities', 21 *Am. U. Int'l L. Rev.*, 461 (2006).

102 J. Gupta and K. Tienhaara, Special Issue on Sustainable Development and Investment, *International Environmental Agreements: Politics, Law and Economics* 6:4 (2006).

103 Bafundo, *supra* note 101, 2006.

104 Bafundo, *supra* note 101, 2006.

105 Paul G. Harris, 'Common but Differentiated Responsibility: The Kyoto Protocol and United States Policy', 7 *N.Y.U. Envtl. L. J.* 27 (1999).

106 Tuula Honkonen, 'The principle of common but differentiated responsibilities in post-2012 climate negotiations', *RECIEL* 18(3) 257 (2009).

107 Gupta, 2006, *supra* note 102.

108 Yoshiro Matsui, 'Some Aspects of the Principle of "Common but Differentiated Responsibilities', *INEA* 2 151 (2002).

109 Matsui, *supra* note 108, 2002.

developing countries may need to be limited to 'incremental costs' only[110] and not be expanded to include all kinds of past perceived 'wrongs'. Fifth, it is also important that the principle should not be interpreted to imply that there are no responsibilities on the part of weaker countries; but that even the weaker countries need to be differentiated in order to assess what kinds of responsibilities they can assume; and that they are also under an obligation to modify their development patterns as far as possible.[111] As Mumma says, "There is no necessary reason why common but differentiated responsibility should mean *no* responsibility".[112] Sixth, while such a principle is needed to protect justice principles and encourage developing countries to come on board, such a principle should not be interpreted unreasonably so that it discourages the developed countries from taking on their own responsibilities. This principle has not yet been elevated to a customary law principle[113] and the way it is interpreted will be critical for determining its future.

> The CBDR principle has not been explicitly interpreted in court decisions. However, there have been decisions where countries are being differentiated based on their level of development, for the Seabed Disputes Chamber was faced with the complex question of how far developing States that sponsored entities were subject to preferential rules. On first appearances, the question would appear to be highly nuanced, as the seabed regime contains numerous provisions which do take into account the interests of developing States. In particular, the Law of the Sea Convention states that '[t]he effective participation of developing States in activities in the Area shall be promoted . . . having due regard to their special interests and needs' (article 148), going on to reference specifically land-locked and geographically disadvantaged developing States. The Chamber thus rightly acknowledges those provisions of the Convention (as affected by the 1994 Implementation Agreement) that do take such considerations into account. Nevertheless, the Chamber focuses on the specific wording of Article 148 which states that such effective participation 'shall be promoted as *specifically provided for* in this Part',[114] thus demarcating those provisions for which no specific mention is made in terms of the level of development. As the Chamber remarks, 'there is no general clause for the consideration of such interests and needs beyond what is provided for'.[115]

Moreover, the Chamber felt it necessary to identify not just the limits of preferential treatment within the regime, but also why differentiation beyond this – in the case of sponsoring developing States – would be inappropriate. Though dressed in legal language, the Chamber's position on this is equally determined by considerations

---

110 Ibid.
111 Albert Mumma and David Hodas, 'Designing a Global Post-Kyoto Climate Change Protocol that Advances Human Development', 20 *Geo. Int'l Envtl. L. R.* 617 (2007–2008).
112 Mumma and Hodas, *supra* note 111, 2008: 631.
113 C. D. Stone, 'Deciphering Sustainable Development' (1994) 69 *Chi.-Kent L. R. 977*.
114 Seabed Disputes Chamber, *supra* note 7.
115 Seabed Disputes Chamber, *supra* note 7.

of policy in seeking to establish clear parameters for a regime at the beginning of its operational existence. Notably, the language of the high seas – and some of the difficulties that have faced that particular maritime zone – is used.

> Equality of treatment between developing and developed sponsoring States is consistent with the need to prevent commercial enterprises based in developed States from setting up companies in developing States, acquiring their nationality and obtaining their sponsorship in the hope of being subjected to less burdensome regulations and controls. The spread of sponsoring States 'of convenience' would jeopardize uniform application of the highest standards of protection of the marine environment, the safe development of activities in the Area and protection of the common heritage of mankind.[116]

Whether the difficulties of regulating ships flying flags of convenience on the high seas is directly analogous to sponsored entities seeking out States 'of convenience' is disputable, though the point that differentiation in standards would undermine overall regulatory uniformity must nevertheless be accurate. The Chamber does acknowledge that levels of development might affect the application of the precautionary approach, but seeks to prevent over-generalisations, preferring instead to note that "What counts in a specific situation is the level of scientific knowledge and technical capability available to a given State in the relevant scientific and technical fields".[117]

5.4 Precautionary Approach

The precautionary approach is one of the key elements of sustainable development and has long been recognized as central to any strategy on sustainable development.[118] It has been described both as 'the most prominent' and 'perhaps the most controversial' development in international environmental law over the past two decades.[119] While the precautionary approach has been referred to in many international instruments, there remains uncertainty as regards its scope and status.[120]

---

116 Seabed Disputes Chamber, *supra* note 7.
117 Seabed Disputes Chamber, *supra* note 7.
118 See Principle 4.1 of the 2002 ILA New Delhi Declaration on the Principles of International Law Relating to Sustainable Development. D. Freestone "The Precautionary Principle" in R. Churchill and D. Freestone, *International Law and Climate Change* (Boston: Gordon and Trotman, 1991) at 25.
119 J. B. Wiener "Precaution" in D. Bodansky, J. Brunnée and E. Hey, eds., *The Oxford Handbook of International Environmental Law* (Oxford, New York: OUP, 2007) at 599.
120 The precautionary approach has been referred to in, for example, the 1987 Montreal Protocol on Substances that Deplete the Ozone Layer, the 1992 UN Framework Convention on Climate Change. The 1992 Convention on Biological Diversity, the 1995 Agreement for the Implementation of the Provisions of the United Nations Convention on the Law of the Sea of 10 December 1982 Relating to the Conservation and Management of Straddling Fish Stocks and Highly Migratory Fish Stocks, the 2000 Cartagena Protocol on Biosafety to the Convention on Biological Diversity, and the 2002 Stockholm Convention on Persistent Organic Pollutants.

At its core, the precautionary approach permits – or even requires – action to prevent harm to the environment in the absence of full scientific evidence about the nature, likelihood and/or extent of harm. It is reflected, most famously, in Principle 15 of the Rio Declaration on Environment and Development as follows:

> In order to protect the environment, the precautionary approach shall be widely applied by States according to their capabilities. Where there are threats of serious or irreversible damage, lack of full scientific certainty shall not be used as a reason for postponing cost-effective measures to prevent environmental degradation.

From this definition it becomes apparent that the precautionary approach, like sustainable development, requires a balancing of different interests, mainly environmental and economic. Where and how this balance is struck explains, at least in part, the source of uncertainty over the scope and status of the precautionary approach. As Wiener notes, applying precaution as a legal concept involves complex issues such as finding 'the optimal balance' between, for example, benefits and costs, safety and innovation, assumptions about vulnerability and resilience amongst many others.[121]

Principle 15 of the Rio Declaration suggests a number of considerations in determining how the balance is to be struck. In the first place, the threshold for action is 'serious or irreversible damage'. Secondly, the measures to which Principle 15 of the Rio Declaration applies are 'cost-effective measures'. This suggests that economic considerations are relevant in determining whether and what precautionary measures are to be taken. This formulation lacks what Nollkaemper referred to as an 'absolutist pretence' – the notion that once a certain risk threshold is met, measures to prevent harm must be taken at all costs.[122] This approach to balancing the need to avoid risk with cost-effectiveness is concretely reflected in, for example, the Kyoto Protocol which, in the face of the risk of serious *and* possibly catastrophic consequences of climate change, settled on clearly insufficient emissions reduction targets because of the economic costs associated with higher reduction targets.[123]

Other instruments establish a different balance. The 1990 Bergen Ministerial Declaration's definition of the precautionary approach, for example, incorporates Nollkaemper's 'absolutist pretence' in that it defines the precautionary approach

---

121   Wiener, *supra* note 119 at 598.

122   A. Nollkaemper "'What You Risk Reveals What You Value' and Other Dilemmas Encountered in the Legal Assault on Risks", in D. Freestone and E. Hey, eds., *The Precautionary Principle and International Law: The Challenges of Implementation* (The Hague: Kluewr, 1991) at 74.

123   For discussion on the relationship between the Kyoto targets and precaution see D. Tladi *Sustainable Development in International Law: An Analysis of Key Enviro-Economic Instruments* (Pretoria: PULP, 2007) at 141–43 and 153–55.

without cost-effectiveness as a qualifier of the measures to be adopted.[124] The 1995 Fish Stocks Agreement adopts a similarly unqualified approach to precaution.[125] Article 6(2) simply states that the "absence of adequate scientific information shall not be used as a reason for postponing or failing to take conservation and management measures".

The Cartagena Protocol on Biosafety, like many other international agreements on sustainable development, reaffirms Principle 15 of the Rio Declaration.[126] However, in the implementation of the advanced informed agreement procedure, the Protocol provides that '[L]ack of scientific certainty due to insufficient relevant scientific information' with respect the adverse impacts of Living modified organisms 'shall not prevent [the Party of Import] from taking decisions, as appropriate, with regard to the import of living modified organisms'.[127] The right to take decisions, either '[a]pproving the import with or without conditions' or 'prohibiting import',[128] appears not to be qualified by cost-effectiveness. Moreover, unlike Principle 15 of the Rio Declaration, the Cartagena Protocol does not require the potential damage to be 'serious or irreversible', but merely speaks of 'potential adverse effects'.

The question may also be asked whether precautionary principle requires or whether it permits action. In the case of the former, once the established threshold of risk is met, action has to be taken while in the case of the latter action may be taken. This question – along with the related question of who bears the burden of proof – was at the heart of the negotiations of the 2010 Nagoya Supplementary Protocol on Liability and Redress.[129]

Even with these contestations, there does appear to be a general understanding of the contours of the precautionary approach as requiring the adoption of measures when a certain threshold of risk to the environment is met. What that threshold is and the extent of the measures are issues that will be clarified as the principle continues to develop in practice and case law.

Whether the precautionary approach is a principle of law or simply a policy approach remains controversial. To the extent that it is found in a treaty, there is

---

124 See para. 7 of the 1990 Bergen Ministerial Declaration on Sustainable Development in ECE Region. See also Article 7 IUCN's Draft International Convention on Environment and Development (Fourth Edition) which refers to precaution as a duty and defines it as follows: '. . . even in the absence of scientific certainty, appropriate action shall be taken to anticipate, prevent and monitor the risks of serious or irreversible environmental harm' (2010).

125 1995 Agreement for the Implementation of the Provisions of the United Nations Convention on the Law of the Sea of 10 December 1982 Relating to the Conservation and Management of Straddling Fish Stocks and Highly Migratory Fish Stocks.

126 Cartagena Protocol/Biosafety Protocol, 39 ILM 1027 (2000). The Third preambular paragraph of the Cartagena Protocol reaffirms 'the precautionary approach contained in Principle 15 of the Rio Declaration'.

127 Arts. 10(6), 11(8) of the Cartagena Protocol. See also Article 11(8) of the Cartagena Protocol.

128 Article 10(3) of the Cartagena Protocol.

129 2010 Nagoya/Kuala Lumpur Supplementary Protocol on Liability and Redress to the Cartagena Protocol on Biosafety. See for discussion of various interests in the negotiations D. Tladi, "Civil Liability in the Context of the Cartegena Protocol: To be or Not to be (Binding)?" 10 (2010) *Int'l Envtl. Agr.: Pol., L. & Econ.* 15.

obviously no controversy. The question arises as to its legal status in cases where it is not reflected in binding instrument.

The approach of the WTO dispute settlement mechanisms to the precautionary approach was first pronounced in the *Beef Hormones dispute*.[130] The WTO Appellate Body made two important findings with respect to the precautionary approach. First, the Appellate Body was not willing to pronounce upon whether the precautionary principle has become a general or customary principle of international law, expressing the view that this was an 'abstract question'.[131] The Panel then suggests that whatever its status in general international law 'the precautionary principle does not, by itself, and without a clear textual directive to that effect' override the provisions of the SPS Agreement.[132] Scholars have noted, however, that the test later adopted for such matters in the *Asbestos dispute*,[133] that of the 'reasonable health official', permits considerable scope for precaution,[134] particularly when read in light of the legitimacy granted to minority scientific views in the *Retreaded Tyres dispute*.[135]

The ICJ, in the *Pulp Mills* case, adopted a similarly conservative approach to the precautionary approach.[136] In response to the substantial arguments of the parties in relation to the precautionary approach, the Court merely stated that

> while the precautionary approach may be relevant in the interpretation and application of the provisions of the Statute, it does not follow that it operates as a reversal of the burden of proof[137]

The Court never shares its view of the legal status of the precautionary approach or, for that matter how it does operate. The decision of the majority stands in stark contrast to the zeal of the separate opinion of Judge Cançado Trindade who is unequivocal that the precautionary principle is a principle of international environmental law.[138] He asserts that the precautionary principle emanates from the 'universal juridical conscience' which is the 'ultimate material "source" of all

---

130   *EC-Measures Concerning Meat and Meat Products (Hormones)* AB-1994-4.
131   Ibid. at 91, 92.
132   Ibid. at 94. While the Appellate Body took the view that precaution 'indeed finds reflection' in the Article 5.7, the Appellate Body did accept that Article 5.7 did not 'exhaust[s] the relevance of the precautionary principle'. The approach of the Appellate Body was followed by a Panel decision in *EC-Measures Affecting the Approval and Marketing of Biotech Products* WT/DS291 of 29 September 2006 wherein the panel held that the 'legal status of the precautionary principle remains unsettled' (at para. 7.88).
133   *EC – Measures Affecting Asbestos and Asbestos-Containing Products* WT/DS135/R and WT/DS135/AB/R.
134   M. C. Cordonier Segger and M. Gehring, "Precaution, Health and the World Trade Organization: Moving toward Sustainable Development" (2003) 29: 1 *Queen's Law Journal* 133.
135   *Brazil – Measures Affecting Imports of Retreaded Tyres* WT/DS332/AB/R.
136   *Case Concerning Pulp Mills on the River Uruguay (Argentina v Uruguay) (Judgment)*, [2010] I.C.J. General List No. 135.
137   Ibid. at para. 164.
138   See Separate opinion of Trindade in the *Pulp Mills* case at, e.g. paras 6, 52, 68 and 220.

Law' and the 'new *jus gentium* our time'.[139] The significance of this classification is that it loosens the grip that the lack of consistent state can have on the development of precaution as a principle of law.

5.5 *Public Participation*

The *1992 Rio Declaration on Environment and Development* established public participation in environmental decision-making as a cornerstone of sustainable development and good governance.[140] The Rio Declaration recognised that providing the public right to access information and to consultation with public authorities ensures transparency and accountability, and creates opportunities for public involvement on issues that impact society. Equally, States should guarantee access to judicial and administrative redress as a means of guaranteeing that these rights are safeguarded.

In this regard both human rights and trade and investment perspectives are possible. Both avenues have generated significant discussion. But equally, one should not dismiss the general relevance of issues of public participation and civil society involvement. Argentina raised the importance of public participation in *Pulp Mills*, with particular reference to the importance of public consultation as a key component of an environmental impact assessment. It has been widely noted that despite the Court's willingness to engage with other aspects of sustainable development and environmental norms, there was no similar eagerness in the respect of broadening obligations of participation and consultation.

The establishment of the *Aarhus Convention on Access to Information, Public Participation in Decision-making and Access to Justice in Environmental Matters*[141] *(Aarhus Convention)* in 1998 represented a monumental step in linking environmental protection with sustainable development and human rights in international law. In effect, the Aarhus Convention combined the Rio principles of public involvement and access to information and justice into a succinct multilateral agreement, which created procedural rights aimed at facilitating a right to a healthy environment. It is unique in that it is focuses exclusively on the obligations of individual States to its own citizens. Access to environmental information[142], public participation[143], and access to justice[144] form the three overarching pillars on which the Aarhus Convention is based.[145]

---

139 Ibid. at para. 52 and 68.
140 Principle 10, Rio Declaration on Environment and Development, UN Conference on Environment and Development, UN Doc. A/CONF.151/5Rev.1, 31 ILM 874 (1992) available at http://www.unep.org/Documents.Multilingual/Default.asp?documentid=78&articl eid=1163.
141 38 ILM 517 (1998) available at http://www.unece.org/fileadmin/DAM/env/pp/documents/cep43e.pdf.
142 Ibid. at Articles 4 and 5.
143 Ibid. at Articles 6, 7, and 8.
144 Ibid. at Article 9.
145 Ibid. at Article 1 establishes, "In order to contribute to the protection of the right of every person of present and future generations to live in an environment adequate to his or her health and well-being,

The Aarhus Convention requires the State to provide public access to environmental information at the request of any individual.[146] Information must be provided without an interest having to be stated.[147] 'Environmental information' includes any information in written, visual, aural, electronic or any other material form on the state of the environment.[148] To facilitate these requirements, the Aarhus Convention provides that State parties must take steps to incorporate these responsibilities into legislation or regulations, and create means by which these obligations can be enforced.[149] Article 6 requires the State to give early, effective and adequate information and to notify the public on environmental matters that are to be decided in order to encourage and maximize public involvement in the decision-making process.[150] States must also implement laws to ensure that the public has redress where its rights to public participation are infringed in any way.[151]

Access to information and justice and public participation was also recognized as one of the seven principles of sustainable development in the 2002 ILA New Delhi Declaration.[152] The New Delhi Declaration recognises public participation as essential to sustainable development and good government as it promotes transparency, accountability and inclusion.[153] To secure public participation, the New Delhi Declaration recognises the importance of the protection of the public's right to seek, access and receive information held by governments and to express opinions and impart ideas.[154] Finally, it establishes access to effective judicial or administrative procedures as essential where harm is or is likely to be suffered by individuals, and to claim compensation.[155]

This section examines how international courts and tribunals have implemented the principle of public participation and access to information and justice such as they are recognized in the New Delhi Declaration. The analysis focuses on judgments of both social and human rights courts and tribunals and economic courts and tribunals. The cases provides useful insight as to the development and scope of these rights in international law and guidelines as to how these rights should be interpreted and applied in future cases.

First, it must be noted that the principles of public participation and access to justice and information have been defined and greatly utilized by the

---

each Party shall guarantee the rights of access to information, public participation in decision-making, and access to justice in environmental matters in accordance with the provisions of this Convention".

146   Ibid. at Article 4
147   Ibid. at Article 4(1)(a). Article 4(4) creates strict exceptions to this rule.
148   Ibid. at Article 3.
149   Ibid.
150   Ibid. at Articles 6–8.
151   Ibid. at Article 9.
152   Int'l Law Ass'n, New Delhi Declaration of Principles of International Law Relating to Sustainable Development, Res. 3/2002 (Apr. 6, 2002), available at http://cisdl.org/tribunals/pdf/NewDelhiDeclaration.pdf.
153   Ibid. at Article 5.1.
154   Ibid. at Article 5.2.
155   Ibid. at Article 5.3.

Inter-American Court of Human Rights (IACHR), European Court of Human Rights (ECHR), the Aarhus Convention Compliance Committee (ACCC) and the African Court on Human and Peoples' Rights (ACHPR).

6. Access to Information

The importance of the right of the public to access information is established in IACHR case of *Claude Reyes et al. v Chile*.[156] There, the IACHR held that State actions should be governed by transparency and accountability, and highlighted the significance of the rule of access to information as a means of establishing this balance and fostering increased democracy.[157] In *Giacomelli v Italy*,[158] the ECHR recognises the significance of the right to access to information by linking it to the importance of government decision-making that first considers the possible harmful impacts of activities on the environment and aims to strike a fair balance between the competing interests.[159] It stated that public access to such information is necessary to enable individuals to assess the danger to which they are exposed in order to formulate an informed opinion on the issue.[160]

The IACHR further explored the full meaning of access to information in *Claude Reyes et al. v Chile*.[161] It found an intrinsic link between the human right to freedom of expression and the right to access to information, as guaranteed by Article 13 of the American Convention on Human Rights[162] which includes "freedom to seek, receive, and impart information and ideas of all kinds."[163] Thus, it the right to access information establishes both the right of the individual to request State-held information, as well as a positive obligation of the State to provide it.

The ACHPR was of a similar view in *Scanlen and Holderness v Zimbabwe*,[164] when it held that the expression, reception, and dissemination of ideas and information are indivisible concepts.[165] Thus, where there is an unlawful restriction to an individual's freedom of expression is also a restriction on the right of all others to receive information and ideas.[166]

---

156 *Claude Reyes et al. v Chile*, No. 151, Judgment of 19 September 2006, Tribunal: Inter-American Court of Human Rights, Year of decision: 2006.

157 Ibid. at para. 86.

158 *Giacomelli v Italy*, No 59909/00, Judgment of 2 November 2006, Tribunal: European Court of Human Rights, Year of Decision: 2006.

159 Ibid. at para. 83.

160 Ibid.

161 *Claude Reyes et al. v Chile*, *supra* note 156.

162 O.A.S.Treaty Series No. 36, 1144 U.N.T.S. 123, entered into force July 18, 1978.

163 Ibid. at Article 13.

164 Comm. 297/2005, 26th ACHPR AAR Annex (Dec 2008 – May 2009), available at http://www.worldcourts.com/achpr/eng/decisions/2009.04_Scanlen_v_Zimbabwe.htm.

165 Ibid. at para. 108

166 Ibid.

Importantly, the IACHR in *Claude Reyes et al. v Chile*[167] provided that information should be provided without the need to provide direct interest or personal involvement in order to obtain the information, a key feature of the Aarhus Convention.[168]

A series of cases emanating from the ECHR have construed an indirect right to access information from articles of the European Convention on Human Rights.[169] In *Guerra and Others v Italy*,[170] the Commission found a breach of Article 8, which provides for the right to respect for an individual's private and family life, where the State failed to disclose information on risks of harmful substances to the public. Similarly, in *McGinley and Egan v UK*[171] the Commission found that Article 8 requires that, where a Government engages in hazardous activities which might have hidden adverse consequences on the health of those involved in such activities, an effective and accessible procedure should be established which enables persons to seek all relevant and appropriate information.[172] In *Oneryildiz v Turkey*,[173] the Commission also recognised the right to be informed of danger from Article 2 of European Convention on Human Rights (right to life).[174]

Courts' View on Exceptions

On the issue of exceptions to the right of access to information, the IACHR provided that States should be governed by a principle of maximum disclosure, and the presumption should be that all information is open and accessible, subject only to a limited set of exceptions.[175] Where the right of access to information does admit restrictions, the IACHR established strict guidelines to determine whether such restrictions would be acceptable. Restrictions imposed on the right of access to information should be:

a)   Established by law to create legal certainty, avoid possible influence of the arbitrary and capricious discretion of the public authorities.[176]

b)   For a purpose which is allowed by the American Convention on Human Rights.[177]

c)   For the general welfare of the public, necessary in a democratic society, and intended to satisfy a compelling public interest.[178]

---

167   *Claude Reyes et al. v Chile, supra* note 17, at para. 77.
168   See *supra* note 141, Aarhus Convention, Article 4(1)(a).
169   Convention for the Protection of Human Rights and Fundamental Freedoms Art. 6.1, 4 November, 1950, 213 U.N.T.S. 221, available at http://www.echr.coe.int/NR/rdonlyres/D5CC24A7-DC13-4318-B457-5C9014916D7A/0/ENG_CONV.pdf
170   Judgment of 19 February 1998, *Reports of Judgments and Decisions* 1998-I.
171   (1999) 27 EHRR 1.
172   Ibid. at para. 101.
173   [2002] ECHR 496 (18 June 2002).
174   Ibid. at para. 90.
175   *Claude Reyes et al. v Chile, supra* note 156, at para. 92.
176   Ibid. at para. 89, 98.
177   Ibid. at para. 90.
178   Ibid. at para. 91.

d) Proportionate to the interest that justifies it and must be appropriate for accomplishing this legitimate purpose.[179]

Ultimately, the least restrictive interpretation of the right should be selected.

The Aarhus Compliance Committee (Compliance Committee) was also of a similar view on restricting limitations to the right to access information. In the *Aarhus Convention Compliance Committee Case Concerning Romania*,[180] the Compliance Committee held that as a general rule, Environmental Impact Assessments (EIAs) should be disclosed in entirety, with the possibility of exempting parts of the EIA as an exception to the rule.[181] In cases where there may be grounds for refusal to do so, these grounds must be interpreted restrictively, taking into account the public interest served by disclosure.[182] Importantly, the reasoning on which such decisions as to whether to exempt parts of the information from disclosure are made should be clear and transparent.[183]

In the *Aarhus Convention Compliance Committee Case Concerning the European Community*,[184] the Compliance Committee stated that a balance must be struck between the competing interests of public interest in disclosing environmental information and the possible harm to economic interests of the developer.[185] Where there is significant public interest, the Aarhus Convention would require disclosure.[186]

Importantly, in *Kenneth Good v Republic of Botswana*[187] the ACHPR adjudicated on the Botswana Immigration Act, which provided that where an individual was expelled from the country, the courts had no power to seek and obtain any information and/or reasons on the grounds of that person's expulsion.[188] The court ruled that circumstances where the information sought is relevant in a trial for the vindication of a right, the right to receive information cannot be withheld for any reason.[189]

7. Public Participation

According to *Claude Reyes et al. v Chile*,[190] the link between facilitating access to information and building the capacity of the public to participate in environmental decision-making, by allowing them to question, investigate and consider whether public functions are being performed justifiably and efficiently.

179 Ibid.
180 ACCC/C2005/15; ECE/MP.PP/2008/5/Add.7, 16 April 2008.
181 Ibid. at para. 30.
182 Ibid.
183 Ibid.
184 ACCC/C/2007/21, ECE/MP.PP/C.1/2009/2/Add.1, 11 December 2009.
185 Ibid. at para. 30.
186 Ibid.
187 Comm. 313/05, 28th ACHPR AAR Annex (Nov 2009–May 2010), available at http://www.worldcourts.com/achpr/eng/decisions/2010.05_Good_v_Botswana.htm.
188 Ibid. at para. 191.
189 Ibid. at para. 193.
190 *Claude Reyes et al. v Chile, supra* note 156, at para. 86.

Proper Notification of the Public

Whether a State has fulfilled its obligation to properly inform the public about proposed activity in an "effective manner" depends on the particular means employed, and the circumstances of the case.[191] The Compliance Committee expanded on this principle in the *Aarhus Convention Compliance Committee Case Concerning Lithuania*.[192] For the public to be informed in an "effective manner," public authorities should implement the best means of informing the public of opportunities to participate which ensures that all those who potentially could be concerned have a reasonable chance to learn about proposed activities and their possibilities to participate.[193] This may entail tailoring the most suitable method of notifying the public to the circumstances of that particular State or area,[194] and providing repeat notifications where necessary.[195]

Further, notification of the public of opportunities to participate in environmental decision-making must take place at an early stage when all options are still open and the public's views can be incorporated into the planning process. Importantly, the time given to the public to consider and review information related to the proposed activity before consultation takes place must be adequate and sufficient to do so. The Compliance Committee explained this position as follows:

> The requirement to provide "reasonable time frames" implies that the public should have sufficient time to get acquainted with the documentation and to submit comments taking into account, *inter alia*, the nature, complexity and size of the proposed activity. A time frame which may be reasonable for a small simple project with only local impact may well not be reasonable in case of a major complex project.[196]

There is no exact calculation to determine the adequacy of the public notification period, and as such a flexible approach to setting sufficient time frames should be adopted.[197] In the *Aarhus Convention Compliance Committee Case*

---

191 *Aarhus Convention Compliance Committee Case Concerning Armenia*, ACCC/C/2009/43, ECE/MP.PP/2011/11/Add.1, April 2011, para. 70.

192 ACCC/2006/16; ECE/MP.PP/2008/5/Add.6, 4 April 2008.

193 Ibid. at para. 67.

194 For example, the Compliance Committee states at para. 67, "Therefore, if the chosen way of informing the public about possibilities to participate in the EIA procedure is via publishing information in local press, much more effective would be publishing a notification in a popular daily local newspaper rather than in a weekly official journal, and if all local newspapers are issued only on a weekly basis, the requirement of being "effective" established by the Convention would be met by choosing rather the one with the circulation of 1,500 copies rather than the one with a circulation of 500 copies."

195 See *supra* note 52, *Aarhus Convention Compliance Committee Case Concerning Armenia*, ACCC/C/2009/43, ECE/MP.PP/2011/11/Add.1, April 2011, para. 70.

196 *Aarhus Convention Compliance Committee Case Concerning Lithuania*, ACCC/2006/16; ECE/MP.PP/2008/5/Add.6, 4 April 2008, para. 67.

197 *Aarhus Convention Compliance Committee Case Concerning Belarus*, ACCC/C/2009/37, ECE/MP.PP/2011/11/Add.2, April 2011, para. 89.

Concerning Armenia[198] the Compliance Committee stated that the time needed from the moment of the notification until the hearing, in which the public concerned would be expected to participate in an informed manner, depends on the size and the complexity of the case.[199] So where in that case, the public was given one week in which to review voluminous, technical EIA documentation for a mining project, the Compliance Committee found that the State failed to give early notice and allow the public to participate in an effective manner.[200]

Scope of Public Participation

In the *Aarhus Convention Compliance Committee Case Concerning France*,[201] the Compliance Committee held that effective participation does not solely depend on the number of inquiries, but on the adequacy of the information given to the public in response to inquiries, and that public participation takes place in a transparent and open manner.[202]

The principle was further explored in the IACHR *Case of the Saramaka People v Suriname*.[203] There, the State failed to conduct environmental or social impact assessments before granting logging and mining concessions on territory possessed by the Saramaka people. In so doing, it failed to consider the special relationship between the Saramaka People and their ancestral territory, and thus the scale of impact the proposed activity would have on that indigenous community. In its judgment, the IACHR expanded on the meaning of States' obligations to facilitate public participation, and in the interest of fairness and equality, the IACHR imposed even more burdensome requirements on the State where indigenous groups are involved. It held that effective participation must include consultation with the community according to its customs and traditions.[204] The IACHR's guidelines on conducting public consultations are instructive.[205] Consultations must:

a) Be in good faith, with the objective of reaching agreement;
b) Be at the early stages of a development or investment plan to allow for consideration and discussion within the community, and not only when the need arises to obtain approval from the community;
c) Include an account of the possible risks, including environmental and health risks; through culturally appropriate procedures;

---

198 ACCC/C/2009/43, ECE/MP.PP/2011/11/Add.1, April 2011.
199 Ibid. at para. 65.
200 Ibid. at para. 67.
201 ACCC/C/2007/22, ECE/MP.PP/C.1/2009/4/Add.1, 8 February 2011.
202 Ibid. at para. 43.
203 *Case of the Saramaka People v Suriname*, Judgment of 28 November 2007, Tribunal: Inter-American Court of Human Rights, Year of Decision: 2007.
204 Ibid. at para. 133.
205 Ibid.

d)   Facilitate constant communication between the parties – the State must both accept and disseminate information; and
e)   Be in accordance with the customs and traditional methods of decision-making of the community.

Further, where the proposed development is likely to have significant impacts within indigenous territories, the State has an additional responsibility to obtain the free, prior and informed consent of that indigenous group, according to the customs and traditions.[206]

The Aarhus Convention Compliance Committee also expanded on the sufficiency of public participation in cases where a fragmented approach has been taken to obtaining permission for a major development, for example where a development entails several permitting decisions. In the *Aarhus Convention Compliance Committee Case Concerning the European Community*,[207] the Compliance Committee implemented a simple test in determining whether the requirement for public participation in environmental decision-making has been properly adhered to: does the permitting decision, or range of permitting decisions, to which all the elements of the public participation procedure apply (set out in Article 6 of the Aarhus Convention[208]), embrace all the basic parameters and main environmental implications of the proposed activity in question?[209] According to the Compliance Committee, the test issue must be examined on a case-by-case basis, and even where public participation has taken place on one environmentally-related permitting decision, if there are permitting decisions which may have adverse environmental impacts for which no public participation has taken place, a State would have failed to fulfil its obligations on public participation under the Aarhus Convention.[210]

8. Access to Justice

Rules of governance that require that the public have access to information and be allowed to participate in decision-making are only so effective as the procedures in place to protect these rights, should they be abrogated or infringed. Thus, individuals must have access to recourse in circumstances where their rights have been violated.

In *Giacomelli v Italy*,[211] the ECHR noted that an individual must have the opportunity to appeal to a court where he finds that his interests have not been properly considered in the decision-making process.[212] In *Claude-Reyes*

---

206 Ibid. at para. 134.
207 ACCC/C/2006/17, ECE/MP.PP/2008/5/Add.10, 2 May 2008.
208 See *supra* note 207, article 6.
209 Ibid. at para. 43.
210 Ibid.
211 *Giacomelli v Italy, supra* note 158.
212 Ibid. at para. 83.

et al. v Chile,[213] the IACHR required that State parties establish effective recourse by law and ensure due implementation.[214] In justifying its position, it stated:

> Safeguarding the individual from the arbitrary exercise of public authority is the main purpose of the international protection of human rights. The inexistence of effective domestic recourses places the individual in a state of defenselessness.[215]

The ACHPR also ruled on the issue to the right to access to justice provided under the African Charter on Human and Peoples' Rights in *Kenneth Good v Republic of Botswana*,[216] concerning sections of the Botswana Immigration Act which prevented any person declared by the President to be a prohibited immigrant from questioning or appealing such declaration.[217] The court held,

> The right to be heard requires that the Complainant has unfettered access to a tribunal of competent jurisdiction to hear his case. It also requires that the matter be brought before a tribunal with the competent jurisdiction to hear the case. A tribunal which is competent in law to hear a case has been given that power by law: it has jurisdiction over the subject matter and the person. Where authorities put obstacles on the way which prevent victims from accessing the competent tribunals or which oust the jurisdiction of judicial organs to hear alleged violations of human rights, they would be denying victims of human rights violations the right to have their causes heard.[218]

The ACHPR further held that the right to a fair trial, which includes the right to be heard, to be informed of reasons and to seek recourse, is an absolute right that cannot be derogated from in any circumstance.[219] As such, certain sections of the Botswana Immigration Act were therefore contrary to Article 7 of the African Charter on Human and Peoples' Rights.[220]

213 *Claude Reyes et al. v Chile, supra* note 17.
214 Ibid. at para. 130.
215 Ibid. at para. 129.
216 Comm. 313/05, 28th ACHPR AAR Annex (Nov 2009–May 2010) available at http://www.worldcourts.com/achpr/eng/decisions/2010.05_Good_v_Botswana.htm.
217 Ibid. at para. 166.
218 Ibid. at para. 169.
219 Ibid. at para. 175.
220 Article 7 of the African Charter on Human and Peoples' Rights provides:

  1   Every individual shall have the right to have his cause heard. This comprises:

   a)   The right to an appeal to competent national organs against acts of violating his fundamental rights as recognized and guaranteed by conventions, laws, regulations and customs in force;
   b)   The right to be presumed innocent until proved guilty by a competent court or tribunal;
   c)   The right to defence, including the right to be defended by counsel of his choice;
   d)   The right to be tried within a reasonable time by an impartial court or tribunal.

As a corollary to the right to access to justice, the ACHPR found that the independence of the judiciary is essential. In *Malawi African Association v Mauritania*,[221] legislation sought to place the authority to try certain criminal matters on three appointed members of the military. The Court held that withdrawing criminal procedure from the Court's jurisdiction and conferring it onto the executive compromises the independence and impartiality of the courts, thereby violating article 7 of the African Charter on Human and Peoples' Rights.[222]

In *Amnesty International v Sudan*,[223] the ACHPR also held that the right to freely choose one's counsel is essential to the assurance of a fair trial.[224] Thus, the establishment of an independent objective system for regulating and licensing advocates is also a necessary requirement of this right.[225]

In *The Mayagna (Sumo) Awas Tingni Community v Nicaragua*,[226] the IACHR went further to emphasise that for a recourse for a breach of a human right to exist, it is not enough that it be established formally by law, but the State must ensure that such recourse is "effective"[227] and it provides "everything necessary to remedy it."[228]

The IACHR judgment in the *Case of the Yakye Axa Indigenous Community v Paraguay*[229] expanded on the meaning of "effective" remedies, and also drew particular references to the context of indigenous groups. In determining whether the remedies provided by the State were "effective", the Court deemed it necessary to first examine whether recourse was formally provided, and then determine whether the recourse could be deemed to be effective.[230] In considering whether recourse was formally provided, the court analysed the various stages of the administrative proceedings required by the State.[231]

Moving on to its consideration of whether "effective" recourse was available, the Court clearly stated that in providing effective protection "the specific characteristics that differentiate the members of the indigenous peoples from

---

2   No one may be condemned for an act or omission which did not constitute a legally punishable offence at the time it was committed. No penalty may be inflicted for an offence for which no provision was made at the time it was committed. Punishment is personal and can be imposed only on the offender.

221   Comm. 54/91, 61/91, 98/93, 164/97, 196/97, 210/98, 13th ACHPR AAR Annex V (1999–2000), available at http://www.worldcourts.com/achpr/eng/decisions/2000.05.11_Malawi_African_Association_v_Mauritania.htm.

222   Ibid. at para. 98.

223   48/90, 50/91, 52/91, 89/93, 13th ACHPR AAR Annex V (1999–2000), available at http://www.worldcourts.com/achpr/eng/decisions/1999.11_Amnesty_International_v_Sudan.htm.

224   Ibid. at para. 68.

225   Ibid.

226   (Ser. C No. 79), Tribunal: Inter-American Court of Human Rights, Year of Decision: 2001.

227   Ibid. at para. 114.

228   Ibid. at para. 113.

229   (Ser. C) No. 125, Judgment of 15 June 2005, Tribunal: Inter-American Court of Human Rights, Year of Decision: 2005.

230   Ibid. at paras 64–5.

231   Ibid.

the general population and that constitute their cultural identity must be taken into account."[232] For a remedy to be effective, it must also allow redress within a "reasonable term", which considers a) complexity of matter, b) procedural initiative of interested party and c) conduct of the judicial authorities.[233] In the instant case, the Court held that a protracted delay of eleven years and eight months that passed was in itself a violation of the right to fair trial.[234] It stated that there is a violation of Article 25 (Right to Judicial Protection) of the American Convention whenever delays in the administrative procedures are produced, not by the complexity of the case, but by the systematically delayed actions of the State authorities.[235] It further held that Article 1(1) (obligation to respect rights and to ensure free and full exercise of those rights and freedoms) places the State under the obligation to ensure that procedures for recourse are accessible and simple and that the bodies in charge of them have the necessary technical and material conditions to provide a timely response to the requests made in the framework of said procedures.[236] This reasoning was also mirrored in IACHR *Case of the Saramaka People v Suriname*.[237]

International courts and tribunals have been particularly active in upholding the right to access to information, public participation and access to redress guaranteed under their respective conventions. These rights are essentially reflected in the Aarhus Convention, and aim at protecting the right of an individual to a healthy environment and promoting sustainable development. The ILA New Delhi Declaration 2002 went even further to and placed an even greater degree of significance and priority on public participation and access to justice by establishing it as one of the seven principles of sustainable development.

Past cases in the IACHR, ECHR, ACHPR and the Aarhus Compliance Committee have produced significant jurisprudence and guidance in determining the scope of the right and circumstances which constitute a violation of such rights. Cases have linked the freedom of access to information as essential to the realisation of the right to freedom of expression. They also underscore the importance of full and free access to information in facilitating the public's ability of the public to participate in environmental decision-making. Due to the proliferation of cases being brought by indigenous groups, the IACHR's decisions are especially instructive on the need to tailor the application of such guarantees to the customs and traditions of indigenous peoples. Courts have also demonstrated the need to give strict protection to the rights of public access and participation and a reluctance to admit restrictions to such rights, save only in exceptional circumstances.

Further, the principles of public participation and access to justice and information have also been defined and activated by the World Trade Organization

---

232 Ibid. at para. 51.
233 Ibid. at para. 65.
234 Ibid. at para. 86.
235 Ibid. at para. 88.
236 Ibid. at para. 102.
237 See *supra* note 203 at paras 177–8.

(WTO) Appellate Body, the North American Free Trade Agreement (NAFTA) Tribunals and the International Centre for Settlement of Investment Disputes (ICSID) Tribunals.

9. Access to information

Access to information, also referred to as transparency, in any dispute settlement system is fundamental to democratic governance today. It includes procedural and substantive transparency. The former relates not only to the publication of awards and access to pre-award submissions from the parties and to decisions made by the tribunal over the course of the proceedings but also to public admittance to the tribunal hearings.[238] The latter relates to the dispute settlement bodies interpreting substantive treaty provisions in light of the transparency principle.

a. Transparency as a principle

The international trade and investment dispute settlement bodies directly linked transparency to the fundamental international law principle of due process and gave transparency a very prominent role in interpreting the relevant substantive legal standards and the WTO Appellate Body in *US-Underwear* dispute pointed out that Article X: 2 of the GATT 1994 "maybe seen to embody a principle of fundamental importance – that of promoting full disclosure of government acts affecting Members and private persons and enterprises, whether of domestic or foreign nationality."[239] It explicitly affirmed the due process dimensions of transparency and further elaborated its essential implication, i.e., "Members and other persons affected, or likely to be affected, by governmental measures imposing restraints, requirements and other burdens, should have a reasonable opportunity to acquire authentic information about such measures and accordingly to protect and adjust their activities or alternatively to seek modification of such measures."[240]

In *US-Shrimp* dispute, the Appellate Body, explicitly stated that Article X:3 of the GATT 1994 establishes minimum standards for transparency and procedural fairness and further argued that the non-transparent and ex parte nature of the internal governmental procedures as well as the fact that countries whose applications are denied do not receive formal notice of such denial, nor the reasons for the denial, and the fact, too, that there is no formal legal procedure for review of, or appeal from, a denial of an application, are all contrary to the spirit, of Article X:3 of the GATT 1994.[241]

---

238 Tienhaara Kyla (2009), *The Expropriation of Environmental Governance: Protecting Foreign Investors at the Expense of Public Policy*, Cambridge University Press, at p. 131.

239 Appellate Body Report, *US-Restrictions on Imports of Cotton and Man-made Fibre Underwear*, WT/DS24/AB/R, 1997, at p. 21.

240 Ibid.

241 Appellate Body Report, *US-Import Prohibition of Certain Shrimp and Shrimp Products*, WT/DS 58/AB/R, 1998, para. 183.

In *Metalclad v Mexico*, the NAFTA Tribunal – an arbitration tribunal established under Chapter 11 of NAFTA – stated that the principle of transparency includes the idea that all relevant legal requirements of one Party for the purpose of initiating, completing and successfully operating investments made, or intended to be made, should be capable of being readily known to all affected investors of another Party.[242] The Tribunal further argued that it is State's "duty to ensure that the correct position is promptly determined and clearly stated so that investors can proceed with all appropriate expedition in the confident belief that they are acting in accordance with all relevant laws".[243]

b. Procedural transparency

Turn to procedural transparency, efforts to increase such transparency have been made in the relevant tribunals.

Access to documents

Even though it codifies the GATT practice of keeping proceedings confidential, the Understanding on Rules and Procedures Governing the Settlement of Disputes (DSU) does include improvements in providing access to information in the World Trade Organization (WTO) dispute settlement. According to the DSU, a party to a dispute may disclose statements of its own positions to the public and shall provide a non-confidential summary of its publication for public disclosure upon request of a Member.[244] In the *Hormones Sanctions disputes* (DS 320 and DS 321), the Appellate Body argued that "public disclosure of Appellate Body reports is an inherent and necessary feature of our rules based system of adjudication."[245]

In the NAFTA case of *Methanex Corpoaration v United States of America*, the Tribunal found that it had no power to accept the Petitioners' requests to receive materials generated within the arbitration, yet, such materials may however be derived from the public domain or disclosed into the public domain within the terms of the Consent Order regarding Disclosure and Confidentiality, or otherwise lawfully.[246] Yet, following the adoption of notes of interpretation regarding access to documents by the Free Trade Commission (FTC) in 2001,

242 *Metalclad Corporation v the United Mexican States*, ICSID, Case No. ARB (AF)/97/1, NAFTA Award of 30 August 2000, para. 76.

243 Ibid.

244 The Understanding on Rules and Procedures Governing the Settlement of Disputes (DSU), Annex 2 of the WTO Agreement, Annex 2 of the WTO Agreement, WTO, 1994, article 18(2).

245 Appellate Body Procedural Ruling, Procedural Ruling of 10 July to Allow Public Observation of the Oral Hearing, *United States – Continued Suspension of Obligations in the EC-Hormones Dispute* (AB-2008-5), *Canada – Continued Suspension of Obligations in the EC-Hormones Dispute* (AB-2008-6), 10 July 2008, para. 5.

246 *Methanex Corpoaration v United States of America*, NAFTA, Decision of the Tribunal on Petitions from Third Persons to Intervene as "Amici Curiae", 2001, para. 47.

each party agreed to make available to the public in a timely manner all documents submitted to, or issued by, a Chapter 11 Tribunal.[247]

In the *Biwater* case, the ICSID Tribunal imposed certain limitations on disclosure of documents in order to preserve the integrity of the process of the time being in its Procedural Order No. 3. [248] The Arbitral Tribunal in Procedural Order No. 5 noticed that the broad policy issues concerning sustainable development, environment, human rights and governmental policy addressed by the petitioners fall within the ambit relevant ICSID Rules (Rule 37 (2)(a)).[249] Yet, it further argued that the broad issues on which the Petitioners are especially qualified are ones which are in the public domain, and about which each Petitioner is already very well acquainted.[250] Accordingly the Petitioners' application for access to the documents filed by the parties was once again denied.

The Tribunal in the *Suez* case argued that the Petitioners propose to offer views to the Tribunal on general issues which *per se* do not require comprehensive information of the factual basis of this case and noted that the NGOs had already gained much information about the case from other sources.[251] Accordingly, the Tribunal considers that the Petitioners can fully carry out that function without access to the record.[252] Nevertheless, the Tribunal points out that "as a general proposition, amicus curiae must have sufficient information on the subject matter of the dispute to provide perspectives, expertise and arguments that are pertinent and thus likely to be of assistance to the Tribunal".[253]

Public hearings

The WTO dispute settlement proceedings being held behind the doors can be traced back to the old GATT era. In response to a joint request by the parties (the US, Canada and EC), the panel hearings of the disputes *US-Continued Suspension of Obligations* and *Canada- Continued Suspension of Obligations* were open to the public which was the first time in GATT/WTO history. The panel kept in mind that "the issue of transparency of panel and Appellate Body proceedings is currently under review as part of the negotiations on improvements and clarifications

---

247 Subject to the reaction of: confidential business information; information which is privileged or otherwise protected from disclosure under the Party's domestic law, and information which the Party must withhold pursuant to the relevant arbitral rules, as applied; NAFTA Free Trade Commission, Notes of Interpretation of Certain Chapter 11 Provisions, 31 July 2001, available at http://www.international.gc.ca/trade-agreements-accords-commerciaux/disp-diff/NAFTA-Interpr.aspx?lang=en&view=d.

248 *Biwater Gauff (Tanzania) LTD. v Tanzania*, Procedural Order NO. 5, ICSID Case No. ARB/05/22, 2007, para. 66.

249 Ibid. at para. 64.

250 Ibid. at para. 65.

251 *Suez, Sociedad General de Aguas de Barcelona, S.A., and Vivendi Universal S.A. v Argentina*, Order in Response to a Petition by Five Non-Governmental Organizations for Permission to Make an Amicus Curiae Submission, ICSID Case No. ARB/03/19, 2007, para. 25.

252 Ibid. at para. 25.

253 Ibid. at para. 24.

of the DSU".²⁵⁴ It recalled "the dispute settlement system of the WTO serves to preserve the rights and obligations of Members under the covered agreements, which included the DSU, and to clarify the existing provisions of those agreements in accordance with customary rules of interpretation of pubic international law"²⁵⁵ and found that open panel hearings are compatible with the DSU.²⁵⁶ Subsequent panels have always agreed to open their hearings when the parties jointly made such a request, without entering again into the question of legality under the DSU.²⁵⁷

The Appellate Body decided to open to the public for the first time an oral open hearing in the *Hormones Sanctions disputes* (DS 320 and DS 321). Canada and several other WTO Members consider that open hearings are an important contribution to the legitimacy and the perception of legitimacy of the WTO dispute settlement system.²⁵⁸ Accordingly, the Appellate Body issued the procedure ruling to allow public observation of the oral hearing, finding that it has the power to authorize the lifting of confidentiality at the joint request of the participants as long as this does not adversely affect the rights and interests of the third participants or the integrity of the appellate process.²⁵⁹

Upon the consent of parties, the hearings of investment disputes could be open to the public under the UNCITRAL and ICSID arbitration rules.²⁶⁰ Canada, the US (in 2003) and Mexico (in 2004) decided to support open hearings in NAFTA investor-state disputes through affirming that it will consent, and will request the consent of disputing investors and, as applicable, tribunals, that hearings in Chapter 11 dispute to which it is a party be open for the public, except to ensure the protection of confidential information, including confidential business information.²⁶¹ Learning from experiences of NAFTA, many bilateral investment

254 Panel Report, *US – Continued Suspension of Obligations in the EC-Hormones Dispute*, WT/DS 320/R, 31 March 2008, para. 7.52.

255 Ibid.

256 Ibid. at para. 7.43–7.53.

257 Request for an Open Appellate Hearing by the European Communities, *US – Continued Suspension of Obligations in the EC-Hormones Dispute* & *Canada – Continued Suspension of Obligations in the EC-Hormones Dispute*, in the World Trade Organization before the Appellate Body, available at http://trade.ec.europa.eu/doclib/docs/2008/july/tradoc_139528.pdf.

258 Appellate Body Report, *US – Continued Suspension of Obligations in the EC-Hormones Dispute*, WT/DS 320/AB/R, 16 October 2008, para. 145.

259 Appellate Body Procedural Ruling, Procedural Ruling of 10 July to Allow Public Observation of the Oral Hearing, *US – Continued Suspension of Obligations in the EC-Hormones Dispute* (AB-2008-5), *Canada – Continued Suspension of Obligations in the EC-Hormones Dispute* (AB-2008-6), 10 July 2008, para. 7.

260 Article 25 (4) of the UNCITRAL Arbitration Rules stipulates that "Hearing shall be held in cameras unless the parties agree otherwise"; Article 32 (2) of the 2006 ICSID Arbitration Rules reads: "unless either party objects, the Tribunal . . . may allow other persons, besides the parties, to attend or observe all or part of the hearings . . .".

261 Office of the United States Trade Representative, NAFTA Commission Announces New Transparency Measures, October 2003, available at http://www.ustr.gov/about-us/press-office/press-releases/archives/2003/october/nafta-commission-announces-new-transparent; Foreign Affairs and International Trade Canada, NAFTA Free Trade Commission Joint Statement: Decade of Achievement, 16 July 2004, available at http://www.international.gc.ca/trade-agreements-accords-commerciaux/agr-acc/nafta-alena/JS-SanAntonio.aspx?lang=en&view=d.

treaties (BITs) or investment chapters in FTAs, e.g., US model BIT and Canadian Model FTA, provided that the tribunal shall conduct hearings open to the public.[262] The Tribunal in the *Suez* case noticed that the *Methanex* case and *UPS* case (both NAFTA cases under UNCITRAL Arbitrations Rules) involved public hearings, both parties having consented to allowing the public to attend the hearings while the crucial element of consent by both parties to the dispute in the case in question was absent.[263] Yet, the Tribunal did argue that "public acceptance of the legitimacy of international arbitral processes, particularly when they involve states and matters of public interest, is strengthened by increased openness and increased knowledge as to how these processes function".[264]

10. Public Participation

The past twenty years have seen a rapid increase in the number of trade disputes which has opened the door to the civil society. In the *US-Shrimp* dispute, the WTO Appellate Body affirmed Member's right to attach amicus curiae brief to its own submissions.[265] As far as separate amicus curiae briefs are concerned, the Appellate Body considered that the panel had the discretionary authority either to accept and consider or to reject information and advice submitted to it, whether requested by a panel or not.[266] In subsequent cases, the Panels often accepted the information submitted by the amici curiae (mainly university professors and environmental or public interest NGOs), yet, the Panel sometimes found it unnecessary to take the amicus curiae briefs into account, e.g., the *EC-biotech* dispute;[267] or invited the parties and third parties to express their views on how it should handle the amicus briefs and decided that it would not further consider the argument of the brief to the extent that the parties reflected those arguments in their written submissions and/or oral statements, e.g., the *US-Zeroing* dispute.[268]

---

262 For instance, Canada-Columbia FTA, Chapter 8, Art. 830 (2), Canada-Peru FTA, Chapter 8, Art. 835 (1)–(2). The US has committed to open hearings in all of its recently negotiated BITs and investment chapters in FTA (with Chile, Singapore, Uruguay, Peru, Colombia, the Central American countries and the Dominican Republic). See Natalie Bernasconi-Osterwalder and Lise Johnson, Transparency in the Dispute Settlement Process: Country Best Practices, The International Institute for Sustainable Development, Feburary 2011, at p. 8.

263 *Suez, Sociedad General de Aguas de Barcelona, S.A., and Vivendi Universal S.A. v Argentina*, Order in Response to a Petition by Five Non-Governmental Organizations for Permission to Make an Amicus Curiae Submission, ICSID Case No. ARB/03/19, para. 4.

264 Ibid. at para. 22.

265 "We consider that the attaching of a brief or other material to the submission of either appellant or appellee, no matter how or where such material may have originated, renders that material at least *prima facie* an integral part of the participant's submission"; Appellate Body Report, *US – Import Prohibition of Certain Shrimp and Shrimp Products*, WT/DS 58/ AB/R, 12 October 1998, para. 89.

266 Ibid. at para. 108.

267 Panel Report, *EC – Measures Affecting the Approval and Marketing of Biotech Products*, WT/DS 291/R, WT/DS 292/R, WT/DS 293/R, 29 September 2006, paras 7.10 and 7.11.

268 Panel Report, *US – Laws, Regulations and Methodology for Calculating Dumping Margins ("Zeroing")*, WT/DS 294/R, 31 October 2005, para. 1.7.

The Appellate Body in the *US-Lead and Bismuth II* case noticed the DSU and the *Working Procedures* are silent on the matter of unsolicited briefs and further found that "we have the legal authority to decide whether or not to accept and consider any information that we believe is pertinent and useful in an appeal".[269] In the *EC-Asbestos* dispute, the Appellate Body in the interests of fairness and orderly procedure, decided to adopt additional procedures which allows any person, whether natural or legal, other than a party or a third party to the dispute, wishing to file a written brief to apply for leave to file such a brief.[270] The Appellate Body in *EC-Sardines* reaffirmed their authority to receive an amicus curiae brief from a private individual or an organization and inferred that they are entitled to accept such a brief from a WTO Member.[271] They further stressed that acceptance of any amicus curiae brief is a matter of discretion, which they will exercise on a case-by-case basis and they could exercise their discretion to reject an amicus curiae brief if, by accepting it, this would interfere with the "fair, prompt and effective resolution of trade disputes".[272]

Civil society involvement in the WTO dispute settlement system has triggered similar developments in international investment law. Amicus curiae briefs have been filed and admitted in the NAFTA and ICSID arbitral tribunals.

Neither the UNCITAL Arbitration Rules nor Chapter 11 of the NAFTA Agreement contain express provision on non-disputing party participation. Following the case law of Iran-US Claims Tribunal and the practice of the WTO Appellate Body, the NAFTA arbitral tribunal in *Methanex* for the first time decided that it had the power to accept amicus briefs. In this case, the Tribunal noticed the Petitioners' argument that there was an increased urgency in the need for amicus participation in the light of the award dated 30th August 2000 in *Metalclad Corporation v United Mexican States* and an alleged failure to consider environmental and sustainable development goals in that NAFTA arbitration.[273] It further emphasized that the case concerned a matter of public interest "not merely because one of the Disputing Parties is a State", but also because its subject matter concerns public interest.[274] The Tribunal also argued that "the Chapter 11 arbitral process could benefit from being perceived as more open or transparent;" and "the Tribunal's willingness to receive amicus submissions might support the process in general and this arbitration in particular; whereas a blanket refusal could do positive harm".[275] Accordingly, the Tribunal allowed the Petitioners to

269   Appellate Body Report, *US-Imposition of Countervailing Duties on Certain Hot-Rolled Lead and Bismuth Carbon Steel Products Originating in the United Kingdom*, WT/DS 138/AB/R, 10 May 2000, para. 39.

270   Appellate Body Report, *EC – Measures Affecting Asbestos and Asbestos-Containing Products*, WT/DS 135/AB/R, 12 March 2001, para. 52.

271   Appellate Body Report, *EC – Trade Description of Sardines*, WT/DS 231/AB/R, 26 September 2002, para. 164.

272   Ibid. at para. 167.

273   *Methanex Corpoaration v United States of America*, NAFTA, Decision of the Tribunal on Petitions from Third Persons to Intervene as "Amici Curiae", 2001, para. 6.

274   Ibid. at para. 49.

275   Ibid. at para. 49.

make amicus written submissions.[276] In October 2011, the Tribunal of the *United Parcel Services* (UPS) largely followed the *Methanex* approach and accepted the amicus curiae brief by the Canadian Union of Postal Workers and the Council of Canadians which represents Canadian postal workers' labor interests.

The NAFTA Free Trade Commission issued a statement on non-party participation in Chapter 11 disputes on 7 October 2003.[277] According to the statement, any non-disputing party that is a person of a Party, or that has a significant presence in the territory of a Party, that wishes to file a written submission with the Tribunal (the "application") will apply for leave from the Tribunal to file such a submission. In determining whether to grant leave to file a non-disputing party submission, the Tribunal will consider, among other things, the extent to which: ". . . (d) There is a public interest in the subject-matter of the arbitration". Relying on this guideline, the NAFTA Tribunal in *Glamis* decided to accept the amicus curiae brief by a tribal community – the Quechan Indian Nation and several NGOs.[278]

The initial ICSID arbitration rules are silent on permitting or prohibiting the submission by nonparties of amicus curiae briefs or other documents. This silence did not prevent tribunals from accepting amicus curiae briefs. The first case in which the Arbitral Tribunal granted a nonparty to a dispute the status of amicus curiae and accepted amicus curiae submission is the *Suez/Vivendi* dispute. In its Order of 19 May 2005, the Tribunal unanimously concludes that Article 44 of the ICSID Convention grants it the power to admit amicus curiae submissions from suitable nonparties in appropriate cases.[279] With respect to "appropriateness", the Tribunal first found that the present case potentially involves matters of public interest as it will consider the legality under international law of various actions and measures taken by governments.[280] It further noticed that in this particular case, the investment dispute centers around the water distribution and sewage systems providing basic services to millions people and as a result may raise a variety of complex public and international law questions, including human rights considerations.[281] Accordingly, the Tribunal found that "this case does involve matters of public interest of such a nature that have traditionally led courts and other tribunals to receive amicus submissions from suitable nonparties".[282]

---

276 The petitioners in this case are the International Institute for Sustainable Development, Communities for a Better Environment and the Earth Island Institute.

277 NAFTA Free Trade Commission, Statement of the Free Trade Commission on non-disputing party participation "Celebrating NAFTA at Ten" NAFTA Commission Meeting, 7 October 2003, available at http://www.international.gc.ca/trade-agreements-accords-commerciaux/agr-acc/nafta-alena/nafta_commission.aspx?view=d (accessed on 11 Feb 2012).

278 *Glamis Gold, Ltd., Claimant v The United States of America*, Respondent, Decision on Application and Submission by Quechan Indian Nation, NAFTA, 16 September 2005, para. 2.

279 *Aguas Argentinas, S.A., Suez, Sociedad General de Aguas de Barcelona, S.A., and Vivendi Universal S.A. v Argentina*, Order in Response to a Petition by Five Non-Governmental Organizations for Permission to Make an Amicus Curiae Submission, ICSID Case No. ARB/03/19, 2005, para. 16.

280 Ibid. at para. 19.

281 Ibid.

282 Ibid. at para. 20.

The Tribunal further argued that the acceptance of amicus submissions would have the additional desirable consequence of increasing the transparency of investor-state arbitration.[283]

This order reflects a tendency toward greater transparency and openness in investment treaty arbitration. This tendency has led to a formal amendment of the ICSID Arbitration Rules in April 2006. The new Arbitration Rule 37 (2) provided that "After consulting both parties, the Tribunal may allow a person or entity that is not a party to the dispute . . . to file a written submission with the Tribunal regarding a matter within the scope of the dispute . . ." In other words, it explicitly permits non-disputing party participation. This new procedural rule is frequently referred in the subsequent cases, for instance, the *Biwater Gauff* case. In *Biwater Gauff*, the Petitioners argued that "this arbitration process goes far beyond merely resolving commercial or private conflicts, but rather has a substantial influence on the population's ability to enjoy basic human rights. Therefore, the process should be transparent and permit citizens' participation."[284] The Arbitral Tribunal has carefully considered each of the conditions in Rule 37 (2) (a), (b) and (c), and it is of the view that "it may benefit from a written submission by the Petitioners, and that allowing for the making of such submission by these entities in these proceedings is an important element in the overall discharge of the Arbitral Tribunal's mandate, and in securing wider confidence in the arbitral process itself."[285] Interesting to note that, in the Award, issued on 24 July 2008, the *Biwater* Tribunal extensively referred to the amicus curiae submission and found the *amici's* observations useful and that the submission informed the analysis of claims.[286]

10.1 The Principle of Good Governance

The principle of good governance has a central place in the New Delhi Declaration as a formative principle in the legal architecture of sustainable development. As the Declaration states, 'good governance is essential to the progressive development and codification of international law relating to sustainable development'. Aspects of this include democratic and transparent decision-making (including the full participation of all major groups), the observation of due process and the respect for human rights, and greater moves towards corporate social and investment responsibility. In and of themselves, each of these themes has been the subject of substantive debate over many years, with progress being seen in numerous ways – though undoubtedly that must be set against the general trend of increased marginalisation of many of the issue raised by sustainable development.

283 Ibid. at para. 22.
284 *Biwater Gauff (Tanzania) LTD., v United Republic of Tanzania*, Procedural Order No. 5, ICSID Case No. ARB/05/22, 2 February 2007, para. 14.
285 Ibid. at para. 50.
286 *Biwater Gauff (Tanzania) LTD., v United Republic of Tanzania*, Award, ICSID Case No. ARB/05/22, 24 July 2008, para. 392.

Though the concept itself is not without conceptual difficulties, there is arguably sufficient clarity around the idea to understand the core of the principle. As the ILA Committee on Legal Aspects of Sustainable Development noted in its 2002 report, 'Its exact contents may not be very clear in the discourse of politics and development studies. Yet, as a legal concept it has found a place in . . . legally relevant documents . . . The concept of good governance can well be instrumental in integrating the various dimensions of the concept of sustainable development'.[287]

Where, perhaps, progress has been much less conspicuous has been in the judicial endorsement of the notion of good governance as a central theme of sustainable development. Nevertheless, though judicial authority is sparse, it is not entirely absent. The 2011 *Seabed Mining Advisory Opinion* utilises the language of good governance, and in two different – but equally important – senses. First, in discussing its own role in the advisory opinion, and implicitly more widely in dispute settlement, the Chamber noted that "[t]he functions of the Chamber . . . are relevant for the good governance of the Area", going on to point out "by answering the questions it will assist the Council in the performance of its activities and contribute to the implementation of the Convention's regime".[288] Although a *sine qua non*, this aspect of good governance of natural resource management is easily forgotten, namely the role of judicial bodies to utilise general principles and the rule of law both to resolve disputes (i.e., its contentious jurisdiction)[289] and, as in the present Advisory Opinion, to assist political bodies in the accomplishment of their duties by acting as an 'independent and impartial body.[290]

Secondly, the Chamber arguably relied upon the tenets of good governance when considering the measures necessary for a sponsoring State to undertake to accomplish *domestically* its international obligations of diligence obligation. A central point was whether a State could achieve its obligation to regulate contractors purely through the means of private law and contractual relations. The Chamber ruled that it could not, relying upon good governance justifications for the enactment of law, over and above mere contracts, and then outlining (within the confines of its judicial role) some of the general principles that should guide the content of the law and regulations. As it says, '[t]he "contract approach" would, moreover, lack transparency. It will be difficult to verify, through publicly available measures, that the sponsoring State had met its obligations'.[291] On the question of the content of such binding rules, the Chamber also gives

---

287 2002 ILA Report, pp. 396–97.
288 *Advisory Opinion, supra* note 70, paras 29–30.
289 T. Stephens, 'Sustainability Discourses in International Courts: What Place for Global Justice?' in D. French (ed.), *Global Justice and Sustainable Development* (Leiden/Boston: Martinus Nijhoff, 2010) 56: 'Fairness and justice, notions that underlie not only sustainability, but also principles of equity that have long been applicable in the resolution of disputes over natural resources . . . there remain many opportunities for their deployment to resolve fractious disputes over natural resources at a time of growing scarcity and accelerating environmental degradation'.
290 *Advisory Opinion, supra* note 70, para. 26.
291 *Advisory Opinion, supra* note 70, para. 225.

some direction to sponsoring States as to the content of the measures which would 'enable it to discharge its responsibilities'.[292] The Chamber is keen to stress it will not interfere in legitimate areas of State discretion; '[p]olicy choices on such matters must be made by the sponsoring State' – to do otherwise would run the risk of the Chamber as a '[j]udicial bod[y] [to] perform functions that are not in keeping with . . . [its] judicial character'.[293] In particular, the Chamber makes comments of certain 'general considerations that a sponsoring State may find useful',[294] which are worth quoting in full:

> . . . the sponsoring State must take into account, objectively, the relevant options in a manner that is reasonable, relevant and conducive to the benefit of mankind as a whole. It must act in good faith, especially when its action is likely to affect prejudicially the interests of mankind as a whole . . . Reasonableness and non-arbitrariness must remain the hallmarks of any action taken by the sponsoring State.[295]

This seems very sensible in tone, if slightly abstract in nature. Undoubtedly, the special nature of the Area as common heritage of mankind has significantly influenced the Chamber in this regard. Thus, it might be thought that it has little general relevance to the due diligence obligation, for instance, of States in regulating transboundary hazards. Nevertheless, one can see similarities with the *dicta* of the International Court of Justice in the *Pulp Mills* case in which it spoke of due diligence being 'an obligation which entails not only the adoption of appropriate rules and measures, but also a certain level of vigilance in their enforcement'.[296] Thus to the extent that the Chamber's references to reasonableness, non-arbitrariness and good faith have generic relevance, this aspect of the Advisory Opinion can be seen to have broader appeal and support the judicial endorsement of good governance more widely.

10.2 The Principle of Integration and Interrelationship

The principle of integration is an essential element of the international law of sustainable development, highlighting the importance of process as well as substance in the attainment of sustainable development goals. As one commentator has said, '[t]o operationalize sustainable development, we need to recognize that one principle – integrated decision-making – holds the other principles together'.[297] The notion of integrating environmental considerations into economic planning can be traced back, on the international level, at least as far back as Principles 13 and 14

---

292 *Advisory Opinion, supra* note 70, para. 227.
293 Ibid.
294 Ibid.
295 *Advisory Opinion, supra* note 70, para. 230.
296 *Case Concerning Pulp Mills, supra* note 136, para. 197.
297 See J. Dernbach, "Achieving Sustainable Development: The Centrality and Multiple Facets of Integrated Decisionmaking" 10 *Ind. J. Global Legal Stud.* (2003) 248.

of the 1972 Stockholm Declaration on the Human Environment, which advocated an 'integrated and coordinated approach to their development planning', also as an important tool 'for reconciling any conflict between economic development and environmental protection. Similarly, though not identical, wording can be found in almost all subsequent international policy documents on the issue, including the 1982 World Charter for Nature,[298] 1987 report of World Commission on Environment and Development,[299] and significantly at the 1992 Rio Conference on Environment and Development in both *Agenda 21*[300] and – in a much abbreviated form – in Principle 4 of the 1992 Rio Declaration, which must be taken to provide the internationally-agreed reference-point on the issue, stating that '[i]n order to achieve sustainable development, environmental protection shall constitute an integral part of the development process and cannot be considered in isolation from it'.

Paragraph 7 of the ILA's 2002 New Delhi Declaration emphasizes that integration is required not only between economic and environmental considerations, but additionally among human rights and social objectives, all of which are components of sustainable development. To this end, decision-making should be integrated both in process and outcome at all relevant levels – global, regional, national, sub-national and local. At the 2006 ILA Toronto Conference, the Committee focused on the Principle of Integration and Interrelationship, suggesting that it may be understood as encompassing three complementary dimensions, referred to as 'systemic', 'institutional' and 'legal' integration. In its 'systemic' dimension, integration is an overarching conceptual framework for sustainable development, a macro-vision whereby integration incorporates the very essence of sustainable development. This perspective can be perceived in Vice-President Weeramantry's opinion in the *Gabčíkovo-Nagymaros* case:

> After the early formulations of the concept of development, it has been recognized that development cannot be pursued to such a point as to result in substantial damage to the environment within which it is to occur. Therefore development can only be prosecuted in harmony with the reasonable demands of environmental protection. Whether development is sustainable by reason of its impact on the environment will, of course, be a question to be answered in the context of the particular situation involved.

It is thus the correct formulation of the right to development that that right does not exist in the absolute sense, but is relative always to its tolerance by the environment. The right to development as thus refined is clearly part of modern international law. It is compendiously referred to as sustainable development'.[301]

---

298 GA Res. 37/7, 28 October 1982, Principle 7: 'In the planning and implementation of social and economic development activities, due account shall be taken of the fact that the conservation of nature is an integral part of those activities'.

298 GA Res. 37/7, 28 October 1982, Principle 7: 'In the planning and implementation of social and economic development activities, due account shall be taken of the fact that the conservation of nature is an integral part of those activities'.
299 World Commission on Environment and Development (WCED); *Our Common Future* (Oxford, OUP, 1987) 62–65.
300 See, in particular, Chapter 8: Integrating Environment and Development in Decision-Making.
301 ICJ Reports (1997) 92.

A further example of this systemic dimension of integration can be seen in the WTO's 2001 Doha Ministerial Declaration: '[w]e are convinced that the aims of upholding and safeguarding an open and non-discriminatory multilateral trading system, and acting for the protection of the environment and the promotion of sustainable development can and must be mutually supportive'.[302]

Systemic integration remains, however, somewhat removed from the practical realities of integration. 'Institutional' integration addresses these more intensively, by promoting the establishment or strengthening of institutional structures and procedures that fully integrate environmental and developmental issues in all spheres of decision-making. In this context, specific mention may be made of the evolution of the environmental impact assessment (EIA) procedure, which as a specific application of the integration principle was given discrete mention within the Rio Declaration,[303] and has evolved and been subsequently refined over the years, in both domestic[304] and international law,[305] as one of the most powerful integrative tools currently available to decision-makers. As Judge Weeramantry said of the role environmental impact assessment should play in the decision-making process, '[o]f course the situation may well be proved to be otherwise and fears currently expressed may prove to be groundless. But that stage is reached *only after* the Environmental Impact Assessment and *not before*'.[306] Environmental impact assessments thus put into practice the theory, and have often proved an effective technique in not only incorporating the range of issues to be considered within the decision-making process, but equally importantly, in addressing them in a proactive, and potentially preventative, manner.

The third and final dimension of the principle is 'legal' integration, in which the concept of integration has the power to harmonize different norms (e.g., rules applicable to international investment protection, on one hand,

---

302 WT/MIN(01)/DEC/1, 20 November 2001, para. 6.

303 See Principle 17: 'Environmental impact assessment, as a national instrument, shall be undertaken for proposed activities that are likely to have a significant adverse impact on the environment and are subject to a decision of a competent national authority'.

304 See J. Holder, *Environmental Assessment: The Regulation of Decision Making* (Oxford: OUP, 2004).

305 Instances include the 1991 Espoo Convention on Environmental Impact Assessment in a Transboundary Context, 1991 Madrid Protocol on Environmental Protection to the 1959 Antarctic Treaty, Annex I and 2001 Draft Convention on Prevention of Transboundary Harm from Hazardous Activities, article 7. K. Gray, 'The Internationalization of Environmental Impact Assessment: Potential for a Multilateral Environmental Agreement' 11 *Colo. J. Int'l Envtl. L. and Pol'y.* (2000) 101. Mention should also be made of the development of other forms of impact assessment including social and human rights considerations.

306 *Request for an Examination of the Situation in accordance with Paragraph 63 of the Court's Judgment of 20th December 1974 in the Nuclear Tests Case (New Zealand v France)* ICJ Reports (1995) 345, emphasis added. H.E. Judge C. G. Weeramantry was, in fact, considering the role the 'principle' of EIA should have in the judicial decision-making process, which is debatable. Nevertheless, the general view expressed as to the importance of EIAs is surely correct. He returned to the issue of EIA in his separate opinion in *Case Concerning Gabčíkovo-Nagymaros Project (Hungary/Slovakia)* (1997) ICJ Reports 111–13, in which he discussed the importance of 'continuing EIAs'.

and international environmental law, on the other) or to serve as a judicial reasoning tool. In these respects, it is important that the language of Principle 4 'lends itself to legal interpretation and practical application', [307] perhaps more so than other principles of sustainable development. Indeed, as evidenced by the references from jurisprudence above, the Principle of Integration has been applied by the International Court, most clearly in the *Gabčíkovo-Nagymaros* case.

The principle has even more expressly been referred to and applied by the Permanent Court of Arbitration, which in the *Arbitration regarding the Iron Rhine Railway (Belgium/The Netherlands)* (2005) noted that:

> [b]oth international and EC law require the integration of appropriate environmental measures in the design and implementation of economic development activities . . . Environmental law and the law on development stand not as alternatives but as mutually reinforcing, integral concepts, which require that where development may cause significant harm to the environment there is a duty to prevent, or at least mitigate, such harm (paragraph 59).

The WTO Appellate Body has explicitly referred to the principle of integration, among others principles of the Rio Declaration, in the *Shrimp dispute*.[308] It did so in interpreting the WTO Ministerial Decision on Trade and the Environment,[309] and the WTO Agreement itself, in the context of its Preamble which refers to sustainable development. As the WTO Appellate Body noted:

> The preamble of the *WTO Agreement* — which informs not only the GATT 1994, but also the other covered agreements — explicitly acknowledges 'the objective of sustainable development' . . .[310]

The WTO's explanatory note in this decision deserves particular attention. The AB refers to the *objective* of sustainable development, explaining that '[t]his *concept* has been generally accepted as integrating economic *and* social development *and* environmental protection'[311] (emphasis added). This is remarkable. It can

---

307 P. Sands, 'International Law in the Field of Sustainable Development' LXV *British Yearbook of International Law* (1994) 338; M. C. Cordonier Segger and A. Khalfan, *Sustainable Development Law: Principles, Practices and Prospects* (Oxford: OUP, 2004) 35–140.

308 *US – Import Prohibition of Certain Shrimp and Shrimp Products* WT/DS58/AB/R, 12 October 1998, footnote 147.

309 Adopted by Ministers at the Meeting of the Trade Negotiations Committee Marrakesh, 14 April 1994.

310 WTO, *US – Import Prohibition of Certain Shrimp and Shrimp Products – Report of the Panel* (15 May 1998) WT/DS58/R; WTO, *US – Import Prohibition of Certain Shrimp and Shrimp Products – Report of the Appellate Body* (6 November 1998) Doc.WT/DS58/AB/R, 123, Note 107.

311 Ibid. WTO, *US – Shrimp–Appellate Body Report* 123.

be argued that the AB recognised in principle the need to integrate all three elements or 'pillars' of sustainable development – social development, economic development and environmental protection, and did so in order to achieve a WTO sustainable development purpose.[312]

Indeed, the Appellate Body's analysis in the *Shrimp dispute* can be seen as an indirect implementation of the principle in a number of ways – its recognition of sustainable development as an objective informing all of WTO law, its interpretation of the term 'exhaustible natural resources' in Article XX(g) GATT to also cover living resources, and its understanding that the US should have examined alternative measures in cooperation with foreign countries before launching an export restriction.

This small accumulation of international jurisprudence relating to the Principle of Integration attests to its relative robustness.

2012 SOFIA GUIDING STATEMENTS

on the Judicial Elaboration of the 2002 New Delhi Declaration of Principles of International Law relating to Sustainable Development

Purpose

The purpose of the Guiding Statements is to provide further elucidation of the 2002 New Delhi Declaration of Principles of International Law relating to Sustainable Development, recognising the significant judicial developments that have occurred over the last 10 years.

Interpretation

The Guiding Statements must be read alongside the 2002 New Delhi Declaration and be considered supplementary to it.

The Guiding Statements have been elaborated to support the continued development of the seven principles of the New Delhi Declaration and thus must not be read restrictively or unduly literally.

The Guiding Statements are to be construed in the spirit of the New Delhi Declaration, recognising that the principles are inter-related and that each principle must be read in the context of the other principles.

The Guiding Statements are not reflective of all developments since the New Delhi Declaration but may be considered as representing key trends and other themes since 2002.

312 See *supra* note 13.

Guiding Statements

1) Recourse to the concept of 'sustainable development' in international case-law may, over time, justify a hardening of the concept itself into a principle of international law, despite a continued and genuine reluctance to formalise a distinctive legal status;

2) Treaties and rules of customary international law should, as far as possible, be interpreted in the light of principles of sustainable development and interpretations which might seem to undermine the goal of sustainable development should only take precedence where to do otherwise would be to undermine territorial boundaries and other fundamental aspects of the global legal order, would otherwise infringe the express wording of a treaty or would breach a rule of *jus cogens*;

3) As a matter of common concern, the sustainable use of all natural resources represents an emerging rule of general customary law, with particular normative precision identifiable with respect to shared and common natural resources;

4) The principle of equity (incorporating notions of intergenerational equity, intragenerational equity and substantive equality) and the goal of the eradication of poverty should, where appropriate, contextualise and inform judicial and quasi-judicial decision-making when matters of sustainable development are raised. Though judicial bodies and quasi-judicial bodies cannot alone address the social, economic, governance and political issues that invariably form key aspects of such disputes, it is nevertheless incumbent upon judicial and quasi-judicial bodies to further such principles of equity and fairness in accordance with their judicial function;

5) The principle of common but differentiated responsibilities has a recognised status in treaty law, case law and State practice but would be strengthened as a normative feature of sustainable development if there was further reliance upon it by judicial bodies, thus allowing the legal principle to consolidate and be legally embedded as distinctive from the political discourse in which it is most often and currently utilised;

6) The precautionary principle has significant and increasingly precise legal implications, notwithstanding ongoing debate surrounding its formal legal status;

7) The principle of public participation and access to information and justice are foundational to sustainable development, and judicial and quasi-judicial bodies must seek to affirm this further in both their substantive decisions and, as applicable, as elements of their own procedure;

8) Though the principle of good governance has remained largely outside the jurisprudence of the International Court of Justice, elements of the principle can be seen in various judicial and quasi-judicial bodies and this should be endorsed more broadly;

9) The principle of integration and interrelationship is the primary means by which courts and tribunals provide an overarching conceptual framework for

sustainable development, and the expectations of standards of due process, integrative decision-making and good faith negotiations (all of which support the principle of integration) should be further strengthened;

10) Environmental impact assessment is a mandatory rule of customary international law and must be recognised by judicial bodies especially in all matters affecting shared and common natural resources, and where there is a risk of transboundary and global environmental harm.

8 The principles of sustainable development in the case concerning *Pulp Mills on the River Uruguay*

Dire Tladi

8.1 Introduction

Sustainable development evolved to facilitate a paradigm shift from one where economic concerns trumped social and environmental concerns to one where all three concerns were accounted for.[1] The facts of the case concerning *Pulp Mills on the River Uruguay* (hereinafter the *Pulp Mills* case), in which Argentina argued that pulp mills constructed by Uruguay on a shared river were harmful quintessentially reflected the tension between the values of sustainable development.[2] In particular, the consistency with sustainable development of the construction of the pulp mills along the river was at issue.

Perhaps no other case since the *Gabčíkovo-Nagymaros* case has afforded the International Court of Justice with the opportunity to develop the principles relating to sustainable development like the *Pulp Mills* case.[3] As with the *Gabčíkovo-Nagymaros* case, the *Pulp Mills* case involves the interpretation of a treaty on the utilization of a shared river – in the *Gabčíkovo-Nagymaros* case it was the River Danube and in the *Pulp Mills* case it is the River Uruguay. Moreover, both cases involve projects with economic benefits which, purportedly for environmental reasons, one state sought to have stopped. While *Pulp Mills* has yet to generate as much attention as *Gabčíkovo-Nagymaros* – particularly the celebrated separate opinion of then Vice-President of the Court Judge Weeramantry in the *Gabčíkovo-Nagymaros* – the *Pulp Mills* case is as revealing in regards to the complexities of sustainable development and the approach of the Court as was the *Gabčíkovo-Nagymaros* case.[4] As with the *Gabčíkovo-Nagymaros* case, the *Pulp*

---

1 Dire Tladi, *Sustainable Development in International Law: An Analysis of Key Enviro-Economic Instruments* (Pretoria: Pretoria University Law Press, 2007) 34.
2 *Case Concerning Pulp Mills on the River Uruguay* [2010] ICJ Rep 14.
3 *Case Concerning the Gabčíkovo-Nagymaros Project (Hungary v Slovenia)* [1997] ICJ Rep 7. See especially the celebrated separate opinion of then Vice-President of the Court, H. E. Judge C. G. Weeramantry.
4 For commentary on the *Gabčíkovo-Nagymaros* case see, e.g. Vaughn Lowe, 'Sustainable Development and Unsustainable Arguments' in Alan Boyle and David Freestone, eds., *International Law and Sustainable Development* (Oxford: OUP, 1999); Owen McIntyre, 'Environmental Protection of International Rivers' (1998) 10 *J. Envtl. L.* 79; Johan G. Lammers, 'Case Analysis: The Gabčíkovo-Nagymaros Case Seen in Particular From the Perspective of the

Mills case produced a number of minority and separate opinions, one or two of which could still receive significant scholarly attention in the future.

Since *Gabčíkovo-Nagymaros*, there have been many developments that have contributed to the development of international law relating to sustainable development. There have been decisions in national, regional and international courts and tribunals on sustainable development.[5] International organizations have adopted and elaborated more instruments encapsulating the principles of sustainable development.[6] Civil society has adopted instruments on sustainable development, including the International Law Association's New Delhi Declaration on Sustainable Development. Numerous books and academic contributions on the subject have been published.[7] There has thus been a wealth of material developed and produced since *Gabčíkovo-Nagymaros* that could have contributed to the ICJ's consideration of the legal arguments in the *Pulp Mills* case. The *Pulp Mills* case was thus an opportunity to contribute to the further evolution of sustainable development as a concept, ideology or principle whose objective is to usher in a new paradigm of integrating of environmental, social and economic considerations.

This chapter provides an analysis of the ICJ's consideration of the principles relevant to sustainable development in the *Pulp Mills* case and, in particular, assesses the contribution of the case to the evolution of sustainable development. While the *Pulp Mills* case touches on a number of interesting international law questions, particularly in relation to the interpretation of treaties and the consequences of breaches of treaty obligations, the purpose of this chapter is limited to principles of sustainable development and how the ICJ interacts with them. I am also not concerned with whether Uruguay did or did not breach any of its obligations or whether there was sufficient evidence of pollution or not. These questions, while relevant for the proper disposal of the case, fall outside the scope of this chapter.

Law of International Watercourses and the Protection of the Environment' (1998) 11 *Leiden J. Int'l L.* 287. See, for commentary on the *Pulp Mills* case Owen McIntyre, 'The Proceduralisation and Growing Maturity of International Water Law' (2010) 22 *J. Envtl. L.* 475.

5 See, as examples of international cases relevant for sustainable development, *Regarding the Iron Rhine ('IJzeren Rijn') Railway (Belgium v Netherlands)* (Arbitral Award); *Advisory Opinion on the Responsibilities and Obligations of States Sponsoring Persons and Entities with Respect to Activities in the Area* (Seabed Disputes Chamber of the International Tribunal for the Law of the Sea).

6 See, e.g. Cartagena Protocol on Biosafety to the Convention on Biological Diversity 2000; Nagoya-Kuala Lumpur Supplementary Protocol on Liability and Redress to the Cartagena Protocol on Biosafety 2010; Stockholm Convention on Persistent Organic Pollutants 2001.

7 See, e.g. Alan Boyle and David Freestone, *International Law and Sustainable Development: Past Achievements and Future Challenges* (Oxford: OUP, 1999); Nico J. Schrijver and Friedl Weiss, *International Law And Sustainable Development: Principles And Practice* (The Netherlands: Martinus Nijhoff Publishers, 2004); David Freestone and Charlotte Streck, eds., *Legal Aspects Of Implementing The Kyoto Protocol Mechanisms: Making Kyoto Work* (Oxford: OUP, 2005); Daniel Bodansky, Jutta Brunnée and Ellen Hey, *The Oxford Handbook of International Environmental Law* (Oxford: OUP, 2007); Duncan French, *Global Justice and Sustainable Development* (The Netherlands: Martinus Nijhoff Publishers, 2010).

8.2 The judgment of the ICJ

8.2.1 The facts

From the judgment of the ICJ the facts can briefly be summarized as follows: The 1961 bilateral treaty between Uruguay and Argentina (hereinafter the Montevideo Treaty) defines the River Uruguay as a boundary between the two countries. Article 7 of the Montevideo Treaty makes provision for the two states to establish a 'régime for the use of the river'. The regime contemplated by Article 7 of the Montevideo Treaty was put in place by the 1975 Statute of the River Uruguay (hereinafter the '1975 Statute'). It is this Statute which Argentina alleged was breached by Uruguay.

It is useful to sketch out a few of the provisions of the 1975 Statute having a bearing on the Court's approach to sustainable development. The purpose of the 1975 Statute is described in Article 1 as being to 'establish the joint machinery necessary for the optimum and rational utilization of the River Uruguay, in strict observance of the rights and obligations arising from treaties and other international agreements in force for each of the parties'. Articles 7 to 12 of the 1975 Statute establish several procedural obligations to meet the objective spelt out in Article 1. Article 7 provides that if one of the Parties plans any project which may 'affect navigation, the régime of the river or the quality of its waters, it shall notify' a commission set up to facilitate coordination between the parties (hereinafter CARU) and the latter should notify the other party. Articles 8, 9 and 10 provide for exchanges between the Parties to determine whether the planned project would be detrimental to the regime of the river. Article 11 provides that if the notified Party comes to the conclusion that indeed the planned project 'might significantly impair navigation, the régime of the river or the quality of its waters', it should notify the other Party and provide information on the aspects of the project that it finds objectionable and the changes that could made to improve the project. Article 12 provides that if, following any consultations, the Parties fail to reach agreement on how to proceed, the dispute settlement mechanism should be followed, i.e. the matter should be referred to the ICJ.

Moreover, under Article 41 of the 1975 Statute, the Parties undertake certain specific substantive obligations. First, the Parties undertake 'to protect and preserve the aquatic environment and, in particular, to prevent its pollution, by prescribing appropriate rules and measures in accordance with applicable international agreements'. In Article 35 the Parties agree to adopt measures to ensure that the management of the soil and woodlands and the use of the groundwater and waters of the river 'do not cause changes which may significantly impair the régime of the river or the quality of its waters'. Article 36 creates an obligation for the Parties to coordinate measures to avoid changes to the ecological balance of the river. Finally Article 27 provides that the right of each Party to use the waters of the river within its jurisdiction 'shall be exercised without prejudice to the application of the procedure' in Article 7 to 12.

Against this background, Uruguay authorized the construction of two pulp mills along the banks of the river, namely the ENCE Mill and the Botnia Mill. It appears from the facts as summarized by the ICJ that Uruguay gave authorization for the construction of the two pulp mills without having fully exhausted the communication process provided for in Articles 7 to 12, although the construction of the ENCE mill was eventually discontinued. In the case of ENCE, CARU received knowledge of the project not from Uruguay but from a Spanish entity formed to build the mill. Furthermore, only after several requests for information on the project were made by CARU did Uruguay transmit to CARU a summary for public release of an environmental impact study. Moreover, Uruguay granted an initial authorization for the construction of the project prior to the submission of the relevant information and, in any event, prior to the approval by and/or consent of either CARU or Argentina.

The Botnia project, it appeared, proceeded much along the same lines as the ENCE project. CARU were informed of the project informally by the representatives of the entity responsible for building the mill. Again it appears that Uruguay granted environmental authorization prior to providing CARU or Argentina with certain information, notwithstanding repeated requests from CARU. Subsequently, and before the conclusion of the consultations, Uruguay authorized the construction of the mill which was completed together with several associated facilities.

8.2.2 Sustainable development in the ICJ's judgment

The ICJ found that Uruguay failed to comply with the procedural obligations to inform CARU and Argentina of the planned activities along the river. However, the Court found that there was no violation of any of the substantive obligations relating to the protection of the environment. It is, however, the manner in which the Court interacts with various provisions of the 1975 Treaty and key concepts related to sustainable development that is the focus of my attention.

That Uruguay had breached its procedural obligations was never in doubt. Indeed it appears that even Uruguay expected the ICJ to find that it was in breach of the procedural obligations.[8] The key issue in dispute was the consequence of the breach of procedural obligations for the substantive obligations and whether the Court should order the cessation of the project. For Argentina, the breach of the procedural obligations implied at the same time a breach of the substantive obligations. Moreover, Argentina argued, based on Articles 1 and 41, that norms of international environmental agreements should be applied in determining whether there were breaches. Responding to these questions, the Court refers to several concepts associated with sustainable development.

The Court refers to 'sustainable development' in the context of assessing the relationship between the procedural obligations and the substantive obligations.

8 See generally Uruguay's prayers in *Case Concerning Pulp Mills on the River Uruguay, supra* note 2 [23].

It notes that under the 1975 Statute, the 'optimum and rational utilization' of the river is to be achieved through cooperation and the procedures laid down in Article 7 to 12. The Court then quotes from its judgment in the *Gabčíkovo-Nagymaros* case in which, having noted that 'this need to reconcile economic development with protection of the environment is aptly expressed in the concept of sustainable development', it opined that 'it is for the Parties themselves to find an agreed solution that takes account of the objectives of the Treaty'.[9] It is apparent that for the Court cooperation is a critical element for the proper implementation of the Treaty and, to this end, the Court continues that 'it is by cooperating that the States can jointly manage the risks of damage to the environment'.

While the Court finds that the two categories of obligations 'complement one another perfectly' and that there is 'functional link' between them, there is a clear sense that it is the procedural obligations, at least in the case under consideration, that are more important or, at any rate, more at issue in the case.[10] Contrasting the two sets of obligations, the Court states that while 'substantive obligations are frequently worded in broad terms, the procedural obligations are narrower and more specific, *so as to facilitate the implementation of the 1975 Statute.*'[11] For the Court, therefore, cooperation, which is the essence of the procedural obligation laid out in Articles 7 to 12, is key for the sustainable management of the River Uruguay. Along this line, the Court considers that the River Uruguay 'can only be protected through close and continuous co-operation between the riparian states.'[12]

The obligation to inform under Article 8 is seen as an integral part of the cooperation referred to by the Court. The critical question is the content of the information and the time when the information should be provided. In considering these questions, the Court refers to the 'principle of prevention', which obliges states to 'use all the means at its disposal in order to avoid causing significant damage to the environment of another State', which it considers to be part of international law.[13] The procedural obligations created in the Statute are thus presented as giving effect to this principle of prevention.[14] It is only through prompt notification that CARU can assess whether the activities could cause

9 Ibid. at 77.
10 Ibid.
11 Ibid. (emphasis added).
12 Ibid. at 81.
13 Ibid. at 101.This principle has strong foundations in international law. See, e.g. *Corfu Channel* case *(United Kingdom v Albania)* [1948] ICJ 15, 124 Reporter 22; *Legality of the Threat or Use of Nuclear Weapons, Advisory Opinion* [1996] ICJ Rep 226. See also *Trail Smelter* case *(United States v Canada)* [1941] Rep Int Arbitr Awards 1905, 1965. This principle forms the basis of a proposal by a group of States to have the General Assembly resolution request an advisory opinion from the International Court of Justice on obligations of State with respect to climate change. The principle is also reflected in Article 194 of the UN Convention on the Law of the Sea. See also Principle 1 of the New Delhi Declaration of Principles of International Law Relating to Sustainable Development; Principle 2 of the Rio Declaration on Environment, New Delhi Declaration, ILA Rep. 2002.; Development and Principle 21 of the Stockholm Declaration on the Human Environment, ibid.
14 *Case Concerning Pulp Mills on the River Uruguay, supra* note 2 [102].

damage to the environment of Argentina and thereby initiate the process to prevent the damage.[15] The Court, based on the principle of prevention, concludes that the notification should be submitted early, as soon as the party intending to initiate the activity is in possession of a 'plan which is sufficiently developed', and certainly before a decision has been made on the environmental viability of the project.[16]

An important question that the Court had to consider was whether, at the end of the consultation period in Article 12, there was an obligation on Uruguay to discontinue the construction of the mills. The dilemma here is clear. To provide for such a 'no-construction' obligation would essentially be to grant a veto to one riparian state over development projects of the other riparian state. On the other hand, to dismiss such an obligation could potentially be to render the process ineffective because the State authorizing the project would have carte blanche to implement unsustainable projects once the period had elapsed. The Court considered that the procedural obligations in the Statute did not create a 'no construction obligation' once the consultation period had elapsed.[17] What the Court does not address, at least not explicitly, is whether the preventative principle in any way affects the obligations of the parties subsequent to the consultation period. In particular if, as the Court had suggested, the procedural obligations are expressive of the preventative principle, what role, if any, should the preventative principle have in interpreting the content and breadth of the parties' obligations, and the consequences of the breach of such obligations?

Argentina had argued that Uruguay was in breach of several substantive obligations including the obligation to contribute to the optimum and rational use of the river (Article 1), the obligation to ensure that the management of the soil and woodlands does not impair the quality of the river (Article 35) and the obligation to prevent pollution and preserve the aquatic environment (Article 41). On each of these the Court found there to be no violation. However, assessing each of these claims provided the Court an opportunity to comment on several sustainable development-related principles.

One of the most important principles considered by the Court, in the context of assessment of the scientific evidence and the burden of proof, was that of precaution. Argentina and Uruguay had made several arguments concerning the precautionary principle, with the former arguing that the precautionary principle implies a reversal of the burden of proof or that the burden applies equally to both parties. The Court's view of 'the precautionary approach' is that 'while [it] may be relevant in the interpretation and application of the provisions of the Statute, it does not follow that it operates as a reversal of the burden of proof.'[18] According to the Court, absent the 1975 Treaty reversing the burden of proof or placing the burden equally on the Parties, the burden remains on the party asserting breach of

15 Ibid. at 105.
16 Ibid. at 105, 120.
17 Ibid. at 157.
18 Ibid. at 164.

the environmental obligations.[19] What the Court does not do is explain how, in its assessment, the precautionary approach applies and how it affects the interpretation of the 1975 Treaty, if at all, and the disposition of the case.

As for sustainable development itself, the Court does refer to it in the course of the judgment. At several places in assessing whether the breach of the procedural violations amounted to a breach of the obligation to contribute to the optimum and rational utilization of the river, the Court stresses the need to balance economic and environmental interests – classic sustainable development-speak. The Court, for example, states that the

> Attainment of optimum and rational utilization requires a *balance* between the Parties' rights and needs to use the river for economic and commercial activities on the one hand, and the obligation to protect it from any damage to the environment that may be caused by such activities.[20]

Elsewhere, the Court notes that the formulation of Article 27 of the Treaty reflects both the 'need to reconcile the varied interests of riparian States' and the 'need to *strike a balance* between the use of the waters and the protection of the river consistent with the objectives of sustainable development'.[21] Finally, on this theme, the Court opines that Article 27 'embodies [the] interconnectedness between equitable and reasonable utilization of a shared resource and the *balance* between economic development and environmental protection that is the essence of *sustainable development*.'[22] However, as with precaution, these references are never integrated into the Court's assessment of the law and facts and, consequently, we are deprived of a glimpse into the Court's attitude towards sustainable development.

Perhaps the most significant contribution of the judgment to sustainable development is the Court's statement on environmental impact assessments. In connection with the obligation to prevent pollution and preserve the aquatic environment, the Court determines that there is a general requirement to conduct environmental impact assessments for planned activities. This requirement, which the Court determines to have gained 'so much acceptance among States' that it now forms part of the corpus of international law, has to be used to interpret the provisions of Article 41 of the 1975.[23] The Court also stated that environmental impact assessments have to be performed prior to the implementation of the project and that once the implementation commences there should be continuous monitoring of the environmental effects.[24] The significance of the Court's conclusion on environmental impact assessments is that while the Court refers to environmental impact assessments in the context of Article 41, it essentially

19 Ibid.
20 Ibid. at 175 (emphasis added).
21 Ibid. at 177 (emphasis added).
22 Ibid. (emphasis added).
23 Ibid. at 204.
24 Ibid. at 205.

endorses the idea as a general requirement of international law in relation to shared watercourses, presumably even outside the confines of treaty law.

As to the content and scope of the environmental impact assessment the Court finds that 'neither the 1975 Statute nor general international law specify the scope and content'.[25] Consequently, the Court decided that 'it is for each State to determine in its domestic legislation. . . the specific content of the environmental impact assessment' taking into account 'the nature and magnitude' of the planned activity as well the likely adverse impact on the environment.[26] With respect to Argentina's arguments that the environmental impact assessment should have considered alternative sites for the mills, the Court adopts a two-track rebuttal.[27] First, consistent with the conclusion that international law does not lay down requirements for the content and scope of the environmental impact assessment, the Court suggests that there is no obligation to consider alternative sites. Second, the Court concludes that it is 'not convinced' that an assessment of alternative was not carried out.[28] The Court adopts a similar approach with respect to the need to consult affected populations, noting first that there was no obligation to consult affected communities and secondly that Uruguay did consult affected communities.[29] While the Court's determination that the requirement for environmental impact assessments was part of customary international law is a significant contribution to the law on sustainable development, the Court could have gone further to ensuring the quality of the environmental impact assessments by setting minimum requirements for the scope and content.

Much of the judgment in relation to the impact of discharges on the quality of the river's effects on biodiversity and air pollution is focused on assessment of the facts and scientific evidence – something this author is not competent to comment on and which, in any event, falls outside the scope of this chapter. Nonetheless, the Court's conclusions in each of those areas provide us a glimmer into the Court's attitude to sustainable development. With respect to phosphorous, for example, having found that the total level of phosphorous exceeds the limits allowed in Uruguayan national legislation the Court determines the contribution of the Botnia mill is proportionately insignificant and that given the remedial action by Uruguay this did not constitute a violation of Article 41.[30] In the same vein, in relation to algal bloom the Court, after a brief summation of the Parties arguments, states that it has not been established 'to the satisfaction of the Court' that algal bloom was caused by discharges from the mill.[31] Similar responses are provided in respect of phenolic substances, nonyphenols and dioxins and furans.[32] With respect to harm to biodiversity, the Court, along the same lines, states that

25 Ibid.
26 Ibid.
27 Ibid. at 210.
28 Ibid.
29 Ibid. at 216, 219.
30 Ibid. at 247.
31 Ibid. at 250.
32 Ibid. at 254, 257, 259.

'the record shows that a clear relationship has not been established' between the mill and detected abnormalities in some fish species. Judges Al-Khasawneh and Simma described the judgment, particularly in relation to the consideration of Article 41, as 'terse and formalist'.[33] While this evaluation relates mainly to the manner in which the scientific evidence was evaluated, it could also be applied to the scant reliance on the principles of sustainable development. The question can be asked, for example, how these assessments would be affected by the application of the 'principle of prevention', the 'precautionary principle' or for that matter the 'objective of sustainable development'.

8.3 Sustainable development at the periphery

While the ICJ *refers* to the 'principle of precaution', 'precautionary approach' and the 'objective of sustainable development', there is a clear discomfort with these principles, or perhaps reluctance to fully embrace them. In particular, the Court never explores how these principles operate, their implications or even how they affect the given set of facts.

The first principle that the Court refers to is the principle of prevention, which as already described, has long standing roots in international law. The Court confirms what it had already determined in the *Advisory Opinion on Threat or Use of Nuclear Weapons,* namely that the principle is part of the body of international law relating to the environment.[34] Beyond a finding that the principle of prevention requires the information on any activity that may cause damage to be provided in a timely manner, the Court does not explore how, in other areas, the principle of prevention may affect the interpretation of the 1975 Treaty. More importantly, the implications of this principle, which the Court accepts to be a principle of customary international law, are not factored at all into the interpretation of the substantive obligations under the 1975 Treaty.

An even thriftier treatment is given to the precautionary principle. Leaving out the references to arguments of the parties, the Court refers to precaution only once.[35] Moreover, even the reference to precaution does not suggest that the Court deems it part of the body of international law, or at best the Court is non-committal. First, the Court refers to it not as the precautionary principle but as an 'approach'. Second, the Court considers that the precautionary approach 'may be' relevant, as opposed to 'is' relevant in the interpretation of the Statute. Third, the Court places emphasis not on how the precautionary principle is (or may be) relevant but rather on what it cannot do, namely operate 'as a reversal of the burden of proof'. The Court's reluctance to explore more fully the impact of precautionary principle on the case at hand is even more startling given that both parties accepted it as a principle of law, although they differed on its implications for the resolution of the case. The result of this approach is that

---

33 *Case Concerning Pulp Mills on the River Uruguay, supra* note 2 in separate opinion of Judge Khasawneh, 5.

34 See *supra* note 13

35 *Case Concerning Pulp Mills on the River Uruguay, supra* note 2 [164].

the Court does not, in considering whether the respective obligations under the 1975 Treaty have been violated, factor in the precautionary principle.

I pause here to refer the separate opinion of Judge Cançado Trindade which was particularly critical of the treatment of precaution and the principle of prevention by the Court. The separate opinion, which was reminiscent of H.E Judge C. G. Weeramantry's famous separate opinion in *Gabčíkovo-Nagymaros,* laments the fact that the Court did not show the same 'zeal and diligence' when dealing with legal principles as it did when assessing the factual and scientific questions.[36] Judge Cançado Trindade is in no doubt that both the precautionary principle and the principle of prevention are general principles of international environmental law and he repeats this assertion at various places in the separate opinion.[37] According to Judge Cançado Trindade these principles ought to have guided the Court in the interpretation and application of the 1975 Treaty, including in the determination of the factual questions.[38]

What flows from the separate opinion of Judge Cançado Trindade is that both principles ought to have been taken into account in determining not only whether the procedural obligations had been complied with, but also whether the substantive obligations had been complied with. This leads to the question of whether the assessments of the Court, both in terms of facts and law, relating to whether the mills would endanger the optimum and rational use of the river, impair the water quality of the river, or lead to pollution of the river and harm the aquatic environment would have been different had the Court factored these principles in more deliberatively. In truth, it is hard to say because the Court never appraises us of its understanding of the implications of the principles.

The precautionary principle illustrates this uncertainty well – the pun is intended. While the separate opinion of Judge Cançado Trindade presents an organized portrait of the law relating to precaution, the reality is closer to a messy collage.[39] What is clear from all the definitions of the precautionary principle is that it involves a balance between benefits, costs, risks, uncertainty, foreseeability, vulnerability and resilience amongst other factors.[40] When and how this balance is struck is less clear. Other uncertainties and contestation involve whether the precautionary principle permits or requires action.

The formulation of the precautionary principle relied on by Judge Cançado Trindade, Principle 15 of the Rio Declaration, is perhaps a good starting point to illustrate the uncertainties. Principle 15, as is now well known, provides that where 'there are threats of *serious or irreversible damage,* lack of *full scientific certainty* shall not be used a reason for postponing *cost-effective measures* to prevent

---

36 Ibid. at 4 in separate opinion of Cançado Trindade. See also the joint dissenting opinion Al-Khasawneh and Simma [27].

37 See, e.g. ibid. at 52, 100, 113 in the separate opinion of Cançado Trindade.

38 Ibid. at 99, 148 in the separate opinion of Cançado Trindade.

39 See generally for discussion of the possible understandings of precaution, the forthcoming report of the ILA Committee on Sustainable Development.

40 See, e.g. Jonathan B. Wiener, 'Precaution' in Daniel Bodansky, Jutta Brunnée and Ellen Hey, eds., *The Oxford Handbook of International Environmental Law* (Oxford: OUP, 2007) 599.

environmental degradation' (emphasis added). This formulation does not have an 'absolutist pretence' – the idea that all environmental risks deserve precautionary response measures at all costs.[41] The formulation is not absolutist, first, in the sense that it applies only to 'serious or irreversible damage' and thus there is a countenance of some level of damage. Second, the qualification of 'scientific certainty' by 'full' suggests a degree of probability or, at least, likelihood of the risk materializing before action is required. Finally, the obligation to take response measures is limited by the fact that only 'cost-effective' measures need be taken. Other international instruments, such as the 1990 Bergen Ministerial Declaration and the 1995 Fish Stocks Agreement, appear to adopt a more absolutist approach to the balancing process.[42]

Some assessment of these questions could have assisted the Court, whatever the final outcome, to provide a more reasoned response to the questions raised by the Parties. Depending on the Court's view on where and how the balance should be struck, the precautionary principle could have assisted the Court's evaluation of whether the mills posed a risk to the environment of the River Uruguay. Moreover, a more explicit reliance on precaution in the assessment of these and other questions in the case would contributed significantly to the clarification of some of the content of precaution as a legal concept.

Twelve years earlier, in the *Gabčíkovo-Nagymaros* case, the Court referred once to 'the concept of sustainable development', prompting H. E. Judge C. G. Weeramantry to pen his famous separate opinion making the case that sustainable development was 'more than a just concept' and that it was 'a principle with normative value'.[43] We have come full circle because in the *Pulp Mills* case the Court is unwilling to affirm sustainable development as a legal norm. The Court rather refers to sustainable development as an 'objective'.[44] More importantly, the value of sustainable development to the Court appears only to be that it is embodied in Article 27 of the 1975 Statute. What is not clear is whether sustainable development is at all relevant in deciphering the content of the Statute or determining the obligations of the parties. The separate opinion of Judge Cançado Trindade, however, refers to sustainable development as one of the principles of

---

41 Andre Nolkaemper, 'What You Risk Reveals What You Value, and Other Dilemmas Encountered in the Legal Assaults on Risks' in David Freestone and Ellen Hey, eds., *The Precautionary Principle and International Law: the Challenge of Implementation* (The Hague: Kluwer Law International, 1996).

42 See Bergen Ministerial Declaration on Sustainable Development in the ECE Region 1990 para. 7; see also Article 6 (2) of United Nations Agreement for the Implementation of the Provisions of the United Nations Convention on the Law of the Sea of 10 December 1982 Relating to the Conservation and Management of Straddling Fish Stocks and Highly Migratory Fish Stocks 1995. See also Cartagena Protocol on Biosafety to the Convention on Biological Diversity, *supra* note 6, which, while reaffirming Principle 15 of the Rio Declaration, itself adopts a different balancing approach. These instruments and their approach to the balancing act are described in the ILA Committee's report.

43 See *Case Concerning the Gabčíkovo-Nagymaros Project (Hungary v Slovenia)*, *supra* note 3 [88] separate opinion of then Vice-President H. E. Judge C. G. Weeramantry.

44 See ibid. at 177.

international environmental law.[45] The reluctance of the Court to acknowledge sustainable development as part of the body of law reflects the doubts and con-testations about the normative nature of sustainable development.[46]

That the Court considers sustainable development as an objective raises the question what the Court understands this objective to mean and how this under-standing influences its assessment of the facts and the law. The Court appears to conceptualize sustainable development as a tool to balance 'economic develop-ment and environmental protection'.[47] This understanding ignores the evolution of sustainable development, away from the binary approach of balancing eco-nomic development and environment, to one which recognizes that sustainable development aspires to *integrate* environmental, economic and social concerns.[48] The Court may well have understood social concerns as being subsumed under economic development, but this obfuscates the fact that while social and eco-nomic development issues are related, they are very different.[49]

In contrast, Judge Cançado Trindade conceptualizes sustainable develop-ment as 'encompassing the fostering of economic growth, the eradication of poverty and the satisfaction of basic human needs (such as those pertaining to health, nutrition, housing, education).'[50] This conceptualization is reflected in the manner that Judge Cançado Trindade takes into account the 'imperatives of human health and the well-being of peoples'.[51] The tendency not to account for social concerns in sustainable discourse – or to account for social concerns as an afterthought – is, unfortunately, prevalent in international law practice and law-making.[52] Judge Cançado Trindade describes the trumping of social and environmental concerns – the trumping of environmental concerns is reflected in the Court's judgment by the thrifty treatment given to precaution and the prin-ciple of prevention – as '*homo oeconomicus*'.[53]

---

45 Ibid. at 6 separate opinion of Cançado Trindade. See also ibid. at para. 132 *et seq.*

46 *Cf.* Lowe, *supra* note 4; C. G. Weeramantry, *Universalising International Law* (The Netherlands: Martinus Nijhoff Publishers, 2004) at 432; Tladi, *Sustainable Development in International Law*, *supra* note 1 at 94 *et seq.*

47 See *Case Concerning Pulp Mills on the River Uruguay*, *supra* note 2 [177]. See also Tim Stephens, 'Sustainability Discourses in International Courts: What Place for Global Justice?' in Duncan French, ed., *Global justice and sustainable development* (The Netherlands: Martinus Nijhoff Publishers, 2010).

48 See also Principle 7 of New Delhi Declaration of Principles of International Law Relating to Sustainable Development 2002. The implications of this move are considered in greater in detail in Tladi, *Sustainable Development in International Law*, *supra* note 1. See also Dire Tladi, 'Fuel Retailers, Sustainable Development and Integration: A Response to Feris' [2008] *Con. Court Rev.* 255.

49 See Tladi, *Sustainable Development in International Law*, *supra* note 1 at 78 *et seq*, especially at 81.

50 See *Case Concerning Pulp Mills on the River Uruguay*, *supra* note 2 at 132 [132] in the separate opinion of Cançado Trindade.

51 Ibid. at 153 *et seq.*

52 See Tladi, *supra* note 1 at 245 *et seq.* Tladi 'Sustainable Development, Integration and the Conflation of Values: The Fuel Retailers Case' in French, *supra* note 48 at 85 *et seq.*

53 *Case Concerning Pulp Mills on the River Uruguay*, *supra* note 2 at 155 in the separate opinion of Cançado Trindade.

The Court is quite clearly *aware* of sustainable development and related principles. However, there is clear unwillingness to fully integrate these concepts into the decision it reaches. The Court is content merely to refer to them, almost symbolically, without integrating them into decision. Thus we are never given a glimpse of how, or for that matter if, any of the principles of sustainable development impacted on, for example, the 'no-construction' obligation question, the impact of the mills on the environment, how the economic benefits of the mills relate to the allege environmental and social hazards and so on.

8.4 Conclusion

The case concerning *Pulp Mills on the River Uruguay* provided the Court with the opportunity to clarify, develop and elaborate the scope, application and even legal status of some important principles relating to sustainable development. The Court's statement that the requirement to conduct environmental impact assessments is part of customary international law is a significant contribution to the law on sustainable development. While the Court could not find its way to setting the parameters for a quality environmental impact assessment through the identification of minimum standards on scope and content, the mere recognition of this requirement as customary international law should not be minimized in the process towards mainstreaming sustainable development in international law.

However, by and large, the Court chose to decide the case without consideration of – much less reliance on – sustainable development-related principles. Whether the decision not to elaborate on sustainable development and related principles was a deliberate choice, whether it was as a result of the uncertainty surrounding the principles (both in terms of scope and legal status) or whether the Court just felt *this case* could be properly adjudicated without dwelling too much on these principles is not clear. Time will tell whether commentators and other courts will interpret the Court's decision not to dwell on sustainable development-related principles as a rejection of their relevance or not. I can only hope that, in assessing the Court's outlook, the separate opinion of Judge Cançado Trindade will not be overlooked.

9 Sustainable development law principles in the *Costa Rica v Nicaragua*[1] territorial disputes

Jorge Cabrera Medaglia and Miguel Saldivia Olave

9.1 Introduction

For the second time in less than two years, on 8 March 2011, the International Court of Justice (ICJ) ruled on a dispute between Costa Rica and Nicaragua. On the first occasion, the case arose from navigational and related rights of Costa Rica on the San Juan River. On the second occasion, the dispute mostly related to the territorial integrity of Costa Rica and to the environmental impacts of some

---

1 Since 2012 several legal developments have taken place: on 22 December 2011 Nicaragua filed an application and instituted proceedings against Costa Rica for 'violations of Nicaraguan sovereignty and major environmental damages on its territory', contending in particular that Costa Rica undertook construction works (a road named 'Route 1856') near the border between the countries along the San Juan River. Nicaragua further claimed that the construction of the road was causing ongoing damage to the river. On 17 April 2013, by two different orders, the ICJ joined the two cases alleging the 'principle of the sound administration of justice and with the need for judicial economy'. On 24 September 2013, Costa Rica filed a new Request for Provisional Measures in response to new and additional works carried out by Nicaragua on the disputed land (opening new channels or caños in the wetland). After holding the hearings on that request, the Court indicated the following provisional measures: 'a) it decided, unanimously, that Nicaragua should refrain from any dredging and other activities in the dispute territory, and should, in particular, refrain from work of any kind on the new two "caños" (channels); b) . . . that Nicaragua should fill the trench on the beach north of the eastern caño within two weeks for the date of the present order, immediately inform the Court of the completion of the filling of the trench and, within one week for the said completion, submit to it a report containing all the necessary details, including photographic evidence; c) it further found, unanimously, that except as needed for implementing the obligation under the previous point, Nicaragua, should (i) cause the removal from the dispute territory of any personnel, whether civilian, police or security and (ii) prevents any such personnel from entering the disputed territory; d) it also found, unanimously, that Nicaragua should cause the removal from and prevent the entrance into the dispute territory of any private persons under its jurisdiction or control; e) it further held, by 15 votes to 1, that, following consultation with the Secretariat of the Ramsar Convention and after giving Nicaragua prior notice, Costa Rica might take the appropriate measures related to the two new caños, to the extent necessary to prevent irreparable prejudice to the environment of the disputed territory and that, in taking that measures, Costa Rica should avoid any adverse effects on the San Juan River; and f) lastly, the Court decided, unanimously, that the parties should regularly inform it, at three month intervals, as to compliance with the above provisional measures'. Finally, the public hearing for the two cases were scheduled to take place on from 14 April 2015 to 24 April 2015.

activities carried out by Nicaragua in the San Juan River and in Costa Rica's land affecting the environment (wetlands, biodiversity and the forest resources). This chapter addresses the environmental impacts of the case and the application of the sustainable development principles.

On November 2010, Costa Rica instituted proceedings in the ICJ against Nicaragua with regard to an alleged 'incursion into, occupation of and use by Nicaragua's Army of Costa Rican territory as well as breaches of Nicaragua's obligations towards Costa Rica'[2] under several international treaties and conventions.

Costa Rica asserted that Nicaragua was not only acting in outright breach of the established boundary regime between the two states, but was also transgressing the core foundational principles of the United Nations, namely the principle of territorial integrity and the prohibition of the threat or use of force against any State in accordance with article 2 of the UN Charter; also endorsed between the parties in articles 1, 19 and 29 of the Charter of the Organization of American States.

In addition, Costa Rica charged Nicaragua with having occupied, in two separate incidents, the territory of Costa Rica in connection with the construction (and the cutting of trees) of a canal across Costa Rican territory from the San Juan River to Laguna Los Portillos, and certain related works of dredging on the San Juan River. Costa Rica states that the 'ongoing and planned dredging and the construction of the canal will seriously affect the flow of water to the Colorado River of Costa Rica, and will cause further damage to Costa Rican territory, including the wetlands and national wildlife protected areas located in the region'.[3]

According to Costa Rica, Nicaragua rejected all calls for withdrawal of its armed forces from the occupied territory and all means of negotiation. Costa Rica alleged that Nicaragua intended not to comply with the Resolution of 12 November 2010 of the Permanent Council of the Organization of American States calling, in particular, for the withdrawal of Nicaraguan armed forces from the border region, by requesting the avoidance of the presence of military or security forces in the area where their existence might rouse tension, in order to create a favourable climate for dialogue between the two nations.

Therefore, Costa Rica requested the ICJ 'to adjudge and declare that Nicaragua is in breach of its international obligations . . . as regards the incursion into and occupation of Costa Rican territory, the serious damage inflicted to its protected rainforests and wetlands, and the damage intended to the Colorado River, wetlands and protected ecosystems, as well as the dredging and canalization activities being carried out by Nicaragua on the San Juan River'.[4]

Meanwhile, in a round of oral observations, Nicaragua stated that the activities it was accused of by Costa Rica took place on Nicaraguan territory and that they

2 Application of the Republic of Costa Rica Instituting Proceedings, 2. Available at: <http://www. icj-cij.org/docket/files/150/16279.pdf> accessed 24 March 2015.
3 Ibid. at 6.
4 Ibid. at 26.

did not cause, nor did they risk causing, irreparable harm to the other party. Nicaragua also asserted that since the said natural channel had become obstructed over the years, it had undertaken to make it once more navigable for small vessels. The country furthermore claimed that the number of trees felled was limited and that it had endeavoured to replant the affected areas, all located on the left bank of the said channel, with ten trees for every one felled.

Finally, Nicaragua indicated that the dredging operations on the San Juan River were made necessary by the progressive sedimentation of its bed and that it not only had a sovereign right to dredge the river, but also an international obligation to do so.

This was not the first time that a decision of the ICJ was requested by Costa Rica. On 29 September 2005, Costa Rica asked the Court to adjudge and declare that Nicaragua was in breach of its international obligations in denying to Costa Rica the free exercise of its rights of navigation and associated rights on the San Juan River. According to Costa Rica, at that moment, Nicaragua had violated, among other things: a) the obligation to allow all Costa Rican vessels and their passengers to navigate freely on the San Juan for purposes of commerce, including communication and the transportation of passengers and tourism; b) the obligation not to impose any charges or fees on Costa Rican vessels and their passengers for navigating on the river; and c) the obligation not to require persons exercising the right of free navigation on the river to carry passports or obtain Nicaraguan visas.[5]

9.2 The environmental implications

Nicaragua's intentions for the San Juan River are not entirely clear. Some hypotheses are the construction of a channel to compete with the Panama Channel, the development of large hydroelectric projects and improving the navigability of the river.

Regardless of these decisions, all of the possibilities could generate different environmental impacts depending on the scope of works. In fact, this is one of the main points of Nicaraguan non-compliance with the international environmental obligations: nobody knows with certainty, beyond the eventual damage, which are really the plans and intentions of Nicaragua.

Costa Rica has developed a highly technical document detailing the damage to the wetlands northeast of the Caribbean. Among the findings include: a) changes to the ecological character of the wetlands in their area of influence of some 225 hectares; b) that the water system (water quality, flora and fauna), resident and migratory birds would be most affected by the actions identified, including the opening of an artificial channel, the flow of sediments and tree felling. Similarly,

---

5 *Case Concerning the Dispute regarding Navigational and Related Rights* (*Costa Rica v Nicaragua*). Summary of the judgment of 13 July 2009. Available at: <http://www.icj-cij.org/docket/files/133/15331.pdf> accessed 24 March 2015.

some of these actions affect the Ramsar Site Wildlife Refuge located in Rio San Juan Nicaragua; and c) to continue the changes in magnitude and extent of the Rio San Juan, which on the conditions that currently exist, confirming that the scenarios for medium and long term that the report develops are likely to become a reality. These scenarios involve a number of negative effects on the environment (hydrology, vegetation, wildlife), each in varying degrees, but in any case with significant and serious impacts.

In the Request for Provisional Measures, Costa Rica added that, as a consequence of the military occupation, Nicaragua destroyed an area of primarily rainforests and fragile wetlands on Costa Rican territory (listed as such under the Ramsar Convention's List) and acted contrary to the International Court of Justice ruling in its judgment of 13 July 2009 and in the first and second Alexander Awards, dated 30 September 30 1897, and 20 December 1897, respectively.[6]

The dredging of the San Juan River by Nicaragua was commenced pursuant to an order of President Ortega of 18 October 2010. The damaging effect of the dredging work breaches Costa Rica's sovereign rights pursuant to the 1858 Treaty of Limits, as authoritatively interpreted in the Cleveland Award and reaffirmed in 2009 by the ICJ. Costa Rica has a right, corresponding to Nicaragua's obligation not to undertake works of improvement, including from within its own territory that would 'result in the occupation, flooding or damage of Costa Rica territory, or in the destruction or serious impairment of the navigation of the said River [San Juan River] or any of its branches'.[7] By commencing dredging in this way, Nicaragua is in breach natural historical course into Laguna Los Portillos.

Nicaraguan officials had indicated that the intention of that country was to deviate some 1,700 cubic meters per second of the water that currently is carried by the Costa Rican Colorado River. In spite of Costa Rica's regular protests and calls on Nicaragua not to dredge the San Juan River until it could be established that the dredging operation would not damage the Colorado River or other Costa Rican territory, Nicaragua nonetheless continued with its dredging activities on the San Juan River and even announced on 8 November 2010 that it would deploy two additional dredges to the San Juan River. The National Port Company (EPN) is to provide one of the new dredges while the other is reportedly still under construction.

In accordance with Costa Rica's position, all of these statements by Nicaragua demonstrate the likelihood of damage to Costa Rica's Colorado River, and to Costa Rica's lagoons, rivers, herbaceous swamps and woodlands. The dredging operation also poses a threat to wildlife refuges in Laguna Maquenque, Barra del Colorado, Corredor Fronterizo and the Tortuguero National Park.

---

6 Request for the Indication of Provisional Measures Submitted by the Republic of Costa Rica. Available at: <http://www.haguejusticeportal.net/Docs/Court%20Documents/ICJ/Costarica%20vs%20Nicaragua%20Instituting%20proceedings.pdf> accessed 24 March 2015
7 Ibid. at 2.

9.3 Legal framework applicable to the dispute

The ICJ was requested to adjudge and declare that, by its conduct, Nicaragua had breached several international treaties and law principles: a) the 1858 Treaty of Limits between Costa Rica and Nicaragua; b) the fundamental principles of territorial integrity and the prohibition of use of force under the Charter of the United Nations and the Charter of the Organization of American States; c) the Arbitral Award made by President Cleveland in 1888; and d) the Ramsar Convention on Wetlands.[8]

But these are only a few group treaties involved in the dispute. Central America has signed and ratified a significant number of legally binding regional instruments as well as numerous statements related to sustainable development. As examples, it is worth noting the following conventions: the Regional Convention for the Management of Natural Forest Ecosystems and Forest Plantation Development; the American Convention on Climate Change; the Central American Convention for the Protection of the Environment; and importantly, the Convention on Priority Protected Areas and Biodiversity Conservation in Central America. Besides these environmental instruments, several countries in Central America have signed legal documents that establish a commitment to sustainable development and in particular to the conservation of biological diversity, including wetlands.

Beyond the above-mentioned international conventions and declarations, in the case of border areas, the principles of the 'soft law' must be applied, particularly in the cases of natural resources shared by two or more States. This point of view is especially useful in the case of the San Juan River, which is a water system under the exclusive sovereignty of Nicaragua, but, under the principles of the soft law, it must be considered as a unit since it is a part of a whole river basin.

For example, a resolution reaffirms the principles contained in the Rio Declaration on Environment and Development to point out that in this Statement: '. . . among other things, it established the sovereign right of states to define their development policies'. It also underlines the precautionary principle (Principle 15 of Rio Declaration), which states:

> [I]n order to protect the environment, the precautionary approach shall be widely applied by States according to their capabilities. Where there are threats of harm serious or irreversible damage, lack of full scientific certainty should not be used as a reason for postponing cost effective measures to prevent the costs of environmental degradation.

This approach requires a preventive policy to protect the natural resources. Therefore, precaution and prevention must be the key principles to avoid or minimize the degradation and deterioration of such resources. As a direct consequence,

---

8 Few references to the obligations under the Convention on Biological Diversity are found, despite the fact that the river was a protected area and that the biodiversity of the territory, especially that of the forest resources, was also impacted by the Nicaraguan activities.

it is worth establishing the principle *in dubio pro natura*, adapted by analogy from other law areas, which is completely 'in harmony with nature.'[9]

While there is no unanimous position on the doctrine concerning these principles, we point out some general conclusions widely accepted by most scholars, founded on treaties and international jurisprudence. For example, consider principles or regulations on shared natural resources, which include:[10]

a) The duty of States to cooperate in the control, prevention, reduction and elimination of adverse environmental effects;
b) The duty of the State not to cause damage to the environment in other states;
c) The duty to conduct an environmental impact assessment before initiating certain activities that affect the environment or natural resources located in other states;
d) The duty to notify, exchange information and consult with other States in the case of activities or projects with significant potential impacts on borders;
e) The duty to develop scientific studies and evaluations;
f) The duty to act in emergencies;
g) Other duties related to the settlement of differences, accountability and non-discrimination.

Related to the above is the duty to inform and consult in good faith (and there still may be other requirements depending on exactly correlated activities). This duty is an instrument established in the Biodiversity Convention. Specifically, article 14 promotes a reciprocal basis, notification, exchange of information and consultation on activities under their jurisdiction or control, which is expected to significantly affect biological diversity of other States or areas beyond their jurisdiction. It also sets out duties to notify in case originating under its jurisdiction imminent or grave danger or damage to biological diversity of other States. It is generally considered that there is a duty under international law to notify, exchange information and consult with other States in the case of activities with significant potential impacts across borders, including an environmental assessment of such projects. The lack of information is exacerbated when considering the importance that both countries have given to the conservation of biodiversity in protected areas located in the boundary. In fact, the activities in the San Juan River are a good example of environmental impacts across borders.

Also, both States had ratified the Central American Protected Areas Convention. This treaty highlights the importance of border strips in protecting natural resources by indicating that the conservation of habitats and biodiversity in boundary waters requires the will of all, including external cooperation at regional and global levels. It also requires each State to commit according

9 Resolution No. 5893–95 Constitutional Court of Costa Rica.
10 These statements are mentioned in the UNEP Guidelines on Shared Natural Resources, 1978, indicating that they have subsequently been collected in a multiple treaties and conventions.

to their capabilities, national programmes and priorities, to take all possible measures to ensure the conservation of biodiversity and its sustainable use and the development of its components within their national jurisdiction, and to cooperate to the extent of its possibilities in border and regional actions.

A declaration on border protected areas signed by the Governments of the Republics of Costa Rica and Nicaragua on 15 December 1990 establishes the International System of Protected Areas for Peace (SIAPAZ is its Spanish acronym) and declares it as the conservation project with highest priority in both countries, because it is 'absolutely [imperative to] protect the largest sample of tropical rainforest that is located on the slope of Central America,' since 'the area has an extraordinary amount of diversity of habitats such as rainforest and riparian, rivers, ponds and wetlands also a fauna of great richness and diversity, and great potential for ecotourism'.[11]

9.4 Provisional measures

In the Application, Costa Rica requests the ICJ as a matter of urgency to order the following provisional measures so as to rectify the presently ongoing breach of Costa Rica's territorial integrity and to prevent further irreparable harm to Costa Rica's territory, pending its determination of this case on the merits:

a) The immediate and unconditional withdrawal of all Nicaraguan troops from the unlawfully invaded and occupied Costa Rican territories;
b) The immediate cessation of the construction of a canal across Costa Rican territory;
c) The immediate cessation of the felling of trees, removal of vegetation and soil from Costa Rican territory, including its wetlands and forests;
d) The immediate cessation of the dumping of sediment in Costa Rican territory;
e) The suspension of Nicaragua's ongoing dredging programme, aimed at the occupation, flooding and damage of Costa Rican territory, as well as at serious damage to and impairment of the navigation of the Colorado River, giving full effect to the Cleveland Award and pending the determination of the merits of this dispute;
f) That Nicaragua shall refrain from any other action which might prejudice the rights of Costa Rica, or which may aggravate or extend the dispute before the Court.

The purpose of this request was to protect a number Costa Rica's rights, namely its right to sovereignty, to territorial integrity and to non-interference with its rights over the San Juan River, its lands and its environmentally protected areas, as well as the integrity and flow of the Colorado River. Costa Rica stated that:

---

11 The International System of Protected Areas for Peace Agreement (SIAPAZ).

[T]he felling of trees, the clearing of vegetation, the removal of soil, and in particular, the construction of an artificial canal accompanying Nicaragua's dredging activities in the territory of Costa Rica, including the illegal deposit of sediments on to Costa Rican territory, breaches Costa Rica's right not to have its territory flooded or damaged in any other way, under the 1858 Treaty of Limits.[12]

The request asked for a provisional measure ordering the withdrawal of Nicaraguan forces in order to prevent the aggravation and/or extension of the dispute. Costa Rica also noted that the urgency of the present request is underscored by the continued damage being inflicted on Costa Rica's territory.

9.5 The ICJs decision and the principles applied

In March 2011, the ICJ ordered Nicaragua and Costa Rica to refrain from sending their security forces to the disputed border area between the two countries, thus meeting a key demand of the Costa Rican government. The Court also determined that, as Costa Rica had asserted, it could be shown that dredging work carried out in the neighbouring Nicaragua San Juan River caused environmental damage. It consequently ordered Nicaragua to stop the activities in the river as Costa Rica's petition.

The Court opined, '[e]ach party shall refrain from sending to, or maintaining in the disputed territory, including the *caño*, any personnel, whether civilian, police or security.'[13] It added that:

Costa Rica may dispatch civilian personnel charged with the protection of the environment to the disputed territory, including the *caño*, but only in so far as it is necessary to avoid irreparable prejudice being caused to the part of the wetland where that territory is situated; Costa Rica shall consult with the Secretariat of the Ramsar Convention in regard to these actions, give Nicaragua prior notice of them and use its best endeavours to find common solutions with Nicaragua in this respect.[14]

After the ICJ's decision, Costa Rica expressed its 'deep satisfaction' with the precautionary measures issued by the ICJ while Nicaragua noted that the opinion clarified that they have not been 'as invaders' and have 'the right to dredge' the San Juan River.

12 Request for the Indication of Provisional Measures Submitted by the Republic of Costa Rica. Available at: <http://www.haguejusticeportal.net/Docs/Court%20Documents/ICJ/Costarica%20vs%20Nicaragua%20Instituting%20proceedings.pdf> accessed 9 March 2016.
13 Decision of ICJ on the request for the indication of provisional measures submitted by Costa Rica in the case concerning *Certain Activities carried out by Nicaragua in the Border Area (Costa Rica v Nicaragua)*. Available at: <http://www.icj-cij.org/docket/files/150/16324.pdf> accessed 24 March 2015 [*Costa Rica v Nicaragua*].
14 Ibid.

Despite divergent interpretations, this decision put into evidence the application of important principles of sustainable development, such as those included in the New Delhi Declaration 2002. Therefore, a sentence's analysis is relevant for the application of these principles in future cases.

1. The duty of States to ensure sustainable use of natural resources.

According to the New Delhi Declaration:

> [I]t is a well-established principle that, in accordance with international law, all States have the sovereign right to manage their own natural resources pursuant to their own environmental and developmental policies, and the responsibility to ensure that activities within their jurisdiction or control do not cause significant damage to the environment of other States or of areas beyond the limits of national jurisdiction.[15]

The Declaration also emphasizes that the States are under a duty to manage natural resources, including those solely within their own territory or jurisdiction, in a rational, sustainable and safe way so as to contribute to the development of their peoples, and adds that 'all relevant actors (including States, industrial concerns and other components of civil society) are under a duty to avoid wasteful use of natural resources and promote waste minimization policies'.[16]

The ICJ applies this principle when it states, 'the disputed territory is moreover situated in the "Humedal Caribe Noreste" wetland, in respect of which Costa Rica bears obligations under the Ramsar Convention'.[17]

According to the decision, 'the Court considers that, pending delivery of the judgment on the merits, Costa Rica must be in a position to avoid irreparable prejudice being caused to the part of that wetland where that territory is situated' and 'for that purpose Costa Rica must be able to dispatch civilian personnel charged with the protection of the environment to the said territory'.[18] In accordance with these statements, the Court estimated that Costa Rica has a duty to protect natural resources in the San Juan River.

2. The principle of good governance is also included within the New Delhi Declaration.

Good governance is essential to the progressive development and codification of international law relating to sustainable development. It commits States and international organizations: a) to adopt democratic and transparent decision-making procedures and financial accountability; b) to take effective measures to combat official or other corruption; c) to respect due process in their procedures

---

15 New Delhi Declaration of Principles of International Law Relating to Sustainable Development, Resolution 3/2002. Available at: <http://www.ila-hq.org/en/committees/index.cfm/cid/25> accessed 24 March 2015 [New Delhi Declaration].

16 Ibid.

17 *Costa Rica v Nicaragua, supra* note 13.

18 Ibid.

and to observe the rule of law and human rights; and d) to implement a public procurement approach according to the WTO Code on Public Procurement.[19]

This principle requires full respect for the principles of the Rio Declaration, the full participation of women in all levels of decision making, and corporate social responsibility and socially responsible investments for a fair distribution of wealth among and within communities.[20]

The ICJ agrees with this principle and accepts that 'the ongoing presence of Nicaraguan armed forces on Costa Rica's territory is contributing to a political situation of extreme hostility and tension' and that 'a provisional measure ordering the withdrawal of Nicaraguan forces from Costa Rican territory is justified so as to prevent the aggravation and/or extension of the dispute'.[21]

3. Prevention. Is one of the principles of international environmental law and it is also applied by the ICJ.

According to Professor Philippe Sands, 'the preventive principle requires action to be taken at an early stage and, if possible, before damage has actually occurred. The principle is reflected in stated practice in regard to a broad range of environmental objectives'.[22]

This principle is reflected in the ICJ's decision. At first, the Court accepts that Costa Rica asked 'as a matter of urgency to order the provisional measures so as to rectify the presently ongoing breach of Costa Rica's territorial integrity and to *prevent* further irreparable harm to Costa Rica's territory'.[23]

Later, the Court stated that 'a provisional measure ordering the withdrawal of Nicaraguan forces from Costa Rican territory is (. . .) justified so as to *prevent* the aggravation and/or extension of the dispute'.[24] However, it should be noted that the Costa Rica submission did not request the application of the precautionary principle and the ICJ did not make any specific reference to this important principle of sustainable international development law.

4. The Polluter-pays principle 'is important for environmental protection, and integration of environmental considerations in economic decisions'.[25] Sands explains that this principle 'establishes the requirement that the costs of pollution should be borne by the person responsible for causing the pollution'.[26] In reference to this principle, the Court cited the third clause of the Cleveland Award of March 22, 1888, which reads:

The Republic of Costa Rica has the right to demand indemnification for any places belonging to her on the right bank of the River San Juan which may

19 New Delhi Declaration, *supra* note 15.
20 Jorge Cabrera, Frederic Perron-Welch and Alexandra Keenan, *Crafting Future Just Biodiversity Laws and Policies* (CISDL Biodiversity and Biosafety Law Programme, 2011) at 11.
21 *Costa Rica v Nicaragua, supra* note 13.
22 Philippe Sands, *Principles of International Environmental Law* (Cambridge: Cambridge University Press, 2003) at 247.
23 *Costa Rica v Nicaragua, supra* note 13
24 Ibid.
25 The New Delhi declaration does not include this expressly as a principle.
26 Philippe Sands, *supra* note 22 at 279.

be occupied without her consent, and for any lands on the same bank which may be flooded or damaged in any other way in consequence of works of improvement.

Although the Court finally does not tackle this idea in this decision, that mention is relevant for the treatment of the international environmental law.

9.6 Conclusion

First, it is worth emphasizing that Nicaragua's sovereignty over the river is not disputed. It has been established by various international awards and agreements in which limits have been set between the countries that Nicaragua assumes both the rights and obligations concerning the use of San Juan River. The sovereignty of a specific country over its natural resources is not a new subject in international law and is embodied in resolutions of the United Nations General Assembly and in several multilateral environmental agreements. The recent ruling of the ICJ referred to the conditions of navigation on the river confirms this conclusion.

This decision is very important for international environmental law, as it captures some of the principles recognized in several multilateral agreements. However, the most important feature of the Court ruling for this chapter is the mention of sustainable development principles set out in the Declaration of New Delhi.

The ICJ addressed the duty to ensure sustainable use of natural resources. In this sense, the Court considers that Costa Rica must be in a position to avoid irreparable prejudice being caused to the part of that wetland where that territory is situated. On the other hand, the Court applies the good governance principle and accepts that the ongoing presence of Nicaraguan armed forces on Costa Rica's territory is contributing to a political situation of extreme hostility and tension.

Therefore, this decision could have potential impacts on the development of the ICJ's jurisprudence on environmental and sustainable development matters.

10 Sustainable development in the judgments of the International Court of Justice

Marcel Szabó

10.1 Introduction

As Durán and Morgera claim, the definition of sustainable development is primarily a construction of international law.[1] Despite this, sustainable development is not something artificial, it is a matter of the definition of sustainable development itself rather than to the concept. Many different interpretations, however, persist among authors and sources of this law. There are multiple uses of sustainability or sustainable development, and no one claims to hold the holy grail of the perfect understanding.[2]

This chapter examines whether the judgments of the International Court of Justice in The Hague (the "ICJ") have fostered and continue to foster the crystallisation of sustainable development principles in the field of public international law. Although some aspects of sustainable development have emerged in important cases before other international courts, such as the *Iron Rhine* case,[3] it is arguably the ICJ that has exerted the greatest impact on the development of global international sustainable development law. Thus, in the following, the most significant judgments of the ICJ are analysed. The bulk of this analysis starts with the *Gabčíkovo-Nagymaros* case, although brief reference is made to several important predecessor cases.

10.2 Pre-*Gabčíkovo-Nagymaros* ICJ jurisprudence

10.2.1 Case Concerning the Continental Shelf (Libyan Arab Jamahiriya v Malta)

In 1985, the ICJ issued its opinion in the *Case Concerning the Continental Shelf (Libyan Arab Jamahiriya v Malta).*[4] The primary issue in the case was

---

1 Durán, Gracia Marin and Morgera, Elisa, *Environmental Integration in the EU's External Relations* (Oxford/Portland, OR: Hart Publishing, 2012) at 34–5.
2 Bulla, Miklós, *A fenntartható fejlődés fogalmi világa* in Vissza vagy hova – Útkeresés a fenntarthatóság felé Magyarországon, Tertia, 2002 at 105.
3 *Arbitration regarding the Iron Rhine (Ijzeren Rijn) Railway between the Kingdom of Belgium and the Kingdom of the Netherlands*, Award of 24 May 2005, UNRIAA XXVII 35. See Baetens, Freya, "The Iron Rhine Case: On the Right Track to Sustainable Development?" in this volume.
4 *Continental Shelf (Libyan Arab Jamahiriya v Malta), Judgment*, ICJ Reports 1985, p. 13.

the appropriate delimitation line of the continental shelf between the states, however in the process the Court had occasion to apply several different principles. One of the essential arguments posed by Libya was that there should be an application of equitable principles to the matter.[5] Further, the Court stated that "[t]he application of equitable principles thus still leaves the Court with the task of appreciation of the weight to be accorded to the relevant circumstances in any particular case delimitation."[6]

Indeed, the Court embraced and applied the concept of equitable principles to the question of how to establish the appropriate boundary delimitation in recognition of its establishment as an important international law principle per se. In this case, the Court used the concept of equitable principles for a heavily fact-driven evaluation under the concept of relevant circumstances.[7]

10.2.2 Case Concerning Maritime Delimitation in the Area between Greenland and Jan Mayen (Denmark v Norway)

Moving on from this, in 1993 the ICJ issued its opinion in the *Case Concerning Maritime Delimitation in the Area between Greenland and Jan Mayen*, another case involving the establishment of the continental shelf boundary between the two states.[8] Again, this case stressed the imperative of applying equitable principles for issues involving boundary decisions.[9] In this case, the Court included the importance of proportionality as a matter of equitable principles rather than as a separate element and intended to be used as part of a "reasonable degree of proportionality" standard.[10]

10.3 Findings of the ICJ in the *Case Concerning the Gabčíkovo-Nagymaros Project*

The ICJ first included the concept of sustainable development in the *Advisory Opinion on Threat or Use of Nuclear Weapons* in 1997, declaring that the principle was part of the body of international law relating to the environment.[11] Nevertheless, the *Gabčíkovo-Nagymaros* dispute was the first case before the ICJ to assess questions of international environmental law and, as a corollary, sustainable development.[12]

---

5 Ibid. at para. 45.
6 Ibid. at para. 48.
7 Ibid. at paras 60–1.
8 *Maritime Delimitation in the Area between Greenland and Jan Moyen, Judgment*, ICJ Reports 1998, p. 38.
9 Ibid. at para. 46.
10 Ibid. at para. 66.
11 *Legality of the Use by a State of Nuclear Weapons in an Armed Conflict*, Advisory Opinion, 1996 ICJ 67 (July 8), para. 29.
12 *Case Concerning the Gabčíkovo-Nagymaros Project (Hungary v Slovakia)* [1997] ICJ Rep. 7.

10.3.1 The legal dispute between Hungary and Slovakia

The case related to the 1977 agreement concluded between the Hungarian People's Republic and the Czechoslovak People's Republic.[13] The purpose of this agreement was to facilitate the construction of a hydraulic power plant system consisting of two locks on the Hungarian-Czechoslovak section of the Danube. According to the 1977 plans, the system included two barrages, one built by the Czechoslovak Republic and another planned at Nagymaros in Hungary. The latter was not built as a result of environmental and technical concerns about the project's feasibility. The Nagymaros construction was suspended by Hungary in 1989 and was closely followed by the cessation of Hungarian work toward the project in Czechoslovakian territory. However, Hungary was unable to convince Czechoslovakia to suspend its work until a thorough environmental examination was conducted.

Czechoslovakia, for its part, was convinced that Hungary intended to withdraw from the project altogether and decided to unilaterally complete the barrage system, while considerably diverging from the original plans described in the treaty. The result of Czechoslovakia's unilateral actions was the creation of "Variant C," the implementation of a barrage system on Slovak soil, which made it possible to divert the Danube without authorisation from Hungary. Additionally, Czechoslovakia intended to operate the envisioned power plant independently regardless of Hungarian reservations. As a result, and due to fears of Czechoslovakia's intensions regarding the Danube, Hungary terminated the 1977 treaty in 1992. In spite of the Hungarian termination, Czechoslovakia diverted the Danube later in 1992, and made the Gabčíkovo barrage operational at the same time. On 1 January 1993, Czechoslovakia ceased to exist, and was replaced by the Czech Republic and Slovakia. The area of concern in this case fell within Slovakian territory. After mediation from the European Union, the parties submitted the dispute to the ICJ, and requested the ICJ to adjudge whether the 1977 treaty remained in force after Hungarian termination, and also if Slovakia was entitled to put into operation by the diversion of the Danube the project elements connected to the Gabčíkovo facility.

10.3.2 Judgment of the International Court of Justice in the Case Concerning the Gabčíkovo-Nagymaros Project

In its judgment of 25 September 1997, the ICJ declared that the suspension of work at Nagymaros and the termination of the 1977 Treaty were unlawful. According to the ICJ's judgment, Czechoslovakia had the right to unilaterally

---

13 Treaty between the Hungarian People's Republic and the Czechoslovak People's Republic concerning the construction and operation of the Gabčíkovo-Nagymaros System of Locks, 16 September 1977.

create the Variant C installations, but it acted unlawfully when it began to operate the system, diverting the overwhelming majority of the flow of the Danube from its original bed and thereby depriving Hungary of its right to an equitable and reasonable share of the frontier watercourse.[14] The Court proclaimed that the existing structures must be jointly operated but that there was no obligation to create or operate additional entities However, the Court did emphasise that the parties should reconsider the environmental impacts of the Gabčíkovo power plant and craft an appropriate solution to the issue of how much water should be discharged into the Old Danube bed and its side branches.[15] Regarding the diversion of the Danube, the judgment recognised *"the continuing effects of the diversion of these waters on the ecology of the riparian area of the Szigetköz"*[16]. As a result, the Court found that there must be a minimum quantity of water required to sustain natural conditions, which should be kept in the original riverbed and in the side arms in order to protect the natural environment, and the specification of which should be equally essential for both Parties. The Court stressed "the great significance that it attaches to respect for the environment; not only for the States but also for the whole of mankind",[17] and explained that it "has no difficulty in acknowledging that the concerns expressed by Hungary for its natural environment in the region affected by the Gabčíkovo-Nagymaros Project related to an 'essential interest' of that State".[18]

The Court took into account the circumstances of the case, which involved contractual issues, the concomitant involvement of *pacta sunt servanda* principles, and also environmental concerns, in its analysis. The Court affirmed the "integrity of the rule *pacta sunt servanda*" and implicitly rejected Hungary's contention that "the previously existing obligation not to cause substantive damage to the territory of another state had [. . .] evolved into an *erga omnes* obligation of prevention of damage pursuant to the precautionary principle".[19] In doing so, the Court denied that environmental law principles could trump treaty law.[20] With respect to state liability law, Hungary referred to the international legal norms of emergency in the hope of proving the existence of grave and imminent peril threatening the environment, an argument that may

---

14 *Case Concerning the Gabčíkovo-Nagymaros Project, Judgment*, para. 78.
15 Ibid. at para. 140.
16 Ibid. at para. 85.
17 Ibid. at para. 53.
18 Ibid.
19 Ibid. at para. 97.
20 It could be noteworthy to mention the observation made by Jan Klabbers, who referred to the Court's pragmatism as the reason for its recognition of the existence of the 1977 treaty: "One of the intriguing parts of the case resides in the fact that the Court was willing to find that the 1977 Treaty continued to be in force, all environmental arguments notwithstanding. "[. . .] The Court must have thought that maintaining it would be the best thing to do in order to help settle the dispute."
    See Klabbers, Jan, "Cat on a Hot Tin Roof: The World Court, State Succession, and the G/N Case", *Leiden J. Int'l L.* 11 (1998) 2, p. 346.

justify derogation from the contractual obligations.[21] During the discussion of this particular issue, the ICJ emphasised that while it can accept the argument and is aware of the fact that environmental protection is an important state interest, it believed that Hungary could not prove the imminent peril of the environment and therefore could not refer to the rules of liability in respect of emergency.[22]

The ICJ judgment clarified that both current and future generations are seriously endangered when mankind ignores the environmental impacts of mechanisation, and technical and industrial development. Therefore, the ICJ found it important to ensure the proper balance between economic development and environmental protection under the rubric of sustainable development. The ICJ explained the obligation imposed by the concept of sustainable development on the parties, including, in this case, conducting environmental impact assessments with respect to the operation of the Gabčíkovo power plant.[23] This was in accord with the ICJ's statements that the concept of sustainable development has customary international law status. In Section 140 of the judgment, the ICJ required consideration of current standards in the course of evaluating environmental risks. By mentioning the terms "vigilance" and "prevention," the ICJ indirectly referred to the concepts of precaution and prevention.[24] However, this reference is only indirect in nature and it is unclear why the ICJ failed to make explicit reference to these concepts.[25]

If we accept that, pursuant to the principle of prevention, an investment which contains a serious environmental risk could be suspended until the joint environmental impact assessment is conducted, then the first action of Hungary's that was claimed to have been unlawful, that is, suspending the construction of the Nagymaros dam, could not have been considered an unlawful action. Consequently, the conduct of Czechoslovakia in deviating from the plans pursuant to the original agreement would have fallen into the category of breach of law, particularly the unilateral construction and putting into operation of the facility after the unilateral diversion of the Danube. In response to this, the termination of the agreement could have been a lawful measure establishing an entirely novel situation in the dispute between the parties.

21 Memorandum of the Republic of Hungary, 2 May 1994, paras 6.56.–6.69.

22 *Case Concerning the Gabčíkovo-Nagymaros Project* case, "[The Court] has concluded that, with respect to both Nagymaros and Gabčíkovo, 'the perils invoked by Hungary, without prejudging their possible gravity, were not sufficiently established in 1989, nor were they "imminent"; and [. . .] Hungary had available to it at that time means of responding to these perceived perils other than the suspension and abandonment of works with which it had been entrusted'" (para. 57 of the judgment).

23 *Case Concerning the Gabčíkovo-Nagymaros Project, Judgment, supra* note 12, para. 140.

24 Ibid.

25 Boyle, A. E., "The Gabčíkovo-Nagymaros Case: New Law in Old Bottles", *Y.Bk. Int'l Envtl. L.* 8 (1997): 13–20, p. 17.

10.3.3 Separate opinion of H. E. Judge C. G. Weeramantry

It is important to discuss the Separate Opinion of H. E. Judge C. G. Weeramantry in the *Gabčíkovo-Nagymaros* case, since this opinion analysed the concept of sustainable development in detail and revealed the aspects of the principle of sustainable development in a broad context. According to Weeramantry's standpoint, the fundamental principle of sustainable development is more than a mere concept because sustainable development is a principle of normative value, playing a major role in deciding the case.[26] In his opinion, sustainable development is defined as the right to development limited by the need to preserve the environment.[27] Pursuant to Weeramantry's opinion, both the right to environmental protection and the right to development form part of international law, although these rights may collide and it is for the principle of sustainable development to resolve the conflict.[28] Sustainable development offers itself as an instrument to strike a balance between human rights, environmental rights and the competing right to economic development. It should be noted that Weeramantry raised the principle of continuing environmental impact assessment[29] and the principle of contemporaneity in the application of environmental norms[30] – notions which the ICJ judgment simply connected to the concept of sustainable development – separately from sustainable development.

10.4 Issues of sustainable development in the *Case Concerning Pulp Mills on the River Uruguay*

On 20 April 2010, the ICJ delivered its judgment in a dispute between Argentina and Uruguay. The *Case Concerning Pulp Mills on the River Uruguay*[31] provided the Court with the opportunity to contribute further to the evolution of sustainable development law and theory. Similar to the *Gabčíkovo-Nagymaros* case, the *Pulp Mills* case centered around the interpretation of a treaty on the utilisation of a shared river, in this instance the River Uruguay. Both cases involved joint projects with significant environmental implications that led one of the parties to stop construction of the project after an agreement had been entered into. And both cases reveal the complexity of sustainable development and the ICJ's approach to it. Since 1997, there have been major developments in international sustainable development law, including the conclusion and entry into force of

---

26 *Case Concerning the Gabčíkovo-Nagymaros Project, Separate Opinion of Vice-President Weeramantry*, *supra* note 12, at paras 88–9.

27 Canelas de Castro, Paulo, "The judgment in the Case Concerning the Gabčíkovo-Nagymaros Project", *Y.Bk. Int'l Envtl. L.* 8 (1997), pp. 21, 28.

28 Separate Opinion of Vice-President Weeramantry, *supra* note 26 at p. 90.

29 Ibid. at paras. 111–13.

30 Ibid. at paras. 113–15.

31 *Case Concerning Pulp Mills on the River Uruguay (Argentina v Uruguay), Judgment*, 2010 ICJ Reports 14.

legal instruments,[32] as well as decisions[33] of national, regional, and international courts and tribunals.[34] Consequently, the ICJ had a larger body of laws, rules and principles upon which to analyze the definition and principles underlying sustainable development and its implementation.

The River Uruguay constitutes the border between Argentina and Uruguay according to a 1961 bilateral treaty. Pursuant to the so-called Montevideo Treaty, the parties established a regime for the use of the river, which was regulated by the 1975 Statute of the River Uruguay. In 2003 and 2005, Uruguay unilaterally issued an authorisation for the construction of two pulp mills along the banks of the river, without having fully exhausted the communication with Argentina under the process laid down in the 1975 Statute. In its judgment, the ICJ found that Uruguay had failed to comply with the procedural obligations necessary to adequately inform Argentina and the Administrative Commission of the River Uruguay (the "CARU") prior to the initial authorisation for the construction of the project. Nevertheless, the Court found that Uruguay did not violate the substantive obligations under the 1975 Statute relating to the protection of the environment. The Court confirmed the obligation of due diligence,[35] and reaffirmed that this obligation "is now part of the corpus of international law relating to the environment".[36] Rejecting Argentina's argument, the ICJ underlined that due diligence is the obligation of conduct rather than one of result.[37]

When assessing the relationship between procedural obligations and substantive obligations, the Court underlined the importance of cooperation, which is a crucial element for the proper implementation of the Treaty by stating that "it is by cooperating that the States can jointly manage the risks of damage to the environment".[38] In this connection, the Court recalled its judgment in the *Gabčíkovo-Nagymaros* case, noted that the "need to reconcile economic development with protection of the environment is aptly expressed in the concept of sustainable development,"

---

32 See, e.g. the 2000 Cartagena Protocol on Biosafety to the Convention on Biological Diversity, the 2010 Nagoya Protocol on Access to Genetic Resources and the Fair and Equitable Sharing of Benefits Arising from the Utilisation to the Convention on Biological Diversity and the International Law Association's New Delhi Declaration on Sustainable Development.

33 See especially the *Arbitration Regarding the Iron Rhine ('Ijzeren Rijn') Railway (Belgium v The Netherlands)*, Arbitral Award of 24 May 2005 and the Advisory Opinion of the Seabed Disputes Chamber of the International Tribunal for the Law of the Sea on matters relating to the Responsibilities and Obligations of States sponsoring persons and entities with respect to activities in the Area, Advisory Opinion of 1 February 2011.

34 Tladi, Dire, "Principles of Sustainable Development in the Case Concerning Pulp Mills on the River Uruguay", *International Development Law Organization Legal Working Paper*, at 2–3. Available at http://www.idlo.int/Documents/Rio/01.%20Pulp%20Mills%20on%20the%20River%20Uruguay.pdf.

35 A state is thus obliged to use all the means at its disposal in order to avoid activities which take place in its territory, or in any area under its jurisdiction, causing significant damage to the environment of another state. *Case Concerning the Pulp Mills on the River Uruguay, Judgment*, para. 10.

36 *Legality of the Threat or Use of Nuclear Weapons*, Advisory Opinion, ICJ Reports 1996 (I), at 242, para. 29.

37 Ibid. at para. 187.

38 Ibid. at para. 77.

and added that "[i]t is for the Parties themselves to find agreed solutions that takes account of the objectives of the Treaty".[39]

In the context of the obligation to inform, the Court referred to the "principle of prevention" as part of international environmental law. Pursuant to the Court's judgment, the principle of prevention obliges states to "use all the means at its disposal in order to avoid causing significant damage to the environment of another state".[40] Therefore, the Court surmised that Uruguay should have submitted the relevant information to the CARU without delay in order to enable the Commission to assess the possible harm to the environment on the territory of Argentina. Without prompt notification, the CARU could not initiate the process to prevent the damage.[41] Nevertheless, the Court failed to address the effects of the preventative principle on the obligations of the parties subsequent to the consultation period, in particular, the role of the preventative principle in interpreting the content of the parties' obligations, as well as the ensuing consequences.[42]

As regards the precautionary principle, Argentina argued that the principle implied a reversal of the burden of proof or a finding that the burden applies equally to both parties. The Court held that "while it may be relevant in the interpretation and application of the provisions of the Statute, it does not follow that it operates as reversal of the burden of proof".[43] Thus, the burden of proof remained on the party asserting the breach of environmental obligations. The Court not only reduced the principle to a simple "approach" that may be relevant to the case, but fails to explain the exact application of the principle.

At this point, we can draw another parallel between the two ICJ decisions. As in the *Gabčíkovo-Nagymaros* case, a number of judges elaborated dissenting and separate opinions to the judgment. The most remarkable was that of Judge Cançado Trindade, who focused his thoughts on general principles of law, including the principle of prevention and the precautionary principle. He was critical of the Court's approach regarding these principles and observes that the ICJ did not show the same "zeal and diligence" in respect of legal principles as it did when it examined the factual and scientific questions.[44] According to him, these principles ought to have guided the Court in the interpretation and application of the 1975 Statute, and should have been taken into account in determining the procedural and substantive obligations of the parties.

39 Ibid. at para. 76.
40 Ibid. at para. 101. The principle is also reflected in, *inter alia*, the *Corfu Channel* case *(United Kingdom v Albania)*, ICJ judgment of 9 April 1949 at 22 and the *Advisory Opinion on the Legality of the Threat or Use of Nuclear Weapons*, Advisory Opinion of the International Court of Justice of 8 July 1996. See also the *Trail Smelter* case *(US v Canada)* (1941) Vol III Reports of International Arbitral Awards 1905–1982 at 1965.
41 *Case Concerning the Pulp Mills on the River Uruguay, supra* note 31 at para. 105
42 Tladi, Dire, "Principles of Sustainable Development in the Case Concerning Pulp Mills on the River Uruguay", op. cit. 6.
43 *Case Concerning the Pulp Mills on the River Uruguay, Judgment, supra* note 31 at para. 164.
44 Para. 4 of the Separate Opinion of Cançado Trindade in the *Case Concerning Pulp Mills on the River Uruguay*. See also the joint dissenting opinion of Judges Al-Khasawneh and Simma, *supra* note 31 at para. 27.

The concept of sustainable development was considered by the ICJ in the context of balancing between economic and environmental interests. This narrow understanding of the concept of sustainable development ignores the fact that social concerns are integral elements of sustainable development and therefore reduces sustainable development to a mere tool of balancing economic development and environmental protection.[45] In his Separate Opinion, Judge Cançado Trindade described sustainable development as "encompassing the fostering of economic growth, the eradication of poverty and the satisfaction of basic human needs (such as those pertaining to health, nutrition, housing, education)."[46] Nevertheless, the Court recognised that each party has the right to make equitable and reasonable use of the shared watercourse for economic and commercial activities. In this regard, the Court noted that Article 27 of the Statute embodied the "interconnectedness between equitable and reasonable utilization of a shared resource and the balance between economic development and environmental protection that is the essence of sustainable development",[47] placing the right of equitable use within the framework of sustainable development.[48]

The most significant contribution of the *Pulp Mills* judgment to the development of international environmental law and the principles governing the law of shared watercourses is the recognition of the environmental impact assessment as a practice that has become an obligation under general international law by reason of its wide acceptance among the states:

> [i]t is the opinion of the Court that in order for the Parties properly to comply with their obligations under . . . the 1975 Statute, they must, for the purposes of protecting and preserving the aquatic environment with respect to activities which may be liable to cause transboundary harm, carry out an environmental impact assessment. . . . In this sense, the obligation to protect and preserve, under . . . the Statute, has to be interpreted in accordance with a practice, which in recent years has gained so much acceptance among States that it may now be considered a requirement under general international law to undertake an environmental impact assessment where there is a risk that the proposed industrial activity may have a significant adverse impact in a transboundary context, in particular, on a shared resource. Moreover, due diligence, and the duty of vigilance and prevention which it implies, would not be considered to have been exercised, if a party planning works liable to affect the régime of the river or the quality of its waters did not undertake an environmental impact assessment on the potential effects of such works.[49]

45 Tladi, Dire, "Principles of Sustainable Development in the Case Concerning Pulp Mills on the River Uruguay", *supra* note 34 at 12

46 Para. 132 of the Separate Opinion of Cançado Trindade in the *Case Concerning Pulp Mills on the River Uruguay*.

47 *Case Concerning the Pulp Mills on the River Uruguay, Judgment, supra* note 31 at para. 177.

48 Boyle, Alan, Pulp Mills Case: A Commentary, p. 4. Available at http://www.biicl.org/files/5167_pulp_mills_case.pdf

49 "As the Court has observed in the case concerning the Dispute Regarding Navigational and Related Rights, 'there are situations in which the parties' intent upon conclusion of the treaty was, or may

In order to prevent pollution and preserve the aquatic environment, environmental impact assessments must be performed prior to the implementation of projects that are likely to cause significant environmental harm. After the commencement of implementation, environmental effects must be continuously monitored.[50]

10.5 Issues of sustainable development in *Whaling in the Antarctic (Australia v Japan)* case

In 2014, the ICJ issued the judgment in the *Whaling in the Antarctic* case.[51] Unlike the prior cases, this case centered on allegations by Australia that Japan had violated the terms of the International Convention for the Regulation of Whaling (ICRW). Due to the nature and location of the contested activities, New Zealand joined the case as a non-party intervenor as well. The primary issues in the case centered on Japan's allowance of whaling of protected species and in legally protected areas under the auspices of a governmentally approved whaling research program.[52] Australia maintained that this program, the Jananese Whale Research Program under Special Permit in the Altantic (JARPA) and its subsequent iterations, JARPA II and JARPA III, were in fact being used to allow commercial whaling in contravention of Japan's ICRW treaty obligations.

Before reaching the question of Japan's research permit system, the Court provided a background on the international legal systems that culminated in the ICRW. This background, beginning in 1931 with the Convention for the Regulation of Whaling, was aimed at ensuring a balance between economic interests in whaling and the "sustainability of the whaling industry."[53] It was founded on the need to harmonise new technological capacities that could lead to advances in whaling ship range and harvest takes with the preservation of whales for future industrial purposes in what would now be viewed as an equitable arrangement.[54]

The Convention's terms were insufficient against the vastly expanding industrial potential and growth of consumer demand for whale-based products.[55] As the Court explained, this resulted in the 1937 International Agreement for the Regulation of Whaling, which was a more thorough agreement in terms of its intended results and in terms of creating a system of permitted and prohibited species for whaling purposes, limitations on harvesting, limitations on seasons

---

be presumed to have been, to give the terms used . . . a meaning or content capable of evolving, not one fixed once and for all, so as to make allowance for, among other things, developments in international law' *Dispute Regarding Navigational and Related Rights (Costa Rica v Nicaragua)*, Judgment, ICJ Reports 2009, p. 242, para. 64). See *Case Concerning the Pulp Mills on the River Uruguay, Judgment, supra* note 31 at para. 204.

50 Ibid. at para. 205.
51 *Whaling in the Antarctic (Australia v Japan: New Zealand Intervening), Judgment,* 2014 ICJ, Reports p. 1
52 Ibid.
53 Ibid. at para. 43
54 Ibid.
55 Ibid.

for allowed whaling activities, and limitations on areas in which whaling could be conducted.[56] Importantly for the *Whaling in the Antarctic* case, the 1937 Agreement created a system under which states could issue permits for those wishing to conduct whaling activities for scientific and research purposes.[57]

Less than a decade later, another whaling treaty was created – the ICRW.[58] The ICRW was, as the Court explained, in some ways a less detailed text than its predecessors in that the bulk of the regulations regarding specific stocks and whaling management practices were placed in the Schedules and subject to readier amendment.[59] Governance of the Schedule terms was vested in large part in the ICRW Commission, which has the ability to issue non-binding but highly persuasive recommendations on whaling stocks and management practices.[60] In addition, the Commission receives information and advice from a specially created Scientific Committee.[61] The Scientific Committee has the ability to evaluate guidelines for the issuance of national special whaling permits for scientific and research purposes and can evaluate the permitting systems in place by ICRW member states. Findings are provided to the Commission as well as the states themselves.[62]

While evaluating the arguments presented by all sides regarding Japan's actions and their relationship to the scientific and research permitting system, the Court explicitly noted that "Australia and Japan have respectively emphasized conservation and sustainable exploitation as the object and purposes of the Convention [ICRW] in the light of which the provisions should be interpreted."[63] The Court found a middle ground in the arguments asserted and "observed that neither a restrictive nor an expansive interpretation . . . is justified. The Court notes that programmes for purposes of scientific research should foster scientific knowledge; they may pursue an aim other than either conservation or sustainable exploitation of whale stocks."[64] In this way, the Court chose to endorse the current ICRW guidelines, which seek to refrain from restricting the ability of scientific knowledge and research to be advanced for the purposes of entire ecosystems by concerns that strictly relate to whale stocks.[65]

Beyond this, the Court refused to enter into the fray of the overall legality of whaling or the need for further regulations in order to preserve whale stocks for future generations. Indeed, the Court explicitly stated that it was "aware that members of the international community hold divergent views about the apropriate policy toward whales and whaling, but it is not for the Court to settle

56 Ibid.
57 Ibid.
58 Ibid. at para. 44.
59 Ibid. at para. 45.
60 Ibid. at paras 45–6.
61 Ibid. at para. 47.
62 Ibid.
63 Ibid. at para. 57.
64 Ibid. at para. 58.
65 Ibid.

these differences."[66] The Court did, however, establish that there are two elements to the permit allowance "for purposes of scientific research," namely that "even if a whaling programme involves scientific research, the killing, taking and treating of whales pursuant to such a programme does not fall within . . . [the ICRW] unless these activities are 'for purposes of scientific research.'"[67]

The Court went on to evaluate the elements of these two requirements. It found that, contrary to an assertion from Australia, there was no requirement that whales be killed for scientific purposes only in the event that a non-lethal method of conducting the desired research is not available.[68] Next, the Court examined the requirement that the action be solely for scientific purposes and created limitations on this concept:

> The Court observes that a State often seeks to accomplish more than one goal when it pursues a particular policy. Moreover, an objective test of whether a programme is for the purposes of scientific research does not turn on individual government officials, but rather on whether the design and implementation of a programme are reasonable in relation to achieving the stated research objectives . . . the Court considers that whether particular government officials may have motivations that go beyond scientific research does not preclude a conclusion that a programme is for the purposes of scientific research . . . At the same time, such motivations cannot justify the granting of a special permit for a programme that uses lethal sampling on a larger scale than is reasonable in relation to achieving the programme's stated research objectives. The research objectives alone must be sufficient to justify the programme as designed and implemented.[69]

The Court then used these standards to conduct an in-depth evaluation of Japan's permitting programs.[70] From the outset, the Court found that "the use of lethal sampling per se is not unreasonable in relation to the research objectives of JARPA II."[71] However, upon consideration of the scientific and non-scientific data offered by Japan, the Court held that "the evidence does not establish that the programme's design and implementation are reasonable in relation to achieving its stated objectives . . . the special permits granted by Japan for the killing, taking and treating of whales in connection with JARPA II are not 'for purposes of scientific research' . . .".[72] Further, the Court agreed with Australia's arguments that Japan had allowed what amounted to commercial fishing of protected species of whales in sanctuary territories, violating additional terms of the ICRW.[73]

---

66 Ibid. at para. 69.
67 Ibid. at para. 71.
68 Ibid. at para. 86.
69 Ibid. at para. 97.
70 Ibid. at paras 98–222.
71 Ibid. at para. 224.
72 Ibid. at para. 227.
73 Ibid. at para. 233.

Throughout the main judgment, the Court did not refer directly to the *Gabčíkovo-Nagymaros* case or the principles contained therein, however it did tacitly endorse sustainabilty in the preservation of whaling stocks through a thorough application of the standards set out in the ICRW. More explicit findings regarding the applicability of sustainable development principles in the *Whaling in the Antarctic* case can be found in the separate opnions of Judge Cançado Trindade and Judge *Ad Hoc* Charlesworth.

Judge Trindade's opinion focused on several aspects of the case, including the applicability of *opinio juris communis*.[74] In this context, he pointed to the *Gabčíkovo-Nagymaros* case as the case which extended international environmental law to treaty interpretation law, moving it away from a sub-field of international law and into a role as an interpretative principle.[75] In conjunction with the *Gabčíkovo-Nagymaros* case, Judge Trindade argued that the steady increase in treaty regimes leading to environmental protection, particularly for endangered species, established considerations of international environmental law as part of *opinio juris communis*.[76] Further, Judge Trindade argued that intergenerational equity principles had a part to play in analysing the Whaling in the Antarctic case, especially as the issues involved would have a direct impact on the ability of future generations.[77] He noted that, although the case issued from *Pulp Mills*, for example, in terms of facts it still touched on the same concepts of intergenerational equity and international environmental law.[78] Judge Trindade concluded this portion of his opinion by noting that "inter-generational equity marks presence nowadays in a wide range of instruments of international environmental law, and indeed of contemporary public international law."[79]

Judge Trindade also addressed the precautionary principle and the principle of prevention, noting that these were included in the memorials and arguments submitted to the Court.[80] He explained:

[d]espite the hesitation of the ICJ (and of other international tribunals in general) to pronounce and dwell upon the precautionary principle, expert writing increasingly examines it, drawing attention to its incidence when there is need to take protective measures in face of risks, even in the absence of corresponding scientific proof. The precautionary principle, in turn, draws attention to the time factor, the temporal dimension, which marks a noticable presence in the interpretation and application of treaties and instruments of international environmental law. In this domain in general, and in respect of the ICRW Convention in particular, there has occurred, with the passing of time, a move

74 Separate Opinion of Judge Cançado Trindade, *Whaling in the Antarctic (Australia v Japan: New Zealand Intervening)*, pt. V.
75 Ibid. at para. 30.
76 Ibid. at paras 38–40.
77 Ibid. at paras 43–44.
78 Ibid. at para. 43.
79 Ibid. at para. 47.
80 Ibid. at pt. VIII.

towards conservation of living marine resources as a common interest, prevailing over State unilateral action in search of commercial profitability.[81]

Judge *Ad Hoc* Charlesworth also focused on the precautionary principle in her opinion.[82] She discussed the *Gabčíkovo-Nagymaros* case and the *Pulp Mills* case as being important for incorporating the precautionary principle into international jurisprudence because they allowed courts, notably the ICJ, to "contemplate[. . .] the interpretation of treaty obligations in light of new approaches to environmental protection."[83] Further, she noted that "treaties dealing with the environment should be interpreted whenever possible in light of the precautionary approach, regardless of the date of their adoption."[84]

10.6 Conclusion

One can agree with the statement of Ida L. Bostian in connection with the *Gabčíkovo-Nagymaros* case: "The Court's decision was not a clear victory for either party."[85] The Gabčíkovo-Nagymaros problem was a particularly sensitive dispute both for Slovakia and Hungary. The ICJ was capable of elaborating a well-balanced, delicate decision, which guarantees that the most fundamental interests of both parties are safeguarded. However, the complexity of the international legal problem – which encompasses significant technical and scientific elements – made it impossible for the Court to provide for a detailed arrangement. The judgment rendered in 1997 may have been perhaps disappointing for many. According to international scholarship, where the additional rights of the Parties are determined, the provisions of international environmental law, international water law and the law of treaties must be considered with equal weight. However, the judgment evidently favours the provisions of the law of treaties to the detriment of the other two areas of law. Thus the Court "missed the opportunity to give further definition to the concept of sustainable development" in the *Gabčíkovo-Nagymaros* case.[86] Jan Klabbers finds it decisive that the Court is aware of the fact that certain determinations of the case will "return and haunt" in other cases as well. Consequently, while the Court introduced and operationalised the concept of sustainable development, it "stopped short of declaring or referring to sustainable development as a norm of customary international law."[87]

---

81 Ibid. at para. 71.
82 Separate Opinion of Judge *Ad Hoc* Charlesworth, *Whaling in the Antarctic (Australia v Japan: New Zealand Intervening)*, para. 6.
83 Ibid. at para. 7.
84 Ibid. at para. 9.
85 Bostian, Ida L., "Flushing the Danube: The World Court's Decision Concerning the Gabčíkovo Dam", *Colorado Journal of International Environmental Law and Policy* 9 (1998) at p. 414.
86 Koe, Adrianna, "Damming the Danube: The International Court of Justice and the Gabčíkovo-Nagymaros Project (Hungary v Slovakia)", *Sydney Law Review* 20 (1998) 4, p. 612.
87 Taylor, Prue, "Case concerning the Gabčíkovo-Nagymaros Project: A Message from the Hague on Sustainable Development", *New Zealand Journal of Environmental Law* 3 (1999), 109–126, p. 110.

Twelve years after the judgment, in the *Pulp Mills* case the ICJ could have resolved the questions of international environmental law and the legal implications of sustainable development that had been left open in the *Gabčíkovo-Nagymaros* judgment.[88] Nevertheless, in 2010 the Court was still reluctant to confirm sustainable development as a legal norm. Rather, the Court referred to sustainable development as an "objective".[89] Despite the Court's significant contribution to the law on sustainable development brought about by the recognition of the requirement to conduct environmental impact assessments as forming part of customary international law, the ICJ did not altogether seize the opportunity to develop, clarify and elaborate the scope, application and the legal status of the principles relating to sustainable development. As Dire Tladi observes, "[t]he Court is quite clearly aware of sustainable development and related principles. However, there is clear unwillingness to fully integrate these concepts into the decision it reaches. The Court was content merely to refer to them, almost symbolically, without integrating them into the decision."[90]

This pattern was affirmed in the 2014 *Whaling in the Antarctic* case, in which the ICJ was perhaps more tacitly willing to take sustainable development principles into account but was unwilling to include them in the textual language of the judgment. However, the separate opinions demonstrate an increasing awareness of principles such as the precautionary approach to other aspects of law on sustainable development.

On the basis of the these cases, we may come to the conclusion that the ICJ will also be careful in the future with respect to its resolutions concerning international environmental law and it will recognise certain aspects of law only if it is absolutely necessary. Commentators agree that the ICJ must pay more attention to environmental issues and it should not be "deterred" from determining the role of the continuously developing norms of international law on sustainable development.[91]

---

88 Trevisan, Lauren, "The International Court of Justice's Treatment of 'Sustainable Development' and Implications for Argentina v Uruguay", *Sustainable Development Law & Policy* 10 (2009) 1, p. 40.

89 *Case Concerning the Pulp Mills on the River Uruguay, Judgment, supra* note 31 at para. 177.

90 Tladi, Dire, "Principles of Sustainable Development in the Case concerning Pulp Mills on the River Uruguay", *supra* note 34 at p. 13.

91 Koe, *supra* note 86 at p. 629.

Permanent Court of Arbitration

11 Developing the judicial habit in nuanced ways through the *Abyei-Sudan* case

Jennifer McKay

Safeguarding the environment is a crosscutting United Nations' activity. It is a guiding principle of all our work in support of sustainable development. It is an essential component of poverty eradication and one of the foundations of peace and security.

Kofi Annan, United Nations Secretary-General, 1997[1]

11.1 Introduction

This chapter provides a detailed analysis of the *Abyei* adjudication which took place in 2009 before the Permanent Court of Arbitration, The Hague.[2] The arbitration was pursuant to an agreement between the Government of Sudan and the Sudan People's Liberation Movement/Army under Article 5 of the Arbitration Agreement that had been negotiated between the Parties prior to the Division of Sudan into two countries. The Arbitration related to a conflict that was non-international in character. International law has rules to protect the environment in international conflict such as Article 23 of Hague 1V[3]. Article 55 of the Geneva Conventions of 1949[4] requires that care be taken to protect the natural environment. Indeed, the arbitration shows that there was not very much deliberate destruction of land, forestry and water assets, despite the conflict being prolonged. Instead, the issues of the arbitration concerned the long-term rights to exploit these assets (both surface and groundwater) and oil. The actual boundary line in the Abyei region was crucial, as this would have an impact on which country would own the assets.

1 <http://www.eoearth.org/article/Regional_cooperation_for_peace_and_sustainable_development_in_Africa> accessed 24 April 2012

2 In the Permanent Court of Arbitration the Hague www.pca-cpa.org: *Abyei Arbitration* (The Government of Sudan/The Sudan People's Liberation Movement/Army), PCA, Award of the Arbitral Tribunal (22 May 2009) <http://www.pca-cpa.org/showpage.asp?pag_id=1306> accessed 24 April 2012.

3 Hague Declaration (1V) Respecting the Laws and customs of war on land Article 22, Annex, sec 2 ch 1; see also J. Cohan, 'Modes of Warfare and Evolving Standards of Environmental Protection Under the International Law of War' (2003) 15 *Flo. J. Int'l L.* 481.

4 Protocol 1 Additional to the Geneva Convention of 12 August 1949, and Relating to the Protection of Victims of International Armed conflicts Dec 12, 1977, 1125 UNTS 609, 6 US T 3516.

The arbitration is, therefore, an example of longer-term thinking about the environment and, *prima facie*, the use of historical evidence to attribute the land to different ethnic groups.

The arbitration was before these international Experts:

Professor Pierre-Marie Dupuy (Presiding Arbitrator)
H.E. Judge Awn Al-Khasawneh
Professor Dr. Gerhard Hafner
Professor W. Michael Reisman
Judge Stephen M. Schwebel

The purpose of this chapter is to examine the outcome of the adjudication and whether it reflects the seven International Law Association's (ILA) principles in relation to sustainable development.[5] The chapter reviews the ways the adjudication was approached and considers whether the aspects of the adjudication illustrates the use of the seven principles which have been discussed earlier in this book, see Chapter 3 by Nico Schrijver. This chapter relies on the New Delhi Declaration,[6] which provides the most current benchmark of important principles of international law on sustainable development. The New Delhi Declaration was based on a comprehensive and balanced decade of study and analysis by the ILA Committee on the Legal Aspects of Sustainable Development. These rules are considered to have a high degree of normative clarity.

The seven principles in the ILA from the New Delhi Declaration are:

1   The duty of States to ensure sustainable use of natural resources;
2   The principle of equity and the eradication of poverty;
3   The principle of the precautionary approach to human health, natural resources and ecosystems;
4   The principle of public participation and access to information and justice;
5   The principle of good governance;
6   The principle of common but differentiated obligations;
7   The principle of integration and interrelationship, in particular in relation to human rights and social, economic and environmental objectives

The most important first point to make is that the *Abyei* arbitration was concerned with applying the Abyei Protocol in the context of a civil war. The Abyei Protocol was the key aspect of an attempt to bring peace to a region that had endured over

---

5 See Nico Shrijver, 'The New Delhi Declaration: Principles of International Law Related to Sustainable Development' in M. C. Cordonier-Segger, C. G. Weeramantry, eds., *Sustainable Justice: Reconciling Economic, Social and Environmental Law* (The Netherlands: Martinus Nijhoff, 2005) 549–60.

6 ILA, 'Declaration of Principles of International Law Related to Sustainable Development', Resolution 3/2002 adopted at the 70th Conference of the International Law Association (New Delhi 2–6 April 2002) (9 August 2002) UN Doc A/CONF.199/8 [hereinafter New Delhi Declaration].

70 years of war.[7] The case had, as its fundamental question, to determine whether a border delimited as part of a Comprehensive Peace Agreement[8] was appropriate to the terms of the Comprehensive Peace Agreement. This border was between the north and south of the then nation of Sudan. The Abyei region is in the midst of this region, and is the pathway[9] between the drier more populated north and the wetter south. The area has been the subject of a long-standing dispute over access to resources, namely water and oil,[10] links to the land, and there has been considerable violence in the region.

The Presiding Arbitrator stated:[11]

> The other aspect is that the Abyei area is contained within one of the oil blocks, and there has been quite a lot of exploration and drilling of oil wells in the area. Now, we were not shown a map of where these oil wells were. We were told our mandate was to define the area in 1905 – of course there were no oil wells in 1905. There was no mechanised farming; there was no railway; there were no towns. If we had taken into consideration these developments since 1905, we would have been violating our mandate. But there is a lot of oil there – the Abyei Protocol stipulates that the oil revenues that come from the sale of oil in the Abyei area be divided between the Misseriya and the Ngok Dinka, the government and the SPLM. If the boundary is defined one way, it puts quite a lot of oil in the Abyei area, and therefore more of that oil revenue has to be shared. If we had accepted the government's claim that the boundary was the river, there would have been no oil revenue to share.

Hence, there were several resource issues overlapping with the ILA Principles. To approach these the PAC states how it would use international and other laws.[12]

The PCA Tribunal was sensitive to the extent to which principles and practices of international law, insofar as they prove applicable, must be adapted to the specific context of this dispute. As the following sections demonstrate, the special character of the Abyei Boundary Commission (ABC), the Abyei Boundary Commission Experts, the object and purpose of the ABC's constitutive instruments, and the international law value of sources, will affect the role which legal principles and precedent from other areas of law play in an arbitral process. Although it is permissible to apply relevant international law where appropriate, the Tribunal will be particularly attentive to the wording, context, object,

---

7 See *Abyei* case, *supra* note 2 at para. 455ff.
8 Signed by the Government of Sudan (GoS) and the Sudan People's Liberation Movement/Army (SPLM/A) on 9 January 2005.
9 See *Abyei* case, *supra* note 2 at para. 345.
10 Jennifer M. McKay, 'The Permanent Court of Arbitration and the Sudanese Peace Process: Legal Issues from the Abeyi Arbitration in reviewing the Mandate of an Ad hoc Body' (2009) 16 *Aus Int'l L. R.* at 232–39.
11 *Abyei* case, *supra* note 2 at para. 271.
12 *Abyei* case, *supra* note 2 at para. 435.

and purpose of the Abyei Protocol, the Abyei Appendix, the Interim National Constitution, and the Arbitration Agreement.[13]

It went on to say that:

> But international law is only one part of the applicable law. The Tribunal is mindful of the entire lex specialis prescribed by the Parties and the inter-relations between its component parts. Article 3(1) prescribes a functional hierarchy among the applicable sources of law that reflects the specific concerns of the Parties: the CPA (particularly those components of the CPA that directly bear upon Abyei within the North-South peace process) takes precedence in application, followed by the Interim National Constitution, followed by "general principles of law and practices." It should also be emphasized that Article 3(2) explicitly calls for the Tribunal to apply the Arbitration Agreement.[14]

The *Abyei* arbitration was concerned with the vital terms of the Arbitration agreement delimiting the Abyei area, and in particular the question of the case was whether the ABC experts exceeded their mandate as per the Comprehensive Peace Agreement (CPA). The mandate was to 'define and demarcate the area of the nine Ngok Dinka Chiefdoms transferred to Kordofan in 1905'.[15] The Experts were tasked to scientifically research, select and weigh such facts on the basis of a formula that was susceptible to several, contradictory interpretations, with a view to arriving at a 'final and binding' decision that 'defined . . . and demarcated' the Abyei area.[16]

The fundamental driver of the *Abyei* arbitration was the desire to achieve peace, which is relevant to the ILA Principles, especially Principles 2, 4, 5 and 7. This leads the author to argue that this arbitration illustrates Principles 2, 4 and 5 in a fundamentally novel way. However, within that context, the arbitration also illustrates several other principles and the integration that is absolutely necessary to achieve sustainable development. Peace is necessary, as is a government that will act to ensure that human rights are protected, respected and fulfilled. The arbitration is also important from a procedural point of view as it is an adjudication between a State and a non-state party. The PCA is an important body for such complex disputes as noted by Crawford and Rest.[17]

---

13 *Abyei* case, *supra* note 2 at para. 435.
14 *Abyei* case, *supra* note 2 at para. 436.
15 See *Abyei* case, *supra* note 2 at para. 3.
16 *Abyei* case, *supra* note 2 at para. 477.
17 James Crawford, 'The Permanent Court of Arbitration and Mixed Arbitration', Remarks of Professor James Richard Crawford SC FBA LLD, University of Cambridge and Matrix Chambers on the occasion of a Celebration of the Centenary of the PCA, The Hague, 18 October 2007; A. Rest, 'Enhanced Implementation of International Environmental Treaties by Judiciary – Access to Justice in International Environmental Law for Individuals and NGOs: Efficacious Enforcement by the Permanent Court of Arbitration' (2004) 1 MqJICEL.

The arbitration concerns all of the seven principles, but is particularly strong on:

2   The principle of equity and the eradication of poverty;
4   The principle of public participation and access to information and justice;
5   The principle of good governance;
7   The principle of integration and interrelationship, in particular in relation to human rights and social, economic and environmental objectives.

This chapter looks at the issue of how these have been applied in the context of a peace agreement at that time and the potential division of the former nation of Sudan.

11.2 The Abyei Protocol and the principles of good governance, public participation and access to information and justice

The Abyei Protocol (AP) was signed on 26 May 2004 and provided for agreed upon principles in administering the Abyei Area upon signing of the peace agreement. Notably, Section 1.1.2 of the AP defined the territory as 'the area of the nine Ngok Dinka chiefdoms transferred to Kordofan in 1905.' The Abyei Area was to be accorded special administrative status and was to be administered by a local executive council elected by the residents of the Abyei Area. These residents were to be dual citizens of Western Kordofan and Bahr el Ghazal, with representation in the two legislatures. Residents were defined as members of the Ngok Dinka community and other Sudanese residing in the Abyei Area.[18]

The AP[19] is one of the six fundamental texts recorded and reconfirmed in the CPA. The chapeau of the CPA states that the parties, Government of Sudan (GoS) and the Sudan People's Liberation Movement/Army (SPLM/A) 'MINDFUL of the urgent need to bring peace and security to the people of the Sudan [. . .],' reached agreement on these:

> [. . .] IN PURSUANCE OF [their] commitment [. . .] to a negotiated settlement on the basis of a democratic system of governance which, on the one hand, recognizes the right of the people of Southern Sudan to self-determination and seeks to make unity attractive during the Interim Period, while at the same time is founded on the values of justice, democracy, good governance, respect for fundamental rights and freedoms of the individual, mutual understanding and tolerance of diversity within the realities of the Sudan.[20]

18 *Abyei* case, *supra* note 2 at para. 113.
19 *Abyei* case, *supra* note 2 at para. 587. The Abyei Protocol is the fourth Chapter of the CPA. The five other chapters include the Machakos Protocol dated 20 July 2002 (Chapter I); the Agreement on Security Arrangements dated 25 September 2003 (Chapter VI of the CPA); the Agreement on Wealth Sharing dated 7 January 2004 (Chapter III of the CPA); the Protocol on Power Sharing dated 26 May 2004 (Chapter II); the Protocol on the Resolution of the Conflict in Southern Kordofan and Blue Nile States dated 26 May 2004 (Chapter V).
20 *Abyei* case, *supra* note 2 at para. 587.

Hence the ILA Principles 2, 4 and 5 are embedded as fundamental premises of the entire process.

The Interim National Constitution further confirms the duty of the Government of National Unity to implement agreements that reflect the human rights of all parties and indeed adopts a human rights based approach since it obliges the government to do this. This is stated below:

> The Duty of the Government of National unity [is] to implement
>
> [. . .] the Comprehensive Peace Agreement (CPA) in a manner that makes the unity of the Sudan an attractive option especially to the people of Southern Sudan, and pave the way for the exercise of the right of self-determination according to Part Sixteen of this Constitution.

In furtherance of these objectives, and duties the Abyei Protocol lays down, at the very beginning of its first section, the following three general principles of agreement on Abyei:

1.1.1 Abyei is a bridge between the north and the south, linking the people of Sudan;

1.1.2 The territory is defined as the area of the nine Ngok Dinka chiefdoms transferred to Kordofan in 1905;

1.1.3 The Misseriya and other nomadic peoples retain their traditional rights to graze cattle and move across the territory of Abyei.[21]

The AP also provided for the establishment of the ABC, which was given the task of defining and demarking the Abyei area.

On 17 December 2004, the Parties signed an 'Understanding on Abyei Boundaries Commission' (Abyei Appendix), which determined the composition of the ABC as follows:

(a) one representative from each of the GoS and the SPLM/A;

(b) 'five impartial experts knowledgeable in history, geography and any other relevant expertise' nominated by the United States, the United Kingdom and the Inter-Governmental Authority on Development (IGAD);

(c) two nominees of the GoS and two nominees of the SPLM/A 'from the present two administrations of the Abyei Area;'

(d) two nominees of the GoS from the Messiriya; and

(e) two nominees of the SPLM/A from the 'neighboring Dinka tribes to the South of the Abyei Area.'

Hence this showed an application of Principles 2 and 5 in the detail of the composition and this is further buttressed by the inclusive processes as described below.

In determining the Abyei Area, the ABC was required 'to listen to representatives of the people of Abyei Area and their neighbours, [as well as to] listen to presentations of the two Parties' and to 'consult the British Archives and other

---

21 *Abeyi* case, *supra* note 2 at paras 588–89.

relevant sources on Sudan wherever they may be available, with a view to arriving at a decision that shall be based on scientific analysis and research.'[22]

Where the application of this process floundered (in the opinion of this author) was the provision that allowed the ABC Experts to determine the rules of procedure of the ABC. This lead to a great number of *ad hoc* processes and data collection methods which were challenged in the Award decisions. The process was unclear and not considered transparent and this undermined Principles 2 and 5.[23]

Hence, the fundamental aspect of the arbitration concerned the two key ILA principles mentioned above – the principle of equity and alleviation of poverty and the principle of good governance. In these, sharing of grazing rights and the dual special administration zone satisfied the ILA principles of equity and alleviation of poverty and good governance. To delve more deeply, the author went on to search for nuances referencing other ILA principles using an adaptation of a legal content analysis approach. This is described and administered below.

11.3 Legal content analysis to capture the nuances of the seven ILA Principles in the *Abyei* arbitration

The author used systematic content analysis of the *Abyei* arbitration[24] supplemented by an *adapted* legal content analysis. The method to achieve the adapted legal content analysis consisted of a number of steps. The first was to read the entire majority judgment and consider the seven principles. Here the author used word search techniques. This technique, for example, makes it possible is able to say that the ILA New Delhi Declaration principles are not mentioned by name and the word 'sustainability' does not appear in the *Abyei* arbitration report.

This prompted the author to consider using content analysis methods as these have been used by the author before[25] and are common in legal scholarship.[26]

Content analysis does not replace traditional legal scholarship but, instead, the aim here is to offer distinctive insights that complement the types of understandings that only traditional analysis can generate.[27] The conventional legal analysis has already been presented above.

For the content analysis the adaptation process first involved using just the *Abyei* arbitration alone. The steps to create the single case content analysis

---

22 *Abyei* case, *supra* note 2 at paras 114, 115–16.
23 Jennifer M. McKay, 'The Permanent Court of Arbitration and the Sudanese Peace Process: Legal Issues from the Abeyi Arbitration in reviewing the Mandate of an Ad hoc Body' (2009) 16 *Aus. Int'l L. R.* at 232–39.
24 M. Hall and R. Wright (no date) systematic content analysis of judicial opinions. <http://epstein.law.northwestern.edu/research/WrightHall.pdf> accessed 17 March 2015.
25 See Adam Gray and Jennifer M. McKay, 'Are utility attitudes to the environment shaped by corporate governance? Assessing the evidence from Australian utility reports' (2006) 11 (1) *Water Utility Management International* 8–11 <http://www.iwaponline.com/wumi/00101/1/default.htm>.
26 See, e.g., D. Zaring, 'The use of foreign decisions by Federal courts an empirical analysis' (2006) 3 *J. Empirical Legal Stud.* 297, at 303.
27 See M. Hall and Ronald Wright, *supra* note 24.

method are shown below in a series of steps. This process, like much innovation in research methods, was a spontaneous self-taught method.[28] This has a worthy pedigree in legal scholarship.

11.3.1 Method to create the adapted legal content analysis

The process was as follows:

Key word searches on key words such as sustainability, ILA, ILA-2 equity (intra generational inter-generational equity, ILA-3 precautionary, ILA-4 public participation, access to information, access to justice, ILA-5 good governance, ILA-6 CDR, and ILA-7 Integration, and human rights.

The results are presented below but discussed under each of the ILA Principles:

WORD/ILA Principle (if applicable)	*Abyei* case majority	Comments majority
Peace	Section 9 of the Abyei Protocol reads: 'Upon signing the Comprehensive Peace Agreement, the Presidency shall, as a matter of urgency, start peace and reconciliation process for Abyei that shall work for harmony and peaceful co-existence in the area.'	Fundamental aspect of the case after 70 years of internal conflict. para. 587, 591, 657.
Sustainability	Nil.	Nil not mentioned.
ILA New Delhi	Nil.	Nil not mentioned.
Intra generational equity ILA Principle 2	Some references in the context of peace.	However it is part of the outcome.
Inter generational equity 2	Sharing of land and water between two groups the basis for the arbitration.	Fundamental aspect.
Equity generally ILA Principle 2	4 mentions para. 203 204–7. ABC Experts delimited the Abyei Area illegitimately based on pure equity and this was challenged by GoS.	See below equity based in evidence of past use. This was prescribed by the Agreement setting up the arbitration but this is only one of several possibilities. The case demonstrates that this principle tends to trump others.

---

28 Ibid. at 6.

Precautionary ILA Principle 3	Nil.	Is alluded to.
Public participation ILA Principle 4	Para. 1251ff lots of local consultation required and done but the methods used were in dispute between the parties. See discussion.	Part of the mandating law and again here the method selected was disputed.
Access to information ILA Principle 4	Para. 12ff. The ABC methods used to seek information was challenged. Hence parties felt it was unfair.	Fundamental aspect.
Access to justice ILA Principle 4	Para. 1251ff and fundamental aspect of the whole process.	Part of the mandating law. But see dissenting view.
Good governance ILA Principle 5	Para. 1251ff a fundamental aspect of the whole process.	Part of the mandating law.
CDR 6	Nil.	Nil.
Integration ILA Principle 7	Alluded to generally but no use of the word.	Nil.
Human rights ILA Principle 7	Para. 1254 and many others on the rights to return citing African Charter and several other cases.	Part of the mandating law.
Fairness of process in the process of the Abyei Experts	Paras 524 and 534 two specific but several reference the real conflict in the case.	Fundamental dispute of the case reconciled using international law cases.
development	Para. 754[29] key references cited.[30]	Used to encompass the three pillars a lot.[31]

29 Source: Data collection by author (September 2011).

30 *Abyei* case, *supra* note 2 at paras 148, 471.

31 Section 1.6 of the CPA affirms the application of the African Charter on Human and People's Rights, which (among other things) guarantees the right of every individual to leave any country including his own, and to return to his country (Article 12(2)) and the right of all peoples to freely pursue their economic and social development according to the policy they have freely chosen. (Article 21(1)). The legal principles of the continuation of traditional rights enabling lifestyles that necessitate trans-boundary migration are consistent with these principles. In Section 2.5 of the CPA, the Parties agree that 'a process be instituted to progressively develop and amend the relevant laws to incorporate customary laws and practices, local heritage and international trends and practices.' Similarly, Section 2.6.6.2 of the CPA requires the National Land Commission to 'accept references on request from the relevant government, or in the process of resolving claims, and make recommendations to the appropriate levels of government concerning: . . . Recognition of customary land rights and/or law.' The references to 'customary laws and practices' and 'customary land rights' in the CPA would seem to include the exercise of traditional rights. Pursuant to Section 3.1.5 of the CPA, land rights are a relevant factor in the allocation and exploitation of natural resources: 'Persons enjoying rights in land

The Table demonstrates that the concepts embodied in the seven ILA Principles were part of the decision making processes. The key focus areas will be discussed below. The dissenting judgment does not impact on this analysis. The reasons are set out below:[32]

> Professor Hafner had the dissenting opinion on the nature of the ABC. In Professor Hafner's view, the ABC is not a "boundary commission" within the contemplation of the Treaty of Lausanne Advisory Opinion. Rather, the ABC's nature is more akin to that of a pure fact-finding body, as its mandate was limited to ascertaining a set of historical facts and arriving at a final and binding judgment based solely on those facts. For Professor Hafner, the fact that the ABC Experts' decision was binding is not sufficient evidence that they possessed any powers beyond those vested in a fact-finding body (Article 35 of the 1907 Hague Convention and Article 24(2) of the PCA Optional Rules for Fact-finding Commissions of Inquiry both provide for the possibility that the decisions of fact-finding bodies can be made binding).

Thus, according to Professor Hafner, the ABC Experts were not empowered to make any decision having an *ex nunc*, constitutive effect. In his view, the final and binding effect of the ABC Experts' Report resulted directly from Article 5 of the Abyei Appendix; it did not result from the mandate of the ABC itself. Furthermore, he does not share the view that the ABC Experts were obliged to delimit the Abyei Area even in the absence of sufficient evidence; a factual non-liquet was one possible decision the ABC Experts could have taken, and they would not have acted *infra petita* had they chosen to do so. Nevertheless, as Professor Hafner agrees, none of the foregoing observations affects the substance of the conclusions drawn by the Tribunal.'

11.4 Public participation in the process of peace

The majority view is analysed below.

The implementation of peace and the ways the ABC Experts implemented their mandate was the real and major concern of the arbitration. Section 3.1.5 of the CPA, required that land rights be a relevant factor in the allocation and exploitation of natural resources: 'Persons enjoying rights in land shall be consulted and their views shall duly be taken into account in respect of decisions to develop subterranean natural resources from the area in which they have rights, and shall share in the benefits of that development.' So this implements ILA

shall be consulted and their views shall duly be taken into account in respect of decisions to develop subterranean natural resources from the area in which they have rights, and shall share in the benefits of that development.'

32 *Abyei* case, *supra* note 2 at paras 484–85.

Principles 4 and 5. However, if the process to determine land rights is flawed then peace is unlikely to be the outcome.

The administration of the ABC Experts was the major aspect of the decision. For example, in para. 149, by arranging interviews without the knowledge of the parties, the GoS argued that the ABC Experts not only deliberately circumvented the agreed work programme, but also demonstrated a propensity to side with the SPLM/A and thus deprived the GoS of the right to a fair procedure. Good governance is challenged here. This is especially so since no information of these meetings was provided to the GoS until the final presentation of the ABC Experts' report. This was a serious departure from a fundamental rule of procedure and constituted, in the view of the GoS, a ground for finding an excess of mandate, since the taking of evidence by the ABC Experts without procedural safeguards and without informing the GoS constituted an excess of mandate. There were no limitations on the rules of gathering evidence as stated in para. 471:

> None of the foregoing provisions of the Parties' agreements or the Rules of Procedure imposed prohibitions or limitations on the ABC Experts' procedural, investigatory, or fact finding actions. Although the constitutive instruments set forth a variety of provisions to grant the ABC Experts affirmative access to different types of information – people, sites, documents, archives – nothing in any of the instruments forbade the ABC Experts from taking further or additional actions insofar as they were, in their reasonable view, necessary for the fulfilment of their tasks. The ABC Experts were not restricted to evaluating the evidence offered by the Parties; they were explicitly authorized to investigate the matters they thought relevant in determining the boundary and, without the necessary participation of the entire ABC, to draft the final report and to present it to the Sudanese Presidency.

The ABC Experts were not lawyers but were individuals known and recognized in the fields of Sudanese and African history, geography, politics, public affairs, ethnography and culture. They were: (1) Mr. Donald Petterson, the former US Ambassador to Sudan from 1992 to 1995, with decades of experience working for the US Foreign Service in Sudan and other countries in Africa; (2) Professor Douglas Johnson, a professor of History at Oxford University who has some 40 years of research experience on Sudan; (3) Professor Godfrey Muriuki, a pre-eminent African historian and professor of African History at the University of Nairobi; (4) Professor Kassahun Berhanu, one of Africa's leading political scientists and a Professor of Political Science at the Addis Ababa University; and (5) Professor Shadrack Gutto, who has published widely on 'subjects of regional and international, legal and political economy' and has been, as of 2008, Professor and Chair of African Renaissance Studies and Director of the postgraduate Centre for African Renaissance Studies at the University of South Africa.

Hence, they used different research methods from these disciplines. A real issue was the lack of specificity in the ways that different constituencies could participate in the discussions that occurred prior to the arbitral panel decision. In the end, the PCA characterised the approach of the ABC Experts as a *tribal approach* and in paragraph 659 stated:

> In light of these objectives, the adoption by the ABC Experts of a predominantly tribal approach, which would result in the inclusion and the participation in the 2011 referendum of most members of the targeted community, the Ngok Dinka, can plausibly be regarded as furthering the stated goals of peace and reconciliation.

There were allegations of partiality.[33] The GoS also argued that evidence of partiality on the part of the ABC Experts could be found in an interview given by Dr. Douglas Johnson, one of the ABC Experts, to the *Sudan Tribune* on 29 May 2006, as well as in the fact that Dr. Johnson was later engaged as an expert consultant by the Government of South Sudan.

Because of such purported lack of impartiality, the GoS argued that its fundamental right to equal and impartial treatment was violated. Further, such considerations are also allegedly indicative of the fact that the ABC Experts did not decide on the basis of 'scientific analysis and research.'

There was argument also about the oral evidence and this was dealt in paragraph 381, as below:

> The SPLM/A argues that, contrary to the GoS's position, oral tradition is considered a valuable source of information by historians, especially in oral or part-oral societies. In addition, courts and tribunals confer a "crucial role" to oral tradition. SPLM/A cites to the Supreme Court of Canada and the Inter-American Court of Human Rights to show that oral tradition of tribal peoples is admitted and relied upon by the courts, "and placed on an equal footing with the types of historical evidence that courts are familiar with, which largely consists of historical documents.

There was a huge debate on witness statements from the point of view of the hearsay rule with the SPLM/A at first denying that the Ngok witness statements have no value on the grounds that they refer to events to which they cannot personally testify. Contrary to the GoS's assertion, hearsay evidence may be admitted in arbitration and tribal knowledge provides "the most reliable proof of the existence of property rights entitled to protection under a state's legal system."[34] As stated in paragraph 717:

> For its part, the GoS has criticized the reliability of witness evidence. This Tribunal agrees that where the witnesses rely on knowledge passed down through one or two generations, the precise dating of the evidence which they supply may sometimes be difficult. Nevertheless, depriving witness

33 *Abyei, supra* note 2 at para. 213
34 *Abyei, supra* note 2 at para. 717

evidence per se of all probative value would be unjustifiable. When defining the historic area of a tribe, an inherently difficult exercise, it is reasonable, and indeed quite logical, to seek information from the tribe members themselves. The ABC was explicitly structured by the Parties to hear such evidence. The Terms of Reference of the ABC, which were agreed upon by the Parties, provided that "[t]he ABC shall thereafter travel to the Sudan to listen to representatives of the people of Abyei Area and their neighbors" and both Parties did rely on witness evidence before the Commission.

The ABC Experts themselves, as specialists, felt they had to consider oral evidence. The Arbitral Tribunal PCA stated in paragraph. 717 that:

> The balanced approach of the Supreme Court of Canada provides useful guidance on the evidentiary value of oral tradition:
> Notwithstanding the challenges created by the use of oral histories as proof of historical facts, the laws of evidence must be adapted in order that this type of evidence can be accommodated and placed on an equal footing with the types of historical evidence that courts are familiar with, which largely consists of historical documents. This is a long-standing practice in the interpretation of treaties between the Crown and aboriginal peoples.

Hence, public participation in the delimitation of the boundaries was a fundamental aspect of the arbitration. The widest possible interpretation of this requirement was debated in the arbitration so the application here was very strong. The need to include all voices and also to accept hearsay and other ways of ensuring full public participation was strengthened.

11.5 Human rights

Human rights were discussed at length and the CPA affirmed the application of the African Charter on Human and People's Rights to the issue at hand. The African Charter on Human and People's Rights guarantees the right of every individual to leave any country including his own, and to return to his country (art 12.2), and the right of all peoples to freely pursue their economic and social development according to the policy they have freely chosen (art 21.1). The legal principles of the continuation of traditional rights enabling lifestyles that necessitate trans-boundary migration are consistent with these principles.

In art 2.5 of the CPA, the Parties agreed that 'a process be instituted to progressively develop and amend the relevant laws to incorporate customary laws and practices, local heritage and international trends and practices.'

The *Abyei* arbitration discussed several decisions of the International Court of Justice (ICJ) on this issue[35] in particular and hence applied the human rights

---

35 *Abyei, supra* note 2 at para. 754

requirements in the context of pre-existing traditional rights. The *Abyei* decision went on to say that:

> The ICJ considered traditional fishing rights and land rights, without how-ever finding them sufficient to allocate title to territory based on the notion of better established effectivités.[36]

The arbitration did not allude to integration through the use of the Charter.

11.6 Conclusion

The analysis of the important decision in the *Abyei* arbitration shows that several key ILA Principles were fundamental even in the context of the overarching objec-tive to create peace. Of these, a crucial one that was discussed at length concerned the public participation in the process. The arbitration gives real definition to this concept as it allows all types of evidence to be used and several types of ways of collecting such information. Indeed, a key aspect of the resolution involved inter-pretation of the underlying documents to ensure that the ABC Experts could independently gather evidence and indeed they could do this individually. The implementation of the processes to gather evidence was a real source of challenge and dispute and there were challenges to the fairness aspects. Hence, in any subse-quent case of this type, it is important that the processes for evidence gathering be made clearer. In this case, the arbitrators did indeed use international legal prec-edents and took a wide view. The guidelines being analysed needed to be clearer. However, this goes to reinforce how seriously the concepts of public participation are taken and that the methods should be agreed up by the parties.

In *Abyei*, human rights were expressly addressed and several cases of the ICJ were used. However, the challenge here in *Abyei* was the presumption that his-torical records would provide an adequate basis for future rights to land, water and oil. The arbitration had to deal with the issue that oil reserves were found afterwards. This brings into sharp contrast this selection of the past attachments to land to determine future access and exploitation rights to oil.

The approach using the content analysis was then able to draw out several other applications of the principles even in the context of civil war. Overall, the arbitration is a powerful lesson on the problems of public participation and how that can be seen as unfair, if the processes are not transparent. Long-term good governance has transparency of decision making processes at its core.

---

36 *Sovereignty over Pulau Ligitan and Pulau Sipadan (Indonesia/Malaysia)*, Judgment, ICJ Reports 2002, at 625; *Maritime Delimitation and Territorial Questions between Qatar and Bahrain, Merits, Judgment*, ICJ Reports 2001, 40. See Series, TMC Asser Press, forthcoming 2009), also available at <www.pca-cpa.org>.

12 The *Iron Rhine* case

On the right track to sustainable development?

Freya Baetens[1]

12.1 Introduction

17 August 1585 – Antwerp, the cultural, economic and financial centre of the Seventeen Provinces and one of the most prosperous cities of north-western Europe, surrenders to the Spanish troops after more than one year of siege. The partition of the northern and southern provinces of the Netherlands is a fact. After the siege, the Dutch fleet on the river Scheldt is kept in position for the next two centuries, blocking the city's access to the sea, cutting it off from international trade and thereby crippling its economy; a traumatic passage in the history of relations between the Netherlands and Flanders.

This all occurred in times long past but once in a while disputes still arise with regard to Dutch–Flemish/Belgian activities in this region. Where the declared focus of the argument used to be on religion (Protestant versus Catholic), both sides now often invoke the protection of the environment as the main reason for their conduct, as illustrated not only by the object of the present chapter, the *Iron Rhine* dispute,[2] but also for example by the debates concerning the deepening of the Westerschelde (the estuary of the Scheldt river).[3] One of the underlying motives for both parties, throughout history, is and has always been economic: the competition between the port of Antwerp (Belgium) and that of Rotterdam (the Netherlands). Hence, during the discussion of the *Iron Rhine* case in general and the sustainable development principle as applied in this dispute in particular, the reader ought to bear in mind that arguments on both sides

1 The author would like to warmly thank Ineke van Bladel and Andrea Varga for their feedback. Regarding potential errors or omissions, the usual disclaimer applies. This paper has been updated until 1 April 2012.
2 *Arbitration regarding the Iron Rhine ("Ijzeren Rijn") Railway between The Kingdom of Belgium and The Kingdom of the Netherlands* (Award of 24 May 2005) UNRIAA XXVII 35.
3 I. van Bladel, 'Schuivende grenzen: nabuurrelaties in het Schelde-estuarium' in G.C. Dohmen and M.C.E.M. Draaisma, *Een kwestie van grensoverschrijding: liber amicorum P.E.L. Janssen* (The Netherlands: Wolf Legal Publishers, 2009) 23–39.

might be informed by other than purely environmental reasons.[4] The presence of such underlying motives does not imply that this case is merely a 'cover' – unable to contribute in a significant manner to the clarification of the status and content of sustainable development principles. On the contrary, it is highly likely that in any given dispute where environmental protection plays a role, other motives will need to be considered as well – so the true value of the *Iron Rhine* case precisely lies in its search for the 'right balance' of sustainable development in its economic and environmental form.

This chapter first addresses the factual background of the *Iron Rhine* dispute, including the questions submitted to the arbitral panel; continuing with an analysis of the award itself, focusing on the treatment of sustainable development principles; and finishing with an assessment of the relevance of this case for the future application of sustainable development principles in other similar cases.

12.2 Factual background

12.2.1 The separation of Belgium and the Netherlands

Music is said to sooth restive souls but Auber's opera *La Muette de Portici* achieved rather the opposite when it ignited revolutionary feelings in the Southern Netherlands against their perceived 'oppressors' from the North. After centuries of separation following the fall of Antwerp, the Southern and Northern Netherlands had been reunited by the five European ruling powers (Austria, France, Prussia, Russia and the United Kingdom) at the 1815 Congress of Vienna, convened after the defeat of Napoleon Bonaparte. This 'United Kingdom of the Netherlands' was however rife with strife from its inception, resulting in another decision of the aforementioned ruling powers convened in the London Conference of 1830 to split the territory up into a northern (the Netherlands) and a southern part (Belgium). The purpose was to maintain the function of the latter as a neutral buffer zone, headed by a German prince (Leopold of Saxe-Coburg-Gotha) who was the uncle of the British Queen Victoria and married to the French Princess Louise of Orléans. Notably, the approval of the Netherlands to this reorganization did not seem of primordial importance which was rather ill-received in The Hague as detectable from the nine-year-delay of King William I in ratifying the *Treaty between Belgium and the Netherlands relative to the Separation of their Respective Territories* [the 1839 Treaty of Separation].[5]

---

4 See, e.g. the highly critical assessment of C. Djeffal, 'The Iron Rhine Case – A Treaty's Journey from Peace to Sustainable Development' (2011) 71 Zaörv 3, 584; C. Warbrick, 'The "Iron Rhine" ("Ijzeren Rijn") Arbitration (Belgium – Netherlands): Its Contribution to International Law' in *PCA Award Series* (The Hague: TMC Asser Press, 2007) 2.

5 Treaty between Belgium and the Netherlands relative to the Separation of their Respective Territories (1838–1839) 88 CTS 426.

12.2.2 *The creation of a Belgian right of transit*

Among other provisions, the Treaty of Separation granted Belgium a right of transit over Netherlands territory so as to allow for a direct link from the Belgian port of Antwerp to Mönchengladbach and Duisburg in the German Rhine basin (Ruhrgebiet) via the Dutch provinces of Noord-Brabant and Limburg. Roads and canals were considered an outmoded means of conveyance by the time an agreement was found to execute this transit right, so the parties opted for a tele-ological interpretation of the treaty terms and organized the construction of a railway track instead – metaphorically named the "Iron Rhine"[6] – as specified in the 1873 Iron Rhine Treaty.[7]

12.2.3 *The construction and use of the Iron Rhine railway*

The Iron Rhine railway was constructed according to the Treaty of Separation as amended by the Iron Rhine Treaty, used intensively from 1879 until the First World War and thereafter intermittently until 1991. The Belgian inter-est in modernizing the route as a multi-track electrified line suitable for more intensive and heavier transport arose even before 1991 – which runs counter to the Dutch economic interests, specifically its Rotterdam-Germany freight route (the 'Betuweroute'). An alternative railway route from Belgium to Germany also exists (the Hasselt-Montzen-Aachen route) but it is substantially longer (210 km as opposed to 160).

During the period of disuse, the section of the 'historic route' on Dutch ter-ritory remained in use as part of the public railway system but the Netherlands designated parts of the area crossed by the Iron Rhine as nature reserves. After a series of informal communications, Belgium formally initiated discussions in 1998 on the use, restoration, adaptation and modernization [together called the 'reactivation'] of the Iron Rhine railway which led to the adoption of a Memorandum of Understanding [MoU] in 2000, providing among others for (i) a joint international study by the three countries involved on the consequences of reactivation and the existence of alternative routes, and (ii) an Environmental Impact Assessment by the Netherlands for the section of the Iron Rhine located on its territory. These studies were completed in May 2001 and concluded that the preferred option would be to maintain the historic route. Disagreement among the parties continued concerning the 'temporary use' of the railway by Belgium (while negotiations and/or works were ongoing) and the allocation of costs (which were due to be significantly higher if the reactivation needed to be in

---

6 This metaphor allegedly originates from Ludolf von Campenhausen, 'Zur Eisenbahn von Köln nach Antwerpen 1833' 7 as cited in C. Djeffal, 'The Iron Rhine Case – A Treaty's Journey from Peace to Sustainable Development' (2011) 71 Zaörv 3, 571 fn7.

7 Convention between Belgium and the Netherlands relative to the Payment of the Belgian Debt, the Abolition of the Surtax on Netherlands Spirits, and the Passing of a Railway Line from Antwerp to Germany across Limburg (1872–1873) 145 CTS 447.

compliance with the Netherlands' environmental protection measures resulting from the re-designation of the area as nature reserve).

12.2.4 The initiation of arbitral proceedings

Both States agreed to submit their differences to an arbitral panel so as to determine the nature and scope of the Belgian transit right and the allocation of costs in light of the Parties' obligations under the relevant treaties and principles of international law as well as under EC law. Belgium's right to make renewed and significantly heavier use of the railway line was not disputed as such by the Netherlands, but the two States did disagree concerning Belgium's alleged entitlement to unilaterally establish the plan for the reactivation; the Netherlands' alleged entitlement to unilaterally enact specific conditions for such a reactivation; and, most importantly, the allocation of the related costs arising therefrom. The arbitral proceedings were conducted pursuant to an Arbitration Agreement between Belgium and the Netherlands, concluded in July 2003. The Arbitral Tribunal constituted to decide this dispute was composed of Judge Rosalyn Higgins (President), Professor Guy Schrans, Judge Bruno Simma, Professor Alfred H.A. Soons, and Judge Peter Tomka. Pursuant to the Arbitration Agreement, the Tribunal was established under the auspices of the Permanent Court of Arbitration, which also served as Registry for the arbitration.

12.3 Award

The Tribunal rendered its final Award on 24 May 2005, which was structured into seven parts: (I) procedural history, background and party submissions; (II) legal basis and scope of Belgium's transit right; (III) the role of European law in the present arbitration; (IV) the Belgian request for reactivation and the MoU of March 2000; (V) measures envisaged by the Netherlands in the light of Article XII of the 1839 Treaty of Separation; (VI) allocation of costs; and (VII) replies of the Tribunal to the questions put by the parties. For the purpose of this chapter – the contribution of this Award to the development and understanding of sustainable development principles – only parts II, V and VI will be discussed in-depth. For a discussion of the other sections of the Award, in particular the highly interesting discussion on European law and the need to avoid trespassing on the prerogatives of the Court of Justice of the EU, the reader is kindly referred to the relevant literature.[8]

8 See, e.g. N. Lavranos, 'The MOX Plant and IJzeren Rijn Disputes: which Court is the Supreme Arbiter?' (2006) 19 LJIL 1, 223–46; I. van Bladel, 'The Iron Rhine Arbitration Case: on the Right Legal Track?: an Analysis of the Award and of its Relation to the Law of the European Community' (2006) 18 *Hague Ybk Int'l L.* 3–22; P. d'Argent, 'De la fragmentation à la cohésion systémique: la sentence arbitrale du 24 mai 2005 relative au "Rhin de Fer" (IJzeren Rijn)' in *Droit du pouvoir, pouvoir du droit: mélanges offerts à Jean Salmon* (Brussels: Bruylant, 2007) 1122–27; C. Warbrick, 'The "Iron Rhine"("Ijzeren Rijn") Arbitration (Belgium – Netherlands):

12.3.1 Legal basis and scope of Belgium's transit right

12.3.1.1 From intertemporal to effective interpretation: whither the intention of the parties?

12.3.1.1.1 IRON RHINE APPLICATION

The Tribunal examined the applicable legal provisions as well as the principles of interpretation it had to apply to the disputed elements in Article XII of the Treaty of Separation. In this Article, the parties had stipulated that:

> In the case that in Belgium a new road would have been built or a new canal dug, which would lead to the Maas facing the Dutch canton of Sittard, then Belgium would be at liberty to ask Holland, which in that hypothesis would not refuse it, that the said road, or the said canal be extended in accordance with the same plan, entirely at the cost and expense of Belgium, through the canton of Sittard, up to the borders of Germany. This road or canal, which could be used only for commercial communication, would be constructed, at the choice of Holland, either by engineers and workers whom Belgium would obtain authorization to employ for this purpose in the canton of Sittard, or by engineers and workers whom Holland would supply, and who would execute the agreed works at the expense of Belgium, all without any burden to Holland, and without prejudice to the exclusive rights of sovereignty over the territory which would be crossed by the road or canal in question. [. . .][9]

The main problem which the Tribunal encountered here was the matter of inter-temporality in the interpretation of treaty provisions. Relying on the meanwhile (in)famous Article 31(3)(c) of the Vienna Convention on the Law of Treaties [VCLT],[10] which allows adjudicatory bodies to consider "any relevant rules of international law applicable in the relations between the parties", the Tribunal not only examined relevant provisions of European law but also of general and environmental international law. The difficulty arising here was the choice between interpreting the obligations and rights of parties according to such relevant rules in existence at the time of concluding the Treaty (i.e. in 1839), at the moment of

---

Its Contribution to International Law' in *PCA Award Series* (The Hague: TMC Asser Press, 2007) 7–15; C. Djeffal, 'The Iron Rhine Case – A Treaty's Journey from Peace to Sustainable Development' (2011) 71 Zaörv 3, 572–77.

9 The Treaty of Separation was concluded in Dutch and French; this English translation is provided by the Tribunal in para. 32 of the Award.

10 Vienna Convention on the Law of Treaties (concluded 23 May 1969, entered into force 27 January 1980) 1155 UNTS 331; the 'systemic integration' principle incorporated in Article 31(3)(c) of the VCLT was elaborately discussed in the UN ILC 'Fragmentation of International Law: Difficulties Arising from the Diversification and Expansion of International Law: Report of the Study Group' (17 July 2006) *GAOR* 61st Session Supp 10, 403 and is often portrayed as a 'master key' solution to all interpretation problems, e.g. at para. 430 of the ILC Fragmentation Report.

the re-designation of the area as a nature reserve by the Netherlands (i.e. 1990s) or when the Tribunal was asked to interpret the Treaty (i.e. 2005).

The Tribunal opted for an evolutive approach, stating that "both international and EC law require the integration of appropriate environmental measures in the design and implementation of economic development activities."[11] It is not denied that the intertemporal rule is relevant for the interpretation of treaty terms, but at the same time, as also held in various other cases, this rule does not require adjudicatory bodies to "be oblivious either to later facts that bear on the effective application of the treaty, nor indeed to all later legal developments."[12] The goal of the interpretative exercise is to ensure an application that renders a treaty effective in terms of its object and purpose, which is particularly relevant in an area where new technical developments relating to the operation and capacity of railways undergo such significant and unforeseeable changes over time.

In the Award itself, the Tribunal does not elaborate on the distinction between the latter two points in time: the rules in existence at the time of re-designation (1990s) as opposed to those at the time of the rendering of the Award (2005). This could affect the legal status of environmental principles as these have undergone significant changes in the meantime, moving from the realm of soft law to that of hard law in the course of the last two decades. In its Interpretation of the Award issued in September 2005,[13] the Tribunal did address this issue, by stating that the obligations of the Netherlands relate to standards "as current Netherlands legislation would require and not as they may have been applicable in 1991".[14] Although this reply specifically related to the financial obligations of the Netherlands with regard to maintenance, it can safely be assumed that for all other purposes, the phrase "contemporary rules of international environmental law" is to be understood as a reference to such rules in existence at the time of the Award rendering.

12.3.1.1.2 DEVELOPMENT OF INTERNATIONAL RULES ON TREATY INTERPRETATION

In the words of Max Huber in the *Island of Palmas* arbitration, the intertemporal rule implies that "a juridical fact must be appreciated in the light of the law contemporary with it, and not of the law in force at the time when a dispute in regard to it arises or falls to be settled."[15] The International Law Commission [ILC]'s

---

11 Iron Rhine Award, *supra* note 2 at para 59.

12 Ibid. referring to *Nationality Decrees Issued in Tunis and Morocco* (1923) PCIJ Ser B, No 4, 24; *Namibia (SW Africa)* (Advisory Opinion) [1971] ICJ Rep 16 at 31; *Aegean Sea Continental Shelf (Greece/Turkey)* (Judgment) [1978] ICJ Rep 3 at 32, para. 77; WTO, *US – Shrimp Import Prohibition of Certain Shrimp and Shrimp Products* (Report of the Appellate Body 12 October 1998) WT/DS58/AB/R (1999) 38 ILM 118, para. 130.

13 *Arbitration regarding the Iron Rhine ("Ijzeren Rijn") Railway between the Kingdom of Belgium and The Kingdom of the Netherlands* (Interpretation of the Award of the Arbitral Tribunal 20 September 2005) UNRIAA XXVII 127.

14 Ibid. at para. 13.

15 *Island of Palmas (Netherlands/USA)* (Award of 4 April 1928) [1949] RIAA vol. II. 839 at 845.

1964 version of Article 69 of the Draft Articles on the Law of Treaties (later: Article 31 of the VCLT) made reference to the intertemporal rule in its explanation of the ordinary meaning of a treaty text, which had to be determined according to "the general rules of international law in force *at the time of its conclusion*" (emphasis added).[16] In further ILC discussions, some members "considered that the interpretation of the treaty may be affected by changes in the general rules of international law" although the majority at that time was of the opinion that this concerned "a question of the modification of the rule laid down in the treaty by a later legal rule rather than one of the interpretation of the terms".[17] Upon re-examination of the provision, this reference to intertemporality was nevertheless omitted because "the relevance of rules of international law for the interpretation of treaties in any given case was dependent on the intentions of the parties" so "that to attempt to formulate a rule covering comprehensively the temporal element would present difficulties".[18] This did not imply that the temporal element became irrelevant, but the Commission considered that it would play its necessary role as part of the good faith element in the interpretation of a treaty term.

Instead (or in addition to) the intertemporal rule, the Tribunal refers to other interpretatory aids which have guided its decision, these being the principle of effectiveness and the intention of the parties. The maxim *ut res magis valeat quam pereat*, perhaps better known as the effectivity principle, entails that the authors of a treaty have a presumed interest to make a treaty provision effective rather than ineffective.[19] The effectivity principle forms an alternative to the teleological approach as it aims to offer an objective evaluation of what functions best in a certain situation, rather than a more subjective assessment of what the parties intended to be the ultimate object and purpose. This idea is not new; under a slightly different nomen (and as an aspect of precisely the teleological approach) it has been referred to as the doctrine of "emergent purpose" which

> is not textual, since the emergent purpose cannot be gathered from the text; nor is it subjective, since it is independent of the original intentions of the parties, and perhaps also of their subsequent attitudes. Rather, it regards the creation of the parties as having acquired a separate existence, at any rate within the necessary limits imposed by the original text.[20]

Such making of an abstraction of the Parties' intentions in the light of what would be most effective – and assuming that such effectiveness is what the Parties were striving for, is for example also present in Judge Higgins' Declaration to

16 ILC, 'Report of the ILC on the work of its Sixteenth Session' (1964) ILCYb vol. II 199, Article 69.
17 Ibid. at 202–03, commentary to Arts. 69–71, para. 11.
18 ILC, 'ILC Draft Articles on the Law of Treaties with Commentaries' (1966) ILCYb vol. II, 222, commentary to Article 27, para. 16.
19 I. Sinclair, *The Vienna Convention on the Law of Treaties*, 2nd edn (Manchester: MUP, 1984).
20 F.G. Jacobs, 'Varieties of approach to treaty interpretation with special reference to the draft convention on the law of treaties before the Vienna diplomatic conference' (1969) 18 ICLQ 2, 318–46, 320.

the *Kasiliki/Sedudu Island* case, where she stated that the task of the ICJ is "to decide what general idea the Parties had in mind, and then make reality of that general idea through the use of contemporary knowledge."[21] It would seem that the Parties to the *Iron Rhine* dispute also recognized the sensibility of this approach as they already accepted the existence of a Belgian right of transit "not of fixed duration" in their 2003 Arbitration Agreement, including a right to adaptation and modernization. The case was thus limited to an examination of the modalities of such right, while not disputing the effect that such interpretation (although not explicit in the treaty and neither deductable from any Party intention at the time of its conclusion) is indeed the only one which allows for an effective exercise of that right.[22] This in turn allowed the Tribunal to adopt a "dynamic and evolutive approach to a treaty that was meant to guarantee a right of commercial transit through time" – reminiscent of the approach in the *Rhine Chlorides* case.[23] However, applying the principle of effectiveness in interpretation does not "entitle a Tribunal to revise a treaty", although this invariably raises the question as to where the boundary lies.[24]

Exploring the principle of systemic integration and Article 31(3)(c) of the VCLT, an approach to interpretation can be discerned which sheds "new light on the position of treaties in the progressive development of international law over time (the so-called problem of 'inter-temporality')."[25] Subsequent developments in international law may affect a treaty in at least two ways, being through an effect on its application (actualization or contemporization) and through an effect on its interpretation (in case of evolutionary concepts). The former effect has been provided with a proviso that such far-reaching application ought to be only allowed for in cases where an intent of the Parties thereto can be established.[26] As it might be difficult for the interpreter to discover concrete evidence of such intent, the ICJ as well as the ILC have accepted that contemporization may also be permissible in cases "where the Parties insert provisions into their treaty which *by their terms or nature* contemplate evolution".[27]

---

21 *Kasikili/Sedudu Island (Botswana/Namibia)* (Judgment) General List No 99 [1999] ICJ 1045.

22 I. van Bladel, 'The Iron Rhine Case and the Art of Treaty Interpretation: The Application of Nineteenth Century Obligations in the Twenty-first Century' in N. Blokker et al., eds., *The Netherlands in Court: Essays in Honour of Johan G. Lammers* (The Netherlands: Martinus Nijhoff, 2006) 13–14.

23 See *supra* note 13, at para. 84 a similar approach was taken in, e.g. the *Case Concerning the Audit of Accounts between the Netherlands and France in Application of the Protocol of 25 September 1991 Additional to the Convention for the Protection of the Rhine from Pollution by Chlorides of 3 December 1976* (Award) [12 March 2004] UNRIAA XXV 267–344.

24 See *supra* note 13, at para. 49; see C. Brown, *A Common Law of Adjudication* (Oxford: OUP, 2007) at 46–47, 51–52; D. French, 'Environmental Dispute settlement: the first (hesitant) signs of spring?' (2006) 19 *Hague Ybk Int'l L.* 7–8.

25 C. McLachlan, 'The Principle of Systemic Integration and Article 31(3)(c) of the Vienna Convention' (2005) 54 ICLQ 2, 282.

26 Ibid. referring to e.g. H. Thirlway, 'The Law and Procedure of the International Court of Justice 1960–1989 Part Three' (1991) 62 BYbIL 1, 57; Jiménez de Aréchaga, 'Report of the International Law Commission on the work of its Sixteenth Session' (1964) ILCYb vol. I 34, para. 10.

27 ILC, 'Report of the International Law Commission on the work of its Fifty-Seventh Session' (2005) A/60/10 219, fn 384, referring to *Case Concerning the Gabčíkovo-Nagymaros Project (Hungary v*

Applying this to the case at hand, it would seem that the Treaty of Separation, if not by its terms, then at least by its nature, falls into this category. The Parties themselves have made a start with this, by already in 1873 interpreting Article XII so as to allow for the construction of a railway, instead of a road or canal. The conclusion of the Iron Rhine Treaty could arguably be seen as a text-book example of "a subsequent agreement between the parties regarding the interpretation of the treaty or the application of its provisions" – a means of interpretation mentioned in Article 31(3)(a) of the VCLT. The extracts of the diplomatic negotiations leading up to the 1839 Treaty of Separation were not considered to qualify as *travaux préparatoires* – subsidiary interpretatory aids under Article 32 of the VCLT – because, although they "may show the desire or understanding of one or other of the Parties at particular moments", they nevertheless do "not serve the purpose of illumination a common understanding as to the meaning of the various provisions of Article XII."[28] The Tribunal adds that it will consider the circumstances of the conclusion (also a subsidiary rule of treaty interpretation under Article 32 of the VCLT) although it is doubtful whether such consideration will have brought any insights into a possible common view of the Parties, as both countries were all but of one mind in 1839.[29]

It would not be impossible that, due to a lack of clear joint intentions at the conclusion of both States, the Tribunal might have implicitly considered the treaty track record which Belgium and the Netherlands have developed in the subsequent 165 years – even more so, as both sides invoked sustainable development grounds to justify their conduct as will be discussed in Section 13.3.2.2 of this chapter. The contemporary treaty practice of both Belgium and the Netherlands shows a progressive willingness to undertake international environmental obligations so although it is quite certain that environmental protection was not in the mind of the Parties in 1839, it is equally certain that it is now – as evidenced by the fact that sustainable development goals were invoked by both Parties in this dispute. The regard for the original intent of the Parties may indeed be too restrictive, as there is always a certain measure of insecurity as to how the law will develop, which States have to accept, even if they cannot foresee any and all consequences. An illustration of this is the wide-spread incorporation of the most-favoured-nation principle in economic treaties, whereby States by definition do not know what the future most-favoured-nation treatment will entail. However, one ought to be aware that the *Iron Rhine* decision does go a step further than, for example, the World Trade Organization [WTO] Appellate

Slovakia) [1997] ICJ Rep 7, at 76–80; Separate Opinion of H.E. Judge C.G. Weeramantry, ibid. at 113–15; *Namibia (Legal Consequences)*, (Advisory Opinion) [1971] ICJ Rep 16, at 31; *Aegean Sea Continental Shelf* case *(Greece v Turkey)* [1978] ICJ Rep 3, at 32.

28 See *supra* note 13 at para. 48.
29 See, e.g. I. van Bladel, 'The Iron Rhine Case and the Art of Treaty Interpretation: The Application of Nineteenth Century Obligations in the Twenty-first Century' in N. Blokker et al., eds., *The Netherlands in Court: Essays in Honour of Johan G. Lammers* (The Netherlands: Martinus Nijhoff, 2006) at 12.

Body in the *Shrimp-Turtle* case.[30] While Article XX GATT contains a reference to environmental protection which is subjected to changes in interpretation as international environmental law develops, the 1839 Treaty of Separation does not include any such reference. The Tribunal still – and in this author's opinion, correctly – decided to interpret its terms in the light of emerging principles of international environmental law.

12.3.1.2 From developing to developed principles

The Tribunal's evolutive approach to treaty interpretation did not solve all interpretative difficulties, since solving the timeframe issue in favour of an application of today's rules still left confusion as to what such current rules precisely entail. In other words, the existence and precise content of the relevant rules, particularly within international environmental law, was disputed. In this regard, the Tribunal noted that there is considerable debate as to what "constitutes 'rules' or 'principles'; what is 'soft law'; and which environmental treaty law or principles have contributed to the development of customary international law."[31]

> Without entering further into those controversies, the Tribunal notes that in all of these categories "environment" is broadly referred to as including air, water, land, flora and fauna, natural ecosystems and sites, human health and safety, and climate. The emerging principles, *whatever their current status*, make reference to conservation, management, notions of prevention and of sustainable development, and protection for future generations.[32] (emphasis added)

Taking a legally binding decision concerning the interpretation of a treaty provision using relevant rules that may not have achieved binding status between the Parties to the dispute could be (and has been in relation to various disputes)[33] open to criticism as it arguably creates new obligations which the parties did not consent to. Anticipating such critiques, the Tribunal relied upon Principle 4 of the Rio Declaration[34] to explain that "[e]nvironmental law and the law on development

---

30 WTO, (Report of the Appellate Body 12 October 1998) WT/DS58/AB/R (1999) 38 ILM 118.
31 Para. 58 of the Award.
32 Para. 58 of the Award.
33 J. Pauwelyn, *Conflict of Norms in Public International Law: How WTO Law Relates to Other Rules of International Law* (CUP, 2003); G. Marceau, 'Fragmentation in International Law: The Relationship between WTO Law and General International Law: A Few Comments from a WTO Perspective' (2006) 17 *Finnish YIL* 5; C. McLachlan, 'The Principle of Systemic Integration and Article 31(3)(c) of the Vienna Convention' (2005) 54 ICLQ 279; F. Baetens, 'Muddling the waters of treaty interpretation? Relevant rules of international law in the *MOX Plant* OSPAR Arbitration and *EC Biotech* case' (2008) 77 *NJIL* 3, 197–216.
34 UN Conference on Environment and Development 'Rio Declaration on Environment and Development' (14 June 1992) UN Doc A/CONF. 151/26/Rev 1 vol I, 3: Principle 4 states that "environmental protection shall constitute an integral part of the development process and cannot be considered in isolation from it".

stand not as alternatives but as mutually reinforcing, integral concepts, which require that where development may cause significant harm to the environment there is a duty to prevent, or at least mitigate, such harm [which] in the opinion of the Tribunal, has now become a principle of general international law".[35] As already set out by the ICJ in the *Gabčíkovo-Nagymaros* case and quoted with approval in the *Iron Rhine* Award, "new norms have to be taken into consideration, and [. . .] new standards given proper weight, not only when States contemplate new activities but also when continuing with activities begun in the past".[36] Thus linking its approach to the early origins of the no-harm rule as set out in the *Trail Smelter* arbitration and referring to the definition of sustainable development in the ICJ's *Gabčíkovo-Nagymaros* case, the Tribunal seems to indicate that its decision is not to be regarded as innovative (and possibly controversial) in its take on environmental protection standards, but on the contrary, a logical step in a decades-old tradition of adjudicatory decision-making.[37]

The reason for this elaboration in terms of timeframe and content, was of course that the Treaty of Separation and the Iron Rhine Treaty remain silent on the question of maintenance, adaptation and modernization of the railway.[38] The question of maintenance had solved itself in practice, as the Netherlands had assumed this burden – presumably as part of its territorial sovereignty – but the adaptation and modernization was a more complex, uncharted problem. The transit right of Belgium as such was not under dispute, but the Parties' disagreement centred around the question whether the reactivation plan was to be considered the creation of a new railway line (in which case, the costs were to be borne by Belgium according to Article XII of the Treaty of Separation) or merely maintenance of the existing line (in which case the expenditure was to be shouldered by the Netherlands – according to Article XI of the Treaty of Separation).[39] The latter Article stipulates that:

> The use of these roads [. . .] which will only be subject to the payment of moderate tolls for the maintenance of these roads, in such a manner that the transit trade will not encounter any obstacles on them and that, in return for the above-mentioned tolls, these roads will be maintained in good state and prone to facilitating trade.

Thus the Tribunal engaged in an extensive examination of both Articles, applying the rule of intertemporal law and the principle of effectiveness to reach the conclusion that the provisions of Article XII remained in principle applicable to the planned adaptation and modernization.[40] The reason for this was that the Belgian request for reactivation of a line long dormant, with a freight capacity considerably

---

35 See *supra* note 13 at para. 59.
36 *Gabčíkovo-Nagymaros Project (Hungary/Slovakia)* [1997] ICJ Rep 7, at 78, para. 140.
37 *Trail Smelter* case *(United States v Canada)* (Decision of 11 March 1941) 3 RIAA 1938.
38 See *supra* note 13 at paras 76–77.
39 See *supra* note 13 at paras 75–76.
40 See *supra* note 13 at paras 74–84.

surpassing the previous arrangement, went beyond mere maintenance of the existing line, although it did not amount to a request for a new line. Insofar as the upgrading costs were concerned, the current international rules were held to be applicable, in the light of the concept of reasonableness.

Juxtaposing two statements of the Tribunal, a certain contradiction seems discernible. On the one hand, the Tribunal held that "[t]he emerging principles, *whatever their current status*, make reference to conservation, management, notions of prevention and of sustainable development, and protection for future generations" (emphasis added), while on the other hand, "there is a duty to prevent, or at least mitigate, such harm [which] in the opinion of the Tribunal, has now become a principle of general international law".[41] In other words, while the Tribunal is indicating that it will take into account a wide range of 'emerging principles', it acknowledges only the no-harm duty as a binding legal principle. Arguably, the Award could be criticized for not being entirely consistent in this aspect: although it is only willing to make an explicit statement with regard to the legal status of one – uncontroversial – principle, it does seem to wish to 'keep its options open' to take a decision partially based on emerging principles which are possibly not legally binding. Taken to its extreme, this could impose new obligations upon Parties which have not consented thereto, if such non-binding principles are 'read into' existing treaty obligations.[42] If principles are still in the emerging stages, they are not (yet) binding hard law and should hence not be applied as if they were.

One possible explanation for the Tribunal's approach could be that it was evidently aware that obligations relating to conservation, management, prevention and sustainable development have in fact been accepted by both Parties to this dispute in the context of their obligations under EC law – so they do in fact form relevant hard law. However, this underlying understanding (if it was present) has not been made explicit; on the contrary, the Tribunal repeatedly indicated that its decision was based on international and domestic Dutch law only, as it was not necessary to rely upon EC law to decide this dispute.[43] It decided to apply international environmental principles *pure sang* rather than in their implemented form, as incorporated in EC law, more precisely through Article 175 EC Treaty (now 192 TFEU), the Habitat Directive and the Birds Directive.[44] That way, the Tribunal succeeded in avoiding allegations of trespassing into the territory of the Court of Justice of the EU, but it simultaneously moved onto more controversial grounds as the legal status of such principles in international law is far less clear than under EC law.

The practical usefulness of sustainable development principles has been doubted because of their vagueness which has been attributed to a perceived

---

41 Ibid. at 58–59.
42 See, e.g. the highly critical assessment of C. Djeffal, 'The Iron Rhine Case – A Treaty's Journey from Peace to Sustainable Development' (2011) 71 Zaörv 3, 579–85.
43 See, e.g. *supra* note 13 at paras 120, 131, 137.
44 Council Directive 79/409/EEC of 2 April 1979 on Conservation of Wild Birds (1979 OJ (L 103)1) Birds Directive; Council Directive No. 92/43/EEC of 21 May 1992 on the conservation of natural habitats and of wild fauna and Flora (Habitats Directive).

lack of consent between States concerning the precise conduct required by such principles.[45] However, the former does not necessarily follow from the latter: States' duties following from general principles are often vague, one could think of for example 'due diligence' or 'due process', as they prescribe an obligation of conduct and not of result. To deduct from such legal nature, that sustainability principles are too vague to be applied, would be one step too far.[46] In this regard, the *Iron Rhine* Tribunal seems to have specifically tried to avoid reading too much into these principles as it focused specifically on preventing or mitigating serious harm to the environment. This application was necessary so as to allow these principles to play a meaningful role in the interpretation of the Treaty at hand, fitting within (as mentioned above) a tradition of decision-making in this type of cases, while still offering a margin of discretion. States remain at liberty to interpret the extent of prevention/mitigation measures required – this requirement could be interpreted differently in future cases for developing States which have no technologically-advanced mechanisms at their disposal to prevent or mitigate environmental damage, in accordance with the common but differential responsibilities principle.

12.3.1.3 Exercise of sovereignty without need for notifying, consulting or obtaining consent?

According to the Tribunal, the Article XII phrase "without prejudice to the exclusive rights of sovereignty over the territory which would be crossed by the road or canal in question" implied that the Netherlands had "forfeited no more sovereignty than that which was necessary for the track to be built and to operate to allow a commercial connection from Belgium to Germany" across Dutch territory.[47] Designation of parts of this territory as a nature reserve "did not in theory constitute a limitation of the right of transit"; thus there was no legal obligation for the Netherlands to obtain Belgian approval, or even consult its neighbour.[48] The Tribunal hence clearly viewed sovereignty as the 'default mode' or *lex generalis*, to which Belgium's contractual transit right

---

45 See, e.g. P. Malanczuk, 'Sustainable development: some critical thoughts in the light of the Rio Conference' in: K. Ginther, E. Denters, P. de Waart, eds., *Sustainable development and good governance* (The Netherlands: Martinus Nijhoff, 1995) 23–52; A. Boyle and D. Freestone, 'Introduction' in: A. Boyle and D. Freestone, eds., *International law and sustainable development: past achievements and future challenges* (Oxford: OUP, 2001) 1–18; V. Pupavac, 'A Critical Review of the NGO Sustainable Development Philosophy' in Z. Yongnian, J. Fewsmith, eds., *China's Opening Society: the Non-State Sector and Governance* (Abingdon: Routledge, 2008) 15–35; R. Pavoni, 'Environmental Rights, Sustainable Development, and Investor-state Case Law: a Critical Appraisal', in P. Dupuy, F. Francioni, E.U. Petersmann, eds., *Human Rights in International Investment Law and Arbitration* (Oxford: OUP, 2009) 525–56.

46 To the contrary: see C. Djeffal, 'The Iron Rhine Case – A Treaty's Journey from Peace to Sustainable Development' (2011) 71 Zaörv 3, 582–85.

47 See *supra* note 13 at para. 87.

48 See *supra* note 13 at para. 95.

formed the *lex specialis* – to be interpreted rather narrowly insofar as it required derogations from the Netherlands' sovereignty.

Two comments can be made here. First, as to the contribution of sustainable development principles to the decision, one could wonder whether the final result would have been different, had the sustainability argument been stronger on the Belgian side. In other words, was the decisive reason to hold that the Dutch measures are not unreasonable restrictions to the transit right the fact that they were within the Dutch legitimate exercise of sovereign rule-making powers (thereby supported by their sustainable objective)? Or, would reliance on the argument of such sovereign rule-making powers not have sufficed, in case such sustainable objectives had been absent? Evidently, this hypothetical question cannot be answered conclusively either way but it is worth considering, before displaying any over-abundant enthusiasm as to the contribution of sustainable development principles to the outcome in the *Iron Rhine* case.

The second comment in this regard relates to the finding of the Tribunal that, in the light of the minimal use and even recent non-use of the railway by Belgium, it was "not unreasonable for the Netherlands to assume that that situation would possibly continue into the near foreseeable future". Had the Netherlands at the time of the re-designation of the Meinweg had reasons to assume that Belgium would propose a reactivation, it "*might have been desirable* on the basis of good neighbourliness to consult with it before the designation" (emphasis added).[49] In other words, even if Belgium had informed the Netherlands in time of its reactivation plans, it would not only not have been legally required (merely 'desirable') to initiate consultations, it would also not even have been strongly advised (merely 'might have been'). Although again, good neighbourliness is a 'vague' general principle imposing an obligation of conduct, it would seem that this phrasing represents a missed opportunity as it goes against recent developments in public international law, which attach increasing importance to notification and consultation before embarking upon projects which affect the exercise of rights by other States. The Netherlands did not have to obtain Belgian permission before re-designating its territory but the Tribunal's dismissal of the Belgian argument that some form of consultation should have taken place prior to re-designation, does not fit within the broader trends developing within international environmental law.[50]

Would this case have been decided differently if Belgium had not interrupted its use of the railway? Most likely this would not have made a difference to the outcome because the re-designation would still have qualified as a legitimate exercise of sovereign regulatory powers in pursuit of sustainable development. The only difference would be that the Netherlands might have been under an obligation to notify, and perhaps consult, Belgium concerning its plans. This is positive news for States who are under the obligation of allowing such use of parts of their territory – and this use is being made without discontinuation. Furthermore, it is

---

49 Ibid. at 95
50 As analysed in e.g. *Pulp Mills on the River Uruguay (Argentina* v *Uruguay)*, Judgment, ICJ. Reports 2010, p. 14

not unthinkable that such arguments could be invoked by States that are acting as respondents in international investment arbitration procedures, where a certain regulatory measure with an environmental purpose is alleged to form a violation of a foreign investor's rights.

12.3.2 Measures envisaged by the Netherlands in the light of the Treaty of Separation

12.3.2.1 Applicable domestic legislation

After having decided that the interpretation of EC law, particularly relating to the system of Trans-European Networks [TEN] and environmental legislation, was not necessary in order to decide the dispute as these rules did not provide the parties with any rights or duties additional to those already included in the 1839 Treaty of Separation,[51] the Tribunal commenced its review of the applicable domestic legislation. Such legislation included most notably the Noise Abatement Act (*Wet Geluidhinder*) and other environmental protection rules. Certain detailed measures specifically relating to the Iron Rhine railway reactivation were stipulated in a document (the Draft Planning Procedure Order) from 2003, prepared by the Netherlands infrastructure manager.[52] The Tribunal found that, as the Netherlands recognised the Belgian right of transit, Belgium equally did not contest the Dutch right to take measures for the protection of the environment and noise abatement, but it refused to bear the financial consequences of such measures, particularly the building of a tunnel in the Meinweg area,[53] as this allegedly amounted to an unnecessary interference with the Belgian transit right.[54] Looking at matters from a different angle, the Tribunal held that the Netherlands was not required "to apply its national legislation and policy with respect to the reactivation of the Iron Rhine railway in a more favourable way than with respect to other railways in the Netherlands, unless such non-discriminatory application would amount to a denial of Belgium's transit right or render the exercise of that right unreasonably difficult."[55]

Applying these principles to the case at hand, the Tribunal reached the conclusion that the measures envisaged by the Netherlands did not amount to a denial or an unreasonable restriction. This finding in principle, however, did not as such have any bearing on the related but distinct question of the allocation of the costs.

---

51 See *supra* note 13 at paras 107–37.
52 See *supra* note 13 at paras 183–84.
53 See *supra* note 13 at para. 193.
54 See *supra* note 13 at para. 187.
55 See *supra* note 13 at para. 204.

12.3.2.2 Sustainable development as a deadlock argument

Interestingly, sustainable development objectives were invoked on both sides to support the legality of the State's conduct. Belgium argued that its request for reactivation was motivated by a desire to protect the environment, as set out in the TEN system provided for in Articles 154 to 156 of the EC Treaty (now Articles 170 to 172 of the TFEU). This system included the Iron Rhine railway in a list of priority projects aimed at supporting more sustainable means of conveyance, by favouring railways over air and road transport.[56] This argument was not examined in-depth by the Tribunal as it held that the consideration of European law was not required in order to reach a solution. The Netherlands equally invoked its pursuit of sustainable development as a legitimate ground for its measures, relying on European law (Habitat Directive and the Birds Directive) as well as sustainable development principles under international law more broadly. In this sense, sustainable development even creates a deadlock – as it could equally be argued that increased railway traffic will reduce more polluting forms of transport such as air and road traffic.

12.3.2.3 Limits of reasonability

The addition of the phrase "unless such non-discriminatory application would amount to a denial of Belgium's transit right or render the exercise of that right unreasonably difficult" is interesting, as it could mean for future cases that may be more black-white that a State could possibly not take more 'weighty' decisions, if this would imply that a right can no longer be exercised. For example, one could imagine a situation in which a State has obtained the right to operate (or, more likely, benefit from the operation of) a nuclear power plant in another State – and the other State decides to close down all nuclear power plants on environmental grounds. This would entail a complete denial of an existing right, although it could reasonably fall within the current context of increased concern regarding power plants after the incident at Fukushima in Spring 2011, as countries such as Germany have in fact enacted such complete shut-downs. Would the existence of a treaty right to co-enjoy the operation of such plants prevail over such significant policy choices, so as to necessitate a differentiation between this particular plant as opposed to others?

Interestingly also, the Tribunal did not venture into *obiter dictum* zone by giving examples of measures which, short of a complete denial of a right, would

---

56 Decision No 1364/2006/EC of the European Parliament and of the Council of 6 September 2006 laying down guidelines for trans-European energy networks and repealing Decision 96/391/EC and Decision No 1229/2003/EC, OJ L 262 (22.9.2006) at 1–23; Communication de la Commission, Une initiative Européenne pour la croissance investir dans les réseaux et la connaissance pour soutenir la croissance et l'emploi, Rapport final au Conseil Européen, COM (2003) 690 final (11.11.2003); Council Regulation (EC) No 2236/95 of 18 September 1995 laying down general rules for the granting of Community financial aid in the field of trans-European networks, OJ L 228 (23.9.1995) 1–7.

be considered unreasonably restricting the exercise of a right. In other words, one still has to guess where the threshold lies as the Tribunal did not give any indication in this respect. On the one hand, it is understandable that the Tribunal preferred to stay 'on safe ground' as it considered this threshold not to be reached in the case at hand. On the other hand, one could criticize the Award in this regard as the Tribunal did not substantiate *why* it did not consider the exercise of Belgium's transit right to be not rendered unreasonably difficult – hence opening up the Award for criticism that it is arguably not sufficiently motivated. For future cases, this part of the Award does not offer extensive guidance.

12.3.3 Allocation of costs

12.3.3.1 Setting out criteria and principles

After having established that (i) Belgium had the right to reactivate the Iron Rhine railway as part of its treaty-guaranteed transit right; and (ii) that the Netherlands had the right to subject the exercise of such right to reasonably restrictive environmental protection measures, the remaining question was: which party has to shoulder the costs for the resulting increase in expenses? Belgium contended that the 1839 Treaty of Separation only prescribed it to bear the costs for the construction of a "new road", that hence, it was up to the Netherlands to finance the reactivation works on Dutch territory, even more so as it had rendered impossible the use of the railway by dismantling part of its infrastructure, failing to provide for maintenance, and interrupting restoration works.[57] The Netherlands disagreed, arguing that Belgium ought to bear the full costs of reactivation, as an obligation inextricably linked to the exercise of its transit right and in accordance with Article XII of the 1839 Treaty of Separation, particularly the words "entirely at the cost and expense of Belgium [. . .] without any burden to Holland."[58]

As the Tribunal had already earlier held that the reactivation was not to be considered a "new road" although it did go beyond mere maintenance and hence fell under Article XII of the Treaty of Separation, it continued its search for a middle ground, in absence of clear treaty provisions regulating such matter. For this purpose, it identified three points of departure: first, in matters beyond what was specifically provided for in the Treaty, the Netherlands' sovereignty remains untouched; second, major railway projects "must today include necessary environment protection measures as an integral component"; and, third, the resulting financial burden should not equal a denial or unreasonable restriction.[59] In other words, the costs were not to be borne by either Party on its own, but had to be subjected to careful balancing, as already informally agreed by the Parties prior to the dispute, as reflections of their equally legitimate needs.

57 See *supra* note 13 at paras 212–15.
58 See *supra* note 13 at paras 216–18.
59 See *supra* note 13 at para. 220.

Referring to the *Nuclear Weapons* Advisory Opinion,[60] the Tribunal pointed out that a growing emphasis is put on the duty of prevention in international environmental law, even though the current case is not a standard example of avoiding harmful transboundary effects in other States' territories. It is rather concerned with "the effect of the exercise of a treaty-guaranteed right of one State in the territory of another State and a possible impact of such exercise on the territory of the latter".[61] The Tribunal hence formulated an analogous argument according to which States exercising their rights under international law, also have to take into account environmental protection considerations. As a result, the environmental protection measures were to be fully integrated into the project and its costs. The Tribunal considered it beyond its competences to determine which measures ought to be taken in this regard and also refrained from specifying in monetary terms how the allocation of costs has to be determined, but instead set out a number of relevant criteria and principles thereto. Belgium had to fund the environmental element of the overall reactivation costs as an integral part of its exercise of the transit right.

Broadly speaking, the Tribunal followed the fragmentation of the Iron Rhine on paper into four segments as set out by the Draft Planning Procedure Order. With respect to segment A and B, the costs of reactivation were to be borne by Belgium, with the exception of certain costs caused by the anticipated development of the Netherlands railway system ("autonomous development"), taking into account the quantifiable benefits for the Netherlands arising from the reactivation.[62] The Tribunal went as far as indicating, for each of the four segments of the Iron Rhine track, where such benefits could arise, although it did not engage in any apportioning of its own. With regard to segment C, the Tribunal decided that if a deviation from the historic route was agreed upon, Belgium would only have to bear the costs of reactivation, while the Netherlands had to pay for the re-routing. Concerning segment D, the costs would in principle have to be borne by Belgium, with the exception of the Meinweg tunnel, for which the costs were to be apportioned in equal parts between the two Parties. The reason for this was that both Parties had contributed to the occurrence of a situation which required much more costly measures: Belgium had not fully informed the Netherlands of its intended intensified use in a timely fashion, while the Netherlands had opted to establish a national park in an area which was already crossed by a railway.[63]

One author quite aptly pointed out the resemblance of the Iron Rhine Tribunal's approach with that of the ICJ in the *North Sea Continental Shelf* case.[64] In the latter case it was first decided that the coastal State has a sovereign right to the continental shelf but as there was no legal principle which determined the precise extension of such right, the ICJ resorted to equity to solve the case.[65]

60 *Legality of the Threat or Use of Nuclear Weapons* (Advisory Opinion) [1996] ICJ Rep (I) 226.
61 See *supra* note 13 at paras 222–23.
62 See *supra* note 13 at paras 227–29.
63 See *supra* note 13 at para. 234
64 C. Djeffal, 'The Iron Rhine Case – A Treaty's Journey from Peace to Sustainable Development' (2011) 71 Zaörv 3, 578–79.
65 *North Sea Continental Shelf (Germany/Netherlands)* [1969] ICJ Rep 3 at 22, paras 19 and 46, para. 83 *et seq.*

Likewise, the *Iron Rhine* Tribunal set out clearly which rules were applicable to the dispute (Article XII of the Treaty of Separation) but then resorted to setting out a number of relevant criteria and principles as guidance for the parties in allocating the costs. This seems to have been the most sensible approach as it responds to what the Parties had asked the Tribunal to do.

12.3.3.2 *Appointment of a committee of experts*

After having set out the applicable guidelines to determine the allocation of costs, the Tribunal held that it was not its task "to investigate questions of considerable scientific complexity as to which measures will be sufficient to achieve compliance with the required levels of environmental protection." [66] Hence, it recommended that the Parties set up a committee of independent experts to determine the costs of the reactivation, of the autonomous development of the Dutch railway system and the resulting quantifiable benefits. This was not a groundbreaking decision, for example also in the *Case Concerning Land Reclamation by Singapore in and around the Straits of Johor*, the Tribunal endorsed an Award on Agreed Terms which mainly reflected the conclusions of an expert group report prescribed earlier by the International Tribunal for the Law of the Sea. It seems wise with risk assessents and cost determinations in general, to leave the matter to experts, as is often already done in economic disputes before the World Trade Organization (e.g. dumping margin calculations) and investor-State arbitrations (e.g. fair market value in expropriation cases).

12.4 Conclusion

Why is this case relevant for sustainable development although it is essentially economic in nature? Because all such disputes are. In this case, the Tribunal did exactly what the Parties asked it to do: it resolved the dispute, searched and found a middle ground – although it had to bend itself from time to time in legally supple positions to achieve this goal. It is very likely that in future cases which involve the application of old treaties, such approach to interpretation will become increasingly prevalent if adjudicators are to allow such treaties to remain relevant, in times where the original intention of the parties lies in a distant blurry past and the contemporary application requires the consideration of many more recent rules. Perhaps one could see this as the legal version of Darwin's natural selection process: treaties either have to be adapted to maintain their effectiveness, or they will perish.

---

66 Para. 235 of the Award.

International Tribunal for the Law of the Sea

13 The *United Nations Convention on the Law of the Sea* (LOSC) and sustainable development jurisprudence

David Freestone and Freedom-Kai Phillips

13.1 Introduction

This chapter provides a brief overview of the 1982 *United Nations Convention on the Law of the Sea* (LOSC),[1] with a focus on its contributions to sustainable development principles and practices as seen in recent jurisprudence. First, a synopsis of key provisions of the LOSC and related international instruments is provided. Second, the 2009 *Southern Bluefin Tuna* case is summarized. Third, the 2011 *Advisory Opinion of the Seabed Disputes Chamber of the International Tribunal on the Law of the Sea* (ITLOS) on the *Responsibilities and Obligations of States Sponsoring Persons and Entities with Respect to Activities in the Area* is discussed, highlighting the requirements for precaution, for international responsibility of States sponsoring sea bed exploration and exploitation activities, and for "due diligence."[2] Fourth, the *Request for an Advisory Opinion Submitted by the Sub-regional Fisheries Commission* (SRFC) of 2015 is also considered, illustrating the international legal responsibility of States for fishing vessels flying their flags and further developing the application of the "due diligence" requirements.[3] Finally, a few conclusions relating to the contributions to sustainable development made by the LOSC and respective jurisprudence are provided.

13.2 The LOSC and sustainable development

Tommy Koh, chair of the final sessions of the Third UN Conference on the Law of the Sea, which finalized the convention text, called it the "Constitution for

---

1 *United Nations Convention on the Law of the Sea*, (10 December 1982), UNTS No. 31363, <http://www.un.org/depts/los/convention_agreements/texts/unclos/unclos_e.pdf>. [LOSC, *Convention*]

2 *Responsibilities and Obligations of States Sponsoring Persons and Entities with Respect to Activities in the Area*, Case No. 17, Advisory Opinion (ITLOS Seabed Disputes Chamber 1 February 2011), 50 ILM (2011), <https://www.itlos.org/fileadmin/itlos/documents/cases/case_no_17/adv_op_010211.pdf>. [ITLOS Advisory Opinion 2011]

3 *Request for an Advisory Opinion Submitted by the Sub-regional Fisheries Commission* (SRFC), Case No. 21, Advisory Opinion (ITLOS, 2 April 2015), <https://www.itlos.org/fileadmin/itlos/documents/cases/case_no.21/advisory_opinion/C21_AdvOp_02.04.pdf>. [ITLOS Advisory Opinion 2015]

the Ocean."[4] It contains 320 Articles with 9 Annexes. Although other treaties cover aspects of the marine environment, either directly or indirectly, the 1982 text is the most comprehensive and many of its provisions are way ahead of their time. The 1982 text has also been supplemented by two Implementation Agreements. The first relates to Part XI of the Convention on seabed mining dates from 1994,[5] and the second *Agreement on Conservation and Management of Straddling Fish Stocks and Highly Migratory Fish Stocks*, from 1995.[6] Although there have been developments in the basic concepts relating to sustainable development since 1982, the LOSC nevertheless provides an important early framework for the conservation of the oceans. Notably, it imposes a unique, unqualified general obligation on States to "protect and preserve the marine environment."[7] This has been interpreted to include living resources,[8] but the Convention does specifically require parties to take measures "necessary to protect and preserve rare or fragile ecosystems as well as the habitat of depleted, threatened or endangered species and other forms of marine life."[9]

The LOSC also lays out the requirements for a detailed and rigorous regime for the prevention, reduction and control of pollution from any source, including atmospheric pollution.[10] States are obliged to establish measures, either individually or jointly, to prevent, reduce, and control "all sources of pollution of the marine environment." This includes "all measures consistent with this Convention that are necessary to prevent, reduce and control pollution of the marine environment from *any source*, using for this, purpose the best practicable means at their disposal and in accordance with their capabilities, and they shall endeavour to harmonize their policies in this connection" (emphasis added).[11] This includes but is not limited to "the release of toxic, harmful or noxious substances, especially those which are persistent, from land-based sources, from or through the atmosphere." It also includes pollution from dumping, from

4   President Tommy Koh. See The Law of The Sea: Official Text of the UN Convention on the Law of the Sea, *supra* note 1, at xxxiii.

5   Agreement Relating to the Implementation of Part XI of the United Nations Convention on the Law of the Sea of 10 December 1982, adopted by the United Nations General Assembly on 28 July 1994: A/RES/48/283 or 28 July 1994, 1836 UNTS 3, ILM 33 (1994), 1309. [Agreement Relating to the Implementation of Part XI of LOSC]

6   Agreement for the Implementation of the Provisions of the United Nations Convention on the Law of the Sea of 10 December 1982 Relating to the Conservation and Management of Straddling Fish Stocks and Highly Migratory Fish Stocks (1995), UNTC No. 37924 [UN Fish Stocks Agreement (UNFSA)]; see also David Freestone and Zen Makuch, "The New International Environmental Law of Fisheries: The 1995 Straddling Stocks Agreement," (1997) 7 *Ybk Int'l Envtl. L.*, at 3–49.

7   LOSC, *supra* note 1, at art. 192.

8   *Southern Bluefin Tuna (New Zealand v Japan; Australia v Japan), Provisional Measures*, Order of 27 August, 1999, ITLOS Reports 1999, 280, at 295, para. 70.
    [*Southern Bluefin Tuna*]

9   LOSC, *supra* note 1, at art. 194(5). States must also cooperate to address conservation and management of living resources in the high seas, at arts 118–19.

10 Ibid. at art. 194ff.

11 Ibid. at art. 194(1). Perhaps an early example of differentiated responsibility?

vessels, or resulting from natural resources exploration on the seabed or subsoil, and other marine installations.[12]

Recognizing the multiple uses and users of the oceans, the LOSC also requires that measures taken by States must not create unjustifiable interference with the lawful activities of other States, may not directly or indirectly transfer the damage from one location to another, and shall address the use of technology and the accidental introduction of species into the marine environment.[13]

In an important and early reference to requirements of environmental reporting, States must also, directly or through the competent international organizations, observe, measure, evaluate and analyse, by recognized scientific methods, the risks or effects of pollution of the marine environment, particularly those activities which they undertake or authorize to determine if these activities are likely to pollute the marine environment. Reports of these observations shall be published and made available to others, and if monitoring indicates potential harm then this must be assessed and the results communicated.[14]

The primary enforcement tool of the LOSC is the principle of flag State responsibility. Every flag State is required to maintain a register of vessels flying its flag, assume jurisdiction over matters relating to, and actions of, the crew, and make certain measures relating to seaworthiness, training, equipment and signaling are established to ensure safety at sea.[15]

The principle of State responsibility also extends to activities undertaken in relation to the exploration and exploitation of the deep sea bed. Under Article 1(1), the seabed, ocean floor and subsoil beyond national jurisdiction is called the "Area." The Area, as well as its mineral resources, are the "common heritage of mankind" and cannot be subjected to national sovereignty.[16] The Area is reserved exclusively for peaceful purposes and activities conducted there shall be for the benefit of mankind and a whole. Exploration and exploitation activities must be conducted under the jurisdiction of the International Seabed Authority (ISA) and States are liable for the acts and activities carried out by their nationals, both legal and natural persons, which may be in breach of the LOSC or ISA rules, except where the State has taken all necessary and appropriate measures to ensure that any entity that it has sponsored complies with its requirements.[17]

The LOSC also abounds with requirements for international cooperation. These include the obligation to cooperate in formulating and elaborating international rules, standards and recommended practices and procedures consistent with this Convention, for the protection and preservation of the marine

---

12 Ibid.
13 Ibid. at arts 195–196.
14 Ibid. at arts 204–206.
15 Ibid. at art. 94.
16 Ibid. at art. 136. Note further: "The general conduct of States in relation to the Area shall be in accordance with the provisions of this Part, the principles embodied in the Charter of the United Nations and other rules of international law in the interests of maintaining peace and security and promoting international cooperation and mutual understanding." Ibid. at art. 138.
17 Ibid. at arts 137, 139.

environment,[18] but also in the development of pollution prevention contingency planning and the exchange of data[19] as well as in relation to management and conservation of fisheries,[20] the illicit traffic of drugs[21] and the suppression of unauthorized broadcasting.[22]

Finally, many regard the compulsory dispute settlement procedures established by the LOSC as its crowning glory.[23] Part XV of the Convention provides a range of fora for the possible settlement of disputes under the Convention, including the International Court of Justice, the ITLOS – the new tribunal established by the Convention – or arbitral proceedings,[24] together with broad procedural rules.[25] A subsidiary body to ITLOS, the Seabed Dispute Chamber, is also established with a special jurisdiction relating to mineral resource exploration or exploitation.[26]

The Second Implementing Agreement to the LOSC – negotiated as it was after the 1992 UN Conference on Environment and Development – includes many of the concepts of sustainable development elaborated there. The 1995 *Agreement on Conservation and Management of Straddling Fish Stocks and Highly Migratory Fish Stocks*,[27] aims to ensure the long-term conservation and sustainable use of these fish stocks.[28] The Agreement gives effect to States' duty to cooperate in conservation and management and establishes certain general principles that are laid out in Article 5. These principles reflect the majority of the tenets of sustainable development; they are (a) adoption of measures to promote and ensure long term sustainability and optimum utilization of straddling fish stocks; (b) use of the best available scientific evidence to design and maintain stock levels; (c) application of the precautionary approach; (d) assessment of fishing impacts on ecosystems as well as target species; (e) adoption of conservation and management measures at an ecosystem level; (f) minimization of pollution, waste, catch by lost or abandoned gear, and catch of non-target species; (g) protection of biodiversity; (h) measures to prevent or eliminate overfishing and excess capacity; (i) consideration of the interests of artisanal and subsistence fishers; (j) collection and dissemination of data concerning fishing activity, vessel

---

18   Ibid. at art. 197.

19   Ibid. at arts 198–200.

20   Ibid. at arts 117–118.

21   Ibid. at art. 108.

22   Ibid. at art. 109.

23   The design of these provisions was the work of the late Professor Louis Sohn, see David Freestone, "A Decade of the Law of the Sea Convention: Is it a Success?" (2007) 39 *Geo. Wash. U. Int'l L. Rev.* (Issue 3: Special Symposium in Remembrance of Professor Louis Sohn) 101–43. [hereinafter Freestone 2007].

24   LOSC, *supra* note 1, at art. 287.

25   Ibid. at arts 279, 286–287, 288–296, Annex VI.

26   Ibid. at arts 186–187, 153, Annex VI (Section 4).

27   Agreement for the Implementation of the Provisions of the United Nations Convention on the Law of the Sea of 10 December 1982 Relating to the Conservation and Management of Straddling Fish Stocks and Highly Migratory Fish Stocks (1995), UNTS No. 37924. [UN Fish Stocks Agreement (UNFSA)]

28   Ibid. at art. 2.

position, target and non-target species caught; (k) promotion and use of scientific research and technologies relating to fishery conservation and management; and (l) implementation and enforcement of conservation and management mechanisms through motoring control and surveillance.[29] States are required to apply the precautionary approach to conservation and management of straddling fish stocks, and exercise caution in cases of uncertain, unreliable or limited information.[30] Its Annex II even lays down for the first time a clear methodology for the application of the precautionary approach to capture fisheries.[31] In implementing the precautionary approach, States shall improve decision-making, apply common guidelines relating to stock condition, develop data collection and research programs, provide for enhanced monitoring for concerned species, and implement caution management measures including modest catch limits.[32]

13.3 Sustainable development principles in LOSC jurisprudence: *Southern Bluefin Tuna* cases *(New Zealand v Japan; Australia v Japan), Provisional Measures* 1999[33]

In 1999, ITLOS was asked by Australia and New Zealand to approve provisional measures to stop Japan continuing its unilateral Experimental Fishing Programme, under which it had substantially increased its catches from those agreed within the context of the tri-lateral 1993 Convention on the Conservation of Southern Bluefin Tuna, and *inter alia* to enjoin Japan to act in accordance with the precautionary principle.

The Southern Bluefin Tuna, *Thunnus maccoyii*, is listed as a highly migratory species in Annex 1 of the 1982 Convention.[34] The fishery started in the early 1950s with landings peaking in 1961 at more than 80,000 tonnes. Despite increased effort, landings fluctuated, with a downward trend to 35,000 tonnes in 1978. After a modest recovery in 1982–83, there was a steady decline to some 14,000 tonnes in 1990 and catches had been less than 20,000 tonnes per annum since. Japan, Australia and New Zealand had been the traditional harvesters and after informal cooperation during the 1980s the three countries began to limit their catches from 1985 to enable the stock to recover, and in May 1993 the three signed the Convention for the Conservation of Southern Bluefin

29   Ibid. at art. 5, paras (a)–(l).
30   Ibid. at art. 6 (1–2).
31   Ibid. at Annex II: Guidelines for the Application of Precautionary Reference Points in Conservation and Management of Straddling Fish Stocks and Highly Migratory Fish Stocks.
32   Ibid. at art. 6 (3–7). See also David Freestone, "Implementing Precaution Cautiously: The Precautionary Approach in the 1995 Straddling Stocks Agreement" in Ellen Hey, ed., *Developments in International Fisheries Law* (The Netherlands: Kluwer Law International, 1999) 287–325.
33   *Southern Bluefin Tuna* case, *supra* note 8, Provisional Measures, Cases 3 and 4.
34   Jean-Jacques Maguire, "Southern Bluefin Tuna Dispute" in Myron Nordquist and John Norton Moore, eds., *Current Fisheries Issues and the Food and Agriculture Organization of the United Nations* (The Hague: Martinus Nijhoff, 2000) 201–24.

Tuna (CCSBT), which came into force in May 1994.[35] In the meantime, vessels from other countries began to fish for the stock and the catch of these vessels – principally Indonesia, Korea and Taiwan – increased from some 500 tonnes in 1988 to nearly 5,000 tonnes in 1996.

The Scientific Committee of the CCSBT used a "virtual population analysis" (VPA) technique to "back-calculate" historical estimates of the stock size, using estimates of the total numbers caught by age during each year from 1969 onwards. This provided a minimum estimate of stock size, not accounting for fish which die from natural causes and those still left in the water, particularly in areas where fishing had not taken place. From these minimum estimates, actual stock sizes were then calculated. As with all such statistical methods however there were significant uncertainties in this method of stock assessment and as a result the scientists disagreed not only about the current stock size, but also about historical estimates of stock size upon which the current calculations were based. Population projections therefore varied widely depending on the interpretation put upon the data, and the reliability of the historical catch-at age data. Although both sides agreed that the stock was at an all-time low (judgment, para. 71), one side (Japan) thought the scientific evidence suggested the stock was about to recover, the other (Australia and NZ) that it was about to collapse completely.

CCSBT scientists had been discussing an experimental fishing programme for some years in order to try and fill some of the gaps in their data. They had not however been able to agree among themselves as to the parameters of such a programme. It is against this background that the Japanese decision in 1998 to implement a three-year unilateral experimental fishing programme should be viewed. In reaching its decision to award Provisional Measures in the case, the Tribunal did not make a qualitative assessment of the scientific evidence. It did not favour one side's science against the other. What it did rather was to recognize that both sides took different views,[36] i.e. that there was scientific uncertainty as to the impact of the experimental fishing programme, just as there was scientific uncertainty about the health of the stock and the necessary measures which might be needed to ensure conservation and optimum utilization. It then ruled that the parties "should act with prudence and caution to ensure that effective conservation measures are taken to prevent serious harm to the stock of southern blue fin tuna." These measures included the cessation of the unilateral experimental fishing programme. The Tribunal did use the word "caution" rather than "precaution" but the order does *de facto* prescribe measures which are precautionary – i.e. the lack of full scientific certainty was not used as a reason for refusing to take action. Indeed, I have previously called this a classic application of precautionary methodology.[37]

---

35 1993 Convention for the Conservation of Southern Bluefin Tuna. UNTS No. 1819.

36 *Southern Bluefin Tuna* case, *supra* note 8, paras 73–74.

37 See further David Freestone, "Caution or Precaution: 'A rose by any other name?'" in "Symposium on the Southern Bluefin Tuna Cases" (2000) 12 *Ybk. Int'l Envtl. L.* at 25–32, 32. The same form of words "caution" rather than precaution was used by the Tribunal in another application for Provisional Measures: *The MOX Plant* case *(Ireland v United Kingdom), Provisional Measures,* Case 10.

13.4 Sustainable development principles in LOSC jurisprudence: *Advisory Opinion on Responsibilities and Obligations of States Sponsoring Persons and Entities with Respect to Activities in the Area* (2011)

On 1 February 2011, the Seabed Dispute Chamber adopted a historic *Advisory Opinion on Responsibilities and Obligations of States Sponsoring Persons and Entities with Respect to Activities in the Area*,[38] in response to a May 2010 request by the Council of the ISA,[39] which among other things defines the responsibilities and obligations of States as sponsors to seabed activities in the Area and the extent of the sponsoring State's liability for a sponsored entity's non-compliance with the Convention.[40] Under the Convention, the Area is established as "common heritage of mankind,"[41] with the ISA governing all exploratory or extractive activities and prospective projects requiring sponsorship of a Party to the Convention. In applying for an exploration or exploitation license, an entity submits two broadly similar areas for consideration. If a license is granted, the ISA determines which area will be allotted to the applicant; the second area is reserved for activities by the ISA through the Enterprise or "in association with developing States."[42] However, the 1994 Agreement Relating to the Implementation of Part XI, which brought the Convention into force, effectively shelved the international body originally designed to carry out such activities for the benefit of mankind.[43] The remaining alternative was for the exploration of these reserved sites by the ISA in association with developing States.

In April 2008, pursuant to this option, Nauru and Tonga – each Pacific small island developing States – submitted a proposal for exploratory activities in reserved areas. Nauru, an island State with a land area of 21 square kilometers, a population of less than ten thousand, and a gross domestic product in 2009 of $34.5 million,[44] and Tonga an archipelagic State with a land area of 747 square kilometers, a population of just over one hundred thousand and a

---

38 Advisory Opinion 2011, *supra* note 2.

39 Request for Advisory Opinion, in Letter from Nii Allotey Odunton, Secretary-General of the International Seabed Authority [ISA], to Tullio Treves, President of the Seabed Disputes Chamber (11 May 2010), <https://www.itlos.org/fileadmin/itlos/documents/cases/case_no_17/Letter_from_ISBA_14_10_2010_E.doc.pdf>. The original request was electronic and certified true copies were forwarded by the ISA legal counsel on 8 June 2010, and received by the ITLOS Registry on the same date [Letter from Nii Allotey Odunton 11 May 2010].

40 This section is adapted from my previous comments, see David Freestone, *Responsibilities and Obligations of States Sponsoring Persons and Entities with Respect to Activities in the Area* "Commentary" (2011) 105 *Am. J. Int'l L.* 755–61 [Freestone 2011].

41 LOSC, *supra* note 1 at art. 137.

42 Ibid. at Annex III, art. 8.

43 Agreement Relating to the Implementation of Part XI of LOSC, *supra* note 5.

44 Bureau of East Asian and Pacific Affairs, U.S. Dep't of State, Background Note: Nauru (11 February 2015), <http://www.state.gov/r/pa/ei/bgn/16447.htm>.

GDP in 2009 of over $319 million,[45] each sponsored an entity to undertake seabed exploration and exploitation, namely, Nauru Ocean Resources Inc. and Tonga Offshore Mining Ltd. The requests were submitted to the ISA Legal and Technical Commission for consideration, but latter postponed, with Nauru on 1 March 2010 requesting the ISA Secretary General seek an Advisory Opinion from the ITLOS Seabed Disputes Chamber clarifying the extent of the liabilities of a State sponsoring "seafloor mining in international waters."[46]

Specifically, Nauru noted that:

> . . . sponsorship of Nauru Ocean Resources Inc. was originally premised on the assumption that Nauru could effectively mitigate (with a high degree of certainty) the potential liabilities or costs arising from its sponsorship. This was important, as these liabilities or costs could, in some circumstances, far exceed the financial capacities of Nauru (as well as those of many other developing States).[47]

Exposure of sponsoring States to "potentially significant liabilities," in the view of Nauru, would effectively preclude developing countries from engaging in seabed exploration and exploitation, in contravention of the basic principles of the Convention.[48] The position identified by Nauru was included in the agenda of the sixteenth session of the ISA Council, which decided, in light of the wishes of many participants, to reformulate the proposal into three more general, but concise questions.[49] Following receipt by the ITLOS register, the President of the Seabed Disputes Chamber invited Parties to the Convention, the ISA, and intergovernmental organizations with observer status at the ISA to submit written statements.[50]

---

45 Bureau of East Asian and Pacific Affairs, U.S. Dep't of State, Background Note: Tonga (27 October 2015), <http://www.state.gov/r/pa/ei/bgn/16092.htm>.

46 Nauru, Proposal to Seek an Advisory Opinion from the Seabed Disputes Chamber of the International Tribunal for the Law of the Sea on Matters Regarding Sponsoring State Responsibility and Liability, UN Doc. ISBA/ 16/C/6 (5 March 2010) [Nauru 2010].

47 Ibid. at Nauru 2010, para. 1.

48 Ibid. at Nauru 2010, para. 5; LOSC, *supra* note 1 at arts 148, 150, 152(2).

49 See ISA Council, Decision Requesting an Advisory Opinion Pursuant to Article 191 of the United Nations Convention on the Law of the Sea, UN Doc. ISBA/16/C/13 (6 May 6 2010), reprinted in Letter from Nii Allotey Odunton 11 May 2010, *supra* note 39, enclosure. "As indicated by the Authority in its written statement and at the hearing, the decision adopted by the Council on 6 May 2010 was taken 'without a vote' and 'without objection.'" ITLOS Advisory Opinion 2011, *supra* note 2 at para. 4 (citing Written Statement of the Authority, para. 2.4, UN Doc. ITLOS/PV.2010/1/Rev.1 (19 August 2010)).

50 Within the time limits, statements were received from Australia, Chile, China, Germany, the Republic of Korea, Mexico, Nauru, the Netherlands, the Philippines, Romania, the Russian Federation, and the United Kingdom, in addition to the Authority, the Interoceanmetal Joint Organization, and the International Union for Conservation of Nature and Natural Resources. Beginning on 14 September 2010, oral proceedings were held, giving an opportunity to speak to all those who had sent statements, as well as the UNESCO Intergovernmental Oceanographic Commission.

13.4.1 Proceedings

Having found that under Article 191 of the Convention it had jurisdiction to render an Advisory Opinion and that the request was admissible,[51] the Chamber moved to the first of the three questions posed by the ISA:

> What are the legal responsibilities and obligations of States Parties to the Convention with respect to the sponsorship of activities in the Area in accordance with the Convention, in particular Part XI, and the 1994 Agreement relating to the Implementation of Part XI of the United Nations Convention on the Law of the Sea of 10 December 1982?

The Chamber first found that the phrase "activities in the Area" did not include every activity associated with seabed exploration and mining.[52] Relying on the wording of the Convention, rather than the nodule and sulfides regulations issued by the Authority,[53] the Chamber found that the phrase included "drilling, dredging, coring, and excavation; disposal, dumping and discharge into the marine environment of sediment, wastes or other effluents; and construction and operation or maintenance of installations, pipelines and other devices related to such activities."[54] Additionally, the Chamber made the important decision that activities in the Area for the purposes of the Convention with respect to Article 139(1) did not include transportation and processing (although these are covered by the regulations).[55]

On the primary question of legal responsibilities and obligations of a State sponsoring such activities, the Convention text is relatively clear. Article 139(1) reads, in pertinent part:

> States Parties shall have the responsibility to ensure that activities in the Area, whether carried out by States Parties, or state enterprises or natural or juridical persons which possess the nationality of States Parties or are effectively controlled by them or their nationals, shall be carried out in conformity with this Part.[56]

---

51 The Chamber declined to comment on whether the difference in wording between the Statute of the International Court of Justice and Article 191 of the 1982 Convention means that, whereas the ICJ has discretion under its statute to render an Advisory Opinion, this same discretion does not exist for the Chamber. Compare LOSC, *supra* note 1 at art. 191 (stating that the Chamber "shall give" Advisory Opinions), with Statute of the International Court of Justice, Art. 65(1) (stating that the Court "may give" an Advisory Opinion).
52 ITLOS Advisory Opinion 2011, *supra* note 2 at paras 83–84.
53 ISA, Regulations for Prospecting and Exploration of Polymetallic Nodules in the Area, <https://www.isa.org.jm/files/documents/EN/Regs/MiningCode.pdf>; ISA, Regulations for Prospecting and Exploration of Polymetallic Sulphides in the Area, <https://www.isa.org.jm/files/documents/EN/Regs/PolymetallicSulphides.pdf>.
54 ITLOS Advisory Opinion 2011, *supra* note 2, paras 86–87.
55 Ibid. at para. 92.
56 LOSC, *supra* note 1 at art. 139(1).

States Parties are obliged to assist the ISA in this regard,[57] and, under Annex III, Article 4(4) of the Convention, State sponsors shall also, "pursuant to Article 139, have the responsibility to ensure, within their legal systems, that a contractor so sponsored shall carry out activities in the Area in conformity with the terms of its contract and its obligations under this Convention."[58] Thus, the sponsoring State must take all measures necessary to ensure the contractor's compliance and those measures must be incorporated in that State's legal system.[59] Having recognized that Article 139 contains an "obligation to ensure," the Chamber itemized the constituent elements of this obligation, pointing out that it is an obligation of conduct rather than result. More specifically, the obligation does not require the contractor's compliance in every case.[60] It is analogous to the obligation of due diligence and of conduct that the International Court of Justice found in the recent *Pulp Mills* case.[61]

Recognizing that "due diligence" may impose more rigorous requirements for a contractor's riskier activities, the Chamber first identified what it termed the "legal obligation" to apply the precautionary approach as found in Principle 15 of the Rio Declaration.[62] Precaution is required by the ISA nodules and sulfides Regulations, but the Chamber went further, seeing the approach as "an integral part of the general obligation of due diligence of sponsoring States, which is applicable even outside the scope of the Regulations" by requiring actions where scientific evidence on the scope and harmful impact of the activities is insufficient but "there are plausible indications of potential risks."[63] Perhaps in its most significant statement, the Chamber recognized "a trend towards making this approach part of customary international law,"[64] which it found in the *Pulp Mills* judgment and which its present opinion further supports.[65] Additional obligations,

---

57 Ibid. at art. 153(4).

58 ITLOS Advisory Opinion 2011, *supra* note 2 at para. 100. This paragraph, however, continues in a way that severely restricts possible answers to question 2: "A sponsoring State shall not, however, be liable for damage caused by any failure of a contractor sponsored by it to comply with its obligations if that State Party has adopted laws and regulations and taken administrative measures which are, within the framework of its legal system, reasonably appropriate for securing compliance by persons under its jurisdiction."

59 Ibid. at para. 118.

60 Ibid. at paras 109–10.

61 *Pulp Mills on the River Uruguay* (*Argentina v Uruguay*), para. 187 (Int'l Ct. Justice 20 April 2010), <http://www.icj-cij.org/docket/files/135/15877.pdf>.

62 Note that the equivocal wording of Principle 15 requires States only to introduce "cost-effective measures" "according to their capabilities." Rio Declaration on Environment and Development, 14 June 1992, UN Doc. A/CONF.151/5/Rev.1 (13 June 1992) [hereinafter Rio Declaration], reprinted in 31 ILM 874 (1992). This wording was reportedly introduced by the United States at the 1992 Rio Conference.

63 ITLOS Advisory Opinion 2011, *supra* note 2 at para. 131.

64 Ibid. at para. 135.

65 See, David Freestone and Ellen Hey, *The Precautionary Principle and International Law: The Challenge of Implementation* (The Hague: Kluwer Law, 1996); David Freestone, "The Marine Environment," in Jonathan B. Wiener, Michael D. Rogers, James K. Hammitt and Peter H. Sand, eds., *The Reality of Precaution: Comparing Risk Regulation in the United States and Europe* (London: Routledge, 2011).

determined to be "direct obligations" which are relevant to meet the due diligence "obligation to ensure" include "best environmental practices," which are required by the ISA sulfides regulations and the standard clauses for exploration contracts.[66] The Chamber found that the "direct obligation" of sponsoring States to conduct environmental impact assessments extended beyond the scope of the ISA regulations.[67] On the broader question of treatment of developing States, the Chamber endorsed the principle of equity, recognizing that enterprises in developing jurisdictions may be established to avoid more stringent regulations elsewhere, and that the spread of sponsoring "States of convenience" would jeopardize the application of the higher standard of environmental protection.[68]

The second question put to the Chamber was, "[w]hat is the extent of liability of a State Party for any failure to comply with the provisions of the Convention in particular Part XI, and the 1994 Agreement, by an entity whom it has sponsored under Article 153, paragraph 2(b), of the Convention?"[69] While this question arguably formed the basis of the most critical aspect of the opinion, it is also the part which has the clearest answer provided by the Convention. Article 139(2) provides that "[w]ithout prejudice to the rules of international law ... damage caused by the failure of a State Party ... to carry out its responsibilities under this Part shall entail liability." However, it continues to say that a "State Party shall not ... be liable for damage caused by any failure to comply ... by a person whom it has sponsored ... if the State Party has taken all necessary and appropriate measures to secure effective compliance."[70] Having already ruled on the first question noting that sponsoring States have a high standard of due diligence,[71] and that the Convention was not a strict liability regime despite arguments to the contrary,[72] the Chamber pointed out that where damages occurred and a sponsoring State failed to take all necessary and appropriate measures to ensure compliance, then the State would be liable, but where a State had discharged its duty a gap in liability would remain, which the Chamber suggested could be filled with the use of a trust fund.[73] In addition, the Chamber indicated that Article 304 of the Convention allowed for the integration of such liability at a future junction through mining regulations.[74]

Finally the third question before the Chamber was, "[w]hat are the necessary and appropriate measures that a sponsoring State must take in order to fulfill its responsibility under the Convention, in particular Article 139 and Annex III,

---

66 ISA, Standard Clauses for Exploration Contract, <https://www.isa.org.jm/files/documents/EN/Regs/Code-Annex4.pdf>.
67 ITLOS Advisory Opinion 2011, *supra* note 2 at paras 145, 148.
68 Ibid. at para. 159.
69 Ibid. at paras 1(2), 164.
70 LOSC, *supra* note 1 at art. 139(2).
71 ITLOS Advisory Opinion 2011, *supra* note 2 at para. 131.
72 Ibid. at para. 189.
73 Ibid. at para. 209.
74 Ibid. at para. 211.

and the 1994 Agreement?"[75] The Chamber found that inherent in the "due diligence" obligation is that the State will ensure that the obligations of the sponsored entity are enforceable.[76] The rules, regulations and procedures under Annex III, Article 21(3) of the Convention are used as minimum standards of stringency for applicable laws environmental or otherwise.[77] These measures cannot simply be contractual arrangements with the sponsored entity. They must be at least as stringent as those adopted by the Authority and certainly no less effective than international rules.[78]

13.5 Sustainable development principles in LOSC jurisprudence: *Request for an Advisory Opinion Submitted by the Sub-regional Fisheries Commission* (2015)

On 2 April 2015, the International Tribunal for the Law of the Sea delivered its first ever Advisory Opinion in response to four questions submitted by the State Parties to the West Africa Sub-Regional Fisheries Commission (SRFC).[79] The Opinion clarifies a number of important issues regarding the obligations of flag States to control the activities of their vessels conducting fishing activities in the exclusive economic zones (EEZs) of other States and their potential liability for failure to do this effectively. It addresses the obligations of an international organization, such as the EU, where vessels flying the flags of the Member States of the organization are fishing under the terms of an access agreement between the organization and a coastal State or States. It also considers the obligations of cooperation under LOSC between coastal States and others engaged in fishing for highly migratory species in the region. The Opinion represents an important further application of the requirements of "due diligence" which were developed by the ITLOS Seabed Disputes Chamber in its 2011 Advisory Opinion.[80]

The West African SRFC was established by a treaty of 29 March 1985 designed to strengthen cooperation among its members regarding the management of the living resources of their EEZs.[81] It has seven member States and is based in Dakar, Senegal.[82] By a supplementary treaty in 1993 (the MAC Convention), the SRFC sought to regulate and harmonize minimum access

---

75 Ibid. at para. 212.

76 Ibid. at para. 239.

77 Ibid. at para. 240.

78 Ibid. at para. 241.

79 ITLOS Advisory Opinion 2015, *supra* note 3.

80 ITLOS Advisory Opinion 2011, *supra* note 2; David Freestone, *Responsibilities and Obligations of States Sponsoring Persons and Entities with Respect to Activities in the LOSC Area* "Commentary" (2011) 105 *Am. J. Int'l L.* 755–61.

81 SRFC, Request for an Advisory Opinion to the International Tribunal for the Law of the Sea – ITLOS, Written Statement, (November 2013), <https://www.itlos.org/fileadmin/itlos/documents/cases/case_no.21/written_statements_round1/C21_19_CSRP_orig_Eng_rev.pdf>.

82 Members are Guinea, Cape Verde, The Gambia, Guinea Bissau, Mauritania, Senegal, and Sierra Leone.

conditions (MAC) for EEZ resources in the sub-region, as well as to implement regional FAO instruments relating to the exercise of hot pursuit and coordination of surveillance. The 1993 MAC Convention was further revised in June 2012; its amended version entered into force on 16 September 2012. The 2012 revised MAC Convention includes innovative provisions including the FAO definition of IUU Fishing,[83] requirements of the 2009 FAO Port State Measures Agreement,[84] acceptance of the precautionary and ecosystem approaches to fisheries and, in an especially interesting provision, its Article 33 specifically provides that "[t]he Conference of Ministers of the SRFC may authorize the Permanent Secretary of the SRFC to bring a given legal matter before the International Tribunal of the Law of the Sea for advisory opinion." Apparently thereby availing itself of the power included within the ITLOS Rules of Procedure to refer "a legal question" to ITLOS.[85]

It was utilizing this provision of the 2012 MAC Convention that the seven State Parties passed a resolution instructing their Secretariat to refer a number of legal questions to ITLOS for an Advisory Opinion. On 27 March 2013 the following questions were referred to the ITLOS Registrar:

1   What are the obligations of the flag State in cases where illegal, unreported and unregulated (IUU) fishing activities are conducted within the exclusive economic zone of third party States?
2   To what extent shall the flag State be held liable for IUU fishing activities conducted by vessels sailing under its flag?
3   Where a fishing license is issued to a vessel within the framework of an international agreement with the flag State or with an international agency, shall the State or international agency be held liable for the violation of the fisheries legislation of the coastal State by the vessel in question?
4   What are the rights and obligations of the coastal State in ensuring the sustainable management of shared stocks and stocks of common interest, especially the small pelagic species and tuna?

On 28 March 2013, the ITLOS Registrar registered the request as Case 21 and notified all the State Parties to LOSC, inviting States Parties, the SRFC and relevant international organizations to present written statements. Twenty-two States Parties and six international organizations made written statements as did

---

83 FAO, International Plan of Action to Prevent, Deter and Eliminate Illegal, Unreported and Unregulated Fishing (2001), <http://www.fao.org/docrep/003/y1224e/y1224e00.htm>.
84 2009 FAO Agreement on Port State Measures to Prevent, Deter and Eliminate Illegal, Unreported and Unregulated Fishing.
85 International Tribunal for Law of the Sea, Rules of the Tribunal ITLOS/9 (17 March 2009), Article 138(1), <https://www.itlos.org/fileadmin/itlos/documents/basic_texts/Itlos_8_E_17_03_09.pdf> [ITLOS Rules, *rules of procedure*]. Article 138(1) permits referral for an Advisory Opinion ". . . on a legal question if an international agreement related to the purposes of the Convention specifically provides for the submission to the Tribunal of a request for such opinion."

the US – a non-Party – and World Wildlife Fund.[86] Oral hearings were held
2–5 September 2014.[87]

13.5.1 Admissibility

Although the ITLOS Seabed Disputes Chamber delivered a major Advisory
Opinion in 2011,[88] this is the first occasion on which the full Tribunal has
been presented with a request for an Advisory Opinion. A number of States
Parties, in their written statements and oral presentations, argued vigorously
against the admissibility of the request, pointing out that neither LOSC
nor the Statute of the Tribunal expressly gives ITLOS jurisdiction to give
Advisory Opinions and that this request did not arise from a legal dispute but
was seeking to give the Tribunal a legislative role beyond the proper functions
of a judicial body.

Article 21 of the Statute establishing the ITLOS, listed as Annex VI of the
Convention, reads:

> The jurisdiction of the Tribunal comprises all disputes and all applications
> submitted to it in accordance with this Convention and *all matters specifically
> provided for in any other agreement which confers jurisdiction on the Tribunal.*
> (emphasis added).[89]

Additionally, Article 16 of the ITLOS Statute obliges the Tribunal to "frame rules
for carrying out its functions. In particular, it shall lay down rules of procedure."[90]
Article 138(1) of the Rules of Procedure for the Tribunal reads:

> The Tribunal may give an advisory opinion on a legal question if an
> international agreement related to the purposes of the Convention specifically
> provides for the submission to the Tribunal of a request for such an opinion.[91]

The Tribunal took the view that there was no reason to interpret the phase in
Article 21 of the Statute – "all matters specifically provided for in any other

---

86 Saudi Arabia, Germany, New Zealand, China, Somalia, Ireland, the Federated States of
Micronesia, Australia, Japan, Portugal, Chile, Argentina, the United Kingdom, Thailand, the
Netherlands, the European Union, Cuba, France, Spain, Montenegro, Switzerland and Sri
Lanka. And the following six organizations: the Forum Fisheries Agency, the International Union
for Conservation of Nature and Natural Resources (IUCN), the Caribbean Regional Fisheries
Mechanism, the United Nations, the Food and Agriculture Organization of the United Nations
and the Central American Fisheries and Aquaculture Organization.
87 Oral presentations were made by Argentina, Australia, Chile, the European Union, Germany, the
Federated States of Micronesia, New Zealand, Spain, Thailand and the United Kingdom, as well
as the SRFC, the Caribbean Regional Fisheries Mechanism and IUCN.
88 ITLOS Advisory Opinion 2011, *supra* note 2; Note that Article 191 of LOSC specifically confers
Advisory Jurisdiction on the Seabed Disputes Chamber.
89 LOSC, *supra* note 1, Annex VI, art. 21.
90 Ibid. at Annex VI, art. 16.
91 ITLOS Rules, *supra* note 85, art. 138(1).

agreement which confers jurisdiction on the Tribunal" – in a restrictive way, so as, for example, only to apply to disputes.[92] The questions – in so far as they related to the regime of the EEZ – fell clearly within the scope of the 2012 MAC Convention and were of a legal nature, justifying a legitimate exercise of the Tribunal's discretionary power to give an Advisory Opinion.[93]

The Tribunal then considered each of the questions in turn: First, "*[w]hat are the obligations of the flag State in cases where illegal, unreported and unregulated (IUU) fishing activities are conducted within the Exclusive Economic Zone of third party States?*"[94] Having stated that the coastal State has the primary responsibility for the policing of foreign vessels fishing within its EEZ,[95] the Tribunal then looked at the provisions of the Convention relating to the obligations of flag States. There has long been debate as to the relevance of the "*duties of the flag State*" set out in Article 94 LOSC to vessels engaged in fishing.[96] Article 94(1) appears to concern itself primarily with the internal order of vessels flying a flag, providing: "every State shall effectively exercise its jurisdiction and control in administrative, technical and social matters over vessels flying its flag."[97] Article 94(2) continues: "in particular every State shall: (a) maintain a register . . .; and (b) assume jurisdiction . . . in respect of administrative, technical and social matters concerning the ship."[98] The remainder of the Article deals with construction and certification of seaworthiness, qualifications of masters, crew, etc., important issues but not specifically related, it has been argued, to the way in which the vessel conducts the activities in which is involved – fishing, marine research and the like.

The interpretation of Article 94 of the Convention by the Tribunal ends this controversy – for it decided that the use of the words "in particular" in Article 94(2) indicated that the list of flag State responsibilities that followed was not exhaustive but only indicative.[99] Hence, it said

> as far as fishing activities are concerned, the flag State, in fulfillment of its responsibility to exercise effective jurisdiction and control in administrative matters, must adopt the necessary administrative measures to ensure that fishing vessels flying its flag are not involved in activities which will undermine the flag State's responsibilities under the Convention in respect of the conservation and management of marine living resources.[100]

Moreover, the Tribunal reminded us that it had found already in the *Southern Bluefin Tuna* cases,[101] that a flag State's obligation under Article 192

---

92 ITLOS Advisory Opinion 2015, *supra* note 3 at paras 54–60.
93 Ibid. at paras 61–69.
94 Ibid. at para. 85.
95 Ibid. at para. 106.
96 Freestone 2011, *supra* note 40.
97 LOSC, *supra* note 1 at art. 94(1).
98 Ibid. at art. 94(2).
99 Advisory Opinion 2015, *supra* note 3 at para. 117.
100 Ibid. at para. 119.
101 *Southern Bluefin Tuna* case, *supra* note 8, *Provisional Measures*, Order of 27 August 1999, ITLOS Reports 1999, 280, at 295, para. 70.

LOSC to "protect and preserve the marine environment" includes "conservation of the living resources of the sea."[102] Flag States are therefore obliged to take the necessary measures to ensure that their nationals and vessels flying their flag are not involved in IUU fishing activities in the EEZ of another State.[103]

When considering exactly what such "necessary measures" might be in relation to flag States overseeing their fishing boats, the Tribunal drew attention to the standard of due diligence required of States in the 2011 Advisory Opinion of the Seabed Disputes Chamber.[104] Although the relationship between a State and an entity that it is sponsoring for mineral exploration or exploitation activities in the Area are not entirely comparable with that between a flag State and its fishing vessels, nevertheless it felt that the same principles are applicable. In the 2011 Advisory Opinion, the Disputes Chamber had said that the "obligation 'to ensure' is not an obligation to achieve, in each and every case, the result that the sponsored contractor complies with the aforementioned obligations. Rather, it is an obligation to deploy adequate means, to exercise best possible efforts, to do the utmost, to obtain this result."[105] The flag State of a fishing boat therefore has a similar obligation of conduct, rather than result. It is under a due diligence obligation "to deploy adequate means, to exercise best possible efforts, to do the utmost", to ensure compliance and to prevent IUU fishing by fishing vessels flying its flag.[106]

Second the Tribunal considered: "*[t]o what extent shall the flag State be held liable for IUU fishing activities conducted by vessels sailing under its flag?*"[107] Despite the fact that neither LOSC nor the 2012 MAC Convention provides guidance on the issue of liability, the Tribunal clearly regarded this as a simpler question. Having held that flag States had an obligation of due diligence to the coastal State to ensure its vessels did not engage in IUU fishing in its EEZ, then if the flag State does not take adequate measures to prevent this, a breach of international State responsibility arises for which the flag State would be liable.[108] Such a breach of "due diligence' does not require a pattern of behaviour; it can be triggered by a single incident. Third, the Tribunal considered: "*[w]here a fishing license is issued to a vessel within the framework of an international agreement with the flag State or with an international agency, shall the State or international agency be held liable for the violation of the fisheries legislation of the coastal State by the vessel in question?*"[109] The Tribunal framed its response to this

---

102 Advisory Opinion 2015, *supra* note 3 at para. 120.

103 Ibid. at para. 124.

104 ITLOS Advisory Opinion 2011, *supra* note 2.

105 Ibid. at para. 110.

106 Ibid.

107 ITLOS Advisory Opinion 2015, *supra* note 3 at para. 141.

108 Ibid. at para. 144; Citing the ILC *Draft Articles on State Responsibility* Article 2: "There is an internationally wrongful act of a State when conduct consisting of an action or omission (a) is attributable to the State under international law, and (b) constitutes a breach of an international obligation of the State." Ibid. at Article 31(1): "The responsible State is under an obligation to make full reparation for the injury caused by the internationally wrongful act."

109 Ibid. at para. 151.

question with two major constraints. First, it would only consider the question in relation to international organizations (as it interpreted the term "agency") which had exclusive competence for the regulation of fishing transferred to them by their member States – which *de facto* means only the European Union – and, secondly, for jurisdictional reasons, only in relation to fishing within the EEZ of the requesting States.[110]

The basic principle is that an international organization that has assumed exclusive competence to regulate fishing has in effect put itself in the place of its member States and assumed the same due diligence obligations which the member States would have had individually.[111] Where the international organization is the only contracting Party to a fisheries access agreement then it must ensure that vessels flying the flags of its Member States comply with the coastal States' fisheries laws and do not conduct IUU fishing activities within their EEZs. If the international organization does not exercise such due diligence, then it is liable for this breach of obligation. Solely liable – the Tribunal thought – although it suggested that the SRFC Member States could request the international organization provide information on whether it or its Member States have responsibility on any specific issue and, if no timely response is received, then the result would be joint and several liability.[112]

Finally, the Tribunal considered: *"[w]hat are the rights and obligations of the coastal State in ensuring the sustainable management of shared stocks and stocks of common interest, especially the small pelagic species and tuna?"*[113] On this wide-ranging final question the Tribunal was effectively able to answer by direct reference to the text of Part V of the Convention. All these rights and duties are comprehensively set out in Articles 61–64 of the Convention, although most of these articles impose an obligation to "cooperate"[114] or to "seek to agree."[115] The Tribunal worked carefully though these provisions to highlight their significance and also to point out the "due diligence" requirements of these hortatory obligations.[116] It also reminded the requesting States that the obligation to cooperate in relation to exploitation of tuna species in the region that is imposed by Article 64(1) does not simply apply to coastal States. The SRFC Member States also have the right to require cooperation from non-Member States whose nationals fish for tuna in the region, "directly or through appropriate international organizations with a view to ensuring conservation and promoting the objective of optimum utilization of such species."[117]

---

110 Ibid. at paras 158–59.
111 Ibid. at para. 172.
112 Ibid. at para. 173; p. 63.
113 Ibid. at para. 175.
114 LOSC, *supra* note 1 at art. 61(2), 64(1).
115 Ibid. at art. 63(1), 63(2).
116 ITLOS Advisory Opinion 2015, *supra* note 3 at paras 189–91, 194–99, 202–3.
117 Ibid. at 67.

13.6 Conclusion

It should be clear from the above that although the 1982 LOSC predates much of the sustainable development debate, the law of the sea regime, of which LOSC forms the keystone, contains already, or has been able to accommodate, the evolving sustainable development concepts – such as those contained in the New Delhi Declaration. While it must be acknowledged that implementation is always a challenge, the LOSC itself contains a number of key sustainable development obligations which have been supplemented by both the 1995 United Nations Fish Stocks Agreement (UNFSA) and by judicial interpretation.

The principle of the *sustainable use of natural resources* is a key aspect of the LOSC regime in terms of the protection and preservation of the marine environment as well as the conservation and management of living resources. The UNFSA takes this approach even further in relation to straddling and highly migratory fish stocks and there is evidence that the precautionary and ecosystem approaches are being taken on board at national and regional levels. There is certainly recognition in the LOSC itself that States may have the sovereign right to exploit natural resources but only in accordance with the duty to protect and preserve the marine environment.[118]

The *equity* concept of the principle of equity and eradication of poverty is reflected in a number of provisions of the LOSC which require, for example, coastal States to take into account the interests of land-locked and geographically disadvantaged States,[119] which have the right "to participate, on an equitable basis, in the exploitation of an appropriate part of the surplus of the living resources of the exclusive economic zones of coastal States of the same sub region or region." By the same token the "common heritage of mankind" status of the Area means activities undertaken there shall be for the "benefit of mankind as a whole, irrespective of the geographical location of States, whether coastal or land-locked, and taking into particular consideration the interests and needs of developing States and of peoples who have not attained full independence or other self-governing status . . ."[120] Income collected by the ISA under Article 82 from levies on the exploitation of coastal States' extended continental shelves shall also be distributed "on the basis of equitable sharing criteria, taking into account the interests and needs of developing States, particularly the least developed and the land-locked among them."[121]

More problematic perhaps is the *principle of common but differentiated responsibilities*. In the 2011 Advisory Opinion of the ITLOS Seabed Disputes Chamber, the Chamber went to some lengths to stress the point that the duties of States sponsoring activities in the Area were the same – equally rigorous – whether they were developed or of developing States – so as to avoid the development of what

---

118 LOSC, *supra* note 1 at art. 193.
119 Ibid. at arts 69 and 70 – referenced elsewhere, e.g. art. 136.
120 Ibid. at art. 140.
121 Ibid. at art. 82(4).

they termed "sponsoring States of convenience" – analogous to "flags of convenience" in the maritime sector. This point was also picked up by the ITLOS 2015 Advisory Opinion when it held that the duties of flag States under Article 94 included the obligation to exercise "due diligence" over the activities of fishing boats to ensure they were not involved in IUU fishing – whatever the nationality of the vessels.[122] This is simply good governance. Having said that, however, Christopher Stone in his examination of the common but differentiated responsibilities argues that, in many ways, the LOSC reflects that principle, though it is not referred to explicitly, as it includes what he call "close cognates."[123]

The principle of the *precautionary approach* is by contrast much easier to find. It has been argued that it is inherent in the text of the LOSC – even though it was not a recognized idea in the 1970s.[124] However, as we have seen above, precaution plays a central role in the 1993 UNFSA. It was applied *de facto* by the ITLOS in the *Southern Bluefin Tuna* and *Moxs Plant* cases and was also utilized as the basis for the due diligence requirements relating to a State's responsibility to ensure compliance with the Convention under Article 139 as interpreted and applied by the Seabed Dispute Chamber and the ITLOS Advisory Opinions.

Fifth, the principle of *public participation and access to information* is found in both the LOSC as well as the Rules of the Tribunal. Article 204 of the LOSC provides for States and relevant international organizations to make available, through publication and dissemination, information and knowledge resulting from marine research and scientific activities.[125] Under the Rules of the Tribunal, copies of the materials submitted by the disputing Parties shall be made available to the public on the opening of oral proceedings or prior.[126] Another important innovation in the 1995 UNSA is the requirement for transparency in regional fishery organizations.[127]

Sixth, the *principle of good governance* is exemplified in the dispute settlement procedures established under Part XV of the LOSC, allowing for transparent reconciliation of disputes in observance of the rule of law. More particularly the rules adumbrated by the ITLOS Seabed Disputes Chamber and the 2015 ITLOS Advisory Opinion relating to the due diligence of States sponsoring activities in the Area or providing flags to fisheries vessels are outstanding examples of the good governance agenda.[128]

---

122 ITLOS Advisory Opinion 2015, paras 137–140.
123 Christopher Stone, "Common but Differentiated Responsibilities in International Law" 2000 98 AJIL 276, 276.
124 David Freestone, "International Fisheries Law since Rio – the continued rise of the Precautionary Principle" in Alan Boyle and David Freestone, eds., *International Law and Sustainable Development.* (Oxford: OUP, 1999) at 135–64, 153. FAO took the view in 1992 that precaution was compatible with LOSC *Legal Issues concerning High Seas Fisheries* FI/HSF/TC/92/8 (FAO Rome June 1992).
125 LOSC, *supra* note 1 at art. 244.
126 ITLOS Advisory Opinion, *supra* note 85 at arts 67, 134.
127 UNFSA, *supra* note 6 at arts 2, 12.
128 ITLOS Seabed Disputes, Proceedings Before the Chamber (2011); ITLOS Advisory Opinion 21 (2015).

Lastly, the principle of *integration and interrelationship* of social, economic and environmental objectives is exemplified in both the substantive provisions balancing extractive rights with obligations relating to environmental protection, as well as in the application of "all necessary and appropriate measures" when considering the extent of liability of a sponsoring State. Provisions of the LOSC which promote *international cooperation*, particularly relating to data sharing and sharing of information necessary to prevent environmental damage,[129] further illustrate the integration of socio-economic and environmental considerations into the Convention.

Overall, despite that fact that the 1982 Convention predates the United Nations Conference on Environment and Development, it can certainly be argued that the sustainable development principles developed since then are well represented in the LOSC regime, either in the 1982 text itself, as interpreted by the ITLOS, or in the regime developed explicitly in the 1995 UNFSA.

---

129 LOSC, *supra* note 1 at art. 200, 242.

14 The interpretation of sustainable development principles in ITLOS

Aline Jaeckel and Tim Stephens*

14.1 Introduction

The International Tribunal for the Law of the Sea (ITLOS) handed down its first judgment in December 1997,[1] and since that time has developed an extensive and impressive body of jurisprudence on environmental issues. ITLOS has not mentioned 'sustainable development' in express terms, but it has engaged with several associated principles for managing the environmental impacts of human uses of the oceans (including, *inter alia*, the precautionary principle and environmental impact assessments).[2]

Unlike other international judicial bodies, ITLOS has a clear mandate to resolve disputes concerning sustainable development. This is by virtue of ITLOS's central role in settling disputes concerning the 1982 United Nations Convention on the Law of the Sea[3] (LOSC), one of the most important multilateral environmental agreements ever concluded. The LOSC was concluded in 1982, well before the term 'sustainable development' entered the lexicon through the landmark 1987 report of the World Commission on Environment and Development.[4] Nonetheless, notions of sustainability clearly animate many aspects of the LOSC, particularly Part XII. Moreover, concepts of sustainability are imbued in the Convention's lengthy Preamble, which refers, among other things, to the need for the 'equitable and efficient utilisation' of the resources of the ocean, the 'protection and preservation of the marine environment', the 'realisation of a just and equitable international economic order', and 'economic and social advancement of all peoples of the world'. Additionally, ITLOS not only has jurisdiction over disputes concerning the LOSC, but has also been conferred jurisdiction under a

---

* The authors acknowledge that some parts of this chapter draw from the contribution by Professor Stephens to the Final Report of the International Law Association Committee on International Law on Sustainable Development (2012).

1 *M/V Saiga (Saint Vincent and the Grenadines v Guinea)* (prompt release) (1997) 110 ILR 736.
2 Gwenaele Rashbrooke, 'The International Tribunal for the Law of the Sea: A Forum for the Development of Principles of International Environmental Law?' (2004) 19 *Int'l J. Mar. & Coastal L.* 515.
3 United Nations Convention on the Law of the Sea, opened for signature 10 December 1982, 1833 UNTS 397 (entered into force 16 November 1994).
4 World Commission on Environment and Development, *Our Common Future* (1987).

host of implementing agreements,[5] including the 1995 Fish Stocks Agreement,[6] which are more explicit in setting out sustainability principles.[7]

This chapter examines the evolution of ITLOS's sustainable development jurisprudence, from the first tentative steps in considering environmental issues in several provisional measures and prompt release cases, to being at the vanguard in the international judicial endorsement of contemporary principles of environmental governance in *Responsibilities and Obligations of States Sponsoring Persons and Entities with Respect to Activities in the Area (Seabed Mining Advisory Opinion)*.[8] ITLOS has developed increasing confidence and familiarity in matters of environmental law, and has made a contribution to a jurisprudence of sustainable development that is of equal (and possibly greater) significance to that of the International Court of Justice (ICJ). In doing so, ITLOS has proven to be successful in integrating or 'mainstreaming' environmental principles in its decisions.[9]

14.2 Sustainable development disputes in the LOSC dispute settlement system

As is well known, the dispute settlement system of the LOSC is distinctive by virtue of its generally compulsory character and the reach of its subject-matter jurisdiction across most aspects of the LOSC.[10] These features were considered important when negotiating the LOSC, so that there was an authoritative, centralised, mechanism for resolving LOSC disputes, thereby minimising the likelihood of parties adopting unilateral interpretations that might undermine the 'package deal' consensus that the LOSC embodies. Part XV contains the key dispute settlement provisions of the LOSC, and refers to the various dispute settlement bodies that may be utilised to resolve LOSC disputes, and the types of dispute that can be litigated. Importantly, the Part XV dispute settlement machinery applies to most provisions of the LOSC that concern living and non-living resources and the protection of the marine environment.

---

5 See Robin Churchill, 'Dispute Settlement in the Law of the Sea: Survey for 2011' (2012) 27 *Int'l J. Mar. & Coastal L.* 517, 545.

6 *Agreement for the Implementation of the Provisions of the United Nations Convention on the Law of the Sea of 10 December 1982 Relating to the Conservation and Management of Straddling Fish Stocks and Highly Migratory Fish Stocks*, opened for signature 4 December 1995, (1995) 34 ILM 1542 (entered into force 11 December 2001) ('Fish Stocks Agreement').

7 Ibid. at art. 5.

8 *Responsibilities and Obligations of States Sponsoring Persons and Entities with Respect to Activities in the Area* (Seabed Dispute Chamber of the International Tribunal of the Law of the Sea, Case No 17, 1 February 2011).

9 Alan Boyle and James Harrison, 'Judicial Settlement of International Environmental Disputes: Current Problems' (2013) 4 *J. Int'l Disp. Settlem.* 245.

10 See further Donald R. Rothwell and Tim Stephens, *The International Law of the Sea* (Oxford: Hart, 2010) ch. 18; Natalie Klein, *Dispute Settlement in the UN Convention on the Law of the Sea* (Cambridge: CUP, 2005); Tim Stephens, *International Courts and Environmental Protection* (Cambridge: CUP, 2009) 41–7.

ITLOS occupies a central role in the LOSC dispute settlement system, but it has no exclusivity of jurisdiction, nor any hierarchical superiority, over other courts or tribunals in dealing with LOSC disputes. Part XV instead gives parties a choice among four judicial institutions – ITLOS, the ICJ, an arbitral tribunal, or a 'special' arbitral tribunal – for dealing with their LOSC disputes. If parties express no preference for one of these, or in the event of a dispute between parties having made different choices, then arbitration is the default option. Of the 60 or so States that have lodged declarations, around half have chosen ITLOS as their first (or equal first) preferred forum for resolving LOSC disputes. It should also be noted that ITLOS does have automatic or default jurisdiction in relation to cases concerning the prompt release of fishing vessels and in applications for provisional measures. Moreover, the Seabed Disputes Chamber within ITLOS has jurisdiction over seabed disputes and may render Advisory Opinions concerning the seabed mining regime. ITLOS has also imitated the ICJ in creating a Chamber for Marine Environmental Disputes under the special chambers mechanism of Annex VI to the LOSC. As with the ICJ's Environmental Chamber, the ITLOS Chamber for Marine Environmental Disputes has never been used. This suggests that States prefer to have disputes involving sustainable development issues resolved by generalist rather than specialist bodies. This also underlines the critical importance of implementing the principle of integration as sustainability issues will almost inevitably be intertwined with other legal questions.

It is through the exercise of its default jurisdiction that ITLOS has had primary opportunity to address important disputes touching on issues of sustainable development. These disputes can be grouped into three separate categories. First, there are the prompt release cases, which have made up the bulk of ITLOS's caseload. Second, there are provisional measures cases. Third, there are advisory opinions that have addressed sustainable development questions most directly. The discussion that follows assesses the products of each of these categories of cases.

14.3 The sustainable development jurisprudence of ITLOS

14.3.1 Prompt release cases

The LOSC enclosed significant areas of the high seas through the Exclusive Economic Zone (EEZ) regime, affording coastal States exclusive sovereign rights and jurisdiction over living and non-living resources up to 200 nautical miles from the territorial sea baselines. In an effort to balance these new entitlements with the rights of other States, the LOSC included an important protection for foreign fishing vessels arrested by coastal States in their EEZ for violating coastal State fisheries laws. Hence, Article 73 provides that coastal States may take enforcement action against foreign fishing vessels in the EEZ, but arrested vessels and their crews are to be 'promptly released on the posting of a reasonable bond or other security.' Additionally, under Article 292, States whose vessels have been arrested may turn to ITLOS (unless another forum is selected, by mutual agreement) for a determination on whether an arrested vessel should be released.

Prompt release cases have made up the largest number of ITLOS's total caseload. As of 2012, there have been nine applications for prompt release. However, not all of these have progressed to the merits stage or involved questions of sustainability. Two prompt release cases were not heard at a merits stage,[11] and a further three have not involved questions relating to unsustainable fishing.[12] This leaves the *Camouco*,[13] *Monte Confurco*,[14] *Volga*[15] and *Juno Trader*[16] prompt release cases, all of which have related to questions of illegal, unregulated and unreported (IUU) fishing. These questions were most pronounced in the *Camouco, Monte Confurco* and *Volga* cases, which arose from arrests of vessels conducting IUU fishing for Patagonian toothfish in the Southern Ocean near Antarctica.

In these three cases ITLOS needed to determine if the financial bond and other conditions set by the arresting States (France in the *Camouco* and *Monte Confurco*, and Australia in the *Volga*) were 'reasonable' for the purposes of Articles 73 and 292 of the LOSC. In doing so, ITLOS emphasised that it needed to have regard to the balance between coastal and flag State interests encapsulated in the LOSC. The attitude of ITLOS to questions of environmental sustainability in the prompt release context is best exemplified by the *Volga*, the most recent prompt release case to raise sustainability issues. The *Volga* was a Russian flagged vessel operating illegally in the Australian EEZ surrounding Heard and McDonald Islands in the Southern Ocean and part of an IUU fishing fleet that had taken thousands of tonnes of the endangered Patagonian toothfish.

In its judgment in the *Volga* case, ITLOS recalled its statements in earlier prompt release cases of the factors that are relevant in assessing whether a bond is 'reasonable', including the gravity of the fishing offences, the potential penalties under the law of the detaining State, the value of the detained vessel and its cargo, and the amount and form of bond set by the coastal State.[17] However, it found that no specific weight was to be given to the problem of IUU fishing in the Southern Ocean affecting a number of States, which was undermining the objectives of the Convention on the Conservation of Antarctic Marine Living Resources (CCAMLR).[18] For its part, Australia had maintained that the regional and global concern about the unsustainability of IUU fishing was directly relevant to assessing what bond was reasonable. ITLOS certainly noted 'international concerns about [IUU] fishing' but went on to indicate that they were not relevant, as

---

11 *Grand Prince (Belize v France)* (prompt release) (2000) 125 ILR 251; *Chasiri Reefer 2 (Panama v Yemen)* ITLOS Case No 9.

12 *M/V Saiga (Saint Vincent and the Grenadines v Guinea)* (prompt release) (1997) 110 ILR 736; *Hoshinmaru (Japan v Russian Federation)* ITLOS Case No 14; *Tomimaru (Japan v Russian Federation)* ITLOS Case No 15.

13 *Camouco (Panama v France)* (prompt release) (2000) 125 ILR 151, (2000) 39 ILM 666.

14 *Monte Confurco (Seychelles v France)* (prompt release) (2000) 125 ILR 203.

15 *Volga (Russian Federation v Australia)* (prompt release) (2003) 42 ILM 159.

16 *Juno Trader (St Vincent and the Grenadines v Bissau)* (prompt release) (2005) 44 ILM 498.

17 *Volga (Russian Federation v Australia)* (prompt release) (2003) 42 ILM 159, [63].

18 *Convention for the Conservation of Antarctic Marine Living Resources*, opened for signature 20 May 1980, 1329 UNTS 48 (entered into force 7 April 1982).

it was only by reference to possible penalties that ITLOS could assess the gravity of fishing offences.[19] This approach was questioned by two judges in dissenting opinions. Judge Anderson and Judge *ad hoc* Shearer argued that the balancing exercise undertaken by ITLOS between coastal States and flag States was artificial unless broader considerations were also addressed, including the obligations under the LOSC to conserve marine living resources and the grave allegations of illegal fishing for endangered fish stocks at the heart of the *Volga* case.[20]

From the *Volga* case it is clear that ITLOS has taken a somewhat circumscribed and procedurally-focused approach to questions of prompt release, treating the Article 292 mechanism as one providing a safeguard mechanism for arrested vessels, and not one in which it is appropriate to deal with substantive matters of sustainable marine resource management. This might appear appropriate given the summary character of the prompt release procedure, however it must be remembered, as Judge Anderson pointed out, that coastal States have a responsibility under the LOSC to conserve and protect marine living resources within their EEZ, particularly if they are endangered.[21] The *Volga* case was decided in 2002, and given the advances made by ITLOS in addressing sustainability questions a decade later in the *Seabed Mining Advisory Opinion*, ITLOS might well approach a prompt release case such as the *Volga* case differently today. To do so would require no revolution in the conceptual framework of factors relevant to determining the reasonableness of a bond. It would simply mean acknowledging that coastal States have the primary responsibility for sustainably managing EEZ fisheries resources, that activities which undermine sustainable fisheries management are inconsistent with the objectives of the LOSC, and that they are properly deterred by the arrest and detention of IUU fishing vessels and the setting of hefty bonds (and other conditions) for the release of vessels.

14.3.2 Provisional measures cases

ITLOS's automatic competence to respond to applications for provisional measures pending the hearing of LOSC disputes on their merits has given rise to several highly significant decisions on questions of sustainable development. Article 290 of the LOSC allows for the making of interim orders either by an agreed court or, failing agreement, by ITLOS in order 'to preserve the respective rights of the parties to the dispute or to prevent serious harm to the marine environment, pending the final decision.' Article 290 makes clear that the provisional measures jurisdiction of ITLOS has a strong environmental objective. It does not exist only to safeguard the rights of parties to a dispute, but was also included in the LOSC so that harm to the marine environment could be prevented. Of

---

19 *Volga (Russian Federation v Australia)* (prompt release) (2003) 42 ILM 159, [68]–[69].
20 *Volga (Russian Federation v Australia)*, dissenting opinion of Judge Anderson (ITLOS Case No 11, 23 December 2002), para. 2; *Volga (Russian Federation v Australia)*, dissenting opinion of Judge *ad hoc* Shearer (ITLOS Case No 11, 23 December 2002), at paras 7–13.
21 See, in particular, LOSC Art 61.

course, this does not mean that ITLOS can entertain any request for provisional measures concerning environmental harm – the request must still be connected with an alleged violation of the LOSC. However, given the expansive reach of Part XII of the LOSC, which seeks to minimise pollution of the marine environment from any source, it is evident that this component of ITLOS's jurisdiction can play an important role in advancing sustainable development objectives.

There have been several applications for provisional measures made to ITLOS, the most recent being in the *Arctic Sunrise* case.[22] Three of these provisional measures cases have addressed questions of environmental protection: the *Southern Bluefin Tuna* case,[23] the *MOX Plant* case,[24] and the *Straits of Johor* case.[25] Although none of these cases successfully moved to the merits, in all three cases ITLOS did render provisional measures orders that took a precautionary approach consistent with the purpose of Article 290 which, as has been observed, operates to protect the legal rights of disputing parties and the marine environment from serious impairment.

The *Southern Bluefin Tuna* case arose from a dispute over the sustainable management of stocks of a highly migratory fishery, southern bluefin tuna, that migrate through the EEZs of a number of States, and across large areas of the high seas in the southern hemisphere. Australia and New Zealand brought the proceedings jointly against Japan, following Japan's decision to conduct a large-scale 'experimental fishing program.' Australia and New Zealand requested the establishment of an arbitral tribunal to hear the dispute and, pending the establishment of the tribunal, that ITLOS make provisional measures orders so that Japan would suspend its experimental program. In terms of substantive law, Australia and New Zealand pointed to several provisions of the LOSC allegedly violated by Japan, including the duty under Article 118 'to cooperate . . . in the conservation and management of living resources of the high seas.'

ITLOS largely accepted the arguments by Australia and New Zealand, and ordered (by eighteen votes to four) that catches of southern bluefin tuna be stabilised at the level recommended by the Commission for the Conservation of Southern Bluefin Tuna, and (by twenty votes to two) that Japan cease engaging in its experimental fishing program. This was an important order from the perspective of sustainable development. ITLOS noted that 'the conservation of the living resources of the sea is an element in the protection and preservation of the marine environment.'[26] In so doing, ITLOS identified the important links between the provisions of LOSC to protect and preserve the marine environment, and those relating to the conservation and sustainable management of fisheries.

---

22 *Arctic Sunrise (Netherlands v Russian Federation)*, (provisional measures) ITLOS Case No 22.
23 *Southern Bluefin Tuna (New Zealand v Japan; Australia v Japan)* (provisional measures) (1999) 117 ILR 148, (1999) 38 ILM 1624.
24 *MOX Plant (Ireland v United Kingdom)* (provisional measures) (2002) 41 ILM 405.
25 *Land Reclamation by Singapore in and around the Straits of Johor (Malaysia v Singapore)* (provisional measures) ITLOS Case No 12.
26 *Southern Bluefin Tuna, supra* note 23 at [70].

ITLOS found that Article 290 was appropriately applied because stocks of southern bluefin tuna were depleted, and conservation measures were necessary to restore them. ITLOS encouraged the parties to 'act with prudence and caution in order to ensure that effective conservation measures are taken.'[27] Although ITLOS did not refer expressly to the precautionary principle, a precautionary approach did structure the approach it took to the case.[28] ITLOS noted that first, scientific uncertainty surrounded the sustainability of catches of southern bluefin tuna; secondly, that it was not able to assess the evidence conclusively; and thirdly, that the situation was sufficiently urgent to require interim measures to safeguard not only the rights of the parties but also to prevent further depletion of southern bluefin tuna stocks.[29]

In the *MOX Plant* case between Ireland and the United Kingdom, ITLOS reaffirmed the 'prudence and caution' formulation adopted in the *Southern Bluefin Tuna* case, but decided that the situation did not demand an order restraining the United Kingdom from undertaking further steps in its plans to commission a new nuclear processing plant. The United Kingdom had begun the process for establishing a plant to produce mixed oxide (MOX) fuels from nuclear waste at the Sellafield facility on the Cumbrian coast on the Irish Sea. Ireland raised a number of objections in relation to this plan, and litigated the dispute in several forums. In relation to the LOSC, Ireland contended that the United Kingdom had not taken measures required under the LOSC to prevent, reduce and control pollution of the marine environment of the Irish Sea from accidental or intended releases of radioactive materials and had not engaged in a proper environmental impact assessment. As with the *Southern Bluefin Tuna* case, the matter never reached the merits stage because of complex jurisdictional issues that involved competition between multiple judicial forums. But unlike the *Southern Bluefin Tuna* case, ITLOS did not give a strong order in favour of the applicant to restrain the proposed activity posing a risk of damage to the marine environment. This was because there was no evidence of any activities occurring in connection with the proposed plant that would have any demonstrable environmental impact in the period pending the establishment of the Annex VII tribunal to hear the merits of the case.[30]

The third provisional measures case with an environmental dimension was the *Straits of Johor* case, and concerned land reclamation work undertaken by Singapore in and adjacent to the Straits of Johor, which is a narrow international

27 Ibid. at [77].
28 See, further, David Freestone, 'Caution or Precaution: A Rose by Any Other Name?' (1999) 10 *Ybk. Int'l Envtl. L.* 15; Jacqueline Peel, 'Precaution: A Matter of Principle, Approach or Process?' (2004) 5 *Melb. J. Int'l L.* 483 and Tim Stephens, *Int'l Ct. & Envtl. Prot.* (2009) 224–27.
29 *Southern Bluefin Tuna, supra* note 23 at [80].
30 For a critical assessment of the order see David VanderZwaag, 'The Precautionary Principle and Marine Environmental Protection: Slipper Shores, Rough Seas, and Rising Normative Tides' (2002) 33 *Ocean Dev. & Int'l L.* 165; Stephens, *supra* note 28 at 235–36.

strait separating Singapore from Malaysia. Malaysia commenced the proceedings seeking the establishment of an Annex VII arbitral tribunal to determine a maritime boundary between the two States, and to declare that Singapore had violated its obligations under the LOSC to protect the marine environment. Unsurprisingly, in light of the prominence given to precaution in the *Southern Bluefin Tuna* and *MOX Plant* cases, the parties referred to this principle in their pleadings in the *Straits of Johor*. Malaysia contended that the principle must direct the application and implementation of the LOSC. In its order, ITLOS did not consider this argument directly, but instead turned its focus to the need for cooperation between the parties to resolve their dispute in such a way as to prevent environmental damage. ITLOS noted that the land reclamation works by Singapore may well have adverse impacts on the marine environment and that 'prudence and caution' required the parties to 'establish mechanisms for exchanging information and assessing the risks or effects of land reclamation works and devising ways to deal with them.'[31] As Judge Anderson explained in his separate declaration, the orders of ITLOS, which required the parties to cooperate to assess and prevent adverse environmental impacts from the land reclamation were 'intended to be constructive guidance to the parties' and were also 'designed to preserve the marine environment.'[32]

14.3.3 Advisory jurisdiction

Undoubtedly the most significant law of the sea case contributing to sustainable development principles is the 'historic'[33] *Seabed Mining Advisory Opinion*, rendered by the Seabed Dispute Chamber (hereafter 'Chamber'). Although based within ITLOS, the Chamber is legally an independent body, in other words, a 'tribunal within a tribunal.'[34] The Chamber has jurisdiction to interpret Part XI of the LOSC and regulations on the exploration and exploitation of minerals at or beneath the international seabed, 'the Area' beyond the limits of national jurisdiction. Such regulations are adopted by the International Seabed Authority (ISA), which administers the Area 'on behalf of mankind as a whole.'[35]

The *Seabed Mining Advisory Opinion* was requested by the ISA Council following concerns by Nauru about the responsibilities and potential liabilities especially of developing States when sponsoring mining activities in the Area.

---

31 *Land Reclamation by Singapore in and around the Straits of Johor (Malaysia v Singapore)* (provisional measures) ITLOS Case No 12, [99].

32 Ibid. at [5] (Declaration of Judge Anderson) [5].

33 David Freestone, 'Responsibilities and Obligations of States Sponsoring Persons and Entities with Respect to Activities in the Area' (2011) 105(4) *AJIL* 755–60, 755.

34 Helmut Tuerk, 'The Contribution of the International Tribunal for the Law of the Sea to International Law' in Alex G. Oude Elferink and Erik Jaap Molenaar, eds., *The International Legal Regime of Areas beyond National Jurisdiction: Current and Future Developments* (The Hague: Martinus Nijhoff Publishers, 2010) 217–30, at p. 221.

35 LOSC, *supra* note 3 Art 153(1).

Although not mentioning sustainable development as such, the case offers insightful observations particularly on the principles of sustainable use of natural resources, precaution, common but differentiated responsibilities, equity and good governance.[36]

One way in which the Chamber developed these principles is by linking them to due diligence. The Chamber noted that the obligations of States who sponsor contractors to carry out mining activities in the Area are twofold. First, States are obliged to exercise due diligence to ensure contractors comply with their obligations. Secondly, sponsoring States have direct obligations including the obligation to assist the ISA, apply a precautionary approach and best environmental practices, conduct environmental impact assessments, and ensure recourse to compensation for damage caused by pollution.[37] These obligations arise under the LOSC and related instruments and exist autonomously, though meeting them is also relevant for complying with the due diligence 'obligation to ensure.'[38] By linking the two, the Chamber illuminated the far-reaching scope of due diligence.

14.3.3.1 Sustainable use of natural resources

Implicitly reinforcing the principle of sustainable use, the Chamber built on the ICJ's interpretation of due diligence in the *Pulp Mills* case.[39] It noted the variable nature of the concept, highlighting that what is considered sufficiently diligent may change in light of new scientific discoveries and that 'the standard of due diligence has to be more severe for the riskier activities.'[40] The Chamber emphasised that due diligence is an obligation to exercise best possible efforts and includes adopting domestic measures.[41]

Equally significant was the endorsement of environmental impact assessment (EIA). The Chamber noted that the obligation of sponsoring States to ensure that mining contractors conduct EIAs is both a direct obligation and an element of due diligence[42] making it applicable beyond the ISA regulations.[43] Additionally, conducting EIAs is a general obligation under customary international law.[44] In this context, the Chamber referred approvingly to the *Pulp Mills* case and applied the ICJ's reasoning in a transboundary context to areas beyond national

---

36 For a detailed discussion, see Duncan French, 'From the Depths: Rich Pickings of Principles of Sustainable Development and General International Law on the Ocean Floor – the Seabed Disputes Chamber's 2011 Advisory Opinion' (2011) 26 *Int'l J. Mar. Coast L.* 525–68, at p. 526.
37 *Seabed Mining Advisory Opinion, supra* note 8 at para. 122.
38 Ibid. at para. 123.
39 Ibid. at para. 115. See *Pulp Mills on the River Uruguay (Argentina v Uruguay)*, Judgment 2010 ICJ Reports p. 14, para. 197.
40 *Seabed Mining Advisory Opinion, supra* note 8 at para. 117.
41 Ibid. at paras 118–20.
42 Ibid. at paras 141–45.
43 Ibid. at para. 150.
44 Ibid. at paras 145, 147–49.

jurisdiction.[45] This exemplifies how sustainable development jurisprudence may be reinforced when advanced in multiple forums. Moreover, it underlines the important linkages between procedural and substantive obligations.

14.3.3.2 Precaution

The *Seabed Mining Advisory Opinion* also constructed a noteworthy extension of precaution. Despite the LOSC containing no explicit reference, the ISA regulations directly require sponsoring States to apply a precautionary approach.[46] However, clearly aiming to extend its legal effect, the Chamber built on the 'implicit' link between precaution and due diligence made in the *Southern Bluefin Tuna* case[47] and identified precaution as an integral element of due diligence. Thus, precaution becomes applicable even to activities not regulated in the ISA regulations.[48] As Duncan French has noted, 'an obligation only contained within subsequent secondary regulations has now been transformed into a fundamental element of the conventional requirement on sponsoring States.'[49] Moreover, the Chamber enunciated a surprisingly low threshold for this element of due diligence, noting that it applies 'where there are plausible indications of potential risks.'[50]

Finally, breaking previous silence on the legal status of precaution, the Chamber recognised the growing number of international instruments incorporating the precautionary approach and found 'a trend towards making this approach part of customary international law.'[51] This rich discussion is the strongest endorsement of precaution to date by an international tribunal and clearly demonstrates the Chamber's willingness to take an evolutionary approach to interpreting law in light of current environmental concerns.

Such an evolutionary approach is also demonstrated in the Chamber's finding that the obligation to apply 'best environmental practices' in general terms has become part of the due diligence obligation.[52] Despite it only being included in the then latest ISA regulations on sulphides,[53] the Chamber found that the

---

45 *Seabed Mining Advisory Opinion*, paras 147–148. See *Pulp Mills on the River Uruguay, supra* note 8 at para. 204.

46 ISA, *Regulations on Prospecting and Exploration for Polymetallic Nodules in the Area* (ISBA/6/A/18, 13 July 2000, as amended by ISBA/19/A/9 and ISBA/19/A/12, 25 July 2013, and ISBA/20/A/9, 24 July 2014), Regulation 31(2); ISA, *Regulations on Prospecting and Exploration for Polymetallic Sulphides in the Area* (ISBA/16/A/12/Rev.1, 15 November 2010, as amended by ISBA/19/A/12, 25 July 2013 and ISBA/20/A/10, 24 July 2014), Regulations 33(2); ISA, *Regulations on Prospecting and Exploration for Cobalt-rich Ferromanganese Crusts in the Area* (ISBA/18/A/11, 27 July 2012, as amended by ISBA/19/A/12, 25 July 2013), Regulation 33(2).

47 *Seabed Mining Advisory Opinion, supra* note 8 at para. 132.

48 Ibid. at para. 131.

49 French 2011, *supra* note 36 at p. 547.

50 *Seabed Mining Advisory Opinion, supra* note 8 at para. 131.

51 Ibid. at para. 135.

52 Ibid. at para. 136.

53 ISA, *Regulations on Prospecting and Exploration for Polymetallic Sulphides in the Area* (ISBA/16/A/12/Rev.1, 15 November 2010, as amended by ISBA/19/A/12, 25 July 2013 and ISBA/20/A/10, 24 July 2014), Regulations 33(2).

first ISA regulations on polymetallic nodules 'should be interpreted in light of the development of the law, as evidenced by the subsequent adoption of the Sulphides Regulations.'[54]

14.3.3.3 Common but differentiated responsibility and equity

The *Seabed Mining Advisory Opinion* also contains an enlightening, albeit implicit, reference to the principle of common but differentiated responsibility. With the common heritage principle being one of the building blocks of Part XI,[55] intra-generational equity and inclusion of developing States feature strongly. The Chamber expressly recognised the relevant provisions ensuring preferential treatment for developing States, yet unambiguously noted that none of these affect a sponsoring State's responsibilities or liability, which 'apply equally to all sponsoring State, whether developing or developed.'[56]

The Chamber recognised the overriding importance of the marine environment as transcending economic differences of States. The Chamber explained the importance of avoiding 'sponsoring States "of convenience"', a reference to a general challenge in the law of the sea in enforcing flag State responsibilities, and which would 'jeopardize uniform application of the highest standards of protection of the marine environment, the safe development of activities in the Area and protection of the common heritage of mankind.'[57]

The Chamber did, however, acknowledge that differences might apply for direct obligations. A case in point is that the ISA regulations include the precautionary approach by direct reference to principle 15 of the Rio Declaration,[58] which in turn requires States to apply precaution 'according to their capabilities.'[59] Yet, the Chamber immediately qualifies the categorisation of States by highlighting that 'the reference to "capabilities" is only a broad and imprecise reference to the differences in developed and developing States.'[60] Advancing a more individualistic approach, the Chamber notes that 'what counts in a specific situation is the level of scientific knowledge and technical capability [. . .].'[61] Thus, the Chamber parts with broad-brush categorisations of States and, whilst expressly recognising the specific provisions to ensure integration of developing States, it places limits on preferential treatment to avoid repeating troublesome constructions from other environmental law regimes.

---

54 *Seabed Mining Advisory Opinion, supra* note 8 at para. 137.
55 LOSC, *supra* note 3 at Arts 136–137.
56 *Seabed Mining Advisory Opinion*, para. 158.
57 Ibid. at para. 159.
58 *Regulations on Prospecting and Exploration for Polymetallic Nodules in the Area*, Regulation 31(2); *Regulations on Prospecting and Exploration for Polymetallic Sulphides in the Area*, Regulations 33(2); *Regulations on Prospecting and Exploration for Cobalt-rich Ferromanganese Crusts in the Area*, Regulation 33(2) *supra* note 46.
59 1992 Rio Declaration on Environment and Development, 31 ILM 874, Principle 15; see also *Seabed Mining Advisory Opinion, supra* note 8 at para. 129.
60 *Seabed Mining Advisory Opinion, supra* note 8 at para. 162.
61 Ibid. at para. 162.

14.3.3.4 Good governance or equity

Lastly, the Chamber endorsed principles of good governance and equity. In a rare judicial articulation of the former, the *Seabed Mining Advisory Opinion* noted that 'the functions of the Chamber [. . .] are relevant for the good governance of the Area.'[62] Moreover, by requiring sponsoring States to take domestic legal and administrative measures[63] in line with the common heritage nature of the regime, the Chamber's decision strengthens both principles. In deciding on domestic measures, States 'must take into account, objectively, the relevant options in a manner that is reasonable, relevant and conducive to the benefit of mankind as a whole.'[64] The Chamber further clarified that merely entering into a contract with the sponsored entity would not fulfil the State's international responsibilities *inter alia* because it would 'lack transparency.'[65] Thus, within the State-centred constraints of international law, the Chamber's approach seeks to ensure that good governance seeps from the international through to the domestic level, so that mining entities live up to their social and environmental responsibilities.

14.3.3.5 Erga omnes *obligations*

Bearing upon several sustainable development principles, one of the Chamber's most important contributions relates to the enforceability of *erga omnes* obligations.

First, the Chamber observed that compensable harm includes 'damage to the Area and its resources constituting the common heritage of mankind, and damage to the marine environment.'[66] This suggests an inclusion of pure environmental harm without direct impact on any particular State. Secondly, in addressing the question of which State may bring a claim against a sponsoring State in the event of environmental harm, the Chamber speculated that the ISA itself may have such entitlement implicitly derived from its obligation to act on behalf of mankind.[67] Granting an international organisation such rights would be a milestone, even under Part XI with its already progressive provisions allowing the ISA legal standing.[68] What is more, the Chamber noted that each State Party may bring a claim, relying on the *erga omnes* nature of the obligation to protect the marine environment in areas beyond national jurisdiction.[69]

With such far-reaching conclusions the Chamber became the first international judicial body to expressly endorse Article 48 of the International Law Commission Articles on State Responsibility,[70] thus accepting, in principle, the

---

62 Ibid. at para. 29.
63 Ibid. at paras 118–20, 218.
64 Ibid. at para. 230.
65 Ibid. at para. 225.
66 Ibid. at para. 179.
67 Ibid. at para. 180; LOSC, Art 137(2), 153(1), 157(2).
68 LOSC, *supra* note 3 at Art 187, Annex IV, Art 37.
69 *Seabed Mining Advisory Opinion, supra* note 8 at para. 180.
70 International Law Commission Articles on Responsibility of States for Internationally Wrongful Acts (2001).

existence of an *actio popularis* for environmental harm to global commons. Given the longstanding doubts over the legal status of Article 48, the *Seabed Mining Advisory Opinion* consolidates its position in international law and may prove to be significant in understanding the capacity of international courts to enforce environmental protection obligations.

14.3.3.6 Evaluation

The *Seabed Mining Advisory Opinion* exhibits an evolutionary approach to environmental legal interpretation. Since the Chamber drew on general international law to support its findings, they will undoubtedly radiate well beyond the seabed mining regime[71] and may greatly support the consolidation of sustainable development principles.

Nevertheless, the stringency of the findings should be understood in the context of Part XI and two aspects in particular. First, the importance the Chamber placed on properly implementing the principle of common heritage of humankind,[72] and secondly, the inherently evolutionary design of Part XI. The ISA possesses regulatory powers to gradually develop regulations for the exploration and eventually exploitation of seabed minerals in parallel with advancing our knowledge of the deep sea environment. Through its advisory jurisdiction, the Seabed Dispute Chamber provides judicial guidance to 'assist the [ISA] Council in the performance of its activities.'[73] Such progressive institutional and procedural elements allow for sustainable development of seabed minerals and protection of the marine environment. The practical effect of the *Advisory Opinion* is proven, *inter alia*, by the fact that the first set of ISA regulations adopted in 2000 have now been updated to reflect the more progressive environmental standards in the later sets of regulations, as envisaged by the *Advisory Opinion*.

14.3.3.7 SRFC Advisory Opinion

In April 2015, ITLOS delivered the first Advisory Opinion by the full Tribunal, in response to the *Request for an Advisory Opinion Submitted by the Sub-Regional Fisheries Commission (SRFC) (SRFC Advisory Opinion)*.[74] The request by the SRFC concerned questions of flag State responsibilities for IUU fishing, as well as rights and obligations of coastal States to sustainably manage shared stocks and stocks of common interest.

There are several features of the *SRFC Advisory Opinion* of relevance to the continued evolution of sustainable development principles in the law of

---

71 French 2011, *supra* note 36 at p. 538.

72 *Seabed Mining Advisory Opinion, supra* note 8 at para. 226.

73 Ibid. at para. 30.

74 *Request for an Advisory Opinion Submitted by the Sub-Regional Fisheries Commission (SRFC)*, Advisory Opinion of 2 April 2015, ITLOS Case No 21. See further Tim Stephens, 'ITLOS Advisory Opinion: Coastal and Flag State Duties to Ensure Sustainable Fisheries Management' (2015) *ASIL Insights* 19(8).

the sea. The first is the very fact that ITLOS assumed jurisdiction to provide the Advisory Opinion, despite questions over its capacity to do so. Neither the LOSC nor the ITLOS Statute makes express reference to ITLOS possessing advisory jurisdiction, however ITLOS concluded that Article 21 of the ITLOS Statute, which forms an integral part of the LOSC, when referring to 'matters' and not only 'disputes' must encompass a capacity to render advisory opinions.[75] As ITLOS has found, decisively, that it does possess plenary advisory jurisdiction over disputes concerning the LOSC this leaves open the opportunity for State Parties to seek guidance from ITLOS on any aspect of the LOSC, including those relating to environmental protection and natural resource management. However, ITLOS did observe that Article 21 of the ITLOS Statute does not itself establish its advisory jurisdiction – rather it is an enabling provision allowing other agreements to confer jurisdiction.[76]

Turning to substantive legal issues, the Tribunal took the opportunity in the *SRFC Advisory Opinion* to reiterate the connection between managing marine living resources and marine environmental protection. It highlighted that the conservation of living resources 'constitutes an integral element in the protection and preservation of the marine environment'[77] as previously found in the *Southern Bluefin Tuna* case.[78]

The Tribunal also observed that 'the ultimate goal of sustainable management of fish stocks is to conserve and develop them as a viable and sustainable resource.'[79] It interpreted 'sustainable management' as meaning 'conservation and development' as referred to in Article 63(1) of the LOSC.[80] In line with this pragmatic but broad goal, the Tribunal found that SRFC Member States must, as with coastal States managing shared fish stocks, adopt conservation and management measures that prevent over-exploitation, maintain or restore stocks at levels that can produce maximum sustainable yields, and are based on the best scientific evidence available and the precautionary approach.[81]

In what could become an important clarification of flag State responsibilities, the Tribunal found that flag States have the 'responsibility to ensure' that their nationals and the vessels flying their flag do not engage in IUU fishing activities and comply with the laws and regulations concerning conservation measures adopted by the coastal State.[82] In referring to the *Seabed Mining Advisory Opinion*, the Tribunal noted that this obligation is one of due diligence and of 'conduct' rather than 'result'. It requires flag States to comply with their obligations under the LOSC, including ensuring enforcement mechanisms to monitor and secure compliance with the State's laws and regulations. 'Sanctions applicable

---

75 *SRFC Advisory Opinion, supra* note 74 at para. 56.
76 Ibid. at para. 58.
77 Ibid. at para. 120.
78 *Southern Bluefin Tuna, supra* note 23 at para. 70.
79 *SRFC Advisory Opinion, supra* note 74 at para. 190.
80 Ibid. at para. 191.
81 Ibid. at para. 208.
82 Ibid. at paras 124–127.

to involvement in IUU fishing activities must be sufficient to deter violations and to deprive offenders of the benefits accruing from their IUU fishing activities.'[83] Importantly, the liability of the flag State arises from its failure to comply with its due diligence obligations, rather than from the vessel conducting IUU fishing activities.[84] However, this could allow for greater pressure on flag States that do not exercise the necessary due diligence in accordance with its responsibilities under the LOSC. As the Tribunal highlighted, it 'is of the view that the SRFC Member States may hold liable the flag State of a vessel conducting IUU fishing activities in their exclusive economic zones for a breach, attributable to the flag State, of its international obligations [. . .].'[85]

14.4 Conclusion

The oceans comprise the vast majority of the Earth's living space and provide crucial ecosystem services, making the sustainable use of marine spaces and resources fundamental for achieving sustainable development. In light of this importance, as well as the dispute settlement framework of Part XV of the LOSC, and in particular its compulsory elements, it can be expected that Part XV will be one of the more important vehicles for the advancement of a jurisprudence of sustainable development.

ITLOS, as the specialised, standing, dispute settlement body established under the LOSC, has evolved into an important authority for juridical support of sustainable development principles. Over time, the Tribunal has markedly changed its language and approach towards marine environmental protection. Early cases on the prompt release of vessels showed a reluctance of ITLOS to consider questions of IUU fishing when deciding the 'reasonableness' of bonds. A more proactive approach was visible in the three provisional measures cases involving significant environmental considerations. ITLOS expressed its support for a precautionary approach towards preventing environmental harm and, on two occasions, ordered the parties to act with prudence and caution in pursuing potentially harmful activities. This language has resonated beyond ITLOS and was referred to by Australia and New Zealand in the proceedings in the *Whaling in the Antarctic* case before the ICJ[86] (although precaution was not addressed by the Court itself in its judgment[87]).

This gradual development in the integration of sustainable development principles in ITLOS jurisprudence reached a high point in the *Seabed Mining Advisory Opinion* rendered by the Seabed Dispute Chamber in 2011. The Chamber explicitly endorsed and extended the obligations to exercise due diligence, adopt a precautionary approach and to undertake environmental impact assessments.

---

83 Ibid. at para. 138.
84 Ibid. at para. 146.
85 Ibid. at para. 147.
86 *Whaling in the Antarctic (Australia v Japan)*, International Court of Justice, Memorial of Australia, 9 May 2011, paras 4.89–4.90; Written Observations of New Zealand, para. 74.
87 Ibid.

Moreover, the *Advisory Opinion* recognised the importance of common but differentiated responsibilities whilst also ensuring the equality of States and their responsibilities and liability when engaging in environmentally harmful activities. The concept of common heritage of humankind, and its inherent notion of equity, was particularly important to the opinion. The *Advisory Opinion* was a step towards giving the common heritage principle concrete meaning in recognising the potential for the ISA to bring a claim against a non-complying sponsoring State. It significantly strengthened the growing acceptance that *erga omnes* obligations to protect the marine environment are enforceable by all parties to an agreement such as LOSC, which embodies a collective scheme to achieve common objectives.

Although arguably not as progressive in character as the *Seabed Mining Advisory Opinion*, the *SRFC Advisory Opinion* sought to strengthen the enforceability of the prohibition of IUU fishing activities. Given this background of successful integration of principles of sustainable development into its decisions, ITLOS is well positioned to advance these principles in its future decisions.

World Trade Organization dispute settlement mechanism

15 Disputes on sustainable development in the WTO regime

Markus Gehring and Alexandre Genest

15.1 Introduction

The global trade treaty regime developed from diplomatic systems to rules-based systems from 1948 onward and evolved from the General Agreement on Tariffs and Trade (GATT 1947)[1] to the World Trade Organization (WTO) in 1995. As the scope of WTO activities has extended beyond purely economic parameters, there has been a growing awareness of the developmental, social, environmental and health implications of trade. Given these nexuses, it is crucial that trade law is informed by a holistic perspective that takes into account potential impacts from a sustainable development point of view.

The infrastructure of sustainable development must reconcile three premises: the trade perspective is adamant that economic liberalization provides the most efficient way of environmental protection and societal betterment; the environmental viewpoint asserts that the status quo is fatally harming natural capital and must be modified; and the development schema prioritizes curtailing the incidence of poverty.

While any single international organization or process would be hard-pressed to address this broad range of challenges alone, measures can certainly be taken to increase the likelihood that the WTO regime supports sustainable development. Indeed, despite that the Doha "Development Agenda" Round of negotiations are stalled, important procedural and substantive progress is nevertheless being achieved through interpretation of WTO Rules by the Dispute Settlement Body (DSB).[2]

At present, the most generally accepted definition of sustainable development is found in the 1987 Brundtland Report,[3] where it is seen as ". . . development

---

1 General Agreement on Tariffs and Trade, Oct. 30, 1947, 61 Stat. A-11, TIAS 1700, 55 UNTS 194.
2 Based on Articles XXII and XXIII of the GATT and the Dispute Settlement Understanding. See Understanding on Rules and Procedures Governing the Settlement of Disputes, Marrakesh Agreement Establishing the World Trade Organization, Annex 2, The Legal Texts: The Results of the Uruguay Round of Multilateral Trade Negotiations 354 (1999), 1869 UNTS 401, 33 ILM 1226 (1994).
3 In 1983, States established the World Commission on Environment and Development (WECD) an independent investigatory body composed of international policy and scientific experts in accordance with UN General Assembly (UNGA) Resolution Res. 38/161. The outcome of the WCED process, the Brundtland Report, led to UNGA Resolution 42/187, which resolved that

that meets the needs of the present without compromising the ability of future generations to meet their own needs."[4] A declaration from the 1992 United Nations Rio Conference on Environment and Development (UNCED) called for "[t]he further development of international law on sustainable development, giving special attention to the delicate balance between environmental and developmental concerns"[5] and "taking into account the special needs of developing countries".[6] The 2002 Johannesburg Plan of Implementation (JPOI), adopted at the World Summit on Sustainable Development (WSSD) in Johannesburg, South Africa, made a collective commitment to "advance and strengthen the interdependent and mutually reinforcing pillars of sustainable development – economic development, social development and environmental protection – at the local, national, regional and global levels."[7] These commitments encompassed the central tenets of the emerging international sustainable development law agenda.

Sustainable development has been enshrined as an explicit object and purpose of over 50 binding international treaties.[8] Most importantly for the purposes of this chapter, sustainable development has been incorporated into the Preamble of the 1994 WTO Agreement.[9] While preambles are not technically legally binding in the same way that operational provisions can be,[10] they can certainly play a role in interpretation of a treaty, particularly in identifying the treaty's object and purpose.

Thus, it is important to understand the intended meaning of the Preamble to the WTO Agreement. In the Preamble, the concept of sustainable development is mentioned in connection with the optimal use of the world's resources. Moreover, it is important to note that the Preamble specifically recognizes the

---

sustainable development "should become a central guiding principle of the United Nations, Governments and private institutions, organizations and enterprises."

4   World Commission on Environment and Development, Our Common Future (1987) 43; see also 'Our Common Future' UN World Commission on Environment and Development Rep (4 August 1987) UN Doc A/42/427.

5   "*Agenda 21* (Annex 2)" in Report of the UN Conference on Environment and Development Vol.I (13 June 1992) UN Doc A/CONF.151/26 (Vol I); 31 ILM 874 [2.10][39.1 (a)].

6   Ibid. at [39.1 (b)].

7   "Johannesburg Declaration on Sustainable Development and Johannesburg Plan of Implementation" in *Report of the World Summit on Sustainable Development* (4 September 2002) UN Doc A/CONF.199/L20 at 5.

8   M.C. Cordonier Segger and A. Khalfan, *Sustainable Development Law: Principles, Practices and Prospects* (Oxford: OUP, 2004) at 45–50, 95–98; see also, for general discussion, D. French, *International Law and Policy of Sustainable Development* (Manchester: Manchester University Press, 2005); J.F. Weiss and N. Schrijver, eds., *International Law and Sustainable Development: Principles and Practice* (Leiden: Martinus Nijhoff, 2004); and A. Boyle and D. Freestone, eds., *International Law and Sustainable Development: Past Achievements and Future Challenges* (Oxford: OUP, 1999).

9   Marrakesh Agreement Establishing the World Trade Organization (signed 15 April 1994, entered into force 1 January 1995) 1867 UNTS 4, 33 ILM 1144, Preamble (WTO Agreement).

10 In general international law the preamble is part of the context in which the international treaty has to be interpreted; see Vienna Convention on the Law of Treaties (singed 23 May 1969, entered into force 27 January 1980) 1155 UNTS 331, 8 ILM 679 (VCLT) Art. 31.

need to raise standards of living and income for people, to protect the environment, and to do so in a way that is consistent with the needs and concerns of developing countries, so that international trade can contribute to these countries' development needs.

Two years later the 1996 Singapore Ministerial Declaration[11] appeared to broaden sustainable development beyond optimal use of natural resources, but also to convey sustainable development as a natural result of liberalized trade. At the Geneva Ministerial Conference in 1998, the WTO and Member States formally recognized that sustainable development is not only related to natural resources or an inevitable result of the economic liberalization process, but is actually one of the goals of the WTO itself.[12]

With this in mind, the remainder of the chapter analyses recent decisions of the WTO DSB which directly impact four variations on the theme of sustainable development: (i) the duty of States to ensure sustainable use of natural resources; (ii) the principle of precautionary approach to human health, natural resources and ecosystems; (iii) the principle of common but differentiated responsibilities; and (iv) the principle of integration and interrelationship, in particular in relation to human rights and social, economic and environmental objectives.

15.2 Duty of States to ensure sustainable use of natural resources and GATT Article XX

15.2.1 Tuna-Dolphin I *(1991) and GATT 1947*

A GATT 1947 Panel report circulated (but not adopted) in 1991 decided a dispute involving Mexico and the United States ("U.S.") and put the spotlight on the linkages between environmental protection policies and trade. Known as the "*Tuna-Dolphin I*" case[13], the GATT 1947 Panel report drew heavy criticism from environmental groups under the impression that trade rules thwarted environmental protection. The facts of the case may be summarized as follows.

In the Eastern Tropical Pacific (ETP), schools of tuna often swim beneath schools of dolphins. When tuna is harvested with mile-long purse seine nets, dolphins are trapped in the nets. They often die unless they are released. In response to this unfortunate consequence of tuna fishing which led to the death

11 "Full implementation of the WTO Agreements will make an important contribution to achieving the objectives of sustainable development." Singapore Ministerial Declaration (18 December 1996) WT/MIN(96)/DEC, 36 ILM 218 online: http://docsonline.wto.org, at para. 16. Please note that the Ministerial declarations are generally political statements and not legally binding upon Members. An exception is the decision to engage in trade negotiations.

12 "We shall also continue to improve our efforts towards the objectives of sustained economic growth and sustainable development." Geneva Ministerial Declaration (20 May 1998) WT/MIN(98)/DEC/1 online: http://docsonline.wto.org, at para. 4.

13 *US – Restrictions on Imports of Tuna (Complaint by Mexico et al.)* (1991), GATT Doc. DS21/R, 39th Supp. B.I.S.D. (1993) 155 online: http://www.wto.org/english/res_e/booksp_e/analytic_index_e/introduction_01_e.htm.

of a great number of dolphins, the U.S. adopted the Marine Mammal Protection Act (MMPA), a law primarily focused on American fishermen which prohibited them from killing dolphins in the course of fishing tuna over and above a permit that specified an authorized number of incidental dolphin kills.[14]

In 1990 the U.S. enacted the Dolphin Protection Consumer Information Act – the "dolphin safe" labelling law, which amended the MMPA. The MMPA was subject to the GATT because it directed the Secretary of Treasury to impose an embargo on all tuna imports from a country if that country exporting tuna to the U.S. could not provide documentary evidence to U.S. authorities proving that its regulatory pro-gramme applicable to incidental takes of marine mammals and its rate of incidental killings were both comparable to that of the U.S. On this basis, the U.S. Government banned tuna imports from Mexico in 1990.

Mexico filed a complaint on the basis that the MMPA violated the GATT and requested the formation of a GATT Arbitral Panel in February 1991. The GATT Panel ruled in favour of Mexico and declared that the MMPA was inconsistent with GATT Article III.

The GATT Panel also refused to justify the MMPA under GATT Article XX, stating that GATT exceptions to protect human or animal life or health (Article XX(b)) or exhaustible natural resources (Article XX(g)) applied only to measures within the jurisdiction of the importing country. GATT prevented trade rules from displaying "extraterritoriality" and did not allow one country to take trade action to enforce its own domestic laws in another country. In other words, a country could not adopt a trade measure to tackle an environmental problem beyond its borders.

Moreover, the MMPA did not qualify as a necessary measure under GATT Article XX(b) given that the U.S. had failed to establish that it had exhausted all reasonably available GATT-consistent options and that the U.S. did not demon-strate that there existed no other less GATT-inconsistent measures.

The GATT Panel also stressed that a trade restriction could qualify under GATT Article XX(g) only if it was "primarily aimed" at the conservation of natu-ral resources and that such a trade restriction could be taken in conjunction with domestic restrictions only if the trade measure was "primarily aimed at rendering effective these restrictions."

The reasoning of the *Tuna-Dolphin I* case implied more generally that no import restriction designed to address environmental concerns outside the juris-diction of a country could be justified under GATT Article XX. Moreover, an environmental measure that addressed internal environmental concerns was faced with passing a stringent test before being justified.

Mexico chose, however, not to seek implementation of that GATT ruling. In any event, under pre-WTO GATT rules the United States would have been able to block the implementation of the ruling by refusing to join in a consensus necessary to its adoption. The *Tuna-Dolphin* report was steeped in fears that

---

14 John H. Knox "The Judicial Resolution of Conflicts Between Trade and the Environment" (2004) 28 *Harv. Envtl. L. Rev.* 1, 6.

environmental concerns would open the gates to a flood of protectionist abuses. The *Tuna-Dolphin* GATT Panel report received general support among GATT members: notably, none of the 11 countries that made third-party submissions sided with the U.S.[15] As a result, the GATT 1947 was viewed by many as disregarding the duty to ensure the sustainable use of natural resources.

15.2.2 The Gasoline and Shrimp-Turtle I cases: GATT Article XX(g) and exhaustible natural resources

The WTO Appellate Body overturned the conclusions of the *Tuna-Dolphin* case in respect of GATT Article XX(g) (measures regarding exhaustible natural resources) in two cases known as "*Gasoline*"[16] and "*Shrimp-Turtle I*".[17] The *Gasoline* case involved U.S. regulations that required U.S. refiners and importers to ensure that their gasoline was at least as clean as it was in 1990. Refiners and importers had to establish an individual gasoline cleanliness baseline for 1990; if available data were insufficient, refiners could use post-1990 data, while importers had to use a statutorily imposed baseline equal to the average cleanliness of all U.S. gasoline in 1990. The statutorily imposed baseline represented a more difficult standard than its own baseline for a refiner or importer whose gasoline was dirtier than average in 1990. Given that the individual baseline option was available to refiners and not importers in a situation of insufficient data, Brazil and Venezuela claimed that the U.S. violated the national treatment principle (GATT Article III) by according less favourable treatment to imported gasoline than to domestic gasoline.

The WTO Appellate Body agreed with the U.S. position, on the grounds of GATT Article XX(g), which was the only issue raised on appeal by the U.S. (Brazil and Venezuela would end up winning the case before the WTO Appellate Body under GATT Article XX's chapeau, as will be seen below.) In its decision, the Appellate Body stated that Article XX(g) did not impose a "least GATT-inconsistent" test to a trade measure dealing with exhaustible natural resources; such a test was relevant only under GATT Article XX(b), as only that provision uses the term "necessary".

The Appellate Body also stated that the requirement that trade measures be "made effective in conjunction with restrictions on domestic production or consumption" under GATT Article XX(g) did not ask of trade measures that they be "primarily aimed at" (*Tuna-Dolphin* case) making domestic measures effective. This requirement, according to the Appellate Body, simply meant "even-handedness in the imposition of restrictions, in the name of conservation, upon

---

15 Ibid.

16 *US – Standards for Reformulated and Conventional Gasoline (Complaint by Brazil and Venezuela)* (1996), WTO Doc. WT/DS2/AB/R (Appellate Body Report), online: http://docsonline.wto. org.

17 *US – Import Prohibition of Certain Shrimp and Shrimp Products (Complaint by India et al.)* (1998), WTO Doc. WT/DS58/AB/R (Appellate Body Report), online:http://docsonline. wto.org.

the production or consumption of exhaustible natural resources". The U.S. met this requirement of even-handedness under GATT Article XX(g) by regulating domestically-produced gasoline as much as imported gasoline. Nevertheless, as will be explained in the next section of this article, the WTO Appellate Body ultimately refused to uphold the U.S. regulations under GATT Article XX's chapeau.

The second opportunity granted to the WTO Appellate Body to overturn the *Tuna-Dolphin* case with respect to GATT Article XX(g) came with the *Shrimp-Turtle I* case. Sea turtles, just like dolphins, are often incidentally captured and drown as a result not of tuna fishing, but rather shrimp trawls. In 1987, the U.S. started requiring that US shrimp trawlers use "turtle excluder devices" (TEDs) in their nets when in areas that show a significant likelihood of encountering sea turtles.

In 1989, the U.S. enacted a law banning the importation of shrimp harvested with technology that may adversely affect sea turtles unless the harvesting nation could certify having a regulatory programme and an incidental sea turtle take-rate comparable to that of the U.S.

This requirement essentially meant that countries among whose waters sea turtles could be found and which harvested shrimp with mechanical means had to impose on their fishermen requirements comparable to those borne by U.S. shrimpers (i.e. the use of TEDs) if they wished to qualify as certified shrimp exporters to the U.S. market. In early 1997, India, Malaysia, Pakistan and Thailand filed a joint complaint against the U.S. ban of their shrimp products. The plaintiff countries argued that the U.S. shrimp ban violated GATT Article XI that prohibits restrictions on imports, which was not disputed by the U.S.

The focus then turned to GATT Article XX(g). The WTO Appellate Body stated that the expression "exhaustible natural resources" includes living organisms such as sea turtles. In reaching this conclusion, the WTO Appellate Body underlined that the expression "exhaustible natural resources", "crafted more than 50 years ago", had to be interpreted in light of "contemporary concerns of the community of nations about the protection and conservation of the environment" and relied on the preamble of the WTO Agreement and its explicit acknowledgment of "the objective of sustainable development" as evidence of such concerns.[18]

The Appellate Body stressed that the preamble to the WTO Agreement, which "reflects the intentions of the negotiators" thereof, "must add colour, texture and shading to our interpretation of the agreements annexed to the WTO Agreement", including the GATT and in this case Article XX(g) thereof.[19] In interpreting GATT Article XX in light of its context and object and purpose, the Appellate Body paid close attention to "[t]he most significant" development with respect to the relationship between trade and the environment, i.e. the Decision of Ministers at Marrakesh to establish a permanent Committee on Trade and Environment (the "CTE"). The Appellate Body pointed to that Decision's statement that

18 *Shrimp-Turtle I* – Appellate Body Report, *supra* note 17 at para. 129. See also *supra* note 17n. 107, where the Appellate Body explained that the concept of sustainable development "has been generally accepted as integrating economic and social development and environmental protection". Ibid.
19 Ibid. at para. 153.

there should not be, nor need be, any policy contradiction between upholding and safeguarding an open, non-discriminatory and equitable multilateral trading system on the one hand, and acting for the protection of the environment, and the promotion of sustainable development on the other

and also to the fact that Ministers took "note" in that Decision of the Rio Declaration on Environment and Development, *Agenda 21*.[20]

The Appellate Body did not specifically overturn the *Tuna-Dolphin* case on the issue of extraterritoriality, but considered that the U.S. trade measures in respect of sea turtles showed a "sufficient nexus" to the U.S. as sea turtles circulated in waters under U.S. jurisdiction. The "sufficient nexus" test constituted a novel approach compared to the *Tuna-Dolphin* case, which did not consider the fact that the dolphins the U.S. aimed to protect also circulated in waters under U.S. jurisdiction. The Appellate Body therefore broadened the reach of GATT Article XX(g) and – albeit indirectly – of extraterritoriality. Moreover the Appellate Body decided that the U.S. shrimp ban related to the conservation of an exhaustible natural resource and that it was made effective in conjunction with similar domestic restrictions. The U.S. shrimp ban therefore met the requirements of GATT Article XX(g).

15.2.3 Gasoline *and* Shrimp-Turtle I: *GATT Article XX's chapeau*

Once a measure qualifies under any of the exceptions provided under GATT Article XX(a) to XX(j), GATT Article XX's chapeau requires in addition that trade measures must not be applied in a manner that constitutes arbitrary or unjustifiable discrimination between countries where the same conditions prevail, or a disguised restriction on international trade, to be justifiable.

In the *Gasoline* case, the U.S. argued before the WTO Appellate Body that it would have encountered administrative difficulties related to verification and enforcement if it had allowed gasoline importers to adopt their own baselines. The U.S. also argued that it would have incurred too heavy a financial burden if it had imposed a uniform statutory baseline on all domestic refiners and importers alike. The Appellate Body rejected these arguments, underlining that the U.S. had not sufficiently attempted to negotiate a solution with Brazil and Venezuela to address the administrative difficulties and that the U.S. had ignored the financial burden it imposed on foreign refiners. The U.S. therefore lost the *Gasoline* case.

In the *Shrimp-Turtle I* case, the U.S. shrimp ban did not meet the requirements of GATT Article XX's chapeau for two main reasons. First and foremost, the U.S. intentionally and effectively coerced foreign governments into adopting "a regulatory programme that is not merely comparable, but rather essentially the

---

20 Ibid. at para. 154. The Appellate Body itself refers to principles embodied in the Rio Declaration on Environment and Development and in *Agenda 21*, which refer to balancing environmental protection and sustainable development with the needs of developing countries.

same" as the U.S. programme to protect sea turtles while harvesting shrimp.[21] Second, the Appellate Body noted that the U.S. did not engage in serious negotiations with the plaintiff countries with a view to negotiate a similar agreement to that reached with Latin American and Caribbean countries (the Inter-American Convention) before enforcing the shrimp ban.[22] The U.S. provided several Latin American and Caribbean countries with technical and financial assistance and longer transition periods; by not offering the same treatment to all WTO members, the U.S. unjustifiably discriminated among WTO members.[23]

The Appellate Body stated in the *Shrimp-Turtle I* case that GATT Article XX's chapeau gives rise to the delicate exercise of drawing an unfixed case-by-case line of equilibrium between the right to invoke an exception under Article XX and the right to demand compliance with substantive provisions under the GATT. In the instant case, the Appellate Body thought that the Inter-American Convention convincingly demonstrated that "an alternative course of action was reasonably open to the United States for securing the legitimate policy goal of its measure, a course of action other than the unilateral and non-consensual procedures of the import prohibition". The Appellate Body stressed that failure on the U.S. part to engage in multilateral negotiations directly caused the unilateralism inherent to the shrimp import ban; according to the Appellate Body, the unilateralism of the U.S. course of action was also revealed by the fact that a government that applied for certification of its shrimp harvesting methods had no formal opportunity to be heard or to respond to any objections raised regarding its harvesting methods.

15.2.4 Shrimp-Turtle II, *GATT Article XX and extraterritoriality*

The issue of extraterritoriality had yet to be openly revisited since the *Tuna-Dolphin I* case. In the *Shrimp-Turtle I* case, the Appellate Body did not specifically overturn the *Tuna-Dolphin I* case on the issue of extraterritoriality, but had established a test whereby trade measures that showed a "sufficient nexus" to the country which adopted the trade measures could be justified.

Further significant developments occurred in the *Shrimp-Turtle II*[24] case. Malaysia submitted a complaint to the WTO on the grounds that the U.S. had failed to comply with the decision in the *Shrimp-Turtle I* case. It raised the continuing unilateralism of the U.S. sea turtle conservation programme. Malaysia attempted to take the reasoning expressed by the Appellate Body in *Shrimp-Turtle I* a step further: the U.S. could not impose any import prohibition in the absence of an international agreement that authorized such actions.

---

21 Ibid. at para. 163.
22 Ibid. at para. 166.
23 See, e.g. *Shrimp-Turtle I* – Appellate Body Report, *supra* note 17 at para. 175.
24 *US – Import Prohibition of Certain Shrimp and Shrimp Products (Recourse to Article 21.5 of the DSU by Malaysia)* (2001), WTO Doc. WT/DS58/AB/RW (Appellate Body Report), online: http://docsonline.wto.org.

In fact, the U.S. had attempted to negotiate an agreement on sea turtle conservation with Malaysia and other countries which had yielded only a non-binding memorandum of understanding that did not discuss trade restrictions. Moreover, the U.S. had amended its programme to address its deficiencies raised in the *Shrimp-Turtle I* case.

In interpreting GATT Article XX's chapeau, the Panel (not overturned by the WTO Appellate Body) referred to sustainable development as found in the WTO Agreement's preamble.[25] The WTO Panel and ultimately the Appellate Body rejected Malaysia's argument, interpreting the *Shrimp-Turtle I* case as requiring of the U.S. that it engage in serious and good faith negotiating efforts on sea turtle conservation with all parties concerned, but not that the U.S. manage to conclude a formal agreement before imposing unilateral trade restrictions. The WTO Panel decided that the U.S. had met this requirement in its efforts to negotiate an agreement with Malaysia and other countries before imposing trade restrictions. The WTO Appellate Body supported the Panel's decision and added that "it is one thing to prefer a multilateral approach" when evaluating the validity of trade restrictions under GATT Article XX, but that "it is another to require the conclusion of a multilateral agreement as a condition of avoiding 'arbitrary or unjustifiable discrimination' under the chapeau of Article XX. We see, in this case, no such requirement."

The WTO Panel, echoed by the Appellate Body, also commented on the fact that although the Appellate Body, in the *Shrimp-Turtle I* case, did not approve of laws that required other countries to enact essentially the same law as that of the importing country, the Appellate Body did "at least implicitly" recognize that GATT Article XX's chapeau did not forbid an importing country from requiring that the laws of exporting countries be "comparable in effectiveness" to the laws of the importing country.

15.2.5 China – Raw Materials, *accession protocols, quantitative restrictions, and GATT Article XX*

The *China-Raw Materials*[26] case concerned four types of export restraint that China, a leading producer, imposed on the export of nine raw materials. The U.S., the European Union (the EU) and Mexico (collectively the "complainants") challenged 40 specific Chinese measures before the WTO Panel[27]. The complainants alleged that these export restraints violated China's commitments under China's Accession Protocol and GATT Article XI and argued that the use of export restraints created scarcity and caused higher global prices for the raw

---

25   *US – Import Prohibition of Certain Shrimp and Shrimp Products Sector, Recourse to Article 21.5 by Malaysia* (Panel Report) (2001) WT/DS58/RW, at para. 5.54.

26   *China – Measures Related to the Exportation of Various Raw Materials* – AB–2011–5 (Appellate Body Reports), WT/DS394/AB/R and WT/DS395/AB/R and WT/DS398/AB/R (30 January 2012).

27   *China – Measures Related to the Exportation of Various Raw Materials* (Panel Reports), WT/DS394/R and Corr.1/WT/DS395/R and Corr.1/WT/DS398/R and Corr.1 (5 July 2011).

materials at issue. They also allegedly provided Chinese domestic industry with a significant advantage by way of a sufficient supply, and lower and more stable prices for the raw materials.

The Panel (upheld by the Appellate Body) found that China's export duties violated its commitments under its Accession Protocol. The Panel also found that certain export quotas imposed by China on some of the raw materials at issue were inconsistent with GATT Article XI. China had maintained that its export restrictions were necessary to conserve the finite resources and to ensure domestic supply, as some of the raw materials at issue face depletion in the near future. China argued that this foreseeable depletion of finite resources constituted a critical shortage for purposes of GATT Article XI:2(a), which authorizes temporary quantitative restrictions to prevent or relieve a critical shortage of foodstuff or other essential products. China argued that the term "temporarily" as used in GATT Article XI:2(a) does not mark a "bright line" moment in time after which an export restriction has necessarily been maintained for too long. Moreover, China argued that Article XI:2(a) and Article XX(g) may apply cumulatively.

The WTO Appellate Body interpreted four expressions found within GATT Article XI:2(a) as follows, which interpretations informed its decision:[28]

(i)   the terms "temporarily applied" refer to measures applied for a "limited time", "in the interim", "to bridge a 'passing need'", but does not entail a time-limit fixed in advance;

(ii) the expression "critical shortage" refers to "those deficiencies in quantity that are crucial, that amount to a situation of decisive importance, or that reach a vitally important or decisive stage, or a turning point";

(iii) the terms "foodstuffs or other products essential" refer to foodstuffs or otherwise absolutely indispensable or necessary products; and

(iv) the expression "to prevent or relieve" means to "alleviate or reduce an existing critical shortage, as well as for preventive or anticipatory measures adopted to pre-empt an imminent critical shortage".

In rejecting China's arguments regarding GATT Article XI:2(a), the Panel relied on the observations that some of China's export restrictions had already been in place for more than a decade, that China could provide no indication of when such restriction would be withdrawn, and that the export restriction would likely have remained in place until the reserves had been depleted.

Based on such observations, the Appellate Body reiterated the conclusions of the Panel that "if there is no possibility for an existing shortage ever to cease to exist, it will not be possible to 'relieve or prevent' it through an export restriction applied on a temporary basis."[29] The Appellate Body further noted that "if a measure were imposed to address a limited reserve of an exhaustible natural resource, such

---

28   *China – Raw Materials* (Appellate Body Reports), *supra* note 27 at paras 323–28.

29   Ibid. at para. 336.

measure would be imposed until the point when the resource is fully depleted."[30] The Panel underlined that the temporary criterion can influence the meaning ascribed to the term "critical" in that "[t]his temporal focus seems consistent with the notion of 'critical', defined as 'of the nature of, or constituting, a crisis'".[31]

The Appellate Body also stated that GATT Articles XI:2(a) and XX(g) serve different functions (temporary measures to relieve or prevent critical shortages of food or other essential products vs. conservation of exhaustible natural resources) and contain different obligations (notably Article XX's chapeau) and cannot be invoked indistinguishably. The Appellate Body did not however preclude the possibility both provisions could apply to a single measure.[32]

As a result, the Appellate Body agreed with the Panel to the effect that China's export restrictions could not be considered "temporarily applied" to address a "critical shortage" within the meaning of GATT Article XI:2(a).[33]

China then argued that certain of its export quotas and duties were necessary for the protection of the health of its citizens and could be justified under GATT Article XX(b). China also argued that certain of its export duties were adopted as conservation measures and could be justified under GATT Article XX(g).

The Panel found that the wording and the context of Paragraph 11.3 of China's Accession Protocol prevented China from invoking GATT Article XX to justify its violations of the obligations contained in Paragraph 11.3.[34] The Appellate Body upheld the Panel on this point and stated that China's WTO-plus obligation "arises exclusively from China's Accession Protocol". As a result, "[h]ad there been a common intention to provide access to Article XX, language to that effect would have been included in Paragraph 11.3 or elsewhere in China's accession protocol."[35]

The Appellate Body reached this conclusion despite having underlined that China's Accession Protocol constitutes "an integral part" of the WTO Agreement, and as such must be interpreted in accordance with the customary rules of interpretation of public international law,[36] including interpretation in light of the WTO Agreement's object and purpose.[37] Referring to the WTO Agreement's Preamble, and recalling its various objectives including sustainable development, the Appellate Body nevertheless stated that "none of the objectives listed above, nor the balance struck between them, provides specific guidance on the question of whether Article XX of the GATT is applicable to Paragraph 11.3 of China's Accession Protocol."[38] Such interpretation prevents the public policy justifications under GATT Article XX from applying to Paragraph 11.3 of China's Accession

---

30 Ibid. at para. 336.
31 Ibid. at para. 7.297.
32 Ibid. at para. 337.
33 Ibid. at para. 344.
34 Ibid. at para. 7.158.
35 Ibid. at paras 293, 307.
36 As requested by Article 3.2. of the DSU.
37 VCLT, *supra* note 10, at art. 31(1).
38 *China – Raw Materials* (Appellate Body Reports), *supra* note 27 at para. 306.

Protocol and arguably does not give full force and effect to the principle of sustainable development codified in the WTO Agreement's Preamble.[39] In any event, according to the Panel, China was unable to demonstrate that certain of its export duties and quotas could reduce pollution caused by raw material extraction or production in order to improve human health under GATT Article XX(b).[40] Moreover, the Panel decided that China had been unable to demonstrate that its export restrictions had been made in conjunction with restrictions on domestic production or consumption of the raw materials and had thus failed to meet the requirements of GATT Article XX(g).[41]

More generally, the Appellate Body's ruling in the *China-Raw Materials* case increases the asymmetrical burden of complying with WTO-plus obligations by preventing acceding countries from invoking public policy justifications under GATT Article XX, even though member States may derogate from their GATT obligations on the basis of Article XX thereof.[42] Moreover, future acceding countries must tread carefully when negotiating and drafting their accession protocols so as to ensure that Article XX is referenced in all those provisions in respect of which they intend to reserve the right to invoke that Article's public policy justifications.[43]

15.3 Principle of the precautionary approach to human health, natural resources and ecosystems

15.3.1 Likeness under GATT Article III and the TBT Agreement

In the *Tuna-Dolphin I* case under GATT 1947, the U.S. had implicitly argued that differential treatment under GATT Article III between tuna that are caught using different techniques did not amount to discrimination since products resulting from different production methods do not constitute "like" products. The GATT Panel rejected this idea and stated that likeness between products must be based on the physical characteristics of the products themselves. The process or production method (PPM) did not represent a valid product differentiation criterion and therefore the U.S. could not embargo tuna imports from Mexico on the basis that Mexican tuna was not produced in accordance with U.S. requirements. All tuna that featured the same physical characteristics had to be treated in the same way, regardless of how it was being caught.

The broader implication of the reasoning adopted by the GATT Panel in the *Tuna-Dolphin I* case was that imports produced according to a sustainable PPM could not be treated differently from imports produced according

---

39 Elisa Baroncini, "An Impossible Relationship – Article XX GATT and China's Accession Protocol in the China – Raw Materials Case", *Bridges Trade BioRes* 6:1 (May 2012) online: http://ictsd. org/news/biores/, at 19–20.

40 *China – Raw Materials* (Panel Reports), at paras 7.512, 7.516.

41 Ibid. at paras 7.512, 7.613.

42 Baroncini, *supra* note 27 at 20.

43 See Bridges Weekly Trade News Digest, Vol. 16, No. 14 (1 February 2012), at 3.

to an unsustainable PPM through trade measures. In other words, differences between products that went beyond their physical characteristics could not be invoked to distinguish products and thus could not serve as a basis for differential treatment. Fortunately, WTO jurisprudence has positively evolved since the *Tuna-Dolphin I* case.

In the "*EC-Asbestos*" case,[44] Canada argued that a French ban on products containing asbestos violated GATT Article III given that asbestos-laden products were "like" substitute products made in France that did not contain asbestos and that this less favourable treatment violated the national treatment principle. The WTO Panel accepted Canada's argument, but the WTO Appellate Body overturned the Panel's decision, stating that the carcinogenic risk posed by a product compared to that of other products constitutes a highly significant physical difference that can be taken into consideration when considering likeness under GATT Article III. Imports of asbestos-laden products (which are carcinogenic) could therefore be banned while their domestic substitutes (which are not carcinogenic, or if so only in a negligible fashion) were being sold as they did not constitute "like" products. The WTO Appellate Body's decision in the *EC-Asbestos* case leaves the door open for health and environmental characteristics of products to be raised when evaluating likeness, although it does not reverse the *Tuna-Dolphin I* case in respect of PPMs.

Most recently in the *US-Clove Cigarettes*[45] case, the Appellate Body decided that for purposes of establishing likeness between products under Article 2.1 of the Agreement on Technical Barriers to Trade (TBT)[46], one should look to the competitive relationship between the products, rather than the purpose of the regulation at issue. However, the Appellate Body did consider that "the regulatory concerns underlying a measure, such as the health risks associated with a given product, may be relevant to an analysis of the 'likeness' criteria under Article III:4 of the GATT 1994, as well as under Article 2.1 of the TBT Agreement, to the extent they have an impact on the competitive relationship between and among the products concerned."[47]

15.3.2 Protecting human health under GATT Article XX(b)

The WTO Appellate Body pronounced itself on the "necessity" criterion within GATT Article XX(b) in the "*EC-Asbestos*" case. The Appellate Body stated that France could not be expected to use any alternative other than a ban given that these

---

44 *EC – Measures Affecting Asbestos and Asbestos-Containing Products*, WT/DS135/AB/R (Appellate Body Report), adopted 5 April 2001.

45 *US – Measures Affecting the Production and Sale of Clove Cigarettes*, WT/DS406/AB/R (Appellate Body Report), adopted 24 April 2012, at para. 116.

46 Agreement on Technical Barriers to Trade, GATT Doc. MTN/FA II-AIA-6, adopted on 15 December 1993, in Final Act Embodying the Results of the Uruguay Round of Multilateral Trade Negotiations, GATT Doc. MTN/FA, 33 ILM 9 (1994).

47 *US – Measures Affecting the Production and Sale of Clove Cigarettes*, WT/DS406/AB/R (Appellate Body Report), *supra* note 45 at para. 119.

other measures would not have eliminated the risk that France intended to eliminate (i.e. presence of asbestos-laden products in the domestic market). The Appellate Body also stressed that "all WTO members have the right to determine the level of protection that they consider appropriate in a given situation". The WTO Appellate Body demonstrated that although a health measure must be the least GATT-inconsistent possible to meet the necessity requirement, this requirement does not prevent a WTO member country from fixing its level of protection as high as desired. Granting such flexibility to countries in choosing their desired level of protection avoids the pitfall whereby trade would bring down environmental protection.

The *Brazil-Retreated Tyres*[48] case was the first where a developing country invoked GATT Article XX(b) against a challenge by an industrialized country, in this case the European Communities. Brazil banned the import of retreated tyres arguing that the large quantities of retreated tyres imported from the EC created environmental problems including dangers associated with mosquitoes that breed in tyres and tyres catching fire. The EC argued that Brazil had not shown that the ban on retreated tyres was necessary to protect human health. In its decision, the Panel underlined the importance of sustainable development.

The analysis under GATT Article XX(b) centered around the exceptions to retreated tyre import ban that Brazil allowed for MERCOSUR (Mercado Común del Sur) countries. The Panel found that the measure generally fulfilled Article XX(b) GATT to protect animal, plant and human life or health, but constituted a disguised restriction on international trade and was thus not justified under Article XX GATT.

The Appellate Body upheld the Panel's conclusion on the applicability of Article XX(b) GATT, but recognized that public health or environmental problems may often be tackled only with a comprehensive policy comprising a multiplicity of interacting measures, and that in the short-term it may be difficult to substantiate the contribution of each measure taken in isolation. Moreover, the Appellate Body recognized that results obtained from such measures can often only be evaluated with the benefit of time.[49] Here the Appellate Body showed particular sensitivity to the potentially long-term sustainability reach of environmental and/or public policy measures and may have further lowered the burden of proof for justifying such measures under the general exceptions provided by GATT Article XX.

15.3.3 Technical regulations and sanitary and phytosanitary measures

15.3.3.1 TBT Agreement and mandatory technical regulations

Essential to protect life, health and the environment, product standards can sometimes appear non-discriminatory on their face while still entertaining protectionist aims. Two GATT/WTO agreements were concluded to curtail the

---

48 *Brazil – Measures Affecting Imports of Retreaded Tyres*, WT/DS332/AB/R (Appellate Body Report), adopted 17 December 2007.
49 Ibid. at [151].

potential trade-restrictiveness of product standards: the TBT Agreement[50] and the Agreement on the Application of Sanitary and Phytosanitary (SPS) Measures.[51] The TBT Agreement's more stringent obligations apply to mandatory technical regulations (as defined under Annex 1.1 of the TBT Agreement), as opposed to standards which are voluntary. The issue of what constitutes a mandatory technical regulation under the TBT Agreement, initially thought as straightforward, recently constituted a question of prime importance in *Tuna-Dolphin II*[52] case.

The *Tuna-Dolphin II* case concerned a labelling scheme for tuna products and constitutes in many ways a continuation of the dispute underlying the *Tuna-Dolphin I* case. Although Mexico had brought claims under both the TBT Agreement and the GATT in the *Tuna-Dolphin II* case, the Panel only considered the claims based on the TBT Agreement. Since the unadopted *Tuna-Dolphin I* GATT Panel report, multilateral cooperation aimed at improving the International Dolphin Conservation Program (IDCP) in the Eastern Tropical Pacific (ETP) progressed steadily. In 1992, the U.S., Mexico, and eight other countries participating in the ETP tuna fishery adopted the La Jolla Agreement[53], which formalized the IDCP into a comprehensive but voluntary program that included advanced requirements related to fishing equipment and practices, training and on-board coverage by independent veterinarians. The U.S. along with the 15 nations participating in the ETP tuna fishery, agreed to the Declaration of Panama in October of 1995, which aimed at making compliance with the La Jolla Agreement mandatory.[54]

In July 1997, the U.S. enacted the International Dolphin Conservation Program Act (IDCPA), which amended the MMPA and implemented the Declaration of Panama. In April 1998, the Agreement on the International Dolphin Conservation Program (AIDCP) was signed by nations participating in the ETP tuna fishery. As a result of these concerted efforts, the U.S. changed its definition of "dolphin safe" from a "method of capture" standard to a "non-mortality or serious injury"

50 Agreement on Technical Barriers to Trade, GATT Doc. MTN/FA II-AIA-6, adopted on 15 December 1993, in Final Act Embodying the Results of the Uruguay Round of Multilateral Trade Negotiations, GATT Doc. MTN/FA, 33 ILM 9 (1994).

51 Agreement on the Application of Sanitary and Phytosanitary Measures, GATT Doc. MTN/FA II-AIA-4, adopted on 15 December 1993, in Final Act Embodying the Results of the Uruguay Round of Multilateral Trade Negotiations, GATT Doc. MTN/FA, 33 ILM 9 (1994) .

52 *US – Measures Concerning the Importation, Marketing and Sale of Tuna and Tuna Products* (Appellate Body Report), WT/DS381/AB/R, circulated to WTO Members 16 May 2012; Panel Report, *US – Measures Concerning the Importation, Marketing and Sale of Tuna and Tuna Products* (Panel Report), WT/DS381/R, circulated to WTO Members 15 September 2011. See also Mark J. Robertson, "The fairy tale of US 'dolphin safe' labelling: False claims, unintended consequences", *Bridges Trade BioRes* 6:1 (May 2012) online: http://ictsd.org/news/biores/; Bridges Weekly Trade News Digest, Vol. 16, No. 19 (16 May 2012); Marie Wilke and Hannes Schloemann, "Tuna-Dolphin: Not-So-Voluntary Labelling?" *Bridges Trade BioRes Trade & Environment Review*, Vol. 5, No. 3 (Autumn 2011), at 5; "Mixed Victory for Mexico as WTO Rules on 'Dolphin Safe' Labelling", *Bridges Trade BioRes* 11:16 (19 September 2011) online: http://ictsd.org/news/biores/.

53 33 ILM 936 (1994).

54 See Robertson, *supra* note 52

standard. However, such change remained in effect only for a few weeks in 2003[55] before being stayed in April 2003[56] and then permanently reversed by a U.S. court first in 2004 and then in 2007.[57]

The *Hogarth* court decision meant that tuna harvested in the ETP by a large vessel using purse seine nets may be labelled "dolphin-safe" only upon certification that no dolphins were killed or seriously injured during the sets in which the tuna were caught and that no purse seine net was intentionally deployed on or used to encircle dolphins during the same fishing trip.[58] By contrast, tuna caught outside the ETP required only a certification that no dolphins were intentionally netted or encircled during the catch. In other words, non-ETP tuna did not require proof that no mortalities or serious injuries to dolphins had occurred.

As a result, the U.S. market remained effectively closed to tuna from Mexico, which is predominantly harvested using purse seine nets, as non-certified tuna is cast aside by the U.S. food supply chain. Mexico challenged the *Hogarth* U.S. court decision and the Dolphin Protection Consumer Information Act (DPCIA) – the "dolphin safe" labelling law which amended the MMPA – and related regulations before the WTO.

In the *Tuna-Dolphin II* case the Appellate Body[59], upholding the Panel's conclusions,[60] decided that the U.S. "dolphin safe" labelling constituted a mandatory technical regulation as defined under Annex 1.1 of the TBT Agreement and thus subject to the TBT Agreement's more stringent obligations, even though complying with the "dolphin safe" label requirements did not constitute a legal prerequisite for importation into the U.S.

The Appellate Body reached this decision based on the finding that the DPCIA established a single and legally mandated definition of the term "dolphin-safe" and prohibited labels that relied on a different standard,[61] including the AIDCP dolphin safe label complied with by Mexican fishermen. The Panel, upheld by the Appellate Body, found that the U.S. DPCIA and its "dolphin-safe" label imposed

---

55 On 31 December 2002, the Secretary of Commerce (through Dr. William Hogarth of the National Oceanic and Atmospheric Administration) made a "final finding" that the "intentional deployment on or encirclement of dolphins with purse seine nets is not having a significant adverse effect on any depleted dolphin stock in the Eastern Tropical Pacific ocean." Taking and Importing of Marine Mammals, 68 Fed. Reg. 2010–11 (15 Jan. 2003).

56 *Earth Island Institute v Evans*, 256 F. Supp. 2d at 1074, which affirmed *Earth Island Institute v Evans*, No. 03-0007, 2004 WL 1774221, at 30–31 (N.D. Cal. 9 Aug. 2004).

57 *Earth Island Institute v Hogarth*, 494 F.3d 757 (9th Cir. 2007) (*Hogarth*).

58 *US – Measures Concerning the Importation, Marketing and Sale of Tuna and Tuna Products* (Appellate Body Report), *supra* note 13 at para. 176; Panel Report, *US – Measures Concerning the Importation, Marketing and Sale of Tuna and Tuna Products* (Panel Report), *supra* note 13 at para. 2.20.

59 *Tuna-Dolphin II* (Appellate Body Report), *supra* note 52 at para. 199.

60 *Tuna-Dolphin II* (Panel Report), *supra* note 52 at para. 7.140.

61 *Tuna-Dolphin II* (Appellate Body Report), *supra* note 52 at para. 199; *Tuna-Dolphin II* (Panel Report), *supra* note 52 at para. 7.144.

labelling requirements "in a binding and exclusive manner"[62] and "prescribed certain requirements that must be complied with in order to make *any* claim relating to the manner in which the tuna was caught in relation to dolphins".[63]

The Panel decided that an otherwise voluntary label acquires a mandatory character through regulation of consumer information as controlling the information that reaches consumers restricts the marketing ability of producers. The Panel underlined that the U.S. DPCIA prohibited any statement relating to dolphins, whether misleading or otherwise, which did not comply with the "dolphin-safe" label requirements, and that the U.S. DPCIA required compliance with the "dolphin-safe" label, "the *only* standard available to address" dolphin safety, "as the exclusive means of asserting a 'dolphin-safe' status for tuna products".[64]

15.3.3.2 Articles 2.4 and 2.5 of the TBT Agreement and international standards

Under the TBT Agreement, international standards must be used as a basis for domestic technical regulations except when such international standards "would be an ineffective or inappropriate means for the fulfillment of the legitimate objectives pursued, for instance because of fundamental climatic or geographical factors or fundamental technological problems" (TBT Agreement Article 2.4).

Moreover, Article 2.5 of the TBT Agreement creates a rebuttable presumption that a technical regulation does not create an unnecessary obstacle to international trade if it is prepared, adopted or applied for one of the previously mentioned legitimate objectives (among others) and if it is in accordance with relevant international standards.

In the *Tuna-Dolphin II* case Mexico had argued that the "AIDCP dolphin-safe definition and certification" constituted an international standard. The Appellate Body was therefore asked to rule on what constitutes an "international standard" for purposes of Article 2.4 of the TBT Agreement.

According to the Appellate Body, "a standard has to be adopted by an 'international standardizing *body'*" [as opposed to an "organization"], "that is, a body that has recognized activities in standardization and whose membership is open to the relevant bodies of at least all [WTO] Members" and on a non-discriminatory basis.[65] According to Mexico, a WTO member state could join the AIDCP upon invitation, a "mere formality".[66]

According to the Appellate Body, "whether a body is 'open' if all WTO Members or their relevant bodies can accede pursuant to an invitation has to be decided on a case-by-case basis" and "[i]t is conceivable that an invitation might indeed be a 'formality' (. . .) if the invitation occurred automatically once

---

62 *Tuna-Dolphin II* (Panel Report), *supra* note 52 at para. 7.144. and see para. 7.112, where the Panel uses the expression "in a binding or compulsory fashion".

63 Ibid. at para. 7.143.

64 Ibid. at paras 7.143–7.144.

65 *Tuna-Dolphin II* (Appellate Body Report), *supra* note 52 at paras 356, 359, 378.

66 Ibid. at paras 386, 398.

a Member or its relevant body has expressed interest in joining a standardizing body." The Appellate Body decided that Mexico had not proven that "the issuance of an invitation occurs automatically once a WTO Member has expressed interest in joining"; the Appellate Body also decided that the fact that the decision to issue an invitation to join the AIDCP had to be made by consensus among AIDCP parties suggested otherwise.

Overruling the Panel, the Appellate Body decided that the AIDCP did not constitute an "international" body for the purposes of the TBT Agreement and that as such, that the "AIDCP dolphin-safe definition and certification" did not constitute a "relevant international standard" under the TBT Agreement.[67]

15.3.3.3 Article 2.1 of the TBT Agreement and discrimination

In the *Tuna-Dolphin II* case the Appellate Body overruled the Panel and decided that the U.S. "dolphin-safe" label provided "less favourable treatment" to Mexican tuna than that accorded to tuna products of the U.S. and other countries by banning the purse seine net fishing practice used predominantly by Mexican fisheries and thus effectively preventing the great majority of Mexican tuna from accessing the U.S. "dolphin-safe" label, in violation of Article 2.1 of the TBT Agreement.

According to the Appellate Body, the differential treatment attributable to not qualifying for the US "dolphin-safe" label affected Mexico's export competitiveness[68] in a way that could not be justified by the objectives put forward by the U.S. and deemed legitimate (i.e. (i) consumer information and (ii) dolphin protection).[69]

The Appellate Body identified the crucial question before it as whether the distinction established by the US "dolphin-safe" label between tuna products containing tuna caught by using purse seine nets in the ETP, on the one hand, and tuna products containing tuna caught by other fishing methods outside the ETP, on the other hand, which distinction caused the detrimental impact on Mexican tuna products, stemmed exclusively from a legitimate regulatory distinction rather than reflecting discrimination.[70] In other words, is such a distinction "calibrated to the likelihood that dolphins would be adversely affected in the course of tuna fishing operations" in and outside of the ETP?

With respect to dolphin mortality arising from tuna fishing outside the ETP, the Appellate Body relied on the Panel's uncontested finding of fact that there were "clear indications that the use of certain tuna fishing techniques *other* than setting on dolphins may also cause harm to dolphins".[71] The Appellate Body also relied on the Panel's uncontested findings of fact that "the *risks* faced by dolphin populations

67 Ibid. at para. 399.
68 Ibid. at paras 235–39.
69 Ibid. at para. 242, citing Panel Report, at para. 7.401.
70 Ibid. at paras 284, 286.
71 Ibid. at para. 247, citing Panel Report, at para. 7.520.

in the ETP are *not* [unique to the ETP]", that the use of certain fishing techniques other than setting on dolphins causes harm to dolphins, and that where "tuna is caught outside the ETP, it would be eligible for the US official label, even if dolphins have in fact been caught or seriously injured during the trip, since there is, under the US measures as currently applied, no requirement for a certificate to the effect that no dolphins have been killed or seriously injured outside the ETP".[72]

The Appellate Body noted that the U.S. "dolphin-safe" label did not address adverse effects on dolphins resulting from the use of other fishing methods predominantly employed to supply the U.S. as vessels fishing outside the ETP only need to have their captain certify that no purse seine net was intentionally deployed on or used to encircle dolphins during the fishing trip. The Appellate Body further cited the Panel in noting that risks to dolphins resulting from fishing methods other than setting on dolphins "could only be monitored by imposing a different substantive requirement, i.e. that no dolphins were killed or seriously injured in the sets in which the tuna was caught."[73] The U.S. argued that it did not impose such a requirement to tuna fishing outside the ETP under its "dolphin-safe" label due to high costs. The Appellate Body and Panel found such argument unpersuasive and inconsistent with the fact that the no dolphin injury or kill requirement would be imposed for the same tuna caught in the same conditions in the same fisheries, where an alternative label would be used.

The Appellate Body concluded that the U.S. DPCIA and "dolphin-safe" label were not "calibrated" to the risks to dolphins arising from different fishing methods in different areas of the ocean, that they were not "even-handed", and that their detrimental impact on Mexican tuna products did not "stem exclusively from a legitimate regulatory distinction". More particularly, "the U.S. measure *fully* addresses the adverse effects on dolphins resulting from setting on dolphins in the ETP, whereas it does 'not address mortality (observed or unobserved) arising from fishing methods other than setting on dolphins outside the ETP'".[74]

15.3.3.4 Article 2.2 of the TBT Agreement and (un)necessary trade-restrictiveness

Technical regulations must not constitute unnecessary obstacles to trade and must not be more trade-restrictive than necessary to fulfill a legitimate objective (TBT Agreement Article 2.2). A non-exhaustive list of legitimate objectives mentions, among others, the environment and the protection of human health or safety and of animal or plant life or health.

The SPS Agreement, which uses language similar to that used by the TBT Agreement, requires parties to adopt and apply SPS measures "only to the extent necessary to protect human, animal or plant life or health" on the basis

72 Ibid. at paras 248–251, citing Panel Report, at paras 7.520, 7.532, 7.552.
73 Ibid. at para. 292, citing Panel Report, at para. 7.561.
74 Ibid. at para. 297, citing Panel Report, at para. 7.544.

of scientific principles and that SPS measures not be maintained without sufficient scientific evidence (SPS Agreement Articles 2.1 and 2.2). As with the TBT Agreement, the SPS Agreement requires countries to use international standards as a basis for their SPS measures and creates a rebuttable presumption of validity for SPS measures that conform to international standards. However, the SPS Agreement allows parties to provide a higher level of protection than that of international standards only if there is a scientific justification or in accordance with a detailed procedure (SPS Agreement Article 3.3). The detailed procedure (which includes conducting a risk assessment) under SPS Agreement Article 5 sets out criteria to identify "the appropriate level of sanitary or phytosanitary protection" and aims to avoid "arbitrary or unjustifiable distinctions" that result in "discrimination or a disguised restriction on international trade" (SPS Agreement Article 5.5). Parties must ensure that SPS measures "are not more trade-restrictive than required to achieve their appropriate level of sanitary or phytosanitary protection, taking into account technical and economic feasibility" (SPS Agreement Article 5.6).

With respect to the requirement that a measure not be more trade-restrictive than necessary to fulfill a legitimate objective (TBT Agreement), or not more trade-restrictive than required to achieve the appropriate level of SPS protection (SPS Agreement), the WTO Appellate Body stated in the *Australia-Salmon* case[75] that a SPS measure will fail this requirement only if there exists a reasonably available alternative that is significantly less trade restrictive and that still achieves the intended level of protection of the party that adopted the SPS measure. The WTO Appellate Body clarified in the *Japan-Agricultural Products* case[76] that the complaining State bears the burden of proving the existence of such an alternative.

In the *Japan-Apples*[77] case, the WTO Panel found that Japan's measure was not based on a sufficient risk assessment as Japan failed to properly analyse the "likelihood" of the disease spreading. The WTO Panel held that the phytosanitary measure at issue was "clearly disproportionate" to the risk identified by Japan on the basis of the scientific evidence.

With respect to relying on international standards, the WTO Appellate Body stated in the *EC-Hormones*[78] case, that even if a domestic SPS measure does not use an international standard as a basis, the burden of proof still remains on the complainant to show that the SPS measure does not comply with the SPS

75 *Australia – Measures Affecting Importation of Salmon (Complaint by Canada)* (1998), WTO Doc. WT/DS18/AB/R (Appellate Body Report), online: http://docsonline.wto.org at para. 194.

76 *Japan – Measures Affecting Agricultural Products (Complaint by the United States)* (1999), WTO Doc. WT/DS76/AB (Appellate Body Report), online: http://docsonline.wto.org (*Japan-Apples*) at para. 126.

77 *Japan – Measures Affecting the Importation of Apples*, WT/DS245/R, adopted 10 December 2003 (Panel Report), upheld by Appellate Body Report WT/DS245/AB/R, at para. 8.198.

78 *EC – EC Measures Concerning Meat and Meat Products (Hormones) (Complaint by Canada and the United States)* (1998), WTO Doc. WT/DS26/AB/R (Appellate Body Report), online: http://docsonline.wto.org (*WTO Appellate Body, Meat Products*).

Agreement. The WTO Appellate Body reiterated this position in respect of the TBT Agreement in the *EC-Sardines*[79] case.

Moreover, the WTO Appellate Body decided in the *EC-Hormones*[80] case that despite the requirement that a domestic SPS measure setting a level of protection higher than that of international standards must rely on a risk assessment, such a SPS measure needs not be grounded in the majority view held by the scientific community – the risk assessment must simply reasonably support the SPS measure.

TBT Agreement Article 2.2 was at the forefront of the recent *Tuna-Dolphin II* case, in which the U.S. put forward two objectives that were deemed legitimate by the Panel (upheld by the Appellate Body on this point): (i) consumer information and (ii) dolphin protection. The Panel considered the list of legitimate objectives in Article 2.2 of the TBT Agreement and found that the consumer information objective fell within the broader goal of preventing deceptive practices, and that the dolphin protection objective related to the protection of animal life or health or the environment.[81]

Mexico had argued before the Panel that the U.S. disposed of a "reasonably available alternative measure" in permitting the use in the U.S. market of the "AIDCP dolphin safe label".[82] According to the Appellate Body, the Panel had to examine the following criteria, among other things, in determining whether the U.S. AIDCP and "dolphin-safe" label "are more trade-restrictive than necessary" within the meaning of Article 2.2 of the TBT Agreement:

> the contribution that the US measure makes to the achievement of its objectives; the trade restrictiveness of the US 'dolphin-safe' labelling provisions; whether Mexico had identified a 'reasonably available' and less trade-restrictive alternative measure, and to compare the degree of the US measure's contribution with that of the alternative measure, which is reasonably available and less trade restrictive, taking account of the risks non-fulfilment would create.[83]

The Appellate Body started its analysis by focusing on the contribution of the AIDCP and "dolphin-safe" label to their stated objectives. Regarding the consumer information objective, the Appellate Body recalled the Panel's finding that the U.S. AIDCP and "dolphin-safe" label "can only *partially* ensure that consumers are informed about whether tuna was caught by using a method that adversely affects dolphins" given that consumers may be misled to think that tuna that was caught using a technique other than purse seine nets does not adversely affect dolphins.[84]

---

79 *EC – Trade Description of Sardines (Complaint by Peru)* (2002), WTO Doc. WT/DS231/AB (Appellate Body Report), online: http://docsonline.wto.org.

80 *WTO Appellate Body, Meat Products, supra* note 24.

81 Tuna-Dolphin II (Appellate Body Report), *supra* note 52 at para. 303, citing Panel Report, at para. 7.437.

82 Ibid. at para. 326, citing Panel Report, at para. 7.566.

83 Ibid.

84 Ibid., citing Panel Report, at paras 7.562, 7.563.

Regarding the dolphin protection objective, the Appellate Body recalled the Panel's finding that the AIDCP and "dolphin-safe" label "may, at best, only partially fulfil their stated objective of protecting dolphins by ensuring that the U.S. market is not used to encourage fishing fleets to catch tuna in a manner that adversely affects dolphins" given that that the DCEPIA and "dolphin-safe" label effectively achieve such objective only within the ETP and, outside the ETP, only regarding purse seine net and high seas driftnet fishing.[85]

The Appellate Body then considered the extent to which the alternative measure proposed by Mexico would fulfil the U.S.'s objectives and decided that the Panel's analysis of whether Mexico had demonstrated that the U.S. the DCPIA and "dolphin-safe" label were "more trade-restrictive than necessary" under TBT Agreement Article 2.2 "was based, at least in part, on an improper comparison."[86] The Appellate Body underlined that "the alternative measure identified by Mexico is *not* the AIDCP regime, as such, but rather the *coexistence* of the AIDCP rules with the US measure." The Appellate Body then split its analysis between tuna harvested *outside* the ETP and tuna harvested *inside* the ETP.

Regarding tuna harvested *outside* the ETP, the Appellate Body stated that "there is no difference between the measure at issue and the alternative measure identified by Mexico, namely, the coexistence of the US 'dolphin-safe' labelling provisions with the AIDCP rules" on the basis that "the geographic scope of application of the AIDCP rules is limited to the ETP", meaning that only the U.S. measure would apply thereto. As a result, the DCPIA and "dolphin-safe" label achieves the U.S. objectives in the same way as the Mexican alternative for tuna harvested *outside* the ETP.

The Appellate Body then turned to tuna harvested *inside* the ETP and stated that the Panel should have focused its analysis on comparing whether the U.S. measures and the Mexican alternative achieve the U.S. objectives to the same degree *inside the ETP*. Here the Appellate Body reiterated findings made by the Panel that "dolphins suffer adverse impact beyond observed mortalities from setting on dolphins[87], even under the restrictions contained in the AIDCP rules." Here, however, the Appellate Body seemed to reframe the Mexican alternative only as the AIDCP rules and not as the *coexistence* of the AIDCP rules with the U.S. measure and finds that since "tuna caught in the ETP by setting on dolphins would be eligible for the 'dolphin-safe' label," the Mexican alternative would contribute to the U.S. objectives "to a lesser degree than the measure at issue, because, overall, it would allow more tuna harvested in conditions that adversely affect dolphins to be labelled 'dolphin-safe'." As a result, the Appellate Body stated that the Panel's analysis was "flawed and cannot stand"[88], disagreed with the Panel's findings that the Mexican alternative

---

85   Ibid. at para. 327, citing Panel Report, at para. 7.599.

86   Ibid. at para. 328.

87   Ibid. at fn 663: "[i]n particular, the Panel considered cow-calf separation; potential muscle injury resulting from the chase; immune and reproductive systems failures; and other adverse health consequences for dolphins, such as continuous acute stress. (See Panel Report, paras 7.491–7.506)."

88   Ibid. at para. 331.

would achieve the U.S.'s objectives "to the same extent" as the U.S. DCPIA and "dolphin-safe" label, and decided that consumers were not more misled under the U.S. DCPIA and "dolphin-safe" label than under the Mexican alternative.

Mexico argued before the Appellate Body that the U.S.'s dolphin protection objective was violated the sixth recital of the preamble of the TBT Agreement. The Appellate Body rejected Mexico's argument by stating that the sixth recital requires that a *measure*, and rather than its objective, must not be applied in a manner that would constitute a means of arbitrary or unjustifiable discrimination between countries where the same conditions prevail or a disguised restriction on international trade.[89]

15.4 Principle of common but differentiated responsibilities

The principle of common but differentiated responsibilities is seen as finding its equivalent in the Special but Differentiated Treatment provisions of nearly all WTO Agreements.

Attempts to facilitate development interests through world trade law were made in the Tokyo Round (1973–1979) and resulted in an "enabling clause" on "Differential and More Favourable Treatment, Reciprocity and Fuller Participation of Developing Countries" (also known as "Special and Differential Treatment"). The enabling clause established an exception to Article I of GATT allowing special and differential treatment for developing countries. Although this double standard has been controversial from inception it has only recently been challenged in the Dispute Settlement Mechanism of the WTO.

In the 1999 *India-Quantitative Restrictions* case, the WTO Panel recalled the WTO preamble in making a statement about the development needs of certain countries, stating:

> . . . we recall that the Preamble to the WTO Agreement recognizes both (i) the desirability of expanding international trade in goods and services and (ii) the need for positive efforts designed to ensure that developing countries secure a share in international trade commensurate with the needs of their economic development. In implementing these goals, WTO rules promote trade liberalization, but recognize the need for specific exceptions from the general rules to address special concerns, including those of developing countries.[90]

Here, the Panel acknowledged a basis for "special and differential" treatment in relation to a country's economic capabilities in reference to the founding document of the WTO. It thus affirmed the legitimacy of special and differential treatment of less developed countries like India within the WTO framework, for instance to

89 Ibid. at para. 339.
90 *India – Quantitative Restrictions on Imports of Agricultural, Textile and Industrial Products* (1999), WTO Doc. WT/DS90/R (Report of the Panel), at para. 7.2.

lawfully utilize protective measures and import restrictions for maintenance of their balance of payments. This opened the way for a number of other cases referring to this principle.

Exploring issues of fair differentiation further, in the *EC-Tariff Preferences* case, the Appellate Body rejected the arguments of the European Communities (EC) that its tariff preferences were based on sustainable development objectives. The 2004 *EC-Tariff Preferences* case[91] related to the scheme of generalized tariff preferences for developing countries. India complained that special preferences based on certain drug arrangements adopted by beneficiary countries were inconsistent with the most-favoured nation clause (Article 1.1 GATT 1994) and could not be justified under the Decision on Differential and More Favourable Treatment, Reciprocity, and Fuller Participation of Developing Countries.[92] Similar provisions exist for environmental and labour rights, but in the end these were not challenged. The Panel found that the EC's scheme was indeed inconsistent with Article 1.1 GATT and could not be justified under the Enabling Clause. This was because developed countries were compelled to grant identical tariff preferences under GSP schemes to all developing countries without differentiation and the Panel found that it should apply to all developing countries. The Appellate Body reversed these last two findings but concluded that the drug criteria, due to a closed list of beneficiary countries and unclear criteria for the selection of these countries, was not covered by the exception.

The EC argued that because the Enabling Clause was designed to fulfill the objectives of the WTO, it should not be interpreted as an exception to Article 1.1 GATT but rather as an incentive for developed countries to confer preferences on their less developed counterparts. The Appellate Body considered this argument and agreed with the initial observation. Indeed, it overturned one of the Panel's findings – interpreting non-discrimination according to the objectives of the GATT and the WTO – and accepted that the differentiation between developing countries according to their needs was possible. The Appellate Body, citing its *US-Shrimp* decision, found that the objectives of the WTO could be fulfilled through "General Exceptions". Indeed, they noted that "the optimal use of the world's resources in accordance with the objective of sustainable development" could be achieved through application of the WTO exceptions, such as Article XX(g) GATT.

However, the Panel in the same case found that the EC could not justify its drug arrangements under Article XX(b) GATT, because it could not prove that its system was designed to protect human health in the European Union. Rather, the Panel agreed with India's argument that increased market access was intended to contribute to sustainable development of the beneficiary countries. As the fight against illicit drug production and exports were deemed to be part of a broader

---

91   *EC – Conditions for the Granting of Tariff Preferences to Developing Countries* (20 April 2004) (Appellate Body Report) WT/DS246/AB/R.

92   *Differential and More Favourable Treatment Reciprocity and Fuller Participation of Developing Countries* (28 November 1979) L/4903, BISD 26S/203.

sustainable development objective (as confirmed by several multilateral instruments and the official justification to the Regulation setting up the EC System), these could not be justified as a measure that only sought to benefit the EC. This decision demonstrates that both the "environmental" and the "development" aspects (including health) are part of the concept of sustainable development that the WTO dispute settlement body recognizes as a WTO objective.

The common but differentiated responsibilities principle operates even in procedural terms, allowing for longer timeframes for compliance. In the 2005 *Mexico-Soft Drinks* case, the WTO Panel was ". . . aware of the crucial importance of the provisions on special and differential treatment in the WTO agreements in general, and of Article 12.11 of the DSU in particular. During the Panel proceedings, the Panel [had] taken into account Mexico's status as a developing country, *inter alia*, when establishing the timetable for the Panel process."[93] Mexico was essentially granted special and differential procedural leeway on the basis of its development status.

In the recent case of *United States-Certain Country of Origin Labelling (COOL) Requirements*, Mexico argued that the U.S. did not take into account Mexico's "special needs as a developing country when preparing and applying the COOL measure" in question.[94] The Panel nonetheless eventually decided that Mexico had not shown enough evidence to demonstrate a violation of the special and differential treatment provision in that context.[95]

In *US-Clove Cigarettes* (2012) case, involving Indonesian clove cigarettes and their alleged discrimination in the U.S. market, Article 2.12 of the TBT Agreement regarding reasonable intervals was at issue. The Panel found that the U.S. interval between the publication and entry into force of its technical regulation on this was inconsistent with Article 2.12, but not that Indonesia's developing country status had been dealt with inconsistently. The Appellate Body further considered that since there were like products in the case, the U.S. measure constituted discrimination against Indonesia on the basis of "treatment no less favourable".[96]

15.5 Principle of integration and interrelationship, in particular in relation to human rights and social, economic and environmental objectives

On a theoretical level, trade is not automatically good or bad for the environment and social development. Rather, the specific contours of international trade rules and regimes and modes of implementation dictate the degree to

---

93 *Mexico – Tax Measures on Soft Drinks and Other Beverages* (2005), WTO Doc. WT/DS308/R (Report of the Panel), at para. 8.234.
94 See *Bridges Weekly Trade News Digest*, Vol. 15, No. 40 (23 November 2011), at 4; see also *Bridges Weekly Trade News Digest*, Vol. 16, No. 12 (28 March 2012), at 11.
95 *US – Certain Country of Origin Labelling (COOL) Requirements* (2011), WTO Docs. WT/DS384/R, WT/DS386/R (Reports of the Panel), at para. 7.68
96 *US – Measures Affecting the Production and Sale of Clove Cigarettes* (2012) (Appellate Body Report), at paras 5, 111, 276–79

which trade advances sustainable development goals. Public international law, the umbrella under which international trade law is situated, can and should adopt a principled approach to ensure that it can deliver on its global objective of sustainable development. Balanced and integrated legal analysis is a prerequisite to ensure that prescriptions resonate with developmental initiatives.

In the 1996 *US-Gasoline* case, the WTO Appellate Body stated that "the General Agreement is not to be read in clinical isolation from public international law."[97] Following this admission of public international law sources, in the 1998 *US-Shrimp* case, the WTO Appellate Body found that the concept of sustainable development "has been generally accepted as integrating economic and social development and environmental protection" and explicitly referred to the Paragraph 4 Rio principle of integration.[98]

In the *EC-Biotech*[99] case, the WTO Panel confirmed that a Panel may consider "other relevant rules of international law when interpreting the terms of WTO agreements if it deems such rules to be informative."[100] It requested

> several international organizations (Codex, FAO, the IPCC Secretariat, WHO, OIE, the CBD Secretariat and UNEP) to identify materials (reference works, glossaries, official documents of the relevant international organizations, including conventions, standards and guidelines, etc.) that might aid us in determining the ordinary meaning of certain terms used in the definitions.[101]

Lastly, in *China-Raw Materials*, the Panel reaffirmed the principle of sovereignty over natural resources, to freely exploit natural resources for development, and GATT Article XX(g), which stresses the need to also regulate these resources in accordance with sustainable development.[102] The Panel concluded that economic development and conservation of resources can indeed operate in harmony and alongside WTO obligations, giving some hope for sustainable development being increasingly integrated into WTO decisions in the future.[103]

15.6 Conclusion

The reasoning of the WTO dispute settlement body in these cases, taken together, demonstrates that the objective of sustainable development has become

---

97   *US – Standards for Reformulated and Conventional Gasoline* (1996) WTO Doc. WT/DS2/9 (Appellate Body Report and Panel Report), art. 31, p. 17.
98   *US – Shrimp* (Appellate Body Report), *supra* note 17 at para. 129, fn 107, fn 147.
99   *EC – Measures Affecting the Approval and Marketing of Biotech Products*, WT/DS291/R, WT/DS292/R, WT/DS293/R, Add.1 to Add.9, and Corr.1 (Panel Report), adopted 21 November 2006.
100 *EC – Biotech,* (Panel Report), *supra* note 99 at para. 7.93.
101 Ibid. at Annex 3, at para. 1596.
102 *China – Measures Related to the Exportation of Various Raw Materials* (2011) (Reports of the Panel), at paras 7.378–7.381.
103 Ibid. at para. 7.381.

an integral part of the world trading system. Legal arguments encompassing an integrated developmental and environmental approach have been made by the parties and accepted by the relevant dispute settlement organs. On the other hand, it is clear that the Panels and the Appellate Body will not accept sustainable development as a trump card. It cannot just be invoked in order to justify non-compliance with established WTO disciplines.

It also shows that sustainable development is not a one-way relationship between developed and developing countries, but rather promotes mutual understanding and can also be successfully employed by both groups. A solid legal understanding of the objective and its underlying principles, as well as the appropriate application of specific facts of each case embedded in a reasoned legal argument is required to make a successful sustainable development argument in world trade law.

Sustainable development is development that can meet the needs of the present without compromising the needs of future generations.

Precaution has been recognized as a valid principle in international law and also as incorporated in the SPS Agreement through careful respect for precautionary interpretation.

With regards to sustainable use of natural resources, the WTO allows such measures but only as exceptions not as a fundamental rule and there is room for improvement. In terms of common but differentiated responsibilities, the equivalent is found in the special but differential treatment provisions, but broader application as a principle in the dispute settlement system has yet to be achieved.

Further, while there are strong commitments to integration, with recognition of the need for balancing integration and mutual support between economic growth, social justice and environmental protection objectives (*US–Shrimp* case), there remains a great deal of space for more substantive integration both in tribunal decisions, and in trade treaties themselves.

16 The principle of good governance in WTO disputes

Jarrod Hepburn

16.1 Introduction

This chapter considers how aspects of the principle of good governance have been manifested in the case law of the World Trade Organization (WTO) over the last 20 years.

The starting point for this inquiry is the 2002 New Delhi Declaration of Principles of International Law Relating to Sustainable Development. The New Delhi Declaration establishes seven principles, including the principle of good governance. The Declaration defines 'good governance', in relevant part, in the following way:

> [The principle of good governance] commits States and international organisations:
>
> a)   to adopt democratic and *transparent decision-making* procedures . . .
> c)   to respect the principle of *due process* in their procedures and to observe the rule of law and human rights . . .[1]

Although there may be many competing definitions of good governance, the elaboration of the principle in the New Delhi Declaration will be adopted here to frame the inquiry into its manifestation in WTO case law.

At the outset, it is important to clarify the scope of this inquiry. Good governance and the WTO have been studied by commentators from a variety of angles. Many of these studies have, for instance, examined elements of good governance as they are manifested in the WTO's own, internal processes.[2] These studies have

---

1 ILA, 'Declaration of Principles of International Law Related to Sustainable Development', Resolution 3/2002 adopted at the 70th Conference of the International Law Association (New Delhi 2–6 April 2002) (9 August 2002) UN Doc A/CONF.199/8 [ND], principle 6 (emphasis added).

2 See, e.g. V. Hughes, 'The Institutional Dimension' in D. Bethlehem *et al.*, eds., *The Oxford Handbook of International Trade Law* (Oxford: OUP 2009) 295–6; M. Orellana, 'WTO and Civil Society' in Bethlehem, M. Matsushita, T. Schoenbaum and P. Mavroidis, *The World Trade Organisation: Law, Practice and Policy*, 2nd edn (Oxford: OUP, 2006) 927–28; P. Van den Bossche, *The Law and Policy of the World Trade Organization*, 2nd edn (Cambridge: CUP, 2008) 148–59.

focused on the operation of the WTO as an institution and the manner in which it makes its decisions or structures its negotiations. In this respect, it has been found wanting by some commentators, who point out a degree of hypocrisy in the fact that the WTO calls for improvements in good governance within its Member States while adopting entirely secretive, non-transparent procedures within its own organisational governance structures.[3]

These internal examinations of the WTO are not, however, the focus here. Instead, the emphasis is on WTO case law – decisions of the dispute settlement Panels and the Appellate Body. As a result of this, the chapter's focus shifts to a more external view, to the utility or instrumental success of the WTO as a tool for achieving good governance at the national level. This is because the WTO's dispute settlement organs are established to resolve disputes brought by one WTO Member State against another. The resulting case-law, as a product of the dispute resolution process, applies to the Member States themselves. A focus on this case-law thus necessarily means a focus on the way in which the WTO imposes good governance on its Member States through its dispute settlement rulings. Thus, in contrast with other literature on good governance and the WTO, this chapter examines the WTO's 'vertical' effect on good governance within its Member States.

A second clarification is also appropriate. It might be observed that the WTO, both as an institution and as a set of substantive rules regulating international trade, is based on principles such as transparency, non-discrimination, and rational, rules-based decision-making.[4] This might suggest that the entire WTO represents a tool for encouraging good governance in its Member States. On this view, it could be said that *every* case from the WTO dispute settlement organs manifests or supports the principle of good governance within Member States in some way, simply by enforcing whichever substantive WTO rule is at issue in the case.

However, this chapter takes a more targeted approach. It selects just two aspects of the broad principle of good governance identified in the New Delhi Declaration – transparent decision-making (here labelled simply 'transparency') and due process – and discusses cases that address these aspects as they impact upon WTO Member States.

Section 16.2 examines the first aspect of good governance, transparency. The cases reviewed ultimately show a wide interpretation of relevant duties in the WTO Agreements. However, the cases also indicate that duties of transparency must be implemented carefully by national authorities to avoid provoking tension with other aspects of good governance such as impartial administration.

Due process in the WTO case-law is examined in Section 16.3 of this chapter, through the lens of cases relating to the duty to give reasons for national administrative decisions. A duty to give reasons is said to be one central element of due

---

3 G. de Burca and J. Scott, 'The Impact of the WTO on EU Decision-Making' in G. de Burca and J. Scott, eds., *The EU and the WTO: Legal and Constitutional Issues* (Oxford: Hart, 2001) 28–29.

4 P. Van den Bossche, *supra* note 3 at 37; World Trade Organization, 'About the WTO – A Statement by the Director-General' <http://www.wto.org/english/thewto_e/whatis_e/wto_dg_stat_e.htm> accessed 25 March 2015.

process in many jurisdictions. WTO case law on reasons, though not extensive, can be seen to encourage improvement in the quality of national decision-making. However, it also emphasises the WTO's own position as part of the national decision-making structure, via its role of international review.

16.2 Transparency in WTO case law

Transparency can have a wide variety of meanings.[5] At one end of the spectrum, as discussed in Dr. Jonathan Bonnitcha's chapter, 'The Principle of Good Governance in the Reasoning of Investor-State Arbitral Tribunals,' some investor-State arbitral tribunals have defined transparency to mean that individuals must know in advance precisely how they will be treated by government authorities, and exactly how discretionary powers will be exercised. Transparency in this chapter is understood in a more limited sense, covering the access to and provision of information about administrative processes and decisions made by government authorities. It is acknowledged that this interpretation of transparency, as an element of the principle of good governance, has interconnections with another of the New Delhi principles, the principle of public participation and access to information and justice.[6] Indeed, the New Delhi Declaration itself states that '[p]ublic participation is essential to . . . good governance',[7] and that '[g]ood governance requires . . . the full participation of women in all levels of decision-making'.[8] Nevertheless, the overall focus remains on the principle of good governance, based on the definition in Principle 6 of the Declaration.

There are various provisions in many of the WTO Agreements that relate to transparency and the publication of information. For instance, Article 63 of the Agreement on Trade-Related Aspects of Intellectual Property Rights (TRIPS Agreement), entitled 'Transparency', requires WTO Member States to publish all laws, regulations, judicial decisions and administrative rulings of general application that relate to intellectual property rights. This publication must be done 'in such a manner as to enable governments and right holders to become acquainted with them',[9] and thereby to know the rules and decision-making procedures that each WTO Member will apply to them. The laws and rulings must also be notified to the WTO Council for TRIPS.

Article 22 of the Subsidies and Countervailing Measures Agreement (SCM Agreement) imposes certain notification obligations on Member States when they decide to initiate an investigation on the imposition of so-called 'countervailing

5 See E. Fisher, 'Transparency and Administrative Law: A Critical Evaluation' (2010) 63 *Curr. Leg. Probl.* 272–314.

6 See New Delhi Principles, *supra* note 1 at 5.

7 Ibid. at 5.1.

8 Ibid. at 6.3.

9 Agreement on Trade-Related Aspects of Intellectual Property Rights, 15 April 1994, Marrakesh Agreement Establishing the World Trade Organization, Annex 1C, 1869 UNTS 299, 33 ILM 1197, art. 63.

duties'.[10] In addition to giving a general public notice, Member States must notify the affected WTO Member and 'other interested parties known to the investigating authority to have an interest therein'.[11] Such 'interested parties' are likely to be producers, located in the affected WTO Member State, of the products against which the countervailing duty would be imposed.

Similarly, the Agreement on Technical Barriers to Trade (TBT Agreement) and the Agreement on Sanitary and Phytosanitary Standards (SPS Agreement) include 'legislated', explicit provisions on transparency in a range of areas. For example, under the TBT Agreement, WTO Members must publish notifications of proposed new technical regulations that may have a significant effect on trade, as well as the objective and rationale of the regulation and the products likely to be affected.[12] Under the SPS Agreement, governments must notify other governments of new or changed SPS measures that may affect trade, and must generally publish all relevant measures.[13]

As noted above, though, the focus of this chapter is on the judicial interpretation of these transparency obligations in WTO case-law. Although case law on the TBT and TRIPS transparency obligations has not yet arisen, the SPS transparency requirements have been examined by the WTO's dispute resolution organs. In the case of *Japan – Agricultural Products II*, the US complained about a measure imposed by Japan relating to the importation of a range of fruits. The measure at issue required certain tests to be done on every variety of the range of fruits before they could be imported to Japan. The tests aimed at preventing the introduction of codling moths, a pest that was claimed to cause serious damage. Amongst other things, the US argued in the case that this testing requirement had not been published by Japan, in violation of Article 7 and Annex B of the SPS Agreement.

At first instance, the Panel began by noting that the publication obligations in Annex B were specified to apply to 'phytosanitary measures such as laws, decrees or ordinances which are applicable generally'.[14] It then observed that Japan's testing requirement was not in fact mandatory or legally enforceable. Rather, as Japan contended, it was only *one* permitted method of demonstrating the safety of imported fruit. The Panel considered whether this non-mandatory nature of the requirement meant that it could not be characterised as a 'phytosanitary regulation' captured by the Annex B obligations. However, adopting a wide view of transparency, the Panel ultimately concluded that the testing requirement *was*

---

10 WTO rules authorise the imposition of these duties effectively in retaliation, following a government's determination that a competitor government is subsidising its domestic industry and thereby artificially lowering the prices of the industry's exports.

11 1867 UNTS 14, art. 22(1).

12 1868 UNTS 120, art. 2.9. The TBT Committee has adopted procedures and forms for making these notifications: see G/TBT/1/Rev.8 of 23 May 2002.

13 1867 UNTS 493, arts 5.8 and 7, and Annex B. As with the TBT Agreement, the SPS Committee has adopted more detailed procedures for making notifications: see G/SPS/7/Rev.2 of 2 April 2002.

14 *Japan – Measures Affecting Agricultural Products* (27 October 1998) WT/DS76/R [8.108].

covered by Annex B because it was a measure that would bring an advantage to an exporter if complied with.[15] The Panel added that the 'general availability to answer any queries' of Japan's authorities was not sufficient to meet publication obligations. Furthermore, the 'highly technical nature' of the testing requirement similarly did not excuse Japan from publishing it.[16]

On appeal, the Appellate Body (AB) agreed with this broad view of the Annex B transparency obligations, and indeed strengthened them by reference to the purpose behind the provisions. Thus, it confirmed that the reference to 'laws, decrees or ordinances' was only illustrative and not an exhaustive list of the kinds of measures subject to the transparency obligations.[17] In addition, the AB noted that Annex B must be interpreted in light of its object and purpose, which was 'to enable interested Members to become acquainted with' the relevant regulations on food safety.[18] This pushed the AB to read Annex B widely and include the non-mandatory testing requirement within the scope of the transparency obligations.

Other WTO agreements also contain transparency provisions and have been the subject of interpretation in WTO case-law. One such case study on transparency comes from the 'sub-regime' within WTO law of anti-dumping. As a basic definition, dumping occurs when one country sells products into another country at below cost price. The WTO Anti-Dumping Agreement regulates the conditions under which national trade authorities can make determinations of when a trading partner country is engaging in dumping, and when anti-dumping duties may be imposed by the target state in retaliation for this. The Agreement places some emphasis on due process and the procedures of decision-making in this area. It also permits intervention by states and (foreign) private traders affected by these dumping determinations.[19]

In *EC – Pipe Fittings*,[20] the AB was called on to interpret Article 6.4 of the WTO Anti-Dumping Agreement Agreement. This provision requires national authorities to give 'timely opportunities for all interested parties to see all information that is relevant to the presentation of their cases'. In its decision, as in *Japan – Agricultural Products II*, the AB gave a wide interpretation to this obligation.

Brazil had argued that the European Communities (EC) had failed to disclose a certain document which explained how it had made a dumping determination adversely affecting Brazilian producers. At first instance, the Panel hearing the case found no violation of Article 6.4. It found, firstly, that the data in the document in question was consistent with other information that *was* disclosed to the relevant parties. Secondly, the document had no 'added value' for the purposes of the EC's investigation. Lastly, and relatedly, the document was not relevant to

---

15 Ibid. at [8.111–12].

16 Ibid. at [8.115].

17 *Japan – Measures Affecting Agricultural Products II* (19 March 1999) WT/DS76/AB/R [105]

18 Ibid. at [106]

19 See generally P. Van den Bossche, *supra* note 2 at ch 6.2.

20 *EC – Anti-Dumping Duties on Malleable Cast Iron Tube or Pipe Fittings from Brazil* (7 March 2003) WT/DS219/R.

the dumping determination, nor was it specifically relied on by the EC in reaching its dumping determination.[21]

On appeal, however, the AB took a different view. In its view, Member States must disclose documents under Article 6.4 not only if they are relevant from the perspective of the national investigating authority, but also if they are relevant to a party's own presentation of its case.[22] This reading of Article 6.4 is perhaps not controversial given the text of Article 6.4 itself, which refers to 'all information that is relevant to the presentation of [interested parties'] cases'. Nevertheless, the AB confirmed a wide understanding of 'relevance'. Furthermore, the AB added, the information need not have been specifically relied on to reach the decision on a dumping determination. In the AB's view, the information does not need any 'added value', as suggested by the Panel; it is simply sufficient that the information was *used* by the authorities during the dumping investigation.[23]

This wider definition adopted by the AB in *EC – Pipe Fittings* has implications not only for other WTO Member States (who are primarily addressed by WTO obligations), but, in this context, also for private traders and producers who are granted rights to participate in national dumping procedures.[24] Like Article 63 of TRIPS mentioned above, the extension of transparency obligations to private parties demonstrates the importance of these obligations not only 'horizontally', between states, but also 'vertically', between states and individuals. Other WTO jurisprudence, such as the *Argentina – Hides and Leather* case discussed below, has also seen Panels highlight this extension to private entities (in the *Hides and Leather* case, under GATT Article X:1).[25] Since it is, by and large, individuals and private entities that are the ultimate objects of the 'governance' exercised by states, the principle of good governance would be limited if its manifestations only applied as between states. It is significant for present purposes, then, that this case law refers to and enforces these transparency provisions in a wide manner. De Burca and Scott suggest another connection to the requirement for 'democratic . . . decision-making procedures' in the New Delhi Declaration's view of good governance. In their view, the WTO's inclusion of private traders represents a model of global deliberative democracy, rather than traditional representative democracy, that encourages 'experimentation and mutual learning' amongst the actors in the system.[26] The WTO case law in this area, then, serves to strengthen both the transparency and the democratic aspects of good governance.

---

21 Ibid. at [7.348].

22 *EC – Anti-Dumping Duties on Malleable Cast Iron Tube or Pipe Fittings from Brazil* (18 August 2003) WT/DS219/AB/R and WT/DSB/M/154 [145].

23 Ibid. at [147].

24 See M. de Bellis, 'The Disclosure of Information: Anti-Dumping Duties and the WTO System' in S Cassese and others, *Global Administrative Law: Cases, Materials, Issues,* 2nd edn, IRPA/IILJ 2008), 80 <http://www.iilj.org/GAL/documents/GALCasebook2008.pdf> accessed 23 March 2015.

25 *Argentina – Definitive Anti-Dumping Duties on Poultry from Brazil* (22 April 2003) WT/DS241/R [11.76].

26 De Burca and Scott, *supra* note 3 at 28.

The importance of the role of private traders in the WTO system was again emphasised in *Argentina – Poultry Anti-Dumping Duties*. This case, brought by Brazil, related in part to the interpretation of Article 12.1 of the WTO Anti-Dumping Agreement. Like the SCM Agreement discussed above, this provision requires national authorities, after they have initiated an investigation that will lead to a dumping determination, to notify both 'the Member or Members the products of which are subject to such investigation' and 'other interested parties known to the investigating authorities to have an interest therein'. Again, these 'interested parties' will normally include exporters from the affected Member State, whose products will become subject to the anti-dumping duties if they are ultimately imposed following the investigation and determination.

Argentina, as respondent in the case, argued that it had satisfied the Article 12.1 obligation because it had notified the relevant Brazilian authorities and had asked for their assistance in identifying and contacting potentially affected exporters in Brazil. It observed that, while it was aware of the interest of certain Brazilian exporters, it did not have contact details for them and so it could not notify them directly.[27] The Panel, however, disagreed with this reading of Article 12.1. It acknowledged that, merely because an interested exporter might have been 'known to the investigation authorities' this does not necessarily imply that sufficient contact details are known. However, in the Panel's view, Argentina should have made 'reasonable efforts' to obtain contact details. 'Sending a letter [to the Brazilian authorities] with only a very general request for assistance, without specifying the exporters for which contact details are required, does not satisfy the need to make all reasonable efforts.'[28]

Again, then, the WTO dispute settlement organs took a broad view of transparency in *Argentina – Poultry Anti-Dumping Duties*, requiring serious positive efforts from member states to fulfil transparency obligations, particularly where private trading parties were involved in the matter.

In another case, though, a WTO Panel has highlighted possible tensions between the principle of transparency and other important principles, such as fairness and impartiality. *Argentina – Hides and Leather* focused on a more general provision on transparency and good governance found in the text of GATT Article X:3. This provision commits Member States to the '*uniform, impartial and reasonable*' application of customs laws. At issue in the case was a measure taken by Argentina to permit representatives of the cow hide tanning industry to be present at customs during the export clearance process. Argentina stated that the intention of this measure was to contribute to the openness of the export process, and to prevent the possibility of fraud arising from inaccurate tariff classifications of the hides and leather being exported. The presence of the industry representatives was provided for because they supposedly had more expertise than Argentine customs officials in classifying the goods for export.[29]

---

27 *Argentina – Poultry Anti-Dumping Duties, supra* note 25 at [7.126].
28 Ibid. at [7.132].
29 *Argentina – Measures Affecting The Export of Bovine Hides and the Import of Finished Leather* (19 December 2000) WT/DS155/R [11.88]. The claimant in the case, the European Communities,

The Panel acknowledged the good intentions of the measure, and did not reject Argentina's claim that it required expert advice to classify the hides for export.[30] However, it focused on the requirement of 'impartiality' in Article X:3. In this respect, the Panel expressed concern about the risk that an *overly* transparent process created an 'inherent danger' of confidential commercial information about particular exporters being discovered by the industry body representatives, who could then use this information to their own advantage.[31] Seen from this perspective, the Argentine customs process thus appeared partial to certain interests in the domestic industry.

Thus, despite the apparently good intentions of the Argentine customs authorities in *Argentina – Hides and Leather*, the Panel ultimately considered that other aspects of good governance – such as the existence of fair procedures that applied impartially to all relevant parties – were more important than transparency here. Alternatively, it could be suggested that Argentina was offering *too much* transparency to particular parties (namely, those represented at the export process) and not enough to others.

16.3 Due process and the duty to give reasons in WTO case law

A second aspect of good governance, relating to due process, has played out in several WTO cases.[32] In these cases, the WTO dispute settlement organs have discussed the duty to give reasons for national administrative decisions. The existence of, and rationales for, this duty have been much discussed in many domestic jurisdictions,[33] while less attention has been paid to it at the international level. However, as noted, consideration of the duty can be found in some WTO decisions, and these decisions are seen to demonstrate important connections between the duty and the principle of good governance.

As with transparency provisions, there are various WTO Agreements that impose a reason-giving duty in explicit form. For instance, Article XVIII of the WTO's plurilateral Agreement on Government Procurement requires State Parties to provide reasons to unsuccessful foreign tenderers for government business as to why their tender was not selected. State Parties must also indicate 'the characteristics and relative advantages of the tender selected as well as the name of the winning tenderer.' As yet, the WTO's dispute settlement organs have not

---

challenged this view on the grounds that 'no particular expertise is required to distinguish between raw or salted hides on the one hand and more processed products on the other' [11.87]. In addition, if Argentina needed specialised expertise, it ought to have trained its own staff.

30 The Panel commented that it would not explicitly rule on this claim. Ibid. at [11.91] at n 378.

31 Ibid. at [11.100].

32 See J. Hepburn, 'The Duty to Give Reasons for Administrative Decisions in International Law' (2012) 61 *Int'l & Comp. L. Quart.* 641.

33 For the debate in the UK, see, e.g. P. Craig, *Administrative Law*, 6th edn, (London: Sweet & Maxwell, 2008) at 403–08; M. Elliott, 'Has the Common Law Duty to Give Reasons Come of Age Yet?' [2011] PL 56.

been called on to consider these particular provisions. However, more can be said about other WTO Agreements – in particular, the Safeguards Agreement and the WTO Anti-Dumping Agreement – that contain either specific reason-giving provisions or more general provisions that *have* been considered by Panels and the AB. In these cases, the WTO adjudicators have read the general provisions to include a duty to give reasons for national administrative decisions.

The Safeguards Agreement allows national authorities to impose duties on particular imported goods in circumstances where the authorities have made a determination that 'serious injury to the domestic industry that produces like or directly competitive products' would arise from the imports.[34] Before making this determination of serious injury, national authorities must conduct an investigation under Article 3.1 of the Safeguards Agreement, and must publish a report 'setting forth their findings and reasoned conclusions' on all pertinent issues. The AB has provided various synonyms for this relatively clear instantiation of a duty to give reasons: authorities must '"give an account of" a "judgement or statement which is reached in a connected or logical manner or expressed in a logical form" . . . "distinctly, or in detail"'.[35] Furthermore, the Article 3.1 obligation is said to mean that, if a safeguards determination is challenged before the WTO organs, reviewing Panels must not be left to deduce for themselves the 'rationale for the determinations from the facts and data contained in the report'.[36]

The fact that a duty to give reasons exists for determinations made under the Safeguards Agreement, then, is clear enough. In the case of *US – Lamb*, though, the AB offered some comments on the reason for the duty's existence, and on its scope, and these comments provide an insight into the intended effect of the duty on good governance in member states.

In particular, the AB in *US – Lamb* commented on the quality of the reasons required to be given by national authorities.[37] In its view, first-instance Panel rulings on a safeguards case must check for a national determination that 'fully addresses the nature, and, especially, the complexities, of the data, and responds to other plausible interpretations of that data.'[38] An explanation is not reasoned or adequate if 'some *alternative explanation* of the facts is plausible, and if the competent authorities' explanation does not seem adequate in the light of that alternative explanation.'[39] These comments suggest that the AB viewed the Safeguards Agreement as underpinned by a goal of improving the quality of domestic decision-making. The existence of a duty to present reasoning for a safeguards determination obliges national authorities to consider all the issues more fully before deciding, and ultimately improves the end result.

---

34 Agreement on Safeguards, 1869 UNTS 154, art. 2.1.
35 *US – Definitive Safeguard Measures on Imports of Certain Steel Products* (10 November 2003) WT/DS248/AB/R [287].
36 Ibid. at [288] (citations omitted).
37 *US – Safeguard Measures on Imports of Fresh, Chilled or Frozen Lamb Meat from New Zealand and Australia* (1 May 2001) WT/DS177/AB/R [106].
38 Ibid.
39 Ibid.

Indeed, the AB's view here could almost be considered as enforcing not only a duty to give reasons, but a duty to have the *best* reason or the *most plausible* reason. This is potentially quite a strong duty, calling on national authorities to consider all plausible alternative explanations for any serious injury suffered by a particular domestic industry. This interpretation from the AB of the Safeguard Agreement's reason-giving requirement thus appears to express significant concern for domestic decision-making processes.

In *US – Line Pipe*, also a Safeguards Agreement case, the AB added to its views from *US – Lamb*. It held that the reasons presented by national authorities for a safeguards determination must be 'clear and unambiguous'. The reasons cannot 'merely imply or suggest an explanation' for the action, but must offer 'a straightforward explanation in express terms.'[40] This holding also suggests an underlying concern in the AB's interpretation of the Safeguards Agreement to improve the quality of national administrative decisions. It is here, then, that the principle of good governance manifests itself via the duty to give reasons.

The cases discussed so far in this section focus on the role of reasons in improving the quality of domestic decisions, at least in the area of trade. However, a more holistic view of the WTO's (admittedly not extensive) case-law on reasons suggests that, for the WTO, this is not the primary role of reasons. Other cases in fact indicate a different, principal role for the provision of reasons in encouraging good governance at the national level. The WTO creates this new role by basing the reasons requirement on the facilitation of international review by its adjudicative organs.

In the case of *US – Steel Safeguards*, the European Communities challenged certain import duties placed on steel products by the US, following an administrative decision by the US International Trade Commission (USITC). Apart from the reasons obligation in Article 3.1, the AB noted Article 4.2(c) of the Safeguards Agreement, and considered that it constituted an 'elaboration of the requirement set out in Article 3.1 . . . to provide a "reasoned conclusion"' for a safeguards determination.[41] It described the obligation in Article 4.2 as an obligation to present a 'reasoned and adequate explanation' for the USITC's decision.[42] Importantly, it then connected this obligation to the effectiveness of its own review process, holding that a WTO Panel could not fulfil its mandated role of objectively assessing national administrative decisions for compliance with WTO obligations without full reasons being given for why those decisions were made.[43] The AB rejected the US argument that the absence of reasons did not necessarily mean that the decision violated substantive WTO obligations. Instead, it considered that, without a sufficient explanation for the decision, the reviewing Panel would have no option but to find a violation.[44]

40 *US – Definitive Safeguard Measures on Imports of Circular Welded Carbon Quality Line Pipe from Korea* (15 February 2002) WT/DS202/AB/R [217].
41 Ibid. at [289].
42 Ibid. at [276].
43 *US – Steel Safeguards, supra* note 35 at [278–79], [288], [298–99].
44 Ibid. at [303].

This reasoning from the AB seeks to ensure that international review by WTO organs be effective, should it occur. The WTO's focus here is less on assisting domestic administrations to make 'good' or 'correct' decisions, and more on enabling its organs to determine whether decisions are in fact good or correct – a 'review rationale' for reasons.

The case of *US – Lamb*, already discussed above, also gave further detail on the requirement to give a 'reasoned and adequate explanation' of a determination of serious injury to domestic industry under Article 4.2 of the Safeguards Agreement. Although this requirement is not directly contained in the text of the Safeguards Agreement, the AB in *US – Lamb* held that it arose from a combination of the obligations in Article 4, on the one hand, and the standard of review to be applied by a Panel in assessing whether WTO Members have complied with their obligations under Article 4, on the other hand.[45] The standard of review, as mandated by Article 11 of the WTO's Dispute Settlement Understanding, requires a Panel to give an 'objective assessment of the matter before it'. This standard lies somewhere between *de novo* review and total deference to the decisions of national administrators. The AB described an objective assessment as having two elements.[46] The first, which the AB labelled the 'formal' element, is an examination of whether national authorities have evaluated all relevant factors. The second, the 'substantive' element, recognises that an evaluation of relevant factors cannot be simply a matter of form, a mere checklist of factors to be ticked off.[47] The evaluation undertaken by national authorities must instead include substantive consideration of how these factors 'have a bearing on' (to use the language of Article 4.2(a)) the situation of the domestic industry. For the AB, the way in which a reviewing Panel ensures compliance with the substantive element is by looking for a reasoned and adequate explanation for the authorities' determination. The existence of this explanation then allows the Panel to determine whether the WTO Member's authorities have complied with their WTO obligations. Importantly, the reasons requirement that the AB places on reviewing Panels will naturally flow downwards to national authorities themselves. Authorities are required to give a reasoned and adequate explanation because the Panels are required to seek one in conducting their review, and Panels will find a breach of WTO obligations if such an explanation is not present. This again supports the view that the WTO's approach to reasons in the sub-regime of safeguards is an instrumental one, aimed most directly at facilitating review by international organs.

In *Thailand – H-Beams*, the review rationale was prominent again. In the case, the WTO was called on to assess reason-giving requirements found not in the Safeguards Agreement but in the WTO Anti-Dumping Agreement. The first instance Panel in the case took an expansive approach to certain obligations in the Agreement. In particular, Article 3.1 of the WTO Anti-Dumping

---

45 *United States – Lamb, supra* note 37 at [105].
46 Ibid. at [103].
47 Ibid. at [104].

Agreement requires national authorities to base certain determinations of injury to a domestic industry on 'positive evidence', and further requires them to conduct an 'objective examination' of various factors in making the determination. Faced with interpreting this obligation, the Panel consulted dictionary definitions of 'positive' and 'objective'. In light of the definition of 'positive' as including 'formally or explicitly stated', and 'objective' as including 'presenting facts uncoloured by feelings', the Panel concluded that Article 3.1 embraced an obligation that the reasoning supporting a determination be 'formally or explicitly stated' in the documents to which interested parties have access from the time of making the determination.[48] The Panel connected this interpretation to the ability for interested parties to challenge national authorities' determinations. It noted that 'without access to the disclosed factual basis and reasoning supporting the determination at least from the time of the final determination, interested parties and WTO Members would be unable to assess whether bringing a WTO dispute settlement complaint relating to the determination would be fruitful.'[49] Given the costs typically associated with making and defending WTO claims, particularly for developing country Members, the Panel viewed it as particularly significant that reasons be given for final determinations. As in *US – Steel Safeguards*, the duty to provide reasons was also an 'essential aspect of the requirements concerning dispute settlement and meaningful Panel review under the DSU and the AD Agreement.'[50] The reasoning as disclosed by national authorities, in other words, was essential as forming the basis of review by a WTO Panel.

The Panel took further support for its argument on reading a reasons requirement into Article 3.1 from Article 12 of the WTO Anti-Dumping Agreement. This provision more explicitly requires national authorities to distribute to interested parties a notice containing 'all relevant information on the matters of fact and law and reasons which have led to the imposition of final measures', as well as 'the reasons for acceptance or rejection of relevant arguments or claims made by the exporters and importers'.[51] For the Panel, Article 12 provided 'important context' for interpreting Article 3.1, indicating the significance attached by WTO Members to the provision of information about national administrative determinations.[52]

On appeal, however, the AB took a different view of the significance of Article 12, and of the width of the obligations expressed by Article 3.1. It preferred to keep what it saw as substantive obligations separate from obligations that it viewed as procedural. Thus, it found that Article 3.1 only dealt with the substantive obligations of WTO Members seeking to impose anti-dumping duties, regulating the evidence that Members were permitted to draw on in

---

48 *Thailand – Anti-Dumping Duties on Angles, Shapes and Sections of Iron or Non-Alloy Steel and H Beams from Poland* (28 September 2000) WT/DS122/R [7.143].

49 Ibid.

50 Ibid. at [7.149].

51 The reasons aspects of Article 12 of the AD Agreement appear not to have been considered in WTO dispute settlement cases, apart from the reference in *Thailand – H-Beams* discussed here.

52 *Thailand – H-Beams, supra* note 48 at [7.151].

making determinations.[53] By contrast, it said, Article 12 established 'procedural and due process obligations' that were certainly important, but could not be read into the substantive provisions of Article 3.1.[54] Since no specific claims of violation of Article 12 had been made in the case, the AB did not further comment on that provision and the rationales behind it. Therefore, while the AB in *Thailand – H-Beams* declined to confirm the Panel's analysis of the utility of reasons for rights of defence and for judicial review, it did not explicitly reject it either.

These cases are an indication in the WTO jurisprudence – and regardless of what the WTO might provide in the texts of its Agreements, in its media statements, its negotiations, etc. – that the WTO views itself, through its role of review, as an instrument of good governance. Irrespective of any effect on the quality of national decisions that might flow from imposing a reasons duty on trade authorities (as suggested by the first set of cases discussed), the WTO in these latter cases contends that reasons must be given in order to allow it to fulfil its designed role of international review. From this perspective, the transparent and reasoned decision-making processes that are essential to good governance in fact include the WTO itself, as one 'quasi-judicial' arm of a multi-level government, stretching from the domestic level to the international level.

Taken together, then, the cases on the duty to give reasons suggest that the WTO sees itself as having a dual role in terms of good governance. Firstly, it aims to enhance good governance directly at the national level, by requiring reasons and thus improving the quality of domestic decision-making. Secondly, it concurrently establishes an international review structure to provide a check on poor national decision-making, once again requiring reasons to support this structure.

16.4 Conclusion

The largely procedural requirements in WTO Agreements for transparency and reason-giving are perhaps seen as less serious targets for a dispute resolution proceeding than the WTO's substantive rules in areas such as import tariffs, dumping, subsidies, safeguards and technical and sanitary regulations. In addition, the relatively clear obligations in these areas to publish certain documents or take certain steps when making trade-related determinations might be thought to contrast with more contestable concepts such as 'like products',[55] 'public morals'[56] or 'exhaustible natural resources',[57] so prominent elsewhere in WTO case law and commentary. Given this, it may not be surprising that the case law interpreting transparency and reason-giving requirements in the WTO Agreements is not extensive.

---

53 *Thailand – Anti-Dumping Duties on Angles, Shapes and Sections of Iron or Non-Alloy Steel and H Beams from Poland* (5 April 2001) [106].

54 Ibid. at [110].

55 General Agreement on Tariffs and Trade 1947, 55 UNTS 194 [GATT] arts I:1 and III:4.

56 Ibid. at art. XX(a); General Agreement on Trade in Services, 1869 UNTS 183 art. XIV(a).

57 GATT, *supra* note 56 at art. XX(g).

Nevertheless, the cases reviewed in this chapter represent a modest but determined approach from the WTO to contribute to the principle of good governance in the area of trade. Wide interpretations of transparency requirements, combined with due process obligations founded on a commitment to improve both directly and indirectly the quality of national decision-making, indicate that WTO case law over the past two decades has provided support for sustainable development through the proactive application of elements of the principle of good governance.

17 The principle of integration in WTO/TRIPS jurisprudence

*Henning Grosse Ruse-Khan**

17.1 Introduction

The notion of sustainable development as a concept in international law has several connotations – as expressed in the International Law Association (ILA) Declaration of Principles of International Law Related to Sustainable Development.[1]

At its core is the principle of integration and reconciliation of economic, social and environmental objectives. In one of the most recognised trade and environment cases in the WTO, the WTO Appellate Body emphasised that the sustainable development objective 'must add colour, texture and shading to our interpretation of the Agreements annexed to the WTO Agreement'.[2] This includes the WTO Agreement on Trade Related Aspects of Intellectual Property Rights (TRIPS). With its articles 7 and 8, TRIPS contains a balancing objective and public interest principles as specific expressions of the principle of integration. In the Doha Declaration on TRIPS and Public Health, all WTO Members stressed the importance of these norms for interpreting TRIPS. Against this background, this chapter analyses the extent to which WTO case law concerning TRIPS has utilised these norms in addressing the manifold intersections between Intellectual Property (IP) protection and other economic, social and environmental concerns.

* This chapter is based on presentations at International Development Law Organisation (IDLO) conference on 'Sustainable Development Principles in the Decisions of International Courts and Tribunals (1992–2012)' (Rome 15–17 June 2011) and a seminar at the Centre for International Law (CIL) on 'The (Non)Use of Treaty Object and Purpose in IP Disputes in the WTO' (National University Singapore, 27 July 2011). The empirical research on the Panel- and Appellate Body reports has been conducted with the help of Anna Mattes and Joerg Hoffman. I am grateful for their support. All errors remain my responsibility.

1 ILA, 'Declaration of Principles of International Law Related to Sustainable Development', Resolution 3/2002 adopted at the 70th Conference of the International Law Association (New Delhi 2–6 April 2002) (9 August 2002) UN Doc A/CONF.199/8 [New Delhi Declaration] <http://www.cisdl.org/sustainable_development/pdf/NewDelhiDeclaration.pdf> accessed 22 August 2011.

2 *US – Import Prohibition of Certain Shrimp and Shrimp Products,* (Appellate Body Report) WT/DS58/AB/R (6 November 1998) para. 153.

The chapter begins with a short review on the principle of integration as the core of the concept of sustainable development. It then provides examples for linkages between the (international) regulation of IP and vital societal interests such as health, environment, trade and a knowledge society. In the following, the relevant treaty provisions addressing such linkages in the WTO law pertaining to IP are examined. The core of this chapter analyses in section 17.5 whether and how WTO Panels and the Appellate Body have, in interpreting the TRIPS Agreement, relied on articles 7 and 8 as primary textual expressions of the object and purpose of TRIPS. The main legal argument is that in the case of TRIPS, integration of other societal objectives functions primarily via treaty interpretation, based on the accepted principles of article 31 of the Vienna Convention on the Law of Treaties (VCLT), and with an important role for TRIPS' object and purpose. The latter is primarily embodied in the balancing objectives of article 7 and the public interest principles of article 8 TRIPS – which together represent IP-specific expressions of the sustainable development objective and its principle of integration. Against this background, Panels have a legal obligation to interpret TRIPS in light of both articles 7 and 8. The hypothesis is that Panels give insufficient, if any, role to the integration provisions of articles 7 and 8 in interpreting TRIPS. The empirical analysis from the first 20 years of TRIPS-related disputes confirms this. While there is only a comparable limited number of TRIPS cases (around seven per cent of all WTO complaints), the 12 reports issued addressed approximately 55 instances where TRIPS provisions or terms where subject to interpretation. In just over half of these were object and purpose addressed in any form; including approximately 15 instances where they have only been mentioned, but not applied. The remaining approximately 15 instances break down in only three cases where articles 7 and 8 have been applied; another three where they have been merely acknowledged; and 9 where other objectives (of TRIPS or its provisions) have been applied. This paints a picture of a quantitatively limited, and qualitatively rather arbitrary, use of TRIPS object and purpose in the interpretation exercise. However, with the high profile dispute over Australia's plain packaging laws underway, one might expect important clarifications on the role of the objectives and principles in TRIPS for reconciling economic interests and health policies.

17.2 The principle of integration as core of the sustainable development concept

For about 40 years now, the notion of integrating (economic and social) development concerns and the protection of the environment has found its expression in international legal instruments. As early as 1972 – and hence long before the term 'sustainable development' gained prominence in the famous Brundtland Report[3] – the Stockholm Declaration on the Human Environment

---

3 Report of the World Commission on Environment and Development, *Our Common Future*, UN Doc. A/42/427 [Brundtland Report].

urged that: "States should adopt an integrated and coordinated approach to their development planning so as to ensure that development is compatible with the need to protect and improve environment for the benefit of their population."[4]

About 20 years later, the 1992 Rio Declaration on Environment and Development[5] embodies a list of 27 principles, which, *inter alia*, focus on integration, and inter-relation of social and economic development and environmental protection.[6] Principle 4 emphasises the role of integration for achieving sustainable development,[7] and principle 25 nicely summarises the notion of integration in the following statement: "Peace, development and environmental protection are inter-dependent and indivisible". In 2002, the World Summit on Sustainable Development (WSSD) placed the notion of sustainable development in the centre of global attention as the main notion to resolve the environment/development dichotomy. The WSSD produced the Johannesburg Declaration on Sustainable Development[8] and the Johannesburg Plan of Implementation.[9] In the former, all participating states assumed:

> a collective responsibility to advance and strengthen the interdependent and mutually reinforcing pillars of sustainable development – economic development, social development and environmental protection – at the local, national, regional and global levels.[10]

4 Stockholm Declaration of the United Nations Conference on the Human Environment, UN Doc. A/Conf.48/14/Rev. 1(1973) [Stockholm Declaration on the Human Environment] principle 13. The Stockholm Declaration calls for such an integration of environmental concerns in development decision-making also in its principle 14 and addresses integrative aspects further in principles 2–5, 8, 9, 11, 12.

5 Report of the United Nations Conference on Environment and Development – Annex I: Rio Declaration on Environment and Development' [Rio Declaration on Environment and Development] (12 August 1992) UN Doc. A/CONF.151/26 vol. I <http://www.un.org/documents/ga/confl51/aconfl5126-1annex1.htm> accessed 22 August 2011.

6 Report of the United Nations Conference on Environment and Development – Annex I: Rio Declaration on Environment and Development (12 August 1992) UN Doc. A/CONF.151/26 vol. I <http://www.un.org/documents/ga/confl51/aconfl5126-1annex1.htm> accessed 22 August 2011.

7 Principle 4 states: 'In order to achieve sustainable development, environmental protection shall constitute an integral part of the development process and cannot be considered in isolation from it'.

8 Johannesburg Declaration on Sustainable Development, adopted at the 17th plenary meeting of the World Summit on Sustainable Development (4 September 2002) A/CONF.199/20 [Johannesburg Declaration] <http://www.un.org/esa/sustdev/documents/WSSD_POI_PD/English/POI_PD.htm> accessed 22 August 2011.

9 The Johannesburg Plan of Implementation <http://www.un.org/esa/sustdev/documents/WSSD_POI_PD/English/POIToc.htm> accessed 22 August 2011, builds on the achievements made since the Rio Summit and aims to expedite the realisation of the remaining goals. To this end, states committed themselves to undertaking concrete measures promoting the integration of the three components of sustainable development – economic development, social development and environmental protection – as interdependent and mutually reinforcing pillars.

10 Johannesburg Declaration, *supra* note 8 at 5.

In the same year, the ILA, based on the work of its Committee on Legal Aspects of Sustainable Development,[11] adopted a Declaration of Principles of International Law Related to Sustainable Development.[12] The Declaration, *inter alia*, contained 'the principle of integration and interrelationship, in particular in relation to human rights and social, economic and environmental objectives'. It considers this principle on integration as 'essential to the achievement of sustainable development' and states that all levels of governance and all sectors of society are encouraged to implement it.[13] The other six ILA principles – such as duty of states to ensure sustainable use of natural resources, the principle of equity and the eradication of poverty, or the precautionary approach to human health, natural resources and ecosystems – address specific economic, environmental and social aspects and balance those. Hence they are expressions of the overarching integration principle.[14]

Also in some of the most prominent decisions of international courts and tribunals on sustainable development, the notion of integration and reconciliation performed a central function. The concept of sustainable development played the role of balancing economic, social and environmental interest in the *Gabčíkovo – Nagymaros* case decided by the International Court of Justice (ICJ);[15] in the Arbitral Award under the auspices of the Permanent Court of Arbitration (PCA) regarding the *Iron Rhine ('Ijzeren Rijn') Railway*;[16] and in the reports of the WTO Dispute Settlement Panel and Appellate Body in the *US – Shrimp*[17] case. Therefore, decisions of courts and tribunals addressing the notion of sustainable development in international law confirm its main role as a principle of integration and reconciliation.[18] The WTO Appellate Body's report in the *US – Shrimp* dispute is of particular relevance since it concerned the operation of sustainable development as a part of the treaty objective of the WTO Agreements. As will be shown below, the approach taken by the Appellate Body already contains the main elements and appropriate guidance for giving effect to such an objective in the context of TRIPS and disputes relating to its implementation.

---

11 The work of the Committee, in particular its two reports, is online available at <http://www.ila-hq.org/en/committees/index.cfm/cid/25> accessed 22 August 2011.

12 New Delhi Declaration, *supra* note 1. For an analysis of the principles in the New Delhi Declaration see M.C. Cordonier Segger and A. Khalfan, *Sustainable Development Law: Principles, Practices and Prospects* (Oxford: OUP, 2004) 96 –171.

13 New Delhi Declaration, *supra* note 1 at para. 7.2.

14 See Henning Grosse Ruse-Khan, 'A Real Partnership for Development? Sustainable Development as Treaty Objective in European Economic Partnership Agreements and Beyond' (2010), vol. 13 (1) *J. Int'l Econ. L.* 139, at 147–8.

15 *Gabčíkovo-Nagymaros Project (Hungary/Slovakia)*, Judgment of 25 September 1997, ICJ Rep 1997, p. 7 <http://www.icj-cij.org/docket/files/92/7375.pdf> accessed 30 March 2012.

16 *Arbitration Regarding the Iron Rhine ('Ijzeren Rijn') Railway* (Belgium/Netherlands), PCA, Award of the Arbitral Tribunal (24 May 2005) vol. XXVII, 35 <http://www.pca-cpa.org/showpage.asp?pag_id=1155> accessed 22 August 2011.

17 See *US – Shrimp, supra* note 2; *US – Shrimp Recourse to Article 21.5 by Malaysia,* (Panel Report) WT/DS58/RW, adopted 15 June 2000.

18 See Grosse Ruse-Khan, *supra* note 14 at 148–50.

From this brief overview follows that basically all documents relating to sustainable development in international law emphasise the principle of integration and reconciliation. The ILA committee described it 'as the very backbone of the concept of sustainable development'[19] and others have identified it as a core principle inherent in that concept.[20] Already the Brundtland Report had explained that sustainable development requires the '*balanced reconciliation and integration of economic, environmental and social priorities*'.[21] This justifies the further analysis on WTO case-law concerning the interpretation of TRIPS to focus on the role of the integration principle. Before that, however, the next section indicates the significant linkages between the protection and enforcement of IP with other societal concerns – be they environmental, social or of economic nature.

17.3 Intellectual property linkages with social, environmental and economic concerns

The international protection of IP – in form of Agreements such as TRIPS – not only affects the global protection of interests of those who engage in the development and production of creative or innovative products and services. Its impact also extends to various economic, social, cultural or environmental objectives which WTO Member States pursue. The debate on patent protection for pharmaceutical products and access to life-saving drugs is probably the most commonly known example of international IP rules impacting on common societal interests (public health) as well as individual human rights (right to health).[22] A different,

---

19 ILA New Dehli Decleration, *supra* note 12 at 7.

20 See P. Sands, 'International Law in the Field of Sustainable Development' (1994) 65 *Brit. Ybk Int'l L.* 303, 336; Nico J. Schrijver, 'The Evolution of Sustainable Development in International Law: Inception, Meaning and Status' (2007) *Recueil des Cours* 217, 362.

21 M.C. Cordonier Segger and M. Gehring, 'Introduction' in M.C. Cordonier Segger and M. Gehring, eds., *Sustainable Development in World Trade Law* (The Hague: Kluwer, 2005) 1, at 5 (emphasis added). In the Brundtland Report, this key principle of 'merging environment and economics in decision making' appears, *inter alia*, as one of seven 'critical objectives' that follow from the principle of sustainable development, see Brundtland Report, *supra* note 3 at para. 72: 'The common theme throughout this strategy for sustainable development is the need to integrate economic and ecological considerations in decision making'.

22 On the TRIPS and public health debate see H. Hestermeyer, *Human Rights and the WTO – The Case of Patents and Access to Medicines* (Oxford: OUP, 2007); M. Varella, 'The WTO, Intellectual Property and Aids – Case Studies from Brazil and South Africa' (2004) JWIP 523; F. Abbott, 'The Doha Declaration on the TRIPS Agreement and Public Health: Lighting a Dark Corner at the WTO' (2002) 5 JIEL 469; D. Matthews, 'WTO Decision on Implementation of Paragraph 6 of the Doha Declaration on the TRIPS Agreement and Public Health: A Solution to the Access to Essential Medicines Problem?' (2004) 7 JIEL 73; for the human rights perspective see ECOSOC, 'The Impact of the Agreement on Trade Related Aspects of Intellectual Property Rights on Human Rights' (27 June 2001) E/CN.4/Sub.2/2001/13; UNHCR Sub-Commission on Human Rights, 'Intellectual property rights and human rights', res 2000/7; on the WTO 'response' see *Ministerial Conference*, 'Doha Declaration on the TRIPS Agreement and Public Health', WT/MIN(01)/DEC/2

more recent illustration is the tension between domestic plain packaging campaigns to address the health risks associated with smoking and the international (IP and investment) rules protecting the tobacco companies' trademarks against 'unjustified'[23] requirements limiting their use.[24] Beyond the TRIPS/Public Health paradigm, patent protection under TRIPS is argued to be in conflict with the Convention on Biological Diversity;[25] digital copyright rules potentially interfere with access to knowledge[26] or the protection of personal data and privacy;[27] trademarks can limit the freedom of expression;[28] seizing goods via border enforcement of IP rights may serve as a significant barrier to trade;[29]

(20 November 2001), as well as *General Council*, 'Decision of 30 August 2003', WT/L/540 and Corr.1 (1 September 2003), and *General Council*, 'Decision of 6 December 2005' WT/L/641 (8 December 2005).

23 See TRIPS art 20 which regulates domestic conditions for trademark use and makes this dependant on, *inter alia*, meeting a justifiability requirement.

24 T. Voon and A. Mitchell, 'Implications of WTO Law for Plain Packaging of Tobacco Products' in Andrew Mitchell, Tania Voon and Jonathan Liberman, eds., *Public Health and Plain Packaging of Cigarettes: Legal Issues* (Cheltenahm: Edward Elgar, 2012); University of Melbourne Legal Studies Research Paper No 554 <http://ssrn.com/abstract=1874593> accessed 30 September 2016.

25 TRIPS *Council Secretariat*, 'The relationship between the TRIPS Agreement and the Convention on Biological Diversity: Summary of Issues Raised and Points Made' (February 2006) IP/C/W/368/Rev.1 <http://www.wto.org/english/tratop_e/trips_e/ipcw368_e. pdf> accessed 21 December 2016; Commission on Intellectual Property Rights (CIPR), 'Integrating Intellectual Property and Development Policy' (London, 2002) ch 4, Traditional Knowledge, Access and Benefit Sharing <http://www.iprcommission.org/papers/pdfs/final_report/Ch4final.pdf> accessed 30 September 2016; M. Chouchena-Rojas, M.R. Muller, D. Vivas and S. Winkler, eds., 'Disclosure Requirements: Ensuring Mutual Supportiveness between the WTO TRIPS Agreement and the CBD' (Geneva: IUCN and ICTSD, 2005)) <http://www.iprsonline.org/resources/docs/Disclosure_req_book. pdf> accessed 30 September 2016; for a recent proposal to amend TRIPS in order to achieve coherence with the CBD see India, Brazil, *et al.* 'Communication on a Proposal to Amend TRIPS' (31 May 2006) WT/GC/W/564.

26 S. Dussollier, Y. Poullet and M. Buydens, 'Copyright and Access to Information in the Digital Environment' (UNESCO Study, Paris 17 July 2000) CII-2000/WS/5; H. Grosse Ruse-Khan, 'Access to Knowledge under the International Copyright Regime, the WIPO Development Agenda and the European Communities' new External Trade and IP Policy' in E. Derclaye, ed., *Research Handbook on the Future of EU Copyright* (Cheltenham: Edward Elgar Publishing, 2009) 575–613.

27 On the issue of protecting personal data and enforcing IP rights see the European Court of Justice (ECJ) judgment of 29 January 2008 in the Case C275/06 *Productores de Música de España Promusicae v Telefónica de España* [2008] ECR I-271, considering that the European law 'does not require member states to lay down an obligation to disclose personal data in the context of civil proceedings'. See also O. Vincents, 'When Rights Clash Online: The Tracking of P2P Copyright Infringements vs the EC Personal Data Directive' (2007) 16 *Int'l J. L. Info. Tech.* 270–96.

28 A. Rahmatian, 'Trade Marks and Human Rights' in P. Torremanns, ed., *Intellectual Property and Human Rights* (The Hague: Kluwer, 2008) 335–58.

29 A prime example here are shipments of generic drugs legally produced in India and destined to Brazil and other developing countries. In transit through ports in the EU, several shipments were detained and some subsequently sent back or destroyed on the basis of alleged patent

and certain exercises of IP rights, especially in licensing agreements, may be anti-competitive or inhibit the transfer of technology.[30]

Furthermore, some of the most relevant contemporary problems facing the global community today link or 'intersect' with IP protection. The current attempts to tackle climate change by strengthening a global regime for the reduction of carbon emissions under the United Nations Framework Convention on Climate Change (UNFCCC)[31], *inter alia*, focus on the transfer of carbon-reducing, 'green' technologies to developing countries. IP protection here can function as an incentive for research, development and production of such technologies, but it may also severely limit the transfer and dissemination of these technologies.[32] In the same vein, ensuring food security is an issue on which IP protection certainly has an impact. Patent and especially plant variety protection can 'incentivise' innovations in agricultural production and offer new technologies, tailored crops or other food-securing solutions to developing countries – while at the same time serving as a potential barrier for the re-use of harvested seeds, as well as the wide distribution of IP protected seeds, plant genes and even crops in general.

These examples for linkages between IP protection and other economic, social and environmental concerns illustrate the significant potential for operating the integration principle. As the next section shows, WTO law in general and TRIPS in particular contain a strong legal basis for such an integrative approach in the interpretation and implementation of IP obligations in the WTO.

17.4 WTO/TRIPS treaty provisions on integration

In the preamble of the 1994 Marrakesh Agreement Establishing the WTO (WTO Agreement), the Contracting Parties recognised:

> that their relations in the field of trade and economic endeavour should be conducted with a view to raising standards of living, ensuring full employment and a large and steadily growing volume of real income and effective demand, and expanding the production of and trade in goods and services, while allowing for the optimal use of the world's resources in accordance with the *objective of sustainable development*, seeking both to protect and preserve the environment and to enhance the means for doing so in a manner consistent with their respective needs and concerns at different levels of economic development.[33]

---

infringements in the transit country; see H. Grosse Ruse-Khan and T. Jaeger, 'Policing Patents Worldwide? EC Border Measures against Transiting Generic Drugs under EC- and WTO Intellectual Property Regimes' (2009) 40 *Int'l Rev. Intell. Prop. & Comp. L.* (IIC) 502.

30   See arts 8 (2), 40 TRIPS as well as the explicit link made in the first of the new EC–ACP regional trade agreements, art 142 (2) of the EC–CARIFORUM Economic Partnership Agreement (EPA).

31   United Nations Framework Convention on Climate Change (UNFCCC), 1771 UNTS 107 <http://unfccc.int/resource/docs/convkp/conveng.pdf> accessed 22 August 2011.

32   For some emerging work on the role of IP in the transfer of 'green' technologies see <http://ictsd.net/programmes/energy/technology/> accessed 22 August 2011.

33   Marrakesh Agreement Establishing the World Trade Organization (WTO) (emphasis added) <http://www.wto.org/english/docs_e/legal_e/legal_e.htm> accessed 23 August 2011. This

WTO Members further confirmed the importance of this objective in the 2001 Doha Declaration initiating the Doha Development Round of trade negotiations by reaffirming their 'commitment to the objective of sustainable development, as stated in the Preamble to the Marrakesh Agreement'.[34]

A prominent example of the operation of this sustainable development objective in WTO law can be found in the *US – Shrimp* dispute concerning the WTO consistency of US trade restrictions imposed on shrimp imports in order to protect sea turtles which may get caught during shrimp fishing. Here, the WTO Appellate Body had to resolve the issue whether sea turtles fall under the general exception provision of article XX(g) GATT which deals with 'exhaustible natural resources'. It referred to the preamble of the WTO Agreement and noted:

> that this language demonstrates a recognition by WTO negotiators that optimal use of the world's resources should be made in accordance with the *objective of sustainable development*. As this preambular language reflects the intentions of negotiators of the WTO Agreement, we believe it *must add colour, texture and shading to our interpretation of the agreements annexed to the WTO Agreement*, in this case, the GATT 1994.[35]

The Appellate Body also noted that '[t]his concept has been generally accepted as *integrating economic and social development and environmental protection*.'[36] But how should the principle of integration 'add colour' to the interpretation of WTO law? Based on the general role for a treaties' object and purpose in the interpretation exercise,[37] the Appellate Body explained that:

> where the meaning imparted by the text itself is equivocal or inconclusive, or where confirmation of the correctness of the reading of the text itself is desired, light from the object and purpose of the treaty as a whole may usefully be sought.[38]

Hence, sustainable development as one element of the multiple objectives of the WTO Agreement guided the Appellate Body's interpretation of the article XX(g) GATT term 'exhaustible natural resources' to include the protection of living species such as sea turtles.

language differs significantly from the original GATT preamble that encouraged GATT contracting parties to engage in a 'full use of the resources of the world'.

34 See WTO *Doha Ministerial Declaration*, WT/MIN (01)/DEC/1 (14 November 2001) para. 6 <http://www.wto.org/english/thewto_e/minist_e/min01_e/mindecl_e.htm> accessed 6 May 2010.

35 WTO Appellate Body Report, *US – Shrimp*, *supra* note 2 at para. 153, (emphasis added).

36 Ibid. at para. 129 (fn 107), (emphasis added).

37 See 'The International Law Commission's Commentary on arts 27 to 29 of its Final Draft Articles on the Law of Treaties', *Ybk Int'l L. Comm'n* (1966), vol. II, 221. For a more detailed analysis on the role of the sustainable development objective for treaty interpretation, see H. Grosse Ruse-Khan, 'A Real Partnership for Development? Sustainable Development as Treaty Objective in European Economic Partnership Agreements and Beyond' (2010) 13 (1) JIEL 139, at 158–67.

38 WTO Appellate Body Report, *US – Shrimp*, *supra* note 2 at para. 114.

The WTO Agreement's preamble and its reference to the sustainable development objective informs not only the appropriate understanding of GATT provisions, but the interpretation of all other agreements annexed to the WTO Agreement. As one of the objectives of the overarching WTO Agreement, it thus also applies in the context of TRIPS. TRIPS itself, however, contains primarily two provisions, which express its object and purpose: according to article 7, which is entitled 'objectives':

> the protection and enforcement of intellectual property rights should contribute to the promotion of technological innovation and to the transfer and dissemination of technology, to the mutual advantage of producers and users of technological knowledge and in a manner conducive to social and economic welfare, and to a balance of rights and obligations.

In essence, this provision encourages an interpretation and implementation of the IP protection TRIPS provides in a balanced, proportional manner contributing to both social and economic welfare.[39] Furthermore, under section one of article 8, describing the 'principles' of TRIPS:

> Members may, in formulating or amending their laws and regulations, adopt measures necessary to protect public health and nutrition, and to promote the public interest in sectors of vital importance to their socio-economic and technological development, provided that such measures are consistent with the provisions of this Agreement.

In a nutshell, this provision advocates an understanding of individual TRIPS provisions – to the extent allowed by the provision's ordinary meaning and its interpretative context – which permits measures necessary to protect public health as well as the promotion of public interests.[40] For the specific linkage between public health and patent protection for medicines, WTO Members have confirmed this understanding in para. 4 of the Doha Declaration on TRIPS and Public Health: they 'affirm that the *Agreement can and should be interpreted and implemented in a manner supportive* of WTO Members' *right to protect public health* and, in particular, to promote access to medicines for all.'[41] To achieve this, WTO Members in para. 5 (a) then emphasise as one of the main tools that all TRIPS provisions

---

39   Article 7 calls for balancing (1) incentives for the 'promotion of technological innovation' with measures for 'the transfer and dissemination of technology'; (2) the interests of 'producers and users of technological knowledge' and, more generally, (3) WTO members' 'rights and obligations'. For a more detailed analysis on the TRIPS objective under art 7 see H. Grosse Ruse-Khan, 'Proportionality and Balancing within the Objectives of Intellectual Property Protection', in P. Torremanns, ed., *Intellectual Property and Human Rights* (The Netherlands: Kluwer, 2008) 161, at 173–78.

40   For a detailed discussion on the ambiguous role of art 8 TRIPS, see H. Grosse Ruse-Khan, 'Policy Space for Domestic Public Interests Measures under TRIPS' (2009) South Centre Research Paper Series No 22 <http://ssrn.com/abstract=1542542> accessed 30 September 2016; P. Yu, 'The Objectives and Principles of the TRIPs Agreement' (2009) 46 *Hous. L. Rev.* 797 <http://ssrn.com/abstract=1398746> accessed 30 September 2016.

41   Doha Declaration on TRIPS and Public Health, *supra* note 22 (emphasis added).

'*shall be read in the light of the object and purpose of the Agreement as expressed, in particular, in its objectives and principles*'.[42] An interpretation based on articles 7 and 8 of TRIPS therefore is the primary (and horizontally applicable)[43] instrument to address linkages between IP and other societal concerns – such as access to medicines. This in turn highlights the overlap between the sustainable development objective in the WTO preamble and the specific TRIPS articles 7 and 8. In essence, both incorporate the integration and reconciliation of economic, social and environmental concerns. Articles 7 and 8 TRIPS hence must be understood as IP-specific expressions of the integration principle. These provisions therefore enhance the legitimacy and importance of an integrative approach to TRIPS interpretation in order to address the linkages between IP protection and other societal concerns.

In sum, the balancing objectives set out in article 7 TRIPS and the public interest principles of article 8(1) TRIPS shall guide the interpretation of every individual TRIPS provision – as much as the general rules of treaty interpretation, in particular the ordinary meaning of the individual treaty terms, allow. This means that, especially in cases of ambiguity, of broad and open treaty language where more than one interpretation is possible, TRIPS provisions can and must be interpreted in accordance with the balancing objective of article 7, giving effect to public interest concerns expressed in article 8.[44] However, giving effect to the objectives and principles of TRIPS, as well as the general sustainable development aim of the WTO preamble, depends on the role of other sources for treaty interpretation. One cannot disregard or override unambiguous language in individual TRIPS provisions,[45] for example on the scope of exclusive rights of copyright, trademark or patent holders in articles 11, 16 and 28 TRIPS.[46] The ordinary meaning of a treaty provision and its context[47] are equally important; with the ordinary meaning serving as a logical starting point for interpretative exercise.[48] Adding 'colour, texture and shading'[49] via the treaties' objectives then

42 Ibid. (emphasis added).

43 Compared to the other TRIPS flexibilities mentioned in para. 5 of the Doha Declaration, an interpretation based on art 7 and 8 affects not only one, but *all* TRIPS provisions.

44 See C. Correa, *Trade Related Aspects of Intellectual Property Rights* (Oxford: OUP, 2007) at 109; ICTSD and UNCTAD, 'Resource Book on TRIPS and Development: An authoritative and practical guide to the TRIPS Agreement' (Geneva, 2005) Part One, ch 6 section 6.

45 See J. Pauwelyn, 'WTO Dispute Settlement: Of Sovereign Interests, Private Rights and Public Goods' in K. Maskus and J. Reichmann, *International Public Goods and Transfer of Technology* (Cambridge: CUP, 2005) at 828.

46 Even though one may find individual terms within these provisions which are open enough for an interpretation which – in appropriate scenarios – gives effect to public interest considerations – see e.g. 'product *obtained directly*' by a patented process in art 28 (2) or '*likelihood of confusion*' in art 16 (1) TRIPS.

47 Context not only includes the complete treaty text including its preamble and annexes but also additional and subsequent agreements and agreed practice on the interpretation and application of treaty provisions; cf Vienna Convention on the Law of Treaties, 1155 UNTS 331 (1969) at arts 31(2), 31(3).

48 It is however 'to be not determined in the abstract, but in the context of the treaty and in light of its objective and purpose' see *Ybk Int'l L. Comm.*, *supra* note 37 at 221; see also M. Lennard, 'Navigating by the Stars: Interpreting WTO Agreements' (2002) 5 (1) JIEL 17, 29.

49 WTO Appellate Body Report, *US – Shrimp*, *supra* note 2 at para. 152.

is a secondary, corrective step[50] whose importance depends on the strength and concreteness of ordinary meaning and context.

Therefore, an explicit and plain wording on how to protect the economic interests of right holders (e.g. the obligation to grant 20 years of patent protection, under article 33 TRIPS) cannot be overcome by the balancing principles in articles 7, and 8 TRIPS or the WTO preamble – even if public health concerns might call for a significant shortening of protection (e.g. to *10* or *15* years in order to encourage generic competition). The decisive question then is how much weight can and should be attached to the objectives in the process of interpretation? Subject to the individual circumstances at hand, the following general guiding principle applies: the more specific the ordinary meaning in the treaties' context is, the less room there is for a significant impact of any modification by the treaties' object and purpose. The more ambiguous, indefinite and multi-layered a provision's common understanding in relation to the treaty is, the more it needs further determination and concretisation by the treaties' objective. Thus, provisions incorporating *broad and open legal concepts* which cannot rely on significant concretisation from their context will not only lend themselves to, but demand, an interpretation which draws heavily on the object and purpose of the international agreement at stake.[51]

The main legal argument here developed is that in case of TRIPS, integration of other societal concerns functions primarily via treaty interpretation, based on the accepted principles of article 31 VCLT, and with an important role for TRIPS' object and purpose. The latter is primarily embodied in the balancing objectives of article 7 and the public interest principles of article 8 TRIPS – which together represent IP-specific expressions of the sustainable development objective and its principle of integration. Against this background, WTO adjudicators have a strong mandate to interpret TRIPS in light of articles 7 and 8 TRIPS. The hypothesis to be verified or falsified in the next section is that they so far have given insufficient, if any, role to the integration provisions of articles 7 and 8 TRIPS in interpreting the Agreement.

17.5 IP-related jurisprudence in the WTO

The WTO has been praised for its effective and relatively quick mechanism of settling disputes amongst WTO Members.[52] It is generally considered to be one of the cornerstones of the multilateral trade order. The system deals with

---

50 I. Sinclair, 'The Vienna Convention on the Law of Treaties', 2nd edn (Manchester: Manchester University Press, 1984) at 130.

51 See Alexander Orakhelashvili, *The Interpretation of Acts and Rules in Public International Law* (Oxford: OUP, 2008) at 344–45; and in the context of the sustainable development objective, see H. Grosse Ruse–Khan, 'A Real Partnership for Development? Sustainable Development as Treaty Objective in European Economic Partnership Agreements and Beyond' (2010) 13 (1) JIEL 139, 162–67.

52 See generally A. Loewenfeld, 'Remedies Along with Rights: Institutional Reforms in the New GATT' (1994) 88 AJIL 477–88.

disputes concerning the rights and obligations of WTO Members under the WTO Agreements and is governed by the WTO Understanding on Rules and Procedures Governing the Settlement of Disputes (DSU)[53] and the specific dispute settlement provisions in other WTO agreements. According to article 64 TRIPS, disputes over the consistency of domestic measures of WTO Members with TRIPS obligations are also governed by the DSU.[54] Disputes are initiated by claims brought by WTO Member States against other WTO Members. After initial consultations (article 4 DSU), the complainant can request the establishment of a Panel[55] (articles 6–8 DSU), which is charged to objectively assess the facts of the case and 'the applicability of and conformity with the relevant covered agreements' (article 11 DSU). The Panel prepares a report, which includes its findings on the consistency of the domestic measure at stake and submits this report to the Dispute Settlement Body (DSB)[56] for adoption (article 16 DSU). The Panel report is automatically adopted, unless all WTO Members in the DSB agree not to adopt it[57] or one of the parties files an appeal to the WTO Appellate Body (article 16 (4) DSU). The Appellate Body[58] reviews cases on issues of law covered in the Panel report and submits its report to the DSB (articles 17, 18 DSU) where again it is automatically adopted unless all WTO Members disagree. To ensure compliance with the Panel and Appellate Body reports, the DSU foresees – as a last resort – the right of the complainant to retaliate against the non-complying member by suspending an equivalent amount of WTO obligations (article 22 DSU).

In a nutshell, article 3 (2) of the DSU nicely summarises the main role and purpose of the WTO dispute settlement system. It provides:

> The dispute settlement system of the WTO is a central element in providing security and predictability to the multilateral trading system. The Members recognize that it serves to preserve the rights and obligations of Members under the covered agreements, and to clarify the existing provisions of those agreements in accordance with customary rules of interpretation of public

---

53 See Understanding on Rules and Procedures Governing the Settlement of Disputes, Annex 2 of the Marrakesh Agreement Establishing the World Trade Organisation, (1994) 33 ILM 1197 *et seq*, in force since 1 January 1995 <http://www.wto.org/english/docs_e/legal_e/28-dsu.pdf>.

54 Technically, art 64 (1) refers to 'Articles XXII and XXIII of GATT 1994 as elaborated and applied by the Dispute Settlement Understanding'. The moratorium in art 64 (2) TRIPS to exclude so called non-violation and situation complaints has so far been extended so that these types of complaints continue not to apply to TRIPS.

55 Panels are composed of three independent experts according to the procedure set forth in art 8 DSU.

56 The DSB is the primary organ of the DSU and consists of representatives of all WTO members (art 2 DSU).

57 This so-called 'negative consensus principle' applies to all main decisions of the DSB and hence ensures that the formally member-driven process nevertheless leads to quick and rule-based decisions made by independent experts.

58 The Appellate Body is composed of seven persons, three of whom serve on a case.

international law. Recommendations and rulings of the DSB cannot add to or diminish the rights and obligations provided in the covered agreements.[59]

17.5.1 Empirical analysis

In the following, the empirical data about TRIPS-related cases under the DSU will be presented in the wider context of WTO dispute settlement. Then, the methodology applied for identifying the reliance of Panels and the Appellate Body on articles 7 and 8 TRIPS (as expressions of the integration principle) will be described and the main findings discussed.

As of March 2015, 490 complaints have been brought to the WTO dispute settlement system.[60] Of those, 34 cases concern, *inter alia*,[61] the TRIPS Agreement.[62] Since 2009 however, no reports have been issued – while the plain packaging dispute that has generated five separate complaints which are heard by one panel is likely to be decided not before later in 2017. For that reason, the analysis presented here focuses on the first 15 years of WTO dispute settlement. Other empirical analysis suggests that in the 1995–2010 period, the main bulk of TRIPS cases fall in first five years (20 cases in 1995–1999), with a constant decline since (only one complaint in 2005–2009; and two, currently not further pursued, complaints brought in 2010).[63] Only about seven per cent of all WTO complaints hence raise TRIPS issues. Those complaints dealing with TRIPS led to nine Panel reports; and of these three were appealed resulting in three Appellate Body reports concerning TRIPS. Contrasted with an average of around 53 per cent of all complaints, which move to the 'Panel-stage',[64] only about 30 per cent of all TRIPS cases are brought to a Panel, which engages in a judicial analysis. More than two-thirds of all TRIPS complaints hence are resolved at the consultation stage.[65] And while usually on average 70 per cent of all Panel reports are appealed,[66] only 33 per cent (three of nine) Panel reports on TRIPS matters reach the Appellate Body.

---

59   DSU, *supra* note 56.
60   For a list of cases, see <http://www.wto.org/english/tratop_e/dispu_e/dispu_status_e.htm> accessed 19 March 2015.
61   One must emphasise that one complaint may raise violations of more than one WTO Agreement.
62   For a list of the 34 cases which cite the TRIPS Agreement in the request for consultations, see <http://www.wto.org/english/tratop_e/dispu_e/dispu_agreements_index_e.htm?id=A26#selected_agreement> accessed 19 March 2015.
63   K. Leitner and S. Lester, 'WTO Dispute Settlement 1995–2010 – A Statistical Analysis' (2011) 14 JIEL 191, at table 5. Compare however the WTO list of TRIPS cases, *supra* note 62 which list one more case in the 2005–2009 period. In that case however, no decision in substance was made on any TRIPS issue.
64   J. Pauwelyn, 'The Dog that Barked but Didn't Bite: 15 Years of Intellectual Property Disputes at the WTO' (2010) 1(2) *J. Int'l Disp. Settlem.* 389, 393.
65   As it appears, also the most recent cases brought in 2010 will be settled without the establishment of a Panel; see Government of India Press Release, 'India EU Reach an Understanding on Issue of Seizure of Indian Generic Drugs in Transit' (28 July 2011) <http://pib.nic.in/newsite/erelease.aspx?relid=73554> accessed 30 September 2016.
66   Pauwelyn, *supra* note 64 at 394.

Table 17.1

Number of complaints from 01 1995 – 08 2011	Complaints raising (inter alia) TRIPS issues	Panel Reports on TRIPS issues	Appellate Body Reports on TRIPS issues
426	29	9	3

There are hence a total of 12 reports by Panels and the Appellate Body dealing with the TRIPS Agreement, which serve as basis for analysing the number of instances when articles 7 and 8 TRIPS were resorted to in the process of treaty interpretation. The following methodology then has been adopted for analysing the use of these two provisions (as TRIPS-specific embodiments of the integration principle):

(1) All 12 TRIPS-related reports are analysed for the number on provisions or terms which have been subject to interpretation by the Panels or the Appellate Body;

(2) In a second step, the 12 reports (including the main arguments of the parties) are scanned by using electronic search tools for passages addressing the following issues:

    a   articles 7 and/or 8 TRIPS (objectives and principles)

    b   the WTO preamble (especially its sustainable development objective);

(3) To contrast this result with reliance on other factors affecting treaty interpretation, further electronic searches look for the number of instances when the term 'object' and/or 'purpose' has been used for purpose of treaty interpretation.

The analysis concerning point (1) reveals that in the 12 TRIPS-related reports a total number of 55 TRIPS provisions or terms have been subject to interpretation by the Panels or the Appellate Body.[67] Of those 55 instances of interpretation, in

---

67 Broken down to the individual Panel reports, the following picture emerges: *India – Patent Protection for Pharmaceutical and Agricultural Chemical Products (US)*, (Panel Report) WT/DS50/RW (5 September 1997): five instances of interpretation; *India – Patent Protection for Pharmaceutical and Agricultural Chemical Products (US* (Appellate Body Report*))* WT/DS50/AB/R (19 December 1997): four instances; *Indonesia – Certain Measures Affecting the Automobile Industry* (Panel Report), WT/DS59/RW (2 July 1998): zero instances (the Panel did not engage in a substantive interpretative analysis of TRIPS as the case was decided on other grounds); *India – Patent Protection for Pharmaceutical and Agricultural Chemical Products* (EC (Panel Report)), WT/DS79/RW (24 August 1998): two instances; *Canada – Patent Protection of Pharmaceutical Products* (Panel Report), WT/DS114/RW (17 March 2000): four instances; *US – Section 110 (5) of the US Copyright Act* (Panel Report), WT/DS160/RW (15 June 2000): five instances; *Canada – Term of Patent Protection* (Panel Report), WT/DS170/RW (15 May 2000): five instances; *Canada – Term of Patent Protection* (Appellate Body Report), WT/DS170/AB/R (18 September 2000) (DS 170): five instances; *US – Section 211 Omnibus Appropriations*

30 cases the interpretation addressed object and purpose – either of the treaty or, in some instances, of the specific provision under interpretation. This includes 15 cases with the mere mentioning of object and purpose of a treaty as relevant for the interpretation exercise – without, however, any further discussion on what the objective of TRIPS may be and how it affects the appropriate understanding of the provision under interpretation.

Regarding the use of article 7 and/or 8 TRIPS as treaty objective in comparison to other objectives relied upon in the interpretation exercise, the following picture emerges:

(1) Application of articles 7 and/or 8 TRIPS: three instances
(2) Mere acknowledgement of articles 7 and/or 8 TRIPS as object and purpose (but without use/application): three instances
(3) Application/use of other objectives:

    a   of TRIPS as a treaty: six instances
    b   of individual provisions or sections of TRIPS: three instances

(4) Mere acknowledgements of treaty object and purpose: 15 instances.

17.5.1.1 Application of Articles 7 and 8 TRIPS

Looking at the three cases where articles 7 and/or 8 TRIPS have been applied in more detail, one finds that in only one of these instances articles 7 and 8 have in fact been used as treaty objectives which function to integrate other societal concerns in the interpretation exercise. In the *Canada – Patents* dispute, two exceptions in the Canadian patent law relating to pharmaceutical patents and the market-entry of generic competitors were scrutinised under TRIPS provisions which contain various open and ambiguous terms that invite an interpretation based on articles 7 and 8. In addition, this is one of the few WTO disputes concerning access to medicines which were decided in adjudication.[68] Although Canada's arguments relied strongly on these provisions as treaty objectives, the Panel in the end did not allow articles 7 and 8 to affect the interpretative result for any of the individual TRIPS terms subject to interpretation. Given the particular importance of this case for the operation of articles 7 and 8, the arguments of the parties and the Panel will be analysed in more detail in section 17.5.2 below.

Act of 1998 (Panel Report)), WT/DS176/RW (6 August 2001): seven instances; *US – Section 211 Omnibus Appropriations Act of 1998* (Appellate Body Report), WT/DS176/AB/R (2 January 2002): six instances; *EC – Protection for Trademarks and Geographical Indications for Agricultural Products and Foodstuffs* (Panel Report), WT/DS290/RW (15 March 2005): six instances; *China – Measures affecting the Protection and Enforcement of Intellectual Property Rights* (Panel Report), WT/DS362/RW (26 January 2009): six instances.

68 The other one being the *India – Patents* case which dealt with India's obligation to provide a so called 'mail-box' system for receiving pharmaceutical patent applications during the years after 1995 (while the transition periods to fully introduce product patent protection for pharmaceuticals were still running).

The second instance concerns the so-called *US – Havana Club* dispute.[69] Here, the European Community (EC) complained about prohibitions in US law concerning the registration or renewal in the US of a trademark, if it was previously abandoned by a trademark owner whose business and assets have been confiscated under Cuban law. Dealing with competing business interests, the dispute does not focus on the balance between economic, social and/or environmental objectives. In relation to article 7, the Panel acknowledged the interpretative role of this provision as expressing the object and purpose of TRIPS, but primarily understood it as a call for the good faith implementation of TRIPS. The Panel stated:

> Moreover, Article 7 of the TRIPS Agreement states that one of the objectives is that "[t]he protection and enforcement of intellectual property rights should contribute . . . to a balance of rights and obligations." We consider this expression to be a form of the good faith principle. The Appellate Body in *United States–Shrimps* stated that this principle "controls the exercise of rights by states. One application of this principle, the application widely known as the doctrine of *abus de droit*, prohibits the abusive exercise of a state's rights and enjoins that whenever the assertion of a right "impinges on the field covered by [a] treaty obligation, it must be exercised bona fide, that is to say reasonably." (. . .) Members must therefore implement the provisions of the TRIPS Agreement in a manner consistent with the good faith principle enshrined in Article 7 of the TRIPS Agreement.[70]

The last instance is one where only articles 8(1) TRIPS has been applied in the *EC – Geographical Indications* dispute which relates to the EC's system of protecting geographical indications (GIs) for agricultural products and foodstuffs. Here, the US and Australia contended that the relevant EC regulations do not provide national treatment with respect to geographical indications and do not provide sufficient protection to pre-existing trademarks that are similar or identical to a geographical indication. The Panel agreed that the EC regulation violates national treatment obligations by demanding, for foreign right holders and products, equivalent GI protection for EC right holders and products in order to obtain GI protection in the EC. It relied on article 8(1) TRIPS in order to explain the absence from the TRIPS Agreement of a general exception provision – such as GATT article XX – which could otherwise justify national treatment violations. According to the Panel, the public interest principles embodied in article 8(1) TRIPS:

> reflect the fact that the agreement does not generally provide for the grant of positive rights to exploit or use certain subject matter, but rather provides for the grant of negative rights to prevent certain acts. This

---

69 *US – Section 211 Omnibus Appropriations Act of 1998*, WT/DS176 (in the following: *US – Havana Club*.

70 *US – Havana Club, supra* note 69 at para. 8.57.

fundamental feature of intellectual property protection inherently grants Members freedom to pursue legitimate public policy objectives since many measures to attain those public policy objectives lie outside the scope of intellectual property rights and do not require an exception under the TRIPS Agreement.[71]

In essence, the Panel used article 8(1) to explain the absence of a general exception provision in TRIPS with the limited scope of IP rights. These are negative rights to prohibit others from the (commercial) use of, for example, a patented drug – but no positive rights to make or sell these drugs on a market without, for example, obtaining regulatory approval or outside the limits set by marketing regulations. While this is an important insight that reveals a critical balance between IP protection and the pursuit of other public policy objectives such as health or the environment, article 8(1) did not function as interpretative device to guide the understanding of TRIPS provisions.

17.5.1.2 Mere acknowledgement of Articles 7 and/or 8 TRIPS as TRIPS object and purpose

Next to these three cases where articles 7 and/or 8 have been applied, there are another three instances where Panels or the Appellate Body have acknowledged them as expressing the object and purpose of TRIPS, but did not apply these provisions for interpretative purposes. The first instance again concerns the *Canada – Patents* dispute[72] and will be dealt with in greater detail in section 17.5.2 below. The second one can be found in the Panel decision on the *US – Havana Club* case. Here, the Panel asserts that the obligation to make certain signs eligible for trademark protection under article 15 TRIPS implies that such signs must be protectable: any other understanding 'would be meaningless and inconsistent with the objectives of the TRIPS Agreement as set out in the preamble and article 7 of the TRIPS Agreement.'[73] The subsequent arguments are then based on the interpretative context of article 15 – with no further discussion on TRIPS' object and purpose.

The third instance of mere acknowledgement of articles 7 and 8 occurred in the *Canada – Patent Term* dispute which deals with rather technical questions on the appropriate calculation of the length of protection for patents granted before TRIPS entered into force. In an important concluding statement the Appellate Body held that:

71 *EC – GIs, supra* note 67 at para. 7.246.
72 The Panel acknowledged that 'both the goals and the limitations stated in Articles 7 and 8.1 must obviously be borne in mind' when interpreting art 30 TRIPS – as well as 'other provisions of the TRIPS Agreement which indicate its object and purposes'; see *Canada – Patents, supra* note 67 at para. 7.26.
73 *US – Havana Club, supra* note 69 at para. 8.49. Given the equation of 'meaningless' with inconsistency with art 7, the Panel's argument seems to reflect its understanding of art 7 as an expression of the good faith principle.

The findings in this appeal do not in any way prejudge the applicability of Article 7 or Article 8 of the *TRIPS Agreement* in possible future cases with respect to measures to promote the policy objectives of the WTO Members that are set out in those Articles. Those Articles still await appropriate interpretation.[74]

The statement is placed right before the report's conclusion as an *obiter dictum* indicating the relevance of articles 7 and 8 for TRIPS disputes on domestic measures promoting public interests. The reference to the policy objectives set out in articles 7 and 8 indicates that those provisions operate to balance objectives such as health or environmental protection with the IP protection TRIPS requires. It hence serves as an important acknowledgement by the highest adjudicative body of the WTO about the role of articles 7 and 8 for a balanced interpretation and implementation of TRIPS and underlines their character as TRIPS-specific expressions of the principle of integration.

17.5.1.3 Application of other objectives and mere acknowledgement of object and purpose

In contrast to the six cases applying or acknowledging articles 7 and 8 as objectives, there are in total nine instances where other goals or principles were used as expressing object and purpose relevant for treaty interpretation. They can be grouped into three cases where the objectives of a specific TRIPS provision have been relied upon, and six instances where the object and purpose of TRIPS as a whole were applied. As to the latter, Panels and the Appellate Body have considered:

(1) 'the need to promote effective and adequate protection of intellectual property rights'[75];
(2) the need for effective protection for pharmaceutical innovations 'as expressed in article 70:8 TRIPS'[76];
(3) the non-discriminatory treatment of foreign right holders as compared to nationals (national treatment)[77];

---

74 *Canada – Patent Term*, supra note 67 at para. 101.

75 See *India – Patents (US)*, supra note 67 at para. 101, which quotes the preamble to the TRIPS Agreement as evidence for this objective.

76 See *India – Patents (EC)*, supra note 67 at paras 7.38–7.39 which states '*In order to achieve the object and purpose of the TRIPS Agreement, as expressed in Article 70.8*, there must be a mechanism to preserve the novelty of pharmaceutical and agricultural chemical inventions which are currently outside the scope of product patent protection and the priority of applications claiming their protection, for the purposes of determining their eligibility for protection by patents after the expiry of the transitional period' (emphasis added).

77 See WTO Panel Report, *EC – GI*, supra note 67 at para. 7.235 where the Panel observed 'The object and purpose of the TRIPS Agreement depends on the obligation in Article 1.3 to accord the treatment provided for in the Agreement to the nationals of other Members, including national treatment under Article 3.1. That object and purpose would be severely undermined if a Member could avoid its obligations by simply according treatment to its own nationals on the basis of close

(4) 'the provision of adequate standards and principles concerning the availability, scope, use and enforcement of trade-related intellectual property rights'[78];

(5) 'minimum standards concerning the availability, scope and use of intellectual property rights'[79]; and

(6) 'a minimum set of procedures and remedies that judicial, border and other competent authorities must have available to them'[80].

These 'objectives' all certainly represent important aims and principles of, or *reason d'être*, for TRIPS. They often find additional justification in its preamble – a place where one can expect the expressions of the object and purpose of a treaty. However, as TRIPS does contain a treaty provision explicitly entitled as 'Objectives', this must, at least together with the preamble, inform the understanding of TRIPS. The fact that in none of the instances above any further reference was made to articles 7 (and/or 8) TRIPS indicates that these provisions have not been taken seriously. In particular in those disputes, which occurred after the Doha Declaration that highlighted articles 7 and 8 as primary expressions of TRIPS object and purpose, one would expect at least a discussion on the role of these provisions.

Equally (if not more) worrisome is the invocation of the object and purpose of an individual provision[81] (or section)[82] instead of the treaty as a whole. Article 31 (1) VCLT is clear on this point: 'A treaty shall be interpreted in good faith in accordance with the ordinary meaning to be given to the terms of the treaty in their context and in the light of *its* object and purpose.'[83] Of course, it is often quite appropriate – as part of the context or the negotiating history – to examine the objective of the individual provision under interpretation or of the section or

---

substitute criteria, such as place of production, or establishment, and denying treatment to the nationals of other WTO Members who produce or are established in their own countries.'

78   See ibid. at para. 7.620. Before invoking this as 'the object and purpose of the TRIPS Agreement, as indicated by Articles 9 through 62 and 70 and reflected in the preamble', the Panel began by recalling that 'The ordinary meaning of the terms in their context must also be interpreted in light of the object and purpose of the agreement.'

79   See ibid. at para. 7.714. The Panel considered this as 'one of the objects and purposes of the Agreement, as highlighted in paragraph (b) of the second recital in its preamble'. The notion of 'minimum standards' of IP protection on which the Panel relies here is part of the wider notion of 'adequate standards and principles' that the Panel addressed earlier in para. 7.620.

80   See *China – IPRs, supra* note 67 at para. 7.214. The Panel referred to these minimum IP enforcement standards as not as object and purpose of TRIPS but as 'major reasons for the conclusion of the TRIPS Agreement' and technically qualified its interpretative analysis as recourse to this supplementary means of interpretation in accordance with art 32 of the VCLT.

81   See *India – Patents (US), supra* note 67 at paras 8.24–8.27 (where the Panel discusses, after referring to ordinary meaning and context, 'the object and purpose of Article 70.8'); and para. 8.57 (where again the same Panel engages in an 'analysis of the context and the object and purpose of Article 70.9').

82   See *US – Havana Club, supra* note 69 at para. 8.97 where the Panel, after discussing the context of the provision under interpretation, referred to 'the object and purpose of the enforcement provisions of Part III' as 'expressed in the Preamble to the Agreement'.

83   VCLT, *supra* note 47 at art. 31(1) (emphasis added).

part of the treaty where it is located.[84] This approach, however, does not relieve the interpreter from taking the treaties' object and purpose as the third element of article 31 (1) VCLT into account.

Finally, there are 15 instances of mere acknowledgement of treaty object and purpose as a relevant part of the interpretation exercise.[85] A good example is the Panel's approach in interpreting the term 'commercial scale' as key threshold for a WTO Member's obligation to foresee criminal sanctions against certain types of IP infringements in the *China – IPRs* dispute. After a general statement on the importance of articles 31–33 VCLT as guiding TRIPS interpretation,[86] the Panel emphasises the three elements of article 31(1) VCLT for interpreting the first sentence of article 61 TRIPS containing the relevant terms at issue: '[t]he Panel will now turn to the terms used in that provision, *read in context and in light of the object and purpose of the Agreement*, to determine the scope and content of that obligation.'[87] After a long, technical examination of the ordinary[88] and contextual meaning[89] of the phrase and a full discussion of the arguments of the parties and third parties,[90] the Panel concludes:

> (. . .) that a "commercial scale" is the magnitude or extent of typical or usual commercial activity. Therefore, counterfeiting or piracy "on a commercial scale" refers to counterfeiting or piracy carried on at the magnitude or extent of typical or usual commercial activity with respect to a given product in a given market.[91]

Although the Panel pledges a VCLT-based interpretation, it nevertheless neglects one key element of the general rule of treaty interpretation in article 31(1) VCLT. With only one brief and general reference to the TRIPS preamble,[92] the Panel in effect pays only lips service to interpreting article 61 'in light of [TRIPS] object and purpose'.[93] As the empirical analysis in this section has shown, this appears as a common problem in WTO adjudication interpreting TRIPS provisions.

---

84 A good example for such an approach is *EC – GIs, supra* note 67 at para. 7.181 where the TRIPS preamble is utilised to explain 'the purpose of the "basic principles" in Articles 3 and 4'.

85 *India – Patents, supra* note 67 at para. 43 *et seq* and para. 55 *et seq:* two instances; *India – Patents, supra* note 67 at para. 7.67 *et seq:* one instance (concerning object and purpose of the transitional arrangements of the TRIPS Agreement); *US – Copyrights, supra* note 67 at paras 6.32, 6.43 *et seq* and 6.107: two instances; *Canada – Patent Term, supra* note 67 at paras 58, 59: one instance (here the Appellate Body does go a bit beyond merely mentioning object and purpose); *US – Havana Club, supra* note 69 at paras 8.15, 8.22 *et seq*, 8.52: three instances; *US – Havana Club, supra* note 69 at paras 240 and 326 *et seq:* two instances; *EC – Geographical Indications, supra* note 67 at paras 7.191 (purpose of art 3.1 TRIPS) and 7.192 (purpose of the TRIPS Agreement): two instances; *China – IPRs, supra* note 67 at paras 7.515 and 7.531: two instances.

86 *China – IPRs, supra* note 67 at para. 7.500.

87 Ibid. at para. 7.515 (emphasis added).

88 Ibid. at paras 7.533–7.538.

89 Ibid. at paras 7.539–7.545.

90 Ibid. at paras 7.546–7.576.

91 Ibid. at para. 7.577.

92 Ibid. at paras 7.530–7.531.

93 VCLT, *supra* note 47 at art. 31(1).

17.5.2 *The* Canada – Patents *dispute*

The TRIPS case that dealt most extensively with articles 7 and 8 and their role for the interpretation of TRIPS provisions is discussed in more detail in this section. The dispute *Canada – Patents*,[94] initiated by the EC against Canada, concerned the TRIPS consistency of two provisions in the Canadian Patent Act, which allowed certain exceptions to the exclusive rights of the patent holder. These exceptions concerned pharmaceutical and other products for which marketing approval is required and authorised the making and use of the patented invention (1) in order to carry out tests necessary to obtain marketing approval for generic versions of the patented drugs (bolar exception); and (2) in order to manufacture and stockpile generic versions for a period of six months before the end of the patent term so that generic copies would be readily available as soon as the patent term of the original drug expired (stockpiling exception). The EC challenged the compliance of these two exceptions with article 27 (1) second sentence and article 30 TRIPS. The former contains specific non-discrimination obligations with regard to the availability and enjoyments of patents.[95] Article 30 TRIPS allows WTO members to foresee exceptions to patent rights in their national laws, under the three conditions that the national exceptions are (1) 'limited'; (2) 'do not unreasonably conflict with a normal exploitation of the patent'; and (3) 'do not unreasonably prejudice the legitimate interests of the patent owner, taking account of the legitimate interests of third parties'. The amount of open and ambiguous terms such as 'unreasonable' and 'legitimate' in article 30 and 'discrimination' in article 27:1, together with the public health objective underlining Canada's exceptions for generic drug producers, should make this dispute the perfect test ground for the influence of articles 7 and 8 on the interpretation of TRIPS provisions.

The following excerpts from the Panel report nicely summarise the arguments of Canada, the EC, as well as the legal reasoning of the Panel on the role of articles 7 and 8 TRIPS:

> 7.24 In the view of Canada, the italicized text of Article 7 above declares that one of the key goals of the TRIPS Agreement was a *balance* between the intellectual property rights created by the Agreement and other important socio-economic policies of WTO Member governments. Article 8 elaborates the socio-economic policies in question, with particular attention to health and nutritional policies. With respect to patent rights, Canada argued, *these purposes call for a liberal interpretation of the three conditions stated in Article 30 of the Agreement,* so that governments would have the necessary *flexibility* to adjust patent rights to maintain the desired balance with other important national policies.

94 *Canada – Patents, supra* note 67 at.
95 The non-discrimination requirement in art 27 (1) and its relationship to arts 7 and 8 will be discussed below.

7.25 The EC did not dispute the stated goal of achieving a balance within the intellectual property rights system between important national policies. But, in the view of the EC, *Articles 7 and 8 are statements that describe the balancing of goals that had already taken place in negotiating the final texts of the TRIPS Agreement.* According to the EC, to view article 30 as an authorization for governments to "renegotiate" the overall balance of the Agreement would involve a double counting of such socio-economic policies. In particular, the EC pointed to the last phrase of article 8.1 requiring that government measures to protect important socio-economic policies be consistent with the obligations of the TRIPS Agreement. The EC also referred to the provisions of first consideration of the preamble and article 1.1 as demonstrating that the basic purpose of the TRIPS Agreement was to lay down minimum requirements for the protection and enforcement of intellectual property rights.

7.26 In the Panel's view, article 30's very existence amounts to a recognition that the definition of patent rights contained in article 28 would need certain adjustments. On the other hand, *the three limiting conditions attached to Article 30 testify strongly that the negotiators of the Agreement did not intend Article 30 to bring about what would be equivalent to a renegotiation of the basic balance of the Agreement.* Obviously, the exact scope of article 30's authority will depend on the specific meaning given to its limiting conditions. The words of those conditions must be examined with particular care on this point. *Both the goals and the limitations stated in Articles 7 and 8.1 must obviously be borne in mind when doing so as well as those of other provisions of the TRIPS Agreement which indicate its object and purposes.*[96]

Assessing this passage and in particular the Panel's reasoning highlighted in italics against the main legal argument in section 17.4 above, one certainly cannot agree with the position of the EC and further needs to criticise several points made by the Panel. Article 7 cannot be viewed as merely declaratory statement of a balance already inserted into the individual norms of TRIPS during the negotiations. Within the process of treaty interpretation, the general rule in article 31 VCLT places the object and purpose of a treaty as elements of interpretation on equal footing next to ordinary meaning and context of the provisions at stake. In the WTO dispute settlement system, this rule serves to 'clarify' the meaning of the WTO Agreements, including TRIPS.[97] A TRIPS provision, explicitly entitled as 'Objectives' of the Agreement, hence guides as expression of its object and purpose, together with the ordinary meaning and context, the interpretation of TRIPS. About one year after the Panel issued its report, all WTO Members confirmed this in of the Doha Declaration. The interplay between article 31(1) VCLT, article 3(2) DSU and the title and text of article 7 therefore stand against perceiving article 7 as mere declaratory

---

96 *Canada – Patents, supra* note 67 at paras 7.24–7.26 (emphasis added).
97 See art 3 (2) of the DSU and the further discussion in section 17.4, *supra* note 53.

statement with no operational value in the interpretation exercise. In this regard, the arguments of the EC are in complete denial of article 31(1) VCLT. Apart from this technical-legal reasoning, also the very objective of balancing itself and the promotion of socio-economic welfare requires this to be tailored towards domestic needs and thus to be performed at the domestic implementation level. As I have argued elsewhere, it is on this stage only where a proportional balance between protection of new innovations and their transfer and dissemination to the public can be performed effectively.[98]

The VCLT principles of interpretation equally stand against the reasoning of the Panel in para. 7.26. While it is correct that the limiting conditions in article 30 TRIPS certainly have to be borne in mind when exercising the balance article 7 calls for, *they in turn have to be interpreted in light of the object and purpose of TRIPS.* Here we may recall that the starting point is the text of the treaty provision and its ordinary meaning.[99] If, giving due regard to the provisions context, that meaning leads to an evident result and leaves little (if any) room for different understandings, the impact of the treaty's objectives is likely to be marginal.[100] If however – as in case of article 30[101] and article 27 (1)[102] – the interpretation of broad and open terms and concepts is at stake, the role of article 7 will be much greater. Contrary to the Panel, the conditions of article 30 as such cannot be relied upon to limit the role of article 7 *a priori.* An even more troublesome aspect is that – although calling for 'both the goals and the limitations stated in Arts 7 and 8.1' to be 'borne in mind' when interpreting the conditions of article 30 TRIPS – the Panel fails to do so in its subsequent analysis. There is no discussion of articles 7 and/or 8 in the examination of the three conditions of articles 30 – although Canada and other third party participants relied heavily on these provisions to support their understanding of the third condition of article 30 TRIPS.[103]

In relation to the alleged inconsistency with the non-discrimination obligation under article 27(1) however, the Panel did address articles 7 and 8. The relevant second sentence of article 27(1) states that:

> Subject to paragraph 4 of Article 65, paragraph 8 of Article 70 and paragraph 3 of this Article, *patents shall be available and patent rights enjoyable without discrimination as to* the place of invention, *the field of technology* and whether products are imported or locally produced.[104]

---

98   See H. Grosse Ruse-Khan, *supra* note 39 at 175–76.

99   Cf. section 17.4, *supra* note 22. See in particular WTO Appellate Body Report, *US–Shrimp, supra* note 2 at 114; *Ybk. Int'l L. Comm., supra* note 37 at 220.

100 It nevertheless should be considered since para. 5 (a) of the Doha Declaration on TRIPS and Public Health requires the objectives to be taken into account for every provision of TRIPS; see section 17.4, *supra* note 22.

101 'Unreasonable conflict', 'normal exploitation', 'legitimate interests of the patent owner' and 'legitimate interests of third parties'.

102 'No discrimination'.

103 See WTO Panel Report, *Canada – Patents, supra* note 67 at para. 7.67.

104 TRIPS, *supra* note 22 at art 30 (emphasis added).

The EC argued that the anti-discrimination rule stated in the italicised language in the text of article 27.1 above not only requires that the core patent rights made available under article 28 be non-discriminatory, but also requires that any exceptions to those basic rights made under articles 30 and 31 must be non-discriminatory as well.[105] Canada advanced two defences to the EC's claim of an article 27.1 violation. First, Canada argued that the non-discrimination rule of article 27.1 does not apply to exceptions taken under article 30. The scope of article 30 would be reduced to insignificance if governments were required to treat all fields of technology the same, for if all exceptions had to apply to every product it would be far more difficult to meet the requirement that article 30 exceptions be 'limited'. It would also be more difficult to target particular social problems, as are anticipated by articles 7 and 8 of the TRIPS Agreement.[106] The Panel disagreed and stated that article 27 does not require all article 30 exceptions to be applied to all products. Article 27 prohibits discrimination as to, *inter alia*, the field of technology – but 'does not prohibit bona fide exceptions to deal with problems that may exist only in certain product areas.'[107] As to the role of articles 7 and 8, the Panel noted:

> Moreover, to the extent the prohibition of discrimination does limit the ability to target certain products in dealing with certain of the important national policies referred to in Articles 7 and 8.1, that fact may well constitute a deliberate limitation rather than a frustration of purpose.[108]

Second, Canada argued that the relevant exception in its Patent Act does not discriminate against pharmaceutical products.[109] Facing the difficult task of giving an appropriate meaning to the term 'discrimination' in articles 27:1, the Panel did not take this opportunity to rely on articles 7 and 8 to 'colour' the understanding of this open and ambiguous term. Instead, after examining briefly its ordinary meaning,[110] the Panel limited itself to defining the concept of discrimination to the extent necessary to resolve the issues of discrimination raised before it.[111] Given that the text of the relevant exception in Canada's Patent Act did not suggest any limitation to a specific field of products or technology, the Panel focused on the notion of *de facto* discrimination. Here it concluded that there was no prove for the adverse effects of section 55.2(1) being limited to the pharmaceutical industry, or that the objective indications of purpose demonstrated a purpose to impose disadvantages on pharmaceutical patents in particular, as is often required to raise a claim of *de facto* discrimination.[112]

---

105 *Canada – Patents, supra* note 67 at para. 7.86.
106 Ibid. at para. 7.89.
107 Ibid. at para. 7.92.
108 Ibid.
109 Ibid. at para. 7.87.
110 Ibid. at para. 7.94.
111 Ibid. at para. 7.98.
112 Ibid. at para. 7.105.

Again, the approach by the Panel is subject to criticism: while acknowledging Canada's arguments on the role of articles 7 and 8 to balance IP protection with other societal interests,[113] the Panel apparently viewed the non-discrimination requirement as limiting that role of articles 7 and 8. As argued above in relation to article 30, also the specific terms of article 27 TRIPS – the prohibition of certain types of discrimination – cannot be utilised to limit the role of the general objectives in article 7 *a priori*. Instead, while a careful assessment of the ordinary meaning of 'without discrimination' may certainly amount to a limited option for giving effect to a balance of interests, it is the terms of article 27 which in turn must be interpreted in light of the object and purpose of TRIPS. Here, the Panel again failed to consider articles 7 and 8 as interpretative tools to shape the appropriate understanding of the term 'discrimination'. It took ordinary meaning and context into account,[114] but then missed the chance to rely on articles 7 and 8 for further shaping the meaning of this open and ambiguous term. In a nutshell, this approach resembles much of what the overall empirical analysis has shown: if at all looking at articles 7 and/or 8, the WTO case law so far has shied away from dealing with these provisions and their role for the interpretation of TRIPS.

17.6 Conclusion

Against the background of legal concept of sustainable development in international law, this chapter has examined how WTO jurisprudence on IP protection has dealt with the principle of integrating economic, social and environmental objectives. Various examples for linkages between IP protection and other societal concerns illustrate the significant potential for operating the integration principle. The main legal argument developed is that in case of the WTO/TRIPS Agreement, integration of societal concerns functions primarily via treaty interpretation – primarily in case of domestic implementation, but also in case of dispute settlement. Such interpretation must be based on the accepted principles of article 31 VCLT and – especially after the Doha Declaration – calls for an important role for TRIPS' object and purpose. The latter is primarily embodied in the balancing objectives of article 7 and the public interest principles of article 8 TRIPS. Together they embody IP-specific expressions of the sustainable development objective and its principle of integration. Against this background, Panels have a strong mandate to interpret TRIPS in light of articles 7 and 8 TRIPS.

The hypothesis has been that WTO adjudication so far has given an insufficient role to the integration provisions of articles 7 and 8 in interpreting TRIPS. The empirical analysis confirms this. While there is only a comparably limited number

113 Ibid. at 25, para. 4.14: The Panel recognised Canada's argument that 'The TRIPS Agreement as a whole was framed so as to achieve balance between competing interests, and to ensure that the assertion of patent rights did not prevent the realization of other important societal objectives. As stated in the first recital of its preamble and in the objectives endorsed by its Article 7, the TRIPS Agreement was not intended to promote patent rights at the expense of legitimate trade, social and economic welfare, and the rights of others.'
114 Ibid. at paras 7.94, 7.98.

of TRIPS cases (seven per cent of all WTO complaints) in the first 15 years of WTO dispute settlement, the 12 reports issued addressed in total 55 instances where TRIPS provisions or terms were subject to interpretation. In only about half of these were object and purpose addressed in any form; including approximately 15 instances where they have only been mentioned, but not applied. The remaining approximately 15 instances break down in only three cases where articles 7 and 8 have been applied; another three where they have been merely acknowledged; and 9 where other objectives (of TRIPS or its provisions) have been applied. This paints a picture of a quantitatively limited, and qualitatively rather arbitrary, use of TRIPS object and purpose in the interpretation exercise.

Why is this so? One cannot do much more than speculate about the exact reasons for not relying on articles 7 and 8 in the interpretation exercise. Initially, a reluctance to resort to teleological interpretations in WTO dispute settlement can be understood in the context of WTO Members' fear of a supranational court interfering with national autonomy by forms of 'judicial activism' and 'overreach'. Any treaty interpretation which claims to focus on the intention of the contracting parties or the ratio underlying a specific rule is likely to trigger objections of arbitrariness of the interpretation.[115] WTO adjudication responding to this fear can however only explain an overall reluctance to resort to object and purpose. It does not offer any reasons why articles 7 (and 8) have been applied in only 20 per cent of cases where object and purpose were addressed. This may of course be due to the fact that often the parties to the dispute did not raise articles 7 and/or 8 TRIPS as (interpretative) arguments. That certainly appears to be the case for a number of disputes, which dealt with more technical-legal questions and where balancing different societal objectives was less apparent.[116] But also in the *Canada – Patents* dispute where Canada did rely heavily on articles 7 and 8 as guiding TRIPS interpretation, the Panel effectively paid only lip service to its own commitment to take these provisions into account in its analysis. In the end, it may well be that also the substantive ambiguity of articles 7 and 8 TRIPS lead WTO adjudicators to shy away from putting them into operation. After the Doha Declaration and with an ever-growing amount of scholarship on these provisions, there is, however, no further reason to be shy.

In sum, the analysis of the WTO Panel and Appellate Body reports indicates that the interpretation of TRIPS, in accordance with all elements recognised under

---

115 As I have argued elsewhere, these concerns about objectiveness and legitimacy should however not prevent an interpreter from resorting to the treaty's object and purpose – as long as the latter is expressed in (as the case with TRIPS) or at least can be derived *from the text of the treaty*. See H. Grosse Ruse-Khan, 'From TRIPS to ACTA: Towards a New "Gold Standard" in Criminal IP Enforcement?' in C. Geiger, ed., *Criminal Enforcement of Intellectual Property: A Blessing Or A Curse?* (Cheltenham: Edward Elgar, 2012) 171–90 <http://ssrn.com/abstract=1592104> accessed 19 March 2015, 17.

116 In the *China – IPRs* case however, the question of what must be the threshold for IP infringing activities to warrant criminal prosecution certainly concerns a balance between social and economic objectives. China nevertheless did not appear to have raised arts 7 and 8 as a justification for more flexibility to determine this threshold in accordance with its domestic societal objectives.

article 31 VCLT and giving due regard to the extra emphasis placed on the objectives of article 7 TRIPS by all WTO Members in the Doha Declaration, is still to be realised in WTO jurisprudence. Although the decision in the *Canada – Patent* dispute predates the Doha Declaration by about one year, nothing really has changed. The approach in the 2009 *China – IPRs* report indicates that there is systemic problem of not taking the object and purpose of TRIPS seriously in the process of treaty interpretation. Panels should come to realise that articles 7 and 8 are not only relevant for public health issues, but shall guide the interpretation of 'each provision of the TRIPS Agreement'.[117]

Given the quasi-exclusivity WTO dispute settlement enjoys over addressing international IP interpretation,[118] there is a definite need for a more detailed, concrete elaboration by WTO adjudicators of the content and implications of articles 7 and 8 TRIPS on the meaning of individual TRIPS provisions. This would certainly advance the overall goal of the WTO dispute settlement system to provide 'security and predictability to the multilateral trading system'.[119] WTO Members would find out how to operate these provisions in TRIPS interpretation and implementation. Taking all main interpretative elements mentioned in article 31 VCLT seriously will also ensure that WTO adjudicators live up to their pledges to follow the 'customary rules of interpretation of public international law'[120]. Sticking to these rules as a whole (and not neglecting certain elements) in turn will underline the 'rule-based' character of the system and add to the objectivity and legitimacy of the interpretation exercise and its result. Looking forward, the plain packaging disputes certainly offer a very good (and closely watched) opportunity for WTO adjudicators to engage in an analysis of articles 7 and 8 that does justice to their importance in balancing private rights and public interests.

---

117 Doha Declaration, *supra* note 22 at para. 5 (a).

118 The jurisdiction over TRIPS disputes is – by virtue of arts 23 (1) and 2 (a) DSU – exclusive *de jure*. By incorporating, *inter alia*, the main substantive provisions of the Paris and Berne Convention into TRIPS, WTO Panels enjoy jurisdiction also over the two classic IP treaties. This jurisdiction is *de facto* an exclusive one since the theoretical option of bringing a case on Paris or Berne Convention rules to the ICJ under art 33 of the Berne Convention or art 28 of the Paris Convention has never been used. Recent trends to litigate compliance with international IP treaty norms, including those of TRIPS, in investor – state arbitration however may pose a challenge to this exclusivity – see H. Grosse Ruse-Khan, Litigating Intellectual Property Rights in Investor-State Arbitration: From Plain Packaging to Patent Revocation, Fourth Biennial Global Conference of the Society of International Economic Law (SIEL) Working Paper No. 2014–21; Max Planck Institute for Innovation and Competition Research Paper No. 14–13; University of Cambridge Faculty of Law Research Paper No. 52/2014 – <http://ssrn.com/abstract=2463711> accessed 19 March 2015.

119 See art 3 (2) DSU, *supra* note 53.

120 See ibid.

18 Elaborating the common but differentiated responsibilities principle in the WTO

Joyeeta Gupta and Nadia Sanchez

18.1 Introduction

The gradually evolving law of sustainable development at the global level[1] has been seen as incorporating the seven key principles adopted in the New Delhi Declaration of 2002.[2] These include the duty of States to ensure the sustainable use of natural resources; the principle of equity and the eradication of poverty; the principle of common but differentiated responsibilities and respective capabilities (CBDR); the principle of the precautionary approach to human health, natural resources and ecosystems; the principle of public participation and access to information and justice; the principle of good governance; and the principle of integration and interrelationship, in particular with respect to human rights and social, economic and environmental objectives. This chapter examines the question – what does the principle of common but differentiated responsibilities mean and what is the diversity of opinion regarding its content in the scientific literature. It considers how the World Trade Organization Panel has interpreted the idea of differential treatment and whether these precedents throw light on the content of the CBDR principle.

18.2 The CBDR and its contested interpretation

International law has always seen equity as an important principle. However, the shape this principle takes is often context-relevant. In treaties dealing with water, equity has been interpreted in terms of how water resources should be allocated among countries.[3] In contrast to discussions with respect to water resources, in

---

1 N. J. Schrijver and F. Wiess, eds., *International Law and Sustainable Development: Principles and Practice* (Leiden: Martinus Nijhoff, 2004).

2 ILA New Delhi Declaration of Principles of International Law Relating to Sustainable Development, 2 April 2002, UN Doc. A/CONF.199/8, 9 August 2002 [New Delhi Declaration].

3 The International Law Association's *Helsinki Rules on the Uses of International Rivers* in 1966 and the UN Watercourses Convention of 1997 (Watercourses Convention) have elaborated on principles of equity. The Watercourses Convention argues that in determining equitable utilization, the parties must take into consideration the 'geographic, hydrographic, hydrological, climatic, ecological and other factors of a natural character; the social and economic needs; the effects of the use of watercourses by one state on another state; existing and potential uses; conservation, protection,

the area of global environmental challenges equity principles have emerged in the form of Common but Differentiated Responsibilities and Respective Capabilities in the Rio Declaration on Environment and Development,[4] the United Nations Framework Convention on Climate Change,[5] and the Convention on Biological Diversity.[6] This elaboration followed the need felt by the international community to use differential treatment in dealing with countries in different stages of development as expressed in the 1982 United Nations Convention on the Law of the Sea[7] and the 1987 Montreal Protocol on Substances that Deplete the Ozone Layer.[8] The idea of differentiation is not only applied in a North-South context but is increasingly being used within regional groupings of developed countries, namely within the European Union and the UN Economic Commission for Europe in the 1988 EC Large Combustion Directive,[9] the 1991 Volatile Organic Compounds Protocol,[10] and the 1992 Maastricht Treaty.[11]

The CBDR principle is particularly relevant in relation to common global environmental problems; where countries have differential roles in contributing to causing the problems as well as different abilities to deal with the impacts of the problem.[12] Although in the early 1990s the recognition of a series of global environmental problems was accompanied by the recognition of the need to differentiate between countries, the literature since then has been quite divided on the issue. While many authors continue to argue that there is a need to differentiate between countries based on the degree to which they have contributed to a problem and their ability to deal with it, and that this is supported by the justice principle[13] and other principles,[14]

---

development and economy of the use of water and the costs of measures taken to that effect; and the availability of alternatives' (Art 6). It argues further that the relevant parties must then decide on the weights that they will assign to the different criteria and then come to an evaluation of how best to divide the responsibilities.

4 United Nations Conference on Environment and Development, UN Doc. A/CONF.151/5/Rev 1 (1992) [Rio Declaration].

5 United Nations Framework Convention on Climate Change (9 May 1992) 1771 UNTS 107.

6 United Nations Convention on Biological Diversity (5 June 1992) 1760 UNTS 79.

7 United Nations Convention on the Law of the Sea (10 December 1992) 1833 UNTS 3.

8 Montreal Protocol on Substances that Deplete the Ozone Layer (16 September 1987) 1522 UNTS 3.

9 EEC Council Directive on the Limitation of Emissions of Certain Pollutants into the Air from Large Combustion Plants (24 November 1988) 88/609/EEC.

10 Protocol to the 1979 Convention on Long-Range Transboundary Air Pollution Concerning the Control of Emissions of Volatile Organic Compounds or their Transboundary Fluxes (18 November 1991) 2001 UNTS 187.

11 Treaty on European Union (7 February 1992) 1759 UNTS 3.

12 Duncan French, 'Developing States and International Environmental Law – The Importance of Differentiated Responsibilities' (2000) 49:1 *Int'l Comp. L. Q.* 35.

13 See, e.g. L. Rajamani, 'The Principle of Common but Differentiated Responsibility and the Balance of Commitments under the Climate Regime' (2000) 9 RECIEL 120; R. Anand, *International Environmental Justice: A North-South Dimension* (Aldershot: Ashgate, 2004); C. Batruch, '"Hot Air" as Precedent for Developing Countries? Equity Considerations' (1998) 17 *UCLA J. Envtl. L. & Pol'y* 45.

14 J. Gupta and N. Sanchez 'The CBDR Principle Elaborated in Relation to Other Principles of Law' in M. C. Bassiouni J. Gomula, P. Mengozzi, J. G. Merrills, R. N. Navia, A. Oriolo, W. Schabas, and

there is a growing group of scholars who argue that recognizing this principle will not help to address the seriousness of the environmental problems and develop appropriate solutions. The notion of 'territorial variation'[15] is seen as unlikely to help address environmental problems like climate change fast enough[16] and 'per capita based variations', i.e. pollution targets that take population size into account are seen as unacceptable because all countries have to reduce their emissions if, for example, climate change is to be addressed.[17] In other words, countries should be assessed in relation to their total and not to their per capita contributions and this would be consistent with the sovereign equality of States.[18] Furthermore, many developing countries are developing rapidly and their contributions to the environmental problems are changing with great speed. Other countries feel that these rapidly developing countries cannot simply claim a right to development. They need instead to integrate environmental challenges into their growth storylines both in relation to the climate change regime[19] and the regime to deal with the depletion of the ozone layer.[20] Furthermore, the size of populations and economies of a handful of developing countries like China, India and Brazil is so great that these can single-handedly affect the effectiveness of treaty implementation if these countries are provided with clauses that reduce the level of mitigation activities expected from them. Finally, making lower demands on States that do not yet have an evolved policy implementation system may lead to greater emissions, which these very States may be unable to control because of their poor governance structures.[21]

Formally speaking, most countries are in support of this principle within the context of global environmental issues. However, the extent to which they are willing to go in interpreting this principle is different. Thus, although the US government formally accepts this principle through its ratification of the United Nations Framework Convention on Climate Change, the Senate's requirement of 'meaningful participation' by developing countries in 1996[22] still underlies US unwillingness to take far-reaching action to reduce its own emissions if key

A. Vigorito, eds., *The Global Community Yearbook of International Law and Jurisprudence, Global Trends: Law, Policy & Justice Essays in Honour of Professor Giuliana Ziccardi Capaldo* (New York: Oceana, 2013) at 23–39.

15 Varying on the basis of contextual differences.

16 M. Weisslitz, 'Rethinking the Equitable Principle of Common but Differentiates Responsibility: Differential Versus Absolute Norms of Compliance and Contribution in the Global Climate Change Context' (2002) 13 *Colo. J. Int'l Envtl. L. & Pol'y* 473.

17 T. B. Adams, 'Is there a Legal Future for Sustainable Development in Global Warming? Justice, Economics and Protecting the Environment' (2003) 16 *Geo. Int'l Envtl. L. Rev.* 77.

18 N. E. Bafundo, 'Compliance with the Ozone Treaty: Weak States and the Principle of Common but Differentiated Responsibility' (2006) 21 *Am. U. Int'l L. Rev.* 461.

19 Gupta, *supra* note 14.

20 Bafundo, *supra* note 18.

21 Ibid.

22 Byrd-Hagel Resolution (Senate Resolution 98), US Congressional Record: October 3, 1997 (senate) p S10308-S10311.

developing countries do not do the same.[23] The decision of Canada, Russia, Japan and New Zealand to not support post-2012 targets on climate change also reflects a similar position.[24]

In the environmental field, the conflicts on interpreting the CBDR principle can lead to some lessons. One can argue first that differentiation will only be fair when clear criteria are presented that outline the basis on which the differentiation occurs.[25] Second, given that societies are dynamic, countries may graduate in and out of the categories in which they were initially placed. Clearly, China is in a very different situation now than it was in 1990, while the situation of Greece has changed rapidly in the last three to four years. The application of the principles should allow these countries to move from one group to another, thereby having an implication on the level of their responsibilities.[26] Third, environment and development problems show clearly that there are some structural problems with our production and consumption patterns and that these need to be considerably modified, chiefly by the developed countries.[27] However, developing countries will need to rapidly shift to new systems of production to avoid institutional and technological lock-in situations creating the same kinds of problems.[28] Fourth, the solution thus far to the problem of different capacities has been to offer developing countries 'new and additional' resources, which are over and above the official development assistance (ODA) being provided to them.[29] Given that such resources are very limited and may be used to justify an unending demand on the developed countries, they were only available for the 'incremental costs'[30] of achieving global benefits (e.g. emission reduction) and not local benefits (e.g. adaptation). However, the resources generated thus far have not been in addition to ODA but have been mainstreamed within ODA. Fifth, '[t]here is no necessary reason why common but differentiated responsibility should mean *no* responsibility'.[31] It should be clear that this principle does not exempt developing countries from responsibilities but rather that its recognition puts them under an awareness of the need to change their development paths and patterns to avoid exacerbating the problem further.[32] Thus, while fairness requires that countries should be differentiated based on specific criteria, such a principle should be interpreted as encouraging countries to become aware of

23 P. G. Harris, 'Common but Differentiated Responsibility: The Kyoto Protocol and United States Policy' (1999) 7 *N.Y.U. Envtl. L. J.* 27.

24 Honkanen discusses the different interpretations of the CDBR in considerable detail. T Honkonen, 'The Principle of Common but Differentiated Responsibilities in Post-2012 Climate Negotiations' (2009) 18 RECIEL 257.

25 Gupta, *supra* note 14.

26 Y. Matsui, 'Some Aspects of the Principle of "Common but Differentiated Responsibilities"' (2002) 2 INEA 151.

27 New Delhi Declaration, *supra* note 2 at Principle 3.4.

28 Matsui, *supra* note 26.

29 See *supra* note 27.

30 Matsui, *supra* note 26.

31 Albert Mumma and David Hodas, 'Designing a Global Post-Kyoto Climate Change Protocol that Advances Human Development' (2008) 20 *Geo. Int'l Envtl. L. Rev.* 619 at 631.

32 Ibid.

their own specific responsibilities the moment they cross the threshold of a certain criteria. This awareness may lead them to reconsider their own growth patterns. While the CBDR principle is not yet a customary law principle, discussions about it and its interpretation indicate that this will remain a cornerstone of environmental law for some time to come.

18.3 Special and differential treatment (SDT) within the WTO

18.3.1 Introduction

We now turn to discuss how differentiation is dealt with in the context of the World Trade Organization (WTO). The trade regime is different from global environmental and developmental regimes – trade regimes have promoted free trade and always opposed discrimination. This means that WTO Member Countries must not discriminate between their trading partners (referred to as the most-favoured-nation clause).[33] Another cornerstone is the national treatment clause, which argues that once imported goods have entered the domestic market, these should be treated as equal to local goods.[34] Although non-discrimination is critical to the trade regime, some limited exceptions are possible. Countries may negotiate a free trade agreement and promote non-discrimination of goods with other members to the agreement; this could imply discriminating against goods provided by those outside the agreement. Countries may allow developing countries special access to markets or raise barriers against products under very limited conditions. Non-discrimination is the rule. However, there has been evolving discussion on the need for special and differential treatment of developing countries to take their concerns into account. These could include privileged access to developed country markets, the right to restrict imports from developed countries, the right to subsidize exports, and flexibility in the application of rules. But these remain contested through the Doha rounds of negotiation. The principle of CBDR is clearly not part of the WTO rules. This section looks specifically at disputes regarding discrimination and differentiation in order to identify if clear precedents have emerged in decisions of the Panels established by the WTO Dispute Settlement Body. Only one case actually mentions the CBDR principle (the *US Shrimp-Turtle* case), while the other cases discuss differentiation between countries based on their 'capabilities'. In other words, the WTO does not seem to emphasize the 'responsibility' side of the equation.[35]

33 General Agreement on Tariffs and Trade (15 April 1994), Marrakesh Agreement Establishing the World Trade Organization 1867 UNTS 154, 33 ILM 1144 [GATT] Art 1; General Agreement on Trade in Services (15 April, 1994), Marrakesh Agreement Establishing the World Trade Organization, Annex 1A, 1867 UNTS 14 [GATS] Art 2.

34 GATT, *supra* note 33 at Art 3; GATS, *supra* n 33, Art 17; Agreement on Trade-Related Aspects of Intellectual Property Rights (15 April 1994), Marrakesh Agreement Establishing the World Trade Organization, Annex 1C, 1869 UNTS 299, 33 ILM 1197 [TRIPS] Art 3.

35 See CISDL-IDLO-ILA Online Resource of Sustainable Development in International Courts and Tribunals, online: <www.cisdl.org> (accessed 18 July 2013).

18.3.2 The Shrimp-Turtle *case*

In the *United States – Import Prohibition of Certain Shrimp and Shrimp Products* (*US Shrimp-Turtle* case) the US had established an import prohibition of shrimp and shrimp products from non-certified countries, i.e. from countries that had not used a certain type of net in catching shrimp.[36] This prohibition affected shrimp and shrimp products from India, Malaysia, Pakistan and Thailand. These countries requested the WTO's Dispute Settlement Body (DSB) to establish a Panel to consider this dispute.

The Panel found that the US prohibition violated GATT Art XI:1.[37] The Appellate Body held that although the US import ban was adopted to help conserve exhaustible natural resources such as the species of turtle often unwittingly caught in the shrimp nets and, thus, covered by the Art XX(g) exception, it could not be justified because it constituted an 'arbitrary and unjustifiable' discrimination under the chapeau of Art XX.[38] The measure constituted 'arbitrary' discrimination because of the rigidity and inflexibility in its applications, and the lack of transparency and procedural fairness in the administration of trade regulations, and it was 'unjustifiably' discriminatory because of its intended and actual coercive effect on the specific policy decisions made by foreign governments that were members of the WTO.[39]

With respect to the CBDR principle, the Appellate Body referred to the concept of capabilities stating that the US failed to take into account the different situations which may exist in the exporting countries and thus failed to pass the 'unjustified discrimination' test by applying the same regime to domestic and foreign shrimp.[40] In order to remove the unjustifiable discrimination, serious good faith efforts must address what caused such discrimination, i.e. an absence of or insufficient negotiation with the Members involved and the unilateral nature of the measure which did not allow for the particular situation of each exporting country to be taken into account.[41] In addition, and referring now to the concept of responsibilities, the Panel urged Malaysia and the United States to:

> . . . cooperate fully in order to conclude as soon as possible an agreement which will permit the protection and conservation of sea turtles to the satisfaction of all interests involved and taking into account the principle that States have common but differentiated responsibilities to conserve and protect the environment.[42]

---

36 *US – Import Prohibition of Certain Shrimp and Shrimp Products* (6 November 1998) WT/DS58/AB/R, DSR 1998: VII, 2755.

37 Ibid. at para. 7.

38 Ibid.

39 Ibid. at para. 172.

40 *US – Import Prohibition of Certain Shrimp and Shrimp Products — Recourse to Article 21.5 of the DSU by Malaysia* (21 November 2001) WT/DS58/AB/RW para. 5.46. See also *supra* note 36, paras 184, 186.

41 Ibid. at para. 5.69.

42 Ibid. at para. 7.2.

This is the only case in which the WTO dispute settlement bodies actually referred to the CBDR.

18.3.3 India: quantitative restrictions to protect balance-of-payment situation

In this case India had maintained quantitative restrictions on the imports of agricultural, textile and industrial products, claiming that these restrictions would help to protect its balance-of-payments situation under GATT Art XVIII.[43] These restrictions included an import licensing system, imports canalization through government agencies and actual user requirements for import licenses.[44] The imported products that were subject to them fell in 2,714 tariff lines,[45] 710 of which were agricultural products.[46] The US considered these restrictions as inconsistent with India's obligations under the GATT.[47] This led to the establishment of a Panel to examine this dispute by the WTO DSB.

The Panel found that India's measures were inconsistent with GATT regulations.[48] It concluded that as India's monetary reserves were adequate, its measures to protect its balance-of-payment situation were not necessary to forestall the threat of, or to stop, a serious decline in its monetary reserves,[49] and that since India was not being required to change its development policy, it was not entitled to maintain its balance-of-payment (BOP) measures.[50] Finally, the Panel found the measures could not be justified because they were not 'measures maintained under balance-of-payments'.[51]

In this case, the Panel provided a rather limited interpretation of the CBDR principle, with a strong focus on the concept of capabilities. According to the Panel, the right to maintain import restrictions is tied to the economic development needs of less-developed country Members. As external and domestic conditions improve, however, a Member must progressively relax its import restrictions.[52] The same emphasis on capabilities is noticed when the Panel refers to the WTO Agreement and its recognition of the need to ensure that developing countries secure a share in international trade commensurate with the needs of their economic development, thus, specific exceptions from the general rules address the special concerns of developing countries.[53]

---

43 *India – Quantitative Restrictions on Imports of Agricultural, Textile and Industrial Products* (22 September 1999) WT/DS90/R, as upheld by the Appellate Body Report, WT/DS90/AB/R, DSR 1999: V, 1799.
44 Ibid. at para. 7.2.
45 Ibid. at para. 2.9.
46 Ibid. at para. 3.67.
47 Ibid. at para. 3.1.
48 Ibid. at para. 5.144.
49 Ibid. at para. 5.184.
50 Ibid. at para. 5.215.
51 Ibid. at para. 5.241.
52 Ibid. at para. 3.206.
53 Ibid. at para. 7.2.

18.3.4 EU: Asbestos

The third case involves France and Canada and subsequently Brazil and is in relation to an environmentally harmful substance – asbestos. France issued a ban on asbestos in 1996. This affected imported asbestos and products containing asbestos and benefitted certain domestic substitutes such as PVA, cellulose and glass ('PCG') fibres and products containing such substitutes.[54] Canada considered this ban as a trade-restrictive measure and issued a complaint before the WTO DSB. Canada argued that the French Government had access to an alternative less trade-restrictive measure to achieve its objective of protecting human health and that any practical difficulties in implementing such a measure should not be considered in assessing whether the measure is reasonably available unless it is clearly established that these practical difficulties make implementation absolutely impossible.[55]

The Appellate Body found that the ban as an 'integrated whole' was a 'technical regulation' and was thus covered by the Agreement on Technical Barriers to Trade (TBT Agreement). Compliance with the ban was then mandatory.[56] It also found that Canada had failed to demonstrate the likeness between asbestos and PCG fibres and between cement-based products containing asbestos and those containing PCG fibres, and, thus, had failed to prove that the measure was inconsistent with Art III:4.[57] The ban was justified as an exception under GATT Art XX(b) and led to neither arbitrary or unjustifiable discrimination, nor constituted a disguised restriction on international trade.[58]

Regarding the CBDR principle, Brazil, intervening as third party, elaborated the idea of capabilities when arguing that in imposing the ban, France did not 'take into account the special development, financial and trade needs' of Brazil or Zimbabwe, as required by Art 12.2 of the TBT Agreement.[59] Nor, it argued, did France ensure that the ban '[did] not create unnecessary obstacles to exports' of chrysotile from Brazil, as required by Art 12.3.[60] According to Brazil, this provided a supplemental reason for arguing that the ban was inconsistent with France's obligations under the TBT Agreement. There is no statement by the WTO with respect to this argument.

---

54 EC – *Measures Affecting Asbestos and Asbestos-Containing Products* (5 April 2001) WT/DS135/R and Add.1, as modified by the Appellate Body Report, WT/DS135/AB/R.

55 Ibid. at para. 224.

56 EC – *Measures Affecting Asbestos and Asbestos-Containing Products* (5 April 2001) WT/DS135/AB/R para. 192 (a).

57 Ibid. at para. 192 (d).

58 Ibid. at para. 192 (f).

59 EC – *Measures Affecting Asbestos and Asbestos-Containing Products* (18 September 2000) WT/DS135/R/Add.1 para. 279.

60 Ibid.

18.3.5 Korea: subsidizing the ship-building industry

This case between the Republic of Korea and the European Communities related to the ship-building industry. The Republic of Korea adopted a number of measures including subsidies to promote its shipbuilding industry. The EC submitted that these measures included subsidies that were prohibited and would affect the trade in commercial vessels.[61] The EC filed a dispute against Korea in 2003.

The Panel found that certain measures were prohibited subsidies, i.e. specific subsidies contingent upon export performance.[62] It also found that certain loans under the 'Pre-Shipment Loan' (PSL) measure were prohibited export subsidies and rejected Korea's defence that they were export credit grants because these loans were given to shipbuilders rather than foreign buyers.[63] The Panel rejected the EC's claims that the debt restructuring of Korean shipyards involved subsidization or that shipyards received subsidies through tax concessions.[64] It also rejected the EC's claim that certain subsidized transactions seriously prejudiced its interests by causing significant price depression.[65] The Panel recommended that Korea withdraw the prohibited subsidies within 90 days.[66]

In this case, the Panel refered to the preamble of the WTO Agreement where it recognizes 'that there is need for positive efforts designed to ensure that developing countries, and especially the least-developed among them, secure a share in the growth in international trade commensurate with the needs of their economic development'.[67] It also cited Art 27 of the Agreement on Subsidies and Countervailing (SCM Agreement) measures, 'subsidies may play an important role in economic development programmes of developing country Members',[68] emphasizing that the SCM Agreement provides substantial special and differential treatment for developing countries, including in respect of export subsidies.[69]

18.3.6 Mexico: taxes on soft drinks

The following case concerned a dispute between the US and Mexico regarding taxes on soft drinks. Mexico had issued tax measures under which soft drinks using non-cane sugar sweeteners were subject to 20 per cent taxes on their transfer and importation and on specific services provided for the purpose of transferring soft drinks and bookkeeping requirements.[70] The US complained that these measures affected US exports which included non-cane sugar sweeteners

---

61 *Korea – Measures Affecting Trade in Commercial Vessels* (7 March 2005) WT/DS273/R.
62 Ibid. at paras 7.205–6.
63 Ibid. at para. 7.328.
64 Ibid. at paras 7.564–6.
65 Ibid. at para. 7.684.
66 Ibid. at para. 8.699.
67 Marrakesh Agreement Establishing the World Trade Organization, *supra* note 33, Preamble.
68 Ibid.
69 Ibid.
70 *Mexico – Tax Measures on Soft Drinks and Other Beverages* (7 October 2005) WT/DS308/R.

such as High Fructose Corn Syrup (HFCS) and beet sugar and soft drinks sweetened with such sweeteners.[71]

The Panel found that the tax measures on soft drinks sweetened with HFCS were inconsistent with GATT rules[72] as these drinks were subject to internal taxes (20 per cent transfer and services taxes) in excess of taxes imposed on like domestic products – i.e. soft drinks sweetened with cane sugar (exempted from those taxes).[73] Regarding non-cane sugar sweeteners such as HFCS, the Panel found that the tax measures were inconsistent with GATT regulations as the 20 per cent tax was applied in a way that afforded protection to domestic production.[74] The Panel also found that Mexico acted inconsistently with GATT regulations by according less favourable treatment to non-cane sugar sweeteners, such as HFCS, (through tax measures as well as bookkeeping requirements) than that accorded to like domestic products (cane sugar).[75]

With regard to the CBDR principle, Mexico alleged that the Panel must take into account that the 'WTO Agreement contains principles and provisions the purpose of which is to grant more favourable treatment to developing countries'.[76] The Panel found that Mexico did not identify any provision – among the provisions that accord special and differential treatment to developing countries – that might permit Mexico to accord less favourable treatment to products of another WTO Member or to discriminate against directly competitive or substitutable products of another Member in favour of domestic production.[77] Additionally, the Panel states that it had 'taken into account Mexico's status as a developing country, *inter alia*, when establishing the timetable for the Panel process, and had accorded flexibility within that timetable for the receipt of Mexico's submissions and responses'.[78]

18.3.7 EC: approval and marketing of biotech products

The following case involved a dispute between the EC and the United States, Canada and Argentina regarding biotech products. The EC had issued a general moratorium on approvals of biotech products, adopted specific measures on the approval of specific biotech products, and EC Member States had adopted safeguard measures to prohibit the import and/or marketing of specific biotech products within the territories of their Member States. The Complainants included the United States, Canada and Argentina, whose agricultural biotech export products were affected by the above EC measures.[79]

---

71 Ibid. at para. 2.6.
72 Ibid.
73 Ibid. at para. 8.7.
74 Ibid. at para. 8.9.
75 Ibid. at para. 8.10.
76 Ibid. at para. 4.148 (citations omitted).
77 Ibid. at para. 4.148.
78 Ibid. at para. 8.234.
79 *EC – Measures Affecting the Approval and Marketing of Biotech Products* (21 November 2006) WT/DS291, 292, 293/R.

The WTO Panel found that a general *de facto* moratorium on approvals of bio-tech products was in effect on the date of Panel establishment, i.e. August 2003.[80] It was general in that it applied to all applications for approval pending in August 2003 and *de facto* because it had not been formally adopted.[81] Approvals were prevented through actions/omissions by a group of five EC Member States and/or the European Commission.[82] The Panel also found that the general morato-rium was not applied in order to achieve the EC level of sanitary or phytosanitary protection but as a procedural decision to delay final substantive approval deci-sions.[83] The general moratorium led to undue delay in the completion of the EC approval procedure conducted in respect of at least one biotech product at issue and thus the EC's measures were inconsistent with the WTO Agreement on the Application of Sanitary and Phytosanitary Measures.[84]

Regarding the CBDR principle in this case, Argentina argued that the EC measures restricted exports of developing country members to the EC[85] and that there is no reference in the EC approval legislation to the special needs of developing country members.[86] The Panel stated that the absence of a reference to developing country needs in the text of the EC approval legislation does not demonstrate that the legislation itself fails to take account of these needs, or that the EC is precluded from taking into account, or has not taken account, of these needs when applying that legislation.[87]

18.3.8 Comparative assessment

Table 18.1 compares the WTO cases that have either directly or indirectly taken differentiation into account.

In the above cases, we can distinguish between cases that aim to protect the environment (the *US Shrimp-Turtle* case) and human health from environmen-tal contamination (the asbestos case and the case on bio-technology) and cases that focus on measures that have no direct relationship to human health or the environment (e.g. the Korea *Commercial Vessels* case, the Mexico *Taxes in Soft drinks* case, and the India *Quantitative Restrictions* case).

In the case on whether the use of specific fishing nets can be required by the US in order to protect the turtle species, the Panel recognized the need to protect the turtles but saw the US measures as unilateral, arbitrary and unjustifiable – and called for greater cooperation between the two States in order to find ways to

---

80 Ibid. at para. 7.1285.
81 Ibid. at para. 7.1272.
82 Ibid. at para. 7.1272 (iii).
83 Ibid. at para. 7.1393.
84 Ibid. at para. 7.1568.
85 Ibid. at para. 7.1608; see also para. 7.1325.
86 Ibid. at para. 7.1609.
87 Ibid. at para. 7.1623. We note, however, that Directive 2001/18 in its 13th preambular paragraph states that the content of the Directive 'duly takes into account' the European Communities' 'international trade commitments'. Argentina did not acknowledge this paragraph.

Table 18.1 A comparative assessment of the WTO cases that to some extent take differentiation into account

Case/ Parties/ Year	Subject	Decision	CBDR-SDT
India – *Quantitative Restrictions* Complainant: US Respondent: India 1999	Quantitative restrictions on imports of agricultural, textile and industrial products that India claimed were maintained to protect its balance-of-payments (BOP) situation under GATT Art XVIII.	Quantitative restrictions inconsistent with GATT Art XI:1; violated Art XVIII:11; not justified under Note Ad Art XVIII:11; and violated Art 4.2 of the WTO's Agreement on Agriculture.	Right to maintain import restrictions was tied to the economic development needs of less-developed country members. However, as external and domestic conditions improved, a Member must progressively relax its import restrictions (para. 3.206). WTO Agreement recognizes the need to ensure that developing countries secure a share in international trade commensurate with the needs of their economic development. WTO rules promote trade liberalization, but recognize the need for specific exceptions from the general rules to address special concerns, including those of developing countries (para. 7.2).

EC – *Asbestos* Complainant: Canada Respondent: EC 2000	France's ban on asbestos: imported asbestos (and products containing asbestos) vs certain domestic substitutes such as PVA, cellulose and glass ('PCG') fibres (and products containing such substitutes).	The ban was covered by the Agreement on Technical Barriers to Trade (TBT Agreement) and compliance with it was mandatory.	Questions to the parties – Reply from Canada: practical difficulties in the implementation of an alternative measure do not exclude that measure as a less trade-restrictive measure (para. 224). Questions to third parties – Reply from Brazil: in imposing the ban, France did not 'take into account the special development, financial and trade needs' of Brazil or Zimbabwe, as required by Art 12.2 of the TBT Agreement. Nor did France ensure that the ban '[did] not create unnecessary obstacles to exports' of chrysotile from Brazil, as required by Art 12.3. This provides a supplemental reason why the ban is inconsistent with France's obligations under the TBT Agreement (para. 279).
US – *Shrimp* Complainant: India, Malaysia, Pakistan, Thailand Respondent: US 2001	US import prohibition of shrimp and shrimp products from non-certified countries (i.e. countries that had not used a certain net in catching shrimp).	US prohibition violated GATT Art XI and constituted 'arbitrary and unjustifiable' discrimination under Art XX.	The US failed to take into account the different situations which may exist in the exporting countries thus failed to pass the 'unjustified discrimination' test by applying the same regime to domestic and foreign shrimp (para. 5.46). The Panel urges Malaysia and the United States to cooperate fully in order to conclude as soon as possible an agreement which will permit the protection and conservation of sea turtles to the satisfaction of all interests involved and taking into account the principle that States have common but differentiated responsibilities to conserve and protect the environment (para. 7.2).

(continued)

Table 18.1 (continued)

Case/Parties/Year	Subject	Decision	CBDR-SDT
Korea – *Commercial Vessels* Complainant: EC Respondent: Korea 2005	Korea's various measures relating to alleged subsidies to its shipbuilding industry.	Panel rejected EC claims that these measures as such were inconsistent with the Agreement on subsidies and Countervailing Measures (ASCM) Art 3.1(a) and 3.2. Certain measures were prohibited export subsidies. Rejected the EC claims that the debt restructurings of Korean shipyards involved subsidization or that shipyards received subsidies through tax concessions. Rejected EC's claim that the subsidized transactions at issue seriously prejudiced its interests by causing significant price depression within the meaning of ASCM Art 6.3(c). The Panel recommended that Korea withdraw the individual APRG and PSL subsidies within 90 days.	Preamble of the WTO Agreement recognizes 'that there is need for positive efforts designed to ensure that developing countries, and especially the least-developed among them, secure a share in the growth in international trade commensurate with the needs of their economic development'. ASCM Art 27 recognizes that 'subsidies may play an important role in economic development programmes of developing country members' providing substantial special and differential treatment for developing countries, including in respect of export subsidies (see fn 128).

Mexico – *Taxes on Soft Drinks* Complainant: United States Respondent: Mexico 2005	Mexico's tax measures under which soft drinks using non-cane sugar sweeteners were subject to 20 per cent taxes on (i) their transfer and importation; and (ii) specific services provided for the purpose of transferring soft drinks and bookkeeping requirements. Tax measures were inconsistent with GATT Art III:2 and Art III:4.	Panel: Mexico has not identified any provision that, referring to its status as developing country, might permit Mexico to accord less favourable treatment to products of another WTO Member than it accords to its own like products or to discriminate against directly competitive or substitutable products of another Member in favour of domestic production (para. 4.148). 'The Panel has taken into account Mexico's status as a developing country, *inter alia*, when establishing the timetable for the Panel process, and has accorded flexibility within that timetable for the receipt of Mexico's submissions and responses' (para. 8.234).
EC – *Approval and Marketing of Biotech Products* Complainant: United States Canada, Argentina Respondent: EC 2006	(i) Alleged general EC moratorium on approvals of biotech products; (ii) EC measures allegedly affecting the approval of specific biotech products; and (iii) EC member State safeguard measures prohibiting the import/ marketing of specific biotech products within the territories of these Member States. Products at issue: Agricultural biotech products from the United States, Canada and Argentina. A general *de facto* moratorium on approvals of biotech products was in effect on the date of Panel establishment. It was not applied for achieving the EC level of sanitary or phytosanitary protection but it was a procedural decision to delay final substantive approval decisions. EC acted inconsistently with the Agreement on the Application of Sanitary and Phytosanitary Measures Annex C(1)(a) and, by implication, Art 8.	Argentina argued that the measure restricts exports of developing country members to the EC (para. 7.1608) and that there is no reference in the EC approval legislation to the special needs of developing country members (para. 7.1609). Panel: the absence of a reference to developing country needs in the text of the EC approval legislation does not demonstrate that that legislation itself fails to take account of these needs, or that the EC is precluded from taking account, or has not taken account, of these needs when applying that legislation (para. 7.1623).

protect the turtles, thus recognizing that there were common but differentiated responsibilities in protecting them.

In the cases concerning environmental products (exported also from the developing countries) that could harm human health in the EC, the French ban on Canadian asbestos exports was upheld and the Panel did not comment on Brazil's argument that France had not accounted for the special development, financial and trade needs of developing country exporters. With respect to bio-tech products, the Panel held that the EC's moratorium and other measures led to unnecessary and inconsistent delays in approving the imports of these products, but that nothing in the EC's legislation implied that it had not taken developing country issues into account.

The remaining three cases focus on the need to differentiate the developing country situation through accepting policies that protected the balance-of-payment situation (e.g. India) and domestic products (e.g. Mexico and the soft drink case and the Korean ship-building industry). In the case of India, the Panel held that as developing countries improve their state of development, they must progressively relax their import restrictions.[88] In the case of Mexico, the Panel found that Mexico had not adequately argued the case of special and differential treatment of developing countries that would justify discriminating against imported products based on the type of sugar used. In the case of South Korea, the Panel found that only some of the measures to promote the shipbuilding industry were prohibited subsidies and recognized that positive measures may be needed to help developing countries 'secure a share in the growth in international trade commensurate with the needs of their economic development.'[89]

18.4 Conclusion

This chapter has examined the literature on the CBDR principle and the evolving interpretation of differential treatment in the experience of the WTO. Within the context of the emerging law of sustainable development, the principle of the CBDR and Respective Capabilities of countries has been adopted with respect to various environmental treaties. However, the literature indicates that there are two schools of thought – one that argues vehemently in favour of such differentiation, and the other that argues that such differentiation may not help to address the environmental problem. One can infer from the literature that differentiation is only justifiable on the basis of clear criteria, when the differentiation is temporary taking the dynamic nature of development into account, when the differentiation does not imply that developing countries have a perverse incentive to prolong the use of outdated technologies, when some kind of assistance (new and additional finance, capacity building, technology transfer) is provided to the developing countries in order to enable their meaningful participation

---

88 *India – Quantitative Restrictions, supra* note 43 at para. 3.206.
89 *Korea – Measures Affecting Trade in Commercial Vessels, supra* note 61 at para. 7.206 fn 128, citing the Preamble of the WTO Agreement.

in addressing problems with a limit on the demand made on the developed countries, and when differentiation does not imply a blanket exemption of responsibility on developing countries.

Within the context of trade, where non-discrimination is a key principle, the notion of special and differential treatment of developing countries is often discussed. It should be noted up-front that the bulk of the relevant cases focuses only on the rapidly developing countries and the emerging markets (e.g. Brazil, Argentina, Mexico, South Korea, India) of which two are members of the OECD (Mexico and South Korea) and does not say anything about issues concerning most of the poorer developing countries who are in many ways the actual beneficiaries of the CBDR principle. The cases directly or indirectly deal with the issue of differential treatment. Only one of the cases studied looks at common and differentiated responsibilities in relation to protecting turtles – and here required the parties to discuss how best to jointly protect the species and rejects the idea of unilateral, arbitrary and unjustifiable use of import restrictions. The other cases focus primarily on the differentiated capacity principle.

The cases on environmental products that could harm human health do not deny that there is a need to differentiate products coming from the developing world, but also do not hold in their favour in relation to asbestos and biotech products. On the other hand, it is clear that the Panel will not allow discrimination against foreign products in relation to domestic products simply because of differentiation arguments (e.g. Mexico case on sugar in soft drinks), but it will accept the need of developing countries to promote their industry in acquiring a share of the international market (e.g. the case of shipbuilding in South Korea). However, the Panel sees such differentiation as temporary and dynamic and needing to respond to changing developing country circumstances (e.g. the case of India's balance-of-payment measures). These precedents help to show that differentiation is seen as important in the WTO context, they define the scope of differentiation and the limits to differentiation, and the need to see these as temporary. However, we believe that these precedents are more useful in terms of highlighting the differentiated capacity of countries to take action, than the differentiated responsibilities. This is logical as trade is structurally different from environmental issues. The literature and cases illustrate that the debate on differentiation continues.

Part IV

Sustainable development in State-to-other dispute settlement mechanisms

Human rights courts

19 The principles of sustainable development in the practice of UN human rights bodies

Stephanie Safdi and Sébastien Jodoin

19.1 Introduction

International human rights law has come to play an increasingly important role in global policies and practices aimed at the realization of sustainable development. For the most part, the rapprochement between human rights and sustainable development has developed in an indirect manner through distinct sets of normative linkages between human rights and the environment on the one hand and human rights and development on the other.[1]

The last 40 years have witnessed the slow, but steady, cross-fertilization of international human rights law with international environmental law.[2] For one thing, both fields recognize that a healthy environment is a necessary precondition for human dignity and the exercise of a range of basic human rights. This was first articulated in Principle 1 of the Stockholm Declaration, according to which '[m]an has the fundamental right to freedom, equality and adequate conditions of life, in an environment of a quality that permits a life of dignity and well-being'.[3] More recently, the UN Human Rights Council (UNHRC) has noted that climate change[4] and environmental damage[5] can have negative impacts on human rights. Regional and international courts and bodies have likewise found that serious environmental damage may amount to violations of

1 There is also a growing trend toward the recognition of links between the human rights and a third pillar of the concept of sustainable development, the international trade regime, which is not discussed in this chapter. See Susan Ariel Aaronson, 'Seeping in Slowly: How Human Rights Concerns are Penetrating the WTO' (2007) 6 *World Trade Rev* 1.

2 See generally Alan E. Boyle and Michael R. Anderson, eds., *Human Rights Approaches to Environmental Protection* (Oxford: OUP, 1996); Romina Picolotti and Jorge Taillant, eds., *Linking Human Rights and the Environment* (Tucson: University of Arizona Press, 2003); Marc Pallemaerts, 'A Human Rights Perspective on Current Environmental Issues and Their Management: Evolving International Legal and Political Discourse on the Human Environment, the Individual and the State' (2008) 1 *Human Rights and International Legal Discourse* 149.

3 'Declaration on the Human Environment' in 'Report of the United Nations Conference on the Human Environment' (Stockholm 5–16 June 1972) UN Doc A/CONF.48/14/Rev 1.

4 Human Rights and Climate Change, UNHRC Res 7/23 (25 March 2009) UN Doc A/HRC/10/L.11.

5 Human Rights and the Environment, UNHRC Res L7 (18 March 2011) UN Doc A/HRC/16/L.7.

the rights to life, health, food, water, property, and culture.[6] With individuals, communities, and indigenous peoples increasingly turning to human rights law to seek recourses and remedies in cases involving environmental issues, this developing body of international law can be expected to continue expanding in scope and significance.

Another point of convergence concerns the role that human rights can play in addressing environmental problems, by providing procedural and substantive standards to guide and strengthen environmental decision-making as well as adjudicative mechanisms to protect rights and address harms.[7] Although it does not refer to human rights as such, Principle 10 of the Rio Declaration avows the importance of public participation, information, and access to justice in environmental matters.[8] The UNHRC has more explicitly affirmed 'that human rights obligations and commitments have the potential to inform and strengthen international, regional and national policymaking in the area of environmental protection, promoting policy coherence, legitimacy and sustainable outcomes'.[9] The human rights field also offers a distinct set of competent courts and institutions with widely accepted legitimacy that can address environmental harms that rise to the level of human rights violations and advance human rights and environmental norms. At the same time, enforcement of human rights can also enhance environmental protection by, for instance, bolstering the role of local communities and indigenous peoples in the control and management of resources.

The enthusiasm for human rights in the environmental field has been most clearly reflected in a growing trend in national and international law toward the creation and protection of new environmental rights. A substantive right to a healthy environment is now included in the constitutions of close to 60 states as well as in regional human rights conventions for Africa and the Americas.[10] Procedural rights in environmental matters have also been developed in many jurisdictions around the world and most notably enshrined in a regional European treaty.[11]

6   Dinah Shelton, 'Human Rights and the Environment: What Specific Environmental Rights Have Been Recognized?' (2007) 35 *Den. J. of Int'l L. & Pol'y* 129.

7   Michael R. Anderson, 'Human Rights Approaches to Environmental Protection: An Overview' in Boyle and Anderson (*supra* note at 2).

8   Declaration on Environment and Development, 'Report of the United Nations Conference on Environment and Development' (1992) UN Doc A/CONF.151/6/Rev.1. See also *Agenda 21*, 'Report of the United Nations Conference on Environment and Development' (1992) UN Doc A/CONF.151/26/Rev.1 [*Agenda 21*], Preamble to Ch 23 ('One of the fundamental prerequisites for the achievement of sustainable development is broad public participation in decision-making.')

9   Human Rights and the Environment, *supra* note 5.

10 See David Boyd, *The Environmental Rights Revolution: A Global Study of Constitutions, Human Rights, and the Environment* (Vancouver, Toronto: UBC Press, 2011).

11 Convention on Access to Information, Public Participation in Decision-Making and Access to Justice in Environmental Matters (adopted 25 June 1998, entered into force 30 October 2001) 2161 UNTS 447.

A relatively more recent trend has seen the human rights and development regimes become increasingly interwoven with one another.[12] The Declaration on the Right to Development, issued by the UN General Assembly in 1986, was the first international instrument to explicitly acknowledge the link between human rights and development. It proclaimed that:

> [t]he right to development is an inalienable human right by virtue of which every human person and all peoples are entitled to participate in, contribute to, and enjoy economic, social, cultural and political development, in which all human rights and fundamental freedoms can be fully realized.[13]

The critical linkages between human rights and development received further recognition in later instruments such as the Vienna Declaration and Programme of Action on Human Rights,[14] the Cairo Declaration on Population and Development,[15] and the Copenhagen Declaration on Social Development.[16] In particular, the Johannesburg Declaration on Sustainable Development embraces a conception of sustainable development that touches upon key issues at the intersection of development and international human rights law, albeit one devoid of explicit rights-based language.[17]

The relationship between human rights and development has both substantive and procedural aspects. Substantively, the UN Committee on Economic, Social, and Cultural Rights (CESCR) has conceptualized poverty as a human rights issue that undermines the effective enjoyment of human rights.[18] This claim has served as the basis for articulating the extra-territorial responsibility of states for the

---

12 See generally Bridgitte Hamm, 'A Human Rights Approach to Development' (2001) 23 *Hum Rts Q* 1005; Henny Helmich, ed., *Human Rights in Development Cooperation* (Paris: OECD Development Centre and Netherlands Institute of Human Rights, 1998); Bard Andreassen and Stephen P. Marks, eds., *Development as a Human Right: Legal, Political and Economic Dimensions*, 2nd edn (Antwerp: Intersentia, 2010).

13 Declaration on the Right to Development, UNGA Res 41/128, 97th Mtg (4 December 1986) UN Doc A/RES/41/128 art 1(1). The Declaration further emphasizes at art 2(3) that States have 'the right and the duty to formulate appropriate national development policies that aim at the constant improvement of the well-being of the entire population and of all individuals, on the basis of their active, free and meaningful participation in development and in the fair distribution of the benefits resulting therefrom'.

14 Vienna Declaration and Programme of Action (adopted by World Conference on Human Rights on 25 June 1993) UN Doc A/CONF.157/23.

15 'Report of the International Conference on Population and Development' (Cairo 5–13 September 1994) UN Pub E.95.XIII.18.

16 'World Summit for Social Development Programme of Action' (1995) UN Doc A/CONF.166/9.

17 UNDESA 'Johannesburg Declaration on Sustainable Development' in 'Report of the World Summit on Sustainable Development: Annex' (26 August–4 September 2002) UN Doc A/CONF.199/20 para 18 (defining sustainable development as including access to clean water, sanitation, adequate shelter, health care, and food security). See also UNDESA 'Johannesburg Plan of Implementation' in ibid. at para 116 (emphasizing access to education) and paras 5, 7(e), 11(b), 54(n), 58(g) (highlighting the importance of cultural diversity).

18 UN Committee on Economic, Social, and Cultural Rights, 'Poverty and the International Covenant on Economic, Social and Cultural Rights' UN Doc E/C.12/2001/10.

full realization of economic, social, and cultural rights in developing countries.[19] Procedurally, the incorporation of human rights considerations and practices into development programming has resulted in the emergence of a more participatory approach to development, emphasizing the importance of empowerment, poverty eradication, and capacity-building.[20] As stated by the UN Development Programme, integrating human rights and human development 'can thus bring significant rewards, and facilitate in practical ways the shared attempts to advance the dignity, well-being and freedom of individuals in general'.[21]

The normative linkages that the field of human rights has maintained with the environmental and development regimes provide fertile ground for understanding and strengthening its role in shaping the global implementation of sustainable development. The key question that remains is whether these concerns can be brought together into a more integrated contribution that embraces the economic, environmental, and social pillars of sustainable development.[22] One fruitful avenue in this direction may be to focus on the types of human rights concerns that cut across the environmental and developmental regimes, namely the substantive standards of human dignity and well-being and the procedural standards of due process, participation, and justice.

In this chapter, we discuss the role and potential of human rights in international sustainable development law with reference to two key principles of sustainable development, one substantive, the other procedural: the duty of states to ensure the sustainable use of natural resources, and the principle of public participation and access to information and justice.[23] We review these principles in light of the practice over the past 20 years of human rights bodies established through the UN Charter,[24] as well as specific UN human rights treaties.[25] We

---

19   Ashfaq Khalfan, 'International Human Rights Law and Levels of Financing for Development' in Marie-Claire Cordonier Segger and Christopher Weeramantry, eds., *Sustainable Justice: Reconciling Economic, Social and Environmental Law* (Leiden: Brill, 2004) at 313.

20   J. K. Boesen and H. O. Sano 'The Implications and Value Added of a Human Rights-Based Approach,' in B. A. Andreassen and S. P. Marks, eds., *Development as a Human Right: Legal, Political and Economic Dimensions (supra* note 12 at 13).

21   UN Development Programme, 'Human Development Report' (2000) 19 <http://hdr.undp.org/en/reports/global/hdr2000/> accessed 28 March 2012.

22   See Dominic McGoldrick, 'Sustainable Development and Human Rights: An Integrated Conception' (1996) 45 *Int'l & Comp LQ* 796.

23   For a list of the principles of international law on sustainable development, see International Law Association, 'New Delhi Declaration of Principles of International Law Relating to Sustainable Development' (2002) 2 *Int'l Envt'l. Agreements: Pol., L. & Econ.* 211 [New Delhi Declaration].

24   These UN Charter-based bodies include the Economic and Social Council (ECOSOC), under which lies the Human Rights Council (UNHRC), formerly known as the Commission on Human Rights, with a Sub-Commission on Prevention of Discrimination and Protection of Minorities.

25   UN treaty-based organs correspond to the six main UN Human Rights Conventions. The first two, the International Covenant on Civil and Political Rights (ICCPR) and the International Covenant on Economic, Social, and Cultural Rights (IESCR), both established in 1966, lay out first- and second-generation rights, respectively. These rights are elaborated and implemented through additional treaty bodies. Those relevant to our analysis include the Committee on the Elimination of Discrimination Against Women (CEDAW), Committee on the Rights of the Child

conclude by reflecting on ways to enhance the relationship between human rights and the pursuit of sustainable development.

19.2 The duty of states to ensure the sustainable use of natural resources

An early expression of the duty of states to limit their natural resource use was articulated in 1972 in Principle 21 of the Stockholm Declaration[26] and furthered by Principle 2 of the Rio Declaration.[27] Together, Principle 21 and Principle 2 affirmed the sovereign right of states to exploit natural resources within their jurisdictions, while limiting this right with the responsibility borne by states to avoid causing damage to the environment of other jurisdictions beyond their boundaries or control.[28] A number of multilateral environmental conventions[29]

(CRC), Committee Against Torture, Committee on the Elimination of Racial Discrimination (CERD), and the Human Rights Committee (HRC).

26 Declaration on the Human Environment, 'Report of the United Nations Conference on the Human Environment' (1972) UN Doc. A/CONF.48/14/Rev. 1 Principle 21 ('States have, in accordance with the Charter of the United Nations and the principles of international law, the sovereign right to exploit their own resources pursuant to their own environmental policies, and the responsibility to ensure that activities within their jurisdiction or control do not cause damage to the environment of other States or of areas beyond the limits of national jurisdiction.').

27 Declaration on Environment and Development, 'Report of the United Nations Conference on Environment and Development' (1992) UN Doc A/CONF.151/6/Rev.1 Principle 2 (adding that states have the 'sovereign right to exploit their own resource pursuant to their own environ-mental *and development* policies . . .' [emphasis added]).

28 The responsibility of States to avoid causing trans-boundary environmental damage is also reflected in international law cases. See e.g. *Trail Smelter Arbitration (United States v Canada)* (1938) 3 RIAA 1911, 1965, reprinted in (1939) 33 AJIL 182, (1941) 3 RIAA 1938, reprinted in (1941) 35 AJIL 684 (recognizing that 'under the principles of international law, as well as the law of the United States, no State has the right to use or permit the use of territory in such a manner as to cause injury by fumes in or to the territory of another or the properties or persons therein, when the case is of serious consequences and the injury is established by clear and con-vincing evidence'); *Corfu Channel* case *(UK v Albania)* [1949] ICJ Rep 4, 22 (affirming in dicta that it is 'every State's obligation not to allow knowingly its territory to be used for acts contrary to the rights of other States').

29 See e.g. African Convention on the Conservation of Nature and Natural Resources (adopted 15 September 1968, entered into force 9 October 1968) 1001 UNTS 3, preamble & art. XVI(1) (b) (affirming that the utilization of natural resources 'must aim at satisfying the needs of man according to the carrying capacity of the environment', and requiring consulting and cooperation between parties where development plans are 'likely to effect the natural resources of another state'); Convention Concerning Protection of World Cultural Property and Natural Heritage (adopted 16 November 1972) UST 40; Lima Convention for the Protection of the Marine Environment and Coastal Area of the South-East Pacific (adopted 12 November 1981, entered into force 19 May 1986) UN Doc UNEP/GC/INF.11, 185; United Nations Convention on the Law of the Sea (adopted 10 December 1982, entered into force 16 November 1994) UN Doc A/CONF.62/122, 21 ILM 1245, art 61 on Conservation of Living Resources (declaring that States 'shall ensure through proper conservation and management measures that the maintenance of the living resources in the exclusive economic zone is not endangered by over-exploitation'); Convention on Biological Diversity (adopted 5 June 1992, entered into force 29 December 1993) 31 ILM 822, preamble ('Affirming that the conservation of biological diversity is a common

and agreements[30] have since expanded this duty. They now hold states to a responsibility to ensure that natural resources are used sustainably, including with regard to impacts solely within states' own jurisdictions.

The duty of states to ensure the sustainable use of natural resources, recognized as Principle 1 of the ILA New Delhi Declaration, is premised on the notion that earth's 'climate system, biological diversity and fauna and flora of the Earth, are the common concern of humankind'.[31] In its contemporary articulation, the principle modifies states' traditional 'sovereign right to manage their own resources' with duties based not only on the necessity to limit trans-boundary harms, but also on inter- as well as intra-generational equity. States must manage their resources 'in a rational, sustainable, safe way so as to contribute to the development of peoples, with particular regard for the rights of indigenous people, and to the . . . protection of the environment, including ecosystems'.[32] This includes 'tak[ing] into account the needs of future generations in determining the rate of use of natural resources'.[33] The principle thereby reflects a growing acceptance of ecological interdependence, the connection between resource use and human rights, and concern for the welfare of future generations.[34]

Over the past several decades, international human rights bodies have articulated the rights-based contours of the principle of sustainable use. While no specific human right to sustainable resource use has been recognized, the principle has

concern of human kind' and '[r]eaffirming also that States are responsible for conserving their biological diversity and for using their biological resources in a sustainable manner').

30 See e.g. International Tropical Timber Agreement (10 January 1994), UN Conference on Trade and Development, UN Doc. TD/TIMBER.2/Misc.7/GE.94-50830, art 1(h) (encouraging 'sustainable utilization and conservation of tropical forests and their genetic resources'); Association of Southeast Asian Nations (ASEAN) Agreement on the Conservation of Nature and Natural Resources (adopted 9 July 1985) <http://www.aseansec.org/1490.htm> accessed 28 March 2012, art 1 (requiring parties to undertake 'the measures necessary to maintain essential ecological process and life-support systems, to preserve genetic diversity, and to ensure the sustainable utilization of harvested natural resources under their jurisdiction in accordance with scientific principles and with a view to attaining the goal of sustainable development').

31 New Delhi Declaration (*supra* note at 23) Principle 1.

32 Ibid.

33 Ibid.

34 For an example of the integration of ecological awareness and intergeneration concerns into international law, see Convention for the Protection of the Marine Environment of the North-East Atlantic (adopted 22 September 1992, entered into force 25 March 1998) *reprinted in* (1993) 32 ILM 1069, preamble ('Recognising that concerted action . . . is essential to prevent and eliminate marine pollution and to achieve sustainable management of the maritime area, that is, the management of human activities in such a manner that the marine ecosystem will continue the legitimate uses of the sea and will continue to meet the needs of present and future generations'). For a commentary on the increasing use and acceptance of such sustainable development principles, see M.C. Cordonier Segger and A. Khalfan, *Sustainable Development Law: Principles, Practices, and Prospects* (Oxford: OUP, 2005) at 97 (commenting that sustainable development principles are broadly seen as legitimate, as 'the changing structure of international law has allowed a multiplicity of actors, both State and non-State, to generate knowledge and participate in the development of sustainable development discourse through domestic and international legal systems').

been connected to an array of first, second, and third generational rights.[35] These rights can impose a powerful backstop on the state's developmental and resource use prerogatives. At the same time, the practice of international human rights bodies reveals the challenges of adjudicating sustainable use standards.

Iterations of a sustainable resource use principle are increasingly present in reports to UN human rights bodies on human rights issues in member countries. Because of the diversity of charter and treaty-based human rights bodies in the UN system and the heterogeneous nature of their texts, there is no monolithic articulation of the principle. Rather, these texts together have outlined important contours of a sustainable resource use principle in its connection to human rights issues in specific contexts. For instance, the 1995 report 'Situation of Human Rights in Cambodia' by Michael Kirby, Special Representative for Human Rights in Cambodia, comments extensively on the 'right to a healthy environment and right to sustainable development'.[36] Like the ILA New Delhi Declaration, Kirby's comments are guided by 'particular attention to vulnerable groups, notably women, . . . and persons belonging to minorities, in particular indigenous peoples'.[37] The report praises Cambodia's accession to the Convention on Biological Diversity, whose safeguards are intended to ensure 'conservation and sustainable use of biological resources' by integrating these requirements into national decision-making.[38]

The Cambodia report illustrates the way in which human rights representatives have drawn on international sustainable development norms to respond to local resource exploitation. It insists that the sovereignty of states imbues them with responsibility to minimize adverse impacts on natural resources and encourage customary use of resources 'compatible with conservation or sustainable use requirements'.[39] Cambodia may breach these duties through the impact of logging concessions and agribusiness on the sustainability of resources and, relatedly, on indigenous communities, who are 'dependent on their environment for their food, cultures, and ways of life'.[40] The report suggests legal reforms to implement sustainability standards and protect the right of present and future communities to natural resources. Commenting on the rights of minorities, it appeals to the Cambodian government to reform its land tenure law and produce 'a sustainable development strategy in consultation with the affected communities'.[41] It also

35 See Dinah Shelton, 'Environmental Rights' (2001) in Donald K Anton and Dinah Shelton, eds., *Environmental Protection and Human Rights* (Cambridge: CUP, 2011) at 130 (explaining that 'those interested in enforcing environmental norms sometimes invoke "existing human rights law and institutions, recasting or applying human rights guarantees" when their enjoyment is threatened by environmental norms').

36 UNHCR 'Situation of Human Rights in Cambodia: Report of the Special Representative of the Secretary-General for Human Rights in Cambodia, Mr. Michael Kirby' (26 February 1996) UN Doc E/CN.4/1996/93, 7.

37 Ibid. at 4.

38 Ibid. at 7.

39 Ibid. at (quoting Convention on Biological Diversity (*supra* note 29)) art. 10(c).

40 Ibid.

41 Ibid. at 25.

recommends that the King of Cambodia enter into a 'trust relationship' with minorities living in remote provinces, which would oblige the government to include communities in decision-making about the disposition of resources, to minimize the impact of economic development, and to compensate communities for the impact of such development where it does occur.[42]

Required periodic reports by countries to the Human Rights Committee also illustrate the dissemination and local adaptation of the sustainable resource use principle. These reports suggest that states themselves may view the sustainability of resources in human rights terms. For instance, a 1992 report by the Colombian government laid out Colombia's efforts to ensure sustainable development of natural resources, such as tropical forests. Colombia's report portrayed the state in its role as both a natural resource and human rights steward. As part of Colombia's broader ecosystem policy, the report noted efforts to ensure the rights to land and resource use by indigenous groups, including the creation of 72 'indigenous reserves'. Colombia would guarantee the rights of indigenous groups to exploit renewable resources within their territories in a 'rational' manner, to be overseen by inspectors.[43]

With this language, Colombia's report manifests some of the interesting tensions implicated by the state's duty to ensure sustainable resource use. Colombia highlights its important obligation to exercise stewardship over natural resources. At the same time, its self-portrayal as the source of rationality with respect to resource use resonates with paternalism with respect to indigenous peoples and implicates their right to self-determination in the control and use of natural resources.[44] It also elides the equally important role that indigenous peoples may play in safeguarding the sustainability of resources as against the state's frequently more exploitative and consumptive practices, such as the logging and agribusiness that Kirby highlighted in his report on Cambodia. Colombia's report aptly sheds light on the need to clarify the relationship between the state's duty to ensure sustainable natural resource use and the host of other human rights that this duty may implicate, including rights to property, culture, and participation in decision-making processes.

The UN human rights bodies have, in fact, connected sustainable resource use to a range of recognized human rights. Connections are predominantly with so-called second-generation social and economic rights, but also with first-generation civil and political rights, as well as with third-generation collective or solidarity rights. A 2004 annual report by the UN Commission on Human

---

42 Ibid. at 22–23.

43 Caroline Dommen, 'Claiming Environmental Rights: Some Possibilities Offered by the United Nations Human Rights Mechanisms' (1999) 11 *Geo. Int'l Envtl. L. Rev.* 1.

44 While not *per se* legally binding, the UN Declaration on the Rights of Indigenous Peoples mirrors the language of human rights treaties, such the ICCPR and IESCR, in recognizing that 'Indigenous peoples have the right to self-determination. By virtue of that right they freely determine their political status and freely pursue their economic, social, and cultural, development.' United Nations Declaration on the Rights of Indigenous Peoples, UNGA Res 61/295, Annex (13 September 2007) UN Doc A/RES/61/295 art 3.

Rights, entitled 'Human Rights and the Environment as Part of Sustainable Development', exemplifies the connection of the sustainable use of natural resources to the fulfilment of a broad array of social and economic rights. According to the report, degradation of environmental resources, including clean water, can jeopardize rights protected under the International Convention on Economic, Social, and Cultural Rights, such as 'the right of everyone to . . . the continuous improvement in living conditions', (Article 11) and 'the right to the highest attainable standards of health' (Article 12).[45]

Treaty-based bodies tend to articulate the principle in connection with the specific rights with which they are charged to safeguard. The Committee on the Elimination of Racial Discrimination (CERD) and the Committee on the Rights of the Child (CRC) have both exposed the disparate impacts of resource exploitation on vulnerable groups. CERD expressed concern in 1995 for Papua New Guinea's human rights violations connected with large-scale mining operations, including adverse effects of environmental degradation on minority groups. Prompted by petitions by the Western Shoshone Nation concerning environmental degradation cause by multinational extractive industries in Western Shoshone territories, the CERD also urged the United States to desist from resource exploitation that harms the rights of indigenous peoples. In a 2006 decision, the CERD called on the United States to 'pay particular attention to the right to health and cultural rights of the Western Shoshone people, which may be infringed upon by activities threatening their environment and/or disregarding the spiritual and cultural significance they give their ancestral lands'.[46]

Similarly, the CRC has expressed concern with the impacts of resource exploitation on children's health, as in an examination of a 1994 report by Belarus.[47] In a 2009 General Comment on Indigenous Children and their Rights Under the Convention, the CRC also emphasized the connection between cultural rights and sustainable resource use. It noted 'that the right to exercise cultural rights among indigenous peoples may be closely associated with the use of traditional territory and the use of its resources'.[48] The interrelationship of human rights means that cultural violations tend to produce violations of other human rights as well. Threats to the 'cultural significance of traditional land and the quality of the natural environment' can thus jeopardize the 'right to life, survival, and development' of indigenous children.[49]

Recently, the UN Human Rights Council has begun to examine aspects of this principle in light of the impacts of climate change on the enjoyment of human rights. The Council's March 2008 Draft Resolution connected climate

---

45 UNCHR, 'Human Rights and the Environment as Part of Sustainable Development' (6 February 2004) UN Doc E/CN.4/2004/87 11.

46 *Decision 1(68) (United States of America)* (11 April 2006) UN ESCOR, CERD, 68th Sess CERD/C/USA/DEC/1 para 8.

47 Dommen (*supra* note at 43) 14.

48 'Indigenous Children and their Rights Under the Convention' (2009) UN Committee on the Rights of the Child, General Comment No 11, CRC/C/GC/11 3.

49 Ibid. at 35.

change to sustainable use principles expressed in rights-based language. The Draft Resolution began from the premise 'that human beings are at the center of concerns for sustainable development and that the right to development must be fulfilled so as to equitably meet the development and environment needs of present and future generations'.[50] In a 2009 annual report, the High Commissioner for Human Rights reported extensively on the threats that climate change will pose to states' ability to fulfil human rights obligation to their citizens by way of its impact on the sustainability of natural resources and the health and integrity of ecosystems. The Commissioner noted the particular vulnerability of women, children, and indigenous groups, and articulated an inter-generational equity sensibility in recognizing children as 'active participants and stewards of natural resources'.[51]

As the climate change reports suggest, adjudicating unsustainable use of natural resources as a human rights abuse is not a straightforward matter despite evident linkages. Developing states that have contributed the least to climate change will be among those struggling the most to fulfil the social and economic rights of their citizens. The government of Spain raised a related concern in a comment responding to Special Rapporteur Fatma Ksentini's 1994 Draft Principles on Human Rights and the Environment.[52] One of Ksentini's proposed principles gave states a duty to 'ensure the right to a secure, healthy, and ecologically sound environment'.[53] Spain wanted to qualify this principle with the condition that states be obliged only 'as far as their economic, financial, and budgetary policies allow'.[54] The qualification highlighted the resistance of many states to the enforcement of administratively demanding positive rights, as well as the need to clarify standards regarding what may constitute a violation.

Adjudication of specific abuses can help to lay out these standards. In this respect, the individual complaint mechanism of the HRC, described in more detail in section 19.3 below, has been instrumental. In the 1988 decision *Ivan Kitok v Sweden,* the HRC affirmed the authority of the state to regulate the sustainable use of natural resources within its borders. Kitok, a member of the Sami 'ethnic minority', alleged that Sweden's 1971 Reindeer Husbandry Act violated his right to culture under Article 27 of the International Covenant on Civil and Political Rights (ICCPR). The Act restricted reindeer breeding to members of recognized Sami villages, a restriction which prevented the

50 'Promotion and Protection of All Human Rights, Civil, Political, Economic, Social and Cultural Rights, Including the Right to Development: Human Rights and Climate Change' (26 March 2008) UN Human Rights Council, A/HRC/7/L.21/Rev.1 2.
51 'Report of the Office of the United Nations High Commissioner for Human Rights on the Relationship between Climate Change and Human Rights' (15 January 2009) UN Human Rights Council, A/HRC/10/61 17.
52 Fatma Zohra Ksentini, 'Draft Principles on Human Rights and the Environment' (1994) UN Commission on Human Rights, E/CN.4/Sub.2/1994/9 Annex 1.
53 Ibid. at Principle 1.2.
54 'Human Rights and the Environment' (31 January 1996) UN Commission on Human Rights, E/CN.4/1996/23 3.

'non-village' Kitok from exercising his 'inherited land and water rights'.[55] The HRC recognized the Act as a legitimate measure 'to restrict the number of reindeer breeders for economic and ecological purposes and to secure the preservation and well-being of the Sami minority'.[56] Ordering the state to reverse the Act's particular application to Kitok, the HRC channelled the resource use controversy into an identity-based conflict concerning the appropriate use of ethnic criteria by the state.

The HRC has also considered standards by which a state's own exploitation of natural resources could be adjudged to violate the cultural rights of ethnic minority and indigenous groups. Beginning in 1992, the HRC considered a series of complaints brought by 'reindeer breeders of Sami ethnic origin' against the Finnish government.[57] The Sami depend predominantly on reindeer husbandry, 'which has traditionally been and remains' the basis of their culture and associated economic livelihood.[58] Complainants alleged that Finland had breached their right to culture by destroying reindeer grazing lands through industrial quarrying, forestry, and the expansion of roads to aid in resource exploitation. In each case, the HRC found that the increasing exploitation of grazing lands did not violate the complainants' right to culture. In the 1996 decision *Jouni E. Lansmän et al v Finland*, the HRC articulated a 'threshold test' to evaluate such claims, according to which resource extraction would transgress Article 27 rights only if 'of such proportions as to deny the authors the right to enjoy their culture in that area'.[59] Though indicating that in the future the cumulative impacts of aggregated exploitative activities could, 'taken together, [. . .] erode the rights of Sami people to enjoy their own culture', the HRC refused to find that the threshold had been crossed in the present case.[60] Instead it asked whether the procedural rights of the complainants – their 'effective participation' in decisions concerning the state's development policy – had been achieved.[61]

The practices of human rights bodies manifest both the potential and the challenges of applying rights-based approaches to sustainable resource use issues. On the one hand, a human rights approach powerfully calls attention to the duty of states to use, as well as to safeguard, natural resources for the benefit of individuals and communities. In this way, a human rights approach can help to integrate a sustainable use principle into the policymaking of states, as well as to prevent and provide corrective action for overly exploitative practices. On the other hand, delineating and enforcing substantive standards for sustainable resource use has proved exceedingly difficult in

---

55   *Ivan Kitok v Sweden* (1988) UN Human Rights Committee, Communication No 197/1985, CCPR/C/33/D/197/1985 5. HRC terminology refers to decisions as 'communications' and complainants as 'authors'.

56   Ibid. at 7.

57   *Ilmari Lansmän v Finland* (1994) UN Human Rights Committee, Communication No 511/1992, CCPR/C/52/D/511/1992 2.

58   Ibid. at 3.

59   *Jouni E Lansman et al v Finland* (1996) UN Human Rights Committee, Communication No 671/1995, CCPR/C/58/D/671/1995 12.

60   Ibid. at 13.

61   Ibid. at 12.

practice. The HRC, for instance, has at once articulated a threshold standard after which the State's resource use violates the rights of individuals and communities and shied away from identifying violations in practice, preferring instead to evaluate complainants' procedural rather than distributive justice claims. The adjudication of particular cases demands a delicate balance of competing interests within resource use decisions. Though the human rights paradigm aims to overcome power imbalances that ordinarily determine such resource use outcomes, realizing this promise in particular cases has proven to be a serious challenge.

Over time, the further presentation and adjudication of complaints may help to clarify and strengthen substantive standards through a human rights assessment of sustainable resource use in context. This will require ensuring access of groups harmed by exploitative resource use to human rights mechanisms. In this sense, the principle of sustainable resource use is intimately connected to the principle of public participation and access to justice, introduced below. The empowerment of indigenous groups and involvement of diverse individuals and communities in decision-making processes can help to prevent overly exploitative resource use. In fact, the challenges associated with the practical implementation of human rights standards in the context of sustainable resource use have led some scholars to suggest that international human rights law is best equipped to provide a focus on the procedural and participatory rights of affected individuals and communities in contexts involving conflicts over the sustainable use of resources.[62]

Notwithstanding the challenges associated with applying the principle in specific cases, the practice of international human rights bodies suggests that the principle of the sustainable use of natural resources should be understood as embracing, and being tied to, an array of human rights belonging to individuals and communities. A human rights approach to sustainable resource use illuminates the human dimensions of excessive resource exploitation – the depredation of civil and political, as well as economic, social, and cultural rights that can ensue. Most importantly, it powerfully illustrates the consequences of unsustainable and inequitable resource use for the dignity, rights, and welfare of individuals and communities, particularly those most vulnerable.

19.3 The principle of public participation and access to information and justice

First enshrined as Principle 10 in the Rio Declaration,[63] the principle of public participation, access to information, and access to justice in environmental and

---

62 See e.g. Alan Boyle, 'The Role of International Human Rights Law in the Protection of the Environment' in Boyle and Anderson (*supra* note at 2) 64 ('Where international law does have much to offer is in the empowerment of individuals and groups, those most affected by governmental policies, and for whom the opportunity to influence decisions and policies is the most useful and direct means of determining the right balance of environmental, social, and economic interests').

63 Declaration on Environment and Development, 'Report of the United Nations Conference on Environment and Development' (1992) UN Doc A/CONF.151/6/Rev.1 Principle 10 ('Environmental issues are best handled with the participation of all concerned citizens, at the

development matters appears in numerous multilateral environmental agreements[64] and instruments.[65] It reflects an increasing international commitment to the use of procedural and participatory approaches to environmental governance.[66]

In its articulation of this principle, the ILA New Delhi Declaration identifies a participatory justice dimension within the sustainable development paradigm and explicitly connects it to the human rights regime.[67] It provides that 'public participation is essential to sustainable development and good governance in that it is a condition of responsive, transparent, and accountable governments' as well as civil society. The principle's orientation is toward the 'empowerment of peoples in the context of sustainable development', including through 'access to effective judicial or administrative proceedings' and recognition of the 'vital role of women'.[68]

The New Delhi Declaration's expression of the principle contains three identifiable dimensions: (1) public participation in decision-making processes, which requires 'effective protection of the human right to hold and express opinions'; (2) access to information 'held by governments and commerce on economic and social policies regarding the sustainable use of resource and protection of the environment'; and (3) access to justice, including non-discriminatory 'access to effective judicial and administrative procedures'.[69] These three dimensions of participatory justice have broad resonance in the human rights domain. UN human rights institutions are increasingly recognizing them as rights, spelling out their content, and applying them to specific environmental and development matters.[70]

relevant level. At the national level, each individual shall have appropriate access to information concerning the environment that is held by public authorities, including information on hazardous materials and activities in their communities, and the opportunity to participate in decision-making processes. States shall facilitate and encourage public awareness and participation by making information widely available. Effective access to judicial and administrative proceedings, including redress and remedy, shall be provided').

64 See e.g. United Nations Convention to Combat Desertification in Countries Experiencing Serious Drought and/or Desertification, Particularly in Africa (adopted 17 June 1994, entered into force 26 December 1996) 1954 UNTS 3 art 10(f); United Nations Framework Convention on Climate Change (adopted 9 May 1992, entered into force 21 March 1994) 1771 UNTS 107 art 6(a)(iii); Aarhus Convention on Access to Information, Public Participation in Decision-Making and Access to Justice in Environmental Matters (adopted 25 June 1998, entered into force 30 October 2001) <http://www.unece.org/fileadmin/DAM/env/pp/documents/cep43e.pdf> accessed 28 March 2012.

65 See generally, *Agenda 21* (*supra* note at 8) Preamble to Ch 23 ('One of the fundamental prerequisites for the achievement of sustainable development is broad public participation in decision-making').

66 See Jonas Ebbesson, 'Participatory and Procedural Rights in Environmental Matters: State of Play' (2009) UNEP-OHCHR High Level Expert Meeting on the New Future of Human Rights and Environment: Moving the Global Agenda Forward <http://www.unep.org/environmentalgovernance/Events/HumanRightsandEnvironment/tabid/2046/Default.aspx> accessed 28 March 2012.

67 New Delhi Declaration (*supra* note at 23), Principle 5 215.

68 Ibid.

69 Ibid.

70 The Aarhus Convention, in its preamble, also affirms these three dimensions of procedural rights – access to information, participation, and justice. It posits that their fulfilment is necessary to ensure 'that every person has the right to live in an environment adequate to his or her health and well-being'

Given the prominent role of participatory justice in human rights norms and institutions, the extensive manifestation of this principle in UN texts related to sustainable development and the environment is unsurprising. Numerous general comments and reports related to sustainable development have articulated the dimensions of this participatory justice principle, often with a democratic and empowerment orientation. Meanwhile, the HRC, in its adjudicative decisions, has sought to implement participatory rights in the context of claims regarding unsustainable natural resource exploitation and the cultural rights of indigenous peoples. These human rights instruments can play a critical role in spelling out the content of participatory justice as well as creating and safeguarding channels for broad participation in decision-making and access to information and justice. Particularly given the difficulties of adjudicating distributive justice, such channels may be essential to ensuring fair outcomes and protecting the array of human rights implicated by natural resource use, control, and distribution.

UN human rights texts have given prominent attention to the importance of the right of communities and individuals to participate in decision-making regarding environmental matters. Special Rapporteur Fatma Ksentini's 1994 Draft Principles on Human Rights and the Environment includes the right to participation, both as a means of fulfilling other rights and as an end in itself. Principle 18 lodges in '[a]ll persons the right to active, free, and meaningful participation in planning and decision-making activities and processes that may have an impact on the environment and development', including a 'right to prior assessment' of proposed activities.[71] According to Ksentini, the principle has both 'individual and collective dimensions; it covers economic, social, cultural and political aspects which give full meaning to the concept of democracy', bridging first, second, and third-generation rights.[72] Ksentini's expression of the right to participation establishes a connection between democracy and human rights. It requires mechanisms for individuals and communities to influence decisions and seek redress of inequitable outcomes, as well as to engage broadly in shaping a society's approach to resource utilization.

Periodic reports and general comments by human rights bodies have since elaborated the right to participation in specific contexts. Kirby's 1996 Commission report on human rights in Cambodia articulated a 'duty' by governments to 'consult [. . .] communities fully', considering 'particular interests within such communities, especially the interests of women'.[73] The report also viewed community participation as essential to 'provid[ing] the political and economic culture

---

and that every person can fulfil the duty to 'protect and improve the environment for the benefit of present and future generations'. Aarhus Convention (*supra* note at 64) preamble.

71 Fatma Zohra Ksentini, 'Draft Principles on Human Rights and the Environment' (*supra* note at 52) Principle 18.

72 Fatma Zohra Ksentini, 'Review of Further Developments in Fields with which the Sub-Commission has been Concerned Related to Human Rights and the Environment' (6 July 1994) UN Commission on Human Rights, UN Doc E/CN.4/Sub.2/1994/9 para 70.

73 Kirby (*supra* note at 36) 23.

necessary to safeguard the fragile environment of Cambodia'.[74] Participation entails the need for greater openness and transparency, as well as the inclusion of communities in designing a society's approach to resource use and to the licensing of resource exploitation.[75]

Meaningful participation in environmental decision-making is closely linked to, and even contingent on, the second dimension of the participatory justice principle – access to transparent and sound information regarding environmental matters. UN human rights bodies have given both of these dimensions enforceable meaning and content as express human rights. Article 19 of the ICCPR recognizes the right to 'receive and impart information and ideas of all kinds',[76] while various instruments, such as the UN Declaration on the Rights of Indigenous Peoples, recognize participation in decision-making as a right.[77] The CESCR has interpreted the right both to information and to participation in decision-making as essential for the realization of economic, social, and cultural rights, including the right to health.[78] According to the Committee, the right to health is an 'inclusive right' but also linked to underlying determinants, such as 'access to health-related education and information' and 'the participation of the population in all aspects of health-related decision-making at the community, national, and international levels'.[79] The HRC has similarly invoked the rights to information and participation as mechanisms for ensuring fair outcomes with regard to specific environmental issues, including the dumping of toxic wastes in poor countries.[80]

---

74 Ibid. at 8.

75 Ibid. at 8–9.

76 International Covenant on Civil and Political Rights (adopted 16 December 1966, entered into force 23 March 1976) UNGA Res 2200A (XXI) <http://www2.ohchr.org/english/law/ccpr.htm> accessed 28 March 2012, art 19.

77 UN Declaration on the Rights of Indigenous Peoples (*supra* note at 44) art 18 (recognizing that 'Indigenous peoples have the right to participate in decision-making in matters while would affect their rights, through representatives chosen by themselves in accordance with their own procedures, as well as to maintain and develop their own indigenous decision-making institutions'). A number of UN instruments protect various attributes of the right to participate, including the UN Convention on the Rights of the Child (adopted 20 November 1989, entered into force 2 September 1990) Office of the High Commission for Human Rights, UNGA Res 4425 <http://www2.ohchr.org/english/law/crc.htm> accessed 28 March 2012. For a discussion of protection of participation rights by the Convention on the Rights of the Child, see UNICEF, 'Rights Under the Convention on the Rights of the Child: Participation Rights: Having an Active Voice' <http://www.unicef.org/crc/files/Participation.pdf> accessed 28 March 2012.

78 The 'right to highest attainable standard of health' is recognized under Article 12 of the ICESCR (adopted 16 December 1966, entered into force 3 January 1976) UNGA Res 2200A (XXI).

79 Committee on Economic, Social, and Cultural Rights, 'General Comment No. 14: The Right to the Highest Attainable Standard of Health' (2000) UN ESCOR, UN Doc E/C.12/2000/4 para 11.

80 UNHRC 'Report of the Special Rapporteur on the Adverse Effects of the Movement and Dumping of Toxic and Dangerous Products and Wastes on the Enjoyment of Human Rights, Okechukwu Ibeanu' (3 September 2009) UN Doc A/HRC/12/26/Add.2 para 13 ('Relevant principles that the Special Rapporteur also considers of great importance to ensuring a human rights-based approach to the management of toxic and dangerous products and wastes in general,

Expressed through a human rights frame, these participatory rights bring social justice and empowerment perspectives to environmental issues. In its 2009 annual report, the HRC linked both access to information and participation in decision-making with the empowerment of vulnerable communities to shape and control their relationship to the environment and environmental risks. The Council noted that 'awareness raising and access to information are critical to efforts to address climate change', enabling those most imminently affected by climate change to manage its risks. Meaningful consultation and participation will become particularly crucial as communities face the need for resettlement.[81] More broadly, 'looking at climate change vulnerability and adaptive capacity in human rights terms highlights the importance of analyzing power relationships' to address 'underlying causes of inequality and discrimination'.[82] The empowerment of individuals and communities, with information and the ability to influence society's decision-making, can develop climate change policy that is more responsive to the needs of vulnerable groups. It can also shift the balance of power to provide them with effective control over processes and outcomes.

The third dimension of the participatory justice principle – access to justice – is a central concern of human rights bodies. The ICCPR commits member states to ensuring that all individuals whose rights have been violated 'shall have an effective remedy', to be determined by 'competent judicial, administrative, or legislative authorities'.[83] The UN Office of the High Commissioner for Human Rights affirmed the general importance of 'effective access to judicial and administrative proceedings, including redress and remedy' in the context of sustainable development in the 2005 Resolution on Human Rights and the Environment as Part of Sustainable Development.[84]

Through several sets of cases, the HRC has filtered sustainable development conflicts through a participatory justice lens. In the 1990 decision *Lubicon Lake Band v Canada,* the HRC declined to consider an alleged violation of the Canadian indigenous band's right to self-determination, protected by Article 1 of the ICCPR, by exploitation of energy resources on its traditional lands. Instead, it considered the Band's claims under Article 27 of the ICCPR, concerning the right to culture. The HRC also declined to engage claims connected to title disputes and ownership of land that Article 1 implicated, instead assessing whether deterioration of lands to which the Band was culturally and physically tied jeopardized its way of life.[85] Though the case effectively discouraged adjudication of

and which he has taken into account in his analysis, are accountability, transparency, access to information and participation').

81   UNHRC, 'Report of the Office of the United Nations High Commissioner for Human Rights on the Relationship between Climate Change and Human Rights' (*supra* note at 51) 25.

82   Ibid. at 26.

83   ICCPR (*supra* note at 76) art 2.

84   UN Office of the High Commission for Human Rights, 'Human Rights and the Environment as Part of Sustainable Development: Human Rights Resolution 2005/60' (20 April 2005) UN Doc E/CN.4/2005/L.10/Add.17 2.

85   *Lubicon Lake Band v Canada* CCPR/C/38/D/167/1984 (10 May 1990).

the Article 1 right to self-determination, it opened an important procedural door for similarly situated indigenous groups to bring claims to the HRC regarding violations of Article 27 cultural rights in connection to natural resource exploitation by the state.

The HRC clarified the centrality of access to justice with respect to sustainable development in the 2001 decision *Anni Äärela and Jouni Näkkäläjärvi v Finland*. As in the *Lansmän* complaints,[86] Sami reindeer breeders alleged that the extension of logging concessions, which were destroying the supply of lichen on which the reindeer fed, threatened the Sami's cultural existence protected by Article 27. The HRC applied the *Lansmän* 'test of whether the impact is "so substantial that it does effectively deny [Article 27 rights]"'.[87] The Committee concluded that it did 'not have sufficient information to draw independent conclusions on the factual importance of the [concession] area to husbandry and the long-term impact on the sustainability of husbandry', and thus on the Sami's Article 27 rights.[88] Instead, it affirmed and ordered a remedy for violations of the petitioners' procedural rights regarding access to justice, as safeguarded through ICCPR Article 14, paragraph 1, concerning equal access to courts. The Committee found that the imposition of a 'substantial cost award' on the plaintiffs by the Finnish Court of Appeals was large enough to impose an effective barrier to their access to justice and accordingly ordered restitution.[89] The Committee also found that the Court of Appeals had violated the complainants' rights regarding equal access to justice by basing its decision on a brief submitted by the government without an opportunity for response.

In reply to a complaint brought by members of the Maori indigenous group against the government of New Zealand, the HRC similarly filtered cultural claims into procedural rights terms. In *Apirana Mahuika et al v New Zealand*, Maori complainants protested a deal extinguishing their traditional fishing rights as an Article 27 violation. The government had entered into an agreement with the Maori Fisheries Negotiators and Commission, under which it subsidized the Maori Commission's purchase of half of the fishing company Sealords, which owned 26 per cent of all fishing quotas established by previous legislation.[90]

86 See discussion of *Jouni E Lansmän et al v Finland* (1996), *supra* note part II.
87 *Anni Äärela and Jouni Näkkäläjärvi v Finland* (2001) UN Human Rights Committee, Communication No779/1997, CCPR/C/73/D/779/1997 4.
88 Ibid. at 9.
89 Ibid.
90 *Apirana Mahuika et al v New Zealand* (2000) UN Human Rights Committee, Communication No 547/1993, CCPR/C/70/D/547/1993. In the 1980s, the government introduced a Quota Management System (QMS), aimed at 'conservation of New Zealand's fisheries resources and for regulation of commercial fishing in New Zealand', which 'allocate[d] permanent, transferable, property rights in quotas for each commercial species within the system'. The Maori subsequently filed a claim with the High Court of New Zealand, protesting that the QMS violated their traditional natural resource use rights affirmed through the 1840 Treaty of Waitangi. In response, through negotiations with four Maori 'representatives', the Government introduced the Maori Fisheries Act of 1989, which transferred 10 per cent of all fishing quotas to the Maori Fisheries Commission to administer on behalf of the tribe. Ibid. at 2.

In return, the Commission signed a settlement on behalf of the Maori people to 'discharge and extinguish, all commercial fishing rights and interests of the Maori', providing that they no longer have legal effect.[91]

In its analysis, the HRC used participatory rights as a way to mediate between the cultural rights of indigenous peoples and consumptive resource use policies. The HRC acknowledged the integral cultural importance to the Maori of natural resource stewardship, which the Maori's traditional fishing rights represented. Yet it also acknowledged the alienability of these rights as well as the government's interest in facilitating commerce. In mediating between these competing demands, the HRC centered its decision on the Maori's right to participate in the decision-making process regarding resource use and control, focusing specifically on the adequacy of the government's consultation with the Maori community. While it questioned the legitimacy of the Maori's representation in the negotiations over their fishing rights, the HRC ultimately decided for the state.[92] The state's attention to the 'cultural and religious significance of fishing for the Maori' in the consultation process and engagement of Maori representatives in decision-making, despite misgivings, was sufficient to extinguish their claims.[93]

Though affirming the powerful role that participatory rights can play in safeguarding cultural integrity and resource rights, the HRC left the standards by which adequate participation can be adjudged rather unresolved. From the standpoint of the Maori, more than mere consultation is needed to make their participation in state processes regarding resource use meaningful and consequential. In addition, the dispute raises important questions regarding the legitimacy of representation by those engaged to speak on behalf of groups like the Maori in determining the future of collective rights.

Other human rights adjudicatory bodies have called attention to development processes, which have lacked participation and consent by affected communities. The CERD, for instance, called on the United States to '[d]esist from all activities planned and/or conducted on the ancestral lands of Western Shoshone or in relation to their natural resources, which are being carried out without consultation with and despite protests of the Western Shoshone peoples'.[94] While these demands are powerful, something more than mere consultation is required to meet the participatory standards articulated by Ksentini[95] or demanded by claimants like the Maori. The CESCR also articulated a much more capacious understanding of participatory rights when it stated that '[p]romoting health must involve effective community action in setting priorities, making decisions,

---

91 Ibid.
92 'The Committee has noted the authors' claims that they and the majority of members of their tribes did not agree with the Settlement and that they claim that their rights as members of the Maori minority have been overridden.' Ibid. at 13.
93 Ibid. at 14.
94 Decision (1) 68 (*supra* note at 46) para 10.
95 Fatma Zohra Ksentini, 'Draft Principles on Human Rights and the Environment' (*supra* note at 52) Principle 18.

planning, implementing and evaluating strategies to achieve better health.'[96] In order for participatory rights to fulfil their promise, they must achieve the broader objectives of the human rights paradigm. As such, they can be a vehicle for empowering marginalized communities, expanding the circle of decision-makers, changing the way that environmental and developmental processes are affected, and even altering our basic normative commitments to orient development processes away from environmental and human rights harms and toward the realization of human dignity.

This human rights approach to sustainable development thus suggests that it is not merely quantity of resources that may be at issue but the nature and quality of control: the human – resource relationship is itself often at stake. While HRC decisions have brought attention to the importance of participatory rights, they have generally upheld the state's understanding of standards for consultation and participation. Accordingly, the frontier of human rights mechanisms from the standpoint of communities may be in elaborating and expanding the content of the participatory right to move it closer to their own vision of empowerment.

The practice of UN human rights bodies elucidates both the potential and the limitations of participatory justice for sustainable development. Understood through the lens of human rights, the principle of public participation insists that participatory rights cannot be traded away or circumvented by more powerful actors in decision-making processes. It thus provides a venue for otherwise marginalized individuals and communities to understand, engage in, and alter development-related decisions and policies that affect them, as well as to seek fair redress and obtain appropriate remedies when harmed. At the same time, it suggests that focusing on procedural rights at the expense of substantive ones can leave communities with little more than the opportunity to be consulted in administrative processes that all too frequently run against their interests.

By contrast, some of the rights enshrined in the UN Declaration on the Rights of Indigenous Peoples advance a much stronger concept of participation that is tied to the dignity, rights, and identity of indigenous peoples and extends beyond participation to embrace the right to free, prior, and informed consent and the principle of self-determination.[97] The HRC has recently begun borrowing from these standards to elaborate the substantive content of the participatory right in adjudicatory decisions. In the 2009 decision, *Poma Poma v Peru*, the HRC found that the state had violated the Article 27 cultural rights of an indigenous claimant from the Aymara community.[98] Water diversion projects by the Peruvian state undertaken to support the continued growth and development of the city of Tacna had substantially degraded the pasturelands on which the Aymara community depend for the grazing of alpacas and llamas, the community's traditional and

---

96 Committee on Economic, Social and Cultural Rights, 'General Comment No 14' (*supra* note at 79) para 54.

97 United Nations Declaration on the Rights of Indigenous Peoples (*supra* note at 44).

98 *Ángela Poma Poma v Peru* (27 March 2009) UN Human Rights Committee, Communication No 1457/2006, UN Doc CCPR/C/95/D/1457/2006.

'only means of subsistence'.[99] The HRC again found that the threshold beyond which a state's legitimate interest in 'promot[ing] its economic development' impedes the 'right of a community to enjoy its own culture' can be measured by whether 'members of the community in question have had the opportunity to participate in the decision-making process . . .'.[100] In a departure from previous decisions, the Committee emphasized that in order for this participation to be 'effective' it requires 'not mere consultation but the free, prior, and informed consent of the members of the community', which Peru had failed to obtain.[101]

The field of indigenous rights provides a useful counterpoint to the practice of the human rights bodies, highlighting the crucial connection between procedural rights and the substantive consequences of development processes for all those who are and will be affected. Intertwining the human rights corpus with the field of indigenous rights may provide powerful reciprocal benefits, particularly with regard to elaborating and enforcing participatory justice. *Poma Poma* suggests that the HRC is indeed already moving in this direction.

Further adjudication, cross-fertilization, and clarification by human rights bodies may help to fill out the standards for meaningful participation in decision-making, access to information, and access to justice. These standards should be judged by whether they empower individuals and communities, enabling them to secure their rights and alter processes sufficient to obtain more just outcomes. In doing so, human rights bodies can give content to the participatory justice principle to guide and strengthen its application throughout international law.

19.4 Conclusion

The authors' analysis of the practice of international human rights bodies with respect to the principles of sustainable use of natural resources and of public participation and access to information and justice reveals both the potential and the challenges of drawing on human rights for the implementation of international law on sustainable development. While human rights relating to the environment or development have provided a core of substantive content for sustainability and have extended the scope of some of its key principles, international bodies have been generally reluctant to engage in the resolution of conflicts regarding competing resource uses and rights and have often focused on procedural issues in deciding concrete cases. At the same time, while procedural human rights have been developed and extended in ways that should strengthen the ability of communities to participate in the realization of sustainable development, these rights have not fulfilled the promise that has been placed upon them by some scholars – they too require serious consideration of competing interests between rights and between rival societal concerns.

This practice seemingly relegates human rights to a procedural shell that has little to contribute to the substance of sustainability. The way forward for enhancing

99   Ibid. at para 3.
100   Ibid. at paras 7.4–7.6.
101   Ibid. at para 7.6.

the contribution of human rights to the pursuit of sustainable development must therefore grapple with the difficult, but fundamental, exercise of balancing rights, both against one another and against other important considerations in law and public policy. In doing so, human rights could fulfil one of the central ambitions of the concept of sustainable development – to reconcile competing economic, social, and environmental interests and objectives – as expressed in its foundational principle of integration.[102]

The importance of balancing and reconciliation is a familiar concern for international human rights law. For one thing, it is generally recognized that all human rights are 'indivisible and interdependent and interrelated' and that '[t]he international community must treat human rights globally in a fair and equal manner, on the same footing, and with the same emphasis'.[103] To the extent that this applies to human rights that relate to both the environment and development, this understanding offers the normative basis for reconciling competing rights within contexts that raise sustainability issues. The potential technique for this reconciliation might be proportionality balancing, which has become the dominant mode of adjudication in domestic, regional, and international human rights regimes.[104] Proportionality balancing refers to the multi-step analytical process through which courts resolve tensions between two sets of applicable constitutional rights, values or interests. As explained above, a form of this proportionality balancing analysis has already been employed by human rights bodies to establish the correct balance between, for instance, resource extraction and cultural rights.[105] There is no reason why it could not be further applied to resolve conflicts at the intersection of economic, social, and environmental rights, provided that these rights are in fact accorded equal status within a given legal system.

In this last regard, the recognition of a stand-alone right to a healthy environment may provide a vehicle for a more balanced reconciliation of economic, social, and environmental rights.[106] In fact, numerous constitutional provisions

---

102 See Sébastien Jodoin, 'The Principle of Integration and Interrelationship in International Sustainable Development Law' in A. Usha, ed., *Environmental Law: Principles and Governance* (Hyderabad: ICFAI University Press, 2008) at 83.

103 Vienna Declaration (*supra* note at 14) para 5.

104 For a general overview of the structure of proportionality balancing, see Alec Stone Sweet and Jud Mathews, 'Proportionality Balancing and Global Constitutionalism' (2008) 47 *Colu. J. Transnat'l L.* 73 at 76 ('First, in the "legitimacy" stage, the judge confirms that the government is constitutionally authorized to take such a measure. (. . .) The second phase "suitability" is devoted to judicial verification that, with respect to the act in question, the means adopted by the government are rationally related to stated policy objectives. The third step "necessity" has more bite. The core of necessity analysis is the deployment of a "least-restrictive means" (LRM) test: the judge ensures that the measure does not curtail the right any more than is necessary for the government to achieve its stated goals. (. . .) The last stage, "balancing in the strict sense," is also known as "proportionality in the narrow sense." If the measure under review passes the first three tests, the judge proceeds to balancing *sensu stricto*').

105 See *Jouni E. Lansmän et al v Finland* (1996) (*supra* note at 59); *Anni Äärela and Jouni Näkkäläjärvi v Finland* (2001) (*supra* note at 87).

106 See generally Boyd (*supra* note at 10).

for the right to a healthy environment inherently invoke proportionality balancing by incorporating references to the right to development,[107] the sustainable or rational use of natural resources or the environment,[108] future generations,[109] and sustainable development.[110] Article 24 of the South African Constitution, for instance, secures its present and future members the right to have their environment protected through measures that at once 'secure ecologically sustainable development and use of natural resources' and simultaneously 'promot[e] justifiable economic and social development.'[111] Operationalizing the right to a healthy environment, so articulated, necessitates the challenging but productive reconciliation of competing constitutional demands in service of environmental and dignitary goals. While it is important to continuously interrogate the efficacy of such constitutional provisions[112], the increasing prevalence of the right to a healthy environment in national constitutions offers a promising vision of the role of human rights in the pursuit of sustainable development worldwide.

As such, the reconciliation of different rights at the intersection of environment and development may not simply amount to a useful contribution to the implementation of sustainable development, it may be seen as the very essence of sustainability. Although referring to differing conceptions of rights, the separate opinions of Justices Weeramantry and Cançado Trindade in key cases before the International Court of Justice reflect the view that rights can play this important role in adjudicating disputes involving sustainable development.

In his separate opinion in the *Gabčíkovo-Nagymaros* case, H.E. Justice C.G. Weeramantry argues that sustainable development 'offers an important principle for the resolution of tensions between two established rights. It reaffirms in the arena of international law that there must be both development and environmental protection, and that neither of these rights can be neglected.'[113] In his separate

---

107   See references to the right to a healthy environment in the following constitutions: Argentina, art 41; Belgium, art 23; Ecuador, art 89; Georgia, art 35; Norway, art 110(b); Paraguay, art 7(1); Portugal, art 66; and South Africa, art 24.

108   See the references to the right to a healthy environment in the following constitutions: Argentina, art 41; Byelorussia, art 46; Cape Verde, art 70; Spain, art 45; Georgia, art 35; Norway, art 110(b); Portugal, art 66; Seychelles, art 38; and Slovakia, art 44(1).

109   See the references to the right to a healthy environment in the following constitutions: Argentina, art 41; Brazil, art 225; Georgia, art 35; Norway, art 110(b); and the Republic of South Africa, art 24.

110   See the references to the right to a healthy environment in the following constitutions: Benin, art 27; Congo, art 35; Ecuador, art 89; Portugal, art 66; Seychelles, art 38; and the Republic of South Africa, art 24.

111   See Constitution of the Republic of South Africa, art 24.

112   See generally Boyd (*supra* note at 10).

113   *Case Concerning the Gabčíkovo-Nagymaros Project (Hungary v Slovakia)* (Separate Opinion of H. E. Justice C. G. Weeramantry) [1997] ICJ Rep 88, 95. He also refers to environmental human rights as well: Ibid. at 114. In another passage, H. E. Justice C. G Weeramantry sums up the substantive conflict underlying the *Gabčíkovo-Nagymaros* case in the following terms: 'The people of both Hungary and Slovakia are entitled to development for the furtherance of their happiness and welfare. They are likewise entitled to the preservation of their human right to the protection of their environment.' Ibid. at 90.

opinion in the *Pulp Mills* case, Justice Cançado Trindade likewise insists on the rights-based dimensions of sustainable development, describing it as a 'link between the right to a healthy environment and the right to development'.[114] He emphasizes the mutual concerns displayed by the protection of human rights and the environment[115] as well as the manner in which human rights have come to adopt an inter-temporal dimension.[116] He considers, moreover, that international law's failure to take into account a number of core foundational principles would inevitably lead to, among other things, 'breaches of rights at stake'.[117]

When considered together, these different legal developments suggest that deciding a case on the basis of the principles of sustainable development is ultimately about confirming, denying, and balancing different, often conflicting rights, whether individual, collective, or intergenerational.[118] They remind us that human rights, just as much as development, can only be sustainable if all rights, whether economic, social or environmental, are given equal emphasis and consideration in both the substance of decisions and the process by which they are reached. Most importantly, a human rights approach to sustainable development requires us to confront the difficult challenges and complex conflicts between different rights and to seek solutions that are fair, just, and equitable.

---

114 *Pulp Mills on the River Uruguay (Argentina v Uruguay)* (Separate Opinion of Justice Cançado Trindade) <http://www.icj-cij.org/docket/files/135/15885.pdf> accessed 28 March 2012, para 132.

115 Ibid. at paras 152–64.

116 Ibid. at paras 115–22.

117 Ibid. at para 193. His summary of the parties' submissions clearly evinces his (and their) view of the importance of rights for this dispute, as reflected in the following passage:

> Uruguay further stated, in its rejoinder, that "[d]evelopment is permitted (indeed, required under Article 1 of the United Nations Covenants on Civil and Political Rights and on Economic, Social and Cultural Rights, among other places) so long as the environment is protected for the benefit of future generations".' In acknowledging its need to improve the 'living conditions' of 'present and future generations of its population', Uruguay argued that 'Argentina has not challenged the right of Uruguay to develop economically, and thus to meet the needs of present and future generations of her citizens.
>
> Ibid. at para 146.

118 See in this regard Sébastien Jodoin, 'Rights, Integrity, and the Principle of Sustainable Development: Dworkinian Reflections on the Sustainability of International Law,' in Michel Morin, Marie-Claire Cordonier Segger, Fabien Gélinas, and Markus Gehring, eds., *Fraternity, Responsibility and Sustainability in Law* (Toronto: Lexis Nexis, 2012) at 703.

20 Sustainable development controversies in the African Commission on Human and Peoples' Rights

Hennie Strydom

20.1 Introduction

In 1981 the Organization of African Union (OAU) adopted the African Charter on Human and Peoples' Rights, also known as the Banjul Charter, which came into force in 1986.[1] Article 30 of the Charter created an African Commission on Human and Peoples' Rights to "promote human and peoples' rights and ensure their protection in Africa". According to its Charter mandate, the Commission was assigned the functions to (a) promote human and peoples' rights; (b) undertake studies and research on African problems in the field of human and peoples' rights; (c) determine principles and rules aimed at solving legal problems relating to human and peoples' rights; (d) cooperate with other African and international institutions concerned with the promotion and protection of human and peoples' rights; (e) ensure the protection of human and peoples' rights in accordance with the conditions laid down by the African Charter; (f) interpret, at the request of a State Party or an institution of the OAU, any provision of the Charter; and (g) perform any other task entrusted to it by the African Heads of State and Government.[2]

The African Charter allows for both State and individual complaints[3] although the formulation in the Charter on individual complaints is far from clear. Article 55 merely mentions "communications other than those of states parties" and in terms of article 58 the Commission can entertain "one or more communications" when they reveal the existence of serious or massive violations of human and peoples' rights. However, over the years the Commission's practice has revealed an acceptance of complaints from both individuals and NGOs.[4] One of the most problematic aspects of the Commission's work is its protective function. In this the Commission has failed due to a variety of reasons. Limited in terms of its Charter functions, the Commission had little leeway, no matter how creative and progressively it could go about in interpreting Charter provisions; it faced chronic

---

1 OAU Doc CAB/LEG/67/3 rev. 5, 21 ILM (1982) 58.
2 African Charter on Human and People's Rights, 21 ILM 58 (1982), art 45.
3 Ibid. at arts 47, 55, 58.
4 See Viljoen *International Human Rights Law in Africa* 2nd edn (Oxford: OUP, 2012) 300–302. See also sources in Alston and Goodman *International Human Rights* (Oxford: OUP, 2013) 1028, 1029.

under-funding from Member States and a concomitant lack of human and other resources; and it plunged itself into controversy by failing to deal effectively with complaints when they were too politically charged or by dealing incoherently and inconsistently with communications and by failing to follow up on its decisions in a more decisive way.[5] The protective work of the Commission was also obscured by the confidentiality rule in the Charter. Under the terms of article 59 (1) all measures taken by the Commission, which could include all findings and reasoning relating to complaints, were to remain confidential until the Assembly of Heads of State and Government decided otherwise.

In 1998, by means of a Protocol to the African Charter, the OAU established an African Court on Human and Peoples' Rights[6] with the specific mandate to complement the protective mandate of the Commission.[7] Two years after the establishment of the Court, the African Union (AU) replaced the OAU as Africa's new regional organization with the objective to, *inter alia*, achieve greater unity and solidarity amongst the States and peoples of Africa and to "promote and protect human and peoples' rights in accordance with the African Charter on Human and Peoples' Rights and other relevant human rights instruments".[8] The Constitutive Act also makes provisions for the establishment of an African Court of Justice, which will be the Court of the AU[9], an institution inspired by the European Court of Justice, and which was to come about by means of its own Protocol in 2003.[10] Since 2004 a process was set in motion to merge the African Human Rights Court with the Court of Justice[11], a move that stalled the functioning of the Human Rights Court and that culminated in the adoption in 2008 of the Protocol on the Statute of the African Court of Justice and Human Rights.[12] Article 2 of this Protocol merged the two Courts into one in the following terms:

> The African Court on Human and Peoples' Rights established by the Protocol to the African Charter on Human and Peoples' Rights on the Establishment of an African Court on Human and Peoples' Rights and the Court of Justice of the African Union established by the constitutive Act of the African Union, are hereby merged into a single Court and established as 'The African Court of Justice and Human Rights'.

---

5 See, *inter alia*, ibid. at 294–297.
6 Protocol to the African Charter on Human and Peoples' Rights on the Establishment of an African Court on Human and Peoples' Rights accessible at http://www.au.int/en/sites/default/files/Protocol_African_Charter_Human_Peoples_Rights_Establishment_African_Court_Human_Peoples_Rights_1.pdf, visited on 11 August 2011. The Protocol entered into force in 2004.
7 Ibid. at art 2. See also Viljoen (*supra* note at 5) at 424, 425, 437, 438.
8 See Constitutive Act of the African Union (2000) art 3(a) and (h).
9 Ibid. at art 18.
10 Protocol of the Court of Justice of the African Union, adopted by the 2nd ordinary session of the Assembly of the African Union, 11 July 2003.
11 For background information on this see Viljoen (*supra* note 4) at 456 *et seq.*
12 Adopted at the 11th ordinary session of the Assembly in Egypt on 1 July 2008.

At the time of writing only three States, Burkina Faso, Libya and Mali, have deposited instruments of ratification, which means that the Human Rights Court is still the forum for claimants seeking binding judicial remedies for human rights violations. However, with its demise as a self-standing human rights court pending, it is unlikely that there will be a rush by litigants to avail themselves of the Court's powers.

It is against this background that the work of the African Commission must be appreciated when we focus on what is perceived to be a landmark case of the Commission, namely *SERAC v Nigeria*[13], and another and more recent one, namely *Centre for Minority Rights Development (Kenya) v Kenya*.[14] In both cases the Commission has broken its longstanding silence on socio-economic rights and in doing so has also ventured into the applicability of sustainable development principles in factual situations where environmental rights and the right to development have played a major role. This is all the more significant in view of the fact that sustainable development and economic integration are seen as an integral part of accelerating the socio-economic development of the African continent by the African Union.[15]

20.2 The *SERAC* case

20.2.1 Factual background

The issues in this case arose from oil exploration activities in Ogoniland which forms part of the coastal plains and the Niger Delta in the south of Nigeria. The Ogoni, a distinct ethnic people, have been living in the area for more than 500 years, making a living from agriculture and fishing in one of the most densely populated areas in Africa. As the largest wetland in the world, the Niger Delta itself is rich in biodiversity and comprises four ecological zones with diverse and delicate ecosystems. The area's curse is its oil resources which attracted oil industrialists about half a century ago. Shell Petroleum Development Corporation (Nigeria) controlled upstream activities while the Nigerian State's National Petroleum Company took control of downstream activities.[16]

This is where the Ogoni peoples' nightmare started. Faced with "inadequate environmental regulations, ineffective policing of legislative measures, oil exploitation and the non-implementation of environmentally sound management practices, greed and corruption on the part of government officials"[17] a massive

---

13 2001 AHRLR 60.

14 IHRR vol 18 No 1 (2011) 254.

15 *Supra* note 8 at arts 3(j), 4(n).

16 For a detailed assessment of the environment in the Delta and the consequences of the oil exploration activities see UNEP *Environmental Assessment of Ogoniland* (2011) accessible at http://www.unep.org, visited on 15 August 2011.

17 Van der Linde and Louw "Considering the interpretation and implementation of article 24 of the African Charter on Human and Peoples' Rights in the light of the *SERAC* communication" (2003) *Afr. Hum. Rts. L. J.* vol 3 at 167, 168–69.

campaign of public protests followed which led to the shut-down of the Shell operation in 1993.[18] In 1996, during the time of military rule in Nigeria, the Social and Economic Rights Action Centre (SERAC), based in Nigeria, and the Centre for Economic and Social Rights (CESR), based in the USA, jointly brought a communication to the African Commission under the terms of the individual complaints mechanism. The communication alleged direct involvement by Nigeria's military government in oil exploration through the state oil company without any regard for the health or environment of the local communities by disposing of toxic wastes into the environment in violation of international environmental standards; that the government had condoned and facilitated these violations by placing the state's security forces at the disposal of the oil companies; that the government failed to monitor the activities of the oil companies or require them to undertake environmental impact assessments and in the process not only withheld information on environmental dangers from the Ogoni communities but failed to allow for proper consultation with affected communities. Of special concern were allegations of attacks by Nigerian security forces aimed at the destruction and burning of Ogoni villages, crops and animals in an attempt to drive the communities off their land. Communications between security forces explicitly confirmed the government-sponsored terror campaign which also explained the complete failure by the government to investigate the attacks.

The impugned conduct constituted a violation of a number of rights in the African Charter. The communication alleged a violation of articles 2 (non-discrimination); 4 (right to life); 14 (right to property); 16 (right to health); 18 (right to a family); 21 (right to dispose of natural resources); and 24 (right to a healthy environment). It is this latter right to which we shall now turn for the purpose of this chapter.

20.2.2 The African Charter and the environment

Article 24 of the African Charter provides as follows: "All peoples shall have the right to a general satisfactory environment favourable to their development". This provision is the first rights-based, binding formulation aimed at the protection of the environment and links the right to a satisfactory environment to a developmental objective. On occasion it was pointed out that the adoption of article 24 in a manner that failed to properly consider its possible implications is "indicative of the failure of the negotiators to foresee the complexity of the inclusion of the right to a satisfactory environment in an international human rights instrument".[19] This is all the more so in view of the extraordinary need for economic development on the African continent and the potential harm economic development, pursued for short-term benefits only, may cause to the environment. It is for these reasons that one expects judicial and even quasi-judicial bodies to pronounce on matters of such importance in a manner that will bring

18 See UNEP report (*supra* note at 16) at 43.
19 Van der Linde and Louw (*supra* note at 17) at 169.

greater clarity to otherwise over-broad and confusing formulations in legal instruments. Whether the African Commission succeeded in this is a matter for debate.

In the admissibility phase[20] of the proceedings before the Commission it was
noted that Nigeria has incorporated the African Charter into its domestic legal system with the result that the Charter rights could be invoked before national courts.[21]
However, it also transpired that the military government had over time ousted the
jurisdiction of the courts by decree in matters involving government-related violations of fundamental rights with the result that the Commission had a fairly easy
task in rejecting the application of the rule on the exhaustion of domestic remedies
in the matter simply because of the inadequacy of such remedies in providing relief
to those whose rights have been violated and to declare the communication admissible. Moreover, despite ample notice and ample time to respond to the situation in
Ogoniland, the government authorities failed to act in any decisive way, which the
Commission treated as the "absence of a substantive response from the respondent state" which meant that the matter had to be decided on the facts "provided
by the complainants and treat them as given".[22] The Commission's treatment of
the adequate remedies requirement is reinforced in General Comment No 9 of
the Committee on Economic, Social and Cultural Rights.[23] There the Committee
required States Parties to use *all* means at their disposal to give effect to the rights
in the Covenant, which must include appropriate means of redress and means of
ensuring governmental accountability are put in place. As far as the status of the
international instrument in the domestic legal order is concerned, it is required that
binding human rights provisions "should operate directly and immediately within
the domestic legal system of each State party, thereby enabling individuals concerned to seek enforcement of their rights before national courts and tribunals".[24]

The merits phase was introduced with an observation by the Commission on
what is generally expected of governments with respect to human rights obligations
under an international human rights instrument. In this regard the Commission
identified four levels of duties States have regardless of the nature of the rights
in question. The first level entails the obligation to respect the right in question
which means that the state should refrain from interfering with the enjoyment of
the right. In the case of socio-economic rights this would entail an obligation "to
respect the free use of resources owned or at the disposal of the individual alone
or in any form of association with others . . . for the purpose of rights-related
needs".[25] The obligation to protect requires the State to act in a positive way,
for instance by taking effective measures to protect rights holders against private
acts of third parties which may constitute a violation of a fundamental right. This
second duty, the Commission pointed out, corresponds with the third, namely
to promote the realization of rights and freedoms. In performing this duty the

20 See African Charter, art 56.
21 *SERAC* (*supra* note at 13) para 41.
22 Ibid. at para 40.
23 UN Doc. E/1999/22, Annex IV (1998).
24 Ibid. at para 4.
25 *SERAC* (*supra* note at 13) at para 45.

State must make sure that individuals are able to freely exercise their rights and freedoms.[26] In the fourth instance the State has a duty to fulfil the rights in question by utilizing the State's machinery for the actual realization of the rights.[27]

At more or less the same time as the Commission involved itself in these issues, a group of more than thirty experts met in Maastricht from 22 to 26 of January 1997 to reflect on the evolution of international law with regard to economic, social and cultural rights. This meeting culminated in the adoption of the Maastricht Guidelines on Violations of Economic, Social and Cultural Rights on which the experts unanimously agreed as reflecting the evolution of developments since 1986, the year in which the Limburg Principles on the implementation of the International Covenant on Economic, Social and Cultural Rights were adopted.[28] In the Maastricht principles mention is made of three different types of obligations States have, namely the obligations to respect, protect and fulfil, and a failure to perform any of these obligations would constitute a violation of the rights in question. This is explained as follows:

> The obligation to respect requires States to refrain from interfering with the enjoyment of economic, social and cultural rights. . . . The obligation to protect requires States to prevent violations of such rights by third parties. . . . The obligation to fulfil requires States to take appropriate legislative, administrative, budgetary, judicial and other measures towards the full realization of such rights.[29]

The Commission was therefore on firm ground when, from the perspective of the different levels of state duty, it argued that the article 24 right to a healthy environment in the African Charter "is closely linked to economic and social rights in so far as the environment affects the quality of life and safety of the individual".[30] In the case put forward by the complainants the right to a clean environment was also linked to the right to physical and mental health in article 16 of the Charter, in which instance it was argued that the Nigerian government violated both rights by directly participating in the contamination of air, water and soil; by failing to protect the Ogoni population from harm caused by the oil companies; and by failing to provide or permit environmental studies to determine the actual or potential health and environmental risks.[31]

The clear obligations imposed upon a State in terms of article 24 of the Charter, namely to take reasonable and other measures to prevent pollution and ecological damage and to secure ecologically sustainable development, are, according to the Commission, also a consequence of article 12 of the ICESCR, to which Nigeria is

26 Ibid. at para 46.
27 Ibid. at para 47.
28 For the Limburg Principles see Leckie and Gallagher, ed., *Economic, Social and Cultural Rights: A Legal Resource Guide* (USA: University of Pennsylvania Press, 2006) at 451.
29 See Leckie and Gallagher (*supra* note 28) at 464, 465, 466.
30 *SERAC* (*supra* note 13) at para 51.
31 Ibid. at para 50.

a party. This provision requires States Parties to take the necessary steps for the full realization of the right to health and for the improvement of all aspects of environmental and industrial hygiene. As regards the complaints in the *SERAC* case, this would mean that:

> The state is under an obligation to respect these rights and this largely entails non-interventionist conduct from the state; for example, to desist from carrying out, sponsoring or tolerating any practice, policy or legal measures violating the integrity of the individual.
>
> Government compliance with the spirit of articles 16 and 24 of the African Charter must also include ordering or at least permitting independent scientific monitoring of threatened environments, requiring and publicising environmental and social impact studies prior to any major industrial development, undertaking appropriate monitoring and providing information to those communities exposed to hazardous materials and activities and providing meaningful opportunities for individuals to be heard and to participate in the development decisions affecting their communities.[32]

State conduct in the *SERAC* case was the direct opposite of what is required in terms of these standards. Not only was there no protection at all, but the State itself, through its security forces, engaged in repressive activities that violated the rights in question. This conduct, the Commission found, also violated article 21 of the African Charter in that the affected communities were prevented from freely disposing, in their own interest, of their wealth and natural resources.[33] The same consequence will be visited upon the State if it fails in its duty to protect its citizens against the harmful conduct of private parties, which, *in casu*, was clear from the Nigerian government's allowing the oil companies to destroy the livelihoods of the Ogoni communities with impunity. In this instance the Commission took its lead from the well-known *Velásquez* case[34] where the Inter-American Court of Human Rights ruled as follows:

> The State is obligated to investigate every situation involving a violation of the rights protected by the Convention. If the State apparatus acts in such a way that the violation goes unpunished and the victim's full enjoyment of such rights is not restored as soon as possible, the State has failed to comply with its duty to ensure the free and full exercise of those rights to the persons within its jurisdiction. The same is true when the State allows private persons or groups to act freely and with impunity to the detriment of the rights recognised by the Convention.[35]

32 Ibid. at para 52, 53. See also principle 10 of the Rio Declaration on Environment and Development (1992).

33 Ibid. at para 55.

34 *Velásquez v Honduras*, Inter-American Court, Series C no 4, Judgment of 29 July 1988. See *SERAC* (*supra* note 13) at para 57, 58.

35 Ibid. at para 176.

20.2.3 Scope and content of the right to a satisfactory environment

The significance of the *SERAC* case firstly is that it has confirmed the right to a satisfactory environment as enshrined in the African Charter, and secondly, that there are specific State duties with regard to the realization of the right that signatory states take upon themselves. The different levels of State duties and what each entails constitute further confirmation of an established international law principle, namely the principle of due diligence, which, *inter alia*, embodies certain preventative steps States are bound to take to prevent harm from occurring in neighbouring States. In the *Pulp Mills* case the International Court of Justice has pointed out that the "principle of prevention, as a customary rule, has its origins in the due diligence that is required of a State in its territory".[36] In the fundamental rights field this principle has been confirmed in the landmark ruling by the Inter-American Court of Human Rights in the *Gonzales* case.[37]

By exposing the inaction of the Nigerian government and the latter's complicity in the violation of the rights concerned, the Commission has also brought to an end the impunity with which the rights have been violated. In this regard one should take note of the 1997 impunity report of the Special Rapporteur to the Sub-Commission on the Prevention of Discrimination and Protection of Minorities.[38] There it was noted that to be complete and effective, "the campaign against immunity must be preceded by a serious and thorough investigation to bring to light the factual sources of the violations and identify the perpetrators and the victims so that the former can be punished and the damage done to the latter can be appropriately remedied".[39] This is what the communication and the findings of the Commission did in the *SERAC* case. The report further mentioned that various international instruments incorporate principles of combating impunity with regard to violations of economic, social and cultural rights and the right to development and then made the rather strange observation that although "the legal framework for the right to a healthy environment is still lacking, that does not prevent it from being included in the existing legal framework", apparently referring to the legal framework that exists for economic, social and cultural rights and the right to development.[40] That there is no reference here to article 24 of the African Charter is even more inexplicable in view of the fact that the Special Rapporteur, where the report dealt with regional human rights instruments, specifically mentioned articles 20 (right to existence), 21 (right to freely dispose of wealth and natural resources), and 22 (right to economic, social and cultural development) of the African Charter.[41]

---

36 *Case Concerning Pulp Mills on the River Uruguay (Argentina v Uruguay), International Court of Justice*, Merits, 20 April 2010, para 101.

37 *Gonzales v Mexico*, Judgment of 16 November 2009, 49 ILM 640 (2010). See also the 2016 Report on Due Diligence in International Law by a Study Group of the International Law Association, available at http://www.ila-hq.org/en/study-groups/index.cfm/cid/1045, accessed on 13 December 2016.

38 UN Doc. E/CN.4/Sub.2/1997/8.

39 Ibid. at para 21.

40 Ibid. at para 23.

41 Ibid. at para 25(a).

What the Commission failed to give guidance on was the nature and content of the right to a satisfactory environment. As a result the substantive meaning of this right remains undefined and its future application probably dependent upon the context in which it will find application. However, the procedural aspects of the right are clearly demarcated in the Commission's analysis and the claimants' entitlement to information, prior consultation, impact assessments and access to a remedy henceforth a notable outcome of the proceedings.[42] In its unequivocal confirmation of the justiciability of the right to a satisfactory environment, the Commission has certainly opened up interesting prospects for other claimants in African countries, but, from a jurisprudential point of view it could have played a more significant role had it given a reasoned exposition of the relevant international and other sources that informed the outcome of its deliberations on the violation of the right to a satisfactory environment. Contrary to Shelton's conclusion, namely that "the Commission took pains to support its analysis and findings through numerous references to the decisions of other global and regional human rights bodies"[43], the Commission's reasoning on the satisfactory environment issue provides very little information on comparative developments.

20.3 The *Enderois* case[44]

20.3.1 Factual background

The Enderois community, comprising approximately 60,000 people, lived for centuries near Lake Bogoria in Kenya where they followed a pastoral way of life in which the lake area formed an integral part of their religious and traditional practices. The community and their way of life came under threat in 1963 when, following independence, the British Crown's claim to Enderois land was transferred to Kenyan county councils which held the land in trust for the community. Under new laws passed in 1973, the Kenyan government established a game reserve around the lake in 1978 and promised affected families of the community alternative fertile land. In addition the community would receive 25 per cent of the tourism revenues and a large portion of the employment opportunities generated by the game reserve. None of this became reality and the community was eventually forced to move to semi-arid land on the periphery of the lake with no access to the places where they used to perform their cultural and religious rites or grazed their cattle. When discussions with the government failed to produce any positive results they commenced action in the national courts only to be told by the Kenyan High Court that matters relating to a community's collective right to property cannot be entertained by the courts. Subsequent to this ruling, parts

---

42 See also Van der Linde and Louw (*supra* note 17) at 175.

43 D. Shelton "Decision regarding communication 155/96, African Commission on Human and Peoples Rights" 96 AJIL (2002) 937 at 941.

44 *Centre for Minority Rights Development (Kenya) and Minority Rights Group International on behalf of Enderois Welfare Council v Kenya*, IHRR vol 18 no 1 (2011).

of the community's land were then sold to third parties and mining concessions were granted without proper consultation with the community, an event that threatened pollution to the waterways which the community depended on.

Against this background, the applicants in the matter brought a complaint on behalf of the Enderois community to the African Commission alleging a violation of articles 8 (freedom of conscience and religion); 14 (right to property); 17 (freedom to take part in cultural life and the right to protect traditional values); 21 (right to freely dispose of wealth and natural resources); and 22 (right to economic, social and cultural development). For purposes of this chapter the focus will be on the violations and findings linked directly or indirectly to articles 21 and 22. Despite numerous reminders to submit arguments on the admissibility of the case, the respondent state failed to cooperate with the result that admissibility became a matter of course and based solely on the applicants' submission.

20.3.2 The preliminary issue of the distinct nature of the community and its right to protection

The respondent State requested the African Commission to determine whether the applicant community could be recognized as a community, sub-tribe or clan on their own. This was an issue in the matter in view of the fact that the respondent state was of the opinion that the Enderois could not be classified as a distinct community in need of special protection in view of the fact that the community formed an integral part of another tribe or tribes.[45]

This issue should be seen in the context of one of the distinctive features of the African Charter, namely the inclusion of *peoples'* rights in addition to individual rights. Apart from the ideological reasons behind this move, such as the insistence of States with socialist inclinations to include a reference to peoples' rights, there was the cultural justification of Leopold Senghor who explained the matter as follows: "We simply meant . . . to show our attachment to economic, social and cultural rights, to collective rights in general, rights which have a particular importance in our situation in a developing country" and added that in Africa "the individual and his rights are wrapped in the protection of the family and other communities".[46] Whatever the historical reasons behind the inclusion of the term, the meaning of 'peoples' in the Charter, is not without controversy. While an ideological understanding of the term as denoting the population of the territorial state still dominates, there is nothing that stands in the way of an interpretation according to which 'peoples' may refer to sub-groups with common characteristics based on language, culture, ethnicity, religion, etc. and not necessarily living in one territorial State.[47] Such an interpretation has the potential of expanding the protection of the African Charter to cover a variety of groups, a development that might not find favour with many states who fear the potential

45 Ibid. at para 145.
46 Quoted in Viljoen (*supra* note 4) at 242.
47 Ibid. at 243.

undermining of their territorial unity and sovereignty through rights-based claims by communities with collective interests. In the *SERAC* case the Commission did not clarify the concept 'peoples' but merely referred to the 'Ogoni people', the 'people of Ogoniland' or the 'Ogoni community as a whole' as the victims of the violation of Charter rights.

A Special Rapporteur mission to Kenya on the situation of indigenous peoples confirmed the problematic nature of the issues involved here. In the Special Rapporteur's subsequent report the following observation was made[48]:

> As in some other African countries . . . the contested use of the term 'indigenous' in Kenya has implications for policy decisions and therefore for the human rights of the concerned populations. From a human rights perspective, the question is not 'who came first' but the shared experiences of dispossession and marginalization. The term 'indigenous' is not intended to create a special class of citizens, but rather to address historical and present day injustices and inequalities . . .
>
> Within this perspective, pastoralists and hunter-gatherers are normally regarded as indigenous peoples in the international context, and they increasingly come to identify themselves as such in many countries, including in Africa. In Kenya they include pastoralist communities such as the Endorois, Borana, Gabra, Maasai, Pokot, Samburu, Turkana, and Somali, and hunter-gatherer communities whose livelihoods remain connected to the forest, such as the Awer (Boni), Ogiek, Sengwer, or Yaaku. Other groups such as the Nubians consider themselves as a minority that has also been marginalized, but in an urban context. They and other minority groups share demands to end discrimination and exclusion with indigenous peoples in Kenya. The Kenya Government normally refers to indigenous and minority groups jointly as 'minorities,' 'marginalized' or 'vulnerable communities.'

Finding clarity on the issues raised here has direct consequences for the rights covered in articles 20 to 24 of the African Charter. In the *Enderois* case, the African Commission adopted the criteria provided by the African Commission's Working Group of Experts on Indigenous Populations/Communities for identifying indigenous peoples.[49] In the Working Group's report the view was put forward that less emphasis should be placed on earlier definitions which focused on aboriginality because such a criterion is difficult to use and not very constructive in the African context. Instead, the focus:

> should be on the more recent approaches focussing on *self-definition* as indigenous and distinctly different from other groups within a state; on a *special attachment to and use of their traditional land* whereby their ancestral

---

48 Report of the Special Rapporteur on the Situation of Human Rights and Fundamental Freedoms of Indigenous People, A/HRC/4/32 Add.3, 15 February 2007, para 9.10.

49 *Enderois* case (*supra* note 44) at para 150.

land and territory has a fundamental importance for their collective physical and cultural survival as peoples; on an experience of *subjugation, marginalization, dispossession, exclusion or discrimination* because these peoples have different cultures, ways of life or modes of production than the national hegemonic and dominant model.[50]

In the same report the Working Group has indicated that the most challenging aspect of the rights of indigenous peoples might be the issue of a collective right which implies an understanding of the term 'peoples'. While this concept has an historical link with colonization and the right to self-determination, in the post-colonial phase of Africa's development, the African Charter "needs to be understood and interpreted in the light of present realities where there is a great need of promotion and protection of the human rights of vulnerable groups and peoples within national states."[51]

In contrast with the stance taken by the UN Special Rapporteur and the Commission's African Working Group, the Kenyan constitution and legal system at the time did not recognize economic, social and cultural rights or the collective rights of indigenous communities. In addition Kenya was not a signatory to the ILO Convention No 169 on Indigenous and Tribal Peoples and has not supported the United Nations Declaration on the Rights of Indigenous Peoples. The line of thinking adopted by the African Commission vindicated, in the first instance, the findings and observations of the Special Rapporteur and the African Working Group. Relying heavily on the elements of self-identification and the Enderois community's relationship with a distinct territory for cultural, religious and economic purposes, the Commission was of the firm view that the Enderois community enjoyed collective rights as a people under the African Charter and is entitled to protection against a violation of their rights by the Kenyan government.[52]

Further inspiration for this conclusion came from the jurisprudence developed by the Inter-American Court of Human Rights. Instructive in this regard are *Moiwana Village v Suriname*[53] and *Saramaka People v Suriname*.[54] In *Moiwana Village*, part of a community was massacred and the rest forcefully driven off their land in the course of military clashes in Suriname in 1986. The impugned conduct, which, according to the facts, was attributed to the State, constituted, *inter alia*, a violation of article 21 of the American Convention on Human Rights which guarantees the right to property. In its assessment of the violation concerned, the Inter-American Court stated as follows:

> [T]his Court has held that, in the case of indigenous communities who have occupied their ancestral lands in accordance with customary practices – yet

---

50 Report of the African Commission's Working Group on Indigenous Populations/Communities, DOC/OS (XXXIV)/345, 14 May 2003, at 63.

51 Ibid. at 75.

52 *Enderois* case (*supra* note 44) at para 154–57.

53 Series C No 124, Judgment of 15 June 2005.

54 16 IHRR 2009, Judgment of 28 November 2007.

who lack real title to the property – mere possession of the land should suffice to obtain official recognition of their communal ownership. That conclusion was reached upon considering the unique and enduring ties that bind indigenous communities to their ancestral territory. The relationship of an indigenous community with its land must be recognized and understood as the fundamental basis of its culture, spiritual life, integrity, and economic survival. For such peoples, their communal nexus with the ancestral territory is not merely a matter of possession and production, but rather consists in material and spiritual elements that must be fully integrated and enjoyed by the community, so that it may preserve its cultural legacy and pass it on to future generations.[55]

The importance of this ruling for the African Commission lies in the fact that the community in question was not even indigenous to the area but only settled there in the nineteenth century however it exercised possession over the land ever since in strict adherence to their customary practices.[56] In this way, the Inter-American Court concluded, the Moiwana community members "possess an 'all-encompassing relationship' to their traditional lands, and their concept of ownership regarding that territory is not centered on the individual, but rather on the community as a whole".[57] A similar approach was followed by the Court in the *Saramaka* case which also involved State interference with the communal property of the Saramaka people, who likewise, were not indigenous to the area but settled there as a consequence of European colonization in the seventeenth century. As a distinct tribal community they require special measures that guarantee the full enjoyment of their rights.[58]

20.3.3 The land tenure issue

Legal title to land is central to the enjoyment of property rights. Without legal certainty of title, freedom to dispose of natural resources and the right to economic development will remain tenuous and open to exploitation. It is for these reasons that the African Commission's engagement with security of land tenure in the *Enderois* case has high significance. The general concerns of the complainants in the case bring the nature and scope of the land tenure issue in focus where they argued before the Commission that indigenous groups' specific form of land tenure creates a particular set of problems, such as the lack of formal title recognition of historic territories, the failure of domestic law to acknowledge communal property rights, and the claiming of legal title to indigenous land by the authorities, which has often led to the displacement of people from their historic territory. Aware of these issues, the African Commission has addressed

55 *Moiwana Village* (*supra* note 53) at para 131.
56 *Enderois* case (*supra* note 44) at para 159.
57 *Moiwana Village* (*supra* note 53) at para 133.
58 *Saramaka* case (*supra* note 54) at para 84, 85.

the complaint from the standpoint that the "first step in the protection of traditional African communities is the acknowledgement that the rights, interests and benefits of such communities in their traditional lands constitute 'property' under the Charter and that special measures may have to be taken to secure such 'property rights'".[59]

In this latter instance the Commission relied on the ruling by the European Court of Human Rights in *Doğan v Turkey*[60] which involves the forceful eviction of the applicants from their unregistered property by security forces in 1994. With reference to the right to peaceful enjoyment of one's possessions in article 1 of Protocol I to the European Convention on Human Rights, the Court concluded that the term 'possessions' is not limited to ownership of physical goods and that other rights and interests constituting assets can be regarded as 'property rights' and henceforth as 'possessions' for purposes of the Convention.[61] In the present matter, the Court mentioned rights over common lands, such as pasture, grazing, forest land and the income derived from stockbreeding and tree-felling, as falling within the provision's ambit of what is referred to as 'possessions'.[62]

Following this approach the African Commission concluded that the obligation in article 14 of the African Charter, namely that the State must guarantee the right to property, entails more than *respecting* the right. What are required are measures that will *protect* the right. Important for the Commission's views in this regard, and on which the Commission relied, was the stance taken by the Inter-American Court on Human Rights in the seminal case of the *Mayagna AwasTingni Community*[63] and the already mentioned *Saramaka* case. The subject-matter of the former case relates to the failure by the respondent government to demarcate and register legal title to the community's communal land; to provide effective measures to secure the property rights of the community to ancestral land and natural resources; and to provide an effective remedy in response to the community's claims in relation to their communal property. The respondent government was also accused of unlawfully interfering with the community's property rights by granting concessions on community land to foreign companies without prior consultation with and the consent of the community.

Pertinent to the matter was, *inter alia*, article 21 of the Inter-American Convention on Human Rights which protects the use and enjoyment of property. Similar to the European Court of Human Rights, the Inter-American Court followed a broad interpretation of the property concept by concluding that:

> Property can be defined as those material things which can be possessed, as well as any right which may be part of a person's patrimony; that concept

---

59 *Enderois* case (*supra* note at 44) para 187.
60 41 EHRR (2005) at 231.
61 Ibid. at para 138.
62 Ibid. at para 139.
63 *The Mayagna (Sumo) AwasTingni Community v Nicaragua*, Inter-American Court of Human Rights, Series C, No 79 (2001).

includes all movables and immovables, corporeal and incorporeal elements and any other intangible object capable of having value.[64]

And making it further clear that:

> Through an evolutionary interpretation of international instruments for the protection of human rights, taking into account applicable norms of interpretation and pursuant to article 29(b) of the Convention -which precludes a restrictive interpretation of rights-, it is the opinion of this Court that article 21 of the Convention protects the right to property in a sense which includes, among others, the rights of members of the indigenous communities within the framework of communal property, which is also recognized by the Constitution of Nicaragua.[65]

In realizing their rights, the members of the community are therefore entitled to claim that the State carry out the delimitation, demarcation and titling of the territory in question and that the State abstains from carrying out, until the delimitation, etc. has taken place, actions that might lead agents of the state, acting with the acquiescence of third parties, to affect the existence, use, enjoyment or value of the communal property. By not having complied with its duties in this regard, the State violated article 21 of the Inter-American Convention.[66] Following the same approach to article 21, the Inter-American Court in the *Saramaka* case confirmed its earlier jurisprudence in this regard by stating that "the State has an obligation to adopt special measures to recognize, respect, protect and guarantee the communal property right of the members of the Saramaka community to said territory".[67]

Apart from the Inter-American jurisprudence, the African Commission also invoked the United Nations Declaration on the Rights of Indigenous Peoples, adopted by General Assembly resolution 61/295 of 13 September 2007.[68] In this instance the African Commission considered as relevant the provisions in the Declaration containing State obligations to provide effective measures preventing any action which has the aim of dispossessing indigenous peoples of their lands and territories (art 8(2)(b)); preventing forceful removal of indigenous peoples from their lands and territories (art 10); guaranteeing the right of indigenous peoples to maintain and strengthen their spiritual relationship with their traditionally owned lands (art 25); guaranteeing indigenous peoples' right to their traditional lands and the right to own, use, develop and control such lands (art 26); and instructing the state to establish and implement, in consultation

---

64 Ibid. at para 144.
65 Ibid. at para 148.
66 Ibid. at para 153. See also Anaya and Crider "Indigenous peoples, the environment, and commercial forestry in developing countries: the case of AwasTingni, Nicaragua" 18 HRQ (1996) 345–67.
67 *Saramaka* case (*supra* note 54) at para 96.
68 See *Enderois* case (*supra* note 44) at para 204.

with the indigenous peoples concerned, a fair, independent, impartial, open and transparent process for the recognition and adjudication of the rights of indigenous peoples in relation to their land, territories and resources (art 27).

From the above developments, the African Commission was in a position to draw the following conclusions with regard to the position of the Enderois community and the rights they are entitled to with regard to their traditional land around Lake Bogoria:

> (1) Traditional possession of land by indigenous people has the equivalent effect as [*sic*] that of state-granted full property title; (2) traditional possession entitles indigenous people to demand official recognition and registration of property title; (3) the members of indigenous peoples who have unwillingly left their traditional lands, or lost possession thereof, maintain property rights thereto, even though they lack legal title, unless the lands have been lawfully transferred to third parties in good faith; and (4) the members of indigenous peoples who have unwillingly lost possession of their lands, when those lands have been lawfully transferred to innocent third parties, are entitled to restitution thereof or to obtain other lands of equal extension and quality. Consequently, possession is not a requisite condition for the existence of indigenous land restitution rights. The instant case of the Enderois is categorised under this last conclusion. The African Commission thus agrees that the land of the Enderois has been encroached upon.[69]

A final matter that deserves attention here are the conditions under which an interference with a property right in terms of article 14 of the African Charter will be justifiable. For this to be the case article 14 requires that the encroachment must satisfy a public need or the general interest of the community and be in accordance with the law. The Commission's point of departure in this instance is that a limitation on rights, to be lawful, must be proportionate to a legitimate need and must follow the least restrictive means possible in the circumstances.[70] In weighing up the interest in pursuing the establishment of a game reserve with the upheaval and displacement suffered by the Enderois community, coupled with the erosion of their property rights, the Commission was unable to find justification for the State's action in the proportionality principle, a finding that was strengthened by the fact that the government could not convince the Commission that alternative means were considered to achieve the objective the government had in mind and which would have been more proportional to the need.[71] In view of the facts of the case and the evidence presented to the Commission, this conclusion is unproblematic. Of some concern though is the Commission's confusion of *public interest* with *state interest* in its analysis of the justification prerequisites in article 14. Here, the Commission starts off by stating

69 Ibid. at para 209.
70 Ibid. at para 214.
71 Ibid. at para 214, 215.

that the public interest test under article 14 is met with a "much higher threshold in the case of encroachment of indigenous land rather than individual private property". In justifying this reasoning, the Commission refers to a 2005 report by the Special Rapporteur of the United Nations' Sub-Commission for the Promotion and Protection of Human Rights where it was stated that "[limitations], if any, on the right to (sic) indigenous peoples to their natural resources must flow only from the most urgent and compelling interest of the state".[72] By equating public interest with state interest the Commission is giving undue prominence to the *salus publica* doctrine in terms of which state interests – as distinct from the common weal – assume an all-encompassing importance in what is supposed to be a balanced accommodation of a plurality of interests of which state interests are but one component. This is exactly the purpose of the common or public interest which becomes possible only where a separation between state and the plurality of non-state entities and their interests is maintained.

The last issue of note raised by the Commission in this regard is the requirement in article 14 that an encroachment must comply with an appropriate legal rule. This means, according to the Commission, that the respondent State must be able to show that the removal of the Enderois community took place in accordance with both Kenyan and international law.[73] Other than relying on the gazetting of the trust land for purposes of a game reserve, the government could provide no other convincing proof that the Enderois trust land became legally extinguished, absolving the state from honouring its legal commitments to the community.[74] As a result the African Commission turned to what it considered to be two remaining elements of the "in accordance with the law" test, namely proper consultation with the affected community and the payment of compensation. In these instances too, the Kenyan authorities were found to be in default. To illustrate what is required of a government in such circumstances, the Commission invoked the safeguards spelled out in the *Saramaka* case.[75] There, the Inter-American Court specified that[76]:

In this particular case, the restrictions in question pertain to the issuance of logging and mining concessions for the exploration and extraction of certain natural resources found within Saramaka territory. Thus, in accordance with Article 1(1) of the Convention, in order to guarantee that restrictions to the property rights of the members of the Saramaka people by the issuance of concessions within their territory does not amount to a denial of their survival as a tribal people, the State must abide by the following three safeguards: First, the State must ensure the effective participation of the members of the Saramaka people, in conformity with their customs and

72 Ibid. at para 212.
73 Ibid. at para 219.
74 Ibid. at para 224.
75 Ibid. at para 227.
76 *Saramaka* case (*supra* note 54) at para 129.

traditions, regarding any development, investment, exploration or extraction plan (hereinafter 'development or investment plan') within Saramaka territory. Second, the State must guarantee that the Saramakas will receive a reasonable benefit from any such plan within their territory. Thirdly, the State must ensure that no concession will be issued within Saramaka territory unless and until independent and technically capable entities, with the State's supervision, perform a prior environmental and social impact assessment. These safeguards are intended to preserve, protect and guarantee the special relationship that the members of the Saramaka community have with their territory, which in turn ensures their survival as a tribal people.

20.3.4 Violation of the right to freely dispose of wealth and natural resources

According to article 21 of the African Charter this right must be exercised in the exclusive interest of the people. In the case of spoliation, a dispossessed people shall have the right to lawful recovery of the property as well as to adequate compensation. To illustrate that a people inhabiting a certain region within a territorial State could also claim under article 21 of the Charter, the African Commission relied on the *Ogoni* case where it was resolved that the right to natural resources contained within traditional lands vests in the people inhabiting the land.[77] The African Working Group has also shown that dispossession of land and natural resources, upon which traditional communities often depend for their survival, has become a major human rights problem, with the result that the protection of rights to land and natural resources have become critical for the survival of subsistence communities and for food security. The protection in question here relates, according to the African Working Group, to articles 20, 21, 22 as well as 24 of the African Charter.[78]

In the *Enderois* case it was argued that the violation of article 21 of the African Charter consists in preventing the community form accessing vital resources in the Lake Bogoria region and in the granting of mining concessions in the area to foreign companies without the community having a share in the natural resources and in the benefits thereof. In their claims the community also argued that article 21 protects the right of the community to the *potential* wealth of their land, which would include revenue derived from tourism, the ruby industry and other possible resources and that since their eviction they have been denied access to these benefits.[79]

In responding to these claims, the African Commission relied, once again, on the jurisprudence of the *Saramaka* case.[80] What deserves special mention here is that in *Saramaka* the legal and constitutional framework of Suriname did not

---

77 *Enderois* case (*supra* note 44) at para 255. See also *Saramaka* case (*supra* note 54) at para 158.
78 African Working Group Report (*supra* note 50) at 11.
79 *Enderois* case (*supra* note 44) at para 124.
80 Ibid. at para 257 ff.

grant property rights to the Saramaka people and furthermore vested ownership of all natural resources in the state. On this basis, the State could claim before the Inter-American Court that it had an inalienable right of exploration and exploitation to such resources. However, besides the law of the State, the customary laws of the Saramaka people entitled them to claim a right over all natural resources within traditional territories.[81] These conflicting positions the Inter-American Court addressed with reference to the duty of signatory States to take special measures in complying with their treaty obligations in respect of the rights of traditional communities and concluded as follows[82]:

> In accordance with this Court's jurisprudence as stated in the Yakye Axa and Sawhoyamaxa cases, members of tribal and indigenous communities have the right to own the natural resources they have traditionally used within their territory for the same reasons that they have a right to own the land they have traditionally used and occupied for centuries. Without them, the very physical and cultural survival of such peoples is at stake. Hence the need to protect the lands and resources they have traditionally used to prevent their extinction as a people. That is, the aim and purpose of the special measures required on behalf of the members of indigenous and tribal communities is to guarantee that they may continue living their traditional way of life, and that their distinct cultural identity, social structure, economic system, customs, beliefs and traditions are respected, guaranteed and protected by States.

On the basis of this understanding of traditional rights over natural resources, the African Commission then draws attention to the concomitant duty of the respondent state in the *Enderois* case to assess whether the restrictions imposed on the community's right to natural resources met with the requirements of article 14. Since the Commission was not apprised of any information in this regard, a violation of article 14 must be found to exist. This finding had implications for the respondent state under article 21 as well. In view of the fact that a justification for the interference with the community's right to natural resources was not established, the restitution and compensation obligations under article 21(2) must consequently be complied with by the respondent State.[83]

20.3.5 *The violation of the right to development*

In article 22 of the African Charter the right of all peoples to economic, social and cultural development is coupled with the State's duty to, individually or collectively, ensure the exercise of the right to development. In the proceedings before the African Commission, the Enderois community alleged a violation of this right by the Kenyan authorities in creating a game reserve on community

---

81 *Saramaka* case (*supra* note 54) at para 119.
82 Ibid. at para 121.
83 *Enderois* case (*supra* note 44) at para 267, 268.

land and in failing to adequately ensure the community's participation in the process through proper consultation. It must be noted that the participation issue is also the subject-matter of an earlier African instrument, namely the African Charter for Popular Participation in Development and Transformation (1990). In this Charter, popular participation is seen as both a means and an end. As an instrument of development, popular participation is essential for a collective commitment to development processes, and as an end in itself, it constitutes a fundamental right of the people to fully and effectively participate in decision-making that affects them.[84]

This view also informed the African Commission's reading of the right to development where it stated that the right is both constitutive and instrumental, or procedural and substantive. In this context the Commission took note of the complainant's arguments in the *Enderois* case, namely that the right to development requires compliance with five main criteria: "it must be equitable, non-discriminatory, participatory, accountable, and transparent, with equity and choice as important, over-arching themes in the right to development".[85] Much of the resulting analysis of the Commission then centred around issues of consultation and choice. With regard to the former, the Commission pointed to a number of deficiencies in the process which rendered consultation with the affected community meaningless. The government refused registration of the community's representative body, confronted the community with a *fait accompli* and failed to fully inform the community members, who were illiterate and lacked understanding of the implications of the project, about the potential consequences of the project for the community. In these circumstances the participation was not free, active and meaningful.[86] In reaching this conclusion the African Commission relied on the findings of the Inter-American Commission of Human Rights in the *Dann* case where for a process of consent that was fully informed it was required, as a minimum condition, that "*all* of the members of a community are fully and accurately informed of the nature and consequences of the process and provided with an effective opportunity to participate individually or as collectives".[87]

On the choice issue it was argued on behalf of the Enderois community that inherent in the right to dispose of natural resources and the right to development is the liberty of action and freedom of choice. Hence, the right to development is about an improvement and increase in capacities and choices, which could not be realized because of the loss of resources and well-being they suffered at the hands of the government's actions in respect of their trust land and their exclusion from effective participation in the game reserve project.[88] These arguments were conceded by the Commission in finding that the Kenyan authorities failed in their

---

84 African Charter for Popular Participation, *supra* note at art 10.
85 *Enderois* case (*supra* note 44) at para 277.
86 Ibid. at para 280–83.
87 *Mary and Carrie Dann v USA*, 10 IHRR 1143 (2003). See *Enderois* case (*supra* note 43) at para 290, 291.
88 *Enderois* case (*supra* note 43) at para 128, 129.

responsibility to include the affected community in the development process, to provide alternative and suitable land and adequate compensation and benefits.[89]

20.4 Conclusion

In the two cases discussed in this chapter, the African Commission developed important guidelines in terms of which government compliance should be measured with regard to sustainable development, access to and the use of natural resources and the taking of protective measures against environmental harm. Of special significance in this regard are the clear formulations on State duties and compliance responsibilities Parties to human rights treaties incur. By invoking case law developments in other regions of the world, most notably in the Americas, the African Commission has clearly demonstrated its willingness to give content to provisions of the African Charter in accordance with an expanding international body of law on the subject-matter. This comparative method has the added value that environmental law principles and notions of sustainable development will increasingly assume a universal meaning and importance in determining whether States have acted with due diligence in responding to the environmental and developmental rights and interests of their citizens.

89 Ibid. at para 298.

21 Sustainable development priorities in the Inter-American Human Rights system

Alexandra Keenan

21.1 Introduction

The New Delhi Principles of Sustainable Development (New Delhi Principles or New Delhi Declaration) recognize, explicitly and implicitly, that aspects of sustainable development intersect in ways that are particular to the circumstances of people's lives and that people must play a part in shaping sustainable societies. The Inter-American Court of Human Rights (the Court) has exemplified these notions in its case law in the past decade, particularly in relation to the rights of indigenous and tribal peoples. The Court relies on the global human rights context to interpret the American Convention on Human Rights[1] (the Convention or American Convention) in a dynamic fashion. This methodology enables its judges to establish links between the environment, culture, spirituality, development and human health – and between generations – that are not clearly evident in the text of the Convention itself.

In the Americas, these connections are perhaps most pronounced in the circumstances of indigenous and tribal peoples, whose holistic relationships with their traditional territories the Court recognizes as crucial to the full exercise of their human rights. As a result, the Court has formed a robust conception of property rights under the American Convention. It has interpreted the Convention's right to property as protecting indigenous and tribal communities' collective right to the secure possession, use and enjoyment of their traditional lands and resources.

The right to property envisioned by the Court also includes the right to exercise a degree of control over the use and development of the land and resources to ensure their continued enjoyment. Indigenous and tribal peoples' dependence upon their ancestral lands and the ecological integrity thereof demands that they participate meaningfully in decisions about where they live and how the land is used. The Court has declined to impose its own solutions and has instead ordered States to consult with affected peoples according to the peoples' own values, traditions, and customary law.

---

1 American Convention on Human Rights (Pact of San José, Costa Rica) (adopted 22 November 1969, entered into force 18 July 1978) OASTS No 36, 1144 UNTS (American Convention).

The Court's strongest expressions of these two New Delhi Principles have been in the realm of indigenous and tribal peoples' human rights, but it would be remiss to ignore developments outside the indigenous and tribal context. While the Court has not recognized similar interrelationships between ecological integrity and the general public's cultural, spiritual and material well-being, it has recognized that sustainable development is a matter of public interest and that the American Convention obliges States to facilitate public participation in development decisions through a robust conception of the right of access to state-held information.

21.2 The principles of public participation and integration

Two of the New Delhi Principles stand out in the Inter-American Court's more recent decisions: the principle of public participation and access to information and justice (Principle 5), and the principle of integration and interrelationship (Principle 7).

The New Delhi Declaration describes public participation as 'a condition for responsive, transparent and accountable governments'.[2] The principle encompasses 'the human right to hold and express opinions and to seek, receive and impart ideas' as well as 'a right of access to appropriate, comprehensible and timely information' without undue hardship in obtaining such access[3] and access to justice.

The principle of integration and interrelationship focuses on the connections between human rights, social and environmental objectives.[4] It seeks a multifaceted approach to principles and rules of international sustainable development law and recognizes that current and future generations' needs are interdependent.[5] The Declaration encourages states to 'resolve apparent conflicts between competing economic, financial, social and environmental considerations' through new or existing institutions.[6] Finally, the Declaration exhorts that each principle be construed in the context of the Declaration as a whole and consistent with the Charter of the United Nations.[7]

21.3 The Inter-American Human Rights System

The Organization of American States (OAS) established the Inter-American Human Rights system with the American Declaration on the Rights of Man in 1948. This Declaration was followed by the Inter-American Convention

---

2 ILA New Delhi Declaration of Principles of International Law Relating to Sustainable Development, 2 April 2002, Principle 5.1.
3 Ibid. at Principle 5.2.
4 Ibid. at Principle 7.
5 Ibid. at Principle 7.1.
6 Ibid. at Principle 7.3.
7 Ibid. at Principle 7.4.

on Human Rights in 1969. Twenty-five members of the OAS have ratified or adopted the Convention.[8]

The Inter-American Commission on Human Rights (the Commission) is an autonomous organ of the OAS and represents all OAS Member States.[9] It investigates complaints or petitions regarding human rights violations and promotes human rights measures. Any person, group or NGO may present a petition to the Commission alleging violations of the American Declaration or the American Convention (in the latter case, if the State is a party to the Convention). The Commission will investigate the complaint. It may then hold a hearing and offer to help the Parties settle the matter before producing a private report containing recommendations. If the State Party fails to remedy the situation in time, the Commission will either prepare a second report or refer the case to the Inter-American Court of Human Rights.

The Court was established in 1979 to apply and interpret the American Convention and related treaties. Its contentious jurisdiction is limited to States that have ratified or adopted the Convention and that have explicitly accepted the Court's jurisdiction.

The Commission can appear before the Court in human rights litigation and may request advisory opinions from the Court on interpretation of the Convention. The Commission is a mandatory party to adjudication before the Court,[10] meaning that parties cannot bring a case before the Court without the Commission's consent. The Commission thus performs a gate-keeping role that restricts the cases and issues that appear before the Court. For example, in *Case of the Saramaka People v Suriname*[11] the Court declined to consider a variety of complaints about the effects of displacement resulting from the construction of a dam because the Commission's application to the Court excluded those particular issues from the debate.[12]

21.4 Interpreting and applying the Convention

Parties to the Convention undertake to respect the rights recognized therein and to adopt measures, legislative or otherwise, to give effect to the Convention's

---

8 Argentina, Barbados, Bolivia, Brazil, Colombia, Costa Rica, Chile, Dominica, Dominican Republic, Ecuador, El Salvador, Granada, Guatemala, Haiti, Honduras, Jamaica, Mexico, Nicaragua, Panama, Paraguay, Peru, Suriname, Trinidad and Tobago, Uruguay and Venezuela. Trinidad and Tobago denounced the American Convention on Human Rights by a communication addressed to the General Secretary of the OAS on May 26, 1998. See Organization of American States (Department of International Law), 'B-32: American Convention on Human Rights' <http://www.oas.org/juridico/English/sigs/b-32.html> accessed 3 April 2012.

9 Inter-American Commission on Human Rights, 'What is the IACHR?' <http://www.cidh.oas.org/what.htm> accessed 3 April 2012.

10 Statute of the Inter-American Court of Human Rights, OAS Res No 448 (IX-0/79), reprinted in Basic Documents Pertaining to Human Rights in the Inter-American System, OEA/Ser.L.V/II.82 doc.6 rev.1 (1992), art 28.

11 *Case of the Saramaka People v Suriname*, Judgment, Inter-American Court of Human Rights Series C No 172 (28 November 2007) (hereinafter *Saramaka*).

12 Ibid. at [11]–[17].

rights and freedoms in accordance with their constitutional processes. Article 1(1) states that:

> The States Parties to this Convention undertake to respect the rights and freedoms recognized therein and to ensure to all persons subject to their jurisdiction the free and full exercise of those rights and freedoms, without any discrimination for reasons of race, color, sex, language, religion, political or other opinion, national or social origin, economic status, birth, or any other social condition.[13]

Article 2 further provides that:

> Where the exercise of any of the rights or freedoms referred to in Article 1 is not already ensured by legislative or other provisions, the States Parties undertake to adopt, in accordance with their constitutional processes and the provisions of this convention, such legislative or other measures as may be necessary to give effect to those rights or freedoms.[14]

The substantive rights in the Convention are considered in conjunction with these two provisions.

In some cases, the legal protections already exist in domestic law, but the State lacks an effective process or the political will to grant effective remedies. In such cases, the Court will refer to Article 25 of the Convention:

1   Everyone has the right to simple and prompt recourse, or any other effective recourse, to a competent court or tribunal for protection against acts that violate his fundamental rights recognized by the constitution or laws of the state concerned or by this Convention, even though such violation may have been committed by persons acting in the course of their official duties.

2   The States Parties undertake:
   a   to ensure that any person claiming such remedy shall have his rights determined by the competent authority provided for by the legal system of the state;
   b   to develop the possibilities of judicial remedy; and
   c   to ensure that the competent authorities shall enforce such remedies when granted.

This provision enables the Court to require that States provide reasonable access to justice – an element of public participation – within their domestic systems. Several cases before the Court alleging violations of the right to property (Article 21) have been based in an abridgment of the State's Article 25 obligation to provide an effective legal regime to protect the right.

---

13 American Convention, *supra* note at art 1.
14 Ibid. at art 2.

An understanding of the Court's interpretation of the American Convention requires some familiarity with its interpretive provisions. Article 29 states that:

> No provision of this Convention should be interpreted as:
>
> a   permitting any State Party, group, or person to suppress the enjoyment or exercise of the rights and freedoms recognized in this Convention or to restrict them to a greater extent than is provided for herein;
>
> b   restricting the enjoyment or exercise of any right or freedom recognized by virtue of the laws of any State Party or by virtue of another convention to which one of the said states is a party;
>
> c   precluding other rights or guarantees that are inherent in the human personality or derived from representative democracy as a form of government; or
>
> d   excluding or limiting the effect that the American Declaration of the Rights and Duties of Man and other international acts of the same nature may have.[15]

Article 29 provides for the use of external aids, including other international instruments, to interpret the rights protected by the Convention. The Court has stated that the normative framework existing at the moment should shape the interpretation of international legal instruments[16] and that this interpretation must evolve.[17] In the *Case of the Mapiripán Massacre v Colombia*[18] the Court reasoned that, based on Article 29 of the American Convention and the rules of the Vienna Convention on the Law of Treaties, human rights treaties must be interpreted according to the existing circumstances rather than their 'original meaning'.[19] Accordingly, elements of domestic and international law external to the Convention can be used to expand its scope into areas that were not initially intended.[20] In particular, treaties and other instruments related to the Convention, as well as the broader Inter-American Human Rights system, should be taken into account when interpreting the Convention.[21] As will be seen, the Court has used this interpretive philosophy to connect protected rights with new concerns, including sustainable development as envisioned in the New Delhi Principles.

---

15   American Convention, *supra* note at art 29.

16   *Interpretation of the American Declaration of the Rights and Duties of Man within the Framework of Article 64 of the American Convention on Human Rights*, Advisory Opinion OC-10/89, Inter-American Court of Human Rights Series A No 10 (14 July 1989).

17   *Case of the Yakye Axa Indigenous Community v Paraguay*, Merits, Reparations, and Costs, Judgment, Inter-American Court of Human Rights Series C No 125 (17 June 2005) (hereinafter *Yakye Axa*) [146].

18   *Case of the 'Mapiripán Massacre' v Colombia*, Merits, Reparations, and Costs, Judgment, Inter-American Court of Human Rights Series C No 134 (15 September 2005) (hereinafter *Mapiripán Massacre*).

19   Ibid. at [37].

20   See Lucas Lixinski, 'Treaty Interpretation by the Inter-American Court of Human Rights: Expansionism at the Service of the Unity of International Law' (2010) 21 EJIL 585, 587.

21   *Yakye Axa* (*supra* note 17) at [126].

The Court often cites international legal instruments that are external to the OAS system, but at the same time, the OAS and its various organs have themselves been making incremental progress towards recognition of indigenous rights as well as the sustainable development aspects of human rights. In 2001, the OAS General Assembly passed a Resolution on Human Rights and the Environment in which it acknowledged that effective recognition of human rights, including full enjoyment of economic, social and cultural rights, could create the conditions for better environmental protection: modified behaviour patterns; reduced environmental impacts of poverty and of unsustainable development patterns; more effective dissemination of environmental information; and more active participation in political processes.[22] An American Declaration on the Rights of Indigenous Peoples is also in progress, the first draft having been approved in 1997.[23]

Finally, Articles 30 and 32 of the Convention delineate the limits on recognized rights:

Article 30. Scope of Restrictions

The restrictions that, pursuant to this Convention, may be placed on the enjoyment or exercise of the rights or freedoms recognized herein may not be applied except in accordance with laws enacted for reasons of general interest and in accordance with the purpose for which such restrictions have been established.[24]

Article 32. Relationship between Duties and Rights

1   Every person has responsibilities to his family, his community, and mankind.
2   The rights of each person are limited by the rights of others, by the security of all, and by the just demands of the general welfare, in a democratic society.[25]

The protected rights are thus restricted by the reasonable legal limits imposed by the sovereign States that are Parties to the Convention.

21.5 Integration, interrelationship, and indigenous rights to sustainable development

The situation of indigenous peoples in the Americas has long been a troubling and controversial topic. The nature of indigenous cultures provided the Court with a way to bring sustainable development principles – and in particular the

---

22 OAS General Assembly, 'Human Rights and the Environment' OEA/Ser G, AG/Res 1819 (XXX1-0/01).
23 Proposed American Declaration on the Rights of Indigenous Peoples (Approved by the Inter-American Commission on Human Rights on 26 February 1997) OEA/Ser/L/V/II.95 Doc 6, art XVIII(2).
24 American Convention, *supra* note at art 30.
25 American Convention, *supra* note at art 32.

principle of interdependence – into the purview of the Convention, as access to traditional territories and the ecological integrity of those territories is closely tied to indigenous peoples' enjoyment of their Convention rights.

As a result, although sustainable development was not contemplated in the text of the Convention, the Court has found a way to incorporate environmental principles into its jurisprudence by indentifying linkages between environmental integrity and health, culture, spirituality, and notions of 'a decent life'. These connections are most obvious – and infringements perhaps the most egregious – in the context of indigenous and tribal peoples.

21.5.1 The Awas Tigni *case: the right to communal property*

In *The Case of the Mayagna (Sumo) Awas Tigni Community v Nicaragua*,[26] the Court considered an indigenous group's opposition to a logging concession on the Community's traditional lands. The Awas Tigni Community's subsistence was based on family farming, communal agriculture, gathering, hunting and fishing, according to a traditional collective form of social organization.[27] In 1996, Nicaragua granted a 30-year concession to the Sol del Caribe, S.A. Corporation for logging within the lands that the Community occupied.[28] In response, the Community claimed collective ownership of the land on which the concession was granted.

The Community's claim was brought under Article 21 of the American Convention:

Art 21. Right to Property

1   Everyone has the right to the use and enjoyment of his property. The law may subordinate such use and enjoyment to the interest of society.
2   No one shall be deprived of his property except upon payment of just compensation, for reasons of public utility or social interest, and in the cases and according to the forms established by law.
3   Usury and any other form of exploitation of man by man shall be prohibited by law.[29]

In interpreting this Article the Court considered that, in the preparatory documents for the Convention, 'private property' was replaced by 'his property'.[30] In consideration of this, and of the principle articulated·in Article 29(b) of the Convention that no provision may be interpreted as restricting the enjoyment of any right or freedom, the Court found that Article 21 protected the rights of

---

26   *The Case of the Mayagna (Sumo) Awas Tigni Community v Nicaragua*, Judgment, Inter-American Court of Human Rights Series C No 125 (17 June 2005) (hereinafter *Awas Tigni*).
27   Ibid. at [103(e)].
28   Ibid. at [103(k)].
29   American Convention, *supra* note at art 21.
30   *Awas Tigni* (*supra* note 26) at [145].

indigenous communities to communal property.[31] Overall, the 'property' protected by Article 21 includes:

> those material things which can be possessed, as well as any right which may be part of a person's patrimony; that concept includes all movables and immovables, corporeal and incorporeal elements and any other intangible object capable of having value.[32]

The Court held that indigenous people's spiritual, cultural and economic reliance on the land, and their inherent right to live freely upon the land, must be recognized,[33] despite the Community not having a real property deed to the lands. It noted:

> Given the characteristics of the instant case, some specifications are required on the concept of property in indigenous communities. Among indigenous peoples there is a communitarian tradition regarding a communal form of collective property of the land, in the sense that ownership of the land is not centered on an individual but rather on the group and its community. Indigenous groups, by the fact of their very existence, have the right to live freely in their own territory; the close ties of indigenous people with the land must be recognized and understood as the fundamental basis of their cultures, their spiritual life, their integrity, and their economic survival. For indigenous communities, relations to the land are not merely a matter of possession and production but a material and spiritual element which they must fully enjoy, even to preserve their cultural legacy and transmit it to future generations.[34]

The Court insisted that indigenous customary law must form part of the analysis and that, according to these customary practices, possession of the land should suffice to grant indigenous communities official recognition and registration of their property rights.[35] The Court declared that the State had an obligation to delimit the territory owned by the Community and grant title to it, as the mere privilege of using the land was insufficient to ensure the Community's permanent use and enjoyment of it.[36]

The Court noted that Nicaragua's Constitution recognizes indigenous communal ownership of lands and peoples' rights to live according to their historical and cultural forms of social organization and to enjoy their natural resources,[37] but that the State did not have an effective procedure for delimiting, demarcating and titling

31   Ibid. at [148].
32   Ibid. at [144].
33   Ibid. at [148].
34   Ibid. at [149].
35   Ibid. at [152].
36   Ibid. at [149], [173.4].
37   Ibid. at [116]–[117].

indigenous communal lands.[38] It found that the Community had a communal property right to the lands they inhabited pursuant to the Constitution and the State had an obligation to delimit, demarcate and title the land to them – and to abstain from carrying out actions in the meantime that might affect the Community's enjoyment of its property.[39]

With this decision, the Court became the first international tribunal to uphold an indigenous group's land and resource rights in a legally binding judgment against a state.[40] Furthermore, it recognized the relationship between indigenous peoples' lands and their cultural, spiritual and material well-being that would pave the way for a progressive interpretation of the property rights protected by the Convention.

21.5.2 *The* Yakye Axa *and* Sawhoyamaxa *cases: the clash with private property rights*

In *Case of the Yakye Axa Indigenous Community v Paraguay*, the Court was called upon to weigh indigenous property rights against private property rights. It held that in conflicts between the two, States must consider the broader importance that ancestral property holds for indigenous communities and the fact that they have rights to the natural resources within their traditional territory.[41]

The Yakye Axa Community has an economy primarily based on hunting, gathering and fishing, and supplemented by farming.[42] Members traditionally moved across a wide geographical area to make use of the available resources. Towards the end of the nineteenth century, large areas of land in the Paraguayan Chaco were sold through the London Stock Exchange, and the Anglican Church established several missions in the area.[43] The Europeans established livestock estates where they employed the indigenous inhabitants of the lands.[44] Living conditions on the estates were often intolerable and Yakye Axa members living on one such estate, Estancia Loma Verde, left in 1986 to relocate to an Anglican resettlement far away, and ecologically very different, from their traditional territory.[45] Upon arrival at the settlement, they found that their living conditions did not improve.[46]

In 1993, the Community began taking steps to reclaim its traditional lands. In 1996, members of the Community began to settle alongside a public road facing the barbed wire fence of Estancia Loma Verde.[47] The Community's attempts

---

38 Ibid. at [127].
39 Ibid. at [153].
40 James Anaya and Claudio Grossman, 'The Case of Awas Tigni v Nicaragua: A New Step in the International Law of Indigenous Peoples' (2002) 19 AJICL 1, 2.
41 *Yakye Axa* (*supra* note 17) at [135].
42 Ibid. at [50.3].
43 Ibid. at [50.10].
44 Ibid. at [50.11].
45 Ibid. at [50.13]–[50.14].
46 Ibid. at [50.15].
47 Ibid. at [50.8].

to claim the territory through the state's administrative processes failed. The national Instituto de Bienestar Rural (IBR) recognized that the Community's claim to the land preceded, and was therefore superior to, private ownership, but the IBR could not request expropriation of the property because the firms owning the claimed land were making rational use of the property and refused to negotiate its sale.[48] Various attempts to effect legislative expropriation of the claimed lands in favour of the Community also failed.[49] The private landowners began clearing land, building and excavating within Estancia Loma Verde,[50] while prohibiting members of the Yakye Axa Community from entering or carrying out other activities inside the estate.[51] Community members had to travel far from the settlement to hunt and fish in other areas.[52] Serious health and nutrition problems affected the ability of the children to perform effectively in school,[53] while the deaths of elders in the community threatened cultural continuity.[54]

In June 1999, the President of the Republic of Paraguay issued a decree declaring a state of emergency regarding the Yakye Axa and acknowledging that the land owners' denial of access to the traditional territory denied the Community 'access to the traditional means of subsistence associated with their cultural identity'.[55] The State offered the Community alternate tracts of land but the Community rejected all of the offers, in some cases because the Community had not been adequately consulted in the selection of the lands and in other cases due to potential conflicts with other indigenous communities occupying the territory.[56]

Article 21 of the American Convention formed the crux of the Court's decision. To interpret Article 21 the Court turned to other treaties, such as the International Labour Organization's (ILO) Convention No. 169, which Paraguay had ratified.[57] Convention No. 169 deals extensively with the right of indigenous communities to communal property. It also provides that States must respect the cultural and spiritual values involved in the relationship with the land that peoples occupy and use, especially the collective aspects of the relationship.[58] Therefore, the close relationship between indigenous peoples and their lands and natural resources must be protected by Article 21 of the American Convention. The Court noted that:

> The culture of the members of the indigenous communities directly relates to a specific way of being, seeing, and acting in the world, developed on

48   Ibid. at [50.37].
49   Ibid. at [50.54]–[50.62].
50   Ibid. at [50.76].
51   Ibid. at [50.85].
52   Ibid. at [50.93].
53   Ibid. at [50.99].
54   Ibid. at [50.111].
55   Ibid. at [50.100].
56   Ibid. at [39.a], [50.61] and [171].
57   Ibid. at [130].
58   Ibid. at [136].

the basis of their close relationship with their traditional territories and the resources therein, not only because they are their main means of subsistence, but also because they are part of their worldview, their religiosity, and therefore, of their cultural identity.[59]

This statement marked the Court's recognition that Article 21 can also include a right to the natural resources located in and on the land.

Paraguay's Constitution provided for indigenous communal ownership of the land, sufficient for conservation and development of their own way of life, and for the right to remain in their territory.[60] Paraguayan law also provided a procedure for making indigenous claims to ancestral territory on private lands.[61] However, the procedures only allowed State bodies to expropriate land that was not under rational use, or to negotiate with the private owners, and left indigenous communities powerless when owners refused to sell land that was demonstrably under rational use.[62] The Court found these procedures to be ineffective and to fall short of the standard required by Article 21 of the Convention.[63]

In connection with Article 25, this shortcoming amounted to an abridgment of Convention rights.[64] To comply with the Convention, States must grant effective legal protection to indigenous peoples that 'takes into account their specificities, their economic and social characteristics, as well as their situation of special vulnerability, their customary law, values, and customs'.[65] The Court emphasized that recognition of indigenous lands, territories and resources must be more than abstract or juridical and must be physically delimited or established to be meaningful.[66] States must consider that indigenous territorial rights and control over their habitat are necessary to their survival as peoples, reproduction of their culture and pursuit of their aspirations.[67] In some cases, private property rights may be restricted in order to preserve cultural identities and could be justified if those affected pursuant to Article 21(2) receive fair compensation.[68]

However, indigenous communal rights will not always prevail.[69] In case of conflict between private property and indigenous communal property, the indigenous communal rights may be restricted if the restrictions are: (a) established by law; (b) necessary; (c) proportional (in the sense of interfering as little as possible with the rights); and (d) in pursuit of a legitimate goal in a democratic society.[70] In order to satisfy Article 21(1) of the Convention the restriction must fulfil

59 Ibid. at [135].
60 Ibid. at [74].
61 Ibid. at [75]–[77].
62 Ibid. at [97].
63 Ibid. at [98] and [103].
64 Ibid. at [61].
65 Ibid. at [63].
66 Ibid. at [143].
67 Ibid. at [146].
68 Ibid. at [148].
69 Ibid. at [149].
70 Ibid. at [144].

something more than a merely useful or timely purpose, and the public interest served by the restriction must be clearly more important than the full enjoyment of the indigenous right.[71]

When land cannot be returned to the indigenous group, compensation will be in order. Article 16(4) of ILO Convention No. 169 suggests that the selection of alternative lands or payment of compensation is not at the sole discretion of the State, but requires a consensus of the people in accordance with its own consultation processes, values, customs and customary law.[72]

The Court explained what was lacking in the state's response to the Community's claims:

> To guarantee the right of indigenous peoples to communal property, it is necessary to take into account that the land is closely linked to their oral expressions and traditions, their customs and languages, their arts and rituals, their knowledge and practices in connection with nature, culinary art, customary law, dress, philosophy, and values. In connection with their milieu, their integration with nature and their history, the members of the indigenous communities transmit this non-material cultural heritage from one generation to the next, and it is constantly recreated by the members of the indigenous groups and communities.
>
> While Paraguay recognizes the right to communal property in its own legal order, it has not taken the necessary domestic legal steps to ensure effective use and enjoyment by the members of the Yakye Axa Community of their traditional lands, and this has threatened the free development and transmission of their traditional practices and culture, in the terms set forth in the previous paragraph.[73]
>
> Paraguay had not obtained the Community's agreement with regard to the offer of alternative lands, and had therefore violated Article 21 of the American Convention.[74]

The Court also considered Article 4 of the Convention (Right to Life) to impose upon States an obligation to generate 'living conditions that are compatible with the dignity of the human person' and 'to take positive, concrete measures geared toward fulfillment of the right to a decent life'.[75] The Yakye Axa's distinctive worldview and relationship with the land and its members' individual and collective aspirations were relevant considerations to whether Paraguay had violated its obligations under Article 4. So, too, was the general duty to respect rights embodied in Article 1(1) and the duty of progressive development in Article 26 of the American Convention, as well as Articles 10 (Right to Health); 11 (Healthy

71   Ibid. at [145].
72   Ibid. at [150]–[151].
73   Ibid. at [154]–[155].
74   Ibid. at [152].
75   Ibid. at [162].

Environment); 12 (Food); 13 (Education); and 14 (the Benefits of Culture) of the Additional Protocol to the American Convention in the Area of Economic, Social, and Cultural Rights[76] and the provisions of ILO Convention No. 169.[77] The Court echoed the sentiment, expressed in the *Awas Tigni* case in accordance with the general rules of interpretation in Article 29 of the Convention, that communal property rights in ancestral lands hold special meaning for indigenous peoples and are important requisites for the preservation and inter-generational transmission of their cultural identity.[78] The Court explicitly recognized the link between the environment, culture and human rights, noting that for indigenous peoples like the Yakye Axa, the land was necessary for performing the traditional subsistence activities that provide the peoples with a 'decent existence' as envisioned by Article 4.

The Court then considered General Comment 14 of the United Nations Committee on Economic, Social and Cultural Rights, to the effect that measures to improve indigenous peoples' access to health services and care should be culturally appropriate, and that 'in indigenous communities, the health of the individual is often linked to the health of the society as a whole and has a collective dimension'.[79]

Special detriment to the right to health, and closely tied to this, detriment to the right to food and access to clean water, have a major impact on the right to a decent existence and basic conditions to exercise other human rights, such as the right to education or the right to cultural identity. In the case of indigenous peoples, access to their ancestral lands and to the use and enjoyment of the natural resources found on them is closely linked to obtaining food and access to clean water. In this regard, said Committee on Economic, Social and Cultural Rights has highlighted the special vulnerability of many groups of indigenous peoples whose access to ancestral lands has been threatened and, therefore, their possibility of access to means of obtaining food and clean water.[80]

The denial of the Community's right to communal property had a negative effect on the members' right to a decent life by depriving them of their traditional means of subsistence, clean water and ability to exercise traditional medicine.[81] The Court found that the State had therefore abridged Article 4(1) of the Convention by not taking measures to improve the conditions affecting community members' ability to have a decent life.[82]

---

76 Additional Protocol to the American Convention on Human Rights in the Area of Economic, Social and Cultural Rights (Protocol of San Salvador) (entered into force 16 November 1999) OAS Treaty Series No 69 (1988).

77 *Yakye Axa (supra* note 17) at [163].

78 Ibid. at [124].

79 Ibid. at [166], citing CESCR, 'General Comment No 14: The Right to the Highest Attainable Standard of Health (Article 12 of the International Covenant on Economic, Social and Cultural Rights)' (2000) UN Doc E/C.12/2000/4 [27].

80 *Yakye Axa (supra* note 17) at [167].

81 Ibid. at [168].

82 Ibid. at [176].

In granting reparations, the Court ordered Paraguay to identify the specific traditional territory of the Yakye Axa and to give it to the Community within three years.[83] If the land was in private hands, the State was to assess whether or not to expropriate the land according to the Court's criteria for restriction of property rights, taking into account the Community's values, practices, customs and customary law.[84] If expropriation was not possible, the State was to give the Community alternative land, sufficient to ensure preservation and development of the Community's way of life, and chosen by consensus with the Community according to the Community's own consultation and decision-making practices.[85]

The Sawhoyamaxa Community is a related Paraguayan indigenous community with a background and grievance very similar to that of the Yakye Axa. In 1991, the Sawhoyamaxa Community commenced a claim for lands within the area it traditionally occupied and used.[86] Most community members left the cattle estates to settle along the wire fences around the claimed land,[87] where they lived in conditions of extreme poverty, without adequate drinking water or services of any kind, and without the ability to grow crops.[88] They entered the claimed lands to hunt, fish and gather for subsistence.[89]

The companies that owned the lands contested the Community's land claim and the Community tried, unsuccessfully, to employ the State's administrative and political process for gaining title to the lands. The companies cut down large forested areas on the estates, despite an injunction against logging.[90]

The Court accepted that the claimed lands were suitable for the Community to continue its current subsistence activities, to survive in the short- and medium-term, and to begin a long-term development process for sustainable subsistence.[91] It also noted that the lack of a guaranteed right to its communal property and the conditions in which the Community was living were detrimental to the survival of its members' way of living, customs and language.[92]

Paraguay did not deny the importance of traditional subsistence activities to the Community's culture or even its right to lands of its own.[93] The dispute concerned the claim to land that was subject to long-standing registered title and whether the success of the Community's claim depended upon possession of the lands - which the Community did not have.[94]

83 Ibid. at [217].
84 Ibid.
85 Ibid.
86 *Case of the Sawhoyamaxa Indigenous Community v Paraguay*, Merits, Reparations, and Costs, Judgment, Inter-American Court of Human Rights Series C No 146 (29 March 2006) (hereinafter *Sawhoyamaxa*) [73(6)], [73(9)].
87 Ibid. at [73(7)].
88 Ibid. at [73(62)].
89 Ibid. at [73(71)].
90 Ibid. at [75(56)].
91 Ibid. at [73(10)].
92 Ibid. at [73(75)].
93 Ibid. at [124].
94 Ibid. at [125]–[126].

The Community claimed a violation of its members' Article 4 right to life and the Court noted that the State's duty to guarantee the right to life obligated it to take all necessary actions to remove the Community from the makeshift settlements and to do everything necessary to keep its members safe while they remained there.[95] The State's measures to ameliorate the situation were inadequate.[96] Because the Community's natural resources were related to its survival and way of life, the primary means of getting members out of the settlements was to return them to their ancestral lands so that they could use and enjoy those resources.[97] Paraguay had failed to provide an efficient administrative procedure to turn that goal into a reality.[98]

In analyzing Article 21, the Court again cited Article 13 of ILO Convention No. 169, which provides that States must respect the special cultural and spiritual relationship with the lands or territories occupied or used by indigenous peoples and 'the collective aspects of this relationship'.[99] Indigenous forms of ownership and possession of land that do not conform with the State's conception of property nevertheless deserve equal protection under Article 21 of the Inter-American Convention, and must receive equal protection in order to make Article 21 meaningful for millions of persons.[100]

Consequently, the close ties of indigenous peoples with their traditional lands and the native natural resources thereof, associated with their culture, as well as any incorporeal element deriving therefrom, must be secured under Article 21 of the American Convention.[101]

The Court recalled its previous decisions, in which it had recognized that traditional possession of land by an indigenous group gives rise to a right equivalent to official recognition and registration of title and an entitlement to restitution in the event that the group is deprived of its lands.[102] It noted that the laws of Paraguay provided for a right to claim restitution of traditional lands, a right which persisted for the duration of the indigenous community's unique spiritual and material relationship with the land and which withstood any denial of access to the land for reasons outside the community's control.[103] In this case, the Sawhoyamaxa Community had continued to carry out traditional activities on the claimed lands – despite being denied access to them – and still considered the lands to be its own, thus maintaining its right to restitution.[104]

The Court considered the restitution of traditional lands to be the best reparation measure in the circumstances and ordered the state to adopt all legislative, administrative or other measures necessary to guarantee the

---

95 Ibid. at [163].
96 Ibid. at [170].
97 Ibid. at [164].
98 Ibid.
99 Ibid. at [119].
100 Ibid. at [120].
101 Ibid. at [121].
102 Ibid. at [128].
103 Ibid. at [130]–[131].
104 Ibid. at [133]–[134].

Community ownership rights over its traditional lands.[105] Following *Yakye Axa*, the Court ordered the State to undertake the 'lawfulness, need and proportionality' analysis and, if restitution of the ancestral lands was not possible, to work with the Community to select alternative lands.[106] It clarified that neither the private holding nor the rational use of the Community's traditional lands would constitute an 'objective and sufficient ground' for denying restitution.[107]

21.5.3 The Saramaka *case: the protection of tribal peoples'* traditional resources

The Court has also recognized that tribal peoples have collective ownership rights in their lands, based on their fundamental relationship with their ancestral territories. This principle was spelled out in *Moiwana Community v Suriname*,[108] in the context of the Maroons of Suriname. The Court again picked up the theme in *Saramaka People v Suriname*.[109]

The Saramaka is a community of Maroons, descendants of slaves who escaped and formed culturally and linguistically distinct communities in the 1700s. Maroons are tribal peoples, meaning non-indigenous peoples that, in the findings of the Court, are socially, culturally and economically distinct from other sectors of the national community and that identify strongly with their ancestral territory and follow their own norms, customs and traditions.[110] The Court recognized that like indigenous peoples, tribal peoples have a right to protection of the natural resources necessary for their survival and development and for the continuance of their way of life, and may require special measures.[111]

The Saramaka have a strong spiritual relationship with the land where they realized their freedom.[112] To use the words of the Court, the land provides 'their social, ancestral, and spiritual essence'.[113] The Community therefore sought recourse under the American Convention when Suriname granted logging and

---

105 Ibid. at [210].
106 Ibid. at [212].
107 Ibid. at [214].
108 *Case of the Moiwana Community v Suriname*, Judgment, Inter-American Court of Human Rights Series C, No 124 (15 June 2005) [133]. The Court ordered the State to 'adopt such legislative, administrative and other measures as are necessary to ensure the property rights of the members of the Moiwana Community in relation to the traditional territories from which they were expelled, and provide for their use and enjoyment of these territories'. Ibid. at [209]. The measures were to be taken with the participation and informed consent of the victims of the Moiwana Village massacre. Ibid. at [210].
109 *Case of the Saramaka People v Suriname*, Judgment, Inter-American Court of Human Rights Series C, No 172 (28 November 2007) (hereinafter *Saramaka*).
110 Ibid. at [79]–[84].
111 Ibid. at [86].
112 Ibid. at [82].
113 Ibid.

mining concessions to private companies on the Saramaka's traditional lands without consulting the group.[114]

Suriname's domestic law does not recognize communal property. Instead, it provides that all natural resources belong to the State.[115] Furthermore, the State had not ratified ILO Convention No. 169, so the Court needed to look elsewhere to interpret Article 21 of the American Convention in that particular context. It found sources in both the International Covenant on Civil and Political Rights (ICCPR) and the International Covenant on Economic, Social and Cultural Rights (ICESCR), both of which Suriname had ratified.[116] Common Article 1 of the ICCPR provides that:

> [a]ll peoples may, for their own ends, freely dispose of their natural wealth and resources without prejudice to any obligations arising out of international economic co-operation, based upon the principle of mutual benefit, and international law. In no case may a people be deprived of its own means of subsistence.[117]

Article 27 of the ICCPR further guarantees minorities a right, 'in community with the other members of their group, to enjoy their own culture, to profess and practise their own religion, or to use their own language'.[118] The Court noted that the UN Human Rights Committee has interpreted this Article to include a right to practice a way of life that is closely tied to territory and natural resources.[119] Relying upon these sources and the fact that the American Convention could not be interpreted to restrict the rights enshrined in the ICCPR, the Court determined that Article 21 of the American Convention protects the Saramaka's right to use and enjoy traditional property according to the group's communal land tenure system, which is tied to a spiritual relationship with traditional lands.[120] This was not the first time that Article 27 of the ICCPR had been considered in this context; the UN Human Rights Committee had previously observed that it may protect the land and resource rights of Suriname's Maroons.[121] The adoption of this principle in a decision of the Inter-American Court made it binding upon the state, which had recognized the Court's jurisdiction pursuant to Article 62 of the American Declaration.

The Court maintained its holding, stated in *Awas Tigni,* that Article 21 entitles indigenous and tribal peoples to title to their land, not merely a privilege to

---

114 Lisl Brunner, 'The Rise of Peoples' Rights in the Americas: The *Saramaka People* Decision of the Inter-American Court of Human Rights' (2008) 7 Chinese JIL 699, 700.

115 Constitution of Suriname (1992), art 41, as cited in Brunner (*supra* note 114) at 700.

116 *Saramaka* (*supra* note 109) at [93].

117 International Covenant on Civil and Political Rights (adopted 16 December 1966, entered into force 23 March 1976) 999 UNTS 171 (hereinafter ICCPR).

118 International Covenant on Economic, Social and Cultural Rights (16 December 1966, entered into force 3 January 1976) 993 UNTS 3 (hereinafter ICESCR).

119 *Saramaka* (*supra* note 109) at [94].

120 Ibid. at [95]–[96].

121 UNCCPR, 'Concluding Observations of the Human Rights Committee: Suriname' (4 May 2004) UN Doc CCPR/CO/80/SUR [21].

use it that is vulnerable to outside interference.[122] As Suriname had not yet given legal effect to the Saramaka's property rights, it was not in compliance with the American Convention.[123]

With respect to the extent of the Saramaka's propery rights, the Court held that it extended to certain natural resources on the land:

> In accordance with this Court's jurisprudence as stated in the *Yakye Axa* and *Sawhoyamaxa* cases, members of tribal and indigenous communities have the right to own the natural resources they have traditionally used within their territory for the same reasons that they have a right to own the land they have traditionally used and occupied for centuries. Without them, the very physical and cultural survival of such peoples is at stake. Hence the need to protect the lands and resources they have traditionally used to prevent their extinction as a people. That is, the aim and purpose of the special measures required on behalf of the members of indigenous and tribal communities is to guarantee that they may continue living their traditional way of life, and that their distinct cultural identity, social structure, economic system, customs, beliefs and traditions are respected, guaranteed and protected by states.[124]

Article 21 protects property not only from expropriation, but also from 'deprivation of the regular use and enjoyment' of it.[125] In the case of indigenous and tribal peoples, this protection would extend to the property necessary to protect the relationship with the environment, including resources traditionally used and necessary for the survival, development and continuation of their way of life.[126]

This protection may extend to resources not traditionally used when the extraction of such resources would degrade the environment and affect the enjoyment of traditional resources, but it is not absolute. Recognizing the necessity of limiting a single group's resource rights in a country of millions, the Court specified that the State may restrict the use and enjoyment of tribal property, but only in accordance with a previously established law; when it is necessary, proportional and pursuant to a legitimate aim in a democratic society; and when it does not deny a community its traditions in a way that endangers the community's survival.[127] Before approving concessions or development plans in the Community's territory, the State must safeguard the Community's survival by: ensuring effective participation by the Community; guaranteeing a reasonable benefit to the Community; and securing an independent social and environmental impact assessment.[128] In coming to this conclusion, the Court cited the United Nations Declaration on the Rights of Indigenous Peoples, which was released just months before the *Saramaka* decision:

122 *Saramaka* (*supra* note 109) at [115].
123 Ibid. at [116].
124 Ibid. at [121].
125 Ibid. at [129], [138]–[140].
126 Ibid. at [122].
127 Ibid. at [127]–[128].
128 Ibid. at [129].

1   Indigenous peoples have the right to determine and develop priorities and strategies for the development or use of their lands or territories and other resources.

2   States shall consult and cooperate in good faith with the indigenous peoples concerned through their own representative institutions in order to obtain their free and informed consent prior to the approval of any project affecting their lands or territories and other resources, particularly in connection with the development, utilization or exploitation of mineral, water or other resources.

3   States shall provide effective mechanisms for just and fair redress for any such activities, and appropriate measures shall be taken to mitigate adverse environmental, economic, social, cultural or spiritual impact.

With the *Saramaka* decision, the Inter-American Court became the first international tribunal to find that a non-indigenous minority group has legal rights to the natural resources within its ancestral lands.[129]

21.6 Indigenous and tribal groups' participation in shaping their land rights

Having found in the foregoing cases that Article 21 of the Convention protects indigenous and tribal peoples' use and enjoyment of their traditional territories and resources and the distinctive material, cultural and spiritual benefits they derive from it, the Court further enunciated that it was a logical extension of Article 21 to protect a right to participate in decision-making about the use and development of those assets. The Court has empowered these groups to determine culturally appropriate land titling and development schemes. It declined to impose forms of compensation and consultation, instead ordering the states to cooperate with the communities themselves to forge solutions that comply with the communities' land rights.

In the *Awas Tigni* case, the Court ordered Nicaragua to 'create an effective mechanism for delimitation, demarcation and titling of the property of indigenous communities' and to do so in consideration of the communities' customary laws, values and customs. The Awas Tigni Community was to enjoy full participation in this process.[130] In *Yakye Axa* and *Sawhoyamaxa*, on the other hand, the Court noted that at times returning land to a community will not be possible and something else will be given in compensation. In such cases, the community must agree to the form of the compensation and must be able to make the decision according to its own consultation procedures, values and customary law.[131]

In *Saramaka*, the Court established that indigenous and tribal groups holding property rights must be fully informed and consulted in good faith at an

---

129   Brunner (*supra* note 114) at 699.
130   *Awas Tigni* (*supra* note 26) at [164].
131   *Yakye Axa* (*supra* note 17) at [217]; *Sawhoyamaxa* (*supra* note 86) at [212]

early stage, long before concessions or development are granted for their territory.[132] They must be given the opportunity to participate in conformity with
their customs and traditions.[133] The State's duty to consult includes an obligation
to accept and disseminate information and to maintain communication with the
affected groups.[134] Free, prior and informed consent will be required for major
projects with major impacts on peoples and much of their territory.[135] In all cases
there must be reasonable benefit sharing or compensation.[136]

The UN Declaration on the Rights of Indigenous Peoples, cited in *Saramaka*,
goes further than the Inter-American Court by requiring 'free and informed consent prior to the approval of any projects affecting their land . . . and any other
resources'.[137] The difference may be explained by the different functions of the
UN Declaration and the American Convention. The former aims primarily to
advance the interests of indigenous peoples worldwide, while the latter deals with
the fair exercise of rights in a context where claims will sometimes conflict and the
region's development needs are a very real consideration.

The Court has given States Parties to the American Convention a framework
for involving indigenous and tribal peoples in decision-making, so as to advance
these groups' participation in the just and sustainable use of their lands. The
binding force of the decisions lends strength to communities' demands for a
voice. What is more, it is a model that is flexible enough to be copied and applied
both throughout and outside of the Americas, in diverse cultural and economic
contexts.

21.7 Integration and public participation outside the indigenous and tribal context

The Court has drawn a bright line, with indigenous and tribal peoples on one
hand, and other minorities on the other. This distinction suggests that the Court
is not prepared to extend the same recognition to the general population's
dependence on the environment and natural resources. However, even if States
are not required to consult proactively with non-indigenous and non-tribal populations, they must foster the conditions in which interested members of the public
may participate in policy-making without undue difficulty. In *Claude Reyes et al v
Chile*,[138] the Court took a step towards ensuring that States offer greater access to
information than they have in the past, particularly with regard to development
projects. In that case, the complainants requested information from the Chilean

---

132 *Saramaka* (*supra* note 109) at [133].
133 Ibid. at [129].
134 Ibid. at [133].
135 Ibid. at [134].
136 Ibid. at [133]–[134].
137 United Nations Declaration on the Rights of Indigenous Peoples, (adopted 13 September 2007)
     UNGA Res 61/295 (Annex) UN Doc A/RES/61/295 art 32(2).
138 *Case of Claude-Reyes et al v Chile*, Merits, Reparations and Costs, Judgment, Inter-American
     Court of Human Rights Series C, No 12 (19 September 2006) (hereinafter *Claude Reyes*).

state about a foreign investment contract for a deforestation project with potentially adverse effects on Chile's environment.[139] The State's Foreign Investment Committee provided only partial disclosure of the information requested.

Chile's Constitution provides for judicial recourse for the arbitrary or illegal denial of, or interference with, the right to live in an uncontaminated environment.[140] The Constitution also guarantees 'the freedom to issue an opinion and to provide information, without any prior censorship of any kind and by any means' and 'to file petitions before the authorities on any matter of public or private interest'.[141] Chilean law further provides for a right to request state-held information about private companies when the disclosure of the information is in the public interest and does not affect the proper functioning of the company or national interest, substantially affect the interests of third parties, or conflict with legal or regulatory provisions establishing confidentiality or secrecy.[142]

The American Convention's provision on freedom of expression is as follows:

Art. 13. Freedom of thought and expression:

1   Everyone has the right to freedom of thought and expression. This right includes freedom to seek, receive, and impart information and ideas of all kinds, regardless of frontiers, either orally, in writing, in print, in the form of art, or through any other medium of one's choice.

2   The exercise of the right provided for in the foregoing paragraph shall not be subject to prior censorship but shall be subject to subsequent imposition of liability, which shall be expressly established by law to the extent necessary to ensure:
     a   respect for the rights or reputation of others; or
     b   the protection of national security, public order, or public health or morals.

3   The right of expression may not be restricted by indirect methods or means, such as the abuse of government or private controls over newsprint, radio broadcasting frequencies, or equipment used in the dissemination of information, or by any other means tending to impede the communication and circulation of ideas and opinions

     [. . .]

The Court held that this Article not only provides for a right to request and circulate information in the hands of the State, but also imposes a correlative obligation on the State to provide access to that information or to justify any restriction on disclosure.[143] It operates according to the 'principle of maximum

139 Ibid. at [66].
140 Ibid. at [57(24)].
141 Ibid. at [57(32)].
142 Ibid. at [57(35)].
143 Ibid. at [77].

disclosure' – the onus being on the state to show that restrictions on information are compatible with Article 13.[144]

The Court agreed in the *Claude Reyes* case that the omitted information was of public interest because it related to a foreign investment contract that caused significant public debate due to its potential environmental impact, and because the request for information sought verification that a State body was complying with its mandate.[145] The Court considered the consensus within the OAS about the importance of access to public information, as well as the references to transparency in government and public participation spelled out in the Inter-American Democratic Charter, the Nueva Léon Declaration, the United Nations Convention against Corruption, the Rio Declaration on Environment and Development, and regional developments in Europe.[146] The Court recognized that access to public information is a prerequisite for representative democracy, which in turn is a defining principle in the Inter-American system, affirmed in the OAS Charter.[147]

The Court continued:

> In this regard, the State's actions should be governed by the principles of disclosure and transparency in public administration that enable all persons subject to its jurisdiction to exercise their democratic control of those actions, and so that they can question, investigate and consider whether public functions are being performed adequately. Access to State-held information of public interest can permit participation in public administration through social control that can be exercised through such access.
>
> Democratic control by society, through public opinion, fosters transparency in State activities and promotes the accountability of State officials in relation to their public activities. Hence, for the individual to be able to exercise democratic control, the State must guarantee access to the information of public interest that it holds. By permitting the exercise of this democratic control, the State encourages greater participation by the individual in the interests of society.[148]

In the Court's view, restrictions on access to State-held information must be established by law and not at the discretion of public authorities; they must be in the general interest; they should be for a purpose consistent with the American Convention; and they must be appropriate and proportionate to the compelling public interest that justifies them.[149]

At the time that the complainants were denied access to the information they sought, there was no law in Chile regulating the restrictions on access to state-held information and the state failed to establish the other elements of the test

---

144   Ibid. at [92].
145   Ibid. at [73].
146   Ibid. at [78]–[81].
147   Ibid. at [84].
148   Ibid. at [86]–[87].
149   Ibid. at [89]–[91].

described above.[150] The complainants' stated intent in requesting the information was to encourage social control of the administration of the deforestation project, and the state's refusal to provide information, as well as its lack of justification for the refusal, hindered the exercise of such control.[151] As a result, the Court concluded that Chile had violated the complainants' right to freedom of thought and expression pursuant to Article 13 of the American Convention.[152]

The Court did not consider Article 23 of the Convention (Right to Participate in Government), although it was argued by the complainants' representative, because it had already canvassed the same issues in its discussion of Article 13.[153]

21.8 Conclusion

The Court has drawn upon a range of international legal instruments and principals to shape its interpretations of the American Convention on Human Rights. The ICCPR and ICESR, the various global instruments concerning the rights of indigenous peoples, and instruments promoting openness and transparency in public information embody a set of ideals concerning the recognition of interdependence and public participation in the context of human rights. The Court stitched together these disparate strands to create legal precedents that are binding on the parties and created robust new expectations around the rights of indigenous and tribal peoples, and to some extent the general public, to take part in decisions that impact the environment upon which they depend.

The case of the indigenous and tribal peoples of the Americas has proven fertile ground for the application of the principles of interdependence and public participation because, as found by the Court on numerous occasions, such peoples' material, cultural and spiritual well-being depends upon the exercise of their traditional subsistence activities while their ability to continue such activities depends in turn on the availability and health of, and their access to and control over, their ancestral lands and resources. The principle of interdependence is also reflected in the communal forms of land ownership that the Court has observed in numerous indigenous and tribal cultures appearing before it.

The Court summed up its approach in *Saramaka:*

> In essence, pursuant to Article 21 of the Convention, States must respect the special relationship that members of indigenous and tribal peoples have with their territory in a way that guarantees their social, cultural, and economic survival. Such protection of property under Article 21 of the Convention, read in conjunction with Articles 1(1) and 2 of said instrument, places upon States a positive obligation to adopt special measures that guarantee members

150 Ibid. at [94]–[105].
151 Ibid. at [99].
152 Ibid. at [103].
153 Ibid. at [107].

of indigenous and tribal peoples the full and equal exercise of their right to the territories they have traditionally used and occupied.[154]

The 'full and equal exercise' of their territorial rights requires that the peoples in question play a meaningful role in making the decisions that will affect their lands, which are the objects of the right. Enhancing the participation by indigenous and tribal peoples in the decision-making processes may prove to have profound impacts on the sustainability of state policies. Outside the realm of indigenous and tribal rights, improved access-to-information procedures, as envisioned by the Court, could strengthen the participation rights of States' citizens on a broader scale.

154 *Saramaka* supra note 109 at [91].

22 Sustainable development principles in the European Court of Human Rights

Armelle Gouritin

22.1 Introduction

The European Convention on Human Rights adopted under the auspices of the Council of Europe in 1950 (hereinafter the Convention)[1] does not mention the word 'environment'. In this context, the European Court of Human Rights (hereinafter the Court) cannot *a priori* rely on a clearly defined environmental legal basis to justify its jurisdiction with regards to cases that evoke sustainable development principles.

Nevertheless, the Court considers the Convention as a living instrument. The Court has adopted a very dynamic approach when admissible cases brought before it have an environmental dimension. To do so, the Court relies on the rights guaranteed by the Convention and has a more or less broad conception of their scope of application. The Court has elaborated a whole body of rules covering environmental issues, relying mainly on the following grounds: right to life (Article 2), prohibition of torture (Article 3), right to a fair trial (Article 6(1)), right to respect for private and family life (Article 8), freedom of expression (Article 10), freedom of assembly and association (Article 11), right to an effective remedy (Article 13), and protection of property (Article 1 of the first Protocol – Article P1-1).

Accordingly (and even though the Court has provided no definition of 'environment'), the Court has undergone a far-reaching development by recognising claims with an environmental component. This is, for example, the case with noise pollution,[2] fumes from waste treatment plants,[3] chemical factories,[4] steel plants,[5]

---

1 Convention for the Protection of Human Rights and Fundamental Freedoms (European Convention on Human Rights, as Amended) 1950. For the European Court of Human Rights' case law, see: 'HUDOC' (*online database*) <http://hudoc.echr.coe.int/sites/eng/Pages/search.aspx#{'documentcollectionid2':['GRANDCHAMBER','CHAMBER']}> accessed 12 January 2014.
2 See, e.g. *Hatton and Others v The United Kingdom* [2003] ECtHR 36022/97. The case concerned noise from the Heathrow airport.
3 See *Lopez Ostra v Spain* [1994] ECtHR 16798/90.
4 See *Guerra and Others v Italy* [1998] ECtHR 14967/89.
5 See *Fadeyeva v Russia* [2005] ECtHR 55723/00.

explosion in a waste collection site,[6] mudslide,[7] agriculture rationalisation,[8] granting of permits,[9] water pollution,[10] fish stocks safeguarding,[11] forest protection,[12] and land planning.[13]

Against this background, it will be demonstrated that the Court's case law solidly guarantees and protects some of the New Delhi Principles endorsed in the 2002 New Delhi Declaration of Principles of International Law Relating to Sustainable Development.[14] Attention will be directed to cases that were decided until the end of 2012.

More specifically, this will be illustrated through the Court's approach to the principle of integration and interrelationship, in particular in relation to human rights and social, economic and environmental objectives (see section 22.2 below), and the principles of participation and access to information and justice (see section 22.3.1 below). It will also be demonstrated that the Court's dynamism is nevertheless limited: the Court is ill-equipped to endorse or protect the intrinsic and collective environmental dimensions of sustainability. These limits are exemplified with the cornerstone issues of future generations as rights holders and the environment's intrinsic value (see section 22.4.1 below).

22.2 The Court as a forum to balance environmental, social and economic objectives: the fair balance requirement

22.2.1 The fair balance requirement and environmental affairs: three hypotheses

In this section, it will be demonstrated that the Court's requirements in terms of fair balance implement the seventh New Delhi Principle (integration principle) and more particularly the first and third paragraphs of that principle:

---

6 See *Öneryildiz v Turkey* [2004] ECtHR 48939/99.
7 See *Ledyayeva and Others v Russia* [2006] ECtHR 53157/99, 53247/99, 53695/00 and 56850/00.
8 See *Håkasson and Sturesson v Sweden* [1990] ECtHR 11855/85.
9 See *Pine Valley Developments Ltd and Others v Ireland* [1991] ECtHR 12742/87.
10 See *Zander v Sweden* [1993] ECtHR 14282/88.
11 See *Posti and Rahko v Finland* [2002] ECtHR 27824/95.
12 See *Papastavrou and Others v Greece* [2003] ECtHR 46372/99.
13 See *Vergos v Greece* [2004]. For a more complete overview see Council of Europe, *Manual on Human Rights and the Environment* (Strasbourg: Council of Europe Publishers, 2012).
14 The New Delhi Declaration was released by the International Law Association Committee on the Legal Aspects of Sustainable Development. New Delhi Declaration of Principles of International Law Relating to Sustainable Development 2002. The seven New Delhi principles are: the duty of States to ensure sustainable use of natural resources; the principle of equity and the eradication of poverty; the principle of common but differentiated responsibilities; the principle of the precautionary approach to human health, natural resources and ecosystems; the principle of participation and access to information and justice; the principle of good governance; and the principle of integration and interrelationship, in particular in relation to human rights and social, economic and environmental objectives.

The principle of integration reflects the interdependence of social, economic, financial, environmental and human rights aspects of principles and rules of international law relating to sustainable development as well as of the interdependence of the needs of current and future generations of humankind. . . . States should strive to resolve apparent conflicts between competing economic, financial, social and environmental considerations.

The fair balance technique is one of the three components of the proportionality requirement.[15] The fair balance requirement aims at assessing whether or not national interference with a right guaranteed (a national authority's measure or the lack of such measure) interferes with the rights guaranteed by the Convention, but nevertheless respect the Convention's requirements. Concretely, the Court finds as a first step that the right has been interfered with, and as a second step, the Court finds the interference not to violate the Convention.

This possibility is provided for in the text of the Convention.[16] As a prerequisite, the interference with the right guaranteed must be possible.[17] In the context of environmental affairs, the rights usually relied upon and which can be interfered with are the right to respect for private and family life (Article 8), freedom of thought, conscience and religion (Article 9), freedom of expression (Article 10), freedom of assembly and association (Article 11) and right to property (Article 1 of the first Additional Protocol).

The requirement that all the interests present in environmental affairs must be duly identified and taken into account, i.e. the fair balance technique, is meant to operate a balance between diverging and conflicting interests. The interests of the community as a whole being achieved through the measure having a legitimate goal on the one hand, and the specific interests of the applicant on the other hand.

This is where the link with sustainable development and the integration principle is made clear. Sustainable development is a concept supposed to reflect an equilibrium between different objectives and interests (economic, social, and environmental) and fair balance is a technique that assesses such equilibrium.[18]

---

15 The proportionality requirement is commonly split among three techniques and requirements. First, the national interference with a right guaranteed by the Convention must be appropriate to attain the legitimate goal pursued by the interference. Second, the interference must be necessary. What is at stake is the whole spectrum of other means that would have enabled the legitimate goal to be attained. Third, the proportionality requirement *stricto sensu* refers to the balancing of the interests actually at stake on a case-by-case basis.

16 See for example Articles 8(2), 10(2), and 11(2).

17 This is not possible for several rights (for example the right not to suffer from slavery - Article 4(1) of the Convention): the mere interference with the right will constitute an infringement of the Convention. This is also the case for the rights guaranteed by Articles 2 (right to life), 3 (prohibition of torture), 7 (no punishment without laws), 1 and 2 of the sixth Additional Protocol (abolition of the death penalty and death penalty in time of war), and 4 of the seventh Additional Protocol (right not to be tried or punished twice).

18 See, e.g. Gerd Winter, 'A Fundament and Two Pillars: The Concept of Sustainable Development 20 Years after the Brundtland Report' in Hans Christian Bugge and Christina Voig, eds.,

Three hypotheses can be distinguished. First, environmental rights (or interests) can ground the interference with the enjoyment of a right guaranteed by the Convention, for example the right to property.[19] Environmental protection has been recognised as a valuable activity, a legitimate goal to justify the interference.[20] This is also true for measures aimed at protecting forests, fish stocks, or introducing a rationalised agriculture. Second, environmental rights (or interests) have been interfered with to realise a legitimate goal (for example the economic well-being of the country). Third, the applicant claims that his/her right has been interfered with due to the lack of appropriate measures being adopted by the national authorities (the so-called positive obligations). This is also an application of the fair balance technique, as made clear by the Court in the *Fadeyeva v Russia* case.[21]

In the three hypotheses, national authorities enjoy a wide margin of discretion in environmental, land planning and industrial policy matters. This is settled case law.[22] The more that national authorities are recognised as having a wide margin of discretion, the more lenient the control of the Court. Hence, as a principle, national authorities enjoy a wide margin of discretion in environmental affairs. This leaves little room for the Court to control whether the proportionality requirement is met.

Also, the Court does not deliver abstract rulings: the Court aims at ensuring the enjoyment of concrete rights. Accordingly, the circumstances of each case are crucial for the ruling. The obligations that bind national authorities and the scope of application of the rights guaranteed very much depend upon the circumstances of each case. For example, the type or seriousness of risk suffered by the environment or humans will be a crucial factor to assess the nature and scope of the obligations binding national authorities.

The fair balance requirement can be conceived of as a technique that ensures the integration principle in three hypotheses that are subsequently reported in the subsections that follow. Environmental protection as an objective: a 'cause' reflecting emerging demands (22.2.2), environmental rights interfered with by a national act or a lack of act justified by economic or social welfare concerns (22.2.3), and environmental rights as a justification of the infringement of human rights that reflect economic or social welfare concerns (22.2.4).

Sustainable Development in International and National Law: What Did the Brundtland Report Do to Legal Thinking and Legal Development, and Where Can We Go from Here? (Groningen: Europa Law, 2008) at 28 'in its three-pillar version the term "sustainable" . . . means that the three aspects shall coexist as equivalent entities. In the case of conflict, they shall be balanced, mutual consideration must be taken and compromise found'. Ibid.

19 See, e.g. *Hamer v Belgium* [2007] ECtHR 21861/03.
20 See, e.g. *Turgut and Others v Turkey* [2009] ECtHR 1411/03.
21 *Fadeyeva v Russia* (*supra* note 5) at [99] 'Legitimate aim. Where the State is required to take positive measures in order to strike a fair balance between the interests of an individual and the community as a whole, the aims mentioned in the second paragraph of Article 8 may be of a certain relevance, although this provision refers only to "interferences" with the right protected by the first paragraph – in other words, it is concerned with the negative obligations flowing therefrom'. Ibid.
22 See, e.g. *Giacomelli v Italy* [2006] ECtHR 59909/00.

22.2.2 *Environmental protection as an objective: a 'cause' reflecting emerging demands*

When it approaches cases that have an environmental dimension and integrates this dimension in the fair balance 'equation', the Court constantly recalls that this dimension has a particular weight. For example, in the *Depalle v France* case, the Court stated: 'The Court reiterates that environmental conservation, which in today's society is an increasingly important consideration . . . has become a cause whose defence arouses the constant and sustained interest of the public, and consequently the public authorities'.[23]

In the *Hamer v Belgium* case, the Court went one step further and added that 'economic imperatives and even some fundamental rights, such as right to property, shouldn't be given priority over environmental protection matters, particularly when the State has adopted environmental regulation'.[24] Similarly, in *Hatton v United Kingdom*, the Court ruled:

> [I]n striking the required balance States must have regard to the whole range of material considerations. Further, in the particularly sensitive field of environmental protection, mere reference to the economic well-being of the country was not sufficient to outweigh the rights of others. The Chamber considered that States were required to minimise, as far as possible, interference with Article 8 rights, by trying to find alternative solutions and by generally seeking to achieve their aims in the least onerous way as regards human rights.[25]

This specific weight granted to the environment should be kept in mind when analysing in more depth the fair balance equation in the two hypotheses distinguished below that reflect the integration principle. They are environmental rights infringed by national interference (or lack of action) on the one hand, and environmental rights or concerns as duly restricting the scope of enjoyment of other rights guaranteed by the Convention on the other hand.

22.2.3 *Environmental rights interfered with by a national act or a lack of act justified by economic or social welfare concerns*

In this hypothesis, the fair balance equation is as follows: on the one hand, the environmental pillar endorsed as an environmental right reflects environmental protection concerns; on the other hand, the State's interference through an act or the refusal to act reflects other concerns. The Court has to assess whether the fair balance requirement is respected when a national authority interfered with environmental rights, either by acting or refusing to act.

---

23 *Depalle v France* [2010] ECtHR 34044/02 [89].

24 *Hamer v Belgium* (*supra* note 19) at [79] *in fine*.

25 *Hatton and Others v The United Kingdom* (*supra* note 2) at [86]. Please note that the Grand Chamber overruled the Chamber's findings, without pronouncing itself on this particular statement.

This point can be illustrated with the *Giacomelli v Italy* case.[26] In this case, the applicant's house was located 30 metres away from a plant for the storage and treatment of 'special waste', classified as either hazardous or non-hazardous waste. The local health authority acknowledged air pollution, soil pollution and risk problems for those living nearby. The plant kept running. The applicant submitted that Article 8 of the Convention had been violated (right to respect for home and private life).

The Court followed a two-step analysis in its assessment of the fair balance requirement. This two-step analysis is expressed in the *Hatton* case (among others) as follows:

> The Court considers that in a case such as the present one, involving State decisions affecting environmental issues, there are two aspects to the inquiry which may be carried out by the Court. First, the Court may assess the substantive merits of the government's decision, to ensure that it is compatible with Article 8. Secondly, it may scrutinise the decision-making process to ensure that due weight has been accorded to the interests of the individual.[27]

Regarding the merits of the national authorities' actions or lack of actions with respect to the environmental substantive right not to suffer from the pollution that amounts to an interference with the right to respect for home, family and private life, the diverging rights and interests can be summarised as follows.

On the one hand, the applicant submitted that the pollution caused disturbance to the health and well-being of all those living in the vicinity of the plant.[28] Recognition by the Court of the right not to suffer from pollution that interferes with the right to enjoy private and family life is settled case law:[29]

> Specifically, Article 8 of the Convention applies to severe environmental pollution which may affect individuals' well-being and prevent them from enjoying their homes in such a ways as to affect their private and family life adversely, even without seriously endangering their health.

This rule applies to several circumstances: noise pollution,[30] fumes from waste treatment plants,[31] chemical factories,[32] steel plants,[33] explosion in a

26 *Giacomelli v Italy* (*supra* note 22).
27 *Hatton and Others v The United Kingdom* (*supra* note 2) at [99].
28 *Giacomelli v Italy* (*supra* note 22) at [70].
29 See, e.g. *Fägerskiöld v Sweden* [2008] ECtHR 37664/04 under 'the law', pt 1.
30 See, e.g. *Hatton and Others v The United Kingdom* (*supra* note 2); *Moreno Gomez v Spain* ECtHR 4143/02.
31 *Lopez Ostra v Spain* (*supra* note 3).
32 *Guerra and Others v Italy* (*supra* note 4).
33 *Fadeyeva v Russia* (*supra* note 5).

waste collection site,[34] water pollution,[35] and sodium cyanide leaking.[36] Similarly, the Court acknowledged an interference in the *Giacomelli* case regarding atmospheric pollution.[37]

On the other hand, the Italian government submitted that the plant processed almost all of the region's industrial waste, 'thereby' ensuring development of the region's industry and protecting the community's health.[38] Accordingly, the interests at stake, still according to the Italian government, were public health protection and the preservation of the region's economic well-being. The company's activities were put forward as of public interest value.[39]

The Court acknowledged the interests at stake. The Court also recalled that Article 8 (and hence environmental rights) can be unduly interfered with by actions or lack of actions.[40] A lack of action can be found to infringe on environmental rights when the State omits proper regulation of activities that can impact environmental rights.[41] To fulfil these obligations, the State has to properly take into account the applicant's interest. This can be checked against the respect for environmental procedural rights. This is what the Court assessed as a second step.[42]

22.2.4 Environmental rights as a justification for the infringement of human rights that reflect economic or social welfare concerns

This situation mainly occurred with environmental concerns that justify an interference with the right to property. Article 1 of the first Additional Protocol to the Convention guarantees the right to property. With the view to illustrating that environmental concerns can override rights reflecting economic or social concerns, reference will be made to two recent cases. In the first one, *Depalle v France*, two kinds of properties are involved: public property and private property. The first one is to take precedence over the second one in so far as it is justified by pursuing environmental protection goals. The second case, *Fägerskiöld v Sweden*, concerns energy policy. Renewable energy policy measures take precedence over private property.

These cases are some of the cases where the Court found environmental concerns to override private property rights. In other cases, the Court dealt with

---

34 *Öneryildiz v Turkey* (*supra* note 6).

35 *Zander v Sweden* (*supra* note 10).

36 *Taskin and Others v Turkey* [2004] ECtHR 46117/99.

37 *Giacomelli v Italy* (*supra* note 22) at [76–7]. Striking enough, the interference with the right not to suffer from a pollution that ultimately affects the right protected under Article 8 of the Convention was not discussed by Italy. This illustrates that this settled case law is no longer discussed.

38 Ibid. at 72.

39 Ibid. at 73.

40 Ibid. at 78.

41 As found among others in the *Tatar* case, the obligations binding States in this respect are listed under paras. at 87–8.

42 This reflects the rule as codified in the *Hatton* case (para 99 reproduced above). Environmental procedural rights are addressed in the subsequent section of this chapter.

(among others) forest protection measures,[43] agriculture rationalisation,[44] fish stocks safeguarding,[45] and land planning.[46]

22.2.4.1 First example: the public maritime domain and protection of the environment overriding private property

The facts in the *Depalle* case can be summarised as follows. The case concerns the modification and withdrawal of temporary occupancy authorisations granted for houses built on the maritime public domain. The withdrawal and modification were grounded, *inter alia*, on environmental protection purposes (more specifically, coastal areas protection). The national authorities also called for restoration measures to be conducted by and at the costs of the applicants. All in all, public property was aimed at guaranteeing environmental protection achievement.

Hence, the case at hand did concern the arbitration between the competing interests in the many uses of coastal areas.[47] The interests at stake in this case can be presented as follows: while the applicant contended that the Court should acknowledge her private property rights and the pecuniary value of the house in question, the State was contending that environmental interests, collective use of coastal areas, and nature conservation can override private property rights (that were, moreover, awarded on a temporary basis).

The Court acknowledged all these interests: environmental interests,[48] collective use,[49] and nature conservation as constituting the legitimate goal of the national interference with right to private property. This last aspect is particularly crucial and worth reproducing:

> The Court cannot agree with the applicant's submission that the aim of the interference was not in the general interest, namely, the protection of the property's designation as public property and of the environment. . . . authorisations have no longer been renewed, with the aim of protecting the seashore and more generally the environment. The Court reiterates that environmental conservation, which in today's society is an increasingly important consideration . . ., has become a cause whose defence arouses the constant and sustained interest of the public, and consequently the public authorities. . . . The protection of coastal areas, and in particular beaches, which are 'a public area open to all', is another example . . . of an

---

43 See, e.g. *Hamer v Belgium* (*supra* note 19); *Papastavrou and Others v Greece* (*supra* note 12).

44 *Håkasson and Sturesson v Sweden* (*supra* note 8).

45 *Posti and Rahko v Finland* (*supra* note 11).

46 *Vergos v Greece* (*supra* note 13).

47 *Depalle v France* (*supra* note 23) ECtHR at [45, 46, 48 and 49].

48 Ibid. at 38: 'the land conservation policy guarantees the protection of the physical integrity of maritime public property and compliance with its designated use'.

49 Ibid. at 40: 'The use of maritime public property may be collective or private. Collective use which allows all citizens to benefit from public property (navigation on watercourses, beaches) is freely exercisable, equally available to all and free of charge'.

area where an appropriate planning policy is required. The Court therefore considers that the interference pursued a legitimate aim that was in the general interest: to promote unrestricted access to the shore, the importance of which has been clearly established.[50]

The Court found the lack of compensation not to amount in this case to an infringement of the fair balance requirement. The Court also noted that if the State had exempted the applicant from the obligations provided in the law concerned, the result would have been 'against the aims of the Coastal Areas Act . . . and undermine efforts to achieve a better organisation of the relations between private use and public use'.[51]

Accordingly, the Court gave environmental protection measures an overriding value in the fair balance equation. The right to private property was not infringed in this case.

22.2.4.2 Second example: sustainable energy measures overriding private property

In the *Fägerskiöld v Sweden* case, the Court had for the first time to assess a situation where wind turbines were concerned. Building permits were awarded to erect wind turbines located 371, 430 and 620 metres from the applicants' house. According to the applicants, the wind turbines emitted a constant and pulsating noise, in addition to (sometimes) a light effect. They found the noise and the light to be very intrusive and disturbing. The measured noise level did not reach the maximum regulatory level of 40 db. The applicants submitted that the wind turbines' operation allowed by national authorities constituted an infringement with their right to property on the one hand, and their right to family and private life on the other.

The interests concerned in this case can be summarised as follows: on the one hand, the applicants claimed that their peaceful enjoyment of property had been interfered with, while the value of their property had been decreased due to the wind turbines operations. On the other hand, the Swedish government put forward the public interest pursued with the granting of the permits: 'energy production in a sustainable society should have the smallest possible impact on the environment and the climate'. The government also emphasised the 'legitimate aim of protecting the economic well-being of the country *and the rights and freedoms of others* by *contributing to the sustainable development of Sweden's natural resources* and ensuring that its citizens could live in a safe and peaceful environment' and 'wind power is a *renewable source of energy* considered to be environmentally friendly and to contribute to the sustainable development of society'.[52]

---

50 Ibid. at 81.
51 Ibid. at 89.
52 *Fägerskiöld v Sweden* (*supra* note 29) under 'the law', pt 1.

The Court endorsed the interests concerned and specified the following regarding the Swedish government's arguments:

> [T]o the Court, there is no doubt that the *operating of the wind turbine is in the general interest as it is an environmentally friendly source of energy which contributes to the sustainable development of natural resources*. It observes that the wind turbine at issue in the present case is capable of producing enough energy to heat between 40 and 50 private households over a one-year period, which is *beneficial both for the environment and for society*.[53]

This is extremely interesting: the Court was taking a position on energy, and more specifically 'green' energy. The legitimate goal being endorsed, the Court then went on and operated the fair balance test. The Court began by spelling out the fair balance equation as follows: 'the Court must have regard to the positive environmental consequences of wind power for the community as a whole while also considering its negative impact on the applicants'.[54] The Court then recalled that States enjoy a wide margin of appreciation in matters raising environmental issues and underlined that 'the nuisance caused to the applicants by the wind turbine cannot be considered so severe as to affect them seriously or impinge on their enjoyment of their property'.[55] The Court refused to qualify the noise at stake as an environmental pollution. The Court also took note of the diverse remedies available to the applicants while 'a constant review of the measures already taken and the opportunity to request further measures are available to the applicants through the Environmental Code'.[56] Following this, the Court found the applicants' submissions to be ill-founded. Their case was found not to be admissible.[57]

The originality of the case lies on the fact that two environmental dimensions can be found here. Noise pollution on the one hand, and the sustainable development of Sweden's natural resources through renewable sources of energy on the other. Hence, the environmental dimension was individual in as much as the applicants complained about noise pollution, and collective in as much the Swedish government put forward sustainable development of Sweden through renewable sources of energies. The Court held in that case that the collective environmental interest was to override the individual one. This kind of case is expected to appear more frequently before the Court with the development of renewable sources of energy infrastructures. Yet, we should recall that each case will be assessed against the concrete situation to be determined on a case-by-case basis (i.e. the level of pollution, the intensity of the pollution, and the duration of the pollution).

Another interesting point in this case is that the Court relied on international standards to assess whether or not the noise could qualify as pollution.

---

53 Ibid. at pt 2.
54 Ibid.
55 Ibid.
56 Ibid.
57 Ibid. at pt 3.

Accordingly, the role of international organisations such as the World Health Organization in the setting of standards is crucial because these standards also cover soil pollution, water pollution and atmospheric pollution.[58] Nevertheless, the outcome of these standards will always, *in fine*, depend upon the specific situation at hand before the Court.

All in all, the Court's case law has given flesh to the integration principle. The fair balance requirement proves to be a technique that calls for an equilibrium between competing environmental, social and economic objectives. The fair balance requirement is a guarantee that the social and economic dimension do not systematically take precedence over the environmental dimension.[59] Another set of New Delhi Principles are enforced by the Court: environmental procedural rights.

22.3 The Court as a forum to guarantee the enjoyment of environmental procedural rights

22.3.1 *Right to access information, participate in decision-making and access justice*

The Court has recognised a broad range of environmental procedural rights that reflect those endorsed in the Aarhus Convention on Access to Information, Public Participation in Decision-Making and Access to Justice in Environmental Matters.[60] Environmental procedural rights found a solid basis with the adoption of the Aarhus Convention that distinguishes three pillars: citizens' access to information, public participation, and access to justice. Environmental procedural rights are either specifically guaranteed by the Convention's provisions (Articles 6 and 14) or unveiled by the Court as stemming from substantive human rights

---

58 For example, the International Agency for Research on Cancer (IARC), a specialised agency of the World Health Organization announced on 17 October 2013 that it has classified outdoor air pollution and particulate matter as carcinogenic to humans (consequently, they are classified as carcinogenic agents that belong to Group 1).

59 Several authors have pointed out that pitfall. See, e.g. M. Fitzmaurice, *Contemporary Issues in International Environmental Law* (Cheltenham: Edward Elgar, 2009) 70–2; Hans Christian Bugge, Christina Voigt and Norges Forskningsråd, eds., *Sustainable Development in International and National Law: What Did the Brundtland Report Do to Legal Thinking and Legal Development, and Where Can We Go from Here?* (Groningen: Europa Law Publishing, 2008) 28: 'However, as the biosphere (although objectively flexible to a certain extent) cannot reflect on itself and its relationship with humans, as it is reckless and uncompromising, the three-pillar concept leads easily to mock compromises. Sacrifices of nature, as commanded by prevailing short term economic or social interests, may become destructive for economy and society in the long'.

60 Aarhus Convention on Access to Information, Public Participation in Decision-Making, and Access to Justice in Environmental Matters 1999. The Aarhus Convention was signed by 35 Member States of the United Nations Economic Commission for Europe (UNECE) and by the European Community at the 'Environment for Europe' ministerial conference in the Danish city of Aarhus on 25 June 1998. It entered into force on 30 October 2001 and now has 44 contracting parties, including the European Union – which succeeded to the European Community – and all its Member States (except Ireland) as well as most countries in transition from Eastern Europe, Central Asia and the Caucasus (except Russia and Uzbekistan).

provisions. The Court unveiled environmental procedural rights that lie upon substantive human rights provisions in (among others) the *Taskin and Others v Turkey* case, where the Court identified some procedural requirements as part of the States' obligations flowing from Article 8 of the Convention:

> The Court reiterates that, according to its settled case-law, whilst Article 8 contains no explicit procedural requirements, the decision-making process leading to measures of interference must be fair and such as to afford due respect for the interests of the individual as safeguarded by Article 8. . . . It is therefore necessary to consider all the procedural aspects, including the type of policy or decision involved, the extent to which the views of individuals were taken into account throughout the decision-making process, and the procedural safeguards available. . . . Where a State must determine complex issues of environmental and economic policy, the decision-making process must firstly involve appropriate investigations and studies in order to allow them to predict and evaluate in advance the effects of those activities which might damage the environment and infringe individuals' rights and to enable them to strike a fair balance between the various conflicting interests at stake. . . . The importance of public access to the conclusions of such studies and to information which would enable members of the public to assess the danger to which they are exposed is beyond question. . . . Lastly, the individuals concerned must also be able to appeal to the courts against any decision, act or omission where they consider that their interests or their comments have not been given sufficient weight in the decision-making process. . . .[61]

Some recent developments in the Court's case law regarding the freedom of expression are important as the Court has recently recognised the right of access to (environmental) information. In the case of *Österreichische Vereinigung zur Erhaltung, Stärkung und Schaffung Eines Wirtschaftlich Gesunden Land - und Forstwirtschaftlichen Grundbesitzes v Austria* delivered on 28 November 1013,[62] the applicant was an association whose aim was to research the impact of transfers of ownership of agricultural and forest land on society and to give opinions on draft laws. The association challenged the refusal of an Austrian regional authority to provide access to information. As reported by the Court, the regional authority approves agricultural and forest land transactions (Regional Real Property Transactions Commissions). The purpose of the approval is 'to preserve land for agricultural use and forestry and, in some of the regions . . . to avoid the proliferation of second homes'.[63]

This case is a landmark case in the field of access to environmental information. Indeed, that the Court had to rule on the refusal to grant access to

---

61 *Taskin and Others v Turkey* (*supra* note 36) at [118–119].
62 *Österreichische Vereinigung zur Erhaltung, Stärkung und Schaffung Eines Wirtschaftlich Gesunden Land - und Forstwirtschaftlichen Grundbesitzes v Austria* [2013] ECtHR 39534/07.
63 Ibid. at 6.

environmental information as the main interference with the rights guaranteed by the Convention.[64] The Court analysed the case on the basis of Article 10 of the Convention (freedom of expression) and Article 13 (right to an effective remedy). The Court found that Article 10 had been violated, but no violation was found with regards to Article 13. The findings of the Court are extremely important regarding the violation of Article 10. The Court first recalls its recent case law and the move towards 'the recognition of a right of access to information'.[65] However, the Court refused to extend this right as to encompass the 'general obligation' to 'either . . . publish all decisions . . . in an electronic database or to provide . . . with anonymised paper copies upon request.'[66]

This movement of the Court towards the recognition of the right of access to information within the scope of Article 10 (freedom of expression) is therefore parallel to the recognition of environmental procedural rights within the scope of Article 8 (right to respect for private and family life) and Article 3 (right to life).

The rationale of the requirement to respect environmental procedural rights is to be found in the fair balance requirement analysed in the previous section. The fair balance requirement calls for the applicant's interests to be duly considered. This can be done if environmental procedural rights are respected. The requirements of the Court in this respect illustrate the sixth and fifth New Delhi Principles, as further exemplified below with regards to risk management obligations.

22.3.2 Risk management: studies, regulation and proof

Risk management is an illustration of the requirements of the Court in terms of environmental procedural rights, and more particularly the sixth New Delhi Principle (good governance) with regards to the obligation 'to adopt democratic and transparent decision-making procedures'. Risk management is also an illustration of the fifth Principle (public participation and access to information and justice).

As recalled in the *Giacomelli* case,[67] environmental procedural rights require appropriate studies and investigations to be conducted. The public must have access to the conclusions of the studies and investigations. The public must also have the possibility to appeal to Courts to challenge a refusal to provide access to these conclusions or the refusal to conduct studies or investigations. In the case at hand, the Court found the Environmental Impact Assessment not to have

---

64 The Court acknowledges this environmental dimension. See, e.g. ibid. at 35.

65 Ibid. at 41.

66 Ibid. at 42. The benchmarks that the Court assessed were 'whether the reasons given by the domestic authorities for refusing the applicant association's request were "relevant and sufficient" in the specific circumstances of the case and whether the interference was proportionate to the legitimate aim pursued' (para 42). In that respect, the Court found that 'the reasons relied on by the domestic authorities in refusing the applicant association's request for access to the Commission's decisions – though "relevant" – were not "sufficient"'. Ibid. at para 47. It can be noted that the Court qualified the aim of preserving land for agricultural use and forestry and in some of the regions to avoid the proliferation of second homes as 'of considerable public interest'. Ibid.

67 *Giacomelli v Italy* (*supra* note 22) at [82–83].

been conducted before the operation of the company's activities, but seven years after the company began its activities.[68] The Italian Ministry of the environment found twice that the plant's operation did not meet environmental regulation.[69] Nevertheless, the administrative authorities had not ordered the closure of the facility, as requested by an administrative judicial authority.[70]

Following this, the Court found environmental procedural rights to be infringed.[71] Accordingly, the Court concluded that the fair balance requirement was not met since the applicant's interest not to suffer from the effects of a pollution caused by a plant could not have been properly acknowledged by national authorities:

> The Court considers that the State did not succeed in striking a fair balance between the interest of the community in having a plant for the treatment of toxic industrial waste and the applicant's effective enjoyment of her right to respect for her home and her private and family life.[72]

Some scholars contend that environmental regulation *per se* creates rights.[73] This approach identifies regulation as a link between environmental affairs and rights. Case law of the European Court of Human Rights indirectly backs this approach. The Court sanctions the lack of appropriate regulation of dangerous activities (as in the *Tatar v Romania* case)[74] and the non-enforcement of this regulation when it does exist (as in the *Öneryildiz v Turkey* case),[75] including when the infringement by a private person was recognised by a national Court but the national authorities did not act to enforce the national

68   Ibid. at 86–88.
69   Ibid. at 89.
70   Ibid. at 92–93.
71   Ibid. at 94: 'It (the Court) considers that the procedural machinery provided for in domestic law for the protection of individual rights, in particular the obligation to conduct an environmental-impact assessment prior to any project with potentially harmful environmental consequences and the possibility for any citizens concerned to participate in the licensing procedure and to submit their own observations to the judicial authorities and, where appropriate, obtain an order for the suspension of a dangerous activity, were deprived of useful effect in the instant case for a very long period'.
72   Ibid. at 97.
73   On this approach see, e.g. K. Hectors, 'The Chartering of Environmental Protection: Exploring the Boundaries of Environmental Protection as Human Right' (2008) 17 *Eur. Energy Environ. Law Rev. European Energy and Environmental Law Review* 165, 165: 'In general, four approaches have been used in legal practice'; ibid. at 166 fn 7: '4) regulatory approach: integration of environmental protection in many policy fields (this approach is the only non rights-based approach)'. See also Marc Pallemaerts and Armelle Gouritin, 'Environmental Rights Standards, the EU's Self Proclaimed Global Green Leadership in Question?' [2011] *La rotezione dei diritti fondamentali: Carta dei diritti UE e standards internazionali* 93, 93–112.
74   *Tatar v Romania* [2009] ECtHR 67021/01 [112]. Similarly, see *Öneryildiz v Turkey* (*supra* note 6) at [89–90].
75   *Öneryildiz v Turkey* (*supra* note 6) at [102].

Court's findings (as in the *Lopez Ostra v Spain* case).[76] It is settled case law that national authorities have the duty to regulate activities and regulation must take into account the specifications of the activities. This obligation governs the licensing, setting up, operation, security and supervision of the activity. This obligation also encompasses the obligation for national authorities to adopt practical measures aimed at ensuring the effective enjoyment of the rights guaranteed by the Convention.[77] This obligation 'indisputably applies in the particular context of dangerous activities'.[78]

Evidence is a cornerstone issue in environmental matters. The Court has constantly emphasised the primary obligation binding national authorities to regulate risk for the environment and human health. This obligation has recently been emphasised by the recognition of the precautionary principle.[79] Indeed, the principle exempts the applicant from the burden of proof: the applicant does not necessarily have to prove the reality and certainty of risk. Nevertheless, the applicant still has to establish the causal link between the effects of the activity (and inherent risks) and the infringement of the right at stake in each case (for example enjoyment of private home, effect on human health, etc.). This causal link is difficult to establish, as the Court itself recognises.[80]

In the *Tatar* case, the Court did refer to the precautionary principle that is affirmed in the fourth New Delhi Principle. The Court first underlined the progressive recognition of the precautionary principle in texts of the European Union. The Court subsequently reported on the case law of the European Court of Justice. This case law establishes that States can adopt measures when there remain uncertainties concerning the existence or extent of risks for human health.[81] Applying the principle, the Court found that the precautionary principle calls for States not to delay the adoption of effective and proportionate measures aimed at preventing the risk of serious and irreversible damages to the environment when scientific or technical certainties are lacking.[82]

In the *Tatar* case, the effect of this principle was at least twofold. On the one hand, the fair balance requirement in its procedural component had been infringed in terms of risk assessment. The economic and social positive (expected) effects flowing from the gold mine activities[83] could not justify the Romanian authorities' granting the company the authorisation to run its activities without having previously debated the risks created for the environment and involving the public in

---

76 *Lopez Ostra v Spain* (*supra* note 3) at [56].
77 *Tatar v Romania* (*supra* note 74) at [88].
78 *Öneryildiz v Turkey* (*supra* note 6) at [89–90]. In the same sense see *Tatar v Romania* (*supra* note 74) at [88].
79 *Tatar v Romania* (*supra* note 74) at 27 pt h and para 109.
80 Ibid. at 103–07.
81 Ibid. at 27 pt h. The Court refers to *United Kingdom of Great Britain and Northern Ireland v Commission of the European Communities* [1998] ECJ C-190/96; *The Queen v Intervention Board for Agricultural Produce* [1998] ECJ C-263/97.
82 *Tatar v Romania* (*supra* note 74) at [109].
83 As highlighted in the Environmtental Impact Assessment conducted in 1993; ibid. at 19.

this debate.[84] The Environmental Impact Assessment conducted in 1993 underlined these risks: they were hence predictable.[85] On the other hand, the Romanian authorities did not adopt the necessary measures that would have protected the interests of the applicants to enjoy a healthy and protected environment.[86]

The Court's case law fully endorses environmental procedural requirements. Similar to the integration principle, the Court has elaborated a whole body of obligations that give flesh to the New Delhi Principles, and more particularly the fifth Principle (principle of public participation and access to information and justice) and the sixth Principle (good governance). This case law also fills a weakness of sustainable development: the implementation deficit.[87] The dynamism of the Court is nevertheless limited by a structural problem: the rights guaranteed largely reflect an individual and anthropocentric approach to human rights. This structural problem is illustrated in the subsequent section.

22.4 The limit of the Court to endorse the New Delhi Principles regarding the intrinsic and collective dimension of the environment

22.4.1 The Court is ill-equipped to endorse the intrinsic and collective dimension of the environment

Another approach to environmental affairs through the human rights lens is the recognition of an autonomous right to a healthy and protected environment.[88] The centre of gravity then lies in the environment having an intrinsic and collective value. The recognition of the autonomous substantial human right to a healthy environment is not unanimous. Some scholars reflect on how to conceptualise this right and other scholars reject this recognition.[89] This rejection echoes the reluctance of governments to recognise the autonomous right in an Additional Protocol to the Convention. Indeed, the initiatives for the adoption of an Additional Protocol to the Convention that would add the right to a 'healthy

---

84 Ibid. at 110 and 115–116.

85 Ibid. at 111.

86 Ibid. at 112.

87 See, e.g. Felix Ekardt, 'Sustainability and a New Concept of Liberty' in Hans Christian Bugge and Christina Voigt, eds., *Sustainable Development in International and National Law: What Did the Brundtland Report Do to Legal Thinking and Legal Development, and Where Can We Go from Here?* (Groningen: Europa Law Publishing, 2008) at 73. Recognising the lack of proper of implementation does not mean that sustainable development does not have a 'judicial function' when interpreting and applying environmental law. On this thesis, see, e.g. Fitzmaurice (*supra* note 59) at 83; Winter (*supra* note 18) at 39 who exposes the 'constructive potential of indeterminacy'.

88 The autonomous human right linked to the environment can be phrased differently. Reference can be made to the right to a clean, healthy, safe, ecologically balanced, stable, viable, sustainable, or protected environment.

89 See, e.g. Christian Tomuschat, *Human Rights: Between Idealism and Realism* (Oxford: OUP, 2003) at 51–2.

and viable' environment in the catalogue of the human rights guaranteed by the Convention have always been contentious and failing.[90]

Against that background, the recognition of the autonomous right temporarily occurred at the judicial level. As a sign of the Court's dynamism, the Court partially recognised the right to a 'healthy and protected' environment in the *Tatar* case.[91] This (temporary) recognition can be seen as a sign of dynamism since the Court went against the above-mentioned reluctance to adopt an Additional Protocol that would add the autonomous right to the catalogue of the rights guaranteed. Nevertheless, even though the Court has acknowledged the right, no obligations that would bind States have been clearly recognised by the Court as specifically flowing from the right to a healthy and protected environment. This is why the temporary recognition can only be said to have been partial. The *Tatar* case did not specify any clear normative content or consequences for this right. This is a central and recurrent conundrum of the right's recognition, be it at the national, regional or international level. In addition, this partial recognition has been temporary: the Court seems to have taken a step backwards in subsequent cases.[92]

Accordingly, the European human rights framework is ill-equipped to address environmental affairs that have a collective dimension or concern the environment's intrinsic value. The European human rights system is strongly criticised for having a predominantly individual approach. The rights guaranteed by the

90 The latest attempt is not expected to be successful. The Parliamentary Assembly of the Council of Europe has adopted in September 2009 a recommendation on a 'draft additional Protocol to the European Convention on Human Rights on the right to a healthy environment' (*Recommendation 1885 (2009)*, Parliamentary Assembly, Council of Europe. Adopted by the Assembly on 30 September 2009 (32nd sitting). *Österreichische Vereinigung zur Erhaltung, Stärkung und Schaffung Eines Wirtschaftlich Gesunden Land – und Forstwirtschaftlichen Grundbesitzes v Austria* (n 62); *Giacomelli v Italy* (*supra* note 22) at 82–3. The reluctance to adopt the Protocol was expressed as soon as one month later in the meeting of the Committee of Experts for the Development of Human Rights (DH-DEV) that took place on 12–14 October 2009 (As reported in 'Overview of the recent case-law of the European Court of Human Rights and the European Committee of Social Rights on the environment', *DH-DEV(2010)02, Steering Committee for Human Rights (CDDH), Committee of Experts for the Development of Human Rights (DH-DEV)*, 3). 'Reservations' were reiterated during the CDDH meeting that took place on 24–27 November 2009. Such a 'cautious' approach is clearly at odds with the ever-growing recognition of the autonomous right in national laws and constitutions, other regional human rights systems such as the African regional human rights framework (African Charter on Human and Peoples Rights 1981, Art 24.), or the Inter-American regional human rights framework (Additional Protocol to the American Convention on Human Rights in the Area of Economic, Social and Cultural Rights 1988, Arts 11-1); and at the global level (as reported, e.g. in José Mendes Bota, 'Drafting an Additional Protocol to the European Convention on Human Rights Concerning the Right to a Healthy Environment' (Committee on the Environment, Agriculture and Local and Regional Affairs of the Parliamentary Assembly, Council of Europe 2009) 12003 under 'II. The gradual recognition of the right to a healthy environment' <http://www.coe.int/t/dghl/standardsetting/hrpolicy/other_committees/GT-DEV-ENV_docs/erec1885.pdf> accessed 12 January 2014.

91 *Tatar v Romania* (*supra* note 74) at [107, 112].

92 See, e.g. *Dubetska* [2011] ECtHR 30499/03 [105]. The Court hereby relates back to its case law prior the *Tatar* case, when assuming that '[t]he Court refers to its well-established case-law that neither Article 8 nor any other provision of the Convention guarantees the right to preservation of the natural environment as such'.

Convention are first and second generation human rights that are primarily meant to protect identified individuals.[93] This is exemplified with the contentious question of future generations as rights holders.

22.4.2 An illustration: the impossibility of recognising future generations as rights holders

The issue of future generations is addressed by the second New Delhi Principle (equity and the eradication of poverty) with regards to the intergenerational dimension of equity.[94] The recognition of future generations as rights holders is *a priori* not possible in the context of the Convention. This impossibility illustrates the limits of the Convention and the Court's jurisdiction: the rights mobilised in cases that have an environmental dimension have a strong individual dimension.

Within the law of the Convention as it is interpreted and applied by the Court, the notion of victim is autonomous. This means that the Court legally defines 'victim' according to its own standards. As a principle, only direct victims of a claimed violation can bring a case before the Court. Some exceptions temper the principle's rigour.

These exceptions prove to be very relevant when it comes to future generations. Indeed, the Court has recognised the status of 'potential victim'. Potential victims are those under threat of having their rights violated (for example there are no doubts that a domestic statute will apply).[95] Furthermore, the victim status can be recognised independently of the materialisation of damage.[96] In other

---

93 On this point, see among others Edith Brown Weiss, *In Fairness to Future Generations: International Law, Common Patrimony, and Intergenerational Equity* (Tokyo: United Nations University; Transnational Publishers, 1988) at 114; Christian Schall, 'Public Interest Litigation Concerning Environmental Matters Before Human Rights Courts: A Promising Future Concept?' (2008) 20 *Envtl. L.* 417; Francesco Francioni, *International Human Rights in an Environmental Horizon* (2011) EJIL 41–55 <http://hdl.handle.net/1814/15944> accessed 13 January 2014, and more particularly at 50 regarding the European Court of Human Rights:

> But in spite of the undeniable progress marked by these judgments toward the opening up of an environmental horizon of human rights, they still fail to achieve the objective of the recognition of an independent right to a decent environment. This is prevented, first, at a substantive level by the purely individualistic conception of human rights still pervading the jurisprudence of the Strasbourg Court. Negative impacts on the environment, even where severe, are relevant only in that they produce an interference with the sphere of rights guaranteed by the convention to 'individuals'. Thus, environmental integrity is not seen as a value per se for the community affected or society as a whole, but only as a criterion to measure the negative impact on a given individual's life, property, private and family life. Secondly, at the procedural level, the individualistic approach followed by the Court excludes the admissibility of public interest proceedings to defend the environment, unless the applicants can show a direct impact of the activities complained of on the sphere of their individual rights.

94 Future generations are also referred to in preamble and Principles 1 and 7 of New Dehli Declaration (*supra* note 14).

95 See, e.g. *Association Ekin v France* [2001] ECtHR 30882/96.

96 See, e.g. *Pine Valley Developments Ltd and Others v Ireland* (*supra* note 9). On the objectivity shift, see, e.g. *Scordino v Italy (No 1)* [2006] ECtHR 36813/97.

words, an individual who claims that the effects of a dangerous activity require the adoption of positive adaptation measures cannot be opposed by the States on the grounds that the effects have not yet occurred. The problem is one of an evidentiary nature and echoes the difficulties mentioned above regarding risk and proof matters. Another exception to the direct victim requirement is the recognition of victims 'by ricochet': the claimed violation concerned victim A as a first step and subsequently concerned victim B as a second step. Victim B is the victim 'by ricochet' (for example the widow of a detainee).

When turning to the specific issue of 'not yet born' persons, the Court denies their recognition as victims[97] although the *Open Door and Dublin Well Woman v Ireland* case had slightly opened the door for such recognition in 1992.[98]

To sum up, if the status of potential victim can fit with the intertemporal feature of intergenerational justice, this status does not extend to future generations.

However, one could argue that the recognition of present generations suffering a not-yet occurred damage matches with the occurrence of damage to be suffered by future generations. Despite the move towards less stringent requirements of qualifying the victim described above, and despite the possibility that the Court would grant environmental rights with a collective nature rather than the currently-applied individualistic dimension, the author does not think that the Court would go so far as to recognise future generations as collective holders of rights guaranteed by the Convention. Once again, these are projections. The Court may retain a very progressive approach, but the author is fairly sceptical.

All in all, it seems that the recognition by the Court of future generations as holders of rights and present generations as holders of obligations towards future generations, is not likely to occur, unless this legal status were to be endorsed by a particular Protocol to the Convention.[99] As another consequence of the predominantly individual nature of the rights guaranteed by the European system, the impossibility for the Court to recognise the environment's intrinsic value can be slightly nuanced.

22.4.3 Some shy steps towards the recognition of the environment's intrinsic value?

The Convention can *a priori* not provide solid grounds to guarantee the protection of the environment's intrinsic value that is reflected in the preamble of the New Delhi Declaration ('the objective of sustainable development involves a comprehensive and integrated approach . . . which aims at the sustainable use of natural resources of the Earth and the protection of the environment on

---

97 See, e.g. *Dayras and Others v France* [2005] ECtHR 65390/01.

98 See, e.g. *Open Door and Dublin Well Woman v Ireland* [1992] ECtHR 14234/88.

99 L. Collins came to the same conclusion for the EU in Lynda Collins, 'Environmental Rights for the Future? Intergenerational Equity in the EU' (2007) 16 *Review of European Community and International Environmental Law* 321, 321–331, 329.

which nature . . . depend(s)') and in the first New Delhi Principle (sustainable use of natural resources), more particularly under the third paragraph of this Principle:

> The protection, preservation and enhancement of the natural environment, particularly the proper management of climate system, biological diversity and fauna and flora of the Earth, are the common concern of humankind. The resources of outer space and celestial bodies and of the sea-bed, ocean floor and subsoil thereof beyond the limits of national jurisdiction are the common heritage of humankind.

If the Court recognised the environment's intrinsic value, it would then be possible to have this value as part of the fair balance equation and possibly be recognised as a peculiar weight when compared to social and economic values.

The Court has slightly recognised the environment's intrinsic value in several instances. For example, the Court acknowledged this value in the *Depalle* case: 'The relevant provisions on unlawful interference with maritime public property no longer refer essentially to navigation but take account of the *protection of coastal areas for their own sake*.'[100] The Court acknowledged the intrinsic value of the environment that is recognised in French domestic statute (i.e. it does not refer to the social or economic interests implied by the activities linked to the coastal areas – for example tourism). This acknowledgement proved instrumental when the Court framed the fair balance equation and established which interests were pursued by the national interference (a statute in this case). Indeed, to find a justification for the national authorities to apply the statute in question 'consistently and more strictly', the Court did then ground itself on this interest ('increasing need to protect coastal areas and their use by the public').[101]

Still, in the *Depalle* case, the Court unveiled another rule when referring to 'overriding' interests that could have overridden the protection of coastal areas for their own sake, namely architectural interest or an interest dictated by a concern to protect the *national heritage*.[102] The Court has not gone further on this point and did not expose what 'national heritage' is to encompass. National heritage may encompass some environmental elements that call for the recognition of the environment's intrinsic value (for example biodiversity). If that were the case, some environmental elements might be recognised as overriding interests when compared to the protection of other environmental elements (here, the protection of coastal areas for their own sake). This point is left open for discussion. The Court may explain or apply the rule unveiled in future cases.

The Court also touched upon the environment's intrinsic value in cases that concern environmental damage. However, the Court does not always make

---

100 *Depalle v France* (*supra* note 23) at [39] (emphasis added).
101 Ibid. at 89.
102 Ibid.

clear to what extent environmental damage has an impact on the obligations of States and the fair balance mechanism. The Court referred to environmental damage and the threshold issue in the *Tatar* case, when it ruled that the precautionary principle calls for States not to delay the adoption of effective and proportionate measures in order to prevent *serious and irreversible damages* to the environment.[103] The Court specified the degree of importance when it comes to preventing damages to the environment: Article 8 of the Convention grounds the *primary duty* for States to set a legislative and administrative framework aimed to effectively *prevent* damages to the environment.[104] Still, in the *Tatar* case, the Court noted that some of the species damaged by the Baia Mare incident were protected and under extinction, while other species did disappear.[105] Accordingly, the interest of not suffering from environmental damage is all the more crucial and given weight. Similarly, the Court refers to 'irreparable damage' in the *Giacomelli* case.[106]

The seriousness of environmental damage also appeared in the *Mangouras v Spain* case.[107] This case concerned the bail applied to the Prestige's Master, Mr Mangouras. In this instance, the level of environmental damage was brought into play when the Court assessed whether the State could justify the setting of the bail ground on the disastrous and large-scale effects of the oil spill disaster. The underlying question was whether environmental damage considered as a fact could be a solid basis to be one of the triggering elements when setting the amount of the bail.

The Court underlined that the 'marine pollution on a seldom-seen scale' had caused 'huge environmental damage',[108] the 'national and international disaster caused by the oil spill', and the 'public outcry'.[109] These factors have been found crucial to recognise as a 'primary objective' the presence of the applicant and hence, one element of the fair balance equation. In this respect, the Court has been particularly eloquent and clear when it referred not to the protection of the environment as an emerging demand as the Court repeatedly mentions in environmental affairs, but to the emerging demand in Europe and internationally 'in relation to environmental offences',[110] and to a 'tendency (*that*) can also be observed to use criminal law as a means of enforcing the environmental obligations imposed by European and international law'.[111] These 'new realities' have to be taken into account in interpreting the provisions of the Convention (Article 5(3) in this case).[112] Furthermore, the Court recognised that environmental

103 *Tatar v Romania* (*supra* note 74) at [109].
104 Ibid. at 88.
105 Ibid. at 27.
106 *Giacomelli v Italy* (*supra* note 22) at [19].
107 *Mangouras v Spain* [2009] ECtHR 12050/04.
108 Ibid. at 88.
109 Ibid. at 85.
110 Ibid. at 86.
111 *Mangouras v Spain* (*supra* note 108).
112 Ibid. at 87.

offences as a means of enforcing environmental obligations reflect 'fundamental values of democratic societies'.[113]

Nevertheless, the Court did limit these factors as factual data that influenced the level of bail since 'the judicial authorities should adjust the amount required by way of bail in line with the level of (*civil and criminal*) liability incurred', and in this case 'large sums of money are at stake'.[114] Accordingly, the amount of bail did guarantee environmental offences provisions' effectiveness. It is possible to regret that the environment's value is slightly reduced to a monetary dimension.

22.5 Conclusion

It has been demonstrated that the Court has elaborated a strong record of rights and obligations that implement some of the New Delhi Principles. Particular attention was paid to the integration principle and environmental procedural rights.

It was recalled that no clearly defined environmental legal basis can be found within the text of the Convention. Also, the attempts to adopt an Additional Protocol that would guarantee the autonomous right to a healthy environment have always failed. Consequently, this hampers the Court from recognising the collective dimension associated with environmental degradation on the one hand (as exemplified with the cornerstone issue of future generations) and the environment's intrinsic value on the other.

Indeed, the Convention was adopted in 1950. At that time, the human rights guaranteed were predominantly of the first and second generation. Environmental concerns emerged later while the legal canvassing in positive law of both the collective dimension of environmental related issues (for example through the rights of future generations) and the environment's intrinsic value are still in their infancy.

In this context, the dynamism of the Court should be acknowledged and welcomed. It should also be underlined that the cases reported in this chapter have all been adjudicated by the Court following the initiative of citizens or groups of citizens. Consequently, it is up to citizens and NGOs to make use of the paths unveiled by the Court in order to enable the Court to settle its case law, deliver new rulings and provide new paths. It can also be inferred from this active role of citizens that they did answer the calls expressed in the Preamble of the New Delhi Declaration to pursue 'the objective of sustainable development in an effective way' and 'to continue the progressive development and, as and where appropriate, codification of international law related to sustainable development.'

113   *Mangouras v Spain* (*supra* note 108).
114   Ibid. at 88.

Investor-State arbitral tribunals

23 The integration principle in ICSID awards

*Antony Crockett**

23.1 Introduction

It is customary for works discussing almost any aspect of investment treaty law and practice to include an introductory remark on the "explosion" in the number of cases referred to arbitration since the late 1990s. According to statistics compiled by the United Nations Conference on Trade and Development (UNCTAD), the number of investor-State cases initiated pursuant to the terms of international investment agreements (IIAs) grew exponentially in the previous decade, reaching a total of 608 by the end of 2014.[1] In some quarters, the extraordinary fecundity of the system is presented as proof that the international rule of law is in the rudest of health.[2] For others, the massive and ongoing growth in the total numbers of treaties and disputes evidences "normless" expansionism, driven by greedy neoliberal corporate lawyers at great cost to the developing world.[3]

A stated objective of many (if not all) IIAs is to contribute to economic development by creating favourable conditions for investment.[4] However, in interpreting and applying the substantive investment protection provisions of IIAs, tribunals

* This chapter is based on a short paper prepared for the IDLO-CISDL conference on *Legal Preparedness for Global Sustainability: Sustainable Development Principles in the Decisions of International Courts and Tribunals, 1992–2012* (IDLO Headquarters, Rome, 16–17 June 2011). The author is grateful to Matthew Weiniger and Audley Sheppard for comments on this chapter and to Alison Farquhar and Timothy Hughes who provided valuable assistance with the original research. The views expressed in this chapter are the personal opinions of the author, who is also responsible for any errors.

1 UNCTAD, *Recent Trends in IIAs and ISDS,* IIA Issues Note No. 1 February 2015 <www.unctad.org/diae> (accessed 26 March 2015), 1. The true total of cases may be slightly higher than UNCTAD statistics reveal due to the fact that it is not compulsory in every case for the initial reference to arbitration, or the final award, to be made public.

2 See, e.g. Stephan Schill, *The Multilateralization of International Investment Law* (Cambridge: CUP, 2009).

3 M. Sornarajah, 'Evolution or revolution in international investment arbitration? The descent into normlessness' in Chester Brown and Kate Miles, eds., *Evolution in Investment Treaty Law and Arbitration* (Cambridge: CUP, 2011).

4 See, e.g. preamble to the United Kingdom Model Agreement for the Promotion and Protection of Investment, Appendix 4 in Campbell McLachlan, Laurence Shore and Matthew Weiniger, *International Investment Arbitration: Substantive Principles* (Oxford: OUP, 2007).

constituted to adjudicate on investor-State disputes have been criticised for being insufficiently sensitive to concerns regarding protection of human rights or the environment.[5] These criticisms have provoked a lively debate amongst scholars and practitioners, mainly focused on the issue of whether treaties or tribunals (or both) are to blame.[6] In this context, regardless of one's point of view, the abundance of awards provides a rich source of jurisprudence for analysis.

This chapter reports on the results of a research exercise which aimed to document the ways in which investment treaty tribunals have interpreted and analysed principles of international law relating to sustainable development reflected in the International Law Association Declaration on the Principles of International Law Related to Sustainable Development (New Delhi Principles) in the period from 1992 to 2012.[7]

Following a brief primer on investor-State dispute resolution under IIAs, the methodology and results of this research exercise are summarised in section 23.2.2 below. It may immediately disappoint the reader to discover that no published awards were identified in which the tribunal cites or otherwise refers to the New Delhi Principles. Section 23.3.2 seeks to strike a more optimistic tone, positing that the decisions of tribunals can be seen, in some cases, as supportive of the New Delhi Principles, in particular the principle of good governance. Section 23.3.2.2 suggests that in order for principles of international law related to sustainable development to play a more active role in the resolution of investor-State disputes, lawyers working in the latter field must become familiar with those principles.

23.2 Terminology, methodology and results

The so-called "system" (or, more pejoratively, "regime") of investor-State dispute resolution has a relatively recent history. The first arbitration pursuant to an IIA was commenced in 1987.[8] The same year, the World Commission on Environment and Development adopted the famous Brundtland Report calling for sustainable development, defined as 'development that meets the needs of the present without compromising the ability of future generations to meet their own needs'.[9] This section provides a very brief overview of the legal framework for investor-State dispute resolution and introduces relevant terminology. It also summarises the

5 See, e.g. Bruno Simma, 'Foreign Investment Arbitration: a Place for Human Rights?' (2011) *ICLQ* 573; Kyla Tienhaara, *The Expropriation of Environmental Governance: Protecting Foreign Investors at the Expense of Public Policy* (Cambridge: CUP, 2009).
6 See, e.g. Michael Waibel, Asha Kaushal, Kyo-Hwa Chung, Claire Balchin, eds., *The Backlash Against Investment Arbitration* (The Hague: Kluwer Law International, 2010).
7 Resolution 3/2002 adopted at the 70th Conference of the International Law Association, held in New Delhi, India 2–6 April 2002, UN Doc. A/CONF.199/8 (9 August 2002).
8 *Asian Agricultural Products v Republic of Sri Lanka* (ICSID Case No. Case No. ARB/87/3, Final Award, 27 June 1990).
9 United Nations, *Our Common Future: Report of the World Commission on Environment and Development*, UN Doc. A/42/427 – Annex 4 (4 August 1987), chapter 2, I.

methodology used by the author to search for references to principles of international sustainable development law in the decisions of investor treaty tribunals and the results of a survey of decisions published from 1992 to 2012.

23.2.1 Investor-State dispute resolution

The vast majority of the total universe of IIAs comprises of bilateral investment treaties (BITs). The former acronym also encompasses multilateral agreements and free trade agreements (FTAs) which include provisions for the protection of foreign investors;[10] the most well-known example of the latter being the North American Free Trade Agreement (NAFTA) signed between Canada, Mexico and the United States. IIAs include substantive obligations governing the conduct of host States vis-à-vis foreign investors and (typically) give qualifying investors a right to commence arbitration against the host State if these standards are breached.

The majority[11] of investor-State disputes are submitted to arbitration pursuant to the Convention on the Settlement of Investment Disputes between States and Nationals of Other States[12] (ICSID Convention). The ICSID Convention was negotiated in the early 1960s under the auspices of the World Bank. The purpose of the Convention was to create a neutral forum for determining disputes between States and foreign investors, particularly in circumstances where domestic legal systems provided inadequate protection for the property rights of foreign investors or otherwise represented a disincentive to foreign direct investment. Although international law imposed substantive obligations on States with respect to the treatment of foreign investors, such obligations were not capable of enforcement (generally speaking) unless the investors' home State exercised rights of diplomatic protection on behalf of the investor.[13]

The ICSID Convention provides a legal framework pursuant to which States consent to submit disputes with foreign investors to arbitration before international tribunals. States are further bound to comply with the decisions (known as "awards") rendered by ICSID tribunals, subject to the possibility of annulment proceedings under Article 52 of the ICSID Convention. Disputes which may be submitted to ICSID include: (i) disputes arising under investment contracts[14] between States and foreign investors, which will typically be governed by the domestic law of the host State; and (ii) disputes arising under IIAs, which will be governed by international law.[15] It is the latter form of dispute which is the focus of discussion in this chapter.

---

10 As used by UNCTAD, the IIA acronym also refers to double taxation treaties.
11 UNCTAD, *supra* note 1 at 7.
12 Signed 18 March 1965, entered into force 14 October 1966, 575 UNTS 159.
13 McLachlan, Shore and Weiniger, *supra* note 4 at 4.
14 Including, for example, concessions to exploit natural resources or to construct and/or operate public infrastructure.
15 See Christoph H. Schreuer, *The ICSID Convention: A Commentary*, 2nd edn (Cambridge: CUP, 2009).

IIAs may also provide for arbitration under the Arbitration Rules of the United Nations Commission on International Trade Law (UNCITRAL).[16] Less frequently, an IIA may allow investors to refer disputes to arbitration pursuant to the rules of a commercial arbitration institution such as the Court of Arbitration of the International Chamber of Commerce (ICC)[17] or the Stockholm Chamber of Commerce (SCC).[18] It is beyond the scope of this chapter to discuss the differences between the rules and sufficient to note one key difference, namely that investor-State arbitration proceedings pursuant to UNCITRAL, ICC or SCC rules may be confidential whereas the registration of a request for arbitration under the ICSID Convention and the status of the arbitration proceedings is published on the internet.[19] However, aside from the possibility of documents in the arbitration being "leaked" by the parties, awards rendered by tribunals determining disputes under IIAs will only be made public if (i) the underlying treaty mandates publication of awards; (ii) the parties agree that the award may be made public; or (iii) the award is made public in the context of enforcement proceedings.

23.2.2 Methodology and results of survey

A sample of awards for the period 1992 to 2012 was obtained from the ICSID website and the investment treaty arbitration database maintained by the University of Victoria.[20] Only final awards published in English were included in the sample. This sample was then subjected to an electronic word search for references to the New Delhi Principles and the words "sustainable development". The electronic search failed to identify any award which referred to the New Delhi Principles. A number of awards were identified which contained the words "sustainable development". Closer inspection revealed that these references were invariably preceded by the words 'International Institute for . . .' and appeared in the award merely to identify, for purposes of citation, an amicus submission prepared by the IISD.[21]

16 See, e.g. Article 13 of the Agreement between the Government of the Kingdom of Cambodia and the Government of the Republic of Singapore on the Promotion and Protection of Investments <http://www.unctad.org/sections/dite/iia/docs/bits/singapore_cambodia.pdf> (accessed 28 February 2012).

17 See, e.g. Article VIII of the Agreement between the Republic of Turkey and the Arab Republic of Egypt concerning the reciprocal promotion and protection of investments <http://www.unctad.org/sections/dite/iia/docs/bits/turkey_egypt.pdf> (accessed 28 February 2012).

18 See, e.g. Article 10 of the Agreement between the Government of the Russian Federation and the Government of the Republic of Lithuania on the promotion and reciprocal protection of investments <http://www.unctad.org/sections/dite/iia/docs/bits/lithuania_russia.pdf> (accessed 28 February 2012).

19 See <http://icsid.worldbank.org > (accessed 28 February 2012). See also, Administrative and Financial Regulations, Regulation 23.

20 See <http://italaw.com/> (accessed 28 February 2012).

21 On the role of an amicus curiae ("friend of the court") in investor-State dispute resolution see, Nathalie Bernasconi-Osterwalder, 'Transparency and Amicus Curiae in ICSID Arbitrations' in

It should be noted that the legitimacy of the investment treaty regime has been questioned based on the alleged reluctance (or refusal) of tribunals to engage with the broader corpus of international law. In 2011, it was reported that Judge Bruno Simma of the International Court of Justice, in an address to the International Council for Commercial Arbitration, had criticised investment treaty arbitrators for failing to pay adequate attention to social and environmental concerns.[22] A pessimist might conclude, based on the crude survey undertaken for the purposes of this chapter, that such criticism is well founded. Of course, it is also relevant to ask the pessimist whether tribunals should be required to engage with principles of international law relating to sustainable development if those principles are not referred to in the parties' submissions.[23]

Notwithstanding the lack of references to the New Delhi Principles in published awards, there are grounds for optimism regarding the question of whether investor-State dispute resolution might be amenable to application of those principles, in particular the principle of integration. In dealing with disputes where investors have challenged measures claimed by the host State to have been introduced in order to protect the environment, tribunals have developed tests and approaches which, consistent with the principle of integration, involve a weighing and balancing exercise which takes into account the rights of investors under IIAs alongside other interests connected with the three pillars of sustainable development, namely economic development, social development and environmental protection.

A caveat required before proceeding to the discussion of the "jurisprudence" is that there is no system of precedent in investor-State dispute resolution, meaning that the decision of one tribunal is not binding upon the next. Nevertheless, it has been argued that a 'system of *de facto* precedent' has emerged as a result of the widespread practice of parties and tribunals who reference previous decisions in their submissions and awards.[24] Many of the awards considered in the following section are frequently cited by tribunals and commentators. Moreover, many of the awards cited have been criticised for giving undue weight to the investor's rights and interests and, by implication, insufficient weight to environmental, social or wider economic concerns.

23.3 The jurisprudence of integration

This section presents a conception of the principle of integration, followed by analysis of a number of awards which, in the author's view, indicate "entry

---

M.C. Cordonier Segger, M.W. Gehring and A. Newcombe, eds., *Sustainable Development in World Investment Law* (Netherlands: Wolters Kluwer, 2011).

22 Sebastian Perry, 'Arbitrators and Human Rights' *Global Arbitration Review* (13 June 2011) <www. globalarbitrationreview.com> (accessed 28 February 2012).

23 This issue is discussed further in Section 23.3.2.2. It was beyond the scope of the research exercise undertaken for this chapter to review the memorials and other submissions of parties for references to the New Delhi Principles; even when awards have been made public, it remains uncommon for the parties' submissions to be published.

24 Schill, *supra* note 2 at 356.

points" for arguments based on the principle of integration, or more broadly on principles of international law related to sustainable development. It is beyond the scope of this chapter to comment on other "entry points," of which there are an increasing number of possibilities,[25] such as explicit references to sustainable development in IIAs.[26] Such references are increasingly included in IIAs in direct response to criticism that investor-State tribunals have failed to take into account the environmental or social aspects of disputes.[27] As disputes arise and are resolved under the "new generation" of IIAs it seems likely that the number of awards directly engaging with legal principles relating to sustainable development will increase.[28]

23.3.1 *The principle of integration*

The New Delhi Principles describe the 'principle of integration and interrelationship, in particular in relation to human rights and social, economic and environmental objectives' as a principle of international law.[29] It is further stated that:

> States should strive to resolve apparent conflicts between competing economic, financial, social and environmental considerations, whether through existing institutions of through the establishment of appropriate new institutions.

In an article discussing sustainable development as a treaty objective and a tool to achieve integration of economic, environmental and social interests, Henning

25 See, Chester Brown, 'Bringing Sustainable Development Issues before Investment Treaty Tribunals' in Cordonier Segger, Gehring and Newcombe, *supra* note 21.

26 For example, State Parties may include a commitment to sustainable development as an objective of the treaty, usually by including some form of preambular reference as appears, for example, in the 2007 Investment Agreement for the COMESA Common Investment Area (the COMESA Agreement) or the 2007 Agreement between Japan and the Republic of Chile for a Strategic Economic Partnership. States may also qualify the substantive obligations in the treaty by reference to States' prerogative to introduce environmental or social legislation, such as Article 20 (8) of the COMESA Agreement which states as follows: 'Consistent with the right of States to regulate and the customary international law principles on police powers, bona fide regulatory measures taken by a Member State that are designed and applied to protect or enhance legitimate public welfare objectives, such as public health, safety and the environment shall not constitute an indirect expropriation.'

27 See, e.g. Barton Legum, 'Lessons Learned from the NAFTA: The New Generation of US Investment Treaty Arbitration Provisions' (2004) 19(2) *Foreign Investment Law Journal* 344.

28 Ibid. See also, John Beechey and Antony Crockett, 'The New Generation of Investment Treaties: Consensus or Divergence?' in Arthur W. Rovine, ed., *Contemporary Issues in International Arbitration and Mediation* (Netherlands: Martinus Nijhoff Publishers, 2009).

29 ILA, *supra* note 7. The other New Delhi Principles are (i) The duty of States to ensure sustainable use of natural resources; (ii) The principle of equity and the eradication of poverty; (iii) The principle of common but differentiated responsibilities; (iv) The principle of the precautionary approach to human health, natural resources and ecosystems; (v) The principle of public participation and access to information and justice; and (vi) The principle of good governance.

Grosse Ruse-Khan describes the principle of integration as an "overarching" expression of the other New Delhi Principles.[30] Tracing the origins of the principle of integration to the Brundtland Report, according to Ruse-Khan, the principle essentially calls for a balanced reconciliation of economic, environmental and social priorities.[31]

Ruse-Khan goes on to argue that the principle of integration is ambiguous, posing two difficult questions:

1   Does the principle of integration, in any given scenario, demand a specific outcome in terms of the outcome of the weighing and balancing exercise that it contemplates?
2   Who, on the international, national or local level, is best positioned to determine the balance?

Both of these questions are particularly apposite in the context of investor-State dispute resolution. First, as has been noted above, investor-State tribunals have been criticised for giving undue weight to investors' interests and/or for failing to take into account environmental or social interests. Secondly, it has been suggested that the typical appointee to an investor-State tribunal (who we assume will typically be an expert in the substantive and procedural aspects of disputes arising under IIA) is not well qualified to deal with questions arising in other specialised fields of international law.[32] The answer this chapter suggests for the first question is in the negative; the principle of integration does *not* tell us how to determine the appropriate balance between economic, environmental or social objectives, but it can guide the decision making process. Something more will be said about the second question in section 23.3.2.2.

23.3.2 The jurisprudence

It is not the objective of the discussion which follows to comment on the merits of the individual decisions discussed. The goal is more modest and is only to identify awards which show us possible entry points for arguments that the economic, environmental or social interests advanced or protected by a measure should be taken into account by a tribunal, alongside the investor's financial interests, including its rights under the IIA. In particular, a number of awards dealing with claims of indirect expropriation and the meaning of the "fair and equitable treatment" (FET) standard are discussed.

---

30 Henning Grosse Ruse-Khan, 'A Real Partnership for Development? Sustainable Development as Treaty Objective in European Economic Partnership Agreements and Beyond' (2010) 13 (1) *J. of Int'l Econ. L.* 139, 148.

31 Ibid. at 145–50.

32 See, e.g. Perry, *supra* note 22, reporting comments by Professor José Alvarez to the effect that the arbitrators appointed in investor-State cases may not be qualified to resolve questions relating to international human rights law.

23.3.2.1 Indirect expropriation

The concept of expropriation is straightforward; expropriation is a "taking" of property by the State for which compensation is required. Most IIAs contain a provision dealing with expropriation. For example, paragraph 1 of Article 1110 of NAFTA provides that:

> No [State] Party may directly or indirectly nationalize or expropriate an investment of an investor of another Party in its territory or take a measure tantamount to nationalization or expropriation of such an investment ("expropriation"), except:
>
> (a) for a public purpose;
> (b) on a non-discriminatory basis;
> (c) in accordance with due process of law and Article 1105(1); and
> (d) on payment of compensation in accordance with paragraphs 2 through 6.

So far so simple. But difficult questions arise, particularly in cases involving "indirect" expropriation where tribunals have held that governments may be liable to pay compensation for introducing regulations which do not amount to a direct taking of an investment (in the sense of divesting the investor of its legal title to property) but which significantly interfere with the investor's property rights such that they may be said to be "tantamount" (or equivalent) to expropriation.[33]

In *Metalclad v Mexico*,[34] the US claimant had commenced construction of a hazardous waste landfill in Mexico after receiving a permit from the federal government. Subsequently, municipal authorities notified the claimant that the construction activities were unlawful as they were being undertaken without a municipal construction permit. The claimant applied for the permit and, pending the authority's decision, completed construction of the landfill. Sometime later, the authority refused the permit and the local governor issued an Ecological Decree declaring the area where the landfill was located as an area for the protection of a rare cactus, both of which actions had the effect of preventing the landfill from being operated. The claimant alleged that the actions of Mexico (through the municipal authorities) violated Article 1110 of NAFTA. The tribunal found in the claimant's favour, determining that the decision to deny the construction permit application on environmental grounds was improper because Mexican law granted exclusive competence in environmental matters to the federal government (i.e. the decision was *ultra vires*). Together with the fact that the federal government had made representations to the claimant that construction could proceed, the absence of a lawful basis for the denial of the construction permit meant that the decision not to issue the construction permit was tantamount to expropriation.

---

33 On the various approaches taken by tribunals to the question of indirect expropriation see, McLachlan, Shore and Weiniger, *supra* note 4 at [8.71]–[8.89].
34 *Metalclad Corporation v Mexico* (ICSID Case No. ARB(AF)/97/1, Award, 30 August 2000).

The *Metalclad* award has subsequently been identified as one of a number of awards which go too far because 'they fail to consider the purpose of a challenged measure when determining whether it constituted an expropriation'.[35] Paragraph 111 of the award, in particular the first sentence, has attracted criticism:

> The Tribunal need not decide or consider the motivation or intent of the adoption of the Ecological Decree. Indeed, a finding of expropriation on the basis of the Ecological Decree is not essential to the Tribunal's finding of a violation of NAFTA Article 1110. However, the Tribunal considers that the implementation of the Ecological Decree would, in and of itself, constitute an act tantamount to expropriation.

It is probably unfair to criticise the *Metalclad* tribunal for this statement, which follows a paragraph where the implication is that the Ecological Decree was adopted precisely in order to prevent operation of the landfill and that this was done in bad faith. Moreover, the quoted statement is made in the context of a finding which the tribunal declares immaterial to the ultimate result. In any event, subsequent cases show that the question of whether a measure has been introduced in good faith and/or for a proper public purpose is a relevant consideration.

In *Methanex v United States*, a Canadian claimant challenged California's introduction of a regulation banning a methanol-based gasoline additive (MTBE) on grounds that it was a dangerous groundwater pollutant. The tribunal in *Methanex* emphasised that the public purpose of the measure was a fundamental issue because 'as a matter of general international law, a non-discriminatory regulation for a public purpose, which is enacted in accordance with due process and which affects, *inter alios*, a foreign investor or investment is not deemed expropriatory and compensable'.[36]

In *Methanex*, a suggestion that evidence of bad faith or improper purpose on the part of the host State is irrelevant to the question of whether a measure violates investor rights under an IIA came from a surprising source. Early in the case, the claimant argued that the Californian ban on MTBE lacked objective scientific justification and was instead introduced as a consequence of lobbying and/or improper payments to Californian government officials by major US producers of ethanol-based additives (which competed with MTBE). While these allegations were ultimately not pursued by the claimant, the following paragraph of an amicus brief filed by the IISD commented on them as follows:[37]

> Methanex should be presumed to be aware of the political culture of the United States of America. This includes the good, and in some cases, the

---

35 Suzanne Spears, 'Making Way for the Public Interest in International Investment Agreements' in Brown and Miles, *supra* note 3 at 277.

36 *Methanex v United States* (Final Award, 3 August 2005), [278].

37 Amicus Curiae Submissions by the International Institute for Sustainable Development (9 March 2004), 2. <http://www.iisd.org/pdf/2004/trade_methanex_submissions.pdf> (accessed 28 February 2012).

less good. There is no doubt that the functioning of the political system of the United States is closely tied to private donations. But this is not new, and this is not, per se, an issue that can be subject to proper litigation under Chapter 11. The United States political system cannot be put on trial in an investor-state arbitration. In so far as Methanex has stated it is not arguing there was any criminal corruption or wrongdoing, it must fit its case into a narrow window between not putting the system on trial as a whole, and its own admission there was no criminal conduct. IISD submits that Methanex has failed to find such a window here.

Civil society organisations can play a valuable role in bringing public interest issues to the attention of tribunals, but they can also be one-eyed in their advocacy on behalf of such interests. Viewed in isolation from the unproven allegations in *Methanex*, the IISD submission appears to argue that a measure procured as a consequence of political donations or lobbying by a domestic competitor of a foreign investor (and lacking a *bona fide* social or environmental purpose) should be immune from challenge in investor-State dispute settlement where the investor was aware of the potential for political corruption. Accepting the IISD argument in *Methanex*, as it is understood here, would undermine the role of IIAs in fostering the principle of good governance reflected in the New Delhi Declaration which mandates, amongst other things, 'democratic and transparent decision-making processes . . . [and] effective measures to combat official or other corruption'.[38]

It has been noted elsewhere that the NAFTA parties responded to the controversy created as a result of early awards finding that regulatory action could constitute indirect expropriation by taking steps to clarify the scope of Article 1110,[39] including by introducing interpretative annexes to their model BITs which emphasise that (except in rare circumstances) non-discriminatory measures which are 'designed and applied to protect legitimate public welfare objectives, such as public health, safety and the environment, do not constitute indirect expropriation'.[40] Similar language has been included in new agreements outside the NAFTA-zone, for example the COMESA Agreement, the Japan-Chile EPA,[41] and the ASEAN Comprehensive Investment Agreement.[42]

---

38 New Delhi Principles, Principle 6. The argument that the focus of investor-State tribunals on due process considerations can contribute to better government decision making is also made by Martins Paparinkis, 'Regulatory Expropriation and Sustainable Development' in Cordonier Segger, Gehring and Newcombe, *supra* note 21. See also, Jonathan Bonnitcha, 'The Principle of Good Governance in the Reasoning of Investor-State Arbitral Tribunals', chapter 25 in this volume.

39 Legum, *supra* note 27.

40 See, e.g. discussion of the US Model BIT in Beechey and Crockett, *supra* note 28 at 15–16.

41 Agreement between Japan and the Republic of Chile for a Strategic Economic Partnership, (signed 27 March 2007) (Japan-Chile EPA) <http://www.mofa.go.jp/policy/economy/fta/chile.html> (accessed 28 February 2012).

42 2009 ASEAN Comprehensive Investment Agreement, Annex 2, <http://www.asean.org/documents/FINAL-SIGNED-ACIA.pdf> (accessed 28 February 2012).

Such language creates a limited safe harbour for environmental or social regulation. [43] A regulatory measure would still need to comply with various conditions in order to be immune from challenge as an indirect expropriation. For example, the objectives pursued must be "legitimate public objectives";[44] the measure must be "designed and applied" to protect a legitimate objective;[45] and the measure must be "non-discriminatory".[46] Moreover, most IIAs (and the tribunal's statement in *Methanex* regarding general international law) continue to emphasise the importance of due process considerations.

In this context, tribunals have also used a proportionality test (in some cases drawing on European Court of Human Rights decisions) to determine whether a regulatory measure constitutes indirect expropriation and which also seeks to take account of the public interest sought to be protected or promoted by a measure. In *Tecmed v Mexico* – a case involving the cancellation of Tecmed's licence to operate a hazardous waste facility following the breach of various conditions imposed by the licence – the Tribunal said:[47]

> After establishing that regulatory actions and measures will not be initially excluded from the definition of expropriatory acts, in addition to the negative financial impact of such actions or measures, the Arbitral Tribunal will consider, in order to determine if they are to be characterised as expropriatory, whether such actions or measures are proportional to the public interest presumably protected thereby and to the protection legally granted to investments, taking into account the significance of such impact . . . There must be a reasonable relationship of proportionality between the charge or weight imposed to the foreign investor, and the aim sought to be realised by any expropriatory measure.

The *Tecmed* Tribunal found that, in cancelling the licence to operate the landfill, the Mexican regulator was predominantly influenced by political motives rather than the cancellation being a proportionate response to the licence breaches which, although they gave the regulator power to cancel the licence, did not call for such a response.

It would be difficult to argue that the various tests adopted by tribunals are inconsistent with the principle of integration in so far as it is correct to conceive of that principle as requiring a weighing and balancing exercise without dictating the substantive outcome of a dispute. The awards discussed in this section demonstrate that the public interest which is sought to be protected (or promoted) by a measure should be taken into account by an investor-State tribunal. However, the awards also emphasise that the public interest protected by the measure does

43 Spears, *supra* note 35 at 279.
44 Japan-Chile EPA, *supra* note 41 at Article 82 and Annex 9.
45 COMESA Agreement, Article 20(8).
46 See, US Model BIT Annex B, Appendix 6 in McLachlan, Shore and Weiniger, *supra* note 4 at 393–416, 415.
47 *Tecnicas Medioambientales Tecmed S.A. v The United Mexican States* (Award, 29 May 2003), [122].

not necessarily outweigh other interests, including the property rights of the investor and the right of the investor to due process. Government measures will not be immune from challenge under IIAs simply because they are ostensibly introduced to protect an environmental and social interest or, more broadly, to promote sustainable development.

23.3.2.2 Fair and equitable treatment

Most IIAs impose an obligation on the host State to accord fair and equitable treatment to foreign investors. Because treaties rarely give further guidance on the content of the obligation, tribunals have applied the FET standard 'in a broad manner, using it as a yardstick for the conduct of the national legislator, of domestic administrations, and of domestic courts.'[48] It has also been noted that tribunals have drawn inspiration from principles of domestic administrative or constitutional law so that, from a conceptual standpoint, the FET standard embodies the concept of the rule of law as it is recognised in domestic systems.[49]

As far as the investor's interests are concerned, several principles are embraced by the FET standard, including but not limited to: (i) protection of the investor's legitimate expectations; (ii) transparency in decision making and due process; and (iii) good faith.[50] On the other hand, the enquiry into whether a breach of the FET standard has occurred does not involve only an assessment of the State's conduct strictly viewed in terms of its impact upon the foreign investor. There are also countervailing factors which must be taken into account, and a "primary element" of this enquiry is the tribunal's evaluation of the public interest factors which are claimed to provide justification for a measure.[51]

In *Saluka v Czech Republic*[52] (a case involving a government decision to force a foreign owned bank into administration) the Tribunal referred expressly to the balancing exercise that must be undertaken between the investor's (financial) interests and the interests of the State in regulating to protect the public interest, saying that an enquiry into whether a measure breached the FET standard required '[a] weighing of the investor's legitimate and reasonable expectations on the one hand and the host State's legitimate regulatory interest on the other'.[53] In this respect, the Tribunal went to some lengths to emphasise that the regulatory framework in a host State must be expected to evolve and that in order to determine whether the FET standards has been breached 'the host State's legitimate right . . . to regulate domestic matters in the public interest must be taken into consideration as well'.[54]

---

48 Schill, *supra* note 2 at 79.
49 Ibid. at 79–80.
50 See, Rudolf Dolzer and Christoph Schreuer, *Principles of International Investment Law* (Oxford: OUP, 2008) 133–47.
51 McLachlan, Shore and Weiniger, *supra* note 4 at 234–35.
52 *Saluka Investments BV (The Netherlands) v The Czech Republic* (Partial Award, 17 Mar. 2006).
53 Ibid. at [305].
54 Ibid. at [306].

However, regardless of the public interest in question, if a measure lacks an objective basis, involves an exercise of government power for improper purposes or has a disproportionate impact upon the foreign investor, there is a risk that the measure will violate the FET standard.[55] At the same time, bad faith is not a requirement for violation of the obligation to accord FET[56] and some commentators argue that broad definitions of the standard have 'given tribunals *carte blanche* to review the laws and regulations of the host state based on the tribunal's notion of fairness and the expectations of investors, neither of which are likely to have regard for principles of sustainable development'.[57]

It is true that the investor's expectations are an important factor to be taken into account by tribunals when determining whether the FET standard has been breached; indeed investor expectations can be the decisive factor. In *Parkerings v Lithuania* the investor operated parking ticket machines and multi-storey car parks in the city of Vilnius. The investor alleged its legitimate expectations included an expectation that Lithuanian laws and regulations relevant to its investment would not subsequently change to its disadvantage.[58] In rejecting the investor's claim, the Tribunal denied that such an expectation was legitimate, saying that 'any businessman or investor knows that laws will evolve over time'.[59] Similarly, investors must anticipate that environmental or social laws will evolve over time and it will not (generally speaking) be legitimate to expect that those laws will not change.

In *Chemtura Corporation v Canada*,[60] a US chemical manufacturer claimed that Canada's decision to ban a lindane-based pesticide violated Articles 1105 (minimum standard of treatment) and 1110 of NAFTA (expropriation).[61] The Tribunal rejected

---

55 McLaclan, Shore and Weiniger, *supra* note 4 at 233–47.

56 *Mondev v USA* (Award, 29 May 2003) [85].

57 Graham Mayeda, 'Sustainable International Investment Agreements: Challenges and Solutions for Developing Countries' in Cordonier Segger, Gehring and Newcombe, *supra* note 19 at 548.

58 *Parkerings-Compagniet AS v Republic of Lithuania* (Award, 11 September 2007).

59 Ibid. at [332].

60 *Chemtura Corporation v Canada* (Award, 2 August 2010), <http://italaw.com/documents/ChemturaAward.pdf> (accessed 28 February 2012).

61 Article 1105 of NAFTA provides that '[e]ach party shall accord to investors of another party treatment in accordance with international law, including fair and equitable treatment and full protection and security'. This provision was the subject of an interpretative note issued by the NAFTA Free Trade Commission (citation below) to the effect that Article 1105 required only treatment in accordance with the 'customary international law minimum standard of treatment of aliens'.

The *Chemtura* tribunal summarises the obligation under Article 1105 of NAFTA as an obligation to ensure investors 'benefit from regulatory fairness', ibid. at [179]. In considering the international minimum standard of treatment, the tribunal in *Chemtura* addressed a disagreement between the parties regarding the extent to which Article 1105 allowed the host State's regulatory agencies a 'margin of appreciation' and concluded that: 'In assessing whether the treatment afforded to the Claimant's investment was in accordance with the international minimum standard, the Tribunal must take into account all the circumstances, including the fact that certain agencies manage highly specialized domains involving scientific and public policy determinations. This is not an abstract assessment circumscribed by a legal doctrine about the margin of appreciation of specialized regulatory agencies. It is an assessment that must be conducted *in concreto*. The Tribunal will proceed to such assessment *in concreto* when reviewing the specific measures challenged by the Claimant', ibid. at [179].

the claimant's allegations that Canada's Pest Management Regulatory Agency (PMRA) had acted in bad faith in banning lindane-based pesticides. Instead, the tribunal made a finding that, as a matter of fact, the measures taken by the PMRA were undertaken in pursuit of Canada's obligations under the Aarhus Protocol on Persistent Organic Pollutants to the 1979 UNECE Convention on Long-Range Transboundary Air Pollution.[62] In arriving at this finding, the Tribunal also took into account that the use of lindane had been banned or restricted in numerous other countries and that lindane had been designated under the Stockholm Convention on Persistent Organic Pollutants.[63]

In future, host States' obligations under environmental treaties, or their failure to pursue socially or environmentally progressive policies, may provide grounds for investor claims. For example, in 2009, the Canadian philanthropist Peter Allard launched a claim under the Canada–Barbados BIT alleging that the Barbadian government had damaged his investment in an environmental reserve by, among other things, failing to enforce domestic environmental regulations and to comply with its obligations under the Convention on Wetlands of International Importance (commonly known as the RAMSAR Convention) and the United Nations Convention on Biological Diversity.[64] Elsewhere, in late-2011, a group of investors in the solar energy sector in Spain notified the Spanish government of their intention to commence arbitration under the investment protection provisions of the Energy Charter Treaty.[65] In the latter case, the investors are challenging the government's decision to retroactively amend laws allowing solar energy producers to charge higher tariffs, laws which were originally introduced to encourage investment in renewable energy projects.

23.4 Conclusion

This chapter has observed that investor-State tribunals have not applied or referred to the New Delhi Principles in their decisions. However, a limited sample of cases has been presented which show that tribunals might be influenced by arguments based on principles of international law related to sustainable development. In particular arguments based upon the principle of integration, which calls for a balanced reconciliation of economic, environmental and social priorities may be likely to find favour with tribunals. The cases discussed demonstrate that the exercise of

See, *Notes on Interpretation of Certain Chapter 11 Provisions* (NAFTA Free Trade Commission, 31 July 2001), <http://www.naftalaw.org/files/NAFTA_Comm_1105_Transparency.pdf> (accessed 28 February 2012). On the relationship between the FET standard and the customary international law minimum standard of treatment of aliens see, Hussein Haeri, 'A Tale of Two Standards: Fair and Equitable Treatment and the Minimum Standard in International Law' (2011) 27(1) *Arbitration International* 27–46.
62 *Chemtura* tribunal, *supra* note 61 at [138].
63 Ibid. at [135]–[136].
64 Notice of Dispute (8 December 2009), <http://graemehall.com/legal/papers/BIT-Complaint.pdf> (accessed 28 February 2012). The current status of this case is unknown.
65 Signed December 1994, entered into force April 1998, <http://www.encharter.org/> (accessed 28 February 2012).

balancing the interests of foreign investors and the State's right to regulate in the public interest is inherent to the reasoning of investor-State tribunals, even if there is no evidence that tribunals have had the principle of integration in mind when undertaking that exercise.

Sustainable development depends upon financial, economic, environmental and social interests being taken into account by policy makers. To the extent that there exist cases in which investor-State tribunals have failed to take such interests into account, or to give them due weight, this should be a cause for concern.[66] Notwithstanding that the awards discussed in this chapter expressly refer to the need to include the public interest amongst the matters to be weighed by a tribunal, arbitrators have been criticised for giving undue weight to the foreign investor's interests.[67]

The principle of integration serves to remind tribunals that sustainable development requires a balanced approach. It is also necessary to recall the conception of the principle of integration as an "overarching" expression of the New Delhi Principles and to acknowledge the potential contribution investor-State tribunals could make to sustainable development in enforcing principles of good governance, including requirements of transparent decision-making and due process. In this context, arguments in favour of granting States a wider margin of appreciation to introduce measures in pursuit of social or environmental priorities often fail to declare an underlying and problematic assumption, namely that governments, unshackled from the restrictions imagined to be created by IIAs, will exercise their newfound discretion, fairly, transparently and, more generally, in a manner consistent with principles of international law pertaining to sustainable development.[68]

Criticism of tribunals for failing to take account of environmental and social interests may also be misplaced where those interests have not been represented by the parties in their submissions. It is unlikely that a majority of the lawyers who regularly advise States and investors in relation to IIAs are familiar with the New Delhi Principles, much less how those principles might bear upon the issues in an investor-State dispute.[69] As more and more IIAs include express references to sustainable development we may hope that this will change.

---

66 It is necessary to be wary of critiques that investor-State dispute resolution is biased towards investors given that the ratio of investor "wins" to State "losses" does not disclose any noticeable favouritism towards investors. See, Simma, *supra* note 5 at 575.

67 See, e.g. K. Miles, 'Sustainable Development, National Treatment and Like Circumstances in Investment Law' in M.C. Cordonier Segger, M.W. Gehring and A. Newcombe, eds., *Sustainable Development in World Investment Law* (The Hague: Wolters Kluwer, 2011) at 293.

68 See also, Grosse Ruse-Khan, *supra* note 30 at 180: concluding that IIAs including sustainable development as an objective will make a contribution to sustainable development 'if and when the contracting parties [i.e. States] are willing to take the role of the sustainable development objective seriously'.

69 This includes the author, who was unaware of the New Delhi Principles prior to being invited to prepare this chapter.

24 The principle of public participation in ICSID arbitrations

Avidan Kent

24.1 Introduction

The principle of public participation and the international documents by which it is demonstrated are not often mentioned directly in investment treaties, or by investment tribunals.[1] But as demonstrated in this chapter, even if not by name, elements of this principle have found their way into the domain of investment treaty arbitration. Moreover the current trend is set towards the increasing application of this principle.

This chapter scrutinises the principle of public participation as it was demonstrated in investment disputes governed by the Arbitration Rules of the International Centre for Settlement of Investment Disputes (ICSID), and a variety of investment treaties (Bilateral Investment Treaties (BITs) or International Investment Agreements (IIAs)). It will be claimed that the partial application of the principle of public participation in these investment disputes represents a compromise between the rationales of investment treaty arbitration on the one hand, and the increasing recognition of the importance of this principle on the other. It will further be claimed that the application of this principle by investment tribunals represents an evolution in the way this principle is being perceived, and a recognition of the public aspect of investment arbitration.

---

1 The term 'sustainable development' does appear in a few investment treaties (most notably in the preamble to NAFTA, preambles to Canadian Foreign Investment Promotion and Protection Agreements (FIPAs) and Free Trade Agreements (FTAs) signed with Peru, Colombia, Panama and Jordan, see also the preamble of the Australia-Chile FTA). Other treaties, while not using the term 'sustainable development' specifically, refer to the goals of sustainable development, see for example the preamble to the United States-Uruguay BIT. It should also be noted that the negotiated EU-Canada Comprehensive Trade and Economic Agreement (CETA) includes references to the Rio Declaration, Johannesburg Declaration and *Agenda 21*, but until this moment it is not clear whether the CETA will include an investor-state arbitration provision. Another example is the FTA between the European Free Trade Association (EFTA) States and Singapore, which makes explicit reference to the Universal Declaration of Human Rights, *infra* note 2.

24.2 The principle of public participation and access to information and justice

24.2.1 *Road to recognition*

The concept of public participation in sustainable development decision-making processes was recognised in several international documents. The modern inception of this concept in the field of international law can be attributed to the 1948 UN Universal Declaration of Human Rights, in which it was stated that: 'Everyone has the right to take part in the government of his country, directly or through freely chosen representatives.'[2] The following 20 years saw an evolution of this concept from a basic human right into a fundamental principle, which includes an element of good governance and development. This evolution was manifested in the 1969 UN Declaration on Social Progress and Development:

> Social progress and development require the full utilization of human resources, including, in particular: [. . .]
>
> (c) The active participation of all elements of society, individually or through associations, in defining and in achieving the common goals of development with full respect for the fundamental freedoms embodied in the Universal Declaration of Human Rights;[3]

The recognition in the concept of public participation was also manifest in other international documents from this period,[4] but as Professor Schrijver mentions, it was not until the conclusion of the Rio Declaration and the UN *Agenda 21* in 1992 that this concept received its recognition as an international 'principle'.[5] Principle 10 of the Rio Declaration on Environment and Development states:

> Environmental issues are best handled with the participation of all concerned citizens, at the relevant level. At the national level, each individual shall have appropriate access to information concerning the environment that is held by public authorities, including information on hazardous materials and activities in their communities, and the opportunity to participate in

---

2 Universal Declaration of Human Rights (adopted 10 December 1948) UNGA Res 217(III) art 21(1).

3 Declaration on Social Progress and Development, UNGA Res 2542 (XXIV) (1969) GAOR 24th Session UN Doc A/RES/24/2542 [UN Declaration on Social Progress and Development] art 5.

4 Most notably the International Covenant on Civil and Political Rights (adopted 19 December 1966, entered into force 23 March 1976) 999 UNTS 171, Can TS 1976 No 47, 6 ILM 368; and the Inter-American Convention on Human Rights (adopted 22 November 1969, entered into force 18 July 1978) 1144 UNTS 123, OAS TIAS No 36.

5 Nico Schrijver, *The Evolution of Sustainable Development in International Law: Inception, Meaning and Status* (Netherlands: Martinus Nijhoff, 2008) at 198.

decision-making processes. States shall facilitate and encourage public awareness and participation by making information widely available. Effective access to judicial and administrative proceedings, including redress and remedy, shall be provided.[6]

Paragraph 23.2 of the UN *Agenda 21* adds:

One of the fundamental prerequisites for the achievement of sustainable development is broad public participation in decision-making. Furthermore, in the more specific context of environment and development, the need for new forms of participation has emerged. This includes the need of individuals, groups and organizations to participate in environmental impact assessment procedures and to know about and participate in decisions, particularly those which potentially affect the communities in which they live and work. Individuals, groups and organizations should have access to information relevant to environment and development held by national authorities, including information on products and activities that have or are likely to have a significant impact on the environment, and information on environmental protection measures.[7]

Following the Rio Declaration and *Agenda 21*, other international documents like the Johannesburg Declaration,[8] the Aarhus Convention (which recalls on Principle 10 of the Rio Declaration)[9] and others,[10] continued to confirm the international community's commitment to the principle of public participation.[11] Former Secretary-General of the United Nations, Kofi A. Annan, has commented with regard to the role of the Aarhus Convention in the solidification of the principle of public participation:

---

6 Rio Declaration on Environment and Development, UN GAOR (1992) UN Doc A/CONF151/26 [Rio Declaration on Environment and Development].
7 See further references to this principle in *Agenda 21*, UN GAOR (1992) 46th Sess, Agenda Item 21, UN Doc A/Conf.151/26 [UN *Agenda 21*] paras 8.3, 8.4(f) and 8.7.
8 See for example Article 26 of the Johannesburg Declaration on Sustainable Development.
9 Convention on Access to Information, Public Participation in Decision Making and Access to Justice in Environmental Matters (adopted 28 June 1998, entered into force 30 October 2011) 2161 UNTS 447, 38 ILM 517, UN Doc ECE/CEP43 [Aarhus Convention].
10 See also the United Nations Convention on Biological Diversity (adopted 5 June 1992, entered into force 29 December 1992) 1760 UNTS 79, 31 ILM 822; United Nations Framework Convention on Climate Change (adopted 9 May 1992, entered into force 21 March 1994) 1771 UNTS 107, S Treaty Doc No 102–38, 31 ILM 849; North American Agreement on Environmental Cooperation (adopted 14 September 1993, entered into force 1 January 1994) 32 ILM 1480; United Nations Convention to Combat Desertification in Countries Experiencing Serious Drought and/or Desertification, Particularly in Africa (adopted 17 June 1994, entered into force 26 December 1996) 33 ILM 1328; review in K. Bottriell and M.C. Cordonier Segger, 'The Principle of Public Participation and Access to Information and Justice' (2005) CISDL *Recent Developments in International Law Related to Sustainable Development Legal Working Paper Series* [Bottriell and Cordonier Segger] 4–6.
11 Aarhus Convention (*supra* note 9).

Although regional in scope, the significance of the Aarhus Convention is global. It is by far the most impressive elaboration of principle 10 of the Rio Declaration, which stresses the need for citizens' participation in environmental issues and for access to information on the environment held by public authorities.[12]

In 2002, the International Law Association (ILA), under the lead of Dr. Kamal Hossain and Professor Nico Schrijver, adopted the ILA New Delhi Declaration of Principles of International Law Relating to Sustainable Development (New Delhi Declaration), in which the principle of public participation is included:

5. The principle of public participation and access to information and justice
5.1. Public participation is essential to sustainable development and good governance in that it is a condition for responsive, transparent and accountable governments as well a condition for the active engagement of equally responsive, transparent and accountable civil society organizations, including industrial concerns and trade unions. The vital role of women in sustainable development should be recognized.
5.2. Public participation in the context of sustainable development requires effective protection of the human right to hold and express opinions and to seek, receive and impart ideas. It also requires a right of access to appropriate, comprehensible and timely information held by governments and industrial concerns on economic and social policies regarding the sustainable use of natural resources and the protection of the environment, without imposing undue financial burdens upon the applicants and with due consideration for privacy and adequate protection of business confidentiality.
5.3. The empowerment of peoples in the context of sustainable development requires access to effective judicial or administrative procedures in the State where the measure has been taken to challenge such measure and to claim compensation. States should ensure that where transboundary harm has been, or is likely to be, caused, individuals and peoples affected have non-discriminatory access to the same judicial and administrative procedures as would individuals and peoples of the State in which the harm is caused.[13]

24.2.2 The principle of public participation: in essence

The principle of public participation is often described as including three parts. The first part of this principle includes the public's right to participate in decision-making processes in which sustainable development issues are involved. This part is derived from the public's right to be actively involved in decisions that affect

---

12 As quoted on the UNECE Website: <http://www.unece.org/env/welcome> accessed 18 March 2012.
13 ILA, 'New Delhi Declaration of Principles of International Law Relating to Sustainable Development' (2002) 49(2) *Netherlands International Law Review* 299 [New Delhi Declaration].

their lives,[14] and the people's right to express their opinion. This part is also intended to act as a means to ensure good, transparent and responsive governance, and to enhance the quality of decisions.[15]

The second part in this typology – access to information – is perceived as a necessary condition for ensuring effective public participation. This part is intended to ensure qualitative and informed participation by the public, and can be viewed as supporting both certain elements of good governance (informed decisions are better decisions), and the public's right to participate in decision-making by fully understanding the discussed subject-matters. Indeed the New Delhi Declaration states that public participation: 'requires a right of access to appropriate, comprehensible and timely information held by governments'.[16]

The third part of the principle of public participation – access to judicial and administrative procedures – is necessary in order to ensure that people, whether local or foreigners, could participate in judicial and administrative processes in which sustainable development-related measures are being discussed, and claim compensation where harm has been done. This third part is relevant for the overall discussion of international investment law, and can be manifested in areas such as impact assessment mechanisms or the regulation of foreign investments. It is, however, less relevant for the discussion over investor-state arbitration and therefore will not be reviewed.[17]

It should be noted however, as an *obiter dictum*, that this situation may change in the future. In a European Parliament report on the future European international investment policy (later adopted as an EU Parliament's Resolution[18]), it was suggested in the 'explanatory statement' that trade unions and civil society organisations should be granted the right 'to submit cases to the courts – the only way for parties' compliance with their social and environmental commitments to be verified'.[19] In the author's view, this suggestion is somewhat incoherent with the role of international investment law,[20] but nevertheless it suggests a wider role

---

14 See preamble to the Aarhus Convention (*supra* note 9); UN *Agenda 21* (*supra* note 7) at para 23.2.

15 New Delhi Declaration (*supra* note 13) at para 5.1.

16 Ibid.

17 Article 5.3 of the New Delhi Declaration states that: 'The empowerment of peoples in the context of sustainable development requires access to effective judicial or administrative procedures *in the State* where the measure has been taken *to challenge such measure and to claim compensation.*' This paragraph specifically refers to the people's right to confront the state before its own courts and tribunals, to challenge its measures, and to demand compensation from the state. This is clearly not within the domain of investor-state arbitrations, and is not related to this system.

18 European Parliament, 'Resolution of 6 April 2011 on the future European international investment policy' (2010/2203(INI)) <http://www.europarl.europa.eu/sides/getDoc.do?pubRef=-//EP//TEXT+TA+P7-TA-2011-0141+0+DOC+XML+V0//EN> accessed 18 March 2012.

19 European Parliament, Committee on International Trade, 'Report on the Future European International Investment Policy' 22 March 2011 <http://www.europarl.europa.eu/sides/getDoc.do?type=REPORT&reference=A7-2011-0070&language=EN> accessed 18 March 2012.

20 The field of international investment law was designed in order to provide guarantees for foreign investors when acting in foreign territories, by ensuring them of fair and non-discriminatory treatment from states. The ability to sue corporations for non-societal/environmental damages is important, but completely unrelated to this system of laws.

for the public in investment treaty arbitration and a *de facto* access to justice, as formulated by the New Delhi Declaration.

Furthermore, in a recent arbitration between Chevron and Ecuador, certain NGOs have claimed that investment arbitration being held simultaneously to litigation in national courts 'block[s] and remove[s] the right of judicial redress' and 'weaken[s] the ability of indigenous peoples and other marginalized communities to access Ecuadorian courts over claims that arise out of the activities of foreign investors.'[21] The petition, however, was rejected by the Tribunal, which stated that the questions raised in the phase in which the petitioners asked to intervene (concerning the Tribunal's jurisdiction) were primarily legal in nature, and had been significantly covered by the parties.[22]

24.3 Public participation in ICSID arbitration

The focus of this chapter is on the role and place of the principle of public participation in investment treaty arbitration. It will concentrate mainly on arbitrations conducted according to the ICSID Arbitration Rules, which is the most common set of arbitration rules in investment treaty arbitration. It is explained that while some elements of the principle of public participation are accepted in investment treaty arbitration (perhaps even accepted as a general rule), other elements, like access to documents and access to hearings, are not yet accepted. This situation, however, is slowly changing as an increasing number of 'new generation' investment treaties now also include provisions with respect to access to documents and access to hearings.

24.3.1 Public participation in ICSID arbitration: a brief history

The last 10 years has seen a proliferation of modern international investment arbitrations. Before the year 2000, investment treaty arbitrations were relatively rare and not much can be learned from the jurisprudence from this time. The petitioners for intervention and participation as amicus curiae in the *UPS* arbitration indeed noted in 2001:

> While the issue of third party intervention in arbitral proceedings is not without precedent, it has very rarely arisen in the modern era of international commercial arbitration. In fact, the issue of third party intervention has either been ignored, or given very low priority by those crafting the international and domestic regimes providing for international commercial arbitration.[23]

---

21 *Chevron Corporation and Texaco Petroleum v The Republic of Ecuador (Petition for Participation as Non-Disputing Parties)* (2010) PCA Case No 2009–23 (UNCITRAL).

22 *Chevron Corporation and Texaco Petroleum v The Republic of Ecuador (Procedural Order No 8)* (2011) PCA Case No 2009–23 (UNCITRAL) [*Chevron, Procedural Order No 8*].

23 *United Parcel Services of America Inc. v Canada (Decision of the Tribunal on Petitions for Intervention and Participation as Amici Curiae)* (2001) UNCITRAL [*UPS, Amici Curiae Decision*] at para 19. The Tribunal agreed with this determination, see ibid. para 40.

The first investment tribunals to address questions of public participation – the *Methanex* and *UPS* Tribunals – indeed had to draw on WTO and Iran-US Claims Tribunals.[24] Lacking any guiding legal sources on the matter, these Tribunals, as explained below, relied on their 'inherent powers' in order to approve the public's participation in these arbitrations.

Following these cases, the North American Free Trade Commission issued a 'Statement of the Free Trade Commission on Non-Disputing Party Participation' in 2003 (NAFTA Statement) in order to regulate this area, most notably approving that nothing in NAFTA prohibits investment tribunals from accepting written submissions from non-disputing parties (NDPs).[25]

In 2005, for the first time under the ICSID Rules of Arbitration, the *Suez* Tribunal accepted a petition made by several NGOs who wished to participate in its proceedings. Due to the lack of relevant guidance from the ICSID Rules, the Tribunal relied on the previous NAFTA cases and the NAFTA Statement, as well as on its own interpretation, in order to deal with questions such as whether participation should be permitted, who should be allowed to participate, and under what conditions.[26]

Following the *Suez* Tribunal's decision, the ICSID Rules of Arbitration were amended and more or less codified the conditions set by the *Suez* Tribunal. Following these amendments, several ICSID tribunals had to decide on petitions, mainly from NGOs (but also from individuals and public authorities, such as the European Commission) who wished to participate in investment treaty arbitrations. These tribunals, as reviewed below, refined and enriched the body of decisions over this matter.

24.3.2 Public participation in investment treaty arbitration: conceptual evolution

Before commencing an in-depth analysis of the application of the principle of public participation in ICSID arbitrations, two preliminary questions concerning the nature of the principle of public participation, and the jurisdiction of investment tribunals, should be discussed.

First, it is important to note that the duty to provide public participation was designed in order to ensure public participation in *decision-making* processes,[27] and is required from *States*,[28] or other sovereign entities. Arbitration processes in this respect can hardly be seen as classic 'decision-making' processes in which policies are being determined. Similarly, it is also difficult to view arbitrators as equivalent to 'states'. In fact, the main idea behind the

---

24 *UPS, Amici Curiae Decision (supra* note 23) at para 64; *Methanex Amici Curiae Decision (supra* note 31) at paras 31–3.

25 *NAFTA Statement (supra* note 46); see also *Methanex Corporation v United States of America (Final Award of the Tribunal on Jurisdiction and Merits)* (2005) UNCITRAL [*Methanex, Final Award*] para 27.

26 *Suez (supra* note 48).

27 See Principle 10 of the Rio Declaration (*supra* note 6); *Agenda 21 (supra* note 7) at para 23.2.

28 New Delhi Declaration's principle specifically mentions 'governments'.

choice of the commercial arbitration model in investor-state arbitrations and the appointment of independent arbitrators, was to distance this process from States' courts and the influence of the sovereign – which is also a party in these disputes. Indeed these quasi-private proceedings were designed so as to provide foreign investors with a non-politicised, commercially natured dispute-settlement mechanism. Therefore, it can be argued, it is unfit to demand 'sovereign' obligations from those who were appointed to ensure independence from the sovereign, and from the concerns a sovereign must consider.

Conversely, it should be remembered that whatever the original objective of the investor-State arbitration process is, the public nature of this system cannot be ignored. Arbitrators in this context are the interpreters of States' administrative measures and *de facto* apply a judicial review of these measures.[29] Furthermore, the subject-matter of these arbitrations can also be of great public importance, and compensation awarded to private investors is paid from tax payers' pockets. Moreover, in their decision, arbitrators can affect States' measures, or even 'chill' a State from regulating a certain area in the future.[30] Therefore, it can be argued, the public aspect of investment treaty arbitration and its influence over States' governance activities cannot be ignored.

Several investment tribunals have agreed in part with this determination[31] and created a distinction between investment arbitrations in which purely contractual matters are discussed, and investment arbitrations that involve issues which are of public importance. In the latter, it was accepted that arbitrators cannot ignore their ability to affect public matters, nor their accountability toward the affected public.

Furthermore, this realisation can also be found in a 'new generation' of investment treaties, which are discussed in more detail below. Most notably in this respect, this trend is likely to continue as the future EU investment policy is expected to include references to public issues such as the promotion of the rule of law, human rights and sustainable development.[32]

---

29 This view is advocated by scholars such as Van Harten: see, for example G. Van Harten and M. Loughlin, 'Investment Treaty Arbitration as a Species of Global Administrative Law' (2006) *Eur. J. Int'l L.* 17 121 [Van Harten & Loughlin] part 4 of this article; Gus Van Harten, *Investment Treaty Arbitration and Public Law* (Oxford: OUP, 2007).

30 Although the existence of the 'regulatory chill' is disputed in this respect, at least in some cases it seems to have taken place. See for example the case of Philip Morris' threat of investment arbitration over Uruguay's anti-smoking rules, in Rory Carroll, 'Uruguay bows to pressure over anti-smoking law amendments' *The Guardian* (London, 27 July 2010) <http://www.guardian.co.uk/world/2010/jul/27/uruguay-tobacco-smoking-philip-morris> accessed 18 March 2012.

31 Such a distinction was indeed made by investment tribunals, see *Suez* (*supra* note 48) 20; *Biwater Gauff*, 2006 (*supra* note 42) 51; *Methanex Corporation v United States of America (Decision of the tribunal on petitions from third persons to intervene as 'Amici Curiae')* (2001) UNCITRAL (North American Free Trade Agreement) [*Methanex Amici Curiae Decision*] para 49.

32 See European Commission, *Communication from the Commission to the Council, the European Parliament, The European Economic and Social Committee and the Committee of the Regions: Towards a Comprehensive European International Investment Policy* COM(2010)343 final, 7.7.2010; European Parliament, *Resolution of 6 April 2011 on the Future European International Investment Policy* (2010/2203(INI)) <http://www.europarl.europa.eu/sides/getDoc.do?pubRef=-//EP//TEXT+TA+P7-TA-2011-0141+0+DOC+XML+V0//

A second issue that should be discussed involves questions of jurisdiction. Can we expect investment arbitrators, who act in accordance to a specific mandate given to them by the parties that appointed them, to consider public considerations such as the principle of public participation? While denying the request of an NGO that asked to join the *Aguas del Tunari* investment arbitration proceedings, the Tribunal stated on this matter:

> The Tribunal appreciates that you, and the organizations and individuals with whom you work, are concerned with the resolution of this dispute. The duties of the Tribunal, however, derive from the treaties which govern this particular dispute.[33]

The Tribunal's answer is indeed supported by Article 42(1) of the ICSID Convention,[34] which opens with the clear instruction: 'The Tribunal shall decide a dispute in accordance with such rules of law as may be agreed by the parties.'[35] While other international tribunals may find in their governing treaties references to sustainable development, or general international law, most investment treaties do not include such references. If states wish arbitrators to consider these elements, they need only instruct them to do so. The clear lack of reference to these sources of international law in investment treaties is therefore noticeable.

These questions of jurisdiction, however, were also (at least partly) answered by both academics and States. For example, some have argued that the wider corpus of international law should apply even when not specifically mentioned by the governing treaties. For instance, based on Article 31(1) of the Vienna Convention on the Law of the Treaties (VCLT), Anne van Aaken argues that a 'good faith' interpretation of investment treaties implies the consideration of other, non-investment international laws by investment tribunals, as these are rooted within the purpose and objectives of IIAs:

> The ICSID Convention was foremost set up under the auspices of the World Bank not in order to protect private property as such but in order to foster development. Therefore, that purpose also needs to be considered, [FN

EN> accessed 18 March 2012.

33 A letter from David Caron, President of the Tribunal, to the representative of Earthjustice, from January 29, 2003 <http://ita.law.uvic.ca/documents/Aguas-BoliviaResponse.pdf> accessed 18 March 2012 [*Aguas del Tunari*, 2003].

34 See also Article 35 of the 2010 UNCITRAL Arbitration Rules: 'The arbitral tribunal shall apply the rules of law designated by the parties as applicable to the substance of the dispute. Failing such designation by the parties, the arbitral tribunal shall apply the law which it determines to be appropriate.'

35 Convention on the Settlement of Investment Disputes Between States and Nationals of Other States (adopted 18 March 1965, entered into force 14 October 1966) 575 UNTS 159, TIAS 6090, 17 UST 1270 [ICSID Convention] art 42(1).

omitted] and this cannot be done by fostering only the mean of development (investment) while neglecting its end (development): means-end rationality has to take into account the costs of achieving an end.[36]

This claim can also be supported from another direction – by Article 31(3)(c) of the VCLT, according to which tribunals shall take into account 'any relevant rules of international law applicable in the relations between the parties.'[37] The International Law Commission (ILC) has stated in this respect:

> although a tribunal may only have jurisdiction in regard to a particular instrument, it must always interpret and apply that instrument in its relationship to its normative environment - that is to say 'other' international law. This is the principle of systemic integration to which article 31 (3) (c) VCLT gives expression.[38]

Article 31(3)(c) can be especially helpful where treaty language specifically refers to issues such as 'sustainable development', or other relevant sources of international law. In such cases,[39] arbitrators could rely on Article 31(3)(c), and through treaty interpretation consider the above mentioned sustainable development treaties and documents as a part of their governing laws. However, it should be noted that this 'window' is not helpful when the parties have specifically addressed an issue, and restricted the public's participation – as is the case in some rules of arbitration.[40]

Both of the discussed 'preliminary issues' – the application of the principle of public participation by the private-by-nature investment tribunals, and the above raised questions of jurisdiction – are important and should not be easily dismissed. For the purpose of this chapter, however, it is sufficient to conclude these issues by stating that whatever the correct answers should be, the amendment of the ICSID Rules and the conclusion of a 'new generation' of investment treaties have already somewhat resolved these issues by accepting several aspects of public participation, and rejecting others. The following part reviews how investment treaty rules and arbitral decisions address questions of public participation, and describes in more detail the current state of affairs.

---

36 Anne Van Aaken, 'Fragmentation of International Law: The Case of International Investment Protection' in Jan Klabbers, ed., *Finnish Yearbook of International Law* Vol XVII (Netherlands: Martinus Nijhoff, 2008).

37 Vienna Convention on the Law of Treaties (adopted 23 May 1969, entered into force 27 January 1980) 1155 UNTS 331, 8 ILM 679 (1969), UN Doc A/Conf.39/27 [VCLT]; Van Aaken (*supra* note 36) at 10.

38 International Law Commission, *Report of the Study Group of the International Law Commission, Fragmentation of International Law: Difficulties Arising from the Diversification and Expansion of International Law*, finalised by Martti Koskenniemi, UN ILC, 58th Sess., UN ILC, 2006, UN Doc. A/CN.4/L.682 [ILC Report] at 212–13.

39 There are not many cases in which such references exist. For examples, see *supra* note 1.

40 ICSID Convention (*supra* note 35) at art 42(1); UNCITRAL Arbitration Rules art 28.

24.3.3 Arbitration under the ICSID Convention

As mentioned, the issues discussed above were resolved by the Member States of the ICSID Convention, which introduced in 2006 a partial version of the principle of public participation into the ICSID Rules of Arbitration. It should be noted however, that the Member States were also aware of the problems embedded in the inclusion of a public-by-nature principle like the principle of public participation in a system like investment treaty arbitrations. As mentioned above, the field of international investment law was designed to encourage foreign investors to invest in foreign territories. It aimed to do so by overcoming an inherent 'lack of trust' foreign investors may have toward foreign governments, by, *inter alia*, assuring foreign investors a non-politicised, efficient and commercially oriented dispute settlement mechanism. Acknowledging the principle of public participation in this respect can be seen as conflicting with a few of the core objectives of the investor-state dispute-settlement mechanism. The public, for example, can apply pressure on foreign investors[41] or even on arbitrators. During the *Biwater* arbitration, the foreign investor complained about the NGOs' campaign (entitled: 'Dirty aid, dirty water. Hands off Tanzania: Stop UK company Biwater's attempt to sue') that was aimed to put a stop to the arbitral proceedings.[42] The Tribunal indeed agreed in this case that public participation might negatively affect the dispute:

> Given the media campaign that has already been fought on both sides of this case (by many entities beyond the parties to this arbitration), and the general media interest that already exists, the Tribunal is satisfied that there exists a sufficient risk of harm or prejudice, as well as aggravation, in this case to warrant some form of control.[43]

Moreover, it is also possible that by opening investment disputes to third parties' participation, parties may lose a 'certain flexibility and informality' which closed proceedings facilitate.[44] As a result, the possibility to compromise and to amicably resolve disputes could be diminished.[45] This is especially harmful in the

41   See opinions of Thomas Wälde in Thomas W. Wälde, '"Equality of Arms" in Investment Arbitration: Procedural Challenges' in Katia Yannaca-Small, ed., *Arbitration Under International Investment Agreements: A Guide to the Key Issues* (Oxford: OUP, 2010) at 161, 178; Yves Fortier in L. Yves Fortier, 'Investment Protection and the Rule of Law: Change or Decline?' Lecture given by L. Yves Fortier on March 17th 2009 at the British Institute of International and Comparative Law <www.arbitration-icca.org/media/0/12392785460140/0732_001.pdf> accessed 18 March 2012 [Fortier].

42   *Biwater Gauff (Tanzania) Ltd. v United Republic of Tanzania (Procedural Order No 3)* (2006), ICSID Case No ARB/05/22 International Centre for Settlement of Investment Disputes [*Biwater Gauff*, 2006] at para 16.

43   Ibid. at 146.

44   Vaughan Lowe, 'Changing Dimension of International Investment Law' (2007) Oxford Legal Studies Research Paper No 4/2007 <http://papers.ssrn.com/sol3/papers.cfm?abstract_id=970727> accessed 18 March 2012 [Lowe] 122.

45   See also Federico Ortino, 'External Transparency of Investment Awards' (2008) Society of International Economic Law Inaugural Conference Paper http://papers.ssrn.com/sol3/papers.cfm?abstract_id=1159899 accessed 18 March 2012 [Ortino] 13.

context of investor-state relationships, which are often long-termed and depend on the maintenance of a proper working relationship.

Furthermore, accepting the principle of public participation in investment disputes increases the cost and prolongs the duration of the process, a fact that stands in contrast to the efficiency goal of this dispute settlement mechanism.[46] Indeed certain rules of arbitration were modified in order to emphasise this feature in light of increasing public participation.[47]

24.3.4 ICSID Rule 37(2): a compromise

The above review presents a certain conflict between the global recognition of the principle of public participation on the one hand, and the rationales embedded in the investor-state arbitration process. The Member States of the ICSID Convention therefore had to balance these conflicting forces. The result of this balancing is Rule 37(2) of the 2006 ICSID Arbitration Rules, which authorises arbitrators to accept submissions of amicus curiae briefs from the public under certain conditions. Rule 37(2) of the ICSID Arbitration Rules provides that the submission must conform to the following general guidelines:

> The non-disputing party submission assists the Tribunal in the determination of a factual or legal issue related to the proceeding by bringing a perspective, particular knowledge or insight that is different from that of the disputing parties;
> The non-disputing party submission addresses a matter within the scope of the dispute;
> The non-disputing party has a significant interest in the proceedings.

Rule 37(2) further indicates that these submissions should not 'disrupt the proceedings or unduly burden, or unfairly prejudice either party.'

Rule 37(2)'s recognition of the principle of public participation can be discovered in its language. First, the Rule specifically welcomes any 'perspective, particular knowledge and insight' which are unrepresented by the parties. This is a direct invitation to the public's participation in places where its position remains unrepresented.

---

46 *Methanex Amici Curiae Decision* (*supra* note 31) at para 50; the *Suez* Tribunals indeed mention the 'extra burden which the acceptance of amicus curiae briefs may place on the parties' as an important consideration when deciding whether to grant a non-party leave to submit amicus curiae briefs. See also in *Biwater Gauff (Tanzania) Ltd. v United Republic of Tanzania (Procedural Order No 5)* (2007) ICSID Case No ARB/05/22 International Centre for Settlement of Investment Disputes [*Biwater Gauff*, 2007] paras 56–9. This consideration is also present in the UNCITRAL Rules, the ICSID Rules, and the relevant NAFTA Free Trade Commission, 'Statement of the Free Trade Commission on non-disputing party participation' (2003) <http://www.international.gc.ca/trade-agreements-accords-commerciaux/assets/pdfs/Non disputing-en.pdf> accessed 18 March 2012 [*NAFTA Statement*].

47 See Article 17(1) of the UNCITRAL Arbitration Rules: 'The arbitral tribunal, in exercising its discretion, shall conduct the proceedings so as to avoid unnecessary delay and expense and to provide a fair and efficient process for resolving the parties' dispute.'

Second, the Rule also acknowledges that public participation can assist the tribunal and enhance the quality of its decisions. Third, the Rule specifically dismisses the need to achieve both parties' consent to the public's participation. The public right to participate is therefore no longer dependent on foreign investors' consent to open a dispute. Last, the Rule does not limit the types of considerations a tribunal must take into account before accepting amicus curiae briefs. For example, tribunals have included the public nature of the dispute[48] as a reason to allow the public's participation.

Rule 37(2), however, represents a compromise, and it does not include several important aspects of the principle of public participation. For example, it remains silent with respect to the subsequent 'right' implied from the principle of public participation – the right to have effective access to information. Furthermore, following the objections of several Member States,[49] the ICSID Rules do not allow open access to the hearings (at least not without the consent of both parties). The representation of third parties in investment disputes was also not included in Rule 37(2), and was rejected by tribunals.

Lastly, Rule 37(2) indicates that these submissions should not 'disrupt the proceedings or unduly burden, or unfairly prejudice either party.' It can be seen that, as in any act of balancing rights and interests, the principle of public participation is also limited and the interests of foreign investors not entirely forsaken.

24.3.5 Other legal instruments

24.3.5.1 UNCITRAL Arbitration Rules

While this chapter focuses primarily on the ICSID Rules of Arbitration, the importance of other legal sources like the UNCITRAL Arbitration Rules, the NAFTA Statement, or the 'new generation' of IIAs, should not be ignored. Indeed the first investment tribunal to accept public participation in investment treaty arbitration – the *Methanex* Tribunal – was governed by the UNCITRAL Rules. The *Methanex* (and the *UPS*) decision was the foundation on which the *Suez* Tribunal (the first ICSID Tribunal to accept public participation) made its decision under the ICSID Rules, a decision which in turn has led to the modification of these Rules.

The UNCITRAL Arbitration Rules do not explicitly refer to the submission of amicus curiae briefs. Article 17 states that the arbitral tribunal 'may conduct the arbitration in such manner as it considers appropriate' and on this basis several

---

48   Before the entering into force of the 2006 ICSID Arbitration Rules, the *Suez* Tribunal mentioned the public nature of the dispute (i.e. where cases are more than 'simply a contract dispute') as a relevant condition. See *Suez, Sociedad General de Aguas de Barcelona S.A. and Vivendi Universal S.A v Argentine Republic (Order in Response to a Petition for Transparency and Participation as Amicus Curiae)* (2005) ICSID Case No ARB/03/19 International Centre for Settlement of Investment Disputes para 20.

49   Antonio Parra, a Preface to Nathalie Bernasconi-Osterwalder, 'Transparency and Amicus Curiae in ICSID Arbitration' in Marie-Claire Cordonier Segger and others, eds., *Sustainable Development in World Investment Law* (Netherlands: Kluwer 2010) at 189.

tribunals have concluded that they have authority to accept amicus curiae briefs.[50] The fact that the recently revised rules did not address this situation implicitly confirms this interpretation.[51]

With respect to open hearings, Article 28(3) states that '[h]earings shall be held in camera unless the parties agree otherwise.' The possibility of changing this rule is being debated by the UNCITRAL Working Group,[52] and the option of favouring open hearings has been raised.[53]

Recently, the UNCITRAL adopted a separate set of rules – the UNCITRAL Rules on Transparency in Treaty-based Investor-State Arbitration (UNCITRAL Rules on Transparency).[54] In these rules, the UNCITRAL member states have taken a far-reaching approach with respect to the principle of public participation. For example, it was decided that with limited exceptions, arbitral hearings shall be opened to the general public.[55] Furthermore, tribunals are instructed to actively facilitate public access to the hearings by making sufficient 'logistical arrangements.'[56]

The UNCITRAL Rules on Transparency also prescribe a broad rule on access to documents. For example, it is stated that a list of documents – including notice of arbitration, statements of claim, transcripts of hearings, orders, decisions, and awards – shall be made available to the general public.[57] It is further instructed that tribunals shall have the authority to make other documents, such as exhibits, publically available.[58]

These rules, if adopted by future parties to investment treaties, will undoubtedly represent a significant step forward with respect to the application of the principle of public participation in investment disputes.

24.3.5.2 NAFTA

Following the *Methanex* and *UPS* arbitrations, in which it was decided that tribunals possess 'inherent powers' to accept NDPs' participation, the

---

50 See for example *Methanex Amici Curiae Decision* (*supra* note 31); *UPS, Amici Curiae Decision* (*supra* note 23).

51 The UNCITRAL Rules were modified in 2010.

52 UNCITRAL, *Report of Working Group II (Arbitration and Conciliation) on the Work of Its Fifty –fourth Session (New York, 7–11 February 2011)* UN Doc A/CN.9/717 [UNCITRAL WG Report 2011] paras 101–14.

53 Ibid. at para 102.

54 See United Nations Commission on International Trade Law, UNCITRAL Rules on Transparency in Treaty-based Investor-State Arbitration (effective date: April 2014), available online: <http://www.uncitral.org/uncitral/en/uncitral_texts/arbitration/2014Transparency.html> [UCITRAL Rules on Transparency]. See more on these rules in Dimitrij Euler, Markus Gehring and Maxi Schere, eds., *Transparency in International Investment Arbitration* (Cambridge: CUP, 2015).

55 Ibid. at art 6.

56 Ibid. at art 6(3).

57 Ibid. at art 3.

58 Ibid.

North American Free Trade Commission issued a Statement of the Free Trade Commission on Non-Disputing Party Participation in 2003 (NAFTA Statement).[59] The NAFTA Statement approved the Tribunal's notion that nothing in NAFTA prohibits them from accepting NDPs' submissions, and provided procedures with regard to such submissions. The NAFTA Statement was likewise referred to (and relied on) by ICSID Tribunals, most notably the *Suez* Tribunal.

24.3.5.3 New generation of IIAs

Another important development with respect to the 'creeping' acceptance of the principle of public participation in investment arbitration is the introduction of what is often described as a 'new generation' of IIAs. These IIAs form a part of the arbitration's governing laws, and are therefore relevant. Unlike the 'old generation' of IIAs, these IIAs are characterised as more supportive of sustainable development goals States' right to regulate, and often also of the public's right to participate in investor-state arbitration proceedings. Examples of these 'new generation' IIAs, can be found in Canadian and US investment treaties.[60] Among the features that can be found in these 'new generation' treaties are references to sustainable development principles; instruction with respect to third parties' participation; explicit references to the State's right to regulate; and clarification regarding the limits of the term 'indirect expropriation'.[61]

The introduction of these 'new generation' IIAs is important with respect to the investment treaty arbitration, as it provides arbitrators with jurisdiction to consider sustainable development principles and includes the interpretation of relevant legal terms (such as the definition of 'investment', 'national treatment', 'fair and equitable treatment', etc.). Furthermore, where these treaties include references to the arbitral procedures, a more open, transparent and participatory process can take place.

A unique example for the 'creeping' acceptance of the principle of public participation can be found in Article 10.21 of the Dominican Republic-Central American FTA (CAFTA-DR), entitled 'Transparency of Arbitral Proceedings'. This article includes, *inter alia,* instructions to make documents such as pleadings, submissions, minutes, orders and awards available to the public, and to open the arbitral hearings to the public. Article 10.20 of the CAFTA-DR also grants the tribunal the authority to accept amicus curiae briefs from third parties. This novel agreement was the source of further development with respect

---

59 *NAFTA Statement* (*supra* note 46).

60 For more detail, see Chester Brown, 'Bringing Sustainable Development Issues before Investment Treaty Tribunals', in Cordonier Segger and others (*supra* note 49); Nathalie Bernasconi-Osterwalder, 'Transparency and Amicus Curiae in ICSID Arbitration' in Cordonier Segger and others (*supra* note 49).

61 Indirect expropriation claims were raised with respect to financial damages suffered by foreign investors as a result of environmental legislation.

to public participation, as based on its provisions, the first publicly webcasted ICSID arbitration proceeding took place in 2010.[62]

24.3.5.4 Evolution in investment treaty jurisprudence

This chapter began with an introduction of the principle of public participation. Following this introduction it was explained that due to the nature of the principle on the one hand, and that of the investment disputes on the other, several tensions may arise. Next, it was asserted that the conflicting powers in this respect are balanced through the compromise embedded in the ICSID Rules of Arbitration, from which a restricted, but nevertheless substantial principle of public participation has emerged.

The next part of this chapter will be dedicated to the evolution of the principle of public participation within investment treaty jurisprudence. It will focus mainly on the cases governed by the ICSID Arbitration Rules. A comparative review of other relevant investment cases will nevertheless be provided.

The following revision will be performed in two parts. The first part will review the tribunals' approaches towards the public's participation in ICSID arbitrations. The second part will scrutinise these tribunals' approaches toward the public's right to access information.

24.3.5.5 Public participation in ICSID-based arbitral decisions

In the past, several representatives of the public (mostly NGOs) have requested to actively participate in investment disputes. Requests for participation included, *inter alia,* the right to submit written amicus curiae briefs at all stages of the arbitration, to make oral presentations, to respond to investors' arguments, to respond to the tribunals' questions, and even requests to join the arbitration as a party to the dispute. This chapter, however, will review two types of participation; the submission of amicus curiae briefs and attempts to join as a party to arbitration. The first is perhaps the most common form of public participation in investment disputes. The second represents the fullest form of public participation, and emphasises the limits of this principle in investment disputes.

24.3.5.6 Amicus curiae briefs

As discussed above, prior to the amendment of the ICSID Rules, the *Aguas del Tunari* Tribunal rejected the participation of several individuals and NGOs in the arbitral proceedings, claiming it did not have the power to accept such an

---

62 ICSID News Release, '*Pac Rim Cayman LLC v Republic of El Salvador* (ICSID Case No ARB/09/12) – Public Hearing' (2010) <http://icsid.worldbank.org/ICSID/FrontServlet?re questType=CasesRH&actionVal=OpenPage&PageType=AnnouncementsFrame&FromPage=A nnouncements&pageName=Announcement60> accessed 18 March 2012.

intervention from a non-party.[63] The Tribunal's decision was relatively short (less than two pages) and no in-depth discussion was provided.

In 2005, however, the *Suez* Tribunal adopted a different approach in this respect.[64] The question of public participation was raised in the *Suez* arbitration following the submission of a 'Petition for Transparency and Participation as Amicus Curiae' by five NGOs. The NGOs claimed that 'the case involved matters of basic public interest and the fundamental rights of people living in the area affected by the dispute in the case'. The petitioners asked both for the right to participate by presenting legal arguments via the submission of amicus curiae briefs, and to have unrestricted access to information (both to hearings and documents). A similar request was also made by a sixth NGO in parallel ICSID proceedings before the same arbitrators.[65]

With respect to the amicus curiae submissions, despite the lack of specific reference in the ICSID Rules of Arbitration and any similar prior decisions in which an ICSID tribunal had accepted similar briefs, the Tribunal concluded that it had the power to accept such briefs.[66] Inspired by the *Methanex* and *UPS* arbitrations and the NAFTA Statement that followed these arbitrations, the Tribunal decided that, according to Article 44 of the ICSID Rules, it was authorised to decide on a matter of procedure where no reference was made to it within the arbitration's governing laws.[67] The Tribunal enumerated three criteria according to which a request for the submission of an amicus curiae brief would be decided:

> a) the appropriateness of the subject matter of the case; b) the suitability of a given nonparty to act as amicus curiae in that case, and c) the procedure by which the amicus submission is made and considered.[68]

The Tribunal emphasised the public nature of the dispute, and the importance of this nature in its decision to allow public participation: '[g]iven the public interest in the subject matter of this case, it is possible that appropriate nonparties may be able to afford the Tribunal perspectives, arguments, and expertise that will help it arrive at a correct decision.'[69]

A second case in which questions of public participation were raised under the ICSID Rules was the *Biwater* arbitration, which was conducted after the acceptance of Rule 37(2) of the ICSID Rules. The question of public participation in this case was raised when five NGOs requested permission to submit

---

63   *Aguas del Tunari*, supra note 33.

64   *Suez* (supra note 48).

65   *Aguas Proviciales de Santa Fe S.A., Suez, Sociedad General de Aguas de Barcelona S.A. and Interaguas Servicios Integrales del Agua S.A. v Argentine Republic (Order in Response to a Petition for Participation as Amicus Curiae)* (2006) ICSID Case No ARB/03/17 International Centre for Settlement of Investment Disputes [*Suez B*].

66   *Suez* (*supra* note 48).

67   *Suez* (*supra* note 48) at para 10; *Suez B* (*supra* note 65) at para 11.

68   *Suez* (*supra* note 48) at para 17.

69   Ibid. at para 21.

amicus *curiae* briefs, to attend oral hearings and to access key documents.[70] In the reasons for the petition, the petitioners mentioned in addition to the conditions of Rule 37(2) (i.e. expertise, relevancy to the dispute, significant interest, etc.), *inter alia,* the 'vital concern to the local community in Tanzania and a wide range of potential issues of concern to developing countries [. . .]'. The petitioners also mentioned that the public nature of this case 'means that the process should be transparent and permit citizens' participation.'

The *Biwater* Tribunal approved the petitioners' request according to the conditions of Rule 37(2). The Tribunal agreed that the petitioners' address mattered within the scope of the dispute and had sufficient interest in the proceedings (although it did not elaborate regarding why these NGOs had 'sufficient interest' in the proceedings). The Tribunal also repeated the *Suez* Tribunal in stating that, considering the public nature of this case, the amicus curiae brief could assist the tribunal in its work.[71] The Tribunal especially emphasised the 'desirable consequence' that the public's participation can contribute to the legitimacy of investment arbitrations.[72]

Following the *Biwater* arbitration, permission to submit amicus curiae written briefs was granted by other ICSID tribunals, most notably to five NGOs in the *Foresti* arbitration,[73] and to the European Commission in the *AES* arbitration.[74] To the best of the author's knowledge, however, any in-depth discussion with respect to these submissions (if such existed), was never made available to the public.

24.3.5.7 Participation as parties

On several occasions, representatives of the public have requested to receive the full status of a party to the dispute, which is perhaps the fullest possible form of public participation in any dispute. The petitioners in the *Tunari* arbitration requested, for example, 'all rights of participation accorded to other parties to the claim'.[75] A similar request was also made in a NAFTA dispute, in which the Canadian Union of Postal Workers and the Council of Canadians asked to receive standing as parties to the *UPS* arbitration.[76] The petitioners argued that they held a direct interest in the arbitration, and therefore requested to be granted with the right to defend their interests. In another NAFTA dispute, the *Merrill Ring* arbitration, a letter sent by the counsel of three non-disputing parties was interpreted

70 *Petition for amicus curiae status,* in *Biwater Gauff v United Republic of Tanzania* ICSID Case No ARB/05/22 International Centre for Settlement of Investment Disputes [*Biwater, Petition for amicus curiae status*].
71 *Biwater Gauff* 2007 (*supra* note 46) at para 52.
72 Ibid. at para 51.
73 *Foresti 2009* (*supra* note 83).
74 *AES* (*supra* note 89).
75 *Tunari, Petition* (*supra* note 125) at 3.
76 *UPS,* Amici Curiae *Decision* (*supra* note 23) at 2.

by the Tribunal as a request to join as party to the dispute.[77] It was claimed that the non-disputing parties had a 'direct and public interest' in the dispute.[78]

These requests, so it seems, went too far, as all three tribunals denied the public's right to join as a party to investment arbitration proceedings. The *Tunari* Tribunal contested that it had no powers to approve any form of public participation without specific instructions from the governing laws.[79] The *UPS* Tribunal likewise denied any authority to accept another party to the arbitration, basing its decision, *inter alia*, on the scope of the consent granted by the parties to the arbitration, and the obligation an arbitral tribunal has to follow the parties' instructions in this respect.[80] The *Merrill Ring* Tribunal repeated the reasoning of the *UPS* Tribunal, and added that the governing laws (the NAFTA and the UNCITRAL Rules) restrict such a participation only for a 'Party and an Investor of Another Party', and therefore do not permit the participation of public representatives as a party to the dispute.[81]

To conclude the tribunals' approach toward the public's participation in ICSID arbitrations, it seems that a pragmatic approach has been applied with respect to public participation. While tribunals agreed to consider some level of public participation, even without specific authorisation to do so (as was the case of amicus curiae submissions prior to 2006 under the ICSID Rules, or prior to 2003 under NAFTA), they have also agreed as to the boundaries of such participation, and agreed that this should not go beyond the submission of written briefs. Again, it seems that this approach reflects a certain balance between the increasing recognition of the public aspect of investment treaty arbitrations on the one hand, and the rationales embedded within the choice of the commercial arbitration model as a mean to resolve investor-state disputes on the other.

24.3.5.8 Access to information in ICSID jurisprudence

Access to information, as explained above, is routinely considered an inherent part of the principle of public participation. It is intended to support public participation and ensure its effectiveness. The most basic aspect of the right to information in the context of investment treaty arbitration is the right to know about an investment dispute. Indeed Vaughan Lowe has commented in this respect:

> It would be a curious paradox if governments could be held liable to pay hundreds of millions of dollars of taxpayers' money in compensation to

---

77 It is doubtful, however, whether the content of this letter actually reflects such a request. The letter is available online: <http://www.appletonlaw.com/files/Merrill/2.%20%20%20Ltr%20 Shrybman%20to%20ICSID-BWA%20re%20Intent%20to%20file%20joint%20sub_27Jun08.pdf> accessed 18 March 2012 [Letter from Steven Shrybmen].

78 Ibid.

79 *Aguas del Tunari*, 2003 (*supra* note 23).

80 *UPS, Amici Curiae Decision* (*supra* note 23) at paras 35–43.

81 *Merrill & Ring Forestry L. P. v Government of Canada (Letter from the Tribunal)* (2008) UNCITRAL.

foreign investors because the government had failed to behave transparently and fairly, by a tribunal whose existence, proceedings and eventual award were kept a secret from those taxpayers.[82]

Another fundamental aspect of access to information regards the publication of investment awards, which is governed by Rule 48 of the ICSID Rules. According to this rule, awards shall be published only with the consent of both parties. The public therefore does not have an inherent right to view these awards.

This chapter, however, will limit its review to issues that were reflected in investment arbitral decisions, most notably access to arbitration hearings and access to arbitration documents.

24.3.5.9 Access to arbitration documents

Access to arbitration documents in investment treaty arbitrations is often requested by NDPs who wish to make their contribution more effective. It is only rarely, however, that these requests are granted by tribunals. Most notably, the *Foresti* Tribunal ordered to allow access to several of the documents submitted to the Tribunal in order to allow NDPs to focus their contributions to the relevant issues by learning the parties' positions.[83] This decision is unique as it allows access to the arbitration documents despite the investor's objections in the case. This case, however, was discontinued and no documents were ultimately disclosed.

The *Suez* Tribunal also mentioned in this respect that '[t]he purpose in seeking access to the record is to enable a nonparty to act as amicus curiae in a meaningful way.'[84] In a later decision, the *Suez* Tribunal repeated this notion, but rejected petitioners' requests to have access to documents, stating that 'the Petitioners have sufficient information even without being granted access to the arbitration record'.[85] The Tribunal also mentioned that its own former decisions, already published on ICSID's website, contained sufficient information regarding the nature of the investor's claims.[86] The Tribunal further mentioned that the petitioners asked to offer views on general issues, and that in any case their role 'is not to challenge arguments or evidence put forward by the parties. This is the parties' role.'[87]

The *Biwater* Tribunal addressed this issue from a different perspective. It claimed that since the NDPs were not party to the dispute, they should concern themselves only with the broad policy issues in which they were qualified to contribute and in which they claimed to be experts. For this reason, it was

82 Lowe (*supra* note 44) at 120.
83 *Piero Foresti, Laura de Carli and others v Republic of South Africa (Letter from the Tribunal to the Parties, from October 5 2009)* (2009) ICSID Case No ARB/05/22 International Centre for Settlement of Investment Disputes [*Foresti 2009*] paras 2.2–3.
84 *Suez* (*supra* note 48) at para 31. The Tribunal however, did not decide on the matter in this decision.
85 Ibid. at para 24.
86 Ibid. para 24.
87 Ibid. at para 25.

explained, they do not need access to arbitration documents.[88] Furthermore, the Tribunal also relied on its refusal to allow transparency in this dispute as a protective measure from the aggravation of the dispute and as ensuring the integrity of the process.

The *AES* Tribunal adopted a different justification for its refusal to allow access to documents, as it denied access to documents based on the lack of the Parties' consent.[89] However, to the best of the author's knowledge the relevant decision was not published.[90] It is therefore difficult to elaborate on this case.

This reluctance to grant access to documents is also reflected in NAFTA-based arbitral decisions, in which the *V.G. Gallo* and *Methanex* Tribunals refused as well to grant NDPs access to documents.[91] Both of these Tribunals have stated that NDPs 'are to be treated by the Tribunal as any other members of the public'[92] and consequently should not receive access to documents which are not already within the public domain.[93]

Interestingly in this respect, as mentioned by the *Biwater* Tribunal, parties to arbitration may publish their own documents if they wish to do so. Due to the 'interest of procedural integrity', however, the Tribunal prohibited the publication of the opposing party's submissions.[94]

24.3.5.10 Access to arbitration hearings

The case of access to arbitration hearings is relatively simple and undisputed. Following the instructions of Article 32 of the ICSID Rules of Arbitration, both the *Suez* and the *Biwater* Tribunals dictated that without the parties' consent, tribunals cannot permit any third party's attendance during the arbitral hearings.[95] The *Biwater* Tribunal further added in this respect that 'the privacy of the arbitral hearing [is] a central element of the arbitral process'.[96] This approach was also repeated by the *Foresti* arbitration.[97] This approach is not unique to ICSID arbitrations, and has also been applied by NAFTA tribunals (*Methanex* and *UPS*

---

88   *Biwater Gauff,* 2007 (*supra* note 46) at para 65.

89   *AES Summit Generation Limited and AES-Tisza Erömü Kft. v Republic of Hungary (Award)* (2010) ICSID Case No ARB/07/22 para 3.22.

90   Procedural Order No 3 of the *AES* arbitration.

91   *V. G. Gallo v Government of Canada (Procedural Order No 1)* (2008) UNCITRAL para 38; *Methanex Amici Curiae Decision* (*supra* note 31) at 46.

92   *Methanex Amici Curiae Decision* (*supra* note 31) at 46.

93   *V.G. Gallo* (*supra* note 91).

94   *Biwater, Procedural Order* 3 (*supra* note 96) at paras 156–57.

95   *Suez* (*supra* note 48) at para 6; *Suez B* (*supra* note 65) at para 7; *Biwater Gauff,* 2007 (*supra* note 46) at 70–1.

96   *Biwater Gauff (Tanzania) Ltd. v United Republic of Tanzania (Procedural Order No. 3)* (2006) ICSID Case No ARB/05/22 International Centre for Settlement of Investment Disputes [*Biwater, Procedural Order* 3] para 124.

97   *Foresti 2009* (*supra* note 83) at para 4.

tribunals), which were governed by the UNCITRAL Rules,[98] according to which hearings are to be held *in camera* unless the parties agree otherwise.

It should be noted however, that several tribunals have agreed that the parties are entitled to discuss the arbitral proceedings freely.[99] This, to a certain extent, can assist the public representatives who wish to achieve information form a certain dispute – especially as the position of these non-disputing parties usually supports the position of the state.

In order to conclude this part, it seems that tribunals' approach towards the public's access to information is even more restrictive than its approach towards the public's participation. This raises questions with respect to the effectiveness of the limited participation the public is entitled to under ICSID disputes. A certain relief in this respect can be found in the fact that under certain conditions, parties are permitted to 'leak' information to the public by speaking about a dispute, or publishing their own submissions. As NGOs often support the position of the State Party in investment disputes, at least some information can be expected to travel to the interested public via the State.

24.4 Public participation in international investment law: substantive law

The principle of public participation, as explained in this chapter, is procedural by nature. It is intended to safeguard a 'process' (the decision-making process), by ensuring the wide and effective participation 'of all concerned citizens, at the relevant level.'[100] However, this principle can be found, albeit in limited manner, in the substantive laws and principles of the international investment regime.

Protecting the principle of public participation under international investment law's substantive rules will safeguard investors' right to participate in environmental decision-making processes. Allowing foreign investors to participate in environmental decision-making processes can promote sustainable development goals. The perspectives of the private sector are necessary in order to create a sustainable legal environment that supports long-term investment. This is especially true with respect to investment in climate-friendly technologies and renewable energies, where private resources are badly needed. Furthermore, as demonstrated in a recent arbitration,[101] investors can also pressure states to enforce their environmental obligations.

---

98 *UPS, Amici Curiae Decision* (*supra* note 23) at para 67; *Methanex, Amici Curiae Decision* (*supra* note 31) at para 42.

99 *Biwater, Procedural Order* 3 (*supra* note 96). The *Biwater* Tribunal cited in this respect other decisions made by the *Metalclad*, the *Amco* and *Loewen* Tribunals: see paras 121–29. The Tribunal has also mentioned that there are several limitations in this respect, like the 'Non-Aggravation/ Non-Exacerbation' of the Dispute: see para 135.

100 Rio Declaration on Environment and Development (*supra* note 6).

101 In a recent case, a Canadian investor who invested in an eco-tourism facility in Barbados, argued that Barbados' failure to enforce environmental laws and commitments, on which he legitimately relied, led to the pollution of his site: see *Peter A. Allard v The Government of Barbados (Notice of Dispute)* (2009) <http://graemehall.com/legal/papers/BIT-Complaint.pdf> accessed 18 March 2012.

It is argued that, under certain circumstances, the principle of public participation can be seen as a part of the 'fair and equitable treatment' (FET) standard of protection. The FET standard can be found in the vast majority of IIAs. Although it is often invoked in investment disputes, the exact meaning of this standard has remained unsettled.[102] However, for the sake of this discussion, it can be said that the FET standard of protection includes principles like due process, non-discrimination, fairness, transparency and the protection of the investor's 'legitimate expectations' at the time of the investment.[103]

Where and how can the principle of public participation fit in this description? First, the FET guarantees some level of transparency in the state's administrative actions.[104] 'Transparency', in this respect, can be seen as supporting the second part of the principle – the right to information. It can be argued therefore, that where decisions are about to affect investors' rights, foreign investors should be permitted access to any relevant information. It should be noted, however, that tribunals and scholars alike view 'transparency' in a more limited manner.[105] According to the dominant view, the term 'transparency' is restricted to sufficient knowledge of the legal framework in which the investor is operating.[106] Internal deliberations, for example, are considered as not included within the FET standard.[107] Stretching this rule to include access to information on decision-making processes, would seem therefore to be excessive.

The FET standard is regarded also as including the principle of due process.[108] The principle of due process is often linked to the concepts of 'denial of justice' and fair procedure.[109] As for the definition of 'due process' in the context of the FET standard, the *Waste Management* Tribunal explained that the lack of due process should be: 'leading to an outcome which offends judicial propriety – as might be the case with a manifest failure of natural justice in judicial proceedings

---

102   Catherina Yannaca-Small, 'Fair and Equitable Treatment Standard in International Investment Law' (2004) OECD Working Papers on International Investment 2004/3 <http://www.oecd.org/dataoecd/22/53/33776498.pdf> accessed 18 March 2012 [Yannaca-Small]; Kenneth Vandevelde, 'A Unified Theory of Fair and Equitable Treatment' (2010) 43(1) New York University Journal of International Law and Politics 43.

103   *Rumeli Telekom A.S. and Telsim Mobil Telekomunikasyon Hizmetleri A.S. v Republic of Kazakhstan (Award)* (2008) ICSID Case No ARB/05/16.

104   *Emilio Agusto Maffezini v Kingdom of Spain (Award)* (2000) ICSID Case No ARB/97/7, para 83; *LG&E Energy Corp. v Argentine Republic (Decision on Liability)* (2006), ICSID Case No ARB/02/1, para 128; *Biwater Gauff (Tanzania) Limited v United Republic of Tanzania (Award)* (2008), para 602.

105   Rudolf Dolzer and Christoph Schreuer, *Principles of International Investment Law* (Oxford: OUP, 2008) [Dolzer and Schreuer] at 133–34; *LESI et al. v People's Democracy Republic of Algeria (Award)* (2008) ICSID Case No ARB/05/3 [*LESI*] para 151.

106   *Metalclad Corporation v The United Mexican State (Award)* (2000) para 76; *Técnicas Medioambientales Tecmed, S.A. v United Mexican States (Award)* (2003) ICSID Case No ARB (AF)/00/2 [*Tecmed*]; Dolzer and Schreuer (*supra* note 105) at 133–34.

107   Vandevelde (*supra* note 102) at 84.

108   Ibid. at 89; Dolzer and Schreuer (*supra* note 105) at 142.

109   *Waguih Elie George Siag v Arab Republic of Egypt (Award)* (2009) ICSID Case No ARB/05/15, para 452; Dolzer and Schreuer (*supra* note 105) at 142–43; Vandevelde (*supra* note 102) at 89.

or a complete lack of transparency and candour in an administrative process.'[110] This principle, as explained by Dolzer and Schreuer, 'may be violated not only by courts but also through legislative or executive action.'[111] For example, failure to provide notification prior to the seizure of the investor's property,[112] or denial of a permit renewal without notification, and consequently also without the investor's ability to 'express its position as to such issue',[113] have been considered a violation of this principle.

Can the obligation to allow 'public participation' be considered as a part of the due process principle? At first glance, this interpretation could be seen as overreaching. It is difficult to argue that 'public participation in decision-making processes' is a natural and obvious part of 'due process'. The practice of 'public participation' is simply not abundant enough to be considered as such. Furthermore, the threshold of the FET standard is relatively high. For example, the *Thunderbird* Tribunal stated that in order to demonstrate a violation of due process, one must show 'administrative irregularities that were grave enough to shock a sense of judicial propriety'.[114] It is, to say the least, doubtful, whether the lack of public participation can be regarded as 'shocking' in this respect.

It should be noted, however, that both the 'transparency' and 'due process' principles are strongly linked to a third component of the FET standard – the protection of the investor's legitimate expectations. The objective of the FET standard is to secure a predictable and stable environment for foreign investors. It is intended, *inter alia*, to ensure that what investors can legitimately expect while making their investment decisions (for example, host state's promises, assurances, or a consistent and stable legal and business environment), will be upheld.[115]

Both 'transparency' and 'due process' are relevant in this respect. 'Transparency' is often viewed as knowledge of the existing legal framework. Based on this knowledge, it is explained, investors should understand beforehand what they can and cannot legitimately expect from host states.[116] Similarly, the breaching of the due process obligation is considered as a violation of what investors have

110 *Waste Management Inc. v The United Mexican State (Award)* (2004) ICSID Case No ARB(AF)/00/3 para 98.
111 Dolzer and Schreuer (*supra* note 105) at 142.
112 *Middle East Cement Shipping and Handling Co. S.A. v Arab Republic of Egypt (Award)* (2002) ICSID Case No ARB/99/6, para 143.
113 *Tecmed* (*supra* note 106) at paras 161–62.
114 *International Thunderbird Gaming Corporation v The United Mexican State (Award)* (2006) UNCITRAL (NAFTA) [*Thunderbird*] para 200. See also *AES Summit Generation Limited and AES-Tisza Erömü Kft v Republic of Hungary (Award)* (2010) ICSID Case No ARB/07/22 [*AES Summit*] para 9.3.40.
115 The protection of foreign investors' 'legitimate expectations' is a recognition in the changing power balance existing between foreign investors and host states. While prior to the investment, states tend to make promises in order to lure foreign investment into their territories, following the making of the investment, states can easily change their policies, according to popular will. The protection of investors' legitimate expectation, therefore, is aimed to protect investors from such changes: see Dolzer and Schreuer (*supra* note 105) at 4–5.
116 Dolzer and Schreuer (*supra* note 105) at 133–34; *LESI* (*supra* note 105) at para 151.

reasonably relied on when making the investment, as a part of the existing legal environment.[117]

Can foreign investors 'legitimately expect' a State to allow public participation in decision making processes, as stipulated in the New Delhi Declaration? The answer to this question, in the author's view, depends on the place from which the claimant derives its 'legitimate expectations', or the source of the obligation investors expect a State to follow. While it remains debatable whether investors can expect a State to refrain from changing its laws,[118] it seems safe to argue that an investor can legitimately expect a State to adhere to its laws, as long as these are valid. This follows from the interpretation given to the term 'transparency', as discussed above. It can therefore be argued that where the principle of public participation is embedded in the State's own laws, foreign investors can legitimately expect the State to allow them to participate in decision-making processes. For example, it is possible that foreign investors operating in States that have ratified the Aarhus Convention and adopted it into their domestic legal systems can rely on the FET standard in order to secure their right to participate in decision-making processes in environmental matters.

An interesting issue in this respect would be the status of less binding State obligations, such as 'soft laws'. The principle of public participation is embedded, as mentioned above, in non-legally binding sources of law, like the Rio Declaration and *Agenda 21*. Can foreign investors legitimately expect States to follow such 'soft law' commitments? Cordonier-Segger and Khalfan have commented in a different context that '[c]ompliance with "soft law" can shape legitimate expectations, and demonstrate good faith.'[119] The author believes that indeed it can be claimed that where States have complied with the principles of public participation in the past, investors can claim that legitimate expectations were formed.

It should be noted, however, that without the background of former compliance and the tradition of state practice, relying on 'soft law' commitments like those mentioned in this chapter cannot be accepted under the FET standard. This is mainly because it is hard to see how investors could have legitimately relied on non-binding statements. Furthermore, accepting this type of claims would be as if these commitments, via the standards of international investment laws, have transformed

---

117   *Waste Management* (*supra* note 110) at para 98. See also the *Tecmed* Tribunal: 'The investor also expects the State to use the legal instruments that govern the actions of the investor or the investment in conformity with the function usually assigned to such instruments', *Tecmed* (*supra* note 106) at 154.

118   The academic discussion concerning the limits of investors' 'legitimate expectations' focuses mainly on the question of whether a state can modify and change its laws, and whether such a change amounts to a breach of investors' 'legitimate expectations'. See, for example, M Sornarajah, *The International Law on Foreign Investment* (Cambridge: CUP, 2010) at 354–55; Kate Miles, 'Sustainable Development, National Treatment and Like Circumstances in Investment Law' in Cordonier Segger and others (*supra* note 49) at 261, 273.

119   Marie-Claire Cordonier Segger and Ashfaq Khalfan, *Sustainable Development Law: Principles, Practices and Prospects* (Oxford: OUP, 2004) at 10.

themselves into 'hard laws'. This transformation is contrary to the intention of the 'law-making' states, and against the very essence of the term 'soft law'.

Moreover, recent investment tribunals have emphasised that when it comes to 'legitimate expectations', states' promises must be specific. The *Total S.A.* Tribunal has offered the following formula in order to measure the strength of investors' claims based on 'legitimate expectations':

> the more specific the declaration to the addressee(s), the more credible the claim that such an addressee (the foreign investor concerned) was entitled to rely on it for the future in a context of reciprocal trust and good faith.[120]

It will therefore be difficult (if not impossible) for a foreign investor to mention such wide 'soft law' declarations, made in international *fora*, as a basis for its own 'legitimate expectations'.

In order to conclude this part, it can be asserted that when former practice exists, or when specific laws apply, the principle of public participation can certainly be viewed as being protected by the FET standard of treatment. It should be noted however, that under the current interpretation of the FET standard, the limits to this conclusion are clear. 'Soft law' sources in this respect cannot be regarded as a source for investors' 'legitimate expectations'. Therefore, the FET standard cannot be viewed as protecting the principle of public participation, based solely on declarations such as those mentioned above.

24.5 Conclusion

24.5.1 The duality of the principle of public articipation

This chapter can be concluded with two final observations. First, as mentioned at the beginning of the chapter, the principle of public participation includes two aspects. The first can be described as the 'human rights' aspect, and is based on the people's right to take a part in the governance of their environment and to affect the decisions that influence their lives.[121] The second aspect of the principle of public participation is related to elements of good governance, and is relied upon in the assumption that public participation enhances the quality of decisions. As explained below, it seems that despite the petitioners' attempts to raise the 'human rights' aspect of the principle in investment disputes, tribunals did not accept that the public had any inherent right to participate, to affect and to be involved in investment disputes, but may only do so in order to support the tribunal's work.

---

120 *Total S.A. v Argentine Republic (Decision on Liability)* (2010) ICSID Case No ARB/04/01 para 121.
121 This right is reflected in documents such as the 1948 UN Universal Declaration of Human Rights (*supra* note 2) and the Aarhus Convention (*supra* note 9).

4 Human rights narrative of petitioners

The petitioners in the *Suez* arbitration attempted, *inter alia*, to rely on the 'human rights' aspect of the principle of public participation. For example, it was mentioned that 'the procedure should be conducted with transparency and the participation of the people interested in its resolution [. . .].'[122] It was also mentioned that Argentina is 'a constitutional and democratic State', and that 'by virtue of fundamental democratic principles that lead to the enjoyment of human rights, the public decisions that affect millions of people cannot be adopted in secrecy nor exclude the opinion of the affected population.' It was further mentioned:

> The right of every person to participate and make their voice heard in cases where the decisions may affect their rights and interests is an integral part of the principles that secure the right to an effective recourse and the guarantee to due legal process. Such guarantees are expressed both in article 18 of the National Constitution and in the most important international law human rights instruments, as the International Covenant on Civil and Political Rights (Art. 14 and 25) and the American Convention on Human Rights (Art. 8 and 25).[123]

A similar narrative was also adopted by the petitioners at the *Foresti* and the *Tunari* arbitrations. The petitioners at the *Foresti* arbitration have stated 'this arbitration gives rise to a number of issues that are of direct concern to South African citizens and the civil society groups that represent them, as well as a wide range of issues of concern to the citizens of all countries.'[124]

Similarly, the petitioners in the *Tunari* arbitration have argued for the right to ensure 'that issues with broad public impacts are resolved through democratic processes that provide for meaningful public participation.'[125]

The petitioners in the *Biwater* arbitration also raised the public nature of the dispute and the importance of public participation to the credibility of the arbitral process ('the public perception can be one of a system unfolding in a secret environment that is anathema in a democratic context'), and the 'potential impacts of the confidentiality order on public access to documents in the case as it evolves.'[126]

---

122 *Petition for transparency and participation as amicus curiae (unofficial translation from Spanish original)* in *Suez, Sociedad General de Aguas de Barcelona S.A. and Vivendi Universal S.A v Argentine Republic*, ICSID Case No Arb/03/19 [*Suez, Petition for transparency and participation as amicus curiae*] 1.

123 Ibid. at 10.

124 *Petition for Limited Participation as Non-Disputing Parties in Terms of Articles 41(3), 27, 39, and 35 of the Additional Facility Rules* in *Piero Foresti, Laura De Carli & Others v The Republic of South Africa*, ICSID Case No ARB(AF)/07/01 [*Foresti, Petition for Limited Participation*] 4.1.

125 *Petition of La Coordinadora para la defensa del Agua Y Vida* and others to the arbitral Tribunal in *Aguas del Tunari S.A. v Republic of Bolivia*, ICSID Case No ARB/02/3 <http://ita.law.uvic.ca/documents/Aguaaboliviapetition.pdf> accessed 18 March 2012 [*Tunari, Petition*].

126 *Biwater, Petition for amicus curiae status (supra* note 70) at 14.

24.5.3 'Utilitarian' narrative of tribunals

But despite the petitioners' attempt to include the 'human rights' aspect in their petitions, investment tribunals have relied on a different, more 'utilitarian' narrative. Tribunals most notably have emphasised the amicus curiae's ability to assist them in achieving their 'fundamental task of arriving at a correct decision in this case'.[127] Amicus curiae, it is explained, is 'an offer of assistance' to the tribunal,[128] rather than a means for greater public participation.[129]

Moreover, even when considering the importance of public participation and transparency in investment disputes, this, as stated by several investment tribunals, was done as a means to enhance the legitimacy of investment arbitration, and not as a means to provide the public with the ability to be involved in the process.

However, this does not mean that the principle of public participation is absent from this narrative altogether. The tribunals' 'utilitarian' approach is indeed a part of this principle, and is reflected as a means to ensure good governance and enhance the quality of decisions. The preamble to the Aarhus Convention, for example, states:

> Recognizing that, in the field of the environment, improved access to information and public participation in decision-making enhance the quality and the implementation of decisions, [. . .][130]

Furthermore, the UN Declaration on Social Progress and Development from 1969 specifically mentions public participation as a means to ensure that '[s]ocial progress and development require the full utilization of human resources'.[131]

24.5.4 Inadequate application of the principle? Or simply a compromise?

If, to conclude this first observation, it can be said that, while the petitioners viewed their participation as a democratic right to be represented, to actively participate and make their voice heard, the tribunals approved such participation only where it was seen to benefit their own work. Thus the tribunals' approach stands in contrast to the New Delhi Declaration, which views the open access to participation by itself as the most desirable tool for guaranteeing good governance. In other words, the 'human rights' aspect is needed in order to ensure good governance and good decisions. The New Delhi Declaration has stated in this respect '[p]ublic participation in the context of sustainable development requires

---

127 *Suez* (*supra* note 48) at para 11; *Suez B* (*supra* note 65) at 12.
128 *Suez* (*supra* note 48) at para 13.
129 Similar narrative was also repeated in the recent *Chevron* arbitration, in which NGOs asked to raise arguments with respect to the tribunal's jurisdiction. The petitioners, however, were rejected. In its decision, the Tribunal recalled the Parties' agreement that they did not believe the amicus curiae would be helpful to the Tribunal, and that the issue of jurisdiction was extensively covered by the Parties. *Chevron, Procedural Order No. 8* (*supra* note 22) at para 18.
130 Aarhus Convention (*supra* note 9).
131 UN Declaration on Social Progress and Development (*supra* note 1) at art 5.

effective protection of the human right to hold and express opinions and to seek, receive and impart ideas.'[132]

It can be said in this respect that by denying the full utilisation of the right to participate, tribunals inherently miss certain voices, ideas and perspectives which might have benefited their decisions.

Nevertheless, the partial application of the principle by tribunals in this respect can also be seen as a compromise, or a balance between the rationales of the investor-State arbitration system and the increasing demands for transparency and good governance. It should not be forgotten that the closed system of investor-State arbitration was designed in order to encourage foreign investment by providing an efficient, non-politicised form of investor-State dispute resolution mechanism. In this light, the current approach applied by tribunals seems more understandable.

24.5.5 *The evolving nature of the principle of public participation*

As discussed at the beginning of this chapter, according to the different variations of the principle of public participation, the principle was designed in order to ensure public participation in *decision-making* processes, and is required from *States*. The acceptance of this principle (albeit a limited version of it) in the field of investment arbitration, both by investment treaties and tribunals, reflects an evolution of this principle, as it is now perceived to be required also from 'quasi-private' tribunals, such as investment tribunals, in order to ensure public participation in areas that indirectly affect the public interest (rather than in classic decision-making mechanisms), such as investment disputes.

This, perhaps, reflects a wider recognition of the changing nature of global governance, and the acceptance of the notion that beside the classic State-based decision-making mechanisms, other forms of governance nowadays determine our living realities. John Ruggie defined a few years ago the 'new global public domain', in which transnational corporations and civil society organisations are taking an increasing part in national and international governance.[133] It could be that, following Ruggie's logic, international tribunals should also be included in this list, and consequently be required to follow principles which are aimed toward governing entities, such as States. As the above discussion shows, such an evolution is already taking place in the practice of investment tribunals and States.

---

132 New Delhi Declaration (*supra* note 13).

133 John Gerard Ruggie, 'Reconstituting the Global Public Domain – Issues, Actors, and Practices' (2004) 10(4) *Eur. J. Int'l Relns.* 499.

25 The principle of good governance in the reasoning of investor-State arbitral tribunals

Jonathan Bonnitcha

25.1 Introduction

Over the past two decades, the concept of good governance has been central to debates about economic and social development. Governance, in this context, refers to the institutions and procedures controlling the exercise of public power within a State. The concept of 'good governance' is more elusive; different international organizations and academic writers have proposed a range of distinct understandings of the characteristics of 'good' governance.[1] While noting these debates, this chapter does not attempt to resolve disagreement about the appropriate understanding of good governance.[2] Rather, it adopts the conception of good governance articulated in the International Law Association's New Delhi Declaration of International Law Relating to Sustainable Development (New Delhi Declaration).

The New Delhi Declaration identifies the 'principle of good governance' as one of seven principles of international law relating to sustainable development. The New Delhi Declaration states that:

> The principle of good governance is essential to the progressive development and codification of international law relating to sustainable development. It commits States and international organizations:

---

1 The World Bank measures perceptions of 'Voice and Accountability, Political Stability and Absence of Violence/Terrorism, Government Effectiveness, Regulatory Quality, Rule of Law, and Control of Corruption' as components of good governance: D. Kaufmann, A. Kraay, M. Mastruzzi, 'The Worldwide Governance Indicators: Methodology and Analytical Issues' (2010) Policy Research Working Paper 5430, <http://siteresources.worldbank.org/INTMACRO/Resources/WPS5430.pdf> accessed 25 April 2011, 4; the United Nations Millenium Declaration suggests that good governance implies 'open, equitable, rule-based, predictable and non-discriminatory' legal regimes, UNGA, 'United Nations Millennium Declaration' (8 September 2000) UN A/res/55/2, [13]; and Dolzer links good governance to legal constraints on 'unprincipled and arbitrary actions' by the State, R. Dolzer, 'The Impact of International Investment Treaties on Domestic Administrative Law' (2006) 37 *Int'l L. and Politics* 952, 953. Despite the commonalities between these three conceptions of good governance there are also clear differences of emphasis between them.
2 For an overview of this debate see V. Nanda, 'The "Good Governance" Concept Revisited' (2006) 603(1) *The ANNALS of the American Academy of Political and Social Science* 269.

(a) to adopt democratic and transparent decision-making procedures and financial accountability;

(b) to take effective measures to combat official or other corruption;

(c) to respect due process in their procedures and to observe the rule of law and human rights; and

(d) to implement a public procurement approach according to the WTO Code on Public Procurement.

Civil society and non-governmental organizations have a right to good governance by states and international organizations. Non-state actors should be subject to internal democratic governance and to effective accountability.

Good governance requires full respect for the principles of the 1992 Rio Declaration on Environment and Development as well as the full participation of women in all levels of decision-making. Good governance also calls for corporate social responsibility and socially responsible investments as conditions for the existence of a global market aimed at a fair distribution of wealth among and within communities.[3]

This is primarily a *procedural* conception of good governance. Most of the sub-principles to which the New Delhi Declaration refers – namely, democratic and transparent decision-making, financial accountability, combatting corruption, due process, the rule of law and fair and transparent procurement processes – concern the institutions and procedures governing the exercise of public power. The New Delhi Declaration then muddies the waters somewhat, by linking good governance to the achievement of substantive objectives such as socially responsible investment and a fair distribution of wealth. These are admirable goals, but they raise issues about the *outcome* of decisions made by non-state actors. Instituting good governance may well be a *means* to achieve such substantive objectives. However, such substantive objectives are distinct from the procedural conception of good governance on which the New Delhi Declaration is based.

This chapter examines the extent to which arbitral tribunals have invoked the principle of good governance, as understood in the New Delhi Declaration,[4] in resolving investor-state disputes arising under international investment treaties (IITs).

25.2 General references to the principle of good governance

There are few direct references to the principle of good governance in the decisions of arbitral tribunals. This may be because the investment treaties under which investor-state claims arise seldom mention the concept of good governance

---

3 ILA, 'New Delhi Declaration of Principles of International Law Relating to Sustainable Development', annex to UN Doc A/57/329.

4 This procedural conception of good governance reflected in the New Delhi Declaration should be distinguished from the substantive conception of good governance discussed in Jonathan Bonnitcha, *Substantive Protection under Investment Treaties: A Legal and Economic Analysis* (Cambridge: CUP, 2014) 42–5. The latter is a broader and, arguably, vaguer conception that incorporates both procedural and substantive sub-principles.

explicitly. However, several tribunals have referred to sub-principles of good governance, as they are understood in the New Delhi Declaration. The following sections catalogue decisions that have invoked specific sub-principles of the principle of good governance.

Notwithstanding the fact that tribunals seldom refer to the principle of good governance, some academic writers have argued that, in interpreting and applying IITs, arbitral tribunals are articulating standards of good governance that apply to states at the international level. For example, Kingsbury and Schill suggest that:

> Investor-State arbitral tribunals implement broadly phrased international standards set out in very similar terms in many investment treaties, and concretize and expand or restrict their meaning and reach through interpretation, so that they increasingly define for the majority of States of the world standards of good governance and of the rule of law that are enforceable against them by foreign investors.[5]

It is not entirely clear whether Kingsbury and Schill share the procedural conception of good governance proposed by the New Delhi Declaration. At one point, they describe their conception as 'process-oriented'.[6] However, they go on to place the principle of proportionality at the centre of their conception of good governance.[7] Application of the principle of proportionality involves review of the strength of the justification for a particular decision on *substantive* grounds and is, therefore, incompatible with a procedural conception of good governance. This conceptual slippage highlights a point made in the previous section – that analysis of whether the decisions of investment treaty tribunals incorporate principles of good governance is only possible if one has first articulated a clear conception of 'good governance'.

Regardless of the conception of good governance on which their claim is premised, Kingsbury and Schill's proposition that investment treaties 'increasingly define world standards of good governance' is clearly a much stronger claim than the argument that arbitral tribunals sometimes invoke sub-principles of the principle of good governance in their reasoning. By drawing attention to particular occasions in which tribunals have referred to elements of the principle of good governance, I do not intend to endorse such a sweeping proposition. To establish that IIT standards constitute 'world standards of good governance' one would need to undertake a much broader survey of the decisions of arbitral tribunals than that attempted in this chapter. Such a survey would need to examine arbitral decisions that *do not* refer to the principle of good governance or its constituent sub-principles (that is, the majority of arbitral decisions) and show that such decisions are, nevertheless, consistent with the principle of good governance.

---

5 B. Kingsbury and S. Schill, 'Investor-State Arbitration as Governance: Fair and Equitable Treatment, Proportionality and the Emerging Global Administrative Law' <http://www.iilj.org/publications/documents/2009-6.KingsburySchill.pdf> accessed 25 April 2012, 2.

6 Ibid. at 18.

7 Ibid. at 18–40.

25.3 Aspects of good governance: transparency

Several arbitral tribunals have referred to the principle of transparency, almost always in the course of determining whether a host State has breached the fair and equitable treatment (FET) standard of an investment treaty. The first mention of transparency was in the *Maffezini v Spain* decision. The Tribunal held that a Spanish State entity's withdrawal of funds from an investor's bank account breached the FET standard of the relevant treaty due to the 'lack of transparency'.[8] However, the Tribunal's conclusion that the FET standard had been breached rested on the fact the investor had not consented to the withdrawal, not that the state had failed to disclose the withdrawal.[9] As such, it is not entirely clear why the tribunal referred to the principle of transparency or what it understood the obligation of transparency to entail.

The tribunal in *LG&E v Argentina* agreed that the FET standard requires a host State to act transparently, but understood this requirement differently to the *Maffezini* tribunal. The *LG&E* decision held that the FET standard requires a State to act transparently in the sense that:

> [A]ll relevant legal requirements for the purpose of initiating, completing and successfully operating investments made, or intended to be made under an investment treaty should be capable of being readily known to all affected investors.[10]

The Tribunal in *Champion Trading v Egypt* applied this same understanding of transparency in a claim brought by a cotton company regarding administrative decrees that determined the sale price of cotton.[11] The Tribunal dismissed the claim, finding that the claimants 'were in a position to know beforehand all rules and regulations that would govern their investments for the respective [cotton] season to come.'[12]

A third, far broader, understanding of a State's obligation to act transparently under the FET standard was articulated in *Tecmed v Mexico*. The Tribunal held that a State is required to treat foreign investors in way that is 'free from ambiguity and totally transparent'.[13] This entails a more exacting obligation on host

---

8   *Maffezini v The Kingdom of Spain*, Award, ICSID Case No ARB/97/7 (13 November 2000) (*Maffezini*) [83].

9   Ibid. at [75]; K. Vandevelde, *Bilateral Investment Treaties: History, Policy and Interpretation* (Oxford: OUP, 2010) 404; A. Newcombe and L. Paradell, *Law and Practice of Investment Treaties: Standards of Treatment* (Netherlands: Kluwer Law International, 2009) 293.

10 *LG&E Energy v Argentina*, Award, ICSID Case No ARB/02/1 (25 July 2007) [128].

11 The claimant originally framed this claim as a breach of the FET provision of the treaty, but later framed it simply as a breach of 'international law'. The tribunal referred to a decision of the WTO Appellate Body and the *Tecmed* tribunal's discussion of the FET standard in addressing the claim. *Champion Trading Company v Arab Republic of Egypt*, Award, ICSID Case No ARB/02/9 (27 October 2006) (*Champion Trading*) [157]–[164].

12 Ibid. at [164].

13 *Técnicas Medioambientales Tecmed v United Mexican States*, Award, ICSID Case No ARB(AF)/00/02 (29 May 2003), (2004) 43 ILM 133 (*Tecmed*) [154].

States than the requirement that laws be capable of being known. An investor may know the law that applies to its investment, yet be faced with ambiguity, either because the terms of the law are not sufficiently precise or because the law confers a degree of discretion on the authorities that administer it. On the facts of the case, the *Tecmed* Tribunal held that the 'ambiguity and uncertainty' relating to the legal situation of a landfill breached the FET standard.[14] This ambiguity did not stem from any lack of clarity about the conditions governing the claimant's licence to operate the landfill, or the fact that the licence was – formally – only of one year's duration. Rather, the lack of transparency in the case stemmed from uncertainty about the way in which an administrative authority would exercise a discretion conferred by clear and certain general laws; specifically, the question of whether the investor's licence would be renewed.[15]

A similar understanding of the obligation of transparency under the FET standard was developed in *Metalclad v Mexico*.[16] One of the reasons for the Tribunal's decision that Mexico breached the FET standard was that it had failed to 'ensure a transparent and predictable [regulatory] framework'.[17] Under Mexican law, which was readily capable of being known, it was not clear whether the approval of the claimant's landfill by federal authorities exempted the claimant from the normal requirement of obtaining a municipal construction permit.[18]

Of these three understandings of transparency – those articulated in *Maffezini*, *LG&E* and *Tecmed*, respectively – the *LG&E* Tribunal's view is the most consistent with wider principles of sustainable development. This understanding of transparency – that transparency requires laws and regulations to be 'capable of readily being known' – is closely linked to the New Delhi Declaration's principle of 'public participation and access to information and justice.' The ability of the public to participate in a system of governance would be significantly reduced if the laws and regulations constituting that system were not capable of being known.

In contrast, there are significant tensions between the *Tecmed* Tribunal's understanding of transparency and other principles identified in the New Delhi Declaration. By prohibiting regulatory agencies from exercising administrative authority in ways that investors cannot predict *ex ante*, the *Tecmed* decision would limit the ability of governments to respond to new information about environmental risks. When new information about environmental harms associated with a particular activity comes to light, the duty to ensure sustainable use and the precautionary principle would both require States to take steps to mitigate that harm. As such, the New Delhi Declaration clearly envisages circumstances in which it will be necessary to alter regulatory arrangements, even if individuals could not have predicted that regulatory change would be necessary.

14 Ibid. at [172].
15 Ibid. at [172].
16 *Metalclad v Mexico*, Award, ICSID Case No ARB(AF)/97/1 (30 August 2000), (2001) 40 ILM 36 (*Metalclad*) [76].
17 Ibid. at [99], [88].
18 Ibid. at [81]–[86].

25.4 Aspects of good governance: corruption

Arbitral tribunals have considered the issue of corruption in two contexts: first, situations in which the host State retaliates against a foreign investor that has refused to pay a bribe requested by the host State; and second, situations in which a foreign investor pays a bribe to the host State and subsequently seeks to invoke the protections of an investment treaty. In the former set of circumstances, tribunals have been unanimous in agreeing that retaliation against an investor for refusing to pay a bribe will breach the FET standard.[19]

The latter set of circumstances raises more complex issues. When the applicable investment treaty contains a clause requiring foreign investments to be made in accordance with domestic law, corruption in the process of procuring or acquiring an investment will preclude a tribunal from exercising jurisdiction.[20] This, at least, was the view taken by the tribunals in *Inceysa v El Salvador* and *Fraport v the Philippines*.[21] Even when the applicable treaty does not contain such a clause, the *Plama v Bulgaria* Tribunal found that illegality in the acquisition of an investment, including payment of bribes by an investor, renders a dispute inadmissible.[22] Similarly, in *World Duty Free v Kenya* – a claim brought under an investment contract rather than an investment treaty – the Tribunal found that corruption rendered the contract on which jurisdiction depended voidable.[23]

These cases illustrate the complexity of integrating principles of sustainable development within existing legal regimes. While tribunals agree that corruption is an anathema to the legal regime established by IITs, it not always self-evident what implementing the New Delhi Declaration's injunction 'to take effective measures to combat official or other corruption' would entail. For example, at least one commentator has argued that an inflexible policy of denying the protection of IITs to investors who have paid bribes of any sort, would have the perverse consequence of allowing States that have forced unwilling investors to make corrupt payments to act with impunity.[24] On the other hand, one might argue that a 'bright line' test that automatically denies investors the protection of an IIT if they have made a corrupt payment is more likely to send a strong signal to investors and their lawyers that, if a government official demands a bribe, the

19 *EDF (Services) Ltd v Romania*, Award, ICSID Case No ARB/05/13, (8 October 2009) [221]; *F-W Oil Interests v Republic of Trinidad and Tobago*, Award, ICSID Case No ARB/01/14 (2 March 2006) [210]–[212].
20 A. J. Menaker, 'The Determinative Impact of Fraud and Corruption on *Investment Arbitrations*' (2010) 25(1) *ICSID Review* 67, 69.
21 *Inceysa Vallisoletana v Republic of El Salvador*, Award, ICSID Case No ARB/03/26 (2 August 2006) [221]; *Fraport AG Frankfurt Airport Services Worldwide v Republic of the Philippines*, Award, ICSID Case No ARB/03/25 (16 August 2007) [401].
22 *Plama Consortium Ltd v Republic of Bulgaria*, Award, ICSID Case No ARB/03/24 (27 August 2008) [135]; similarly, *Phoenix Action, Ltd v Czech Republic*, Award, ICSID Case No ARB/06/5 (15 April 2009) [101].
23 *World Duty Free v The Republic of Kenya*, Award, ICSID Case No ARB/00/7 (4 October 2006) [188].
24 D. Bishop, 'Toward a More Flexible Approach to the International Legal Consequences of Corruption' (2010) 25(1) *ICSID Review* 63, 65.

only acceptable course of action is for the investor to refuse to pay the bribe and to fall back on its protections under the applicable IIT. Issues that are still more complex arise in determining the appropriate standard of proof to be applied when an allegation of corruption is raised[25] and the question of whether corruption should be addressed as a question of jurisdiction or admissibility phase of proceedings.[26] These questions about the implications of a commitment 'to take effective measures to combat official or other corruption' all remain to be resolved by arbitral tribunals.

25.5 Aspects of good governance: due process and the rule of law

The principles of due process and the rule of law are, themselves, complex and contested concepts. The New Delhi Declaration does not elaborate on the meaning of these concepts. This poses considerable challenges for an inquiry into the extent to which arbitral tribunals draw on the conception of good governance proposed in the New Delhi principles. This chapter adopts relatively narrow conceptions of both due process and the rule of law – understanding 'due process' to refer to ideas of procedural fairness in the conduct of administrative proceedings and the 'rule of law' to refer the set of formal and institutional characteristics of legal systems articulated in Raz's seminal work.[27] However, it is important to note that others have proposed very different conceptions of the rule of law in the context of debate about investment treaty arbitration.[28]

The NAFTA case *Chemtura v Canada* is perhaps the most important of cases dealing with requirements of due process under the FET standard. The case concerned a Canadian ban on pesticides containing lindane; the claimant was a producer of such pesticides. The events leading to the ban were triggered by the US government's decision to prohibit the import of lindane-treated canola seed.[29] The claimant made two principal allegations: that Canadian administrative review of the use of lindane that led to the ban was a sham, motivated by avoiding trade complications with the US rather than legitimate health and environmental concerns; and that the process by which the review was conducted was flawed.[30] The tribunal dismissed the first claim on the facts.[31] However, it accepted that, even if the administrative procedure leading to the ban of lindane had been conducted in good faith, it could still have

---

25 C. Partasides, 'Proving Corruption in International Arbitration: A Balanced Standard for the Real World' (2010) 25 *ICSID Review* 47, 48.

26 R. Kriendler, 'Corruption in International Investment Arbitration: Jurisdiction and the Unclean Hands Doctrine' in K. Hóber, A. Magnusson and M. Ohrstrom, eds., *Between East and West: Essay in Honour of Ulf Franke* (New York: Juris Publishing, 2010) at 323.

27 J. Raz, 'The Rule of Law and Its Virtue' (1977) 93 *The Law Quarterly Review* 195.

28 Vandevelde, *Bilateral Investment Treaties* (*supra* note 9) at 2; S. Schill, 'Fair and Equitable Treatment, The Rule of Law and Comparative Public Law' in S. Schill, ed., *International Investment Law and Comparative Public Law* (Oxford: OUP 2010) at 159.

29 *Chemtura Corp v Government of Canada*, Award (2 August 2010) (*Chemtura*) [13].

30 Ibid. at [133].

31 Ibid. at [143].

breached the claimant's right to procedural fairness under the FET standard.[32] It held that the review process should be assessed 'as a whole' taking into account the subsequent procedures that constituted 'an additional opportunity offered to the claimant to put forward its position'.[33] The claimant advanced a range of contentions, including that: it had not been given sufficient notice of the review; it had not been given sufficient practical opportunities to make submissions; the review did not incorporate adequate scientific evidence; and that the review was not completed in a timely manner. The Tribunal found a degree of factual support for some of the claimant's contentions, particularly the argument that the claimant lacked opportunities to make submissions to the original review. However, it felt that these facts did not reach the threshold of 'procedurally improper behaviour . . . which was both serious in itself and material to the outcome of its inquiry' that would amount to a breach of the FET standard.[34]

Several other decisions are consistent with the threshold that procedural impropriety must be both serious in itself and material to the outcome of administrative proceedings to breach the FET standard. The Tribunal in *AES v Hungary* held that:

> [I]t is not every process failing or imperfection that will amount to a failure to provide fair and equitable treatment. The standard is not one of perfection. It is only when a state's acts or procedural omissions are, on the facts and in the context before the adjudicator, manifestly unfair or unreasonable (such as would shock, or at least surprise a sense of juridical propriety) . . . that the standard can be said to be infringed.[35]

The relevant element of the claimant's FET claim turned on an assessment of the procedures by which the government implemented regulated pricing in the electricity industry. While the Tribunal held that there were 'procedural shortcomings', the most serious being the tight deadlines for comment on the draft price decrees, it held that these did not rise to the level of breaches of FET.[36] The Tribunal noted that claimants had been given an opportunity to comment on the draft decrees that would be applied to them; that, notwithstanding the tight deadlines, they had been able to make comments; that the Ministry considered the claimant's comments and, at times, had adjusted the decrees accordingly; and that the claimants had the opportunity to seek review of the process in Hungarian courts.[37]

In *Lemire v Ukraine*, the claimant alleged that a series of administrative decisions relating to the award of radio licenses under tender were unfair.[38] In

---

32 Ibid. at [145].

33 Ibid.

34 Ibid. at [148].

35 *AES Summit Generation Ltd v Republic of Hungary*, Award, ICSID Case No ARB/07/22 (23 September 2010) [38].

36 Ibid. at [66].

37 Ibid. at [50]–[69].

38 *Lemire v Ukraine (II)*, Decision on Jurisdiction and Liability, ICSID Case No ARB/06/18 (14 January 2010) (*Lemire II*) [315].

considering the claims, the Tribunal held that the FET standard did not place a general obligation on the licensing authority to provide reasons for its decisions.[39] However, the licensing authority repeatedly awarded licenses to politically powerful individuals, notwithstanding the claimant's uncontested evidence that it better satisfied the criteria for award of particular licenses.[40] In this context, the licensing body's failure to state reasons for its decisions was central to the Tribunal's decision that the licensing authority's decision-making procedures had breached the FET standard.[41]

In *Middle East Cement v Egypt*, the procedure by which an administrative seizure and sale of a ship owned by the claimant was executed was deemed to have breached the FET standard. The serious procedural shortcoming in the case was that the authorities did not notify the claimant that the ship would be seized, even though claimant's and its lawyer's addresses were known to the authorities.[42] In *Thunderbird v Mexico*, the Tribunal held that the procedure by which the Mexican regulator had determined that Thunderbird's machines did not comply with gaming legislation satisfied the FET standard, as the claimant had been given an opportunity to be heard and present evidence.[43] In *PSEG v Turkey*, the Tribunal held that 'continuous and endless' changes in the legislation governing an investment, and in the interpretation and implementation of that legislation by the Turkish authorities, breached the FET standard.[44]

A distinct line of decisions have examined the extent to which the FET standard requires a host State to act lawfully. In the NAFTA case *ADF v US*, the claimant alleged that an administrative authority's failure to comply with the terms of its empowering statute breached the FET standard.[45] The Tribunal held that 'something more than simple illegality or lack of authority under domestic law of a State is necessary' to breach the FET standard.[46] In another NAFTA case, *GAMI*, the claimant argued that the failure of the Mexican sugar industry regulator to fully implement the pricing and quota regulations that governed the industry breached the FET standard. The Tribunal held that a 'failure to fulfil the objective of administrative regulations without more does not necessarily rise to a breach of international law.'[47] It found that the claimant had not proved that the regulator had a 'simple and unequivocal' duty to achieve the objectives of the regulatory regime, nor that regulator had made an '"outright and unjustified

39 Ibid. at [394].

40 Ibid. at [384].

41 Ibid. at [419]–[420].

42 *Middle East Cement v Egypt*, Award, ICSID Case No ARB/99/6 (12 April 2002) [143].

43 *International Thunderbird Gaming v United Mexican States*, Arbitral Award (26 January 2006) [198].

44 *PSEG Global v Republic of Turkey*, Award, ICSID Case No ARB/02/5 (19 January 2007) [250]–[254].

45 *ADF Group v United States of America*, Award, ICSID Case No ARB(AF)/00/1 (9 January 2003) [190].

46 Ibid. at [190].

47 *GAMI Investments v Mexico*, Final Award (15 November 2004) [97].

repudiation" of the relevant regulations'.[48] These two decisions are consistent with the threshold defined in *Chemtura* – that procedural unfairness, here a failure to comply with domestic law, must be both serious and material in order to breach the FET standard.

The extent of a requirement of lawfulness was further explored in the decision *Noble v Romania*. The Tribunal held that the FET standard precluded a state from treating an investment in an arbitrary manner.[49] It quoted the ICJ's decision in *ELSI* to explain that arbitrariness, in this context, referred to:

> Not so much something opposed to a rule of law, as something opposed to the rule of law . . . It is a wilful disregard of due process of law, an act which shocks, or at least surprises, a sense of juridical propriety.[50]

The Tribunal held that commencement of insolvency proceedings against the claimant was not arbitrary, because the proceedings were 'initiated and conducted according to the law and not against it'.[51] The suggestion that unlawfulness must be wilful appears to introduce a requirement of intent. However, the following phrase – which affirms that arbitrariness includes action that surprises juridical propriety – appears to leave the possibility open that serious disregard of national law would breach FET, even if an intention to ignore national law were not established.

Taken together, these decisions show an emerging consensus on due process and the rule of law. These decisions can be explained and justified by the principle articulated in *Chemtura* – that procedurally improper treatment of an investment which is both serious in itself and material to the investor would amount to a breach of the FET standard.[52] The principles articulated in these decisions both reflect and elaborate ideas of procedural fairness in the conduct of administrative proceedings.

That said, it is also important to recognize the limits of the incorporation of the principle of due process into arbitral reasoning. There are several other situations in which tribunals have concluded that States have breached the FET standard. They include cases in which a State has failed to respect an investor's legitimate expectations,[53] and cases in which a State has acted in a way that is (in the tribunal's view) substantively unreasonable or disproportionate.[54] The

---

48 Ibid. at [110], [103].

49 *Noble Ventures v Romania*, Award, ICSID Case No ARB/01/11 (12 October 2005) (*Noble Ventures*) [182].

50 Ibid. at [176], citing *Elettronica Sicula SpA (United States of America v Italy)* (Judgment) [1989] ICJ Rep 15, [128].

51 *Noble Ventures (supra* note 49) at [178].

52 *Chemtura (supra* note 29) at [148].

53 For more detailed discussion of the elements of the FET standard see: Newcombe and Paradell (*supra* note 9) at 275; R. Dolzer and C. Schreuer, *Principles of International Investment Law* (Oxford, OUP, 2008) 133; C. McLachlan, L. Shore and M. Weiniger, *International Investment Arbitration: Substantive Principles* (Oxford: OUP, 2007) 226.

54 Bonnitcha, *Substantive Protection under Investment Treaties (supra* note 4) at 210–27.

Chemtura decision provides a degree of clarity on the question of when a failure to provide procedural fairness to an investor will breach the FET standard. The doctrinal principles articulated in that case are also consistent with a number of decisions that examine when a failure to act lawfully will breach the FET standard. However, the *Chemtura* decision and the principles articulated in it do not provide an overarching theory of the full range of circumstances in which the conduct of a state would breach the FET standard.

25.6 Conclusion

Arbitral tribunals have referred to a number of different sub-principles of the New Delhi Delcaration's principle of good governance. This chapter has identified several references to sub-principles concerning transparency, corruption and due process in the reasoning of arbitral tribunals. The majority of these references occur in the course of arbitral analysis of whether a host state has breached the FET standard owed to a foreign investment.

This review of arbitral decisions also illustrates the challenges of integrating principles of sustainable development into established legal regimes. While there seems to be a degree of consensus that the FET standard requires host States to act transparently, tribunals have come to remarkably different views about what the obligation to act transparently requires. In the author's view, at least one of these interpretations, that proposed by the *Tecmed* tribunal, is difficult to reconcile with other principles articulated in the New Delhi Declaration. A second interpretation that derived from the *Maffezini* decision does not provide an internally consistent understanding of the principle of transparency itself. In my view, only the understanding of transparency proposed in the *LG&E* decision is both internally coherent and consistent with the New Delhi Declaration.

Difficulties of a different sort arise with respect to corruption. Although arbitral tribunals share a common understanding of what constitutes corruption – an understanding that is consistent with the principles of the New Delhi Declaration – integrating this principle into the procedural and substantive rules of investment arbitration raises a series of complex doctrinal questions. The answers to these questions are still being worked out by arbitral tribunals.

Perhaps the most significant progress in integrating principles of good governance into arbitral reasoning has been made through reference to principles of procedural fairness in disputes under the FET standard. In this chapter, it has been argued that recent decisions illustrate an emerging consensus that procedurally improper behaviour which is both serious in itself and material to the investor would amount to a breach of the FET standard.[55] This standard, which was articulated in the *Chemtura* decision, is capable of explaining and justifying a range of other arbitral decisions that examine the standard of due process that states owe to foreign investors under IITs. The New Delhi Declaration does not define what is meant by 'due process' and 'the rule of law'. However, the *Chemtura* standard

55 *Chemtura* (*supra* note 29) at [148].

is, at least, consistent with the narrow understandings of due process and the rule of law proposed in this chapter.

Finally, it is far from clear that IITs and the legal constraints they impose on States can be said to constitute 'world standards of good governance'. While several arbitral awards have considered sub-principles of good governance, the majority of arbitral decisions do not refer to sub-principles of good governance. Moreover, few, if any, awards have explicitly referred to a general principle of good governance in justifying their interpretation and application of investment treaties. In this light, generalized claims about IITs and good governance should be treated with caution. Any claim that investment arbitration constitutes a regime of good governance would need to be based on a clearly articulated and justified conception of the principle of 'good governance'. The claim would need to be supported by a thorough and comprehensive review of arbitral reasoning, including analysis of cases in which tribunals *do not* refer to principles and sub-principles of good governance. There would be considerable obstacles to sustaining such a claim. As argued elsewhere, certain strands of arbitral reasoning – notably, more expansive interpretations of the doctrine of legitimate expectations – impose unjustifiable constraints on host state regulatory action.[56] Such decisions are difficult to reconcile with any conception of good governance. At this stage, the better view is that integration of the principle of good governance into the reasoning of investor-State arbitral tribunals is partial, incomplete and contested, and, to the extent it has occurred, that there is considerable complexity in the nature of integration.

---

56 Bonnitcha, *Substantive Protection under Investment Treaties* (n 4) 288.

Regional courts and dispute settlement mechanisms

26 The principle of integration for sustainable development in European policy and jurisprudence

Marie-Claire Cordonier Segger and Markus Gehring

26.1 Introduction

The principles of integration and precaution, as exemplified in European Union (EU) policies, treaties and jurisprudence, may signal a commitment to sustainable development in principle and practice. This chapter explores the evolution and substance of sustainable development principles in the EU through an exploration of key treaties and jurisprudence. First, sustainable development is briefly defined and conceptually positioned in the progressive unification of the EU. Second, the principle of integration for more sustainable development, as seen in policies and treaties and as interpreted and applied in the European Court of Justice (ECJ) and the Court of Justice of the European Union (CJEU). The sustainable development principle of precaution is explored through its interpretation and application by the ECJ and CJEU. Finally, observations and critical thoughts are provided relating to interfaces of sustainable development, integration and the precautionary principle. On the whole, the principles of integration and precaution allow for integrated decision-making, coordinated environmental policy and adoption of preventative measures in cases of scientific uncertainty in support of sustainable development.

26.2 The EU's commitment to sustainable development: sustainable development briefly defined

As a concept, sustainable development emerges from a general aspiration to a global responsibility, for "the interdependent societies and economies, the environment and natural resources, and the conditions of humanity."[1] Conceptually maturing out of the Stockholm Declaration (1972), which established the responsibility of

---

1 Marie-Claire Cordonier Segger and H.E. Judge C.G. Weeramantry, "Introduction to Sustainable Justice: Implementing International Sustainable Development Law" in Marie-Claire Cordonier Segger and H.E.Judge C.G. Weeramantry, eds., *Sustainable Justice*, (Leiden and Boston: Martinus Nijhoff, 2005), p. 2. [Cordonier Segger and Weeramantry 2005]

the international community to sustainably manage transboundary ecosystems,[2] and the Brundtland Report (1987), which recognized the interdependence of environmental and socio-economic challenges grounding sustainable development as a policy objective,[3] the concept signals a strategic shift in human development thinking. In other words, sustainable development "provides a 'conceptual bridge' between the right to social and economic development, and the need to protect the environment."[4]

The importance of sustainable development in Europe has been emphasized repeatedly by European institutions. In 2001, the European Commission, borrowing the Brundtland definition of sustainable development mentioned above, affirmed that "sustainable development is a global objective" and that "the European Union has a key role in bringing about sustainable development."[5] Also, in 2005 the European Commission affirmed that "[t]he essence of the European Union is to work for *sustainable development* as an overarching objective that aims at meeting the needs of the present without compromising the ability of future generations to meet their own needs"[6] with sustainable development providing the foundations for of the Union's promotion of international growth.[7] In a 2006 joint statement, sustainable development was also discussed in the context of poverty eradication.[8] The document affirms that "[t]he primary and overarching objective of EU development cooperation is the eradication of poverty in the context of *sustainable development*"[9] where sustainable development includes "good governance, human rights and political, economic, social and environmental aspects."[10]

Sustainable development is a notion that also appears prominently in the European treaties. Article 2 of the Treaty establishing the European Community

---

2   UN, "Stockholm Declaration on the Human Environment" (16 June 1972), http://www. unep.org/Documents.Multilingual/Default.asp?documentid=97&articleid=1503. [Stockholm Declaration]

3   World Commission on Environment and Development, *Our Common Future* (Oxford: OUP, 1987), http://www.un-documents.net/our-common-future.pdf. [Brundland Report]

4   Cordonier Segger and Weeramantry 2005, *supra* note 1, pp. 2–3.

5   EC, Communication from the European Commission, *A Sustainable Europe for a Better World: A European Union Strategy for Sustainable Development*, COM(2001)264 (15 May 2001), p. 2, http://eur-lex.europa.eu/LexUriServ/LexUriServ.do?uri=COM:2001:0264:FIN:EN:PDF. [EC, COM(2001)264]

6   EC, Strategic Objectives 2005–2009, *Europe 2010: A Partnership for European Renewal Prosperity, Solidarity and Security*, COM(2005) 12 (26 January 2005), p. 8 (emphasis added), http://eur-lex.europa.eu/legal-content/EN/TXT/PDF/?uri=CELEX:52005DC0012&from =EN. [EC, COM(2005) 12]

7   COM(2005) 12, *supra* note 6, p. 12.

8   EC, Joint statement by the Council and the representatives of the governments of the Member States meeting within the Council, the European Parliament and the Commission on European Union Development Policy: "The European Consensus" OJ C 46/01 (24 February 2006), The European Consensus on Development, para 1, http://eur-lex.europa.eu/legal-content/EN/ TXT/PDF/?uri=CELEX:42006X0224(01)&from=EN. [EC, 2006/C 46/01]

9   EC, 2006/C 46/01, *supra* note 8, para 5 (emphasis added).

10   EC, 2006/C 46/01, *supra* note 8, para 7.

(as amended by the Treaty of Amsterdam) introduced sustainable development as an objective of the Union:

> The Community shall have as its task, by establishing a common market and an economic and monetary union and by implementing common policies or activities (. . .), to promote throughout the Community a harmonious, balanced and *sustainable development* of economic activities, a high level of employment and of social protection, equality between men and women, sustainable and non-inflationary growth, a high degree of competitiveness and convergence of economic performance, a high level of protection and improvement of the quality of the environment, the raising of the standard of living and quality of life, and economic and social cohesion and solidarity among Member States.[11]

Sustainable development is enshrined as a core principle of the Treaty of the European Union (TEU). The *Preamble* of the TEU refers to sustainable development as one of the principles that should inspire the promotion of economic and social progress of the EU peoples.[12] Article 3 recognizes that the Union shall "work for the *sustainable development* of Europe" through promotion of balanced economic growth, progressive social growth and environmental protection,[13] and contribute to "peace, security, the *sustainable development* of the Earth, solidarity and mutual respect among peoples, free and fair trade, eradication of poverty and the protection of human rights, in particular the rights of the child, as well as to the strict observance and the development of international law, including respect for the principles of the United Nations Charter."[14] Additional references to sustainable development in the TEU are contained in Article 21(2) on the Union's external action, requiring cooperation in the development and pursuit of common policy for the Union to "foster the *sustainable economic, social and environmental development* of developing countries, with the primary aim of eradicating poverty" and "to help develop international measures to preserve and improve the quality of the environment,"[15] and "the sustainable management of global natural resources, in order *to ensure sustainable development*."[16]

---

11 European Communities, Treaty of Amsterdam Amending the Treaty of the European Union, The Treaties Establishing the European Communities and Certain Related Rights, (1997), Article 2 (emphasis added), http://www.europarl.europa.eu/topics/treaty/pdf/amst-en.pdf [Treaty of the EC 1997].

12 EC, Consolidated Versions of the Treaty on the European Union and the Treaty of the Functioning of the European Union (Lisbon Version), OJ 2010/C 83/01 (30 March 2010), *Preamble*, http://eur-lex.europa.eu/legal-content/EN/TXT/HTML/?uri=CELEX:C2010/0 83/01&from=EN [Treaty of EU 2010] [TFEU 2010].

13 Treaty of EU 2010, *supra* note 12, Article 3(3).

14 Ibid. at art 3(5) (emphasis added).

15 Ibid. at art 21(2)(d).

16 Ibid. at art 21(2)(f) (emphasis added).

Several references to sustainable development are also contained in the Treaty on the Functioning of the European Union (TFEU).[17] Article 11 provides that "[e]nvironmental protection requirements must be integrated into the definition and implementation of the Union policies and activities, in particular with a view to promoting *sustainable development*".[18] Title XX of TFEU is entirely dedicated to the environment.[19] Specifically, Article 191(1) provides that:

> Union policy on the environment shall contribute to pursuit of the following objectives: preserving, protecting and improving the quality of the environment, protecting human health, prudent and rational utilisation of natural resources, promoting measures at international level to deal with regional or worldwide environmental problems, and in particular combating climate change.[20]

Finally, the Charter of Fundamental Rights of the European Union also refers to sustainable development. The *Preamble* provides that the Union seek "to promote balanced and sustainable development" through strengthened protections for fundamental human rights.[21] Additionally, Article 37 on environmental protection refers to the EU's commitment to sustainable development in these words:

> A high level of environmental protection and the improvement of the quality of the environment must be integrated into the policies of the Union and ensured in accordance with the principle of *sustainable development.*[22]

26.3 The ILA sustainable development principle of integration in EU policies and treaties

The principle of integration has been core to the legal fabric of the EU since the Single European Act,[23] with the European approach to integration instructive in nature,[24] and sustainable development recognized as an objective of the EU in

---

17 Ibid.
18 Ibid. at art 11 (emphasis added).
19 Ibid. at art 191–93.
20 Ibid. at art 191(1) (emphasis added).
21 EC, Charter of Fundamental Rights of the European Union, OJ 2010/C 83/02 (30 March 2010), *Preamble*, http://eur-lex.europa.eu/legal-content/EN/TXT/PDF/?uri=OJ:C:2010:08 3:FULL&from=EN [EU Charter of Fundamental Rights 2010].
22 Ibid.
23 European Communities, Treaties establishing the European Communities, Treaties amending these Treaties Single European Act (1987), http://europa.eu/eu-law/decision-making/treaties/pdf/treaties_establishing_the_european_communities_single_european_act/treaties_establishing_the_european_communities_single_european_act_en.pdf [Single European Act].
24 M. Pallemaerts, M. Herodes and C. Adelle, "Does the EU Sustainable Development Strategy Contribute to Environmental Policy Integration" EPIGOV Paper No. 9, Ecologic-Institute for International and European Environmental Policy: Berlin, https://www.researchgate.net/publication/242272825_Does_the_EU_Sustainable_Development_Strategy_Contribute_to_

the 1997 amendments to the treaties establishing the European Communities.[25] Article 11 of the TFEU, as amended by the Lisbon Treaty (formerly Article 6 EC Treaty), as mentioned, enshrines the principles of integration and sustainable development.[26] It is a recognized principle, at the European level, that environmental considerations must be integrated into Union policies and activities, including those related to trade and to development.[27] While a full discussion of European legal intricacies is not within the scope of this chapter, it can be noted that the 'integration principle' is not new to Europe. Originally reflected in former Article 130r(2) of the EU Treaty, which stipulated that preventative actions which address environmental damage and ensure that polluter pays components in the policies of the Community,[28] integration has, as Professor Marc Pallemaerts argued, simply been "given far greater prominence and a clear finality by virtue of being directly linked to the promotion of sustainable development."[29] In Europe, "environmental integration is the main means of promoting sustainable development."[30]

In 1998 the Cardiff Process was initiated to integrate environmental consideration into policy measures with the European Commission highlighting:

> Most of our environmental problems have their origins in current practices in sectors such as agriculture, transport, energy and industry and we must look to these areas for their solution . . . A credible response to the legal obligation of the Treaty requires that the Community equips itself with the necessary tools. Adherence to the integration requirement is in principle subject to judicial control by the European Court of Justice . . .[31]

Environmental_Policy_Integration_State-of-the-Art_Report [Pallemaerts, Herodes, Adelle]; I. von Homeyer, "Experimentalist Environmental Governance in the EU: Complex Challenges, Recursive Policy-Making, International Implications" (Berlin Conference on the Human Dimensions of Global Environmental Change, 22–23 February 2006, Berlin, Germany).

25 Treaty of the EC 1997, *supra* note 11, Article 1(2), 2; see Article 2 ". . . the following objectives: . . . to achieve balanced and sustainable development". Article 2 of the further mandates the Community to, *inter alia*, "promote a harmonious, balance and sustainable development of economic activities." See M. Pallemaerts, "The EU and Sustainable Development: An Ambiguous Relationship" in M. Pallemaerts and A. Azmanova, eds., *The European Union and Sustainable Development: Internal and External Dimensions* (Brussels: VUB Press, 2006), 24; Presidency Conclusions, Rhodes European Council, 2–3 December 1988, Annex 1, para 1: "Sustainable development must be one of the overriding objectives of all Community policies."

26 TFEU 2010, *supra* note 12, at art 11 (emphasis added).

27 European Union, *Sustainable Development in the European Union: 2015 Monitoring Report of the EU Sustainable Development Strategy* (Luxembourg: Publications Office of the European Union, 2015), http://ec.europa.eu/eurostat/documents/3217494/6975281/KS-GT-15-001-EN-N. pdf [EU 2015 SD Report].

28 Single European Act (1986), *supra* note 8, Article 130r(2) at 1040.

29 M. Pallemaerts, *The European Union and Sustainable Development: Internal and External Dimensions* (Brussels: IES, 2006) 25. [Pallemaerts 2006].

30 Pallemaerts 2006, *supra* note 29.

31 EC, Communication from the Commission to the European Council of 27 May 1998 on A Partnership For Integration: A Strategy for Integrating the Environment into EU Policies

Additionally, the EU undertook integration of environmental factors into EU external relations, including new economic agreements, and giving added weight to these social dimensions. The EC Strategy for Integrating Environment into EU Policies reaffirms the importance of the integration principle in the EU, noting the challenge facing the Community is defining a development agenda which aims to achieve sustainable development in an integrated and holistic way achieving socio-economic, developmental and environmental objectives in tandem.[32]

To secure integration in these areas, the Cardiff Process[33] involved designing new sustainable development strategies intended to 'mainstream' environmental considerations into different sectors of the European economy such as fisheries,[34] energy,[35] and transportation.[36] By 1999 the Commission had recognized a direct link between the integration principle, the objective of sustainable development in international economic agreements and trade law, and the use of sustainability assessments as a tool to achieve this integration, with a particularly awareness to the challenges faced by developing countries in the trade liberalization context.[37] The 2000 Lisbon Strategy was proposed to integrate environmental issues

(Cardiff, June 1998) [COM(1998) 333 – Not published in the Official Journal], at 3, http://eur-lex.europa.eu/legal-content/EN/TXT/?uri=URISERV:l28075. [Cardiff Strategy].

32 Cardiff Strategy, *supra* note 31, at 5–6.

33 Commission Working Document, "From Cardiff to Helsinki and beyond: Report to the European Council on integrating environmental concerns and sustainable development into Community policies" SEC(1999) 1942, 24 November 1999; Commission Communication, "Integrating Environmental Considerations into other Policy Areas – a Stocktaking of the Cardiff Process" COM(2004) 394 final, 1 June 2004.

34 EC, Communication from the Commission to the European Council, "Elements of a Strategy for the Integration of Environmental Protection Requirements into the Common Fisheries Policy" COM (2001) 143 (16 March 2001), http://eur-lex.europa.eu/LexUriServ/LexUriServ.do?uri=COM:2001:0143:FIN:EN:PDF; See K. Van den Bossche and N. van der Burgt, "Integrating Environmental Concerns into the European Common Fisheries Policy" in M. Pallemaerts in M. Pallemaerts and A. Azmanova, eds., *The European Union and Sustainable Development: Internal and External Dimensions* (Brussels: VUB Press, 2006) 237; C. Coffey, *Integrating Environment into the Common Fisheries Policy* (London: London Institute for European Environmental Policy 2000) 5.

35 Communication from the Commission, Strengthening Environmental Integration within Community Energy COM(1998) 571, http://aei.pitt.edu/3371/1/3371.pdf; Policy; A. Hadfield, "The Role of Energy Policy in Sustainable Development: Greening the Environment and Security Energy Supply" in M. Pallemaerts and A. Azmanova, eds., *The European Union and Sustainable Development: Internal and External Dimensions* (Brussels: VUB Press, 2006) 217. EC, Directive 2001/77/EC of the European Parliament and of the Council of 27 September 2001 on the promotion of electricity produced from renewable energy sources in the internal electricity market, OJ L 283/33 (2001), http://eur-lex.europa.eu/legal-content/EN/TXT/PDF/?uri=CELEX:32001L0077&from=EN.

36 Commission Staff Working Paper, Integrating Environment and Sustainable Development into Energy and Transport Policies: Review Report 2011 and Implementation of Strategies, SEC (2001) 502, Brussels, 21 March 2001.

37 Commission Working Paper on "Mainstreaming of Environmental Policy", submitted to the Cologne European Council SEC (1999) 777.

with economic policy,[38] and the Commission, in accordance with the Directive on Environmental Impact Assessment, began assessments for the elaboration of Community policies and plans, as treaty negotiation instruments represent plans that could affect the environment.[39] Growing out of the Cardiff Process, the EC interpretation of this integration principle has evolved over the past decade and can be traced through various Strategies, Communications of the EC, Decisions of the European Council, as well as binding Directives and Regulations, each with a place in European law and policy.[40]

In the launch of the 2001 *Sustainable Development Strategy for Europe* (SDS),[41] the operational aspects of integration were highlighted and the Council was asked "to finalise and further develop sectoral strategies for integrating environment into all relevant Community policy areas."[42] However, the principle of integration was extended in the final approved SDS, with recognition that it is "based on the principle that the economic, social and environmental effects of all policies should be examined in a coordinated way and taken into account in decision-making."[43] The Commission recommended early in the policy discourse that "careful assessment of the full effects of a policy proposal must include estimates of its economic, environmental and social impacts inside and outside the EU."[44] The final SDS calls for mechanisms in the Commission's action plan for better

38 European Parliament, Lisbon European Council 23 and 24 March 2000, Presidency Conclusions (2000), http://www.europarl.europa.eu/summits/lis1_en.htm; Commission Communication "Bringing Our Needs and Responsibilities Together-Integrating Environmental Issues with Economic Policy" COM (2000) 576, 20. Sept. 2000, http://eur-lex.europa.eu/LexUriServ/LexUriServ.do?uri=CELEX:52000DC0576:EN:HTML.

39 EC, Directive 2001/42/EC of the European Parliament and of the Council of 27 June 2001 on the Assessment of the Effects of Certain Plans and Programmes on the Environment OJ 2001 L 197/30 at Art. 2(a), Art. 3(1) to (5), http://eur-lex.europa.eu/legal-content/EN/TXT/PDF/?uri=CELEX:32001L0042&from=EN [Directive 2001/42/EC]; The instructions to negotiate European Union trade treaties are (i) subject to preparation by an authority at the regional level, and (ii) required by administrative provisions once European negotiating instructions have been issued, they are also likely to have significant environmental effects, as discussed in Chapter 2 above; See also European Commission, *Handbook for Trade Sustainability Impact Assessment* (Strasbourg: European Commission, External Trade, March 2006), http://trade.ec.europa.eu/doclib/docs/2006/march/tradoc_127974.pdf.

40 G. de Burca, "The Constitutional Challenge of New Governance in the European Union" (London: UCL: Current Legal Problems Series, November 2002), http://eucenter.wisc.edu/OMC/Papers/deburca.pdf.

41 Presidency Conclusions, Göteborg, 15 and 16 June 2001 SN 200/1/01 REV 1, http://www.consilium.europa.eu/en/european-council/conclusions/pdf-1993-2003/g%C3%96teborg-european-council--presidency-conclusions-15-16-june-2001/ [Presidency Conclusions, Göteborg]; See also Commission Communication, *A Sustainable Europe for a Better World: A European Union Strategy for Sustainable Development*, COM(2001) 264, *supra* note 5.

42 Ibid. at para 32.

43 Ibid. at para 22.

44 EC, COM(2001)264, *supra* note 5, at 6, noting that "The Commission will submit an action plan to improve regulation to the Laeken European Council in December. This will include mechanisms to ensure that all major legislative proposals include an assessment of the potential economic, environmental and social benefits and costs of action or lack of action, both inside and outside the EU. The Council and Parliament should amend legislative proposals in the same spirit."

regulation, which is mainly internal, "to ensure that all major policy proposals include a sustainability impact assessment covering their potential economic, social and environmental consequences".[45] However, one year later in 2002, the EU also adopted a Global Partnership for Sustainable Development Strategy, with a prominent role for integration in external relations noting the need for a systematic approach to socio-economic policy formulation.[46] The Strategy further highlights that some EC development cooperation policies "already have a fully integrated approach to sustainable development . . . In many cases, however, environmental considerations could be analysed more systematically."[47]

Strategic Environmental Impact Assessments (EIAs) were identified by the EU as a procedural way to implement the integration principle in trade law and policy.[48] The EC's 2002 Communication on Impact Assessments[49] stressed that EIAs would be required for negotiating guidelines for international agreements that have an economic, social or environmental impact.[50] The Commission sought to base its decisions on sound analysis of potential impacts, and a balanced appraisal of available policy instruments.[51] The Commission argued that by doing this, it was "delivering on its Göteborg commitments to implement sustainable development and to establish a tool for sustainable impact assessment."[52] In addition the EIA policy dovetailed well with the EC's Framework for the External Dimension of Sustainable Development,[53] with respect in the world economy,[54] which reports:

45 Presidency Conclusions, Göteborg, *supra* note 41, at para 24.

46 EC, Communication from the Commission to the Council, the European Parliament and the Economic and Social Committee, "Integrating Environment and Sustainable Development into Economic and Development Co-operation Policy: Elements of a Comprehensive Strategy" COM(2000)264 (2000), http://eur-lex.europa.eu/legal-content/EN/TXT/PDF/?uri=CELE X:52000DC0264&from=EN. [EC, COM(2000)264].

47 Ibid. at 46.

48 Regulation (EC) No 2493/2000 of the European Parliament and of the Council of 7 November 2000 on measures to promote the full integration of the environmental dimension in the development process of developing countries, Official Journal L 288 of 15.11.2000, http://eur-lex.europa.eu/legal-content/EN/TXT/HTML/?uri=URISERV:l28086&from=EN; Communication from the Commission of 13 February 2002: Towards a global partnership for sustainable development COM(2002) 82 final, http://aei.pitt.edu/37769/1/COM_(2002)_82-final.pdf; EC, COM(2000)264, *supra* note 46.

49 EC, Commission Communication on Impact Assessment, Brussels, COM (2002) 276, http://eur-lex. europa.eu/LexUriServ/LexUriServ.do?uri=COM:2002:0276:FIN:EN:PDF. [EC, COM(2002)276]

50 Directive 2001/42/EC, *supra* note 39; EC, Implementing Activity Based Management in the Commission, SEC (2001) 1197, http://ec.europa.eu/transparency/regdoc/rep/2/2001/EN/2-2001-1197-EN-6-0.Pdf; EC, Action plan "Simplifying and improving the regulatory environment" COM(2002)278, http://eur-lex.europa.eu/legal-content/EN/TXT/PDF/?uri =CELEX:52002DC0278&from=EN. [Better Regulation Action Plan]

51 EC, COM(2002)276, *supra* note 49.

52 Ibid.

53 C. Bretherton and J. Vogler, *The European Union as a Global Actor* (London: Routledge, 1999) 83.

54 Single European Act, *supra* note 8, at art 177. Article 177 of the EU Treaty specifies that the EC development cooperation policy shall foster "the smooth and gradual integration of developing countries into the world economy."

Developing countries can be integrated into the world economy through trade and regional economic integration . . . negotiations in this area should take full account of the needs of developing countries and of the objective of sustainable development . . . the EC has initiated an environment and sustainability review of the [WTO Millennium Round] . . .[55]

Several practical measures are underlined as tools for integration to achieve sustainable development, including: (i) Europe's Generalised System of Preferences (GSP), which allows for additional preferential treatment to countries that respect minimum social and environmental standards,[56] (ii) the Communication on Public Procurement, which integrates a chapter on the environment and on social issues,[57] and (iii) Protocol 10 to the *Lomé IV Convention*, as the first formal international agreement acknowledging the need for forest-certification systems for trade in tropical wood, based on internationally harmonized criteria and indicators.[58] As the Strategy notes:

> To be conducive to sustainable development, the regulatory framework should preserve the ability of host countries to regulate transparently and in a non-discriminatory way, the activity of the investors, foreign and domestic alike, on their respective territory and to pursue a stable business climate. This is particularly important to developing countries. In this respect, traditional provisions on special and differential treatment, such as exemptions and exceptions, or longer transitional periods, for developing countries may no longer suffice. Rather, the environment and sustainable development should be built into the regulations so that they can be implemented and applied by all countries.[59]

This policy direction was strengthened after the 2002 World Summit on Sustainable Develoment (WSSD). In the 2006 Renewed Sustainable Development Strategy (RSDS), the Council recognized that "the principle that sustainable development is to be integrated into policy-making at all levels,"[60] and committed to

---

55 EC, COM(2000)264, *supra* note 46.
56 EC Regulations No. 3281/94 and 1256/96 and Commission Communication COM (97)534/4 "Special Incentive Arrangements Concerning Labour Rights and Environmental Protection", October 1997.
57 Commission Communication "Public Procurement in the European Union" COM (98)143 final of 11 March 1998, http://ec.europa.eu/internal_market/publicprocurement/docs/green-papers/com-98-143_en.pdf.
58 EC, Agreement Amending the Fourth ACP-EC Convention of Lomé (Signed 4 November 1995) ACP-CE 2163/95, OJ L 156/3, Protocol 10, https://ec.europa.eu/europeaid/sites/devco/files/revised-lome4convention-1998_en.pdf. [Lomé IV].
59 EC, COM(2000)264, *supra* note 46.
60 Council of the European Union, Review of the EU Sustainable Development Strategy (EU SDS): Renewed Strategy, 10117/06 (9 June 2006), para 10, https://www.etuc.org/IMG/pdf/st10117.en06.pdf. [EU SDS 2006].

"promote sustainable development in the context of the WTO negotiations."[61] Additionally, the Council further mandated that:

> all EU institutions should ensure that major policy decisions are based on proposals that have undergone high quality Impact Assessment (IA), assessing in a balanced way the social, environmental and economic dimensions of sustainable development and taking into account the external dimension of sustainable development and the costs of inaction[62]

EU law and policy has continued to develop in this direction. Sustainable development was policy the basis of the 2007 reform of the Common Agricultural Policy of the European Union.[63] The Council in December 2009 conducted a second review of the SDS, highlighting progress made in mainstreaming SDS into external policies,[64] and confirming that sustainable development continued to be fundamental policy objective of the EU under the Lisbon Treaty,[65] with the President also re-affirmed that the SDS will "continue to provide a long-term vision and constitute the overarching policy framework for all Union policies and strategies."[66] In the EU's 2009 Regulation on its Generalised System of Preferences at Article 2, an exception is granted to guarantee special market access for goods and services from "beneficiary countries and territories" listed in Annex I (developing countries) which demonstrate "sustainable development and good governance."[67] At Article 8, the EU usefully details and further defines this commitment to sustainable development as, *inter alia*, having "ratified and effectively implemented all the conventions listed in Annex III,"[68] having provided "an undertaking to maintain the ratification of the conventions and their

---

61 EU SDS 2006, *supra* note 60, at p. 20.

62 Ibid. at para 11.

63 See EC, Green Paper, Adapting to Climate Change in Europe: Options for EU Action COM (2007) 354 final, 29 June 2007, at 14, http://eur-lex.europa.eu/legal-content/EN/TXT/HTML/?uri=URISERV:l28193&from=EN.

64 Commission Communication, "Mainstreaming Sustainable Development into EU Policies: 2009 Review of the European Union Strategy for Sustainable Development" COM(2009) 400 (24 July 2009), http://eur-lex.europa.eu/LexUriServ/LexUriServ.do?uri=COM:2009 :0400:FIN:en:PDF.

65 Council of the European Union, 2009 Review of the EU Sustainable Development Strategy (EU SDS): Presidency Strategy, 16818/09 (1 December 2009), http://register.consilium.europa. eu/doc/srv?l=EN&f=ST%2016818%202009%20INIT. [EU SDS 2009].

66 EU SDS 2009, *supra* note 65, at p.2.

67 EC, Council Regulation (EC) No 732/2008 of 22 July 2008 applying a scheme of generalized tariff preferences for the period from 1 January 2009 to 31 December 2011 and amending Regulations (EC) No 552/97, (EC) No 1933/2006 and Commission Regulations (EC) No 1100/2006 and (EC) No 964/2007, Official Journal L 211 , 06/08/2008 P. 0001–0039, Article 2 and 8, http://eur-lex.europa.eu/LexUriServ/LexUriServ.do?uri=OJ:L:2008:211:00 01:0039:EN:PDF [No 732/2008, *Generalised System of Preferences*]; The actual effect of this provision is limited, due to most countries already being tariff free under the terms of the Lome Convention.

68 No 732/2008, *supra* note 67, at art 8(1)(a).

implementing legislation and measures," and accepting "regular monitoring and review of its implementation record in accordance with the implementation provisions of the conventions it has ratified."[69] In 2010 the EU passed the 'Europe 2020' as an inclusive strategy for sustainable development which builds upon pre-existing strategic initiatives and establishes the mutually supportive principles of knowledge-centric smart, sustainable, and inclusive growth to guide the development agenda over the following decade.[70]

26.4 The ILA sustainable development principle on integration in EU court cases

The principle of integration has also been occasionally be used to determine competences in the EU and to balance environmental protection objectives against other competing fundamental values. As Advocate General Bot noted when summarized the case law in joined cases C204/12 to C208/12 *Essent Belgium NV v Vlaamse Reguleringsinstantie voor de Elektriciteits- enGasmarkt*:

> Express elevation of environmental protection to the level of an imperative requirement relating to public interest that may be invoked in order to justify measures that restrict the freedoms of movement even where such measures are discriminatory would, in my view, contribute to ensuring its pre-eminence over other considerations.
>
> Theoretical justification for such an outcome can, it seems to me, be found in the principle of integration, according to which environmental objectives, the transverse and fundamental nature of which have been noted by the Court,[71] should be taken into account in the definition and implementation of European Union policies. Although that principle does not require that priority should always be given to environmental protection, it does mean that the environmental objective may be routinely balanced against the European Union's other fundamental objectives.[72]

In the seminal case of *First Corporate Shipping AG* Advocate General Léger explained further the relationship of sustainable development and integration stating that 'sustainable development' is not equivalent to environmental interests

---

69 Ibid. at art 8(1)(b).

70 Commission Communication, "Europe 2020: A Strategy for Smart, Sustainable and Inclusive Growth" COM(2010) 2020 (3 March 2010), http://ec.europa.eu/eu2020/pdf/COMPLET%20EN%20BARROSO%20%20%20007%20-%20Europe%202020%20-%20EN%20version.pdf. [Europe 2020].

71 *Commission of the European Communities* v *Council of the European Union*, Case C-176/03, Judgment, EU:C:2005:7879, para 41–2, http://curia.europa.eu/juris/liste.jsf?language=en&num=C-176/03. [C-176/03].

72 A.G. Bot in Joined Cases C-204/12 to C-208/12, *Essent Belgium NV v Vlaamse Reguleringsinstantie voor de Elektriciteits- enGasmarkt*, 8 May 2013, ECLI: EU:C:2013:294, para 95–7 ; Jans, H. J., and Vedder, H.H.B., *European Environmental Law*, 4th edn (Groningen: European Law Publishing, 2011) 23.

being systematically preferred by the Community in accordance with Article 3 of the EC Treaty, but rather involves a necessary balance between various often competing interests being reconciled.[73] Advocate General Léger goes on to note the normative development in the EU including: (i) identification of its genesis originating in a Communication of the Commission of 24 March 1972 which stressed the importance of respecting the principle of 'integration' in implementation; (ii) indication that alignment of economic activities and environmental protection across the Community is in line with Article 2 of the EEC Treaty; (iii) explanation that 'sustainable development' which was defined by the Brundtland Report (1987) as "development which meets the needs of the present without compromising the capacity of future generations to meet their needs," and necessitating a coordinated policy response; and (iv) illustration that Article 130r(2) aims to reconcile 'sustainable development' through 'integration' requiring Community legislature to harmonize environmental measures based on a common integrated policy strategy.[74] Finally, in discussing the application of these principles, Advocate General Léger specified that policy design and implementation must observe the "objective of 'sustainable development' and the principle of 'integration'" based on an informed assessment of human activates in the area and a reconciliation between conservation of natural habitats and the necessary consequences to economic activities.[75]

The principle of integration has also been interpreted by the European Court of Justice (ECJ) in scoping Members legal obligations to undertake impact assessment.[76] In the 2010 *Wallonia Cases* the Advocate General of the ECJ noted that "[the environmental assessment of legislative measures] requires the contracting parties to endeavour to ensure that environmental, including health, concerns are *considered and integrated* to the extent appropriate in the preparation of their proposals for policies and legislation that are likely to have significant effects on the environment, including health. The aim in this context is . . . *to integrate the environment into the considerations in some form or other . . .*"[77] As noted by the

---

73 *The Queen v Secretary of State for the Environment, Transport and the Regions ex parte First Corporate Shipping Ltd, interveners: World Wide Fund for Nature UK (WWF) and Avon Wildlife Trust*, Case C-371/98 ECLI:EU:C:2000:108 (7 November 2000), http://curia.europa.eu/juris/liste.jsf?language=en&num=C-371/98# [First Corporate Shipping AG]; Opinion of Advocate General Léger delivered on 7 March 2000, para 54. [Leger Opinion].

74 Léger Opinion, *supra* note 73, para 55-7.

75 Ibid. at 58.

76 *Sweden v Commission of the European Communities* et al., Case T 229/04, (11 July 2007), http://curia.europa.eu/juris/showPdf.jsf?text=&docid=62401&pageIndex=0&doclang=EN&mode=lst&dir=&occ=first&part=1&cid=294508.

77 Opinion of Advocate General Kokott delivered on 4 March 2010, *Terre Wallonne ASBL (C-105/09) and Inter-Environnement Wallonie ASBL (C-110/09) v Régionwallonne*, ECR 2010 00000, para 44, http://curia.europa.eu/juris/liste.jsf?language=en&num=C-105/09# [Opinion, ECJ Wallonia Case]; Council Decision 2008/871/EC of 20 October 2008 on the approval, on behalf of the European Community, of the Protocol on Strategic Environmental Assessment to the 1991 UN/ECE Espoo Convention on Environmental Impact Assessment in a Transboundary Context (OJ 2008 L 308, p. 33) (emphasis added).

Court in *Wallonia*, "Significant effects on the environment can therefore be taken fully into account only if they are assessed in the case of all preparatory measures which may result in projects subsequently implemented having such effects."[78]

The Court of Justice has had certain limited occasions to interpret the objective of sustainable development. While over 224 judgments make reference to 'sustainable development,' the great majority of these cases react only in relation to a certain treaty article or directive/regulation. In other words, arguments based on the sustainable development objective, or which explain more thoroughly the idea of sustainable development, are limited to a few cases before 2012. In *Commission of the European Communities* v *Council of the European Union* Advocate General Ruiz-Jarabo Colomer explains that the concept of sustainable development as used in the EC Treaty is often linked to that of environment, thus:

> [a]lluding to a human dimension which cannot be overlooked when mention is made of protecting and improving the environment. In the geophysical medium which our natural surroundings represent, quality of life asserts itself as a citizenship right emanating from various factors, some of them physical (the rational use of resources and *sustainable development*) and some more intellectual (progress and cultural development).[79]

Advocate General Léger, in an earlier decision, discusses the objectives of sustainable development inherent in the common policy on the environment as needing to be "understood in the light of the rule that natural resources must be used in a rational manner. The emphasis here is on the necessity of implementing measures to preserve the quantity of natural resources."[80] In *Calí & Figli v SEPG*, Advocate General Cosmas in his opinion offers a definition of sustainable development as "development that meets current needs without prejudicing the ability of future generations to meet their needs," essentially adopting an idea reminiscent of those employed by the Brundtland Commission.[81]

Finally, in *Commission v Council*, the Commission asked the CJEU to annul the 2004 Council decision implementing the Joint Action 2002/589/ (the 'contested decision') in the area of Common Foreign and Security Policy mandating a European Union contribution to the Economic Community of West African States (ECOWAS)'s Moratorium on Small Arms and Light Weapons, and to

78 Opinion, ECJ Wallonia Case, *supra* note 77, at para 35.
79 Opinion of Advocate General Ruiz-JaraboColomer, Case C-176/03, *supra* note 71, at para. 66 (emphasis added).
80 *Kingdom of Spain v Council of the European Union*, Case C-36/98, Opinion of Advocate General Léger delivered on 16 May 2000, at para 77, http://curia.europa.eu/juris/liste.jsf?language=en&num=C-36/98.
81 *Diego Calí & Figli Srl v Servizi ecologici porto di Genova SpA (SEPG)*, Case C-343/95, Opinion of Advocate General Cosmas delivered on 10 December 1996, http://curia.europa.eu/juris/showPdf.jsf?text=&docid=100778&pageIndex=0&doclang=en&mode=req&dir=&occ=first&part=1&cid=600868. [Calí & Figli v SEPG].

declare it illegal and inapplicable.[82] The *Preamble* of the contested decision made a reference to sustainable development[83] and it was thus successfully argued by the Commission that this measure is not just a security measure but rather a development cooperation measure.[84] Up to 2012, in essence, judges have continued to respect the integration principle for sustainable development, in interpreting treaties and laws, and in clarifying the competences of the Union. While the case law does not yet correspond to the importance of sustainable development in the Treaties, is can safely be concluded that it is one of the principles that should inspire the activities of the various European institutions across sectors.

European institutions and legislation alike seem to have in mind a more all-encompassing idea of sustainable development. In fact, both in the treaties and in the CJEU jurisprudence, sustainable development as an informing principle or objective is recurrent not only in relation to the environment, but also with reference to economic growth and social policies and issues. With regards to this, the Commission has explained that there are three inter-related components in sustainable development: economic, social, and environmental.[85] Moreover, European Union institutions seem to be concerned about sustainable development both within European borders, and in the wider world as well (particularly, less developed countries).

26.5 The ILA sustainable development principle of precaution in EU court cases

The precautionary principle, which originates from Principle 15 of the Rio Declaration, was initially incorporated into the European framework via the Maastricht Treaty,[86] and is now found in Article 191(2) of the TFEU.[87] While listed under the Title XX relating to environment, the precautionary approach has been interpreted to apply to all actions relating to health and safety.[88] In *Sandoz*,

82 See case C-91/05 *Commission of the European Communities v Council of the European Union*, Judgment of the Court of 20 May 2008, para. 1.

83 "[t]he excessive and uncontrolled accumulation and spread of small arms and light weapons poses a threat to peace and security and reduces the prospects for sustainable development particularly in West Africa".

84 See case C-91/05 *supra* note 82, at para. 19.

85 Communication from the Commission to the European Parliament, the Council, the Economic and Social Committee and the Committee of the Regions "Towards a Global Partnership for Sustainable Development" COM(2002) 82 final, p. 6.

86 Treaty of Maastricht on European Union, OJ C 191 (29 July 1992), at Article 109i, 130r, http://europa.eu/eu-law/decision-making/treaties/pdf/treaty_on_european_union/treaty_on_european_union_en.pdf. [*Maastricht Treaty*].

87 TFEU 2010, *supra* note 12, at art 191(2): "Union policy on the environment shall aim at a high level of protection taking into account the diversity of situations in the various regions of the Union. It shall be based on the precautionary principle and on the principles that preventive action should be taken, that environmental damage should as a priority be rectified at source and that the polluter should pay."

88 *Artegodan GmbH v Commission of the European Communities*, Case T-74/00, 2002 E.C.R. II-04945, (28 November 2002) at para 183, http://eur-lex.europa.eu/legal-content/EN/TXT/PDF/?uri=CELEX:62000TJ0074&from=EN.

a pre-Maastricht case which focused on a State's ability to restrict the sale vitamin fortified food,[89] the Court of Justice in interpreting the free movement of goods provision recognized the ability of a State to require adequate proof of the safety of goods prior to market access.[90] In upholding the State's procedural discretion, the Court invoked the precautionary principle in principle if not in name. Following *Sandoz*, the precautionary principle was used to initiate various regulatory actions including: on industrial actions, costumer products, pharmaceuticals, and genetically modified organisms.[91]

While the TFEU makes reference to the precautionary principle, little further definition was provided by 2012. The preeminent case, *Pfizer Animal Health SA v Council* provides summary of applicable jurisprudence, specifies a procedure for evaluating scientific evidence in law making, and defines the evidentiary threshold of 'hypothetical risk' applicable to precaution.[92] First, the Court recognizes the longstanding legal validity of proactive institutional measures grounded in the precautionary approach in instances of scientific uncertainty relating to risks to human health.[93] Second, noting that the precautionary principle is invoked inevitably in cases of scientific uncertainty,[94] the Court stressed that to satisfy the precautionary principle, the preventative measures while not "fully demonstrated by conclusive science" is nonetheless adequately supported by available scientific data.[95] Third, in assessing the standard of risk relative to invoke the precautionary principle, the Court notes the need for a risk, based not on "mere hypotheses" nor requiring scientific confirmation.[96] This 'hypothetical approach' to risk is assessed by the public authority based on the specific circumstances and taking into account the possible adverse impacts, available remedies, and available scientific data.[97] Finally the Court reaffirmed the importance of deference to the

---

89 Case 174/82, Sandoz BV, 1983 E.C.R. 2445, at para 11, 20, http://stl.pku.edu.cn/wp-content/uploads/2014/04/5Patrick.pdf. [Sandoz].

90 *Sandoz, supra* note 89, at para 21–3.

91 Veerle Heyvaert, "Facing the Consequences of the Precautionary Principle in European Community Law" (2006) *European Law Review* 185, http://users.uoa.gr/~gdellis/IIA/2_Heyvaert2.pdf.

92 Case T-13/99, *Pfizer Animal Health SA v Council*, 2002 E.C.R. II- 03305, at para 160, http://curia.europa.eu/juris/showPdf.jsf?text=&docid=47642&pageIndex=0&doclang=en&mode=lst&dir=&occ=first&part=1&cid=629818. [*Pfizer*]

93 Ibid. at para 114–15, 139; See: *United Kingdom v Commission*, Case C-180/96, [1998] ECR 1-2265, para 100, [BSE judgment]; *National Farmers' Union and Others*, Case C-157/96, [1998] ECR I-2211, para 64. [NFU judgment]; *Fedesa and Others*, Case C-331/88, [1990] ECR I-4023; *Mondiet*, Case C-405/92 [1993] ECR I-6133; *APAS*, Case C-435/92, [1994] ECR I-67; *Spain v Council*, Case C-179/95, [1999] ECR I-6475; *Greenpeace France and Others*, Case C-6/99, [2000] ECR I-1651); By the Court of First Instance see in particular: *Bergaderm and Goupil v Commission*, Case T-199/96 , [1998] ECR II-2805; *P Bergaderm and Goupil v Commission*, Case C-352/98, [2000] ECR I-5291; The order of 30 June 1999 in *Pfizer Animal Health v Council*, C-13/99, [1999] ECR II-1964; The order of the President of the Court of First Instance of 30 June 1999 in *R Alpharma v Council*, Case T-70/99, [1999] ECR II-2027).

94 *Pfizer, supra* note 92, para 142.

95 Ibid. at para 144.

96 Ibid. at para 146.

97 Ibid. at para 152–53.

public authority noting that where the precautionary principle is applied, the fact that there remains scientific uncertainty or an inability to conduct a risk assessment does not inhibit a pubic authority to take preventative measures where such measures appear essential.[98]

In *Waddenvereniging and Vogelsbeschermingvereniging*, the Court in considering the environmental impact of mechanical cockle fishers in relation to Article 6 of the EU Habitats Directive,[99] found that where "doubt remained as to the absence of adverse effects . . . the competent will have to refuse authorization."[100] In light of the conservation objectives of the site, the competent national authority was found correct to only to authorize activity where it can be made certain there will be no adverse impacts.[101] The EU jurisprudence illustrates two key points: (i) the standard underlying the precautionary principle is defined by applicable legislation (i.e. The Habitats Directive, TFEU) and (ii) where uncertainty about the risks exists, the range of acceptable precautionary measures will be broad.

26.6 Conclusion

Certain lessons can be drawn from the experience of European law and policy in using the integration principle and the precautionary principle to promote more sustainable development. It is clear that sustainable development is a confirmed treaty objective of the EU. To achieve this objective, it is a well-recognized principle of European Law that environmental protection requirements must be integrated into the definition and implementation of the Union policies and activities, in particular with a view to promoting sustainable development. This principle as enshrined originally in the Treaty Establishing a European Community (EC Treaty) at Article 6, now found at Article 11 of the TFEU (Lisbon Treaty), has been given effect through many measures and regulations of the EU.[102] The principle of precaution is similarly established.

The principles are applied in process and substance to the external relations of the EU, and is relevant to the interpretation of the EU's economic policies, decisions and treaties. As noted, the EU was only required to integrate environmental considerations into its policies and actions, and this remains the focus of the Treaty provisions themselves. However, in practice over the past decade since the 2002 WSSD shaped the external dimensions of their SDS, the EU has

---

98 Ibid. at para 382, 386.

99 Council Directive 92/43/EEC of 21 May 1992 on the conservation of natural habitats and of wild fauna and flora (OJ 1992 L 206). [Habitats Directive].

100 *Landelijke Vereniging tot Behoud van de Waddenzee and Nederlandse Vereniging tot Bescherming van Vogels v Staatssecretaris van Landbouw, Natuurbeheer en Visserij, Coöperatieve Producentenorganisatie van de Nederlandse Kokkelvisserij UA*, Case C-127/02, [2004] ECR I-7448, para. 57, http://curia.europa.eu/juris/liste.jsf?language=en&num=C-127/02. [*Waddenvereniging and Vogelsbe schermingvereniging*].

101 *Waddenvereniging and Vogelsbeschermingvereniging*, *supra* note 100, para 59.

102 Treaty of EU, TFEU 2010, *supra* note 12; EU Charter of Fundamental Rights 2010, *supra* note 21; Pallemaerts, Herodes, Adellem *supra* note 24.

increasingly emphasized that both environmental *and social* considerations must be identified and taken into account. This point has been re-affirmed in 2002, 2006, 2007 and 2009, by both the Commission and Council, in numerous strategies, communications, and even regulations.[103] Furthermore, the EU SDS and other related policies identify EIA as a main procedural instrument for integration and precaution. Such EIAs are required for all international negotiations that might have economic, environmental or social impacts, such as new trade agreements. The measures in the EU's trade agreements may be interpreted in light of their commitment to integrate social and environmental dimensions into economic development. The EU has sought exceptions and exemptions from trade and investment rules to provide regulatory flexibility and accommodate environment and social development interests. Recently, the EU has been going further, committing through cooperation and trade incentives such as the GSP to promote improved environment and social standards for trading partners,[104] and even negotiating new instruments to enhance trade and investment in more sustainable goods and services.[105] Taken as a whole, these developments appear encouraging.

However, in light of the key tensions, it must be noted that while precaution can prevent risky activities current EU policies stop short of *requiring* the EC to actually mitigate the negative environmental impacts identified in SIAs, a position that appears less than fully respectful of the precaution principle, and the integration principle laid out in global policy debates, and in the *Iron Rhine* decision.[106] The EIA process must identify potential impacts, and the EC is obliged to report on what will be done. But in the way that Article 11 of the TFEU has been interpreted, the EU does not, at present, yet seem to *require* substantive measures be taken to ensure that negative environmental and social impacts are actually mitigated, or even significantly reduced. As noted in the EU Communication on Impact Assessment, "Impact Assessment is an aid to decision-making, not a

103 Current Sustainable Development Strategy (2006): European Council DOC 10917/06; 2009 Review of the EU Sustainable Development Strategy COM (2009) 400; Commission Communication "On the Review of the Sustainable Development Strategy: A Platform for Action" COM(2005) 658 final; Commission Communication "Draft Declaration on Guiding Principles for Sustainable Development" COM(2005) 218 final, 25.5.2005; Commission Communication "The 2005 Review of the EU Sustainable Development Strategy: Initial Stocktaking and Future Orientations" COM(2005) 37, 9.2.2005.

104 EC Regulations No. 3281/94 and 1256/96 and Commission Communication COM (97)534/4 "Special Incentive Arrangements Concerning Labour Rights and Environmental Protection", October 1997; Laura Beke and Nicolas Hachez, "The EU GSP: A Preference for Human Rights and Good Governance? The Case of Myanmar" (March 2015) KU Leuven Working Paper No. 155, https://ghum.kuleuven.be/ggs/publications/working_papers/new_series/wp151-160/wp155-beke-hachez.pdf.

105 Lomé IV, *supra* note 58, Protocol 10; European Commission, *Trade, Growth and World Affairs: Trade Policy as a Core Component of EUs 2020 Strategy* (November 2010), http://trade.ec.europa.eu/doclib/docs/2010/november/tradoc_146955.pdf.

106 *Award in the Arbitration regarding the Iron Rhine ("Ijzeren Rijn") Railway between the Kingdom of Belgium and the Kingdom of the Netherlands*, decision of 24 May 2005, Reports of International Arbitral Awards XXVII pp.35–125, http://legal.un.org/riaa/cases/vol_XXVII/35-125.pdf.

substitute for political judgment."[107] At present, "[a]n impact assessment will not necessarily generate clear cut conclusions or recommendations. It does, however, provide an important input by informing decision-makers of the consequences of policy choices."[108] As such, it seems that the EU is bound to conduct an *ex ante* assessment of a new economic agreement, examining both impacts in Europe and in the partners and also to explain what measures are being taken to address environmental and social challenges that have been identified in the assessment.[109] But it is not required to mitigate the social or environmental problems that the change in rules occasioned by the accord might cause.

Are precaution and integration only procedural in the EU after all, or are there also substantive mechanisms, at least for economic law and policy, provisions that can be adopted in a trade or investment treaty to accommodate trade-related environmental and social concerns? Current European experience does offer certain insights vis-à-vis integration of environmental and social concerns achieve sustainable development.

First, in the European context, guided by a binding integration principle, economic growth is not meant to cause direct material environmental damage through increases in unsustainable economic development activities, and this principle is slowly extending to social development in practice. Nor are direct normative impacts that encourage disallowing or 'chilling' environment and social development laws and measures expected. Rather, European law and related policies require the EC to conduct sustainability impact assessments, attempt to provide exceptions and exemptions in economic policies, and call for measures to ensure that economic policies, environment and development are mutually supportive. Second, in the context of the integration principle, Europe economic policies and agreements are not intended to create incentives for economic growth that will add to serious environmental and social problems which already exist at the domestic level. Rather, at least in European law and related policies, there is an emphasis on the need for development cooperation, for technical assistance, and for international dialogue to ensure that economic policy and law will achieve sustainable development objectives, and will strengthen related social and environmental standards and laws in each sector.

Third, in the context of both precaution and integration principles, economic policies and treaties are not intended to encourage unsustainable growth in highly polluting or exploitative sectors, or stimulate – through pollution havens and other developments – the spread of industries that are being phased out of

---

107 EC, COM(2002)276, *supra* note 49.

108 Ibid. at 49.

109 Ibid. at 49., noting that: "Sometimes the impact assessment may point towards a preferred basic approach and the optimal policy instrument early in the process. Subsequent analysis will then focus on improving the effectiveness of the proposal in terms of changes introduced to key design parameters or stringency levels. It may also identify accompanying measures to maximize positive and minimize negative impacts. The reasons for the most preferred policy option will be clearly outlined in the Impact Assessment Report. Alternative instruments that meet the same set of policy objective(s) should always be considered at an early stage in the preparation of policy proposals."

most developed country economies. Rather, European law and policy calls for increased trade and investment in cleaner low-carbon technologies, in environmental goods and services, and in sustainably managed natural resources such as forest products. Indeed, the European GSP Regulations provide direct market access incentives aimed specifically at encouraging sustainable development and good governance in developing countries. Up to 2012, such steps appear to move beyond procedural questions of impact assessment or policy coherence, and into substantive legal measures to encourage sustainable development through new economic rules granting market access.[110] This suggests that rather than imposing external standards on developing country partners through sanctions, the EU may be taking initial steps to link the ratification and implementation of multilaterally negotiated accords on environment, human rights and other aspects of sustainable development with economic policy and preferences granted. While inevitably progress remains, the integration and precautionary principles are alive and well in EU legislation and jurisprudence in support of broader sustainable development principles.

---

110 See, in preparation, COM(2004) 461 final: Communication from the Commission to the Council, the European Parliament and the European Economic and Social Committee of 7 July 2004 entitled "Developing Countries, International Trade and Sustainable Development: The Function of the Community's Generalized System of Preferences (GSP) for the Ten-year Period from 2006 to 2015."

27 The principles of integration and precaution in the European legal regimes

Zsuzanna Horváth

27.1 Introduction

Both principles of integration and precaution have their roots in international environmental law serving sustainable development. Although sustainable development has not yet reached the status of a legally binding norm or a principle of international customary law, there are several international treaties and soft law instruments accepting and expressing the need for economic and social development, which is 'sustainable' in the sense that it reconciles developmental interests with the sound management of environmental resources on which development depends, so that it can last over the long term. On the other hand, there are further principles widely accepted in international law, the aim of which is to promote sustainable development, for example in the area of environmental protection.[1] They are expressed in international treaties and national legislation, in soft law documents, like declarations, or various strategy papers, and they are often used by international and national courts as a basis for their judgments. Some of these principles aiming to reach sustainable development are so generally accepted and supported that they are being recognized as customary international rules.[2]

The 2002 New Delhi Declaration of Principles of International Law Relating to Sustainable Development adopted by the ILA Resolution 3/2002 identified seven principles of international law the application and further development of which would enhance the effectiveness of efforts in pursuing sustainable development. Among these, the general principle of integration is fundamental for the achievement of sustainable development, since it strongly connects economic and social development with environmental protection. Among the more special ones, the precautionary approach is also considered as a key principle in this respect, since it requires early action in preventing damages in the environment

---

1 For a detailed review of the origins, development and status of sustainable development in international law see Marie-Claire Cordonier Segger, 'Sustainable Development in International Law' in Hans Christian Bugge and Christina Voigt, eds., *Sustainable Development in International and National Law* (Groningen: Europa Law Publishing 2008).
2 Ibid. at 163.

and human health even in the absence of scientific certainty on the consequences of economic activities.[3]

Sustainable development and many of the supporting principles grouped around this concept are also generally accepted and promoted in the European Union: several policy documents, hard and soft law instruments, have been adopted by the EU institutions in order to reconcile and balance economic, social and environmental interests in various fields of the European integration. Also, the European Courts show readiness to apply these principles in interpreting provisions of primary and secondary sources of EU law, in answering questions put by national courts in preliminary ruling procedures, in deciding on the legality of the EU institutions' acts or in judging the Member States' infringements in application of EU law.

In 2005, within the framework of its sustainable development process, the EU adopted a declaration on guiding principles that were to govern its strategy. The integration of environmental considerations into economic and social policies and the precautionary principle are also included within the 10 principles identified.[4]

The aim of this chapter is to show how the principles of environmental integration and precaution emerged in EU law and how they are understood and interpreted by EU institutions, scholars and EU Courts, through the examination of EU Treaties and the most important case law of the European Court of Justice and the General Court (the former Court of First Instance). For an understanding of the legal and judicial interpretations and application of these principles and of the role they play in fostering environmental protection and sustainable development in the EU, the most important policy documents will also be examined.

27.2 Sustainable development, its key objectives and guiding principles in the European Union

27.2.1 Sustainable development in EU policy documents

The concept of sustainable development was initially formulated as a political priority in its Fifth Environmental Action Programme entitled 'Towards Sustainability' adopted in 1993,[5] following the United Nations Conference on Environment and Development held in Rio de Janeiro in 1992. The Fifth

---

3 ILA Resolution 3/2002: *New Delhi Declaration of Principles of International Law Relating to Sustainable Development*, in ILA, 'Report of the Seventieth Conference', New Delhi (London: ILA, 2002) <http://www.ila-hg.org> accessed 5 October 2016 (New Delhi Declaration).
4 European Council, *Declaration on Guiding Principles for Sustainable Development*, Annex I to the Presidency Conclusions of the Brussels European Council 16 and 17 June 2005, 10255/1/05REV 1, 2005, at 28–30. See also the Commission's Communication on the draft declaration, COM(2005) 218.
5 Resolution of the Council and the Representatives of the Governments of the Member States on the Community programme of policy and action in relation to the environment and sustainable development ('Towards Sustainability' – the Fifth Environmental Action Programme), OJ C 138, 17 May 1993 1.

Environmental Action Programme explicitly refers to the Rio Declaration which lists several principles, and to Agenda 21, the programme for action to reach sustainable development, both adopted by the Rio Conference.[6] Thus, it might be considered as the implementation of the *Agenda 21*, at the EU level. The programme calls sustainable development a 'principle', lifting it into the range of the EU environmental policy principles. However, it is clear from the wording that the EU considered sustainable development as a policy and strategy goal for not only its environmental but also other EU policies. It states that the 'word "sustainable" is intended to reflect a policy and strategy for continued economic and social development without the detriment of the environment and the natural resources on the quality of which continued human activity and further development depend'. The Programme recalls the definition given by the World Commission on Environment and Development (WCED) Bruntland Report word by word, according to which 'Sustainable development is development that meets the needs of the present without compromising the ability of future generations to meet their own needs',[7] which has become the most often cited definition, and which has been reinforced by the Principle 1 and 3 of the Rio Declaration. The drafters consider the Programme a 'turning point for the Community' since 'the reconciliation of environment and development is one of the principal challenges facing the Community and the world at large in the 1990s'. They designed it:

> Not for the Community alone, nor one geared towards environmentalists alone. It provides a new approach to the environment and to economic and social activity and development, and requires positive will at all levels of the political and corporate spectrums, and the involvement of all members of the public active as citizens and consumers in order to make it work.[8]

The Sixth Environmental Action Programme of the Union entitled 'Our Future, Our Choice' is also based on the concept of sustainable development; it forms 'a basis for the environmental dimension of the European Sustainable Development Strategy'.[9] In its draft, the Commission considers sustainable development as 'a major opportunity for post-industrial Europe', and it states that 'sustainable development is more than a clean environment. The social and economic

---

6 See 'The Rio Declaration on Environment and Development' and the '*Agenda 21*' introduced and commented by Stanley P. Johnson, *The Earth Summit, The United Nations Conference on Environment and Development (UNCED)* (London: Graham & Trotman, 1993).

7 Report of the World Commission on Environment and Development, *Our Common Future*, Chapter 2: Towards Sustainable Development, point 1, UN Doc. A/42/427, <http://www.un-documents.net/ocf-02.htm#I> accessed 9 April 2011.

8 The Fifth Environmental Action Programme of the EU, *supra* note 6 at 12, 18.

9 1600/2002 Decision of the European Parliament and of the Council laying down the Sixth Community Environment Action Programme, Art. 2, OJ L 242, 10 September 2002, 1.

implications of environmental action must be taken into account when pursuing sustainable development'.[10]

The EU started to develop its Sustainable Development Strategy in 2000, when the European Council in Lisbon 'set itself a new strategic goal for the next decade: to become the most competitive and dynamic knowledge-based economy in the world, capable of sustainable economic growth with more and better jobs and greater social cohesion'. It presented a 10-year programme and action plan, which was based, first of all, on the development of the economic and social pillar.[11] In 2002 the European Council in its Gothenburg meeting adopted the Sustainable Development Strategy of the European Union, which completed the Lisbon Strategy by including an environmental dimension, according to which sustainable development 'requires dealing with economic, social and environmental policies in a mutually reinforcing way' and that this strategy 'is based on the principle that the economic, social and environmental effects of all policies should be examined in a coordinated way and taken into account in decision-making'.[12] According to the Commission, the EU Sustainable Development Strategy 'recognizes that in the long term, economic growth, social cohesion and environmental protection must go hand in hand'.[13] By adding the missing environmental dimension to the concept, the EU accepted the same 'three pillar approach' which was strongly emphasized by the Johannesburg Declaration on Sustainable Development adopted at the World Summit on Sustainable Development in 2002, and which considered economic development, social development and environmental protection as 'interdependent and mutually reinforcing pillars of sustainable development'.[14]

Based on the Commission's stocktaking of progress made in this area,[15] the EU strategy was renewed in 2006. The Renewed EU Sustainable Development Strategy highlighted that 'many unsustainable trends in relation to climate change and energy use, threats to public health, poverty and social exclusion, demographic pressure and ageing, management of natural resources, biodiversity loss, land use and transport still persist and new challenges are arising', therefore it required urgent action. The European Council reinforced the EU commitment to sustainable

10 Commission Communication on the Sixth Environment Action Programme of the European Community, Environment 2010: Our Future, Our Choice, COM (2001) 32, Brussels, 24 January 2001, 1, at 11.

11 Presidency Conclusions, Lisbon European Council, 23–24. March 2000, see 'The Way Forward' point I.5 <http://www.consilium.europa.eu/uedocs/cms_data/docs/pressdata/en/ec/00100-r1.en0.htm> accessed 9 April 2011.

12 European Council, Presidency Conclusions – Göteborg, 15 and 16 June 2001, SN 200/1/01 REV 1.

13 Commission Communication, A Sustainable Europe for a Better World: A European Strategy for Sustainable Development, COM (2001) 264, Brussels, 15 May 2001, at 2.

14 The Johannesburg Declaration on Sustainable Development, at point 5. At point 8 it reaffirms the Rio commitment <http://www.un.org/jsummit/html/documents/summit_docs/131302_wssd_report_reissued.pdf> accessed 9 April 2011.

15 See, e.g. Commission Communication on the Review of the Sustainable Development Strategy, A Platform for Action, COM (2005) 658, Brussels, 13 December 2005.

development, which 'is an overarching objective of the European Union set out in the Treaty, governing all the Union's policies and activities'. The renewed strategy aims, *inter alia*, at a continuous improvement of quality of life for present and future generations, promotion of effective management of natural resources, economic prosperity, environmental protection and social cohesion. The new strategy reproduces the principles and objectives adopted in 2005, and furthermore sets out tasks and describes necessary actions for various policy fields.[16]

In 2009, the strategy was reviewed again, with a view to mainstream it into EU policies. The Commission, in reflection of the economic and financial crisis affecting all sectors, considered it crucial to 'turn the crisis into an opportunity to address financial and ecological sustainability and develop a dynamic low-carbon and resource efficient, knowledge-based, socially inclusive society'. The focus is on 'green growth', since green measures help to revive the economy and create jobs, stimulate new technologies and reduce the impact on climate change, the depletion of natural resources and the degradation of ecosystems. After giving an overview of the progress in the EU strategy, the Commission states that at the EU level, sustainable development is primarily promoted in the context of individual EU policies, and the EU strategy itself plays a central role in promoting the overall objective and guidance for them. Taking sustainable development into the future, the strategy should focus, *inter alia*, on a low-input economy, energy and resource efficient technologies, sustainable transport and shifts towards sustainable consumption behaviour, intensified environmental efforts for the protection of biodiversity, water and natural resources. It emphasizes that 'degradation of ecosystems not only reduces the quality of our lives and the lives of future generations, it also stands in the way of sustainable, long-term economic development.'[17] Adopting these findings and suggestions for the future, the European Council repeatedly stated that the current developments in many respects are not sustainable and that the limits on the carrying capacity of the earth are being exceeded. The European Council urges the necessary reform of the EU Sustainable Development Strategy, which remains a long term vision and an overarching policy framework providing guidance for all EU policies and strategies, with a time frame up to 2050.[18]

Since the 10-year period for the implementation of the EU Lisbon Strategy ended in 2010, a new strategy for jobs and growth was put forward, entitled 'Europe 2020'. This new strategy is intended to move European economies out from the crisis and to lift the EU onto a new, more sustainable growth path. Three priorities of 'Europe 2020' are defined: smart growth – development of an economy based on knowledge and innovation; sustainable growth – promoting a more

16 European Council, Presidency Conclusions – 15/16 June 2006, 10633/1/06 REV 1, at point 17. See for details, Council of the European Union, Review of the EU Sustainable Development Strategy (EU SDS) – Renewed Strategy, 10917/06, Brussels, 26 June 2006.
17 Commission Communication, Mainstreaming sustainable development into EU policies: Review of the European Union Strategy for Sustainable Development, COM (2009) 400, Brussels, 24 July 2009, at 1–2, 13–15.
18 European Council 2009 Review of the EU Sustainable Development Strategy, Presidency Report 16818/09, Brussels, 1 December, 2009.

resource efficient, greener and more competitive economy; and inclusive growth – fostering a high-employment economy delivering social and territorial cohesion. For the achievement of this aim, the Commission proposed headline targets for the employment rate, investments for research and development, education and fighting poverty, and developed 'flagship initiatives'.[19] Adopting the 'Europe 2020', the European Council emphasized the importance of financial stability and structural reforms to put the economy back on the path of sustainable growth.[20] It might be noted here that although the new strategy aims at sustainability in the European development, it lays more stress on the economic objectives than on the social and environmental ones. It would be important to find a better synergy between the cross-cutting priority strategies of the European Union, such as the 'Europe 2020' and the Sustainable Development Strategy.[21]

27.2.2 Key objectives and guiding principles for sustainable development

The 2006 review of the EU Sustainable Development Strategy is based on the objectives and principles adopted in 2005; these have been repeatedly endorsed by subsequent policy documents. The Commission and the Council defined four key objectives for sustainable development: environmental protection; social equity and cohesion; economic prosperity; and meeting international responsibilities. Ten principles for guiding the EU sustainable development policy have been defined: promotion and protection of fundamental rights; intra and intergenerational equity; open and democratic society; involvement of citizens; involvement of business and social partners; policy coherence and governance; policy integration; the use of best available knowledge; the precautionary principle; and the polluters pay principle.

27.2.3 Sustainable development in the EU Treaties[22]

The Preamble of the Treaty on European Union (TEU) in its recital 9 refers to the three pillars of sustainable development, as the objective of the Union:

> Determined to promote economic and social progress for their peoples, taking into account the principle of sustainable development and within the context of the accomplishment of the internal market and of reinforced cohesion and environmental protection, and to implement policies ensuring

---

19 Commission Communication on Europe 2020: A Strategy for Smart, Sustainable and Inclusive Growth, COM (2010) 2020, Brussels, 3 March 2010, at 3–4, 8–9.

20 European Council, Conclusions, EUCO 13/10, Brussels, 17 June 2010.

21 According to the Commission, merging of these strategies does not seem feasible given the different roles they fulfil, see *supra* note 18, at 13–14. The Council also called for the enhancement of the links and synergies between the two strategies, see *supra* note 19.

22 Treaty on the European Union (TEU) and Treaty on the Functioning of the European Union (TFEU) (as resulted from the Lisbon Treaty amendments, signed on 13 December 2007 and entered into force on 1 December 2009), European Union, *Consolidated Treaties, Charter of Fundamental Rights* (Luxembourg: Publications Office of the European Union 2010).

that advances in economic integration are accompanied by parallel progress in other fields.

According to Article 3 of the TEU:

> The Union . . . shall work for the sustainable development of Europe based on balanced economic growth and price stability, a highly competitive social market economy, aiming at full employment and social progress, and a high level of protection and improvement of the quality of the environment (paragraph 3). 'In its relations with the wider world, the Union shall . . . contribute to the sustainable development of the Earth' (paragraph 5).

There is only one reference to the concept of sustainable development in the Treaty on the Functioning of the European Union (TFEU) in Article 11 on the integration of environmental requirements into the Union's policies, 'with a view to promoting sustainable development'. Sustainable development, as a principle or objective, however, is not mentioned in the Environment Title of the TFEU, where Article 191 lists the objectives, principles, and parameters for the environmental policy of the Union.

It should be mentioned here that Article 6 of the TEU accepted the Charter of Fundamental Rights of the European Union as having the same legal value as the Treaties. Grouping around the solidarity rights, this Charter refers to sustainable development as a principle, under the title Environmental protection (Article 37): 'A high level of environmental protection and the improvement of the quality of the environment must be integrated into the policies of the Union and ensured in accordance with the principle of sustainable development'.

27.3 Integration of environmental requirements into other EU policies

27.3.1 International origins

The principle of environmental integration has its roots in the international environmental policy. The 1972 Stockholm Declaration already called for an integrated approach: according to Principle 13:

> In order to achieve a more rational management of resources and thus to improve the environment, States should adopt an integrated and coordinated approach to their development planning so as to ensure that development is compatible with the need to protect and improve environment for the benefit of their population.[23]

---

23 UNEP, Stockholm Declaration of the United Nations Conference on the Human Environment, Principle 13, <http://www.unep.org/Documents.Multilingual/Default.asp?DocumentID=97 &ArticleID=1503&l=en> accessed 9 April 2011.

The 1992 Rio Declaration formulated as Principle 4 that '[i]n order to achieve sustainable development, environmental protection shall constitute an integral part of the development process and cannot be considered in isolation from it'. *Agenda 21* contains a whole chapter (Chapter 8) on integrating environment and development in decision-making, in which it explains the objectives and activities for policy-making, legislation, use of economic instruments, environmental accounting and for means of implementation.[24] The Johannesburg Declaration on Sustainable Development and the Johannesburg Plan of Implementation adopted at the follow up World Summit on Sustainable Development in 2002, reaffirming the commitments expressed in the Rio Declaration and in *Agenda 21*, are strongly permeated by the requirement not only of the integration of environmental requirements into other fields, but of the integration among all the three pillars of sustainable development.[25]

The ILA New Delhi Declaration of Principles of International Law Relating to Sustainable Development presented at the Johannesburg World Summit is a comprehensive collection of the most important guiding principles of international law on sustainable development.[26]

The New Delhi Declaration entitles the Principle 7 as '[t]he principle of integration and interrelationship, in particular in relation to human rights and social, economic and environmental objectives'. It reflects the interdependence among various aspects of sustainable development, which represents a broader understanding of the integration principle than that of requiring the integration of environmental requirements into other – first of all economic – policies. According to the Centre for International Sustainable Development Law (CISDL) commentary on the integration principle,

> States should ensure that social and economic development decisions do not disregard environmental considerations, and not undertake environmental protection without taking into account relevant social and economic implications'. This emphasizes the responsibility of environmental policymakers and regulators as well, so as to duly calculate the impact of environmental decisions on social and economic policies, which is called the 'reverse sustainable development obligation.[27]

---

24 'Rio Declaration on Environment and Development', and '*Agenda 21*' Report of the United Nations Conference on Environment and Development (Annex I) UN Doc A/CONF.151/26 (Vol I). See *supra* note 7.

25 Johannesburg Declaration on Sustainable Development and Johannesburg Plan of Implementation, adopted at the 17th plenary meeting of the World Summit on Sustainable Development (4 September 2002) A/CONF.199/20 <http://www.un.org/esa/sustdev/documents/WSSD_POI_PD/English/POI_PD.htm> accessed 5 October 2016.

26 See *supra* note 4. See also Marie-Claire Cordonier Segger, 'Sustainable Development in International Law' *supra* note 2, and the 'Commentary' by Nico Schrijver in Marie-Claire Cordonier Segger and H.E. Judge Christopher Gregory Weeramantry, eds., *Sustainable Justice Reconciling Economic, Social and Environmental Law* (Leiden: Martinus Nijhoff, 2005) 549–52.

27 Text of Brief Commentaries, at point 7 <http://cisdl.org/public/docs/new_delhi_declaration.pdf> accessed 9 April 2011.

The integration principle is considered as a general principle that 'serves as the very backbone' of the concept of sustainable development.[28]

The integration principle is aimed at not only by policy declarations but by several international treaties and agreements. It is furthermore referred to by decisions of international courts.[29]

27.3.2 *The development of the integration principle in the European Union*

The concept of integration appeared for the first time in the First Environmental Action programme of the European Community, although it was not listed as one of the then 11 principles of its newly established environmental policy. Rather, it was formulated as a requirement for the Community activities to take account of concern for the protection and improvement of the environment, in the elaboration and implementation of these policies.[30] The Third Action Programme, by listing those policy fields where greater awareness of the environmental dimension could be achieved, called for the creation of an overall strategy for integration.[31] The Fifth Action Programme required a considerable change in almost all major policy areas of the EU to achieve sustainable development. The full integration of environmental protection requirements into the definition and implementation of other Community policies was considered as the necessary instrument, a 'basic strategy' in bringing about these changes. For the selected sectors (manufacturing industry, energy, transport, agriculture and tourism) having a particularly significant impact on the environment as a whole, it set out tasks and fixed targets.[32] The Sixth Action Programme is strongly based on the necessity of the integration of environmental requirements into all policies and actions and of the contribution to the sustainable development in the EU and also in its future Member States. Among its strategic approaches it emphasizes the necessity of further efforts for integration of environmental protection requirements into the preparation, definition and implementation of EU policies and activities in different policy sectors.[33]

---

28 See the ILA Final Conference Report New Delhi 2002 'Fifth and Final Report Searching for the Contours of International Law in the Field of Sustainable Development' at 7 <http://www.ila-hq.org/en/committees/index.cfm/cid/25> accessed 9 April 2011.

29 For example, the UN Framework Convention on Climate Change, or the UN Convention on Biological Diversity. For an analysis see Sébastien Jodoin, The Principle of Integration and Interrelationship in Relation to Human Rights and Social, Economic and Environmental Objectives, CISDL Draft Working Paper Montreal, 2005 <http://www.worldfuturecouncil.org/fileadmin/user_upload/papers/CISDL_P6_Integration.pdf> accessed 9 April 2011.

30 OJ C 112, 20 December 1973, 1, at 10–11.

31 OJ C 139, 13 June 1977, 1, at 5–6.

32 The Fifth Environmental Action Programme, *supra* note 5. The Decision 2179/98 on the revision of the programme listed the environmental integration among its key priorities, and urged for a more consistent approach in its implementation. OJ L 275, 10 October 1998, 1, at 3–6.

33 The Sixth Environmental Action Programme entitled 'Environment 2010: Our Future, Our Choice', *supra* note 10 at 2–5.

The EU started to develop its integration strategy, the so-called 'Cardiff Process', in 1998, with the aim to put the integration requirement – already enshrined by the Treaty – into practice. The Commission stated that the traditional vertical approach of environmental regulation could only partly solve the problems, and that the integration of environmental considerations into other polices is no longer an option but an obligation. Therefore it called for a new strategy based on horizontal approach providing for guidelines for the EU institutions to properly integrate environmental dimension into other policies. These include, *inter alia*, integrating the environment into all activities by the Institutions; a review of existing policies; and introduction of strategies for action in key areas.[34] In June 1998 the European Council in its meeting in Cardiff adopted the integration strategy, and invited 'all relevant formations of the Council to establish their own strategies for giving effect to environmental integration and sustainable development within their respective policy areas.'[35] It called the Transport, Energy and Agriculture Councils to start this process.[36] Later on further sector strategies were developed in the field of enterprises (industry), development, internal market, economic and financial affairs, trade and external relations, fisheries, cohesion policy, employment, research and economic recovery. In 2004 the Commission evaluated the results of the Cardiff Process for the first time, giving a detailed analysis of integration strategies and measures adopted so far for their implementation. This stocktaking, while presenting positive results, admitted that this process suffered from several shortcomings and therefore, should be revitalized. The Commission called for an improvement of consistency of these strategies, for a strengthening of political commitment, for an improvement of implementation and review mechanisms, for clearer priorities, and for adopting a strategic forward looking approach.[37] The Cardiff Process has contributed to the lifting of integration higher in political agenda within the EU. The progress made in this area is regularly discussed at European Council meetings, and, because of their interrelations, together with the results of the EU Sustainable Development Strategy. Therefore, the strengthening of the integration process is called for in almost all political documents in relation to sustainable development.

27.3.3 The integration principle in the EU Treaties

The integration principle was inserted into the EC Treaty for the first time by the Single European Act in 1987, when the amended Treaty acknowledged the Community's competence in environmental policy, and established a 'constitutional basis' for action at European level. In the Environment Title, Article

---

34 Commission Communication, Partnership for Integration: A Strategy for Integrating Environment into EU Policies, Cardiff – June 1998, COM (98) 333, Brussels, 27 May 1998.

35 European Council, Presidency Conclusions, Cardiff, 15–16 June 1998, SN 150/1/98 REV 1, at point 34.

36 Ibid. at point 34.

37 Commission, Integrating Environmental Considerations into Other Policy Areas: A Stocktaking of the Cardiff Process, COM (2004) 394, Brussels, 1 June 2004, at 31–32.

130r paragraph 2 was formulated without using the word 'integration'; it stated that 'environmental protection requirements shall be a component of other Community policies'. The Maastricht Treaty amendments in 1992 reformulated the wording as 'environmental protection requirements must be integrated into the definition and implementation of other Community policies'. The 1999 Amsterdam Treaty amendments further strengthened the role of environmental policy among the other policies of the EU: it defined sustainable development, the high level of protection and the improvement of the quality of the environment as objectives for the EU. The Amsterdam Treaty gave more weight to the principle of integration by moving it from the Environmental Title to the front of the Treaty, where the principles for the EU are listed, and by adding the promotion of sustainable development as the final objective of the integration principle in Article 6. Consequently, environmental integration cannot be considered as a goal in itself, but a means to achieve sustainable development.[38]

The Lisbon Treaty amendments, which came into force in 2009, have not changed either its position in the Treaty or the definition of the provision on the integration principle. According to Article 11 of the TFEU, 'Environmental protection requirements must be integrated into the definition and implementation of the Union's policies and activities, in particular with a view to promoting sustainable development.' The accommodation of the integration requirement at such a prominent place of the Treaty shows its general character,[39] referring not only to environmental but to all other sector policies. Integration can still be considered as the most important principle governing the EU environmental policy, since it strongly links the environmental policy and all the other policies of the EU together.[40] Indeed, it reflects the recognition that environmental policy alone cannot improve the environment, the degradation of which is caused by other – mainly economic – policies, such as industry, agriculture, transport and so on. To reduce the harmful effects of these policies on the environment a continuous 'greening' of these policies is needed.[41] The integration of environmental considerations into other policies means that those policies have to set and achieve environmental objectives as their own ones, within their sector specific objectives.

According to the wording of Article 11 TFEU the integration requirements seem to be narrower in its scope than the understanding of the principle in international documents mentioned above. However, it should be added, that this

---

38 In an evaluation of achievements of sustainable development in the EC policies, Ludwig Krämer suggests a reconsideration of this Treaty requirement, since sustainable development and environmental protection can only be achieved by a better and more serious implementation of the integration requirement, see 'Sustainable Development in EC Law' in Hans Christian Bugge and Christina Voigt, *supra* note 2, at 394.

39 André Nolkaemper, 'Three Conceptions of the Integration Principle in International Environmental Law' in Andrea Lenschow, ed., *Environmental Policy Integration, Greening Sectoral Policies in Europe* (London: Earthscan 2002) 28–31.

40 Ludwig Krämer, *EC Environmental Law*, 6th edn (London: Sweet & Maxwell, 2007) 390.

41 Ibid. at 21.

provision has to be read in conjunction with the Article 191 TFEU, which lists the objectives, principles and parameters that are to be taken into account in preparing EU environmental policy. These together constitute the 'environmental requirements',[42] among which the economic and social development of the Union as a whole and the balanced development of its region have to be underlined here.

The wording of the Article 11 TFEU indicates that integration is more than a political guideline: it is a rule that must be applied.[43] It is widely accepted that the principle is addressed not only to the EU institutions when they formulate policy measures and adopt legal acts, but also to the Member States when they implement EU legislation or when they are allowed to depart from EU rules applying safeguard measures provided by the Treaty.[44] Although the academic interpretations vary on the question of whether the integration requirement in the Treaty is a legal obligation or a political guideline,[45] it is accepted that environmental objectives and principles do not have a priority over other policies; there is a need to find a balance between them. This means that the same weight has to be given to environmental protection as to the other sector specific objectives of the EU. In conflict situations the most important question is, perhaps, enforceability: to what extent integration requirements bind the institutions, and whether an act that does not integrate environmental requirements can be considered void. The case law of the European Courts shows that the EU institutions have wide discretionary power in the application of environmental principles, thus challenging the legitimacy of an act will only be successful in exceptional cases.[46]

27.3.4 Application of the integration principle by the European Court of Justice

The European Court of Justice (ECJ) plays an important role in the development of European environmental law, accepting and strengthening its central role in the European economic and political integration. By accepting the European Community's environmental competence, balancing the economic interest in free movement of goods and environmental interests, broadening the legal basis for environmental acts, and strengthening the implementation of environmental law by the Member States, the ECJ shows its strong commitment towards environmental protection. Therefore, it has been considered as an environmental

---

42 Ludwig Krämer, *supra* note 38 at 21, Jan H. Jans and Hans H.B. Vedder, *European Environmental Law*, 3rd edn (Groningen: Europa Law Publishing 2008) 17, 46–50.

43 Gerd Winter, 'The Legal Nature of Environmental Principles in International, EC and German Law' in Richard Macrory, ed., *Principles of European Environmental Law* (Groningen: Europa Law Publishing, 2004). For the overall analysis of the principle, see Nele Dhondt, *Integration of Environmental Protection into other EC Policies* (Groningen: Europa Law Publishing, 2003).

44 Nele Dhondt, *supra* note 43, at 47–48.

45 Ibid. at 81–98.

46 Ludwig Krämer, *supra* note 40 at 22; Nele Dhondt, *supra* note 43 at 183.

tribunal.[47] Through the recognition of environmental principles as legal principles, in particular the integration principle, it has enhanced the legal status of the environment.[48] Although the ECJ has not yet annulled a European secondary legal act because of non-application of the integration principle, it has had many occasions to interpret the meaning and role of the principle, first of all in defining a proper legal basis for EU acts and secondly in the scope of the legislator's discretion in applying environmental requirements provided by the Treaty.

The *Chernobyl I* case[49] belongs to the first cases in which the ECJ referred to the integration requirement of the Treaty. The Court had to decide on the proper legal basis of a measure having environmental (and other) objectives. Greece contested the legality of the Council Regulation 3955/87 on the conditions of imports of agricultural products from third countries following the accident at the Chernobyl nuclear power-station,[50] which included a possibility to prohibit the importation of products exceeding the maximum permitted level of contamination. Greece claimed that the Regulation should have been based on Article 130s of the EC Treaty (now Article 192 TFEU) on environmental policy, instead of Article 113 of the EC Treaty (now Article 207 TFEU) on common commercial policy, since, as Greece asserted, the objective of the Regulation was exclusively the protection of the health of the public against the consequences of the nuclear accident. The Court pointed out that the choice of the legal basis might influence the content of the measure, as the procedural requirements of the enabling provisions were different (qualified majority voting under Art. 113, and the participation of the Parliament and the ECOSOC under Art. 130s). Given that these differences entail not purely formal consequences, the appropriate choice of the legal basis is of importance in the assessment of the legality of a measure. The Court held that 'the choice of the legal basis for a measure must be based on objective factors, which are amenable to judicial review'. The Court stated that the Regulation aimed at the safeguarding of the health of consumers on the one hand, and the regulation of trade between the EC and third countries, on the other. The Court declared that the fact that maximum permitted levels of contamination were fixed in the Regulation to protect public health, and that the protection of health was also an objective of the EC environmental policy, meant that it could not remove the measure from the sphere of the common commercial policy. The Court held that Articles 130r and 130s, which conferred powers to the EC to act in environmental matters, left intact EC powers in other fields even if the measure pursued at the same time environmental protection objectives. The Court referred to the integration principle:

---

47   Philippe Sands, 'The European Court of Justice: An Environmental Tribunal?' in Han Somsen, ed., *Protecting the European Environment: Enforcing EC Environmental Law* (London: Blackstone, 1996).

48   Ludwig Krämer, 'Thirty Years of EC Environmental Law' in Han Somsen, ed., *The Yearbook of European Environmental Law*, vol 2 (Oxford: OUP, 2002) 161.

49   *Hellenic Republic v Council* C-62/88 [1990] ECR I-1527 (*Chernobyl I*).

50   OJ L 371, 30 December 1987 at 14.

Moreover, that interpretation is confirmed by the second sentence of Article 130r (2), pursuant to which 'environmental protection requirements shall be a component of the Community's other policies'. That provision, which reflects the principle whereby all Community measures must satisfy the requirements of environmental protection, implies that a Community measure cannot be a part of Community action on environmental matters merely because it takes account of those requirements.[51]

In this judgment, the ECJ pointed out the essence of the integration principle, that is, environmental policy objectives, such as safeguarding human health, have to be pursued not only by environmental policy, but by other policies of the EU; the principle obliges institutions when they adopt legislation in various policies, e.g. in EU commercial policy. Thus, through the integration principle, environmental protection might be ensured by acts adopted within the other policy sectors.

The *Titanium dioxide* case[52] also concerns the choice of the proper legal basis. The Commission asked for the annulment of Directive 89/428 on waste from the titanium dioxide industry,[53] the aim of which was to harmonize national programmes for the elimination of such waste. The Directive was based on the (then) new Article 130s of the EC Treaty (now Article 192 TFEU) in the Environment Title.[54] The Commission argued that this was the wrong legal basis, since the 'main purpose' or 'centre of gravity' of the Directive was to improve the conditions of competition in the TiO_2 industry, thus it concerned the establishment and functioning of the internal market, and therefore, it should have been based on the (then) new Article 100a (now Article 114 TFEU). The Council considered that the 'centre of gravity' of this measure was the elimination of the pollution caused by waste from the TiO_2 manufacturing process, which is one of the objectives referred to in Article 130r of the EC Treaty (now Article 191 TFEU); thus, this was the correct legal basis.

Similarly to the *Chernobyl I* case, the ECJ stated that:

> In the context of the organization of the powers of the Community the choice of the legal basis for a measure may not depend simply on an institution's conviction as to the objective pursued but must be based on objective

---

51 *Chernobyl I, supra* note 49 at para 20.
52 *Commission v Council* C-300/89 [1991] ECR I-2867 (*Titanium dioxide*).
53 Directive 89/428 on procedures for harmonizing the programmes for the reduction and eventual elimination of pollution caused by waste from the titanium dioxide industry OJ L 201, 14 July 1989, 56.
54 In 1983, the Commission based its original proposal on the Article 100 and 235 of the EC Treaty. After the entry into force of the Single European Act in 1987, which inserted the Title on the Environment and the new provisions on harmonization into the Treaty, the Commission changed the legal basis to Article 100a. The Council adopted the Directive on the basis of the new environmental Article 130s.

factors which are amenable to judicial review ... Those factors include in particular the aim and content of the measure.

The Court held that the contested Directive had the twofold aim to harmonize national programmes for the reduction and elimination of pollution caused by TiO$_2$ waste, that is, to protect the environment, on the one hand, and to establish greater uniformity of production conditions and therefore of conditions of competition in the TiO$_2$ industry on the other. Since the disparities between the laws of the Member States concerning the treatment of that waste had an impact on production costs, it might distort the competition. The Court emphasized the importance of the increased role of the Parliament in the legislation, reflecting the fundamental democratic principle of the peoples' participation in the decision-making[55] (Article 100a provided for the cooperation procedure, while Article 130s allowed it to be consulted only).

The Court referred to the integration principle in Article 130r (2), 'environmental requirements shall be a component of the Community's other policies', which 'implies that a measure cannot be covered by Article 130s merely because it also pursues objectives of environmental protection'. Finally, the Court observed that Article 100a (3) required the Commission to take as a base the high level of environmental protection in its proposals for the approximation of the laws of the Member States which have as their object the establishment and functioning of the internal market. 'That provision thus expressly indicates that the objectives of environmental protection referred to in Article 130r may effectively be pursued by means of harmonizing measures adopted on the basis of article 100a'.[56]

The importance of this judgment for the integration principle in the EU lies in the fact that it reinforces its role as a bridge between economic and environmental interests. The harmonization of different national rules is the primary measure aiming at the elimination of barriers to the establishment and functioning of the internal market. The legal basis for harmonization had been widely used for environmental measures well before the Treaty amendment by the Single European Act, which established the competence for the European Community in environmental policy. The *Titanium dioxide* judgment indicates that measures in various economic and other policy areas, adopted under the harmonization provisions of the Treaty, have to follow environmental requirements; that the legislator has to meet the objective of the high level of protection; and furthermore, that the legal basis for harmonization can be used even after the constitutional establishment of the environmental competence of the Community. This latter obviously extends the range of measures, and gives more opportunity to the EU legislator to act in favour of environmental protection.

55 *Titanium dioxide, supra* note 52 at para 20. For comments on this point see Barents, René, *The Internal Market Unlimited: Some Observations on the Legal Basis of Community Legislation*, (1993) 30:1 CMLR, at 95–96; Ida J. Koppen, *The Role of the European Court of Justice in the Development of the European Community Environmental Policy*, EUI Working Paper (Florence, 1992) EPU No. 92/18 at 25.
56 C-300/89, *op cit* at para 24.

In the *Bettati v Safety Hi-Tech* case[57] the ECJ had to interpret Article 130r of the EC Treaty (now Article 191) and the legal nature of its environmental requirements. The question was the validity of Regulation 3093/94 on ozone depleting substances[58] in the light of environmental objectives and principles set in Article 130r of the EC Treaty. Article 5 of the Regulation prohibited the use of HCFC compounds that deplete the ozone layer. Safety Hi-Tech alleged that the Regulation in question was invalid: the prohibition of the use of HCFCs for fire-fighting was illegal under Article 130r of the EC Treaty since the Council had not observed the objective, the principles and the criteria of that provision, and thus it exceeded the bounds of its discretion. The Council contended that Article 130r granted it a wide discretion regarding the measure it chose to adopt in order to implement environmental policy, and that the Court is not entitled to review the exercise of its discretion. It held that a measure would be illegal only if it were manifestly inappropriate for the aim pursued. The ECJ held that judicial review was possible in light of Article 130r, albeit within certain limits. The ECJ cited almost the entire text of Article 130r on environmental objectives, principles and parameters,[59] although it left out the third sentence of Art. 130r (2) on integration, despite the fact that the Advocate General explicitly referred to it. The reason might be that the judgment was given in July 1988, when the Amsterdam Treaty, which removed the principle to the new Article 6 EC, had already been signed (but was not in force yet). This omission, however, does not mean that the Court excluded the principle from being used as a criterion of validity.[60] According to the ECJ, '[t]hat provision thus sets a series of objectives, principles and criteria which the Community legislature must respect in implementing environmental policy'.[61] The ECJ added that:

---

57 *Bettati v Safety Hi-Tech* C-341/95 [1998] ECR I-4355.

58 Regulation 3093/94 on substances that deplete the ozone layer, OJ L 333, 22 December 1994, 1. This Regulation implemented the Vienna Convention on the protection of the ozone layer and the Montreal Protocol on ozone depleting substances in the Community.

59 Article 130r(1) objectives: 'preserving, protecting and improving the quality of the environment; protecting human health; prudent and rational utilization of natural resources; promoting measures at international level to deal with regional or worldwide environmental problems'. Article 130r(2) principles: 'Community policy on the environment shall aim at a high level of protection taking into account the diversity of situations in the various regions of the Community. It shall be based on the precautionary principle and on the principles that preventive action should be taken, that environmental damage should as a priority be rectified at source and that the polluter should pay. Environmental protection requirements must be integrated into the definition and implementation of other Community policies.' Article 130r(3) conditions (parameters): 'In preparing its policy on the environment the Community shall take account of: available scientific and technical data; environmental conditions in the various regions of the Community; the potential benefits and costs of action or lack of action; the economic and social development of the Community and the balanced development of its regions.'

60 See Nele Dhondt, *supra* note 43, at 169.

61 *Bettati v Safety Hi-Tech*, *supra* note 57, at para 34.

However, in view of the need to strike a balance between certain of the objectives and principles mentioned in Article 130r and of the complexity of the implementation of those criteria, review by the Court must necessarily be limited to the question of whether the Council, by adopting the Regulation committed a manifest error of appraisal regarding the conditions for the application of Article 130r of the Treaty.[62]

The ECJ refused the argument of Safety Hi-Tech that the Regulation – since it did not prohibit the use of halons, which are more harmful than HCFCs – did not ensure the protection of the environment as a whole, and failed to ensure a high level of protection. The ECJ pointed out that 'Article 130r is confined to defining the general objectives of the Community in the matter of the environment' and that '[r]esponsibility for deciding what action is taken is conferred by the Council by Article 130s'. The ECJ stated that '[i]t does not follow from those provisions that Article 130r (1) of the Treaty requires the Community legislature, whenever it adopts measures' relating to a specific aspect of the environment, 'to adopt at the same time measures relating to the environment as a whole'. The ECJ pointed out that the Regulation, 'in the light of scientific evidence', constituted more stringent control measures on the use of HCFCs than those deriving from the Community's international obligations, therefore it met the requirement of the high level of protection. Furthermore, the ECJ held, that the high level of protection required by the Treaty didn't necessarily mean 'the highest [level] that is technically possible'.[63] The Court recalled that Member States might take more stringent protective measures under Article 130t (now Article 193 TFEU).

This judgment clearly shows that the ECJ is ready to review the legality of EU acts in light of objectives principles and conditions of the EU environmental policy listed in the Treaty. This reinforces, on the one hand, that according to the integration principle the environmental requirements have to be taken into consideration not only by the policymaker but by the legislator, and, on the other hand, that besides the objectives and principles, the 'conditions' (parameters) belong to the 'environmental requirements' as well. This judgment also shows that the ECJ accepts quite a wide discretion for the legislator in the appraisal of 'environmental requirements', in other words in the application of the integration principle.

There are further cases where the Court only mentions or does not refer explicitly to the principle, in spite of the fact that the Advocate General uses it as a strong argument in its opinion. One example is the *PreussenElectra* case[64] where the Court was asked whether the German system regulating the purchase of electricity produced from renewable energy sources was compatible with Article 30 of the EC Treaty (now Article 34 TFEU), which prohibits restrictions on the free movement of goods. The Court referred to the EU programme on the promotion of renewable energy resources under its international obligations stemming from the Kyoto

---

62   Ibid. at para 35.
63   Ibid. at paras 41–42, 46–47.
64   *PreussenElectra* C-379/98 [2001] ECR I-2099.

commitments, and to the integration principle[65], in the sense that environmental considerations justified discriminatory measures towards private undertakings. The Court did not interpret the principle. The Advocate General held that:

> Of particular importance is Article 6 (now Article 11 TFEU), which now provides that: 'Environmental protection requirements must be integrated into the definition and implementation of the Community policies referred to in Article 3 (now Article 2-6 TFEU)' including therefore the internal market, and which adds: 'in particular with a view to promoting sustainable development.'

As its wording shows, Article 6 is not merely programmatic; it imposes legal obligations. Special account must therefore be taken of environmental concerns in interpreting the Treaty provisions on the free movement of goods. Moreover, harm to the environment, even where it does not immediately threaten – as it often does – the health and life of humans, animals and plants protected by Article 36 of the Treaty (now Article 36 TFEU), may pose a more substantial, if longer-term, threat to the ecosystem as a whole. It would be hard to justify, in these circumstances, giving a lesser degree of protection to the environment than to the interests recognized in trade treaties concluded many decades ago and taken over into the text of Article 36 of the EC Treaty, itself unchanged since it was adopted in 1957.[66]

Another example is the *Stichting Greenpeace* case[67] in which Greenpeace and other environmental organizations and private persons asked the Court of First Instance (now the General Court) to annul the Commission's decision on financing by the EU Fund the construction of power stations in the Canary Islands, claiming that the environmental impact assessment required for such operations under the EU Directive 85/337 had not been taken. The applicants stated that the Commission's decision was contrary to EU environmental policy, and that it breached its 'dual' obligation to monitor the implementation of the EU law by Spain. The Court considered the application inadmissible, stating that the applicants were not 'directly and individually concerned' by the contested decision, which is required by the Treaty for private persons to initiate procedures before the European Courts. In the appeal case, the findings of the ECJ were the same, based on its settled case law; it dismissed the appeal on grounds of the lack of *locus standi*.[68] These decisions of the Courts have been widely criticized, and considered as a missed opportunity to assess the compliance of the Commission's decision with the integration requirement.[69] Another aspect for questioning these conclusions of the Courts was raised, according to which the integration requirement of the Treaty may be regarded as addressing

---

65 Ibid. at paras 74–76.
66 Opinion of Advocate General Jacobs in case *PreussenElectra* C-379/98 [2001] ECR I-2103, at paras 231–32.
67 *Stichting Greenpeace and Others v Commission* T-585/93 [1995] ECR II-2205.
68 *Stichting Greenpeace and Others v Commission* C-321/95P [1998] ECR I-1653.
69 Donth, *supra* note 43, at 160.

all EU institutions, including the judiciary; thus, they were under an obligation to take a more integrated approach. The opinion of Advocate General Cosmas in the appeal case underlined the importance of the integration principle:

> by observing that the Treaty provisions concerning the environment are not mere proclamations of principle. Paragraph 1 of Article 130r may refer in general terms to the pursuit of objectives to which Community policy must contribute in the sector of the environment, and paragraph 2 may trace the general principles of that policy, but the last sentence of the first subparagraph of paragraph 2 of Article 130r of the Treaty appears to impose on the Community institutions a specific and clear obligation which could be deemed to produce direct effect in the Community legal order. It expressly states that: 'Environmental protection requirements must be integrated into the definition and implementation of other Community policies.[70]

The Advocate General pointed out that 'that obligation has not remained a "dead letter" but has been imported into secondary Community law, and indeed in the context of legislation on the financing by the Community of certain actions having an impact on the environment.' He quoted Article 7 of Regulation 2052/88, which provided that measures financed by the Funds shall be in keeping with Community policies, including those concerning environmental protection. Therefore, his opinion was that 'in so far as the financing of the works for the construction of the two power stations in the Canary Islands is concerned, the Commission was obliged to take into consideration the aspect of environmental protection'. Furthermore, the Advocate General underlined that:

> observance, in the present case, of the Commission's specific and clear obligation to take into account the safeguarding of environmental interests . . . is not of concern solely to the Commission but is also of relevance for certain individuals. The latter may seek judicial protection in the event of non-compliance with that obligation, provided of course that they satisfy the procedural requirements in that connection.[71]

Consideration of these arguments might lead to the conclusion that not only the Commission but also the Court breached the integration principle as well.[72] The importance of the Advocate General's opinion lies in emphasizing the binding nature of the integration principle, compliance with which is a specific and clear obligation stemming from the Treaty. On the other hand, non-compliance with the integration principle by the legislator justifies an action for annulment initiated by individuals at European Courts.

---

70 Opinion of Advocate General Cosmas in case *Stichting Greenpeace and Others v Commission* C-321/95P [1998] ECR I-1654 at para 62.
71 Ibid. at paras 63, 65.
72 Donth, *supra* note 43 at 162.

27.4 Principle of precaution in the European Union

27.4.1 International origins

Similarly to the integration principle, the principle of precaution has its roots in international environmental policy and law. The formulation of the principle is a consequence of the industrial, technological and scientific development of the last decades, which besides contributing to the well-being of humans, often entails serious, harmful consequences for the environment and human health. These new types of risks caused, e.g. by various chemicals or by genetically modified organisms, are not predictable to one hundred per cent certainty. Prevention of environmental harm is one of the most important principles generally accepted in international, European and national environmental policies and laws from the very beginning of their establishment and development. The principle of precaution reinforces the necessity of prevention by going a step further: it requires an anticipatory thinking from decision-makers, an early preparation for potential, uncertain threats, in situations where no definitive scientific proof exists as to the occurrence and nature of environmental harm, such as its seriousness, durability, reversibility or cumulative effects. In these situations preventive actions cannot be postponed awaiting scientific certainty. The precautionary principle shows an important turning point in the development of environmental law in response to the necessity for early action to prevent risk in the face of scientific uncertainty.[73]

Reference is often made to the German national environmental law as one origin of the precautionary principle. Indeed, the concept of '*Worsorgeprinzip*' emerged in the late 1970s; its meaning might be interpreted as a kind of 'foresight' bringing a new, more careful approach to environmental protection in situations of the lack of scientific certainty.[74]

The most often cited source of international law in this field is the Rio Declaration on Environment and Development, Principle 15:

> In order to protect the environment, the precautionary approach shall be widely applied by States according to their capabilities. Where there are threats of serious or irreversible damage, lack of full scientific certainty shall not be used as a reason for postponing cost-effective measures to prevent environmental degradation.[75]

In fact, the precautionary concept appeared even earlier in the 1980s, for example, in relation to the protection of the North Sea ecosystems against waste

---

73 Nicolas de Sadeleer calls this progress as a 'genuine paradigm shift' and an 'important milestone in risk reduction' in *Environmental Principles from Political Slogans to Legal Rules* (Oxford: OUP, 2002) 91.

74 See, e.g. Sonja Boehmer-Christiansen, 'The Precautionary Principle in Germany: Enabling Government' in Timothy O'Riordan and James Cameron, eds., *Interpreting the Precautionary Principle* (London: Earthscan, 1994) 32–6.

75 'The Rio Declaration on Environment and Development' in Stanley P. Johnson, *supra* note 7 at 120.

dumping. Participants of the third international conference in their Declaration stated that they:

> Will continue to apply the precautionary principle, that is to take action to avoid potentially damaging impacts of substances that are persistent, toxic and liable to bioaccumulate even where there is no scientific evidence to prove a causal link between emissions and effects.[76]

Starting from the adoption of the Rio Declaration, various international conventions requiring precautionary action have been signed and the principle has been further strengthened and clarified by international soft law documents. Some examples are the 1992 UN Framework Convention on Climate Change, the 1992 UN Convention on Biological Diversity, the 1992 OSPAR Convention on the Protection of the Marine Environment of the North-East Atlantic, or the 2000 Cartagena Protocol on Biosafety.[77] One of the most expressive examples among these sources is the UN Framework Convention on Climate Change. It defines the precautionary principle as a guiding principle:

> The Parties should take precautionary measures to anticipate, prevent or minimize the causes of climate change and mitigate its adverse effects. Where there are threats of serious or irreversible damage, lack of full scientific certainty should not be used as a reason for postponing such measures, taking into account that policies and measures to deal with climate change should be cost-effective so as to ensure global benefits at the lowest possible cost. To achieve this, such policies and measures should take into account different socio-economic contexts, be comprehensive, cover all relevant sources, sinks and reservoirs of greenhouse gases and adaptation, and comprise all economic sectors. Efforts to address climate change may be carried out cooperatively by interested Parties.[78]

Despite the various understandings and interpretations of the content and the legal status of the precautionary principle and the lack of its clear definition, it is widely accepted as an evolving principle of general customary international law since it is provided for by international treaties, soft law instruments, many states

---

76 Ministerial Declaration of the Third International Conference on the Protection of the North Sea, The Hague, 8 March 1990 <http://www.ospar.org/html_documents/ospar/html/3nsc-1990-hague_declaration.pdf> accessed 9 April 2011.

77 For an outline of the development of the precautionary principle in international law see, e.g. Markus W. Gehring and Marie-Claire Cordonier Segger, 'Precaution in World Trade Law: The Precautionary Principle and Its Implications for the World Trade Organization'<http://www.cisdl.org/pdf/brief_precaution_trade.pdf> accessed 15 December 2016; Claudia Saladin, 'Precautionary Principle in International Law' (2000) 6 *International Journal of Occupational and Environmental Health* 270 <http://www.sehn.org/pdf/ppep.pdf> accessed 9 April 2011.

78 Art 3 para 3 of the UN Framework Convention on Climate Change <http://unfccc.int/essential_background/convention/background/items/1349.php> accessed 9 April 2011. The European Union joined the Convention by Decision 94/69, HL L 33, 2 July 1994, 11.

apply it within their domestic laws, and it is increasingly invoked by international courts including the European Courts.[79]

One important aspect in the precautionary approach concerns the reversal of the burden of proof. According to the traditional approach those who oppose an activity have to prove that it does cause environmental damage. The precautionary principle, however, shifts the burden of proof on those who wish to carry out an activity requiring them to prove that it will not cause harm to the environment.[80]

The New Delhi Declaration[81] considers the precautionary approach to human health, natural resources and ecosystems as being central to sustainable development, committing not only states but international organizations and civil society 'to avoid human activity which may cause significant harm to human health, natural resources or ecosystems including in the face of scientific uncertainty'. This approach includes accountability for harm caused, prudent planning, thorough environmental impact assessment, which may result in refusal of an authorization for a possible harmful activity, and placing of the burden of proof on the persons who wish to carry out such activities. The Declaration calls for an appropriate risk management, and also for reliance on an up-to date, independent and transparent scientific judgment, and the availability of judicial or administrative review. Of importance is the warning for the avoidance of economic protectionism in the principle's application.

27.4.2 The development of the precautionary principle in the European Union

At the European level the precautionary principle first appeared in 1993, when the Fifth Environmental Action Programme of the EU stated that 'the guiding principles under this programme derive from the precautionary approach'.[82] The Sixth Environmental Action Programme intends to reinforce the principle in a way that '[G]reater focus on prevention and the implementation of the precautionary principle is required in developing an approach to protect human health and the environment', and that the programme shall be based, *inter alia*, on these principles.[83]

---

79 See, for example, Philippe Sands, *Principles of International Environmental Law* (Manchester: Manchester University Press, 1995) at 212; de Sadeleer, *supra* note 72 at 317–19; Owen McIntyre and Thomas Mosedale, 'The Precautionary Principle as a Norm of Customary International Law' (1997) 9 *J. Envtl. L.* 221; James Cameron, 'The Status of the Precautionary Principle in International Law' in Timothy O'Riordan and James Cameron, eds., *Interpreting the Precautionary Principle* (London: Earthscan 1994).

80 Sands, *supra* note 78, at 212.

81 New Delhi Declaration, *supra* note 4.

82 Fifth Environmental Action Programme, *supra* note 6, at 24. The Decision 2179/98 on the revision of the programme mentions the principle in connection with hazardous chemicals, *supra* note 33 at 11.

83 Sixth Environmental Action Programme, *supra* note 10, at 1, 3.

At the same time as the Fifth Environmental Action Programme was adopted the Maastricht Treaty entered into force, which broadened the principles of the Environmental Title in the EC Treaty by introducing the precautionary principle. Article 130r paragraph 2 (now Article 191 paragraph 2 TFEU) provided that 'Community policy on the environment shall aim at a high level of protection . . . It shall be based on the precautionary principle and on the principles that preventive action should be taken . . .'

Neither the EU environmental action programmes nor the Treaty provisions define the precautionary principle. Given the considerable differences between various interpretations of its meaning and responsibilities stemming from the principle, it is difficult for policymakers and legislators to balance conflicting interests in situations of potential risks to humans and the environment. Trying to clarify these issues, the Commission adopted guidelines for the application of the precautionary principle. The Commission outlined its approach, trying to find a common understanding of risk assessment and management, and also to avoid unwarranted recourse of the principle as a disguised form of protectionism.[84] The Commission broadened the scope of the principle, considering precaution as a general principle which should be applied not only in environmental protection but in other fields:

> [In] specific circumstances where scientific evidence is insufficient, inconclusive or uncertain and there are indications through preliminary objective scientific evaluation that there are reasonable grounds for concern that the potentially dangerous effects on the environment, human, animal or plant health may be inconsistent with the chosen level of protection.

The Commission emphasized the importance of a preliminary risk assessment, the political responsibility in determining the acceptable level of risk, and the possible reversal of the burden of proof placing the responsibility on the manufacturer to produce the scientific evidence. The Commission considers proportionality, non-discrimination, consistency, the cost-benefit analysis and the re-examination of measures in light of scientific developments as general principles for the application of precaution.[85]

The precautionary principle is increasingly reflected in EU environmental legislation with or without explicit mentioning; some examples are the Directives on industrial emissions (the integrated pollution prevention and control), on GMOs, on baby food, the Habitats Directive, the Regulations on ozone

---

84 Commission Communication on the precautionary principle, COM (2000) 1, Brussels, 2 February 2000.

85 For the critical analysis of the Communication, *inter alia*, on the risk assessment, and on the questions remained unanswered, see e.g. David Vogel, 'The Politics of Risk Regulation in Europe and the United States' in H. Somsen, ed., *The Yearbook of European Environmental Law*, vol 3 (Oxford: OUP, 2003) 25–6; see also, e.g. Wybe Th. Douma, 'The Precautionary Principle in the European Union' (2000) 9 RECIEL 132 at 141–43.

depleting substances, and on chemical substances (REACH).[86] The European Courts often have to interpret provisions of these EU legal acts.

27.4.3 The application of the precautionary principle by the European Court of Justice (ECJ) and by the General Court (the Former Court of First Instance - CFI)

The case law of the European Courts involving the application of the precautionary principle can be grouped around cases dealing with environmental issues,[87] and around cases that concern health and food safety issues. Although the TFEU provides for the precautionary principle only in relation to environmental policy, the scope of its application has been extended to other policies that involve scientific uncertainty, primarily to protect human health, which is one of the objectives of EU environmental policy. This resulted, to a great extent, from the innovative interpretation of the principle by the European Courts.[88] The Commission's above-mentioned communication reinforced this more general character of the principle. In this group of cases[89] the risk to human health posed by chemicals,

---

86 Directive 2010/75 on Industrial Emissions (Integrated Pollution Prevention and Control), *OJ L* 334, 17 December 2010, 17; Directive 2001/18 on the deliberate release into the environment of genetically modified organisms, OJ L 106, 17 April 2001, 1; Directive 1999/39 amending Directive 96/5/EC on processed cereal-based foods and baby foods for infants and young children, OJ L 124, 18 May 1999, 1; Directive 92/43 on the conservation of natural habitats and of wild fauna and flora OJ L 206, 22 July 1992, 7; Regulation 2037/2000 on substances that deplete the ozone layer, OJ L 244, 29 September 2000, 1; Regulation 1907/2006 concerning the Registration, Evaluation, Authorisation and Restriction of Chemicals (REACH), establishing a European Chemicals Agency, OJ L 396, 30 December 2006, 1.

87 Examples: *Lirussi* C-175/98 and 177/98 [1999] ECR I-6881 (waste management – temporary storage); *ARCO Chemie Nederland* C-418/97 and C-419/97 [2000] ECR I-4475 (concept of waste); *Fornasar* C-318/98 [2000] ECR I-4785 (definition of hazardous waste, more stringent national measures); *Waddenzee*, C-127/02 [2004] ECR I-7405 (conservation of natural habitats, concept of plan or project).

88 Nicolas de Sadeleer points out that in the 'genuine environmental cases' uncertainties are far more important, given the difficulties of predicting the reactions of ecosystems to ecological risks (e.g. climate change). In many cases on health protection, however, the European Courts have to deal with internal market issues, i.e. the free movement of goods – like GMOs, medicinal products, food additives – therefore the Courts seem to endorse a stricter approach. See 'The Precautionary Principle in EC Health and Environmental Law' (2006) 12 *Euro. L. J.* 139.

89 Examples: *Greenpeace France*, C-6/99 [2000] ECR I-1651; *Bergaderm and Goupil v Commission*, C-352/98 P [2000] ECR I-5291 (and T-199/96 [1998] ECR II-2805) (public health, carcinogenic compound in a bronzing product); *Pfizer Animal Health v Council*, T-13/99 [2002] ECR II-3305 (additive in feedingstuffs – transfer of resistance to antibiotics from animals to humans); T-70/99 *Alpharma v Council* [2002], ECR II-3495 (additive in feedingstuffs – transfer of resistance to antibiotics from animals to humans); *Artegodan v Commission*, T-74,76,83,84,85,132,137,141/00 [2002] ECR II- 4945 (medicinal products for human use); *Monsato Agricoltura Italia*, C-236/01 [2003] ECR I-8105 (novel food, food from GMO maize, national restriction on trade); *Commission v Denmark*, C-192/01 [2003] ECR I-9693 (vitamins and minerals in foodstuffs, prohibition on marketing, public health); *Sweden v Commission*, T-229/04 [2007] ECR II-2437 (paraquat in plant protection products, protection of human and animal health).

cosmetic products, medicines, food and feed additives, etc. is at issue, which naturally attracts high concern. It also raises several questions of the preliminary assessment of risk. Beside the ECJ, the General Courts (the former CFI) plays an important role in shaping the precautionary principle with the result of establishing it as a general principle of European Law.

27.4.3.1 Environmental protection issues

One of the most important cases on nature protection is the *Waddenzee* case,[90] where the Court interpreted the Habitats Directive[91] in light of the precautionary principle. The case concerned the authorization of fishing activities in the nature protection area of the Dutch Waddenzee. Nature protection associations claimed that mechanical cockle fishing causes damage to the flora and fauna and reduces the fish stock for birds resulting in a decline in their population. The ECJ found that this fishing activity fell within the concept of 'plan' or 'project' under the Habitats Directive, which requires Member States take appropriate steps to avoid the deterioration of habitats and significant disturbance of the species in designated sites. According to Article 6 (3) of the Habitats Directive a project likely to have a significant effect may be authorized only after a specific environmental impact assessment demonstrates that the project will not adversely affect the integrity of the site and its conservation objectives. The Court stated that 'such a risk exists if it cannot be excluded on the basis of objective information'. This follows from 'the precautionary principle, which is one of the foundations of the high level of protection pursued by Community policy on the environment . . . by reference to which the Habitats Directive must be interpreted'.[92] The Court followed: 'in case of doubt as to the absence of significant effects such an assessment must be carried out'. The assessment of risk must be made in light of the characteristics and specific environmental conditions of the site. The authorization can only be given where the assessment demonstrates the absence of risk in light of the best scientific knowledge. 'Where doubt remains as to the absence of the adverse effect on the integrity of the site . . . the competent authority will have to refuse the authorisation'. The Court stated that 'the authorisation criterion . . . of the Habitats Directive integrates the precautionary principle'. A less stringent authorization criterion could not as effectively ensure the fulfilment of the conservation objectives.[93]

In the *Bluhme* case[94] the ECJ had to decide on a Danish wildlife measure prohibiting the import of any species of bee other than subspecies *Appis Mellifera Mellifera* (an indigenous brown bee specie) into the island of Læsø. The Court here had to balance the economic interests in free movements of goods and the

---

90   *Waddenzee, supra* note 87.
91   Directive 92/43 on the conservation of natural habitats and of wild fauna and flora OJ L 206, 22 July 1992, 7.
92   *Waddenzee, supra* note 89 at para 44.
93   Ibid. at para 49, 57–59, 61.
94   *Bluhme*, Criminal proceedings against Ditiev Bluhme, C-67/97 [1998] ECR I-8033.

environmental interests in protection of the health and life of animals. Article 36 of the EC Treaty (now Article 36 TFEU) allows restrictions on imports and export of goods justified, *inter alia*, on grounds of the protection of health and life of humans, animals or plants, provided that these measures meet certain conditions (prohibition of arbitrary discrimination or disguised restriction of trade). Notwithstanding the fact that in this case the risk of extinction of this subspecies was not proven by scientific evidence, the ECJ applied the precautionary approach without explicitly mentioning it. The Court considered that 'measures to preserve an indigenous animal population with distinct characteristics contribute the maintenance of biodiversity by ensuring the survival of the population concerned.'[95] The ECJ referred to the Rio Convention on Biological Diversity, which endorses the principle in its Preamble '[n]oting also that where there is a threat of significant reduction or loss of biological diversity, lack of full scientific certainty should not be used as a reason for postponing measures to avoid or minimize such a threat'.[96]

The *Fornasar* case[97] concerned the definition of hazardous waste and the possibility of a Member State applying more stringent measures than those contained in the EU legislation.[98] The ECJ referred to the environmental provisions of Article 175 of the EC Treaty (now Article 192 TFEU) used as a legal basis for the Directive, the intention of which was to implement the principles of prevention and precaution. It stated that:

> By virtue of those principles, it is for the Community and the Member States to establish a framework to prevent, reduce, and, in so far as is possible, eliminate from the outset the sources of pollution or nuisance by adopting measures of a nature such as to eliminate recognised risks.

The Court held that the Directive and the Decision at issue did not prevent Member States from classifying as hazardous waste items other than those featured on the list established by the Council Decision, and thus, from adopting more stringent protective measures in order to prohibit the abandonment, dumping or uncontrolled disposal of such waste. This follows also from Article 176 of the EC Treaty (now Article 193 TFEU) itself.[99] Since the origin and the component substances of the waste concerned could not be identified with certainty, it obviously posed an unpredictable harm to human health and the environment. Advocate General Cosmas underlined the binding nature and the general character of the precautionary principle, according to which the Community must take

95 Ibid. at para 33. See also the opinion of Advocate General Fennell, who refers to the precautionary principle, [1998] ECR I-850, at para 32.
96 Convention on Biological Diversity <http://www.cbd.int/convention/text/> accessed 5 October 2016.
97 *Fornasar, supra* note 86.
98 Directive 91/689 on hazardous waste, OJ L 377, 12 December 1991, 20; and Decision 94/904 establishing a list of hazardous waste OJ L 356, 31 December 1994, 14.
99 *Fornasar, supra* note 86, at para 37, 46, 51.

action even where there is not an existing but a potential risk to the environment. He pointed out that:

> Of particular interest for the resolution of this case is the reference to a specific (negative) manifestation of the precautionary principle. It implies that the competence of public authorities to adopt for a particular purpose the measures deemed necessary to avert a risk to the environment cannot be restricted, particularly where this risk has not been ascertained or 'charted' by prior regulation. In other words, determining in advance and in a limitative manner the circumstances requiring the intervention of public authorities to avert a specific risk to the environment, even if it is impossible to define that risk in advance in a concrete manner, would be contrary to the precautionary principle.[100]

27.4.3.2 Health protection issues

The *BSE ('mad cow disease')* case[101] is also an example of when the ECJ applied the precautionary approach, albeit without an explicit reference.[102] This case belongs to the early application of the precautionary principle by the ECJ in health protection issues. Here the UK contested the legality of the Commission's decision, which prohibited the export of bovine animals and other derived products from the UK to the Member States and to third countries because of the BSE disease.[103] Neither the SEAC (British scientific body) nor the Scientific Veterinary Committee of the EU could exclude the possibility of transmission of the disease to humans (known as Creutzfeldt-Jacob disease) on the basis of available scientific evidence. The ECJ again underlined the wide measure of discretion that the EU legislature enjoys in defining the nature and extent of the adopted measure, and stated that the Court 'must restrict itself . . . to examining whether the exercise of such discretion is vitiated by a manifest error, or a misuse of powers or whether the Commission did not clearly exceed the bounds of its discretion'.[104] The ECJ acknowledged that when the decision was adopted, there was great uncertainty as to the risks posed by these products. It stated that '[w]here there is uncertainty as to the existence or extent of risks to human health, the institutions may take protective measures without having to wait until the reality and seriousness of those risks become fully apparent.' The Court referred to the environmental

---

100 Opinion of the Advocate General Cosmas in *Fornasar* case [2000] ECR I-4785 at paras 32–4. It must be noted, that his opinion was that the Directive 91/689 did not implement the environmental objectives of the Treaty properly, and that it infringed the principles of prevention and precaution. See at paras 44–6.

101 *UK v Commission*, C-180/96 [1998] ECR I-2265.

102 Further examples are: *Mondiet*, C-405/92 [1993] I-6133 (conservation of fishery resources, prohibition of driftnets); *Santona Marshes*, C-355/90 [1993] ECR I-4221 (conservation of wild birds – special protection areas); *APAS*, C-435/92 [1994] I-67 (conservation of wild birds – hunting season).

103 Commission Decision 96/232 on emergency measures to protect against bovine spongiform encephalopathy OJ L 78, 28 March 1996, 47.

104 *UK v Commission*, *supra* note 100, at para 60.

provisions of the Treaty, especially to the objective of protecting human health, the principle of the high level of protection the preventive action and the integration of environmental requirements into other EU policies.[105] Although the reasoning of the Court (and also of the Commission) clearly reflects the application of the precautionary approach, explicit reference is not made to this principle.[106] The judgment raised the issue of the difference between the principles of prevention and precaution. Views on this question vary, although a greater number argue that while both require action at an early stage, precaution is wider than prevention, since prevention does not require protective measures in case of insufficient scientific evidence.[107] The decisive factor is scientific uncertainty.

In the *Greenpeace France* case[108] the Court interpreted the Directive 90/220 on GMO in the light of the precautionary principle.[109] Alleging the infringement of the principle, Greenpeace sought the annulment of the authorization of the marketing of GMO maize. The aim of Directive 90/220 was to protect human health and the environment regarding the deliberate release of GMOs into the environment; it provided for an authorization procedure, which involved, *inter alia*, a risk assessment and the Commission's favourable decision as a precondition. The question was whether the national authority had discretion not to give its consent for the marketing of GMO products after the favourable decision of the Commission. The ECJ held that the system of notification is based on the precautionary principle. It stated that the 'observance of the precautionary principle is reflected' in the whole system of authorization provided by the Directive via strict notification and information requirements, and by allowing Member States provisionally to restrict or prohibit the use/sale on their territory of a product which received consent where it has justifiable reasons to consider that it constitutes a risk to human health or the environment.[110] The Court pointed out that the system of protection – Articles 4, 12(4), 16 – implied that the Member State could not be obliged to give its consent if in the meantime it had new information that led it to consider that the product may constitute a risk to human health and the environment. In such cases it must immediately inform the Commission and the other Member States.

The *Artegodan* case[111] is one of the most important in the series of cases in which the General Court (the former Court of First Instance – CFI) had to

---

105 Ibid. at paras 98–100.
106 This judgment was strongly criticized because of the missed opportunity to demonstrate the usefulness of applying the principle. See, e.g. Douma, *supra* note 85, at 137; Dhondt, *supra* note 43, at 151.
107 Cf. Krämer, *supra* note 40, at 25.
108 *Greenpeace France*, C-6/99 [2000] ECR I-1651.
109 Directive 90/220 on the deliberate release into the environment of genetically modified organisms, OJ L 117, 8 May 1990, 15. At the time of the delivery of the judgment the precautionary principle was not spelled out in its text. It has been repealed by the Directive 2001/18, OJ L 106, 17 April 2001, 1, which is now based on the principle, and is required to take it into account in the implementation, see Preamble (8) and Article 1.
110 *Greenpeace France*, *supra* note 108, at para 44.
111 *Artegodan v Commission*, T-74, 76, 83, 84, 85, 132, 137, 141/00 [2002] ECR II- 4945.

interpret the precautionary principle. Several firms sought the annulment of the Commission's decisions ordering Member States to withdraw marketing authorizations of medicinal products for human use that contained certain amphetamine substances. The Commission referred to a negative scientific opinion.[112] The applicants claimed, *inter alia*, the infringement of Directives on the authorization of medicinal products in the EC. The CFI found that there was a lack of any new scientific data or information on the harmfulness of these substances; thus, the contested decisions were in breach of Directive 65/65,[113] and so it annulled them. The CFI underlined the 'general principle identified in the case law, that protection of public health must unquestionably take precedence over economic considerations'.[114] The CFI stated that in case of scientific uncertainty the competent authority must assess the medicinal product in accordance with the precautionary principle. When the CFI clarified the origin and the content of the principle, it stated that in environmental matters Article 174 (2) of the EC Treaty (now Article 191 (2) TFEU) established the binding nature of the principle,[115] and that Article 174 (1) (now Article 191 (1)) objectives included the protection of human health.

Although the precautionary principle is mentioned in the Treaty only in connection with environmental policy, it is broader in scope. It is intended to be applied in order to ensure a high level of protection of health, consumer safety and the environment in all the Community's spheres of activity.

These requirements are:

> Expressly integrated into the definition and implementation of all Community policies and activities under the Article 6 EC [now Article 11 TFEU] and Article 152 (1) EC [now Article 168 (1) TFEU on the integration of health protection into other policies] respectively.[116]

From this the Court concluded that:

> The precautionary principle can be defined as a general principle of Community law requiring the competent authorities to take appropriate measures to prevent specific potential risks to public health, safety and environment, by giving precedence to the requirements related to the protection of those interests over economic interests. Since the Community institutions are responsible, in all their spheres of activity, for the protection of public health, safety and the environment, the precautionary principle can be

---

112 Opinion of the Committee for Proprietary Medicinal Products of the European Agency for the Evaluation of Medicinal products.

113 Directive 65/65 (as amended) on the approximation of provisions laid down by law, regulation or administrative action relating to proprietary medicinal products OJ 22, 9 February 1965, 369, English spec edn, 1965–1966, 24.

114 *Artegodan, supra* note 110, at para 173.

115 Ibid. at para 182.

116 Ibid. at para 183.

regarded as an autonomous principle stemming from the above mentioned Treaty provisions.[117]

The CFI referred to the *BSE* judgment for the possibility to take preventive measures in case of scientific uncertainty. It notes how, in the judgment, the Court 'implicitly applied' the precautionary principle in the review of proportionality. The CFI held that where scientific evaluation did not make it possible to determine the existence of a risk with sufficient certainty, the competent authority had to provide solid and convincing evidence which, while not resolving the scientific uncertainty, might reasonably raise doubts as to the safety and/or efficacy of the medicinal product.[118] The importance of this judgment lies, in large part, with the CFI accepting the general, autonomous character of the principle of the EU, allowing its application in spheres where the EU Treaties do not expressly provide for it, which is justified also by the integration requirement of the Treaty.[119]

The CFI reinforced its approach towards the interpretation and the conditions for the application of the precautionary principle in later cases, for example, in the *Pfizer* case concerning the withdrawal of authorization by the Council of the use of certain additives (antibiotics) in animal feed. The use of these substances involved a 'possibility' of having adverse effects on human health. The CFI, in reference to the earlier case law of the ECJ and CFI, stated that by reason of the precautionary principle the Community institutions may take protective measures without having to wait until the reality and seriousness of risks to human health and the environment become fully apparent. The CFI went further, stating that 'a risk assessment cannot be required to provide the Community institutions with conclusive scientific evidence of the reality of the risk and the seriousness of the potential adverse effects'. However it underlined the requirement of a thorough risk assessment before the adoption of protective measures, which cannot be based on a purely hypothetical approach. The CFI stated that 'it is for the Community institutions to determine the level of protection which they deem appropriate for society.'[120]

In the *Paraquat* case[121] the validity of Commission Directive 2003/112 on plant protection product was assessed by the CFI[122] in the light of the precautionary principle. The aim of the measure was to include paraquat as an

---

117   Ibid. at para 184.

118   Ibid. at paras 185, 192.

119   de Sadeleer, *supra* note 87 at 143; Joanne Scott, 'The Precautionary Principle Before the European Courts' in Richard Macrory, ed., *Principles of European Environmental Law* (Groningen: Europa Law Publishing, 2004) 53–5.

120   *Pfizer*, *supra* note 88, at paras 139–42, 151–53, 155–56, 164. For the same statements see also the *Alpharma* and *Monsato* cases, *supra* note 88.

121   *Sweden v Commission*, T-229/04 [2007] ECR II-2437 (*Paraquat*).

122   Council Directive 91/414 concerning the placing of plant protection products on the market *OJ* L 230, 19 August 1991, 1 Commission Directive 2003/112 OJ L 321, 6 December 2003, 32 amending it to include paraquat as an active substance.

active substance within plant protection products. According to the text of the contested Directive certain uses of paraquat pose an unacceptable risk to the operator, and also to the life of certain animals and birds.[123] The assessment of the available scientific evidence obviously showed that the scientific information was inadequate for the estimation of the extent of the risk for human and animal health. The CFI pointed out that Directive 91/414 required that in light of current scientific and technical knowledge, it must be possible to expect that the use of plant protection products will not have any harmful effects on human health. The Court stated that:

> It follows from that provision, interpreted in combination of the precautionary principle, that in the domain of human health, the existence of solid evidence, which while not resolving scientific uncertainty, may reasonably raise doubts as to the safety of a substance, justifies, in principle . . . [its] refusal . . . The precautionary principle is designed to prevent potential risk. By contrast, purely hypothetical risks, based on mere hypotheses that have not been scientifically confirmed, cannot be accepted.[124]

This statement justifies protective measures in case of strong suspicion of harmful effects, but precludes the abuse of the application of precautionary principle for protectionism.

The *Afton Chemical* case[125] concerned the validity of Directive 2009/30 limiting the use of specific metallic additives (such as MTT) in fuels in the light of the precautionary principle. These additives might raise the risk of damage to human health. As the ECJ stated, at the time of the adoption of the Directive 'the European Union legislature was faced with serious doubts, in the absence of adequate and reliable scientific data, as to whether MTT was harmless for health and the environment.' The ECJ repeatedly stated that where it is impossible to determine with certainty the alleged risk because of the lack of reliable scientific assessment, but the likelihood of real harm to public health persists, the precautionary principle justifies the adoption of restrictive measures. Furthermore, the Court was of the opinion that:

> The European Union legislature could justifiably take the view that the appropriate manner of reconciling the high level of health and environmental protection and the economic interests of producers . . . was to limit the content of MMT in fuel . . . while providing for the possibility . . . of revising those limits on the basis of the results of assessment.[126]

---

123   Preamble to the Directive 2003/112, Recitals (4)–(5).
124   *Parquat, supra* note 120, at paras 160–61.
125   C-343/09 *Afton Chemical Limited v Secretary of State for Transport* ECR [2010] I-07027.
126   Ibid. at paras 59–64.

A similar interpretation of the conditions for the application of the precautionary principle is given in the *Gowan* case,[127] where the validity of Commission's Directive 2006/134 restricting the use of fenarimol in plant protection products was at issue. This substance has potential endocrine disrupting properties, although, the available scientific evidence, again, was insufficient. Gowan challenged the reliance of the precautionary principle as a justification for the restrictions imposed on the use of fenarimol. The ECJ quoted the objective of health protection at a high level and the precautionary principle of the EU environmental policy, and the environmental integration principle. Furthermore it cited the Article 168 TFEU stating that:

> Requirements relating to the protection of human health are a part of all the policies and actions of the Union and must therefore be taken into account in the implementation of the common agricultural policy by the institutions of the Union.

Based on this dual integration requirement, the ECJ stated that, '[t]he precautionary principle applies where the institutions of the Union take measures to protect human health under the common agricultural policy'.[128]

In a recent case brought by the *Commission against France*,[129] the national prior authorization scheme for processing aids and foodstuffs was investigated by the ECJ in the light of the EU food law and of the precautionary principle. The French system constituted a measure restricting the marketing of such goods lawfully manufactured or marketed in other Member States. France argued that the aim of the contested scheme was the high level of health protection governed by the precautionary principle. Although the ECJ found that the French measure was in breach of the proportionality principle, it held that in the absence of harmonization measures Member States can decide at which level they intend to ensure the protection of health and life of humans, which 'discretion is particularly wide' in case of scientific uncertainty as to certain substances used in the preparation of foodstuffs. Therefore, 'it must be acknowledged that a Member State may, under the precautionary principle, take protective measures without having to wait for the reality and the seriousness of those risks to be fully demonstrated'. The ECJ reaffirmed that:

> Where it proves to be impossible to determine with certainty the existence or extent of the alleged risk because of the insufficiency, inconclusiveness or imprecision of the results of studies conducted, but the likelihood of real harm to public health persists should the risk materialise, the precautionary

---

127   *Govan Commércio Internacional e Serviços Ltᵈᵃ v Ministero della Salute*, C-77/09. ECR [2010] I-13533.

128   Ibid. at paras 71–72. The Court referred to the former cases concerning the application of the precautionary principle in the sphere of the common agricultural policy, e.g. C-157/96 *National Farmers' Union and Others* [1998] ECR I-2211; *Monsato* case, *supra* note 88; *BSE* case, *supra* note 96.

129   *Commission v France* C-333/08 ECR [2010] I-00757.

principle justifies the adoption of restrictive measures, provided they are non-discriminatory and objective.[130]

The Court held that the assessment of the risk cannot be based on purely hypothetical considerations, and that:

> A correct application of the precautionary principle presupposes, first, identification of the potentially negative consequences for health of the proposed use of processing aids, and, secondly, a comprehensive assessment of the risk to health based on the most reliable scientific data available and the most recent results of international research.[131]

The *Raffinerie Mediterranee* case[132] concerned the interpretation of the polluter pays principle and Directive 2004/35 on environmental liability with regard to the prevention and remedying of environmental damage.[133] The question was, *inter alia*, whether national legislation allowing the national authorities to impose certain requirements as conditions for authorization for the use of areas of land in the *Priolo* Site of National Interest was compatible with the provision of the Directive. The national measures provided for criteria, procedures and rules for the safety, decontamination and environmental reinstatement of polluted sites. The applicants in the main proceeding asserted that the contested measures violated their right to property. The Italian Government, however, considered that the authority's practice to set the condition of the implementation of environmental remedial measures for the use of land was consonant with the precautionary principle. The ECJ held that the competent authorities of the Member States might identify and require measures to prevent and remedy environmental damage. The ECJ recalled that according to the case law of the ECJ:

> While the right of property forms part of the general principles of EU Law, it is not an absolute right and must be viewed in relation of its social function. Consequently, its exercise may be restricted, providing that those restrictions in fact corresponds to objectives of general interests pursued by the European Union and do not constitute disproportionate and intolerable interference, impairing the very substance of the rights guaranteed.

The Court pointed out that protection of the environment was one of those objectives.[134] The Court stated that such a national measure:

---

130   Ibid. at para 93.
131   Ibid. at para 92.
132   *Raffinerie Mediterranee (ERG) Spa and Others v Ministero dello Sviluppo economico and Other Authorities*, C-379/08 and C-380/08 ECR [2010] I-02007.
133   OJ L 143, 21 April 2004, 56.
134   Ibid. at paras 80–81.

Must be justified by the objective of preventing a deterioration of the environmental situation in the area in which those measures are implemented or, pursuant to the precautionary principle, by the objective of preventing the occurrence or resurgence of further environmental damage on the land belonging to the operators which is adjacent to the whole shoreline at which those remedial measures are directed.[135]

27.5 Conclusion

Environmental integration and precaution became guiding principles for European environmental policy. The European Courts contributed to the development of these principles in clarifying their meaning, the responsibilities they entail and the legal consequences of their non-respect. From the case law developed in this area so far, the following conclusions may be drawn:

Both environmental integration and precaution can be considered as general principles of European Union law because their scope extends to policy areas outside environmental protection. They require the application of further environmental principles and objectives, notably the integration principle transposes environmental principles into other EU policies, while the precautionary principle strengthens the principle of high level of protection of the environment and human health. These principles reinforce the application of each other: the principle of integration requires the application of precautionary approach, and vice versa. The preprinciple requires other policies to take more thorough preventive measures at an early phase to protect the environment and human health. Overall, these principles help to balance conflicting interests/principles and serve as instruments for the interpretation of law, for example by playing a key role in defining environmental obligations.

Further, these principles serve as instruments for the interpretation of law: they play a key role in defining environmental obligations. The application of these principles contributes to the revision and updating of relevant legal measures. The legality/validity of secondary norms may be assessed in the light of these principles; legal acts have to be consistent with them. Additionally, the principles are binding upon the institutions of the EU and also upon Member States when they implement EU law and have enabling functions for the EU institutions to act in the exercise of their competences, even when there is no specific reference made to these principles in the secondary law. Member States may rely on these principles when they wish to derogate from EU law, according to the Article 30 on free movements of goods, Article 114 (4)–(5) and (10) on harmonization measures, Article 191 (2) and 193 on environmental policy. These principles may justify restrictions on basic rights in order to protect general inter such as protection of human health and the environment. Finally, these principles help to develop new principles, such as protection of future generations

135 Ibid. at paras 90–92.

and protection of the global environment; thus they give legal significance to the principle of sustainable development.

The case law developed so far on these principles shows that they are not fully-fledged yet, and that further clarifications are needed for their better understanding and more effective application. It is clear, however, that the integration of environmental requirements and the precautionary principle plays a key role in strengthening EU environmental policy, increasingly making it possible to give priority to protection of non-material interests over economic ones. The implementation and enforcement of these principles contributes to the achievement of sustainable development.

28 The emergence of sustainable development jurisprudence in South Asia

Sumudu Atapattu

28.1 Introduction

The adoption of the *Our Common Future* report by the World Commission on Environment and Development almost 25 years ago heralded a new era in international environmental law, and it would not be wrong to refer to 'sustainable development' as one of the most influential terms of our times. Proposed as a possible solution to the increasingly polarized debate on economic development and environmental protection,[1] sustainable development has attracted perhaps as much scholarly debate[2] as the debate on globalization in recent years.

From a rather vague and 'slippery' concept,[3] sustainable development has matured into an umbrella term encompassing both substantive and procedural components.[4] Its evolution within a rather short span of time is 'remarkable' with some scholars focusing their analysis principally on international legal instruments for sustainable development.[5] Despite this remarkable development, the definition of sustainable development remains rather vague and embryonic; several attempts have been made, over the years, to flesh out its parameters with the Rio Declaration on Environment and Development being the most ambitious attempt to date. Another, lesser known, though not any less important, attempt was the New Delhi Declaration of Principles of International Law Relating to Sustainable Development adopted by the International Law Association in 2002.[6]

This chapter seeks to discuss the emergence of sustainable development jurisprudence in South Asia. The courts in South Asia have been instrumental in

---

1 See *Our Common Future, Report of the World Commission on Environment and Development* (Oxford: OUP, 1987).

2 See Sumudu Atapattu, *Emerging Principles of International Environmental Law* (New York: Transnational Publishers, 2006) for a list of writers on this topic.

3 See Robert John Araujo, 'Rio+10 and the World Summit on Sustainable Development: Why Human Beings Are the Center of Concerns', (2004) 2 *Geo. J. I. & Pub. Pol'y* 201.

4 See *supra* note 2, particularly chapter 2.

5 See M.C. Cordonier Segger and A. Khalfan, *Sustainable Development Law: Principles, Practices and Prospects* (Oxford: OUP, 2004). Charles Di Leva, 'Emerging Principles of International Environmental Law', book review (2007) 101 AJIL 933.

6 Available at: http://cisdl.org/tribunals/pdf/NewDelhiDeclaration.pdf

expanding the concept of rights in South Asia by interpreting existing rights in a very expansive manner. This chapter discusses some of the seminal cases in South Asia and evaluates to what extent the cases have contributed to the development of a sustainable development jurisprudence in the region. The Supreme Court of India has been the most active judiciary in the region and its influence on other courts in the region has been considerable.

In a nutshell, the principles endorsed by the New Delhi Declaration are: the sustainable use of natural resources; the principle of equity (encompassing both inter- and intra-generational equity) and the eradication of poverty; the common but differentiated responsibility principle; the precautionary principle; public participation, access to information and access to justice; the principle of good governance; and the principle of integration and inter-relationship.[7] Many of these principles are already part of international law relating to human rights and environmental law, while others are emerging.[8] It is not the intention here to discuss these principles in length or their evolution; rather, attention will be paid to how these principles have been articulated by courts in India, Pakistan, Bangladesh, Nepal and Sri Lanka. It is fitting that this chapter looks at a region that boasts of an ancient civilization that led a very sustainable way of life many centuries ago, as was acknowledged by H.E. Judge C.G. Weeramantry in his separate opinion in the *Case Concerning Gabčíkovo-Nagymaros Project*.[9] The emphasis on the cases from India should not be taken as an acknowledgement that the Supreme Court of India is more superior to its counterparts in the region – rather, the emphasis acknowledges the pioneering role that the Supreme Court of India has played over the years; moreover, the cases from India greatly outnumber the cases from other countries in the region.

28.2 Cases from India

The Supreme Court of India is considered a pioneer in the field of environmental protection in South Asia, interpreting the right to life clause in the Indian Constitution[10] in an expansive manner. It has interpreted the right to life to include the right to be free from pollution, the right to a clean environment, and procedural rights relating to the environment. Moreover, the Court has imported principles from international environmental law stressing that the polluter pays principle, sustainable development, and the precautionary principle are all applicable in India. In

---

7 Ibid. Of course, this is a non-binding instrument, but it has benefited from 10 years of painstaking work by the ILA. See Nico Schrijver, 'The New Delhi Declaration of Principles of International Law Relating to Sustainable Development, Commentary' in M.C. Cordonier Segger and C.G. Weeramantry, eds., *Sustainable Justice: Reconciling Economic, Social and Environmental Law* (Leiden: Martinus Nijhoff, 2005) 549.

8 The present author has written on five of such emerging principles: sustainable development, precautionary principle, polluter pays principle, environmental impact assessment and procedural rights, and common but differentiated responsibility principle, see *supra* note 2.

9 *Case Concerning the Gabčíkovo-Nagymaros Project (Hungary v Slovakia)* ICJ Reports (1997) 7.

10 Article 21 of the Indian Constitution.

MC Mehta v Kamal Nath[11] the Court extended the public trust doctrine to cover *all* ecologically important lands, including freshwater, wetlands and riparian forests, not just navigable waters.

The first case in a long line of cases was *Subhash Kumar v State of Bihar*[12] where the Court articulated:

> The right to life is a fundamental right under article 21 of the Constitution and it includes the right of enjoyment of pollution-free water and air for full enjoyment of life. If anything endangers or impairs that quality of life in derogation of laws, a citizen has the right to have recourse to article 32 of the Constitution for removing the pollution of water or air which may be detrimental to the quality of life.[13]

The trend set by this case has been followed and expanded in subsequent cases. In many of these cases, the Court had to strike a balance between economic development and protecting the right of people to live in a clean environment – in other words, achieving sustainable development. The *Vellore Citizens' Welfare Forum v Union of India* (1996)[14] case involved environmental damage and a public health hazard caused by tanneries in the State of Tamil Nadu. The Court stressed that while the tanneries brought in a considerable amount of foreign revenue and generated employment, the industry had no right to destroy the ecology and create a health hazard. It noted that: "[s]ustainable development, and in particular the polluter pays principle and the precautionary principle, have become part of customary international law."[15]

In *Karnataka Industrial Areas Development Board v Sri C. Kenchappa and Others* (2006),[16] the Court reiterated the principle of sustainable development and referred to the Stockholm Declaration as the "Magna Carta of our environment."[17] The Court discussed the history of international environmental law, paying extensive attention to the provisions of the Rio Declaration. It noted that in keeping with the principle of sustainable development, a serious effort has been made "to strike a golden balance between industrial development and ecological preservation."[18] The Court referred to its decision in *AP Pollution Control Board II v MV Nayudu* (2001)[19] where it observed that the right to have access to drinking water is fundamental to life and it is the duty of the State under Article 21 (of the Constitution) to provide clean drinking water to

11 WP (C) No 182 of 1996. Most of the cases referred to in this chapter are available at eLaw, Environmental Law Alliance Worldwide, http://www.elaw.org/node/1849.
12 AIR 1991 SC 420.
13 Ibid.
14 5 SCC 647 (1996).
15 Ibid.
16 AIR 2006 SC 2038, decided 5 December 2006.
17 Ibid.
18 Ibid.
19 Decided 27 January 1999.

its citizens. The Court further noted that there is a need to balance the right to a healthy environment and the right to sustainable development. Similarly, in *Narmada Bachao Andolan v Union of India*,[20] the Court noted that water is a basic human need and is part of the right to life enshrined in Article 21 of the Indian Constitution. The Court reiterated the importance of the precautionary principle, sustainable development and the polluter pays principle as well as the public trust doctrine. In *Intellectuals Forum, Tirupathi v State of AP* (2006)[21] the Court acknowledged the importance of the public trust doctrine in achieving sustainable development. The Court referred to Principle 4 of the Rio Declaration and stressed the need for rational management of resources and the adoption of an integrated and coordinated approach to development planning.

In *Research Foundation for Science v Union of India* (2003),[22] the Supreme Court of India stated that industrialization has had the effect of generating huge quantities of hazardous waste: "[t]hese and other side effects of development gave birth to a principle of sustainable development so as to sustain industrial growth."[23] With regard to the relevant legal principles the Court noted:

> The legal position regarding applicability of the precautionary principle and polluter pays principle which are part of the concept of sustainable development in our country is now well settled. In Vetiore [sic] Citizens' Welfare Forum vs. Union of India & Ors. [(1996) 5 SCC 647], a three Judge Bench of this Court, after referring to the principles evolved in various international conferences and to the concept of "sustainable development", *inter alia*, held that the precautionary principle and polluter pays principle have now emerged and govern the law in our country, as is clear from Articles 47, 48-A and 51-A(g) of our Constitution . . . These principles have been held to have become part of our law. Further, it was observed in Vellore Citizens' Welfare Forum's case that these principles are accepted as part of the [sic] customary international law and hence there should be no difficulty in accepting them as part of our domestic law. Environmental concerns have been placed at same pedestal as human rights concerns, both being traced to Article 21 of the Constitution of India. It is the duty of this Court to render justice by taking all aspects into consideration. It has also been observed that with a view to ensure that there is neither danger to the environment nor to the ecology and, at the same time, ensuring sustainable development, the Court can refer scientific and technical aspects for an investigation and opinion to expert bodies.[24]

The Court also noted that the rights to information and community participation for the protection of environment and human health is also a right that flows

20 10 SCC 664 (2002).
21 AIR 2006 SC 1350.
22 WP 657/1995 (2003).
23 Ibid.
24 Ibid.

from Article 21 of the Indian Constitution and that the authorities must motivate public participation.

In the case of *S. Jagannath v Union of India*[25] which involved the issue of shrimp farming and its negative impacts on the environment including loss of biodiversity and mangroves, salinization, and pollution from effluents, the Court discussed the relevance of sustainable development and quoted from its decision in *Vellore Citizens' Welfare Forum v Union of India*:[26]

> The traditional concept that development and ecology are opposed to each other is no longer acceptable. 'Sustainable Development' is the answer. In the international sphere, 'Sustainable Development' as a concept came to be known for the first time in the Stockholm Declaration of 1972. Thereafter, in 1987 the concept was given a definite shape by the World Commission on Environment and Development in its report called 'Our Common Future.' . . . Finally came the Earth Summit held in June 1992 at Rio . . . During the two decades from Stockholm to Rio 'Sustainable Development' has come to be accepted as a viable concept to eradicate poverty and improve the quality of human life while living within the carrying capacity of the supporting ecosystems. . . . We have no hesitation in holding that 'Sustainable Development' as a balancing concept between ecology and development has been accepted as a part of the customary international law . . .
>
> Some of the salient principles of 'Sustainable Development,' as culled out from Brundtland Report and other international documents, are Inter-Generational Equity, Use and Conservation of Natural Resources, Environmental Protection, the Precautionary Principle, Polluter Pays Principle, Obligation to Assist and Cooperate, Eradication of Poverty and Financial Assistance to the developing countries. We are, however, of the view that 'the Precautionary Principle' and 'the Polluter Pays Principle' are essential features of 'Sustainable Development.'[27]

The Court reiterated the importance of sustainable development in the case of *Smoke Affected Residents v Municipal Corporation of Greater Mumbai and Others*[28] where it had to deal with the health impact of vehicular pollution in the city of Mumbai. It referred to its decision in *MC Mehta v Union of India and Others*[29], which dealt with vehicular pollution in New Delhi:

> Articles 39(e), 47 and 48A by themselves and collectively cast a duty on the State to secure the health of the people, improve public health and protect and improve the environment. It was by reason of the lack of effort on the

25 WP 561/1996.
26 (1996) 5 SCC 647: JT (1996) 7 SC 375, *supra* note 14.
27 Ibid.
28 WP 1762/1999 (decided 10 April 2002).
29 Order dated 5 April 2002.

part of the enforcement agencies, notwithstanding adequate laws being in place, that this Court has been concerned with the state of air pollution in the capital of this country. Lack of concern or effort on the part of various governmental agencies had resulted in spiraling pollution levels. The quality of air was steadily decreasing and no effective steps were being taken by the administration in this behalf.

One of the principles underlying environmental law is that of sustainable development. This principle requires such development to take place which is ecologically sustainable. The two essential features of sustainable development are the precautionary principle and the polluter pays principle.[30]

Thus, elaborating on the precautionary principle, the Court noted that the 'auto policy' must focus on measures to anticipate, prevent and attack the causes of environmental degradation; where there is a lack of adequate information, we must lean in favour of environmental protection by refusing rather than permitting activities likely to be detrimental. This means that unless an activity is proved to be environmentally benign, it is to be presumed to be environmentally harmful. It further requires us to make informed recommendations which balance the needs of transportation with the need to protect the environment and reverse the large-scale degradation that has resulted over the years, priority being given to the environment over economic issues.

The case of *MC Mehta v Union of India*[31] dealt with industrial pollution affecting the famous world heritage site – the Taj Mahal. The petitioner argued in this case that foundries and other hazardous industries in the vicinity of the Taj Mahal are causing acid deposition thereby causing both internal and external damage to the monumental building. The Court noted that, aside from being a cultural heritage site, it is in itself an industry, attracting over two million tourists every year. The Court noted that:

The objective behind this litigation is to stop pollution while encouraging development of industry. The old concept that development and ecology cannot go together is no longer acceptable. Sustainable development is the answer. The development of industry is essential for the economy of the country, but at the same time the environment and the ecosystems have to be protected. The pollution created as a consequence of development must be commensurate with the carrying capacity of our ecosystems.[32]

It again referred to its decision in *Vellore Citizens' Welfare Forum v Union of India*[33] where extensive reference was made to sustainable development, the precautionary principle and the polluter pays principle, noting that these are now well-established

---

30 Ibid.
31 WP 13381/1984 (decided 30 December 1996).
32 Ibid.
33 (1996) 5 SCC 647 *supra* note 14.

principles of Indian law. The importance of procedural rights was discussed in the case of *People's Union for Civil Liberties and Another v UOI and Others* (2005)[34] where the Court noted that the right to information is a facet of 'speech and expression' enshrined in Article 19 and thus, the right to information is indisputably a fundamental right.

The case of *Thilakan v Circle Inspector of Police, Cherpu Police Station and Others*[35] involved the business of providing earth for land filling for various development projects. Although there was no legal requirement for the owner of the land to obtain a permit to remove earth from his own property, the Court articulated a very important principle here: "[n]o man can claim absolute right to indulge in activities resulting in environmental degradation in the land owned by him." It referred to the decision in *State of Tamil Nadu v Hind Stone*,[36] where the Court endorsed both intra and inter-generational equity principle:

> Rivers, Forests, Minerals and such other resources constitute a nation's natural wealth. These resources are not to be frittered away and exhausted by any one generation. Every generation owes a duty to all succeeding generations to develop and conserve the natural resources of the nation in the best possible way. It is in the interest of mankind. It is in the interest of the nation.[37]

The Court then referred to its decision in *MC Mehta v Kamal Nath*[38] where it articulated:

> The concept of sustainable development is now part of our environmental law, in view of various decisions of the Apex Court. The competing claims of the present generation for development and also the claims of future generations to inherit a healthy environment have to be balanced. While exploiting the resources, the capacity of the environment to repair and replace, has also to be taken note of. If a tree is cut and removed, for another tree to grow to the same size, it may take several years. If a bucket of soil is removed, to generate the same, the earth may take a few hundred years. The same is the case of other natural resources also. The length of time only varies. The revenge of mother earth has started displaying in the form of earthquakes, tsunamis, unusually wild cyclonic storms etc. Therefore, it is high time that we think of putting a stop to the defiling and degrading of mother earth.

It also referred to its decision in the *Vellore Citizens'* case[39] where the Court held that the precautionary principle and the polluter pays principle are essential

34   Case No: Appeal (civil) 4294, date of judgment, 6 January 2004.
35   W. P. (C) No. 24627 of 2007(F), decided 23 October, 2007.
36   1981 (2) SCC 2054.
37   Ibid.
38   1997 (1) SCC 3886.
39   See *supra* note 14.

features of the concept of sustainable development. The Court stated that the precautionary principle in the context of municipal law means:

(i)   Environmental measures must anticipate, prevent and attack the causes of environmental degradation.

(ii) Where there are threats of serious and irreversible damage, lack of scientific certainty should not be used as a reason for postponing measures to prevent environmental degradation.

(iii) The 'onus of proof' is on the actor or the developer/industrialist to show that his action is environmentally benign.[40]

The Court then concluded that:

> In view of the above and other judgments, the principle of sustainable development and the doctrines of 'polluter pays' and 'precautionary principle' are part of our environmental law, which is built around Article 21 of Constitution of India. The conditions impugned in this Writ Petition are necessary to protect the environment. If every land owner, driven by profit motive, is to dig his land to win sand, no land except pits will be left for the future generations.[41]

Similarly, in *Chinnappa*,[42] the Court reiterated that sustainable development is essentially a policy and strategy for continued economic and social development detrimental to the environment and natural resources. While providing for the present, we need to take account of the future – we owe a duty to future generations. We must learn from our mistakes in the past so that they can be rectified for a better present and future. The Court noted that the government has a duty under Article 21 of the Constitution to protect the environment, and that sustainable development and the precautionary principle are the salutary principles that govern the law of the environment. In addition, the Court stated that unless there is an inconsistency, the Courts must give due regard to international conventions when interpreting domestic law. The Court also highlighted the importance of environmental impact assessment reports.

In *TN Godavarman Thirumulpad v Union of India*[43] the Court reiterated the importance of sustainable development in the context of protecting natural resources:

> Forests are a vital component to sustain the life support system on the earth. Forests in India have been dwindling over the years for a number of reasons, one of them being the need to use forest area for development activities

---

40   Ibid. The 'polluter pays principle' was held to be a sound principle by the Court in *Indian Council for Enviro-Legal Action v Union of India*, 1996 (3) SCC 212.

41   See *supra* note 38.

42   *K.M. Chinnappa v Union of India*, UP 202/1995 (decided 30 October 2002).

43   WP 202/1995, decided 26 September 2005.

including economic development. Undoubtedly, in any nation development is also necessary but it has to be consistent with protection of environment and not at the cost of degradation of environment. Any programme, policy or vision for overall development has to evolve a systemic approach so as to balance economic development and environmental protection. Both have to go hand in hand. In ultimate analysis, economic development at the cost of degradation of environment and depletion of forest cover would not be long lasting. Such development would be counter productive. Therefore, there is an absolute need to take all precautionary measures when forest lands are sought to be directed for non forest use.[44]

The importance of the precautionary principle was endorsed by the Court in the case of *AP Pollution Control Board v Professor MV Nayudu (retired) and Others*:[45]

The 'uncertainty' of scientific proof and its changing frontiers from time to time has led to great changes in environmental concepts during the period between the Stockholm Conference of 1972 and the Rio Conference of 1992. In Vellore Citizens' Welfare Forum vs. Union of India and Others[46] Kuldip Singh, J. after referring to the principles evolved in various international Conferences and to the concept of 'Sustainable Development,' stated that the Precautionary Principle, the Polluter-Pays Principle and the special concept of Onus of Proof have now emerged and govern the law in our country too, as is clear from Articles 47, 48–A and 51–A(g) of our Constitution . . .

Noting that the precautionary principle has replaced the assimilative capacity principle, the Court pointed out:

A basic shift in the approach to environmental protection occurred initially between 1972 and 1982. Earlier the concept was based on the 'assimilative capacity' rule as revealed from Principle 6 of the Stockholm Declaration . . . The said principle assumed that science could provide policy-makers with the information and means necessary to avoid encroaching upon the capacity of the environment to assimilate impacts and it presumed that relevant technical expertise would be available when environmental harm was predicted and there would be sufficient time to act in order to avoid such harm . . . In the World Charter for Nature, 1982, the emphasis shifted to the 'Precautionary Principle,' and this was reiterated in the Rio Conference.

The Court pointed out that the precautionary principle is based on the theory that it is better to err on the side of caution than risk irreversible environmental

---

44 Ibid.
45 Decided 27 January 1999.
46 1996 (5) SCC 647.

harm. It then elaborated on its parameters and the need to reverse the burden of proof in some instances:

> The principle of precaution involves the anticipation of environmental harm and taking measures to avoid it or to choose the least environmentally harmful activity. It is based on scientific uncertainty. Environmental protection should not only aim at protecting health, property and economic interest but also protect the environment for its own sake.
>
> The precautionary principle suggests that where there is an identifiable risk of serious or irreversible harm . . . it may be appropriate to place the burden of proof on the person or entity proposing the activity that is potentially harmful to the environment. . . . It is also explained that if the environmental risks being run by regulatory inaction are in some way 'uncertain but non-negligible,' then regulatory action is justified . . . In such a situation, the burden of proof is to be placed on those attempting to alter the status quo. They are to discharge this burden by showing the absence of a 'reasonable ecological or medical concern.' That is the required standard of proof.[47]

The importance of environmental education prompted the decision of the Supreme Court of India in the *MC Mehta v Union of India and Others* (1991).[48] This is one of the cases in a long line of cases in India that used the human rights framework to provide redress for environmental damage as well as to prevent further damage to the environment. The petitioner in this case relied on Article 51A(g) of the Constitution of India which requires every citizen to protect and improve the natural environment, including forests, lakes, rivers and wildlife, and to have compassion for living creatures. In order to fulfil this obligation, the petitioner argued that people needed to be better educated about the environment. The Court pointed out that although law is a regulator of human conduct no law can work effectively unless it is accepted by people in society:

> No law works out smoothly unless the interaction is voluntary in order that human conduct may be in accordance with the prescription of law it is necessary that there should be appropriate awareness about what the law requires and there is an element of acceptance that the requirement of law is grounded upon philosophy which should be followed. This would be possible only when steps are taken in an adequate measure to make people aware of the indispensable necessity of their conduct being oriented in accordance with the requirements of law.[49]

Noting that in a democratic polity dissemination of information is the foundation of the system, and that there is a general acceptance that protection of the

47 See *supra* note 45.
48 WP 860/1009 (Decided 22 November 1991).
49 Ibid.

environment is an indispensable necessity for life to survive on earth, the Court made the following directions:

- Require cinema halls, touring cinemas and video parlors to exhibit free of cost at least two slides or messages on the environment in each show. The Ministry of Environment should prepare appropriate slide material for this purpose.
- The Ministry of Information and Broadcasting should produce short information films on the environment.
- The University Grants Commission shall take steps to prescribe a course on the environment and every Education Board shall take steps to enforce compulsory education on the environment.

This case highlights the important role played by information and education in protecting the environment and synthesizes two streams of law – the enjoyment of human rights, indeed the very survival of people, with the protection of the environment – and demonstrates how one framework can be used to seek redress in relation to another, to further articulate its parameters and to even define new rights through the expansive interpretation of existing rights.

As Jona Razzaque points out, the Supreme Court of India has used the right to life clause in a diversified and creative manner.[50] First, it has been interpreted to include a right to a wholesome environment (starting with *CharanLal's* case[51]). Secondly, it has been interpreted as including a right to a livelihood, a better standard of living, hygienic conditions in the workplace and leisure. Thirdly, the public trust doctrine that has been used to protect and preserve public land[52] was extended to all natural resources in the *Kamal Nath's* case,[53] discussed above.

28.3 Cases from Bangladesh

As in India, the Constitution of Bangladesh does not embody a right to a healthy environment. Unlike India, however, it does not refer to the environment in the Directive Principles. This has not stopped its judiciary, however, from interpreting the right to life clause in an expansive manner. This section will discuss seminal decisions of the Supreme Court of Bangladesh.

In *Dr Mohiuddin Farooque v Bangladesh, represented by the Secretary, Ministry of Irrigation, Water Resources and Flood Control*,[54] the Supreme Court of

---

50 See Jona Razzaque, 'Human Rights and the Environment: The National Experience in South Asia and Africa,' Joint UNEP-OHCHR Expert Seminar on Human Rights and the Environment, January 2002, Geneva: Background Paper No 4. See also, U.C. Banerjee, 'The Doctrine of Sustainable Development: A Discussion' in *Sustainable Justice: Reconciling Economic, Social and Environmental Law, supra* note 7, at 47.

51 AIR 1990 SC 1480.

52 Ibid.

53 See *supra* note 11.

54 49 Dhaka Law Reports (AD) 1 (1997).

Bangladesh considered whether the "fundamental right to life included the protection and preservation of the environment, the ecological balance and an environment free from pollution essential for the enjoyment of the right to life."[55] While the Court noted that the Bangladesh Constitution does not contain a provision akin to Article 48A of the Indian Constitution (which imposes a duty on citizens to protect the environment), it pointed out that Articles 31 and 32 on the right to life, encompass within their ambit several other rights:

> Articles 31 and 32 of our constitution protect right to life as a fundamental right. It encompasses within its ambit, the protection and preservation of environment, ecology free from pollution of air and water, sanitation without which life can hardly be enjoyed or omission contrary thereto will be violative of the said right to life.[56]

Relaxing the requirements relating to standing, the Court noted:

> The expression 'any person aggrieved' [within the meaning of Article 102 of the Bangladesh Constitution] is not confined to individually affected persons only but it extends to the people in general, as a collective and consolidated personality. If an applicant bonafide espouses a public cause in the public interest he acquires the competency to claim hearing from the court. . . . Being a public sector subject, flood control and control of river and channel flows is a matter of public concern.[57]

This trend has been followed in subsequent cases.[58] The space given by the Court in this case has opened the door to similar litigation in Bangladesh and the Courts have developed a robust body of law on environmental issues.

In the case of *Dr. Mohiuddin Farooque v Bangladesh and Others*[59] the Court referred to several principles of the Rio Declaration, including Principles 3 and 10:

> Principle 10 above seems to be the theoretical foundation for all that have been vindicated in the writ petition and also provides a ground for standing. In this context of engaging concern for the conservation of environment, irrespective of the locality where it is threatened, I am of the view that a national organization like the appellant, which claims to have studied and made research on the disputed project, can and should be attributed a threshold standing as having sufficient interest in the matter, and thereby regarded as a person aggrieved to maintain the writ petition . . .[60]

55 Ibid.
56 Ibid.
57 Ibid. Referred to in Parvez Hassan and Azim Azfar, 'Securing Environmental Rights Through Public Interest Litigation in South Asia,' (2004) 22 *Va. Envtl. L. J.* 215.
58 See cases *infra*.
59 Civil Appeal No. 24 of 1995, 17 BLD (AD) 1997, Vol. XVII, Page 1 to 33; 1 BLC (AD) (1996) 189–219.
60 Ibid.

Relaxing the principle of *locus standi* has been one of the innovative approaches taken by the Court, which has greatly facilitated people's access to the Court. In this regard, the Court articulated:

> In the face of the statements in the writ petition BELA is concerned with the protection of the people of this country from the ill-effects of environmental hazards and ecological imbalance. It has a genuine interest in seeing that the law is enforced and the people likely to be affected by the proposed project are saved. This interest is sufficient enough to bring the appellant within the meaning of the expression 'person aggrieved'. The appellant should be given locus standi to maintain the writ petition on their behalf.[61]

In *Farooque v Government of Bangladesh*[62] involving industrial pollution, the Court referred to the seminal decision of the Indian Supreme Court in the case of *Rural Litigation and Entitlement Kendra v State of UP*.[63] "This environmental disturbance has however to be weighed in the balance against the need of lime stone quarrying for industrial purposes in the country and we have taken this aspect into account while making this order."[64] In this case, several committees were appointed and their reports were considered by the Supreme Court. In the final judgment, the Court considered the questions as to whether mining operations can be allowed to continue without adversely affecting environment or ecological balance or causing hazard to people or land. The Supreme Court of India answered as follows:

> It is for the Government and the Nation and not for the Court, to decide whether the deposits should be exploited at the cost of ecology and environmental considerations or the industrial requirement should be otherwise satisfied.
>
> We are not oblivious of the fact that natural resources have got to be tapped for the purpose of social development but one cannot forget at the same time that tapping of resources have to be done with requisite attention and care so that ecology and environment may not be affected in any serious way there may not be any depletion of water resources and long term planning must be undertaking to keep up the national wealth. It has always to be remembered that these are permanent assets of mankind and are not intended to be exhausted in one generation.[65]

Hassan and Asfar note the importance of the contribution made by Bangladesh Environmental Lawyers Associations (BELA) and other environmental lawyers in Bangladesh:

61 Ibid.
62 WP No 891 (1994), *In the matter of: An application under Article 102(1) and (2) of the Constitution of the People's Republic of Bangladesh,* available at: http://www.elaw.org/node/2578
63 AIR 1987 SC 2426.
64 Ibid.
65 Ibid.

The success of the Bangladesh Environmental Lawyers Association in this case shows that the opening it achieved for public interest litigation in Farooq has led to effective advances. It is apparent that the linkage between human rights and environmental concerns seen elsewhere in the subcontinent also exists in Bangladesh, where the superior courts are planning a similar role in keeping the judicial avenue open where the executive route has been blocked.[66]

28.4 Cases from Pakistan

A similar trend can be seen in Pakistan. Pakistan's Constitution does not contain any reference to the environment either in the Bill of Rights (which is rarely seen in Constitutions adopted prior to 1980) or in the directive principles chapter (which seems to be the situation in countries discussed here). Hassan and Asfar note that in Pakistan the only reference to the environment is in a schedule to the Constitution which says that ecology may be the subject of legislation by both the provinces as well as the Federation.[67]

Undeterred by this lack of reference, the lawyers for the petitioners in *Shehla Zia and Others v WAPDA*[68] relied on the extensive jurisprudence in India that recognized that the right to life included the right to a decent quality of life. They also relied on the constitutionally guaranteed right to dignity under Article 14 of the Pakistani Constitution. The Pakistani Supreme Court held that a wide meaning should be given to the word 'life' to enable a man not only to sustain life but also to enjoy it:

> The word 'life' has not been defined in the Constitution but it does not mean nor can it be restricted only to the vegetative or animal life or mere existence from conception to death. Life includes all such amenities and facilities which a person in a free country is entitled to enjoy with dignity, legally and constitutionally.
>
> At this stage it may be pointed out that in all the developed countries great importance has been given to energy production. Our need is greater as it is bound to affect our economic development, but in the quest of economic development one has to adopt such measures which may not create hazards to life, destroy the environment and pollute the atmosphere.[69]

With regard to scientific uncertainty, the Court noted that the precautionary principle should be applied and that a balance should be struck between economic progress and prosperity, minimizing possible hazards. Thus, the Court confirmed that a policy of sustainable development should be adopted. The

---

66 See Hassan and Asfar, *supra* note 57.
67 Ibid.
68 PLD 1994 SC 693.
69 Ibid.

Court pointed out that the Rio Declaration "would serve as a great binding force and [. . .] create discipline among the nations while dealing with environmental problems:"[70]

> The concern for protecting environment was first internationally recognized when the declaration of United Nations Conference on the Human Environment was adopted. . . . Thereafter it had taken two decades to create awareness and consensus among the countries when in 1992 the Rio Declaration was adopted. Pakistan is a signatory to this declaration . . . the principle so adopted has its own sanctity and it should be implemented, if not in letter, at least in spirit. . . . The Rio Declaration is the product of hectic discussion among the leaders of the nations of the world and it was after negotiations between the developed and the developing countries that an almost consensus declaration had been sorted out. Environment is an international problem having no frontiers creating transboundary effects. In this field every nation has to cooperate and contribute and for this reason the Rio Declaration would serve as a great binding force and to create discipline among the nations while dealing with environmental problems . . .[71]

The Court then articulated the importance of the precautionary principle:

> Principle No. 15 envisages rule of precaution and prudence. According to it if there are threats of serious damage, effective measures should be taken to control it and it should not be postponed merely on the ground that scientific research and studies are uncertain and not conclusive. It enshrines the principle that prevention is better than cure. It is a cautious approach to avert a catastrophe at the earliest stage. Pakistan is a developing country. It cannot afford the researches and studies made in developed countries on scientific problems particularly the subject at hand. However, the researches and their conclusions with reference to specific cases are available, the information and knowledge is at hand and we should take benefit out of it. In this background if we consider the problem faced by us in this case, it seems reasonable to take preventive and precautionary measures straightaway instead of maintaining status quo because there is no conclusion finding on the effect of electromagnetic fields on human life. One should not wait for conclusive finding as it may take ages to find it out and, therefore, measures should be taken to avert any possible danger and for that reason one should not go to scrap the entire scheme but could make such adjustments, alterations or additions which may ensure safety and security or at least minimise the possible hazards.[72]

70 Ibid.
71 Ibid.
72 Ibid.

The decision in *Shehla Zia's* case has been cited with approval in many subsequent cases. In *Salt Miners Labor Union v Industries and Mineral Development*[73] the Supreme Court, citing *Shehla Zia*, articulated that "the right to have unpolluted water is the right of every person wherever he lives."[74]

The influence of the Indian Supreme Court on cases in the region including Pakistan is also a significant development. In *Dr Amjad H. Bokhari v Federation of Pakistan*,[75] the Supreme Court of Pakistan referred specifically to several seminal cases decided by the Indian Supreme Court: *Vellore Citizens Welfare Forum v Union of India and Others*,[76] *MC Mehta v Kamal Nath and Others*,[77] and *Indian Council for Enviro-Legal Action and Others v Union of India and others*.[78] The Court noted that the Supreme Court of India has, over the years, awarded compensation by applying the polluter pays principle against the offender (i) to reverse the environmental damage and (ii) to compensate the victims.

The Court also referred to its previous decision in the *Shehla Zia* case and noted: (i) that right to a clean environment was included in the right to life guaranteed in Article 9 and right to dignity guaranteed in Article 14; (ii) that international trends and practices shape national obligations; and (iii) the importance of the Rio Declaration on Environment and Development and the precautionary principle.[79]

In the case of *Anjun Irfan v Lahore Development Authority*,[80] the Supreme Court of Pakistan relied on its counterparts' decision in *S. Jagannath v Union of India and Others*[81] discussed above:

> We are of the view that before any shrimp industry or shrimp pond is permitted to be installed in the ecology [sic] fragile coastal area it must pass through a strict environmental test. There had to be a high powered 'Authority' under the Act to scrutinize each and every case from the environmental point of view. There must be an environmental impact assessment before permission is granted to install commercial shrimp farms. The conceptual framework of the assessment must be broad-based primarily concerning environmental degradation linked with shrimp framing [sic]. The assessment must also include the social impact on different population strata in the area. The quality of the assessment must be analytically based on superior technology.

---

73 1994 SCMR 2061.

74 Ibid.

75 Constitutional Petition 45/2003, *Amicus Curiae* by Parvez Hassan.

76 See *supra* note 14.

77 See *supra* note 11.

78 WP 967/1989 (Decision 8 July 2011).

79 The Court further referred to several international instruments that were applicable to the case including, the Law of the Sea Convention, MARPOL convention, Convention on Safety of Life at Sea and several IMO regulations.

80 PLD 2002 Lahore 555.

81 AIR 1997 SC 811.

It must take into consideration the intergenerational equity and the compensation for those who are affected end [sic] prejudiced.[82]

The reach and the significance of *Shehla Zia's* case is summarized by Hassan and Azfar as follows:

> Perhaps the most important legacy of Shehla Zia to date is that it has provided the public with an almost unfettered right to bring environmentally-related grievances to the superior and subordinate courts. Prior to Shehla Zia, and particularly because of the lack of environment-specific provisions in the Constitution, procedural hurdles of 'standing to sue,' and the constitutional requirement of being an 'aggrieved person,' provided insurmountable hurdles to even the most valid causes of action. Hopefully, Shehla Zia has irrevocably changed all of this. Within a constitutional scheme that holds the law handed down by the Supreme Court and High Courts binding on the subordinate courts, every court in the country is bound to consider environmental complaints on their respective merits. This is a victory whose significance cannot be over-emphasized.[83]

28.5 Cases from Nepal

Similar to other countries in South Asia, Nepal has also been influenced by the legal developments in the region. In the landmark case of *Surya Prasad Sharma Dhungel v Godawari Marble Industries and Others*,[84] the Supreme Court of Nepal held that a clean and healthy environment is part of the right to life clause under Article 12(1) of the Nepal Constitution:

> Good environment is one of the prerequisites for a personal life. But the dust, minerals, smoke and sands emitted by the said factory have excessively polluted the springs water and nearby water bodies, land and atmosphere of the said area, thus continuously deteriorating the health, life, education and profession of the research experts of the petitioner institute, the students of St. Xavier's school, the laborers working in the industry and their family members and ultimately the local inhabitants. While blasting dynamites, crushing stones and transporting boulders and marble, even the minimum security measures have not been adopted or granted neither by the industry nor the government. No measure has been adopted to halt the negative impact and loss on the environment. The respondent industry has no constitutional and legal right to endanger others' life. The local Panchayat including all the respondents are equally responsible for keeping quiet and not

---

82 See *supra* note 78.
83 See *supra* note 57 (footnotes omitted).
84 WP 35/1992 (1995.10.31), available at: https://www.elaw.org/node/1849

implementing any legal measure to thwart this type of unauthorized activity of the industry.[85]

The Court further articulated in this case:

> Since clean and healthy environment is an indispensable part of a human life, right to clean, healthy environment is undoubtedly embedded within the Right to Life. It is clear that the constitutional perimeter in which the applicant had filed the writ petition, has been substantively changed form (sic) the commencement of Article 26 (4) of the Constitution of the Kingdom of Nepal 1990, because this Article has taken environmental conservation as one of the basic Directive Principles of the State.[86]

The Court also acknowledged the importance of sustainable development, stating that while industry is the foundation of development of a country, it is essential to maintain environmental balance along with industrial development:

> It is essential to establish balance between the need to provide continuity to developmental activities and priority to the protection of the environment . . . Development is for the interest, prosperity of human being. Therefore, life of human being is the end. Development is the means to live happily; human beings cannot live a clean and healthy life without a clean and healthy environment. Therefore, safety of the environment is the means. Environment protection measures should be initiated taking into account this fact.[87]

In a more recent case, the Supreme Court of Nepal elaborated on the significance of drinking water for the purpose of maintaining public health. In *Prakash Mani Sharma and Others v Nepal Drinking Water Corporation and Others*,[88] the Court, while not explicitly recognizing that drinking water is a fundamental right, nonetheless held that providing pure drinking water is a responsibility of the welfare state.

In *Prakash Mani Sharma v His Majesty's Government Cabinet Secretariat and Others*,[89] the Court held that a healthy environment is a prerequisite for the protection of personal freedoms under the Constitution. Relying on the concept of sustainable development, the Court acknowledged that environment and development should proceed harmoniously and environmental protection cannot be ignored for the sake of development:

---

85 Ibid.
86 Ibid.
87 Ibid.
88 2237/1990 (10 July 2001), summary available at Environmental Law Alliance Worldwide, http://www.elaw.org/node/1383.
89 WP 2237/1990 (11 March 2003), summary available at Environmental Law Alliance Worldwide, http://www.elaw.org/node/1594.

The freedom of personal liberty of every citizen is constitutionally guaranteed under the Article 12(1) of the Constitution of the Kingdom of Nepal 1990. Henceforth, citizens are no doubt entitled to enjoy this fundamental right to the greatest extent. Personal freedoms at large can only be protected by a healthy environment and it is an unquestionable fact that a polluted environment deprives the right to life protected under the constitution and the laws. That is why the state has a primary obligation to protect the right to personal liberty by mitigating environmental pollution as much as possible. As Article 26(4) of the Constitution provides that the state shall give priority to the protection of the environment and also to prevent its further damage due to development activities by increasing the awareness of the general public about environmental cleanliness, the state is responsible to continue implementing the right to personal liberty under the Art 12(1) of the Constitution. In addition, the respondent government is also charged with an obligation under Section 9(2) of the Treaty Act 1990 to implement provisions of international conventions concerning environment . . . Additionally, the present world community has deemed the right to development as a third generation right. The demand for rapid development also cannot be ignored. Especially a country left behind by the wave of the development like Nepal requires an accelerated development process. At the same time, the state also has an obligation to protect the environment taking into account the negative impact of development upon the environment. Therefore, development and environment should proceed harmoniously. This court is also aware of the respondent's inability to launch environmental protection programs as per the demand of the petitioner due to the constraints of resources and technology. Nevertheless, environmental destruction cannot be encouraged in the name of development.[90]

As in the above-mentioned Indian cases, Nepalese Courts have expanded the right to life clause, as well as the right to personal liberty to include a right to a clean environment. They have also relaxed the traditional notions of *locus standi* and relied on international environmental concepts such as sustainable development and the precautionary principle to support their novel interpretation of protected rights.

28.6 Cases from Sri Lanka

While there have been several important judgments of the Supreme Court of Sri Lanka articulating environmental rights, the *Eppawala Phosphate Mining* case[91] is the most far-reaching case in terms of its vision, the use of international environmental law, and the discussion of the importance of an environmental impact assessment and public participation. Given the far-reaching nature of the judgment, considerable attention will be paid to this case.

90   Ibid.
91   *Tikiri Banka Bulankulame and Others v Secretary, Ministry of Industries and others*, 3 Sri LR 243 (2 June 2000).

One distinguishing feature of the Sri Lankan Constitution must be pointed out here. Unlike in other countries in the region, the current Sri Lankan Constitution does not contain a right to life clause. It may be recalled that the judiciaries in India, Bangladesh, Nepal and Pakistan used the right to life clause to articulate environmental rights, expanding it to encompass many other rights within its ambit, including the right to be free from pollution, the right to a decent standard of living, the right to be free from contamination, the right to water, and the right to a healthy environment. The Sri Lankan judiciary has, by contrast, used the right to equality clause embodied in Article 12(1) of the Constitution to articulate environmental rights. This feature deserves scrutiny and analysis in its own right.

The Court has also been receptive to the use of international environmental law principles in adjudicating national cases. In *Gunaratne v Homagama Pradeshiya Sabha*,[92] the Supreme Court noted that public participation and transparency are essential if sustainable development is to be achieved. These principles have since then gained ground internationally.

The *Eppawala Phosphate Mining* case[93] arose out of a proposed agreement between the Government of Sri Lanka and Freeport McMoran, USA (hereinafter the Company) in respect of developing a deposit of phosphate rock at Eppawela in the North Central Province of Sri Lanka. This agreement granted, among others, the sole and exclusive right to the Company to search and explore for phosphate and other minerals. The petitioners in this case were residents of Eppawela who were engaged in cultivation and owned land there. They alleged that several of their rights guaranteed under the Constitution would be violated if the proposed agreement were to be implemented. The rights invoked were: right to equality,[94] the freedom to engage in a lawful occupation, profession, trade or business,[95] and the freedom of movement and of choosing one's residence within Sri Lanka.[96] They further alleged, relying on the analysis of several reports and experts, that the proposed project would be an environmental and economic disaster.

Justice Amerasinghe, writing the opinion of the Court, noted that "the organs of the state are guardians to whom the people have committed the care and preservation of the resources of the people."[97] He said, referring to the Indian Supreme Court judgment in *MC Mehta v Kamal Nath*[98] that while the natural resources of people are held in trust for them by the Government, this did not mean that the Court had no role to play. Justice Amerasinghe noted that the public trust doctrine is rather restrictive in scope and that the principle of shared responsibility[99] is better suited to apply to natural resources and the environment.

---

92 (1998) 2 Sri LR 11 (3 April 1998).

93 See *supra* note 91.

94 Article 12(1) of the 1978 Constitution of Sri Lanka, available at: http://www.priu.gov.lk/Cons/1978Constitution/Introduction.htm.

95 Ibid. at article 14(1)(g).

96 Ibid. at article 14(1)(h).

97 See *supra* note 91.

98 See *supra* note 11.

99 While the Court indicated that it is the responsibility of everybody, not just the government, to protect the environment, it did not further elaborate on this principle.

Article 27(14) of the Constitution imposes a duty on the State to "protect, preserve and improve the environment for the benefit of the community." Moreover, Article 28(f) places a duty on the people of Sri Lanka to protect nature and conserve its riches.

The proposed agreement acknowledged that some residents presently living in the exploration area may have to be relocated in order to proceed with mining if the company determines so and the company would pay the costs of relocation. At no point, however, were these residents consulted or the plan of possible relocation divulged. While it was argued on behalf of the respondents that the proposed agreement related only to feasibility studies and not mining itself, the Court took the view that the totality of the agreement must be considered in order to decide whether there is an imminent infringement of the petitioners' protected rights.

Relying on Principle 2 of the Rio Declaration and Principle 21 of the Stockholm Declaration, Justice Amerasinghe agreed that the State has the right to exploit its own resources pursuant to its own environmental and development policies. Referring to Principle 14 of the Stockholm Declaration[100] and Principles 1[101] and 4[102] of the Rio Declaration the Court held that the proposed agreement must be considered in light of these principles. The fact that these are non-binding instruments did not deter the Court:

> Admittedly, the principles set out in the Stockholm and Rio De Janeiro Declarations are not legally binding in the way in which an Act of our Parliament would be. It may be regarded merely as 'soft law'. Nonetheless, as a Member of the United Nations, they could hardly be ignored by Sri Lanka. *Moreover, they would, in my view, be binding if they have been either expressly enacted or become a part of the domestic law by adoption by the superior Courts of record and by the Supreme Court in particular, in their decisions.*[103]

The Court noted that while the petitioners did not oppose the utilization of the deposit, they feared that the scale of exploitation envisaged under the proposed agreement could lead to the supplies being exhausted too quickly and cause serious environmental harm affecting the health, safety, livelihood and cultural heritage of the petitioners. The petitioners further submitted that "the phosphate deposit is a non-renewable natural resource that should be developed in a prudent and sustainable manner in order to strike an equitable balance between the needs of the present and future generations of Sri Lankans."[104]

---

100 Principle 14 deals with rational planning.
101 Principle 1 states that human beings are at the center of concerns for sustainable development.
102 Principle 4 embodies the principle of integration and provides that environmental protection shall constitute an integral part of the developmental process.
103 See *supra* note 91 at 274–75 (emphasis added).
104 Ibid. at 276. Justice Amerasighe relied extensively on international environmental law principles in elucidating the meaning of sustainable development.

Drawing inspiration from H.E. Judge C.G. Weeramantry's separate opinion in the *Hungary v Slovakia* case,[105] Justice Amerasinghe referred to the need to balance the needs of the present generation with those of posterity. Sustainable development *does not* mean that further development must be halted:

> In my view, the human development paradigm needs to be placed within the context of our finite environment, so as to ensure the future sustainability of the mineral resources and of the water and soil conservation ecosystems of the Eppawala region . . . Due account must also be taken of our unrenewable (sic) cultural heritage. Decisions with regard to the nature and scale of activity require the most anxious consideration from the point of view of safeguarding the health and safety of the people, naturally, including the petitioners, ensuring the viability of their occupations, and protecting the rights of future generations of Sri Lankans.[106]

The petitioners also alleged that if the proposed mining activity were to proceed, it could affect many historic temples and other monuments of archaeological value as well as ancient irrigation networks of the North Central Province. This is in an area of historical significance, which has been acknowledged by the National Science Foundation as well as the National Academy of Sciences. Moreover, establishing a factory for the production of phosphoric acid and sulphuric acid in this historic area has the potential to cause considerable environmental damage. The Court drew attention to Principle 17 of the Rio Declaration and articulated the importance of the Environmental Impact Assessment (EIA) process:

> This is an important procedural rule designed to facilitate the preventive (Principles 6 and 7 of Stockholm) and precautionary (Principle 15 of Rio) principle already mentioned above. I would like to remind the persons concerned, especially the Central Environmental Authority, that an environmental impact assessment exercise can identify the potential threats of a proposed activity or project, and that this information can then be used to modify the proposed activity in order to take these threats into account. Remedial measures can also be introduced in order to mitigate or reduce any perceived detrimental impacts of the project. In this sense, therefore, an environmental impact assessment exercise contemplated by the National Environmental Act can be instrumental in establishing exactly which areas of the proposed project, or activity require precautionary or preventive measures in order to ensure the overall environmental viability of the project.[107]

---

105   See *supra* note 9.
106   See *supra* note 91 at 279.
107   Ibid.

Justice Amerasinghe noted that in this case the salutary provisions of the law relating to notification and publication of EIAs have not been observed. He further noted that the provision in the proposed agreement that the law of the country will be complied with is superfluous given the fact that every person, whether natural or corporate, must comply with the laws of the republic as they are governed by the rule of law:

> What has been attempted here is to contract out of the obligation to comply with the law and to substitute a procedure for that laid down by the law. It was assumed that by a contractual arrangement between the executive branch of the government and the Company, the laws of the country could be avoided. *That is an obviously erroneous assumption, for no organ of Government, no person whomsoever, is above the law.*[108]

Noting that the proposed agreement sought to circumvent the safeguards in the National Environmental Act the Court was of the view that:

> There is no way under the proposed agreement to ensure a consideration of development options that were environmentally sound and sustainable at an early stage in fairness both to the project proponent and the public. Moreover, the safeguards ensured by the National Environmental Act and the regulations framed thereunder with regard to publicity have been virtually negated by the provision in the proposed agreement regarding confidentiality. I would reiterate what was said by this Court in Gunaratne v Homagagma Pradeshiya Sabha (1998) namely, that publicity, transparency and fairness are essential if the goal of sustainable development is to be achieved.[109]

The Court thus essentially rejected the confidentiality provisions in the proposed agreement as being contrary to the goal of sustainable development. It stressed the importance of procedural principles and referred to Principle 10 of the Rio Declaration, which embodies the principles of access to information, public participation and access to remedies. The Court noted that Principle 10 calls for better citizen participation in environmental decision-making and access to environmental information "for they can help to ensure greater compliance by States of international environmental standards through the accountability of their governments."[110]

The Court further noted that, in this case, the proposed agreement made no reference to an EIA. The law prescribes the procedure to be followed and when it should be followed, for good reason. Project proponents cannot decide

108 Ibid. at 314 (emphasis added).
109 Ibid. at 316.
110 Ibid.

when to comply with the law. The proposed agreement sought to substitute an extraordinary procedure for the proposed project, which contravened the provisions of the National Environmental Act and its regulations, and in turn, effectively excluded public awareness and participation as embodied in the law as well as in Principle 10 of the Rio Declaration.[111]

This judgment is fascinating in many respects: the extensive use of international environmental law principles in the judgment, including those that are embodied in soft law instruments; the use of existing rights in an expansive manner to articulate environmental rights; and the use of the fundamental rights machinery in relation to an imminent infringement of a right thereby averting a possible environmental disaster in the future. This case is a classic example of the use of multiple disciplines to support the creative interpretation of existing rights.

In the case of *Mundy v Central Environmental Authority and Others*[112] the Supreme Court of Sri Lanka referred to the Court of Appeal decision where the latter concluded:

> Courts have to balance the right to development and the right to environmental protection. While development activity is necessary and inevitable for the sustainable development of a nation, unfortunately it impacts and affects the rights of private individuals, but such is the inevitable sad sacrifice that has to be made for the progress of a nation. Unhappily there is no public recognition of such sacrifice which is made for the benefit of the larger public interest which would be better served by such development. The Courts can only minimize and contain as much as possible the effect to such rights . . .[113]

The Court referred to H.E. Judge C.G. Weeramantry's separate opinion in the *Hungary v. Slovakia* case,[114] which provides a detailed discussion of sustainable development and its relevance in the modern commercially advancing society. Justice Weeramantry also referred to the principle of trusteeship of earth resources, in other words the concept of 'public trust', which has been followed as invaluable by Indian Judges in several landmark judgments.

The Supreme Court dismissed the writ applications, in the exercise of its discretionary powers, holding that:

---

111 The Court declared that an imminent infringement of the fundamental rights of the petitioners embodied in Articles 12(1) (right to equality), 14(1)(g) (freedom to engage in a lawful occupation), and 14(1)(h) (freedom of movement and choosing one's residence) has been established. The Court directed the respondents to desist from entering into any contract relating to the Eppawala phosphate deposit. It directed the third respondent (Geological Survey and Mines Bureau) to do a comprehensive study relating to the locations, quantity and quality of the deposit in consultation with the National Academy of Sciences of Sri Lanka and the National Science Foundation and to publish the results of this study. The Court further directed the project proponent to obtain the approval of the CEA according to law.

112 SC Appeal 58/2003, SC minutes 20 January 2004.

113 Ibid.

114 See *supra* note 9.

[When balancing the competing interests] the conclusion necessarily has to be made in favour of the larger interests of the community who would benefit immensely by the construction of the proposed expressway . . . the adoption of the Combined Trace would undoubtedly result in irreversible damage to the eco-system in the Bolgoda Wetland area. Therefore the only option is to adopt the Final Trace which . . . will result only in the displacement of affected people in that area . . . the obligation to the society as a whole must predominate over the obligation to a group of individuals, who are so unfortunately affected by the construction of the expressway.[115]

The case of *Sugathapala Mendis and Raja Melroy Senanayake v Chandrika Bandaranayake Kumaratunge and Others*[116] involved the public trust doctrine and acquisition of public land for private purposes. The Court quoted the decision in *Bandara v Premachandra*[117] where it was held that the public trust doctrine must be upheld not only for purposes of good governance but also for sustainable economic development of the country especially for the economically challenged, the disadvantaged and the marginalized.

Referring to the EIA prepared for this project the Court pointed out that the land that was alienated to Asia Pacific is home to nine threatened species of animals. If the Urban Development Authority (UDA) was sincere about the environmental safety of the project, it should have at least investigated the viability of mitigatory measures to determine whether these species could be adequately preserved. While some deliberation had been done on flood control, there had been little concern expressed in relation to degradation of fauna and flora and long-term effects of development on the ecosystem, microclimate and the surrounding water table. Pointing out that only one page has been devoted in the EIA report to monitoring activities which is hardly sufficient for an area home to endangered species, the Court referred to the Indian Supreme Court decision of *Vellore Citizens' Welfare Forum v Union of India*[118] which analysed the need to balance the impact of development projects on the environment:

Where there is an identifiable risk of serious or irreversible harm, it may be appropriate to place the burden of proof on the person or entity proposing the activity that is potentially harmful to the environment. The burden of proof in such cases is therefore placed firmly on the developer or industrialist who wishes to alter the status quo . . .[119]

---

115 See *supra* note 113.
116 SC Application No 352/2007, SC Minutes 8/10/2008. There were several intervenient petitioners in this case. Excerpts from Sumudu Atapattu, 'Judicial Protection of Human Rights' in *Sri Lanka: State of Human Rights 2010* (Colombo: Law & Society Trust).
117 1994 1 Sri LR 301.
118 See *supra* note 14.
119 See *supra* note 117.

This is a clear reference to the precautionary principle, a cardinal principle of international environmental law.[120] The Court also referred to the Indian Supreme Court decision in *AP Pollution Control Board v Nayudu*[121] where the Court stressed that preservation of the environment is a goal that must be sought for its own sake, not simply because of economic or other benefits: "[t]he environment must not only be protected in the interest of health, property and economy, but also for its own sake. Precautionary duties are triggered not only by concrete knowledge of danger but also by a justified concern or risk potential."[122]

The Court also referred to the case of *People United for Better Living in Calcutta v State of West Bengal*[123] where that Court discussed the efforts made in the US to give a monetary value to wetlands taking into account the various functions they contribute, including water purification and as a habitat for species. The Court was of the view that the UDA saw this land as being valuable because of its developmental potential "and not as a valuable natural resource providing both environmental and long-term economic benefits in its unaltered state."[124]

With regard to the role that the former President played in this case, the Court pointed out that the Constitution requires the President to uphold and defend the Constitution, which includes responsibilities concerning the country's sustainable development. The Court also noted that similar duties are vested with Ministers. The Court referred to the need to comply with the rule of law when exercising Presidential power in a very harsh manner:

> While the exercise of Presidential power is a duty that must accord with the Rule of Law, such compliance should also come from one's own conscience and sense of integrity as owned to its People. This means that whilst they can use their private power and their private property in an unfettered manner when granting any privileges and favors . . . their public power must only be used strictly for the larger benefit of the People, the long term sustainable development of the country and in accordance with the Rule of Law.[125]

28.7 Conclusion

The far-reaching nature of environmental jurisprudence in South Asia has prompted some scholars to advance the critique that judges are engaged in judicial activism usurping the functions of the legislature (and the executive in some instances) particularly in India.[126] While there may be some truth in

---

120 See Sumudu Atapattu, *supra* note 2, chapter 3.
121 (1992) 2 SCC 718.
122 Ibid.
123 AIR 1993 Calcutta 215.
124 See *supra* note 116.
125 Ibid. Emphasis in original.
126 See Varun Gauri, 'Fundamental Rights and Public Interest Litigation in India: Overarching or Underachieving?' (2010) 1 *Indian J. L. & Econ.* 71; Lavanya Rajamani, 'Public Interest

this argument, it can also be argued that a directive from the Supreme Court is exactly what is needed in situations where government agencies are ineffective or inefficient or simply do not care about the plight of people. As Rajamani points out, "[t]he Court has transformed itself, through the exercise of its public interest jurisdiction, into an arena in which political, social and economic battles are fought, and socio-economic justice is delivered."[127] While it is beyond the scope of this chapter to discuss the merits and demerits of public interest litigation as a tool, suffice it to note that without public interest litigation, the developments relating to human rights and environmental rights would not have been possible in many parts of the world. It has been articulated, on the positive side, that "[j]udicial activism and PIL has long been acknowledged as a testament to Indian democracy, and an invaluable tool in addressing executive action,"[128] while on the negative side, it has been argued that the Court merely substitutes executive governance with judicial governance and "the Court has over time developed into a policy evolution fora, a role it is ill-equipped to play."[129]

While accepting that public interest litigation (PIL) can be abused, overused and misused, Puvimanasinghe, however, points out the merits of PIL:

> In the South Asian region as a whole, public interest litigation has been useful in injecting an informed, participatory, and transparent approach to the processes of development, and to governmental and private sector actions involving public resources. It has provided a voice to persons who would otherwise be unheard. Through PIL, multiple sectors and stakeholders become involved in the development process, as envisaged in the idea of sustainable development.[130]

While there is no doubt that the Indian Supreme Court has been the pioneer in this field without which developments in other countries may not have been possible, the Courts could not have engaged in this uphill struggle alone. It is the combination of several factors that led to the groundbreaking judgments that were given birth to in this region; a vibrant civil society, a far-sighted legal profession willing to take chances,[131] and a judiciary willing to relax rigid

---

Environmental Litigation in India: Exploring Issues of Access, Participation, Equity, Effectiveness and Susainability' (2007) 19 *J. Envtl. L.* 293 available at: http://jel.oxfordjournals.org/content/19/3/293.full

127 See Rajamani, *supra* note 126 at 294. She further notes that "where there is a vacuum in governance, the court rushes to fill it."

128 See Rajamani, *supra* note 126, at 319.

129 Ibid.

130 See Shyami Fernando Puvimanasinghe, 'Sustainable Development in the Courts: Towards a Jurisprudence of Sustainable Development in South Asia: Litigation in the Public Interest' (2009) 10 *Sus. Dev. L. & Pol'y* 41.

131 A few committed individual lawyers and a few NGOs have played the role of watchdog in these countries often sacrificing their lucrative law practices – MC Mehta of India, Dr. Mohiuddin Farooque of Bangladesh, Lalanath de Silva of Sri Lanka and Prakash Mani Sharma of Nepal are

legal principles and incorporate international law in their judgments, have all contributed to this success. It is no secret that relaxing the principles relating to *locus standi* to facilitate public interest litigation has contributed significantly to these developments. It is noteworthy that these judges have been bold enough to incorporate international law principles in their judgments (including those in soft law instruments) and adopt expansive interpretations to existing rights to encompass rights that were not originally included. In this regard it is interesting to note what the Supreme Court of the Philippines articulated in relation to environmental rights in the *Minors Oposa Case*:[132] "these basic rights need not even be written in the Constitution for they are assumed to exist from the inception of mankind."[133]

Another observation merits mention here – judicial activism in South Asia seems to be confined to a few judges of the Supreme Court and is not endemic to the institution as a whole. This is certainly true of the Sri Lankan Supreme Court where the ground-breaking judgments seem to have emanated from one or two judges of the Court. Once these judges retired, the judgments of the Court seemed to have reverted to its former mediocre level. This is disconcerting as the untiring efforts of their predecessors can fall by the wayside if the principles articulated by these far-sighted judges are not incorporated and re-affirmed in later judgments.

The cases surveyed above demonstrate that sustainable development and related principles, both substantive and procedural, are now firmly entrenched in the law of South Asia. This development would not have been possible without the innovative approach adopted by the judiciary in the region. The pioneering role played by the Indian Supreme Court has had a huge influence in other countries in the region. Despite political and ideological differences in inter-governmental relations, the courts in neighbouring countries have not hesitated to quote with approval decisions of the Indian Supreme Court. This is a fascinating development. The courts in the region have also relied on international environmental law principles, freely importing these principles into national law, undeterred by the fact that some of these principles are not even fully entrenched in international law or are contained in soft law instruments. Sustainable development, the polluter pays principle, the precautionary principle and the inter-generational equity principle, the public trust doctrine and procedural principles have played significant roles in these cases. As articulated by Justice Banerjee: "[s]ustainable development is not a fixed state of harmony but rather the process of change in which the exploitation of resources, the direction of investment, the orientation of technological development and institutional change are made consistent with future as well as present needs."[134]

some examples. The NGOs include the Environmental Foundation of Sri Lanka and Bangladesh Environmental Lawyers Association (BELA).

132 *Minors Oposa v Secretary of the Dept of Env't & Natural Res.* (1993) 33 ILM 173, 178.
133 Ibid.
134 See *supra* note 50 at 53.

It is encouraging to see the innovative approach adopted by countries in South Asia (this includes the legal profession, the judiciary and civil society) of using an existing legal framework creatively to seek redress in another area of law and to articulate rights that are not explicitly mentioned in the Bill of Rights. Despite criticisms of judicial activism, there is no doubt that these cases have contributed to the development of law in this area in a significant manner. While judges cannot, in principle, deviate from the confines of the constitutional provisions, these cases have amply demonstrated how existing rights can be creatively and expansively interpreted to encompass rights that were not necessarily envisioned by the framers of the original document, thereby making it a truly living document.

29 Sustainable development principles in the Caribbean Court of Justice

Danielle Turnquest Moulton and Stephanie Forte

29.1 Introduction

The Caribbean Court of Justice (CCJ) is a unique regional judicial institution having the power to adjudicate cases in two separate jurisdictions within the Caribbean region.[1] In its Original Jurisdiction, the CCJ is an international court, applying the rules of international law to settle disputes concerning the interpretation and application of the Revised Treaty of Chaguaramas (RTC).[2] In exercising its Appellate Jurisdiction, the CCJ decides on municipal law issues as a final court of appeal for some Member States of the Caribbean Community.[3]

The CCJ has only begun to establish its jurisprudence although it is already clear that principles such as precaution play an important role in the CCJ's analysis. The CCJ as an institution promotes several principles of sustainable development listed in the New Delhi Declaration, including the principle of public participation and access to information and justice, and the Court may be called upon to deliberate issues relating to the duty of States to ensure sustainable use of natural resources. These principles enable the Court to adjudicate matters in which the precautionary approach to human health, natural resources and ecosystems may be invoked before it as a relevant principle. Under Article 65 of the RTC, the Caribbean Community must take "the precautionary principle and those principles relating to preventive action" into account in formulating measures in relation to the environment.

This chapter will discuss the application of the precautionary principle in the courts of the States of the Caribbean region and the Caribbean Court of Justice, in particular how the precautionary principle has affected fisheries management and law in the Caribbean region. In section 29.2 we will discuss the history and the evolution of the precautionary principle. In section 29.3 we will discuss the development of fisheries management through international instruments,

---

1 Duke E. Pollard, *The Caribbean Court of Justice: Closing the Circle of Independence* (Kingston: The Caribbean Law Publishing Company, 2004); Winston Anderson, *Principles of Caribbean Environmental Law* (USA: Environmental Law Institute Press, 2012) 17.
2 Revised Treaty of Chaguramas Establishing the Caribbean Community (CARICOM) including the CARICOM Single Market and Economy 2259 UNTS 293 (signed 5 July 2001, entered into force 2 April 2002); Agreement Establishing the Caribbean Court of Justice (signed 14 February 2001, entered into force 23 July 2002) 2255 UNTS 319, Articles XII(1) and XXV.
3 New Delhi Principles 1, 4, and 5; CCJ Agreement, Article III(2); RTC, Articles 58, 60, 65, 211, and 222.

national policy and case law. In section 29.4 we will analyse the precautionary approach as it relates to fisheries management. In section 29.5 we will discuss Caribbean regional approach to fisheries management and how their categorisation as SIDS impacts their approach to fisheries management. In Section 29.6 we will argue for the aggressive application of the precautionary principle to fisheries management in order to safeguard the economic future of the Caribbean region. Our discussion will canvas national decisions in the Caribbean which analyse the precautionary principles including the cases of *Fishermen and Friends of the Sea v The Environmental Management Authority and Atlantic LNG Company of Trinidad and Tobago*[4]; *People United Respecting Environment (PURE) et al. and Environmental Management Authority*[5]; *and Delapenha Funeral Home Limited v The Minister of Local Government.*[6] It is anticipated that the Court will have recourse to such decisions of national tribunals as persuasive authority when deciding cases in its Original Jurisdiction. The chapter concludes with possibilities for the application of the precautionary principle in the adjudication of fisheries management issues in the CCJ.

29.2 The precautionary principle

Judge Weeramantry in the case concerning the *Nuclear Tests Case (New Zealand v France)* opined in his dissenting argument that "the law cannot function in the protection of the environment unless a legal principle is involved to meet this evidentiary difficulty and environmental law has responded with what has become known as the precautionary principle."[7] The emergence of the precautionary principle within international environmental law is a salient development for sustainable development and environmental protection. Its widespread recognition and implementation has resulted in a contentious debate on whether it has achieved the status of being a norm of customary international law.[8]

29.2.1 The history and development of the "precautionary principle"

The "Vorsorgeprinzip" – a framework principle of German environmental policy emerging in the 1970s – marks the conceptual origins of the precautionary principle. Vorsorge literally meant "beforehand or prior care or worry," and carries overtones of caution and foresight.[9] The principle was used in the context of German air pollution regulation and justified the implementation of incremental emission reduction policies designed to tackle acid rain, global warming and the

---

4 TT [2004] HC 113.
5 TT [2009] HC 133.
6 JM [2008] SC 72.
7 *Request for an Examination in the Nuclear Tests (New Zealand v. France)* case, I.C.J. Reports 1995, p. 342
8 For example, the Supreme Court of India in the cases *A.P. Pollution Control Board v Nayadu*, 1999, S.O.L., Case no.53, at para 27 and *Vellore Citizens Welfare Forum v Union of India* [1996] Supp. 5 S.C.R. 241, declared the precautionary principle as a norm of customary international law.
9 N. Morag-Levine. "Is Precautionary Regulation a Civil Law Instrument? Lessons from the History of the Alkali Act" (2011) 23 *J. Envtl. L.* 1, 1.

pollution of the North Sea.[10] These policies were implemented in the absence of conclusive evidence on causal links between exposure to particular pollutants and identifiable environmental harms.[11] The rejection of the traditional "assimilative capacity approach" paved the pathway for the principle.[12]

The principle was first introduced in 1984 at the First International Conference on Protection of the North Sea, and since then has been integrated into numerous international conventions and agreements, the most prominent being the Rio Declaration on Environment and Development[13] and others including, the Maastricht Treaty on the European Union[14], the Cartagena Convention, the United Nations Framework Convention on Climate Change[15] and the Convention on Biological Diversity.[16]

29.3 The development of international fisheries management

29.3.1 The evolution of international fisheries management

The traditional approach to fisheries management was to be reactive to management problems after they reached crisis levels.[17] The rationale for the international response to the development of fisheries management was the collapse of fisheries through overexploitation of fish stocks due to poor management.[18] The collapse of the cod fishery of Atlantic Canada is one of the most dramatic examples within international environmental law of a failure in fisheries management.[19]

---

10 Germany advocated for the principle to become a cornerstone of European environmental policy in the 1980s.

11 UNESCO. "The Precautionary Principle," (2005) 9. The principle specifically related to technological standards thereby promoting the development of cleaner industrial processes.

12 The "assimilative capacity approach" was a reactive approach based upon the belief that scientific method could accurately determine the assimilative capacity of the environment and therefore once determined sufficient time would remain to address the problem. However, the failure of this approach was due to the fact that this conclusive scientific evidence would come too late and therefore create a situation where damage became irreversible. The application of the precautionary principle meant a shift in favour of a bias towards safety and caution. O. McIntyre and T. Mosedale, "The Precautionary Principle as a Norm of Customary International Law" (2007) 9 *J. Envtl. L.* 221, 221. See also D. Freestone, "The Road to Rio: International Environmental Law After the Earth Summit" (1994) 6 *J. Envtl. L.* 193, 211.

13 Rio Declaration on Environment and Development. 16 June 1972. Available at http://www.unep.org/Documents.multilingual/Default.asp?DocumentID=78&ArticleID=1163, (accessed November 2011).

14 Maastricht Treaty on the European Union, 7 February 1992, available at http://www.europarl.europa.eu/parliament/archive/staticDisplay.do?id=77&pageRank=6&language=EN, (accessed November 2011).

15 UN Framework Climate Change Convention, available at http://unfccc.int/key_documents/the_convention/items/2853.php (accessed November 2011)

16 United Nations Convention on Biological Diversity, opened for signature June 5, 1992, 1760 UNTS 79, 143.

17 Boyle and Freestone, eds., *International Law and Sustainable Development* (Oxford: OUP, 1999) 160.

18 C.W. Clark, T. Lauck *et al.* "Implementing the Precautionary Principle in Fisheries Management through Marine Reserves." (1998) 8 *Ecological Application Supplement* 1, S72, S72.

19 Ibid.

The working definition of fisheries management in the *FAO's Technical Guidelines for Responsible Fisheries* is[20]:

> The integrated process of information gathering, analysis, planning, consultation, decision-making, allocation of resources and formulation and implementation, with enforcement as necessary, of regulations or rules which govern fisheries activities in order to ensure the continued productivity of the resources and the accomplishment of other fisheries objectives.[21]

The Food and Agriculture Organization (FAO) created by the UN in 1945 was a means of promoting the establishment of regional fisheries bodies, and of monitoring and coordinating their activities. The FAO's primary responsibility as it relates to fisheries rests on Article 1(2) of the FAO Constitution.[22] The FAO Conference adopted the FAO Code of Conduct for Responsible Fisheries[23] unanimously on 31 October 1995. The aim of the Code is to outline: principles and international standards of behaviour for responsible practices with a view to ensuring the effective conservation, management and development of living aquatic resources, with due respect for the ecosystem and biodiversity.

The conclusion of United Nations Convention on the Law of the Sea (UNCLOS) in 1982 formally ushered in a new era in world fisheries management.[24] Under the Convention, coastal States were allowed the opportunity to extend their management jurisdiction over fishery resource from 12nm to 200nm, as it was estimated that 90 per cent of the harvested resources would be located in the Exclusive Economic Zone (EEZ).

In 1995, the UN adopted the Agreement for the Implementation of the Provisions of the United Nations Convention on the Law of the Sea of 10 December 1982 relating to the Conservation and Management of Straddling Fish Stocks and Highly Migratory Fish Stocks (UNFSA)[25], which was the elaboration of Articles 63(2) and 64 of UNCLOS. UNFSA was an effort to curb rising conflicts and unilateral actions regarding rights and duties of States to exploit and manage straddling and highly migratory fish stocks. The 1995 Straddling and Highly Migratory Stocks Agreement provided for the first time a framework for regional agreements on fisheries management. The Agreement therefore broke

---

20 FAO Fishery Resources Division and Fishery Policy and Planning Division. Fisheries management. FAO Technical Guidelines for Responsible Fisheries. No. 4. Rome, FAO. 1997. 82.

21 Cochrane, K.L., ed., "A Fishery Manager's Guidebook: Management Measures and Their Application." FAO Fisheries Technical Paper. No. 424. Rome, FAO. 2002. 231.

22 Constitution of the FAO. 16 October 1945.

23 FAO Code of Conduct for Responsible Fisheries. 31 October 1995.

24 United Nations Law of the Sea Convention. 10 December 1982. Available at http://www.un.org/depts/los/convention_agreements/texts/unclos/UNCLOS-TOC.htm (accessed November 2011).

25 The Agreement for the Implementation of the Provisions of the United Nations Convention on the Law of the Sea of 10 December 1982 relating to the Conservation and Management of Straddling Fish Stocks and Highly Migratory Fish Stocks (UNFSA). UNTS vol. 2167.

new ground in international fisheries law more generally, by incorporating new environmental principles, provisions on compliance and enforcement and duty of States to cooperate.[26]

29.4 The precautionary approach to fisheries management

As stated before, Principle 15 of the Rio Declaration is the most widespread definition of the principle. Principle 15 states:

> In order to protect the environment, the precautionary approach shall be widely applied by States according to their capabilities. Where there are threats of serious or irreversible damage, lack of full scientific certainty shall not be used as a reason for postponing cost-effective measures to prevent environmental degradation.[27]

However, there are many variations of the Rio Declaration statement on the precautionary principle. Freestone defines the essence of precaution as:

> the precautionary approach . . . is innovative in that it changes the role of scientific data. It requires that once environmental damage is threatened action should be taken to control or abate possible environmental interference even though there may still be scientific uncertainty as to the effects of the activities.[28]

Before we continue the analysis, we must address the debate on whether there is a difference between the precautionary principle and the precautionary approach. There is no consistency in its use in international law documents and texts. However, it may be said that there are two versions of the principle, the "strong" precaution and the "weak" precaution. The strong version suggests that precaution is mandatory and certain activities should be prohibited if there is no proof that it will do no harm; while the weak version suggests that a lack of absolute certainty is not a justification for preventing an action that might be harmful to human health or the environment.[29] Another theory is that the main

26 T. Henriksen, G. Honneland and A. Sydnes, *Law and Politics in Ocean Governance: The UN Fish Stocks Agreement and Regional Fisheries Management Regimes* (Leiden; Boston: Martinus Nijhoff Publishers/Brill Academic Publishers, 2006) 1.

27 See note 13.

28 Boyle and Freestone, eds., *International Law and Sustainable Development* (Oxford: OUP, 1999).

29 An often quoted strong version is the Wingspread Version Statement. "When an activity raises threats of harm to human health or the environment, precautionary measures should be taken even if some cause and effect relationships are not fully established scientifically. In this context the proponent of the activity, rather than the public, should bear the burden of proof . . . the process of applying the precautionary principle must be open, informed and democratic and must include potentially affected parties. It must also examine the range of alternatives, including no action." The wording of the precautionary principle in most international agreements, including the UNFCCC, and declarations, such as the Rio Declaration is considered "weak." In

difference between the two concepts is that the precautionary approach takes into consideration the social and economic considerations of its application.[30] Also, another theory suggests that the precautionary approach is more flexible, and open to technological innovations, whereas the precautionary principle has more of a hard-line negative undertone.[31] According to the authors Birnie and Boyle, the distinction is trivial and in fact the terms should be taken as synonymous and interchangeable.[32] Due to the fact that in its most extreme form the precautionary principle has been used to ban a type of technology or industry activity, this has created concern about the implications of that attitude towards fisheries.[33] The precautionary approach is more appropriate to the context of fisheries as it is flexible and takes into consideration social and economic considerations, along with the essential requirement of ensuring sustainability of natural resources.[34]

Jurisprudence on the application of the precautionary approach to fisheries management is still developing. *Southern Bluefin Tuna* was the first time that the precautionary approach was applied to fisheries.[35] It is relevant as it provides a guide to substantial fisheries management, such as how to protect stocks and it also demonstrates implications for the dispute settlement mechanism of UNCLOS.[36] In the context of fisheries, the precautionary approach must be applied to: fishery management, fishery research, fishery technology and species introduction. For the purposes of this chapter, we will be focusing on the precautionary principle as it relates to fishery management, although with the understanding that the other aspects of fisheries will inform management.

The FAO states, regarding the application of the precautionary approach that:

> management according to the precautionary approach exercises prudent foresight to avoid unacceptable or undesirable situations, taking into account that changes in fisheries systems are only slowly reversible, difficult to control,

operational terms, a "strong" precautionary principle places the burden of proof of non-harm to the technology developers, while a "weak" precautionary principle places the same burden of proof to technology regulators. J. Morris, *Rethinking Risk and the Precautionary Principle* (Oxford: Butterworth-Heinmann, 2000) 1.

30 S.M. Garcia. "The Precautionary Approach to Fisheries Management and Implications for Fishery Research, Technology and Management." Proceedings, 5th NMFS NSAW. 1999. NOAA Tech. Memo. NMFS-F/SPO-40, 65.

31 See note 30.

32 P.W. Birnie and A.E. Boyle. *International Law and the Environment* (New York: OUP, 2002).

33 See note 30.

34 Ibid.

35 It is the first case heard by the International Tribunal for the Law Of the Sea (ITLOS); in the case they ordered Japan to cease experimental fishing.

36 It was the first time that the ITLOS heard a fishery dispute. It also illustrates how States can maintain their commercial interests without breaching international obligations. *The Southern Bluefin Tuna Cases*, see (1999) 38 ILM, 1624–1656; www.un.org/Depts/los/ITLOS/Tuna_cases.htm (accessed November 2011).

not well understood, and subject to change in the environment and human values.[37]

The precautionary approach as it relates to fisheries management is defined in: (i) Code of Conduct for Responsible Fisheries (CCRF) and (ii) UNFSA. The CCRF is a voluntary, non-binding agreement, while the UNFSA is now a binding agreement amongst signatory States.[38] Article 7.5.1 of the FAO's CCRF[39] is equivalent to Articles 6.1 and 6.2[40] of the UNFSA, where it is stated that the

---

37   FAO. "Precautionary Approach to Capture Fisheries and Species Introductions." FAO Technical Guidelines for Responsible Fisheries. No. 2. (Rome, FAO. 1996).

38   Page 675. A precautionary approach may be considered as implicit in UNCLOS, and is certainly explicitly detailed in UNFSA.

39 1   States [Nations] should apply the precautionary approach widely to conservation, management and exploitation of living aquatic resources in order to protect them and preserve the aquatic environment. The absence of adequate scientific information should not be used as a reason for postponing or failing to take conservation and management measures.

   2   In implementing the precautionary approach, States should take into account . . . uncertainties relating to the size and productivity of the stocks, reference points, stock condition in relation to such reference points, levels of distribution of fishing mortality and the impact of fishing activities, including discards, on non-target and associated or dependent species as well as environmental and socio-economic conditions.

   3   In the case of new or exploratory fisheries, States should adopt as soon as possible cautious conservation and management measures, including . . . catch limits and effort limits. Such measures should remain in force until there are sufficient data to allow assessment of the impact of the fisheries on the long-term sustainability of the stocks, whereupon conservation and management measures based on that assessment should be implemented. The latter measures, should, if appropriate, allow for the gradual development of the fisheries.

   4   If a natural phenomenon has a significant adverse impact on the status of living aquatic resources, States should adopt conservation and management measures on an emergency basis to ensure the fishing activity does not exacerbate such adverse impact. States should also adopt such measures on an emergency basis where fishing activity presents a serious threat to the sustainability of such resources. Measures taken on an emergency basis should be temporary and should be based on the best scientific information available.

40 1   States shall apply the precautionary approach widely to conservation, management and exploitation of straddling fish stocks and highly migratory fish stocks in order to protect the living marine resources and preserve the marine environment.

   2   States shall be more cautious when information is uncertain, unreliable or inadequate. The absence of adequate scientific information shall not be used as a reason for postponing or failing to take conservation and management measures.

   3   In implementing the precautionary approach, States shall:

      (a)   improve decision-making for fishery resource conservation and management by obtaining and sharing the best scientific information available and implementing improved techniques for dealing with risk and uncertainty;

      (b)   apply the guidelines set out in Annex II and determine, on the basis of the best scientific information available, stock-specific reference points and the action to be taken if they are exceeded;

      (c)   take into account, *inter alia,* uncertainties relating to the size and productivity of the stocks, reference points, stock condition in relation to such reference points, levels and distribution of fishing mortality and the impact of fishing activities on non-target and associated or dependent species, as well as existing and predicted oceanic, environmental and socio-economic conditions; and

precautionary approach is to be applied to the conservation, management and exploitation of living aquatic resources in order to protect them and preserve the aquatic environment; and that "the absence of scientific information should not be used as a reason for postponing or failing to take conservation and management measures." The FAO's CCRF highlights that the emergency basis should be of last resort, temporary and based upon the most exhaustive scientific evidence. The UNFSA precautionary approach focuses on sustainability through improved data collection and techniques for dealing with risk and scientific uncertainty.

Two pieces of legislation aptly illustrate the incorporation of the precautionary approach as it relates to fisheries. One is the US Gilchrest-Farr Fisheries Recovery Act section 46, which defines the precautionary approach as:

> (a) exercising additional caution in favour of conservation in any case in which information is absent, uncertain, unreliable, or inadequate as to the effects of any existing or proposed action on fish, essential fish habitat, other marine species, and the marine ecosystem in which a fishery occurs; and (b) selecting and implementing any action that will be significantly more likely than not to satisfy the conservation objectives . . .

This is a good example of how the precautionary approach can be incorporated into fisheries Acts within the Caribbean region. Another piece of legislation that addresses the precautionary approach and fisheries is the US Magnuson-Stevens Fishery Conservation and Management Act.[41] Given the Caribbean's

(d) develop data collection and research programmes to assess the impact of fishing on non-target and associated or dependent species and their environment, and adopt plans which are necessary to ensure the conservation of such species and to protect habitats of special concern.

4   States shall take measures to ensure that, when reference points are approached, they will not be exceeded. In the event that they are exceeded, States shall, without delay, take the action determined under paragraph 3 (b) to restore the stocks.

5   Where the status of target stocks or non-target or associated or dependent species is of concern, States shall subject such stocks and species to enhanced monitoring in order to review their status and the efficacy of conservation and management measures. They shall revise those measures regularly in the light of new information.

6   For new or exploratory fisheries, States shall adopt as soon as possible cautious conservation and management measures, including, *inter alia*, catch limits and effort limits. Such measures shall remain in force until there are sufficient data to allow assessment of the impact of the fisheries on the long-term sustainability of the stocks, whereupon conservation and management measures based on that assessment shall be implemented. The latter measures shall, if appropriate, allow for the gradual development of the fisheries.

7   If a natural phenomenon has a significant adverse impact on the status of straddling fish stocks or highly migratory fish stocks, States shall adopt conservation and management measures on an emergency basis to ensure that fishing activity does not exacerbate such adverse impact. States shall also adopt such measures on an emergency basis where fishing activity presents a serious threat to the sustainability of such stocks. Measures taken on an emergency basis shall be temporary and shall be based on the best scientific evidence available.

41 It established a national Fishery Conservation Zone (FCZ) extending seaward boundaries of the coastal States to 200 nm and exclusive US fishery management authority over fish resources within the

socio-economic dependence on fisheries, this Act may very well be instructive for the Caribbean case, particularly as it reflects a strong commercial slant, with an apparent bias towards commercial interest. The Act does not provide for precautionary closures due solely to scientific uncertainty unless they can be justified by scientific information, assessed according to specific criteria, temporally limited and not overly detrimental to commercial interests without sufficient, measurable environmental goals.[42]

The precautionary principle is not defined in the Treaty of the European Community and prescribes it only once – to protect the environment. The Communication from the Commission on European Communities on the precautionary principle, states:

> in practice, its scope is much wider, and specifically where preliminary objective scientific evaluation, indicates that there are reasonable grounds for concern that the potentially dangerous effects on the environment, human, animal or plant health may be inconsistent with the high level of protection chosen for the Community.[43]

The precautionary approach is explicitly mentioned in the RTC and there are varying approaches to fisheries management in legislation within the region.[44] However in the Agreement establishing the Caribbean Regional Fisheries Mechanism (CRFM) reference is made to the precautionary approach as a principle by which the mechanism should be guided and the provision is Article 5(c), where it states as a principle "encouraging the use of precautionary approaches to sustainable use and management of fisheries resources.[45]

29.4.1 Uncertainty in fisheries management

There is a substantial amount of uncertainty regarding fisheries management and scientists have continually attempted to address the issue. This must be explored because the precautionary approach is based upon the parameters of scientific certainty, and the ability of fishery science to produce certainty will heavily impact the parameters of the precautionary approach.

FCS with the exception of highly migratory tunas. It was established in 1976 and created eight Fishery Management Councils for the conservation and orderly utilisation of the fishery resources of the US.

42 For example, if the Council decides to close down a fishery, the decision it must first be based on the best scientific information, secondly include criteria and a timetable by which to assess the benefit of the closure and thirdly it is based on the Council's assessment of the benefits and impacts of closure. This is an example of the precautionary approach towards fisheries at work; it is a stronger standard than the weak version of the precautionary principle.

43 Commission on European Communities. "Communication from the Commission of the Precautionary Principle," http://ec.europa.eu/dgs/health_consumer/library/pub/pub07_en.pdf, (Brussels, 2000) (accessed November 2011).

44 The Agreement Establishing the Caribbean Community including the CARICOM Single Market Economy, 4 July 1973, Articles 60 and 65.

45 The Agreement Establishing the Caribbean Regional Fisheries Mechanism, 4 February 2002.

The nature of fisheries lends itself to uncertainty. There is uncertainty regarding the stock, such as how to predict how the stock may behave.[46] The scientific understanding and capacity to predict future status is limited by several factors such as: the "fluid" properties of fisheries, the limited knowledge on genetic stock structure and impacts of fishing on resources genetics; the complexity of the interactions between species and gears and fisheries; the poor quality of the available fishery data; the limitation of scientific models and research funds, and the fluctuations of economic parameters.[47] This leads to a degree of uncertainty in information upon which decision-makers must act.

The principle of "best scientific evidence" is found in several instruments relating to fisheries management. In UNCLOS, Article 61 states that the best scientific evidence must be incorporated into management and conservation measures taken in the EEZ. The Preamble to the General Assembly Resolution 44/225, states that for regulatory measures, the best available scientific evidence data and analysis must be used. However, there is no sense of the quantitative nature of best scientific evidence. Additionally, regarding the quality of the data as the best available, it could be that based upon the resources available, that it is of low quality. The UNFSA speaks to the principle of "best scientific evidence," and as does the *Southern Bluefin Tuna* case.

Therefore, given that it is clear that fisheries science tends to be uncertain, we must reassign the parameters of the application of the precautionary approach in order not to make it detrimental towards fisheries. Particularly, given the Caribbean situation where often they lack the resources for conducting proper fisheries science and research, there must be a relaxation of the standard of application of the precautionary approach found, for example, in States within Europe and North America.

As mentioned earlier, one of the biggest concerns in relation to the application of the precautionary approach to fisheries management is whether it may result in the wide-scale closing down of fisheries wherever uncertainty exists. Safeguarding commercial interests creates a tight conflict between exploitation of the fish stock and its protection through the precautionary approach. The nature of the precautionary principle outside of fisheries management is to err on the side of action; and even in the face of a lack of full scientific evidence, precautionary measures should be taken. It is important to note, as mentioned by the authors of Birnie and Boyle, that:

> Although the precautionary approach may have led the parties to other conventions to impose a ban or moratorium on ocean dumping, high seas whaling, and driftnet fishing, when applied to straddling and highly migratory fisheries it has resulted only in more cautious criteria for exploitation and management of stocks and for evaluating long-term impacts, but not a ban or moratorium on fishing.[48]

46 These include sampling variability and biases; uncertainty and long-term fluctuations in stock productivity, dynamics and structure, recruitment, mortality and growth and interactions with other species.
47 See note 30.
48 See note 24, at 119.

Therefore, the precautionary approach has never resulted in a ban or moratorium on fishing, rather, only an increased cautiousness.[49] It must be mentioned that a moratorium is the strongest form of the precautionary approach, although it is not necessarily a negative action. A moratorium is imposed as an emergency resort and can be imposed for a positive purpose such as to encourage the regeneration of a species.

There are two prominent moratoriums that have affected the Caribbean region: the CITES moratorium on Queen Conch in 2003 and the moratorium on sea urchins in Barbados in 1996. It may be instructive to briefly detail the effects of the 1992 moratorium placed on Atlantic Cod. This resulted in 20,000 workers losing their employment, and as it was an industry that had existed for 400 years, it had a strong impact on several other industries, such as truck drivers and grocery owners. One could therefore understand why a strict application of the precautionary approach strikes fear in the minds of stakeholders in fisheries.

29.5 Carribean Small Island Developing States (SIDS) and fisheries management

The Caribbean is defined based upon colonial legacy such as the Commonwealth or "Anglophone," "Dutch", "French", and "Latin America," and based upon regional entities such as the Caribbean Community (CARICOM), the Organisation of Eastern Caribbean States (OECS), Wider Caribbean Region (WCR) and the Association of Caribbean States (ACS). This chapter defines the Caribbean as referring to CARICOM Member States. In this chapter, we refer to the CARICOM Member States and also acknowledge their categorisation as Small Island Developing States (SIDS). Fisheries management must be heavily considered within the region, particularly given the fact that there are three major species which contribute to food security and economic independence of the society, on the endangered list due to overexploitation and poor fisheries management, these are: the Queen Conch, the Spiny Lobster and the Nassau Grouper.[50]

29.5.1 Special considerations for Small Island Developing States of the Caribbean and fisheries management

Article 5.2 of the FAO Code of Conduct, the Special Requirements of Developing Countries addresses the special needs of developing states in fisheries management, and recognizes that:

> In order to achieve the objectives of this Code and to support its effective implementation, countries, relevant international organizations, whether governmental or non-governmental, and financial institutions should give

49 See note 24, at 676.
50 See CITES Appendix II.

full recognition to the special circumstances and requirements of developing countries, including in particular the least-developed among them, and small island developing countries . . . especially in the areas of financial and technical assistance, technology transfer, training and scientific cooperation and in enhancing their ability to develop their own fisheries as well as to participate in high seas fisheries, including access to such fisheries.

The countries of the Caribbean region are SIDS, and therefore should be considered through the lens of these special requirements regarding Fisheries. The 1998 High-Level Panel of External Experts on Fisheries made reference to several issues faced by SIDS in fisheries management, including: the ability to obtain fair share of exploitation of resources; the difficulties with sustainable management of their resources; and monitoring, control and surveillance (MCS). These issues will be an increasingly major issue for the future management of fisheries, which is the issue most relevant to the discussion within this chapter.[51]

The introduction of the *FAO Code of Conduct* states:

Fisheries, including aquaculture, provide a vital source of food, employment, recreation, trade and economic well-being for people throughout the world, both for present and future generations and should therefore be conducted in a responsible manner.

As is the case with several regions within the world, there is a strong socio-economic case for fisheries in the Caribbean region. The importance of fisheries to the Caribbean is mainly food security and socio-economic considerations. The region is heavily dependent upon fisheries for food security and economic survival. Milton Haughton, the Deputy Executive Director of CRFM, Belize notes that:

Fisheries is an important source of livelihood and sustenance for the people of the region, contributing towards food security, poverty alleviation, employment, foreign exchange earnings, development and stability of rural and coastal communities, and culture, recreation and tourism.[52]

The contribution to economies is through fish exports and revenues, and in some territories fishing access fees.[53] Fisheries provide significant employment opportunities, particularly for the most disadvantaged groups within society such as women, and people from rural and low-income backgrounds. The fishery sector provides stable direct and indirect employment for approximately 182,000 persons

---

51 FAO, Committee on Fisheries. "Future Challenges in World Fisheries and Aqua Culture," 23rd session, Rome, Italy, 15–19 February 1999.

52 M. Haughton, "Fisheries Subsidy and the Role of Regional Fisheries Management Organisations: The Caribbean Experience." Available at http://www.unep.ch/etu/Fisheries%20Meeting/submitted Papers/MiltonHaughton.pdf (accessed November 2011)

53 This is more relevant for the Pacific islands where foreign fishing fleets pay to fish in the EEZ's of these territories.

in the African Caribbean Pacific (ACP) states.[54] At the national level across the region, fisheries is an important contributor to Gross Domestic Product (GDP) of many countries, as well as an important foreign exchange earner. Table 29.1[55] below illustrates the importance of fisheries to the CARICOM Sector.

It is noteworthy that the per capita consumption of most CARICOM countries is above the global average of 16.4 kg (2006), and when compared to the 2005 global average for developing countries (13.8 kg per capita), only Haiti is below that average. This high per capita consumption exists despite the fact that fish is not always the cheapest source of animal protein in the region.[56]

In the Caribbean the impact of fisheries subsidies must be addressed as subsidies result in overexploitation. Sustainable fisheries must achieve full potential catch value, whilst also ensuring the preservation of the fisheries. Caribbean governments give subsidies without enough regulation, and this is a crucial aspect of fisheries management.

29.5.2 The regional approach to fisheries management

Table 29.2 below illustrates that the Caribbean SIDS generally focus on marine capture fisheries, and that inland capture and aquaculture is a non-industry for some, and/or dramatically pales in comparison to marine capture.[57] Marine capture fisheries are fisheries where fin (fishes) and non-fin (lobsters, shrimps etc.) are captured in their natural habitat. Aquaculture refers to marine life reared in a controlled and confined environment which may be located, for example, in a river or reservoir.

We must establish the rationale for the necessity of a Caribbean regional approach to fisheries management. The obligations under UNCLOS as it relates to conservation, management and utilisation of living resources are clear. The core articles relating to fisheries are Articles 61 and 62 that deal with conservation, management and utilisation of living resources within the EEZ. Article 123 calls for regional cooperation on enclosed or semi-enclosed seas to "coordinate the management, conservation, and exploration and exploitation of the living marine resources of the sea" and "to protect and preserve the marine environment." The definition of an enclosed or semi-enclosed sea found in Article 122 is applicable to the Caribbean, and therefore provides the basis for regional cooperation on fisheries. Other references to regional cooperation can be found in Article 63 which deals with straddling stocks, Article 64 which deals with highly migratory species and Articles 69 and 70 which deals with the rights of landlocked or geographically disadvantaged states.

---

54 See *supra* note 40, ibid.
55 Caribbean Agribusiness: Fisheries. Table 29.1, available at http://174.123.68.234/primary-dropdown/fisheries#_ftn1, (accessed November 2011).
56 Ibid.
57 In the original version of the table, other regions are included and therefore may be referenced for comparative purposes.

Table 29.1

Country	Contribution of fisheries to GDP (%)	Number of fishers	Total number of fishing boats	Fisheries production 2008 (000kg)	Fish import 2008 (000kg)	Fish export 2008 (000kg)	Total human consumption (tonne)	Per Capita
Antigua and Barbuda	1.70 (2003)	1,088 (2004)	728 (2004)	3,521.0	761.2	37.7	3,530 (2003)	48.3 (2003)
Barbados	0.90 (1990)	2,200 (2000?)	955 (NFSO 2002)	2,711.5	5,788.3	168.0	11,090 (2003)	41.1 (2003)
Belize	3.00	3,000–4,000 (2002?)	552 (NFSO 2002?)	4,150.0	8.3	0	3,625 (2003)	14.2 (2003)
Dominica	2.00 (1994)	2,338	1100 (NFSO 2000)	. . .	8.7	1.4	1,596.8 (2000)	20.24 (2003)
Grenada	2.10 (1994)	1,240 (–)	n/a	2,378.5	725.4	537.5	4,172 (203?)	52.2 (2003?)
Guyana	6.63 (2002)	5,644 (2002?)	>1300 (2004)	61,000.0	9.2	61,000.0	34,642 (2003)	45.7 (2003)
Haiti	. . .	50,000	. . .	. . .	. . .	. . .	21,342 (2003)	2.6 (2003)
Jamaica	0.41 (2001)	15,336 (2004)	4274 (2004)	15,825.0	9,791.2	448.5	49,465 (2003)	18.7 (2003)
St. Kitts and Nevis	0.45 (1994)	650	n/a	363.1	461.5	101.2	1,495 (2003)	35.6 (2003)
St. Lucia	0.75	2,059	690 – most motorised (NFSO 2006)	1,510.2	574.6	0	4,753 (2003)	31.9 (2003)
St. Vincent and the Grenadines	0.90	2,500	600 – most motorised (NFSO 1999)	794.5	0	0	1,711 (1999)	15.1 (1999)
Suriname	0.75	5,169	1150 (NFSO 2006)	24,062.7	4.7	20,877.0	7,124 (2003)	16.3 (2003)
Trinidad and Tobago	0.09	5,100	2184 (NFSO 2003)	14,471.1	2,395.6	2,29.0	18,257	14
Sources	CRFM	CRFM Unless stated	CRFM Unless stated	LMDC	LMDC	LMDC	NFSO	NFSO

Data for 2006 unless stated

. . . Denotes no data

CRFM: Caribbean Regional Fisheries Mechanism; NFSO: National Fisheries Sector Review; FAO, LMDC: Landell Mills Development Consultants 2011

Table 29.2* 1996 Fish catches and aquaculture production in Member States and observers of the Alliance of Small Island States (AOSIS) and Other Small Island Developing States (SIDS)

Area/State	Marine capture (tonnes)	Inland capture (tonnes)	Aquaculture (tonnes)	Total (tonnes)	Marine as percent of total
Caribbean					
Antigua and Barbuda	530	250	0	780	68
Bahamas	9 862	0	24	9 886	100
Barbados	3 439	0	0	3 439	100
Belize	977	0	1 004	1 981	49
Cuba	73 529	6 762	28 467	108 758	68
Dominica	840	0	4	844	100
Grenada	1 577	0	. . .	1 577	100
Guyana	44 110	700	190	45 000	98
Jamaica	12 133	710	3 100	15 943	76
St Kitts and Nevis	216	0	4	220	98
St Lucia	1 271	0	3	1 274	100
St Vincent and the Grenadines	1 300	0	0	1 300	100
Suriname	12 999	150	1	13 150	99
Trinidad and Tobago	12 793	0	12	12 805	100
Sub-total	**175 576**	**8 572**	**32 809**	**216 957**	**81**
Non AOSIS members					
Bahrain	12 940	0	0	12 940	100
Dominican Republic	12 606	1 205	789	14 600	86
Haiti	5 514	500	0	6 014	92
Sub-total	**31 060**	**1 705**	**789**	**33 554**	**93**
Total AOSIS	*484 574*	*25 527*	*39 801*	*549 956*	*88*
Total SIDS	*515 634*	*27 232*	*40 590*	*583 456*	*88*
World Total	*88 195 676*	*7 533 151*	*34 116 249*	*129 865 076*	*68*
AOSIS as percentage of **World**	*0.55*	*0.34*	*0.12*	*0.42*	–
SIDS as a percentage of World	*0.58*	*0.36*	*0.12*	*0.45*	–

*   FAO. "Fisheries and Aquaculture Issues in Small Island Developing States" Available at http://www.fao.org/docrep/meeting/X0463E.htm#TAB3, (accessed November 2011).

29.5.3 Regional fisheries management regimes, treaties, legislation and policy

Regional Fisheries Management Regimes are international institutions established by States, identifying common gains in working together to overcome collective-action problems related to the management of regional fisheries.[58] A variety of definitions exist for what qualifies as a regional mechanism under international fisheries law.[59] There are several such existing regional mechanisms including the Caribbean Regional Fisheries Mechanism (CRFM); the Integrated Caribbean Regional Agricultural and Fisheries Development Program – Fisheries Component (CARIFORUM); the Caribbean Large Marine Ecosystem (CLME); the CARICOM Fisheries Unit and the UNEP Caribbean Environment Programme (CEP). The Action Plan of the Caribbean Environment Programme as well as the Cartagena Convention and its Protocols address the issue of fisheries management. As mentioned before, The Agreement to the CRFM already includes the precautionary approach.

As mentioned before, there are provisions with the Revised Treaty of Chaguaramas that speak directly the fisheries issue. Chapter 4, Part 2, specifically Article 60 addresses fisheries management and development within the Caribbean region. There are other provisions, which though they did not speak specifically of fisheries, were nonetheless applicable to fisheries.[60]

One of the most significant developments in the regional approach to fisheries in recent times is the formulation of the Caribbean Community Common Fisheries Policy and Regime (CCCFP). Article 5 of the Agreement Establishing the CCCFP provides that the "fundamental principles" that shall guide the implementation of the Policy include the application of the precautionary approach to fisheries management. Articles 4.2 and 23 incorporate the dispute resolution system of the RTC, which creates the potential for the CCJ to consider the precautionary principle in its analysis. It demonstrates the regional seriousness of addressing the issue of fisheries. In order to create a deeper understanding of the possibilities of the Caribbean Common Fisheries Policy and Regime, the European Union's Common Fisheries Policy and its associated regulations should be considered as a comparative model for development.

All OECS Member States have enacted fisheries law that directly speaks to fisheries management that generally makes provision for regional cooperation in fisheries

---

58 See *supra* note 18, 2.

59 Article 8(1) of UNFSA states that coastal States and distant water fishing nations (DWFNs) shall pursue cooperation either directly or through appropriate sub-regional or regional fisheries management organisation or arrangements. This largely reiterates Article 63(2) and 64 of UNCLOS except for the reference to arrangements. The distinction between the different possible types of regional mechanisms is obscure and reflects that there is no single format of regional management that can fit all geopolitical and biophysical conditions. See ibid.

60 These other provisions address broader social and economic policies such as movement of good, services, freedom of establishment and non-discrimination of community nationals.

management and the governmental approach.[61] Some of the other CARICOM States such as Jamaica possess a Fishing Industry Act, which does not speak much to fisheries management, and others such as Haiti and Suriname lack adequate national fisheries legislation. There is the Caribbean Fisheries Development and Training Institute Act.[62] In most countries the State plays a key role in fisheries policy by regulating management and conservation of the resources through direct intervention in the implementation of policies through development programmes. It is possible to identify different fisheries administrative structures.[63] The fisheries sector does not generally receive high priority in some territories, and the organisation of fishermen into cooperatives can play a vital role in promoting development of the sector.[64]

Another aspect of fisheries management is the States of the Caribbean taking action to fulfil their commitments to the sustainable development of biodiversity and natural resources in Conventions to which many are signatories such as the Convention on Biological Diversity (CBD), the Convention on the International Trade in Endangered Species of Wild Fauna and Flora[65] (CITES) and the Protocol concerning Specially Protected Areas and Wildlife[66] (SPAW Protocol). As mentioned earlier Caribbean States are managing endangered species in the region such as the Queen Conch, the Spiny Lobster and the Nassau Grouper. CITES establishes regulations that help to protect a fishery by insuring that the animal is being harvested at a level consistent with its natural population growth. The Queen Conch was listed to Appendix II of CITES in 1992 and provides a good complement to national programmes.[67] The region's commitment to Conventions such as CITES assist in the implementation of better fisheries management, particularly for endangered species.

Socio-economic monitoring is present within the Caribbean region, and is a method by which research is conducted on Caribbean fisheries. This is mentioned because it demonstrates a mechanism by which the Caribbean utilises its minimal resources in order to conduct research on fisheries. The concept refers to a monitoring system that will allow analysis of the state of development of local fishing communities and will allow for the development of predictive scenarios and forecasts based upon projected changes in the environmental and socio-economic context.[68] There are several socio-economic monitoring mechanisms present within the Caribbean and conducted by Caribbean fisheries.[69]

---

61 These include the 1984 Fisheries Act of St. Lucia, the Jamaica Fishing Industry Act.

62 Caribbean Fisheries Development and Institution Act, 1975, Chapter 39:53, Act 59.

63 It should be stressed that due to the small-scale nature of fisheries in the Caribbean, the fisheries administration schemes should reflect to comparatively limited living resources in EEZ and not be so elaborate to use more bureaucratic resources than necessary. Ibid.

64 See *supra* note 50, at 19.

65 Convention on the International Trade of Endangered Species (CITES), 1 July 1975.

66 Protocol concerning Specially Protected Areas and Wildlife (SPAW Protocol), 18 June 2000.

67 Nancy Daves, "CITES: A Tool for Regulation of International Trade in Spiny Lobster." Proceedings of the 60th Gulf and Caribbean Fisheries Institute 5–9 November 2007 Punta Cana, Dominican Republic.

68 A. Sanders. *SocMon*. October 2010. Issue 2, p.1.

69 Oistins in Barbados; Dublanc, Colihaut and Bioche fishing villages in St. Peter, Dominica; Booby Island in Nevis, and Grenville in Grenada. Cena, Maria. "Socio-economic Monitoring by Caribbean Fisheries Authorities." SocMon training workshop. May–June 2008.CERMES: UWI Cavehill.

29.5.4 Prospects and pitfalls of the precautionary approach to fisheries management in the Caribbean

In order for the precautionary principle to be invoked there is a two-stage process; there must be (i) a threat of "serious or irreversible" damage and (ii) a lack of full scientific uncertainty.[70] Critics often refer to the scientific uncertainty, vagueness and adverse effects of the precautionary approach as major concerns. Sustainable development is often cited as a benefit of the precautionary approach. The principle is not based on scientific certainty in the causal link between the harm and the effect; rather it is a preventative approach that errs on the side of safety in order to avoid any potential damage to the environment. This is not meant to be an exhaustive exposition on the prospects and pitfalls of incorporating the principle in fisheries management in the Caribbean; however due to constraints of space, we will discuss two prospects and two pitfalls.

The judgment of the Honorable Justice Stollymeyer in *Fishermen and Friends of The Sea v Environmental Management Authority and Atlantic LNG*[71] presents an interesting commentary of the precautionary principle within the Caribbean context. In *Fishermen*, the Honourable Justice Stollmeyer shared a significant perspective in terms of the contextual application of the precautionary principle. He says as economic and social conditions vary from territory to territory that the principle:

> cannot be transported lock, stock and barrel from one to another. That law must always be looked at in the light of prevailing local circumstances and adapted suitably, assuming this to be possible at all.

He commented that even though Trinidad and Tobago may be considered as socially and economically developed to a greater extent than others, that the human, financial, physical or other conditions and resources do not equate to that of Europe or North America and therefore "the high standards set and met there may not be realistic in the context of conditions and resources here." He also states that this difference in standard that the Natural Environmental Policy (NEP) refers to is "serious irreversible" environmental damage as opposed to "serious or irreversible." The implication of this judgment is that the precautionary principle in the Caribbean is to illustrate the linkage between the socio-economic state of Caribbean countries and the challenges that they face in implementing the precautionary approach.

There are several prospects and pitfalls to the implementation of the precautionary approach to fisheries management within the Caribbean region. we will discuss two prospects and two pitfalls.

The economies of many of the countries of the region are highly dependent upon the marine environment for food security and economic survival, primarily

---

70 J. Tickner and C. Raffensperger. "The Precautionary Principle in Action: A Handbook." First edition, available at http://www.biotech-info.net/handbook.pdf (accessed November 2011) 3–4.
71 2004 HC 113.

through tourism and fishing. These major economic sectors are the first to be affected as a result of degraded ecosystems such as coral reefs, mangrove forests and sea grass beds. Therefore, one advantage is that the tourism and fishing industries will benefit from the well-managed ecosystems. It is this advantage that forms the backbone of this chapter. The precautionary principle applied to the Caribbean context will result in better fisheries management and will therefore positively contribute to the economies of Caribbean States, which are dependent on the marine environment through tourism and fishing.[72]

Another prospect is the sustainable development of the natural resources and biodiversity of the Caribbean. Much of the coastal area of the Caribbean is susceptible to land and marine-based pollution. The precautionary approach will contribute towards achieving sustainable development which is a commitment that several countries of the region have made by supporting international instruments such as the Convention on Biological Diversity and the Rio Declaration. The concept of the ecosystem approach to fisheries (EAF) is the way to achieve sustainable development within the context of fisheries. The two concepts of ecosystem management and fisheries management converge in order to ensure a balance between human and ecological well-being.[73] The fact is that ecosystems and fisheries affect each other and the purpose of the EAF is:

> to plan, develop and manage fisheries in a manner that addresses the multiple needs and desires of societies, without jeopardizing the options for future generations to benefit from the full range of goods and services provided by marine ecosystem.[74]

The application of the precautionary approach towards ecosystem approach to fisheries has the potential to impact positively on the achievement of sustainable development in the region.

One pitfall of the precautionary approach is that it may impose a heavy economic burden and prove costly to legitimately include in fisheries management in the Caribbean.[75] For example, conducting fisheries research such as monitoring fish stocks proves to be very costly in an already under-resourced environment. In designing precautionary methods, it is important to understand that, particularly in the Caribbean context with small-scale fisheries there will be a low level of compliance and enforcement may be excessively costly. Therefore,

---

72 UNEP, "Relevance and Application of the Principle of the Precautionary Action to the Caribbean Environment Programme." Secretariat paper approved by the CEP Meeting of Experts and the Third Meeting of the Parties to the Cartagena Convention, November 1992, UN OCA/CAR WG.10/INF.

73 FAO Fisheries and Aquaculture Department. FAO Technical Guidelines for Responsible Fisheries 4 Supplement 2. "Fisheries Management: The Ecosystem Approach to Fisheries," (2003) available at ftp://ftp.fao.org/docrep/fao/005/y4470e/y4470e00.pdf, (accessed November 2011).

74 Ibid.

75 A. Wildavsky, *But Is It True? A Citizen's Guide to Environmental Health and Safety Issues* (Cambridge: Harvard University Press, 1996).

the precautionary approach must reasonably be adapted to the Caribbean situation and be cognisant of the lack of resources for the implementation of the precautionary approach. Additionally, it may be beneficial that financial and compensatory schemes be provided for the Caribbean SIDS in order that they may implement the precautionary approach with greater resources. The FAO Programme of Fisheries Assistance to SIDS is a model that other donor entities could follow. The programme, *inter alia*, aims to improve the sustainable development and management of these fisheries.[76]

Another pitfall is the uncertainty and vagueness of the approach. We will not delve into as much detail in this section because we have already discussed that the precautionary approach has varying formulations, including weak and strong applications; this suggests vagueness and inconsistency. However, we would like to provide a counter-argument that the nature of the approach can very well be defined in practice by decision-makers and does not necessarily have to be a pitfall because it should be clear that the essence of the precautionary approach is towards sustainability.

29.6 Reflections

In light of our discussion on the advantages and disadvantages of the precautionary principle in fisheries management within the Caribbean and the discussion of the regional approach we will present a few observations.

29.6.1 Precautionary principle and EIAs

In the context of the Caribbean, it is important to realise that this would not be our first experience with applying the precautionary principle since in the execution of Environmental Impact Assessments (EIA's) we are currently implementing the principle within the Caribbean. An EIA is a key aspect of large-scale planning activities in the Caribbean, for example hotel and condominium development. It is an information-gathering exercise conducted by the developer and other bodies in order to allow the local planning agency to understand the environmental

---

76 The purpose of the Programme is to enable SIDS to adopt and implement policies and measures to ensure that the capacity of their fisheries administrations is enhanced; that fisheries resources are conserved, managed, developed and utilised in a rational manner; that national food security is enhanced; and that the utilisation of fisheries resources continues to contribute to national economic and social development on a sustainable basis. The FAO Programme, which is consistent with the fisheries provisions of the 1984 Programme of Action for the Sustainable Development of Small Island States, has a tight focus and will address six areas that have been identified by island States as being of high priority. The six areas are: institutional strengthening and national capacity building; enhanced conservation and management of EEZ fisheries; improved post-harvest fish management and marketing; Strengthening the economic role of national fisheries industries and the privatisation of fisheries investments, and aquaculture and inland fisheries conservation, management and development.
  See FAO, "Fisheries and Aquaculture Issues in Small Island Developing States," available at http://www.fao.org/docrep/meeting/X0463E.htm#TAB3, (accessed November 2011).

impact of the development and therefore make a decision on whether or not to approve the development.[77] An EIA uses the precautionary principle as the basis for its rationale, that of considering if there will be "serious or irreversible" harm done to the environment. There have been several Caribbean cases on the issue of the EIA, these include: the *Northern Jamaica Conservation Association v Jamaica Environment Trust et al.*[78]; *Delapenha Funeral Home Limited v The Minister of Local Government*[79]; *Fishermen and Friends of the Sea v The Environmental Management Authority and Atlantic LNG Company of Trinidad and Tobago*[80]; *People United Respecting Environment (PURE) et al. and Environmental Management Authority*[81] and *People United Respecting Environment (PURE) et al. and Environmental Management Authority.*[82]

The National Environmental Policy (NEP) of Trinidad mentions the precautionary approach and states "government policy will adhere to the principle that if there are threats of serious irreversible damage, lack of full scientific certainty will not be used as a reason for postponing measures to prevent environmental degradation." This is a reference to the precautionary approach within an Act from a Caribbean territory and is therefore an example of how it may further be incorporated throughout other territories.

In many ways the prospect of incorporating the precautionary principle will not be completely new to the Caribbean, as we have been implementing the principle in conducting the Environmental Impact Assessments (EIAs). Upon a reading of the afore-mentioned case law, the Justices demonstrate a keen understanding of the precautionary principle; the Caribbean experience in this regard with the principle is therefore translatable to fisheries management.

29.6.2 *Future directions*

1   The precautionary principle can be incorporated in existing frameworks described in the "regional approach" section of this chapter. Several of the frameworks have the spirit of the precautionary approach and with an explicit guiding philosophy, this will demonstrate a commitment to this internationally-recognised principle, therefore ensuring that Caribbean States are adhering to their international commitments. It is commendable that the precautionary principle is incorporated into the Caribbean Community Common Fisheries Policy, and explicitly included in the Revised Treaty of Chaguaramas. The existing regional programmes of the Action Plan of CEP also provide important opportunities for implementation of a precautionary approach. Additionally, the fisheries legislation of the Caribbean territories

77 S.G. Moss, *Environmental Impact Assessment for Sustainable Development in the Commonwealth Caribbean: An Overview* (Cavehill: UWI Faculty of Law Library, 1992).
78 JM [2006] SC 49; JM [2006] SC 65.
79 JM [2008] SC 72.
80 TT [2004] HC 113.
81 TT [2009] HC 133.
82 Ibid. at HC 134.

should take instruction from the US legislation discussed above – the Magnuson-Stevens and Gilchrest-Farr Acts – which explicitly reference the precautionary approach.

2   The Caribbean SIDS lack resources to adequately implement the precautionary approach. Cost should be minimised to the fishing communities and governments of the Caribbean, due to their status as SIDS. Financial support, such as concessionary financing and compensatory schemes should be established by international donor agencies and governments in order that these SIDS may implement the precautionary approach to fisheries research and management adequately, particularly, monitoring, control and surveillance.

3   The precautionary approach should be applied to fisheries subsidies. It is clear that Government subsidies are not regulated with an eye towards sustainable development, and a precautionary approach to issuing subsidies would therefore help to achieve this commitment made by Caribbean States under several international instruments. Additionally the Revised Treaty, being a trade-related treaty should create a provision specifically aimed at addressing the regulation of fisheries subsidies through the incorporation of the precautionary approach.

29.7 Conclusion

While the jurisprudence of the Caribbean Court of Justice in the area of sustainable development is still emerging and many issues have not yet been explored before the regional court, it is likely that the Court will have opportunity to incorporate considerations of sustainable development in case law in the future. We foresee future case law and judicial reasoning of the Court involving and invoking principles 1, 4 and 5 of the New Delhi Declaration in particular considering and applying the precautionary principle, States' sustainable use of natural resources and access to justice as is evident from, inter alia, case law in national decisions and the provisions of the RTC.

30 Application of principles of sustainable development in the Mekong dispute settlement

Phan Tuan Hung and Alexander Kenny

30.1 Introduction

Amongst the world's largest rivers, the Mekong is the longest river in Southeast Asia, stretching for over 4,300 km. Originating in the Tanghia Shan Mountains of Tibet, it passes through the Chinese province of Yunnan, Myanmar, Laos, Thailand, Cambodia, and Vietnam. The rich biodiversity along the Mekong is comparable to that of the Amazon[1], and it is home to approximately 1,100 species of fish, as well as the giant Mekong Catfish, the Irrawaddy dolphin, and the giant freshwater stingray, weighing up to almost 600 kg.[2]

While the Mekong Agreement and its Commission is distinctly inter-governmental, the practices used for 'soft' dispute settlement and negotiation could easily be characterized as engaging individuals, sub-national entities and civil society, among other interested Parties in processes represented by the mechanism.

This chapter provides an overview of certain elements of the Mekong Agreement and the Mekong River Commission (MRC), as well as an analysis on the extent to which four key New Delhi Declaration sustainability principles are reflected in the Mekong Agreement. The analysis draws on hydropower dam development in the region, due its potential benefits and impacts on the environment and peoples of the Mekong Basin and the disputes it has generated. It concludes that, in particular, the New Delhi Declation principles of *the Precautionary Approach to Human Health; Natural Resources and Ecosystems;* and *Public Participation and Access to Information and Justice* are only weakly reflected in the Mekong Principles and related Procedures. Furthermore, as the MRC does not have power of enforcement, the extent to which these principles are realized in practice depends to a large extent on national regulations, will of riparian countries and engagement of non-state actors in the process.

---

1 MRC, About the Mekong, The Land and Its Resources, See http://www.mrcmekong.org/about_mekong/about_mekong.htm.

2 See http://www.worldwildlife.org/places/greater-mekong.

30.2 Mekong River Basin

In the Northern reaches of the Mekong in China and Myanmar, the Mekong is known as the Lancang, and passes through the Hengduan Mountain ranges and gorges.

The Lower Mekong River Basin (Cambodia, Lao PDR, Thailand and Vietnam) is home to approximately 60 million people, amounting to over 40 per cent of the populations of these countries.[3] There are over 100 different ethnic groups living in the basin, making it one of the most culturally diverse regions of the world. The people depend heavily on the aquatic resources of the river and its wetlands, and poverty and food insecurity remain a deep concern, with one-third earning less than a few dollars per day.[4]

The Mekong River Basin is one of the most productive inland fisheries in the world[5], and the largest inland fishery in the world, as it is estimated to account for approximately 25 per cent of global freshwater catch[6]. Not only does it support an economically vital fisheries sector, but it also contributes directly to food security for the poor and is a crucial source of protein in local diets – in 2010 it was estimated that about two-thirds of the rural population of the Lower Mekong Basin, or about 40 million people, were directly involved in wild fish capture.[7]

The Mekong River also serves as an important navigation and trade route, especially as the road system in the Mekong Basin remains sparse in many areas of Cambodia and Laos – more than one-third of riverside populations of Cambodia and Laos live further than 10 km from a year-round road[8]. There are 25 major ports on the Mekong River and, except for a 14 km stretch around the Khone Falls near the Lao-Cambodia border, until recently almost the entire length of the river was navigable for nearly 8 months of the year, although this will no longer be the case as the construction of the Xayaburi Dam in Lao progresses (the first lower Mekong mainstream dam).[9]

30.3 Hydropower dam development in the Mekong River Basin

Dam construction on the Mekong River, as well as its numerous tributaries, remains a source of controversy within the region. Although the Lower Mekong is still not dammed, the Xayaburi dam in Lao is currently under construction

---

3 Ti Le Huu and Lien Nguyen Duc, Water Resources Section, Division of Environment and Sustainable Development, UN-ESCAP, Mekong Case Study, 2.

4 MRC, About the Mekong, People, Livelihoods and Water, http://www.mrcmekong.org/about_ mekong/people.htm.

5 I. G. Baird (2009). The Don Sahong Dam: Potential Impacts on Regional Fish Migrations, Livelihoods and Human Health (PDF). POLIS Project on Environmental Governance, University of Victoria.

6 http://wwf.panda.org/what_we_do/where_we_work/greatermekong/.

7 Mekong River Commission (2010). State of the Basin Report, 2010 (PDF). MRC, Vientiane, Laos.

8 International Network of Basin Organizations: http://www.inbo-news.org/IMG/pdf/State_of_ Mekong_basin_2003_2.pdf.

9 Source: http://www.mrcmekong.org/about_mekong/water_work.htm.

and 11 more mainstream Mekong dams are proposed for the Cambodia and Lao-Thai stretches of the Mekong.[10] Furthermore, according to the 2011 MRC Basin Development Plan, tributaries to the Lower Mekong Basin will power 70 dams by 2030.

The People's Republic China (PRC) has already built a number of dams in the upper section of the river (where the Mekong is named the Lancang) with further mainstream dam development planned. These include the Manwan dam (completed in 1996), the Dachaoshan Dam (2003)[11], and Xiaowan Dam (2010), and the Jinghong Dam (2014), with more dams planned. Downstream countries have repeatedly objected to dam-building on the Mekong by the PRC due to downstream impacts.

In the Lower Mekong Basin mainstream river, two projects have recently received the most attention: the Xayaburi and Don Sahong dams in Lao. Other proposed dams are in very early planning stages. The Xayaburi dam, the first mainstream dam in the Lower Mekong Basin, has been a source of particular controversy not only due to its potential environmental and social impacts, but also due to the process preceding dam development, for its per-ceived unequal benefits and export of electricity to Thailand, and for the precedent it may set for further mainstream dam development in the region. The plan submitted to the MRC was objected to by both Cambodia and Vietnam. Despite the lack of consensus with other member states, as required as a part of the MRC Procedures on Notification, Prior Consultation and Agreement (PNPCA), the Xayaburi dam construction proceeded. The Don Sahong dam is a current focus of dispute, as detailed further in this chapter, after the Lao Government submitted notification to proceed with the dam in 2013.[12]

Dams along Mekong tributaries have also caused considerable controversy, objected to not only by civil society and impacted communities in the case of the Pak Mun dam in Thailand, but also by government via the MRC on the basis of transboundary impacts, such as in the case of the Sesan dams in Vietnam, upstream of Cambodia.

Dam proponents point to the huge energy demand projections of the region, and the potential for hydropower to fuel economic development with benefits to poverty alleviation, as well as their potential to fulfil the energy needs in Lao and Cambodia, where a large proportion of the population remain unconnected to the grid. They argue that hydropower development is a relatively low-impact energy development option which does not contribute significantly to carbon emissions, and can have multiple other benefits for the local population, includ-ing flood and drought control, and irrigation.

10 Long P. Pham, Viet Ecology Foundation, Lancang – Mekong Initiative (Viet Ecology Foundation), http://www.vietecology.org/Article.aspx/Article/64.
11 Quang M. Nguyen, P.E., Hydrologic Impacts of the PRC's Upper Mekong Dams on the Lower Mekong River, June, 2003.
12 See http://www.mrcmekong.org/news-and-events/news/lao-pdr-submits-notification-on-don-sahong-hydropower-project/.

Critics of dam construction, on the other hand, point both to the environmental impacts of dams on the river and on biodiversity, with resulting resettlement, livelihood and other social impacts, especially on the poor and indigenous peoples who are more vulnerable and dependent upon the river's resources, as well as to larger macroeconomic impacts on the productivity of fisheries and downstream agriculture dependent upon sediment deposits and flows. Critics also point to the uneven benefits of hydropower development, as well as inadequate public participation and weak influence of affected neighbouring country governments in decision-making. They argue that power development in the Mekong Region is non-participatory, with environmental and social impacts outweighing benefits, and suggest lower impact alternative energy development and energy efficiency.

There remains significant uncertainty regarding the full extent of both intra- and international impacts of proposed dams on the Mekong River. One study indicated that if 12 proposed dams are built, between 550,000 to 880,000 tons of annual fish catch will be lost by 2030.[13] The report of Strategic Environmental Assessment (SEA) of Hydropower on the Mekong mainstream launched by MRC in October 2010 studied the potential impacts of the planned dams in both the upper and lower basins. One estimated impact is that the Mekong will bear significant reductions in the transport of sediment. For example, sediment loads in Mekong may reduce by 70 per cent, from the peak of 90Mt/year to 20Mt/year in Chiang Saen and Vientiane[14], with resulting impacts on biodiversity, fisheries, and agriculture.

The Mekong Agreement and the MRC and its Secretariat support principles and processes which aim to address these concerns, although they are hampered by weak powers of enforcement and a lack of clarity regarding the implementation of its sustainability principles and dispute resolution processes.

30.4 Legal and institutional framework for cooperation and dispute settlement in the Mekong River Basin

30.4.1 The Mekong Agreement

The Agreement on the Cooperation for the Sustainable Development of the Mekong River Basin (the Mekong Agreement) aims to address the common water management and economic development interests of Cambodia, Lao PDR, Thailand and Vietnam. Signed in 1995, the Mekong Agreement established the MRC and contains provisions related to the use and protection of the Mekong River and its resources. Cambodia, Lao PDR, Thailand, and Vietnam are members of the MRC, while the PRC and Myanmar are partners.

In the Mekong Agreement, Member States commit:

13 MRC, Strategic Environmental Assessment of Hydropower on the Mekong Mainstream, Final Report, October 2010 at 69.
14 MRC – SEA report 2010.

to cooperate and promote in a constructive and mutually beneficial manner in the sustainable development, utilization, conservation and management of the Mekong River Basin water and related resources for navigational and non-navigational purposes, for social and economic development and the well-being of all riparian States, consistent with the needs to protect, preserve, enhance and manage the environmental and aquatic conditions and maintenance of the ecological balance.

As Dialogue Partners, there is limited involvement of the PRC and Myanmar with the MRC. In 2002, the PRC signed an agreement on the provision of hydrological information on the Lancang/Mekong River, providing water level data in the flood season from two stations located on the Upper Mekong in the PRC, which are inputs to the MRC's flood forecasting system.[15]

30.4.2 Principles and procedures

The Mekong Agreement incorporates several principles of international water law as they have been defined in international agreements and conventions, including the 1997 UN Convention on the Non-Navigational Use of International Watercourses, which has been signed by all MRC member states with the exception of the PRC.

Key sustainability and dispute resolution principles include:

- the obligation to not cause significant harm;
- the principle of prior notification;
- the obligation to protect natural resources and ecological balance; and
- the obligation of reasonable and equitable use of water resources for both the mainstream and the tributaries.[16]

Under the framework of Mekong Agreement, the Mekong Joint Committee (one of the three permanent bodies of the MRC) has issued procedures to guide the implementation of the Agreement.

These include:

- Procedures for Data and Information Exchange and Sharing, approved in 2001
- Procedures for Water Use Monitoring, approved in 2003;
- Procedures for Notification, Prior Consultation and Agreement, approved in 2003;
- Procedures for Maintenance of Flows on the Mainstream, approved in 2006;
- Procedures for Water Quality, approved in 2011.

15 See section 2.2.
16 See section 3.1.

30.4.3 Mekong River Commission

The MRC is mandated "to cooperate in all fields of sustainable development, utilisation, management and conservation of the water and related resources of the Mekong River Basin". The MRC replaced the Mekong Committee (Committee for Coordination of Investigations of the Lower Mekong Basin), established in 1957.

As a part of its mandate, the MRC is involved in fisheries management, the promotion of safe navigation, irrigated agriculture, watershed management, environment monitoring, flood management and hydropower. The MRC is also supporting the Basin Development Plan, a joint basinwide planning process for the Lower Mekong Basin countries, and the basis of the MRC's Integrated Water Resources Development Programme.

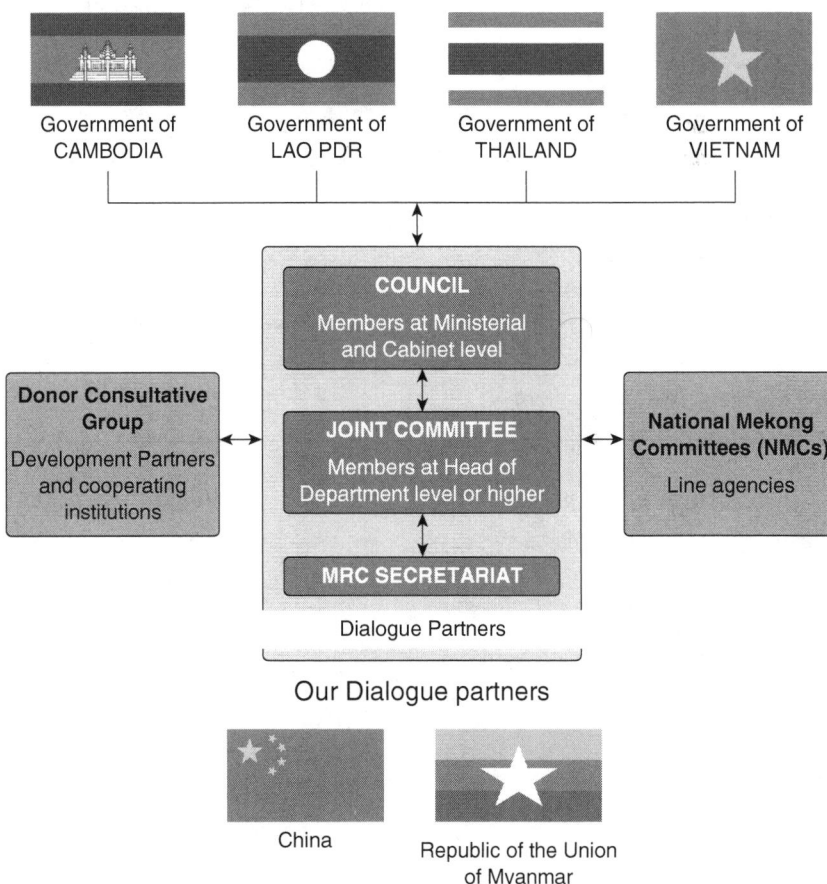

Figure 30.1 Mekong River Commission structure
Source: Mekong River Commission

The MRC is funded by contributions from aid donors, as well as from the four member countries. Formal consultation with the donor community is carried out through an annual Donor Consultative Group meeting.

30.4.4 MRC permanent bodies

The MRC consists of three permanent bodies: the Council, the Joint Committee, and the Secretariat.

30.4.4.1 The Council

The Council, which meets once a year, consists of one member from each country at the ministerial or cabinet level. The Council makes policy decisions and provides other necessary guidance concerning the promotion, support, cooperation and coordination of joint activities and programmes in order to implement the 1995 Agreement. The Council has overall governance of the MRC.

30.4.4.2 The Joint Committee

The Joint Committee is composed of senior officials of the four countries at no less than Head of Department level, and is supported by line agencies, including the Ministry of Foreign Affairs. It implements decisions made at the yearly Council meetings.

30.4.4.3 The MRC Secretariat

The MRC Secretariat is the operational arm of the MRC. It provides technical and administrative services to the Joint Committee and the Council, which is under the direction of a CEO who is appointed by the Council. Under the supervision of the Joint Committee, the CEO is responsible for the day-to-day operations of around 155 professional and general support staff. The MRC Secretariat is co-hosted in two locations, the Office of the Secretariat in Vientiane (OSV) and the Office of the Secretariat in Phnom Penh (OSP). The main counterparts for MRC activities in the four member countries are the National Mekong Committees (NMCs).[17]

30.4.5 Cooperation framework for dispute resolution

Articles 34 and 35 of the Mekong Agreement define the MRC's dispute resolution mechanism. The MRC is mandated to make "every effort to resolve the issue" (Art. 34), but no details are provided regarding how this is to be done in practice. When the solution of a specific issue is not found, it can be referred to

17 See FAO Aquastat http://www.fao.org/nr/water/aquastat/basins/mekong/print1.stm.

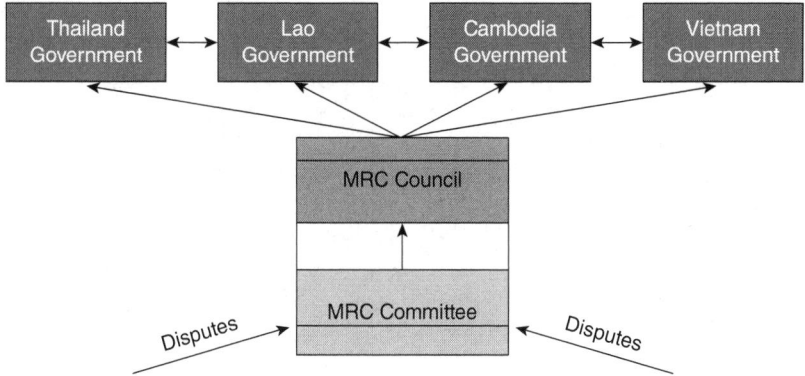

Figure 30.2 MRC dispute resolution process
Source: Author

bilateral negotiations among riparians or a mutually agreed upon external party can be asked for assistance (Art. 35).

In principle, disputes are first processed by the MRC Committee. If no result is reached, the riparian countries can proceed to the MRC Council. However, the MRC bodies do not have power of enforcement. Critically, there are no further details in the Mekong Agreement on the dispute resolution process. Overall, the MRC's provisions for dispute resolution remain vague and indicate a "lack of well-functioning and reliable dispute resolution mechanisms"[18]. Member States tend to resolve differences via bilateral negotiations.

With regards to hydropower development and operations, the lack of clear dispute resolution processes has been particularly evident, as Member Countries have not been able exert much influence on decisions via the MRC or with reference to the Mekong Agreement. In fact, the MRC SEA Report purports that the MRC has "no mechanism for basin-wide regulation of hydropower or other forms of sector development on the Mekong mainstream". The report recommended to "develop new regional institutional mechanisms to plan and manage multi-sector development on the Mekong mainstream" and "develop capacity of existing institutions to regulate, monitor and enforce compliance for hydropower".[19]

The lack of MRC procedures and enforcement has been displayed with regard to three controversial hydropower development projects: Xayaburi and Don Sahong in Lao, and the Se San River in Vietnam. The establishment of a MRC initiated mechanism to address disputes over dams in the Se San River Basin,

18 Susan Schmeier, Water Papers, Resilience to Climate Change: Induced Challenges in the Mekong River Basin – *The Role of the MRC*, (Washington: World Bank, 2011) 2011 at 30.
19 MRC, MRC – SEA Hydropower, *supra* note 13 at 139.

a tributary to the Mekong, largely failed and no agreement could be reached between Cambodia – whose communities are downstream of the dams claimed to be affected – and Vietnam[20]. Some observers claim that interventions and initiatives of the Asian Development Bank may have "further weakened MRC's role in mitigating collective action problems related to the use of water resources in the Mekong River Basin".[21]

Lao's plans for the Dong Sahong Dam project (near the Khone Falls which forms an historic and natural border between the two countries, as the Mekong is not navigable at that point) have led to tensions with Cambodia, which fears negative impacts on fisheries, among multiple other potential biodiversity and environmental impacts. The Cambodian Government protested against the project by sending an official letter to the Lao Government, and at the January 2014 Council meeting, consensus could not be reached regarding whether the dam was subject to Procedures on Notification, Prior Consultation and Agreement. Lao argued that, since the dam would be situated on a channel of the mainstream, it is not a mainstream dam and therefore not subject to PNPCA – and that no consultation is needed – although other Member States disagree. As of 2015, the dam is scheduled for completion by 2018, although the dispute is still pending and has been referred to the Ministerial level.

Although there was no dispute regarding whether the Xayaburi dam was subject to the PNPCA (as all mainstream dams are), construction still began without agreement by Vietnam and Cambodia, nor, in their view, adequate consultation. Lao does not claim that the Mekong Agreement is not binding, but rather that it has adhered to it and the PNPCA, although other Member Countries disagree with the Lao interpretation of the PNPCA.

30.5 Cooperation principles in the Mekong River Basin and the New Delhi Declaration Principles

30.5.1 Cooperation principles of the Mekong Agreement

Member States must cooperate in all fields of sustainable development, utilization, management and conservation of the water and related resources of the Mekong River Basin including irrigation, hydropower, navigation, flood control, fisheries, timber floating, recreation and tourism, with the purposes of optimizing the multiple-use and mutual benefits of all riparians and minimizing the harmful effects that might result from natural occurrences and man-made activities.[22]

---

20 Ibid.
21 See Schmeier, *supra* note 18.
22 Mekong Agreement, *supra* note 13 at ch. III art. 1.

The Mekong Agreement also sets cooperation principles – the sustainable development principles of the Mekong River Basin, explained in the Chapter II (Objectives and Principles of Cooperation).

The Mekong Cooperation Principles pertain to the:

1   Protection of the environment and ecological balance;
2   Sovereign equality and territorial integrity;
3   Reasonable and equitable utilization;
4   Maintenance of flows on the mainstream;
5   Prevention and cessation of harmful effects;
6   State responsibility for damages;
7   Freedom of navigation;
8   Emergency situations.

The following sections summarize the cooperation principles listed above.

30.5.1.1 Protection of the environment and ecological balance

The Mekong Agreement emphasizes the responsibilities of riparian countries in the protection of the environment, natural resources, aquatic life and conditions, and the ecological balance of the Mekong River Basin from pollution or other harmful effects resulting from any development plans and uses of water and related resources in the Basin.

30.5.1.2 Sovereign equality and territorial integrity

Article 4 of the Mekong Agreement is for riparian countries to "cooperate on the basis of sovereign equality and territorial integrity in the utilization and protection of the water resources" of the Mekong River Basin. However, by underlining "sovereign equality", the Agreement ignores the geographical position of members as upstream or downstream states.[23]

In addition, another challenge to the sustainable development of the Mekong River Basin is the large difference among riparian states in their socio-economic development status, with Vietnam, and especially Thailand, having reached a relatively high level of economic, social, and human development, but with Laos and Cambodia still facing the challenges of less developed countries. Different levels of development are associated with different interests in the use and/or the protection of the river and its resources, thus increasing the conflicts among river use and related plans of the states.

---

23 Bernard J. Wohlwend, The Emerging Principles and Rules of International Water Resources Law, *http://www.bjwconsult.com/EMERGING.PDF*, at 9.

Table 30.1 Framework for prior notification, prior consultation and prior agreement

	Mainstream		Tributaries, including Tonle Sap lake
	Dry season	Wet season	
Inter-basin diversion	Specific Agreement	Prior consultation	Notification
Intra-basin use	Prior consultation	Notification	

30.5.1.3 Reasonable and equitable utilization

The Rules for Water Utilization and Inter-basin Diversion provide for "notification" and "prior consultation", aiming to use the waters of Mekong River in a reasonable and equitable manner in the states' respective territories.

Notification, meaning the "timely providing information by a riparian to the Joint Committee on its proposed use of water",[24] is required for proposed uses on the tributaries, including the Tonle Sap Lake, and for intra-basin use on the mainstream during the wet season.

Prior consultation, which aims at arriving at an agreement by the Joint Committee, is required for any proposed inter-basin diversion during the wet season from the mainstreams, and for intra-basin use during the dry season. Any inter-basin diversion project must be agreed upon by the Joint Committee through a specific agreement for each project prior to any proposed diversion.

Member States must notify the Joint Committee in a timely manner as well as provide additional data and information to the Joint Committee that would allow other Members to discuss and evaluate the impact of the proposed use. The notification/prior consultation documents shall be copied to each National Mekong Committee. In the case of prior consultation, Member States are given the opportunity to comment, evaluate and reply, and request additional information.[25]

But these options may not apply to the notification process. The time frame for prior consultation is six months from the date of receiving documents and can be extended by the Joint Committee. During this time, the proposing state is not allowed to implement the proposed project.

However, prior consultation is neither a right to veto the use nor a unilateral right to use water by any riparian without taking into account other riparians' rights.[26]

---

24 The notification shall include feasibility study report, implementation plan, schedule and all available data (section 4.2.1 of NCA).
25 Ibid. at sects 4.3.2.b, 5.3.2.b, 5.4.1, 5.4.2.
26 Ibid. at sect. 1; Mekong Agreement, *supra* note 13 at arts 5.B.1b, 5.B.2a.

30.5.1.4 Maintenance of flows on the mainstream

It is provided that Mekong countries agree to cooperate to maintain the flows on the mainstream in the case of diversions, storage releases, or other actions of a permanent nature, except in the cases of historically severe droughts and/or floods:

1   of not less than the acceptable minimum monthly natural flow during each month of the dry season;
2   to enable the acceptable natural reverse flow of the Tonle Sap to take place during the wet season; and,
3   to prevent average daily peak flows greater than what naturally occur on the average during the flood season.

30.5.1.5 Prevention and cessation of harmful effects

Article 7 of the Mekong Agreement States that riparian countries are responsible to "make every effort to avoid, minimize and mitigate harmful effects that might occur to the environment, especially the water quantity and quality, the aquatic (eco-system) conditions, and ecological balance of the river system, from the development and use of the Mekong River Basin water resources or discharge of wastes and return flows".

Where one or more States is notified with proper and valid evidence that it is causing substantial damage to one or more riparian countries from the use of and/or discharge to water of the Mekong River, that State or States shall cease immediately the alleged cause of harm until such cause of harm is determined.

However, States do not have the obligation to foresee and prevent the possibility of harmful effects that may impact the other basin States. Only when the State is "notified with proper and valid evidence" that substantial damages are being caused to other countries, then that State may take the responsibility of ceasing the alleged harm. In Article 7 we also do not see the responsibility of compensation or recovery in case actual damages occur.

30.5.1.5.1 INFORMATION SHARING AND DATABASES

The Prevention and Cessation of Harmful Effects principle requires information-sharing in order to be effective. The Procedures for Data and Information Exchange and Sharing adopted by the Mekong Council in 2011 provides regulations on data and information-sharing, requiring that Member States cooperate in sharing data and information in a constructive and mutually beneficial way to ensure the sustainable development of the Mekong Basin.

The data and information required to share are "necessary" to implement the Mekong Agreement. While not determining the "necessary" data or information, the procedure for data, information, exchange and sharing lists 12 major groups of information, including: topography, natural resources, agriculture, navigation and transport, flood management and mitigation, infrastructure, urbanization/industrialization, environment/ecology, administrative boundaries, socio-economy, and tourism.

The MRC Secretariat now hosts seven regional databases:

- meteorological and hydrological database;
- water resources database;
- groundwater database;
- water quality database;
- social and economic database;
- forestry database;
- wetland database.

These databases have not been completely developed with full data and information, and Member States are to contribute further certain data and information.

30.5.1.6 State responsibility for damages

Where harmful effects cause substantial damage to one or more riparians from the use of and/or discharge to waters of the Mekong River, the concerned State shall determine all relative factors, the cause, extent of damage and responsibility for damages caused by that State in conformity with the principles of international law relating to state responsibility. The Members are also required to "address and resolve all issues, differences and disputes in an amicable and timely manner by peaceful means" as provided in Articles 34 and 35 of the Mekong Agreement, and in conformity with the Charter of the United Nations.

30.5.1.7 Freedom of navigation

The Mekong Agreement confirms the principle of freedom of navigation for all members in Article 9 for transportation and communication to promote regional cooperation and to satisfactorily implement projects under the Mekong Agreement. The Member States have the obligation of keeping the Mekong River free from obstructions, measures, conduct and actions that might directly or indirectly impair navigability, interfere with this right or permanently make it more difficult. Riparians may issue regulations applicable within their territories, particularly in sanitary, customs and immigration matters, police and general security.

30.5.1.8 Emergency situations

Emergency notification is addressed through Article 10 of the Mekong Agreement. Whenever a Party becomes aware of any special water quantity or quality problems constituting an emergency that requires an immediate response, it shall notify and consult directly with the Party(ies) concerned and the Joint Committee without delay in order to take appropriate remedial action.

30.5.2 New Delhi Declaration Principles

The International Law Association Committee on the Legal Aspects of Sustainable Development released the 2002 New Delhi Declaration on the Principles of International Law Related to Sustainable Development, composed of seven principles to "help to resolve conflicts related to sustainable development, and support the balanced integration of laws and policies at the intersection of international environmental, social and economic law".[27]

The Principles are:

1 the duty of states to ensure sustainable use of natural resources;
2 the principle of equity and the eradication of poverty;
3 the principle of common but differentiated responsibilities;
4 the principle of the precautionary approach to human health, natural resources and ecosystems;
5 the principle of public participation and access to information and justice;
6 the principle of good governance;
7 the principle of integration and inter-relationship, in particular in relation to human rights and social, economic and environmental objectives.

30.6 Comparison of principles in the Mekong Agreement and the New Delhi Declaration

There is overlap between the UN Charter and principles in the Mekong Agreement, and therefore similarities with the New Delhi Declaration (as the UN principles are part of original sources of the New Delhi Declaration). In many cases, a single principle of the New Delhi Declaration (or aspects of the principle) appears in multiple principles and procedures of Mekong Agreement.

This chapter identifies four principles of the New Delhi Declaration which can also, to an extent, be found in principles in the Mekong Agreement. The following sections provide a brief overview of the relationship between the four principles and principles of the Mekong Agreement, including how they translate in practice.

30.6.1 The duty of states to ensure sustainable use of natural resources

In the Mekong Agreement, Member States are required to protect the environment and the ecological balance, and ensure the reasonable and equitable use of the Mekong resources, to maintain the flows of the mainstream Mekong River, to prevent or cease harmful effects, and to bear responsibility for alleged damages.

---

27 These principles emerge from the Brundtland Report and the 1992 Rio Declaration.

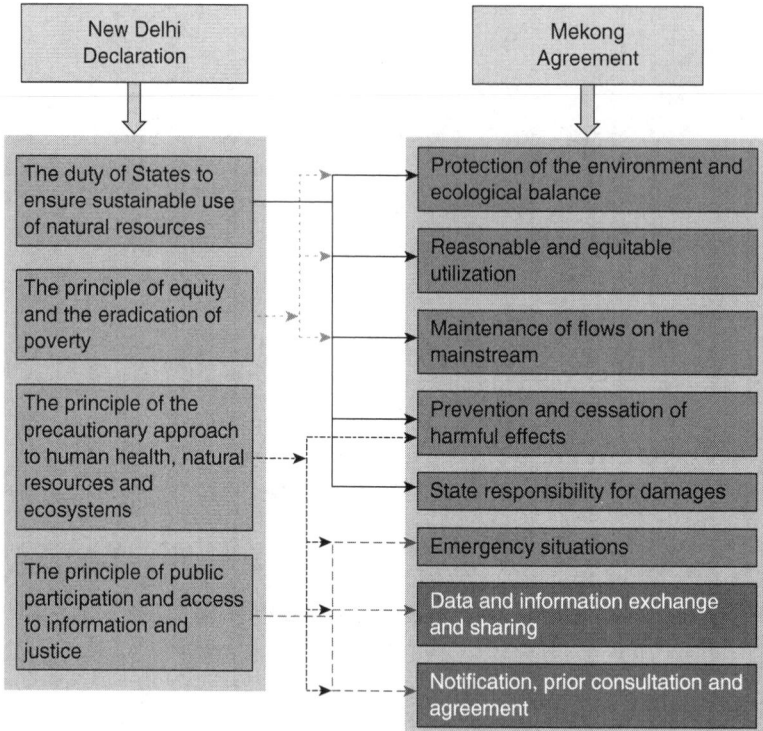

Figure 30.3 Linkages between the principles of the Mekong Agreement and the
New Delhi Declaration

Source: Mekong River Commission

However, the Mekong Agreement is not very explicit regarding how resources are to be sustainably used (with the exception of specific guidance regarding river flow).

Neither the New Delhi Declaration nor Mekong Agreement mention the duty of states in compensation and/or recovery of the damages to the natural resources caused by their own actions or policies.

30.6.2 The principle of equity and the eradication of poverty

The Mekong Agreement does not explicitly mention equity and the eradication of poverty. However, the Agreement supports this principle by acknowledging *"natural assets of immense value to all the riparian countries for the economic and social well-being and living standards of their peoples"*[28] and then requiring their

---

28 Mekong Agreement, *supra* note 13, at preamble, ch. I.

protection in principles relating to Mekong flow, environment, water quality and ecological systems.

30.6.3 The principle of the precautionary approach to human health, natural resources and ecosystems

The Mekong Agreement has two principles potentially relating to the precautionary approach: the principle of prevention and cessation of harmful effects, and the emergency situation. The precautionary principle is also supported in the PNPCA as well as data and information-sharing and exchange.

Although the Mekong Agreement principles listed above can support the precautionary principle, its fulfilment requires more than what is included in these principles. First, adequate studies need to be undertaken, including Environmental Impact Assessments (EIAs) and also Strategic Environmental and Social Impact Assessments (SEAs) which examine not only specific projects but larger development plans as well, consisting of a number of potential projects. While there has been progress on SEAs in the region, with three SEAs related to power development already completed, SEAs are still not required in national laws or in the Mekong Agreement. By adopting a higher level analysis, SEAs could shed greater light on basin-wide and transboundary impacts.

The MRC SEA (2010), as a result of both its assessment of potentially large and irreversible damage to the Mekong River Basin from mainstream hydropower development as well as its recognition that current studies provide an inadequate understanding of the extent of these impacts, referred to the precautionary principle in its recommendation to impose a 10-year moratorium on mainstream dam development, to allow for further studies to be conducted – however, this was not put into effect.

EIA practice in the Lower Mekong Basin countries is also perceived by some observers to be highly inadequate, and rarely resulting in the cancellation of a project, but only in some cases to modifications.[29] The EIA of the Pak Mun dam in Thailand did result in relocation of the proposed dam site, but without further study of the potential impacts at the new site. There are also claims of conflict of interest, such as in the case of the Xayaburi dam, where the same consulting company conducted the EIA as well as aspects of its engineering.[30]

---

29 Mekong River Dams: National Laws to Address Environmental and Human Rights Issues, and Obstacles to Enforcement. Earth Right's International Mekong Legal Advocacy Institute (MLAI) 2009. See https://www.earthrights.org/sites/default/files/publications/Mekong-River-Dams-MLAI_0.pdf.

30 Nonetheless, a peer review of the EIA report conducted by a French company hired by the Government of Lao found that the project was compliant with MRC guidelines. See the case study for the IWRM toolbox "Mekong River, Public Participation in Hydropower Development: Does it Matter?". See http://www.gwp.org/Global/ToolBox/Case%20Studies/Americas%20and%20 Caribbean/CS_463_Mekong_Hydropower_full%20case%20(3).pdf

As detailed in the previous section, the principle of prevention and cessation of harmful effects does not impose the obligation on a state to prevent the potentially irreversible damage to the other basin states. It is only responsible to cease harm after damage has occurred to other countries – after notification "with proper and valid evidence". The emphasis on inter-state impacts is also not consistent with the scope of the precautionary principle, which applies equally to intra-state damage.

The Procedures for Notification, Prior Consultation and Agreement provide an avenue for the application of the precautionary principle when related to inter-state impacts, as neighbouring countries may not agree to development which would cause their environment irreversible harm. However, most observers believe that this procedure has not been successfully implemented in the case of the Xayaburi dam, which went ahead without agreement by other member states.

While the Emergency Situation principle does also emphasize prevention of harm and not just its cessation, it relates more to impacts from dam operation or construction (such as impacts on river flows during either the blockage or release of water) than on overall impacts from the development of a dam.

30.6.4 The principle of public participation and access to information and justice

Although the Mekong Agreement aims to facilitate Member Countries' participation in the other Members' projects by, *inter alia*, giving comments, evaluation, requesting for additional information according to the Procedures on Notification and Prior Consultation, it provides no opportunity to other stakeholders, such as local communities, organizations or individuals, to provide input into states' water use decisions. Regarding information access, Member States can study the MRC Secretariat's databases, and are also asked for support and contributions to strengthen databases. However, National Mekong Committees decide which further information is available to national stakeholders at consultations, and therefore access to information beyond the MRC databases (such as EIAs) is dependent on the will of member states.

The Mekong Agreement does not specifically mention stakeholder or public participation in decision-making, although the MRC has initiated a number of studies, guidelines and principles to enhance meaningful public participation in decision-making. Furthermore, the MRC definition of stakeholders includes those generally excluded from the decision-making.

Nevertheless, in 2009 the MRC concluded that "public participation has not been mainstreamed within MRC programmes and governance" due to a "lack of implementation tool and processes, limited political will by MRC riparian governments, and lack of understanding of the true benefits of engaging diverse stakeholders in decision-making around water resources development and management in the LMB".[31]

This conclusion is supported by further hydropower development in the region and a lack of meaningful public participation. For example, with regards to the Xayaburi dam development, public consultations were not conducted in Lao, where the dam would be located, as they are not explicitly required under the PNPCA Guidelines. Although they were considered necessary by the PNPCA Joint Council Working Group it concluded that public participation was a national matter.[32]

The PNPCA for the Xayaburi dam did include a number of stakeholder consultations in the other countries of the Lower Mekong Basin in January and February 2011. Results supported the 2010 Strategic Environmental Assessment to impose a 10-year moratorium on mainstream dam development, but these and other suggestions were not integrated into decision-making at the national or regional level.[33]

A case study for the IWRM ToolBox found that there is little or no link between the public consultations and government approvals of projects – in other words, that public participation is not meaningful – but rather that the "two processes appear to be undertaken in parallel but exclusive of each other". The case study concludes that "if the link between stakeholder consultation results and government approvals of projects is not addressed, the social and environmental losses would be far outweigh its economic gains for the people of the Mekong River Basin".[34]

30.6.5 The principle of common but differentiated responsibilities

This principle in the New Delhi Declaration does not appear in the Mekong Agreement, which confers the same responsibilities to all Members. All Members are equalized by the principle of sovereign equality, despite the natural tendency for upstream states to generate greater impacts on the downstream states than vice versa. Secondly, the different development status of each country is not reflected in differentiated responsibilities, despite the much higher levels of development in Vietnam and Thailand in comparison to Lao and Cambodia.

---

31 MRC 2009. Stakeholder Participation and Communication Plan for Basin Development Planning in the Lower Mekong Basin. See http://www.mrcmekong.org/assets/Other-Documents/BDP/SPCP-Final-July-2009-Final.pdf.

32 MRC 2011a, Prior Consultation Project Review Report, Available: http://www.mrcmekong.org/assets/Publications/Reports/PC-Proj-Review-Report- Xaiyaburi-24-3-11.pdf

33 See the case study for the IWRM toolbox entitled "Mekong River, Public Participation in HydroPower Development: Does It Matter?" available online at http://www.gwp.org/Global/ToolBox/Case%20Studies/Americas%20and%20Caribbean/CS_463_Mekong_Hydropower_full%20case%20(3).pdf.

34 Ibid.

30.7 Conclusion

The sustainable development principles of the New Delhi Declaration are only weakly reflected in the Mekong Agreement, in particular the principles of public participation and access to information and justice, and the precautionary approach to human health, natural resources and ecosystems. Their application is further weakened by a lack of clear guidelines, processes and procedures, the lack of enforcement capability of the MRC, and the lack of influence of member countries' over other countries' Mekong River Basin development plans.

A key challenge for sustainable use of Mekong River Basin water resources is that the influence of the MRC is limited to only the lower Mekong River Basin, and not the upper basin where China and Myanmar are pursuing ambitious hydropower development plans.

Regarding both local and transboundary impacts, more effective inclusion of civil society and indigenous peoples in decision-making, greater access to information, and a more careful application of the precautionary principle could mitigate environmental and social impacts and result in more equitable and sustainable outcomes.

Dispute resolution mechanisms in international organizations

31 Sustainable development concerns at the Aarhus Convention Compliance Committee

Andriy Andrusevych and Caroline Jo

31.1 Introduction

The compliance mechanism under the Convention on Access to Information, Public Participation in Decision-Making and Access to Justice in Environmental Matters (1998, the Aarhus Convention) is well-documented in academic literature. The compliance mechanism was established by the First Meeting of the Parties of the Aarhus Convention in 2002 by Decision I/7 "Review of Compliance." The mechanism aims to promote and improve compliance with the Aarhus Convention by the Parties. A key element of the compliance mechanism is the Compliance Committee set up to review compliance by Parties.

The Compliance Committee consists of nine members who serve in their personal capacity (not representing any Party). The Committee can consider "cases" triggered in three possible ways: a communication from the public, a submission from a Party, or a referral from the Secretariat of the Convention. So far, no referrals and only one submission have been made; all other cases have been initiated by a communication from the public. Here, we define a case as a dispute requiring consideration by the Committee of the state of compliance by a particular Party with its obligations under the Convention and involving a public hearing.

Since its establishment in 2002 by the First Meeting of the Parties of the Aarhus Convention, the Committee has dealt with numerous issues related to the practical implementation of the Convention by the Parties. In many cases, the Committee had to interpret and apply Convention provisions, as well as its own rules of procedures, to specific situations brought to its attention. Accordingly, substantial case law was developed by the Committee during 2004–2011.[1]

This chapter analyses the case law of the Aarhus Convention Compliance Committee for the period between 2004 and 2011 in the context of some principles of the New Delhi Declaration.

---

1 A. Andrusevych, T. Alge, C. Konrad. eds., *Case Law of the Aarhus Convention Compliance Committee (2004–2011)*, 2nd edn (RACSE, Lviv, 2011) at 5.

31.2 New Delhi principle 5 and Aarhus pillars

The Aarhus Convention stands on three "pillars," namely access to information, public participation and access to justice, provided for under its Articles 4–9.[2] This chapter comprises three sections dealing with respective pillars.

31.2.1 Access to environmental information

31.2.1.1 Relevant provisions

Paragraph 5.2 of the New Delhi Declaration reads:

> Public participation in the context of sustainable development requires effective protection of the human right to hold and express opinions and to seek, receive and impart ideas. It also requires a right of access to appropriate, comprehensible and timely information held by governments and industrial concerns on economic and social policies regarding the sustainable use of natural resources and the protection of the environment, without imposing undue financial burdens upon the applicants and with due consideration for privacy and adequate protection of business confidentiality.

The Aarhus Convention key relevant articles are Article 1 "Objective" (recognizing the right to access to environmental information), Article 2 "Definitions" (definition of environmental information, public and public authorities), Article 4 "Access to Environmental Information" and Article 5 "Collection and Dissemination of Environmental Information." The Convention sets detailed requirements for each of the key elements of access to environmental information, including:

(i)   broad definitions of environmental information (Art. 2.3), public authorities (Art.2.2) and public (Art. 2.4);
(ii) procedural elements for providing information upon request (such as timing, form, etc.) and justified reasons for denial (Art.4.3 and 4.4.);
(iii) obligations of the state to possess (collect) environmental information, as well as to regularly distribute it voluntary (Art.5).

The Aarhus Convention does not limit access to information to the participation process: access to information is its own stand-alone pillar, namely the first pillar of the Convention. Some issues related to access to information relevant for public participation in decision-making are also covered by Article 6 "Public Participation in Decisions on Specific Activities", as discussed in the relevant subsection on public participation below.

The Aarhus Convention does not deal as such with the right to freedom of speech (as reflected in the first sentence of the paragraph 5.2 of the New Delhi

---

2 The Aarhus Convention. Implementation Guide (New York: United Nations, 2000) at 5.

Declaration). Some relevant elements are discussed in the introductory part, in particular prohibition of persecution and harassment.

31.2.1.2 Compliance Committee case law

The Compliance Committee dealt with access to information in 19 out of 58 cases (33 per cent)[3] and majority of those cases also involved other provisions of the Convention. The Committee's case law on access to information provisions focused on the following issues:

(i)   establishment of a clear, transparent and consistent framework on access to information;
(ii) the form, ways and timing of provision of information;
(iii) applicability of positive silence concept;
(iv) grounds for refusal to provide information;
(v)   delegation of functions to private entities;
(vi) costs and fees.

31.2.1.2.1 ESTABLISHMENT OF A CLEAR, TRANSPARENT AND CONSISTENT FRAMEWORK

In most cases the Compliance Committee did not focus on specific violations by the government, but the underlying reasons. In this context the Committee even stated in the EC case that "it does not consider in every instance where [a government] makes an erroneous decision when implementing the requirements of article 4, this should lead the Committee to adopt a finding of non-compliance".[4] In other words, one mistake does always not count. What really matters is the underlying reason, which in many cases was linked to failure to establish a clear, transparent and consistent framework. This includes lack of clear regulation and guidance with regard to the obligations of bodies performing public functions to provide information,[5] failure to provide clear instructions,[6] failure to transpose excused by superiority of international agreement,[7] and lack of clarity or detail in the domestic legislation.[8]

31.2.1.2.2 FORM, WAYS AND TIMING OF PROVISION OF INFORMATION

The environmental information shall be provided in the form requested. Failure to provide information in electronic form (CD), when it was actually available in such form, was considered by the Compliance Committee as not in line with this requirement, especially because provision in other forms was much

---

3 A. Andrusevych, T. Alge, C. Konrad, eds., *Case Law of the Aarhus Convention Compliance Committee (2004–2011),* 2nd edn (RACSE, Lviv 2011) at 206–8.
4 ECE/MP.PP/C.1/2009/2/Add.1, para. 33.
5 Ibid. at para. 27.
6 Alvaro Umana, ed., *The World Bank Inspection Panel: The First Four Years (1994–1998)* (Washington, D.C.: World Bank, 1998).
7 ECE/MP.PP/2008/5/Add.10, para. 58.
8 ECE/MP/PP/C.1/2005/2/Add.3, para. 34.

more expensive[9]. Providing "copies" of information, required by Article 4.1 of the Convention, was interpreted as a requirement that whole documentation be close to the residence of the requester or entirely in electronic form, if the requester lives in another city.[10] Making information generally available, for example through putting it on websites, does not mean that each of the requests shall be answered.[11]

The Convention sets a requirement of providing information as soon as possible, at the latest within one month with a possibility of an extension for another month if the volume and complexity of the information justify such extension. However, there is an obligation to provide an answer within two months from the time the request was made and extensions are included within this time limitation.[12]

31.2.1.2.3 POSITIVE SILENCE CONCEPT

In the context of access to information, the Committee held that the Convention prohibits application of "positive silence" concept for information requests.[13] While tacit agreement may be an acceptable legal technique in some cases, the right to information can be fulfilled only if public authorities actively respond to the requests for information.[14] These considerations are of special importance for situations where information was made publicly available (e.g. on the Internet) and it may be wrongfully assumed to be already provided and, therefore, no response provided to a request.

31.2.1.2.4 GROUNDS FOR REFUSAL TO PROVIDE INFORMATION

Ungrounded refusal to provide information is probably the most frequent violation of the access to information right. While the Aarhus Convention sets detailed requirements on grounds and procedure for refusal, its practical implementation has led to numerous clarifications by the Compliance Committee. In relation to environmental impact assessment (EIA) studies, the Committee held that they cannot be exempted as a matter of general practice – even if there are concerns over intellectual property contained in them – without violating Article 4[15]. In a way, this approach prohibits an approach whereby a general exemption from disclosure is set by a law for certain type of information and, therefore, requiring a case-by-case approach to a procedure for determining the grounds for refusal. The issue of ownership of EIA information is not of relevance.[16]

---

9 ECE/MP.PP/C.1/2009/8/Add.1, para. 70.
10 ECE/MP.PP/C.1/2010/4/Add.2, para. 61.
11 Ibid. at para. 57.
12 See *supra* note 9 at para. 74.
13 See *supra* note 10 at para. 58.
14 Ibid.
15 ECE/MP.PP/2008/Add.7, paras. 28–30.
16 ECE/MP.PP/2005/Add.3, para. 31.

The Committee used such strict interpretation of the Convention's provisions in other situations, too. While recognizing that the Convention protects legitimate economic interest (Article 6.4 (d)), the Committee stated that by no means can this be interpreted as allowing release of information only in case of "no harm" to such interest.[17] It pointed to the need to seek balance between public interested served and harm to economic interests resulting from disclosure of environmental information as required by Article 4.4.

31.2.1.2.5 DELEGATION OF FUNCTIONS TO PRIVATE ENTITIES

The case law of the Compliance Committee includes several interpretations concerning delegation of functions by public authorities to private entities. These include so called "onward referral", a concept of forwarding request of information, or referring the requester to an agency which possesses the information requested. In the opinion of the Compliance Committee the applicability of onward referral in the context of paragraph 4.5 is legitimate but requires that two conditions are met.

The first condition for onward referral is that the request for information is referred to another public authority[18]. This is also true for cases where developers hold such information and referrals are made to such private entities which, in these situations, should be treated as public authorities.[19] What is important is that the Committee, therefore, assumes that developers (companies) can be treated as private authorities, in contrast with public participation obligations where full reliance on the developer cannot be considered as being in line with the Convention. The second condition to be met under Article 4.5 is that onward referral does not compromise compliance with the obligations under Article 5.2 (a)–(b).[20] The reasoning for this finding was that even when there is a delegation of public authority function to a private entity there is still an obligation for the relevant public authority to have access to information on how the delegation is carried out.[21] This is particularly important where environmental issues are concerned.

31.2.1.2.6 COSTS AND FEES

Provision of some environmental information may be difficult, especially when its volume is large. Yet, the information must be provided regardless of its volume.[22] This does not mean, of course, that fees may not be applied and the Convention allows this. However, the fees must reasonable and the relevant case law requires that fees for copying shall be comparable with applicable commercial rates. In particular, the Compliance Committee held that charging 2.05 Euros per page is too

17 ECE/MP.PP/2009/Add.1, para. 30.
18 ECE/MP.PP/2011/Add.2, para. 66.
19 Ibid.
20 Ibid. at para. 69.
21 Ibid.
22 See *supra* note 16 at para. 33.

much compared to 0.03 Euros per page in commercial copy-centres and, therefore, means non-compliance with the requirements of the Aarhus Convention.[23]

31.2.2 *Public participation*

31.2.2.1 *Relevant provisions*

Paragraph 5.1 of New Delhi Declaration reads:

> Public participation is essential to sustainable development and good governance in that it is a condition of responsive, transparent and accountable governments as well as a condition for the active engagement of equally responsive, transparent and accountable civil society organizations, including industrial concerns and trade unions. The vital role of women in sustainable development should be recognised.

The Aarhus Convention's relevant key articles are Article 1 "Objective (recognizing the right to public participation in decision-making), Article 6 "Public participation in decisions on specific activities", Article 7 "Public participation concerning plans, programmes and policies relating to the environment" and Article 8 "Public participation during the preparation of executive regulations and/or generally applicable legally binding normative instruments".

Compared to the New Delhi Declaration, the scope of public participation under the Aarhus Convention is narrower, since all relevant procedures apply to "environmental" or related decision-making, while the New Delhi Declaration speaks about public participation in the context of sustainable development and good governance. No doubt these two concepts are much wider than just related to environment. In fact, the negotiations of the so-called Strategic Plan of the Convention produced a rather weak provision on "exploring possibilities for the development of measures under the Convention to ensure greater opportunities for public participation in policy formulation and implementation contributing to sustainable development"[24]; extending application of the Aarhus principles to "sustainable development" areas met strong opposition from many EU countries.

The Convention, on the other hand, sets firm and detailed rules for public participation procedures, especially in relation to specific decisions (projects). The Convention clearly distinguishes between three "levels" of decision-making: project level (e.g. construction of roads), strategic level (plans, programmes and policies) and legislative (preparation of draft legal instruments). Relevant requirements, grouped by articles of the Convention, for public participation and their implementation are discussed in this section, including scope of application, notification to the public, access to information related to decision-making, procedures for providing comments, etc.

---

23 See *supra* note 9 at para. 79.
24 ECE/MP.PP/2008/2/Add.16, para. 11.

Clearly, the public participation pillar of the Aarhus Convention is closely linked to access to information and access to justice pillars. In particular, Article 4 on access to environmental information shall also be applied to information related to participation in decision-making (e.g. grounds for refusal to information).

31.2.2.2 The Compliance Committee case law

The Compliance Committee dealt with public participation in 31 out of 58 cases (53 per cent)[25]. There was only once a case where the Committee confronted Article 8 (public participation during the preparation of executive regulations and/or generally applicable legally binding normative instruments), yet the Committee decided not to consider the issue at all. Therefore, there is no case law on implementation of this article.

The Committee's case law on public participation dealt with provisions of Article 6 and Article 7 and touched upon various elements, including:

(i) boundaries between project level decisions and decisions on plans or programs;
(ii) public participation in tiered (multiple) decision-making;
(iii) transfer of obligations and reliance on developer in ensuring public participation;
(iv) public participation in environmental impact assessment (EIA) and strategic environmental assessment (SEA);
(v) participation by foreign public;
(vi) "right to veto" and taking account of public participation;
(vii) land planning decisions.

31.2.2.2.1 BOUNDARIES BETWEEN PROJECT LEVEL DECISIONS AND DECISIONS ON PLANS
OR PROGRAMS

Where the decision in question was subject to a discussion whether it falls under Article 6 (project level) or Article 7 (plan or programme), the Compliance Committee would always choose a different option: to discuss the peculiarities of the case regardless of applicability of Article 6 or Article 7, but in light of those obligations (provisions) which apply to either project or plan/programme. Since Article 7 (on plans and programmes) makes a reference to paragraphs 3, 4 and 8 of Article 6, the Compliance Committee usually opted to discuss compliance with those paragraphs.

At the same time, in some cases the Compliance Committee commented on the issue of boundaries between project level decisions and plans/programmes, especially where the issue of access to justice was discussed. While public participation requirements can be effectively dealt with in many cases by using the approach described above, access to justice requirements depend

---

25 A. Andrusevych, T. Alge, C. Konrad, eds., *Case Law of the Aarhus Convention Compliance Committee (2004–2011)*, 2nd edn (RACSE, Lviv 2011) at 206–8.

on how a decision is categorized. Therefore, in some cases the Committee had to comment on this issue. First, the Committee observed that the Convention itself does not establish a precise boundary between Article 6-type decisions and Article 7-type decisions.[26] Second, it said that the label of the decisions in the domestic law of a party is not decisive when determining how to categorize a decision under the Convention, but rather its legal functions and effects.[27]

31.2.2.2.2 PUBLIC PARTICIPATION IN TIERED (MULTIPLE) DECISION-MAKING

In most cases an activity is permitted via a multiple (tiered) decision-making process, which may include project-siting decisions, licensing, construction permit, operational permit, emissions permit, etc. This is especially true for large or complex activities, which are the core of Annex I to the Convention.

The Compliance Committee observed that Article 6 does not require that full range of public participation requirements set out in paragraphs 2 to 10 of the article be applied for each and every decision whether to permit an activity covered by paragraph 1.[28] A decision must first of all be environment-related (having implications for the environment), although this is not spelled out in Article 6. In making this important interpretation, the Committee relied on the title of the Convention which uses the words "in environmental matters."[29] At the same time, it will not be sufficient to apply public partici-pation procedure only to one permitting decision (stage) unless the decision embraces all significant environmental implications of the activity in ques-tion. Therefore, critical importance rests on examination as to what extent a decision indeed "permits" the activity.[30] The Committee proposed to use a "significance test"[31] on a case-by-case basis: a permitting decision (range of decisions) shall embrace all the basic parameters and main environmental implications of the proposed activity. If there are other environment-related permitting procedures (decisions), to which a fully-fledged public participa-tion process, capable of changing basic parameters or affecting environmental aspects of the activity, is not applied, then such a system does not correspond to standards set by Article 6 of the Convention.

A core criterion for public participation in decisions on specific activities is that it is provided at an early stage "when all options are open and effective public participation can take place".[32] Bearing this in mind a party can decide which range of options is to be discussed at each stage of the decision-making.

26 ECE/MP.PP/C.1/2006/2/Add.1, para. 28; ECE/MP.PP/C.1/2007/4/Add.1, para. 65.
27 ECE/MP.PP/C.1/2006/4/Add.2, para. 29.
28 ECE/MP.PP/2008/5/Add.10, para. 41.
29 Ibid.
30 Ibid. para. 42.
31 Ibid. para. 43.
32 Article 6, paragraph 4 of the Aarhus Convention on Access to Information, Public Participation in Decision-making and Access to Justice in Environmental Matters, 2161 UNTS 447 (1999).

If a decision to permit was taken without public involvement, providing for public participation in other subsequent decision-making cannot be considered as meeting the requirements of the Convention.[33]

31.2.2.2.3 TRANSFER OF OBLIGATIONS AND RELIANCE ON DEVELOPER IN ENSURING PUBLIC PARTICIPATION

In some countries, for example of Eastern Europe, Caucasus and Central Asia, public participation is often run by developers (proponents of specific activities). While putting some of the obligations in relation to providing access to information is considered legitimate, as discussed above, transfer of obligations to ensure public participation is subject to several limitations.

Some obligations under Article 6 implicitly require that certain functions are performed only by public authority (e.g. that comments should be submitted to relevant public authority).[34] Reliance solely on the developer for providing for public participation is not in line with the Aarhus Convention.[35] However, the Committee notes that this does not mean that the responsibility of performing some or even all of the above functions related to public participation should always be placed on an authority competent to issue a permitting decision.[36] Yet, neither the developers, nor the consultants hired by them, can ensure the impartiality necessary to guarantee proper conduct of public participation.[37] It is not possible for the public authority to transfer the obligation to take public comments into account to developer only.[38] Instead, the public authority will retain an obligation to ensure that these comments are taken into account during the decision-making process

31.2.2.2.4 PUBLIC PARTICIPATION IN ENVIRONMENTAL IMPACT ASSESSMENT (EIA)

The Convention does not require environmental impact assessment as such. It does require applying relevant provisions of the Convention if public participation is required by national EIA legislation (paragraph 20 of Annex I). On several occasions the Committee acknowledged the importance of environmental assessment – both in form of EIA and strategic environmental assessment (SEA) – for the purpose of improving the quality and effectiveness of public participation.[39] However, it is unclear why the Committee reached a conclusion that "under the Convention, public participation is a mandatory part of the EIA."[40]

33 ECE/MP.PP/2011/11/Add.1, para. 76.
34 ECE/MP.PP/2011/11/Add.2, para. 77.
35 ECE/MP.PP/2008/5/Add.6, para. 78.
36 ECE/MP.PP/2011/11/Add.2, para. 78.
37 Ibid. at para. 80.
38 Ibid. at para. 96.
39 ECE/MP.PP/C.1/2009/8/Add.1, para. 83.
40 ECE/MP.PP/C.1/2009/8/Add.1, para. 82.

31.2.2.2.5 PARTICIPATION BY FOREIGN PUBLIC

The Convention prohibits discrimination on citizenship, nationality or place of registration (in case of legal persons). Based on this provision, the Committee considered that foreign or international non-governmental organizations which expressed their interest in particular decision-making shall be considered as concerned members of the public,[41] therefore granting them all rights related to access to information, public participation and access to justice in relation to a permitting decision on specific activities falling under Article 6. Similarly, the Committee found that exclusion of foreign citizens and persons without citizenship from the possibility to found and participate in an NGO might constitute disadvantageous discrimination against them.[42] At the same time, when it comes to obligations that stem from such interpretation, the Committee reasonably notes that there are no provisions or guidance in or under Article 6, paragraph 2, on how to involve the public in another country in relevant decision-making, and that such guidance seems to be needed, in particular, in cases where there is no requirement to conduct a transboundary EIA; the matter is therefore outside the scope of the Espoo Convention.[43]

31.2.2.2.6 "RIGHT TO VETO" AND TAKING ACCOUNT OF PUBLIC PARTICIPATION

Effective public participation depends on how outcomes are taken into account. It is often wrongfully perceived that the concept requires "consent" from the public. The Committee noted on several occasions that the requirement to take into account does not amount, under the Convention, to the right of the public to veto the decision.[44] Nor does it mean an obligation to accept all comments, reservations or opinions submitted.[45] Yet, a system where comments of the public are routinely disregarded or not accepted on their merits, without any explanation, would not be in line with the Convention.[46]

31.2.2.2.7 LAND PLANNING DECISIONS

In several cases the Committee acknowledged that decisions on land use planning[47] and designation of lands for specific activities[48] fall under requirements of Article 7 as plans.

41 ECE/MP.PP/C.1/2005/2/Add.3, para. 26.
42 ECE/MP.PP/C.1/2005/2/Add.5, para. 16.
43 See *supra* note 8 at para. 28.
44 See *supra* note 39 at para. 98.
45 Ibid. at para. 99.
46 Ibid. at para. 101.
47 ECE/MP.PP/C.1/2007/4/Add.1, para. 72.
48 ECE/MP.PP/C.1/2006/2/Add.1, para. 25.

31.2.3 Access to justice

31.2.3.1 Relevant provisions

Paragraph 5.3 of the New Delhi Declaration reads:

> The empowerment of peoples in the context of sustainable development requires access to effective judicial or administrative procedures in the State where the measure has been taken to challenge such measure and to claim compensation. States should ensure that where transboundary harm has been, or is likely to be, caused, individuals and peoples affected have non-discriminatory access to the same judicial and administrative procedures as would individuals and peoples of the State from which the harm is caused if such harm occurred in that State.

The Aarhus Convention key relevant article is Article 9 "Access to justice." This article sets key obligations in three major areas:

(i) access to justice to challenge violations of access to information requirements (Art. 9.1);

(ii) access to justice to challenge procedural or substantive legality of a decision, act or omission subject to public participation procedure (Art. 9.2);

(iii) access to justice to challenge acts or omissions by private persons or public authorities which contravene provisions of its national law relating to environment (Art. 9.3).

In addition, the Convention sets certain requirements for access-to-justice procedures. They must be fair, equitable, timely and not prohibitively expensive. They must also provide adequate and effective remedies and be carried out by independent and impartial bodies. The Convention further requires information on access to justice procedures to be disseminated and encourages the development of assistance mechanisms to remove or reduce financial and other barriers.[49]

31.2.3.2 The Compliance Committee case law

The Compliance Committee dealt with access to justice in 38 out of 58 cases (66 per cent).[50] Therefore, it is the most sensitive and, possibly, least implemented pillar of the Convention. While the Convention deals in detail with relevant obligations on access to justice, it is probably the weakest pillar of the Convention

---

49 The Aarhus Convention, Implementation Guide (New York: United Nations, 2000) at 124.
50 See *supra* note 3 at 206–8.

today. The perception of the Convention as an "environmental" treaty worsens the situation since its implementation is usually coordinated by environmental authorities which have little intersection with the court system, or court procedure and regulations.

31.2.3.2.1 SOME GENERAL OBSERVATIONS

In some cases the Committee made observations or interpretations in relation to Article 9 in general or relating to several provisions of it. It made it clear that access means a possibility to access the court with your case. Access to justice does not mean you must be satisfied with a court decision. Having an adverse court decision does not in itself necessarily translate into a denial of access to justice.[51] A decision of the court must be enforced, otherwise it violates access to justice requirements provided by the Convention, since Article 9 implies that a court decision is binding and must be complied with.[52]

31.2.3.2.2 PRESUMPTION OF ACCESS

On some occasions the Committee dealt with restriction imposed on members of the public or the concerned members of the public to access review procedures. There is a general trend in the Committee's case law to lean towards "presumption of access" (as opposed to presumption of no access). For example, while recognizing that parties may determine what constitutes a sufficient interest under paragraph 2 Article 9, it emphasized the requirement to do so with the objective of giving the concerned members of the public wide access to justice.[53] Similarly, when accessing criteria for standing for non-governmental organizations under paragraph 3 of Article 9 it decided that the provision shall be read in conjunction with Articles 1–3 and in light of the preamble[54] of the Convention[55]. In the opinion of the Committee the Parties are not obliged to establish a system of popular action (*actio popularis*) in their national law, but they also may not introduce or maintain such strict criteria that they effectively bar all or almost all environmental organizations from challenging acts or omissions that contravene national law relating to the environment.[56] Access to such procedures should thus be the presumption, not the exception[57]. Based on these interpretations, the Committee

---

51 ECE/MP.PP/C.1/2005/2/Add.2, para.27.
52 The Committee refers to paragraph 1 of Article 9, but the interpretation shall be equally applicable to the Article as such, ECE/MP.PP/C.1/2009/6/Add.3, para. 35.
53 ECE/MP.PP/C.1/2006/4/Add.2, para.33.
54 Relevant sentence of the preamble reads: "effective judicial mechanisms should be accessible to the public, including organizations, so that its legitimate interests are protected and the law is enforced".
55 See *supra* note 53 at para. 34.
56 Ibid. at para. 35.
57 Ibid.

considered that application of "Plaumann test" to environmental and health issues prevents all members of the public from being able to challenge decisions or regulations in such cases before the European Court of Justice.[58]

Access to justice must be provided when it is effectively possible to challenge the decision permitting the activity in question[59]. Reliance on judicial discretion may result in inadequate implementation of the access to justice provisions[60] and may, therefore, require establishing timing requirements by a legislature. While the Committee did not support the argument that access to justice after construction starts is meaningless, it considered that lack of access to justice to challenge a permitting decision is not in compliance with the Convention.[61]

Requirement of fairness of the access to justice procedures was repeatedly addressed by the Committee. It found that "fairness" (under Article 9.4) "refers to what is fair to the claimant, not the defendant, a public body".[62] It went even further by introducing the idea that public interest shall be accounted for when awarding costs by the courts in cases where the public is pursing environmental concerns that involve public interest.[63] Failure to notify about a court hearing or communicate a court decision violates the requirement of a "fair" procedure.[64]

Wide discretion from legislature to courts to ensure that costs are not prohibitively expensive may lead to considerable uncertainty regarding costs to be faced where claimants are legitimately pursuing environmental concerns that involve the public interest,[65] as in England and Wales. This violates the requirement to ensure that procedures are not prohibitively expensive.[66]

31.3 Equity and human rights

The principles of equity and related environmental human rights, as reflected in the New Delhi Declaration, can be found in the preamble of the Aarhus Convention, which starts by recalling principle 1 of the Stockholm Declaration. The preamble of the Convention recognizes that adequate protection of the environment is essential to human well-being and the enjoyment of basic human rights, including the right to life itself. It also recognizes that every person has

---

58 ECE/MP.PP/C.1/2011/4/Add.1, para. 86.
59 ECE/MP.PP/C.1/2009/8/Add.1, para. 112.
60 ECE/MP.PP/C.1/2010/6/Add.3, para. 139.
61 ECE/MP.PP/2008/5/Add.10, para. 56.
62 ECE/MP.PP/C.1/2010/6/Add.2, para. 45.
63 Ibid. at para. 46.
64 ECE/MP.PP/C.1/2006/4/Add.1, para. 29.
65 See *supra* note 53 at para. 135.
66 Ibid.

the right to live in an environment adequate to his or her health and well-being, and the duty, both individually and in association with others, to protect and improve the environment for the benefit of present and future generations.

In the context of equity and human rights, Article 1 of the Convention ("Objective") is of outmost importance. Notably, the seventh and related preambular paragraph uses the term "benefit" underlined in the New Delhi Declaration.

Article 1 reads:

> In order to contribute to the protection of the right of every person of present and future generations to live in an environment adequate to his or her health and well-being, each Party shall guarantee the rights of access to information, public participation in decision-making, and access to justice in environmental matters in accordance with the provisions of this Convention.

It is the clearest statement in international law to date of a fundamental right to a healthy environment.[67] Reference to "future generations" clearly reflects inter-generational equity approach.

The Committee dealt directly only once with Article 1 of the Convention (case regarding Ukraine). In assessing the claim of the communicant that by violating various procedural requirements Ukraine violated relevant rights of the people, the Committee noted that "a non-compliance with the operative provisions of the Convention is not in conformity with the objective of the Convention as defined in article 1".[68] However, there is nothing in the text of the Aarhus Convention defining part of it as "operative provisions.[69] It seems that the Committee made such interpretation in light of the title of the article: "Objective".

This approach may be subject to legitimate criticism. The main question should be whether Article 1 creates a binding legal obligation and what is the legal substance (meaning) of the obligation. It is rather clear that all provisions of the Convention create a binding legal obligation. On another occasion the Committee noted that the preamble, while being an important aid to interpreting the Convention, does not in itself create binding legal obligations.[70] In relation to the text of the Article of the Convention, such a conclusion would need significant argument.

67 See *supra* note 1 at 29.
68 ACCC/S/2004/1; ECE/MP.PP/C.1/2005/2/Add.3, para. 36.
69 See *supra* note 3 at 11.
70 ECE/MP.PP/C.1/2011/2/Add.10, para. 68.

31.4 Conclusion

There is significant practice developed by the Compliance Committee of the Aarhus Convention in relation to all three elements of Principle 10 of the Rio Declaration and Principle 5 of the New Delhi Declaration.

The cases reveals various issues of practical implementation of access to information, public participation and access to justice principles. Therefore it provides important guidance for governments, academia, practitioners, and civil society on how to shape future instruments and enforce current ones.

Numerous interpretations by the Compliance Committee give an important stimulus for further thinking and research which, hopefully, will lead to wider recognition and better enforcement of the right of every person of present and future generations to a healthy environment.

32 Sustainable development priorities in World Bank Inspection Panel decisions

Sabine Schlemmer-Schulte *

32.1 Introduction

In September 1993, the World Bank[1] established the Inspection Panel by decision of its Executive Directors.[2] The Inspection Panel[3] was created to provide the Bank's Board of Executive Directors with independent judgment to help resolve major differences related to Bank-financed projects that adversely affect rights and interests of third party non-state actors because the Bank failed to follow its operational policies and procedures in the design, appraisal, or implementation of its operations. The three-member Inspection Panel hears complaints brought to it by an affected party (other than a single individual) in the territory of a borrower of an International Bank for Reconstruction and Development (IBRD) loan or an International Development Association (IDA) credit alleging that its rights or interests have been materially and adversely affected by an action or omission of the Bank in the application of its operational policies and procedures.

Since its inception, the Inspection Panel, which can be best qualified as an accountability mechanism with increasingly *de facto* quasi-judicial character,[4] has

---

* The author wishes to thank Carrie Stafford, J.D., Esq. for her excellent research assistance.

1 Unless the context indicates otherwise, the terms "World Bank" or "Bank" refer to both the International Bank for Reconstruction and Development (IBRD) and the International Development Association (IDA).

2 See Resolution No. 93-10 IBRD, Resolution No. 93-6 IDA, The World Bank Inspection Panel, 22 dated September 1993 (hereinafter Resolution Establishing the Panel) available at http://site resources.worldbank.org/EXTINSPECTIONPANEL/Resources/ResolutionMarch2005.pdf. For a comprehensive record of the history of the creation of Inspection Panel, see Ibrahim F.I. Shihata, *The World Bank Inspection Panel*, 1st edn (World Bank, 1994); *The World Bank Inspection Panel: In Practice*, 2nd edn (Geneva: World Bank: 2000). The Bank reviewed its experience with the Panel twice. In connection with the two reviews, the Bank's Executive Directors clarified and amended the Panel's functions. For the clarifications under the first review which took place in 1996, see http://siteresources.worldbank.org/EXTINSPECTIONPANEL/Resources/1996ReviewResolution.pdf. For the clarifications resulting from the second review completed in 1999, see http://siteresources. worldbank.org/EXTINSPECTIONPANEL/Resources/1999ClarificationoftheBoard.pdf. See also Sabine Schlemmer-Schulte, "Introductory Note to the Conclusions of the Second Review of the World Bank Inspection Panel", 39 *International Legal Materials* 243–51 (2000).

3 For information on the Inspection Panel, see ibid.

4 In this respect, it should be emphasized that the Panel does not offer remedies in the strict sense. Contrary to courts that enforce liability of wrongdoers under domestic law concepts, and

received over 70 requests for inspection, a few of which fell clearly outside its mandate and were therefore not registered.[5] The registered requests concern mainly infrastructure, energy, environmental, land reform projects, and a couple of adjustment or development policy operations. In most requests, non-compliance with the Bank's so-called safeguard policies and procedures covering primarily environmental issues and social interests of affected people was alleged by the requesters. In roughly half of the requests registered, the Panel undertook investigations.

Recently, the World Bank Inspection Panel celebrated its 15th anniversary.[6] To date, with more than four times as many requests for investigations as its age received, and nearly three times as many investigations as its age undertaken, the Panel's case record is remarkable and improved the Bank's operational performance considerably. Encouraged by the Bank's example, other International Financial Institutions (IFIs) copied the World Bank Inspection Panel more or less closely and introduced their own inspection mechanisms.[7] This proliferation of inspection functions as well as their successful work has strengthened the "rule of law" inside International Organizations (IOs) which, by virtue of their traditional legal framework, largely escape comprehensive checks and balances as known by states or private corporations under domestic and international law.

One of the major aspects of the Panel's promotion of the "rule of law" inside IOs lies in the Panel's impact on World Bank operational standards. These standards are entirely a product of the Bank's internal decision-making process. The latter consists of Management initiating the adoption of operational standards and the Board of Executive Directors approving the proposed standards.[8]

judicial bodies that declare subjects of international law responsible for violations of international law, the Panel's function is limited to a finding for wrongdoings by the Bank without its reports representing decisions binding on the Bank. For a discussion of the concepts of accountability, liability, and responsibility, see Sabine Schlemmer-Schulte, "The World Bank, Its Operations, and Its Inspection Panel" *Recht der Internationalen Wirtschaft* (RIW), 175–81 (1999).

5 For a chronology of requests, see a summary of all requests received by the Panel available http://web.worldbank.org/WBSITE/EXTERNAL/EXTINSPECTIONPANEL/0,,contentMDK:2024 0657~menuPK:495328~pagePK:64129751~piPK:64128378~theSitePK:380794,00.html.

6 See Accountability at the World Bank: The Inspection Panel at 15 Years available at http://siteresources.worldbank.org/EXTINSPECTIONPANEL/Resources/380793-1254158345788/InspectionPanel2009.pdf. For records of earlier anniversaries, see Accountability at the World Bank: The Inspection Panel – 10 Years On available at http://siteresources.worldbank.org/EXTINSPECTIONPANEL/Resources/TenYear8_07.pdf , and *The World Bank Inspection Panel: The First Four Years (1994–1998)*. Alvaro Umaña ed. (The World Bank: 1998).

7 By now, seven IFIs including the Asian Development Bank (ADB), the African Development Bank (AfDB), the European Bank for Reconstruction and Development (EBRD), the Inter-American Development Bank (IDB), the International Finance Corporation (IFC), the International Monetary Fund (IMF), and the Multilateral Investment Guarantee Agency (MIGA) have established, or are in the process of establishing, an inspection function.

8 See Article V, Section 4(b) and Article V, Section 5(b) IBRD Articles of Agreement available at http://web.worldbank.org/WBSITE/EXTERNAL/EXTABOUTUS/ORGANIZATION/BODEXT/0,,contentMDK:20049557~menuPK:64020025~pagePK:64020054~piPK:6402040 8~theSitePK:278036~isCURL:Y,00.html. See also Article VI, Section 4(a) and Article VI, Section 4(b) IDA Articles of Agreement available at http://web.worldbank.org/WBSITE/EXTERNAL/EXTABOUTUS/IDA/0,,contentMDK:20052323~menuPK:115747~pagePK:51236175~piPK: 437394~theSitePK:73154,00.html.

The standards are designed to assist the Bank in realizing its ultimate purpose of promoting economic and social development in its borrowing members.[9]

Over time, the set of operational policies[10] has grown into an impressive body of development finance law which, to a large degree, mirrors the Sustainable Development Principles as adopted by the International Law Association (ILA) at the 70th Conference of the ILA in New Delhi, India in April 2002 (ILA New Delhi Declaration of Principles of International Law Relating to Sustainable Development – or the New Delhi Principles).[11] While the Bank insists from a legal perspective that it is only bound by its founding charter – and for interpretation purposes the 1969 Vienna Convention on the Law of Treaties – and agreements it enters into with borrowing members as well as the lending policies, i.e. standards it designs itself for its operations but is not bound by any other general international law (treaty, custom, or general principles of international law, even *jus cogens*),[12] let alone emerging principles of international law such as the New Delhi Principles, the Bank's own standard setting actions are amazingly in sync with the trends towards more sustainability for economic and social development identifiable by actions in other spheres of the global community.

The Bank's Inspection Panel used its competencies to sharpen the Bank's operational policies' teeth along the lines of the spirit of the New Delhi Principles. While the Panel, like the Bank's charter organs, is only bound by the resolution that establishes it – as clarified and/or amended by the two reviews – and the overarching rules of the Bank's charter, the Panel deliberately took a progressive approach in interpreting the Bank's operational standards broadly and, on occasion, borrowing from general international law instruments that the

---

9 See Article I IBRD Articles of Agreement and Article I IDA Articles of Agreement.

10 For details about the genesis, nature, and the Panel's impact on the Bank's operational policies, see *infra* under 32.2.3.

11 See ILA Resolution 3/2002, published as Annex in UN Doc. A/57/329 available at http://daccess-dds-ny.un.org/doc/UNDOC/GEN/N02/534/20/PDF/N0253420.pdf?OpenElement.

12 While many scholars have long criticized and deplored the fact that the Bank, like other IOs, does not accept the notion to be bound by general international law, the Bank's position is absolutely justifiable under international law as *de lege lata*. For details of the Bank's position, see Ibrahim F.I. Shihata, *The World Bank in a Changing World*, Vol. II (The Hague: Martinus Nijhoff, 1995) 563–64. For scholarly views that take a view different from the Bank, see Henry G. Schermers and Niels Blokker, *International Institutional Law*, 3rd edn (Leiden: Martinus Nijhoff, 2001) at 982–84 (including references to further scholarly writings critical of the IOs stance). For a broader discussion of an IO's accountability and liability, see Karel Wellens, *Remedies against International Organizations* (Cambridge: CUP, 2002). For a scholarly view that agrees with the Bank from a legal perspective but urges the Bank to voluntarily subject itself to more accountability for policy reasons, see Karen Hudes and Sabine Schlemmer-Schulte, "Accountability in Bretton Woods" 15 *ILSA J. Int'l & Comp. L.* 501–31 (2009). The lack of IO accountability led to two noteworthy efforts to change the sad state of international law. See the Recommended Rules and Practices formulated by the ILA Committee on Accountability of International Organizations reproduced in the Committee's Final Report at the 2004 Conference in Berlin, Germany, available at http://www.ila-hq.org/download.cfm/docid/6b708c25-4d6d-42e2-8385dada752815e8. See also the ILC (International Law Commission) Draft Articles on Responsibility of International Organizations, UN Doc. A/CN.4/L. 778 (2011), available at http://untreaty.un.org/ilc/sessions/63/A%20 CN4%20L778%20E advance.pdf.

Bank typically need not follow for the benefit of the people and communities in the Bank's client countries, i.e. developing countries in which people live on less than \$2/day.[13]

32.2 The development finance context in which the Inspection Panel operates

32.2.1 The evolution of the World Bank: from brick-and-mortar financier to global policy-maker

As a response to the great depression of the interwar period, the World Bank was established after WWII to finance reconstruction in Europe and promote productive economic development in Bank members through the mobilization of private capital to enable members' industries to trade, and the IMF was set up to administer a new multilateral monetary system facilitating liberal trade among nations.[14] After a brief period of lending to members in Europe financing a variety of essential imports including the restocking of inventories, imports of foodstuffs, raw material, and fuel, the Bank began to focus on its original mission of financing specific productive projects of reconstruction and economic development. Throughout the 1950s and 1960s, the Bank financed projects to improve the infrastructure, industry, and agriculture in borrowing members. From the end of the 1960s and throughout the 1970s, the Bank added the social sectors (health, nutrition, population, and education) as a second focus to its development finance. In the 1980s, the Bank expanded its project range further by adding environmental and gender perspectives to its development finance.

13 The Bank caters to developing countries which include middle-income countries with a gross national income (GNI) per capita of between \$10,000 and \$1,000 per year, and low-income countries with a GNI per capita below \$1,000 per year. These countries are *de facto* dependant on Bank and IMF loans because they cannot attract private capital (foreign investment etc.) unless a Bank or IMF financed structural adjustment program is in place. Structural adjustment programs concentrate on the following measures: (i) liberalization of trade, financial, and capital markets, (ii) privatization of public sectors, (iii) deregulation for private sector activities, and (iv) austerity in terms of government spending for social sector purposes (i.e. spending cuts with respect to education, housing, healthcare. Since the 1990s, these programs are typically accompanied by governance and institutional reform measures, e.g. administrative, judicial, and legal reforms. The macroeconomic and governance reforms to be undertaken by Bank and IMF aid recipients, also called "Washington Consensus" measures because required by DC based aid institutions have been criticized by economists and lawyers because they have net led to sustainable growth. For an economist's perspective, see Joseph E. Stiglitz, *Globalization and Its Discontents* (London: Penguin Books, 2002). For a legal perspective, see Sabine Schlemmer-Schulte, "Sovereign Debt: The Argentine Bonds Case" in Andreas Fischer-Lescano, Hans-Peter Gasser, Thilo Marauhn and Natalino Ronzitti, eds., *Frieden in Freiheit – Peace in Liberty – Paix en Liberté: Festschrift Michael Bothe* (Zurich: Nomos, 2008) at 971, 1011–19.

14 For an overview of the World Bank and the IMF, see Sabine Schlemmer-Schulte, "International Bank for Reconstruction and Development" in Rüdiger Wolfrum, ed., *Max Planck Encyclopedia of Public International Law* (Oxford: OUP, 2012).

During the 1970s, the Bank began recognizing that economic development, or growth, (in terms of gross domestic product (GDP) per capita), could not necessarily be had in the medium- and long-term solely by financing brick-and-mortar projects in borrowing members, or investing in the social sectors. Therefore, the Bank moved gradually and also fully into an area that became known as structural adjustment lending, in 2004 renamed development policy lending. Since the 1980s, the Bank has hence engaged in non-project lending, and supported macroeconomic structural and sectorial adjustment programs in its borrowing members. Under these structural and sectorial adjustment programs, Bank members have to take measures to liberalize trade, liberalize the financial and capital markets, privatize the public sector, and deregulate. Since the 1990s, adjustment programs have also been used by the Bank to promote good governance and the rule of law. For Bank purposes, good governance or institutional programs are geared towards organizing an efficient management by the respective Bank member of its economic and social resources. Numerous legal reform, judicial reform, and administrative reform programs have been financed by the Bank in this vein. Overall, adjustment program financing, or development policy program financing, tends to make up for about half of the Bank's financial assistance. With adjustment lending/development policy lending being the second major focus of the Bank's lending activities, it qualifies as *de facto* policy-maker in developing countries.

32.2.2 *The Panel: a compliance mechanism*

As an independent, investigatory body, the Panel is, despite the quasi-judicial format of its process, in the first place an accountability mechanism but not a court of law.[15] The Panel accords people adversely affected by the Bank's violation of its own development assistance standards new, formal rights: people have standing before the Panel to lodge complaints. As conceived under the Resolution establishing it, the Panel does not offer a direct remedy.[16] Standing in the long

---

15 For an analysis of the nature of the Inspection Panel, see Sabine Schlemmer-Schulte, "The World Bank, Its Operations, and Its Inspection Panel," 3 *Recht der Internationalen Wirtschaft* 175 (1999); S. Schlemmer-Schulte "The World Bank Inspection Panel as Model for Other IOs" in Niels M. Blokker and Henry G. Schermers, eds., *Proliferation of International Organizations – Legal Aspects* (The Hague, Kluwer Publishing, 2001), at 483 *et seq.;* and, comprehensively, Ibrahim F.I. Shihata, *The World Bank Inspection Panel: In Practice*, 2nd edn (Geneva: World Bank, 2000).

16 It may however be noted that the Panel does not attribute new, material rights to people. Accountability by the Bank vis-à-vis people who are adversely affected by Bank failures related to its financing of development projects thus falls in principle still short of the protection accorded under remedial concepts such as liability under domestic law and responsibility under international law. While accountability ensured by the Panel does not provide a remedy, i.e. does not include a right to remedial measures and will not result in a corresponding enforceable court judgment, Bank Management responses to Panel investigations correcting mistakes by the Bank made in the design, appraisal, and supervision of project implementation often amounted to *de facto* remedies for the benefit of project-affected people. Typically Bank responses led to changes in the borrowers' implementation of Bank-financed projects, thus providing indirectly for remedies to project-affected people.

tradition of international law that, in the absence of enforcement of international treaties or custom by states, introduced compliance mechanisms instead,[17] the Panel's investigation of the performance of the Bank is a novelty in the history of international organizations. As a compliance mechanism, the Panel, although not a remedial mechanism, is by virtue of the prominent place it occupies in the context of Bank operations in a position to contribute to the resolution of problems in the design and implementation of Bank-financed development projects for the benefit of people adversely affected by these projects. Typically, Bank Management and the Bank's Board have decided to take corrective measures and redesign and/or make changes in the implementation of a project when a complaint is successfully filed with the Panel, i.e. when the Panel investigation found Bank failures to "follow [the Bank's] own policies and procedures . . . with respect to the design, appraisal and/or implementation of a project financed by the Bank."[18]

17 Historically, ensuring performance on the international plane started with the control of compliance by States with international humanitarian agreements some 100 years ago. See The Hague Convention for the Pacific Settlement of International Disputes of 29 July 1899 and The Hague Convention for the Pacific Settlement of Disputes of 18 October 1907 establishing commissions of inquiry to investigate wartime incidents between belligerent or neutral states. After World War II, compliance by states with human rights, trade, and environmental obligations became one of the main pieces of efforts in the international community to make international law effective. For a discussion of compliance with international human rights law, see generally Henry J. Steiner and Philip Alston, *International Human Rights in Context: Law, Politics, Morals*, 2nd edn (Oxford: OUP, 2000), and Rudolf Bernhardt and John Anthony Jolowicz, eds., *International Enforcement of Human Rights* (Netherlands, Springer, 1987); on compliance and enforcement of European human rights law, see generally Jochen Abr. Frowein and Wolfgang Peukert, 2nd revised edn, *Europäische Menschenrechtskonvention* (Berlin: EMRK-Kommentar, 1996); on compliance and enforcement of human rights in the Inter-American context, see Thomas Buergenthal, "The Inter-American Court of Human Rights" 76 AJIL 231 (1982), and J.S. Davidson, The Inter-American Court of Human Rights (London: Dartmouth Publishing, 1992); on compliance and enforcement of trade law, see John Jackson, *The World Trade Organization: Constitution and Jurisprudence* (London: Royal Institute of International Affairs, 1998), Chapter 4 on dispute settlement, and Ernst-Ulrich Petersmann, *The GATT/WTO Dispute Settlement System: International Law, International Organizations and Dispute Settlement* (London: Kluwer Law International, 1996); on compliance and enforcement of environmental law, see Harold K. Jacobson and Edith Brown Weiss, "Strengthening Compliance with International Environmental Accords: Preliminary Observations from a Collaborative Project" in 2 *Global Governance* 1 (1995), and Edith Brown Weiss, "National Compliance with International Environmental Agreements" in Proceedings of the 91st Annual Meeting of the ASIL (1997) 56–9.

18 See Resolution Establishing the Inspection Panel, *supra* note 2 at para. 12. It may be noted that the Panel's function is to check on the Bank's compliance with its own policies. It is not the Panel's job to check on the borrower or any private sub-contractor of the borrower. However, since the Bank has to supervise the borrower's implementation of the project, inevitably failures of the borrower and its agents in conjunction with project implementation may be discovered when looking at the Bank's performance in terms of supervision as a logical prerequisite for a finding of supervision failures by the Bank. Potential Panel activity has heightened staff awareness while supervising the borrower and also led to an increasing willingness of Bank staff to remind the borrower of correcting mistakes in project implementation. In other words, the fear of Panel activity has in practice had the healthy effect that cures of implementation mistakes were prescribed even though these could not have been subject of the conclusions of Panel reports.

In a revolutionary departure from the typical paradigm of Bank responses to Panel findings, the Bank recently went beyond redesigning a project or instructing the borrower to implement the project in line with Bank policies. In connection with Bank failures related to the Albania Coastal Zone Project (Inspection Panel Request of 30 June 2007) detected by the Panel, the Bank took it upon itself to directly address the harm incurred by project-affected people. Since the Bank had even failed to include a covenant pertaining to compensation and assistance for involuntarily resettled people (as required under the Bank's policy on involuntary resettlement) into the loan agreements with the borrower, the Bank decided to commit its own resources to address the harm. The Bank's commitment in this case included financial assistance for the costs of competent legal assistance in pursuing judicial recourse for compensation. While the lack of a direct remedial nature of the Panel process remains a bone of contention for people adversely affected by Bank-financed projects because, aside from the Panel process, other remedies are not available for them,[19] the Bank's move in the Albania Coastal Zone Project indicates the possibility that it may in the future not only continue remedying project situations directly but be willing to amend the Resolution Establishing the Panel and add a remedial feature to the Panel process itself.

While the Panel's objective to measure Bank compliance with applicable standards is to some extent similar to checking compliance in other areas of international

19 These people cannot bring actions against the Bank in the domestic courts of a borrowing member country based on the concept of liability under the member country's law. Such actions could not be heard by local courts because the Bank benefits in connection with its project lending operations from immunity. In addition, such actions would fail on the merits. No contracts claim can be established as the affected people do not have any contractual relationship with the Bank. No basis for an action in tort exists either since the Bank is only supervising the project's implementation but not involved in any on-site execution of the project. The Bank thus cannot have caused the harm people suffered as required for a tort law claim. People also cannot bring actions against the Bank in an international court under the concept of international responsibility. There is no international judicial forum before which individuals could bring claims against the Bank for violation of international legal standards even if a country would espouse such a claim against the Bank. Furthermore, the merits of such claims for violation of international legal standards could hardly be established. A finding of a violation of Bank policies in the design, appraisal, or implementation of a Bank-financed project in the Panel process does in principle not reflect a violation of general international legal standards. It would finally be difficult to show causality between Bank actions and the harm potentially suffered by individuals because the borrowing country, and not the Bank, is responsible for execution of the project. For a more detailed analysis of possible actions of project beneficiaries against the World Bank and a distinction in this context between the concepts of accountability, liability, and international responsibility, see S. Schlemmer-Schulte, "The World Bank Inspection Panel as Model for Other IOs" in Niels M. Blokker and Henry G. Schermers, eds., *Proliferation of International Organizations: Legal Aspects* (The Hague: Kluwer Publishing, 2001) at 483 *et seq.*; for a detailed discussion of the inapplicability of the US concept of lender's liability to the World Bank, see Ibrahim F.I. Shihata, *The World Bank Inspection Panel: In Practice*, 2nd edn (World Bank: 2000), Chapter 5, at 254 *et seq.*; and on the Bank's immunity, ibid. at Chapter 5, at 241–52. For a discussion of the limitations of the jurisdiction of the International Court of Justice (ICJ) in connection with IOs, see Jerzy Sztucki, "International Organizations as Parties to Contentious Proceedings before the International Court of Justice" in A.S. Müller et al., eds., *The International Court of Justice: Its Future Role After Fifty Years* (The Hague: Martinus Nijhoff Publishers, 1997) at 141.

law (e.g. human rights and environmental law), it differs from the monitoring of compliance in these other areas in a major respect. The Bank's compliance relates formally to internal policies and procedures, i.e. rules created by the Bank itself for its operational work of financing development, not to international standards created by states in the form of treaty law. While legally separate, there is, however, some cross-fertilization between the Bank's compliance with internal standards and international standards. The Bank's internal standards include primarily environmental, social, and other safeguard standards, e.g. requiring environmental assessments, protecting indigenous peoples, or safeguarding against resettlement. The substance of Bank standards is not necessarily identical with international standards, but the latter have often inspired the former. As a result, the Bank's insistence on compliance of the aid recipient with its policies indirectly promotes compliance with international standards of the respective fields, although aid is not strictly conditioned on compliance with the international treaty standards. The Panel's investigation of compliance with respective Bank standards thus reinforces the Bank's indirect role in the transformation of human rights into reality.[20] Occasionally, Bank policies refer directly to international treaty standards in the instance of which the influence of the latter on Bank policies becomes particularly evident.[21] Moreover, the Panel has, in a bold stance on Bank lending policies, argued that Bank policies imply certain international human rights standards agreed under treaties or custom by states.[22]

32.2.3 The Panel's effect on the Bank's operational standards: *authoritative interpretation* in dubio pro *sustainable development*

The first 10 years of Panel activities have primarily entailed clarifications of the Panel process either in conjunction with specific requests or in the context of the two, more comprehensive, reviews of the Panel.[23] These years may therefore, with some justification, be called the decade of institutional clarifications which were useful in fine-tuning and highlighting the Panel's current nature as well as provoking debates over further reforms of the Panel. What has gone more unnoticed in this decade of institutional clarifications, although it is as important an issue as the institutional questions related to the Panel, is the Panel's impact on Bank policies.

---

20 For a discussion of the interplay between international economic, social, environmental, and cultural human rights treaty standards and Bank policies in the Panel's context, see Sabine Schlemmer-Schulte, "The World Bank Inspection Panel: A Record of the First International Accountability Mechanism and Its Role for Human Rights" 6 *Washington College of Law of American University Human Rights Brief* 1, 67, 20 (1999).

21 See, e.g. Operational Policy 4.01 Environmental Assessment which in para. 3 states that the Bank takes, for the purposes of environmental assessment of the projects it finances, into account the "obligations of the country [it lends to] . . . under relevant international environmental treaties and agreements."

22 See discussion of protecting requesters' anonymity and their right to free speech in connection with the Chad/Cameroon Pipeline Project *infra* under III. 5.(c).

23 For a comprehensive discussion of the Panel's evolution, see Ibrahim F.I. Shihata, *The World Bank Inspection Panel: In Practice*, 2nd edn (Geneva: World Bank, 2000).

Under the Resolution establishing it, the Panel can only be seized based on requests related to failures by the Bank to follow its own operational policies and procedures with respect to the design, appraisal, or implementation of a Bank-supported project.[24] The Bank's operational policies and procedures are thus the applicable standards for Panel investigations. The Resolution Establishing the Inspection Panel defines what constitutes operational policies and procedures for Panel purposes. According to the Resolution, operational policies and procedures include the Bank's "Operational Policies [OPs], Bank Procedures [BPs], and Operational Directives [ODs], and similar documents issued before these series were started."[25] Guidelines, Best Practices, and similar documents or statements are, however, explicitly excluded from the category of policies and procedures for purposes of Panel investigations.

Major policies and procedures as well as their amendments are approved by the Board of Executive Directors. Upon Board approval, Bank Management lays out their details in OPs, BPs, or, formerly, in ODs.[26] These documents constitute instructions from Bank Management to staff in accordance with the Board approved policies that led to their issuance. Operational policies and procedures are contained in the Operational Manual.[27] Volume I of the Manual includes all policies and procedures regarding strategies and financial or business products, and Volume II of the Manual contains those policies and procedures that relate to project requirements.[28]

---

24 It may be noted that issues related to the Bank's policies procurement of goods and services laid out in its Procurement and Consultant Guidelines are explicitly outside the scope of the Panel's jurisdiction. See Resolution Establishing the Panel, *supra* note 2 at para. 14(b).

25 The Bank's body of operational policies and procedures has undergone three major reformulation and streamlining exercises. At the end of the 1980s after an internal reorganization, the old body of manual statements and policy notes was gradually transformed into ODs. In addition, new ODs on important subject-matters such as environmental and poverty impacts of Bank-financed projects were issued. In the early 1990s, a second initiative to streamline and simplify the Bank's policies and procedures was taken which resulted in a process called conversion. In the course of that process, ODs were reformulated as OPs and BPs. The third review related to a harmonization effort of the policies of development banks including the World Bank and the major regional development banks, i.e. the African Development Bank, Asian Development Bank, and the Inter-American Bank end of the 1990s and beginning 2000s. A much regretted result of the harmonization of policies of the major development banks was the conversion of the old World Bank OD on mandatory consultations with NGOs in connection with certain projects into a GP (Good Practice) on the topic which, as the document name already indicates, gives a good practice recommendation to consult with NGOs but makes consideration of consultations no longer compulsory.

26 See *Shihata, supra* note 23 at 41–46.

27 The Bank's Operational Manual including current versions of World Bank policies is accessible on the Bank's website. See generally www.worldbank.org, or, more specifically, http://web.world bank.org/WBSITE/EXTERNAL/PROJECTS/EXTPOLICIES/EXTOPMANUAL/0,,menuP K:64142516~pagePK:64141681~piPK:64141745~theSitePK:502184,00.html. Most of the earlier versions of Bank policies are reproduced in Annex II of Shihata, *The World Bank Inspection Panel: In Practice*, 2nd edn (World Bank: 2000), at 345 *et seq.*

28 Volume I covers the topical areas of country focus, sector/thematic strategies, financial products and instruments, and partnership arrangements (in particular co-financing and trust funds). The financial or business products of the Bank include specific and sector investment loans, financial

None of the categorizations regarding the business products or the policies in the Operational Manual has an impact on the work of the Panel. Anything Bank staff is required to follow under OPs, BPs, and ODs falls within the jurisdiction of the Panel, with the exception of procurement matters.

The Panel has had a considerable effect on the Bank's policies and the practice developing under these policies. The Panel's contribution in this respect took two forms: (i) suggesting its own interpretations of the policies and procedures to be complied with by Management in the concrete cases in which the Panel is seized; and (ii) suggesting policy changes in contribution to the broader policy discussion on improving development effectiveness as a result of the Panel's experience with investigations in concrete cases. The Panel's progressive analysis of Bank policies beyond the narrow literal application of these policies with a view of the policies' overall spirit as well as the Bank's overall objective has promoted the sustainable development aspect of Bank policies over the economic growth oriented aspect and has nurtured the general policy debate along the same lines.[29]

32.3 Sustainable development principles in World Bank Inspection Panel decisions

32.3.1 *The duty of states to ensure sustainable use of natural esources*

The Nepal Arun III Proposed Hydroelectric Project was the first Bank-financed project in connection with which the Panel received a request for an investigation in 1994. A group of Nepalese citizens claimed that the Bank had violated a number of policies in connection with the planned infrastructure project whose objective was to address the lack of electricity in Nepal where, at the time, only 9 per cent of the population had access to power. In particular, the requesters argued that the Bank had violated its policy on indigenous peoples. The latter Bank policy, like New Delhi Principle No. 1 that establishes a duty to ensure sustainable use of natural resources,

---

intermediary loans, emergency recovery loans, technical assistance loans, structural and sector adjustment loans, rehabilitation loans, hybrid loans (part investment, part adjustment), debt and debt service loans, learning and innovation loans, guarantees, technical assistance, grants, and country economic and sector work. Volume II includes safeguard policies (e.g. environmental, indigenous peoples, involuntary resettlement, forestry, and international waterways policies), economic project analysis, fiduciary aspects of Bank operations (e.g. procurement guidelines), financial aspects and management of operations (i.e. project supervision, monitoring and evaluation), and contractual aspects of the financial agreements. The table of content of the Operational Manual including links to specific Bank policies in Volume I and Volume II is available at http://web. worldbank.org/WBSITE/EXTERNAL/PROJECTS/EXTPOLICIES/EXTOPMANUAL/0,,m enuPK:64701637~pagePK:51628525~piPK:64857279~theSitePK:502184,00.html.

29 The Panel's active stance towards policies ultimately rests on a liberal interpretation of its own mandate, a prerogative that is only subject to the Board's final authority to interpret the Panel's mandate. The Panel's approach follows the established paradigm of international courts and tribunals and organs of international organizations that determine their own competence. For a general discussion of powers of IOs and organs within these organizations, see Schermers and Blokker, see *supra* note 23 at 139 *et seq.*

aims in connection with the obligation regarding sustainable use of natural resources to protect, among others, the rights of indigenous peoples. The question in this first request before the Panel was whether or not the Bank's policy on indigenous peoples would apply to the population living in the Arun valley in which the hydroelectric power plant was to be built. The Nepalese Federation of Nationalities described the valley as having 24 distinct ethnic groups but the Panel noted that "[w]e are not dealing . . . with a kind of isolated tribal group untouched by modernity that some would argue is foreseen in the [Bank's policy]."[30] Under the Bank's policy:

> [t]he terms "indigenous peoples," "indigenous ethnic minorities," "tribal groups," and "scheduled tribes" describe social groups with a social and cultural identity distinct from the dominant society that makes them vulnerable to being disadvantaged in the development process. . . . Indigenous peoples can be identified in particular geographical areas by the presence in varying degrees of . . . characteristics [including] . . . close attachment to ancestral territories and to the natural resources in these areas, self identification and identification by others as members of a distinct cultural group, an indigenous language, often different from the national language, presence of customary social and political institutions, and primarily subsistence oriented production.[31]

While some groups such as the Rai communities might have, on the basis of anthropological surveys, easily qualified as indigenous peoples given their difference in culture and life-style from mainstream Nepalese society and their difficulty dealing with changes resulting from the hydroelectric project, other ethnic groups would have easily adjusted to the changes coming with the project and therefore not easily met the Bank policy definition of indigenous peoples. The Panel opted for a broader construction of the definition of indigenous peoples which Bank Management accepted.

The China Western Poverty Reduction Project aimed at reducing absolute poverty in certain areas of China, assisting approximately 1.7 million people by providing a safe water supply, and improving social services (such as health and education), electricity connection, and quality of local roads. The project purported to benefit over 60,000 poor farmers on the hillsides of Eastern Qinghai Province who practised high altitude rain fed culture. The land they lived on was eroding because of high population pressure and could no longer sustain them. The project envisioned the voluntary resettlement of farmers from the eroded hillsides to a dry land area in a Tibetan and Mongol autonomous area some 450 km to the West. While the project would have alleviated pressures on farmers on the eroding hills to the East as well as farmers resettled to the West, as a result of the relocation

---

30 See the World Bank Inspection Panel's Investigation Report regarding the Nepal Arun III Hydroelectric Project (21 June 1995), para. 110.
31 See 1991 OD 4.20 Indigenous Peoples, paras. 3 and 5. See also OP 4.10 Indigenous Peoples which replaced the 1991 OD 4.20 in 2005.

of more than 60,000 poor farmers to the West, the Chinese population in the area of the Tibetan and Mongol autonomous area would have increased and made Tibetans and Mongolians an even more marginal minority there. The Panel found that, contrary to the requirements of the Bank's policy on indigenous peoples, several national minorities in the Tibetan and Mongolian area – the Hui, Mongol, Tibetan, Tu, and Salar – were lumped together in the project even though they were culturally different from each other with respect to their local patterns of social organization, religious beliefs, and resource use. Not treating them separately effectively denied these different ethnic groups the protection of their minority cultural traditions as required under Bank policy. Moreover, the cultural dilution as a result of resettlement of Chinese into the Tibetan and Mongolian area jeopardized the status of the Mongolian and Tibetan autonomous area. According to the Panel, that status, although not explicitly referred to in the Bank's policy on indigenous peoples, would be implicitly protected as part of indigenous peoples' societal values and organization.

The Uganda Bujagali Falls Power Projects contemplated to address the lack of access to electricity in Uganda of over 90 per cent of Uganda's population. The projects involved the installation of a 200-MegaWatt run-of-the-river power plant at the Bujagali Falls, a small reservoir, and a dam as well as the construction of approximately 100 km of transmission lines and associated substations. In 2001, a couple of local NGOs and individuals submitted a request for inspection. The request claimed that the Bank had overlooked the cultural significance of the Bujagali Falls, its value for ecotourism, the difficulties in connection with the resettlement of people living on the shore of the falls, and the inappropriateness of Uganda's legal obligations under the power purchase agreement with the private sector investors involved in the project guaranteed by the Bank. The Panel found that the Bank had violated both its policy on cultural property and its policy on natural habitat. These Bank policies reflect the New Delhi Principles in that they are concerned with the protection, preservation and enhancement of the natural environment and the conservation of indigenous or cultural property including unique natural sites to which religious value attaches. Under the Bank's policy on cultural property, the Bank normally declines to finance projects that will significantly damage non-replicable cultural property,[32] and, in the instance of Bank-financed projects benefits being greater than the loss or the damage to cultural property, the Bank will insist on the relocation, preservation, and restoration on alternative sides.[33] The private sector company involved in the project claimed that the chief priest and spirit medium of the Bujagali Falls site which had a highly religious significance for Uganda's 2.5 million Busoga people had agreed to a relocation of the river's spirits. The Panel however heard from the chief priest at a public hearing that "a [spirit] is [not] like a goat that can be transferred from place to

---

32 See 1986 OPN 11.03 para. 2(a). See also OP 4.11 Physical Cultural Resources which replaced the 1986 OPN 11.03 in 2006.
33 See 1986 OPN 11.03 para. 2(b) and (c).

place[.] The spirits [on the contrary] would never allow the dam to be built."[34] The Bank's policy on natural habitat defines critical natural habitat as an area critical from the perspective of biological diversity and which is recognized in this respect and protected by traditional local people.[35] Management therefore argued that the Bank's policy does not apply to purely non-biological features, and thus to a waterfall and a rock. The Panel insisted, with the Board of Directors' concurrence, that the Bujagali Falls area contains not just a waterfall and a rock, but secret trees and other ecological functions and features that are of cultural significance and, therefore, qualify as natural habitat in the Bank policy's sense. Moreover, under the Bank policy on natural habitats, "[t]he Bank does not support projects that . . . involve the significant conversion or degradation of critical natural habitats."[36] When there are no feasible alternatives for the project and no feasible alternatives, the Bank takes mitigation measures such as minimizing habitat loss, or other forms of mitigation measures including the conservation of other natural habitats as an offset.[37] However, while Bank Management had stressed the importance of the Kalagala Falls as a valid natural habitat offset, the Panel found that Uganda had assumed no obligation to preserve these Falls as an offset.

The Chad–Cameroon Petroleum Development and Pipeline Project set an unprecedented framework to transform all the revenue wealth into direct benefits for the respective national economies. For example, out of the net revenues allocated to Chad, 10 per cent of the royalties and dividends from the project were designated to be held in trust for future development endeavours. Five per cent were earmarked for regional development in the oil-producing area, and a substantial proportion of the royalties was devoted to education services, health services, social services, rural development, infrastructure, and environmental and water resource management. By design, therefore, the project reflected New Delhi Principle 1's objective to ensure sustainable use of natural resources. An international consortium of oil companies financed the bulk of the project, while the Bank and the International Finance Corporation (IFC, i.e. the World Bank's private sector lending arm) contributed a small portion to it. Shortly before the Panel was seized with the matter in March 2001, the international media reported that the government of Chad had purchased weapons with part of a US$25 million bonus paid by Chevron and Petronas, members of the consortium of oil companies. Chad had thus broken its promise to the Bank on how it would spend its income from the oil project. In light of mounting pressures from the media as well as the pending request for an investigation by the Panel, the Bank froze the debt relief program for Chad until the government stopped further spending of oil funds and made all government expenditures more transparent. The Bank relied for its retaliation against Chad on General Conditions Applicable

---

34 See Marc Larcey, Traditional Spirits Block a $500 Million Dam Plan in Uganda, *New York Times* (13 September 2001).

35 See 1995 OP 4.04 Annex A. See also 2001 OP 4.04 Natural Habitats which replaced the 1995 OP 4.04 version.

36 See 1995 OP 4.04 para. 4.

37 See 1995 OP 4.04 para. 5.

to Loan and Guarantee Agreements which permit the Bank to suspend or cancel the borrower's rights to withdraw from any loan account in the instance of the borrower's nonperformance under a loan covenant.

In connection with the Democratic Republic of Congo Transitional Support for Economic Recovery Credit Operation, the Bank funded regulatory reform of the logging concession system in Congo and the land-use zoning in the forest areas. Representatives of the indigenous Pygmy peoples in Congo submitted the request for inspection to the Panel in 2005. The Panel found that Bank, in flagrant violation of its policy on indigenous peoples, had even failed to identify the Pygmy peoples as an affected indigenous population during the design phase of the forest-related components of the project. As indigenous people are described in the Bank's policy, the Pygmy peoples were closely attached to their ancestral territories and the natural resources in these areas[38] in that they relied on the forests almost entirely, including for wood and charcoal, bush meat, forest fruit, honey, planned medicines, and other non-timber forest products.

In connection with the Cambodia Forest Concession Management and Control Pilot Project, the Panel's investigation into the Bank-financed forest operations in Cambodia led to a finding of a violation by Management of the Bank's policy on forestry.[39] For future reference, the Management's response to the Panel investigation articulated a series of "lessons learned," and set forth a new framework for Natural Resource Management (NRM) to strengthen and enrich the Bank's efforts to address the full range of social, environmental, and economic issues involved in forest-related initiatives, including crucial issues of land tenure rights, communities living in and around the forests, participation, and transparency, a move tipping the balance of natural resource operations in favour of sustainable use of natural resources, in line with the first New Delhi Principle.

32.3.2 *The principle of equity and the eradication of poverty*

The Brazil Land Reform Poverty Alleviation Project promised to provide loans on favourable terms to impoverished farmers and labourers to enable them to form cooperative associations for buying their own small tracts of land and acquiring the materials necessary to plant and harvest their own crops. These lands would be either acquired in the marketplace from willing sellers or be available as a result of expropriation of larger farms under a constitutionally mandated agrarian reform program. In 1997, a number of local NGOs and individuals filed a request with the Panel asserting, among others, that the Bank had violated its policy on poverty reduction. Specifically, the requesters claimed that the farmers

---

38 See 1991 OD 4.20 Indigenous Peoples para. 5(a). See also the 2005 OP 4.10 Indigenous Peoples which replaced the 1991 OD 4.20.

39 See 1993 OP 4.36 Forestry which in para. 1(a) states that the Bank does not finance commercial logging operations in primary tropical forests. Paras. 1(b)–(f) of that policy require the Bank when financing projects affecting non-tropical forests to design forestry operations from a conservationist and sustainable management perspective. See also the 2002 OP 4.36 Forests which replaced the 1993 OP 4.36.

would be unable to repay their loans and that the prices of property sought to be acquired had risen sharply, making their purchase impossible for the impoverished farmers and labourers. The requesters' assertion went right to the heart of the Bank's mission which, interpreting the Bank's charter and as laid out in the Bank's "Number One," overarching policy on poverty reduction, "is sustainable poverty reduction."[40] Both the Bank's major purpose as taken from its charter as well as its "Number One" policy appear to be the spitting image of the second New Delhi Principle. As the Bank's policy states further "[p]overty encompasses lack of opportunities (including capabilities), lack of voice and representation, and vulnerability to shocks. The Bank's support for poverty reduction is focused on actions . . . to increase opportunity, enhance empowerment, and strengthen security."[41] On the basis of an extensive desk study, the visits to the project area and meetings with numerous beneficiaries and local officials, the Panel concluded that the project was improving the lives of poor farmers in the region as a general matter. In a bold stance, the Panel construed the notion of "poverty reduction" to be consistent with certain loan terms and certain types of land acquisition as part of the project. In particular, the Panel was uncomfortable with the fact that expropriated lands were subject to purchases by the impoverished farmers and labourers, a practice that the Panel believed would encourage unfair profit taking and other forms of corruption. Furthermore, the Panel was uncomfortable that the loan terms under which the farmers borrowed money to purchase land included floating interest rates rather than fixed interest rates. In response to the Panel's reaction, the Brazilian government and Bank Management confirmed that lands that could be expropriated under the agrarian reform would not be purchased under the project, and that the loan terms would be revised to provide for low fixed interest rates.

The Argentina Special Structural Adjustment loan was designed to improve Argentina's social services infrastructure and the quantity of those services, as well as to strengthen the financial sector and improve the regulatory framework. The loan was disbursed in three tranches. One of the conditions for the second tranche was that the borrower's overall budget for certain social programs would be maintained at a certain level, while others would be cut. In 1999, an NGO representing beneficiaries of Pro Huerta, a local food security program that helped the poor maintain small vegetable gardens to produce food for their own consumption, filed a request with the Panel. The requesters asserted that the Bank's policy on poverty reduction was violated since the Pro Huerta program, which was specifically included in the loan agreement as one of the programs to be structurally adjusted, was about to be cut by nearly 65 per cent, an action that contravened the "social budget condition" of the Bank loan to Argentina.

---

40 See 1991 OD 4.15 Poverty Reduction para. 1, first sentence. The 1991 OD 4.15 was replaced by the 2004 OP 1.00 Poverty Reduction. See also 2004 OP 1.00 Poverty Reduction para. 1, first sentence.

41 See 1991 OD 4.15 Poverty Reduction para. 1. The 1991 OD 4.15 was replaced by the 2004 OP 1.00 Poverty Reduction.

In reaction to the Panel's field visit, the Argentine Ministry decided to allocate another US$1.5 million in lottery revenues to the Pro Huerta program. The requesters felt that the total of funds now allocated to the operations of the local food program were adequate. Because the potential harm claimed by the requesters had been averted, the Panel did not recommend a formal investigation.

The Uganda Bujagali Falls Power Projects, an energy generating infrastructure project primarily financed by private sector companies but backed by a Bank partial risk guarantee, also raised issues of consistency with the Bank's overarching mission of poverty reduction, and more specifically, compliance with its policy on economic evaluation of investment operations.[42] Under the project, the government of Uganda and the private investor had entered into a power purchase agreement. This agreement included a clause requiring that the Ugandan government buy all the power that could potentially be produced, based on the plant's capacity, at a fixed price in US Dollars for 30 years, regardless of whether the power was actually produced or needed. The Panel found that, while the project met the criterion of economic acceptability because the expected present value of the project's net benefits was not negative and was higher than the expected net present value of mutually exclusive project alternatives,[43] the project's sustainability was questionable. According to the Bank's policy on economic evaluation of investment operations, the Bank assesses the "robustness," i.e. sustainability, of the project "with respect to economic, financial, institutional, and environmental risks."[44] In terms of economic analysis of the project which is necessarily based on uncertain future events and inexact data and, therefore, inevitably involves probability judgments, the Bank considers "the sources, magnitude, and effects of the risks associated with the project by taking into account the possible range in the values of the basic variables" and assesses "the robustness of the project outcome with respect to changes in these values."[45] The Bank's comprehensive risk assessment ultimately serves the purpose of reducing the risk of failure of the project. The Panel's report highlighted the two strategic risks of the power purchase agreement to Uganda and its guarantors: the shortfall in the projected demand for electricity, and the non-affordability of the electricity rates. The Panel suggested additional risk mitigation measures to provide flexibility and a mutually acceptable way of sharing and reducing stranded costs. The Panel also showed that 10 per cent per year depreciation of the Ugandan currency against the US Dollar could double the electricity tariff to Ugandan consumers over seven years to the equivalent of 13 to 15 cents wholesale. The Panel questioned whether these tariff levels would be affordable for Uganda's population and pointed out that the effects of currency depreciation should have formed part of the risk analysis with regard to affordability of the project in the initial appraisal document.

---

42 See 1994 OP 10.04 Economic Evaluation of Investment Operations.
43 See the discounted expected present net value and net cost related requirements spelled out in para. 1 of the 1994 OP 10.04 Economic Evaluation of Investment Operations.
44 See ibid. at para. 5.
45 See ibid. at para. 6.

32.3.3 *The principle of common but differentiated responsibilities*

With its involvement in the Global Environment Facility (GEF)[46] and the Prototype Carbon Fund, a trust fund created under the Kyoto Protocol,[47] the Bank participates in actively financing the implementation of international environmental agreements that, among others, incorporate the third New Delhi Principle, i.e. rest on the principle of common but differentiated responsibilities. However, only a few of the projects financed under these special trust funds have been subject to an Panel investigation, and none have seriously raised the issues of common but differentiated responsibilities. By and in themselves, Bank support of GEF and Prototype Carbon Fund projects are reflective of direct financial support by the Bank to enable developing countries to address environmental pollution and continue to industrialize while at the same time, as polluters, paying for it.[48]

32.3.4 *The principle of the precautionary approach to human health, natural resources and ecosystems*

The Nepal Arun III Proposed Hydroelectric Project, the subject of the first request for inspection submitted to the Inspection Panel in 1994, raised issues of compliance with the Bank's policy on environmental assessment, a policy that reflects the New Delhi Principle of the precautionary approach. Under the Bank's environmental assessment policy, it requires environmental assessment of projects as a general matter.[49]

> The environmental assessment evaluates the project potential environmental risks and impacts in the area in its area of influence, examines project alternatives, identifies ways of improving project selection, siting, planning, design, and implementation by preventing, minimizing, mitigating, or compensating for adverse environmental impacts and enhancing positive impacts, and includes the process of mitigating and managing adverse environmental impacts throughout project implementation.[50] The environmental assessment takes into account the natural environment . . . , human health and

---

46 For details on the GEF, see Laurence Boisson de Chazournes, L. Boisson de Chazournes, «Le Fonds pour l'Environnement Mondial: Recherche et Conquête de son Identité» XLI *Annuaire Français de Droit International* 612–32 (1995).

47 For details on the special trust fund created under the Kyoto Protocol, see David Freestone, "The World Bank's Prototype Carbon Fund: Mobilizing New Resources for Sustainable Development" in Sabine Schlemmer-Schulte and Ko-Yung Tung, eds., *Liber Amicorum Ibrahim F.I. Shihata: International Finance and Development* (Leiden: Brill, 2001).

48 An interesting recent project funded by the GEF and one in which a request for an investigation was brought before the Panel concerned the Brazil Paranà Biodiversity Project. At issue were in particular the Bank's policies on environmental assessment, natural habitats, and forestry.

49 See 1990 OD 4.00 Environmental Assessment para. 1. The 1999 OP 4.01 Environmental Assessment replaced 1990 OD 4.00.

50 See 1990 OD 4.00 Environmental Assessment para. 2.

safety, social aspects (involuntary resettlement, indigenous peoples, and cultural property), and trans-boundary and global environmental aspects . . . in an integrated way.[51]

In connection with the Arun project, the Panel found that the Bank did not follow the comprehensive scheme of the policy on environmental assessment. Instead, the assessment "followed a piecemeal approach that had recognizable sequence, but did not fully comply with [the policy]."[52] The Panel noted several inadequacies including the Bank's inclination to proceed with the appraisal and negotiation portions of the project before completing the environmental assessment of the Valley route, and inadequate efforts to promote the use of local labour. The Panel also expressed concern about whether the proper institutional structures for managing the environmental impact of the project (such as forest conservation management and measures addressing natural disasters such as floods and road washouts) would come into operation before construction of the hydroelectric power plant began.

The Argentina/Paraguay Yacyretà Hydroelectric Project concerned the world's longest earthen dam, a power plant, a powerhouse, a reservoir, spillways with drainage, and diversion canals. In 1996, a local NGO submitted a request for inspection to the Panel on behalf of itself and people living in Encarnación, Paraguay. The request claimed that, because of Bank failures in filling the reservoirs, the groundwater supplies used for drinking water became contaminated. In addition, the sanitation system had been affected through discharge of untreated sewage into the stagnant waters. Moreover, the project implementation had destroyed island communities as well as ecosystems. Farmland had been flooded and crops destroyed. Fish migration had been disrupted. As a result of the project's adverse socioeconomic impacts, jobs had been lost as well as sources of income for those involved in fishing, ceramics, and bakery. Last but not least, the people living close to the dam suffered from health problems such as respiratory infections and skin and intestinal parasites. The Panel's inspection found that there was a lack of institutional support for the implementing agency of the project. In particular, financial shortages were the major reason for the difficulties in implementing the environmental mitigation measures. The Panel assessed the reservoirs and biodiversity programs as deficient, and determined that the linkages between environmental and health effects were not well established. Furthermore, there was a lack of complete hydro-geological studies, a failure to monitor the impact of the reservoir on lands and soils, problems with the creation and management of compensatory reserves, and a lack of outside review of environmental management plans.

The China Western Poverty Reduction Project allowed the Panel to stress the time and geographical dimensions of the environmental assessment of the Bank-financed project. The Panel found that the environmental assessment undertaken

51 Ibid. at para. 3.
52 See the World Bank Inspection Panel's Investigation Report regarding the Nepal Arun III Hydroelectric Project (21 Jun 1995), para. 73.

by Bank Management did not distinguish between short-term impacts versus those that would occur only in the future. In the Panel's view, the assessment "fail[ed] completely to place the project in proper time frames."[53] Further, looking at the project documentation, the Panel found a "high level of ambiguity, uncertainty, and inconsistency in the use of the term 'project area,'"[54] resulting from the lack of reliable maps. Although the Bank's policy on environmental assessment explicitly states that "adverse environmental impacts . . . may affect an area broader than the sites or facilities subject to physical works,"[55] the Panel noted that Bank Management in the particular case had excluded many areas, people, and communities who were affected by the project from the performed environmental assessment because of the Bank's inadequate definition of "project area." The Panel also found Management's decision to classify the project as Category B not in compliance with the Bank's policy on environmental assessment because out of the 12 types of projects listed on the Category A – the category to which the strictest assessment standards apply – 8 were found within the China Western Poverty Reduction Project and 4 within the component related to the move-in-area of resettled farmers in the West. Another concern pertains to the consideration of project alternatives. The Panel found that "[o]ne of the most noticeable and significant weaknesses of the environmental assessments [in the China Western Poverty Reduction Project] is that investment and project alternatives are neither identified nor systematically compared."[56] In particular, the Panel noted that there was no "systematic study of *in situ* alternatives to resettlement . . . for the national minorities affected within the . . . area [in the West into which the farmers from the eroding hillsides in the East would move]."[57] The Panel also found that precautionary guideline measures under further Bank policies, notably the policy on dam safety[58] and pest management,[59] had not been fully complied with. Despite the occurrence of two serious earthquakes in the project area in the past, Bank Management's environmental assessment lacked a reference to the seismicity of the project area. In terms of pest management, the Panel noted that Bank Management did not currently possess the details of pest management program.

The issue of a proper determination of the "project area" in order to duly assess any adverse impact by the project on people in an environmental assessment as prescribed by Bank policy also played a role in the Panel's investigation into the Pakistan National Drainage Program. This large-scale drainage system was designed to alleviate problems of water saturation and salinization in agricultural lands in the

---

53 See the World Bank Inspection Panel's Investigation Report regarding the China Western Poverty Reduction Project (28 April 2000), para. 52.
54 See ibid. at para. 50.
55 See 1990 OD 4.01 Environmental Assessment para. 8(a).
56 See *supra* note 53 at para. 130.
57 See ibid. at para. 136.
58 See 1996 OP 4.37 Safety of Dams. The 2001 OP 4.37 Safety of Dams replaced the 1996 OP 4.37 Safety of Dams.
59 See 1998 OP 4.09 Pest Management.

northern areas of the Sindh province. The drainage and irrigation systems transformed the natural flow of the Indus River into the Arabian Sea. The drainage and irrigation system included a tidal link which ran through areas occupied by local people and communities as well as through an interconnected series of freshwater lakes that were crucial both ecologically and for fisheries. The Panel found in its 2005 report that the design of the lower drainage system created significant adverse impact and risks for the local population, especially a heightened risk of dangerous flooding caused by a combination of heavy upland rains and storms coming in from the sea. For example, some parts of the tidal link structures were failing as a result of heavy rains and an offshore cyclone in 2003. The flooding resulted in loss of life and large-scale damage to the lands and surrounding communities. The Panel noted that these adverse impacts were not adequately identified, assessed, and mitigated by the Bank's project team. The major reason for this was the apparent over-focus by the Bank on the project's intended beneficiaries, that is the upstream farmers, and not on the downstream people put at risk by the new system.

The issue of categorization of projects in connection with environmental impact assessments reappeared in connection with the Democratic Republic of Congo Transitional Support for Economic Recovery credit operation and the related forest operations. Bank Management had claimed that "technical assistance operations for institutional strengthening are usually classified as Category C [– the category with the lowest standards for environmental assessment purposes – under the Bank's environmental assessment policy]. Where such a categorization results in designs or plans that, when implemented, may have potential impact, they may be given a classification higher than C, normally B."[60] The Panel took issue with categorizing projects for environmental assessment based solely on direct physical impacts. In the Panel's view,

> the financing of policy and institutional reforms in a sensitive sector like the forests of the Democratic Republic of Congo, and related advice and technical assistance, can lead to highly significant environmental and social impacts, even if it does not involve direct financing of the mechanical and organizational tools for industrial logging . . . [For example, the project] could end up officially approving industrial concession rights in millions of hectares of primary tropical forest where many local communities and indigenous peoples are found.[61]

32.3.5 The principle of participation and access to information and justice

Issues of public participation and access to information as enunciated in the fifth New Delhi Principle have frequently come up in connection with Bank-financed projects. The Bank's policies on environmental assessment, indigenous peoples, and involuntary resettlement contain mandatory provisions on consultations

---

60 See the Bank's Management Response at page 25 reproduced in an Annex to the World Bank Inspection Panel's Investigation Report (31 August 2007).
61 See ibid. at para. 360.

of people possibly adversely affected by Bank-financed projects. Disclosure of pertinent information on these projects during the project design and implementation phases is equally required under the three mentioned policies. Issues in terms of the effective protection of the human rights to hold and express opinions and to seek, receive and impart ideas invariably play a role in connection with consultations of project-affected people. And access to justice issues most often take the format of compensation of displaced indigenous peoples and/or involuntarily resettled peoples as a result of Bank-financed projects under respective Bank policies.

32.3.5.1 Consultations with project-affected people

The Argentina/Paraguay Yacyretà Hydroelectric Project, as it involved the settlements of quite a number of people to make way for the reservoir, dam, and power plant, triggered the provisions of mandatory consultations with project-affected peoples under the Bank's policies on environmental assessment[62] and involuntary resettlement.[63] The Panel found that the process of continued participation of affected people had been neglected. The Panel noted a lack of participation by affected people and local authorities in the project-related activities and a tendency by Bank supervision missions to ignore or take lightly the concerns of local people. In particular, the Panel's review found that the number of people to be involuntary resettled – originally estimated to be 50,000 – had ultimately increased to at least 70,000 people. In the Panel's view, the project's weak programs of social communication and lack of adequate identification of vulnerable groups who required special assistance appeared to be the cause of the Bank's of miscalculation in terms of the number of people that needed to be resettled.

32.3.5.2 Disclosure of information

Access to information is vital for project-affected people in order to raise their concerns regarding Bank-financed projects in a meaningful way. In connection with the China Western Poverty Reduction Project, the Panel learned that the project-affected people had only been provided with very limited information about the project. In fact, 93 per cent of the project-affected people that had responded to surveys by the Bank had learned of the project through Chinese government propaganda rather than information provided by the Bank in compliance with its policy on disclosure of operational information.[64] More specifically,

---

62 See 1999 OP 4.01 Environmental Assessment paras. 14–15. The earlier OMS 2.36 Environmental Assessment equally required such consultations.
63 See 1990 OD 4.30 Involuntary Resettlement para. 8 and 2001 OP 4.12 Involuntary Resettlement para. 6(a)(ii).
64 See the 1994 World Bank Policy on Disclosure of Information and related OP/BP 17.40. The 1994 policy on disclosure of information has been amended twice since its first adoption in 1994; in 2002 and, most recently, in 2010.

the Bank's first released project information document was four months behind schedule, and the document failed to adequately discuss the minorities to be affected by the project.

In connection with the Uganda Bujagali Falls Hydropower Projects, the Panel found that the Bank had not disclosed an internal report of 2001 entitled "The Economic Review of the Bujagali Hydropower Project," a document that contained operational information and should have been disclosed for the purposes of meaningful consultation under the Bank's policy on disclosure of information. In connection with the same project, the Panel discussed the issue of nondisclosure of the power purchase agreement between the private company sponsoring the project and the Ugandan government. Although the Bank's policy on disclosure of information did not explicitly make the disclosure of documents relating to a private sector operation mandatory, the Panel noted that the disclosure of the power purchase agreement was critical for the public to understand and participate in an informed discussion. The Panel encouraged the Bank's Executive Directors to clarify in the Bank's policy on disclosure of operational information what type of documents should be made accessible to the public in connection with Bank-supported private sector operations.

The Panel also guarded its own right under the Resolution Establishing the Panel to access all "pertinent records" of the Bank for the purposes of performing its investigatory functions.[65] For example, in connection with the Chad pipeline project and the Albania Integrated Coastal Zone Management and Clean-Up Project, the Panel faced difficulties in accessing project related information held by Bank Management. In the latter instance, a special problem consisted in the failure by a Bank fact-finding mission to uncover and accurately report on material facts relating to the demolition of homes of families living in the southern coastal area of Albania. Also, Bank Management stated that, at the time of project approval, the government had agreed to a moratorium on demolitions in the coastal area until such time as criteria and conditions were put in place to ensure protection of the rights and interests of affected people. In the course of its investigation, the Panel discovered that no such moratorium existed and that Management had misrepresented the facts not only to the Panel, but also in the project appraisal document. The Panel documented all of these errors of fact in its final investigation report and contributed by its disclosures to a correction of Bank failures and remedial actions for the benefit of those harmed by them.

32.3.5.3 *Freedom of speech*

The China Western Poverty Reduction Project allowed the Panel to influence the way in which the borrower under Bank policies had to conduct meaningful consultations with project-affected people. In the absence of any explicit

65 See Resolution Establishing the Panel, *supra* note 2 at para. 21.

reference to the method that was proposed by the Panel in connection with this project, the Panel found that non-confidential questionnaires were used in surveys to be completed by people who would be resettled as they required respondents to list their names.[66] The Panel did not opine on the request's allegation that expressions of disapproval of Han Chinese settlement in traditionally Tibetan populated areas have been treated [by the Chinese government] as counter-revolutionary. It also refrained from couching its preference for confidential methods of surveying project-affected people in human rights terms. But the Panel noted that the Bank had a responsibility to guarantee confidentiality of the respondents where "there is even a perception of potential adverse effects that could result from a truthful statement of opposition to this Bank financed project."[67]

The Chad Petroleum Development and Pipeline Project prompted the Panel to take a more explicit stance on the human right to hold and express opinions in connection with Bank-financed projects. In their request launched in 2001 with the Panel, the requesters alleged the Bank's failure to apply its policies on proper governance and human rights. Specifically the requesters alleged that the Government of Chad had indulged in political repression, coercion, and torture, which had stifled free and open debate and inhibited the requesters and other elements of civil society from participating in the design and implementation of the projects under consideration. In the absence of either a specific Bank policy on human rights or an explicit reference to human rights in the Bank's policy provisions on mandatory consultations with project-affected people, the Panel considered basic respect for human rights to be embedded in various policies of the Bank, in particular those on local consultation. While the Panel emphasized that assessing the status of human rights in a borrowing Member Country in general was not in its mandate, the Panel felt it was appropriate to examine whether human rights violations in Chad were such as to impede the implementation of the project in accordance with the Bank's policies. In the Panel's view, human rights violations as severe as in Chad called into question compliance with Bank policies on informed and open consultations.

Since the Chad pipeline case, the Panel has protected the poor and marginalized peoples' human right to a voice in the development process and reported the risk of retaliation, intimidation, or even imprisonment to the highest authorities

66 It may be noted that the Panel has from the beginning in its own operations kept requesters' names and identities confidential whenever asked for. Thus, the Panel did not make names and identities of requesters available to Management in connection with the requests for inspection related to the Nepal Arun project, the Argentina/Paraguay project, the NTPC project, and the Lesotho/South Africa project, among others. The extension of guarding people's confidentiality to the consultations of project-affected people under Bank policies on participation seems natural in light of the Panel's practice concerning its own investigations. See Shihata, see *supra* note 2 at 62–4.
67 See *supra* note 53 at para. 29.

to limit the negative ramifications on all peoples' desires to put forth claims in connection with Bank-financed projects.[68]

32.3.5.4 Access to justice and compensation claims

The Nepal Arun III Proposed Hydroelectric Project, like most Bank-financed huge infrastructure projects of that kind, raised the social issues associated with involuntary resettlement. This Bank policy, in its various reiterations, acknowledges that development projects that displace people involuntarily generally give rise to "severe economic, social, and environmental problems."[69] Involuntary resettlement may cause severe long-term hardship, impoverishment, loss of jobs and income, assets, shelter and more. In recognition of the serious hardships which may result from relocation, the Bank's policy on involuntary resettlement emphasizes that involuntary resettlement should be avoided or minimized where feasible.[70] Where displacement is unavoidable, displaced persons should be compensated for their losses at full replacement cost, assisted with the move, supported during the transition period in the resettlement site, and assisted in their efforts to improve their former living standards, income-earning capacity, and production levels, or at least to restore them based on resettlement plans.[71] In connection with the Arun project, the Panel found that "the resettlement issue on [certain parts of the] Route had suffered abuse by neglect" and that the interests of farmers along that route had been affected by an inadequate compensation system. The farmers received only cash, but were never provided with any form of rehabilitation. Also, the change of the access road drove down the value of the lands in the Valley, causing adverse effects on those whose lands were partially taken.

The Bangladesh Jamuna Multipurpose Bridge Project involved the construction of a 4.8 km bridge over the Jamuna River. This wide, meandering watercourse is constantly shifting its path because of silt accretion and other factors, and thus the efforts to tame it sufficiently to construct a permanent overpass were a major undertaking. In 1996, the Panel received a request from a group of individuals who lived on a series of islands (known locally as "chars") in the middle of the river channel. The requesters were concerned that the

---

68 Further examples of cases in which the Panel stood up against pressures or reprisals faced by requesters as a fundamental concern for human rights include the 2000 Uganda Bujagali Falls Hydropower Project, the 2006 Brazil Paranà Biodiversity Project, and the 2009 Mumbai India Urban Transport Project.

69 See 1990 OD 4.30 Involuntary Resettlement para. 1. The earlier OMS 2.33 Involuntary Resettlement from the 1980s as well as the later 2001 OP 4.12 Involuntary Resettlement preceding and succeeding OD 4.30 respectively contain similar statement.

70 See 1990 OD 4.30 Involuntary Resettlement para. 3(a) and 2001 OP 4.12 Involuntary Resettlement para. 2.

71 See *supra* note 69 at para. 3(b); OP 4.12 Involuntary resettlement, *supra* note 69 at paras. 6(a)(iii), 6(b), 6(c).

engineering works designed to manage the course of the river would result in increased flooding and erosion of the islands and perhaps even wash away some of their homes entirely.

In conjunction with the Jamuna Bridge Project, the issue was whether the notion of "displaced persons" included not only owners of and permanent residents on land claimed for project completion but extended also to people with contact of lesser legal value to such land. The then applicable 1990 version of the Bank's policy on involuntary resettlement was not yet as explicit in terms of impacts covered for compensation purposes as its later 2001 successor version which was, in fact, much influenced by the Panel's inquiry into the matter.[72] Management had initially not paid attention to the char people on the islands in the river. In its review of the case, the Panel noted that the construction of a river channel through river alignment in preparation of the bridge was likely to result in destruction or permanent flooding of the islands on which the char dwellers lived and earned a living. The Panel concluded therefore that the char dwellers should receive compensation for the potential losses incurred by them. The Panel's approach clarified that even people temporarily living on land which is usurped for the implementation of a Bank-financed project have a right to compensation under the Bank's resettlement policy.

The India NTPC (National Thermal Power Corporation) Power Generation Project concerned a heavy industry complex in the Singrauli region of Central India. The intensive thermal power development program financed by the Bank had led to continual displacement of poor villagers to make way for the huge, coal-fired power generating plants. Environmental and health hazards also resulted from the project (e.g. fly ash from the coal used for operating the plants disposed in ponds, large-scale of purchases of land resulting in deforestation, severe mercury and chromium poisoning, and dust pollution). The Panel found that, as the requesters had alleged, Bank Management's attention to the policy on involuntary resettlement had been marginal in comparison to the overall objectives of the project. Bank Management had largely overlooked that NTPC was completely disregarding the rights of the people it was displacing. Villagers were being forcibly removed from their homes and resettled in urban areas completely unsuited to their mode of living. They were being given lump sum cash payments in lieu of being provided with permanent jobs or training programs to enable them to maintain their livelihood. NTPC's failure to upgrade existing ash ponds or to consider backfilling of ash and existing open cast mines resulted in involuntary resettlements that could have been avoided, as large tracts of land were acquired by NTPC for new ash ponds.

In connection with the Nigeria West Africa Gas Pipeline project which involved the construction of a 678 km pipeline to transport natural gas from Nigeria to

---

72 See OP 4.12 Involuntary resettlement, *supra* note 69 at para. 3 which now extends to "the involuntary taking of land resulting in relocation or loss of shelter, loss of assets, or access to assets, or loss of income sources or means of livelihood, whether or not the affected persons must move to another location, or the involuntary restriction of access to legally designated parks and protected areas resulting in adverse impact on the livelihoods of the displaced persons."

the neighbouring countries of Benin, Togo, and Ghana, the Panel found that Bank Management had not complied with the Bank's policy on involuntary resettlement. Bank Management had not ensured that the livelihood of people who involuntarily lost assets was restored. In particular, the Panel noted that there had been a factor of 10 error in calculating compensation due to resettled people, leading to compensation significantly below the true value of land.

32.3.6 *The principle of good governance*

In addition to the above-mentioned cases in which the Panel lent its support to the protection of the human rights of free speech and compensation for takings of land resulting in relocation, loss of shelter, and sources of income (as defined by Bank lending policies rather than international human rights treaties), the Panel promoted further human rights ideals embodied in the New Delhi Principle of Good Governance. The Panel promoted due process in connection with adverse impacts of Bank action, i.e. financing of development projects in borrowing members, by interpreting the scope of its jurisdiction broadly. The Panel also opined on takings by borrowing governments which took place outside the context of the implementation of a concrete Bank-financed project but rather triggered some general approaches by the Bank to certain domestic affairs by members that contravene principles of good governance.

The Panel had the opportunity to clarify that the scope of its jurisdiction covered both investment as well as adjustment/development policy operations. According to the Resolution Establishing the Panel, the Panel answers to requests relating to Bank failures "with respect to the design, appraisal and/or implementation of a project financed by the Bank."[73] The issue of the meaning of the term "project" as used in the Resolution Establishing the Panel arose in discussions between the Panel and Bank Management in relation to the request concerning the Bangladesh Jute Sector Adjustment Credit filed in 1995. It was then agreed that the term "project" as used in the Resolution has the same meaning as used in the Bank's practice. In the Bank's practice, the term "project" pertains to the Bank's financing of "specific projects" rather than non-project lending which the Bank is only allowed to engage in in "special circumstances" under its Charter.[74] While the term "project" is not limited to the typical physical projects for construction, industry, agriculture, and the like, and would cover a list of items under a so-called program loan in that there would still be the allocation of resources for specific productive purposes, the Bank's practice never considered structural adjustment lending for regulatory and institutional reform purposes as a project form of lending. Despite the Bank's practice limiting the term "project" to non-adjustment lending operations and despite legal issues raised in connection with the proposal to subject adjustment lending operations to inspection

---

73 See Resolution Establishing the World Bank Inspection Panel, para. 12, third sentence.
74 See IBRD Articles of Agreement, Art. III, Section 4(vii) and IDA Articles of Agreement, Art. V., Section 1(b).

investigations,[75] the Panel went ahead and investigated Bank failures related to adjustment programs in addition to investment projects, thereby enforcing the rights of project-affected people and allowing for Panel inquiries into the bigger picture of macroeconomic and institutional policies of the Bank.

Similarly, the Panel clarified that its jurisdiction extended to projects in which the Bank serves as guarantor rather than direct lender. In connection with the Uganda Bujagali Hydropower Projects financed through a partial risk guarantee by the Bank, IFC, and private sector support, Bank Management contended that the Panel had no jurisdiction over the partial risk operations because of the private sector nature of these operations in respect to which the Resolution Establishing the Panel would be unclear. Management noted further that the role of the guarantor is merely to appraise and assess the risks of an existing operation as opposed to cooperating with the borrower in the design and implementation of an operation in the financing of a public sector project. Management acknowledged nevertheless that Bank policies and procedures were generally applicable to the Bujagali project. The Panel took the opportunity to assert its jurisdiction over a private sector guarantee operation underwritten by the Bank and, thus, to confirm a broader scope for its work than argued by Management, interpreting the absence of an explicit exclusion of private sector work from the Panel's investigations under the Resolution establishing it as indicative that no restriction to its jurisdiction applied. In the Panel's view, the Resolution establishing it accorded to it the power to investigate compliance by Management with all policies and procedures with respect to all Bank-financed projects no matter which type of project is concerned as long as a policy itself did not explicitly limit its application. Moreover, in the absence of language excluding their application to private sector guarantees, the Panel found the Bank's safeguard policies on environmental assessment, natural habitat, safety of dams, and involuntary resettlement, and consultation with affected people applicable to the guarantee operation.

In connection with the second complaint received by the Panel on behalf of two Greek citizens in March 1995, the Panel inquired into the taking by the Government of Ethiopia of the Greek citizens' property without compensation.[76] In their complaint, the requesters alleged that the Bank (IDA) had violated a specific Bank policy by continuing to lend to Ethiopia, despite the latter's failure to compensate them for the expropriation some 20 years earlier of property belonging to the family of the requesters. According to the Bank's policy on disputes over defaults on external debt, expropriation, and breach of contract, the Bank has to take a borrowing country's position with respect to an alien's expropriated property into account in its lending if this position is substantially affecting the country's international credit standing.[77] While the Panel decided that it would

---

75 See Shihata, *supra* note 2 at 37–41.

76 See Ethiopia Compensation for Expropriation and Extension of IDA Credits to Ethiopia.

77 See 1986 OMS 1.28 on Disputes over Defaults on External Debt, Expropriation, and Breach of Contract requiring the Bank "not to lend for projects in a country if it considers that the position taken

not register the request because the requesters had failed to exhaust local remedies for their compensation claim and consequently had not shown a *prima facie* way that the failure of the government to compensate them was caused by the Bank's continued lending to Ethiopia, the Panel nevertheless discussed the fact of a possible human rights violation by a borrowing member country in the form of an illegal expropriation and, thereby, made the facts of that possible human rights violation known.[78]

In connection with the Lesotho/South Africa Phase 1B of Lesotho Highlands Water Project, the Panel had another opportunity to opine on an unlawful expropriation situation. As in the Ethiopia case, the Panel reached the conclusion that an investigation was not unwarranted in the absence of a causal link between the alleged Bank failure to follow the policy on disputes over defaults on external debt, expropriation, and breach of contract and the alleged unlawful expropriation. For the purposes of an analysis of the eligibility of the request, the Panel nevertheless delved into the facts of the allegation on unlawful expropriations. According to the requesters, six companies registered in Lesotho and South African nationals who were shareholders in the Lesotho companies, had been deprived of their mining rights without fair, full, and prompt compensation. The alleged facts including the fact that one of the requesters had immediately obtained an interim court order setting aside cancellation of the leases, while the main proceedings in court regarding the validity of the lease cancellations continued, became known.

32.3.7 The principle of integration and interrelationship, in particular in relation to human rights and social, economic and environmental objectives

A number of Bank policies themselves reflect the New Delhi Principle of Integration. For example, the Bank's policy on economic evaluation of investment operations acknowledges the interdependence of social, economic, financial, environmental and other human rights aspects implicitly by requiring the Bank to undertake a balancing test between the economic benefits of Bank-financed

---

by it with respect to alien owners of expropriated property is substantially affecting its international credit standing." See also 1996 OP 7.40 Disputes over Defaults on External Debt, Expropriation, and Breach of Contract which reads

[t]he Bank recognizes that the country may expropriate property of aliens in accordance with applicable legal procedures, in pursuance in good faith of a public purpose, without discrimination on the basis of nationality, and against payment of appropriate compensation. When there are disputes over expropriations that, in the opinion of the Bank, the country is not making reasonable efforts to settle and that are substantially harming the country's international credit standing, the Bank considers whether to continue lending for new projects in the country.

78 It may be noted that Management argued that the request fell outside the scope of the Panel's jurisdiction not for lack of causation but for lack of a situation in which the Bank failure to observe policies related to a Bank-financed project.

projects and the potential environmental and social harms resulting from them.[79] The Panel focused on such balancing type of test in its analysis of the extent to which Bank Management had failed to comply with the Bank's safeguard policies in connection with Bank-financed infrastructure projects. For example, according to the Panel, one of the fundamental problems of the Argentina/Paraguay Yacyretà Hydroelectric Project was an imbalance between the execution of the civil and electromechanical work, and the resettlement and environmental measures to be undertaken in tandem. While the former were, at the time of the Panel's review, 99.8 per cent complete, less than a third of the environmental and resettlement plans had been completed. In the Panel's view:

> [t]his imbalance is dramatically illustrated by the fact that the reservoir was filled prior to completion of the agreed environmental and resettlement measures which resulted in negative environmental impacts and placed populations living in low-lying areas on both sides of the reservoir at higher risk for prolonged period of time. This action . . . has caused risks of serious health hazards through exposure [of people] to unsanitary conditions and poor water quality. Other risks include potential loss of sustainable livelihood for loss of high quality clay and fish resources.[80]

32.4 Conclusion

The World Bank is governed by a set of "truly avant-garde policies and procedures."[81]

> These policies have been carefully designed to ensure that Bank investments, while leading to economic development and growth, do not do so at the expense of poor and marginalized people and the environment. Sustainable growth with justice is a key objective of the Bank . . . and it is precisely through the Inspection Panel that a process exists to ensure that the safeguards embodied in Bank policies are adhered to and that, in case of noncompliance, corrective measures are initiated.[82]

Indeed, the World Bank Inspection Panel has tremendously strengthened the "rule of law" for the benefit of people affected by Bank-financed projects since its inception. The Panel has ensured that the Bank's impressive development finance standards which reflect the New Delhi Principles in many respects are effectively applied in connection with Bank operations. Invariably, the Panel has pushed these standards beyond their literal narrow meaning, at all times stressing the sustainable

79 See OP 10.04 Economic Evaluation of Investment Operations, paras. 5–7.
80 See the World Bank Inspection Panel's Review of Problems and Assessment of Action Plans (16 September 1997) at 4.
81 Werner Kiene, "An Introduction from the Panel Chair", in *Accountability at the World Bank: The Inspection Panel at 15 Years* (Washington, D. C.: World Bank, 2009) at ix (2009).
82 Ibid.

development angle over the economic growth angle or the more traditional Bank view of development.

Some may accuse the Panel of "judicial activism" in stretching the meaning of Bank lending policies as well as stretching its own jurisdiction. However, the latter is firmly consistent with the generally accepted concept of any international judicial body's *compétence de la compétence* to determine its jurisdiction. And, the former recalls the longtime practice of the European Court of Justice's jurisprudence to breathe human rights into the European Communities' treaty body at a time the respective legal framework was basically silent in terms of human rights. While the Panel's stretches may not have always been based on state of art of legal interpretation – although fixes of substandard legal analysis are available – the Panel is justified from a policy perspective to stretch its jurisdiction for the benefit of both its immediate client, the Board of Executive Directors, but also for its ultimate clients, the people adversely affected by Bank-financed projects, in light of the fact that the Bank operates very much in a vacuum from the perspective of accountability of the institution. The Panel certainly contributes greatly to the Bank's reputation as Number One promoter of sustainable development. The Panel would have an even greater impact on sustainable development as supported by Bank projects if it were given greater autonomy and powers to directly decide on remedial measures.

33 Principles on sustainable development in the NAAEC Commission on Environmental Cooperation

*Dane Ratliff**

33.1 Introduction

The adoption of the North American Agreement on Environmental Cooperation[1] ("NAAEC" or the "Agreement") as a side agreement to the North American Free Trade Agreement[2] ("NAFTA"), was in no small measure due to efforts of concerned citizens who sought greater environmental protection in the NAFTA regime.[3] Public participation appears to have directly influenced the development of the NAAEC's own regime, including the many transparency and good-governance provisions in the NAAEC, which will be a central feature of this chapter. The prevailing fear as the NAFTA was being negotiated was that liberalized trade under NAFTA, particularly with Mexico, would engender a "race to the bottom", whereby industry would seek to relocate to "pollution havens" in Mexico, which had the least stringent environmental and labour regulations of the three NAFTA Parties.[4] The result of such an exodus of business, so the logic ran, would

---

* The views expressed herein are those of the author as an academic, and do not necessarily reflect the views of the CEC Secretariat. The author is the former Director of the NAAEC Submissions on Enforcement Matters Unit.

1 North American Agreement on Environmental Cooperation, U.S.-Can.-Mex., 14 Sept. 1993, 32 ILM 1480 [hereinafter NAAEC].

2 North American Free Trade Agreement, U.S.-Can.-Mex., Dec. 17, 1992, 32 ILM 289 and 605 (1993) [hereinafter NAFTA].

3 Robert Housman, "The North American Free Trade Agreement's Lessons for Reconciling Trade and the Environment", 30 *Stan. J. Int'l L.* 379 (1994), 381–84. See also Tseming Yang, Ignacia S. Moreno, James W. Rubin, and Russell F. Smith III, "Free Trade and the Environment: The NAFTA, the NAAEC, and Implications for the Future", 12 *Tul. Envtl. L. J.* 405 (1999), 420–22. Available at: http://digitalcommons.law.scu.edu/facpubs/715.

4 Ibid. See Yang (et al.) *supra* note 3 at 411–12, where they state,

> In the United States, environmental groups and members of Congress believed that Mexico's environmental laws and their enforcement were less stringent than in the United States. They feared that free trade would exacerbate a preexisting 'pollution haven' in Mexico by encouraging relocation of United States industry. Environmentalists feared that the relocation of American industry to Mexico would also create pressure to downgrade environmental norms in the United States. Critics of free trade generally argued that such downward pressure would occur, in part, because investors would seek to reduce the costs of environmental compliance by relocating industry to Mexico.

be that Canada and the US would likewise have to lower their environmental and labour standards to remain competitive.[5] In an attempt to prevent such potential negative impacts of trade liberalization on the environment, and to ensure a degree of upward harmonization of standards in environmental laws and regulations, the NAAEC included provisions requiring each Party to, for example:

(i) (Article 3) "ensure that its laws and regulations provide for high levels of environmental protection and [. . .] strive to continue to improve those laws and regulations";

(ii) and, (Article 4) "ensure that its laws, regulations, procedures and administrative rulings of general application respecting any matter covered by this Agreement are promptly published or otherwise made available in such a manner as to enable interested persons and Parties to become acquainted with them";

(iii) moreover, (Article 5) "with the aim of achieving high levels of environmental protection and compliance with its environmental laws and regulations, each Party shall effectively enforce its environmental laws and regulations through appropriate governmental action";

(iv) and further, to (Article 6) "ensure that persons with a legally recognized interest under its law in a particular matter have appropriate access to administrative, quasi-judicial or judicial proceedings for the enforcement of the Party's environmental laws and regulations";

(v) and, to (Article 7) "ensure that its administrative, quasi-judicial and judicial proceedings referred to in Articles 5(2) and 6(2) are fair, open and equitable".[6]

In the foregoing Articles, the NAAEC operationalized several of the central tenets of sustainable development that are the subject of this book, and which were articulated in the International Law Association's ("ILA") 2002 New Delhi Declaration of Principles of International Law relating to Sustainable Development.[7] A brief summary of the SD Principles found in the NAAEC is

---

5 Ibid. See also, Linda J. Allen, "The North American Agreement on Environmental Cooperation: Has It Fulfilled Its Promises and Potential? An Empirical Study of Policy Effectiveness", 23 *Colo. J. Int'l Envtl. L. & Pol'y* 121 (2012), at 123, where she states,

> The principal concern identified for NAFTA was the potential for liberalized trade to give rise to pollution havens in Mexico as industries relocated to take advantage of lax enforcement of environmental laws in that country, with possible pollution spillovers along the U.S.–Mexico border. *Other concerns were subsequently identified, including* the use of trade regime rules to challenge legitimate domestic environmental regulations and standards as non-tariff barriers to trade, *the downward harmonization of environmental laws and standards as trading partners strive for common standards*, the accelerated exploitation of natural resources due to liberalization of certain sectors, and a general increase in levels of pollution due to economic growth [emphasis added].

6 See NAAEC, *supra* note 1.

7 "ILA New Delhi Declaration of Principles of International Law Relating to Sustainable Development", 2 *Int'l Envtl. Agreements: Politics, Law and Econ.* 211 (2002).

in order here. NAAEC Article Three's call for upward harmonization of environmental laws among the three Parties accords with the Principle of good governance, including on "progressive development of international law relating to sustainable development" and respect for due process and observation of the rule of law. NAAEC Article Four's progressive approach to transparency by publishing information about laws, regulations, and judicial decisions, accords with the Principle on "Public Participation and Access to Information and Justice". NAAEC Article Five's directive to enforce environmental law accords with the good governance principle and accountability as does NAAEC Article Six's access to justice provisions. NAAEC Article Six's access to justice provisions and NAAEC Article Seven's call for access to justice and fairness likewise accords. Before delving further into the NAAEC, it would be useful to consider the form of and mechanisms in the Agreement where such principles operate.

The NAAEC, often referred to as the "NAFTA side agreement", is not a protocol to the NAFTA nor does it in general depend on the NAFTA for its operation, although elements of it, such as Articles 10(3)(b) and 10(6), establish formal coordination with the NAFTA on environmental matters, and one of the overarching objectives of the Agreement is to "support the environmental goals and objectives of the NAFTA".[8] A review of the NAAEC's implementation ten years after its entry into force, concluded that there were however few concrete results of coordination with the NAFTA Free Trade Commission, noting:

> The NAAEC represented a political acknowledgment that sustainable development requires the integration of environmental and trade considerations. A decade after negotiating the NAAEC, however, the Parties still pursue

---

8 See NAAEC Objective 1(d). NAAEC Article 10(3)(b) provides: "The Council shall strengthen cooperation on the development and continuing improvement of environmental laws and regulations, including by: without reducing levels of environmental protection, establishing a process for developing recommendations on greater compatibility of environmental technical regulations, standards and conformity assessment procedures in a manner consistent with the NAFTA." NAAEC Article 10(6) provides for more robust cooperation: "The Council shall cooperate with the NAFTA Free Trade Commission to achieve the environmental goals and objectives of the NAFTA by:

a)   acting as a point of inquiry and receipt for comments from non-governmental organizations and persons concerning those goals and objectives;

b)   providing assistance in consultations under Article 1114 of the NAFTA where a Party considers that another Party is waiving or derogating from, or offering to waive or otherwise derogate from, an environmental measure as an encouragement to establish, acquire, expand or retain an investment of an investor, with a view to avoiding any such encouragement;

c)   contributing to the prevention or resolution of environment-related trade disputes by:

  (i)   seeking to avoid disputes between the Parties,

  (ii) making recommendations to the Free Trade Commission with respect to the avoidance of such disputes, and

  (iii) identifying experts able to provide information or technical advice to NAFTA committees, working groups and other NAFTA bodies;

d)   considering on an ongoing basis the environmental effects of the NAFTA; and

e)   otherwise assisting the Free Trade Commission in environment-related matters."

their trade and environmental policies largely separately, rather than through the CEC.[9]

Despite the latter critique, the latter review of NAAEC implementation concluded that the NAAEC had in fact been successful in conducting assessments of the impact on the environment of trade under NAFTA, and in so doing the Agreement was deemed to have fulfilled part of its mandate by promoting transparency, and by supporting the environmental goals and objectives of NAFTA.[10]

The NAAEC is a stand-alone treaty in public international law terms, and in accordance with Article 2(1)(a) of the 1969 Vienna Convention on the Law of Treaties[11] (VCLT), it is "an international agreement concluded between States in written form and governed by international law [. . .] whatever its particular designation". It was indeed concluded by States (VCLT Article 6), and the heads of State, Government, and Ministers of Foreign Affairs involved had the appropriate "full powers" to "perform all acts relating to the conclusion of a treaty", and moreover they intended to "express the consent of the State to be bound by a treaty" (VCLT Article 7). NAAEC Part V also contains a binding dispute resolution mechanism, which foresees potential financial penalties in case of a "persistent pattern of failure [by a Party] to effectively enforce its environmental law".[12] The NAAEC is thus not a toothless framework agreement or a form of "soft law", rather it contains binding legal obligations for the Parties, and assigns the Parties rights and duties, just as it does the constituent parts of the intergovernmental organization ("IGO") it creates.[13]

NAAEC Article 8 establishes the "Commission for Environmental Cooperation" ("CEC") the IGO which is comprised[14] of: "the Council"[15], which is the Commission's governing body made up of each Party's highest level environmental official; the Secretariat[16], comprised of a professional staff led by an

---

9 *Ten Years of North American Environmental Cooperation: Report of the Ten-Year Review and Assessment Committee to the Council of the Commission for Environmental Cooperation* (15 June 2004), at 25, Commission for Environmental Cooperation, online at: http://www.cec.org/Page.asp?PageID=122&ContentID=2616 (last visited 29 August 2015).

10 Ibid. at 26, where the Report discusses the CEC's work on assessing the effects of trade on the environment stating, "[. . .] observers have praised the CEC's work as 'producing a cutting-edge analysis methodology'. This alone is one of the CEC's major achievements."

11 Vienna Convention on the Law of Treaties, May 23, 1969, art. 31, 1155 U.N.T.S. 331 [hereinafter Vienna Convention].

12 See NAAEC Article 22(1). The dispute resolution provisions are contained in NAAEC Articles 22–36.

13 The NAAEC Parties' governing body, known as "the Council" adopted Council Resolution 13-03, which for the first time formally recognized that the Commission for Environmental Cooperation is an international organization. *See* Council of the Commission for Environmental Cooperation, *Resolution 13-03* (9 August 2013), C/C.01/13/RES/03/Final, online at: http://www.cec.org/Page.asp?PageID=122&ContentID=25683&SiteNodeID=1197&BL_ExpandID=566 (last visited 29 August 2015).

14 See ibid. at Article 8(2).

15 See ibid. at Articles 9 and 10.

16 See ibid. at Articles 11–15.

executive director, and which provides technical, administrative and operational support to the Council and Council working groups, as well as administering the citizen submissions process; and, the Joint Public Advisory Committee[17] ("JPAC"), composed of 15 citizens (five from each country), which advises the Council on any matter within the scope of the NAAEC, and serves as a source of information for the CEC Secretariat.[18]

The NAAEC includes many avenues for public participation, which are described in more detail in section 33.3 below.[19] The CEC Secretariat outlines its basic approach to public participation as follows:

> Given the importance of public participation in conserving, protecting, and enhancing the environment, the CEC must implement appropriate mechanisms for distributing information, and to educate and consult with the public of North America on the activities of its three components: the Secretariat, the Council, and JPAC.
>
> The CEC promotes informed public participation by:
>
> - Distributing information to the public through JPAC
> - Seeking the advice of the National and Governmental Advisory Committees in promoting informed public participation
> - Informing the public of ongoing activities through CEC publications
> - Obtaining information from the public on a specific issue via questionnaires, interviews, forums, meetings, seminars, etc.
> - Consulting with the public on a specific issue through workshops, round tables, electronic discussion groups, and outreach programs
> - Preparing and distributing reports to assist the public in evaluating follow-up decisions.[20]

The above public participation methods help ensure that the work of the CEC is relevant and close to the public. Yet, arguably the most potent method of public participation (and transparency) in the NAAEC is enshrined in Articles 14 and 15, which allow for submission of an assertion to the Secretariat that one (or more) of the Parties is failing to effectively enforce its environmental law, and provide for the Secretariat to further consider such assertions when certain criteria are met. The next section describes the structure and function of the submissions on enforcement matters, or "SEM", process.

17 See ibid. at Article 16.
18 More information regarding the current activities of the CEC and its mission can be found on the organization's website: www.cec.org.
19 It is beyond the scope of this chapter to discuss in depth the CEC's various public participation methods, but for an excellent comparative overview, see "Malgosia Fitzmaurice, Public Participation in the North American Agreement on Environmental Cooperation", 52 ICLQ (April, 2003), 333–68.
20 Commission for Environmental Cooperation, *Framework for Public Participation in CEC Activities*, available online at: http://www.cec.org/Page.asp?PageID=122&ContentID=937&SiteNodeID=536&BL_ExpandID=568 (last visited 30 August 2015).

33.2 The public submissions on enforcement matters ("SEM") process

33.2.1 Structure and operation

Much has been written about the operation and effectiveness of the SEM process,[21] and thus this section merely provides an overview of how a submission is initiated and processed. NAAEC Articles 14 and 15 set out the procedure for filing a submission, how the submission will be processed, and what timelines apply. The Secretariat in a recent determination succinctly mapped out the submission procedure as follows:

> Articles 14 and 15 of the NAAEC provide for a process allowing any person or non-governmental organization to file a submission asserting that a Party to the Agreement is failing to effectively enforce its environmental law. The Secretariat initially considers submissions to determine whether they meet the criteria contained in NAAEC Article 14(1) and the *Guidelines for Submissions on Enforcement Matters under Articles 14 and 15 of the* [NAAEC] (the "Guidelines"). When the Secretariat determines that a submission meets the criteria set out in Article 14(1), it then determines, pursuant to the provisions of NAAEC Article 14(2), whether the submission merits a response from the NAAEC Party named in the submission. In light of any response from the concerned Party, and in accordance with NAAEC and the Guidelines, the Secretariat may notify the Council of the CEC that the matter warrants the development of a factual record, providing its reasons for such recommendation in accordance with Article 15(1). Where the Secretariat decides to the contrary, or where certain circumstances prevail, it proceeds no further with its consideration of the submission.[22]

The Guidelines for Submissions on Enforcement Matters under Articles 14 and 15 of the North American Agreement on Environmental Cooperation[23] include a diagram (reproduced as Figure 33.1, below) showing the possible stages throughout a submission's lifecycle, and the applicable timelines.

As noted, the Secretariat may ultimately recommend a "factual record", and in such case it determines, *inter alia*, whether, in light of the Party's response,

---

21 For a list of several such articles see John H. Knox and David L. Markell, "Evaluating Citizen Petition Procedures: Lessons from an Analysis of the NAFTA Environmental Commission", 47 *Tex. Int'l L. J.* 505 (2012), at note 9. Available at: http://diginole.lib.fsu.edu/lawscholarship/61. It should however be noted that the Secretariat of the CEC is not, as the article title suggests, the "NAFTA" environmental commission, rather the CEC operates independent of the NAFTA.
22 See SEM-13-002 (*Louisiana Refinery Releases*), Article 14(1) Determination (12 August 2013), Secretariat of the Commission for Environmental Cooperation, available online at: http://www.cec.org/Page.asp?PageID=2001&ContentID=25588&SiteNodeID=548&BL_ExpandID=502.
23 The Guidelines are available on the Commission for Environmental Cooperation website at: http://www.cec.org/Page.asp?PageID=1212&SiteNodeID=210&BL_ExpandID=880.

THE SUBMISSIONS ON ENFORCEMENT MATTERS PROCESS

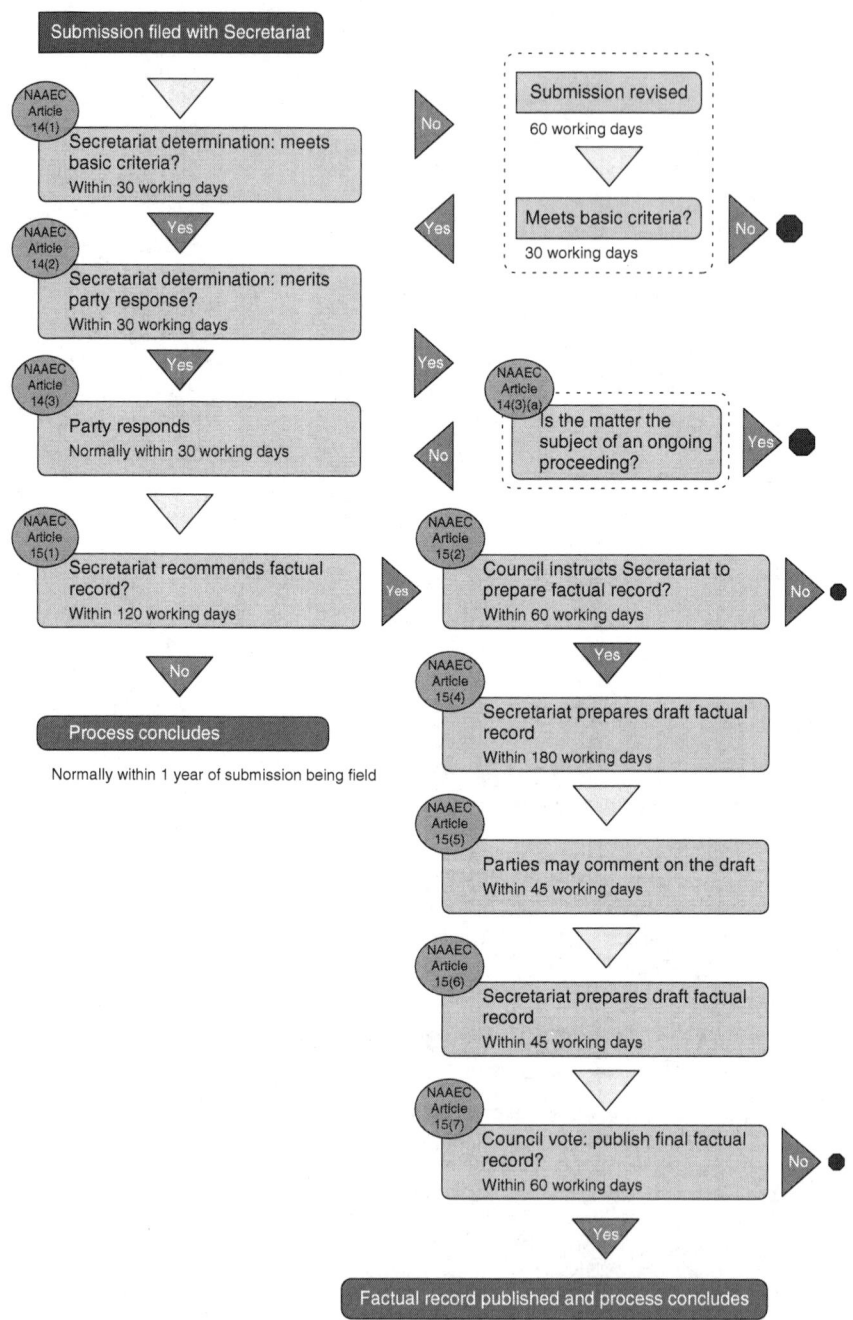

Figure 33.1 Flowchart of the SEM process

central open questions raised by the submitter remain that would warrant the development of a factual record.[24] According to NAAEC Article 15(2), the Council then votes on the Secretariat's recommendation, and if two-thirds of the Parties agree, the Secretariat will be instructed to develop a factual record. In gathering information for a factual record, the Secretariat may take into account information provided by the Parties, independently gathered expert information, and public input.[25] The Secretariat, in drafting a factual record, acts as a neutral administrator considering all sides of the matter at hand, and does not draw conclusions as to whether a Party has failed to effectively enforce its environmental law, rather leaves it to the public to decide on the meaning of the facts presented, and what follow-up to take, if any.[26] The Secretariat presents a draft factual record to the Council, and the Council may comment on the accuracy of the draft within 45 days (NAAEC Article 15(5)). The Secretariat then submits a final factual record to the Council, incorporating Party comments "as appropriate", and Council has 60 days to vote whether to make it public by a two-thirds majority vote (NAAEC Articles 15(6) and (7) respectively). The Council has never voted to withhold publication of a factual record,[27] and there has until the last few years been an apparent deference to the Secretariat's recommendations that factual records are warranted. However, observers of the SEM process have questioned the process' overall effectiveness in delivering on the transparency objectives of the Agreement, in part due allegedly to Council interference and structural defects (see Knox and Markell, *supra* note 21, at 524):

24 See NAAEC Article 15(1). Whether the response has adequately addressed the submitter's assertions, and whether there are central open questions about the assertions after the response, are some of the factors in the Secretariat's decision to recommend a factual record or not. See for example, SEM-09-005 (*Skeena River Fishery*), Determination under Article 15(1) (12 August 2011), at para. 34.

25 NAAEC Article 15(4) provides that:

> In preparing a factual record, the Secretariat shall consider any information furnished by a Party and may consider any relevant technical, scientific or other information:
>
> a) that is publicly available;
> b) submitted by interested non-governmental organizations or persons;
> c) submitted by the Joint Public Advisory Committee; or
> d) developed by the Secretariat or by independent experts.

26 Ibid. at Article 15(3) states, "The preparation of a factual record by the Secretariat pursuant to this Article shall be without prejudice to any further steps that may be taken with respect to any submission." The Parties have recently agreed that the Party's laws that were the subject of a factual record will report after one year following the publication of a factual record, on any actions taken to follow-up the matter at issue in a factual record. The latter follow-up process, although it would enhance transparency and public participation, is voluntary, and thus far has not resulted in every factual record issued after this Council decision was taken having been followed.

27 The CEC's "Registry of Submissions" page provides access to all publicly available information regarding submissions, including Council Resolutions to approve or deny the Secretariat's recommendations to develop a factual record, and/or to make public a factual record. Online at: http://www.cec.org/Page.asp?PageID=751&SiteNodeID=250.

The procedure is structurally biased in favor of the governments. It provides them rights that the submitters do not have: the governments may comment on a draft factual record before it is finalized; they may decide whether it may be published at all; and, most important, they may choose not to authorize it in the first place. Moreover, the governments have used their powerful position to tilt the playing field even more in their favor. Individual governments have sometimes declared part or all of their responses to be confidential or failed to cooperate with Secretariat inquiries in the course of preparing the factual record. Acting together in the Council, they have often delayed making decisions, as explained above, so that factual records are finally released many years after the submissions on which they were based.

In that connection, over the last two years the Council has voted against nearly all the Secretariat's recommendations that a factual record is warranted.[28] In the 20-year history of the process prior to the afore-mentioned Council terminated submissions, there had only been one other vote against recommendation of a factual record, and that was 15 years hence[29]. The Council has at the time of writing been taking a more negative approach to the Secretariat's recommendations in favour of developing a factual record, and this despite the Secretariat's providing the same meticulous reasoning and thorough research in support of all its recommendations as it has always done. Moreover, the Council has recently begun to question the Secretariat's inherent powers, such as those regarding termination of a submission or not due to the existence of pending proceedings.[30] The Council's recent *en masse* denials of Secretariat

28 See Council Resolution 14-04, online at: http://www.cec.org/Page.asp?PageID=122&ContentID=25784&SiteNodeID=1312&BL_ExpandID=566, noting that a factual record is not warranted with respect to SEM-11-03 (Protection of Polar Bears); Council Resolution 14-09, online at: http://www.cec.org/Page.asp?PageID=122&ContentID=25823&SiteNodeID=1312&BL_ExpandID=566, noting that a factual record is not warranted with respect to SEM-12-001 (BC Salmon Farms); Council Resolution 15-01, online at: http://www.cec.org/Page.asp?PageID=122&ContentID=25838&SiteNodeID=1330&BL_ExpandID=566, noting that a factual record is not warranted with respect to SEM-10-002 (*Alberta Tailings Ponds*); and, Council Resolution 15-02, online at: http://www.cec.org/Page.asp?PageID=122&ContentID=25859&SiteNodeID=1330&BL_ExpandID=566, noting that a factual record is not warranted with respect to SEM-13-001 (*Tourism Development in the Gulf of California*).

29 See Council Resolution 00-01, noting that a factual record is not warranted with respect to SEM-97-003 (*Quebec Hog Farms*), online at: http://www.cec.org/Page.asp?PageID=122&ContentID=1135&SiteNodeID=275&BL_ExpandID=566.

30 See *supra* note 27, Council Resolution 12-001 (*BC Salmon Farms*), where Canada and Mexico in the appended *Reasons for Council Instructions, by a Two-Thirds Vote, Regarding Submission SEM-12-001 (British Columbia (BC) Salmon Farms)* are of the opinion that the Secretariat must, on simple notice to the Secretariat that a pending proceeding exists pursuant to NAAEC Article 14(3)(a), cease and desist from any further analysis of a submission, and terminate the submission:

> The NAAEC and the Guidelines are very clear on the steps to be taken following the Party notification: the Secretariat is required to proceed no further with the submission and promptly notify the Council and Submitter that the submission file has been terminated without prejudice to the submitter's ability to file a new submission. *The Secretariat is neither directed nor authorized (explicitly or implicitly) by the NAAEC or the Guidelines to perform an additional analysis of a Party's notification, including assessing the validity of the pending proceedings addressed in such notification* [emphasis added].

recommendations that a factual record is warranted, coupled with attempts at diminution of the Secretariat's inherent powers, lends credence to arguments that the Council can reduce the effectiveness of the SEM process, and thereby also hinder the transparency provisions and SD Principle equivalent of the NAAEC.

33.3 Transparency and public participation in the NAAEC, SEM process

The transparency, public participation, and accountability principle on sustainable development permeate the NAAEC and especially the SEM process. This section will explore how the Agreement requires transparency, public participation, and accountability from the various organs of the CEC, and how these provisions accord with the tenets of sustainable development.

33.3.1 Provisions of the agreement

In the Preamble to the NAAEC, the Parties emphasize "the importance of public participation in conserving, protecting and enhancing the environment". It is suggested there that transparency is essential to meaningful participation, which in turn is central to the operation of the cooperative approach to sustainable development emphasized in the title and objectives[31] of the Agreement. An objective in Article 1 of the Agreement is to ". . . (h) promote transparency and public participation in the development of environmental laws, regulations and policies; . . .", and the fact that any person or organization resident in North America can initiate the SEM process[32], is evidence of the commitment to implementing this objective. The foregoing provisions of the NAAEC, give effect to the conditions in the New Delhi Declaration's Principle on Transparency and Public Participation, which states that:

> Public participation is essential to sustainable development and good governance in that it is a condition for responsive, transparent and accountable governments as well a condition for the active engagement of equally

The United States on the other hand, in its separate *Statement of the United States of America Explaining Its Position and the Reasons for Its Vote Regarding Submission SEM-12-001 (British Columbia (BC) Salmon Farms)* supported the Secretariat's decision regarding pending proceedings, and voted in favour of the Secretariat's development of a factual record:

> The United States therefore believes that neither proceeding is on the same matter as the submission, and consequently that a factual record on the submission would not duplicate effort or interfere with either proceeding. In addition, neither of these proceedings is being 'pursued by the Party' as stipulated in Article 45.3(a) of the NAAEC. Accordingly, the United States sees no basis upon which Article 14.3(a) of the NAAEC could be invoked in this instance to claim that the submissions process should halt with respect to SEM-12-001. Finally, because the Response does not address the substance of the submitters' assertions, the United States believes that questions are raised in the submission that have not been addressed by the Response and that could form the basis for a factual record.

31 Cooperation is explicit in the objectives listed in Article 1, paragraphs (b), (c), (g) and (f).

32 See NAAEC Article 14(1)(f).

responsive, transparent and accountable civil society organizations, including industrial concerns and trade unions. The vital role of women in sustainable development should be recognized.[33]

Specific transparency requirements are likewise embedded in the Article 4 obligation that each NAAEC Party "ensure that its laws, regulations, procedures and administrative rulings of general application respecting any matter covered by this Agreement are promptly published or otherwise made available in such a manner as to enable interested persons and Parties to become acquainted with them". Transparency also contributes to the overall functioning of the CEC in Articles 9(4)[34], 9(7)[35], 10(5)(a)[36] and notably, in Article 21(1)[37] which requires the Parties to cooperate with the Secretariat in providing information when officially requested. The general rule in favour of transparency is also underscored by the fact that there are limited exceptions to the rule spelled out in Article 39[38] (Protection of Information). In the event that differences might arise among the Parties' transparency practices, Article 10(1)(d) may be of assistance, as "[t]he Council . . . shall . . . (d) address questions and differences that may arise between the Parties regarding the interpretation or application of this Agreement".

33.3.2 *Commentary/background to the NAAEC*

The NAAEC emerged from an atmosphere of public participation in international law making,[39] and in the early days of the institution, there was rich public debate and commentary on its function, with various bodies and scholars having expressed opinions, for example:

33 See ILA New Delhi Declaration, *supra* note 6.

34 NAAEC Article 9(4) provides, "The Council shall hold public meetings in the course of all regular sessions. Other meetings held in the course of regular or special sessions shall be public where the Council so decides."

35 Ibid. at Article 9(7) provides, "All decisions and recommendations of the Council shall be made public, except as the Council may otherwise decide or as otherwise provided in this Agreement."

36 Ibid. at Article 10(5)(a) provides, "The Council shall promote and, as appropriate, develop recommendations regarding: public access to information concerning the environment that is held by public authorities of each Party, including information on hazardous materials and activities in its communities, and opportunity to participate in decision-making processes related to such public access".

37 Ibid. at Article 21(1) provides, "On request of the Council or the Secretariat, each Party shall, in accordance with its law, provide such information as the Council or the Secretariat may require, including: (a) promptly making available any information in its possession required for the preparation of a report or factual record, including compliance and enforcement data; and (b) taking all reasonable steps to make available any other such information requested."

38 Ibid. at Article 39(1) provides, "Nothing in this Agreement shall be construed to require a Party to make available or allow access to information:
(a) the disclosure of which would impede its environmental law enforcement; or
(b) that is protected from disclosure by its law governing business or proprietary information, personal privacy or the confidentiality of governmental decision making."

39 See Housman, *supra* note 3.

(i) "Public participation is the lifeblood of the CEC;"[40]

(ii) "[P]ublic participation should be approached [by the CEC] in its broadest sense;"[41]

(iii) "CEC activities should be conducted in an open and transparent fashion, so as to promote spontaneous participation by the public, to create relationships of mutual trust;"[42]

(iv) "Public participation was built into the structure of the Commission, not added as an afterthought;"[43]

(v) "The public will be actively involved [in the CEC's work] through the Secretariat, which will support the Council in its daily operations;"[44]

(vi) "By far the most innovative and substantial mechanism created within the NAAEC for fostering transparency and public participation is the citizen submission process provided for in Articles 14 and 15. Until relatively recently, international law only recognized State actors making claims against other State actors on the international stage. The 'whistleblower' provisions of Article 14 of the NAAEC are innovative in allowing citizens to directly access and participate in the Commission's decision-making processes;"[45]

(vii) "The purpose of the [SEM] process, therefore, is not to apply explicit sanctions based on the information in a factual record, but rather to engage the 'court of public opinion' by shining an international spotlight on perceived domestic enforcement issues and thereby avoiding the feared trilateral 'race to the bottom' that could result from opening trade between the Parties;"[46]

(viii) "Citizens play a significant role in the process by guiding that spotlight and contributing information regarding their concerns as related to the enforcement issues under examination. In bringing the facts out into the open, it is expected that the Parties to the NAAEC will become more accountable and thus more effective in their enforcement measures"[47]; and,

40 North American Institute, "Chairman's Statement," *Workshop: The North American Commission for Environmental Cooperation–Early Implementation. Report and Recommendations* (Vancouver, BC: March 1994).

41 Framework for Public Participation in Commission for Environmental Cooperation Activities (Oct 1999) available at http://www.cec.org/about-us/public-engagement-and-transparency/framework-public-participation-cec-activities (accessed Dec 7, 2012) [Framework].

42 Ibid.

43 Janine Feretti, "Innovations in Managing Globalization: Lessons from the North American Experience", 15 *Geo Int'l Envtl Law Rev* 367, 374 (2003)

44 North American Institute. "Keynote Address, Honourable Tom MacMillan [former Canadian Minister of Environment, 1985–88]," Workshop: The North American Commission for Environmental Cooperation–Early Implementation. Report and Recommendations (Vancouver, BC: March 1994).

45 Environmental Law Institute, *Final Report: Issues Related to Articles 14 and 15 of the NAAEC* (Washington, DC: 31 Oct 2003) at 3 [*Final Report*].

46 David L. Markell, "The Citizen Spotlight Process", 33 *Envtl F.* (Mar/Apr 2001) quoted in *Final Report, supra* note 45.

47 David L. Markell, "The CEC Citizen Submission Process: On or Off Course?", in Markell ed., *Greening NAFTA: The North American Commission for Environmental Cooperation* (2003) quoted in *Final Report, supra* note 45.

(ix) A fundamental purpose of the citizen submission process was "to enlist the participation of the North American public to help ensure that the Parties abide by their obligation to enforce their respective laws".[48]

Commenting on the transparency and public participation objectives of the NAAEC and how these contribute to sustainable development, two eminent scholars wrote that:

> [T]he objectives of NAAEC extend well beyond any trade-related matter and embrace trilateral cooperation for the improvement of the North American environment. [. . .] NAAEC's enumerated objectives . . . include tri-national cooperation for environmental conservation and protection, sustainable development, intergenerational equity, an emphasis on compliance and enforcement, the avoidance of new trade barriers, the development and enactment of economically efficient measures, and pollution prevention. Moreover, *transparency and public participation are presented as keys to accomplishing these goals.*[49]

Echoing the good governance principle, these same scholars also note that in the adoption of the NAAEC there was discussion of a need for international organizations to adopt "democratic and transparent" procedures:

> [U]nderlying public concern for the "greening" of NAFTA is a preoccupation with transparency and public participation. . . . [I]t is widely believed in the environmental NGO community that a more open set of institutions would be increasingly sensitive to environmental issues . . .[50]

33.3.3 Council's commitment to transparency

The Council has expressed its commitment to transparency and public participation in the cooperative work program and implementation of the SEM process, for example in the following Resolutions:[51]

(i) **Council Resolution 99-06 – *Adoption of the Revised Guidelines for Submissions on Enforcement Matters Under Articles 14 and 15* (28 June 1999)**

---

48 Raymond MacCallum, Comment, "Evaluating the Citizen Submission Procedure Under the North American Agreement on Environmental Cooperation" 8 *Colo. J. Int'l Envtl. L. & Pol'y* (1998) 395, 400.

49 Pierre Marc Johnson and Andre Beaulieu, *The Environment and NAFTA: Understanding and Implementing the New Continental Law* (Washington, DC: Island Press, 1996), 142 (emphasis added).

50 Ibid. at 162.

51 All CEC Council Resolutions can be viewed online at: http://www.cec.org/Page.asp?PageID=749&SiteNodeID=263&BL_ExpandID=566.

... RECOGNIZING that the revisions are designed to improve transparency and fairness of the public submissions process and are consistent with Article 11(4) of the North American Agreement on Environmental Cooperation (the "Agreement") and the Council's commitment to a process that honors the Secretariat's decision-making role under Article 14 of the Agreement ...

(ii) **Council Resolution 00-09 – *Matters Related to Articles 14 and 15 of the Agreement* (13 June 2000)**

... RECOGNIZING the need for transparency and public participation before decisions are made concerning implementation of the public submission process under Articles 14 and 15 of the NAAEC;

(iii) Council also reaffirmed a commitment to transparency in **Council Resolution 01-06 – *Response to the Joint Public Advisory Committee (JPAC) Report on Lessons Learned regarding the Articles 14 and 15 Process* (19 June 2001)** where it

... COMMITS to providing a public statement of reasons whenever it votes not to instruct the Secretariat to prepare a factual record.

(iv) **Council Resolution 02-01 – *Instruction to the Secretariat of the CEC to make public the Factual Record regarding the assertion that Mexico is Failing to Effectively Enforce Articles 134 and 170 of The General Law on Ecological Balance and Environmental Protection* (SEM-98-007) (*Metales y Derivados*) (7 February 2002)**

... AFFIRMING its commitment to a timely and transparent process.

Council Resolutions instructing the Secretariat to make public final factual records generally include some form of the latter clause, underscoring the historical presumption of Party cooperation with and transparency in the SEM process.[52]

52 For example, see: Council Resolution 03-03 – Instruction to the Secretariat of the Commission for Environmental Cooperation to make public the Factual Record for Submission SEM-99-002 (*Migratory Birds*); Council Resolution 00-04—Instruction to the Secretariat of the Commission for Environmental Cooperation to make public the Factual Record regarding the assertion that Canada is failing to effectively enforce s. 35(1) of the *Fisheries Act* with respect to certain hydro-electric installations in British Columbia, Canada (SEM-97-001); Council Resolution 02-01 – Instruction to the Secretariat of the Commission for Environmental Cooperation to make public the Factual Record regarding the assertion that Mexico is Failing to Effectively Enforce Articles 134 and 170 of The General Law on Ecological Balance and Environmental Protection SEM-98-007 (*Metales y Derivados*); Council Resolution 03-06 – Instruction to the Secretariat of the Commission for Environmental Cooperation to make public the Factual Record for Submission SEM-98-006 (*Aquanova*); Council Resolution 03-12 – Instruction to the Secretariat of the Commission for Environmental Cooperation to make public the Factual Record for Submission SEM-00-004 (*BC Logging*); Council Resolution 03-13 – Instruction to the Secretariat of the Commission for Environmental Cooperation to make public the Factual Record for Submission SEM-97-006 (*Oldman River II*); Council Resolution 03-14 – Instruction to the Secretariat of the Commission for Environmental Cooperation to make public the Factual Record for Submission SEM-98-004 (*BC Mining*); Council Resolution 03-15 – Instruction to the Secretariat of the Commission for Environmental Cooperation to make public the Factual Record for Submission SEM-97-002 (*Río Magdalena*); Council Resolution 04-07 – Instruction to the Secretariat of the

33.3.4 JPAC's advice to Council

The JPAC has frequently advised the Council on the need for more transparency and public participation. Regarding the latter, in May 1999, JPAC advised the Council that it was:

> convinced that the input of indigenous peoples within the CEC is both nec-essary and valuable. JPAC also recognizes the need to better involve other groups whose access to the CEC process has been similarly limited. JPAC is of the opinion, however, that the input of indigenous peoples is particularly critical and should be the subject of focus for the CEC.
>
> JPAC, therefore:
>
> ENCOURAGES Council to continue emphasizing the need for refin-ing and strengthening capacity building efforts within the CEC programs in order expand the involvement of the North American public, including indigenous peoples;
>
> RECOGNIZES that the National Advisory Committees (NACs) provide an entry point for the public and that this link should be further developed for indigenous peoples; . . .[53]

Later in 1999, having conducted a review of the Draft Framework for Public Participation, the JPAC advised the Council[54] to adopt the draft framework into the CEC's activities. The Framework contains an entire section on transparency and accountability, and states that, "CEC activities should be conducted in an open and transparent fashion, so as to promote spontaneous participation by the public, to create relationships of mutual trust".[55] In 2001, when faced with proposals for limiting the scope of factual records and requir-ing that the Secretariat submit a work plan to the Council prior to undertaking the development of a factual record, JPAC expressed in Advice to Council 01-07 "its frustration" and registered its "strong and considered objection" to these proposals since they would "violate Council's reaffirmation in Council

Commission for Environmental Cooperation to make public the Factual Record for Submission SEM-00-005 (*Molymex II*); Council Resolution 05-09 – Instruction to the Secretariat of the Commission for Environmental Cooperation to make public the Factual Record for Submission SEM-00-006 (*Tarahumara*); Council Resolution 07-02 – Instruction to the Secretariat of the Commission for Environmental Cooperation to make public the Factual Record for Submissions SEM-02-001 (*Ontario Logging*)/ SEM-04-006 (*Ontario Logging II*); Council Resolution 07-03 – Instruction to the Secretariat of the Commission for Environmental Cooperation to make public the Factual Record for Submission SEM-02-003 (*Pulp and Paper*).

53 JPAC Advice to Council J/99-05 Re: Expanding the Involvement of the North American Public, Including Indigenous Peoples in the Work of the Commission for Environmental Cooperation (18 May 1999).

54 In JPAC Advice to Council J/99-06 Re: Draft Framework for Public Participation in the Commission for Environmental Cooperation's Activities (18 May 1999).

55 Draft Framework for Public Participation in Commission for Environmental Cooperation Activities (May 1999). See s 3.3, "Transparency and Accountability" and also, s 3.2, "Efficiency and Timeliness."

Resolution 00-09 of its commitment to improve transparency".[56] JPAC then requested, in Advice 01-09, a public review of these proposals "in the interests of transparency".[57]

This commitment to transparency is reiterated in Advice to Council 03-05 and 04-03, in which JPAC admonishes Council in Resolution 00-09 to "increase transparency and public participation in the citizen submissions process".[58] Moreover, in 2002, the JPAC recommended to Council, "[a] work plan must be made available to the public at the same time as it is provided to the Parties".[59] JPAC also stated in Advice to Council 11-04, "[a] more effective SEM process [. . .] will [. . .] contribute to the sense of fairness and transparency that are at the heart of the NAAEC". Similarly, JPAC expressed, "[t]he prevailing public perception is that the credibility [in the SEM process] has been seriously eroded, primarily because of [. . .] resistance to full transparency [. . .]".[60] In the latter connection, JPAC has often shed light on the discrepancy between the Parties' statements in favour of transparency, and their actions which tend to undermine it. For example, in a letter dated 28 April, 2004 Donna Tingley, a former JPAC Member, wrote:

> The Council's resolutions limiting the scope of factual records and rulings on the sufficiency of information provided in submissions, in conjunction with the Council's decision to delay public review of its decision to define the scope of factual records and subsequent delays in conducting a review of this resolution appear to: 1) Jeopardize the commitment to increase transparency & public participation in the citizen submission process; 2) Violate the object & purpose, or "spirit" of Council Resolution 00-09 (which was a hard-fought compromise designed to allow the process to move forward and re-establish public confidence).[61]

Observers of the process have also noted that the Council's repeated failure to undertake its SEM process obligations in a timely fashion discourages potential submitters, because by delaying votes on Secretariat recommendations, or publication of a factual record, public confidence in the ability of the process to address

---

56 JPAC Advice to Council J/01-03/ADV/01-07 *Re: Citizen Submissions on Enforcement Matters under Articles 14 & 15 of NAAEC* (23 October 2001).

57 JPAC Advice to Council J/01-04/ADV/01-09 *Re: Request to Conduct a Public Review of Two Issues Concerning the Implementation and Further Elaboration of Articles 14 and 15* (30 November 2001).

58 JPAC Advice to Council J/03-05 *Re: Limiting the Scope of Factual Records and Review of the Operation of CEC Council Resolution 00-09 Related to Articles 14 and 15* (17 December 2003); see also JPAC Advice to Council J/04-03/ADV/Final, *Re: Review of the Operation of Council Resolution 00-09 on Matters Related to Articles 14 and 15 of the Agreement* (23 August 2004).

59 JPAC Advice to Council J/ADV/02-07/Rev.1 *Re: Work Plan Issue Related to Submissions under Articles 14 and 15* (2 May 2002), under the Heading "Transparency."

60 JPAC Advice to Council J/11-04/ADV/Final *Re: Submissions on Enforcement Matters (SEM) and Cross Border Movements of Chemicals in North America* (7 December 2011).

61 On file with the CEC Secretariat.

their assertions is shaken.[62] In response to such critiques, the Parties directed that the Guidelines be revised during the so-called "SEM Modernization Process",[63] and the Secretariat's SEM Unit and JPAC worked closely with Party representatives to include transparency and public participation enhancing provisions. Regarding transparency in the SEM modernization process the Council stated that (Press Release: CEC Council Adopts New Guidelines for Public Submissions on Enforcement Matters Unit):

> To promote transparency, the revised SEM Guidelines call for key SEM documents to be available in the three languages of the Commission on its website. Additionally, Council will provide written explanations for its factual record instructions, which will be posted on the CEC website. Moreover, Council members have committed to provide the Joint Public Advisory Committee (JPAC) with information on any new developments and actions taken regarding matters raised in a concluded submission.

As an additional tool for increasing public participation in the SEM process, the Secretariat's SEM Unit's then Director spearheaded the creation of an online portal to facilitate submissions, and assisted the Parties in creating an online tool to track the timeliness of submissions.[64] In the latter connection, since the establishment of the new process deadlines and the SEM Online Tracker, the Parties have more often than not significantly exceeded the Guidelines' allotted time to complete key steps in the SEM process, whereas the Secretariat has mostly acted well within the timelines.[65] Moreover, since the adoption of the Guidelines, the

---

62 Responding to question 12 of a JPAC questionnaire on the SEM process in 2012, which asked previous submitters how long it took for a submission to be processed, and whether that amount of time was considered reasonable, the submitter in SEM-99-002 (*Migratory Birds*) stated:

> The delay came between the Secretariat's request to prepare a factual record and the Council's vote instructing the Secretariat to prepare it. This took 331 days. Considering how frequently the Parties meet, this delay is unwarranted. If this was an isolated delay, further action would not be warranted. However, Council has frequently delayed votes instructing the Secretariat to prepare factual records. In Lake Chapala II, for example, Council took 876 days to vote. In Coal Fired Power Plants, it took 679 days. *These delays are inexcusable. They significantly erode public confidence in the process. Moreover, they delay possible solutions to the problem alleged by submitters* [emphasis added].

See *JPAC Questionnaire on Submitters' Experience with the Citizen Submission Process under NAAEC Articles 14 and 15*, at *International Environmental Law Project SEM-99-002 (Migratory Birds)*, Question 12 response, CEC Website, available online at: http://www.cec.org/Page.asp?PageID=834&ContentID=25124&SiteNodeID=1307&BL_ExpandID=567#Q10.

63 See "CEC Council Adopts New Guidelines for the Public Submissions on Enforcement Matters Process" (12 July 2012), CEC Website, available online at: http://www.cec.org/Page.asp?PageID=122&ContentID=25245&SiteNodeID=1204.

64 The SEM Online Portal can be accessed via the CEC website, here: http://www.cec.org/semportal/Public/Default.aspx?lang=en, and the SEM Compliance Tracker can be accessed via the CEC website, here: http://www.cec.org/sem-tracker/tracker.html.

65 Under Guideline 19.4 Council should normally vote within 60 working days on whether to instruct the Secretariat to prepare a factual record. Not once since adoption of the revised Guidelines has

Parties have neglected to provide the required explanations as to why they failed to meet procedural timelines, thus falling short of their commitments to transparency and timeliness made in the "SEM Modernization Process".[66] The JPAC has also neglected to demand transparency from the Council in the form of such written explanations concerning tardy votes on factual records.

33.3.5 Stages in the SEM Process where transparency is required

There are several areas in the SEM process where actions by the Parties, the Council, and the Secretariat are required in order to ensure transparency in the SEM process. These include:

(i) Admissibility of a submission.
(ii) Notification that exceptional circumstances exist to provide a response within 60 days.
(iii) Notification of pending proceedings.
(iv) Voting on secretariat recommendation for factual record.
(v) Designation of confidential information.
(vi) Provision of information for a factual record pursuant to Article 21(1)(a). And,
(viii) Follow-up to factual record.

33.3.5.1 Admissibility of a submission

The Secretariat has consistently held that Article 14(1) is not intended to be an "insurmountable screening device", which means that the Secretariat will interpret every submission in accordance with the Agreement and the Guidelines, yet without an unreasonably narrow interpretation and application of the Article 14(1) criteria.[67] In that connection, and in order to increase

---

Council voted within the 60 day deadline, and in the case of most submissions Council has doubled or tripled the deadline, for example: *Sumidero Canyon II* took 127 working days; *Wetlands in Manzanillo* took 199 working days; *Protection of Polar Bears* took 122 working days; *BC Salmon Farms* took 138 working days; *Alberta Tailings Ponds* took 115 working days; *Tourism Development in the Gulf of California* took 159 working days. Although the word "normally" in the Guidelines indicates that the deadlines aren't binding, Guideline 19.9 requires a written explanation as to why a deadline couldn't be met. The Council has failed to provide any such written explanations. Thus it appears that until the time of writing the "normal" course of business would actually require more than 60 working days for Council to vote on whether to instruct the Secretariat to prepare a factual record. Information on the afore-mentioned submissions may be found on the Secretariat's website at the Submissions on Enforcement Matters registry: http://www.cec.org/Page.asp?PageID=751&SiteNodeID=250.

66 Guideline 19.9 stipulates that, "Where the Council or a Party is unable to meet any applicable deadline, it should provide to the Secretariat a written explanation of the reason(s) for such and identify the date by which it plans to complete the relevant action; the Secretariat is to then so inform the Submitter. Where the Secretariat is unable to meet any applicable deadline, it should provide the Submitter and Council with an explanation of the reason(s) for such and identify the date by which it plans to complete the relevant action."

67 SEM-97-005 (*Biodiversity*), Determination pursuant to Article 14(1) (26 May 1998); SEM-07-005 (*Drilling Waste in Cunduacán*), Determination pursuant to Article 14(3) (8 April 2009).

transparency the Secretariat has maintained that: Article 14(1) has a relatively low threshold for admissibility, compared with a domestic legal proceeding or formal dispute resolution;[68] submitters should not be expected to present information that may be in the possession of a Party;[69] it is not anticipated that submitters conduct an exhaustive search for information;[70] and the submission procedure does not list means of proof,[71] nor does it establish procedural rules for conducting evidentiary proceedings.[72]

Party responses often include arguments as to why a submission is purportedly inadmissible,[73] or and why the Secretariat should not have proceeded to consider the submission.[74] The introduction of such arguments tends to shift the process from an administrative third-party facilitated one, toward an adversarial one, because the Secretariat is placed in a defensive posture and must provide reasoning in its determinations that responds to such objections. This changes this type of argumentation from the Parties the focus of an Article 15(1) determination away from the submitter's assertions and Party response, to a Party's procedural objections against admissibility or the Secretariat's authority. The latter arguments moreover increase the complexity of documents for the lay reader, thus frustrating the Agreement's transparency and public participation objectives. If the Parties wish to increase transparency through the SEM process as they have stated they do,[75] Party responses should simply focus on providing as much information as possible concerning their environmental law enforcement actions in the context of the submitter's assertions.

33.3.5.2 Notification that exceptional circumstances exist to provide a response within 60 days

Article 14(3)(a) provides that:

> The Party shall advise the Secretariat within 30 days or, in exceptional circumstances and on notification to the Secretariat, within 60 days of delivery of the request:
>
> (a) whether the matter is the subject of a pending judicial or administrative proceeding, in which case the Secretariat shall proceed no further [. . .]

Guideline 9.2 repeats the "in exceptional circumstances and on notification to the Secretariat" language. It is clear that when a Party notifies the Secretariat

---

68 SEM-97-003 (*Quebec Hog Farms*), Notification pursuant to Article 15(1) (29 October 1999), pp. 6–7, <http://goo.gl/PCOlS> (viewed on 24 January 2012).
69 SEM-04-005 (*Coal-fired Power Plants*), Determination pursuant to Article 14(1) (16 December 2004), p. 10, <http://goo.gl/ea4eH> (viewed on 6 January 2012).
70 Ibid. at 11.
71 SEM-09-001 (*Transgenic Maize in Chihuahua*), Determination pursuant to Article 15(1) (20 December 2010), §58.
72 Ibid.
73 See NAAEC, *supra* note 2 at art. 14(1).
74 See ibid.
75 See ibid. at art. 1(h).

under Article 14(3) that exceptional circumstances exist such that 60 days to respond is necessary, the Party in question should also in the interests of transparency describe what these "exceptional circumstances" are that prevent the Party from giving notification within 30 days.

It should also be underscored that in accordance with Guideline 6.2, submitters have 30 days to file a revised submission to the Secretariat and that no extension is given to them. The Secretariat SEM Unit has even terminated submissions when a revised submission is not filed within 30 days after request.[76]

During the SEM modernization process and negotiation of the revised Guidelines, the Secretariat SEM Unit advocated that revised Guideline 9.2 require a Party to state why "exceptional circumstances" exist that would prevent filing of a response within the 30-day period, but this suggestion was not adopted. To date the Parties have also not provided transparency as to why exceptional circumstances, with few exceptions, are almost always invoked by them at that stage of the proceedings.

33.3.5.3 Notification of pending proceedings

As noted above, Article 14(3)(a) provides that a Party may provide in a response "whether the matter is the subject of a pending judicial or administrative proceeding . . ." For the purposes of Article 14(3), the definition of "a judicial or administrative proceeding" is included in Article 45(3).

33.3.5.3.1 NARROW CONSTRUCTION OF ARTICLE 14(3)

The Secretariat's analyses of pending proceedings under Article 14(3) have consistently stated that the question of whether judicial or administrative proceedings are pending should be construed narrowly to give full effect to the object and purpose of the NAAEC.[77] Notification of pending proceedings under Article 14(3) does not lead to an "automatic" termination of the process; rather the Secretariat has always considered the following factors when analyzing a proceeding notified under Article 14(3):

(i)   whether the proceeding in question qualifies as a judicial or administrative proceeding in accordance with Article 45(3)(a);

(ii) whether it is being pursued *by the Party* in a timely fashion and in accordance with its law;

(iii) whether the proceeding is related to the same matter addressed in the submission; and,

---

76 For example, in SEM-02-005 (*ALCA Iztapalapa*), the Submitter did not provide a revised submission within the 30 days, and the process was terminated. In another matter, after filing submission SEM-03-004 (*ALCA Iztapalapa II*) the submitter indicated that it did not have enough resources to send a revised submission by courier.

77 See NAAEC, *supra* note 1 at art. 1.

(iv) whether the proceeding invoked by the Party in its Response appears to have the potential to resolve the matter(s) raised in the submission.

The Secretariat conducts such analysis in the interests of providing greater transparency to the public regarding any extant proceedings that concern "the same matter" at issue in the submission.

33.3.5.3.2 CONSIDERATION OF POTENTIAL INTERFERENCE AND DUPLICATION OF EFFORTS

Guideline 7.5(a) provides that the Secretariat consider whether "requesting a response to the submission is appropriate if the preparation of a factual record on the submission could duplicate or interfere with private remedies that are been pursued or have been pursued by the Submitter". In practice, this means that the Secretariat may take a different position from a court dealing with a particular case filed in a submission.

As stated in previous determinations, the Secretariat is not a court or tribunal and the SEM Process is not adversarial. Secretariat determinations are not binding on the Parties or submitters; factual records are not rulings or judicial opinions and the Secretariat has no curial powers. Secretariat determinations do not bind the Parties and factual records never include a finding on the asserted failure to enforce an environmental law:

> Therefore, it is not evident how the Secretariat's proceeding with review of a matter under Article 14, or recommending a Factual Record pursuant to Article 15 could actually "interfere" with ongoing domestic proceedings in the same way that conflicting court judgments could.[78]

It is thus submitted that Guideline 7.5(a) be carefully applied in favour of the public interest in transparency in the SEM process and that a narrow construction of Articles 14(3)(a) and 45(3) be given to Guideline 9.4 as stated above.

33.3.5.4 Scoping of a factual record

Article 15(2) authorizes the Council to instruct the Secretariat to develop a factual record by a two-thirds vote. Guideline 10.4 explicitly reaffirms that Council action is required and that a majority is sufficient to proceed. No unanimity is required.

In practice, the Council has, on several occasions, redefined the scope of a factual investigation recommended by the Secretariat, often without outlining the reasoning behind Council's decision. The Agreement does not anticipate the Council limiting the scope of a factual record and a contextual reading of Article 15(2) authorizes the Council only to vote on whether or not to instruct the Secretariat to prepare a factual record. A scholar commenting on the SEM Process stated:

78 SEM-07-001 (*Minera San Xavier*) Determination pursuant to Article 14(3) (15 July 2009), §44.

To suggest that the power to "oversee" the Secretariat gives the Council a role in respect of matters relating to the Secretariat where no such explicit role has been given would render unnecessary those provisions in the Agreement that make certain Secretariat responsibilities subject to Council direction and control. It would be contrary to accepted principles of treaty interpretation under which an interpretation should not be adopted that renders provisions of a treaty meaningless.[79]

In Council Resolution 10-05, authorizing the preparation of a factual record respecting Submission SEM-06-005 (*Species at Risk*), the Council decided to limit the number of species under consideration without providing reasons for doing so. Other scope-limiting Council Resolutions have purported to:

(i) list questions that a factual record must address;[80]
(ii) list items in the context of a submission that a factual record shall include;[81]
(iii) define the geographical area subject to the factual record;[82]
(iv) dismiss the environmental law in question;[83]
(v) define cases to which a factual record shall be limited;[84]
(vi) consider whether a submission contains sufficient information;[85] and
(vii) include proceedings or new information not included in a Party response.[86]

None of the above-mentioned situations included an explanation of the Council's reasons for limiting the scope of the factual record, and including such reasons would be in the interests of transparency, and encourage public confidence in the process.

79 Donald M. McRae, "Information Developed by Independent Experts and the Authority of the Secretariat of the Commission for Environmental Cooperation" (February 2007)(McRae paper), §63 (citing the WTO Appellate Body in *United States – Standards for Reformulated and Conventional Gasoline* (WT/DS2/AB/R 29 April 1996): "An interpreter is not free to adopt a reading that would result in reducing whole clauses or paragraphs of a treaty to redundancy or inutility.") The above excerpt and reference from the McRae paper is cited in a memorandum from the SEM Director to the Chair of the JPAC (30 January 2001).
80 Council Resolution 08-03, Authorizing a factual record for submission SEM-04-005 (*Coal-fired Power Plants*).
81 Council Resolution 04-05, Authorizing a factual record for submission SEM-03-005 (*Montreal Technoparc*).
82 Council Resolution 08-01, Authorizing a factual record for submission SEM-03-003 (*Lake Chapala*).
83 Council Resolution 06-07, Authorizing a factual record for submission SEM-04-007 (*Quebec Automobiles*); Council Resolution 08-01, authorizing a factual record for submission SEM-03-003 (*Lake Chapala*).
84 Council Resolution 01-10, Authorizing a factual record for submission SEM-99-002 (*Migratory Birds*).
85 Council Resolution 03-05, Deferring vote of a factual record for submission SEM-02-001 (*Ontario Logging*).
86 Council Resolution 08-01, *supra* note 83.

Limitation of the scope of a factual record should be avoided by the Council, except in such cases where the Secretariat has clearly made an egregious error in its recommendation for a factual record as transparency of the process is thereby frustrated. Considering the plain language of the Agreement in its context, only two voting scenarios are contemplated at the Article 15(2) stage:

(i) based on a two-thirds or unanimous vote, the Council instructs the Secretariat to develop a factual record; or,
(ii) based on a two-thirds or unanimous vote, the Council instructs the Secretariat not to develop a factual record.

However, since the Council considers that it is authorized by the NAAEC to limit the scope of a factual record, there often appears to be a third scenario:

(iii) based on a two-thirds or unanimous vote, the Council instructs the Secretariat to develop a factual record *on parts of the Notification* and the Council provides its reasons.

A distinction should be drawn between a Council Resolution that authorizes a factual record on parts of a recommendation and a Council Resolution redefining what a record should include.

33.3.5.5 *Designation of confidential information*

Article 39(2) of the Agreement and Guideline 17.2 allow any Party to classify or designate any information as confidential. Normally, confidential information designated in a Party response relates to pending proceedings and occasionally has classified information related to environmental compliance.[87] On other occasions, confidentiality has been invoked by a Party when providing information for a factual record.[88]

When considering information classified by a Party as confidential, the Secretariat has redacted those sections from the public version of a determination. As a result, the Secretariat has dismissed a Submission without providing reasons to the Submitter based on confidential claims, while providing its reasons solely to the Party.[89]

In some cases, otherwise publicly available information provided by a submitter has even been classified as confidential by a Party in a Response.[90]

Transparency as a principle of sustainable development law should guide any Party decision to redact information in the Articles 14 and 15 process, and accordingly:

---

87 See SEM-09-002 (*Wetlands in Manzanillo*), Response pursuant to Article 14(3) (12 October 2010).
88 SEM-03-003 *supra* note 83.
89 SEM-09-001 (*Transgenic Maize in Chihuahua*), Determination pursuant to Article 15(1) (20 December 2010), §157; SEM-05-001 (*Crushed Gravel in Puerto Peñasco*), Determination pursuant to Article 15(1) (24 October 2005) at 12; and, SEM-08-001 (*La Ciudadela Project*) Determintion pursuant to Article 15(1) (12 August 2010), §48.
90 SEM-09-002 (*Wetlands in Manzanillo*), Response pursuant to Article 14(3) (12 October 2010).

(i) confidentiality should only apply where information has already been classified under the Party's domestic laws and procedures;

(ii) the Party should always provide a summary of confidential information to be
disclosed publicly in a timely manner, in the spirit of current Guideline 17.3; and,

(iii) there should be recognition that under a Party's laws, information may be
declassified over time and thus, available to the public.

33.3.5.6 *Provision of information for a factual record pursuant to Article 21(1)(a)*

Under Article 21(1) the Secretariat may request and gather information for
development of a factual record. The words "promptly making available"
(Article 21(1)(a)) and "taking all reasonable steps" (Article 21(1)(b)) are used in
the Agreement. Guideline 11.1 lists various sources of information, including
"information . . . furnished by a Party", that the Secretariat "will consider".

The Secretariat has found itself in situations where requests for information are answered with arguments that such information is confidential and
as a result cannot be included in a factual record;[91] that the Secretariat has
no authority to request information because the Party considers it exceeds
the scope of a factual record;[92] or simply, no information is provided at all.[93]
When the Secretariat finds itself not being able to provide information, it
reports that fact in a factual record:

> The Secretariat consulted the [Party] on other means of proof available to
> the [authority] and why they were not considered at the investigation stage.
> When no response was forthcoming, the Secretariat asked [the Party] to
> provide an explanation in the event that it could not legally respond to the
> request; however, no explanation was obtained.[94]

No deadline is established in Guideline 11 and as a consequence, a request
for information from the Party may never be received. The need for timely
provision and receipt of information for a factual record is underscored by
the words "promptly making available" and "taking all reasonable steps" in
Article 21(1). It is recommended that a timeline, similar in length to the
30 days provided in Article 14(3), be incorporated in any future revised
version of Guideline 11. It is also submitted here that the Secretariat may
file independent requests for information before any department, agency or
government body of the Party in question.

---

91 SEM-03-003 *supra* note 83.
92 Ibid.
93 SEM-04-005 *supra* note 83.
94 SEM-02-005 (*ALCA Iztapalapa*) Factual Record at 65–66.

33.3.5.7 Follow-up to factual record

As noted above, the publication of a factual record is considered the final step in the Articles 14 and 15 process. A factual record does not include opinions or comments on the quality of environmental law enforcement by a NAAEC Party. Most importantly, it does not include a determination on whether a Party is failing to effectively enforce its environmental law. It is a document providing neutral information on assertions concerning effective environmental law enforcement practices with respect to a situation identified by a member of the public in North America, in accordance with Article 14(1). Although the submission is closed with the publication of a factual record, NAAEC Article 15(3) does foresee that further steps "may be taken with respect to any submission". Following up on the situation at issue in the submission after publication of the factual record would give better effect to the objectives of the Agreement, and publicly demonstrate the Parties' commitment to constantly improving their environmental law enforcement through public participation.[95]

During the Guidelines revision process, a member of JPAC suggested that a Council resolution instructing the Secretariat to publish the final factual record could provide that, once published, the subject-matter of the submission be subject to further review by an independent expert group, by JPAC, or by some other body. The Parties did not adopt that suggestion, but did publicly commit to providing follow-up one year after the publication of a factual record. To date, such follow-up has yet to take place in any coordinated and public manner.

33.4 Conclusion

The factual Record for Submission SEM-96-001 (*Cozumel*) is often cited as a successful example of the SEM process and in particular, as a model of transparency and efficiency. Taken as a whole, it took less than two years to be completed and at the end, effective environmental change on the matters raised in the submission was reported by the Submitters. Determinations issued during the process were timely because they addressed only admissibility criteria, and analyzed facts raised in the Submission and in the Response. The factual record is only 41 pages (without annexes) and has 102 footnotes.

The Parties have the opportunity to guide the process towards a more simple, effective and transparent SEM process. By taking lessons from and studying the New Delhi Principles on Sustainable Development, the NAAEC could be implemented in a manner that will benefit present and future generations and improve environmental law development and enforcement through greater transparency and public participation.

95 The JPAC has also made suggestions respecting follow-up: See JPAC Advice to Council J/08-01/ ADV/Final, *Re: Submissions on Enforcement Matters: From Lessons Learned to Following up Factual Records* (27 February 2008), para 6 (http://cec.org/Page.asp?PageID=122&ContentID=958&SiteNodeID=290&BL_ExpandID=).

34 Principles of inter-generational equity, public participation and good governance in the Inter-American Development Bank's oversight mechanism

Alexandra Harrington and
Valentina Duran

34.1 Introduction

Throughout this volume, a number of sustainable development principles have been examined in a variety of subject and regional contexts. This chapter adds to the discussion by introducing an evolving system of organizational oversight that incorporates the principles of inter-generational equity, public participation and good governance.

The Inter-American Development Bank (IDB) functions as the regional development financing entity for States in the Latin American and Central American Region.[1] The IDB finances infrastructural projects and projects that promote social, economic, cultural and environmental growth as well as projects aimed at strengthening the rule of law and governance within Member States, including public and private projects.[2] These projects can be solely funded by the IDB or can be co-funded with public and/or private funders.

In its current Institutional Strategy, it is explained that the IDB's function is to balance sustainable growth and decreases in poverty with the needs of "vulnerable" States and the need to establish economies that attract private investment.[3] With this in mind, the IDB has recognized the inter-connectedness inherent in sustainability and has embraced this as a way to connect other policy areas such as gender issues and diversity.[4] The IDB specifically recognizes the dangers of climate change to the region and to each of its Member States and seeks to finance projects that counteract climate change impacts and are geared toward mitigation and adaptation.[5] This policy supports the principle of inter-generational equity in itself by ensuring that funding decisions do not harm future generations or, where there will be some degree of immediate harm, the goal is to ensure long-term benefit to current and future generations in order to promote equity.[6]

---

1   Update to the Institutional Strategy 2010–2020 (Washington, D.C.: Inter-American Development Bank, 2015) vi.
2   Ibid. at 7–8.
3   Ibid. at v.
4   Ibid. at 4.
5   Ibid. at 9.
6   See ibid.

This chapter examines the ways in which the IDB's policies are subjected to oversight in ways that reflect the importance of the sustainable development principles of inter-generational equity, public participation, and good governance. Although these principles might be tacitly incorporated into the IDB's oversight structure and complaint evaluations, this in no way downplays the vital role of inter-generational equity, public participation and good governance in the IDB system. Instead, it can be seen as indicating the adaptability of these principles even in areas where they are not expressly incorporated into governing rules and regulations.

34.2 Independent Consultation and Investigation Mechanism

Throughout the course of the IDB's history, the drive for transparency, accountability and ensuring compliance with the terms of the organization's requirements and lending policies has increased.[7] As part of this path toward openness and public engagement, the IDB created the Independent Consultation and Investigation Mechanism (ICIM) in 2010.[8] The foundational and operational concept of the ICIM relies heavily on its ability to function as an independent oversight entity that is able to review the IDB's decision-making process from a third-party perspective.[9] In this way, there is an attempt to balance the interests of the IDB as a funding entity for beneficial projects with the interests of the communities and areas that are the intended beneficiaries of the funded project.[10]

The ICIM's primary role is to investigate allegations regarding the awarding of IDB funding and subsequent harms that result from the funded projects.[11] However, the ICIM is intended as the body of last resort for those alleging harms and wrongdoing – there is a clear preference for settling issues that arise within the framework of the standard IDB management system.[12] Even when complaints rise to the ICIM level, there are two available tiers of review, and typically a complaint will start at the less onerous tier.[13]

The first tier of entrance into the ICIM system is the Consultation Phase. The goal of this phase is conciliation, and it is established "to provide [. . .] an opportunity for the Parties to address the issues raised . . . in a voluntary, flexible and collaborative manner."[14] The second tier in the ICIM system is the Compliance Review Phase, the goal of which is to "offer [. . .] an investigative process related to the issues raised . . . to establish whether the Bank has failed to comply with any of its Relevant Operational Policies and whether that has caused Harm to the Requesters."[15] There are a number of specific, topic- and population-focused

---

7 Policy of the Independent Consultation and Investigation Mechanism (Washington, D.C.: Inter-American Development Bank, 2015) 5.
8 Ibid.
9 Ibid.
10 Ibid.
11 Ibid.
12 Ibid.
13 Ibid. at 6.
14 Ibid.
15 Ibid.

IDB policies that can be used as the basis for a complaint before the ICIM[16] – for the purposes of this chapter some of the most important aspects of these policies address indigenous communities, environmental issues, disaster risk management, access to information and concerns over the impacts of community relocation when needed to complete Bank-funded projects.[17]

The ICIM provides a solid structure within which to evaluate issues of funding and operational compliance for the IDB. However, it must be noted that the ICIM is limited in its scope and must wait for a complaint to be brought by a willing group of complainants rather than having the ability to review IDB operations and take investigative action where it finds appropriate. As discussed below, there have been cases of credible threats to the lives and livelihoods of those who might complain to the ICIM. Although these actions have been attributed to entities receiving funding rather than the IDB, the potential for harm may pose a limit on the extent to which public participation in the consultative process and the ICIM process occurs in a meaningful way. This potential further undermines the principle of good governance – particularly in terms of the prevention of corruption and the protection of human rights – and the principle of inter-generational equity by threatening to undermine the integrity of current development on future generations.

34.3 IDB operational policies

As noted above, the IDB's decisions are subject to review under a number of Operational Policies that relate to subject-specific content. Below are the Operational Policies which have been most examined by Compliance Review Panels throughout the ICIM's history.

34.3.1 Access to Information Policy

In 2010, the IDB implemented its Access to Information Policy (AIP) with the goal of establishing "its transparent use of funds," and creating a more open relationship between the IDB, other funders, project leaders, involved communities and other stakeholders.[18]

There are four principles that govern and inform the AIP and, consequentially, the ICIM. These principles are 1) maximization of access to information, 2) creating narrow and clear exceptions for IDB activities and decisions, 3) creating "simple and broad" access to information on the IDB's activities, and 4) creating and supporting explanations for IDB decisions on access to information and for the right to review these decisions.[19]

In order to implement these principles, the AIP sets standards for implementation. For Principle 1, the standard is that the IDB "reaffirms its commitment to

---

16 Ibid. at 7.
17 Ibid.
18 Access to Information Policy (Washington, D.C.: Inter-American Development Bank, 2010) 1.
19 Ibid. at 3–4.

transparency in all of its activities and therefore seeks to maximize access to any documents and information that it produces and to information in its possession that is not on the list of exceptions."[20] For Principle 2, the standard is that "[a]ny exceptions to disclosure will be predicated upon the possibility, narrowly and clearly defined, that the potential harm to interests, entities or parties arising from disclosure of information would outweigh the benefits, that the Bank is legally obligated to non-disclosure, or has received information with the understanding that it will not be disclosed."[21] For Principle 3, the standard is that the IDB's "[g]uidelines for maximizing access to information will include clear and cost-effective procedures and timelines for processing requests and will be based on use of a system for classifying information according to its accessibility over time."[22] Finally, for Principle 4, the IDB's standard is that it will provide a full and clear explanation of reasons for denial of requests for information, and that it will also establish an appeals mechanism that can be used in the event that the requester believes that the request was denied in error.[23]

The AIP itself is a clear attempt to implement the principle of public participation at the IDB level and is laudable in this regard. While other aspects of IDB funding and operational policies require the IDB to encourage – and indeed ensure – that national and local laws are complied with by those who implement the project as well as the IDB itself, the AIP has no such requirement for access to information. As such, the AIP misses an opportunity to ensure transparency and public access to information at the national level by failing to address the need for national and local governments to comply with dedicated laws for this.

34.3.2 Environment and Safeguards Compliance Policy

The Environment and Safeguards Compliance Policy (ESCP) was implemented in 2006 as the most recent iteration of the IDB's environmental policy statement.[24] It explicitly notes the impacts of the Rio Declaration and sustainable development *per se* on the IDB's environmental policies and explains that it

> takes into account current changes and realities that influence environmental sustainability . . . [and] recognizes the need to enhance conditions for social and economic development and the important role that sound management of natural resources and the environment plays in this process.[25]

Further, the ESCP incorporates key sustainable development instruments such as the Rio Declaration, Agenda 21 and the Johannesburg World Summit on

---

20 Ibid. at 3.
21 Ibid.
22 Ibid. at 4.
23 Ibid.
24 Environment and Safeguards Compliance Policy (Washington, D.C.: Inter-American Development Bank, 2006).
25 Ibid. at 2–3.

Sustainable Development.[26] In terms of scope, the ESCP "encompasses cultural, social, and economic aspects" relating to the environment, "identifies environment as a dimension of development to be maintained and internalized across all sectors," and affirms "the Bank's commitment to adopt measures that promote corporate environmental responsibility."[27] The ESCP's objectives focus on three areas – encouraging and supporting the development of environmental sustainability as a core element of Member State policy, promoting corporate environmental responsibility, and, essentially for the ICIM, "ensuring that all Bank operations and activities are environmentally sustainable."[28]

The ESCP's central policy implementation methods are centered on two areas, environmental policy mainstreaming and environmental safeguards.[29] Mainstreaming centers on including environmental concerns and principles throughout the IDB's own practices and procedures as well as encouraging similar measures in Member States and in specific projects.[30] The IDB's policies regarding environmental safeguarding are of particular relevance and highlight the place that environmental concerns have in Bank operations. As the ESCP explains,

> [i]n line with sustainable development practices, the Bank takes a general precautionary approach to environmental impacts. . . . [it] favors avoiding negative environmental impacts; when impacts are unavoidable, Bank-financed operations require mitigation measures; and for impacts that cannot be fully mitigated, compensation or offsets should be implemented.[31]

Throughout the ESCP there is an emphasis on the importance of environmental impact assessments (EIA) and the ESCP establishes three levels of classification to indicate the depth of EIA required for a project.[32] Category A projects are those "likely to cause significant environmental and associated social impacts, or have profound implications affecting natural resources."[33] These projects require EIAs or similarly focused assessments in order for the IDB to consider providing funding.[34] Even if funding is provided for a Category A project, the IDB is to continue its oversight of environmental and associated practices and impacts, for example boards or other forms of oversight.[35] Category B projects are those "likely to cause mostly local and short-term negative environmental and associated impacts and for which effective mitigation measures are readily available."[36] These projects typically will require an environmental assessment of some form and require the creation and implementation of an environmental and social management

26 Ibid. at 3.
27 Ibid.
28 Ibid. at 3–4.
29 Ibid. at 4.
30 Ibid.
31 Ibid. at 8.
32 Ibid. at 9.
33 Ibid.
34 Ibid.
35 Ibid.
36 Ibid.

plan.[37] Category C projects are those "likely to cause minimal or no negative environmental and associated social impacts."[38] These projects typically will not require an EIA or other form of assessment to be conducted however they will be subject to routine IDB oversight for compliance and environmental practices.[39]

The ESCP is a significant contribution to the principle of inter-generational equity by ensuring that the short and long term aspects of a project are to be assessed and, where possible, subject to mitigation. The complaints below demonstrate that, in application, the terms of the ESCP in relation to EIAs are not evenly applied because of vague conceptions as to appropriate public participation – specifically consultations with stakeholders and local communities. This creates the opportunity for communities to be disenfranchised from full information regarding and/or participation in public discussions on projects.

34.3.3 Disaster Risk Management Policy

In 2007, the ICIM implemented the Disaster Risk Management Policy (DRMP) to mitigate the potential for damage to the environment and local communities in its funded projects.[40] The stated purpose of the DRMP is "to guide the Bank's efforts to assist its borrowers in reducing risks emanating from natural hazards and in managing disasters, in order to support the attainment of their social and economic goals."[41]

In order to implement the policy, the IDB is required to conduct appropriate evaluations and to withhold funding approval from a project which "would increase the threat of loss of human life, significant human injuries, severe economic disruption or significant property damage related to natural hazards."[42] Included in the analysis for the DRMP are elements to determine whether there is a significant risk of disaster promotion as a result of the project and, if the determination is positive, the potential for prevention and mitigation measures that could be used.[43] In the event of a disaster during the course of the project – natural or otherwise – the DRMP requires the IDB to continuously assess and update its funding plans and terms in order to further the overall policy purpose.[44] These assessments can be negative – such as revoking or downsizing project funding – but also can be positive – for example the provision of additional funding to ensure that the project is able to withstand similar future disasters.[45]

Disasters are by their nature unpredictable and the DRMP reflects an attempt to ensure that the adequate measures are taken to prevent and mitigate disasters to

---

37 Ibid.
38 Ibid.
39 Ibid.
40 Disaster Risk Management Policy (Washington, D.C.: Inter-American Development Bank, 2007).
41 Ibid. at 2.
42 Ibid. at 4.
43 Ibid. at 6.
44 Ibid.
45 Ibid. at 6–7.

the extent possible. Absent from the discussion, however, is a clear sense of how the principle of inter-generational equity underpins the construction of disaster assessment in the DRMP. This is perhaps best illustrated by the vague understanding of the timeline of disasters to be prevented/mitigated and how far into the future the project must look in order to satisfy the terms of the DRMP.

34.3.4 Operational Policy on Indigenous Peoples

The IDB implemented the Policy on Indigenous Peoples in 2006. The goal of this Policy is to ensure that the IDB

> recognizes the need to consolidate conditions that enable indigenous peoples to exercise the right to participate effectively in determining their own political, economic, social and cultural future within the framework of participation in democratic systems and of the construction of multicultural states.[46]

There are two set policy objectives. The first focuses on supporting the identity of indigenous peoples, including their ability to exert governance powers, and the second focuses on "safeguard[ing] indigenous peoples and their rights against adverse impacts and exclusion in Bank-funded development projects."[47]

Due to the nature of indigenous peoples as rights holders and also as citizens of IDB Member States, the Policy recognizes the place of the IDB as uniquely positioned to encourage and protect the rights of indigenous peoples on several levels. Under the Policy, this requires the IDB to act as a facilitator of dialogue and development between indigenous communities and States/regions in which they are located.[48] Part of this involves incorporating the views and voices of indigenous communities in development and funding decisions.[49]

The Policy requires that the IDB take steps to ensure prevention and mitigation of harms to indigenous communities from the projects it funds.[50] To this end, when deciding whether to fund a project it is required that the IDB

> will require and verify that the project proponent conduct an evaluation to determine the seriousness of potential adverse impacts on physical and food security, lands, territories, resources, society, rights, traditional economy, way-of-life and identity or cultural integrity of indigenous peoples, and to identify the indigenous peoples affected and their legitimate representatives and internal decision-making procedures. This evaluation will include preliminary consultations with potentially affected indigenous peoples.[51]

---

46 Operational Policy on Indigenous Peoples (Washington, D.C.: Inter-American Development Bank, 2006) 1.
47 Ibid.
48 Ibid. at sect. IV.
49 Ibid.
50 Ibid. at sect. IV (B).
51 Ibid. at 4.4(a) (i).

Similar to the DRMP, the Policy, which intends to incorporate some aspect of future generations, is unclear as to the extent to which the principle of inter-generational equity must be incorporated in project reviews of potential harms and benefits. Additionally, while the project proponent is required to include an examination of potential impacts on indigenous communities, the extent of community involvement in this examination is vague, making it difficult to fully incorporate the principle of public participation.

34.4 ICIM Reviews

34.4.1 The Pando-Monte Lirio Hydroelectric Power Plant Review, Panama, 2012

In the Pando-Monte Lirio Hydroelectric Power Plant Review (Pando-Monte), the ICIM was asked to review the IDB's funding and support for two hydroelectric dams that were part of a larger, 19 hydroelectric project for Panama.[52] The IDB's initial decision to fund the project was made as part of its dedication to ensuring clean energy projects were developed in Central America.[53]

The complaint was brought by a coalition of local farmers, clergy and religious leaders, and environmental and social activists on the grounds of potential environmental and social impacts from the project that were in violation of the IDB's lending policies.[54] This coalition was particularly concerned that the project would impact on a river which was

> central to the history, the ecology, and the socio-economic fabric of the region . . . [and that] in spite of the creation of employment and related value added by this and similar projects, the Requesters fear that these changes will adversely affect their lives and those of their families and children.[55]

Specifically, the coalition alleged that potential environmental damage, damage to the quality of drinking water, damage to the quality of water used for agricultural purposes, increased flooding potential in the local area, extinction of fish and other biodiversity in the region, and an overall imbalance to the ecological and economic conditions in the region.[56] They also stated their fears and concerns that the overall design and structure of the dam designs were flawed and alleged that the IDB was at least partially responsible for this by tacitly approving the plans through approving funding[57]. In this sense, the complaint was itself focused on the preservation of future generations and of inter-generational equity

---

52   Independent Consultation and Investigation Mechanism Compliance Review PM-MICI001-2010, "The Pando-Monte Lirio Hydroelectric Power Project" (2012) 10.
53   Ibid.
54   Ibid.
55   Ibid. at 13.
56   Ibid. at 14.
57   Ibid. .

by highlighting the impacts that the claimed project deficiencies would have on the ability of children to benefit from the culture and biodiversity associated with their communities. The complaint was also founded in the complainants' beliefs that, of all the funders and governmental entities involved in the project, the IDB was a trusted leader in Panama and in terms of "contributing to sustainable and equitable development."[58]

Throughout the Review, the Panel heavily weighed the interests of development as well as the communities that would be impacted by the development and those advocating for environmental concerns in the areas.[59] From the outset, the Panel noted that within the IDB itself there were vocal protests that the decision to fund the project required more environmental and other information, yet ultimately it was decided to go forward despite these concerns.[60] These findings and admissions can be seen as promoting transparency and good governance within the IDB system by placing emphasis on the importance of the rule of law – regardless whether at the national or international organization level. Further, these findings underscored the importance of socially responsible investment, an essential element of the principle of good governance, by emphasizing the need for the IDB to follow its own protocols when issues of environmental and social impacts were involved.

In terms of environmental damage allegations, the Panel determined that the IDB did not in fact comply with the ESCP and that in "[d]eviating from its tradition of sustainable development practice, the Bank did not take the usual precautionary approach to dealing with potential environmental impacts."[61] Further, the Panel determined that there had been no required assessment of alternatives that would prevent/mitigate environmental damage and that the benefits of continuing on despite the likely environmental damage had not been established.[62] This, in turn, affected the adequacy of the EIA.[63] As noted in the paragraph above, this implicated the principle of good governance by highlighting the IDB's failure to invest in a socially responsible manner where serious issues of sustainability – and, thus, inter-generational equity – were involved.

Additionally, the Panel determined that the IDB had failed to comply with the ESCP by not adequately performing assessments as to the impact of the project on the biodiversity of the region and on the integrity of the river to be harnessed for hydroelectric power.[64] Specifically, the Panel noted that the public hearings held in regard to the project included invitations to select invited participants, rather than the public in general.[65] In terms of consultation and public participation, the Panel agreed with the complaint's allegations that there had been insufficient

58 Ibid. at 16.
59 See ibid.
60 Ibid. at 18.
61 Ibid. at 20.
62 Ibid.
63 Ibid.
64 Ibid. at 21.
65 Ibid. at 23.

local consultation regarding the project and that the EIA, when produced, did not adequately reflect the concerns raised by the local community.[66] The Panel found these inconsistencies yet also recognized the potential importance of the project if properly assessed and implemented. This embraces the principle of public participation, particularly in an instance where the threat to the community was existential, because the right to express opinions, an essential human right, was denied to members of affected communities. By validating the harms caused by the provision of incomplete information to the affected communities, the Panel's determination further implicated the principle of public participation.

This complaint represented the first time that an ICIM Panel issued a report, along with a set of findings and recommendations, according to the system established by the IDB. With this in mind, the Panel offered the IDB guidance as to how to bring funding into compliance with its Operational Policies in the event it decided to proceed with the project.[67] The Panel noted that it was important to examine the IDB's actions and the complainants concerns "as an incentive for learning for the Bank as a whole."[68] Further, the Panel discerned the opportunity to use the complaint as a method to review the strategic programs of the IDB and its lending practices rather than one particular case.[69]

These recommendations focused on curing the inherent flaws in the EIAs and other assessments as well as assisting local authorities in their capacities to monitor the projects.[70] Additionally, the Panel provided suggestions for future IDB scrutiny of funding – particularly public–private funding ventures – to ensure compliance with IDB Operational Policies.[71]

The Panel's future recommendations had a number of areas of focus. One of the most important was on "enhancing the synergies between the Bank's public and private sector ventures".[72] The importance of this was highlighted by the Panel through the lens of the Pando-Monte case. It opined that, had these synergies been implemented for the Pando-Monte project, the need for review would have been far less since many of the issues brought before the Panel could have been addressed and fixed prior to this.[73] Indeed, the Panel found "that this absence of complementarities between public and private sector development efforts is partially responsible for the observed flaws."[74]

Another essential observation and recommendation for the IDB's funding operations came in terms of "strategic sequencing," which the Panel deemed an essential element of private funding decisions that is missing from public funding

66 Ibid.
67 Ibid. at 27.
68 Ibid. at 28.
69 Ibid.
70 Ibid.
71 Ibid. at 28.
72 Ibid.
73 Ibid.
74 Ibid.

decisions more often than not.[75] The Panel noted that the type of public–private project that was at issue in Pando-Monte was likely to increase in use in the future, requiring the IDB to face similar funding and compliance issues. With this in mind, the Panel stated that such future projects "need to have an assured success rate . . . with respect to their adherence to often complicated safeguard policies,"[76] and that "the IDB might need to develop a more consistent strategy for sequencing its financial engagements and better exploit synergies between its public and private sector portfolios."[77]

Within the limitation of its parameters as an oversight body for the IDB alone rather than the entire project, the Panel's findings and recommendations were ground-breaking. However, to the extent that these findings provided recommendations for curing issues within the Pando-Monte project, the Panel did not ensure the complete application of the principles of inter-generational equity, public participation or good governance because it failed to highlight the option of cancelling the IDB's funding of the project. This provided precedent for serious violations of IDB policies that incorporated essential tenets of sustainable development principles not proving fatal to funding, which can weaken the place of sustainable development principles in funding decisions.

34.4.2 Marena Renovables Wind Project Review, Mexico, 2015

In the Marena Review, the Panel examined the IDB's funding decisions and activities in regard to a large, privately owned wind farm project in the Mexican State of Oaxaca.[78] Ownership of the wind farm was private as authorized by, and with permission from, local and national authorities.[79] From the beginning, the project was designated by the IDB as a Category A project under the ESCP due to the high likelihood of significant negative environmental and social impacts in the region.[80]

The complaint was brought by residents of the area affected, with specific focus on the impacts of the project on their traditional cultural practices and methods of living.[81] Specifically, the complaint claimed that there was harm to 1) self-government and safety due to threats from those involved in the project; 2) the communities' unique cultural ties with and relationships to the land, which was being (or would be) impacted by the project, including aspects of biodiversity; and 3) their cultural identity, as related to the land, and their ability to practice culturally important ceremonies that are connected to land impacted by

---

75 Ibid.
76 Ibid.
77 Ibid.
78 Independent Consultation and Investigation Mechanism Compliance Review ME-MICI002-2012, "Marena Renovables Wind Power Project" (2015) 1.
79 Ibid.
80 Ibid.
81 Ibid.

the project.[82] The impacts on the land held notable significance to the complainants due to their traditional cultural practice of communal landholding.[83]

From the outset, the Panel deemed that there were flaws with the application of various IDB Operational Policies in the handling of the Marena project.[84] This was noted in the Panel's initial finding that, overall,

> [t]hose omissions resulted in the project being notable mainly for the opacity of its preparation and execution, in clear violation of the principles of transparency that distinguish the IDB Group. The Bank's Operational Policies clearly state the information disclosure obligations and the time at which such disclosure should occur; nevertheless, in the case of the "Marena Renovables Wind Project," the Bank omitted to comply with them, and no legitimate reasons were found for such omission.[85]

The Panel was particularly concerned with the character of the project and the precedent it would set as well as the impacts it would have. As was noted, "[t]his project was a first in multiple arenas: the first located in close proximity to the ocean, the first to be built on land actively under communal management . . . and the first to be inaccessible by land due to territorial conflict among communities."[86] Due to this, identifying the "social impacts, the mitigation plan, the raising of awareness, and socioculturally appropriate consultation with the affected population was extremely important."[87]

While the Panel determined that the classification of the project as a Category A project was correct, it also found that the IDB did not begin with the proper examination of impacts and mitigation.[88] This meant that, when the IDB eventually did seek to address these issues, its efforts were remedial rather than proactive and were ineffective.[89]

Further, although an EIA was conducted with some degree of thoroughness, the Panel found issues in the methods of inclusion during the consultation process and in the post-EIA consultation process.[90] In making this assessment, the Panel highlighted the importance of consultation with affected communities in terms of understanding the potential issues for the project and in terms of building good will and communication.[91] Not only did this constitute a violation of the ESCP, it also was found to be a violation of the AIP.[92] These findings highlight the place of

82 Ibid.
83 Ibid. at 2.
84 Ibid.
85 Ibid.
86 Ibid.
87 Ibid.
88 Ibid. at 44.
89 Ibid.
90 Ibid. at 45.
91 Ibid.
92 Ibid. at 51.

public participation and good governance in the Panel's decision-making process in terms of providing access to project-held information and ensuring that the essential rights of freedom of opinion and transparency were incorporated. In this context, they can be seen as highlighting inter-generational equity since the concerns expressed by the complainants related not only to the current generation but also to future generations and their abilities to enjoy the same relationship with the land and their culture.

Moving beyond interpretation of the IDB's policies, the Panel noted that the IDB failed to require the local authorities and corporate borrowers to comply with Mexican national and local environmental laws.[93] This in turn undermined the legality of the project as well as the good faith of the IDB as a lender that is required to ensure the observance of relevant laws as part of its lending evaluations.[94] In this finding, the Panel can be seen as invoking tenets of good governance and holding the IDB to them since it required that the Mexican government comply with the rule of law and that the IDB ensure the national government complied with the rule of law. Further, the Panel's findings can be seen to endorse the right of citizens to have both national governments and international organizations uphold the law as part of the principle of good governance.

In terms of compliance with the IDB's Operational Policy on Indigenous Peoples, the Panel found that there were violations due to the lack of comprehensive consultation and the lack of good faith in negotiations with indigenous communities.[95] Specifically, the Panel found that the IDB violated the Operational Policy on Indigenous Peoples, "neglected to consider the cultural impacts on the communities," and violated the essential decision-making structure of the communal land holding indigenous communities affected.[96] Such violations were of import as the project area was located within territory where at least half the population was classified as belonging to one of several possible indigenous communities.[97] Of particular concern to the Panel was the presence of the Ikoot community in the area, as it is one of the rare indigenous communities in the region that is solely dependent on fishing for subsistence rather than agriculture.[98] As such, the Panel was keen to ensure protections for this community and its traditional ways of life and livelihood.[99] Together, this directly relates to the concept of preserving and honouring inter-generational equity since the complainants sought to protect traditions for the current and future generations, thereby endorsing the rights of future generations to share in the benefits of their traditional lands and culture.

Each ICIM Compliance Review report is a separate entity and does not function as binding authority for future complaints, however the Panel noted that

93 Ibid. at 46.
94 Ibid.
95 Ibid. at 58.
96 Ibid.
97 Ibid. at 13.
98 Ibid. 13–14.
99 Ibid.

Compliance Review reports do have persuasive authority in its recommendations section.[100] Combining the established facts of the Marena Review and the recommendations from previous panels in different complaints, the Panel recommended that the IDB solidify its operations to include assessments of the social impacts of projects.[101] In this vein, the Panel made the following observations:

> The social license to operate – that is, the acceptance or approval of a project by a local community – is emerging as a critical factor for the success of development projects. Increasingly, companies view the attainment of the social license as an important aspect of the management of environmental and social risks. Furthermore, going beyond the minimum regulatory requirements is an important component of establishing a company's reputation. We respectfully suggest taking measures to enhance the framework of the Operational Policies in their social perspective.[102]

Overall, the Marena Panel finding is an important step for the recognition of the IDB's place as an oversight body for the implementation of national and local laws at the beginning of a project and for the importance of involving indigenous community landholders in project evaluations. However, it must be noted that the scope of the Panel's review was temporally limited to the period prior to and immediately following the award of funding for the project. As such, the Panel was unable to make findings that would indicate the place of the principles of inter-generational equity, public participation and good governance in the IDB's continuing oversight requirements for projects in the post-award stages.

34.4.3 *Panama Canal Expansion Program, Panama, 2015*

The Panama Canal Review presented the Panel with issues related to the potential expansion of the Canal and its offshoots.[103] After an initial review, the IDB determined that the expansion was a Category A project and began to undertake the appropriate evaluations.[104] According to the Panel, the Category A determination was in compliance with the ESCP.[105]

One of the primary issues for the Panel was whether the IDB complied with the terms of the DRMP when assessing and attempting to mitigate the seismic impact of the project.[106] The Panel found that there were submissions from experts and others regarding the known potential seismic impacts from the project however the IDB did not include the seismic issue or potential mitigation

100 Ibid. at 6.
101 Ibid.
102 Ibid. at 61.
103 Independent Consultation and Investigation Mechanism Compliance Review PN-MICI002-2001, "Panama Canal Expansion Program" (2015) 5.
104 Ibid.
105 Ibid.
106 Ibid. at 1–2.

efforts in its disaster risk assessment.[107] This was found to result in harm to the complainants, particularly in terms of fear of seismic activities and their potential gravity in the future.[108] As a result of these findings, the Panel recommended that the IDB conduct a full assessment of disaster risks associated with the project – including seismic risks – and require the client to take necessary steps to mitigate detected risks.[109] The Panel further recommended that the IDB's future findings be made public so that those potentially affected by the project would have the opportunity to understand how mitigation efforts are used.[110] In this way, the Panel brought the principle of public participation to the future of the project through the requirement of transparency before and after findings were made. Additionally, the principle's endorsement of the human right to access information including that related to the environment was also tacitly endorsed in these findings and recommendations.

There were two instances in which the Panel was called upon to assess the IDB's compliance with its policies in regard to water. In terms of the ESCP, the Panel examined whether the expansion project would cause shortages and threats to long-term water sustainability for human consumption in the project area.[111] Although the Panel credited the IDB with recognizing water sustainability as an issue for the project, it found that the IDB failed to thoroughly evaluate the issue before making an environmental determination for the project.[112]

As a result, the Panel found that the complainants were at risk of water access issues – and at the extreme level perhaps even a disaster – without identified mitigation options.[113] The consequence of this finding was a recommendation that the IDB complete an assessment of the water sustainability issue and that this assessment be made publicly available.[114] These findings and recommendations impact directly on the principle of public participation as well as inter-generational equity, as much of the concern regarding water here related to the ability of current and future generations to have adequate and safe access to it in the long-term. An assessment of this ability could not be made without access to information – including that related to environmental and social concerns – from the project proposing entity, again highlighting the role of the principle of public participation.

The Panel also examined the question of whether there was a proper assessment of the impact of development within a watershed area under the Operational Policy on Indigenous Peoples.[115] This included the potential for expropriation of land that was tied to the complainants' cultural and economic lives.[116] While the

---

107 Ibid.
108 Ibid. at 2.
109 Ibid.
110 Ibid.
111 Ibid. at 3.
112 Ibid.
113 Ibid.
114 Ibid.
115 Ibid. at 4.
116 Ibid. at 15.

Panel concluded that the IDB had not fully failed to comply with the terms of the Policy, it still recommended that the IDB facilitate measures to ensure that those living in the affected areas not be harmed by the project development.[117] As a result, the Panel's determination can be seen as attempting to require inter-generational equity elements be incorporated into future decisions regarding the project by imparting concerns over the benefits to be enjoyed by future generations and how they would be impacted by the project.

The Panama Canal Panel sought to ensure a balance between a potentially vital development project and the needs and safety of the affected communities and the environment. In rendering its findings and recommendations, the Panel was adamant about elements of the principles of public participation and good governance being necessary elements for proper evaluation under the IDB's operating principles. However, while the Panel was firm in its endorsement of the need to ensure proper assessments regarding the impacts of the project on areas that are key to the principle of inter-generational equity, it was less forthcoming in its elaboration of how such impacts were to be weighed and mitigated.

34.5 Conclusion

In creating and empowering the ICIM, the IDB significantly advanced the place of the principles of inter-generational equity, public participation and good governance in its funding decisions and project selection processes.

The ICIM is a unique tool among regional banks in that it has a two-step process for lodging and evaluating complaints that starts with efforts at conciliation prior to quasi-judicial review. This allows for the settling of complaints where possible – thus allowing the decision-making of the bank to change in a less adversarial and more holistic way. At the same time, the availability of a quasi-judicial system allows for an impartial review of the IDB's practices that not only provides findings and recommendations for the particular complaint but also provides general recommendations for changes to or strengthening of IDB policies and practices.

As a relatively new entity, decisions at the Consultation and Compliance Review levels are not numerous. However, the Compliance Panel Reviews already provide insights into the ways in which these panels will tacitly endorse and apply sustainable development principles to ensure that the IDB's projects comply with its own Operational Policies and with the IDB's overall goals, as well as applicable local and national laws. The work of Compliance Review Panels to date demonstrates a commitment to not only apply the Operational Practices but further to move forward and change the IDB's policies or, where appropriate, adopt new policies. A primary example comes from the Pando-Monte Review, in which the Panel recommended that the IDB's future lending practices take into account the increasing importance for public–private funding strategies.

In this way, the Compliance Review panels have served and will continue to serve as conduits of the principles of inter-generational equity, public participation and good governance into many areas of law and policy.

117 Ibid. at 4.

Part V
Conclusion

35 Judicial deliberations and progress on sustainable development

Marie-Claire Cordonier Segger, Alexandra Harrington and Francesse Joy Cordon

35.1 Introduction

Over the past three decades, international disputes and adjudication on sustainable development questions have become more prevalent, with certain discernable trends. The decisions of international courts and tribunals on sustainable development are increasingly sophisticated recognizing the environmental, social and economic dimensions of the questions before them, and demonstrating a grounding in the principles identified in the 2002 ILA New Delhi Declaration of Principles of International Law Relating to Sustainable Development, as annexed to the outcomes of the 2002 World Summit on Sustainable Development.

Such progress in the application of these principles is evident not just in decisions rendered by the International Court of Justice but also in the decisions of other international tribunals and dispute settlement bodies. These tribunals and dispute settlement bodies range from international to regional bodies and cut across specialty area that relate to sustainable development, including trade, human rights and the environment.

The international rule of law, and the particular role of the judiciary in its process, is increasingly important in matters of sustainable development. Judgments of international courts, tribunals and other quasi-judicial bodies are of special significance, both in what is said (and how it is said), and in what is included (and what is omitted). The most respected and widely cited decisions offer signals to guide future international expectations and understandings when economic, human rights and environmental priorities intersect or appear to collide.

Building on existing literature that mainly focuses on particular pillars of sustainable development – economic, environmental or social – in international adjudication and decision-making, this volume has brought fields together in their areas of intersection. It has done this by considering the last three decades of international dispute resolution from an integrated perspective, similar to the one adopted in the United Nations 2015 Sustainable Development Goals, which emerged from a process of consensus building that has developed over time from before the 1972 UN Conference on the Human Environment through the 1992 UN Conference on Environment and Development, the 2002 World Summit on Sustainable Development, and the 2012 UN Conference on Sustainable Development, among other processes.

This concluding chapter brings the volume together by: (i) summarizing and highlighting the trends in the use of sustainable development principles in international courts and tribunals; (ii) drawing lessons from the plethora of relevant decisions in order to consider the potential for similar application of these principles in treaties and their dispute settlement, including under the compliance mechanisms of the Paris Agreement; and (iii) charting a way forward for future legal scholarship and practice on sustainable development.

35.2 Linking the Sustainable Development Goals, the principles of international law on sustainable development and the Sofia Guiding Statements on judicial elaboration of the principles

International legal regimes develop in an interactional manner over decades.[1] Their progress, and evolution, is iterative. As noted throughout this volume, in debates that began prior to the adoption of the 1972 Stockholm Declaration and continued through the 1987 Brundtland Commission's Legal Experts Group on Principles of International Law for the Protection of the Environment and Sustainable Development, the 1992 Rio Declaration, the 2002 World Summit on Sustainable Development Johannesburg Plan of Implementation, and in several international experts' reports and other processes, States and legal scholars have sought to identify principles of international law on sustainable development. In 2002, the International Law Association's Committee on the Legal Aspects of Sustainable Development, after 10 years of study, drew the outcomes of these global debates together in its 2002 ILA New Delhi Declaration on Principles of International Law relating to Sustainable Development as a Resolution of its 70th Biennial Conference in New Delhi, India. The Declaration drew together profound legal analysis of the international jurisprudence up to that time and careful review of many international treaties that sought to promote sustainable development in their object and purpose.[2]

This volume notes that in the ILA New Delhi Declaration, seven principles of international law are highlighted, which characterize treaties related to sustainable development and are reflected in the decisions of international courts and tribunals on sustainable development. States have a duty to respect the following principles: (1) sustainable use of natural resources whereby States have

---

1   On interactional accounts of international law, see J. Brunée and S.J. Toope, *Legitimacy and Legality in International Law* (Cambridge: CUP, 2010); and J. Brunée and S.J. Toope, 'International Law and Constructivism: Elements of an Interactional Theory of International Law' (2000) 39 *Colu. J. Trans'l. Law* 19, 19–74. See also J. Brunée and S. J. Toope, "Persuasion and Enforcement: Explaining Compliance with International Law" (2002) XIII *Finnish Ybk Int'l L.* 1, 1–23. And see J. Brunée, "Coping with Consent: Lawmaking under Multilateral Environmental Agreements" (2002) 15 *Leiden J. Int'l L.* 1, 1–52.

2   See M.C. Cordonier Segger and A. Khalfan, *Sustainable Development Law: Principles, Practices and Prospects* (Oxford: OUP, 2004).

sovereign rights over their natural resources, and a corresponding duty not to cause (or allow) undue damage to the environment of other States in the use of these resources; (2) inter- and intra-generational equity and the eradication of poverty; (3) common but differentiated responsibilities and respective capabilities; (4) the precautionary approach to human health, natural resources and ecosystems, transferring the burden of proving lack of significant harm from an undertaking to the proponent, in cases of scientific uncertainty; (5) public participation, backed by access to information and justice; (6) good governance, with measures to support rule of law, coherence and anti-corruption; and perhaps most telling (7) integration and interrelationship of human rights and social, economic and environmental objectives. This last principle may sometimes be called (in short-hand) a 'principle of sustainable development', holding that States must take into account the environmental and social (including human rights) aspects of economic plans or projects, integrating related measures and costs, to promote more sustainable development. To avoid confusion, however, it can also be identified as 'the integration principle.'

The analysis in this volume demonstrates that these non-exhaustive 'sustainable development principles' are gaining certain recognition by States and other actors in international law. Many are not yet recognized as binding rules of customary international law, and in some cases, they might never be. However, they are increasingly recognized as principles and also made operational in binding international treaties, forming part of international law and policy in the field of sustainable development. In this way, the principles are operationalized and legitimized even if not part of a binding treaty regime.

Indeed, the ILA New Delhi Declaration itself notes that "sustainable development is now widely accepted as a global objective and that the concept has been amply recognized in various international and national legal instruments, including treaty law and jurisprudence at international and national levels." In this way, the New Delhi Declaration assisted in resolving long-standing debates as to the status of sustainable development in international law. Rather than one principle of international law that all development must be sustainable, there are several principles, which collectively seek to promote more sustainable development as an object or purpose. These principles are recognized in many laws and treaties, and are used to guide the interpretation and implementation of legal instruments that aim to promote sustainable development. They are also found guiding the institutions, regulators, and authorities which work to comply with international laws.

This view, adopted in the New Delhi Declaration, has been validated in international policy. In 2012, the United Nations Conference on Sustainable Development called upon countries to agree to a series of time-bound global objectives and targets, building on the 2000 Millennium Development Goals (MDGs) and called on all countries and stakeholders, including through their international treaty bodies and organizations, to assist in achieving these goals. By 2015, these universal 'Sustainable Development Goals' (SDGs) had been adopted in the United Nations. In the United Nations General Assembly Resolution *Transforming our World: The 2030 Agenda for Sustainable Development*, the UN and its Member States agreed on 17 SDGs and 169 related time-bound targets and specific means of implementation.[3] Iteratively, as expert law and governance reviews by the United Nations Environment Programme and the Centre for International Sustainable Development Law (CISDL) have demonstrated, these SDGs and their targets can be found in the object and purpose of many important international treaties in the field of sustainable development.[4]

35.3 Sustainable development principles in international courts and tribunals

The principles identified in the New Delhi Declaration have also begun to be increasingly used by judges and authorities to reach decisions and resolve conflicts in international courts and tribunals. These principles are also informing the reasoning of quasi-judicial, informal dispute settlement bodies such as the accountability mechanisms of the World Bank and the regional development banks.

In 2003, the International Law Association formed a second learned committee of international experts, each nominated as a leading authority of their country on law and sustainable development, for the purpose of analysing the legal status and implementation of the norms in international courts and tribunals. As explained earlier in this volume, this further ILA Committee on International Law on Sustainable Development, through a new decade of legal research, comparative analysis and debate, drafted the *2012 Sofia Guiding Statements on the Judicial Elaboration of the 2002 New Delhi Declaration of Principles of International Law Relating to Sustainable Development* (Sofia Guiding Statements) to provide interpretative guidance for dispute settlement bodies seeking a better understanding of ways to reflect the New Delhi Principles in their decisions. The Committee's final report, adopted by the biennial Conference of the ILA in Sofia, Bulgaria, provided conclusions on the state of application by international courts and tribunals of the New Delhi sustainable development principles. The analysis of the Committee of the most relevant jurisprudence, including the 2010 decision by the International Court of Justice (ICJ) in *Pulp Mills on the River Uruguay*, underscored the need for a principled approach to sustainable development in international jurisprudence and decisions, *viz*:

> [t]he relationship between sustainable development and global justice is a nuanced one . . . However, between States with actual disputes, poised on the brink of either debilitating conflict or peaceful settlement of their differences, a commitment to global justice will not provide a sound legal basis for a decision, as such, to be taken by judges and lawyers.[5]

---

3 A/RES/70/1.

4 See M.C.Cordonier Segger and E. Mrema, eds., *The Contribution of International Law, Policy and Governance to the Sustainable Development Goals*, Issue Briefs (Montreal and Nairobi: CISDL/UNEP, 2016).

5 ILA Report (2010) 805.

This volume shares much of the analysis that was carried out by the international experts on the Committee, considering decisions of international courts and tribunals across four decades from 1972 to 2012 and across geography and subject matter.

The analysis suggests, in essence, that the first principle mentioned in the New Delhi Declaration, the duty of States to ensure sustainable use of natural resources, represents an emerging rule of general customary law, with particular normative precision identifiable regarding shared and common natural resources. Its contours elaborated by the International Court of Justice (ICJ), this principle is relevant to the rules of transboundary resources management, and also to international law addressing humanitarian, scientific and boundary issues, as reflected in the 1996 *Advisory Opinion on the Legality of the Threat or Use of Nuclear Weapons*, discussed throughout, and in the 2004 *Advisory Opinion on the Legal Consequences of the Construction of a Wall in the Occupied Palestinian Territory* (discussed in Chapter 7). Indeed, in the 2011 ICJ Decision in *Costa Rica v Nicaragua* (Chapter 9), Costa Rica alleged that Nicaragua's acts of cutting trees, constructing a canal in Costa Rican territory and dredging along the San Juan River caused serious damage to its internationally protected wetlands and would affect the water flow into the Colorado River in Costa Rica. It bears emphasis that Costa Rica also asked the ICJ, in 2005, to declare Nicaragua guilty of violating international law by denying Costa Rica navigation and other rights on the San Juan River. The dispute illustrated the need for States to respect the sustainable use of natural resources and the ability of good governance principles to ease conflicts over territorial integrity and natural resources. The decision of the ICJ to nominate the Ramsar Convention on Wetlands of International Importance, a venerable treaty for optimal use of the world's wetlands ("the source of sustainable development"), to which both disputing countries were Parties, in a scientific advisory role in the resolution of the conflict, was particularly apposite.

Similarly, the World Trade Organization Dispute Settlement Body (WTO DSB) has found the duty of States to ensure sustainable use of natural resources relevant to its decisions under the WTO Agreements, also reflecting elements of the common but differentiated responsibilities, precaution, and integration principles, in resolving disputes related to trade, the environment and sustainable development (Chapter 18). For instance, in the 1998 *US – Import Prohibition of Certain Shrimp and Shrimp Products (US – Shrimp)* case,[6] while a WTO Panel found the US import prohibition of shrimp and shrimp products from countries that did not use a certain fishing net which excluded endangered sea turtles could constitute an "arbitrary and unjustifiable" discrimination under Article XX of the General Agreement on Tariffs and Trade (GATT),[7] the prohibition was within the Article XX(g) exception in view of the ban's objective of helping conserve exhaustible natural resources like the turtle species often inadvertently caught in shrimp nets.

United Nations human rights bodies and regional human rights courts' jurisprudence helped interpret this principle, along with other sustainable development

---

6 WTO, *United States – Import Prohibition of Certain Shrimp and Shrimp Products* (6 November 1998) WT/DS58/AB/R, DSR 1998:VII, 2755.

7 Ibid. at para. 7.

principles, as being inextricably linked with the international human rights regime. With the growing recognition of a healthy environment as a necessary precondition for the full enjoyment of human rights, the human rights bodies have accepted arguments that causing environmental degradation can violate human rights, especially indigenous rights, and conversely, that measures to safeguard human rights can improve environmental protection (Chapter 19). For instance, the African Commission on Human and People's Rights, in two landmark cases – *Social and Economic Rights Action Centre (SERAC) v Nigeria*[8] and *Centre for Minority Rights Development (Kenya) v Kenya*[9] – drew on case law developments in the Americas and other regions of the world in taking sustainable development principles into account (Chapter 20). This illustrates not only the place that sustainable development principles have before such bodies but also the portability of regional court decisions to other courts that are seeking to incorporate human rights and sustainable development into meaningful jurisprudence.

Second, aspects of the principle of equity and the eradication of poverty have come to be reflected in decisions of the ICJ and other international courts. As noted in the Sofia Guiding Statements, equity incorporates notions of inter-generational equity, intra-generational equity and substantive equality, while the goal of poverty eradication should, where appropriate, contextualise and inform judicial and quasi-judicial decision-making when matters of sustainable development are raised. Though judicial bodies and quasi-judicial bodies cannot alone address the social, economic, governance and political issues that invariably form key aspects of such disputes, it is nevertheless incumbent upon judicial and quasi-judicial bodies to further such principles of equity and fairness in accordance with their judicial function. This is an instance in which judicial and quasi-judicial bodies are uniquely placed to serve their mandates while also serving as champions of equity and fairness across generations and regardless the status of those involved in matters at hand.

Indeed, in the *Case Concerning Gabčíkovo-Nagymaros Project (Hungary/Slovakia)* (1997) (Chapter 10), the ICJ regarded the obligation of due diligence as "part of the corpus of international law relating to the environment".[10] This and subsequent decisions manifest the ICJ's willingness to consider the principles of equity and sustainable use of natural resources, along with public participation, good governance and transparency, and integration, and the consequences of such adoption in future disputes coming before the ICJ. The Court upheld the right of Hungary and future generations to an equitable share of the Danube River course. The Court also ordered the Parties to conduct further consultations and assessments on the effects of the Gabčíkovo power plant. In his separate opinion, H.E. Judge C.G. Weeramantry stated, "[s]ustainable development is thus not merely a principle of modern

---

8 2001 AHRLR 60.

9 IHRR vol 18 No 1 (2011) 254.

10 *Legality of the Threat or Use of Nuclear Weapons*, Advisory Opinion, ICJ Reports 1996 (I), p. 242, para. 29.

international law. It is one of the most ancient of ideas in the human heritage."[11] Judge Weeramantry's sage words - and the sentiment behind them - have become a beacon for the place of sustainable development in judicial and quasi-judicial settings across the globe.

Equity, together with the principles of public participation and access to information and justice, good governance, and integration were also brought to bear by the tribunal in the *Abyei-Sudan* case (Chapter 11), especially during the peace negotiations and determination of the allocation of sharing rights and the dual special administrative zone in this wartorn area. In this case, the Permanent Court of Arbitration also appears to take account of several New Delhi principles on sustainable development in order to determine the resolution of the dispute.

Third, as noted in the Sofia Guiding Statements, the principle of common but differentiated responsibilities (CBDR) has a recognized status in treaty law, case law and State practice but would be strengthened as a normative feature of sustainable development if there was further reliance upon it by judicial bodies, thus allowing the legal principle to be understood and legally embedded as distinctive from the political discourse in which it is most often currently utilized. This volume has demonstrated the ways in which CBDR has been and can be used by and before judicial bodies. As the volume highlights, there is a strong place for CBDR in future courts and tribunals and, thus, as a reinforcing mechanism for the essential qualities of sustainable development principles.

ITLOS, which has jurisdiction over disputes concerning the 1982 United Nations Convention on the Law of the Sea and the agreements concluded under its aegis, serves as a welcoming jurisdiction for cases concerning sustainable development. ITLOS has interpreted and taken CBDR into account, along with other sustainable development principles such as precaution, the duty to ensure sustainable use of natural resources, and good governance, in deciding the cases before it and in granting provisional measures. Such cases actually offer several of the leading international judicial statements on the interpretation of the principles of sustainable development. For instance, in the *Responsibilities and Obligations of States Sponsoring Persons and Entities with Respect to Activities in the Area (Seabed Mining Advisory Opinion)* (Chapters 13, 14), ITLOS acknowledged the differences among States in performing their direct obligations with respect to the Common Area.

Further, within the WTO framework, this principle finds certain elements of reflection in the Special but Differential Treatment provisions of almost all WTO agreements and therefore the resolution of various WTO disputes (Chapter 15). As discussed above in this volume, which considered the WTO's controversial application of CBDR in various cases, certain elements can be learned from WTO analysis. For instance, the WTO Panel in *India – Agricultural Products*,[12] concerned the right to set import restrictions that considered the economic development of

---

11 ICJ Reports (1997) 110.
12 WTO, *India – Quantitative Restrictions on Imports of Agricultural, Textile and Industrial Products* (22 September 1999) WT/DS90/R, as upheld by the Appellate Body Report, WT/DS90/AB/R, DSR 1999:V, 1799.

less-developed country members. The principle, according to the analysis in Chapter 15, is subject to limits for discrimination to be justifiable: (i) when differentiation is only temporary; (ii) when differentiation does not imply a perverse incentive to prolong the use of outdated technologies; (iii) when developing countries are provided with some form of assistance to allow for their meaningful participation in solving problems; and (iv) when differentiation does not translate to a blanket exemption from responsibility on the part of developing countries.

Fourth, as noted in the Sofia Guiding Statements, the principle of the precautionary approach to human health, natural resources and ecosystems, has significant and increasingly precise legal implications, notwithstanding ongoing debate surrounding its formal legal status, and is linked to the recognition of requirements to conduct environmental impact assessments (EIAs) as obligations under international law in certain circumstances. In the 2009 *Pulp Mills on the River Uruguay (Argentina v Uruguay)* decision (Chapters 7 and 10), the ICJ held that EIAs are generally necessary for major development projects under the obligations of general international law, including customary international law. EIAs must be performed prior to project implementation, and upon commencement, monitoring of environmental consequences must be continuous. On the other hand, as discussed above, the WTO, while affirming elements of the precautionary principle as a principle of international environmental law, did not find the need to pronounce on its general status in customary law, instead finding a certain limited reflection of the principle in the WTO Agreement on Sanitary and Phytosanitary Measures at Article 5.3.

In addition to the ICJ and WTO, the PCA, ITLOS, and regional tribunals have also applied the precautionary principle to resolve disputes submitted before them. For instance, in the *Seabed Mining Advisory Opinion* (Chapter 14), ITLOS applied precaution in requiring States to mandate EIAs and conduct due diligence. The tribunal also enjoined States to take the necessary precautionary measures in pursuing potentially harmful commercial enterprises. The Caribbean Court of Justice and courts in the Caribbean region have applied the precautionary principle, particularly in the management of fisheries and ocean resources in the region (Chapter 29). State Parties to the Mekong River Commission have applied this principle in a diplomatic setting in order to resolve hydropower dam development disputes and other controversies concerning the Mekong River environment and local communities (Chapter 30). As noted above, however, given the Mekong River Commission's lack of enforcement powers, the promotion of sustainable development principles largely depends on national laws and regulations, and the engagement of non-state actors.

Fifth, as noted in the Sofia Guiding Statements, the principle of public participation and access to information and justice, is foundational to decision-making on sustainable development, and judicial and quasi-judicial bodies are beginning to reflect greater transparency in both their substantive decisions and, as applicable, as elements of their own procedures. International human rights, as reflected in the American Convention on Human Rights, have guided the Inter-American Court of

Human Rights to resolve conflicts related to economic development, the environment, culture, spirituality, development and human health, particularly in relation to indigenous and tribal peoples' rights, and many of these decisions illustrate the relevance of public participation and integration (Chapter 21). Significantly, the Court construed the right to property granted under this convention as including the right to exercise control over the use and development of land and resources to ensure their constant enjoyment. The indigenous and tribal peoples' dependence upon their ancestral lands and their ecological integrity necessitates their meaningful participation in decisions concerning the use of these lands. By validating the place of such communities and peoples before judicial and quasi-judicial bodies, this principle provides a greater understanding of the spiritual and communal depths of the sustainable development principles per se.

Provisions on access to information, transparency and public participation have been gradually incorporated into the International Centre for Settlement of Investment Disputes (ICSID) Convention Arbitration Rules and several investment treaties and agreements, suggesting opportunities for a more frequent and widespread application of the principle of public participation (Chapter 24). To illustrate this evolution, *Methanex Corporation v United States of America*, governed by the UNCITRAL Arbitration Rules which allow the arbitral tribunal to "conduct the arbitration in such manner as it considers appropriate,"[13] and *UPS* tribunals[14] recognized the public's right to participate in the arbitration proceedings. In 2003, the North American Free Trade Commission issued a "Statement of the Free Trade Commission on Non-Disputing Party Participation". In 2005, the *Suez* tribunal, following the then-ICSID Convention Arbitration Rules, allowed NGOs to participate in the proceedings and defined the conditions under which the public may participate, which conditions were then crystallized in the amended ICSID rules.

Such practices further crystallized in 2014, as UNCITRAL issued the UNCITRAL Rules on Transparency in Treaty-based Investor-State Arbitration.[15] Certain new international investment agreements provide for public participation and other sustainable development principles – changing the global governance landscape, by providing opportunities for transparency to the private sector and civil organizations alike.

Public participation, along with other sustainable development principles, has played an increasingly distinguished role in resolving disputes in international organizations. The Aarhus Convention Compliance Committee mostly handles cases submitted by the public, and by 2012, almost 60 cases addressed access to information. The Compliance Committee's interpretation of environmental

---

13 UNCITRAL Arbitration Rules, Article 17.

14 *Methanex* and *UPS*.

15 United Nations Commission on International Trade Law, UNCITRAL Rules on Transparency in Treaty-based Investor-State Arbitration (effective date: April 2014), available online: <http://www.uncitral.org/uncitral/en/uncitral_texts/arbitration/2014Transparency.html>.

justice may shape the future application of this sustainable development principle in protecting the right of present and future generations to a healthy environment.

Chapters in this volume have considered more than a decade of experience in the accountability and claims mechanisms of the World Bank and certain regional development banks. Allowing persons adversely affected by bank-financed projects to file grievances with these accountability mechanisms permits the financial institutions to resolve complaints among the project proponent, the affected persons, and the bank to review its compliance with its own operational policies and rules. The World Bank Inspection Panel's experiences may have inspired similar systems in the other banks (Chapter 32). The Inter-American Development Bank (IADB) has developed an accountability mechanism – the IADB's Independent Consultation and Investigation Mechanism (as discussed in Chapter 34). Review of the cases submitted to this accountability mechanism and lessons learned in its decisions offers new understandings of how the IADB's development mission, combined with its own standards and sustainability policies, assists in assimilating certain sustainable development principles, particularly access to information, public participation and access to justice.

Significantly prodded by efforts to improve environmental protection in the North American Free Trade Agreement (NAFTA) regime, the North American Agreement on Environmental Cooperation (NAAEC) contains provisions expressing the sustainable development principles. The NAAEC Commission for Environmental Cooperation, the dispute resolution mechanism under the NAEEC, handles claims of non-enforcement of the NAAEC and imposes monetary penalties in case of a "persistent pattern of failure [by a Party] to effectively enforce its environmental law"[16] (Chapter 33).

Sixth, the principle of good governance has been reflected in WTO decisions (Chapter 16). A review of relevant WTO case law including *Japan – Agricultural Products II*,[17] *EC – Pipe Fittings*,[18] *Argentina – Hides and Leather*,[19] *Argentina – Poultry Anti-Dumping Duties*,[20] *US – Lamb*,[21] *US – Line Pipe*,[22] and *US – Steel*

---

16 *See* NAAEC Article 22(1). The dispute resolution provisions are contained in NAAEC Articles 22–36.

17 *Japan – Measures Affecting Agricultural Products (Complaint by the United States)* (1999), WTO Doc. WT/DS76/AB (Appellate Body Report).

18 WTO, *European Communities – Anti-Dumping Duties on Malleable Cast Iron Tube or Pipe Fittings from Brazil* (7 March 2003) WT/DS219/R.

19 WTO, *Argentina – Measures Affecting the Export of Bovine Hides and the Import of Finished Leather* (19 December 2000) WT/DS155/R [11.88].

20 WTO, *Argentina – Definitive Anti-Dumping Duties on Poulty from Brazil* (22 April 2003) WT/DS241/R [11.76].

21 WTO, *United States – Safeguard Measures on Imports of Fresh, Chilled or Frozen Lamb Meat from New Zealand and Australia* (1 May 2001) WT/DS177/AB/R [106].

22 WTO, *United States – Definitive Safeguard Measures on Imports of Circular Welded Carbon Quality Line Pipe from Korea* (15 February 2002) WT/DS202/AB/R [217].

Safeguards,[23] and *Thailand – H-Beams*,[24] demonstrates increased attention to the WTO DSB and Appellate Body's growing application of the principle of good governance, especially its transparency and due process or reason-giving components, in the trade law arena.

This principle of good governance specifically the recognition of transparency in relation to the fair and equitable treatment (FET) standard, corruption and due process, also finds relevance in investor-state disputes (Chapter 16). For instance, in *Técnicas Medioambientales Tecmed v United Mexican States*, the ICSID tribunal ruled that a State should treat foreign investors in a 'free from ambiguity and totally transparent' manner.[25] In *Metalclad v Mexico*, the ICSID tribunal found that Mexico breached the FET standard by, *inter alia*, failing to "ensure a transparent and predictable [regulatory] framework".[26] Corruption in the process of procuring an investment precludes an ICSID tribunal from exercising jurisdiction, as seen in *Inceysa v El Salvador* and *Fraport v the Philippines*.[27] In *Chemtura Corporation v Canada*, the *ad hoc* NAFTA arbitral tribunal held that "procedurally improper" treatment of an investment which was "both serious in itself and material to the outcome of its inquiry" would amount to a breach of the FET standard.[28] The extent however to which investor-state arbitral tribunals have applied this principle may be viewed as partial, incomplete and contested. These investment-focused cases have generated a good deal of meaning for the principle of good governance. Going forward, however, it must be remembered that the principle is intended to have a much larger scope and that these early decisions can assist in the development of the principle before bodies having jurisdiction beyond investment.

Seventh, as noted in the Sofia Guiding Statements, the principle of integration and interrelationship, in particular in relation to human rights and social, economic and environmental objectives, is a key norm adopted by courts and tribunals for sustainable development, and has begun to be linked to expectations of standards of integrative decision-making and good faith negotiations. The principle, reflected in the 1992 Rio Declaration among others, requires economic decision-making to integrate environmental and social (including human rights) considerations, to the point that the proponents of economic plans or projects must consider environmental and social mitigation costs to be integral to

---

23 WTO, *United States – Definitive Safeguard Measures on Imports of Certain Steel Products* (10 November 2003) WT/DS248/AB/R [287].

24 WTO, *Thailand – Anti-Dumping Duties on Angles, Shapes and Sections of Iron or Non-Alloy Steel and H Beams from Poland* (28 September 2000) WT/DS122/R [7.143].

25 *Técnicas Medioambientales Tecmed v United Mexican States*, Award, ICSID Case No ARB(AF)/00/02 (29 May 2003), (2004) 43 ILM 133 [154].

26 *Metalclad v Mexico*, Award, ICSID Case No ARB(AF)/97/1 (30 August 2000), (2001) 40 ILM 36 [99], [88].

27 *Inceysa Vallisoletana v Republic of El Salvador*, Award, ICSID Case No ARB/03/26 (2 August 2006) [221]; *Fraport AG Frankfurt Airport Services Worldwide v Republic of the Philippines*, Award, ICSID Case No ARB/03/25 (16 August 2007) [401].

28 *Chemtura Corporation v Canada* (Award dated 2 August 2010), <http://italaw.com/documents/ChemturaAward.pdf> [148].

the project itself, rather than elements which can be externalized. This principle has been increasingly recognized and reflected in the decisions of the ICJ and the PCA, than in the WTO Panel and Appellate Body decisions, and also in the jurisprudence of international human rights bodies. In itself, the spectrum of judicial and quasi-judicial bodies applying the principle serves to further the principle by demonstrating the ability of sustainable development to be integrated across boundaries and subject matter.

The ICJ, in its *Gabčíkovo-Nagymaros* case, recognized that the "need to reconcile economic development with protection of the environment is aptly expressed in the concept of sustainable development"[29]. In the *Iron Rhine* award, the PCA Arbitral Tribunal explained more directly that since:

> the Stockholm Conference on the Environment in 1972 there has been a marked development of international law relating to the protection of the environment. Today, both international and EC law require the integration of appropriate environmental measures in the design and implementation of economic development activities. Principle 4 of the Rio Declaration on Environment and Development, adopted in 1992[30] which reflects this trend, provides that "environmental protection shall constitute an integral part of the development process and cannot be considered in isolation from it." Importantly, these emerging principles now integrate environmental protection into the development process. Environmental law and the law on development stand not as alternatives but as mutually reinforcing, integral concepts, which require that where development may cause significant harm to the environment there is a duty to prevent, or at least mitigate, such harm . . . This duty, in the opinion of the Tribunal, has now become a principle of general international law . . .[31]

This determination was directly relevant for the decision of the Tribunal in this case, which found that "the reactivation of the Iron Rhine railway cannot be viewed in isolation from the environmental protection measures necessitated by the intended use of the railway line. These measures are to be fully integrated into the project and its costs."[32]

Further, in the *US – Shrimp* case, the WTO Appellate Body concluded that the concept of sustainable development is "generally accepted as integrating economic and social development and environmental protection," explicitly referring to the principle of integration (Chapter 15).[33] The WTO Panel and Appellate Body has applied the integration principle in balancing the protection of intellectual property

---

29 *Case Concerning the Gabčíkovo-Nagymaros Project (Hungary/Slovakia), Separate Opinion of Vice President Weeramantry*, [1997] ICJ Rep. 7, para. 140.

30 31 ILM 874, at p. 877.

31 *The Iron Rhine arbitration* (Belgium/Netherlands) Award of May, 24 2005, online: Permanent Court of Arbitration <http://www.pca-cpa.org/showfile.asp?fil_id=377>, at paras 58–59.

32 Ibid. at 223.

33 WTO, *US-Import Prohibition of Certain Shrimp and Shrimp Products*, WT/DS58/AB/R, para 129, fns 107, 147 (12 October 1998).

rights with other economic, environmental and social interests, by interpreting the Agreement on Trade Related Aspects of Intellectual Property Rights (TRIPS) in light of the balancing objectives laid down in Article 7 and the public interest principles enshrined in Article 8 thereof (Chapter 17). In *Canada – Patents*,[34] which most significantly applied Articles 7 and 8 of TRIPS, the WTO Panel recognized the import of these provisions in balancing intellectual property rights with public interest concerns.

Investment treaty tribunals seldom consider it necessary to explicitly refer to the New Delhi Declaration sustainable development principle of integration in their decisions. But where matters of environment and development arise, they have manifested a positive stance towards integration and good governance (Chapter 25). The inclusion of 'integration' arguments on sustainable development in the pleadings of lawyers representing States and investors can influence the deliberations of tribunals in weighing societal concerns against foreign investors' interests especially with regards to government public policy priorities related to the environment, social justice or poverty reduction.

In Europe, the European Court of Justice and the European Court of Human Rights (Chapter 26) jurisprudence demonstrate judicial leadership in respect for sustainable development principles, especially the principles of integration, public participation, and precaution. Environmental considerations and sustainable development principles are embodied in the European Union (EU) policies and treaties, and in the decisions of the European Court of Justice (Chapter 26). Integration and public participation have been featured in the jurisprudence developed by the European Court of Human Rights, which has evolved fundamental rules on environmental issues founded mainly on rights enshrined in the European Convention on Human Rights such as the right to life (Article 2), prohibition of torture (Article 3), right to a fair trial (Article 6(1)), right to respect for private and family life (Article 8), freedom of expression (Article 10), freedom of assembly and association (Article 11), right to an effective remedy (Article 13), and protection of property (Article 1, First protocol) (Chapter 26). The advancements made by such human rights courts highlight the need for balance between environmental and economic interests. Meanwhile, integration and precaution, among others, have emerged as general principles of EU treaties, laws and policies, including the Declaration on Guiding Principles for Sustainable Development, and appeared prominently in European Court of Justice and General Court jurisprudence (Chapter 26). Although not yet fully-fledged, these principles are being increasingly recognized and operationalized in the European jurisprudence, and suggest potential for further advances.

Sustainable development principles have also materialized in the domestic decisions of South Asian courts, especially those of the courts in India, Bangladesh, Pakistan, Nepal and Sri Lanka (Chapter 28). It is worth emphasizing that Indian jurisprudence pioneered the recognition of sustainable development law and principles in the region. A few of its most seminal cases include *M.C. Mehta v Kamal*

34 *Canada – Patent Protection of Pharmaceutical Products*, WT/DS114/R, fn 66 (17 March 2000).

Nath, where the Court extended the public trust doctrine to all ecologically important lands, freshwater, wetlands and riparian forests, and not just navigable waters; *Vellore Citizens' Welfare Forum v Union of India* (1996), where the Court held "[s]ustainable development, and in particular the polluter pays principle and the precautionary principle, have become part of customary international law"; and *M.C. Mehta v Union of India,* where the Court addressed the industrial pollution affecting the Taj Mahal.[35]

In essence, this volume concludes, there is a rich and growing jurisprudence in relation to sustainable development. Further, there are signs of increasing openness across many international courts and tribunals to the resolution of disputes through reference to principles of sustainable development in international law.

35.4 Potential application of sustainable development principles in the Paris Agreement on Climate Change and its Compliance Committee

The acceptance of sustainable development principles by international courts and tribunals may exert certain inter-actional influence on the development of international treaties, establishing legitimacy, and providing persuasive authority which informs the negotiations that shape and agree on new international obligations. If increasing acceptance and adoption of their precepts within international treaty law is any indication, the New Delhi Principles can be argued to have been well-chosen. For indeed, global acceptance and application of the New Delhi Principles in international law *can* be observed across new or ongoing treaty law negotiations on sustainable development.

A potent illustration is found in the 2015 Paris Agreement on climate change.[36] After nearly 17 years of deadlock, 197 Parties to the UN Framework Convention on Climate Change (UNFCCC) concluded a new international agreement on climate change at the 21st Conference of the Parties to the UNFCCC (COP21) in Paris on 12 December 2015.[37] Sustainable Development Goal 13 to take urgent action to combat climate change and its impacts will be implemented in part through the new Paris Agreement, even as the SDG 13 itself acknowledges that the UNFCCC is the primary international, intergovernmental forum for negotiating the global response to climate change. Other SDGs, for instance on energy, water, hunger, poverty, biodiversity and innovation, are also highly relevant to the treaty's objectives.

The treaty aims to "strengthen the global response to the threat of climate change in the context of sustainable development and efforts to eradicate poverty." Parties hope to hold increases in global temperatures well below 2°C, pursuing efforts toward a 1.5°C limit; to increase adaptation to climate impacts and foster

---

35 WP 13381/1984 (decided 30 December 1996).
36 This section shares thoughts with M.C. Cordonier Segger et al, "Advancing the Paris Agreement on Climate Change for Sustainable Development", *Camb. J. Int'l & Comp. L.,* 2017.
37 Paris Agreement, 12 December 2015, UN Doc. FCCC/CP/2015/L.9/Rev.1.

resilience; and to harness finance flows for low-greenhouse gas (GHG) emissions and climate-resilient development. The Paris Agreement sets a 'high ambition' framework for progressively more important climate mitigation, adaptation and finance commitments by countries, backed by measures for intergovernmental cooperation on loss and damage, forests and land management, technology development and transfer, education and capacity building, with a fit-to-purpose framework of transparency, peer review, stock-taking and compliance support. Adopting a 'bottom up' approach, it builds on submissions of climate action plans to the UNFCCC by 188 countries, as Nationally Determined Contributions (NDCs) to the global response to climate change. The rapid entry into force of the Agreement on 04 November 2016, with over 120 ratifications by January 2017, underscores the importance of the Accord.

Commitments to promote more sustainable development permeate the Paris Agreement and its Adoption Decision. Indeed, the Decision begins by welcoming UNGA Resolution A/RES/70/1 on the global Sustainable Development Goals (SDG), particularly Goal 13,[38] and acknowledging that climate change is a common concern of humankind. The Decision also recognizes that when taking action on climate change, States must respect, promote and consider their human rights obligations; the right to development; the rights of indigenous peoples, children and others in vulnerable situations; gender equality and empowerment; and inter-generational equity. It acknowledges the need to promote universal access to sustainable energy in developing countries, as well as the deployment of renewables, especially in Africa. Important sustainable development principles such as transparency and public participation, integration of environmental concerns and human rights into economic decision-making, good governance, precaution, inter-generational equity, CBDRRC, and sustainable use of natural resources such as energy, are reflected in the Preamble to the Adoption Decision.[39]

---

38 *Transforming our World: The 2030 Agenda for Sustainable Development*, United Nations, 2015. Sustainable Development Goal 13 is to take urgent action to combat climate change and its impacts, and the targets include to: Strengthen resilience and adaptive capacity to climate-related hazards and natural disasters in all countries; Integrate climate change measures into national policies, strategies and planning; Improve education, awareness-raising and human and institutional capacity on climate change mitigation, adaptation, impact reduction and early warning; Implement the commitment undertaken by developed-country Parties to the United Nations Framework Convention on Climate Change to a goal of mobilizing jointly $100 billion annually by 2020 from all sources to address the needs of developing countries in the context of meaningful mitigation actions and transparency on implementation and fully operationalize the Green Climate Fund through its capitalization as soon as possible; Promote mechanisms for raising capacity for effective climate change-related planning and management in least developed countries and small island developing States, including focusing on women, youth and local and marginalized communities. Sustainable Development Goal 13 acknowledges that the United Nations Framework Convention on Climate Change is the primary international, intergovernmental forum for negotiating the global response to climate change.

39 See Cordonier Segger, *supra* note 36; John H. Knox, "Linking Human Rights and Climate Change at the United Nations" (2009) 33:2 *Harv. Entl. L. Rev.* 477 and John H. Knox, "Climate Change and Human Rights Law" (2009) 50:1 *Va. J. Int'l L.* 163.

The Paris Agreement seeks to set in place a universally acceptable framework to limit climate change to well below 2°C, pursuing efforts toward a 1.5°C limit, to support adaptation and resilience, and to mobilize climate finance, equitably promoting sustainable development and poverty eradication, as countries work to address climate challenges domestically while also struggling to elaborate their international cooperative. In essence, the Paris Agreement presents a core triangle of obligations:

(i)   countries must take nationally determined, quantifiable and progressive action for climate mitigation and adaptation;
(ii) these actions are incentivized by changes in financial flows and related technology transfer, capacity building, education and other cooperative measures; and
(iii) enforcement is achieved through transparency and reporting, peer review, periodic stocktaking, public participation and compliance mechanisms, in effect, a bottom-up "pledge-and-review" regime.

The treaty[40] and its Adoption Decision[41] aim to achieve climate mitigation, adaptation and finance through a series of cooperative frameworks and mechanisms, each of which establishes different legal rights and obligations for Parties, and explicitly makes provision for the needs of developing country Parties, especially the most vulnerable. These multilateral mechanisms, some of which link directly to previous CoP Decisions or flow from experience under the Kyoto Protocol, while others are shared with the UNFCCC itself, seek to support Parties to (i) achieve nationally determined contributions to mitigation and adaptation (NDCs), through (ii) mobilization of resources, (iii) transparency, global stocktaking, facilitative dialogue, and review, (iv) a sustainable development mechanism and non-market approaches, (v) technology transfer, and (vi) further implementation measures, such as capacity-building, education, and awareness of compliance and dispute settlement.

The Paris Agreement adopts the UNFCCC rules of procedure and secretariat (Article 16 and Article 17), its governance structure, including subsidiary body for scientific and technological advice (UNFCCC Article 9) and the subsidiary body for implementation (UNFCCC Article 10), the arrangements for voting and observer participation (Article 18, Article 19), and its dispute settlement mechanism (Article 24, see also UNFCCC Article 14). The mechanism to facilitate implementation of the Agreement and promote compliance is established at Article 15.1. This mechanism is structured as an expert-based and facilitative committee, and operates on a transparent, non-adversarial, and non-punitive way, according to procedures being defined by the first Meeting of the Parties to the Paris Agreement (CMA). The Compliance Committee shall pay particular attention to the respective national capabilities and circumstances of Parties.

---

40 While a certain ambiguity may exist on this point, the Paris Agreement can be seen as a Treaty in the sense of Art 2(a) of the Vienna Convention on the Law of Treaties (VCLT). One indication is need for ratification for its entry into force.
41 Adoption Decision, 12 December 2015, UN Doc. FCCC/CP/2015/L.9/Rev.1.

The Compliance Committee shall consist of 12 members with recognized competence in relevant scientific, technical, socio-economic or legal fields, to be elected by the CoP on the basis of equitable geographical representation, with two members each from the five regional groups of the United Nations and one member each from the small island developing States (SIDS) and the least developed countries (LDCs), taking gender balance into account (Adoption Decision, paragraph 103). While the 'rulebook' for the new Compliance Committee was still under development in 2017, through the first CMA, there is great potential for its deliberations to incorporate, and demonstrate, respect for the New Delhi principles of international law on sustainable development.

While all Parties, including those with the least historical contributions to global emissions, begin to play a role in emissions reduction, they also benefit from new investment and collaboration for low-GHG pathways for sustainable development and poverty eradication. As an important instrument in the climate regime, the Paris Agreement holds all the hallmarks of a sustainable development accord.[42] Indeed, the Paris Agreement is predicated upon an expectation that, if NDCs can be shaped and supported by peer review and public awareness, new scientific data on risks, actual impacts, and greater political attention will lead to ever-higher ambition from all levels of governments, along with non-State actors in the private sector and civil society. Some hope that countries, perhaps in clubs with higher ambition, can move towards setting and achieving absolute emissions reduction targets, diversified enhanced mitigation actions, or arrangements among donors and beneficiaries to address key sectors. The former would seek to bind Parties to attain net zero emissions levels over the long term through a standard that is quantifiable. The latter would set higher ambition, whether or not remaining recalcitrant actors also accept such actions as obligatory.

Making the most of this new environment and adapting traditional forms of international law-making under framework treaties accordingly is proving essential to establishing effective responses to climate change under international law. Many countries plan to reform their laws and institutions across diverse economic, environmental and social sectors in order to respond to the challenges of climate mitigation, resilience, technology, finance and accountability.[43] There is thus a pressing need for innovative legal knowledge, expertise and capacity building. An understanding of the principles of international law on sustainable

---

42 See M.C. Cordonier Segger and A. Khalfan, *Sustainable Development Law: Principles, Practices and Prospects* (Oxford: OUP, 2004). See also C. Voigt, *Sustainable Development as a Principle of International Law: Resolving Conflicts Between Climate Measures and WTO Law* (Leiden: Brill, 2009).

43 See for instance: Robert Kibugi, "Mainstreaming Climate Change into Public Policy Functions: Legal Options to Reinforce Sustainable Development of Kenya" (2012) 8 *Fla. A & M UL Rev.* 205., Robert Kibugi, "Legal Options for Mainstreaming Climate Change Disaster Risk Reduction in Governance for Kenya" in Koh Kheng-Lian, ed., *Adaptation to Climate Change, ASEAN and Comparative Experiences* (Singapore: World Scientific Publishing Co. Pte. Ltd., 2015), J.R.T. Villarin, M.A.Y. Loyzaga and A.G.M. La Viña, "In the Eye of the Perfect Storm: What the Philippines Should Do about Climate Change", Working Paper, 8 July 2008.

development, how they can be interpreted and applied by dispute settlement bodies in the interpretation of treaty obligations and by compliance committees and other international mechanisms, may be useful in this regard.

As countries craft the Paris Rulebook and advance efforts to implement the Paris Agreement, including through the presentation of new and more ambitious NDCs and the adoption of domestic laws designing their transition to a low-carbon economy, a profound comprehension of its sustainable development objective, principles and parameters will be paramount. As recognized in the treaty itself, new legal research, education, awareness, capacity building and technical assistance, especially in LDCs and SIDS, but also in high per capita emission countries, will be essential to ensure the success of the commitments undertaken in Paris, the avoidance of climate change's most dangerous consequences, and the transformation of the world's economies, societies and ecosystems towards sustainability.

35.5 Future pathways

International law evolves with caution, and reliance upon the New Dehli Principles on sustainable development remains a work-in-progress for most international adjudication and dispute settlement bodies. The principles are only beginning to shape international decision-making processes and have only started to influence remedies, including access to justice, and the measures by which aggrieved Parties can seek clean water and air, compensation for the taking of their property, resettlement assistance, or the quality of life required for human dignity. It is possible, perhaps even likely, that further 'sustainable' developments in international law will occur through the jurisprudence and determinations of international courts, tribunals and other international dispute settlement bodies over time. This volume, based on decades of research and debate in the International Law Association which led to the Sofia Guiding Statements, and other related discussions among jurists, experts and academics, seeks to contribute to this process. As legal scholarship, it aims to advance our understanding of the law, guide practising jurists in developing their arguments on the basis of these principles, and potentially support international and domestic judges and decision-makers in their invaluable efforts to peacefully resolve disputes and settle claims involving intersections of economic, social and environmental priorities. The reasoning of international courts and tribunals documented in this volume may also inform the future work of authorities and legislators in drafting, enacting and reforming their laws and institutions, as well as the essential efforts of policy makers in crafting new policies and action plans in relation to sustainable development.

The guideposts of international adjudication are still evolving, along with the ever-changing international legal system, legal and policy frameworks, institutions and governance mechanisms. As international principles of law on sustainable development are adopted and interpreted by trusted courts and tribunals, they signal the gradual efforts of entire societies, countries and indeed global communities towards higher levels of responsibility, sustainability and – in the end – justice.

Regional and international courts, tribunals and other dispute settlement bodies are developing jurisprudence. International financial institutions, such as regional and multilateral development banks, with their periodic review of their policies, rules of procedure and decisions, are taking up their own role in the interpretation and respect for the advancing body of policies, rules and jurisprudence.

The current volume illustrates the progress made in the application of sustainable development principles and how they have, over the past four decades in particular, replace an important part of the substance of international law, through their reflection in the most controversial and crucial decisions around the world. Clearly, while the forward strides have been tempered by certain backward stumbles, the judges and authorities presiding over myriad international dispute settlement bodies have contributed immensely to the furtherance of international law on sustainable development.

In the early chapters of this volume, particularly Chapter 6 on sustainable development challenges in international dispute settlement, we highlighted certain challenges confronting the consistent application of sustainable development principles and harmonization within the fragmented international law regime – global governance, treaty deadlocks, overlaps, and overload, and desperately under-resourced implementation and compliance architecture – and expressed our hope that judges stand ready to take on these challenges. It is an honour, as scholars and jurists, to bear witness to myriad judiciaries' knowledge, wisdom, and valour as they face and overcome such challenges. While a great deal of further effort may be needed to truly reconcile a desire for economic development with the human rights and environmental imperatives of our times, the first steps are being taken. Courageously, by millions of citizens and practitioners, by thousands of leaders and legislators, by hundreds of judges and scholars, the international law on sustainable development is advancing. The trends are discernable, traceable and indeed, hopeful. An ever-clearer identification, definition and interpretation of the principles of international law on sustainable development can be expected from the important decisions of courts and tribunals in the near future. For a balanced, integrated and *just* reconciliation of economic, environmental and social dimensions of development, in the interests of present and future generations, our judiciaries can and will be part of the diversity of emergent solutions.

Afterword

Kamal Hossain

This volume dealing with different aspects of sustainable development is welcome soon after the adoption of the United Nations Declaration on Sustainable Development Goals (SDGs) by the UN Summit in September 2015. It will be a valuable addition to analytical discussions on different legal aspects of sustainable development, which will complement the work done by the International Law Association's Committee on Legal Aspects of Sustainable Development, and its successor committee. These contributions should set at rest the skepticism about whether sustainable development can properly be regarded as a legal concept. The challenge of change which societies face in different stages of development needs a framework which would identify and analyze the different facets and the key elements of each facet. The considerable body of juristic writing recognizes the multifaceted character of the concept, which continues to broaden and deepen over time.

The UN Declaration views the SDGs as integrated and indivisible, and as aimed to balance three dimensions of sustainable development – economic, social and environmental. Juristic writings would contribute to a better understanding of the different dimensions of the complex concept. These necessary if appropriate policies and strategies are to be devised to realize sustainable development. The steady evolution of the concept and the recognition of its many dimensions is evident from the formulation of the 17 goals in the UN Declaration. Special attention needs to be paid to goal number 16, which in very clear terms identifies democracy and the rule of law to be essential for building peaceful and inclusive societies, for providing access to justice for all, and for effective, accountable and inclusive societies at all levels.

Sustainable development goal number 16 powerfully reaffirms the critical importance of curbing violence and terrorism as essential for achieving sustainable development. To achieve this objective, due importance must be given to promotion of the rule of law at the national and international levels, to ensure equal access to justice for all, and the promotion and enforcement of non-discriminatory laws and policies for sustainable development. By 2030, States should be expected to significantly reduce illicit financial and arms flows, to strengthen the recovery and return of stolen assets, to combat all forms of organized crime, and to reduce corruption and bribery in all their forms. They should further aim to develop effective, accountable and transparent institutions, and ensure responsive, inclusive, participatory and representative decision-making at all levels. This would require strengthening of relevant national institutions by ensuring public access to information and protection of fundamental freedoms in accordance with national legislation and international agreements, and international cooperation for building capacity at all levels.

This volume is a valuable addition to the literature on sustainable development, which emphasizes the critical importance of the rule of law as being essential, especially in light of the SDGs. The rule of law would aim to secure inclusive economic growth, eradication of poverty and hunger, and full realization of all human rights and fundamental freedoms, including the right to development.

The progressive development of the law relating to sustainable development calls for consensus building around values which should be shared and reflected in making of laws and policies at the national, regional and global levels.

Selected bibliography

E. Agius, ed., *Future Generations and International Law* (London: Earthscan Publications, 1998)

P. Alston, "Conjuring up New Human Rights: A Proposal for Quality Control" (1984) 78 *A.J.I.L.* 607

P. Alston, "Making Space for New Human Rights: The Case of the Right to Development" (1988) *Harv. Hum. Rts. Y.B.* 3

P. Alston, "The Fortieth Anniversary of the Universal Declaration" in J. Berting *et al.*, eds., *Human Rights in a Pluralist World, Individuals and Collectivities* (1990)

P. Alston, ed., *Peoples' Rights* (Oxford: Oxford University, 2001)

P. Alston and G. Quinn, "The Nature and Scope of States Parties' Obligations under the International Covenant on Economic, Social and Cultural Rights" (1987) 9 *Hum. Rts. Q.* 156

C. F. Amerasinghe, *Principles of the Institutional Law of International Organizations*, 2nd edn (Cambridge: Cambridge University Press, 2004)

O. Anaedu and L. Engfeldt, "Sustainable Development Governance" Paper prepared by the World Summit for Sustainable Development Governance Working Group Vice-Chairs Ositadinma Anaedu and Lars-Goran Engfeldt (New York: WSSD, 2002)

S. Arrowsmith, *Government Procurement in the WTO* (The Hague: Kluwer Law International, 2002)

A. Asouzu, *International Commercial Arbitration and African States: Practice, Participation and Institutional Development* (Cambridge: Cambridge University Press, 2001)

S. Atapattu, "Sustainable Development: Myth or Reality? A Survey of Sustainable Development under International Law and Sri Lankan Law" (2001) 14 *Geo. Int'l Envtl. L. Rev.* 265

M. Austen and T. Richards, *Basic Legal Documents on International Animal Welfare and Wildlife Conservation* (The Hague: Kluwer Law International, 2000)

J. E. Austin and C. E. Bruch, *The Environmental Consequences of War: Legal, Economic, and Scientific Perspectives* (Cambridge: Cambridge University Press, 2001)

I. Ayres and J. Braithwaite, *Responsive Regulation: Transcending the Deregulation Debate* (Oxford: Oxford University Press, 1992)

S. Baker, M. Kousis, D. Richardson and S. Young, eds., *The Politics of Sustainable Development* (London: Routledge, 1997)

K. Banks, "Civil Society and the North American Agreement on Labor Cooperation" in J. Kirton and V. Maclaren, eds., *Linking Trade, Environment and Social Cohesion: NAFTA Experiences, Global Challenges* (Aldershot: Ashgate, 2002)

K. Bastmeijer, *The Antarctic Environmental Protocol and Its Domestic Legal Implementation* (The Hague: Kluwer Law International, 2003)

U. Baxi, "The Development of the Right to Development" in J. Symonides, ed., *Human Rights: New Dimensions and Challenges* (Ashgate: Ashgate, 1998)

C. Bellmann, G. Dutfield and R. Meléndez-Ortiz, *Trading in Knowledge: Development Perspectives on TRIPS, Trade and Sustainability* (London: Earthscan/ICTSD, 2003)

E. Benvenisti, "Domestic Politics and International Resources" in M. Byers, ed., *The Role of Law in International Politics: Essays in International Relations and International Law* (Oxford: Oxford University Press, 2000)

J. M. Bergerat, "Tripping over Patents: Aids, Access to Treatment and the Manufacturing of Scarcity" (2002) 17 *Conn. J. Int'l L.* 157

G.A. Bermann, "Taking Subsidiarity Seriously: Federalism in the European Community and the United States" (1994) 94 *Colum. L. Rev.* 331

M. Bowman and A. Boyle, *Environmental Damage in International and Comparative Law: Problems of Definition and Valuation* (Oxford: Oxford University Press, 2002)

M. Bowman and C. Redgwell, *International Law and the Conservation of Biological Diversity* (The Hague: Kluwer Law International, 1995)

A. Boyle and M. Anderson, eds., *Human Rights Approaches to Environmental Protection* (Oxford: Clarendon Press, 1996)

A. Boyle and D. Freestone, eds., *International Law and Sustainable Development: Past Achievements and Future Challenges* (Oxford: Oxford University Press 1999)

D. Brack, "Multilateral Environmental Agreements: An Overview" in H. Ward and D. Brack, eds., *Trade, Investment and the Environment* (London: Royal Institute of International Affairs and Earthscan, 2000)

D. Bradlow, "A Test Case for the World Bank" (1996) 11 *Am. U. J. Int'l L. & Pol'y* 247

D. Bradlow, "Social Justice and Development: Critical Issues Facing the Bretton Woods System: The World Bank, the IMF, and Human Rights" (1996) 6 *Transn'l. L. & Contemp. Probs.* 47

H. Breitmeier, "International Organisations and the Creation of Environmental Regimes" in O. Young, ed., *Global Governance: Drawing Insights from the Environmental Experience* (Cambridge: MIT Press, 1997) at 87–114

J. L. Brierly, *Law of Nations*, 6th edn (Oxford: Clarendon Press, 1963)

N. Brower and J. Brueschke, *The Iran-United States Claims Tribunal* (The Hague: Kluwer Law International, 1998)

R. Brown, "Transboundary Environmental Impacts in a European Context" (1997) 3 *Eur. Env't* 80

E. Brown Weiss, *In Fairness to Future Generations: International Law, Common Patrimony, and Intergenerational Equity* (New York: Transnational, 1989)

E. Brown Weiss, "Environmentally Sustainable Competitiveness: A Comment" (1993) 102 *Yale L. J.* 2123

E. Brown Weiss, "International Environmental Law: Contemporary Issues and the Emergence of a New World Order" (1993) 81 *Geo. L. J.* 675

E. Brown Weiss, "The Emerging Structure of International Environmental Law" in N. J. Vig and R. S. Axelrod, eds., *The Global Environment: Institutions, Law, and Policy* (Washington: Congressional Quarterly, 1999) at 98

E. Brown Weiss, P. C. Szasz and D. B. Magraw, *International Environmental Law: Basic Instruments and Reference* (New York: Transnational, 1992)

I. Brownlie, *Principles of Public International Law* (Oxford: Oxford University Press, 1998)

J. Brunnée and S. J. Toope "International Law and Constructivism: Elements of an Interactional Theory of International Law" (2000) 39 (1) *Colum. J. Transn'l L.* 19

J. Brunée and S. J. Toope, "Environmental Security and Freshwater Resources: Ecosystem Regime Building" (1997) *A.J.I.L.* 26 at 40

W. Burns, "The International Convention to Combat Desertification: Drawing a Line in the Sand?" (1994) 16 *Mich. J. Int'l L.* 831

L. K. Caldwell, *International Environmental Policy* (Durham: Duke University Press, 1996)

L. K. Caldwell, "Beyond Environmental Diplomacy" in J. E. Carroll, ed., *International Environmental Diplomacy* (Cambridge: Cambridge University Press, 1988) at 16

J. Cameron, "International Law and the Precautionary Principle" in T. O'Riordan, J. Cameron and A. Jordan, eds., *Reinterpreting the Precautionary Principle* (London: Cameron May, 2001)

J. Cameron and J. Abouchar, "The Status of the Precautionary Principle in International Law" in D. Freestone and E. Hey, eds., *The Precautionary Principle and International Law: The Challenge of Implementation* (The Hague: Kluwer Law International, 1996)

J. Cameron and J. Abouchar, "The Precautionary Principle: A Fundamental Principle of Law and Policy for the Protection of the Global Environment" (1991) 14 *B.C. Int'l & Comp. L. Rev.* 1

J. Cameron, P. Demaret & D. Geradin, eds., *Trade and The Environment: The Search For Balance* (London: Cameron May, 1994)

P. D. Cameron and D. Zillman, *Kyoto: From Principles to Practice* (The Hague: Kluwer Law International, 2001)

L. Campiglio, L. Pineschi and D. Siniscalco Treves, eds., *The Environment After Rio: International Law and Economics* (Boston: Graham & Trotman, 1994)

A. A. Cancado Trindade, ed., *Human Rights, Sustainable Development and the Environment* (San José, Costa Rica: Instituto Interamericano de Derechos Humanos, 1992)

M. Cappelletti, M. Seccombe and J. Weiler, eds., *Integration through Law* (New York: W. de Gruyter, 1986)

A. Cassese, *International Law* (Oxford: Oxford University Press, 2001)

J. G. Castel, A. L. C. de Mestral and W. C. Graham, *The Canadian Law and Practice of International Trade* (Toronto: Montgomery, 1991)

Center for International Sustainable Development Law, Legal Brief: *International Environmental Governance for Sustainable Development* (December 2001), online: <http://www.cisdl.org>

Centre for International Sustainable Development Law, Legal Brief: *Sustainable Competition Law* (10 September 2003) online: <http://www.cisdl.org>

W. B. Chambers, ed., *Inter-linkages: The Kyoto Protocol and the International Trade and Investment Regimes* (Tokyo: United Nations University Press, 2001)

S. Charnovitz, "Regional Trade Agreements and the Environment" (1995) 37:5 *Environment* 95

W. Choi, *'Like Products' in International Trade Law: Towards a Consistent GATT/WTO Jurisprudence* (Oxford: Oxford University Press, 2003)

R. Churchill and V. Lowe, *The Law of the Sea* (Oxford: Oxford University Press, 1999)

B. Clark, "Environmental Impact Assessment (EIA): Scope and Objectives" in *Perspectives on Environmental Impact Assessment* (Dordrecht: D. Reidel Publishing Co, 1984)

W. C. Clark, "A Transition towards Sustainability" (2001) 27 *Ecology L. Q.* 1021

M. H. Clayton and N. J. Radcliffe, *Sustainability: A Systems Approach*, (London: Earthscan, 1996)

M. Colchester, *Salvaging Nature Indigenous Peoples, Protected Areas and Biodiversity Conservation* World Rainforest Movement and World Wildlife Fund Discussion Paper 55 (Geneva: United Nations Research Institute for Social Development, 1994)

H. Collins, "The Voice of the Community in Private Law Discourse" (1997) 3 *Eur. L. J.* 407

M. C. Cordonier Segger, "Significant Developments in Sustainable Development Law and Governance: A Proposal" (2004) *United Nations Natural Resources Forum* 28:1

M. C. Cordonier Segger "Sustainability and Corporate Accountability Regimes: Implementing the Johannesburg Summit Agenda" (2003) *RECIEL* 12:3

M. C. Cordonier Segger and A. Khalfan, *Sustainable Development Law: Principles, Practices and Prospects* (Oxford: Oxford University Press, 2004)

M. C. Cordonier Segger *et al.*, *Social Rules and Sustainability in the Americas* (Winnipeg: IISD / OAS, 2004)

M. C. Cordonier Segger *et al.*, *Ecological Rules and Sustainability in the Americas* (Winnipeg: IISD / UNEP, 2002)

M. C. Cordonier Segger *et al.*, *Trade Rules and Sustainability in the Americas* (Winnipeg: IISD, 1999)

M. C. Cordonier Segger *et al.*, "Prospects for Principles of International Sustainable Development Law after WSSD: Common but Differentiated Responsibilities, Precaution and Participation" (2003) 12:3 *RECIEL*

M. C. Cordonier Segger *et al.*, "A New Mechanism for Hemispheric Cooperation on Environmental Sustainability and Trade" (2002) 27:2 *Columbia Journal of Environmental Law* 613

M. C. Cordonier Segger, "Sustainable Development in the Negotiation of the FTAA – The Free Trade Area of the Americas: Issues and Visions for the Future, Inter American Perspectives" (2004) 27 *Fordham Int'l L. J.* 1118

M. C. Cordonier Segger and N. Borregaard, "Sustainability and Hemispheric Integration: A Review of Existing Approaches" in C. Deere and D. Esty, eds., *Greening the Americas*, (Boston: MIT Press, 2002)

M. C. Cordonier Segger and M. Leichner Reynal, eds., *Beyond the Barricades: The Americas Trade and Sustainability Agenda* (Aldershot: Ashgate, 2005)

M. C. Cordonier Segger and M. Gehring, "Precaution, Health and the World Trade Organisation: Moving toward Sustainable Development" (2003) 29 *Queen's L. J.* 133

D. Cooper, "The International Treaty on Plant Genetic Resources for Food and Agriculture" (2002) 11 *RECIEL* 1

J. Crawford, ed., *Rights of Peoples* (Oxford: Oxford University Press, 1992)

J. Crawford, *The International Law Commission's Articles on State Responsibility: Introduction, Texts and Commentaries* (Cambridge: Cambridge University Press, 2002)

M. Craven, *The International Covenant on Economic, Social and Cultural Rights: A Perspective on Its Development* (Oxford: Clarendon, 1995)

Crucible Group II, *Seeding Solutions, Volume 1. Policy Options for Genetic Resources, People, Plants, and Patents Revisited* (IDRC and IPGRI, 2000)

A. D' Amato and S. K. Chopra, "Whales: Their Emerging Right to Life" (1991) 85 *Am. J. Int'l L.* 1

K. Danish, "International Environmental Law and the 'Bottom-Up' Approach: A Review of the Desertification Convention" (1995) 3 *Ind. J. Global Leg. Stud.* 133

W. J. Davey,. "The WTO Dispute Settlement System" (2000) 3:1 *J. Int'l Econ. L.* 15

M. Decleris. *The Law of Sustainable Development: General Principles, A Report for the European Commission* (Brussels: European Commission, 2000)

C. Deere, *Net Gains: International Trade, Sustainable Development and Fisheries* (Washington: IUCN – World Conservation, 1999)

K. de Feyter, *World Development Law: Sharing Resources for Development* (Antwerp: Intersentia, 2001)

C. de Fontaubert, *Achieving Sustainable Fisheries: Implementing the New International Regime* (Gland: IUCN, 2003)

P. J. I. M. de Waart, "Securing Access to Safe Drinking Water through Trade and International Migration" in E. Brans *et al.*, eds., *The Scarcity of Water: Emerging Legal and Policy Responses* (The Hague: Kluwer Law International, 1997) at 116–17

J. C. Dernbach, "Sustainable Development as a Framework for National Governance" (1998) 49 *Case W. Res.* 1

D. Devuys, "Sustainability Assessment: The Application of a Methodological Framework" (1999) 1:4 *Journal of Environmental Assessment Policy and Management* 459

E. Dewailly, A. Nantel, J. P. Weber and F. Meyer, "High Levels of PCBs in Breast Milk of Inuit Women from Arctic Québec" (1989) *Bull. Environ. Contam. Toxicol.* 43

E. Dinerstein, D. M. Olson, D. J. Graham, A. L. Webster, S. A. Primm, M. P. Bookbinder, G. Ledec and World Wildlife Fund, *A Conservation Assessment of the Terrestrial Ecoregions of Latin America and the Caribbean* (Washington: WWF & World Bank, 1995)

J. M. Djossou, *L'Afrique, le GATT et l'OMC: Entre territoires douaniers et régions commerciales*, (Sainte-Foy: Presses de l'Université Laval, 2000)

F. Dodds, ed., *Earth Summit 2002: A New Deal* (London: EarthScan, 2002)

C. Dommen and P. Cullet, *Droit International de L'Environment, Textes de base et référence* (The Hague: Kluwer Law International, 2001)

M. Drumble, "Poverty, Wealth and Obligation in International Environmental Law" (2002) 76 *Tul. L. Rev.* 843

P. Duncanson Cameron, *Competition in Energy Markets: Law and Regulation in the European Union* (Oxford: Oxford University Press, 2002)

P. Dupuy, "Soft Law and the International Law of the Environment" (1991) 12 *Mich. J. Int'l L.* 420

W. Durbin, *A Comparison of the Environmental Provisions of the NAFTA, the Canada-Chile Trade Agreement and the Mexican-European Community Trade Agreement* (New Haven: Yale Centre for Environmental Law and Policy, 2000)

G. Dutfield, *Intellectual Property Rights, Trade and Biodiversity* (London: Earthscan, 2000)

A. Echols, *Food Safety and the WTO: The Interplay of Culture, Science and Technology* (The Hague: Kluwer Law International, 2001)

R. H. Edwards and S. N. Lester, "Towards a More Comprehensive World Trade Organisation Agreement on Trade Related Investment Measures" (1997) 33 *Stan. J. Int'l L.* 169

A. Eide, C. Krause and A. Rosas, eds., *Economic, Social and Cultural Rights,* 2nd rev. ed. (Norwell: Kluwer Academic Publishers, 2001)

J. A. Ekpere, "TRIPs, Biodiversity and Traditional Knowledge: OAU Model Law on Community Rights and Access to Genetic Resources" (2003) 7:5 *Bridges Journal* 11

D. Esty, *Greening the GATT: Trade, Environment and the Future* (Washington: Institute for International Economics, 1994)

D. C. Esty and D. Geradin, "Market Access, Competitiveness, and Harmonization: Environmental Protection in Regional Trade Agreements" (1997) 21 *Harv. Envtl. L. Rev.* 265

T. F. M. Etty and H. Somsen, *Yearbook of European Environmental Law* 4 (Oxford: Oxford University Press, 2004)

European Commission, *Communication from the European Commission on the Precautionary Principle* COM 1 (2000), WTO doc. WT/CTE/W/147G/TBT/W/ 137 (27 June 2000)

D. P. Fidler, *International Law and Infectious Diseases* (Oxford: Clarendon Press, 1999)

D. P. Fidler, "The Future of the World Health Organisation: What Role for International Law" (1998) 31 *Vand. J. Transnat'l, L.* 1079

D. Fidler, "Trade and Health: The Global Spread of Disease and International Trade" (1997) 40 *Germ. Y. B. Int'l L.* 30

D. Fidler, "Return of the Fourth Horseman: Emerging Infectious Diseases and International Law" (1997) 81 *Minn. L. Rev.* 771

D. Fidler, "International Law and Global Public Health" 48 *U. Kan. L. Rev.* 1

D. Fidler, "A Globalized Theory of Public Health Law", 30 *J. L. Med. & Ethics* 150

C. Ford, "Judicial Discretion in International Jurisprudence: Article 38(1)(C) and 'General Principles of Law'" 5 *Duke J. of Comp. & Int'l L.* 35–86 (1994)

E. Fox, "Anti-trust and Regulatory Federalism: Races Up, Down and Sideways" (2000) 75 *N.Y.U. L. Rev.* 1781

E. Fox, "Competition Law" in A. Lowenfeld, International Economic Law (Oxford: Oxford University Press, 2002) at 340–83

J. Fox and L. Brown, *The Struggle for Accountability: The World Bank, NGOs, and Grassroots Movements* (Cambridge, MA: MIT Press, 1998)

F. Francione, *Environment, Human Rights and International Trade* (Oxford: Hart, 2001)

T. M. Franck, *Fairness in International Law and Institutions* (Oxford: Oxford University Press, 1995)

D. Freestone and E. Hey, eds., *The Precautionary Principle and International Law: The Challenge of Implementation* (New York: Kluwer International, 1996)

D. French, "Developing States and International Environmental Law: The Importance of Differentiated Responsibilities" (2000) 49 *International & Comparative Law Quarterly* 35

L. Frischtak, *Antinomies of Development: Governance Capacity and Adjustment Responses* (Washington, D.C.: World Bank, 1993)

P. Gallagher, *Guide to the WTO and Developing Countries* (The Hague: Kluwer Law International, 2000)

F. V. Garcia-Amador, "The Proposed New International Economic Order: A New Approach to the Law Governing Nationalization and Compensation" (1980) 12 *Lawyer of the Americas* 1

D. B. Gatmaytan, "Half a Landmark Case: Reflections on *Oposa v Factoran*" (1994) 6 *Philippine Natural Resources Law Journal* 30

I. Gavil, F. Burhenne-Guilmin, A. G. M. La Viña and J. D. Werksman in cooperation with A. Ascencio, J. Kinderlerer, K. Kummer and R. Tapper, *Antitrust Law in Perspective: Cases, Concepts and Problems in Competition Policy* (St. Paul: Thomson West, 2002) 38

M. Gehring and M. C. Cordonier Segger, "The WTO Asbestos Cases and Precaution: Sustainable Development Implications of the WTO Asbestos Dispute" (2003) 15 *Oxford J. Envtl. L.* 289

M. Gehring and M. C. Cordonier Segger, eds., *Sustainable Developments in World Trade Law* (The Hague: Kluwer Law International, 2005)

K. Gent, "Deutsches Stromeinspeisungsgesetz und Europäisches Wettbewerbsrecht" (1999) *Energiewirtschaftliche Tagesfragen – Zeitschrift für die Elektrizitäts – und Gasversorgung* 854 –58

D. Gerber, *Law and Competition in Twentieth-Century Europe: Protecting Prometheus* (Oxford: Oxford University Press, 2001)

D. Gervais, *The TRIPS Agreement: Drafting History and Analysis* (London: Sweet & Maxwell, 1998)

M. Ghezuhly *et al.*, "International Health Law" (1998) 32 *Int'l L.* 539

C. Giagnocavo and H. Goldstein, "Law Reform or World Reform: The Problem of Environmental Rights" 35 *McGill L. J.* 345

K. Ginther, E. Denters and P. J. I. M. de Waart, eds., *Sustainable Development and Good Governance* (The Hague: Kluwer Law International, 1995)

E. Gitli and C. Murillo, in C. Deere and D. Esty, eds., *Greening the Americas* (Boston: MIT Press, 2002)

M. Goransson, "Liability for Damage to the Marine Environment" in A. Boyle and D. Freestone, eds., *International Law and Sustainable Development: Past Achievements and Future Challenges* (Oxford: Oxford University Press, 1999)

D. G. Goyder, *EC Competition Law* 4th edn (Oxford: Oxford University Press, 2003)

P. Grady and K. Macmillan, *Seattle and Beyond: The WTO Millennium Round* (Ottawa: Global Economics Ltd and International Trade Policy Consultants Inc., 1999)

K. R. Gray, "International Environmental Impact Assessment" (2000) 11 *Colo. J. Int'l Envtl. L. & Pol'y* 83

D. A. Grossman, "Warming Up To a Not-So-Radical Idea: Tort-Based Climate Change Litigation" (2003) 28 *Colu. J. Envtl. L.* 1

L. Guruswamy and B. Hendricks, *International Environmental Law* (St. Paul, Minn.: West, 1997)

A. Guzman, "Why LDCs Sign Treaties that Hurt Them: Explaining the Popularity of Bilateral Investment Treaties" (1998) 38 *Va. J. Int'l L.* 639

G. Handl, *Multilateral Development Banking: Environmental Principles and Concepts Reflecting General International Law and Public Policy* (The Hague: Kluwer Law International, 2001)

G. Handl and R. E. Lutz, *Transferring Hazardous Technologies and Substances* (The Hague: Kluwer Law International, 1990)

X. Hanqin, *Transboundary Damage in International Law* (Cambridge: Cambridge University Press, 2003)

D. Harris and S. Livingstone, eds., *The Inter-American System of Human Rights* (Oxford: Clarendon, 1998)

G. Hartkopf and E. Bohne, *Umweltpolitik, vol. 1: Grundlagen, Analysen, und Perspektiven* (Opladen: Westdeutscher Verlag, 1983)

R. L. Heathcote, *The Arid Lands: Their Use and Abuse* (Tokyo: United Nations University, 1983)

D. Held, *Models of Democracy* (Stanford: Stanford University Press, 1987)

K. Helmore and N. Singh, *Sustainable Livelihoods: Building on the Wealth of the Poor* (Bloomfield: Kumarian Press, 2001)

G. Hermes, *Staatliche Infrastrukturverantwortung:rechtliche Grundstrukturen netzgebundener Transport- und Übertragungssysteme zwischen Daseinsvorsorge und Wettbewerbsregulierung am Beispiel der leitungsgebundenen Energieversorgung in Europa* (Tuebingen: Mohr Siebeck, 1998)

J. A. Hernandez, "How the Feds are Pushing Nuclear Waste on Reservations" (1994) *Cultural Survival Quarterly* 40

G. Herrmann, "The Role of UNCITRAL" in I. Fletcher, L. Mistellis and M. Cremona, eds., *Foundations and Perspectives of International Trade Law* (London: Sweet & Maxwell, 2001) 28–36

L. Herz, "Litigating Environmental Abuses Under the Alien Tort Claims Act: A Practical Assessment" (2000) 40 *Va. J. Int'l L.* 545

J. E. Hickey, Jr., and V. R. Walker, "Refining the Precautionary Principle in International Environmental Law" (1995) 14 *Va. Envtl. L. J.* 423

K. Hitchcock, "International Human Rights, the Environment, and Indigenous Peoples" (1994) 5 *Colo. J. Int'l Envtl. L. & Pol'y* 1

H. Hofbauer, G. Lara and B. Martinez, *Health Care: A Question of Human Rights, Not Charity* (Mexico City: FUNDAR, 2002)

J. Holder, *Environmental Assessment: Legal Regulation of Decision Making* (Oxford: Oxford University Press, 2003)

J. Holmberg, *Defending the Future: A Guide to Sustainable Development* (London: Earthscan, 1988)

S. Horton, "Peru and ANCOM: A Study in the Disintegration of a Common Market" (1982) 1 *Texas International Law Journal* 17

D. Hunter, J. Salzman and D. Zaelke, *International Environmental Law and Policy*, 2nd edn (New York: Foundation Press, 2003)

D. Hunter, J. Sommer and S. Vaughan, *Concepts and Principles of International Law* (Nairobi: UNEP, 1998)

G. Hyden and M. Bratton, eds., *Governance and Politics in Africa* (Boulder: Lynne Rienner Publishers, 1993)

IBRD, *International Bank for Reconstruction and Development Operational Policy* 4.01 (Washington: IBRD, 1999)

IBRD, *The Convention on the Settlement of Investment Disputes: Documents Concerning the Origin and Formulation of the Convention* (Washington: IBRD, 1970)

ICTSD, "Comercio y medio ambiente en los acuerdos regionales" (1999) 2:1 *Puentes Entre el Comercio y el Desarollo Sostenible* (Quito: ICTSD/FFLA, 1999)

E. V. Iglesias, *El nuevo rostro de la integracion regional en America Latina y el Caribe* (Washington: Inter-American Development Bank, 1997)

Inter-American Development Bank, *Integration and Trade in the Americas* (Washington: IADB, 1996)

International Council on Human Rights Policy, *Duties sans Frontières: Human Rights and Global Social Justice* (Geneva: ICHRP, 2003)

International Institute for Sustainable Development (IISD), *Impoverishment and Sustainable Development* (Winnipeg: IISD, 1996)

International Law Commission (ILC), *Draft Articles on the Non-Navigational Uses of International Watercourses*, UN Doc. A/46/10 (1991); UN Doc. A/CN.4/L492 & Add. 1 (1994)

International Monetary Fund, *Code of Good Practices on Fiscal Transparency: Declaration of Principles* (1998) 16 April 1998, 37 ILM 942

International Union for Conservation of Nature and Natural Resources, *An Explanatory Guide to the Cartagena Protocol on Biosafety* (Cambridge, UK: International Union for Conservation of Nature and Natural Resources and FIELD, 2003)

Iran–United States Claims Tribunal Reports (Cambridge: Grotius, 1981–1993)

J. H. Jackson, *The Jurisprudence of GATT and the WTO* (Cambridge: Cambridge University Press 2000)

J. Jackson, *The World Trading System: Law and Policy of International Economic Relations*, 2nd edn (Boston: MIT Press, 1997)

H. K. Jacobson and E. Brown-Weiss, "Strengthening Compliance with International Environmental Accords: Preliminary Observations from a Collaborative Project" (1995) 1 *Global Governance* 119

H. K. Jacobson, *Networks of Interdependence: International Organisations and the Global Political System*, 2nd edn (New York: Knopf, 1984)

W. Jaeger, *Regulierter Wettbewerb in der Energiewirtschaft* (Baden-Baden: Nomos, 2002)

M. Janis, R. Kay and A. Bradley, *European Human Rights Law: Texts and Materials* (Oxford: Oxford University Press, 2000)

R. Jennings, "What Is International Law and How Do We Tell It When We See It?" (1981) 37 *A.S.D.I.* 59

A. L. Jernow, "*Ad Hoc* and Extra-conventional Means for Human Rights Monitoring" in P. C. Szasz, ed., *Administrative and Expert Monitoring of International Treaties* (New York: Transnational, 1999)

P. Jha and F. J. Chaloupka, eds., *Tobacco Control in Developing Countries* (Oxford: Oxford University Press, 2000)

P. Kahn, "Contrats d'Etat et Nationalisation – Les Apports de la Sentence Arbitrale du 24 Mars, 1982" 109 *J. Droit Int'l* 844 (1982)

B. Kingsbury, "The Concept of Compliance as a Function of Competing Conceptions of International Law" (1998) 19 *Mich. J. Int'l L.* 345

A. Kirchner, *International Marine Environmental Law: Institutions, Implementation and Innovations* (The Hague: Kluwer Law International, 2003)

C. Kirkpatrick, *The Impact of the Uruguay Round on Least Developed Countries' External Trade: Strengthening the Capacity of LDCs to Participate Effectively in the World Trade Organization and to Integrate into the Trading System* (Manchester: Manchester University Press, 1998)

J. Kirton, and V. Maclaren, eds., *Linking Trade, Environment, and Social Cohesion: NAFTA Experiences, Global Challenges* (Aldershot: Ashgate, 2002)

A. Kiss, "The Implications of Global Change for the International Legal System" in E. Brown Weiss, ed., *Environmental Change and International Law* (Tokyo: United Nations University Press, 1992) 319–25

A. Kiss and D. Shelton, *International Environmental Law*, 2nd edn (New York: Transnational Publishers, 1994)

A. Kiss and D. Shelton, *Judicial Handbook on Environmental Law (Draft)* (Nairobi: UNEP, 2004)

A. Kiss, D. Shelton and K. Ishibashi, *Economic Globalization and Compliance with International Environmental Agreements* (The Hague: Kluwer Law International, 2003)

N. Klein, Dispute Settlement in the UN Convention on the Law of the Sea (Cambridge: Cambridge University Press, 2004)

T. Klindt, "Die Umweltzeichen "Blauer Engel" und 'Europäische Blume' zwischen produkt-bezogenem Umweltschutz und Wettbewerbsrecht" (1998) *Betriebsberater* 545

H. H. Koh, "Why Do Nations Obey International Law?"(1997) 106 *Yale L. J.* 2599

P. Konz, C. Bellmann, L. Assuncao and R. Melendez-Otiz, *Trade, Environment, and Sustainable Development Views from Sub-Saharan Africa and Latin America: A Reader* (Geneva: UNU/IAS & ICTSD, 2000)

M. Koskenniemi, "Breach of Treaty or Non-Compliance? Reflections on the Enforcement of the Montreal Protocol" (1992) 3 *Y.B. Int'l Envtl. L.* 123

A. Kothari, "Beyond the Biodiversity Convention: A View from India" in V. Sanchez and C. Juma, eds., *Biodiplomacy: Genetic Resources and International Relations* (Nairobi: ACTS, 1994) 67

F. V. Kratochwil, *Rules, Norms and Decisions. on the Conditions of Practical and Legal Reasoning in International Relations and Domestic Affairs* (Cambridge: Cambridge University Press, 1989) 201

F. Kratochwil, and J. G. Ruggie, "International Organisation: A State of the Art on an Art of the State" (1986), 40(4) *Int'l Org.* 753 at 768

K. Kummer, *International Management of Hazardous Wastes: The Basel Convention and Related Legal Rules* (Oxford: Oxford University Press, 1995)

J. Kurtz, "A General Investment Agreement in the WTO? Lessons from Chapter 11 NAFTA and the OECD Multilateral Agreement on Investment" (2002) 23 *Journal of International Economic Law* 713-789

W. M. Lafferty and J. Meadowcroft, *Implementing Sustainable Development: Strategies and Initiatives in High Consumption Societies* (Oxford: Oxford University Press, 2000)

B. Lal Das, *The WTO Agreements: Deficiencies, Imbalances and Required Changes* (London: Zed Books, 1998)

W. Lang, ed., *Sustainable Development and International Law* (London: Graham & Trotman/Martinus Nijhoff, 1995)

M. Langford, A. Khalfan, C. Fairstein, and H. Jones, *Legal Resources for the Right to Water: International and National Standards* (Geneva: COHRE, 2004)

H. Lauterpacht, *The Development of International Law by the International Court* (London: Stevens, 1958)

J. W. Le Deuc, "World Health Organization Strategy for Emerging Infectious Diseases" (1996) 275 *J.A.M.A.* 318

S. Lederberg, R.E. Shope, S.C. Oak, eds., *Emerging Infectious Diseases: Microbial Threats to Health in the United States* (Washington D.C.: Institute of Medicine, National Academy Press, 1992)

A. L'Hirondel and D. Yach, "Develop and Strengthen Public Health Law" (1998) 51 *World Health Stat. Q.* 79

A. Lindroos, *The Right to Development* (Helsinki: The Erik Castren Institute of International Law and Human Rights Research Reports, 1999)

M. Lovei and P. Pillai, *Assessing Environmental Policy, Regulatory and Institutional Capacity: A World Bank Policy Note* (Washington: World Bank, 2003)

V. Lowe, "Sustainable Development and Unsustainable Arguments" in A. Boyle and D. Freestone, eds., *International Law and Sustainable Development: Past Achievements and Future Challenges* (Oxford: Oxford University Press, 1999)

V. Lowe, "The Politics of Law-Making: Are the Method and Character of Norm Creation Changing?" in M. Byers, ed. *The Role of Law in International Politics: Essays in International Relations and International Law* (Oxford: Oxford University Press, 2000)

A. F. Lowenfeld, *International Economic Law* (Oxford: Oxford University Press, 2002)

S. Lyster, *International Wildlife Law: An Analysis of International Treaties Concerned with the Conservation of Wildlife* (Cambridge: Cambridge University Press, 1985)

R. Mackenzie, D. H. Meadows, D. L. Meadows, and J. Randers, *An Explanatory Guide to the Cartagena Protocol on Biosafety* (Cambridge: IUCN, 2003)

G. F. Maggio, "Inter/intra-Generational Equity: Current Applications under International Law for Promoting the Sustainable Development of Natural Resources" (1997) 4 *Buff. Envtl. L. J.* 161

G. F. Maggio and O. J. Lynch, *Human Rights, Environment, and Economic Development: Existing and Emerging Standards in International Law and Global Society* (World Resources Institute, 1996)

K. E. Mahoney and P. Mahoney, eds., *Human Rights in the Twenty-first Century: A Global Challenge* (The Hague: Kluwer Academic Publishers, 1993)

H. Mann and K. von Moltke, *NAFTA's Chapter 11 and the Environment: Addressing the Impacts of the Investor-State Process on the Environment* (Winnipeg: International Institute for Sustainable Development, 1999)

842   *Selected bibliography*

G. Marceau, *Anti-Dumping and Anti-Trust Issues in Free-Trade Areas* (Oxford: Clarendon Press, 1994)

E. Marden, "The Neem Tree Patent: International Conflict over the Commodification of Life" (1999) 22 *Boston Col. Int'l & Comp. L. Rev.* 2:279

S. Marks, "Emerging Human Rights: A New Generation for the 1980s?" (1980–81) 33 *Rutgers L. Rev.* 435

J. Mathis, *Regional Trade Agreements in the GATT/WTO Article XXIV and the Internal Trade Agreement* (The Hague: T.M.C. Asser Press, 2002)

M. Matsushita, "International Cooperation in the Enforcement of Competition Policy" (2002) *Washington University Global Studies Law Review* Vol. 1:463

M. Matsushita, T. J. Schoenbaum and P. C. Mavroidis, *The World Trade Organization: Law, Practice, and Policy* (Oxford: Oxford University Press, 2004)

P. McAuslan, "Good Governance and Aid in Africa" (1996) 40 *J. Afr. L.* 168 at 168–82

S. McCaffrey, *The Law of International Watercourses: Non-Navigational Uses* (Oxford: Oxford University Press, 2003)

C. McCrudden, "International Economic Law and Human Rights: A Framework for Discussion of the Legality of 'Selective Purchasing' Laws under the WTO Government Procurement Agreement" (1999) 2:1 *J. Int'l Econ. L.* 3

C. McCrudden, "Labour Rights Revisited: International Investment Agreements and the Social Clause Debate" in M. Irish, ed., *The Auto Pact: Investment, Labour and the WTO* (New York: Aspen, 2003)

H. McGoldrick, "Sustainable Development and Human Rights: An Integrated Conception"(1996) 45 *Int'l & Comp. LQ.* 796

H. McGoldrick, "Sustainable Development: The Challenge to International Law" (1994) *RECIEL* 3

D. H. Meadows, D. Meadows and J. Randers, *Beyond the Limits* (New York: Universe Books, 1972)

R. Meléndez-Ortiz and C. Bellmann, "Commerce international et développement durable" in L. Mills and I. Serageldin, eds., *Governance and the External Factor* (Washington: World Bank, 1992)

C. Milner and O. Morrisey, "Measuring Trade Liberalization in Africa" in M. McGillvray and O. Morrisey, eds., *Evaluating Economic Liberalization. Case-Studies in Economic Development* 4 (New York: St. Martin's Press, 1999/London: Macmillan Press, 1999)

B. Moldan and S. Billharz, *Sustainability Indicators: Report of the Project on Indicators of Sustainable Development* (Chichester: John Wiley, SCOPE 58, 1997)

J. Mommsen, *The Age of Bureaucracy: Perspectives on the Political Sociology of Max Weber* (Oxford: Oxford University Press, 1974)

M. Moore, *Doha and Beyond: The Future of the Multilateral Trading System* (Cambridge: Cambridge University Press, 2004)

D. Morrow, "Poverty Reduction Strategy Papers and Sustainable Development" (Workshop on Poverty and Sustainable Development, Ottawa, January 2001)

S. Morton, *Progress Toward Free Trade in the Western Hemisphere Since 1994* (La Jolla: Institute of the Americas, 1998)

B. Müller, *Equity in Climate Change: The Great Divide* (Oxford: OISE, 2002)

A. Munro and M. W. Holdgate, eds., *Caring for the Earth: A Strategy for Sustainable Living* (Geneva: IUCN, 1991)

S. Murphy, "The ELSI Case: An Investment Dispute at the International Court of Justice" (1991) 16 *Yale J. Int'l L.* 391

E. Neumayer, "Multilateral Agreement on Investment: Lessons for the WTO from the Failed OECD Negotiations" (1999) 46 *Wirtschaftspolitische Blätter* 618–28

E. C. Nieuwenhuys and M.M.T.A. Brus, *Multi-lateral Regulation of Investment* (The Hague: Kluwer Law International, 2001)

A. Nikiforuk, *The Nasty Game: The Failure of Environmental Assessment in Canada* (Canada: Sierra Club, 1997)

A. Nollkaemper, "The Precautionary Principle in International Environmental Law: What's New Under the Sun?" (1991) 22 *Marine Pollution Bulletin* 3

S. Nooteboom and K. Wieringa, "Comparing Strategic Environmental Assessment and Integrated Environmental Assessment" (1999) *Journal of Environmental Assessment Policy and Management* Vol. 1 No. 4 441

M. Nordquist and J. Norton Moore, *Current Marine Environmental Issues and the International Tribunal for the Law of the Sea* (Leiden: Martinus Nijhoff, 2001)

H. Nordström and S. Vaughan, *Trade and Environment, WTO Special Study 4* (Geneva: WTO, 1999

North American Commission for Environmental Cooperation, *Assessing Environmental Effects of the North American Free Trade Agreement (NAFTA): An Analytic Framework (Phase II)* and *Issue Studies* (Montreal: NACEC, 1999)

OAS, *Acuerdos de comercio e integracion en las Americas: Un compendio analitico* (Washington: OAS, 1997)

OAS, *Human Rights: How to Present a Petition in the Inter-American System* (Washington: OAS, 2000)

S. Oberthür and H. E. Ott, eds., "Developing Country Participation (Articles 10, 11)" in *The Kyoto Protocol: International Climate Policy for the 21st Century* (Berlin: Springer Verlag, 1999)

OECD, *Freight and the Environment: Effects of Trade Liberalisation and Transport Sector Reforms* (Paris: OECD, 1997)

OECD, *Policies to Enhance Sustainable Development* (Paris: OECD, May 2001)

OECD Secretariat, "Timing and Public Participation Issues in Undertaking Environmental Assessments of Trade Liberalisation agreements", (paper presented at Workshop on *Methodologies for Environmental Assessment of Trade Liberalization Agreements*, Paris: OECD, October 1999)

P. N. Okowa, "Procedural Obligations in International Environmental Agreements" (1996) *Brit. Y.B. of Int'l L.* 275

P. N. Okawa, *State Responsibility for Transboundary Air Pollution in International Law* (Oxford: Oxford University Press, 2000)

T. A. O'Keefe, "An Analysis of the Mercosur Economic Integration Project from a Legal Perspective" (1994) 28:2 *The International Lawyer* 28, 439

J. Oloka-Onyango, "Human Rights and Sustainable Development in Contemporary Africa: A New Dawn, or Retreating Horizons?" (2000) 6 *Buff. Hum. Rts. L. Rev.* 39

M. K. Omalu, *NAFTA and the Energy Charter: Treaty Compliance with Implementation and Effectiveness of International Investment Agreements* (The Hague: Kluwer Law International, 1999)

T. O'Riordan, A. Jordan and J. Cameron, eds., *Reinterpreting the Precautionary Principle* (London: Cameron May, 2001)

T. Padoa-Schioppa, *Regulating Finance: Balancing Freedom and Risk* (Oxford: Oxford University Press, 2004)

R. A. Painter, "Human Rights Monitoring: Universal and Regional Treaty Bodies" in P. C. Szasz, ed., *Administrative and Expert Monitoring of International Treaties* (New York: Transnational, 1999)

M. Pallemaerts, "The Future of Environmental Regulation: International Environmental Law in the Age of Sustainable Development: A Critical Assessment of the UNCED Process" (1996) 15 *Journal of Law & Com.* 623

D. Palmeter and P. C. Mavroidis, "The WTO Legal System: Sources of Law" (1998) 92 *A.J.I.L.* 398

D. Palmeter and P. C. Mavroidis, *Dispute Settlement in the World Trade Organization: Practice and Procedure* 2nd edn (Cambridge: Cambridge University Press, 2004)

C. Parry, *The Sources and Evidences of International Law* (Manchester: Manchester University Press, 1965)

S. Patandin, P. C. Dagnelie, P. Mulder, E. Op de Coul, J. E. Van der Veen, N. Weisglas-Kuperus and P. J. J Sauer "Dietary Exposure to Polychlorinated Biphenyls and Dioxins from Infancy to Adulthood: A Comparison between Breast-feeding, Toddler, and Long-term Exposure." (1999) 107 *Environ.Health Perspect* 45

J. C. N. Paul, "The United Nations Family: Challenges of Law and Development: The United Nations and the Creation of an International Law of Development" (1995) 36 *Harv. Int'l L. J.* 307

W. Pearce and G. D. Atkinson, "Capital Theory and Measurement of Sustainable Development: An Indicator of 'Weak' Sustainability" (1993) 8 *Ecological Economics* 103–8

F. Perrez, "The Relationship between Permanent Sovereignty and the Obligation Not to Cause Transboundary Environmental Damage" (1996) 26 *Environmental Law* 1187

F. Perrez, "The World Summit on sustainable Development: Environment, Precaution and Trade – A Potential for Success and/or Failure" (2003) 12:3 *R.E.C.I.E.L*

F. Perrez, *Cooperative Sovereignty: From Independence to Interdependence in International Environmental Law* (The Hague: Kluwer Law International, 2000)

E. U. Petersmann, "From the Hobbesian International Law of Coexistence to Modern Integration Law: The WTO Dispute Settlement" (1998) 1:2 *J. Int'l Econ. L.* 175

B. J. Plotkin, "Mission Possible: The future of the International Health Regulations" (1996) 10 *Temp. Int'l & Comp. L. J.* 503

G. Posser, *Grundfragen des Abfallrechts: Abgrenzung von Produkt/Abfall und Verwertung/ Beseitigung* (München: C. H. Beck Verlag, 2001)

S. Prakash, "Towards a Synergy between Intellectual Property Rights and Biodiversity" (1999) *Journal of World Intellectual Property* 2:5

R. Pritchard, *Economic Development, Foreign Investment and the Law* (The Hague: Kluwer Law International, 1996)

D. Quist and I. Chapela, "Transgenic DNA Introgressed into Traditional Maize Landraces in Oazaca, Mexico" (2001) 414 *Nature* 541

Rat von Sachverständigen für Umweltfragen, *Umweltprobleme der Nordsee* (Stuttgart: Kiepenheuer & Witsch, 1980)

J. Razzaque, *Public Interest Environmental Litigation in India, Pakistan and Bangladesh* (The Hague: Kluwer Law International, 2004)

J. Rein, "International Governance through Trade Agreements: Patent Protection for Essential Medicines" (2001) 21 *N.W. J. Int'l L. & Business* 379

C. Reynaud, *Labour Standards and the Integration Process in the Americas* (Geneva: ILO, 2001)

B. Rich, *Mortgaging the Earth: The World Bank, Environmental Impoverishment, and the Crisis of Development* (Boston: Beacon Press, 1994)

J. Richardson, *Environmental Regulation through Financial Organisations: Comparative Perspectives on the Industrialised Nations* (The Hague: Kluwer Law International, 2002)

M. Rodriguez-Mendoza, "The Andean Group's Integration Strategy" in *Integrating the Hemisphere: Perspectives from Latin America and the Caribbean* (Bogota: Inter-American Dialogue, 1997)

N. Roht-Arriaza, "Shifting the Point of Regulation: The International Organisation for Standardization and Global Lawmaking on Trade and the Environment" (1995) 22 *Ecology L.Q.* 479

R. Rosencranz, R. Campbell and D. A. O'Neil, "Rio Plus Five: Environmental Protection and Free Trade in Latin America" (1997) *Georgetown International Environmental Law Review* 9

G. Roth, *Umweltbezogene Unternehmenskommunikation im deutschen und europäischen Wettbewerbsrecht* (Frankfurt: P. Lang, 2000)

G. Roth and C. Wittich, eds., *Max Weber, Economy and Society: An Outline of Interpretive Sociology* (Berkeley: University of California Press, 1968)

L. Ruessmann, "Putting the Precautionary Principle in Its Place: Parameters for the Proper Application of a Precautionary Approach and the Implications for Developing Countries in Light of the Doha WTO Ministerial" (2002) 17 *Am. U. Int'l L. Rev.* 905

N. de Sadeleer, *Environmental Principles: From Political Slogans to Legal Rules* (Oxford: Oxford University Press, 2002)

M. Salazar Xirinchas, *Towards Free Trade in the Americas* (Washington: OAS/Brookings Institute, 2002)

G. P. Sampson, *Trade, Environment and the WTO: The Post-Seattle Agenda*, Overseas Development Council Policy Essay No. 27 (Washington: ODC, 2001)

P. Sands, *Principles of International Environmental Law: Frameworks, Standards and Implementation* 1st edn (Manchester: Manchester University Press, 1996)

P. Sands, *Principles of International Environmental Law* 2nd edn (Cambridge: Cambridge University Press, 2003)

P. Sands, "International Law in the Field of Sustainable Development" (1994) 65 *Br. Yrbk. of I.L.* 303

P. Sands, "European Community Environmental Law: The Evolution of a Regional Regime of International Environmental Protection" (1991) 100 *Yale L. J.* 2511

A. Sarokin and J. Schulkin, "Environmental Justice: Co-evolution of Environmental Concerns and Social Justice" (1994) 14 *The Environmentalist* 121

O. Schachter, *Sharing the World's Resources* (Bangalore: Allied, 1977)

T. Schoenbaum, "International Trade and Protection of the Environment: The Continuing Search for Reconciliation" (1997) 91:2 *American Journal of International Law* 281

N. Schrijver, *Permanent Sovereignty over Natural Resources: Balancing Rights and Duties* (Cambridge: Cambridge Univ. Press 1997)

N. Schrijver and F. Weiss "Editorial" 2 *International Environmental Agreements: Politics, Law and Economics* 2 2002, 105–108

H. Schreuer, *The ICSID Convention: A Commentary* (Cambridge: Cambridge University Press, 2001)

R. A. Sedjo, "Ecosystem Management: An Unchartered Path for Public Forests" (1995) 10 *Resources for the Future* 1

I. Seidl-Hohenveldern, *International Economic Law*, 3rd edn (The Hague: Kluwer Law International, 1999)

A. Seidman, R. Seidman and T. Walde "Building Sound National Frameworks for Development and Social Change" (1999) 4 *C.E.P.M.L. & P. J.* 1

S. K. Sell, "TRIPS and the Access to Medicines Campaign" (2002) 20 *Wis. Int'l L. J.* 481

S. Shaw and R. Schwartz "Trade and Environment in the WTO: State of Play" (2002) 36 *J.W.T.* 129

F. I. Shihata, "The World Bank and the Environment: A Legal Perspective" (1992) 16 *Maryland Journal of International Law and Trade* 1

F. I. Shihata, "The World Bank and the Environment: Legal Instruments for Achieving Environmental Objectives" in I. F. I. Shihata, *The World Bank in a Changing World*, Vol. II (Leiden: Martinus Nijhoff Publishers, 1995)

D. A. Silien, "Human Rights Monitoring: Procedures and Decision-Making of Standing United Nations Organs" in P. C. Szasz, ed., *Administrative and Expert Monitoring of International Treaties* (New York: Transnational, 1999) 83

N. Singh and R. Strickland, eds., *From Legacy to Vision: Sustainability, Poverty and Policy Adjustment* (Winnipeg: International Institute for Sustainable Development, 1996)

A. M. Slaughter, "Governing Through Government Networks" in M. Byers, ed., *The Role of Law in International Politics: Essays in International Relations and International Law* (Oxford: Oxford University Press, 2000)

B. Sohn, "The Stockholm Declaration on the Human Environment" (1973) *Harv. Int'l L. J.* 423

M. Sornarajah, *The International Law on Foreign Investment* 2nd edn (Cambridge: Cambridge University Press, 2004)

R. N. Stavins, ed., *Economics of the Environment*, 4th ed. (New York: W.W. Norton & Company, 2000)

H. Steiner and P. Alston, *International Human Rights in Context: Law, Politics, Morals*, 2nd edn (Oxford: Oxford University Press, 2000)

P. L. Stenzel, "Can NAFTA's Environmental Provisions Promote Sustainable Development?" (1995) 59 *Alb. L. Rev.* 43

J. Stiglitz, *Globalization and Its Discontents* (London: Penguin Books, 2002)

O. Stokke, *Governing High Seas Fisheries: The Interplay of Global and Regional Regimes* (Oxford: Oxford University Press, 2001)

C. D. Stone, *Should Trees Have Standing? Legal Rights for Natural Objects* (Los Altos, California: William Kaufmann, Inc., 1974)

A. O. Sykes, "Trips, Pharmaceuticals, Developing Countries, and the Doha 'Solution' " (2002) 3 *Chi. J. Int'l L.* 47

P. C. Szasz, "Introduction" in P. C. Szasz, ed., *Administrative and Expert Monitoring of International Treaties* (New York: Transnational, 1999)

C. Tan. "Tackling the Commodity Price Crisis Should be WSSD's Priority" (Malaysia: Third World Network, 2002) online: < http://www.twnside.org.sg/title/jb14.htm>

L. Taylor, "Making the World Health Organization Work: A Legal Framework for Universal Access to the Conditions for Health", (1992) 18 *Am. J. L. & Med.* 301

L. Taylor, *An International Regulatory Strategy for Global Tobacco Control*, (1996) 21 *Yale J. Int'l L.* 257

A. L. Taylor and D. W. Bettcher, "WHO Framework Convention on Tobacco Control: A Global 'Good' For Public Health" (2000) 78:7 *Bulletin World Health Organization* 920-9

J. C. Thomas, "Investor-State arbitration under NAFTA Chapter 11" 37 (1999) *The Canadian Yearbook of International Law* 99–137

S. Thomas-Nuruddin, "Protection of the Ozone Layer: The Vienna Convention and the Montreal Protocol" in P. C. Szasz, ed., *Administrative and Expert Monitoring of International Treaties* (New York: Transnational, 1999) 113

U. P. Thomas, "The CBD, the WTO, and the FAO: The Emergence of Phytogenetic Governance" in P. G. LePrestre, ed., *Governing Global Biodiversity: The Evolution and Implementation of the Convention on Biological Diversity* (Aldershot: Ashgate, 2002) 177

M. Thornton., "Since the Breakup: Developments and Divergences in ANCOM's and Chile's Foreign Investment Codes." (1983) 1 *Hastings International and Comparative Law Review* 7

A. Timoshenko, *Environmental Negotiator Handbook* (The Hague: Kluwer Law International, 2003)

A. Tolentino, "Good Governance Through Popular Participation in Sustainable Development" in K. Ginther, E. Denters and P. J. I. M. de Waart eds., *Sustainable Development and Good Governance* (The Hague: Kluwer Law International, 1995)

K. Tomasevksi, *Responding to Human Rights Violations 1946-1999* (The Hague: Martinus Nijhoff, 2000)

S. J. Toope, "Emerging Patterns of Governance" in M. Byers, ed., *The Role of Law in International Politics: Essays in International Relations and International Law* (Oxford: Oxford University Press, 2000) 91

J. Trebilcock, "What Makes Poor Countries Poor? The Role of Institutional Capital in Economic Development" in E. Buscaglia, W. Ratliff and R. Cooter, eds., *The Law and Economics of Development* (London: JAI Press Inc., 1997) 15

P. Trepte, *Regulating Procurement: Understanding the Ends and Means of Public Procurement Regulation* (Oxford: Oxford University Press, 2004)

T. Treves, "The Settlement of Disputes According to the Straddling Stocks Agreement of 1995" in *International Law and Sustainable Development: Past Achievements and Future Challenges*, A. Boyle and D. Freestone, eds. (Oxford: Oxford University Press, 1999)

J. P. Townsend, *Price, Tax and Smoking in Europe* (Copenhagen: World Health Organization, 1998)

A. Trouwborst, *Evolution and Status of the Precautionary Principle in International Law* (Kluwer Law International: The Hague, 2002)

T. C. Trzyna, ed., *A Sustainable World: Defining and Measuring Sustainable Development* (Sacramento: California Institute of Public Affairs, 1995)

D. Tussie and P. I. Vasquez, "The FTAA, MERCOSUR and the Environment" (1997) 9:3 *International Environmental Affairs: A Journal for Research and Policy*

M. Ul-Haq, *Reflections on Human Development* (Oxford: Oxford University Press, 1995)

United Nations Commission on Human Rights, *Joint Report by the Independent Expert on Structural Adjustment Programmes and the Special Rapporteur on Foreign Debt*, UN ESCOR, 2000, UN Doc. E/CN.4/2000/51

United Nations Conference on Trade and Development and General Agreement on Tariffs and Trade Secretariat, *An Analysis of the Proposed Uruguay Round Agreement with Particular Emphasis on Aspects of Interest to Developing Countries* (Geneva: UNCTAD/GATT Secretariat, 1993), MTN.TNC/W/122

United Nations Conference on Trade and Development, *Newly Emerging Environmental Policies with a Possible Trade Impact: A Preliminary Discussion – Report by the UNCTAD Secretariat* (New York: United Nations, 1995)

United Nations Conference on Trade and Development, *Trade and the Environment: Issues of Key Interest to the Least Developed Countries* (New York: United Nations, 1997)

United Nations Development Programme, *Capacity Development for Governance for Sustainable Human Development* (New York: UNDP, 1996)

United Nations Development Programme, *Human Development Report 2000* (Oxford: Oxford University Press, 2000)

United Nations Environment Programme, *Final Report of the Expert Group Workshop on International Environmental Law Aiming at Sustainable Development*, UNEP/IEL/WS/3/2, (1996)

United Nations Environment Programme, *International Environmental Governance SS.VII/1, Report of the Governing Council on the Work of Its Seventh Special Session/Global Ministerial Environment Forum* (13–15 February 2002) UNEP/GCSS.VII/6, Annex I

United Nations Environment Programme, *Goals and Principles of Environmental Impact Assessment* (Nairobi: UNEP, 1987)

United Nations Environment Programme (UNEP) and International Institute for Sustainable Development (IISD), *Environment and Trade: A Handbook* (Winnipeg: IISD/UNEP, 2000)

United Nations Environmental Programme, *Environmental Impact Assessment; Issues, Trends and Practice* (Geneva: UNEP, 1996)

United Nations ESCOR, Commission on Human Rights, Sub-commission on Prevention of Discrimination of Minorities, *Review of Further Developments in Fields with Which the Sub-Commission Has Been Concerned, Human Rights and the Environment*: Final Report prepared by Mrs. Fatma Zohra Ksentini, Special Rapporteur, UN Doc. E/CN. 4/Sub.2/1994/9 (1994)

United Nations High Commissioner for Human Rights and the United Nations Environmental Programme, *Meeting of Experts on Human Rights and the Environment*, 14-15 January, 2002: Conclusions, online: OHCHR, www.unhchr.ch/environment/conclusions

United Nations Secretary-General, *Follow-up to Johannesburg and the Future Role of the CSD* 18 February 2003 E/CN.17/2003/2

United Nations University, *Sustainable Development Governance: The Question of Reform: Key Issues and Proposals* (Tokyo: United Nations University Institute for Advanced Studies, 2002)

United States Centers for Disease Control and Prevention, *Addressing Emerging Infectious Disease Threats: A Prevention Strategy for the United States* (1994)

P. Uvin and I. Biagiotti, "Global Governance and the 'New' Political Conditionality" (1996) 2 *Global Governance: A Review of Multilaterism and International Organisations* 377

G. Van Calster, "Green Procurement and the WTO: Shades of Grey" 11 (3) *RECIEL* 3

J. L. Varela, "Regional Trends in International Law and Domestic Environmental Law: The Inter-American Hemisphere" in S. J. Rubin and D. C. Alexander, eds., *NAFTA and the Environment* (The Hague: Kluwer Law International, 1996)

D. Vignes, "Protection of the Antarctic Marine Fauna and Flora: The Canberra Convention and the Commission Set Up by It" in F. Francioni and T. Scovazzi, eds., *International Law for Antarctica* (The Hague: Kluwer Law International, 1996)

R. B. von Mehren and P. Nicholas Kourides, "International Arbitrations between States and Foreign Private Parties: The Libyan Nationalization Cases" (1981) 75 *Am. J. Int'l L.* 476

K. von Moltke, "International Commission and Implementation of Law" in J. E. Carroll, ed., *International Environmental Diplomacy* (Cambridge: Cambridge University Press, 1988) at 90

K. von Moltke, *International Environmental Management, Trade Regimes and Sustainability* (Winnipeg: International Institute for Sustainable Development, 1996)

K. von Moltke, *The Organisation of the Impossible* (Winnipeg: International Institute for Sustainable Development, 2001)

K. von Moltke, *An International Investment Regime? Implications for Sustainable Development* (Winnipeg: International Institute for Sustainable Development, 2000)

K. von Moltke, "The *Vorsorgeprinzip* in West German Policy," Appendix 3, Royal Commission on the Environment, Twelfth Report (Berlin: RCE, 1988)

D. Vogel, *Trading Up: Consumer and Environmental Regulations in a Global Economy* (Cambridge: Harvard University Press, 1995)

M. E. Wojcik et al., "AIDS in National and International Law" (Proceedings of the Ninety-Sixth Annual Meeting of the American Society of International Law, 16 March 2002) (2002) 96 *Am. Soc'y Int'l L. Proc.* 320

S. Watson, J. E. Flynn and C. Conwell, *Completing the World Trading System: Proposals for a Millennium Round* (The Hague: Kluwer Law International, 1999)

A. Weale, "Ecological Modernisation and the Integration of European Environmental Policy" in J. D. Liefferink, P. D. Lowe and A. P. J. Mol, eds., *European Integration and Environmental Policy* (Cambridge: Cambridge University Press, 1993)

A. Weale, G. Pridham, M. Cini, D. Konstadakopulos, M. Porter and B. Flynn, *Environmental Governance in Europe: An Ever Closer Ecological Union?* (Oxford: Oxford University Press, 2000)

J. H. H. Weiler, *The EU, the WTO and the NAFTA Towards a Common Law of International Trade* (Oxford: Oxford University Press, 2000)

A. Westin, *Environmental Tax Initiative and International Trade Treaties* (The Hague: Kluwer Law International, 1997)

C. G. Weeramantry, "Right to Development" (1985) *Indian J. I. L.* 482

B. Weintraub, "Science, International Environmental Regulation, and the Precautionary Principle: Setting Standards and Defining Terms" (1992) 1 *N.Y.U. Envtl. L. J.* 173

R. Wesseling, *The Modernisation of EC Antitrust Law* (Oxford: Hart, Studies in European Law and Integration, 2000)

D. A. Wirth, "The Rio Declaration on Environment and Development: Two Steps forward and One Back, or Vice Versa?" (1995) 29 *Ga. L. Rev.* 599

World Bank, *A Framework for the Design and Implementation of Competition Law and Policy* (Paris: World Bank and OECD, 1999)

World Bank, *Development in Practice Series: Curbing the Epidemic; Governments and the Economics of Tobacco Control* (Washington: World Bank, 1999)

World Bank, *The State in a Changing World* (Washington: World Bank, 1997)

World Bank, *Governance: The World Bank's Experience* (Washington: World Bank, 1994)

World Bank, *World Bank Operational Manual on Poverty Reduction*, OD 4.15 (December 1991) (Washington: World Bank, 1991)

World Bank, *World Development Report 2000/01* (Oxford: Oxford University Press, 2001)

World Bank, *Sub-Saharan Africa: From Crisis to Sustainable Growth* (Washington: World Bank, 1989)

World Bank, *Social Indicators of Development* (Washington: World Bank, 1995)

World Bank, *World Development Indicators*, CD-ROM (Washington: The International Bank for Reconstruction and Development/The World Bank, 1999)

World Bank, *World Development Report: Knowledge for Development* (Oxford: Oxford University Press, 1999)

World Bank, *The World Bank Inspection Panel, Resolution 93-10*, online: World Bank http://www.worldbank.org/html/ins- panel/operatingprocedures.html

World Commission on Environment and Development, *Our Common Future* (Oxford: Oxford University Press, 1987)

World Health Organization, *World Heath Report 1999: Making a Difference* (Geneva: World Health Organisation, 1999) 78

World Health Organization, "Revision of the International Regulations: Progress Report" (January 1999) 74 *Weekly Epidemiology Rec*

World Health Organization, "Economics of Tobacco Control" (20 August 1999) WHO Doc. A/FCTC/WG1/2

World Health Organization, (July 1998) 78 *Weekly Epidemiology Rec*

World Health Organization, "International Health Regulations" (25 July 1969) *International Health Regulations*, 3rd ann. edn, 91983

World Health Organization and World Trade Organization, *WTO Agreements and Public Health: A Joint Study by the WHO and the WTO Secretariat* (WTO/WHO, 2002)

World Resources Institute, *Global Biodiversity Strategy* (Washington: WRI, 1992)

World Trade Organisation Working Group on the Interaction between Trade and Competition Policy, *Overview of Members' National Competition Legislation – Note by The Secretariat*, WT/WGTCP/W/128/Rev.2, 4 July 2001

World Trade Organisation Secretariat, *Trade, Development and the Environment* (The Hague: Kluwer Law International, 2000)

F. Yamin, "Biodiversity, Ethics and International Law" (1995) 71:3 *International Affairs* 529

F. Yamin and J. Depledge, *The International Climate Change Regime: A Guide to Rules, Institutions and Procedures* (Cambridge: Cambridge University Press, 2004)

K. Ziegler, Völkerrechtsgeschichte (München: C. H. Beck Verlag, 1994)

D. M. Zillman, A. Lucas & G. Pring, *Human Rights in Natural Resource Development* (Oxford: Oxford University Press, 2002)

Index

Note: The following abbreviations have been used – *f* = figure; *n* = note; *t* = table

endangered species 116, 195, 278, 320, 675, 696; international law 34*n16*, 36
Enderois community (Kenya); community's collective right to property 478–9; community's right to protection 479–82; land tenure 482–7; right to development 488–90; right to freely dispose of wealth and natural resources 487–8; *see also* human rights
Energy Charter Treaty 552
energy resources 57, 60, 607, 632–3, 801–2, 804; access to justice 762; equity principle 753–4; good governance 590, 591; hydro power 800–3, 818; nuclear power 111–12, 312, 337, 345, 628–9; precautionary principle 806, 809; public participation 574, 586, 810; sustainable use of natural resources 747–50; thermal power 800–1, 802–3, 808; wind power projects 523–5, 803–6
environment: definition 60, 306
Environment and Safeguards Compliance Policy (ESCP) (Inter-American Development Bank) 796–8, 801, 803, 804
Environmental Action Programmes (European Union) 617–19, 624, 637*n82*, 638
Environmental Cooperation, North American Commission for 25
environmental development *xli–xlii*, 2*n4*, 5*n20*, 9, 31–3
environmental education 660
environmental impact assessments (EIAs) 17, 18, 42, 85, 241, 254, 745; energy resources 633–5, 801, 820; fisheries management 322, 699–701; indigenous and tribal people 508–9; integration 603, 604–5, 606, 608–9, 613, 614*n109*; judicial elaboration 181, 196, 201–2, 215, 219, 221, 237*n306*; marine and coastal environments 339; nuclear processing 345; precautionary principle 637, 640, 754–7; public participation 729, 731, 732, 758; pulp mills 818; refusal to provide information 726–7; risk management 527, 528*n71*, 530; rivers and river infrastructures 248–50, 260, 270, 271, 705, 717*n30*; seabeds

and seabed mining 329, 347–8, 354, 818; South Asia 658, 666–7, 672–3, 674, 675; transboundary disputes 274*n49*, 275, 280; transit rights 299–300; wind power projects 804–5; World Bank 745
Environmental Management Group (EMG) 51*n75*
environmental principles 12*n42*, 236, 597–8, 622–3, 735; development of 41, 47, 49, 57, 64, 66; human rights 447, 451; process of agreement 84, 86–7; South Asia 653, 655, 659, 670, 671, 672; sustainable justice and 112, 117; *see also* principles of international law
environmental protection *xli–xlii*, 9*n37*, 14, 47, 54, 85; as an object 519, 619; community's right to 271, 479–82; fair balance requirement 518*n21*, 711; indigenous people 479–82; precautionary principle 640–2, 668–9; recognition of intrinsic value 533–6; transit rights and 298, 307, 314
environmental refugees 111
environmental rights 21–2; international courts and tribunals 138*n48*
environmental and social impact analysis/plan (ESIA/ESAP) 805, 807, 816, 817, 821
equity principle 1–2, 12, 17, 18, 34, 43; advisory opinions 182, 716; African region 814–15; dispute resolution mechanisms 733–6, 751–4; economic power 113; European Bank for Reconstruction and Development (EBRD) 805–6; exclusive economic zones (EEZs) 336; guiding statements 178; 240; human rights 670; judicial deliberations 816–17; judicial interpretations and applications 204–8, 267, 278, 349–50; natural resources 274; political conflict 287, 288–9; as a principle 87, 104, 105, 188, 284; reasonable and equitable utilization 711, 712*t*; seabeds and seabed mining 329; sovereign rights 711; water resources 425; *see also* fair and equitable treatment (FET); poverty eradication
erga omnes concept 121, 202, 269, 350–1